Mexico TravelBook™

2001 Edition

AAA Publishing
1000 AAA Drive, Heathrow, Florida 32746-5063

Published by:
AAA Publishing
1000 AAA Drive
Heathrow, FL 32746-5063

Send written comments to:
Mexico Editor
Publishing Product Development
Box 66, 1000 AAA Drive
Heathrow, FL 32746-5063

**For advertising rates and
circulation information call:**

(407) 444-8280

Cover photos:

Main photo
Tile roof and cathedral, Oaxaca
© Ernesto Rios Lanz / Sexto Sol

Cover insert photo
Tarahumara Indian / © John Neubauer

Spine photo
Puerto Vallarta / © Wolfgang Kaehler

Printed in the USA by
Quebecor World,
Buffalo, NY

Printed on recyclable paper.
Please recycle whenever possible.

Stock #5022

Contents

Practical Information

Selected Destinations

For Your Information

Mexico TravelBook

Regions

Maps

Indexes

Lodging Classification Photo Credits

How to Use This Book

The AAA Mexico TravelBook has one goal—to make your trip smoother and more enjoyable by providing you with the most up-to-date travel facts and information available.

Before You Depart

The front section of the TravelBook provides the background you need in four different information categories. *Mexico the Country* describes the nation's geography, history, economy, people, architecture, art, music and dance, literature, food and drink, and native celebrations, plus a sampling of outdoor recreational opportunities.

Planning Your Trip offers practical tips. Among the subjects covered are when to go, what to pack, what you may bring and making lodging reservations. *Arriving in Mexico* has information about transportation options, as well as border crossing and temporary vehicle importation procedures for both U.S. and Canadian citizens.

Traveling Within Mexico touches upon health, personal safety, currency, tipping, mail and phone service, the highway system, and whom to contact for assistance in an emergency. Recommendations for purchases to commemorate your trip are given, along with an overview of customs regulations and a description of items that U.S. and Canadian residents may bring out of the country when departing.

Mexico's Travel Regions

This section presents cities and places of interest, as well as lodging and restaurant listings, for the eight regions identified on the map on page 34. Each region is introduced by a brief description and a map graphic showing its location within the country. Descriptions of cities, towns and places within each region are presented alphabetically; the heading includes the name of the city, town or place and the state in which it is located.

Listings of AAA-RATED hotels, motels and restaurants within each region also are presented alphabetically by city or town. For information about how to use these listings, *see "About Lodgings and Restaurants," page 42.* Recreational vehicle sites are listed at the back of the TravelBook under *About Campgrounds.*

Acapulco, Cancún, Guadalajara, Mexico City and Puerto Vallarta receive expanded descriptive treatment, with detailed information pertaining to transportation, visitor services, attractions, dining, shopping, nightlife, sightseeing and recreational opportunities.

Maps accompany selected cities and places. For an orientation map of Mexico that locates cities, towns and places with descriptive write-ups, *see pages 78-79.* Coordinates (for example, A-3) following city, town and place headings relate to the orientation map. Lodging and restaurant spottings on the city maps show the location of properties in that city. Also available to members is the AAA map of Mexico, a detailed road map of the entire country, and AAA's Triptik routing series.

Other TravelBook features include *Speaking of Spanish*, a handy compendium of words and phrases helpful to the Mexican traveler; *Fiestas and Holidays*, a listing of national and local celebrations; a temperature chart showing monthly highs, lows and precipitation for selected cities; a driving distances map; a chart showing metric conversions for miles per hour, temperatures, liquid measures and linear measures; and a page showing representative highway signs.

There are six indexes. The *Points of Interest Index* lists attractions, events and places or things to see that are described in more detail under the city and town write-ups. Index entries are presented under specific subject categories. To find out more about a particular entry, simply note its page number and turn to the corresponding location in the text. The *Alphabetical Listing of Cities, Towns and Places* index designates the page on which information about each begins. Finally, there are four specialized accommodations indexes: the *Bed & Breakfast Lodgings Index*, the *Country Inns Index*, the *Historical Lodgings & Restaurants Index* and the *Resorts Index*.

Acknowledgments

The information in this publication was reviewed for accuracy at press time. However, changes inevitably occur between annual editions. We regret any inconvenience resulting from these circumstances, but they are beyond our control. To help us maintain the best service and provide a superior publication, your suggestions are welcomed. Write directly to: Mexico Editor, Product Development, AAA Publishing, Box 66, 1000 AAA Dr., Heathrow, FL 32746-5063; fax (407) 444-8389.

MEXICO THE COUNTRY

Palace of Fine Arts, Mexico City ©Chris Sharp

At the beginning of the 21st century, Mexico—a country where political and social upheaval have historically been the rule, not the exception—stands at a crossroads of sorts. At the dawn of the 1990s it was poised to take a leap from developing nation to recognized world player. Then a quick succession of setbacks—a guerrilla uprising, a political assassination and a devastating currency devaluation, all in 1994—threatened to rip apart hard-won stability. But this is par for the course in a nation where change has been dramatic and rapid.

Perhaps nowhere else on Earth is there such a difference between old and new, between the traditional past and the unpredictable future. Timeless "Mexican" images still exist, of course. Donkeys amble down dusty paths, and ancient ruins stand silhouetted against the sky. But for every small village where a herd of goats comprises the local traffic, there is a vehicle-choked freeway. And for every local market displaying live chickens, handwoven baskets and piles of vegetables, there is a glitzy mall offering the latest upscale merchandise. Mexico is truly a study in contrasts.

Contrast also is evident in the class divisions that define Mexican society. The passage of the North American Free Trade Agreement (NAFTA) in 1992 pointed to new economic opportunities. But the Indian revolt that occurred in the state of Chiapas less than 2 years later was a blunt reminder that many Mexican citizens still endure horrible living conditions. The extremes of wealth and poverty can be shocking—20 minutes away from Cancún's glittering resorts are windowless, thatch-roofed huts with dirt floors. And in bursting-at-the-seams Mexico City, world-class hotels coexist with sprawling shantytowns that lack running water.

But despite living in a country where day-to-day existence often is filled with hardship, the Mexican people are always eager to show Mexico off to visitors. A rich cultural heritage is proudly showcased in elaborate fiestas and time-honored celebrations that take place practically year-round. An equally rich historical legacy unfolds at a wealth of pre-Hispanic ruins, most of which benefit from careful and ongoing restoration. And although a Third World way of life is still the norm for many people, visitors benefit from a strong and growing first world of hotels, restaurants and related amenities. This makes Mexico not only a wonderfully varied but a comparatively easy nation to explore.

NATURAL FEATURES

Mexico, while part of North America, also marks the transition from that vast continent's topographic and climatic extremes to the more uniformly tropical features of Central America and the Caribbean basin. Although its sun-scorched deserts and jagged mountain ranges look harsh, they also possesses an austere beauty. And not all is geographically forbidding—there are verdant valleys, cool highlands and mile after mile of sandy, palm-fringed beaches.

Roughly triangular in shape, Mexico narrows from an expanse of 1,300 miles across its northern frontier to a mere 140 miles at the Isthmus of Tehuantepec. Two peninsulas are appendages to the mainland. **Baja (Lower) California** is a tongue of land extending southeastward and parallel to the northwest Pacific Coast for nearly 800 miles. The **Yucatán Peninsula** comprises Mexico's easternmost region.

Most of the country consists of hills or mountain ranges broken by level plateaus; the plateaus in turn are carved into many canyons and valleys. Central Mexico is a vast elevated landscape dominated by high mountains to the east and west, many of which are of volcanic origin. The east coast is low and flat, but in the state of Veracruz the lofty mountains advance almost to the coast. The northwestern coastal plain is another relatively flat area, broken in parts by low hills and mountains.

The Sierra Madre comprises three great mountain ranges. The **Sierra Madre Oriental** and the **Sierra Madre Occidental** form the eastern and western boundaries of the central plateau region. The **Sierra Madre del Sur** frames the Pacific coast through the states of Guerrero and Oaxaca.

The height of the mountains is accentuated by deep valleys and canyons, which can plunge more than 1,500 feet below the general level of the plateau. At the bottom of some of these canyons the climate and vegetation are subtropical and distinctly different from conditions at the canyon rim. This is particularly true of the **Copper Canyon** area in the state of Chihuahua. Shadowed by the lofty Sierra Madre Occidental, it is a breathtaking complex of gorges formed by eons of erosion, volcanic activity and earthquakes. The name comes from the rust coloring of many of the canyon walls.

There are hundreds of volcanic peaks in Mexico; in the state of Michoacán alone there are more than 80. Volcanoes active in the last half century or so include Volcán de Fuego de Colima, near the city of the same name; Paricutín, near Uruapan but now dormant; and El Chichonal. Born in the fall of 1943 when a cornfield suddenly erupted, Paricutín grew more than 1,700 feet in 10 months. In 1982 the long-dormant volcano El Chichonal spewed a billion tons of ash and rock across a wide area near the small town of Teapa in southeastern Mexico.

A recent increase in seismic activity has been noted within **Popocatépetl**, at 17,883 feet Mexico's second highest peak. Although snow perpetually covers its upper flanks, Popocatépetl has historically spewed ash over extensive areas. Tests conducted in 1994 measuring sulfur dioxide emissions showed the volcano to be among the world's five or six most active, although scientists cannot predict whether this is a significant

---

Did You Know?

- Mexico ranks 14th in size among the world's countries.

- The Mexican coastline is nearly four times longer than the combined coasts of California and Florida.

- Mexico is divided into 31 states. The largest, Chihuahua, is slightly smaller than Oregon; the smallest, Tlaxcala, is slightly larger than Rhode Island.

- One-quarter of Mexico's total population lives in or around Mexico City.

- There are four mountain peaks within Mexico greater than 15,000 feet in elevation. The tallest, the 18,850-foot extinct volcano Citlaltépetl, is the third-highest point in North America.

- The Western Hemisphere's youngest volcano, Boquerón, is on an island south of the Baja California Peninsula. It was formed in 1952.

- Mexico is a young nation, gaining independence from Spain 45 years after the United States broke free of England.

- With an estimated population of some 100,000,000, Mexico is the most populous Spanish-speaking country in the world.

indication of any future activity. Over time, dozens of villages have sprouted up on Popocatépetl's lower slopes, but as with earthquakes, most Mexicans treat the possibility of an erupting volcano as simply a fact of life.

The backbone of Baja California consists of several westward-sloping mountain ranges. **Sierra de San Pedro Mártir** dominates the northern part of the peninsula; **Sierra de la Giganta**, the southern part. In the former, the peak **Picacho del Diablo** attains an elevation of 10,073 feet, Baja's highest point. The Yucatán Peninsula, on the other hand, is primarily flat or rolling; its highest point is barely 1,000 feet above sea level. Much of the subsurface rock is limestone, and subterranean erosion has produced many sinkholes (cenotes), some of which are used as natural swimming pools. For a more detailed description of each peninsula's geography as well as its human history, *see the separate listings "A Baja Overview" and "A Yucatán Overview" under Baja California and Yucatán Peninsula, respectively.*

THE COASTS

Mexico has four distinct coastal regions. The Baja California Peninsula, bathed by both the Pacific Ocean and the Sea of Cortés (Gulf of California), is marked by numerous bays and coves, as is the northwestern mainland coast. Further south, Pacific breakers crash against the feet of the Sierra Madre Occidental and the Sierra Madre del Sur. The Pacific Coast cities of Manzanillo and Acapulco boast fine natural harbors.

The eastern coastal plain along the Gulf of Mexico is essentially featureless. The flat terrain is characterized by broad beaches, swamps and palm-lined lagoons. Sandbars and lagoons also are features of the western and northern coasts of the Yucatán Peninsula. The peninsula's eastern coast borders the Caribbean Sea and is marked by extensive coral reefs. The islands of **Cozumel** and **Mujeres** are off its northeast corner. Powdery sands and clear, aquamarine waters are the Yucatán's greatest natural resource.

CLIMATE

Since roughly half of Mexico lies below the Tropic of Cancer, elevation has the biggest effect on temperatures. The seacoasts and the adjacent lower altitudes of the interior are warm to hot all year. The average annual temperature in these areas ranges from 77 to 82 F. Summer maximums in Baja California, the northwestern mainland deserts and parts of the Yucatán Peninsula can rise to over 100 F. Warm temperate conditions

---

Fast Facts

AREA: 1,972,554 square kilometers (761,603 square miles).

POPULATION: 100,000,000 (estimated).

CAPITAL: Mexico City, D.F.

HIGHEST POINT: Citlaltépetl (Pico de Orizaba), Ver., 5,747 meters (18,850 feet).

LOWEST POINT: south of Mexicali, B.C., 13 meters (43 feet) below sea level.

LANGUAGE: Spanish; some 50 Indian languages and many more dialects are spoken outside of major cities and towns. English is widely spoken, particularly in larger cities and at resorts.

ENTRY REQUIREMENTS: See "Arriving in Mexico," page 52.

CURRENCY: The monetary unit is the peso. The exchange rate in August 2000 was about 9.0 pesos=$1 U.S., although the rate is subject to small daily fluctuations.

BANK HOURS: Banks are open Mon.-Fri. 9-1:30; in some larger cities, they may reopen 4-6 and are open Sat. 10-1:30. Some of the large hotels and shops will change money, although at varying rates. Banks are closed on all national holidays, and also may close to celebrate local holidays.

BUSINESS HOURS: Shops are generally open Mon.-Sat. 10-7; some in smaller towns close for an hour or two in the afternoon. Shop hours may not always correspond to what is advertised. In resort areas hours are often extended into the evening and stores are open on Sun. Shopping malls are generally open daily; they are closed Jan. 1, Good Friday, May 1 (Labor Day) and Dec. 25. In most cities, businesses operate Mon.-Sat. 9-7; many are closed from 2-4 for the traditional long lunch break.

TAXES: Mexico levies a 15 percent value-added (I.V.A.) tax on all goods and services. The tax is supposed to be included in the posted price or rate; double check if you feel you are being doubly charged.

NATIONAL HOLIDAYS: New Year's Day; Constitution Day, Feb. 5; Birthday of Benito Juárez, Mar. 21; Holy Week (Semana Santa), Good Friday through Easter Sunday; Labor Day, May 1; Battle of Puebla (Cinco de Mayo), May 5; Independence Day, Sept. 16; Day of the Race (Columbus Day), Oct. 12; President's Report to Congress, Nov. 1; Day of the Dead, Nov. 1-2; Anniversary of the Mexican Revolution of 1910, Nov. 20; Feast Day of the Virgin of Guadalupe, Dec. 12; Christmas, Dec. 25. Banks, government offices and most stores are closed. Offices also may close the week between Christmas and New Year's Day.

are found at altitudes ranging from 3,000 to 6,000 feet, with average annual temperatures ranging from 63 to 70 F. From about the 7,000-foot elevation upwards is the cool zone, with average annual temperatures ranging from 59 to 61 F.

Most of the country's annual rainfall normally occurs from June through September or October. The country as a whole receives inadequate precipitation, although rain is heavy along the lower Gulf of Mexico coast, in the southwestern corner near Guatemala and on the seaward slopes of mountains in portions of the southeast. Summer rains in the central plateau region tend to refresh the atmosphere; they also may aggravate pothole problems in the cities. In addition, the narrow, twisting roadways in mountainous areas can become very slippery when wet. Baja California and the northwest receive scant precipitation, and irrigation is needed for agriculture. For average monthly high and low temperatures and precipitation amounts for representative cities, *see pages 68-69.*

Severe weather in Mexico is related to normal meteorological patterns and the country's topography. Earthquakes pose the greatest danger. The great quake of September 1985 toppled buildings and killed more than 10,000 in Mexico City. In September 1995—just a few days prior to the tenth anniversary of that tremor—another major earthquake, centered in the state of Guerrero about 200 miles south of the capital, destroyed adobe houses in remote villages and rattled the nerves of the metropolitan area's 21 million residents. A more benign occurrence is smog, which can plague such major urban centers as Mexico City and Guadalajara during the dry winter.

History

Mexican history has been particularly tumultuous, encompassing cultural peaks as well as the suffering borne out of conquest, war and subjugation. At a time when much of Europe was decidedly primitive, civilizations in the New World were carving out sophisticated architectural, scientific and artistic achievements. The ruins of pyramids, palaces and temples all bear witness to the highly developed skills of the Olmec, Maya, Toltec, Aztec and other cultures that flourished, in some cases, more than a thousand years before the Spanish arrival. Some waged war; all trafficked and explored, leaving behind a fascinating historical legacy. Remnants of these ancient civilizations are scattered throughout central and southern Mexico.

Beginnings

No one knows for sure from where the native peoples of Mexico originally migrated. The likeliest theory is that successive tribes from Asia made their way across a former bridge of land

Chichén Itzá   ©John Neubauer

spanning the Bering Strait and slowly pushed south by way of Alaska. The earliest recorded signs of human habitation in the Americas date to 9500 B.C. Somewhere around 5000 B.C., in the valley of Tehuacán southeast of present-day Mexico City, a straggling community of seed gatherers discovered how to domesticate maize, becoming farmers in the process and beginning the establishment of permanent villages. With the advent of other skills, such as weaving and pottery making, trade between settlements commenced. In time, the stage was set for the next level of societal development—the building of cities.

By the **Pre-Classic Period**, which began around 1500 B.C., a stable farming lifestyle had developed over most of what archeologists refer to as Mesoamerica (the region stretching from Mexico's central plateau south to Costa Rica). Mesoamerica's first advanced civilization reached its height along the Gulf of Mexico coast of what is now the states of Veracruz and Tabasco, although little is known about the people, the **Olmecs**.

Olmec culture—which attained its greatest prominence from 800 to 400 B.C.—produced an early version of a calendar and a written language later refined by the Maya. The Olmecs' greatest achievement, however, was in sculpture. The facial expressions of their colossal, carved stone heads resemble both a jaguar and a human infant. The Olmecs also produced exquisite jade figurines. The reason for their decline remains a mystery, although the theory that the Maya descended from them has considerable support. All of Mexico's great civilizations, in fact, shared links based on religious belief and artistic expression, despite flowering in different locations and developing different languages and customs.

THE CLASSIC PERIOD

The **Classic Period**, from about 200 B.C. through the eighth century, produced Mexico's first noteworthy urban civilizations. Around 100 B.C. construction was begun on the pyramids at **Teotihuacán**, approximately 49 kilometers (30 miles) northeast of present-day Mexico City. One of this country's great historical puzzles is the origin of that ancient city, which may have had 200,000 inhabitants at its peak around A.D. 500. The name, meaning "place where the gods dwell," was bestowed by the Aztecs; by the time they arrived the city had long been abandoned. Teotihuacán's enormous Pyramid of the Sun is one of the most impressive ruins in all Mexico. Frescoes and other examples of artwork that adorned Teotihuacán's religious monuments are on display at Mexico City's National Museum of Anthropology.

Many historians consider the **Maya** to be the crown jewel of pre-Columbian cultures. They developed the mathematical concept of zero and produced a calendar that enabled their priests to predict eclipses and plot the movements of the solar system. In contrast to these refined achievements, the Maya also participated enthusiastically in brutal games, human sacrifice and ritual bloodletting, which they believed helped them to communicate with the gods. They were warlike as well, staging raids on other peoples to secure victims for their sacrificial rites. The vast Maya empire, first centered in Guatemala and the state of Chiapas, spread north to the Yucatán Peninsula by the seventh century. Important Maya centers were **Bonampak**, **Chichén Itzá**, **Cobá**, **Dzibilchaltún**, **Edzná**, **Kohunlich**, **Palenque**, **Tulum**, **Uxmal** and **Yaxchilán**.

Also during this period, the **Zapotecs** established themselves in southern Mexico's Valley of Oaxaca. They created the ceremonial center of **Monte Albán**, which eluded discovery by the Spanish *conquistadores*. Zapotec society was presided over by priests who dwelled in seclusion yet maintained firm control over their subjects. Later, when the **Mixtecs** emerged and took over Monte Albán, the Zapotecs retreated to nearby **Mitla**. Both cities exhibited a highly refined artistic sensibility, a characteristic shared by most of the Classic Period cultures. Monte Albán's renowned Tomb 7, excavated in 1932, yielded a spectacular trove of finely crafted riches.

INVASION AND SACRIFICE

During the **Postclassic Period**, from about the 10th century up until 1500, militarism supplanted the religious aristocracy. Such warlike tribes as the **Toltecs** invaded from the north, developing their own culture. The ruins of Tula in the state of Hidalgo bear witness to their artistry; in fact, the Aztecs later used the term "Toltec" to refer to a person of great skill.

Other tribes infiltrated the valleys of central Mexico during this period, including the **Huastecs**, the **Totonacs** and the **Texcocoans**. Although most of these peoples practiced idolatry and human sacrifice, the Texcococan ruler **Netzahualcóyotl** stood out for his belief in one all-powerful god and a dedication to music and the arts.

In the early 1300s the fierce, nomadic Mexica, now known as the **Aztecs**, drifted down from the northwest. Driven by prophetic decree, they moved from place to place in search of a location where they would see an eagle perched on a cactus pad, clutching a serpent in its beak. According to legend, that spot was an island in the middle of Lake Texcoco, within the Valley of Mexico. The Aztecs soon dominated other tribes and villages in this region, and in 1325 founded the city of **Tenochtitlán**, which was later to become Mexico City.

Aztec civilization was well advanced by the beginning of the 16th century. In addition to being skilled at picture-writing and sculpture, they created three calendars based on a 52-year world life cycle; ran schools for the sons of nobles, for warriors in training, and for youths taught music and dance; and cultivated a variety of plants for medicinal purposes.

Like the Maya, Aztec religious ceremonies revolved around the savage cult of human sacrifice. Elaborate monuments were erected to honor a complex pantheon of gods and deities, and much human effort was devoted to waging war or extracting tribute from tribes that had been subjugated. The Aztec empire became so ruthlessly powerful that only the **Tlaxcalans**, a defiantly independent group, remained outside their control. Ironically, it was Aztec dominance that led to their undoing at the hands of the Spanish *conquistadores*.

THE SPANISH CONQUEST

In the late 15th and early 16th centuries, Spanish explorers were making inroads into the New World, discovering Caribbean islands and points along the North and South American coasts. **Francisco Hernández de Córdoba** discovered the Yucatán Peninsula in 1517, landing at Cape Catoche. One year later **Juan de Grijalva** explored the Mexican coastline west from the Yucatán to the vicinity of Veracruz. In the course of trading with the Indians Grijalva heard tales of fabulous riches that were to be found in the interior.

In 1519, an expedition set out from Cuba under **Hernán Cortés** to conquer the uncharted territory. At the time Cortés was a 34-year-old colonist and landowner living in Cuba. His expedition consisted of several hundred Spanish soldiers, gunpowder, some horses and dogs, and a contingent of Cuban Indians to bear supplies—woefully inadequate, it seemed, to conquer the mighty Aztec empire. But shortly after the expedition landed on the island of Cozumel, the Spaniards were given 20 maidens as a gift. One of them, known as Malintzin by the Indians, was baptized as Marina and called **Malinche**. Malinche became Cortés' mistress as well as his interpreter, as she spoke both Maya and Náhuatl, the Aztec language—giving him a crucial tactical advantage. A shipwrecked Spaniard rescued by Cortés, Jerónimo de Aguilar, also proved an informative ally.

Cortés and his troops reached the little island of San Juan de Ulúa, in the harbor on which the city of Veracruz now lies, and established the first Spanish settlement in Mexico a short distance up the coast. From there they proceeded toward the Aztec capital, encountering only scattered resistance along the way. Rumors of their approach frightened **Moctezuma**, the ruler of Tenochtitlán; a superstitious believer in religious omens, he thought Cortés to be the god Quetzalcóatl, whom myths had decreed would return one day to conquer Mexico (see box p. 404).

The expedition reached Tenochtitlán on Nov. 8, 1519. Cortés was received reluctantly by Moctezuma and remained until the following June. The emperor was persuaded by Cortés—as crafty as he was ruthless—to reside with the Spaniards, thus becoming a voluntary hostage. The populace finally revolted on June 30. Moctezuma was killed, allegedly by his own followers, and Cortés and his men were driven out. The grim battle, in which hundreds of Spanish troops

For Your Information

MEDIA: Mexico City's *The News* is a daily English-language paper available from major hotels in the capital. You should be able to pick up *USA Today* in big cities or resorts. The Sanborn's chain, represented in the larger cities, carries English-language magazines. Hotels usually provide free magazines that list what is happening around town; most hotels also offer U.S. TV channels. Some radio stations in larger cities broadcast in English.

ATTRACTION SCHEDULES: Due to Mexico's sheer size and diversity it it difficult to monitor the operating hours of many attractions. Before setting out for a day of sightseeing, check with the front desk at your hotel regarding schedules for local museums, archeological sites or historic buildings. Other information sources include taxi drivers, tourist offices and city hall. Many museums are open 9-5 and are closed on Monday. Admission fees are inexpensive (usually less than $5).

CUSTOMS: Most citizens are rather formal in their dealings with strangers, and very polite as well; try to respond in kind. Mexicans love children and family unity is revered, so your own kids should feel quite at home. Cultural expression is proudly displayed, and most people have an enthusiastic enjoyment of the arts.

Many older Mexicans are very conservative, and provocative or skimpy dress—on men or women—is frowned upon if worn in churches or other inappropriate places. When sightseeing, dress with both comfort and common sense in mind. Mexican men also love to charm, and female travelers may receive openly admiring

looks or remarks. If such behavior is bothersome, it's best to simply ignore it rather than to get angry, and to minimize or eliminate overtures by dressing conservatively.

PUBLIC RESTROOMS: Take advantage of those in hotels, restaurants, airports or bus stations wherever possible, as public restrooms otherwise are difficult to find. Those in out-of-the-way places, particularly at gas stations, often have primitive plumbing and are definitely not up to the standards of public restrooms in the United States. Always carry a roll of toilet paper and a small bar of soap; both of these necessities can be in short supply away from your hotel.

POLICE: Few tourists ever run into trouble with the law, but you may need to ask police for directions or seek assistance for other reasons. While there are officers who go out of their way to be helpful, other encounters—mainly with regard to alleged traffic violations—can be quite exasperating or even intimidating, especially if you don't speak fluent Spanish. Always cooperate if stopped, but try to resolve the situation right away.

RESOURCES: Bilingual telephone operators provide emergency information as well as details about lodgings, transportation and sightseeing. In Mexico City, phone (5) 250-0123 or 250-0151; elsewhere in Mexico, phone 01 (800) 903-9200; from the United States, phone (800) 482-9832. Brochures and general information are available from Mexico Tourism, (800) 44-MEXICO.

and thousands of Cortés' Indian allies lost their lives, is memorialized in history as *La Noche Triste*, or "Night of Sadness."

Cortés retreated to Tlaxcala, where he and his survivors re-equipped themselves for another siege. A fleet of boats was built for use in attacking the island city. Strengthened by additional allies, Cortés returned the following year. After more than 2 months of fighting, the Spanish demolished Tenochtitlán and executed the last Aztec emperor, **Cuauhtémoc**.

Several factors helped bring about Tenochtitlán's downfall, including superior weaponry, the Spaniards' desire for wealth and the introduction of contagious diseases for which the natives had no immunity. But none was as important as Cortés' ability to recruit tribes who chafed under Aztec domination. Destroying the Aztec empire gave Spain the infamous distinction of wiping out hundreds of years of Indian achievements in Mesoamerica.

COLONIAL RULE

Spain consolidated its holdings in the New World through a series of expeditions that ranged south to the Gulf of Honduras and north toward the Baja California Peninsula. Most of the adventurers who led the forays—such as **Nuño de Guzmán**, who explored the area comprising the present-day states from Michoacán northwest to Sinaloa—were cruel and ruthless. Although Mexico was conquered by these soldiers of fortune, it was governed by Spain's bureaucracy—a succession of viceroys under the Spanish kings. Beginning in 1535 and for nearly 300 years thereafter, all Spanish possessions in North and Central America collectively existed as a colony called New Spain.

The Spanish reign was insignificant politically but momentous socially. Mexico's colonial cities, its grand cathedrals and most of its historic buildings were constructed during the colonial era. On Tenochtitlán's ruins was built Mexico City, laid out, as were all Mexican towns, in a grid anchored by a central plaza—a pattern based on the cities of Spain. The country's natural resources were tapped, and economic activity increased with the introduction of cattle, horses and wheat, as well as the opening of trade routes to the Orient.

It was the mother country, however, that benefitted. The gold and silver so hungrily sought by the *conquistadores* either went to the feudal estates built in Mexico or into the Spanish coffers. The crown controlled every aspect of colonial life but put little effort into developing an infrastructure of roadways and bridges that would help tie the far-flung colony together. Arable land, rather than being owned by individual farmers, was divided into huge parcels and worked by Indians.

Spanish colonists, in fact, treated the Indians as virtual slaves. In addition to farming, they were recruited for building construction and labor in the mines. Spain justified its continued presence in Mexico on the basis of converting the natives—considered barbarians—to Christianity. The church thus played a singular role throughout colonial history. Augustinian, Dominican and Franciscan friars (and later the Jesuits) all journeyed to New Spain to minister and to teach, founding missions in the depths of the wilderness. Over the course of 3 centuries more than 10,000 churches were built, a legacy that can be seen in practically every Mexican town today.

But although the friars' motives were just, exploitation won out. Most of the Spanish colonists were interested only in accumulating wealth, not in improving overall conditions in the vast outpost off which they profited. Over the course of colonial rule, rigid societal classes emerged. Indians were the lowest class, but only slightly higher were the *mestizos*, of mixed Spanish and Indian blood. Creoles, the product of Spanish parents but born in Mexico, were still kept out of society's highest echelon, which was reserved for those born in Spain of racially undoubted parentage. By the turn of the 19th century, these distinctions had bred widespread divisiveness.

INDEPENDENCE AND ITS AFTERMATH

The push for independence began with secret meetings in three central Mexican cities: Morelia, Querétaro and San Miguel de Allende. The revolutionary movement plotted to have Spain's downfall coincide with the rising of Nueva España ("New Spain"), an independent nation. **Don Miguel Hidalgo y Costilla**, the pastor of a parish church in the town of Dolores Hidalgo, was the first great leader of the movement to overthrow Spanish rule. Father Hidalgo was an intriguing mix of flawed cleric (he sired several children) and committed champion for Indian rights. He joined a group of like-minded intellectuals—chief among them **Ignacio Allende**, a Creole aristocrat and army official—who were intent on securing Mexico's freedom.

Word of the conspiracy leaked to Spanish rulers, forcing the fight to begin early. Around midnight on Sept. 15, 1810, Hidalgo gathered his parishioners together and to the accompaniment of a clanging church bell issued *Grito de Dolores*, a stirring declaration that became the rallying cry of those struggling for freedom. The band of revolutionaries took the towns of Celaya and Guanajuato and then retreated north, hoping to enlist the aid of the United States. But Hidalgo and two of his chief officers, Allende and Ignacio Aldama, were captured outside the city of Chihuahua and executed in 1811. Dying in disgrace as a failed rebel and defrocked priest, he is revered today as the father of Mexican independence.

Another priest, **José María Morelos y Pavón**, assumed Hidalgo's mantle. Morelos also dreamed of a free Mexico, and his skill as a military leader put him in a good position to advance the cause. He and his well-trained band of guerrillas captured the city of Chilpancingo, in the state of Guerrero. In 1813, a congress of patriots there formally declared Mexico's independence. Morelos subsequently managed to escape capture at Cuautla and took the southern stronghold of Oaxaca before falling to royalist forces in the provincial capital of Valladolid. He was executed in 1815; Valladolid was renamed Morelia in his honor.

Leadership of the revolution passed to one of Morelos' lieutenants, **Vicente Guerrero**. The fighting dragged on until September 1821, when Guerrero and former Royalist officer **Agustín de Iturbide** entered Mexico City with a plan that declared Mexico an independent constitutional monarchy. The last Spanish viceroy returned to Spain, and shortly thereafter Iturbide crowned himself emperor of Mexico. His empire lasted only a few months, however; the Mexican republic was proclaimed on Dec. 6, 1822, by **Gen. Antonio López de Santa Anna**. Santa Anna later became president, and Iturbide was exiled.

A new constitution drafted in 1823 proclaimed Mexico a federal republic. But freedom brought its own problems, with the government changing hands more than 30 times over a 30-year period. One of the key figures during this era of upheaval was Santa Anna, a charismatic but ideologically unfocused military leader who was president of the country no less than 11 times between 1833 and 1854. Yet he seemed as incapable as the other dictators and generals who successively ruled the nation to bring about a modernized economy and reverse 3 centuries of social inequity.

The internal chaos left Mexico ripe for foreign intervention, and both Spain and France mounted invasions. Mexico's greatest loss, though, occurred at the hands of the United States. Texas—then a Mexican territory—wished to declare itself an independent republic. This sparked the battle for the Alamo, a former mission turned military compound in San Antonio, in 1836. Although Mexico won that conflict, Santa Anna was captured by U.S. Gen. Sam Houston less than 2 months later; in exchange for his freedom he agreed to grant Texan independence. In 1845 the United States voted to annex Texas, redefining its borders to include Mexican territory in what is now New Mexico and California. Mexico, resisting this aggressive expansionist policy, refused to give up the land, and the Mexican-American War soon began.

American troops landed at the port of Veracruz in 1847, occupying the city and killing many civilians. From there they proceeded to Mexico City, following the route Hernán Cortés had taken more than 300 years earlier. In September, U.S. forces entered the capital, staging their final victorious battle at Chapultepec Castle, site of a Mexican military college. The following year the **Treaty of Guadalupe Hidalgo** was signed. Its terms required Mexico to cede its territories north of the Rio Grande, an enormous area encompassing the present-day states of Arizona, New Mexico, California, Nevada, Utah and part of Colorado. A devastating and humiliating blow, the war is remembered at the **Monumento de los Niños Héroes** (Monument to the Child Heroes) in Chapultepec Park, a memorial to the bravery of the young cadets who died defending their country.

THE JUAREZ YEARS

Another period of upheaval followed the U.S. invasion of Mexico, this time focusing on the church. With the advent of Spanish rule, the clergy grew to control much of Mexico's wealth and governing power. But an emerging middle class of educated professionals began to chafe under the church's restrictions. They advocated freedom of speech, the press and education, and pressed for laws designed to separate church and state—all reforms aimed at moving Mexico in a more liberal direction, and all opposed by the church and conservatives determined to maintain the old ways.

One of the leaders of the reform movement was **Benito Juárez**, a Zapotec Indian of humble origin. Taken in at a young age by a family in the city of Oaxaca, he put his resulting education to good use, becoming an attorney and then embarking on a career in politics. Juárez served as the Oaxaca state governor from 1847-52. In 1857, when he was both vice-president of Mexico and president of the Supreme Court, a new liberal constitution was adopted. It called for the separation of church and state and the right to freedom of worship, among other reforms. By the time Juárez assumed the presidency in 1858, opposition between liberals and conservatives had touched off the 3-year War of Reform, one of the most violent in Mexican history. The government toppled, and Juárez himself barely escaped execution. For several years he was unable to reinstate his liberal regime.

Meanwhile, France, England and Spain were prepared to once again take advantage of Mexico's political turmoil, and more specifically to extract payment for huge foreign debts the country had built up. The United States resented this intrusion but was embroiled in its own civil war. Ships from all three nations converged on the port of Veracruz early in 1862. England and Spain ultimately withdrew their challenges, but

French emperor **Napoleon III**, seeking an addition to his empire, marched on Mexico with the enthusiastic backing of Mexican conservatives.

The French army was given a rude reception—and soundly defeated in battle—at Puebla in May 1862 (an event which gave rise to today's *Cinco de Mayo* festivities, celebrated on or around May 5 both north and south of the border). However, a battery of reinforcements occupied Mexico City the following year, driving out Juárez. The new regime needed a royal ruler, and the offer was extended to **Archduke Maximilian** of Hapsburg, a relative of Napoleon III. Maximilian was crowned emperor of Mexico and "ruled" for 3 years while the Juárez government was still in disarray.

Maximilian and his wife **Carlota**, a Belgian princess, embraced their new empire, but the Austrian archduke had no practical governing experience—sorely needed in a country wracked by conflict and neglect. Furthermore, he angered conservative backers by refusing to repeal reform laws. By 1865 the U.S. Civil War was over, and Juárez was receiving American assistance. The looming Franco-Prussian War began to siphon Napoleon III's troops out of Mexico. Carlota set off for Europe to enlist support for her husband's floundering government; when it was denied, legend has it she went insane. By 1867 the empire was bankrupt.

Maximilian was captured and executed by a firing squad at Querétaro; Juárez once again assumed the presidency, leading the country until his death in 1872. Juárez's intelligence, vision and refusal to compromise principles have invited comparisons to Abraham Lincoln, and today he remains the most admired of Mexico's presidents.

REVOLUTION AND REFORM

At the end of Juárez's presidency Mexico was a nation with a democratic government. It also was a nation where poverty and illiteracy were endemic, modes of transportation were woefully underdeveloped, and the economy desperately needed a shot in the arm. From 1876 until 1910, **Porfirio Díaz**—a general under Juárez—ruled Mexico as a dictator. His policies brought momentous changes. Thousands of miles of railroad track were laid, new factories were built, ports were modernized, and improved methods of communication linked the cities. Foreign investment, which Díaz actively courted, was responsible for much of the progress.

Although some Mexicans prospered during the Díaz regime, an overwhelming majority did not. Peasant farmers had their land taken away, while a few wealthy landowners controlled vast amounts of acreage. Prices were controlled, which meant the average citizen could not afford even the most basic items of food and clothing. Meanwhile, the upper class minority wore fine fashions to attend performances of the opera and the symphony held in grandiose public buildings. A ubiquitous military presence suppressed banditry but also silenced any voices of discontent. The rich continued to get richer, the poor ever more destitute.

Growing opposition to the Díaz dictatorship precipitated the bloody, protracted Revolution of 1910, which lasted for a decade. By the time Díaz was re-elected to yet another term in 1910, he was 80 years old and had ruled the country for 34 years. **Francisco I. Madero**, a northern landowner, called for the overthrow of Díaz, garnering fervent support among revolution-minded peasants. Rebel groups materialized seemingly overnight; within months Díaz was forced out of the country and Madero was elected president.

Unfortunately, the end of the Díaz regime did not bring about a period of political stability. Madero was assassinated in 1913, and over the next several years the beleaguered office of the presidency was filled by **Victoriano Huerta, Venustiano Carranza** and **Alvaro Obregón**, among others. Conditions were anarchic; armies recruited women and young boys, cities were burned, and approximately one out of eight Mexicans lost their lives. The issues fueling the disorder were underscored by the guerrilla activities of two revolutionary leaders—**Pancho Villa** and **Emiliano Zapata**.

Villa, born Doroteo Arango, was essentially a bandit, although he understood the hardships endured by the peasant majority. Villa joined Madero's uprising against Díaz, becoming a valuable asset due to his fundamental knowledge of northern Mexico's land and people. Following Madero's assassination, Villa joined forces with Carranza to overthrow the repressive dictatorship of Huerta. But after a falling out with Carranza, he retreated to the desolate mountains of the north, where he engaged in banditry and guerrilla warfare. Villa retired to a ranch near Parral, Chih., in 1920 and was himself assassinated there (by Mexicans) 3 years later.

Zapata was Villa's southern counterpart, the son of a *mestizo* peasant. Uncultured but intelligent, he devoted his life to achieving two simple objectives: democracy for the nation, and a redistribution of land from the government-controlled haciendas back to the people. Zapata drafted the Plan of Ayala, which called for the seizure of stolen land appropriated by the haciendas and its redistribution in the form of *ejidos*, or small cooperative farms. With his wide-brimmed sombrero and big, drooping mustache, Zapata looked every inch the revolutionary hero as he roamed the countryside carrying out land takeovers under the banner *"tierra y libertad"* (land and liberty). He was ambushed and shot to death in 1919 by a Carranza general.

In 1917, a new constitution was adopted, establishing a democratic system of government composed of legislative, executive and judiciary branches. Carranza, however, was reluctant to implement the broad reforms it dictated, and widespread social unrest continued. When he tried to force the election of a handpicked successor to the presidency, an armed rebellion took place and Carranza fled the capital; he was captured and murdered en route to Veracruz.

Although it took time for the political storms to subside, the Revolution carried Mexico into a new age. The days of looking to Europe for cultural inspiration were over, as a strong national identity took their place. For the first time, all of Mexico's peoples—white, *mestizo*, Indian—were embraced. Historians explored the country's pre-Hispanic roots; writers and artists extolled the common man. This spiritual awakening proved vital to the rebuilding of the nation.

MEXICO UNDER THE PRI

Social and economic change continued under the dominant political party, known as the **Institutional Revolutionary Party** (Partido Revolucionario Institucional), or PRI, founded in 1929. The onset of the Great Depression caused the value of the peso to plummet, but a fruitful period of reconstruction began with the peaceful election of **Gen. Lázaro Cárdenas** in 1934. Cárdenas fulfilled many of the 1910 Revolution's ideals. He broke up the huge land holdings that were a holdover of the hacienda system, thus realizing Zapata's dream of returning Mexican land to the people. With the strengthening of unions, worker wages crept upward. Government funds were allotted for education and health care in rural areas. The Cárdenas administration also expropriated foreign-owned oil companies, paving the way for the creation of Pemex, the government-controlled oil monopoly.

Industrial growth was rapid during the 1940s and '50s, and women belatedly won the right to vote in 1954. The 1968 Summer Olympics in Mexico City put the new Mexican prosperity on world view, although the games were tarnished before they began when the police violently suppressed student protests, killing an estimated 300 to 400 people.

The 1970s brought record oil revenues, but excessive borrowing set Mexico up for serious economic trouble when oil prices plummeted in the early '80s. Austerity measures, including the devaluation of the peso, were instituted to combat galloping inflation and the country's huge foreign debt. Many working-class Mexicans saw their standard of living reduced drastically, and the gulf between massive numbers of poor and the very wealthy few grew wider.

Governmental stability in the 20th century instilled a sense of greater national unity and improved the quality of life for most Mexican citizens. However, the PRI's firm control of governmental, labor and trade organizations made it difficult for independent voices to be heard. Cracks began to appear in the party's formerly seamless structure by the time **Carlos Salinas de Gortari**, a Harvard-educated economist, began a 6-year presidential term in 1988. He was elected amid allegations of fraud and with barely half of the popular vote—by far the narrowest PRI victory since the party's inception—over **Cuauhtémoc Cárdenas**, of the leftist Democratic Revolutionary Party (PRD) and the son of beloved former Mexican president Lázaro Cárdenas.

SEARCHING FOR STABILITY

The year 1994 was Mexico's most politically turbulent period since the 1910 Revolution. In January, Indian guerrillas led by the enigmatic Subcomandante Marcos and calling themselves the **Zapatista National Liberation Army**—in honor of revolutionary leader Emiliano Zapata—occupied several towns in the mountainous, undeveloped state of Chiapas, demanding more land and a measure of self-rule for their communities. The rebellion, which left more than 100 dead over 12 days, underscored the fact that large numbers of poor Indian farmers were not sharing in the country's prosperity.

Deeply ingrained class divisions, the very real specter of widespread poverty and the PRI's dominance were major issues in the 1994 presidential race, one of the most competitive in Mexico's history. **Ernesto Zedillo**, a Yale-educated economist, won by a wide margin against a second challenge from Cárdenas in a $700 million campaign to ensure clean results.

A historic shift in the balance of power occurred in July 1997, when Cárdenas won a landslide decision in Mexico City's mayoral race over the PRI candidate—the first time since 1928 that the office had been opened up for election rather than filled by a presidential appointee. The ruling party also lost its majority in the lower house of the National Congress, ending a nearly 70-year monopoly.

The 2000 presidential election showed further evidence that Mexico is perhaps standing on the verge of lasting political change. **Vicente Fox** of the National Action Party (PAN) won a decisive victory over the PRI's candidate, Francisco Labastida, dethroning the country's ruling political dynasty. It was the first time in more than a century that an opposition candidate had been elected.

ECONOMY

Mexico's leading industries are oil, tourism, mining, manufacturing, electronics and textiles. The automobile industry in particular has become one of the country's leading manufacturing sectors. Huge oil and natural gas reserves are located in the coastal Gulf of Mexico region and in the state of Chiapas. Most oil is shipped to the

Young market vendor in Cupilco, Tabasco   ©John Neubauer

United States; other customers include Canada, Japan and France. Paradoxically, reliance upon this natural resource was largely responsible for the economic crisis of the early 1980s, when oil prices fell and Mexico's foreign debt ballooned.

Tourism is perhaps the industry with the greatest potential for future growth. The Mexican government has taken the initiative in specifically developing naturally scenic areas—in particular, the beaches along the Caribbean and Pacific coasts—in order to attract foreign visitors. The most spectacular success story thus far is Cancún, a state-of-the-art resort that is Mexico's No. 1 tourist destination. Much effort also has gone into ongoing restoration of the country's wealth of archeological ruins and the protection of its diverse natural environments—not only for the enjoyment of visitors but to stimulate local economies.

Silver has been mined since colonial times; Mexico is the world's largest producer. Other leading resources in this mineral-rich country are copper, sulfur, zinc, tin, gold, manganese, coal and iron ore. Although mining has always been important to Mexico's economy, the industry has a slow growth rate. Fishing also has long been an important but chiefly local industry. Large-scale commercial fishing operations are based along the Gulf of Mexico, particularly in the waters off the state of Campeche.

Agricultural productivity is a difficult proposition in Mexico due to the rugged topography, poor soils, erratic rainfall and declining rural population. Coffee is grown in the lush highlands of the state of Veracruz, and irrigated lands produce significant amounts of tomatoes, sugar cane, tropical fruits and winter vegetables for export. Because subsistence agriculture is neglected, however, basic foodstuffs such as corn and cereals must be imported.

Northern Mexico in particular has benefited from the proliferation of *maquiladora* industries along the U.S. border—those that import raw materials and parts for assembly into finished products that are then exported. *Maquiladoras* are flourishing in other parts of the country as well: Such products as leather goods, clothing and small-scale equipment are begun in the United States and finished in Mexico. All of these industries take advantage of cheaper Mexican labor, and large-scale assembly plants also are able to sidestep stringent U.S. environmental standards.

The Salinas administration took bold steps to restructure Mexico's economy following the economic problems of the 1980s. Key industries previously owned and operated by the government were privatized, resulting in a more market-oriented system, lessening protectionism and boosting exports. These policies had a moderating effect on inflation, which was less than 10 percent annually by the early 1990s.

NAFTA's Passage

In December 1992 President George Bush, Mexican President Carlos Salinas de Gortari and

Canadian Prime Minister Brian Mulroney signed the historic **North American Free Trade Agreement** (NAFTA). The agreement advocated eliminating restrictions on the flow of goods, services and investment in North America, thus creating a free trade zone among the United States, Canada and Mexico to aid as an impetus in generating economic growth. NAFTA also marked the first time in the history of U.S. trade policy that an overall trade agreement directly addressed environmental concerns.

After passage in both the U.S. Senate and House of Representatives, NAFTA officially took effect Jan. 1, 1994, although the elimination of all manufacturing and agricultural trade restrictions is expected to take 10-15 years.

THE PESO'S DEVALUATION

Capping 1994's political turmoil was the devaluation of the peso in December 1994, which quickly led to a 40 percent plunge in the currency's value by early 1995. Dubbed the "Tequila Effect," Mexico's monetary crisis sent shock waves throughout Latin American financial markets and ruined the Salinas administration's reputation for economic reform. Inflation surged, thousands of small businesses closed and the country was pushed into a deep recession.

The United States contributed $20 billion to an international financial aid package in early 1995 to help prop up the faltering economy. The peso's downfall even cut deep into a hallmark of Mexican *machismo*: Job cutbacks and shrinking expense accounts forced many wealthy businessmen and politicians to say *adios* to their mistresses. But economic recovery began in earnest in 1996, and by 1997 Mexico had fully repaid its debt to the United States.

The peso's value has never really recovered to pre-devaluation levels, hovering at around 10 pesos to the U.S. dollar since 1998. Greater tourist buying power was somewhat dampened by a 1995 increase in the value-added (I.V.A.) tax from 10 to 15 percent. Even so, visitors with dollars to convert will find a country eager to accept them.

PEOPLE

The Mexican people are a vibrant and complex group, despite being the product of a historical legacy that is in many ways tragic and divisive. And just as the country is a land of extremes—from baked desert to dripping jungle, from craggy mountain to swampy coast—there are differences among the people as well. You'll likely encounter both ostentatious wealth and startling poverty, impeccable politeness and stony indifference, gracious manners and leering *machismo*.

THE INDIGENAS

When Hernán Cortés arrived in 1519, the land now comprising Mexico was inhabited by some 15 to 20 million people, a number of whom were under the savage domination of the Aztecs. Many lived in the elevated plateau region of central Mexico, where the weather and soil were most favorable for agriculture. By 1521, a handful of Spanish *conquistadores* had toppled the vast Aztec empire and went on to subjugate an entire country; their sweeping destruction of pre-Hispanic achievements ranks as one of history's great cultural calamities.

After the Conquest, Spaniards came to New Spain, amassed riches and returned to the mother country. The Indians, meanwhile, were put to work in the silver mines, toiled in fields or performed backbreaking manual labor constructing lavish cathedrals and public buildings, laboring side by side with Africans brought into the country for the same purpose. Although the Spanish contributed only minimally to growth—during 300 years of rule only about 300,000 settled in Mexico—a combination of introduced diseases, cultural upheaval and strict suppression decimated the natives.

The Indians, or *indígenas*, living in Mexico today—an estimated 15 percent of the total population—are direct descendants of the Aztec, Maya and other ancient civilizations. These natives speak a primary language other than Spanish, and many might express surprise if referred to as "Mexican." Some are small groups living in self-sufficient isolation; others occupy large territories. While it is convenient for the sake of categorization to lump all Indians together, Mexico's native peoples are characterized by linguistic and cultural differences that can be as distinct as those defining Norwegians and Italians.

Approximately 50 of the numerous ethnic groups populating Mexico at the time of the Spanish arrival remain in existence. They include the **Tarahumara**, who dwell in the Copper Canyon region of northwest Mexico; the **Yaqui,** in the state of Sonora; the **Huichol** and the **Tarasco**, near and along the central Pacific coast; the **Nahua** and the **Otomí**, in the central plateau region; the **Zapotec** and the **Mixtec**, in the state of Oaxaca; the **Chamula**, **Tzeltal** and **Tzotzil**, in the state of Chiapas; the **Huastec**, along the eastern Gulf of Mexico coast; and the **Maya**, throughout the Yucatán Peninsula.

The status of *indígenas* in today's Mexico, unfortunately, is not much better than it was during the colonial era. Poverty is a chronic, debilitating fact of life for more than three-quarters of the country's Indian communities, including many in the economically challenged states of Chiapas, Guerrero and Oaxaca. Indian rights—particularly the demand for self-rule—has been a thorny issue for the Mexican government since the January 1994 uprising led by the Zapatistas. Life is still hard for "Mexico's most forgotten people," as many *indígenas* refer to themselves, but their plight has garnered international attention and forced ongoing government negotiations.

MESTIZOS AND THE "THOUSAND FAMILIES"

The great majority of Mexicans—75 percent—are *mestizos,* of mixed European and Native American descent. They have perhaps the strongest sense of national identity, although occupying various levels of prosperity and social standing. The small percentage of citizens of purely European ancestry—some 10 percent of the population and often referred to as the "Thousand Families"—control the country's political power and economic wealth, just as the Spanish did more than 3 centuries earlier.

There are signs of change, however. The PRI's 1997 political defeats came largely at the hands of the youth vote. An estimated 65 percent of the population is under age 30, and this new generation of Mexicans may prove to be as influential on the nation's economics and culture as the baby boomers have been in the United States.

Mexico is the second most populous country in Latin America after Brazil. Within its 31 states and the Federal District live nearly 100 million citizens—up from just 30 million in 1950. But over the last 35 years the fertility rate has fallen dramatically, and this generational shift has resulted in a trend toward smaller families that will have far-reaching social and economic effects.

LANGUAGE

Spanish is the official language, and Mexico is the world's most populous Spanish-speaking country. Indian dialects are still spoken, mostly in the Yucatán Peninsula and in the states of Chiapas, Oaxaca, Veracruz, Guerrero, Michoacán, Nayarit, Chihuahua and Sonora. For *indígenas* Spanish, if spoken at all, is a second language. Mexico also is a country where any attempt to speak Spanish, no matter how halting, is usually welcomed by the locals. When words won't come, gestures can express a world of meaning.

THE MEXICAN CHARACTER

Many Mexicans have a strong streak of fatalism. The country has weathered hurricanes, erupting volcanoes and severe earthquakes, particularly the one that leveled parts of Mexico City in 1985. More telling is the violence associated with history. Aztec ceremonies revolved around blood-spattered human sacrifice, with hearts literally torn from victims' chests. The Spanish conquest wiped out entire cities. Post-independence Mexico endured war, revolution, assassination and civil strife. Death is thus both honored and mocked in such celebrations as the **Day of the Dead**, when decorated sugar skulls are sold, costumed children bear mock coffins in street parades and families pay tribute to deceased members in front of lavish home altars.

El Caracol (The Snail) is a notable ruin at Chichén Itzá, the Yucatán Peninsula's best-known archeological site.   ©Chris Sharp

But despite a tumultuous past, Mexicans know how to have fun. They give priority to family and holidays. On weekends, city dwellers exit the concrete jungle en masse for beaches, parks and lakeside resorts. A minor saint's day is reason enough to hold a fiesta, and the birthday of a national hero or the date commemorating an important historical or religious event merits a major celebration.

ARCHITECTURE

Mexico is particularly rich with reminders of its earliest architects' work. Innumerable archeological sites—some little more than a few earthen mounds or a crumbling platform, others the spectacular remains of cities—have left behind intriguing clues related to the puzzle of their abandoned cultures.

EARLY BUILDERS

The first great architects were the Maya. They constructed numerous ceremonial centers connected by straight, wide roadways of crushed limestone called *sacbe*. Their buildings took three main forms: the pyramid, often with a temple capping the summit; the palace, consisting of a central court surrounded by chambers; and the ball court, a wide, flat area used for playing a mysterious but presumably sacred ball game.

Another early site is the ceremonial center of **Teotihuacán**, northeast of present-day Mexico City. Researchers have never been able to determine who built the city, although it was later inhabited by the Toltecs. Teotihuacán featured architecture on a monumental scale. Pyramids with sloping sides created an impression of great mass. They were adorned with stucco reliefs, murals and the carved heads of gods that frequently resembled animals. The Zapotecs, who dominated the Valley of Oaxaca in southern Mexico, created **Monte Albán**, a ceremonial center on top of a hilltop they flattened themselves. Its ball court, raised platforms and temples bear the influence of Teotihuacán, Maya architects and the Pre-Classic Olmec people, who inhabited the coastal regions of the present-day states of Tabasco and Veracruz.

Mexican pyramids did not necessarily resemble the familiar form of the Egyptian variety—a square base with four sloping, triangular sides meeting at the top. Created essentially as religious monuments, they frequently had steps built into the sides. Exterior carvings not only served as decoration but also depicted historical and mythological events. The ceremonial centers from which these pyramids rose were dedicated to fanciful gods and paid tribute to the priest rulers who presided over rigidly hierarchical societies.

The medium of choice was stone, a common building material in Mexico and one suitable for long-lasting creations. Frequently employed was a porous, volcanic rock known as *tezontle*, also used by the Aztecs. Although the sheer scope of the structures is awe-inspiring, other archeological remnants—for example, the free-standing arch at Labná, on the Yucatán Peninsula—hint at the direction in which the Maya and other early architects might have headed.

Subsequent tribes such as the Toltecs, Mixtecs and Aztecs expanded on the architectural themes developed by the great Classic civilizations. Pyramids and palaces continued in importance, serving the needs of highly complex religious ceremonies. It was a period of military maneuvers and violent conquest, and the murals, carvings and bas-reliefs applied as decoration depicted scenes of war and human sacrifice.

EUROPEAN INFLUENCE

The arrival of Spain in the early 16th century brought an abrupt end to Indian achievements, as most of the existing civilizations were destroyed. The conquerors frequently chose such razed ground as the place to begin their own construction. The Spanish conquest ushered in a 300-year period during which ecclesiastical architecture predominated, often imitating prevailing European trends.

Augustinian, Dominican, Franciscan and Jesuit friars built churches throughout Mexico as part of a large-scale attempt to convert the natives to Christianity. These structures, distinguished by thick walls and simple interiors with vaulted ceilings, were impressively fortified to serve as protection against Indian attack. A monastery built around an enclosed patio was usually connected to the church. Decoration also served an educational purpose, as frescoes and stone carvings vividly depicted the symbolic themes of the new religion.

Several decorative motifs were developed to enhance the aesthetics of the buildings themselves. A combination dome and tower often was used; the dome, constructed of arched masonry, frequently was covered with colorful tiles arranged in geometric designs. Plateresque decoration foreshadowed the more extravagant flourishes of the 17th and 18th centuries. The word comes from the Spanish *platero,* or silversmith, and the delicate ornamentation that often was placed around doorways or entrances resembled silverwork designs. The **Convento de San Agustín Acolman** (Convent of San Agustín Acolman) in the town of Acolman, México, and the doorway of the **Casa de Montejo** (Montejo House) in Mérida, Yucatán, are two good examples of the Plateresque style.

The wealth amassed from Mexico's silver and gold mines and from the huge sugar-producing

© John Neubauer

haciendas (plantations) led to a spate of ostentatious construction in the 17th and 18th centuries. The baroque style, characterized by lavish ornamentation, came into popularity, and baroque cathedrals began springing up in the central plazas of cities throughout the country. Notable examples are the **Catedral Metropolitana** (Metropolitan Cathedral) and the **Iglesia de Santo Domingo** (Church of Santo Domingo) in Mexico City and the **Cathedral of the Immaculate Conception** in Puebla.

The ultimate baroque expression was a Mexican development known as Churrigueresque, or ultra-baroque. It was named after Spanish artisan José de Churriguera, whose own work, curiously, was much more restrained. Buildings exploded with carved geometric forms, leafy vines, frolicking cherubs, scrolls and other imaginative accents, often to the point that formal structure seemed an afterthought.

The style extended inside as well, and Churrigueresque interiors were a cornucopia of extravagant embellishment, often executed in gold. The overall intent was literally to knock one's eyes out. Stunning examples of this ornate style are the **Iglesia de San Francisco Xavier** (Church of San Francisco Xavier) in Tepotzotlán, México; the **Iglesia de Santa Clara** (Church of Santa Clara) and the **Iglesia de Santa Rosa de Viterbo** (Church of Santa Rosa de Viterbo), both in the

city of Querétaro; the **Cathedral** in the city of Zacatecas; and the interior of the **Iglesia de Santo Domingo** (Church of Santo Domingo) in the city of Oaxaca.

Another form used in Mexico during this period was *mudéjar,* derived from the Spanish Moors. The *mudéjar* style also favored lavish decoration; interiors and exteriors were plastered with colored tiles. Puebla is particularly noted for churches with intricate tiled designs; a secular example is the **Casa de los Azulejos** (House of Tiles) in Mexico City, a former mansion occupied since 1919 by a Sanborn's restaurant.

After the excesses of the Churrigueresque, something had to give. The end of the colonial era saw a return to the more restrained neoclassic style. Buildings often incorporated several styles of architecture, however. Sometimes more than a century passed before work was finished; as a result, influences overlapped, particularly on the larger cathedrals. Mexico City's massive Metropolitan Cathedral took 240 years of off-and-on construction to complete; its facade shows is primarily baroque but also exhibits neoclassic elements, while the ornamentation of the altars is Churrigueresque.

During much of the the 19th century Mexican life was disrupted by war and political turbulence, and architectural development was given short shrift. When relative prosperity returned under dictator Porfirio Díaz, a new round of public buildings appeared, mostly massive structures in a variety of styles that again imitated what was happening in Europe. Mexico City's **Palacio de Bellas Artes** (Palace of Fine Arts) was designed and executed by Italian architects following classic blueprints. Mérida's ornate mansions took on a Parisian influence, as wealthy hemp exporters strove to emulate the refined atmosphere of that French city.

THE MODERN ERA

The early 20th century found Mexican architects struggling for a style to call their own. Attempts at monumentality produced such misguided curiosities as the gigantic statue of José María Morelos, a hero of the Mexican War of Independence. Built on an island in Lake Pátzcuaro, it depicts an ungainly-looking figure reaching toward the sky. Skyscrapers began to sprout in industrial centers like Mexico City and Monterrey, but their functional steel and concrete construction tended to resemble the tall buildings found in any big city.

In the last half of the century, innovative architecture has resulted from the combination of old and new elements. The **National University of Mexico** (UNAM) in San Angel, a southern suburb of Mexico City, was an attempt to create a central campus by integrating facilities into a landscape of barren volcanic rock. Many of the principal campus buildings are covered with colorful mosaics in patterns that recall Mexico's pre-Hispanic cultures. The modernist complex attracted international attention when it opened in the 1950s.

Also in Mexico City is the **National Museum of Anthropology**. This outstanding museum is designed with great open spaces; its centerpiece is a rock patio shaded by a ceiling with support lent by a single column. The style is contemporary, while at the same time reminiscent of the past. Other examples of the old/new blend are evident at the luxury end of hotel construction that has taken place over the past 2 decades or so. In megaresorts like Acapulco and Cancún, a property in the shape of an ancient pyramid will offer palatial appointments and every up-to-the-minute convenience.

One of the latest examples is the **National Center of the Arts**, inaugurated in 1994. The complex, south of downtown Mexico City, contains separate schools of music, film, drama and dance, as well as a library, theater, concert hall and a multimedia arts center. It was planned by Mexican architect Ricardo Legorreta, with contributions from six other architects. The center incorporates such futuristic forms as a central tower studded with exaggerated window frames and painted a vivid orange. A lecture hall, on the other hand, employs a cruciform layout that echoes the mission churches built during the colonial era. Some critics questioned constructing a showy complex at the expense of addressing some of the country's social needs, but there is no doubt that the buildings themselves represent an emerging architectural style that is distinctly Mexican.

ART

Although sizable remnants of pre-Hispanic Mexican architecture survive today, the same unfortunately cannot be said of that era's art. Early painters used walls as their canvases; the ravages of time and the elements—not to mention destruction by the Spaniards—obliterated much of the work of Mesoamerican artists. Museums are today's repositories. The **National Museum of Anthropology** in Mexico City contains the country's finest and most comprehensive pre-Hispanic collection, both original objects and reproductions. Mexican artistic expression varies significantly when viewed from the perspective of three broad historical periods: pre-Hispanic, colonial and post-independence.

SERVING SOCIETY

The various Mesoamerican civilizations, while spanning more than 2,000 years and differing as to specifics of location, duration and identifying features, were still unified in several overall respects. Authoritarian governments were based upon a religious framework; a strict hierarchical organization was followed; and economic self-sufficiency depended upon the successful harvesting of corn. Kings and priests were the rulers, and the rigid societies over which they presided were not conducive to experimentation or innovation. But in a social structure where everyone had his or her place, sculptors, potters and other artisans were free to focus on developing their skills.

Most Mesoamerican art was functionally decorative, adorning the exteriors of temples and pyramids. Creative self-expression was not unknown, even if it tended to result in likenesses of gods and mythical figures. The Pre-Classic **Olmecs**, best known for their monumental stone heads, also produced miniature jade carvings. Artisans in the ceremonial center of **Teotihuacán** fashioned painted pottery and stone masks inlaid with precious gems. The **Zapotecs** of the Valley of Oaxaca created ornamental urns, often in the form of gods whose clothing, jewelry and headdresses were rendered in great detail.

The greatest artistic achievements of the **Maya** were architectural, although they also were accomplished potters, sculptors (of jade figurines) and painters; the most famous examples of the latter skill are the murals at **Bonampak**, in the jungles of southeastern Chiapas state. Another important Maya art form was the *codice*, a document that combined painting and pictographic writing. *Codices* described wars and other historical events and were applied to animal skins or papyrus-like parchment sheets. Sadly, almost all of them were burned under the orders of the Spanish conquerors.

Building decoration—often incorporating such militaristic images as human warriors, eagles, jaguars and plumed serpents—characterized much **Toltec** art. Another typical Toltec motif was the reclining chac-mool figure, equipped with a receptacle for holding hearts torn from sacrificial victims. Discovered at a number of different archeological sites, the figure has become a familiar representation of Mesoamerican sculpture. Warlike imagery reached its apex with the **Aztecs**, who continually engaged in conflict and conquest until they themselves were vanquished.

THE COLONIAL PERIOD

With the establishment of New Spain and the beginning of 3 centuries of colonial rule, painting and sculpture revolved almost entirely around religious themes, in keeping with the Spanish desire to inculcate the doctrines of the Catholic church. Artistic creativity was poured into the construction of imposing cathedrals, replete with elaborate decoration both inside and out. For the most part, transplanted Spanish painters copied the styles of European masters; it wasn't until the 18th century that Indian artists and Mexican-born Spaniards began to make their creative mark. One of the colonial period's most celebrated painters was **Miguel Cabrera**, a Zapotec Indian whose prolific output filled Mexican churches. His contemporary, **José Ibarra**, emulated the Spanish master Bartolomé Esteban Murillo.

The turbulent post-independence years produced few noteworthy talents. One noteworthy figure was landscape painter **José María Velasco**, one of the first Mexican artists to focus on his own country as a subject. **José Guadalupe Posada**, a Guadalajaran engraver and political satirist, became known in the late 19th century for his humorous caricatures of ordinary citizens and national figures.

AFTER THE REVOLUTION

It was in the 20th century that an indisputably Mexican form of art emerged, and its catalyst was the Revolution of 1910. Just as that bloody upheaval eventually resulted in a new sense of nationalism, Mexico's 20th-century masters turned their backs on European imitation and instead began to examine their own traditions and pre-Hispanic roots. Leading the way were three muralists—**Diego Rivera**, **José Clemente Orozco** and **David Alfaro Siqueiros**. Although they differed stylistically, each man echoed the spirit of the revolution, the importance of the common worker, and Mexico's place in the modern world.

Mérida dancers in traditional dress   ©Chris Sharp

Rivera, probably the most celebrated of the three, created works of social and political propaganda. Many of his murals are on display in the **Palace of Fine Arts**, the **Ministry of Public Education** and the **Diego Rivera Mural Museum**, all in Mexico City. Orozco, a zealous patriot as well as a recluse, created paintings with similar themes that were distinguished by a dynamic intensity. Some of this native Jaliscan's best-known works can be seen at the **Cabañas Cultural Institute** and the **Government Palace**, both in Guadalajara.

Siqueiros, the most artistically innovative, also was the most passionately committed to social reform, going to jail on on more than one occasion for engaging in revolutionary activities. His work is on view at Mexico City's **Polyforum Siqueiros**. Another important 20th-century artist, **Rufino Tamayo**, first gained recognition abroad. A Zapotec Indian influenced by cubism, Tamayo depicted Mexican themes but was less explicitly political than his three contemporaries.

Women artists have had a harder time achieving recognition in Mexico's *machismo*-dominated culture. Despite that handicap, the country's best-known modern artist, male or female, may well be **Frida Kahlo**. A childhood victim of polio, and severely injured in a bus accident at age 18, Kahlo lived a life of pain, which often was reflected in her bizarrely surrealistic self-portraits. She was married to Diego Rivera for 25 years, and both artists were committed to preserving Mexico's rich indigenous heritage. The **Frida Kahlo Museum**, in the Mexico City suburb of Coyoacán, occupies an adobe house that was her lifelong residence.

Mexico's contemporary artists employ a diversity of styles to celebrate their own cultural roots. Some of the most original work these days is coming out of Oaxaca, a thoroughly Indian city and capital of the same-named state in south-central Mexico. One of the leaders of the current Oaxacan movement is **Francisco Toledo**, a Zapotec Indian who studied under Tamayo. The work of Toledo, **Sergio Hernández** and other Oaxaqueños incorporates nature, myth, historical fact and symbolic fantasy, sometimes all in the same painting. Their range of technique is equally broad, employing tortoise shells as well as the painter's traditional canvas.

MUSIC AND DANCE

To a Mexican, a love of music is as fundamental a pleasure as the loving bonds of family. The country's musical traditions are exceedingly rich and abundantly varied. As with architecture and art, styles have tended to originate elsewhere before being assimilated and frequently adapted to suit the national preferences: passion, romance and insistent rhythms. Popular folk and dance music in particular vividly evokes the sights, sounds and moods of the country.

A broad distinction can be made between the music of Mexico's *indígena* and *mestizo* groups. Indian musical expression is ceremonial in nature, linked to religious rituals or village fiestas. Within the dominant, mixed *mestizo* population, on the other hand, music has a genuinely mass appeal that is strengthened by a healthy recording industry, ceaseless radio play and impromptu performances that enliven the central plazas of practically every town in the country.

FROM MARIMBA TO MARIACHI

Little is known about what sort of sounds were created by pre-Hispanic civilizations. Music, singing and dancing did, however, play a large role in daily ceremonial life. The mesmerizing beat of the drum was foremost among ancient instruments. Drums were fashioned out of clay, wood, bones and turtle shells. Rattles complemented the beat, and simple reed or clay flutes added a melodic counterpoint. It may well have sounded similar to what can be heard in some Indian villages today.

Spanish *conquistadores* and the missionaries who followed them imported European culture, which began to have an influence on native song and dance. Folk orchestras began to accommodate new instruments, chief among them various types of guitars. The son (also called **huapango**), a driving dance rhythm with plenty of instrumental flourishes, is the basic form of *mestizo* music. Regional styles have different names, such as **son huasteco** (northeastern Mexico), **son jarana** (the Yucatán Peninsula), **son jarocho** (around Veracruz) or **son mariachi** (the state of Jalisco). Whatever the region, the guitar is the lead instrument, replaced by violin in the huasteco style and harp in the jarocho style.

Another of Mexico's traditional sounds is that of the **marimba**, a percussion instrument similar to a xylophone. When struck with small rubber mallets, the marimba's hardwood bars produce clear, breezy-sounding tones. Marimba music is most commonly heard in southern Mexico and Guatemala, where on fiesta days town plazas resonate with lively rhythms, sputtering firecrackers and all manner of merriment.

Popular Mexican songs have long evoked the trials and tribulations of daily life. The **corrido**, a folk narrative descended from Spanish balladry, emerged during the turbulent period of the 1910 Revolution and served as a news service of sorts in the days before radio. In exchange for a meal, wandering minstrels would travel from one rural town to another, singing songs about historical events, heroes, villains and the travails of unrequited love. The **canción** (literally, song or lyric) was usually a slow, unabashedly sentimental ballad appealing to the passionate aspect of Mexican character. No less dramatic were the

rancheras, nostalgic paeans to home and country originally sung by Mexican cattlemen, thus giving them a sort of country-and-western flavor.

The music most emblematic of Mexico is the sound of the **mariachis**. The custom of hiring a group of professional musicians to play at weddings, birthdays and other special occasions began in the state of Jalisco; "mariachi" is said to be an adaptation of the French word *mariage*. Mariachi bands deck themselves out in the costumes of the *charro*, or Mexican cowboy: tight-fitting pants, wide-brimmed sombreros and lots of silver spangles. Today they can be found all over Mexico—regaling foreign tourists in flashy Cancún, playing to homesick laborers in border towns, or serenading the object of a young suitor's desire—all for a fee, of course.

Mariachi bands started out playing guitars, violins and harp, with the harp later replaced largely by the brassy sound of trumpets. The style reached its peak in the 1950s, when Mexican matinee idols in Hollywood films sang their love songs to the strains of mariachis. The two best places for visitors to see them in action today are **Plaza Garibaldi** in Mexico City and **Plaza de los Mariachis** in Guadalajara. A mariachi band worth its salt will be able to reel off an astonishing variety of songs, from long-established classics to customer requests in styles from achingly sad to irresistibly upbeat—and all delivered with undeniable heart and soul.

With the shrinking of the global village over the last couple of decades, Mexico—like many countries throughout the world—has been exposed to a tidal wave of Americanized pop culture. In the cities, radios, bars and dance clubs *(discotecas)* blare the latest pop, rock and hip-hop. 'N Sync, Ricky Martin, Christina Aguilera and other international acts are as popular here as anywhere. But despite the invasion, music with a Mexican feeling continues to thrive.

Norteña, appropriately, originated in the working-class *cantinas* and speak-easies of the northern border area. Springing from the corrida tradition of lyric-driven balladry, norteña songs often spin tales involving small-time thieves, drug runners, illegal immigrants and other antiheroes who buck a system they consider crooked. Musically, norteña is like a Mexican polka, with the accordion typically the lead instrument.

Cumbia, a seductive, danceable import from the Caribbean, was the most popular music in Mexico in the 1980s; the songs are distinguished by their flirtatious lyrics, often spiced with double entendres. Equally danceable **salsa**, which originated in Cuba and Puerto Rico and is influenced by jazz and rock, is popular as well. **Banda** is currently booming in Mexico. These musicians play various popular styles, all arranged with an emphasis on brass and percussion. Concerts given by brass bands fill parks and town halls throughout the country.

All of these influences—spliced together with bits of American rock 'n' roll, pop, country, jazz and rap—combine to produce **tejano**, a cross-cultural musical blend embraced by Americans of Mexican descent. The center of tejano music is Texas (specifically, the gulf coast city of Corpus Christi), although its popularity extends south of the border as well. Tejano's rising star, a young woman named Selena who was sometimes referred to as the "Mexican Madonna," actually hailed from Corpus Christi and was taught Spanish by her father to further her career. Selena was about to break into the English-language market when she was murdered in 1995 by her fan-club president.

POLE FLYERS, HATS AND LITTLE OLD MEN

Rich in history and spectacle, native folk dances are one of Mexico's most enjoyable traditions for visitors. They include those that predate the Spanish arrival, as well as European dances adapted to suit the Mexican character. Although the *conquistadores* initially tried to eradicate what they viewed as simply pagan rites, Franciscan and Dominican missionaries encouraged the continuation of Indian dances and wove these age-old rituals into their ongoing efforts to convert the natives to the Catholic church. The symbolism may have been changed—substituting Moors and Christians in place of warring tribes, for instance—but the costumes and movements remained essentially the same.

Like musical styles, folk dances vary by region. Around Papantla in the state of Veracruz, Totonac Indians still perform the flying pole dance, originally a ceremony meant to appease the rain gods. Five elaborately costumed, daredevil young men climb to a small platform atop a pole. Four of them leap from this lofty perch with ropes tied to their ankles, circling the pole as they spin through the air. The fifth dancer stays on the revolving platform, beating a drum and playing a flute. Thirteen revolutions are made in all, symbolizing the number of months in the Aztec calendar. The flying pole dance—like a few other *indígena* rituals—has shed its original meaning in the process of becoming a tourist spectacle, albeit an unfailingly entertaining one. Today, performing groups known as the **Voladores de Papantla** (Papantla Flyers) execute their crowd-pleasing acrobatics at various locations throughout the country—for pesos, not rainstorms.

In the northern states of Sonora and Chihuahua, Yaqui and Tarahumara Indians perform the **deer dance**, a ceremony once meant to impart good luck on the hunt. A dancer in this vivid re-enactment may even wear the stuffed head of a deer. **Los Viejitos**, the "Dance of the Little Old Men," originated in the state of Michoacán. It is danced by young boys wearing masks carved to resemble the visages of elderly men. The dancers begin by moving arthritically in a parody of old age; by the end, however, their pace has enlivened considerably.

Popular traditional dances are based, not surprisingly, on Spanish steps. Perhaps the one most widely known and closely associated with the country is the **Jarabe Tapatío**, or Mexican hat dance. The costumes for this passionate interlude are flamboyant: for men, the silver-embroidered shirt and trousers and wide-brimmed sombrero of the horseman *(charro)*; for women, the national costume, a *china poblana* dress. The dance ends with the man's sombrero placed on the floor and the couple parading around it.

Aside from going to an actual village fiesta, the best place to observe the amazing variety and colorful theatrics of Mexican native dance is to attend a performance of the world-famous **Ballet Folklórico** at Mexico City's Palacio de Bellas Artes *(see "Concerts" under Mexico City, page 326)*. The Ballet Folklórico of the University of Guadalajara performs in that city's Degollado Theater. Folkloric dance troupes also tour the nation's cities. Hotels in Cancún, Acapulco, Puerto Vallarta and other beach resorts often present "Mexican Fiesta" nights that include a dinner buffet and dance performances. While these professional companies may be more along the lines of a floor show, their presentations are nevertheless a vibrant and colorful re-enactment of the real thing.

LITERATURE

When the *conquistadores* destroyed Maya and Aztec pyramids and temples in the course of their march through Mexico, they also did away with much of the country's linguistic heritage. Evidence suggests that pre-Hispanic civilizations had developed an extensive body of literature; for example, the writings of the poet-king **Netzahualcóyotl** of the pre-Aztec kingdom of Texcoco. The Spaniards, however, considered these and other documents, such as the Maya *codices* (hieroglyphic picture books) to be profane, and many of them were torched.

Although the first printed book appeared in 1535, a body of Mexican literature was very slow to develop. Spanish domination was oppressive, and there was little toleration for any written work save theological dogma. Some of the first non-religious writings were historical accounts of the Conquest. Spanish bishop **Diego de Landa**, the man singularly responsible for the destruction of the *codices*, authored "*Relación de las Cosas de Yucatán*," an account of Maya society in the immediate post-Conquest period. Historian **Bernal Díaz**, who accompanied

Hernán Cortés, wrote a fascinating eyewitness account of the Conquest, *"Historia Verdadera de la Conquista."*

Non-academic literature had to wait until the 17th century. Taxco-born **Juan Ruiz de Alarcón** was one of that era's distinguished playwrights, but perhaps the most celebrated author of the period was **Sor Juana Inés**. As a child Sor Juana demonstrated a remarkable intellect, but the colonial regime literally could not handle a woman with such ability. She entered a convent, an environment that allowed her to study science, art and literature. Sor Juana is remembered chiefly as a poet; her love poems were notable for their sensual overtones and feminist slant.

What is generally acknowledged as the first Mexican novel was published in the midst of the country's struggle for freedom—*"El Periquillo Sarniento,"* written by **José Fernández de Lizardi** under the pseudonym El Pensador Mexicano (The Mexican Thinker). An implied criticism of the status quo manifested in the author's ironic tone turned up in other novels of this period, which often had a historical backdrop. One of the first books to describe the country's natural charms was "Life in Mexico," a mid-19th-century travelogue written by **Frances Calderón de la Barca**, the Scottish wife of an early Spanish ambassador to Mexico.

20TH-CENTURY WRITERS

It was not until after the 1910 Revolution that Mexican writers began to receive international recognition. Their themes often dealt with the search for a national identity after a century of political and societal upheaval. Perhaps the most highly regarded was Nobel prize-winning essayist **Octavio Paz**, who died in 1998. His *"El Laberinto de la Soledad"* ("The Labyrinth of Solitude"), a book-length essay ruminating on the modern Mexican character, addressed—like many of his writings—the paradoxes inherent in the contrast between Indian and Spanish heritages. The most widely known outside Mexico is **Carlos Fuentes**, whose novels are representative of a literary movement known as magic realism. Blurring the distinctions between past and present and fantasy and reality, magic realism was defined by the work of **Juan Rulfo**, whose novel *"Pedro Páramo"* depicts one man's investigation of his father's memory.

Contemporary authors are just as likely to explore Mexican themes. "Like Water for Chocolate," by **Laura Esquivel**, is the romantic tale of a woman determined to win back her true love after he marries her sister; it was adapted into a hugely popular arthouse film. And squarely aimed at the masses are the pop-culture *revistas*, serialized "novels" covering a range of subjects from romance to science fiction. They share several characteristics with comic books, notably color pictures, running plots and a pulpy style of writing.

FOOD AND DRINK

Authentic Mexican dishes have many influences, among them Maya, Aztec, Spanish, French, Moorish and even Chinese. There is much more to the cuisine, however, than the commonly mistaken notion that it is always hot. Many items that are in use throughout the world originated in Mexico. Corn is the country's greatest contribution to global cookery, but the list also includes tomatoes, chocolate, avocados, squashes, beans, pumpkins, chilies and turkeys (the only bird bred in pre-Hispanic Mexico).

Corn, the centerpiece of the Indian diet, took on an almost magical significance in many cultures, being used in religious rituals and ceremonies. Called *teoxintle* until the Spaniards renamed it *maíz*, the different corn varieties enabled native cooks to put this versatile vegetable to assorted uses—grinding kernels to make tortillas, thickening soups, creating beverages.

Squash and beans were other basic foodstuffs, providing practical as well as nourishing applications. Gourds, for example, were fashioned into handy household items. The cacao bean, from which chocolate is made, was so valued that the Indians used it for money, and hot chocolate whipped into a fragrant froth was at one time a drink quaffed only by the upper classes. Another native plant highly prized in pre-Hispanic kitchens was the nopal (prickly pear) cactus. Its juicy fruit was cooked and added to soups and stews, or stuffed with meat. Nopal cactus pads are a common sight in Mexican markets today.

It was with chilies, however, that early cooks could fully utilize their creative talents. Using the entire chile ensured maximum firepower, while removing the veins or seeds lessened the fiery impact. Although eaten alone as a garnish, chilies most often contributed to sauces—either **salsa**, made from a combination of ingredients, or **mole** (MOH-leh), a blend of chilies.

All of this native bounty must have mesmerized the Spanish *conquistadores* who arrived in Mexico. Bernal Díaz, a historian who marched with Hernán Cortés, described the *tianguis* (marketplace in the Aztec language) at Tlatelolco, an important trading center located just north of present-day Mexico City. Wild game included pigeon, duck, rabbit, deer, boar and iguana. From fresh water came frog legs and the larvae of water gnats. Many of the exotic fruits, vegetables and herbs—among them chilies, avocado, cilantro, cumin, papaya, mango, guava and jicama—the Spaniards had never before seen.

The Spanish themselves influenced the native cuisine, introducing cattle, sheep, goats, pigs, chickens, sugar, olive oil, rice, citrus fruits, lettuce, pepper, cinnamon and other products. Many of Mexico's most enduring dishes were developed in the Spanish convents by nuns, who had the time and patience to painstakingly combine spices, herbs and chilies into complex sauces. Eggs, lard, sugar and milk formed the basis for pastries and candies, as well as new, improved versions of the traditional tortilla. The invading French also added to the culinary mix. Wine, butter and cream added a refined touch to sauces, and such herbs as dill and mustard lent flavor to French soufflés, omelettes and pâtes.

MEXICAN STAPLES

Corn anchors the Mexican diet. The **tortilla**, also common in Central America, is as ubiquitous in Mexico as a hamburger in the United States. This thin pancake made of coarse cornmeal appears in many guises. A basket of warm flour tortillas frequently replaces bread or rolls on a Mexican table. **Tacos** are rolled tortillas stuffed with beef, pork, chicken or cheese and customarily seasoned with avocado, onion, lettuce and chile sauce. When served with tomato sauce, soft rolled tacos are called **enchiladas**.

Crisp fried tortillas spread with minced chicken, meat or salad are called **tostadas**. Tortilla dough turnovers filled with cheese are **quesadillas**; when filled with potato, pork sausage (chorizo) or fried beans and then fried in fat, they are **empanadas**. **Tamales** are a mixture of corn and rice dough filled with bits of chicken, pork or sweets, wrapped in corn husks or banana leaves and then steamed. **Tortas**, the Mexican counterpart of sandwiches, are prepared with a small loaf of bread called **telera** or **bolillo** and then filled with different meats, lettuce, onion, tomato, cheese and avocado.

Other prevalent dishes are those made of either **frijoles** (beans) cooked in various ways or rice combined with vegetables, chicken livers, plantains or eggs. **Guacamole** is a salad or side dish that consists of mashed avocado seasoned with onion, hot peppers and tomato.

FESTIVE AND REGIONAL FARE

The nation's favorite special preparation is **mole de guajolote**, turkey served with a rich, thick sauce made from various chilies, peanuts, spices, sesame seed and unsweetened chocolate. As many as 30 different ingredients, all of which must be ground or pureed, may go into the sauce's preparation.

Another distinctly Mexican concoction is **chiles rellenos**, or stuffed chilies. A dark green chili pepper—not the sweet bell variety popular in the United States—is stuffed with cheese or ground meat, fried in a coating of egg batter and then simmered in tomato sauce. A variation of this dish is called **chile en nogada**. Instead of tomato sauce, the chili (stuffed with beef, pork and

fruits) is covered with ground fresh walnuts and a pureed white cheese similar to cream cheese. When sprinkled with red pomegranate seeds and garnished with parsley, the dish represents the red, white and green colors of the Mexican flag. It is frequently served in conjunction with independence celebrations during the month of September.

If you're fond of gastronomic adventure, Mexico has some exotic choices. At the time of the Spanish arrival, the staple diet of the Indians included such items as grasshoppers, ant eggs, rats, armadillos, monkeys, parrots and rattlesnakes. Fine restaurants in Mexico City and Oaxaca still offer insect dishes, including grasshoppers, ant eggs and the worm—crisply fried—found on the maguey plant, from which tequila is made. **Huitlacoche** is a black fungus that grows on ears of corn; it has been cultivated as a delicacy since before the Conquest and is often served with crepes. In the northern part of the country, broiled goat (*cabrito*) is popular.

Different areas of Mexico are known for their style of cooking or for specific dishes. In and around Veracruz the specialty is **huachinango a la Veracruzana**, red snapper broiled in tomato sauce and served with onions, olives and capers. Acapulco and other Mexican seaside towns are famous for their **ceviche** (say-VEE-cheh). Pieces of raw fish or shellfish are marinated in lime juice for at least 8 hours, "cooking" the fish. Chopped tomatoes and onions, chilies and such herbs as cilantro are then added to this dish, which is served chilled and often as an appetizer. In Baja California and the northwestern coastal cities, lobster and shrimp are scrambled into eggs, or replace chicken and pork as tamale fillings.

Historical and geographical isolation have had perhaps their greatest impact on regional cuisine in the Yucatán Peninsula. Here the food has Cuban, Caribbean, European and Asian influences. The fiery habanero chile common in Yucatecan cookery grows nowhere else in Mexico. **Achiote**, the seed of the annatto tree, is the primary ingredient of a pungent spice with a distinctive orange-red color that seasons pork, chicken or fish cooked *pibil* style—sort of a distant relative of American barbecue.

Yucatecan menus offer such authentic dishes as **cochinita pibil**, suckling pig rubbed with achiote, wrapped in banana leaves and baked in an underground oven; **puchero**, a Sunday supper staple of chicken, pork, carrots, squash, cabbage, bananas and sweet potatoes simmered in broth flavored with cilantro and sour orange juice, the whole garnished with radishes; and **huevos motuleños**, a filling breakfast dish featuring a tortilla covered with refried beans, topped with a fried egg and smothered with tomato sauce, peas, diced ham and shredded cheese, usually served with slices of fried banana.

Soups and Desserts

Soups are tasty and varied. Mexican chicken soup is laden with chunks of chicken, rice, vegetables and often sliced avocado. Rich cream soups are made from such unlikely vegetable by-products as squash blossoms. **Pozole**, a hearty soup native to the state of Jalisco but popular in many parts of Mexico, incorporates hominy and pork or chicken in a flavorful broth. Shredded lettuce, chopped onions, strips of fried tortilla and splashes of lime juice are frequently tossed in. This stewlike concoction also takes on red or green hues from the addition of ancho chilies or green tomatoes mixed with various greens, respectively. **Note:** Most Mexican chilies are hot, and some are incendiary. If in doubt about their firepower, ask, "Es muy picante?" ("Is it very hot?").

Desserts are not the focal point of a good Mexican meal. Many are overwhelmingly sweet. **Flan** (browned custard), which is widely served, is a Spanish creation. Although there is a large variety of egg-based, pudding-like sweets, a better choice would be one of the country's tropical fruits, such as papaya, passion fruit, pineapple or mango. Remember to avoid those that are unpeeled. Mexican confections, or **dulces**, are most often fruit-flavored hard candies, sugar-glazed fruits in their natural form or little cakes made of honey, grated coconut, almonds and other ingredients. Some restaurants feature good ice cream *(helado)*.

Beverages

A good way to begin the day in Mexico is to have a steaming cup of coffee. **Café de olla** is flavored with cinnamon and sugar, although you'll have to ask for cream (which usually turns out to be evaporated milk). Espresso and cappuccino are widely available—and undistinguished instant is frequently served in restaurants—but Mexicans favor **café con leche**, a combination of strong black coffee and hot milk that is often poured into a tall glass. Another favorite is Mexican hot chocolate, which is not as sweet as the American version.

Freshly squeezed fruit juices are inexpensive and refreshing. Ask for a **licuado** (fruit shake) made with bananas or papayas. Also inexpensive are soft drinks, the ubiquitous Coca-Cola as well as local brands (**refrescos**). They are not only safe to drink out of the can but one of the few luxuries that the country's poorer citizens can afford. Tehuacán, in the state of Puebla, is famous for bottled mineral waters made with and without natural fruit flavors. Local bottling plants draw from the mineral springs around the city.

Cerveza (beer) is as ubiquitous as Coke *("Coca")*. Two Mexican varieties—Corona and Tecate—are sold everywhere (the latter is the country's No. 1 cheap alcoholic beverage). Qual-

ity brews like Dos Equis and Bohemia are appreciated throughout the world.

Mexico's viticultural history was relatively late in developing. Although pre-Hispanic peoples enjoyed fermented beverages, those derived from the grape were not among them. Spanish colonists introduced the first vine cuttings, and Mexican wines soon began competing with those of the homeland. A marauding insect almost destroyed the grape crop in the late 19th century, but plague-resistant cuttings from California were grafted onto the diseased ones, saving the wine industry. Today almost 80 percent of all domestic vintages are produced in the state of Baja California. Other major wine-producing areas are in the states of Aguascalientes, Querétaro and Zacatecas.

From the several varieties of the maguey (mah-GAY) plant, a cactuslike jack-of-all-trades, come highly intoxicating liquors that are uniquely Mexican. **Tequila** is the quintessential one, traditionally downed from a salt-rimmed glass and immediately followed by a bite into a lime wedge. Bottles of **mezcal** from the vicinity of Oaxaca sometimes include a worm that lives on the plant. Other alcoholic beverages produced from the maguey are **comiteco** (Chiapas), **charanda** (Michoacán), **sotol** (Chihuahua) and **bacanora** (Sonora).

Pulque, manufactured in central Mexico from the maguey's unfermented juice, has less of a kick and is considered to have both nutritious and medicinal properties. **Colonche** is prepared in the states of Aguascalientes, Guanajuato, Jalisco and San Luis Potosí with fermented fruit from the prickly pear cactus. **Rompope** originated in the state of Puebla as a family beverage for festive occasions. Similar to eggnog, its ingredients include milk, egg yolks, sugar, vanilla, cinnamon and a dash of rum.

Dining Tips

In large cities, restaurants serving top-quality French, Italian or Continental cuisine are easy to find. But it's worth the effort to seek out places that focus on traditional Mexican cooking, which is not necessarily the tacos and enchiladas so common north of the border. Native foods can be found in smaller restaurants called *cenadurías, taquerías* or *merenderos*, which cater more to Mexican customers than to foreign tourists. In such establishments diners can order **carne en su jugo** (meat in its juice), tamales and a great variety of **antojitos** (snacks). The sign "Antojitos Mexicanos" indicates that these and other specialties are on the menu. An added bonus at these country-style restaurants are the shows, accompanied by mariachi music, often put on for diners.

Another way to sample local fare is to buy it off the street. Even the smallest town square will have vendors selling roasted meat, cut-up fruit,

Calavera figure   ©John Neubauer

over 2 or 3 hours are not nearly as common as they were a few decades ago. This is particularly true in the capital, where the vast majority of working-class citizens can afford only the barest culinary basics and lengthy business lunches are viewed as needlessly extravagant.

Gracious service is the rule rather than the exception. When you're ready for the check, simply say *"la cuenta, por favor"* ("the check, please"). Making scribbling motions on your hand to imply writing is commonly recognized international sign language.

Regardless of the establishment, always ask about policies and double check the total amount of the bill. You might assume, for example, that there are free refills for coffee when in actuality you'll be charged for each cup you drink (a free second cup is more common at breakfast). Some restaurants may compute the tab by adding up the number of glasses and plates on the table. The 15 percent I.V.A. service tax may be added (sometimes the charge is 17 percent, which includes local tax); again, double check the individual amounts. This does not take the place of a tip, so leave what you think is appropriate, usually 10 to 20 percent of the bill.

CELEBRATIONS

Perhaps the clearest view into the heart of a nation is through its celebrations. This is especially true in Mexico, with its distinctive yet endlessly varied blending of Indian and Hispanic cultures. Each town has its own traditions, stemming from centuries of ancestral practices and beliefs combined with the Christian influences introduced by the Spaniards.

FIESTAS

The country's most dynamic—and ubiquitous—special event is the **fiesta**. A fiesta takes place somewhere in Mexico every day of the year, in the tiniest villages and the biggest cities. There's much to celebrate; in addition to observing national holidays and such countrywide fiestas as Carnaval and the Day of the Dead, every town salutes its patron saint's day.

Fiestas take on myriad forms, but almost every one includes a parade. The procession is usually in association with a revered religious image but also can be secular in nature, often capped off by fireworks. Music, dancing and an array of local edibles are essential elements. Costumed dancers may portray historical, mythological or imagined happenings to the accompaniment of indigenous instruments. Sometimes there are regional or folkloric dances representative of the area or state; mariachi or harp ensembles are the usual accompaniment. The Yucatán, for example, has its evocative *jaranas*, danced by couples in white

soft drinks, sweets or other edibles. Levels of sanitation, however, vary greatly, and the advice of most veteran travelers who stay healthy is to avoid street vendor offerings.

For those accustomed to an early breakfast, Mexican restaurants are not particularly accommodating; many don't open until around 9 a.m. Markets, however, normally open early and are good places to pick up something for a morning meal. Another tip: Buy croissants or sweet rolls at a bakery the night before and have your own breakfast before starting the day.

Because many Mexicans make something of a ceremony out of meals, restaurant service tends to be slower than in the United States. If you follow the Mexican schedule for dining, you will have lunch no earlier than 2 p.m., cocktails at 7 p.m. and dinner at 9 or 10 p.m.

Lunch, or *la comida*, is the main meal of the day (*el almuerzo* also means lunch but tends to be a late morning snack eaten on the run). Many restaurants still offer a *comida corrida*, or lunch special, which usually includes soup, a main course, a dessert and coffee. For those on a budget, making lunch the big meal of the day is the most economical way to dine. As fast food becomes ever more common (there are more than 50 McDonald's restaurants in Mexico City alone) and the traditional midday siesta increasingly a thing of the past, multicourse meals drawn out costumes to the lilting sound of a band. Yucate-can fiestas, called *vaquerías*, brim with joy and merrymaking.

On a more official note is the observance of **Independence Day** on Sept. 16, commemorating the 1810 proclamation of the *Grito de Dolores,* a rallying cry for freedom from Spain, by Father Miguel Hidalgo y Costilla. The town of Dolores Hidalgo, where Father Hidalgo read the *Grito* from his parish church, still figures prominently in Independence Day festivities. The biggest celebration by far, however, is in Mexico City, where the huge *Zócalo* swarms with crowds and fireworks fill the air.

Religious Observances

Some of the Mexico's loveliest traditions center on Christmas, despite the American influence of Santa Claus and Christmas trees. Foremost are the **posadas**, which take place for 9 days beginning Dec. 16 and represent the search for an inn *(posada)* in preparation for the holy birth. Bearing candles and figures of Mary and Joseph, guests circle a house begging for a place to stay, but are refused until the Pilgrims are identified. After that the party begins, with hot punch, sweets and the breaking open of *piñatas*. More and more, gift giving is on Dec. 25, although in smaller towns presents are still exchanged on the traditional Twelfth Night, or Epiphany (Jan. 6).

Another Christmas season tradition is the presentation of **pastorelas** in public plazas, schools and theaters. Based on the events immediately before Jesus' birth, they often have a comic touch. Over time *pastorelas* have come to include in their cast of characters such historical figures as Aztec emperor Cuauhtémoc and revolutionary Emiliano Zapata, who take part as if they had lived during that first Nativity.

Mexico precedes the Lenten season with an uproarious celebration of **Carnaval**. Festivities usually begin on the Saturday before Ash Wednesday and end on Shrove Tuesday night, often with the burning of a papier-maché figure of Juan Carnaval to signal the beginning of Lent. Carnaval is particularly exuberant in Mazatlán and Veracruz.

The Lenten season culminates in **Semana Santa** (Holy Week) from Palm Sunday to Easter Sunday, which is marked by solemn *pastorelas* or a re-enactment of the Passion from Judgment to Resurrection. The young man chosen to portray Jesus undergoes rigorous preparation for his role, which in some places includes being whipped and then tied to a cross. Again, the observance often ends with the burning of a papier-maché figure, this time Judas. Many Holy Week celebrations also venerate the Virgin Mary, with processions bearing some form of her image.

Laughing at Death

Mexico's best-known celebration, one in which both Indian and Catholic traditions blend into a unique expression of love for the deceased, is *Los Dias de Muertos,* or **Days of the Dead**, which are celebrated on Nov. 1 and 2. A straightforward approach to the uncomfortable subject of mortality, the holiday—celebrated in Mexico for centuries—mixes mourning with macabre humor and pagan rites with the Catholic observances of All Souls' and All Saints' days.

Day of the Dead celebrations are similar to, although more serious than, the celebration of Halloween north of the border. But as with Christmas, the American influence has become pervasive, and some Mexican traditionalists worry that the proliferation of Halloween parties in Mexico City and elsewhere, as well as the sale of "spooky" items like vampire masks and plastic jack-o-lanterns, threatens to overshadow the meaning of their own holiday.

Families may honor departed loved ones by telling stories, eating candy skulls or even camping all night in the local cemetery, decorating gravesites, praying and sharing memories. The holiday tends to be downplayed by the wealthier and more educated segments of Mexican society as superstitious ritual or quaint religious holdover, although much of the country continues to explode each November with food, drink, flowers and skeletal figures (which are known as *calaveras;* literally, "skull"). The most traditional Day of the Dead celebration takes place on the island of Janitzio, in Lake Pátzcuaro, although local and regional variations abound.

The popular belief that the dead are permitted to visit their living kin provides the latter a chance to prepare sometimes ostentatious culinary offerings, which usually include sweet loaves of *pan de muerto* (bread of the dead). A lavish *ofrenda*, or altar, could include candles, mementos, pictures of the departed, a bottle of favorite liquor, dancing skeletons, a portrait of the Virgin of Guadalupe and a display of marigolds *(zempoalxóchitl)*, known as the "flower of the dead." Everyone sings, dances and prays, simultaneously sending up and accepting the inevitability of death.

Note: Many Mexicans travel during Holy Week and the Christmas holidays, and visitors should make hotel reservations in advance if planning to be in the country during those times. Local transportation systems tend to be jam-packed during Holy Week. For a listing of representative fiestas, fairs and celebrations in Mexico, *see "Fiestas and Holidays," page 446.*

OUTDOOR RECREATION

SPECTATOR SPORTS

The earliest known sport played in Mexico was a form of ball game; the ruins of courts on which it was played exist at various archeological sites. While the rules are unknown, it is believed that the final outcome for some of the players was death. Fortunately, today's organized recreational activities are decidedly safer. The national sport is **soccer**, played practically the entire year at Mexico City's Azteca Stadium and in other large cities. **Baseball** and **football** also are popular.

Bullfighting was introduced by the Spaniards shortly after the Conquest. More spectacle than sport, the bullfight, or *corrida de toros*, is an elaborate ceremony that begins with a parade and ends with the flamboyantly attired matador taking a—presumably—triumphant tour of the ring to the accolades of spectators while a team of mules drags away the dead bull. In between is a series of encounters between man and beast, kept thrilling by the matador's dramatic skill and by the continual goading of the animal with viciously barbed lances. While bullfighting is very much a part of Mexican lore, those with an aversion to such brutality would be better off not attending. Bullfights can be seen throughout the country but are regularly scheduled in Mexico City, Guadalajara and Tijuana.

Equally spectacular but more humanitarian are the Mexican **rodeos** called *charreadas*. The *charro*, a gentleman cowboy, competes in various displays of skill. These events, usually held on Sunday mornings, feature colorful costumes, music and a general air of showmanship; charro associations from all over Mexico compete. Guadalajara has some of the best exhibitions. **Jai alai**, an exciting game similar to squash that often is accompanied by spirited betting, is played countrywide but particularly in Mexico City and Tijuana. **Competitive cycling, horse racing** and **cockfights** (the last supposedly illegal) all take place in various locations; check at your hotel desk or consult the local tourist office for details.

GOLF, TENNIS AND RIDING

The horse was considered a strange, frightening beast to superstitious Aztecs who first laid eyes on the steeds brought over by Hernán Cortés. These fears were overcome, and today Mexicans are enthusiastic riders. **Horseback riding** is an invigorating way to explore the arid, beautifully scenic stretches of northern Mexico, and this part of the country has a number of stables and ranches that rent horses and arrange riding expeditions. Another popular activity is horseback riding along the beach, available at Acapulco, Mazatlán, Puerto Vallarta and along both coasts of Baja California.

Most **golf** courses are located at the coastal resorts, although Mexico City, Guadalajara and Monterrey also have them. The Los Cabos area is particularly known for well-maintained courses with challenging layouts. Many courses are private and can be played by visitors only if they are accompanied by a member. Hotel-owned courses give preference to guests. Your hotel also might be able to arrange access to a nearby facility. Generally, golf in Mexico is expensive, and even better courses may not be up to U.S. standards. If you intend to play, bring your own clubs if possible; purchasing equipment is even more expensive than playing.

Tennis courts are plentiful in resort areas. Equipment can be rented but varies in quality; again, serious players should bring their own.

THE LURE OF THE WATER

Mexico has some wonderful beaches along its Pacific and Caribbean coasts. The major resorts all offer the usual water sports, from **water skiing** and **windsurfing** to **sailing** and **parasailing**, and any necessary equipment is easily rented. Pay close attention to local warnings regarding surf conditions; many Pacific beaches have dangerous undertows and strong currents. In addition, some ocean waters can be polluted.

Snorkeling is best around Cancún and the islands of Cozumel and Isla Mujeres. The clear, shallow waters here brim with brilliantly hued fish and intricate coral formations. The Baja California and Pacific coasts are more suitable for **scuba diving**, although Baja's Pacific waters are quite cold and the diving spots tend to be hard to reach. La Paz, in southern Baja on the Gulf of California, and Guaymas, on the northwestern mainland coast, have inviting waters, equipment rentals and resort facilities. Other good bases for snorkeling and scuba explorations are Puerto Vallarta, situated amid the coves, rock formations and underwater ledges of the Bay of Banderas; Ixtapa/Zihuatanejo, where offshore rock formations create a variety of underwater sites; and Bahías de Huatulco, with nine lovely bays to explore.

Note: If you're taking scuba lessons or have a referral letter from your home training center, check to make sure that the instructor or dive center you choose in Mexico holds U.S.-recognized certification, such as NAUI, PADI, SSI or YMCA.

While **surfing** has little appeal to most Mexicans, American surfers claim that the country's Pacific breakers are some of the best. Accessible spots include the beaches in the vicinity of Cabo San Lucas at the southern end of Baja California; around Mazatlán and south toward San Blas; and at Puerto Escondido, west of Bahías de Huatulco. Those pursuing surfing opportunities in Mexico should keep in mind that very few boards are available for rent.

Mexico's National Parks

Mexico's natural beauty is one of its greatest assets. Until fairly recently, however, economic development had relentlessly chipped away at nature's resources, resulting in deforestation, air and water pollution, and the extinction of fragile wildlife. Although the march of progress means that these issues will likely remain serious ones, the numerous environmental groups that have formed in Mexico over the last decade have focused the government's attention on the need to preserve the environment, both flora and fauna.

A good way to experience Mexico's varied landscapes is to visit one of the national parks which are scattered throughout the country. In northwest Mexico, **Cumbres de Majalca National Park** rises abruptly from the surrounding ranchlands, encompassing unusual geological formations positioned amid oak and evergreen forests. Camping and lodging facilities are available. The park is 30 kilometers (19 miles) north of the city of Chihuahua via Mex. 45, then another 20 or so miles northwest on an improved gravel road. North America's fourth highest waterfall can be seen at **Basaseáchic Falls National Park**, about 280 kilometers (175 miles) west of Chihuahua via Mex. 16. The falls plunge some 800 feet into an open cylinder formed by huge rock columns. The spray nourishes pine trees growing at the base of the falls, and a marked footpath allows hikers access to the bottom of the canyon. At the top there are basic camping facilities.

Far more forbidding is **Pinacate Desert National Park**, a 600-square-mile protected reserve of wind-sculpted sand dunes, volcanic craters and shimmering lava deposits near the Arizona border in northwestern Sonora state. NASA astronauts have used the area as a training ground for lunar landings. The entrance is off Mex. 2, about 50 kilometers (31 miles) west of the border town of Sonoita. Visitors must register and are restricted to the Cerro Colorado and Elegante Crater areas. A guided tour is the best way to see this desolate region.

Several national parks are located in Mexico's central highlands area, within a day's distance of Mexico City. **Iztaccíhautl-Popocatépetl (Izta-Popo) National Park** surrounds the "Smoking Mountain" and the "White Lady"—Mexico's second and third tallest peaks, respectively. The park road, winding through densely forested ravines, offers frequent views of these perpetually snowcapped volcanoes. Spanish conqueror Hernán Cortés and his troops passed between them on their way to the Aztec capital of Tenochtitlán; the soldiers gathered sulphur from Popocatépetl's crater to make gunpowder. The park is reached by a paved road branching east off Mex. 115, just south of the town of Amecameca.

La Malinche National Park is at the foot of Matlalcuéyetl, a volcanic peak in the state of Tlaxcala that ascends to 14,632 feet. Campgrounds, lodges, picnicking areas, hiking trails, food services and sports facilities are set among pine woods. From the road to the park lodge there are excellent views of the surrounding region. The park is 13 kilometers (8 miles) east of the town of Apizaco via Mex. 136 to a paved turnoff, then about 10 kilometers (6 miles) south following signs for La Malinche.

For adventurers there is **Lagos de Montebello National Park**, in far southeastern Mexico on the Guatemalan border. On sunny days the pine forests are reflected on the surface of lakes, with water colors ranging from brilliant turquoise to leaden gray. Also within the national park are the lesser-known Chincultic ruins. Little has been excavated, except for one temple set high up on a steep cliff. Even so, the commanding view of cornfields and forested mountain ridges from its summit is worth the trip. Travel agencies in San Cristóbal de las Casas offer day trips to the lakes and the archeological zone. To reach them by car, proceed south from San Cristóbal on Mex. 190 to the village of La Trinitaria, then take the road heading east. While standard tourist amenities are in short supply, this region offers breathtaking scenery and a fascinating glimpse into the bygone culture of the Maya people.

Other national parks, in addition to those mentioned above, are described under the nearest listed city or town in the section of the TravelBook covering Mexico's travel regions.

Getting Back to Nature

The most popular areas for **camping** are in Baja California and along the Pacific Coast beaches of the mainland. The desolate beauty of Baja is often accessible only via four-wheel-drive vehicle; campers straying off the beaten path should be experienced and properly equipped.

Some of Mexico's national parks permit camping as well. Many offer a backdrop of cool pine forests or sparkling lakes, as well as good **hiking** trails and scenic spots for **picnicking**. Two popular parks that are a short distance from Mexico City are Desierto de los Leones (Desert of the Lions) and La Marquesa (Parque Nacional Miguel Hidalgo y Costilla). For listings of AAA-RATED campgrounds and trailer parks, *see "About Campgrounds," beginning on page 484.* **Note:** Avoid camping at deserted beaches or in other isolated areas, where banditry tends to occur.

For the prodigiously fit, Mexico has several challenging peaks for **mountain climbing**. Organized expeditions are available to volcanoes Popocatépetl and Iztaccíhuatl, near Mexico City, and to Citlaltépetl (Pico de Orizaba), in the state of Veracruz. The easiest and most popular climb is Popocatépetl. Needless to say, experience is essential. Major equipment is available in Mexico, but plan on bringing personal items (backpack, footwear, sleeping bag). Do not attempt to climb during the rainy season, June through September. For further information, contact the Club de Exploraciones de México (Exploration Club of Mexico), Juan Mateos #146, Mexico City, D.F.

Fishing

Mexico offers some of the best deep-sea **fishing** in the world, particularly around the southern tip of Baja California, in the Gulf of California, along the Pacific coast and off the eastern coast of the Yucatán Peninsula; its excellence is attested to by the numerous tournaments held each year. As with hunting, Mexican authorities are taking greater steps to preserve the country's natural resources, and a catch-and-release policy is advocated for sports anglers.

Locations noted for their deep-sea fishing opportunities include Acapulco for pompano, barracuda and shark; Cabo San Lucas for blue and striped marlin, sailfish and swordfish; Cancún and Cozumel for sailfish, swordfish, marlin, dolphin and barracuda; Ensenada for yellowtail; Guaymas for marlin, sailfish, dolphin and yellowtail; La Paz and Loreto for marlin and sailfish; Los Mochis and Topolobampo for marlin, sailfish, pompano and roosterfish; Manzanillo for sailfish; Mazatlán for sailfish and marlin; Mulegé for snook; and Puerto Vallarta for sailfish, marlin, bonito, red snapper and shark.

Rivers and lakes contain many varieties of freshwater fish. A man-made lake near Valle de Bravo, in the state of México, is known for black bass and trout. Bass also is the lure at Vicente Guerrero, another man-made lake in the state of Tamaulipas. El Novillo Dam, east of Hermosillo in the state of Sonora, has good bass fishing. Whitefish, esteemed as a national delicacy, can be caught in Lake Catemaco, in the state of Veracruz; Lake Chapala, in the state of Jalisco; and Lake Pátzcuaro, in the state of Michoacán.

Fishing regulations, which apply to both freshwater and saltwater species, are not complicated—the only requirement is a license. A Mexican Sportfishing License covers all types of fishing and is valid anywhere in Mexico. If you intend to fish in Baja California or Pacific waters, contact the California office of the Secretaría de Pesca (Mexican Department of Fisheries) in San Diego for an application; phone (619) 233-6956, fax (619) 233-0344.

License fees vary depending on boat size and time spent fishing (1 day to 1 year). They range from about $15 to $30 but are subject to change; contact the Department of Fisheries for updates. The cost is the same whether the angler is alone or part of a tour group. Everyone aboard private boats in Mexican waters must have a fishing license regardless of age and whether or not they are fishing. Licenses are not transferable. Skin divers and scuba divers who fish need a license as well.

Spear fishing is legal only with hand-held or spring-powered spears. The taking of certain species is prohibited; the list includes abalone, lobster, shrimp, pismo clams, cabrilla, totoaba, oysters and sea turtles. It is illegal to sell, trade or exchange any fish caught.

The maximum catch per day varies by species. Generally authorized maximums are 10 fish caught per day, but not more than five of the same species. Catches of marlin, sailfish and swordfish are limited to one per day per species; catches of tarpon, dolphin (mahi-mahi), roosterfish and shark are limited to two per day per species. To preserve game species, many of Mexico's top sport fishing destinations emphasize a catch-and-release policy.

Major hotels and independent companies at the resorts and in port cities can arrange fishing expeditions or provide boats and gear for hire. All non-resident private boats entering Mexican waters must obtain certification and a temporary boat permit from the Mexican Department of Fisheries in San Diego, a Mexican consulate office or a customs broker.

PLANNING YOUR TRIP

Planning for a Mexican vacation first depends on whether you'll be driving your own vehicle around the country, flying to one destination only, or flying to one destination and then driving a rental car to another. If you drive your own vehicle, specific regulations govern its temporary importation across the border. There's also your day-to-day, on-the-road itinerary to consider. Flying eliminates many of these additional details, particularly if a travel agency or tour operator is handling the logistics.

Trip cost will largely be determined by your agenda. If you want frills or as many of the comforts of home as possible, travel exclusively by air or take a guided package tour; stay at internationally recognized hotels or all-inclusive resorts; and eat and shop at establishments that cater primarily to tourists. Your vacation will be essentially hassle-free, but it also could be very expensive. But if you are willing to put up with the occasional lumpy bed or misguided detour and don't mind a few unexpected departures from an otherwise orderly schedule, you will not only reduce expenses but experience Mexico on a much more intimate level.

While not essential, a knowledge of Spanish is helpful. English is spoken widely, especially in large cities and at the popular beach resorts. Elsewhere, Mexicans who work in hotels, restaurants or other aspects of the tourism industry usually speak and understand basic English. Shop owners and market sellers likely will be familiar with numbers, which is helpful when bargaining.

Out-of-the-way places, particularly Indian villages and rural areas in the Yucatán Peninsula and southern Mexico, are another story. But if you know some words or phrases in the native tongue, Mexicans tend to overlook a visitor's halting pronunciation and mixed tenses. Speak slowly, distinctly and be patient if you have trouble making yourself understood. Where some knowledge of the language is necessary, the "Speaking of Spanish" section in this book provides words and phrases that identify common needs.

Keep in mind that the high-school Spanish many Americans learned—and promptly forgot—is based on the Castilian form of the language. Expressions that are innocuous in one Spanish-speaking country can take on an offensive tone in another. Practice is the only way to pick up such nuances.

MEXICO TRAVEL REGIONS

Tourism is big business in Mexico; the country welcomes more than 20 million visitors annually, and the 1994 currency devaluation means those with U.S. dollars can find some very good travel bargains. But no visitor takes on all of Mexico in one vacation. And with its sheer size and enormous variety, who would want to?

This book divides Mexico into eight regions (color-coded on the *Mexico Travel Regions* map), with geography the primary determining factor. Different parts of the country provide varying levels of visitor amenities and offer different things to see and do—so whether you're contemplating a first visit or embarking on the latest of many, a knowledge of what each region offers can be an aid in trip planning.

Travel Advisories

The U.S. Department of State issues Consular Information Sheets and Travel Warnings concerning serious health or security conditions that might affect U.S. citizens. They can be obtained at U.S. embassies and consulates abroad, regional passport agencies in the United States and from the Citizens Emergency Center, 2201 C St. NW, Room 4811, Department of State, Washington, D.C. 20520; phone (202) 647-5225, fax (202) 647-3000. For the latest information about travel advisories or warnings, consult the Bureau of Consular Affairs home page; the website address is **travel.state.gov/.**

Consular Information Sheets provide information about entry requirements, currency regulations, health conditions, security, political disturbances, areas of instability and drug penalties. A Travel Warning is issued when the situation in a country is dangerous enough for the Department of State to recommend that Americans not travel there.

In addition, travelers are urged to remain abreast of regional events and to contact their AAA/CAA travel agent or air or sea carrier for the latest updates.

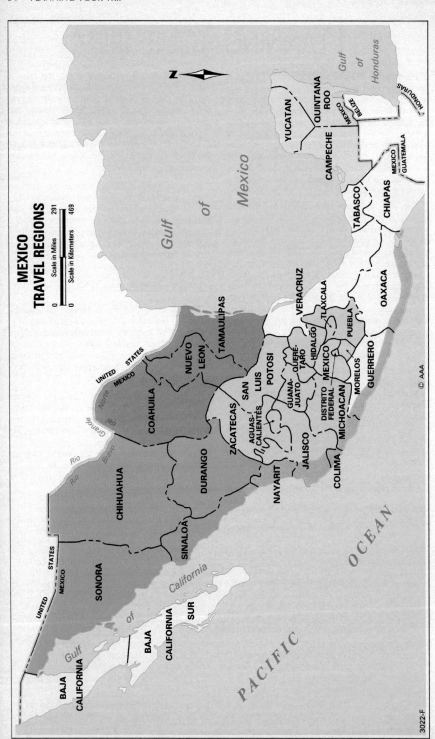

MEXICO
TRAVEL REGIONS

Scale in Miles
0   291

Scale in Kilometers
0   469

© AAA

3022-F

MEXICAN STATE CHART

State	Abbreviation	Area (sq. miles)	Population	Capital
AGUASCALIENTES	Ags.	2,112	888,444	Aguascalientes
BAJA CALIFORNIA	B.C.	26,996	2,241,029	Mexicali
BAJA CALIFORNIA SUR	B.C.S.	28,369	387,430	La Paz
CAMPECHE	Camp.	19,619	668,715	Campeche
CHIAPAS	Chis.	28,653	3,637,142	Tuxtla Gutiérrez
CHIHUAHUA	Chih.	94,571	2,895,672	Chihuahua
COAHUILA	Coah.	57,908	2,227,305	Saltillo
COLIMA	Col.	2,004	415,313	Colima
DISTRITO FEDERAL	D.F.	571	8,520,090	Mexico City
DURANGO	Dgo.	47,560	1,449,036	Durango
GUANAJUATO	Gto.	11,946	4,478,673	Guanajuato
GUERRERO	Gro.	24,819	2,994,365	Chilpancingo
HIDALGO	Hgo.	8,038	2,166,122	Pachuca
JALISCO	Jal.	31,211	6,161,437	Guadalajara
MEXICO	Mex.	8,245	12,222,891	Toluca
MICHOACAN	Mich.	23,138	3,925,450	Morelia
MORELOS	Mor.	1,911	1,496,030	Cuernavaca
NAYARIT	Nay.	10,417	903,886	Tepic
NUEVO LEON	N.L.	25,067	3,684,845	Monterrey
OAXACA	Oax.	36,275	3,286,175	Oaxaca
PUEBLA	Pue.	13,090	4,792,156	Puebla
QUERETARO	Qro.	4,420	1,297,575	Querétaro
QUINTANA ROO	Q.R.	19,387	772,803	Chetumal
SAN LUIS POTOSI	S.L.P.	24,351	2,247,042	San Luis Potosí
SINALOA	Sin.	22,520	2,509,142	Culiacán
SONORA	Son.	70,290	2,183,108	Hermosillo
TABASCO	Tab.	9,756	1,817,703	Villahermosa
TAMAULIPAS	Tamps.	30,650	2,628,839	Ciudad Victoria
TLAXCALA	Tlax.	1,551	911,696	Tlaxcala
VERACRUZ	Ver.	27,683	6,856,415	Jalapa
YUCATAN	Yuc.	14,827	1,617,120	Mérida
ZACATECAS	Zac.	28,283	1,332,683	Zacatecas

Source: National Institute of Statistics and Geography (INEGI), 1997

Following are brief regional summaries, with the Mexican states (or portions of states) that comprise each region listed at the end of its descriptive summary.

YUCATAN PENINSULA

The Yucatán Peninsula's Caribbean coast boasts **Cancún** (Mexico's beach of choice) and the island of **Cozumel** (one of the world's foremost dive sites) as part of a 100-mile stretch of sand and offshore coral reefs. The peninsula also has numerous archeological sites, notably the remains of three great Maya cities: **Chichén Itzá, Uxmal** and the seaside ruins of **Tulum.** The European-flavored city of **Mérida** is, like much of the Yucatán, strongly Indian in character. **States:** *Campeche, Quintana Roo, Yucatán.*

BAJA CALIFORNIA

Although much of the Baja peninsula is inhospitable wilderness, it also is a rapidly developing tourist region. The seaport of **Ensenada** is popular for weekend getaways (and the bustling border metropolis of **Tijuana** for day visits); at the opposite end of the peninsula are the resort towns of **Cabo San Lucas** and **San José del Cabo. States:** *Baja California, Baja California Sur.*

NORTHWESTERN MEXICO

This vast, environmentally harsh but scenic region has long been considered somewhere to get through in order to reach more hospitable points south. This is still primarily the case, although a few spots on the eastern Gulf of California coast, such as **Guaymas, Puerto Peñasco** and **San Carlos,** offer beaches and sport fishing opportunities. **States:** *Chihuahua, Durango, Sinaloa, Sonora.*

NORTHEASTERN MEXICO

Much of northeastern Mexico is simply uninterested in tourism, and the Gulf coast beaches are a far cry from their more developed—and prettier—counterparts along the Caribbean and Pacific shores. However, the easy accessibility and hybrid culture of the major border cities—**Nuevo Laredo, Reynosa** and **Matamoros**—attracts visitors, as does **Monterrey's** big-city sights and amenities. **States:** *Coahuila, Nuevo León, Tamaulipas.*

THE PACIFIC COAST

The "Mexican Riviera" is a year-round resort destination. Not all of the hundreds of miles of coastline is developed by any means, but it is uniformly spectacular, with wide sand beaches and rolling breakers backed by impressive mountains. The well-known vacation choices are **Puerto Vallarta, Acapulco, Mazatlán, Ixtapa/Zihuatanejo, Manzanillo, Puerto Escondido** and **Bahías de Huatulco.** There are some off-the-beaten-track alternatives as well. **States:** *Colima, coastal Guerrero, coastal Jalisco, coastal Michoacán, Nayarit, coastal Oaxaca, southern coastal Sinaloa.*

MEXICO CITY AND VICINITY

Home to one-fifth of the nation's population, metropolitan Mexico City is a formidably congested metropolis and international business center. It pulses with all the excitement—and displays all the social and economic extremes—inherent to one of the world's biggest cities. The capital offers centuries of history, marvelous museums, world-class restaurants and sophisticated nightlife to balance the terrible traffic and daunting pollution. Nearby **Cuernavaca** and the ruins of **Teotihuacán** offer sightseeing options as well as a chance to escape the urban jungle. **States:** *México, Morelos.*

CENTRAL MEXICO

Much of the interior comprises an area known as the central highlands, which has the coolest weather and contains some of the largest population centers in the country. The "colonial cities" of **Guadalajara, Guanajuato, Morelia, Puebla, Querétaro, San Miguel de Allende, San Luis Potosí** and **Zacatecas** are distinguished by traditional, Old World downtown plazas, richly decorated churches and streets lined with stately old buildings. It is here that the Spanish historical and cultural legacy is most strongly evident. **States:** *Aguascalientes, Guanajuato, Hidalgo, Jalisco, Michoacán, Puebla, Querétaro, San Luis Potosí, Tlaxcala, Zacatecas.*

SOUTHERN MEXICO

This region extends south from the central highlands and the Gulf coast area around the port of **Veracruz,** which is known for its seafood and partying atmosphere. If you want to explore a part of Mexico off the usual tourist itineraries, consider **San Cristóbal de las Casas**, situated in the midst of scenic mountains, or **Oaxaca,** a city of culture and charm. **Taxco,** in northern Guerrero, is the southernmost—and one of the most visited—of Mexico's "colonial" cities. **States:** *Chiapas, Guerrero, Oaxaca, Tabasco, Veracruz.*

DESTINATIONS

Generally speaking, Mexico's priciest destinations are its big beach resorts. For the first-time visitor, they offer the exotic lure of a foreign country without too much cultural displacement. One will find American fast-food joints as well as thatch-roofed seafood shacks—and a large proportion of locals who speak English. Cancún, Puerto Vallarta, Acapulco and Ixtapa all fall into this category, as do the somewhat less expensive Cabo San Lucas, Mazatlán, Manzanillo and Bahías de Huatulco.

Also pricey is Mexico City, which is not a place for those seeking laid-back relaxation. Museum lovers, however, will find some truly outstanding ones that exhibit the artistic and historical treasures associated with Mexico's long history.

At the opposite end of the price scale are the less developed areas—parts of the Yucatán and Baja California peninsulas, the states of Oaxaca and Chiapas, the **Copper Canyon**—that provide a maximum of scenic splendor and local flavor and a minimum of pampering. Those with a taste for adventure and no need for luxury will relish the opportunity to camp along a deserted stretch of beach or explore little-visited archeological ruins.

Ecotourism—getting close to nature at relatively remote and unspoiled areas—is a global trend also gaining popularity in Mexico among travelers and tour operators alike. There is growing recognition that preserving the environment benefits tourism as well. In addition to Mexico, the Central American countries of Belize, Guatemala and particularly Costa Rica are popular ecotourism destinations. A bewildering number of tour companies offer specialized excursions based around biking, diving, hiking, kayaking and other activities. Consult a travel agency for details.

The Mexican government has promoted ecological awareness in various ways. In recent years, several areas, such as the **Sian Ka'an Biosphere Reserve** in the state of Quintana Roo, have been given protected status as a refuge for a rich variety of indigenous flora and fauna. **The El Rosario Monarch Butterfly Sanctuary, in** the wooded mountains west of Mexico City, is a protected reserve for the insects, which annually migrate by the millions to the central Mexican highlands. In the **Gulf of California** commercial fishing is strictly regulated in order to protect the sport fishing industry, and a catch-and-release policy is advocated. Whales, which migrate to Baja's Pacific coast each winter, also are protected.

There is ongoing debate as to whether ecotourism preserves or damages fragile natural environments, and whether the demand for ecologically oriented travel alternatives outstrips the country's ability to intelligently manage them. For travelers accustomed to a high level of comfort, an ecotour may not be a wise choice. But for those who prefer unspoiled environments and scientific authenticity over fine dining and five-diamond accommodations, Mexico offers some intriguing choices—from backpacking through the otherworldly moonscapes of the Baja desert to birdwatching expeditions along the northern Yucatán coast.

Perhaps the best bet for combining affordable and acceptable comfort with the pleasure of experiencing new cultural perspectives is a visit to one of the interior cities. Such colonial cities as Guanajuato, Querétaro, San Miguel de Allende, Taxco and Zacatecas, built by the Spanish, have fascinating historical and architectural legacies. Often overlooked on tourist itineraries is Morelia, the capital of Michoacán and perhaps the city in Mexico most reminiscent of Spain. Residents

El Arco is a natural rock formation at the southern tip of the Baja peninsula.   ©John Neubauer

of Oaxaca, San Cristóbal de las Casas and Mérida produce some of the best native handicrafts in Mexico. Guadalajara offers big-city amenities, Mexican atmosphere and Western familiarity, the last resulting in part from a large resident population of American retirees.

General tourist information on a variety of subjects can be obtained from **Fax Me Mexico**, a 24-hour service coordinated by the Tourist Promotion Council of Mexico, a non-governmental public relations firm. By dialing (541) 385-9282, users can receive a directory of subjects, from overviews of major city and regional destinations to helpful advice on trip planning. By following the phone prompts, up to five different documents will be faxed at one time. Call (800) 44-MEXICO—(800) 446-3942—for phone information.

WHEN TO GO

When to go is as important a consideration as where to go. From a weather standpoint, the dry season—October through May—is the best time to visit most of the country. Rainfall patterns, however, vary greatly. In the highland region of central Mexico afternoon showers are likely at any time from June through September, but over a large portion of northern—and especially northwestern—Mexico, rain is infrequent throughout the year. In Chiapas and the normally wet coastal areas, heavy rains can wash out roads or cause mudslides. Much of northwestern Mexico and Baja California is uncomfortably hot in the summer; in the coastal regions summer heat is exacerbated by high humidity. Conversely, fall and winter evenings in high-altitude locations can get quite nippy.

December through February or March is the high season at Mexico's beach resorts, and accommodation rates at the major tourist destinations, such as Cancún and Puerto Vallarta, are at their peak. April through November is the off season, when rates come down and crowds let up. Each resort has its own timetable; Cancún, for example, is crowded with U.S. spring breakers during March and April.

Easter week is perhaps the most popular time of the year for Mexican families to vacation, and if you'll be visiting then hotel reservations will invariably need to be made in advance. Many Mexicans also travel over the Christmas holiday period and during such major national celebrations as the *Fiesta of the Virgin of Guadalupe* on Dec. 12. For good weather, lower cost and crowd avoidance, a general rule of thumb is to go in the spring or fall.

Weather Notes

Mexico encompasses some 760,000 square miles, extends over 17 degrees of latitude and across 30 degrees of longitude, and varies in elevation from sea level to more than 18,000 feet above. This wide range of terrain guarantees a correspondingly wide range of climatic conditions. The weather in Mexico can be oppressively sultry or refreshingly cool, extremely dry or persistently rainy. Because much of the country lies within the tropics, altitude rather than latitude tends to determine the temperature. Two characteristics more or less stand out: a large number of hours of annual sunshine, and distinct wet and dry seasons.

Many of Mexico's population centers, including Mexico City, Guadalajara and Puebla, as well as other inland cities like Guanajuato, Morelia, Oaxaca and Querétaro, are at altitudes that give them springlike weather year-round. Northwestern cities such as Chihuahua and Hermosillo experience greater seasonal extremes. Here summers are sizzling, while temperatures during winter can drop below freezing and occasional light snow falls. The range between daily high and low temperatures often exceeds 30 degrees. Cancún, Acapulco, Puerto Vallarta and other coastal resorts, on the other hand, show little temperature variation from month to month and smaller daily ranges. The nicest weather in these cities is from November through March, when humidities are fairly low and little rain falls.

Severe weather and natural disasters in Mexico are sporadic in nature. Localized heavy rains—particularly in low-lying, tropical coastal areas—can cause flooding, bridge washouts and mud or rock slides that adversely affect transportation. Occasional hurricanes affect the eastern Yucatán Peninsula, the lower Gulf of Mexico coast and the Pacific coast between Mazatlán and Acapulco. Pacific storms also can strike the southern part of the normally arid Baja California Peninsula. As in other mountainous countries, earthquakes are an ever-present possibility and cause the most catastrophic damage. A strong quake in June 1999 killed more than 15 people, damaged churches and other historic buildings in the colonial cities of Puebla and Cholula, and sent Mexico City residents fleeing into the streets as high-rise buildings swayed. The great majority of visitors, however, will hopefully never experience these tremors.

Mexico Tourism Board Offices

LOS ANGELES *2401 W. Sixth St. (Mexican Consulate Building, 5th floor), 90057; (213) 351-2069*

NEW YORK *31 East 63rd St., Third floor, 10021; (212) 821-0314, (800) 446-3942*

VANCOUVER, B.C. *999 W. Hastings St., Suite 1110, V6C 2W2; (604) 669-2845*

You may want to time your arrival to coincide with a significant annual event, such as Oaxaca's *Guelaguetza* celebration in July or Guanajuato's *Festival Cervantino* (International Cervantes Festival) in October. The whole country celebrates occasions like *Independence Day* (Sept. 15 and 16) and the *Day of the Dead* (Nov. 1 and 2). And almost every day of the year some village or town honors its patron saint or commemorates a historical occasion.

All things considered, one of the nicest times to visit is in November: Temperatures are moderate, summer rains have turned much of the normally brown landscape a lusher green, and the peak holiday season is still a month away.

CALLING MEXICO

Trip planning may necessitate making phone calls to Mexico for the purpose of setting up hotel reservations, obtaining information about special events, etc. When calling Mexico from the United States and Canada, first dial 011 (the international access code), then 52 (the country code), then the city/area code (for example, 4 for San Miguel de Allende), and finally the local phone number. While major hotels in tourist areas normally employ English-speaking staffs, a basic knowledge of Spanish will come in handy should you encounter an exception.

Note: Area codes in Mexico are in transition. At press time most had been changed to one digit, followed by a seven-digit local number. Guadalajara, Mexico City and Monterrey have no area code; all local numbers are eight digits, beginning with 3, 5 and 8, respectively. However, area codes are expected to revert back to two- and three-digit numbers beginning sometime in 2001.

PACKING HINTS

Heed the old adage to "pack light." The weather in most areas ranges from mild to warm, and consequently you will not need a great deal of clothing. Bring items that are comfortable and easy to care for. In Mexico City and other high-altitude areas, a light coat is a good idea during the winter months, a sweater or jacket for other times. Sweaters also can ward off the chill of air conditioning, which can be icy in those establishments that have it. Lightweight summer clothing is necessary in tropical areas, which include practically all of the coastal lowlands.

Although Mexico is not a particularly formal country, neither is it lacking in modesty. Some of the native peoples are very conservative, and revealing clothing on either sex is frowned upon, regardless of the heat. Away from the main tourist areas women will attract much unwanted attention by going braless or wearing very short skirts or otherwise provocative attire.

Slacks or jeans are fine for sightseeing and shopping. Shorts and/or bathing suits are more appropriate at the beach and in cosmopolitan cities than they are in small towns or outlying areas, although personal comfort should be the deciding factor. If you plan to dine in an upscale restaurant, it's a good idea to keep casual evening clothes (a sports jacket and tie for men, a dress or suit for women) on hand. Bring a raincoat or umbrella for the rainy-season months of June through September.

A pair of sturdy, comfortable walking shoes is essential for exploring ruins, hiking through forests or climbing up hills, and even for walking the frequently cobblestoned streets of cities and towns. A luggage cart can be useful if you'll be traveling by bus, as stations in smaller towns rarely have porters, and it can save money at airports. For those who plan to be on the go much of the time, a shoulder bag may be more appropriate than a suitcase; make sure it fastens securely.

Take an extra pair of sunglasses, a good sunscreen, insect repellent (absolutely necessary in lowland and coastal areas and not always available in Mexico), a vacuum or plastic bottle for drinking water, eyedrops to ease discomfort from wind or glare, and a combination pocketknife with bottle opener and corkscrew attachments. Mexican pharmacies carry aspirin and other standard toiletry items, but you should bring your own prescription drugs. Toilet paper is often missing in out-of-the-way restrooms; bring several rolls, and always try to carry at least one. Purchase film and batteries before you leave, as they are more expensive in Mexico. Another useful item is a bathtub plug; in many hotel rooms they are missing or don't fit properly.

Electrical current in Mexico is 110-volt, 60-cycle AC—the same as in the United States and Canada—which permits the use of such small standard appliances as shavers, travel irons or hair curlers. In smaller towns, electricity may be weak or even unavailable, so bring a small flashlight and disposable razor.

WHAT MAY BE TAKEN INTO MEXICO

If you're driving across the border, your baggage will be examined at the customs checkpoint. Although there's always the possibility that this procedure can turn into an ordeal of exasperating interactions with customs officials—or time-consuming additional inspections at customs or immigration substations—it has been streamlined for the most part. Each vehicle must pass through a "traffic light" signal system. After submitting a customs declaration form or oral declarations, the driver presses a button that activates a randomly flashing signal. If the light flashes green no further action is taken; if it flashes red your luggage will be inspected, regardless of previous declarations made to customs officials. By law, if the signal is not operating properly no inspections are allowed unless the previous declaration involves goods on which fees are required.

Airline passengers receive a customs declaration form (printed in English) on the flight listing all items that can be brought into Mexico duty-free and without prior authorization. The form should be filled out and is submitted to customs officials upon arrival at the entry point. At some airports (for example, Mexico City's), after retrieving your luggage you'll stop at a similar signal and press a button that activates a randomly

---

Selected Mexican Consulate Offices in the United States and Canada

ARIZONA

NOGALES—Consul de Mexico, 571 N. Grand Ave., 85621; (520) 287-2521

PHOENIX—Consul General de Mexico, 1990 West Camelback Rd., Suite 110, 85015; (602) 242-7398

TUCSON—Consul de Mexico, 553 S. Stone Ave., 85701; (520) 882-5595

CALIFORNIA

LOS ANGELES—Consul General de Mexico, 2401 W. Sixth St., 90057; (213) 351-6800

SAN DIEGO—Consul General de Mexico, 1549 India St., 92101; (619) 231-8414

SAN FRANCISCO—Consul General de Mexico, 870 Market St., Suite 528, 94102; (415) 392-5554

DISTRICT OF COLUMBIA

WASHINGTON, D.C.—Consul de Mexico, 2827 16th Street N.W., 20009; (202) 736-1000

FLORIDA

MIAMI—Consul General de Mexico, 1200 N. W. 78th Ave., Suite 200, 33126; (305) 716-4979

GEORGIA

ATLANTA—Consul General de Mexico, 2600 Apple Valley Rd., 30319; (404) 266-2233

LOUISIANA

NEW ORLEANS—Consul General de Mexico, 2 Canal St., Suite 2240, World Trade Center, 70130; (504) 522-3597

MASSACHUSETTS

BOSTON—Consul de Mexico, 20 Park Plaza, Suite 506, 02116; (617) 426-8782

MISSOURI

ST. LOUIS—Consul de Mexico, 1015 Locust St., Suite 922, 63101; (314) 436-3233

NEW MEXICO

ALBUQUERQUE—Consul de Mexico, 400 Gold St. S.W., Suite 100, 87102; (505) 247-2139

NEW YORK

NEW YORK—Consul General de Mexico, 27 East 39th St., 10016; (212) 217-6400

PENNSYLVANIA

PHILADELPHIA—Consul de Mexico, 111 S. Independence Mall, Suite 310, 19106; (215) 922-4262

TEXAS

AUSTIN—Consul General de Mexico, 200 E. Sixth St., Suite 200, 78701; (512) 478-2866

BROWNSVILLE—Consul de Mexico, 723 E. Elizabeth St., 78521; (956) 542-4431

CORPUS CHRISTI—Consul de Mexico, 800 N. Shoreline Blvd., Suite 410 (North Tower), 78401; (361) 882-5964

DALLAS—Consul General de Mexico, 8855 N. Stemmons Frwy., 75247-3855; (214) 630-7341

EL PASO—Consul de Mexico, 910 E. San Antonio St., 79901; (915) 533-3644

LAREDO—Consul de Mexico, 1612 Farragut St., 78041; (956) 723-6360, 723-6369

SAN ANTONIO—Consul General de Mexico, 127 Navarro St., 78205; (210) 227-9145

UTAH

SALT LAKE CITY—Consul de Mexico, 230 W. 400th St. S., 2nd floor, 84111; (801) 521-8502, 521-8503

WASHINGTON

SEATTLE—Consul de Mexico, 2132 Third Ave., 98121; (206) 448-3526, 448-6819

CANADA

VANCOUVER—Consul General de Mexico, 1177 W. Hastings St., Suite 710, British Columbia V6E 2K3; (604) 684-1859

flashing stoplight. If the light flashes green you may proceed; if it flashes red your luggage will be inspected.

Note: Complaints regarding treatment by customs officials may be registered by contacting the Comptroller and Administrative Development Secretariat (SECODAM). Phone (5) 604-1240 or 480-2000 in Mexico City, 01 (800) 001-4800 out of Mexico City.

MONEY

Up to $10,000 in U.S. currency and traveler's checks (or the equivalent in other currencies) may be taken into Mexico. It is advisable to have the bulk of funds in traveler's checks. U.S. traveler's checks, particularly those issued by the most recognized institutions, are normally easy to cash. It may be more difficult to cash Canadian currency and traveler's checks, so many Canadian travelers convert their money into U.S. currency beforehand.

Small-denomination traveler's checks and also a fair amount of cash come in handy when traveling in Baja California and the more remote areas of mainland Mexico. When presented with sufficient identification, major credit cards are accepted in the larger cities provided that the credit card company normally operates in Mexico.

You can make your dollars go further by exchanging them only as you need them. Exchange rates are posted at hotel front desks, currency exchange offices and banks. Banamex and Bancomer are two of the largest Mexican banks; most cities and towns have branches of one or the other.

If you transport or cause to be transported (including by mail or other means) more than $10,000 in currency or negotiable instruments such as traveler's checks into or out of the United States, you must file a copy of Customs Form 4790 with the U.S. Customs Service, P.O. Box 7407, Washington, D.C. 20229.

PERSONAL ITEMS

You may take with you into Mexico duty free clothing and other personal items. The allowance includes jewelry, perfume, toiletries, one pair of binoculars, books and magazines (in a quantity that does not indicate them to be the object of commercialization), and medicines for personal consumption (accompanied by prescriptions as appropriate and in accordance with quantities prescribed).

Unless acceptable proof of prior ownership is presented upon return to the United States, duty may be required on personal articles that are foreign-made. This proof can be a bill of sale, insurance policy, jeweler's appraisal or original receipt of purchase. Items with serial numbers or other permanently affixed identification can be registered with the nearest customs office before

departure. The certificate of registration will facilitate re-entry into the United States should any question of prior possession arise.

PHOTOGRAPHIC EQUIPMENT

One still or movie camera with up to 12 rolls of unused film, as well as one video recording camera and 12 blank cassettes, are admissible; this includes the camera's power source. Foreign-made cameras can be registered at the point of departure to prove that they were not purchased in Mexico. Airline passengers should have all photographic film hand-inspected at boarding points to ensure against damage from baggage inspection equipment at check-in locations.

Note: Photography must not be for commercial purposes. Tripods and flash equipment require special permits for use at archeological sites, museums and monuments.

CB RADIOS

Three channels are designated for tourist use—9, 10 and 11. Channel 9 is for emergencies and motorist assistance; channel 10 is for communication among visitors; channel 11 is for obtaining local directions and information. A permit is not required to bring a CB radio into Mexico. A permit is required, however, for the temporary importation and use of a ham radio. Permits may be obtained at border crossing points.

U.S. amateur radio licenses are not valid in Mexico. A permit issued by the Secretaría de Comunicaciones y Transportes (Ministry of Communications and Transports) is required for the importation and use of amateur radio equipment. For further information write the American Radio Relay League, 225 Main St., Newington, CT 06111; phone (860) 594-0200.

PETS

Dogs and cats should be left at home because of special inspections and the possible refusal of hotel operators to allow pets in their establishments. However, if you must take your dog or cat into Mexico, you are required to have a veterinarian's *signed* and dated certificate (Pet Health Certificate for dogs and cats) stating the pet is in good health and stating inoculation against rabies and distemper. This certificate, available from a veterinarian's or county health department office, can be obtained up to 2 weeks prior to the date the animal enters Mexico. It is extremely difficult to temporarily import animals other than dogs or cats.

Inoculation certificates are necessary to re-enter the United States if the pet has been out of the country more than 30 days. Dogs can be left at kennels in Laredo, El Paso, Brownsville or Tucson while their owners are traveling in Mexico. The leaflet "Pets and Wildlife" can be obtained by writing U.S. Customs, P.O. Box 7407, Washington, D.C. 20044.

WEAPONS

Strict regulations govern the temporary importation of firearms and ammunition into Mexico. Tourists are not permitted to import pistols, revolvers, automatic firearms or weapons of any type. Technically this includes all knives (pocket and Swiss Army knives, as well as switchblades and other knives that could be classified as weapons). Although tourists are not likely to be fined or incarcerated for bringing in knives normally used for camping purposes, it may be safer to purchase such a knife while in Mexico.

U.S. citizens are most often arrested for firearms possession in border areas, but arrests have been made in every part of the country—including on private boats in Mexican territorial waters. Ignorance of the law in no way guarantees leniency or prevents prosecution. The only way to legally import firearms and ammunition into Mexico is to secure a permit in advance from the nearest Mexican consulate office.

DRUGS

The possession, use or sale of illegal drugs in Mexico is extremely risky. Mexican law, to which tourists in Mexico are subject, deems that trafficking in and/or possession of illegal drugs is a federal offense. All such cases are prosecuted rigorously by the Mexican government regardless of the nature of the drug. During the extensive trial process, which could possibly last more than a year, offenders are not eligible for bail; if found guilty, they are ineligible for parole.

If you require medicines containing habit-forming drugs or narcotics, take precautions to avoid any misunderstanding. Properly identify all drugs, carry only the necessary quantity and have with you a prescription or written statement from a physician. These safeguards will also help to avoid potential customs problems upon return to the United States.

OTHER DUTY-FREE ITEMS

Also allowed are a tent and camping equipment; fishing tackle; two tennis rackets; a pair of skis; a new or used laptop computer; a portable radio/cassette player; a portable television set; a VCR; up to 20 CDs or cassettes; two laser disks; a musical instrument that can normally be carried by one person; a portable typewriter; and up to five used toys (if the tourist is a minor). The duty-free limit for the above items is usually per person or per each family member. Also admissible are gifts or items up to a total value of $300 (provided none are restricted) if arriving by air or sea, $50 if arriving by land. These duty-free limits apply per each crossing or arrival. There are no restrictions on the containers in which items are imported.

Each tourist, provided that he or she is not a minor, may bring in 3 liters of wine or another alcoholic beverage and two cartons of cigarettes, 25 cigars or 200 grams of loose tobacco. Recreational vehicle owners can bring in kitchen, dwelling and/or bedroom furniture or utensils, a videocassette player and a bicycle (with or without motor).

Tourists are *not* permitted to bring any type of live animal, fresh food products of animal or vegetable origin, or plants, flowers or fruits into Mexico. Canned fruit or vegetables are allowed.

ABOUT LODGINGS AND RESTAURANTS

AAA Tourism Editors annually evaluate every lodging establishment listed in this publication at least once every year. Their rigorous evaluation helps ensure that all properties meet AAA's exacting standards for quality.

USING LODGING LISTINGS

To use this book most effectively, read the sample lodging listing along with the explanation of terms used. The location given to pinpoint a facility is based on major reference points (most often highway junctions). When calling any Mexican lodging from the United States, first dial 011 (the international access code), then 52 (the country code), then the area code and local phone number *(see "Calling Mexico," p. 39)*.

In-room amenities are designated by icons *(see the "What the Icons Mean" box)*. All showers are tub showers unless otherwise noted. Where the term "movie" is denoted in the listing, guests can view the movie through a TV channel; there may be an additional charge. If the listing includes the icon "No Cable TV," the available channels are likely to have programs in Spanish

---

The lodgings with ⓕⓨⓘ in place of diamonds are included as an "information only" service for members. The icon indicates that a property has not been rated for one or more of the following reasons: too new to rate; under construction; under major renovation; not inspected; or may not meet all AAA requirements. Listing prose will give insights as to why the ⓕⓨⓘ rating was assigned.

only. Lodgings with satellite TV also may have only Spanish-language channels.

If parking is provided on the premises at no charge, it is not mentioned in the listing. Other parking conditions, such as no parking available, off-site parking, street parking only or off-site valet parking, and any charges, are specifically noted in the listing. Service charges are not shown unless they are $1 or more, or at least 5 percent of the room rate.

Note: Some lodgings in this book may not be evaluated due to their remote location. They do not meet AAA's standards for a diamond rating, but are the best available in an area of touristic interest. These listings are presented for information only and are designated by the "FYI" icon *(see opposite page).*

GUEST SAFETY

Due to unique conditions in Mexico, AAA does not require deadbolt locks on guest room entry and connecting room doors, secondary locks on sliding doors or viewports on guest room entry doors. Difficulty in obtaining hardware and individual styles of conducting business are some of the reasons why AAA has delayed the implementation of its security requirements in Mexico.

However, if a property listed in this publication meets AAA's security requirements at the time of the evaluation, the phrase "meets AAA guest room security requirements" appears in the listing. Tourism Editors view a percentage of rooms at each property. Because it is not feasible for them to evaluate every room in every lodging establishment, AAA cannot guarantee that there are working locks on all doors and windows in all guest rooms.

① SAMPLE LODGING LISTING

AAA | **EDEN PLAZA**
▽▽▽ *Motor Inn* ((987)6-2244
All Year $130-$150 XP $30
Location: 3 km n of San Miguel, on beach road. Fax: 987/22-666. **Facility:** Across from the Caribbean with pedestrian foot bridge access to beach and water facilities. Large attractive rooms. Includes a secluded cluster of thatched-roof cabanas, with separate sitting area and terrace with hammock. Meets AAA guest room security requirements. 208 units. Some whirlpool units. 3 stories, interior corridors. **Terms:** F12; 5 day cancellation notice, package plans. **Amenities:** voice mail, honor bars, hair dryers. *Some:* safes. **Dining:** dining room, restaurant, deli, 7 am-11 pm, $6-$10, cocktails. **Leisure Activities:** 2 pools, wading pool, beach access, swimming, scuba diving, snorkeling, fishing. **Fee:** windsurfing, scuba & snorkeling equipment, charter fishing, scuba instruction, lighted tennis court. **Guest Services:** [MAP] meal plan available, gift shop, valet laundry. *Fee:* area transportation. **Business Services:** conference facilities. **Cards:** AE, MC, VI.

SOME UNITS
🛇 🍽 ⊠ 🏊 ✕ 🎥 / 💻 🖨 /
FEE

② SAMPLE RESTAURANT LISTING

AAA | **PABLO'S GRILL**
▽▽▽ ▽▽▽ *Mexican* (981/6-2343
D $12-$22
Location: On beach at Punta Cancun; in Camino Real Cancun. **Hours:** 6:45 pm-midnight. **Reservations:** suggested. **Features:** No A/C; casual dress; cocktails & lounge; entertainment; valet parking. Fun-filled gastronomical tour through regions of Mexico, its customs, foods and people. Among the must-visit Cancun restaurants. High energy fun. Authentic Mexican food all made with fresh, quality ingredients. Colorful, artistic presentations. Excellent for families. **Cards:** AE, CB, DI, MC, VI.

✕

②

RATES AND DISCOUNTS

Rate lines: The rates listed for approved properties are provided to AAA by each lodging and represent the regular (rack) rate for a standard room. Rates are rounded to the nearest dollar and do not include taxes. Multiple rate lines are used to indicate a seasonal rate difference.

Rate lines show respectively—from left to right—the following information: the dates the rates in that line are effective; any meal plan included in the rate; the two-person rate charged; the extra person (XP) charge; and, if applicable, the family plan indicator. (**Note:** The two-person rate is the only rate shown in order to accommodate this book's two-column listing format.)

Meal plans are designated by CP (Continental Plan of pastry, juice and another beverage), ECP (Expanded Continental Plan offering a wider variety of breakfast items), BP (Breakfast Plan of full breakfast), AP (American Plan of three meals daily), MAP (Modified American Plan of two meals daily) or EP (European Plan, where rate includes room only). Family plan indicators are designated by F17 (children 17 and under stay free), D17 (discount for children 17 and under), F (children stay free) or D (discounts for children). The stipulated age may vary; the establishment also may limit the number of children to whom the family plan applies.

Most—although not all—hotels post their current rates in pesos at the front desk. If there is a rate card posted in the room, the rate shown on it will likely *not* be current. Any violations of posted rates should be reported along with documentation—either the bill itself or a photocopy—to AAA/CAA so that a full investigation can be made on your behalf. **Note:** For convenience, all rates are quoted in approximate U.S. dollars.

WHAT THE ⓐ MEANS

Lodgings and restaurants approved by AAA are eligible for the Official Appointment Program, which permits display and advertising of the ⓐ emblem. The ⓐ next to a listing printed in bold type identifies that property as an Official Appointment establishment with a special interest in serving AAA/CAA members. The ⓐ sign helps travelers find dependable accommodations.

ACCESS FOR THE DISABLED

Qualified properties listed in this book have symbols indicating they are fully accessible, semi-accessible or meet the needs of the hearing impaired. This two-tiered mobility standard was developed to meet varying degrees of accessibility needs.

Fully accessible properties meet the needs of those who are significantly disabled and utilize a wheelchair or scooter. A fully accessible lodging will provide at least one guest room meeting the designated criteria. A traveler with these disabilities will be able to park and access public areas, including restrooms, check-in facilities and at least one food and beverage outlet. A fully accessible restaurant indicates that parking, dining rooms and restrooms are accessible.

[SAVE] Semi-accessible properties meet the needs of those who are disabled but do have some mobility. Such travelers would include people using a cane or walker, or a disabled individual with good mobility but a limited arm or hand range of motion. A semi-accessible lodging will provide at least one guest room meeting the designated criteria. A traveler with these disabilities will be able to park and access public areas, including restrooms, check-in facilities and at least one food and beverage outlet. A semi-accessible restaurant indicates that parking, dining rooms and restrooms are accessible.

This symbol indicates a property with the following equipment available for hearing-impaired travelers: TDD at front desk or switchboard; visual notification of fire alarm, incoming telephone calls, door knock or bell; closed caption decoder available; text telephone or TDD available for guest room use; telephone amplification device available, with shelf and electric outlet next to guest room telephone.

The criteria used by AAA do not represent the full scope of the Americans With Disabilities Act of 1990 Accessibility Guidelines (ADAAG); they are, however, consistent with the ADAAG. AAA/CAA members can obtain from their local club the brochure "AAA Accessibility Criteria for Travelers With Disabilities," which describes specific criteria pertaining to the fully accessible, semi-accessible and hearing-impaired standards.

Note: Although ADAAG criteria apply only to U.S. properties, AAA Tourism Editors endeavor to apply these guidelines to properties in Mexico as well. Always phone ahead to fully understand an accommodation's offerings. Properties that do not fully comply with these exacting accessibility standards may still offer design features that meet the needs of some guests with disabilities.

According to the Americans With Disabilities Act (ADA), businesses that serve the public are prohibited from discriminating against persons with disabilities who are aided by service animals. Businesses must permit guests and their service animal entry, as well as allow service animals to accompany guests to all public areas of a property. A property is permitted to ask whether the animal is a service animal or a pet, or whether a guest has a disability. The property

LODGING EVALUATION CRITERIA

Regardless of the diamond rating, properties listed by AAA are required to provide:

- clean and well-maintained facilities
- a well-kept appearance
- hospitable staff
- comfortable furnishings and pleasant decor

Each guest room is required to have:

- comfortable beds and good quality bedding
- at least one chair
- adequate illumination at each task area
- adequate towels and supplies

Lodging Reservation and Deposit Definitions

RESERVATION: A temporary hold on lodgings, usually until 4 or 6 p.m. on the arrival date.

RESERVATION CONFIRMATION: Once the reservation process is complete, a "confirmation number" is assigned to the guest for future reference. When ample notice is given, a copy of the reservation details and confirmation number is mailed to the guest.

CREDIT CARD GUARANTEED RESERVATION: When reserved lodgings have been secured with a credit card number, the room will be held for the first night regardless of arrival time, but will be billed to the credit card if the guest fails to arrive at all (is a "no show"). Credit card guarantees usually pertain to the first night only.

RESERVATION DEPOSIT: These funds are collected from the guest in advance of arrival to secure reserved lodgings. A reservation deposit can be in the form of cash, check, money order, credit card transaction or other means to transfer funds. One or more days' payment may be required, depending on the length of the stay.

PREPAID RESERVATION: Reserved lodgings that are fully paid in advance of arrival.

CANCELLATION POLICY: Published terms/conditions set by the lodging by which the guest can cancel a reservation and recover all, or a portion of, the deposit/full payment. Sometimes a "service charge" or "handling fee" is levied regardless of how far in advance the reservation was cancelled.

CANCELLATION NUMBER: Upon receipt of a cancellation, it is customary for lodgings to assign a "cancellation number" that is given to the caller for future reference.

may not, however, ask questions about the nature of a disability or require proof of one. No fees or deposits (even those normally charged for pets) may be charged for the service animal. **Since properties in Mexico may not observe these guidelines, it is important that individuals traveling with service animals contact a business in advance and ascertain its policy.**

AAA does not evaluate recreational facilities, banquet rooms or convention and meeting facilities for accessibility. Call a property directly to inquire about your needs for these areas.

Making Reservations

It is a good idea to obtain confirmed reservations for accommodations at beach resorts and in most other Mexican cities during the peak travel seasons—roughly speaking, December through March at the resorts and June through August at the inland cities. Reservations are imperative for the week preceding and following Easter.

Always make lodging reservations before leaving home. A AAA Travel Agency can make reservations for members and will provide written confirmation if you request it. Establishments usually allow you to guarantee reservations without a deposit through the use of a major credit card (American Express, MasterCard or VISA). The card also is generally accepted for final payment, although you might be required to submit

a check to guarantee your reservations absolutely. As a rule, a room reserved without a deposit will be released if it is not claimed by a specified time (usually 4-6 p.m.), unless the establishment agrees in advance to a late arrival time. Resorts invariably require a deposit.

When making reservations, you must identify yourself as a AAA/CAA member. Give all pertinent information about your planned stay. Request written confirmation to guarantee all of the following: type of room, rate, dates of stay, and cancellation and refund policies.

Most establishments give full deposit refunds if they have been notified at least 48 hours before the normal check-in time. Listing prose will note if more than 48 hours' notice is required for cancellation. However, when making reservations, confirm the property's deposit, cancellation and refund policies. Some properties may charge a cancellation or handling fee. When this applies, "cancellation fee imposed" will appear in the listing. If you cancel too late, you have little recourse if a refund is denied. When an establishment requires a full or partial payment in advance, and your trip is cut short, a refund may not be given. **Note:** Age restrictions may apply.

When canceling reservations, call the lodging immediately. Document the date and time you called, the cancellation number if there is one, and the name of the person who handled the cancellation. If your AAA/CAA club made your reservation, allow them to cancel for you as well so you will have proof of cancellation.

When you are charged more than the maximum rate listed, question the additional charge. If management refuses to adhere to the published rate, pay for the room and submit your receipt and membership number to AAA/CAA within 30 days. Include all pertinent information: dates of stay, rate paid, itemized paid receipts, number of persons in your party, the room number you occupied and a list of any extra room equipment used. A refund of the amount paid in excess of the stated maximum will be made if our investigation indicates that unjustified charging has occurred.

If you find your room is not as specified, and you have written confirmation of reservations for a certain type of accommodation, you should be given the option of choosing a different room or finding one elsewhere. Should you choose to go elsewhere and a refund is refused or resisted, submit complete documentation to your local AAA/CAA club office *within 30 days*, including your reasons for refusing the room and copies of your written confirmation and any receipts or canceled checks.

HOTEL/MOTEL FIRE SAFETY

Because of the highly specialized skills needed to conduct professional fire safety evaluations, AAA Tourism Editors cannot assess fire safety. Listed properties with smoke detectors in guest rooms, as well as those offering the added protection of automatic sprinkler systems, are identified by one of two symbols *(see the sample listing)*. At each establishment whose listing shows one of these symbols, a sampling of rooms has been evaluated to determine that this equipment is in place.

What The Icons Mean

Member Values

(AAA) or **(AA)** Official Appointment

[fyi] Informational listing only

Member Services

(✈) Airport transportation

(🐕) Pets allowed

(🍴) Restaurant on premises

(🍴•) Restaurant off premises (walking distance)

(24🍴) 24-hour room service

(🍸) Cocktail lounge

(👶) Child care

Accessibility Features

(♿) Fully accessible

(♿) Semi-accessible

(🚿) Roll-in showers

(👂) Hearing impaired

Leisure Activities

(🏊) Outdoor pool

(🏊) Indoor pool

(🏊) Indoor/outdoor pool

(💪) Health club on premises

(💪•) Health club off premises

(🎯) Recreational activities

In-Room Amenities

(✗) Non-smoking rooms

(🌡) No air conditioning

(☎) No telephones

(📺) No cable TV

(🎬) Movies

(VCR) VCR

(📻) Radio

(☕) Coffee maker

(📟) Microwave

(🗄) Refrigerator

(DATA PORT) Data port/modem line

Availability

If an in-room amenity is available only on a limited basis (in some but not all rooms), the term "SOME UNITS" will appear above those icons.

SOME UNITS

♿ 👂 💪 🎬 VCR ☕ / 🗄 DATA PORT ✗ /

Additional Fees

Fees may be charged for some of the services represented by the icons listed here. The word "FEE" will appear below each icon when an extra charge applies.

SOME UNITS

♿ 👂 💪 🎬 VCR ☕ / 🗄 DATA PORT ✗ /

FEE   FEE   FEE

The Lodging Diamond Ratings

AAA Tourism Editors evaluate and rate each lodging based on the overall quality and services offered at a property. The size, age and overall appeal of an establishment are considered as well as regional decorating and architectural differences.

While guest services are an important part of all diamond ratings, they are particularly critical at the four and five diamond levels. A property must provide a high level of service, on a consistent basis, to obtain and support the four and five diamond rating.

Properties are world-class by definition, exhibiting an exceptionally high degree of service as well as striking, luxurious facilities and many extra amenities. Guest services are executed and presented in a flawless manner. The guest is pampered by a professional, attentive staff. The properties' facilities and operation help set industry standards in hospitality and service.

Properties are excellent and display a high level of service and hospitality. They offer a wide variety of amenities and upscale facilities in the guest rooms, on the grounds and in the public areas.

Properties offer a degree of sophistication. Additional amenities, services and facilities may be offered. There is a noticeable upgrade in physical attributes, services and comfort.

Properties maintain the attributes offered at the one diamond level, while showing noticeable enhancements in room decor and quality of furnishings.

Properties offer good but modest accommodations. Establishments are functional, emphasizing clean and comfortable rooms. They must meet the basic needs of comfort and cleanliness.

THE RESTAURANT DIAMOND RATINGS

AAA Tourism Editors are responsible for determining a restaurant's diamond rating based on established criteria.

These criteria were established with input from AAA trained professionals, members and restaurant industry experts. They are purposely broad to capture what is typically seen throughout the restaurant industry at each diamond rating level.

Often renowned, these establishments impart a world-class and opulent, adult-oriented experience. This is "haute cuisine" at its best. Menus are often cutting edge, with an obvious dedication to use of only the finest ingredients available. Even the classic dishes become extraordinary under the masterful direction of highly acclaimed chefs. Presentations are spectacular, reflecting impeccable artistry and awareness. An expert, formalized staff continuously anticipates and exceeds guest expectations. Staff members' unfailing attention to detail appears effortless, well-rehearsed and unobtrusive. Undoubtedly, these restaurants appeal to those in search of the ultimate dining experience.

Examples include renowned dining rooms associated with luxury lodgings, or exclusive independent restaurants often found in metropolitan areas.

These establishments impart a luxurious and socially refined experience. This is consistent fine dining. Menus typically reflect a high degree of creativity and complexity, featuring elaborate presentations of market-driven or traditional dishes. A cultured, professional and highly proficient staff consistently demonstrates a profound desire to meet or exceed guest expectations. Restaurants of this caliber are geared to individuals with an appetite for an elite, fine-dining experience.

Examples include dining rooms associated with luxury lodgings, or exclusive independent restaurants often found in metropolitan areas.

These establishments impart an increasingly refined and upscale, adult-oriented experience. This is the entry level into fine dining. Creative and complex menus offer a blend of traditional and trendy foods. The service level is typically semi-formal with knowledgeable and proficient staff. Routinely these restaurants appeal to the diner in search of an experience rather than just a meal.

Examples include high-caliber, chic, boutique and conventional restaurants.

These establishments provide for dining needs that are increasingly complex, but still reasonably priced. They typically exhibit noticeable efforts in rising above the ordinary in many aspects of food, service and decor. Service is typically functional yet ambitious, periodically combining informal style with limited self-service elements. Often well-suited to traditional, special occasion and family dining.

Examples include a varied range of specific concept (theme) and multi-purpose establishments.

These establishments appeal to a diner seeking good, wholesome, no-nonsense eating at an affordable price. They typically provide simple, familiar and unadorned foods served in a sensible, casual or self-service style. Often quick service and family oriented.

Examples include coffee shops, diners, cafeterias, short order and modest full service eateries.

LODGING CLASSIFICATIONS

AAA Tourism Editors evaluate lodgings based on classification, since all lodging types by definition do not provide the same level of service and facilities. Thus, hotels are rated in comparison to other hotels, resorts to other resorts—and so on. A lodging's classification appears beneath its diamond rating in the listing.

Hotel — *full service*
Usually high-rise establishments, offering a wide range of services and on-premise food/beverage outlets, shops, conference facilities and recreational activities.

Motel — *limited service*
Low-rise or multi-story establishment offering limited public and recreational facilities.

Country Inn — *moderate service*
Similar in definition to a bed and breakfast, but usually larger in size, with a dining facility that serves at least breakfast and dinner.

Resort — *full service*
Offers a variety of food/beverage outlets and an extensive range of recreational and entertainment programs—geared to vacation travelers.

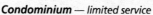

Bed & Breakfast — *limited service*
Usually smaller, owner-operated establishments emphasizing an "at home" feeling. A continental or full, hot breakfast is served and included in the room rate.

Condominium — *limited service*
Apartment-style units or homes primarily owned by individuals and available for rent. A variety of room styles and decor treatments, as well as limited housekeeping service, is typical.

Motor Inn — *moderate service*
Single or multi-story establishment offering on-premise food/beverage service, meeting and banquet facilities and some recreational facilities.

Complex — *service varies*
A combination of two or more types of lodging classifications.

Lodge — *moderate service*
Typically two or more stories with all facilities in one building. Rustic decor is common. Usually has food/beverage service.

Apartment — *limited service*
Primarily offers temporary guest accommodations with one or more bedrooms, a living room, a full kitchen and an eating area. Studio apartments may combine the sleeping and living areas into one room.

Cottage — *limited service*
Primarily individual housing units that may offer one or more separate sleeping areas, a living room and cooking facilities.

Ranch — *moderate service*
Often offers rustic decor treatments and food/beverage facilities. Entertainment and recreational activities are geared to a Western theme.

LODGING SUBCLASSIFICATIONS

The following are subclassifications that may appear along with the classifications listed above to provide a more specific description of the lodging.

Suite
One or more bedrooms and a living room/sitting area, closed off by a full wall. Note: May not have a partition bedroom door.

Extended Stay
Properties catering to longer-term guest stays. Will have kitchens or efficiencies and may have a separate living room area, evening office closure and limited housekeeping services.

Historic
Properties must meet one of the following criteria:
- Be listed on the National Register of Historic Places
- Be designated a National Historic Landmark
- Be located in a National Register Historic District

Classic
Renowned and landmark properties, older than 50 years, known for their unique style and ambience.

ARRIVING IN MEXICO

CROSSING THE BORDER

All U.S. and Canadian tourists entering Mexico by land must stop at the international border to show proof of citizenship, pay a fee to have their tourist card stamped, and complete the necessary forms if temporarily bringing a vehicle into the country. Hours of operation for Mexican customs and immigration offices at major border crossing points are as follows:

CALIFORNIA/MEXICO
Calexico/Mexicali—Daily 24 hours
San Diego/Tijuana—Daily 24 hours

ARIZONA/MEXICO
Douglas/Agua Prieta—Daily 24 hours
Lukeville/Sonoita—Daily 6 a.m.-midnight
Nogales/Nogales—Daily 24 hours

TEXAS/MEXICO
Brownsville/Matamoros—Daily 24 hours
Del Rio/Ciudad Acuña—Daily 24 hours
Eagle Pass/Piedras Negras—Mon.-Fri. 8-8, Sat. 10-2
El Paso/Ciudad Juárez—Daily 24 hours
Laredo/Nuevo Laredo—Daily 24 hours
McAllen/Reynosa—Daily 24 hours

PROOF OF CITIZENSHIP

U.S. and Canadian tourists traveling to Mexico must carry proof of citizenship. A valid (unexpired) passport is the most convenient, since it ensures problem-free re-entry into the United States, serves as a photo ID and facilitates many transactions, such as cashing traveler's checks. The U.S., Canadian and Mexican governments also recognize a birth certificate, which must be a certified copy with a raised seal from the government agency that issued it. A driver's license, baptismal certificate or voter registration card is *not* considered proof of citizenship.

You can request a passport application form by contacting the National Passport Information Center; phone (888) 362-8668. Comprehensive passport information and application forms also are available on the U.S. State Department website; the address is **travel.state.gov**.

It's a good idea to carry an extra copy of your birth certificate, as well as keeping a record of your passport number. Make two photocopies of your passport identification page and other personal documents before leaving home. Leave one set at home, and carry the other set with you in a separate place from your actual documents.

Those persons holding dual U.S./Mexican citizenship should be prepared to travel into and out of both countries with the proper documentation required by both countries. This includes a Mexican passport to travel into and out of Mexico as a Mexican citizen. U.S. citizens who also are Mexican nationals are considered Mexican by local authorities, which may hamper U.S. government efforts to provide consular protection should it be necessary.

TOURIST PERMITS

The Mexican government imposes a 170-peso (at press time, approximately $18 U.S.) tourist entry fee for each visitor entering Mexico for pleasure or on business. The fee must be paid in order to have your tourist permit validated if you plan to remain anywhere in Mexico for more than 72 hours, or stay less than 72 hours and travel beyond the 26-kilometer (16-mile) border zone.

If you're entering Mexico by land it is advisable to obtain your tourist permit prior to leaving the United States. The government-issued permit (commonly referred to as a tourist card, but actually a form) is available upon presentation of proof of citizenship from Mexican consulates in the United States and Canada (*see page 40*) or immigration offices at official points of entry. If you're arriving by air, it is distributed on the flight; if you're arriving by cruise ship, it is distributed upon disembarking.

If arriving by land, the tourist entry fee is paid at a branch of any bank operating in Mexico (a list of banks at which the fee can be paid is shown on the back of the tourist permit form). Upon payment the permit is stamped with an official "Fee Paid" designation. (Although the fee may be paid at any time prior to leaving the country, it is recommended that it be paid at the border.) If arriving by air, the fee is included in the price of the ticket charged by the airline. If arriving by cruise ship, the fee is collected upon disembarking or is included in the purchase price of a cruise, but only if the stay is longer than 72 hours. **Note:** All visitors are required to produce verification of payment by showing the "Fee Paid" stamp on their tourist permit upon departing Mexico.

Exemptions are as follows:

—Visitors traveling by land or sea anywhere in Mexico and staying less than 72 hours

—Visitors traveling by land to destinations within the 26-kilometer (16-mile) border zone, regardless of length of stay

—Those visiting as students (as defined by Mexican immigration laws)

—Visitors traveling by land beyond the border zone and staying more than 72 hours but limiting their visit to the following routes/destinations: Tijuana to Ensenada, B.C.; Mexicali to San Felipe, B.C.; Sonoita to Puerto Peñasco, Son.; Ciudad Juárez to Paquime, Chih.; Piedras Negras to Santa Rosa, Coah.; or Reynosa to China, N.L., and Reynosa to Presa Cuchillo, Tamps.

Certain concessions are granted to those visiting Mexico on a recurring basis. Tourists entering by land should keep their validated tourist permit showing proof of payment, which allows unlimited visits within the permit's 6-month validity period. Business travelers entering by land should keep their validated business entry card (not a tourist permit) as proof of payment, which grants unlimited visits within a 30-day period. **Note:** Any person traveling in Mexico on business with only a tourist permit is subject to a fine. For further information contact the Embassy of Mexico, 1911 Pennsylvania Ave. N.W., Washington, D.C. 20006; phone (202) 728-1600.

When applying for a tourist permit, minors (under age 18) traveling without their parents— i.e., alone or with friends or relatives—must present proof of citizenship (a valid passport or birth certificate) and a notarized, signed letter of consent from their parents granting permission for the minor to travel in Mexico. If the minor's parents are divorced or separated, the letter must be accompanied by divorce or separation papers, or proof of sole custody. Even if one parent goes along, a minor must submit from the absent parent a notarized, signed letter of consent, or when applicable, divorce, death certificate or guardianship papers.

Canadian citizens, including parents, traveling abroad with a minor should be prepared to document their legal custody of that child. If a minor is traveling with a friend or relative, the individual with the minor must have a notarized letter of consent from both parents (including a telephone number) or a custody document. In all cases it is important for the minor to have a valid Canadian passport. Mexican citizens living in the United States must go to the Mexican consulate nearest their place of residence and sign the legal documents granting permission for the minor to travel in Mexico.

The single-entry tourist permit is valid for up to 180 days and must be returned to Mexican border officials upon leaving Mexico. A multiple-entry permit allows unlimited entry into Mexico within the 180-day period. If a tourist permit is not used within 90 days of issuance it becomes void. Carry your tourist permit with you at all times while in Mexico. If you lose it, a duplicate can be obtained from local immigration officials.

You *must* be out of the country by the end of the validity period, or you will be subject to a fine. Extensions of up to 90 additional days can be obtained from Mexican immigration officials only when a physician verifies that you are too ill to travel.

ARRIVING BY AIR

There are international airports in or near the resorts of Acapulco, Bahías de Huatulco, Cancún, Cozumel, Ixtapa, Cabo San Lucas/San José del Cabo, Mazatlán and Puerto Vallarta, as well as in Mexico City, Guadalajara, Monterrey and Mérida, among other cities. These airports receive regular flights from the United States as well as some charter flights. Major Mexican cities that receive direct U.S. flights are so identified in their descriptive listing. **Note:** Unlike nonstop service, a direct flight stops at least once and may involve changing planes.

The following major international airlines serve Mexico:

Aero California, (800) 237-6225

Aeroméxico, (800) 237-6639

www.aeromexico.com

Alaska Airlines, (800) 252-7522

www.alaskaair.com

American Airlines, (800) 433-7300

www.americanair.com/

America West Airlines, (800) 235-9292

www.americawest.com/

Continental Airlines, (800) 525-0280

www.flycontinental.com/

Delta Airlines, (800) 241-4141

www.delta-air.com/

Mexicana Airlines, (800) 531-7921

www.mexicana.com

TWA, (800) 221-2000

www.twa.com/

United, (800) 241-6522

www.ual.com/

The two major domestic airlines are Mexicana and Aeroméxico, with flights linking the resorts and larger cities to Mexico City. Smaller regional airlines operate in different parts of the country. Aeromar serves central Mexico, Aviacsa the Yucatán Peninsula and southern Mexico, and Taesa mainly northern Mexico. Other regional airlines include Aerocaribe, Aerocozumel and Aero Guadalajara. Traveling between destinations within the country often involves changing planes in Mexico City. Schedules, fares and routes all are subject to change. Smoking is generally prohibited on all international flights; check with the appropriate Mexican carrier regarding its smoking policy.

Airports almost always offer fixed-rate transportation via bus, minivan or taxi to downtown or hotel zone areas. Usually there is a booth at the airport where you can purchase a ticket or voucher. You also may have the option of riding in a private car (which costs more) or sharing the ride (and paying less). For safety reasons, never hail an unmarked cab outside the terminal.

There are frequent flights to Mexico from such "gateway" cities as Dallas/Fort Worth, Houston, Los Angeles and Miami. A bewildering array of fares, vacation packages and promotions also are available, and it often pays to search for a bargain. AAA/CAA members can obtain fare and schedule information and make reservations through AAA Travel Agencies. When making reservations, be sure you confirm all flights at least 72 hours prior to departure—particularly the return leg of a round trip.

Charter flights, while offering low fares, also are subject to the greatest number of restrictions. The charter operation can cancel a flight up to 10 days before it is scheduled to depart; if *you* cancel, you may not be able to recoup your money. When considering a charter flight, review the refund policy and contract stipulations carefully.

Car Rentals

U.S. rental cars generally cannot be driven across the border into Mexico. One exception is Hertz, which permits designated vehicles rented at airport facilities in San Diego, Tucson and Yuma to be taken across the border; special paperwork is required. Enterprise Rent-a-Car also allows rental vehicles to be driven into Mexico, contingent upon the purchase of Mexican automobile insurance; however, the policy varies according to the Enterprise location.

If you're flying into Mexico but plan on taking a side trip from your main destination, renting a car is an easy way to sidestep dealing with unfamiliar local transportation. AAA/CAA members can reserve a rental car through their local club; it is recommended that you make all necessary arrangements prior to your departure.

The major U.S. franchises are located in the larger cities. There are numerous Mexican companies as well, but although their rates are cheaper the vehicles may be less reliable. Overall, the cost of renting a car in Mexico is at least, if not more, expensive than in the United States.

It's also advisable to prepay for the vehicle in advance. Most companies require a credit card; some will accept a cash deposit, although the amount is likely to be hefty. A U.S. or Canadian driver's license is acceptable. The usual minimum age limit is 25; special restrictions may be placed on drivers above a certain age. If you want such extras as air conditioning or automatic transmission, make sure you know what the additional cost will be. Also take your itinerary into account when deciding how long to rent. While most companies will allow you to rent in one location and drop off at another, the drop-off charge can be quite steep. Request that a copy of

the reservation confirmation be mailed to you; this should reduce the chance of overcharging, since the rate will be printed on the confirmation slip.

Booking a vehicle in advance simplifies matters, but it may not guarantee the make and model of your choice when you arrive. Many Mexican rental vehicles are Volkswagen Beetles, and if one is unavailable a company may try to send you elsewhere or charge for an upgrade. Inspect the car carefully before you drive off the lot. Check the windshield for cracks; the windshield wipers; the body and fenders for dents, rust, etc.; the head and taillights; the tires for wear and pressure; and note any missing items, such as the gas cap or floor mats. Seat belts and a fire extinguisher are required by law. A thorough inspection is well worth the time, as you will be charged for anything that is perceived damaged or missing.

Mexican automobile insurance is required; it is provided by the rental company and figured into the total cost of the contract. Standard contracts normally include both liability coverage and collision coverage after payment of a deductible. Obtaining an optional collision damage waiver (CDW) will cost more but means that you won't have to pay the deductible (which can be in excess of $2,000) in the event of an accident. While the extras add up, they're worth it for peace of mind—an accident a thousand miles away from home in a foreign country can be a traumatic experience. Look into what your own automobile insurance covers—it might, for example, take care of damages to a rental car.

Keep the rental company's toll-free emergency number handy in case you run into trouble on the road. And when you return the vehicle, remember to fill the gas tank; the refueling charge will be much more expensive than any pump.

Arriving By Personal Vehicle

If you're driving into Mexico, a little advance preparation can prevent crossing the border from becoming a lengthy process. AAA club offices at border locations can provide Mexican automobile insurance to members. Automobile Club of Southern California and California State Automobile Association offices also provide for members the forms required to bring a vehicle into the country (the temporary vehicle importation permit and the promise to return vehicle form). ACSC offices include an instruction sheet explaining how to fill out the forms.

Following are the locations of AAA border offices. (**Note:** The Chula Vista office is 8 miles north of the Baja California border.)

YUMA, ARIZONA
AAA Arizona
1045 S. 4th Ave. (85364)
Mon.-Fri. 8:30-5
(520) 783-3339

CHULA VISTA, CALIFORNIA
Automobile Club of Southern California
569 Telegraph Canyon Rd. (91910-6495)
Mon.-Fri. 9-5, Sat. 9-1
(619) 421-0410

EL PASO, TEXAS
AAA Texas
1201 Airway Blvd., Suite A-1 (79925)
Mon.-Fri. 9-6, Sat. 9-1
(915) 778-9521

LAREDO, TEXAS
AAA Texas
7100 N. San Bernardo Ave., Suite 101 (78041)
(I-35, Del Mar exit 4)
Mon.-Fri. 9-6, Sat. 9-1
(956) 727-3527

TEMPORARY IMPORTATION OF VEHICLES

Both a temporary vehicle importation permit and a promise to return vehicle form are required for vehicle travel beyond 26 kilometers (16 miles) of the mainland border. These documents are **not** required on the Baja California Peninsula (the states of Baja California and Baja California Sur), unless the vehicle is put on a ferry bound for the mainland. In the state of Sonora, a free "Sonora Only" pass good for 6 days can be obtained at the 21-kilometer (13-mile) immigration checkpoint on Mex. 15 south of Nogales. A sticker is placed on the vehicle, which must be returned to the same booth where you obtained it when departing Sonora. If you plan to drive beyond the Sonora state border, a temporary vehicle importation permit and windshield sticker also must be obtained (*see below*).

To obtain these documents from a Mexican consulate or an immigration office at an official point of entry, the vehicle owner must be 18 years of age or older, have a valid U.S. or Canadian driver's license, present proof of citizenship (passport, birth certificate or affidavit of citizenship), and provide proof of ownership (the original current registration) for each vehicle being taken into Mexico. Information on the application for temporary vehicle importation must match the information on the promise to return form; the same requirements apply to both.

The temporary importation permit is generally issued for 90 days; extensions of up to 90 days can be obtained from Mexican immigration officials. Only one permit will be issued per person, for one motorized vehicle at a time. It should be carried with you (not left in your car) at all times while in the country. If the permit or the promise

to return vehicle form is lost or stolen, replacement documentation can be issued by Mexican customs offices to the vehicle importer as long as a certified document is obtained from the U.S. Embassy (U.S. residents) or the Canadian Embassy (Canadian residents) or one of their consulates attesting to the loss.

At the point of entry (mainland border crossings or transporting a vehicle by ferry from Baja California to the mainland), an $11 (plus tax) administrative fee must be paid using a major credit card (American Express, MasterCard or VISA). The card must be in the registered owner's name and issued by a U.S. or Canadian bank or lending institution. Cash, checks, money orders or a credit card issued by a Mexican bank will not be accepted. The fee can be paid only at a Banjército (Bank of the Army) branch office. A sticker is then applied to the vehicle's windshield.

In addition to the completed temporary vehicle importation permit and promise to return vehicle form, the following documents must be presented at the point of entry: acceptable proof of citizenship, a valid driver's license, a tourist permit and a current vehicle license/registration receipt, which should be carried in the car at all times while in Mexico. (Carry a copy of the registration receipt, not the original.)

Note: The temporary importation permit *must* be presented *at* the border. "Second border" stops at the 26-kilometer (16-mile) point (a checkpoint for proper documents and dutiable goods) will *not* accept the $11 administrative fee or issue a windshield sticker.

For leased or company-owned vehicles, a notarized letter of authorization (printed on stationery showing the company's or leasing agency's letterhead) that permits the driver to take the vehicle out of the United States or Canada and into Mexico is required, and an employee ID card must be presented. If the vehicle is not fully paid for, a letter from the lienholder authorizing use of the vehicle in Mexico for a specified period must be presented. Rented vehicles require a rental agreement and a notarized affidavit from the rental car company stating the company's permission to bring the car into Mexico. The same name must appear on the rental agreement and on the temporary vehicle importation permit.

If the owner does not have or does not wish to use a major credit card, a bond—based on the value of the vehicle—must be posted with a Mexican bonding firm (Afianzadora) at the point of entry. However, this is a costly procedure that involves much paperwork.

For the temporary importation of two vehicles, at least two persons must travel as tourists, and separate permits must be obtained for each vehicle. For example, one individual will not be allowed with both a car and a motorcycle, even if he or she owns both vehicles. One of the vehicles must be registered to another qualified driver in the same party, or a second person can obtain a permit for the additional vehicle by presenting a notarized affidavit of permission from the owner.

It is not mandatory for a group of people arriving in Mexico in the same vehicle to leave in the same vehicle; however, the individual who obtained and filled out the temporary vehicle importation permit must leave the country in the same vehicle in which he or she arrived. Drivers crossing and recrossing the border need not obtain a new temporary vehicle importation permit with each crossing, provided that the initial permit is still valid.

The temporary importation permit, promise to return form and windshield sticker **must be returned to Mexican customs officials at the border for cancellation,** either before or on the expiration date shown on the promise to return vehicle form and *prior to* re-entering the United States. Those failing to comply will be fined. There is no set fine; the amount can be up to the total value of the vehicle, and there is the possibility that the vehicle could be confiscated. You also will be denied subsequent entry into Mexico until the fine is paid.

The regulations for automobiles also apply to recreational vehicles. Equipment and luggage should be packed to permit easy customs inspection. Vehicles exceeding 3 metric tons in weight require a special permit, as do buses. If in doubt as to how your vehicle will be classified, consult the nearest Mexican consulate office before starting your trip.

Trailers and motor homes can only stay in Mexico 6 months unless they are left in bond at an authorized trailer park. Such trailer parks have placed a bond with the nearest Mexican customs office, making them responsible for the storage of the recreational vehicle.

When you pay the administrative fee and enter Mexico with your own vehicle, a guarantee must be signed on your credit card, giving the Mexican government authority to track down the owner or driver if the vehicle is left behind. If a fine is incurred, it may be charged against the credit card. Should your vehicle become incapacitated, arrangements to leave without it can be made through the U.S. Embassy or one of its consulates, or through a Mexican customs (Aduana) office. **Note:** The Mexican government does not provide facilities for storing an automobile if you have to suddenly leave the country. It can be left with friends, but no one will be able to drive it; Mexican law dictates that a personal vehicle cannot be driven unless its owner is present.

Hacienda (the Mexican Treasury Department) has the authority to confiscate any vehicle that has been illegally imported into the country. Hacienda also has the authority to confiscate a vehicle whose owner (or driver) cannot produce the proper temporary vehicle importation documentation. **Note:** It is illegal for a foreigner to sell a motor vehicle in Mexico.

INSURANCE

U.S. automobile insurance is *not* valid in Mexico. It must be replaced by insurance from a Mexican company. While some American companies may extend their coverage a certain number of miles from the border or number of days in Mexico, *only* a Mexican automobile liability policy is acceptable as evidence of financial responsibility if you have an accident in that country.

Arrange for a policy with full coverage issued through a reliable Mexican insurance company with complete adjusting facilities in cities throughout the country. AAA offices in border states can provide Mexican automobile insurance to members. Automobile Club of Southern California and California State Automobile Association offices will issue Mexican automobile insurance documents for rented vehices under the following conditions: The rental car is driven only in the states of Baja California and Baja California Sur, the 16-mile (26-kilometer) border zone along the Mexican mainland, or the Mex. 8 "tourist route" from Lukeville, Ariz. to Puerto Peñasco, Son.

Unlike the prevailing tenet of U.S. and Canadian law, Mexican law is based on the Napoleonic Code, *which presumes guilt until innocence is proven.* As a result, *all* parties (operators of vehicles) involved in an accident in Mexico are detained for assessing responsibility. If the accident involves no personal injury, the drivers may be asked to go with the attending officer to the police station to complete the necessary accident report, and the vehicles will usually be impounded for investigation. Once blame is established, the negligent driver's vehicle will remain impounded until he or she pays the damages.

If the accident causes injury or death, the operators will be jailed until the authorities determine who was at fault. Then only the responsible driver will remain incarcerated until he or she guarantees restitution to the victims and payment of the fine imposed for causing the accident (under Mexican law an automobile accident is a criminal offense).

A Mexican insurance policy is recognized by the authorities as a guarantee of proper payment for damages according to the terms of the policy. When presented, it can significantly reduce red tape and help to bring about an early release. However, a Mexican insurance policy may not prevent a motorist from actually being detained *if* he or she is involved in an accident that results in injury or death.

Note: Automobile Club of Southern California border offices in California, New Mexico and Texas offer optional coverage with their policy that provides professional legal services necessary to deal with Mexican authorities. Under this coverage, a bond will be submitted in order to obtain the release of the automobile and the freedom on bail of the insured party who is involved in legal proceedings.

If an accident in which a driver is at fault results in damage to government property, such as road signs, safety fences, light or telephone poles, toll stations, street pavement or sidewalks, he or she must pay for the repairs needed even if no other vehicle was involved or no injury or death occurred.

All accidents or claims *must* be reported before leaving Mexico. If you need assistance with a claim, you should obtain it *only* from an authorized agent or adjuster of the insurance company that issued the policy. Official release papers should be kept as evidence that the case is closed, especially if the car shows obvious damage from the accident.

The Mexican government has no minimum requirement for insurance; the agent will help you obtain the coverage best suiting your needs. If you obtain Mexican insurance through a AAA club office, the policy will be written by the day, with a discount for more than 30 days' coverage, and will be issued immediately upon application. Call ahead to determine what specific information (vehicle ID number, included accessories, etc.) is needed so that the policy can be accurately written. Towed vehicles *must* be identified in the policy; if not, the policy can be declared void.

Rates are based on the current value of the vehicle; towed vehicles are covered separately. Policies are written in both English and Spanish. In the event of a disagreement, the Spanish text will prevail. Read your policy carefully before entering Mexico to discern what is and isn't covered. Most companies, for example, do not include lawyer's fees to defend the policyholder against criminal charges, although adjusters in the larger cities may keep lawyers on a retainer who will act on behalf of the insured free of charge.

Personal accident insurance, baggage insurance and medical coverage are all wise investments. AAA members should check with their local club regarding the availability of these services.

TRAVEL TO CENTRAL AMERICA

Anyone driving through Mexico en route to Central American countries, and intending to drive back through Mexico into the United States, must have a U.S. passport and the appropriate visa for each country visited. If tourism is the sole purpose of the trip and the 180-day travel limit has not been exceeded, it shouldn't be necessary to return the temporary vehicle importation permit, the promise to return vehicle form and the windshield sticker at the Mexico/Guatemala or Mexico/Belize border; all three documents should be retained and then returned to customs officials when departing Mexico.

Following are the current entry requirements for U.S. and Canadian citizens traveling to Central America; for additional information, contact the nearest Mexican consulate office or the U.S. consulate in Matamoros prior to departing the United States.

Belize—A visa is not required for visits of less than 3 months; visits of more than a month require a permit from Belizean immigration officials. A passport is required, as is proof of sufficient funds and proof of onward passage.

Costa Rica—A visa is not required. A passport or acceptable proof of citizenship is required, as is a tourist permit, proof of sufficient funds and proof of onward passage.

El Salvador—A visa and proof of onward passage are required. Visitors must have at least 6 months' continued validity on their passport and may be required to submit a notarized employer letter.

Guatemala—A passport and tourist permit both are required, as is proof of sufficient funds and proof of onward passage. **Note:** For safety reasons, visitors entering the country by motor vehicle along the coastal route are advised to use the Talismán/El Carmen border crossing (Mex. 200) rather than the crossing between Ciudad Hidalgo and Tecún Umán (the crossing used by most commercial traffic).

Honduras—Visitors are strongly advised to have a visa. Proof of sufficient funds and proof of onward passage also is required.

Nicaragua—A visa is not required for U.S. visitors; it is required for Canadian visitors. A passport is required for all visitors and must have at least 6 months of continued validity after the dates of stay in Nicaragua. Proof of sufficient funds and proof of onward passage also is required.

Panama—A passport, tourist permit and proof of onward passage are required. Tourist cards with a 30-day validity period are available from airlines that serve Panama.

TRAVELING WITHIN MEXICO

FOR ASSISTANCE

Special needs frequently require a special kind of help, particularly when you are visiting a foreign country. The following sources of aid are suggested for travelers to Mexico.

MEDICAL ASSISTANCE

Ask at your hotel desk or consular office for the name and address of the nearest hospital and English-speaking doctor. Several Mexican and U.S. companies offer medical evacuation service by air; the U.S. Embassy in Mexico City provides a list of these firms. Tourist publications often print names and addresses of local hospitals. Most Mexican cities and towns also have a Cruz Roja (Red Cross) facility. For additional medical aid information, *see the "In Case of Emergency" box under the listing for Mexico City, page 301, and "The Informed Traveler" boxes under the listings for Acapulco, page 227, Guadalajara, page 355, Puerto Vallarta, page 271, and Cancún, page 91.*

LEGAL DIFFICULTIES

Assistance often is provided by Protección al Turista (Tourist Assistance). Offices are in Ensenada, Mexicali, Rosarito Beach, San Felipe, Tecate and Tijuana on the Baja California Peninsula and in the capital of each state on the mainland, normally in the same building that houses the state tourism office. The U.S. Embassy and Mexican consulate offices in the United States and Canada can provide lists of attorneys who speak English. Procuraduría Federal del Consumidor (Federal Consumer Protection Agency) offices are in all state capitals and other major cities.

If you run into problems with the police in Mexico, Tourist Assistance recommends that the following steps be taken:

—Observe or ask for the officer's name (most police wear nameplates), badge number, department (federal, state or municipal), and vehicle number.

—Go to the nearest police station to pay any traffic-related fine and ask for a receipt.

—Write out the nature of the complaint and mail it to the Tourist Assistance Director.

Although the vast majority of tourists return home without encountering any legal difficulties, you could be arrested for breaking laws you didn't know about or for what would be considered a minor offense in Canada or the United States. For example, if you are involved in a traffic accident that causes injury you will automatically be taken into police custody, regardless of who is at fault. If detained or arrested, you should contact one of the following organizations:

The United States Embassy. For U.S. consular services in Mexico City, phone 01 (5) 209-9100 and ask for Citizens Services.

GOVERNMENT OFFICIALS

Visitors who encounter trouble or require emergency services while in Mexico should contact the appropriate office of the State Tourism Department or, if there is no office nearby, notify local police. Outside major cities, Mexican government authority rests with the *delegado*, an elected official who presides over emergencies and civil or legal disputes. This individual can be found at the *delegación municipal* or *subdelegación*. Offices are often at the *palacio municipal* (city hall); ask at your hotel desk for directions. In isolated rural areas, authority is usually vested in an appointed citizen who reports to the nearest *delegado*. Tourist crime, however, occurs rarely in out-of-the-way places, so it shouldn't be necessary to resort to the last measure.

The Secretaría de Turismo (the Ministry of Tourism, or SECTUR) in Mexico City staffs a 24-hour hotline that can offer information regarding what laws protect visitors and where to turn for assistance. Operators are bilingual. In Mexico City, phone (5) 250-0123 or 250-0151; elsewhere in Mexico, phone 01 (800) 903-9200 (toll-free long distance); from the United States, phone (800) 482-9832. Within Mexico, this hotline also can be used to summon the Green Angels. *See "Phone Service," page 71,* for additional information about making telephone calls within Mexico.

Your embassy or consulate. By international law, you have the right to call a consular officer *(see "Embassies, Consulates and Consular Agencies," page 59).* **Note:** The long distance access code for the United States and Canada from within Mexico is 95 (station to station). For Mexico from within the country the code is 91.

The International Legal Defense Counsel. This association allows access to a worldwide network of reputable attorneys. Their address is ILDC, Packard Bldg., 111 S. 15th St., 24th Floor, Philadelphia, PA 19102; phone (215) 977-9982.

SECODAM, or the Comptroller and Administrative Development Secretariat, can help with complaints and also provides information about all government bureaus. Phone (5) 604-1240 or 480-2000 in Mexico City, 01 (800) 001-4800 elsewhere within Mexico.

Embassies and consulates advise and assist their nationals in case of accident, serious illness or death. Consular agents can help in such matters as lost passports. Important travel information, compiled by the U.S. Embassy in Mexico City, is contained in the brochure "Tips for Travelers to Mexico." Obtain a copy before your trip by enclosing $1 and writing the Superintendent of Documents, U.S. Government Printing Office, Washington, D.C. 20402, or the Consumer Information Center, Pueblo, CO 81009.

STATE DEPARTMENT SERVICES

The U.S. State Department's Overseas Citizens Services office deals with such problems as notifying home if you are caught in a natural disaster or political disturbance, delivering emergency messages, making emergency money transfers and providing emergency loans. In these and other instances, have friends or family phone (202) 647-5225 (24 hours). Information also is provided for nonemergency questions. For emergency situations dealing with minors, contact the Office of Children's Issues; phone (202) 736-7000.

Note: Regulations prohibit tourists from sending *collect* wires outside Mexico. Collect telephone calls can be made from any Mexican city to U.S. and Canadian points and to several other countries.

Embassies, Consulates and Consular Agencies

Note: If calling from outside Mexico, dial 01152 before the area code and phone number. The U.S. Embassy's fax number is 01152 (5) 208-4178; the website address is www.usembassy-mexico.gov/. Office hours vary but are indicated where known.

U. S. EMBASSY:

Mexico City, D.F., Paseo de la Reforma #305, Col. Cuauhtémoc, (5) 209-9100; Mon.-Fri. 8:30-5:30

CANADIAN EMBASSY:

Mexico City, D.F., Av. Schiller #529, Col. Polanco, (5) 724-7900; Mon.-Fri. 8:30-2

U. S. CONSULATES:

Ciudad Juárez, Chih., (16) 11-3000, after hours (16) 28-5559; Mon.-Fri. 8-4:45

Guadalajara, Jal., Progreso #175 at Avenida López Cotilla, (3) 825-2998 or 825-2700; Mon.-Fri. 8-4:30

Hermosillo, Son., Calle Monterrey #141 Pte., (62) 17-2375 or 17-2382; Mon.-Fri. 8-4:30

Matamoros, Tamps., Avenida Primera #2002, (88) 12-4402; Mon.- Fri. 8-noon and 1-5

Mérida, Yuc., Paseo Montejo #453 at Avenida Colón, (99) 25-5011; Mon.-Fri. 7:30-4

Monterrey, N.L., Avenida Constitución #411 Pte., (8) 345-2120; Mon.-Fri. 8-5

Nuevo Laredo, Tamps., Allende #3330, Col. Jardín, (87) 14-0512; Mon.-Fri. 8-12:30 and 1:30-5

Tijuana, B.C., Calle Tapachula #96, Col. Hipódromo, (66) 81-7400; Mon.-Fri. 8-4:30

U. S. CONSULAR AGENCIES:

Acapulco, Gro., Costera Miguel Alemán #121 (in the Hotel Acapulco Continental Plaza), (74) 81-1699 or 69-0556; Mon.-Fri. 10-2

Cabo San Lucas, B.C.S., Boulevard Marina and Pedregal #1, (114) 3-3566; Mon.-Fri. 10-noon

Cancún, Q.R., Plaza Caracol, 2nd floor (Boulevard Kukulcán, Km 8.5), (98) 83-0272; Mon.-Fri. 9-1 and 3-6

Ixtapa, Gro., Plaza Ambiente (Office 9), (755) 3-1108; Mon.-Fri. 10-2

Mazatlán, Sin., Rodolfo T. Loaiza #202, Golden Zone (in the Hotel Playa Mazatlán), (69) 16-5889; Mon.-Thurs. 9-1

Oaxaca, Oax., Calle M. Alcalá #201 (Office 206), (951) 4-3054; Mon.-Fri. 9-2

Puerto Vallarta, Jal., Vallarta Building, Plaza Zaragoza, (322) 2-0069; Mon.-Fri. 9-2

San Luis Potosí, S.L.P., calles Francisco P. Mariel and V. Carranza, (4) 812-1528; Mon.-Fri. 9-1

San Miguel de Allende, Gto., Dr. Hernández Macías #72, (4) 152-2357; Mon. and Wed. 9:30-1 and 4-7, Tues. and Thurs. 4-7

CANADIAN CONSULATES:

Acapulco, Gro., Costera Miguel Alemán #121 (in the Hotel Acapulco Continental Plaza), (74) 85-6621; Mon.-Fri. 9-1

Cancún, Q.R., Plaza Caracol, 2nd floor (Boulevard Kukulcán, Km 8.5), (98) 83-3360; Mon.-Fri. 9-5

Guadalajara, Jal., Aurelio Aceves #225 on Minerva Circle (in the Fiesta Americana Guadalajara), (3) 625-3434, ext. 3005; Mon.-Fri. 10-1

Puerto Vallarta, Jal., Av. Hidalgo #226, (322) 2-5398; Mon.-Fri. 9-1

Tijuana, B.C. (66) 84-0461; Mon.-Fri. 9-1

Mexico's Highways

Mexico forever seems to be in the midst of a massive road-building program. Many of the old roads follow ancient Indian causeways or the cobblestoned *caminos carreteros* (carriageways) of colonial days. But new construction continues, and bypasses and loop roads are becoming standard features around cities and towns that have narrow streets and heavy traffic.

A network of toll highways *(autopistas)* covers most parts of the country. Most of the newer tollways are four-lane, have road shoulders and comparable in quality to U.S. highways. Emergency roadside phones often are spaced about every 2 kilometers (1.25 miles) along toll roads, and many are patrolled by the Green Angels as well. For the most part, toll roads are safe, speedy and scenic. Tolls are on the expensive side, however—so much so that the highways are often all but deserted because Mexican motorists can't afford to use them.

Do not expect most free roads in Mexico to compare to the Interstate highway system in the United States. Following the dictates of mountainous terrain, nontoll roadways are mostly rolling or winding, although there are many straight and/or level stretches in northern Mexico and the Yucatán Peninsula. Some of them have a sandpaper texture that affords better traction on curves but is wearing on tires.

Each Mexican state is responsible for the maintenance of its roads, and some are better kept than others. Weather conditions, especially heavy rains, and such natural occurrences as mud or rockslides can keep roadways in disrepair. Lanes tend to be narrow, and shoulders are either narrow or nonexistent.

Roads in Mexico are generally not marked as clearly as those in the United States. Signs for turns and route directions will sometimes consist of city or town names only. Ideally, route numbers are posted every 5 kilometers (3 miles) on small roadside markers, but these also can be few and far between.

If you plan to drive little-used or unpaved roads, inquire locally about conditions before heading out. Even a good map may not be accurate regarding the conditions of unpaved or ungraded routes; deep sand "roads" can stall even a four-wheel-drive vehicle, and seasonal downpours can render unpaved roads impassable. Put a protective covering over your luggage to keep out dust, and store camera equipment in plastic bags.

Driving Precautions

Above all, motorists in Mexico should heed this advice: **Do not drive after dark if at all possible**. Few roads are equipped with street lights, and night visibility is poor. Vehicles, which are sometimes driven with no headlights, might suddenly swerve to your side of the road to avoid potholes (which become invisible after dark). Bicycles without lights or reflectors are ridden, and pedestrians commonly use the roads at night. In addition, the Green Angels *(see the "Emergency Road Service" subheading)* stop patrolling at 8 p.m. If you intend to cover a certain distance during any one day, get an early start and estimate your total driving time on the side of caution. *Never* pull off the road to sleep.

The possibility of robbery is another reason to curtail driving after dark. Bandits are likely to target foreign vehicles and have been known to pose as stranded motorists or police officers, so it's never a good idea to stop and offer assistance if you're unsure of the situation. You must stop, however, at designated police checkpoints *(see "Law Enforcement" below)*.

Livestock—principally cattle, goats and donkeys—may unexpectedly appear on rural roadways, even during the day and along those that are fenced. Slow down and give them a wide berth. Furthermore, animals will be almost invisible on unlighted roads at night—and can cause tremendous damage to your vehicle if they are struck.

Always be alert to road conditions and other drivers. Bus, truck and other drivers who are familiar with local routes will drive faster and negotiate maneuvers more boldly than tourists, who will likely find the highways more narrow, winding and weathered than those in the United States.

On some main corridors truck traffic is moderate to heavy, and truckers may drive aggressively or inconsiderately. If a truck begins to pass on a two-lane road, be prepared to pull off onto the gravel or graded dirt flanking the road surface if necessary to give the truck adequate room. Exercise caution; along the sides of roadways without shoulders there often is a full or partial covering of brush or undergrowth. Be particularly careful if you are attempting to pass a slow-moving truck—the driver isn't likely to pull over to give you more maneuvering room. Also be on the lookout for vehicles that are temporarily stopped in the roadway, particularly in rural areas.

Signaling one's intentions can convey a different meaning in Mexico. What American and Canadian drivers would interpret as an indicated left turn—a flashing left taillight—can also mean an invitation to pass on the left. Attempt to pass only when it can be done safely. If making a left turn off a two-lane roadway where there is no separate left-turn lane, the driver is expected to pull over to the right as far as possible and wait for traffic to clear before making the turn.

Heed the signals given by other drivers as well. When an oncoming truck flashes its headlights a couple of times, the driver is warning you to slow down or pull over. Since this signal is usually made when both you and the truck are approaching a one-lane bridge or narrow section of the road, you had better comply—the truck driver generally will not.

Speed bumps *(topes)* and potholes *(baches)* constitute perhaps the greatest danger to motorists on Mexican highways. Speed bumps are at the entrance to almost every town, no matter how small, and also can be encountered within towns. They are prohibited on open sections of road and on toll roads, except at the entrance to toll stations. Warning signs will say *Topes* or *Vibradores* and give the distance in meters. Instead of words, some *topes* signs show a picture symbol and the distance in meters. Some speed bumps may not be preceded by a warning sign. *Topes* are raised cobblestone bumps that can damage the underside of a vehicle unless negotiated at a very slow speed (in other words, you basically must come to a stop). *Vibradores* are both lower and wider than *topes*.

Potholes are a particular problem along older free (nontoll) roadways and are exacerbated during the summer rainy season. Short-term maintenance may be nothing more than filling the pothole with sand or dirt. As some can be large enough to swallow a tire, caution is advised wherever potholes occur.

In the downtown sections of larger cities there are likely to be a number of one-way streets. Instead of signs, small arrows on the side of buildings or on lampposts often will indicate traffic direction. Follow the flow; if in doubt as to whether you are driving in the right direction, note which way parked vehicles are facing.

Recreational Vehicle Travel

Recreational vehicle travel should be confined to the main highways. Do not park in isolated areas or camp along the highway or on beaches. Vehicles left unattended should be securely locked, with the shades or curtains drawn and all equipment (bicycles, chairs, etc.) removed from the outside. Never sleep in any vehicle parked along the roadside.

Propane gas is obtainable by vacationers traveling in recreational vehicles more than 50 kilometers (30 miles) below the U.S. border. This policy ensures that tourists who use propane for their engines, stoves and heaters will have an adequate supply.

For a listing of AAA rated recreational vehicle sites, *see "About Campgrounds," pages 484-489.*

Gasoline, Oil and Repairs

All gas stations in Mexico are concessions granted by the federally run oil company, Pemex. Fuel prices are fixed by the government. Be sure you are charged the correct amount; make sure the pump is at zero before having your tank filled; know just how many gallons/liters your tank holds; and keep smaller denominations of pesos in case attendants run out of change. Stations on major routes are spaced at adequate intervals but occasionally run out of supplies; it's a good idea to always keep your gas tank at least half full.

Most Pemex stations sell two grades of unleaded *(sin plomo)* gas: "Magna," dispensed from green pump handles, is the cheaper of the two; the premium grade is dispensed from red pump handles. Pemex stations no longer offer Nova (leaded) gas, although diesel fuel is available. The quality of the fuel tends to be somewhat lower than comparable U.S. unleaded grades. Stations are full service; let the attendant fill the tank, but make sure he zeroes out the pump. Tipping is customary; a few pesos is fine.

Since unleaded pump nozzles in Mexico are sometimes larger than those in the United States, it's a good idea to keep a funnel in the car. Remember that pumps in Mexico register liters, not gallons; 10 liters is equal to about 2.5 gallons. For conversion information, *see the metric chart*

Did You Know?

- Green traffic lights in Mexico flash three times just before they turn yellow.

- If you become lost in an unfamiliar city or town, ask a local taxi driver for directions or have him lead you where you want to go; it can save a lot of headaches. A knowledge of Spanish is helpful in these situations, and agree on a price first.

- Motorists stopped at red lights in cities will often be approached by people attempting to earn money by washing windshields. If you're not interested, mouth the words *"no tengo dinero"* or shake your head "no" and rub your thumb and index finger together—the international symbol for "I have no money."

- In small towns, signs announcing *topes* (speed bumps) can appear suddenly, and not just at the entrance to town. Heed the warnings if you're driving; you basically have to slow to a stop to avoid scraping the underside of your vehicle on these exaggerated bumps.

Driving Restrictions In Mexico City

Due to continuing air pollution caused by emissions released by the enormous number of vehicles, driving in the Mexico City metropolitan area, including the Distrito Federal (Federal District) and parts of the state of México, is restricted 1 day a week based on the last digit of a vehicle's license plate. The restrictions do not apply from 11 p.m. to 5 a.m. They are in effect until further notice and apply to all vehicles, regardless of license plate origin—not just those with Mexican tags. Foreign drivers unaware of the driving restrictions face potentially heavy fines—up to $300—and possible impoundment of their vehicle. For additional information *see the "Don't Drive Today" box on page 294.*

on page 452. Stations with a "GasoPLUS" sign accept credit cards of the same name for gasoline purchases, but otherwise you'll have to pay cash, so keep peso amounts handy.

Service stations and private garages carry oils made in Mexico by foreign companies and by Pemex. Its brand, Brio, comes in several grades which are indicated by the color of the can; gold, black and blue are the best.

If your own vehicle or a rental car requires routine maintenance or major repairs while on the road, there are plenty of automotive repair shops (indicated by signs that say *taller mecánico*) in most parts of the country. Make sure you have a complete understanding about any work to be done as well as its cost. If a part must be ordered there could be additional expense and long delays, as permission from Mexican customs is needed to import parts. A knowledge of Spanish is usually necessary when negotiating with car repair shops, and it could be difficult finding a mechanic familiar with the make and model of your vehicle. Also keep in mind that businesses in Mexico may close from around 2-4 p.m. for *siesta.*

EMERGENCY ROAD SERVICE

The idea of having a vehicle breakdown in Mexico can be unnerving, but motorists unfortunate enough to find themselves stranded do have a resource: the **Green Angels**. Since 1960, these crews have patrolled major highways throughout the country. "Angeles Verdes" are identified by their distinctive green uniforms and green-and-white pickup trucks. Most Green Angel patrols are linked to some 40 base stations; routes are patrolled daily 8-8.

Green Angels personnel are carefully selected and should be familiar with the facilities along their routes. Services offered include vehicle mechanical aid, towing, adjustment or changing of tires, road condition information, medical first aid and protection. Motorists pay for the cost of automobile parts, gasoline and oil, but service is rendered free of charge. A tip is customary, although not required. Although all crew members

are supposed to be bilingual, a knowledge of Spanish will still come in handy.

To enlist the assistance of a crew, pull completely off the highway and lift the hood of your vehicle. Contact the Secretaría de Turismo (the Ministry of Tourism, or SECTUR) to obtain help or to have a crew dispatched; phone their national hotline, 01 (800) 903-9200 (toll-free long distance within Mexico). In and around Mexico City, phone 01 (5) 250-8221, ext. 130 or 250-8555, ext. 297.

If you break down in a remote area, it may be necessary to hail a passing motorist, or preferably a bus or truck driver, and ask that he or she stop at the nearest available location to place the call. You also may be able to use one of the emergency telephones found along most of the newer toll highways and also along some older roads. Since Green Angel crews constantly cover their assigned sector, however, the chances are good that a patrol will soon locate you. Unfortunately, repairs are another matter *(see the "Gasoline, Oil and Repairs" subheading).*

ROAD SIGNS

Road signs are a mix of international picture symbols and signs in Spanish. A sign saying *Via Corta* indicates a short or alternate route. Toll roads are designated by the word *cuota* (and also by the letter "D" following the route number), nontoll roads by *libre*. Right turns on red are prohibited unless a sign is marked *Continua*. A sign with the word *Retorno* means a U-turn is permitted. Signs often posted just before entering small towns are *Poblado Proximo* (upcoming town), *Disminuya su Velocidad* (reduce your speed) or those that show the maximum speed limit allowed.

Common signs along highways include *Arbochate el Cinturon* (Buckle Your Seat Belt) and *No Deje Piedras Sobre el Pavimento* (Don't Leave Stones on the Pavement); the latter refers to the common practice of placing rocks in the road to denote a hazard or disabled vehicle. Some intersections without traffic signals have signs that say *Ceda el Paso a un Vehiculo* (Cede the Right of Way to One Vehicle); they are posted on each intersecting road and indicate that one vehicle at a time may proceed.

Be careful when approaching bridges. Those marked *Un Solo Carril* or *Puente Angosto* are narrow, one-way bridges. When two cars approach such a bridge from opposite directions, the first driver to flick his or her headlights has the right-of-way. The other should pull to the side of the road, allowing the first driver to cross. Although not a regulation, it is a general practice.

PARKING

If possible, schedule daily activities so that your car does not have to remain unattended for any length of time. Heed "no parking" signs, which depict a red circle with a diagonal line superimposed over a capital "E." Illegally parked cars will be towed, or their license plates will be removed. Recovering either item can result in a nightmare of time, expense and frustration. If in doubt, park in a guarded lot rather than on the street. Never leave valuables in plain sight in a parked vehicle.

On a one-way street, make certain your vehicle is parked on the left side, not the right. Parking on the street also likely means being approached by a youngster who will offer to watch your vehicle while you're gone. This often is a good idea, since the couple of pesos you hand over are a small price to pay for peace of mind. If a group of boys appears on your return, however, pay only one.

LAW ENFORCEMENT

On main highways the speed limit is generally about 100 km/h (60 mph) or as posted. In many cities the limit is about 40 km/h (25 mph); in some small towns it may be as low as 30 km/h (18-20 mph). Always obey the speed limit; while local police are generally lenient toward tourists who commit minor traffic violations, they make an exception in the case of speeding.

In Mexico City and those parts of the state of Mexico falling within the greater metropolitan area (particularly north and east of the Federal District), motorists with foreign license plates may be stopped by police for alleged driving infractions. If you commit an infraction and recognize it, accept the *boleta de infracción* (ticket) without arguing.

If you are stopped and did not do anything wrong, however, do not give in to a demand for graft. Take the officer's number and ask to speak with his *jefe* (HEH-feh), or boss, or to be taken to the nearest *delegación de policía* (police station) to explain your situation. In Mexico City, the Secretaría de Turismo (the Ministry of Tourism, or SECTUR) may be able to provide assistance if you feel you have been unfairly accused of a traffic violation; phone (5) 250-0123 or 250-0151. Elsewhere in Mexico, phone 01 (800)

903-9200 (toll-free long distance), or contact the nearest state tourism department.

Note: Motorists in northwestern Mexico—primarily those heading north toward the border—may occasionally be stopped by narcotics police, members of the military or inspection station personnel who are searching for arms or, more likely, drugs. These individuals may also speak only Spanish, which can make the situation stressful for those not fluent in the language. While you should cooperate fully—even if it means explaining in English that you do not speak Spanish—by all means report any unfair treatment to the U.S. Embassy in Mexico City or to the nearest Mexican consulate office upon your return home. Such checkpoints are most likely to occur from Sinaloa north through Sonora, although they are a possibility practically anywhere in the country.

BUS SERVICE

Mexico has a well-developed bus system, and this is an economical way to travel around the country. More than a dozen Mexican bus lines maintain frequent express service from U.S. border points to most cities. Although service is less extensive in Baja California, buses travel practically everywhere. Among the major lines are **Autobuses de Oriente** (ADO), **Enlaces Terrestres Nacionales** (ETN), **Transportes del Norte** (TN) and **Estrella de Oro**.

Most of these companies offer both first-class (*primera*) and "deluxe" service (referred to as *ejecutivo, lujo, primera plus* and similar terms). The quality is comparable to first-class U.S. bus service, and frequently includes such amenities and extras as air conditioning, reclining seats, footrests, restrooms, movies, free snacks and beverages, as well as controlled 95 km/h (60 mph) speed. They also make few—sometimes no—stops and carry fewer passengers. For long trips, bring your own food—in case you don't want to eat in the restaurant where the bus stops—drinking water and a roll of toilet paper. Seats on first-class buses are normally reserved in advance. Smokers take note: Smoking is not permitted on first-class and "deluxe" buses.

Note: Travel only during the day; avoid overnight trips. First-class and "deluxe" buses use toll highways and are less likely to encounter incidents of robbery or assault.

Second- and third-class buses should by no means be compared to U.S. lines. You can hail one of these buses just about anytime and anywhere simply by standing at the side of the road and waving, and they're certainly a great way to experience local life. However, they make interminable stops, the vehicles themselves are frequently antiquated and can be unpleasantly hot, and you may have to share your seat with a pig or chicken. Furthermore, they cost only slightly less than first-class or "deluxe" buses, and without the convenience of making advance reservations.

Many Mexican cities have one central bus station (*Central Camionera or Central de Autobuses*), which may or may not be near the main plaza or center of town. The various bus lines maintain offices at the central station. In some cities there may be several stations in different locations that serve specific companies or destinations. If you're unsure where to go, ask for the *estación del autobús* and give your destination. For trips between major cities, purchase a reserved-seat ticket from the station in advance; this is imperative for long weekends, and around school holidays, holiday seasons and important fiestas.

Note: Round-trip fares are not sold. Although buses frequently run behind schedule, be punctual—yours might depart the second it's supposed to. Routes, fares and departure times are always subject to change, and the only way to obtain this information is directly from the station. English is not likely to be spoken, so write your destination down and make certain you're getting on the right bus. Mexican bus schedules usually indicate whether the bus is *local* or *de paso* (which means it is en route from another location). *Directo* or *expresso* indicate a nonstop route. *Salida* means departure; *llegada,* arrival.

Do not use local buses for in-town transportation; a taxi, although more expensive, is safer. Exceptions are buses that travel specifically to tourist attractions; while these may be slow, they allow you to relax and enjoy the scenery.

The American bus line **Greyhound Lines Inc.** provides limited schedule and fare information for major Mexican buslines and can ticket passengers to most U.S. border cities, in addition to Tijuana. Once across the border, passengers make arrangements with a Mexican busline. Often there are buses that shuttle between the U.S. and Mexican stations. From Mexico City, bus trips to points of interest throughout the country are easily arranged; the major buslines operate out of four huge terminals located in the northern, southern, eastern and western sections of the city.

One option to using buses as your main means of on-the-road transportation is to take a guided motor coach tour. Prior to 1991, U.S. and Canadian visitors were required by law to use Mexican buses and take Mexican tours once they crossed the border. Restrictions on bus travel have eased, and American buses now are able to make the entire journey. Such U.S. companies as **Gray Line Tours** offer trans-border bus excursions from several hours to several days' duration that visit various parts of Mexico. Contact a travel agency for details.

Rail Service

Passenger rail service in Mexico has declined as "deluxe" (first-class) bus service becomes more and more common. Private companies now operate Mexican trains, and there is only one class of service: regular first class (*única primera*), which consists of a reclining seat (there are no longer berths or private rooms). If you want to see the country while someone else does the driving, bus travel is recommended. One popular tourist train trip is the **Chihuahua al Pacífico** railway, which runs through the rugged Sierra Madre Mountains and the spectacularly scenic Copper Canyon region of northwestern Mexico (*see Copper Canyon listing under Northwestern Mexico*).

Ferry Service

A private company, **Grupo Sematur**, operates regularly scheduled ferry service between the Mexican mainland and Baja California. Round trips connect the ports of Santa Rosalía-Guaymas, La Paz-Topolobampo (Los Mochis) and La Paz-Mazatlán. Reservations, necessary at all times, should be made at least 1 week in advance (at least 1 month if your departure date is during a holiday period). **Note:** Although reservations can be made from the United States or within Mexico by phone, as well as in person at one of the ferry offices, a knowledge of Spanish will be necessary.

Expect frequent changes in schedules and rates. It is advisable to reconfirm the rate as well as space availability before you depart. Normally, ferries depart Santa Rosalía on Wed. and Sun. at 8 a.m. and Guaymas Tues. and Fri. at 8 a.m.; sailing time is about 8 hours. Ferries depart La Paz Wed.-Mon. at 8 p.m. and Topolobampo (Los Mochis) Mon.-Sat. at 9 a.m.; sailing time is about 9 hours. Ferries depart from both La Paz and Mazatlán Sun.-Fri. at 3 p.m., with Sat. sailings during holiday periods; sailing time is about 19 hours. Within Mexico, current schedule and fee information may be obtained by calling 01 (800) 696-9600 (toll-free long distance).

Note: If you plan on transporting a vehicle from Baja California to the Mexican mainland, it is necessary to obtain a temporary vehicle importation permit. Although permits are supposed to be available at Baja ferry offices, they rarely are. To avoid frustration and disrupted travel plans, obtain the permit at the border.

When applying for a vehicle permit, acceptable proof of citizenship, the *original copy* of the current registration and an authorized letter of permission from the lienholder (if a vehicle is not fully paid for) all must be presented for each vehicle being transported (including motorcycles). For additional details *see "Temporary Importation of Vehicles," page 55.*

The ferry office in La Paz is at Guillermo Prieto and 5 de Mayo, 2 blocks southeast of Plaza Constitución. It is open Mon.-Fri. 7-1 and 4-6, Sat.-Sun. 8-1. The ferry terminal is at Pichilingue, the deep-water port for La Paz, about 16 kilometers (10 miles) north of the city. In Santa Rosalía, the ferry office is in the terminal building on Mex. 1, just south of the main entrance into town. In Topolobampo, Guaymas and Mazatlán, offices are at the ferry terminal.

In the state of Quintana Roo, a daily ferry carries passengers and vehicles from Puerto Morelos to Cozumel; however, variable schedules can cause long waiting periods. Passenger boats also make several daily trips to Cozumel from Playa del Carmen. In addition, daily passenger trips run from Puerto Juárez, just north of Cancún, to Isla Mujeres; daily passenger/vehicle trips run from Punta Sam to Isla Mujeres. *See Cancún listing, page 93, and the separate listings for Playa del Carmen and Puerto Morelos under Yucatán Peninsula.*

HEALTH CONCERNS

Sanitation and hygiene in Mexico have improved considerably in the last several decades. Several endemic infectious diseases have been eradicated, and today life expectancy at birth is 70 years for men, 78 years for women. Reasonable precautions will eliminate serious health risks for almost all foreign visitors.

VISITING HIGH-ALTITUDE AREAS

If you live in or are used to a lower altitude, you may need a short adjustment period when visiting areas above 1,525 meters (5,000 feet). Don't push yourself too hard; a light diet and reduced intake of alcoholic beverages are recommended. Move about in a leisurely fashion for the first few days. If you're affected by the altitude (headache or nausea), rest quietly until you feel comfortable; it may take from 12 to 36 hours before you feel better. Another health consideration at high altitudes is overexposure to the sun; use a suntan lotion that has an effective sunscreen agent.

Persons with weak hearts or of very advanced age should consult their physician before undertaking prolonged visits to cities at high elevations. Travelers with specific health concerns should inquire about recommended immunizations or medications to carry with them.

Acute Mountain Sickness (AMS), which can strike at altitudes of 2,450 meters (8,000 feet) or more, is the body's way of coping with reduced oxygen and humidity. Also known as altitude sickness, its symptoms include headaches, double vision, shortness of breath, loss of appetite, insomnia and lethargy. Some people complain of temporary weight gain or swelling in the face, hands and feet. Even those used to high altitudes may feel the effects of AMS. If symptoms strike, stop ascending. A quick descent will alleviate the discomfort.

The negative reaction of your body to changes in altitude is lessened if you're in good physical shape and don't smoke. Ascend gradually, eat light but nutritious meals and drink plenty of bottled water. Alcohol consumption may aggravate AMS symptoms if they occur.

Note: The elevation for city and place descriptions is given when it is over 762 meters (2,500 feet).

AIR QUALITY

As is common when traveling anywhere in the world, a change in weather or lifestyle can particularly affect the health of elderly visitors, young children or those who suffer from cardiac or respiratory conditions. Mexico City's dense traffic and air pollution, conditions present in any large metropolis, are factors that nevertheless should be taken into consideration. Air pollution also is a factor in Guadalajara and Monterrey.

Mexico City's location is partly responsible for its pollution problem: More than 7,000 feet above sea level, it is situated at the bottom of a valley ringed with mountains. Despite the unfavorable geography, a thin atmosphere and an estimated 3.5 million vehicles on the streets, federal and city authorities continue to take steps toward a cleaner environment.

EATING AND DRINKING

Follow the cardinal rule for fruits, vegetables and seafood: Do not eat anything that has not been peeled by you, or that cannot be cooked or boiled. Avoid unpasteurized dairy products as well. Otherwise, take every opportunity to enjoy regional dishes, which are described in more detail under "Food and Drink" in the *Mexico the Country* section of this book. Avoid food sold by street vendors, but at the better restaurants in Cancún, Mexico City, Puerto Vallarta and other cities where tourism is big business, virtually anything on the menu can be enjoyed without fear.

Mexican restaurants traditionally do not have a separate nonsmoking area. One exception is Vips, a restaurant chain that is casual, bright, modern, clean, efficient and springing up everywhere.

Bottled water in liter or smaller sizes is sold throughout Mexico at gas station convenience stores, grocery stores and shops catering to tourists. Chemical disinfecting tablets also are available from pharmacies and supermarkets. If the hotel has its own purification system, tap water can be used for brushing your teeth or rinsing contact lenses; ask to make sure, and also ask about the ice dispensed by ice machines. Most hotels routinely provide bottled water for drinking (some may charge for it when you check out). If in doubt about the water in smaller towns, ask for *agua purificada*. Remember that this includes ice cubes. If you find yourself in an area where bottled water is not available, boil water vigorously for one full minute to kill disease-causing organisms.

These precautions should serve to ward off the most common visitor ailment, diarrhea (which Mexicans call *turista*). Bed rest and a liquid diet (unsweetened tea is best) will cure most cases. If these preventive measures fail, see a doctor. There are physicians, surgeons, specialists, good hospitals and Mexican Red Cross clinics in all the major cities and larger towns. In many villages, the Instituto Mexicano del Seguro Social (IMSS), the Instituto de Seguridad y Servicios Sociales de los Trabajadores del Estado (ISSSTE) and the Secretaría de Salud run clinics or hospitals where visitors can receive medical assistance. Most of the better hotels have house doctors; if not, your hotel manager or the local police will help you find medical assistance. It's not a good idea to buy over-the-counter antibiotics.

DISEASES

The risk of contracting typhoid or cholera is minimal, despite sporadic cholera outbreaks. Vaccinations will offer protection in areas off the tourist itinerary, where running water and drainage systems frequently are inadequate, but vaccinations should not be considered a substitute for caution in selecting food and drink. In the case of cholera or other intestinal ailments, this means avoiding raw or undercooked seafood and cold seafood dishes.

Malaria and the mosquitoes that transmit the disease are unpredictable at best in sections of Mexico, depending on such local conditions as weather, altitude, mosquito control efforts and the prevalence of disease. Mosquitos also can spread dengue fever. In coastal areas, the risks of being bitten are greater. Use mosquito repellent (brands containing DEET are said to be the most effective) if you plan on spending time outdoors, and try to avoid being out at dusk, when mosquitos are most likely to bite.

The following states have a risk of malaria outside urban areas: Campeche, Chiapas, Guerrero, Michoacán, Nayarit, Oaxaca, Quintana Roo, Sinaloa and Tabasco. Consult your physician or local health department before leaving for information on the status of malaria risk and the advisability of taking a preventive drug.

Tourists arriving in Mexico from yellow fever-infected areas must have a yellow fever vaccination certificate; tourists arriving directly from the United States or Canada are not required to have the certificate.

The Centers for Disease Control and Prevention (CDC) in Atlanta operates a hot line with international health requirements and health recommendations for foreign travelers. Topics include general vaccinations, food and water guidelines and current disease-outbreak reports. A touch-tone phone is needed for the daily 24-hour service; phone (404) 332-4559. For faxed information, dial 404-332-4565, request an international directory and select the desired documents for the area you are visiting. The website address is **www.cdc.gov/**.

PERSONAL SAFETY

Violent crime in Mexico has increased drastically—by some estimates, as much as 80 percent—since 1994. The skyrocketing crime rate has been blamed on several factors: a criminal justice system that investigates few crimes and punishes even fewer perpetrators; law enforcement officers in tacit partnership with organized criminal activity (and out-of-work former soldiers and police who turn to such activity); rising unemployment fueled by economic hardship; and the ever-growing gap between rich and poor that makes crime an increasingly lucrative career option.

The Mexico City metropolitan area, where an estimated 21 million people are crammed together, has been hit especially hard. Armed attacks have occurred there in broad daylight, and kidnappings for ransom have made national headlines. Tijuana and Ciudad Juárez—both centers of the flourishing border drug trade—have seen violent crime escalate. Political instability in the states of Guerrero and Chiapas has led to sporadic violence (although not directed at foreigners). But other cities, including such tourist destinations as Cabo San Lucas, Cancún, Puerto Vallarta and San Miguel de Allende, have few crime problems.

To counteract Mexico's current high-profile reputation as a dangerous place, the Ministry of Tourism has set up a website, "Safe Travels in Mexico," that provides information relating to street crime and security issues, as well as safety tips for specific regions and cities. The "Travel Tips" link offers practical advice concerning driving, sightseeing and airports. The address is **www.safemexico.com**.

Regardless of the destination, sound judgment should prevail; the same behaviors one would use at home to maintain personal safety also apply here. For example, it is very important to look and act confident rather than bewildered when out in public. But don't flaunt expensive watches, jewelry or clothing; those most likely to be targeted for robbery or assault are easily identifiable as tourists or as individuals who are well-off or wealthy.

Avoid putting your wallet in a back pocket or wearing a purse with a shoulder strap that can be grabbed by a passerby. Petty thieves and pickpockets use a razor to slash pockets or bags, so keep your belongings close to you at all times. Put cameras in briefcases or bags with a chain-reinforced strap. Stash traveler's checks and cash in different places; for example, in money belts and extra pockets sewn inside clothing. Keep photocopies of passports, credit cards and other documents in a separate place from the originals. Be very cautious around ATM machines. If possible, use one during the day inside a large commercial facility; avoid nighttime transactions at glass-enclosed street machines.

If you're driving, do not leave valuables in plain view in your car; stow possessions out of sight. Use parking lots or garages whenever possible. Parking areas are designated by a sign with the word "Estacionamiento" and the international symbol of a red circle with a capital "E" inside. Always lock your car, roll up the windows and park in a well-lighted area. If traveling by bus or train, be especially careful at the station; never leave your luggage unattended, and lock all items together with a chain or cable if possible.

As crime is an unfortunate byproduct of widespread poverty, highway robberies do occur, particularly outside of tourist areas and in the southern part of the country. To avoid becoming a target, don't drive at night, stick to toll or major highways where possible, and above all do not pull off the road to sleep. Camp in designated national parks or at RV sites rather than along lonely beaches or other unsupervised wilderness areas.

In less-traveled areas of Mexico—particularly near the northern and southern international borders in Sonora and Quintana Roo, respectively, and in the states of Chiapas, Guerrero and Oaxaca—motorists may be stopped at military checkpoints and approached by official-looking men who request identification and ask where you are going. If you are stopped at a roadblock, remain calm and polite, comply with instructions, speak as little Spanish as possible, and get badge numbers and names. If asked to hand over your wallet, give them *only* the proper identification; if necessary, remove all your money first. Report any irregularities to the appropriate Department of Tourism or consular office.

Poorly paid police, particularly in and around Mexico City, may intimidate foreign motorists into paying "fines" for minor infractions. You could also encounter a situation in which you are charged with an infraction that you are certain you did not commit. Such a situation can be both frightening and infuriating, but if it happens, try to remain calm. Ask to be shown documentation of the rule you violated. Request to speak with someone of higher authority if necessary, and be

ware of "plainclothes policemen"; insist on seeing identification. Very obviously writing down all the details of the incident—name, badge number, the nature of the alleged violation, the exact location where it occurred—may help defuse the situation. Avoid handing over an original driver's license, car rental contract, vehicle registration or any other document; always carry photocopies.

If resistance provokes further trouble, ask for the ticket, pay it at a bank and claim a receipt. To register a complaint, contact the Secretaría de Turismo (the Ministry of Tourism, or SECTUR) in Mexico City; phone (5) 250-0123 or 250-0151, or 01 (800) 903-9200 (toll-free long distance within Mexico).

Women, either traveling alone or with others, normally do not need to take special precautions, but there are a few things that should be kept in mind. While ethnic or sexual stereotyping is unfortunate, it can occur. Female travelers who look obviously foreign, or those with fair skin and hair, may attract unsolicited attention. If this happens, the best response is no response. In *cantinas*, bars with a macho, often hard-drinking male clientele, female customers are unwelcome. Sexual assault is not out of the question, particularly in Mexico City. In bars and nightspots (even those in areas frequented by tourists) avoid accepting a drink from a stranger; it may be drugged.

CURRENCY

The monetary unit is the peso (its symbol is the dollar sign, or $). One peso equals 100 centavos. There are 10¢, 20¢ and 50¢ coins; peso coins are in denominations of $1, $2, $5, $10, $20 and $50. Bills are in denominations of 20, 50, 100, 200 and 500 pesos. The 10¢, 20¢ and 50¢ coins are not often used, but they come in handy as spare change to give to the needy, if you're so inclined, or to help facilitate souvenir purchases at markets. Hang on to smaller denomination bills and coins as you accumulate them, or exchange a dollar amount that will yield small-denomination coins or bills.

Cash payments for amounts that include centavos are rounded off to the nearest 10 centavos. An item costing 11.52 pesos, therefore, would be rounded off to a cash payment of 11.50 pesos; an item costing 11.56 pesos would be rounded off to a cash payment of 11.60 pesos. Check and credit card payments will show the exact amount and must be paid in that amount. Credit card charges are converted into dollars by the bank issuing the card, usually at a favorable bank rate.

In border cities and some tourist resorts, prices in Mexican currency may carry the abbreviation

MAXIMUM/MINIMUM TEMPERATURES - RAINFALL

(TEMPERATURES ARE IN FAHRENHEIT, RAINFALL IN INCHES)

	JAN.	FEB.	MAR.	APR.	MAY	JUNE	JULY	AUG.	SEPT.	OCT.	NOV.	DEC.
ACAPULCO,												
GUERRERO	88/72	88/72	88/72	88/73	90/76	90/77	91/77	91/77	90/76	90/76	90/75	88/73
	.3	.1	.1	.1	1.1	10.4	8.9	10.4	15.0	6.3	1.9	.3
CHIHUAHUA,												
CHIHUAHUA	64/36	69/39	75/44	82/53	89/59	93/66	89/66	88/65	85/60	80/52	72/42	65/36
	.3	.1	.1	.1	.4	1.4	3.0	3.1	2.0	.7	.2	.3
CANCUN,												
QUINTANA ROO	83/67	84/67	86/69	89/72	90/73	90/75	90/75	91/75	89/75	87/74	85/71	83/69
	3.5	2.2	1.6	1.6	4.6	7.0	4.3	5.9	9.0	8.6	3.8	4.3
CUERNAVACA,												
MORELOS	78/55	81/56	85/59	86/62	85/63	81/62	79/60	79/60	77/60	78/58	79/57	78/55
	.5	.2	.2	1.1	2.7	10.3	10.0	9.0	9.8	3.7	.8	.1
DURANGO,												
DURANGO	66/40	70/43	75/46	81/51	84/56	85/60	81/59	79/59	77/57	76/52	72/46	66/42
	.4	.2	.1	.1	.3	2.0	3.8	3.8	3.3	1.3	.3	.4
GUADALAJARA,												
JALISCO	74/44	78/46	82/49	86/53	88/57	84/61	79/60	79/59	78/59	78/54	77/48	74/46
	.5	.2	.2	.3	1.0	6.4	9.8	7.6	5.8	2.3	.4	.5
GUANAJUATO,												
GUANAJAUTO	70/46	73/48	77/51	81/54	82/57	79/58	77/57	77/57	75/57	75/54	73/49	70/47
	.5	.1	.2	.8	1.3	5.0	4.7	4.6	4.7	1.7	.6	.4
LA PAZ,												
BAJA CALIFORNIA SUR ..	73/55	76/55	79/56	85/59	88/65	93/66	96/74	96/75	94/74	90/69	83/62	76/57
	.6	.1	.1	0	0	.1	.5	1.4	2.5	.5	.2	.8
MAZATLAN,												
SINALOA	73/63	73/62	74/63	77/66	81/71	85/77	86/78	87/78	86/78	85/76	80/70	75/65
	.6	.2	.1	.1	0	1.2	6.0	8.0	8.9	2.9	.5	.6
MERIDA,												
YUCATAN	82/64	84/64	89/68	92/70	92/72	91/73	91/73	91/73	89/73	86/71	83/67	82/65
	1.2	1.1	.6	.6	2.9	5.1	5.0	6.0	7.7	4.4	1.4	1.4

Maximum/Minimum Temperatures - Rainfall
(Temperatures are in Fahrenheit, Rainfall in Inches)

	JAN.	FEB.	MAR.	APR.	MAY	JUNE	JULY	AUG.	SEPT.	OCT.	NOV.	DEC.
MEXICO CITY,												
Distrito Federal	70/42	74/44	78/48	80/51	80/52	77/54	74/52	74/52	72/52	72/49	71/45	69/43
	.4	.1	.4	1.1	2.0	4.9	6.1	6.0	5.3	2.1	.6	.2
MONTERREY,												
Nuevo Leon	68/48	73/52	79/56	86/64	89/68	92/71	94/72	93/72	87/69	81/63	74/55	70/50
	.5	.8	.6	1.1	1.4	2.5	1.8	3.8	5.9	3.3	.9	.4
MORELIA,												
Michoacan	70/45	73/47	77/51	80/54	81/58	77/59	74/58	74/57	73/57	73/53	72/49	70/46
	.6	.2	.2	.7	1.7	5.7	6.6	6.1	5.2	2.3	.6	.5
PUEBLA,												
Puebla	71/44	73/46	77/51	79/53	78/55	75/55	74/54	74/54	73/54	74/51	73/47	71/44
	.3	.2	.2	1.1	2.7	5.7	5.0	6.3	6.2	2.8	.9	.2
QUERETARO,												
Queretaro	73/44	77/46	82/51	86/55	87/57	84/58	81/57	81/57	79/56	78/52	76/48	74/45
	.6	.2	.3	.7	1.8	4.4	4.9	4.1	3.5	1.6	.4	.3
SAN CRISTOBAL DE LAS CASAS,												
Chiapas	68/40	70/40	72/43	73/45	72/48	71/51	71/50	70/50	70/50	69/48	69/44	68/40
	.3	.3	.7	2.2	4.5	9.4	6.5	6.8	9.5	4.8	1.4	.5
SAN LUIS POTOSI,												
San Luis Potosi	71/43	74/45	82/50	86/53	86/56	82/58	80/56	81/56	77/56	75/51	74/47	71/44
	.3	.2	.1	.5	1.3	2.4	1.3	2.0	2.7	.9	.4	.3
TAXCO,												
Guerrero	78/55	82/58	87/62	89/64	87/65	80/64	79/62	78/62	77/62	78/61	78/59	77/58
	.5	.5	.2	.7	4.1	10.9	9.9	11.5	10.2	4.2	.9	.2
TIJUANA,												
Baja California	68/43	68/45	69/47	72/50	74/53	76/57	82/61	83/64	82/60	79/55	74/49	70/45
	1.6	1.3	1.1	.6	.2	0	0	0	.2	.2	1.2	1.3
VERACRUZ,												
Veracruz	76/65	77/66	79/69	83/73	86/76	87/77	88/75	88/76	87/75	85/73	82/70	78/67
	.8	.6	.7	.6	2.5	10.6	15.1	11.7	13.8	6.8	2.4	1.1

"m.n." (moneda nacional); prices in American currency, "dlls." (dollars). As a general rule, Mexican establishments rendering services to tourists quote and charge in pesos. Information sheets showing pictures of Mexican coins and bills are normally available at airports and border crossings, or appear in tourist publications.

Note: As a convenient reference, any prices or rates appearing in this book are quoted in approximate U.S. dollars unless stated otherwise. In August 2000, the exchange rate was approximately 9.0 pesos to the dollar. However, the peso is a floating currency subject to small daily fluctuations.

Many banks in U.S. border cities handle currency exchanges, but rates are not likely to be as favorable as those offered by banks and airports south of the border. Although the services offered by Mexican banks are being upgraded, many exchange dollars for pesos only during morning business hours.

Credit cards should cover almost all hotel, restaurant and store charges, as well as airline tickets for flights within Mexico. (**Note:** Gasoline purchases cannot be charged unless you have a GasoPLUS credit card—issued only in Mexico—which can be used at Pemex gas stations.)

Automated teller *(caja permanente)* machines are available in major cities and resort areas; most accept the widely honored Cirrus and PLUS cards. Expect peso denominations in return, and to be charged a service fee by your bank for each transaction. Using an ATM card avoids the commission charged by banks for exchanging traveler's checks into pesos (and the exchange rate is often better), but there is always the possibility that travelers will be forced to withdraw money. Make all ATM transactions during daylight hours, preferably at machines inside commercial establishments.

Unfortunately, the threat of purse or wallet snatching is ever present in crowded areas or a busy marketplace. Keep your money and important documents separate. Consider depositing surplus currency and jewelry in hotel vaults. When out in public, ignore remarks from strangers such as "What's that on your shoulder?" or someone yelling "Thief!" in a crowded area—both may be setups used by pickpockets or scam artists to distract your attention or trick you into revealing where you carry your money.

TIPPING

Casas de cambio (private money exchangers) usually offer a better rate of exchange for dollars (cash or documents). These exchange offices often are located next to big hotels in cities, or in malls in resort areas. A driver's license is needed to cash U.S. traveler's checks. Currency exchange also is a standard service at hotel front desks; call the hotel or hotels at which you'll be staying just prior to your trip to see what exchange rate is being offered. Trying to find the best rate usually boils down to a matter of convenience, since differences are normally minimal. If you're shopping around for the best rate or trying to save pennies a pocket calculator will come in handy.

If you're using traveler's checks, exchange only what you think you'll need for the next day or two. Keep in mind that all Mexican banks charge a service fee or commission to exchange dollars for pesos; beware of banks that charge a flat fee per traveler's check cashed. Traveler's checks denominated in pesos can be purchased at banks and currency exchange offices in the United States and will be easier to cash in small towns and areas away from tourist centers.

While tipping is virtually universal, the matter of whom, when and how much to tip varies. In Mexico, waiters, maids, porters and other workers whose wages are low must rely to a great extent on tips for their living. Let your conscience be your guide, and don't hesitate to reward outstanding service or penalize poor service.

Percentages for hotel and restaurant staff are similar to those in the United States and Canada. In restaurants, make sure that a service charge has not already been added onto the bill. Taxi drivers are not usually tipped unless they've performed some special service, such as waiting while a bit of shopping is done. Gas station attendants, however, expect a tip. Sightseeing tour guides should be tipped. There also are individuals whom you would not normally tip at home but should in Mexico; for example, theater ushers, washroom attendants and parking attendants.

Economic reality makes it necessary for some Mexicans to resort to begging as a means of survival. Women or children will ask for coins on the street or outside the town cathedral. Another frequently employed location, particularly in larger cities, is a busy intersection. Here an entire family may gather—washing windshields or even putting on an impromptu performance in costume—in return for small change from motorists stopped at the red light. Whether to give under such circumstances is up to the individual, of course, but considering the very real poverty with which many people must cope, any gift will be much appreciated.

Street vendors can be ubiquitous, particularly in the main plazas of towns, at archeological sites and other places where tourists are likely to be, and at beaches where vending is not prohibited. If you do decide to purchase something from a roving vendor, be very discreet; otherwise you will be inundated by insistent hawkers pushing everything from fruit to straw baskets. If you don't intend to buy, firmly communicate your lack of interest.

Young children frequently will offer special services to visitors. Even if it is performed in an unsolicited manner—for example, cleaning your windshield while you're stopped at a red light—compensation is expected. Again, if you are not interested in what a child is offering, whether it be carrying your bags at the airport or promising to guard your car while you shop or see the sights, be very firm about declining.

Youngsters also will charm coins or other gifts out of visitors, and it may be hard to resist these overtures. If you do succumb, hand something directly to a child. Children have been killed running across busy streets to pick up "gifts" tossed from car windows. Better yet, buy some pieces of fruit or other inexpensive foods at the local market. A few clothing items, pencils, pens or simple toys can be packed along with your own personal belongings if you enjoy contributing such gifts to the needy.

MAIL SERVICE

All letter mail to Mexico travels by air. First class mail service from Mexico to other countries is by air; parcel post and second class mail is by land. If you want to send mail from Mexico, use post mail only in those cities with airline service. **Note:** Mail service is notoriously slow, and mail can take up to a month to reach destinations in the United States, even that marked "via air mail." Do not expect postcards, letters or packages to arrive back home before you do.

Postal codes in Mexican addresses should be placed before the name of the destination town or city, as in the following example: Hotel Imperial, Avenida Guadalupe #210, 45040 Guadalajara, Jal., Mexico.

ADDRESSES

If you've ever had difficulty hunting down an address in almost any large city in the United States, prepare for the same possibility in Mexico. Street names tend to change mysteriously on either side of a town's main square, or capriciously after traversing several blocks. Street signs may be outdated or even nonexistent. Addresses frequently do not include numbers. All of this can be frustrating if trying to locate an out-of-the-way shop or restaurant; however, there are some general guidelines that can be relied on to aid in the search.

Although used where known in this book for purposes of clarification, designations such as *avenida* and *calle* usually are not posted, and streets are referred to by name only. That name may include a compass direction—*Nte.* or *Norte*, *Sur*, *Pte.* or *Poniente* and *Ote.* or *Oriente* for north, south, east and west, respectively. When an address includes *s/n* it means there is no number. In numbered addresses, the number follows rather than precedes the name. Addresses on main routes outside of cities or towns will often be stated in terms of the number of kilometers from town; for example, *Km. 18 a Mérida*.

Sprawling urban areas (Guadalajara and Monterrey, for example) have their own inscrutable logic regarding street names and configurations, and trying to find something outside of well-known tourist areas can turn into an adventure. In a class of its own is Mexico City, where an estimated 1,500 new thoroughfares are carved out of the metropolitan area each year and existing streets are renamed with dizzying regularity.

Streets in smaller cities are usually laid out in a simple grid pattern radiating from the central plaza (technically, only the square in Mexico City is referred to as the *zócalo*). Specific locations within the core downtown area can thus be pinpointed relatively easily in terms of the number of blocks north, south, east or west of the plaza.

If you need to ask directions from someone on the street, you may be steered off course; Mexicans tend to improvise rather than admit they don't know. But again, there are certain strategies that can increase your chances of success. Keep questions brief and to the point, and ask them with a smile; most people will be happy to try and help. Women who were brought up not to talk to strangers may ignore you, and don't bother asking a child, particularly if your Spanish is rusty. Maps are not likely to be understood; pointing is more direct. If you ask how long it will take to reach a specific destination, or what the exact distance is, remember that the answer is likely to be subjective.

PHONE SERVICE

Making telephone calls within and out of Mexico is not the hassle it once was, but keep two things in mind: Calling from your hotel, while convenient, is likely to be expensive; and using public phones, while less expensive, can be frustrating. If you do not speak fluent Spanish, local calls to businesses, police stations or public service agencies can easily grind to a halt. And busy signals are commonplace; if a call must be made and you experience difficulty getting through, keep trying.

If you want to connect directly to an international destination without speaking to an operator, use your calling card and the access code for your long-distance carrier. AT&T's USA DIRECT number is 001 (800) 462-4240. Similar services are offered in Mexico by MCI, 001 (800) 674-7000, and Sprint, 001 (800) 877-8000. To avoid having expensive hotel surcharges tacked on to your bill, don't call from your room. Some hotels may block one or more access code numbers if you try to call from the room; if that is the case, make the call from a public pay phone with a U.S. calling card. (**Note:** Some hotels add a charge for local calls made from the room in addition to the hefty surcharge placed on all international calls. Inquire when you check in whether local calls are extra.)

There are very few strictly coin-operated public pay phones left in Mexico. Most public phones are labeled Telmex, the name of the national telephone company, and are part of a system called Ladatel—literally, long distance *(lada)* telephone. Ladatel phones allow direct dialing without operator assistance and are less expensive than making phone calls from a hotel room. Local calls also can be made from Ladatel phones.

There are several types of Ladatel phones. Some have a coin slot that accepts pesos in the appropriate denomination and a slot in which to insert a disposable Ladatel phone card. Others have two slots—one for the phone card and one for Mexican bank credit cards (Banamex, Bancomer or Carnet). Some phones also accept U.S. telephone calling cards. (**Note:** When calling from a Ladatel phone, a Ladatel phone card is necessary to connect with the local phone system in order to then use a calling card. Ladatel phone cards can be purchased in various peso denominations at most pharmacies and gas station minimarkets, as well as from machines at airports and bus stations.)

A number of coins may be required if the call is lengthy, and it's easier to simply insert a phone card rather than feed the necessary pesos into the phone. The card is left in the slot while the call takes place. If the call does not go through, the card is returned. If the call is for less time than the value of the card, it is returned with a credit amount shown. If the call is still in progress when the card's value has been used up, the phone will beep and another card must be inserted to continue the call. Some phones have a digital display window that monitors the cost of the call.

When calling long distance from one Mexican location to another, dial 01 (the access code), then the area code, then the local phone number. (**Note:** Mexican phone numbers shown in this book include only the area code and the local number, not the access code that must also be dialed if making a long-distance call.) Local calls in Mexico do not require dialing the area code.

Telmex is currently converting all local numbers in Mexico to seven or eight digits from the current five, six or seven digits (a process expected to be completed in December 2000). Numbers which had two- or three-digit area codes (123/4-5678, 12/34-5678) now have one-digit area codes (1/234-5678). Guadalajara, Mexico City and Monterrey have eight-digit local numbers and no area code (1234-5678). The change affects only local calls; long distance calls (both within and from out of the country)

still require dialing the area code plus the phone number. The change also does not affect dialing 800 numbers. (**Note:** Phone numbers in this edition show the old area code format. However, at press time area codes were expected to be changed again—back to two- and three-digit numbers—beginning sometime in 2001.)

Free tourist publications usually include numbers for hotels, restaurants, attractions, travel agencies, airlines and so forth, as well as emergency and general information numbers. For additional assistance, consult a Telmex directory.

If you have a problem trying to make a specific local or long-distance call, enlist the aid of an operator; there are few recordings advising callers of phone number or area code changes. To reach a long-distance operator within Mexico, dial 020; for directory assistance, dial 040; for emergency assistance, dial 060. Keep in mind that English is not likely to be spoken.

To reach an English-speaking international operator, dial 090. To make an international call to the United States or Canada, dial 001, then the area code and phone number. Calling collect is the least expensive option. If you call from your hotel room, however, you may be charged even if the call is not accepted.

TIME ZONES

Most of Mexico's states are on Central Standard Time. Exceptions are the states of Nayarit, Sonora, Sinaloa and Baja California Sur, which are on Mountain Standard Time, and Baja California, which is on Pacific Standard Time.

In 1996, the entire country began observing daylight savings time ("summer time," or "La Hora de Verano") from the first weekend in April through the last weekend in October.

BEST BUYS

Rare indeed is the visitor who can resist buying a Mexican-handcrafted item to take home. Generations of families have not only made their living but perpetuated tradition by producing both practical and artistic objects, and the astute shopper can acquire purchases of real beauty and worth through a combination of careful selection and skillful bargaining.

WHERE TO LOOK AND WHAT TO LOOK FOR

Mexican crafts are available at indoor and outdoor public markets; at fixed-price, government-run stores bearing the FONART logo; and at tourist-oriented boutiques and shops in hotels, malls and at resorts. Markets will offer the greatest variety of goods as well as the greatest concentration of shoddy merchandise. The standardized offerings at FONART outlets will enable you to compare cost and quality for various kinds of crafts from all over the country. Boutiques are often expensive, but they offer a relaxed, air-conditioned atmosphere if you can't take the cacophony of the markets on a hot day.

Whatever the item, prices can be low or moderate for adequate work in traditional styles or very expensive for fine artistry and design. Bargaining in markets or the private homes of artisans is one way to bring down prices. You could begin by offering no more than half the stated price; then come up very slowly. Experiment with different techniques; an offer to pay in cash or a feigned lack of interest could sway an otherwise unyielding shopkeeper. Also helpful is a knowledge of basic Spanish, including the words for numbers.

Don't succumb to impulse buys at the craft markets; the same earthenware jug being pushed by one persistent vendor may be available for less four stalls away. It pays to shop around, first checking out merchandise you're interested in to see if vendors are quoting different prices for the same item, or what the general going price seems to be. You'll then be in a much better position to bargain if someone offers a "slashed price" or "special rate" that really isn't. Also compare locations; identical handicrafts sold in Cancún, for example, may be less on nearby Isla Mujeres. Try to save at least some souvenir shopping for the end of the trip, when you'll have a better idea of local prices and there is less likelihood of purchases being lost or broken.

Generally, the reputation of the shop will indicate the quality of the goods; you'll need a sharper eye when buying at a market or from a roadside stand. Since souvenirs and gifts often provide the longest-lasting memory of a trip to Mexico, you should examine all purchases for quality and authenticity. Silver that is genuine sterling bears the numerals ".925"—which certifies that it is at least 92.5 percent pure—and the symbol of the manufacturer, which is usually two letters—for example, MH. If in doubt, don't buy. Inspect leather articles to determine that they are all leather, rather than a thin piece glued over plastic or cardboard.

A smart purchase of metalcraft, pottery, baskets or textiles depends on your judgment of quality. Be certain that copper vessels are actually copper, not iron sprayed with copper that later flakes off. Handles are often the weak spots on baskets. Woven goods may contain synthetic fibers; check the material carefully if you want something that's genuinely handcrafted. It is prohibited by law to import anything made of tortoiseshell into the United States. Also be aware that the export of gold coins, including gold coins that have been incorporated into jewelry, is prohibited unless you have obtained an export permit.

At some archeological sites you may find people selling objects they've supposedly found. Refuse these offers; the exportation from Mexico of antiques or items which may be described as national treasures is against the law. Reproductions are available in craft shops; be sure they include wording stating they are not genuine.

This colorful hodgepodge in San Cristóbal de las Casas is typical of sidewalk markets throughout Mexico. ©John Neubauer

DUTY-FREE SHOPPING

In addition to crafts and other native items, border cities and some resorts also offer goods produced outside Mexico. Tijuana in particular attracts hordes of tourists with itchy fingers and open wallets. Here you can buy French perfume, Italian shoes, fine liquor and cheap trinkets—sometimes all on the same street. With imported goods, make sure you know the comparable price in the country of origin, as not everything is a bargain.

Note: Items sold in duty-free shops are intended for export and are free of duty and taxes only in Mexico; if your purchases exceed your personal exemption, these items may be subject to duty. For additional information about customs regulations, see "What U.S. Citizens May Bring Back."

REGIONAL SPECIALTIES

Various cities and towns in Mexico excel in one or more crafts, which can be purchased not only at the point of origin but in shopping meccas like Mexico City, Guadalajara and Oaxaca. Taxco, an old colonial mining town in the state of Guerrero, is the place to search out **silver** articles. **Gold filigree jewelry**—incorporating designs based on treasures found in the tombs of the Monte Albán ruins—is a specialty of the state of Oaxaca. Several towns in the state of Michoacán, particularly Santa Clara del Cobre, are known for **copper** items; **tin metalwork** can be found in San Miguel de Allende, in the state of Guanajuato. High-quality **gemstones**, including opals, amethysts, topaz and agate, are available in Querétaro, in the state of Querétaro, and the nearby towns of San Juan del Río and Tequisquiapan. These should be purchased only in reputable stores.

Pottery is one of Mexico's biggest craft industries. The Oaxaca area is known for its distinctive greenish-black pottery. Artisans in the Yucatán Peninsula produce brightly painted designs. The Guadalajara suburbs of Tlaquepaque and Tonalá are other pottery centers. **Ceramics** utilizing blue talavera tiles are a specialty of Puebla. **Lacquered trays** of polished black, inlaid with gold-leaf patterns, can be found at shops in Pátzcuaro, Uruapan and Morelia, all in the state of Michoacán; **lacquered chests** and other decorative items are crafted at Olinalá, an isolated mountain village northeast of Acapulco.

Woven goods incorporate distinct styles, depending on who is doing the weaving. Good bargains can be found on *sarapes*, a woolen or cotton blanket worn like a poncho; *rebozos*, a rectangular piece of cloth similar to a shawl; *huipils* (ee-PEEL), brocaded blouses created in amazing variety; and *guayaberas*, pleated shirts for men that originated on the Yucatán Peninsula. Other items include **blankets, rugs** and strawwoven **Panama hats. Note:** Since it can be con-

sidered offensive for foreigners to wear native costumes, wait until you get home before putting on such clothing articles.

Hand-blown glass can be had in Guadalajara, Monterrey and Mexico City. **Wood furniture** in Spanish colonial styles is a specialty of San Miguel de Allende and Cuernavaca. Paracho, in the state of Michoacán, is famous for the production of **guitars** and other stringed instruments. Oaxaca and the Copper Canyon area of northwestern Mexico are noted for woven **baskets**. *Huaraches* (leather sandals) and other **leather goods** are sold in most parts of Mexico. Boutiques in the coastal resorts offer many lines of stylish, casual **sportswear**, often by well-known international designers.

DEPARTING MEXICO

If you entered Mexico with a car or any other motor vehicle, you must leave the country with that vehicle. See "Temporary Importation of Vehicles," page 55. Applicable documents (temporary vehicle importation permit, promise to return vehicle form and windshield sticker) may be collected at an interior inspection point, but usually they are returned to Mexican immigration and customs officials at the border. Be sure to return all documents if you do not plan to re-enter Mexico on a multiple-entry tourist permit. U.S. customs offices at the major border crossing points are open daily 24 hours; an exception is the Otay Mesa crossing, just east of Tijuana International Airport, which is open daily 6 a.m.-10 p.m. **Note:** Motorists traveling north to the U.S. border are subject to official Mexican agricultural inspections at stations along the highways. All fruits, vegetables, houseplants and other plant matter will be inspected.

If departing by air, call the airline at least 24 hours prior to departure to confirm reservations and departure time. **Note:** Mexico charges an airport tax of around $17 or the equivalent in pesos on international departing flights, which is usually included in the price of your ticket; check with the airline to make certain.

Cruise ship passengers returning from Mexico to the United States are required to pay a $6.50 customs user fee; this is generally included in the ticket price.

Returning U.S. citizens must present to U.S. customs officials valid proof of citizenship, either a valid passport or a birth certificate; the latter must be a certified copy from the government agency that issued it. A passport is required for returning naturalized citizens; it also is recommended that naturalized citizens note their naturalization certificate numbers to facilitate re-entry into the United States.

A Customs Declaration form should be prepared before you pass through U.S. customs. An oral declaration may be given to the customs inspector if all articles acquired abroad are accompanying you and do not exceed your allowable duty-free exemption. A written declaration is required for items exceeding your personal exemption in total retail value, and for more than one liter (33.8 fl. oz.) of alcoholic beverages, 200 cigarettes (one carton) or 100 cigars.

To expedite the process, keep sales slips handy and have all your purchases in one bag if possible. You must declare to customs officials items both in your possession and acquired during your trip, including:

- items purchased
- items given to you while abroad, such as wedding and birthday gifts or inherited items
- items purchased in duty-free shops or on board a carrier
- items you have been asked to bring back for another person
- items for which repairs or alterations were made, even if free of charge
- items you intend to sell or use in a business

The price actually paid for each item must be stated on your customs declaration form in U.S. currency or its equivalent in the country of acquisition and must include any value added tax (VAT) if it was not refunded prior to arrival.

The helpful booklet "Know Before You Go" lists and explains all U.S. customs regulations and those of many other agencies as well. Write to the U.S. Customs Service, P.O. Box 7407, Washington, D.C. 20044.

WHAT U.S. CITIZENS MAY BRING BACK

EXEMPTIONS

Each visitor to Mexico may bring back, duty free, articles not exceeding $400 in retail value from a stay abroad of at least 48 hours. Duty must be paid on all items in excess of this amount. The exemption is allowed once every 30 days. A $200 exemption is granted if you cannot claim the $400 exemption because of the 30-day or 48-hour limitations. It may include 50 cigarettes, 10 cigars, 150 milliliters (4 fl. oz.) of alcoholic beverages or 4 fl. oz. of perfume containing alcohol. This individual exemption may not be grouped with other members of a family on one customs declaration.

Special regulations apply to gifts; *see "Gifts" below*. Articles purchased and left for alterations or other reasons do not qualify for the $400 exemption when shipped at a later date. Duty must be paid when the shipment is received; it cannot be prepaid. Personal-use shipments valued at less than $200 are duty free.

RESTRICTED OR PROHIBITED ARTICLES

Certain items considered injurious or detrimental to the general welfare of the United States are prohibited entry by law, including lottery tickets, narcotics and dangerous drugs, obscene articles and publications, seditious and treasonable materials, hazardous articles (fireworks, dangerous toys, toxic or poisonous substances) and switchblade knives.

To prevent the introduction of plant and animal pests and diseases, the agricultural quarantine bans the importation of certain fruits, vegetables, plants, livestock, poultry and meats. All food products brought into the United States must be declared. If you attempt to conceal agricultural items, you can be fined $50-$100. The U.S. Department of Agriculture also prohibits the importation of any kind of pet obtained in Mexico.

Endangered or threatened wildlife species or products made of any part of these species are generally prohibited, unless you have a permit issued by the U.S. Fish and Wildlife Service. This includes products made from sea turtles, as well as all ivory and ivory products made from elephant or marine mammal ivory. If you are thinking of returning to the United States with any purchased articles made of fur, any animal skin other than cowhide leather, whalebone or any product manufactured wholly or in part from any type of wildlife, write to the U.S. Fish and Wildlife Service, Division of Law Enforcement, P.O. Box 3247, Arlington, VA 22203-3247 for information about regulations before you go.

Such live birds as parrots, parakeets or birds of prey, widely available on the market in Mexico, can be brought into the United States subject to inspection by the U.S. Department of Agriculture. Birds must be quarantined upon arrival for at least 30 days in a USDA-operated facility at the owner's expense. Quarantine space must be reserved in advance; for information contact a USDA office.

To be taken out of Mexico, cultural artifacts or property items such as pre-Columbian monumental and architectural sculpture or murals, clay figurines, original paintings and other works of art (not handicrafts) will need an export certificate. Valuable religious and archeological relics are the property of the Mexican government and may not be taken out of the country.

Goods purchased in Mexico but originating in Cuba, Iran, Iraq, Libya or North Korea are not admissible. Gold coins, medals and bullion may be brought into the United States, but such items originating in or brought from these same countries are prohibited.

One foreign-made article of a type carrying a protected U.S. trademark—for example, cameras, binoculars, musical instruments, jewelry or watches—may be brought into the United States under your personal exemption, provided the article accompanies you for private use and is not sold within 1 year of importation. Some perfumes are limited to one bottle; a few are prohibited altogether. If you intend to purchase perfume, be sure to inquire about trademark restrictions beforehand. *See "Personal Items," page 41,* for safeguards to consider when entering Mexico with foreign-made articles.

For additional information regarding restricted items, write for the free booklet "Travelers' Tips," available in English, Spanish, Italian or Japanese from the U.S. Department of Agriculture, Washington, D.C. 20250. For information about permits allowing the importation of some restricted articles, contact the nearest U.S. Department of Agriculture Animal and Plant Health Inspection Service office or write to APHIS, U.S. Department of Agriculture, 6505 Belcrest Rd., Hyattsville, MD 20782; phone (301) 734-8645.

ALCOHOLIC BEVERAGES

The federal government permits each resident who is 21 years of age or older to bring into the United States one liter of alcohol duty free once every 30 days. However, most states restrict the quantity of alcoholic beverages that may be imported, and state law prevails if you arrive in a state that permits a lesser amount than what you have legally brought into the United States. For this reason it is important to know the import limits of your state of residence as well as the state of entry.

Taxes imposed on alcoholic beverages (which include beer and wine as well as distilled spirits) vary by state; miniature bottles are prohibited. Since these regulations can be quite complex, verify them before your trip if you intend to bring alcoholic beverages back with you.

GIFTS

Gifts accompanying you across the U.S./Mexico border are considered to be for personal use and are included in the $400 exemption.

Gifts sent in packages with a total retail value not exceeding $100 may be sent to friends or relatives in the United States free of U.S. customs duty or tax, provided that no recipient receives more than one gift shipment per day. Gifts may be sent to more than one person in the same package if they are individually wrapped and labeled with the name of the recipient. Perfumes valued at more than $5 retail, tobacco products or alcoholic beverages may not be included in gift packages. The designation "Unsolicited Gift," the name of the donor and the retail value of the contents must be clearly marked on the outside.

Consolidated gift parcels should have listed on the outside the names of the recipients and the value of each gift. However, the safe arrival of gifts sent through the mail cannot be guaranteed.

It also is possible to ship gifts through a broker. If you choose to do so, always obtain the name of the customs broker at the border who will handle the shipment. Make sure you understand the shipping arrangements and fees involved before signing the contract. (**Note:** Customs brokers are not U.S. Customs employees, and brokers' fees are based on the cost of delivery services, not the value of the items shipped. If the fee seems excessive in relation to the value of the shipment, opt to take purchases across the border with you if at all possible.)

DUTIES

A flat rate of duty of 10 percent is applied to the first $1,000 worth (fair retail value) of merchandise in excess of your customs exemption of $400. The sales receipt functions as proof of value. Family members residing in one household and traveling together may group articles for application of the flat-duty rate. Articles must accompany you to the U.S. border. The flat-duty rate may be taken only once every 30 days.

Articles over the initial $1,000 flat-duty limit are dutiable at the rate applicable to the articles. Under the terms of the North American Free Trade Agreement, the United States offers a preferential rate of duty to many imports originating in Mexico; these items must be listed on the Customs Declaration form if returning by air or sea or declared orally if returning by land. The final authority on duty-free items and duty rates for other items is the U.S. customs official at the border.

Payment of duty is required uopn arrival for articles accompanying you and may be paid in U.S. currency; by personal check in the exact amount of the duty; or by government check, money order or traveler's check if not exceeding the duty amount by more than $50. MasterCard and VISA are accepted at some locations.

WHAT CANADIAN CITIZENS MAY BRING BACK

Canadian residents who have been outside Canada **at least 48 hours** may bring back, duty and tax free, articles not exceeding $200 (Canadian) in retail value. This exemption can be claimed any number of times a year. After an absence of **7 days or more** Canadian residents may bring back duty and tax free goods up to $500 in value. The $500 exemption may be claimed regardless of any $200 exemption taken on a previous trip and requires a written declaration; the two exemptions may **not** be combined at one time.

Canadian residents can claim duty- and tax-free entry for articles (excluding tobacco products or alcoholic beverages) that do not exceed a total value of $50 upon return from each trip abroad of at least 24 hours. In general, items brought into Canada under a personal exemption must be for personal or household use, souvenirs, or gifts for friends or relatives.

The following limitations apply to either the $200 or $500 exemption: 50 cigars, 200 cigarettes, 14 ounces (400 grams) of tobacco and 400 tobacco sticks, as well as 40 ounces (1.1 liters) of wine or liquor *or* 300 ounces (8.5 liters) of beer or ale (equivalent to 24, 12-ounce bottles/cans). All exemptions are individual and may not be combined with another person's to cover an article valued at more than the maximum exemption. You may be requested to prove the length of your visit outside Canada. Dated sales receipts for goods or services received constitute valid proof and should be kept.

All declared goods associated with the $200 personal exemption must accompany the purchaser to the Canadian border; declared goods associated with the $500 personal exemption may follow the purchaser by mail. Gifts sent to friends or relatives from Mexico do not count against a resident's personal exemption as long as a gift is valued at no more than $60 Canadian and does not consist of alcoholic beverages, tobacco products or advertising matter. Make sure a gift card is enclosed to avoid misunderstanding. Since parcels to be shipped must first be examined by Mexican government customs officials, consider having a customs broker or a forwarding agent handle these important details before you leave Mexico.

Canada grants to residents who have been abroad at least 48 hours a special 8 percent combined duty and GST (Goods and Services Tax) rate on the next $500 value in goods (except tobacco and/or alcohol) in excess of maximum exemptible amounts, provided the goods are of Mexican origin. Regular duties apply on any amount over that. For detailed information concerning specific duty rates and prohibited articles, consult Canadian customs before leaving on your trip.

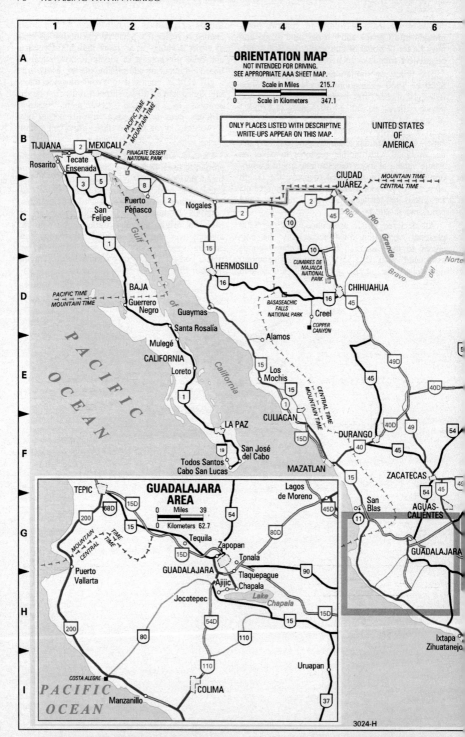

ORIENTATION MAP

NOT INTENDED FOR DRIVING.
SEE APPROPRIATE AAA SHEET MAP.

0   Scale in Miles   215.7

0   Scale in Kilometers   347.1

ONLY PLACES LISTED WITH DESCRIPTIVE
WRITE-UPS APPEAR ON THIS MAP.

UNITED STATES
OF
AMERICA

TIJUANA   MEXICALI

Rosarito

Tecate
Ensenada

PINACATE DESERT
NATIONAL PARK

PACIFIC TIME
MOUNTAIN TIME

San
Felipe

Puerto
Peñasco

Nogales

CIUDAD
JUÁREZ

MOUNTAIN TIME
CENTRAL TIME

Río

Río

Grande

Bravo

del

Norte

Gulf

HERMOSILLO

CUMBRES DE
MAJALCA
NATIONAL
PARK

CHIHUAHUA

BAJA

of

Guerrero
Negro

Guaymas

Santa Rosalía

Mulegé

BASASEACHIC
FALLS
NATIONAL PARK

Creel

COPPER
CANYON

CALIFORNIA

Loreto

California

Alamos

Los
Mochis

CENTRAL TIME
MOUNTAIN TIME

P A C I F I C

O C E A N

LA PAZ

San José
del Cabo

CULIACAN

DURANGO

Todos Santos
Cabo San Lucas

MAZATLAN

ZACATECAS

PACIFIC TIME
MOUNTAIN TIME

San
Blas

AGUAS-
CALIENTES

GUADALAJARA AREA

TEPIC

0   Miles   39

0   Kilometers   62.7

Lagos
de Moreno

GUADALAJARA

MOUNTAIN
TIME

CENTRAL
TIME

Tequila

Zapopan

Tonala

Puerto
Vallarta

GUADALAJARA

Ajijic

Tlaquepaque

Chapala

Jocotepec

Lake

Chapala

COSTA ALEGRE

Uruapan

P A C I F I C

O C E A N

Manzanillo

COLIMA

Ixtapa
Zihuatanejo

3024-H

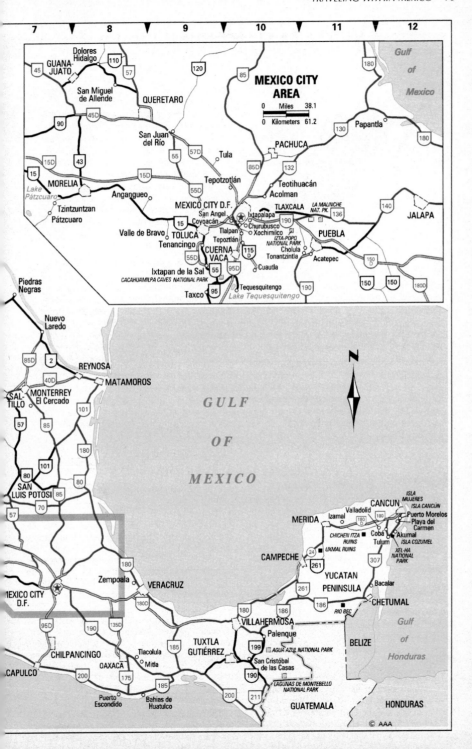

MEXICO CITY AREA

0 Miles 38.1
0 Kilometers 61.2

Gulf of Mexico

GUANAJUATO
Dolores Hidalgo
San Miguel de Allende
QUERETARO
San Juan del Río
Tula
PACHUCA
Papantla
MORELIA
Lake Pátzcuaro
Tzintzuntzan
Pátzcuaro
Angangueo
Tepotzotlán
Teotihuacán
Acolman
TLAXCALA
LA MALINCHE NAT. PK.
JALAPA
MEXICO CITY D.F.
San Angel
Coyoacán
Tlalpan
Churubusco
Xochimilco
Ixtapalapa
Tepoztlán
IZTA-POPO NATIONAL PARK
Cholula
Tonantzintla
PUEBLA
Acatepec
Valle de Bravo
TOLUCA
Tenancingo
CUERNAVACA
Ixtapan de la Sal
CACAHUAMILPA CAVES NATIONAL PARK
Cuautla
Tequesquitengo
Lake Tequesquitengo
Taxco

Piedras Negras
Nuevo Laredo
REYNOSA
MATAMOROS
SALTILLO
MONTERREY
El Cercado
SAN LUIS POTOSI

GULF

OF

MEXICO

N

ISLA MUJERES
ISLA CANCÚN
CANCUN
Valladolid
MERIDA
Izamal
Puerto Morelos
Playa del Carmen
CHICHEN ITZA RUINS
Cobá
Tulum
Akumal
ISLA COZUMEL
UXMAL RUINS
XEL-HA NATIONAL PARK
CAMPECHE
YUCATAN PENINSULA
Bacalar
CHETUMAL
RIO BEC
Zempoala
VERACRUZ
Gulf of Honduras
MEXICO CITY D.F.
VILLAHERMOSA
Palenque
BELIZE
CHILPANCINGO
Tlacolula
OAXACA
Mitla
TUXTLA GUTIÉRREZ
AGUA AZUL NATIONAL PARK
San Cristóbal de las Casas
ACAPULCO
Puerto Escondido
Bahias de Huatulco
LAGUNAS DE MONTEBELLO NATIONAL PARK
GUATEMALA
HONDURAS

© AAA

Yucatán Peninsula

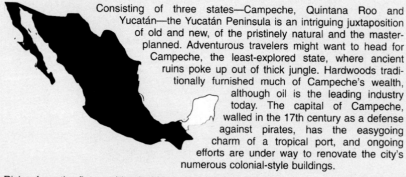

Consisting of three states—Campeche, Quintana Roo and Yucatán—the Yucatán Peninsula is an intriguing juxtaposition of old and new, of the pristinely natural and the master-planned. Adventurous travelers might want to head for Campeche, the least-explored state, where ancient ruins poke up out of thick jungle. Hardwoods traditionally furnished much of Campeche's wealth, although oil is the leading industry today. The capital of Campeche, walled in the 17th century as a defense against pirates, has the easygoing charm of a tropical port, and ongoing efforts are under way to renovate the city's numerous colonial-style buildings.

Rising from the flat scrubland of Yucatán state are the magnificent archeological sites of Chichén Itzá and Uxmal, must-sees on any Yucatán traveler's itinerary. Legacies of Maya civilization, these ceremonial centers contain monumentally scaled buildings created without benefit of such basics as the wheel, metal tools or proven beasts of burden. And among the small Indian villages dotting the Yucatán's rolling hills, one bona fide city stands out: Mérida, one of the first cities to be built by the Spanish. Ornate mansions, fine old buildings and lively plazas combine to give this vibrant capital a distinctly European feel—despite the exotic flowers and sultry heat.

Quintana Roo, which occupies the eastern part of the peninsula, was almost wholly isolated from the rest of the country until the completion of two roads (Mex. 180 and Mex. 186). Today, however, most of Quintana Roo's visitors fly in, and their destination of choice is Cancún, which as recently as the late 1960s was a sleepy, unknown fishing village. No more—hordes of spring breakers, winter-weary gringos and beach lovers have made this sun-splashed resort one of the world's top tourist destinations.

A Yucatán Overview

The Yucatán (yoo-cah-TAHN) Peninsula has always seemed somewhat detached from the rest of Mexico. A combination of geographic, ethnographic and historical factors have combined to produce this feeling, which exists among the people inhabiting the Yucatán even today—most think of themselves as *yucatecos* first, Mexicans second.

The peninsula also is a land of contrasts. It encompasses Mexico's most popular tourist destination—the resort playground of **Cancún**—as well as some of the country's oldest and most impressive archeological ruins.

Geography

The first Spaniards who arrived at the Yucatán's eastern shore in the early 16th century believed it to be a huge island in between the Caribbean Sea and the Gulf of Mexico. Certainly the region's physical characteristics, which are more similar to the state of Florida than to the rest of Mexico, could qualify it as a separate country.

Though often perceived as being Mexico's southernmost region, the peninsula is in fact the country's eastern frontier. The city of **Mérida** is farther north than Guadalajara, Puebla and Mexico City. And while much of the Mexican mainland is a series of valleys alternating with rugged mountains, the Yucatán is an essentially featureless plain of limestone frosted with a meager layer of soil.

Another difference is altitude. The vast plateau of central Mexico lies more than a mile above sea level, and the titanic Sierra Madre mountain ranges have peaks taller than 15,000 feet. In contrast, the Yucatán Peninsula's highest elevations—an undulating region of hills near the border of Campeche and Yucatán states known as the Puuc—do not even reach 1,000 feet.

The peninsula has almost no river systems, although there are some small lakes in the southern part of the state of Quintana Roo. Surface water that seeps through the porous limestone collects underground or fills cenotes (sinkholes), which function as natural swimming pools. Climatically, the Yucatán shares with much of Mexico a pattern of erratic rainfall. Much of the state of Yucatán is dry to the point of being desertlike, and the chief vegetation is thorny, inhospitable scrub. Elsewhere, such as in the southern parts of Campeche and Quintana Roo, abundant rainfall produces stands of thick jungle. **Sian Ka'an Biosphere Reserve** *(see Tulum listing)*, covering more than a million acres, is a protected haven for diverse plant and animal species.

The peninsula's most exploitable natural resource is its eastern coastline, which is lined with gorgeous white-sand beaches fronting the aquamarine Caribbean. Two offshore islands, **Cozumel** and **Isla Mujeres** *(see separate listings)*, are surrounded by warm, clear waters that teem with myriad species of tropical and game fish. One of the world's longest unbroken barrier reefs, which has been the undoing of many ships over the centuries, stretches along the Caribbean coast. The wealth of fishing, diving, snorkeling, swimming and boating opportunities, along with a number of Maya archeological ruins, have combined to make tourism the Yucatán's most profitable industry, and its cities and shores are now visited by multitudes of foreigners.

HISTORY

It wasn't always so. As early as 400 B.C., the ancient Maya civilization was beginning to evolve in the state of Chiapas, Belize, most of Guatemala and parts of Honduras. Its origin remains one of history's puzzles, although it is believed that the Maya were descended from the Olmec, whose own civilization flourished along Mexico's lower gulf coast in what is now the state of Tabasco. Over a period of time roughly parallel to the rise of the Roman Empire, the Maya developed their own sophisticated civilization—and bizarre, blood-spattered rites.

The years from about 300 to 900 A.D., known as the Classic Period, were the height of Maya achievement. It was during this time that the magnificent ceremonial center at **Palenque** *(see separate listing under Southern Mexico)* was constructed. Monumental pyramids were constructed over a wide portion of Mesoamerica, from the Yucatán Peninsula to present-day Honduras, and the Maya devised a complex writing system, mastered mathematic principles and created highly accurate astrological calendars. At some point during the ninth century, however, Palenque and other cities in Guatemala, Belize and Honduras were abandoned.

An increasing number of archeologists, anthropologists, linguists and other experts are conducting research at Maya sites in an effort to try and understand why these civilizations collapsed. While the information gathering has produced inevitable disagreements, scientific minds do seem to agree that the Maya were not a peaceful

Rattlesnake carvings (seen over this doorway at Uxmal) were considered by the Maya to be a fertility symbol. ©Chris Sharp

3026-H

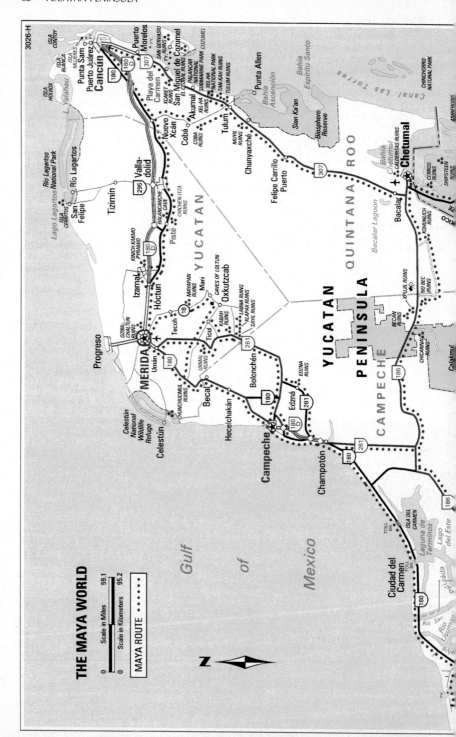

THE MAYA WORLD

Scale in Miles
0   59.1

Scale in Kilometers
0   95.2

MAYA ROUTE • • • • • •

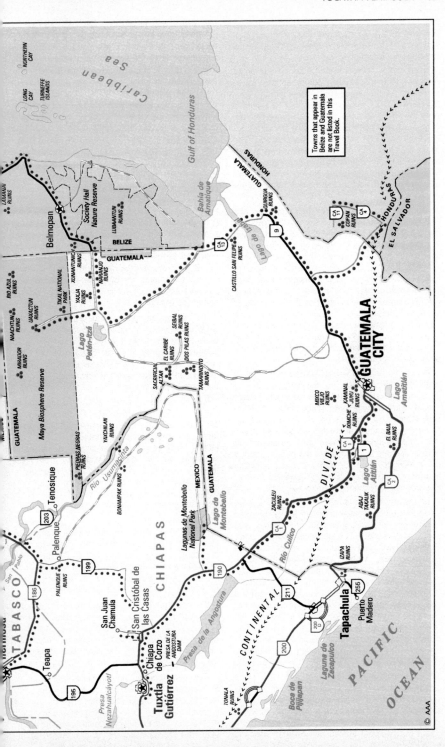

people, as had once generally been believed. Torture and human sacrifice, in fact, were an integral part of Maya society, from sporting events to religious ceremonies.

Even when compared to today's widespread societal violence, some commonplace Maya practices evoke shudders. Bloodletting—grotesque forms of self-mutilation that produced a flow of droplets presented as offerings to the gods—was routinely indulged in by the ruling aristocracy as well as the common citizen. The Maya ball game, in which two teams endeavored to keep a heavy rubber ball in constant motion, often ended with the losing players being decapitated or even trussed up and bounced down pyramid steps.

Most archeologists have theorized that the Maya's simple hierarchy—a sharp social division between the small but powerful ruling class and the poor peasants—resulted in a mass revolt against the elite and the resultant downfall of society. Recently a new theory has been postulated. Excavations of burial tombs carried out at Caracol, an archeological site in western Belize near the Guatemalan border, suggest the existence of a large "middle class." This group may have lived in a manner similar to that enjoyed by nobility, although their economic and political status is not to be equated with the idea of the modern-day middle class.

If not middle-class revolt, several other factors could have contributed to the collapse of the great Maya cities in Central America. Widespread warfare was one likely cause. Another was large-scale exploitation of the fragile rain forest environment, in which slash-and-burn agricultural techniques may have depleted the natural jungle, opening up the land to the ravages caused by prolonged drought. Finally, overpopulation and unproductive land use may have led to malnutrition and eventually, starvation.

Following the downfall of Palenque, Copan, Tikal and other major cities, the Maya migrated northward into the Yucatán Peninsula (the present-day states of Campeche and Yucatán). Between 1000 and 1500, such major cities as **Chichén Itzá, Cobá, Dzibilchaltún, Edzná, Mayapan, Tulum** and **Uxmal** were built. The focus of Maya civilization moved from the observance of elaborate religious rituals toward commercial, governmental and militaristic concerns. Some cities functioned as trade centers between the Caribbean and gulf coasts and Mexico's interior, as the Yucatán Peninsula was infiltrated by such tribes as the Putun Maya (later known as the Itzae), the Cocom and the Xiu.

The squabbling among these different factions set the stage for Spanish conquest. While Hernán Cortés was busy conquering Mexico's interior, Francisco de Montejo the Elder sailed from Spain in 1527 and landed at Cozumel. Montejo met with fierce resistance as he tried repeatedly to subdue the Maya, who conducted war with a vengeance. In 1540 his son continued the long campaign to add the Yucatán Peninsula to Spain's crown. When the leader of the Xiu dynasty finally capitulated to the invaders, effective resistance was largely ended. Despite sporadic rebellions, the Maya were slowly overwhelmed. One of the atrocities committed under Spanish authority was the mass burning in 1562 of the *codices*, priceless picture books describing Maya history and religion.

While Spanish coffers were growing fat with the gold and silver mined from the highlands of central Mexico, the Yucatán offered no such riches. During the 17th and 18th centuries the peninsula languished as a steamy colonial outpost, its coasts plagued by French and English pirates. The few Spaniards who settled around Mérida and other colonial outposts grew sugar cane and raised cattle. Meanwhile, the Maya not killed by protracted warfare with the *conquistadores* succumbed to European-introduced diseases or were ruthlessly enslaved on the Spanish haciendas (plantations).

The Yucatecan spirit of independence asserted itself anew when Mexico broke free from Spain in 1821. For the next 2 years the Yucatán was an autonomous entity. It joined Mexico in 1823 but seceded again in 1846, as Mexico and the United States battled over disputed territories along the northern frontier.

The bloody War of the Castes, a racially motivated conflict in which Maya rebels rose up against their oppressors, began in 1847. Indians under the inspiration of "talking crosses" attacked Mexican government troops attempting to subjugate the Yucatán Peninsula; the crosses allegedly protected the rebels. The first cross, carved from a cedar tree, appeared in the town of Felipe Carrillo Puerto, then called Chan Santa Cruz; others were placed in neighboring villages.

Although the Maya claimed most of the peninsula by 1848, long-ingrained patterns superseded military strategy, and they abruptly left the field of battle to plant fields of corn. By this time, Mexican government troops had intervened, and the rebels were pushed to the southeastern corner of what is now the state of Quintana Roo.

The disruptive wars of the mid-19th century destroyed many of the sugar haciendas. As a result, Spanish and European settlers turned to henequén, a spiny-leaved member of the agave family, as a cash crop. The hardy plant thrived in the hot, dry conditions of the northern peninsula.

Henequén plantation owners became wealthy. Still isolated from the rest of Mexico due to a lack of transportation, they turned to Europe for cultural guidance. Many henequén barons lived in Mérida, and the city, with its opulent marble mansions, became known as the "Paris of the

The Maya Route

Enormous temples, intricately sculpted structures, lofty volcanoes, tropical rain forest—all are traversed by La Ruta Maya (The Maya Route), that region of Mesoamerica which includes all of Belize, most of Guatemala, portions of Honduras and El Salvador, and all or part of the Mexican states of Campeche, Chiapas, Quintana Roo, Tabasco and Yucatán.

Maya civilization began more than 2,000 years ago and reached its zenith between A.D. 300 and 900. At the same time Europe was suffering through the Dark Ages, the Maya people enjoyed a creative flowering more advanced than any of their contemporaries in the known world. They built temples and ceremonial centers that continue to evoke wonder; developed an astronomical calendar and predicted both solar and lunar eclipses; pioneered the mathematical concept of zero; and evolved a highly refined hieroglyphic writing system. The Maya also were accomplished artists, historians and road builders.

For reasons that are still unknown, major ceremonial centers such as Palenque and Tikal were abandoned by the early 10th century, as Maya civilization shifted northward to the Yucatán Peninsula and such cities as Chichén Itzá and Uxmal. Between about 1200 and the Spanish arrival in the early 16th century, El Mundo Maya (The Maya World) toppled; the exact causes remain a mystery. It is theorized that warlike invaders from the north, dissension between peasant farmers and the elite, a change in focus from religious to militaristic concerns, overpopulation, drought and crop failure all had varying degrees of impact.

By the time Francisco Hernández de Córdoba discovered the Yucatán Peninsula in 1517, the once-mighty civilization retained little of its former glory, and the population had dwindled. The first Spanish stronghold in the region was established in 1542 at Mérida; the last Maya city to surrender was Tayasal, Guatemala, in 1697. The Maya retreated to the jungles of Quintana Roo, where fierce revolts continued through 300 years of Spanish domination. Even after Mexico won freedom from Spain, the Yucatán twice declared its independence.

Maya descendants today number about 2 million in Mexico and Central America and speak more than 20 different dialects. In some small villages, the na—an oval-shaped, thatched-roofed hut with sascab (lime dirt) floors—is still the principal dwelling. Several hundred Lacandón Indians who live in the hot, humid lowlands of the state of Chiapas are perhaps the nation's citizens most secluded from and least influenced by modern life. For these people, timeless traditions have managed to survive.

In an effort to promote and preserve the cultural, historical and environmental heritage of El Mundo Maya, the governments of Mexico, Guatemala, Belize, Honduras and El Salvador are endeavoring to transcend political boundaries in order to unite their archeological sites and colonial cities. Funding will help the countries sponsor ongoing excavations and promote low-impact tourism. Tour companies catering chiefly to European visitors offer package trips to the more accessible sites. To protect native species of flora and fauna, several biosphere reserves have been created, most notably Sian Ka'an.

The Maya Route covers a 120,000-square-mile area from the Isthmus of Tehuantepec, Mexico's narrowest point, through the Yucatán Peninsula and south to Honduras and El Salvador. The "route" is actually a loosely tied-together network of existing roadways. These range from modern toll roads to unpaved dirt trails that can become a quagmire during rainy weather. The main highways are Mex. 186, which runs east-west across the southern portions of Quintana Roo and Campeche; Mex. 307, which runs north-south along Quintana Roo's Caribbean coastline; and Mex. 180, which connects Cancún with Mérida before traveling southwest along the Gulf of Mexico coast. In addition, Mex. 180-D is a toll route roughly paralleling Mex. 180 between Cancún and Mérida. Other roads branching off these highways are adjuncts to the route. Note: For any road trips, make certain the vehicle you drive—whether rented or your own—is in top condition. Away from the cities, much of this part of Mexico remains primitive.

West." However, virtual enslavement of the landless majority by a privileged few again led—in the Yucatán as well as other parts of Mexico—to conflict, namely the Revolution of 1910.

MODERN YUCATAN

Synthetic fibers have diminished the demand for henequén, although the plant is still raised commercially, along with corn and tropical fruits like bananas and coconuts. In the early 1960s, improved transportation links were instrumental in joining the Yucatán to the rest of Mexico. Mex. 186 was completed from Villahermosa to Chetumal, near the southeastern Caribbean coast. A rail line was extended from Coatzacoalcos, on the gulf coast at the northern end of the Isthmus of Tehuantepec, into the upper Yucatán, and air service drastically cut travel time. The advent of international tourism has most transformed the peninsula. The Yucatán's spectrum of activities—from birdwatching at isolated jungle lagoons to shopping at exclusive resort boutiques—appeals to a variety of budgets and lifestyles.

The Yucatecan people—direct descendants of the Maya—are one of Mexico's largest indígena groups. They live throughout the peninsula, particularly in the state of Yucatán, and their short stature, dark-skinned complexions and sculpted cheekbones bear unmistakable witness to their forebears. Maya dialects are as readily spoken as Spanish, although residents employed in the tourist industry usually speak some English as well. Yucatecans are friendly; don't be afraid to ask for the time or for directions, but return the kindness with a smile and a thank-you. You could also try thanking in Maya, which (spelled phonetically) is "dios boteek." Always ask first if you wish to photograph one of the local people; this can be done as simply as holding up your camera and saying *"por favor"?*

Outside of the cities, villages can look strikingly primitive. An oval-shaped, whitewashed hut, frequently windowless, might sit neatly in the shade of fruit trees or next to a field of henequén plants. Hammocks, cooler in the tropical heat, are often used instead of beds. Yucatecan women wear a *huipil*, a shift dress of white cloth that is often embroidered; everyone wears leather *huaraches* (sandals).

The rich cultural and historical legacy of Maya civilization is being preserved through **La Ruta Maya**, or The Maya Route, which encompasses a 120,000-square-mile area stretching east from the Isthmus of Tehuantepec and embracing the entire Yucatán Peninsula as well as the countries of Belize and Guatemala and parts of Honduras and El Salvador.

AKUMAL, QUINTANA ROO (G-12)

The diving center of Akumal is off Mex. 307 about 26 kilometers (16 miles) north of Tulum. Although it is centered around several expensive resort complexes, you don't need to be a guest in order to enjoy the long, curving, shell-covered beach or swim in the clear bay. Yellow blight has killed many of the coconut palms, but Akumal is still a lovely place. Area dive shops offer courses and certification. Deep-sea fishing for the likes of giant marlin and sailfish is another attraction. **Yalkú**, just north of Akumal, a protected lagoon ideal for snorkeling; admission is charged.

The heart of town, with its small grocery stores and eateries, is laid-back and friendly, more akin to the humble fishing village Akumal once was. Here families can refuel and enjoy the area's natural attributes along with local residents.

CAMPECHE, CAMPECHE (G-10)

Capital of the state of the same name, Campeche (kahm-PEH-cheh) is the largest city between Villahermosa and Mérida. Its waterfront, dotted by offshore oil rigs, is the base of Mexico's largest gulf coast shrimp fleet.

Hernández de Córdova and his *conquistadores* stopped in this area in 1517 to obtain fresh water. Founded in 1540 by Don Francisco de Montejo, the city flourished from the export of hardwoods and dyewoods to Europe. One of the foremost cities of New Spain in the mid-16th century, Campeche preserves buildings that date from this period in its old San Francisco section. One such structure was the house where Montejo planned his conquest of the Yucatán.

Campeche's most remarkable attraction is a massive 1.5-mile hexagonal wall with eight fortresses that was erected for protection against repeated sackings by pirates in the 16th and 17th centuries. Begun in 1686, the fortification took 18 years to build.

Fuerte de la Soledad (Fort Soledad), 3 blocks north of the ancient Puerta del Mar entranceway, has been converted into a museum displaying Maya artifacts, an arms collection and exhibits on colonial history. On the outskirts of the city is one of the most impressive of all the fortresses, **Fuerte de San Miguel** (Fort San Miguel). Its moat supposedly contained crocodiles.

Fuerte de San Carlos (Fort San Carlos), a government-sponsored handicrafts market today, has intriguing secret underground passageways. Linked to many houses in the city, the tunnels provided a hiding place for women and children when pirate ships came to plunder. Most passageways are sealed with bricks, but guides offer tours into the fort's basement for a small fee. The roof of Fort San Carlos, still equipped with ancient cannon, offers a spectacular view of the gulf.

Among the words coined in Campeche is *campechano*, used to describe a pleasant, easygoing person. Local tradition has it that the word "cocktail" originated here centuries ago because

English pirates were served drinks adorned by palm fronds resembling cocks' tails. Happily, the root of Campeche's name, taken from the Maya words *kim* and *pech*, meaning "serpent" and "tick," has no modern application.

Though the city is studded with ancient walls and fortresses, it also contains such buildings as the **Government Palace** and the **Legislative Palace**, respectively referred to as "the jukebox" and "the flying saucer" for their modern architecture, which blends surprisingly well with the native buildings. Local markets sell such handicrafts as panama hats and articles made of alligator skin. The regional cuisine includes such exotic dishes as shark stew.

Other points of interest include the 1540 **Franciscan Cathedral**, the oldest convent church in the Yucatán Peninsula; the 1546 **Convent of San Francisco**, the site of one of the first masses in Campeche; the Temple of San Francisquito, which now houses the **Instituto Cultural Campechano** (Campeche Cultural Institute); and the **Casa del Teniente del Rey** (House of the King's Lieutenant), which contains colonial furnishings. Alameda Park's **El Puente de los Perros** (Bridge of Dogs), a colonial bridge guarded by carved stone dogs, honors the Dominican missionaries called the "Dogs of God" for their zealous hounding of converts.

The State Tourism Bureau (Coordinación de Turismo del Estado) provides tourist information; phone (981) 6-6767 or 6-6068. ADO (Autobuses de Oriente) offers "deluxe" bus service.

Several destinations are nearby. Seybaplaya, Sihoplaya and Acapulquito to the south offer swimming beaches. In Hecelchakán, 54 kilometers (33 miles) northeast via Mex. 180, the **Museo Camino Real** displays exquisite Jaina Island clay figurines.

Edzná, a classic Maya city first inhabited in 600 B.C., is 45 kilometers (28 miles) southeast of Campeche via a new road. Within its 3.5-square-mile area, some of which is overgrown, are the 98-foot-tall **Templo de los Cinco Cuerpos** (Temple of Five Stories) and many outlying ruins. This is the state's principal archeological zone.

Roadways within the state of Campeche are primarily two-lane and somewhat wider than average. Roads to the archeological zones are well marked and maintained. Some shoulders drop off into deep trenches to aid drainage during the period of heavy summer rains.

WHERE TO STAY

HOTEL DEL MAR
Hotel ☎ 981/6-2233

All Year $80-$90 XP $5
Location: Center; facing the gulf. Av Ruiz Cortines 51 24000. Fax: 981/1-1618. **Facility:** Modern style; all rooms with balcony. Walled pool area. 148 units. *Bath:* some combo or shower only. 6 stories, interior corridors. **Terms:** F14. **Dining & Entertainment:** dining room, restaurant, 7 am-2 am, Sun-Wed to 11 pm, $6-$12, cocktails, nightclub, entertainment. **Leisure Activities:** wading pool, exercise room. **Guest Services:** gift shop, valet laundry. **Business Services:** conference facilities, administrative services. *Fee:* PC, fax. **Cards:** AE, CB, DS, MC, VI.

SOME UNITS

CANCUN, QUINTANA ROO

Cancún's metamorphosis from drowsy fishing village to vacation paradise is a true Cinderella story. Less than 30 years ago tourists were almost unknown; those of the camera-toting, sightseeing variety—if they visited the Yucatán Peninsula at all—opted for the Maya ruins at Chichén Itzá or the sultry charm of Mérida. Mexico's Caribbean coastline was left to two types of visitors. Serious skin and scuba divers, who more often than not belonged to some exclusive organization, chartered private planes to take them to hidden coves or secluded, rocky shores. Equally serious beach bums had miles of palm-studded stretches almost to themselves. The rich, the famous and those in search of the perfect tan all went to Acapulco.

Until 1961 the Yucatán was almost completely isolated from the rest of Mexico. In that year, however, completion of a highway across the southern part of the peninsula to Chetumal, the

Fast Facts

LOCATION: Just off the northeastern tip of the Yucatán Peninsula.

POPULATION: 450,000 (estimated).

AREA CODE: 9.

WHAT'S THERE: Beaches boasting powdery sand and clear, beautifully blue-green water; excellent snorkeling and scuba diving off the islands of Cozumel and Isla Mujeres and along the Caribbean coast; some of Mexico's most lavishly appointed hotels; abundant shopping and dining opportunities; easy accessibility to Chichén Itzá, Tulum and other Yucatán archeological sites.

❶ Best Western Plaza Caribe	⓰ Hotel Presidente	㉚ The Club Grill
❷ Calinda America Cancún	Inter-Continental Cancún	㉛ Coral Reef
❸ Calinda Viva Cancún	⓱ Hotel Sierra Cancún	㉜ Cote Sud
❹ Camino Real Cancún	⓲ Hyatt Cancún Caribe	㉝ Fantino
❺ Cancún Palace	⓳ Hyatt Regency-Cancún	㉞ La Brisa
❻ Caribbean Villages Cancún	⓴ Le Meridien	㉟ La Dolce Vita
❼ Casa Maya Hotel	㉑ Marriott CasaMagna Cancún	㊱ La Habichuela
❽ Condo Hotel Kin-Ha Cancún	㉒ Miramar Mision Cancún	㊲ La Joya Restaurant
❾ Continental Plaza Cancún	㉓ The Ritz-Carlton Cancún	㊳ Lorenzillo's
❿ Crown Paradise Club	㉔ Sheraton Cancún Resort & Towers	㊴ Maria Bonita
⓫ Fiesta Americana Condesa Cancún	㉕ Sunset Lagoon Hotel & Marina	㊵ Mikado
⓬ Fiesta Americana Grand Coral Beach	㉖ Westin Regina Resort Cancún	㊶ Restaurant El Calamar
⓭ Hilton Cancún Beach & Golf Resort	㉗ Blue Bayou	㊷ Restaurant Los Pericos
⓮ Holiday Inn Express	㉘ Carlos 'n Charlie's	㊸ Rosato Ristorante
⓯ Hotel Calinda Beach	㉙ Casa Rolandi's	㊹ Savio's

Quintana Roo state capital, opened it up. Things changed forever when FONATUR, the government agency responsible for developing Mexico's tourism potential, determined that the azure waters, fine-grained sand and natural beauty of a spit of land lying off the peninsula's northeastern tip were prime ingredients for the creation of a resort playground.

Bridges were built connecting both ends of this barrier island to the mainland. Drainage and electricity were provided. With these basics in place, the design of Cancún—an area once home to the Maya and later a refuge for pirates—was placed in the eager hands of developers.

At the beginning of the 1970s, Cancún didn't even show up on maps. A building boom began in the mid-1980s. The permanent population, the majority of whom serve the tourist industry and who hail from all over Mexico, has mushroomed from the original handful of fishermen. Some 3 million visitors arrive annually, about 90 percent of them from the United States and Canada.

Cancún is Mexico's most popular tourist destination for several reasons. Vacationers flock here for the year-round warm weather; for constant sea breezes and the tropical sunsets; for fishing, diving and boating; for the opportunity to spend large sums of money in fancy restaurants, upscale boutiques and flashy nightspots; and last but not least, to soak up sun on the beach. Cancún is a spring break hotspot, a major convention city, a getaway for honeymooners and a convenient base from which to explore the rest of the Yucatán.

Ciudad Cancún (Cancún City), located on the mainland, is Cancún's commercial and business backbone. **Isla Cancún** (Cancún Island), an elbow-shaped sandbar nearly 15 miles long but just a quarter-mile wide, is separated from the mainland by narrow causeways at either end (blink and you'll miss them). In between are the calm waters of **Laguna Nichupté** (Nichupté Lagoon). The island's seaward side fronts Mujeres Bay from Ciudad Cancún east to **Punta Cancún** (Cancún Point). The point is the crook of the elbow; south of it the shoreline faces the open Caribbean.

All of Cancún Island is occupied by the **Zona Hotelera** (Hotel Zone), which consists almost entirely of tourist services. It boasts some 25,000 hotel rooms, fine restaurants, loud nightspots, pricey shopping, a championship golf course and recreational opportunities from water skiing to windsurfing.

The newness so evident in the Hotel Zone contrasts starkly with the rundown villages and centuries-old Maya ruins found in other parts of the Yucatán. The big hotels are Cancún's real "sights," dazzling the eye with public areas awash in marble, tropical plants and dramatically lit art. Architecturally, the more recently built hotels take their cue from Mexico's ancient pyramids and temples.

The juxtaposition of Subway and Dunkin' Donuts outlets (just two of many familiar U.S. franchises) with the big, sweeping resorts makes for a slightly surreal atmosphere. It's all accentuated by the changing hues of the Caribbean surf. Everything is etched under sunlight bright enough to make sunglasses a full-time accessory.

Often linked with Cancún in the minds of travelers, **Cozumel** (see separate listing) is a separate destination with its own agenda. Lying south of Cancún and about 12 miles offshore opposite the mainland town of Playa del Carmen, it is Mexico's largest populated island. Deservedly popular with divers, the waters off Cozumel are unsurpassed for their clarity and for the variety of brilliantly colored marine life that inhabit them. A somewhat lower-cost alternative to Cancún, it attracts laid-back sun seekers who aren't interested in wild nightlife or a hectic schedule.

Isla Mujeres (see separate listing), a tiny island 4 miles off the Yucatán Peninsula's easternmost tip, lies just north of Cancún opposite mainland Puerto Juárez. The name, which means "Island of Women," is believed to have been coined by Spanish explorers who arrived to find an abundance of statues sculpted in female forms, a ceremonial legacy left behind by the Maya. This was another favored refuge for pirates due to its isolated location. Recent growth is related directly to tourism, although Isla Mujeres is less developed and even more casual

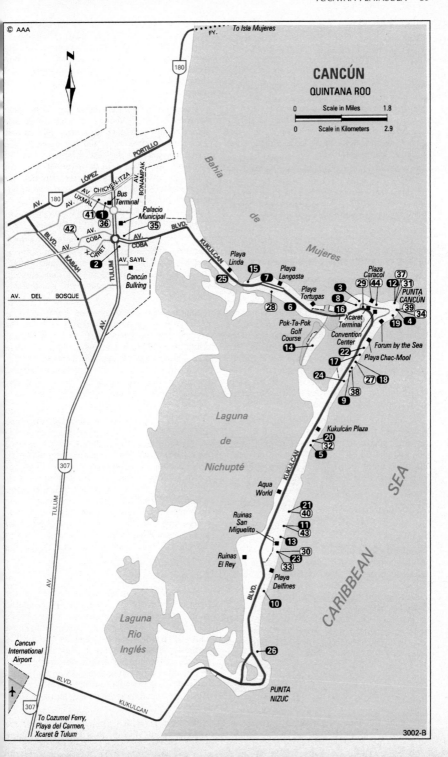

© AAA

N

To Isla Mujeres

180

CANCÚN
QUINTANA ROO

| 0 | Scale in Miles | 1.8 |
| 0 | Scale in Kilometers | 2.9 |

Bahia

de

Mujeres

PORTILLO

LÓPEZ
AV. CHICHÉN-ITZA
AV. BONAMPAK
AV. 180
AV. UXMAL
Bus Terminal
Palacio Municipal
(41)(1)
(36)
(42)
AV. COBA
(35)
BLVD.
KUKULCAN
(2)
X.-CARET
AV. TULUM
AV. SAYIL
AV. COBA
Cancún Bullring
AV. DEL BOSQUE
BLVD. AV. KABAH

Playa Linda
(15)
(25)
Playa Langosta
(7)
Playa Tortugas
(3)
(8)
(6)
(16)
(28)
Playa Caracol
Plaza Caracol
(29)(44)
(37)
(12)(31)
PUNTA CANCÚN
(39)
(34)
(19)(4)
Xcaret Terminal
Convention Center
(14)
Pok-Ta-Pok Golf Course
(22)
(17)
Forum by the Sea
Playa Chac-Mool
(24)
(27)(18)
(38)
(9)

Laguna
de
Nichupté

Kukulcán Plaza
(20)
(32)
(5)
KUKULCAN

Aqua World
(21)
(40)
Ruinas San Miguelito
(11)
(43)
(13)
Ruinas El Rey
(30)
(23)
(33)
Playa Delfines
BLVD.
(10)

Laguna Rio Inglés

Cancun International Airport
307

BLVD.
KUKULCAN

(26)

PUNTA NIZUC

SEA

CARIBBEAN

TULUM
AV.
307

To Cozumel Ferry,
Playa del Carmen,
Xcaret & Tulum

3002-B

than Cozumel. The crystal-clear waters off the island are great for snorkeling.

Big, glamorous, fast-paced Cancún, on the other hand, holds little appeal for the vacationer seeking a tranquil hideaway. Its traditional image has been a fairly economical one, with plenty of tour packages offering discounted airfares and lodgings. But the sophisticated, upscale traveler also is courted via such plush retreats as the Fiesta Americana Grand Coral Beach, the Ritz-Carlton and the latest arrival, Le Meridien, which opened in December 1998.

This is not the "real" Mexico: English is commonplace (although Spanish might be offered first), fast food proliferates, and the glare of neon replaces historical and cultural shadings. The pervasive Americanization is comforting for those who are hesitant about vacationing in a foreign country, who desire a higher level of amenities or who want fewer hassles than are routinely encountered in Mexico's less-developed areas.

Cancún also faces a familiar dilemma: the specter of resort development taking over the coastline to the south. Already on the drawing board is a plan to develop the now-isolated stretch of southern Quintana Roo coastline between Punta Herrero and Xcalak (near the Belize border) for ecologically oriented tourism. The "Costa Maya" will feature small resorts of no more than 50 units spread out along the shore. Nature is protected, however, in such places as the 1.5-million acre **Sian Ka'an Biosphere Reserve,** also in southern Quintana Roo.

Despite the environmental concern, there's no denying that Cancún's popularity gives a boost to the Mexican economy. Planeloads of satisfied vacationers embrace it for what it is—a combination of natural beauty and modern facilities tailor-made for the pursuit of indulgence.

APPROACHES

BY AIR

Cancún International Airport is on the mainland off Mex. 307, about 16 kilometers (10 miles) southwest of downtown Ciudad Cancún and about 10 kilometers (6 miles) from the southern end of Cancún Island. It receives regular flights from major cities in the United States and Mexico; many are daily. Aeroméxico, (98) 84-1186, American, (98) 86-0129, Continental, (98) 86-0006, Mexicana, (98) 83-4881, and Northwest, (98) 86-0444, offer direct flights from U.S. cities. **Note:** There are no direct flights from Canada to Cancún; most major U.S. airlines meet connecting flights from Canada in Dallas, Houston and New York. To confirm schedules, contact the appropriate airline or a travel agency. For additional information about airlines *see "Arriving by Air," page 53.*

Aerocaribe and Aerocozumel (both affiliated with Mexicana) are regional airlines with service to Cancún from various Mexican cities. They fly to nearby Yucatán destinations, including Chichén Itzá, Cozumel, Mérida and Playa del Carmen, as well as to Oaxaca. For information phone (800) 531-7921.

The airport is not very large but can be quite crowded, especially during the winter high season. Renting a luggage cart costs $1. Airport staff hand out free maps and brochures for the popular regional tourist destinations, so you can pick these up if you need the information. Don't exchange dollars for pesos at the currency exchange office; you'll get a better rate at your hotel. The office is handy for changing Mexican currency back into dollars when you leave, although you'll be shortchanged by the rate.

All arriving passengers pass through Mexican customs; make sure your declaration form is properly filled out. Each arrival must press a button. If the light flashes green you may proceed; if it flashes red your luggage will be routinely checked.

Shuttle service via minivan (*colectivos*) is available from the airport to the Hotel Zone. The average fare is around $10 per person—less costly than taking a taxi, which can run more than $20 depending upon your location. *Colectivos* do not provide service back to the airport, making a cab ride necessary upon departure. Cabs affiliated with the bigger hotels often have a fixed rate for service to the airport.

Confirm your reservation and departure time with your airline at least 24 hours prior to departing Cancún. For international flights, arrive 2 hours before scheduled departure time to be on the safe side. The airport has a number of souvenir shops if you want to make last-minute purchases; prices are a bit steep, but U.S. dollars are accepted. Prices for merchandise sold at the duty-free store—mostly liquor, cigars and perfume—aren't that much of a bargain. **Note:** At press time the departure tax was about $17, although this fee is often incorporated into the price of the ticket.

BY CAR

Mexico's easternmost city is located at the Yucatán Peninsula's northeastern tip. From the west, Mex. 180 via Veracruz, Villahermosa, Campeche and Mérida is the preferred route; it ends at Punta Sam, north of Cancún. From Villahermosa, an alternate route is Mex. 186 east to Escárcega, Camp., and then north on Mex. 281 to Champotón. It carries heavy truck traffic and has very few gas stations or mechanical services. This route should only be driven during daylight hours.

Mex. 180 is two lanes between Mérida and the small town of Hoctún. Four-lane toll highway

Mex. 180-D begins at Hoctún and roughly parallels Mex. 180 for a distance of about 240 kilometers (150 miles). All of Mex. 180-D is in very good condition, lightly traveled and quicker than Mex. 180, which passes through towns—but also isolated if you happen to break down.

Kilometer markers are along the right side of the road, and there are regular intervals, indicated by signs, to make a U-turn *(retorno)*. Signage is good (both speed limit and mileage signs and the international blue highway signs). Toll plazas are located at the Chichén Itzá exit and at the Yucatán/Quintana Roo state line (which also is a customs checkpoint). At press time, toll charges totaled about $17. There are only a few gas stations along the length of the route, so make sure your tank is always at least half full.

Mex. 180-D ends about 16 kilometers (10 miles) west of the airport; follow the sign that says "Cancún/Puerto Juárez" to stay on the mainland, or the sign "Tulum/Aeropuerto" to get to the Hotel Zone.

An access route to Cancún from the south is Mex. 307, which begins about 19 kilometers (12 miles) west of Chetumal off Mex. 186 in southern Quintana Roo and proceeds north through Bacalar and Tulum. The section of Mex. 307 from Tulum north to Cancún, which closely parallels the Caribbean coast and offers access to several beach resorts, is known as the **Cancún-Tulum Corridor**.

A highway branching northwest at Tulum offers access to the Cobá archeological zone and joins Mex. 180 at the town of Nuevo Xcán—a distance of about 85 kilometers (53 miles). It saves time and mileage if you want a more direct route from Tulum to Mérida.

By Bus

The bus terminal is in downtown Ciudad Cancún at the intersection of avenidas Tulum and Uxmal, in front of the Plaza Caribe Hotel. First- and second-class buses arrive regularly from various points on the Yucatán Peninsula, including Chetumal, Chichén Itzá, Mérida, Playa del Carmen, Tulum and Valladolid. Frequent "deluxe" service is available from Mérida, with stops en route at Chichén Itzá and Valladolid. For additional information about buses *see "Bus Service," page 63*.

By Cruise Ship

Cancún has no docking facilities for cruise ships. Only an occasional ship stops offshore from Playa Tortugas, at Km 7 on Boulevard

The Informed Traveler

Media

The *Miami Herald* and *USA Today* are available in the bigger hotels. Radio Turquesa (105.1 FM) offers English-language news, weather and information about local events. Local FM station 93.1 broadcasts American rock and Spanish commercials.

Most hotels have a cable TV system that offers the ABC, CBS, NBC and Fox networks via a U.S. affiliate, such staples as CNN and ESPN, and HBO or another movie channel, in addition to Spanish-language channels.

Weather

Cancún is warm year-round, although constant sea breezes temper the summer heat. Several of the big hotels have open-air public areas that can be uncomfortable (even with breezes) because of the high humidity.

The sun is intense, especially when it reflects off the water; use an appropriate sunblock for any long-term exposure. The beaches are warm enough for swimming all year. Rain can fall in any month, although May through October is the likeliest time. The greatest chance for hurricanes or other unsettled weather is in September and October.

Shorts and T-shirts are what most visitors wear; casual but stylish resort wear is appropriate at the nicer restaurants or for an evening out. Pack a sweater for the occasional cool winter day or air-conditioned summer interior, depending on the time of year you visit.

Staying Safe

Tourist crime is not prevalent, and using regular common sense should be the only precaution necessary. Car break-ins can occur in the Hotel Zone's shopping areas; don't invite one by leaving valuables in plain view. Be vigilant when walking in Ciudad Cancún after dark.

In Case of Emergency

To lodge a complaint with the Procuraduría del Consumidor (Consumer Protection Agency), phone (98) 84-2369. For municipal police assistance phone (98) 84-1913; the station is on Avenida Tulum next to City Hall. To reach traffic police phone (98) 84-0710. If you lose your tourist card, contact the Immigration Office, avenidas J.C. Nader and Uxmal in Ciudad Cancún; phone (98) 84-1404.

For 24-hour emergency medical assistance contact the Red Cross (Cruz Roja), Avenida Yaxchilán #2, phone (98) 84-1616; the small hospital Total Assist, Calle Claveles #5, phone (98) 84-1058 (English-speaking doctors); or Hospital Americano, at Calle Viento #15 (off Avenida Tulum south of Avenida Cobá), phone (98) 84-6133. All of these facilities are in downtown Ciudad Cancún.

Kukulcán; passengers are ferried to land. If you're on a ship that docks at Cozumel and want to spend some time in Cancún, you'll be tendered from Cozumel to Playa del Carmen, about a 45-minute drive south of Cancún (or check with your ship's shore excursion desk to see if they offer a Cancún package). Depending on the length of shore leave, you could squeeze in a shopping trip or a visit to one of the beaches. **Note:** If you arrange a shore excursion through the ship it will wait for you; if you arrange it yourself the ship won't wait. Keep timing in mind.

GETTING AROUND

CITY LAYOUT

The main streets in downtown Ciudad Cancún (referred to as El Centro) are east-west **Avenida López Portillo**, the in-town section of Mex. 180, which extends from the western city limits northeast to Puerto Juárez and Punta Sam; and north-south **Avenida Tulum**, the in-town section of Mex. 307, which runs south toward the airport. **Avenida Cobá** parallels López Portillo several blocks west and becomes Boulevard Kukulcán as it enters the Hotel Zone. Most souvenir shops, stores and restaurants are along or near Tulum and Cobá.

Ciudad Cancún is divided into districts called *super manzanas*, each containing several blocks unified by a central square or park. It is the city's business center; hotels cater to business, local and budget-minded travelers.

Boulevard Kukulcán (also called Paseo Kukulcán, but often referred to simply as "Kukulcán") runs the length of Cancún Island and is the only main traffic artery. It actually begins at Avenida Bonampak, on the eastern edge of Ciudad Cancún. Past **Punta Nizuc** (Nizuc Point), the island's southern tip, Kukulcán runs into southbound Mex. 307 at the overpass leading to the airport. **Note:** The speed limit along most of Kukulcán is 40 km/h (25 mph) and is strictly enforced; the limit increases to 60 km/h (40 mph) at the southern end of the island. Where u-turns are permitted, signs in the median say *retorno*.

The approach to the Hotel Zone from the airport is not impressive—a two-lane road lined with tropical scrub and tacky billboards. Once Cancún Island is reached, however, Kukulcán becomes a landscaped, four-lane divided highway. The first glimpse of the aquamarine Caribbean is stunning.

Most of the Caribbean side is lined with big hotels set back from the road, and views of the water are few. There are no residential areas on the island; its accommodations, restaurants, shopping areas, nightspots and expensive timeshare condominiums all target vacationers. Kukulcán's four lanes divide briefly to encompass Cancún Point, the elbow of the island's "seven" configuration.

Numbered addresses are rarely given for places in the Hotel Zone; instead, median kilometer markers (from Km 1 on the mainland east of downtown to Km 25 south of Nizuc Point) indicate locations. Directions also are given in reference to well-known landmarks or hotels. Because there is only one road, it's almost impossible to get lost.

RENTAL CARS

It's not really necessary to rent a car while staying in Cancún; bus and taxi service is frequent. You'll need one if you plan a day or overnight trip down the coast to Tulum or to one of the Yucatán archeological sites and don't want to be part of an organized tour. The quality of most regional roads is very good. Do not underestimate the amount of time it will take to arrive at your destination, and avoid driving on secondary roads after dark.

Rates are on the expensive side; you'll save money by reserving a car in advance of your arrival. Arranging for pickup and drop-off at the airport will eliminate taxi fares. Make certain you fully understand the terms of any rental contract. If the car only has half a tank of gas when you pick it up, you can return it with half a tank; double check before you drive off. Check the car carefully to make sure the spare tire is inflated, all tire jack parts are included (lift up the spare tire compartment cover and remove them from the sleeve), and inventory for nicks and dents. **Note:** License plates on rental vehicles say "renta," marking you as a visitor.

Hertz is one of several rental car agencies available, with offices at the airport, downtown Ciudad Cancún and on Kukulcán in the Cancún Point area. AAA/CAA members enjoy exceptional discounts through Hertz for vehicles booked in the United States or Canada. Consult your local AAA/CAA club or phone Hertz, (800) 654-3080.

BUSES

"Ruta 1" and "Ruta 2" buses (marked "Hoteles" on the windshield) run regularly from the mainland to the southern end of the Hotel Zone and back daily 6 a.m.-midnight. The "Ruta 8" bus goes to Puerto Juárez and Punta Sam for the ferries to Isla Mujeres. Fares are inexpensive—2 pesos (about 20c) in Ciudad Cancún, 4 pesos (about 40c) on Cancún Island. You'll need Mexican currency; exact change isn't necessary. The Hotel Zone has frequent designated stops, and drivers also can be flagged from hotel driveway entrances along Kukulcán. Using the bus is much cheaper than taking a cab, especially If you're staying at the southern end of the Hotel Zone.

Visitor Services

Guided Tours

The most popular day excursions from Cancún are to Xcaret, Xel-Há and Tulum, all south along the Caribbean coast. Guided tours to Chichén Itzá, Cobá and Uxmal also are available. There are numerous in-town tour operators, but many hotels have a travel agency on site or a concierge who can help with tour arrangements.

Gray Line Cancún, Calle Robalo #30, offers motorcoach tours to various regional points of interest; phone (98) 87-2450. Bus tours to Xcaret leave daily at 9 and 10 a.m. from the Xcaret terminal next to the Fiesta Americana Grand Coral Beach; phone (98) 83-3143 or 83-3144. Aqua World (see attraction listing) offers a Cozumel tour aboard the Caribbean Princess that includes shopping, sightseeing, snorkeling, lunch, a beach buffet and round-trip transportation. Daily departures are at 8 a.m.; phone (98) 85-2288.

Information Sources

Cancún Tips, a magazine with easy-to-read maps and information about restaurants, shopping, entertainment, sightseeing and local services, is available at most hotels, the airport and the state tourist office. Cancún Tips Tourist Guide is a booklet containing maps, useful phone numbers and lots of general information. Yucatan Today focuses on Mérida and the state of Yucatán. Pick up these and other free tourist-oriented publications and maps at the airport when you arrive.

Staff members of Cancún Tips magazine operate information booths at the airport, in the Plaza Caracol shopping center (Hotel Zone) and in Ciudad Cancún at the corner of avenidas Tulum and Chichén Itzá. The State Tourism Office is at Avenida Tulum #26 (between avenidas Cobá and Uxmal next to Banco Inverlat); phone (98) 84-8073. The Cancún Convention and Visitors Bureau is at avenidas Nader and Cobá; phone (98) 84-6531.

The post office building (Correo) is at avenidas Xel-Há and Sunyaxchén, a couple of blocks west of Avenida Yaxchilán; open Mon.-Fri. 8-7, Sat. 9-1.

Currency Exchange

Casas de cambio (currency exchange offices) and banks are along Avenida Tulum in downtown Ciudad Cancún. Offices also are located in the Hotel Zone malls and in the vicinity of Cancún Point. Most banks are open Mon.-Fri. 9-1:30; currency exchange normally is confined to the morning hours. Since the rates offered by exchange offices, banks and hotels normally don't differ that much, exchanging dollars boils down to a matter of convenience. Convert only what you'll need for bus and taxi fares, souvenir purchases and so forth.

Buses are likely to be crowded during the morning and evening, when mainland locals use them to get to and from work.

The Linea Verde bus line offers round-trip excursions (paquetes turísticos) to such popular destinations as Chichén Itzá, Cozumel and Xcaret. Departures are from the main bus terminal in downtown Ciudad Cancún.

TAXIS

Picking up a cab directly at your hotel is the most convenient, but they also tend to have the highest rates. Some hotels list fares to various destinations at the front entrance; if not, ask the doorman. Better hotels will arrange "payouts," putting cab fares on the bill so they show up on your credit card receipt as a recorded expense. Taxis within the Hotel Zone are very expensive; it can cost $5 or more to ride from a hotel at the southern end to one at the northern end, compared to about 40c on the Kukulcán bus.

Green city taxis can be hailed on the street in Ciudad Cancún. All cabs are controlled by the local government, so the driver should be able to provide a rate list if asked. If you're going from the Hotel Zone to Ciudad Cancún, Puerto Juárez or Punta Sam, take the Kukulcán bus to the mainland, then a taxi to your destination, since the city taxis have a cheaper rate structure than the Hotel Zone taxis. To lodge a complaint or report lost articles phone (98) 88-6990.

FERRIES

Enclosed, air-conditioned passenger ferries run between Puerto Juárez, about 3 kilometers (2 miles) north of Cancún, and Isla Mujeres hourly from around 6 a.m. to 6 p.m. The trip takes 15-20 minutes; one-way fare is about $2.20. Local "Ruta 8" buses make the short trip along Avenida Tulum in Ciudad Cancún to the Puerto Juárez public dock; you can also get there by taxi.

A passenger/car ferry operates daily, weather permitting, between Punta Sam, about 5 kilometers (3 miles) north of Puerto Juárez, and Isla Mujeres. The trip takes about 45 minutes. The first departure is around 7:15 a.m.; the last, around 8:15 p.m. Double-check departure times at the public ferry dock. There are separate fees for vehicles and pasengers. For additional information about ferry schedules, see "What To Do—Sightseeing" below, and the separate listings for Playa del Carmen and Puerto Morelos.

PARKING

There are very few municipal parking lots in Ciudad Cancún or the Hotel Zone. Park on city streets at your own discretion. If you've rented a car or are driving your own vehicle, keep it in the hotel lot—most of them are guarded—and use buses or cabs for local excursions.

WHAT TO SEE

AQUA WORLD is at Km 15.2 on the lagoon side of Boulevard Kukulcán (opposite the Melía Cancún Hotel). This large, modern marina functions as an all-purpose recreation center, organizing deep-sea fishing, jungle tour, diving and snorkeling excursions. Equipment also is available for parasailing, windsurfing, jet skiing and wave running (the last by means of a small, jet-powered boat).

The *Cancún Queen* is a paddlewheeler that cruises through the mangroves lining Nichupté Lagoon. Dinner in the air-conditioned dining room is followed by dancing to live band music on the top deck. The *Snorkel and Jungle Tour* navigates lagoon waterways en route to Paradise Island and snorkeling in the vicinity of a coral reef. Safety is stressed, and life jackets, snorkeling equipment and lunch are provided. Aqua World's *Sub See Explorer* is an air-conditioned, submarine-like boat with large glass windows built into the sides for underwater viewing of fish, coral formations, rays, turtles and other local marine life. The vessel also tours the island; lunch and a beverage are included.

Facilities include a water sports shop, snack and beverage stand, restrooms and parking areas. Scuba diving instruction is available. The staff is uniformed, nametagged and bilingual. Aqua World is open daily 6:30 a.m.-9:30 p.m. The *Cancún Queen* cruise departs the marina daily at 6:30 p.m. The *Sub See Explorer* departs daily on the hour 9-3. Fees for each activity vary; ages 3-11 pay half the adult rate for the *Cancún Queen* and *Sub See Explorer* cruises. Arrange cruise excursions or fishing trips in advance; Aqua World sales kiosks are located in most major hotels. AE, MC, VI. Phone (98) 85-2288, fax (98) 85-2299.

CANCUN CONVENTION CENTER is at Km 8 on Boulevard Kukulcán near Cancún Point. It was rebuilt after being damaged in 1988 by Hurricane Gilbert. The complex offers a variety of performing arts events and provides extensive convention, exhibition and office space in addition to shops and restaurants. The highlight of the four-story building is a huge ballroom overlooking the Caribbean. Paintings and sculptures by local artists are on display in public areas. A small museum, the **Museo Arqueológico de Cancún**, is next to the center and exhibits a collection of pre-Hispanic artifacts gathered from around the

state. Museum open Tues.-Sat. 9-7, Sun. 10-5. Admission is about $1.75; free to all Sun. and holidays.

LAGUNA NICHUPTE (Nichupté Lagoon) lies between the Hotel Zone and the mainland. It contains a combination of fresh and salt water. A few small islands are within the lagoon, and peninsulas punctuate the shoreline. Two smaller lagoons connected to Nichupté by narrow waterways: **Laguna Bojórquez**, at the northeastern end, and **Laguna Rio Inglés**, at the southwestern end. Local tour operators offer day and evening cruises of Nichupté, which is the residence of many different bird species; hotels usually can make the necessary arrangements.

RUINAS EL REY (El Rey Ruins) are on the lagoon side of Boulevard Kukulcán at Km 17; watch for signs. Although much smaller than other Yucatán archeological sites, the ruins are a nice change of pace from the pervasive newness. They are proof that many Mayas were sailors and fishermen, navigating the sea to Central America and possibly some of the Caribbean islands.

The small ceremonial center contains temple platforms and a few larger buildings sitting amid stands of banana plants and other jungle growth. The discovery of skeletal remains at this site indicates it might once have been used for human burial or sacrifice. There is a separate entrance to the ruins, which are surrounded by the Caesar Park Beach & Golf Resort. Open daily 8-5. Admission is charged; free to all Sun.

Close by, on the Caribbean side of Kukulcán at Km 16.5, is **San Miguelito**, another Maya site that consists of a small building anchored by stone pillars.

SIAN KA'AN BIOSPHERE RESERVE—*see Tulum.*

TULUM RUINS—*see Tulum.*

XCARET—*see Playa del Carmen.*

XEL-HA NATURAL PARK—*see Tulum.*

WHAT TO DO

DINING

Restaurants in Cancún range from hole-in-the-wall casual to casually elegant, and food covers the bases from fast-food burgers and fries to Yucatecan specialties. Cost will be the likely factor in your dining choices.

Many hotel restaurants on Cancún Island offer standard Continental dishes of reliable quality and predictable expense. Most hotels go to great lengths to keep their guests on the premises, and some may charge for meals whether they are eaten or not. Dress is usually casual but not unkempt (no shorts or T-shirts). Gracious, professional service and candlelit, romantic settings are the norm. Do not expect much in the way of local cookery, although exotic house specialties take advantage of fresh seafood and tropical fruits. Dinner for two (excluding drinks, wine and tip) can run upwards of $60.

In addition to the hotel restaurants, Cancún Island has representatives of such U.S. and Mexican franchises as **Houlihans, Ruth's Chris Steak House** and **Carlos 'n Charlie's**. For the homesick there are numerous American fast-food outlets, although prices are higher than in the United States and Canada.

Perhaps the best place in the Hotel Zone for a full-blown Mexican dining experience is **Maria Bonita**, next to the Camino Real Cancún hotel. The wildly colorful dining areas, which have views of the Caribbean, are furnished with hand-painted chairs and decorated to reflect various regions of Mexico. The staff dresses up as notable figures from Mexican history, service is gracious, musicians stroll among the diners, and the culinary details extend to such extras as flavored butters artfully wrapped in tamale corn husks. It all makes for a festive evening.

An excellent breakfast choice is the Mexican chain **Vips**, on Kukulcán across from the Forum by the Sea shopping complex. A coffee shop and casual restaurant, it has reliably good, reasonably priced food served in a bright, cheery atmosphere. Try one of the filling Mexican breakfasts, such as *bistec de pollo encebollado* (chicken cutlets pounded thin and sauteed with onions), served with *chilaques* (tortilla strips, salsa and cheese with a dollop of sour cream), a side of refried beans, a basket of *pan dulce* (lightly sweetened breads), toast, a glass of fruit juice and good American-style coffee—all for around $4.

Avenida Tulum in Ciudad Cancún is lined with eateries, and most have outdoor tables. Establishments compete for business by displaying the house specialty at the door and even posting an employee outside to lure customers. It adds up to a noisy street spectacle that you may not want to put up with while dining. Look for places where locals congregate if you want authentically prepared *sopa de lima*—soup with a chicken broth base, vegetables and a tangy dose of fresh lime juice—or *poc-chuc*, spicy marinated pork grilled with onions. Montejo, brewed in Mérida, is the beer of choice. **Los Almendros**, downtown at avenidas Bonampak and Sayil, offers authentic Yucatecan dishes and has a picture menu to simplify ordering.

Restaurants in the large hotels use purified water for cooking and for washing produce; inquire about this health procedure specifically at places on the mainland. In general, avoid ice cubes in drinks unless you know purified water has been used. For a list of AAA-RATED establishments in Cancún, *see the Lodgings & Restaurants section*.

SHOPPING

Shopping in Cancún's Hotel Zone usually focuses on pricey merchandise or T-shirts and beach supplies. While one can find a wide range of Mexican handicrafts, prices are some of the most expensive in the country. As a duty-free zone, however, Cancún offers potential bargains on international items. It pays to shop around for crafts and souvenirs, as merchants compete vigorously for tourist dollars. Examine any merchandise carefully before buying; quality can vary greatly.

In Ciudad Cancún, a variety of shops and open-air craft markets line Avenida Tulum. **Kihuic**, near the intersection with Avenida Cobá, is a block-long flea market with stalls offering handicrafts, knickknacks, marble chess sets, men's *guayabera* shirts, *huipil* (ee-PEEL) dresses and Panama hats. Bargaining is expected at the markets; never offer to pay the initial asking price.

The enclosed, air-conditioned Hotel Zone malls are every bit as sleek as their U.S. and Canadian counterparts. Elegant **Plaza Caracol**, one of the largest, is at Km 8.5 across from the Cancún Convention Center. Cool marble walls and floors are the setting for some 200 shops and boutiques offering jewelry, designer clothing, resort wear, silver and decorative art. An outdoor section has more shops, along with restaurants and currency exchange offices. At Km 13 is **Kukulcán Plaza**, which has a similar mix of boutiques, plus a fast-food court. For kids there's a bowling alley, movie theater, a video and laser game entertainment center, and an outdoor play area (at the mall's southern end). **Forum by the Sea**, Km 9 next to the Hotel Krystal Cancún, is the newest; it has Tommy Hilfiger, Bvlgari Berger Jewelry and other specialty boutiques, restaurants (including Rainforest Café) and the Cancún branch of the Hard Rock Café. **Flamingo Plaza**, Km 10.5 on Kukulcán (lagoon side), contains several duty-free stores and boutiques, a gym, a currency exchange office and numerous fast-food outlets.

Three smaller shopping centers in the vicinity of Plaza Caracol are **Terramar Plaza**; **Mansión Costa Blanca**, where the shops sell designer clothing; and **Plaza Lagunas**, which specializes in casual sportswear. Handicrafts, jewelry and clothing are available at **Plaza La Fiesta**, a bit farther down Kukulcán. If you enjoy haggling (in English) with persistent craft vendors, browse the stalls at the **Mercado de Artesanías Coral Negro** (Flea Market), a white stucco building on Kukulcán (lagoon side) just south of the convention center. **Plaza Nautilus** is on the mainland, on the lagoon side of Kukulcán between Km 3 and 4 (opposite Playa Linda).

Most of the mall stores are open daily 10-8 or 10 p.m. Outside the Hotel Zone many stores observe the traditional *siesta* and close for a few hours in the afternoon (usually 2-5); most are closed on Sunday. The sales tax is 10 percent, which may be waived at some shops if you pay in cash.

BEACHES

Spectacular beaches are Cancún's main claim to fame. Cancún Island's Caribbean-facing shoreline is edged with golden-colored, tiny-grained sand. Composed of innumerable microscopic plankton fossils, it remains cool to the feet despite the strong sun. A gorgeous counterpoint is provided by the ever-shifting colors of the sea, which range from the opalescent green of the shallows to sky-blue wave swells to vivid turquoise at the horizon.

The beaches along the northern side of the island fronting Bahía Mujeres (Mujeres Bay) are narrower but have the same velvety sand. The water here is calm and shallow, the sandy bottom is mostly free of rocks, and beaches are regularly raked to clear them of seaweed. The Caribbean beaches are wider and more dramatic, with occasional crashing breakers and dangerous undertows.

The best beaches are in front of the big hotels. All beaches in Mexico, however, are federally owned property and therefore public, even stretches that may seem like they are on hotel property (although you can't use hotel facilities if you're not a guest). Heed the flags posted to indicate surf conditions. Green or blue flags indicate safe conditions for swimming; yellow, caution; and red or black, dangerous.

The "inner" coast of Cancún Island borders saltwater **Nichupté Lagoon**. Nichupté, lined in some places with stands of mangrove, doesn't have the Caribbean's beauty, but the calm water is ideal for scuba diving and water skiing.

The following designated public beaches are described in the order they appear along Cancún Island, beginning at the top of the island's "seven" configuration after leaving the mainland. *See map page 89.*

PLAYA LINDA is just before the bridge over Canal Nichupté, at Km 4. Boat tours embark to Isla Mujeres from the pier here, and there are several gift, snack and dive equipment shops.

PLAYA LANGOSTA is next to the Casa Maya Hotel at Km 5. The beach is close to several yacht clubs, water sports facilities, a seaplane base, shops and restaurants. Tour boats leave from the dock here.

PLAYA TORTUGAS, near the Intercontinental Presidente Cancún at Km 6, is frequented by locals and tourists staying downtown.

PLAYA CARACOL is close to the Fiesta Americana Grand Coral Beach and the Xcaret bus terminal. Further east is Cancún Point, the crook of the Cancún elbow. The very tip of the point, behind the Camino Real hotel, is where Mujeres Bay meets the open Caribbean. Isla Mujeres is visible in the distance. Waves crash against the rocks and send up plumes of spray on the Caribbean side, while just around the point the water is calm, shallow and translucent. Note the change in hues from steely blue to soft turquoise. A lone *palapa* hut offers a nice vantage point from which to contemplate the open sea.

Reaching the point is an easy walk from the Camino Real's beachfront through shallow water and scattered rocks (wear nonslip shoes). Stand on the point and face west for a lovely view that takes in the peach exterior of the Fiesta Americana hotel, vividly colored water and coconut palms rustling in the breeze.

PLAYA CHAC-MOOL, at Km 9.5, is another popular stretch not associated with one of the big hotels. Washed by the intensely hued Caribbean surf, it has sand that is incredibly powdery.

PLAYA DELFINES is at Km 17 at the southern end of the Hotel Zone, opposite the El Rey ruins. The wide stretch of sand here is far from the action and as a result provides a more relaxed setting for swimming and beachcombing.

A Hotel Zone beach   ©Chris Sharp

SIGHTSEEING

People come to Cancún not to sightsee but to sun, swim, eat, party and relax. There are options, however, particularly if you consider the surrounding area. One diversion is exploring the length of the Hotel Zone. Walk through the public and pool areas at a few of the big resorts. Buses marked "Hoteles" stop frequently along Boulevard Kukulcán, so use them to get from one place to another (keep in mind that you must pay bus fare each time you reboard).

Daytime cruises ply Nichupté Lagoon and the waters around Cancún Island, Cozumel and Isla Mujeres. Prices range from around $30-$50 per person. Boat operators and itineraries change, so check with your hotel or a local travel agency to see what's available. **Aqua World** *(see attraction listing)* offers a Cozumel trip that includes round-trip transportation and a cruise to Isla Mujeres that includes time for shopping, lunch and relaxing at the beach; for information phone (98) 85-2288. The 340-person capacity *Dolphin Express* cruiser also travels to Isla Mujeres; activities include shopping, snorkeling and dolphin observation at the **Pirate's Village** facility on the island. Cruises depart daily at 10 a.m. from the **Playa Langosta Pier**, next to the Casa Maya Hotel at Km 5 on Boulevard Kukulcán. For reservations and information phone (98) 83-1488.

If you would rather explore Isla Mujeres on your own, take one of the commercial water taxis that leave from the public dock at **Puerto Juárez**. There are approximate hourly departures in each direction daily beginning around 6 a.m. to around 6 p.m. The enclosed, air-conditioned boat holds about 30 passengers and docks at the northern end of the island; the trip takes 15-20 minutes. Schedules are posted at both docks but are subject to changes or delays; double-check the final departure time when you arrive at Isla Mujeres. One-way fare is 22 pesos (about $2.20) and is collected after you board. Crowds are a distinct possibility depending on the time of year.

Ferry service to Isla mujeres also is available from the Fiesta Americana Coral Beach Cancún hotel. Departures are at 9 a.m., 11 a.m. and 1 p.m., with returns at 10 a.m., noon and 2 p.m.

A few miles north of Puerto Juárez is **Punta Sam**, from which a car/passenger ferry departs for Isla Mujeres several times daily (weather permitting). Because Isla Mujeres is so small, however, a car isn't necessary for routine day trips or an afternoon at the beach. Passengers not transporting a vehicle can use the Punta Sam ferry as well.

For those who want an underwater adventure, the **Atlantis** is a 65-foot, battery-powered silver submarine. The air-conditioned, pressure-controlled cabin accommodates 48 passengers for a 45-minute undersea tour at a depth of about 50 feet. Large portholes running the length of the sub offer views of rhythmically swaying fan corals and a variety of marine life. (**Note:** Entering the sub involves climbing down steep stairs.) Children under age 4 are not permitted, and the trip is not advised for those prone to motion sickness. A boat departs (weather permitting) from the **Playa Linda Pier**, Km 4 on Kukulcán, for the sub site off Isla Mujeres. A fee is charged (half price for ages 4-12). Phone (98) 83-3021.

Extending south from Cancún is a 100-mile stretch of Caribbean coastline sprinkled with scenic beaches and protected by a series of offshore coral reefs. The region, sometimes referred to as the "Mayan Riviera," is traversed by Mex. 307, also known as the **Cancún-Tulum Corridor**, which offers access to a growing number of resorts and ecologically oriented attractions. While organized tours frequent such tourist spots as the Xcaret and Xel-Há marine parks, driving offers greater flexibility and the opportunity to see secluded spots the tour buses don't visit.

Note: Mex. 307 is a four-lane divided highway as far south as the vicinity of Tulum, with road expansion continuing to the south. However, improvements such as roadside kilometer markers and pavement markings are yet to be completely implemented throughout the stretch. Drivers should observe the speed limit—80 km/h (50 mph); many motorists tend to drive too fast for conditions. Almost all points of interest are a kilometer or so east of Mex. 307 via dirt or rutted roads; they are denoted by crude signs as well as prominent billboards. Mileage signs ("Chetumal 360") are posted in kilometers.

From Cancún, it takes a little less than 2 hours to reach Tulum. South from the Boulevard Kukulcán junction the highway is lined with tropical scrub and an occasional thatch-roofed hut. The turnoff for **Puerto Morelos** *(see separate listing)* is about 36 kilometers (22 miles) south of Cancún; this rustic outpost attracts snorkelers, divers and anglers to a large offshore coral reef. The poverty of many locals is underscored by the scattered houses along the highway, which have thatched roofs, open doorways, dirt floors and no windows. The turnoff for **Punta Beté**, about 58 kilometers (36 miles) south of Cancún, leads to a private, jungle-lined beach sheltered by reefs and rocky lagoons; despite a few accommodations and a campground, the atmosphere is delightfully serene.

The turnoff to **Playa del Carmen** *(see separate listing)*, is about 68 kilometers (42 miles) south. This funky town is a laid-back alternative to Cancún's size and pace. While there are condominiums, paved streets and other creeping signs of affluence, most visitors come for the simple thatched-roof restaurants, hammocks slung between palm trees, craft stalls and campgrounds. Also here is Playacar Club de Golf, a public, 18-hole course designed by Robert Von Hagge.

The turnoff for **Xcaret** *(see Playa del Carmen)* is about 72 kilometers (45 miles) south. Once a peaceful cove, it has been transformed into an all-day waterside theme park with an ecological slant. The highlight here is an underground river that flows through a series of caves to the beach; swimmers don life jackets and float along with the current.

The most popular day-trip excursion in the Mexican Caribbean is the organized bus tour to Xcaret from Cancún; this also is the most convenient way to visit the park. Colorfully painted buses depart for Xcaret from the Xcaret terminal, a large thatch-roofed building on Boulevard Kukulcán in the Hotel Zone (next to the Fiesta Americana Grand Coral Beach hotel). There are two tour packages; both include round-trip transportation and park admission. Buses depart from the terminal daily at 9 and 10 a.m.; the ride takes about an hour. Tickets can be purchased at the terminal. The cost for the day trip alone (returning to Cancún around 6 p.m.) is about $50; for the day trip plus dinner and the folkloric show "Xcaret at Night" (returning to Cancún around 9:30 p.m.), about $70. Phone (98) 83-3143 or 83-3144.

Ten kilometers (6 miles) beyond Xcaret is the turnoff to **Paamul**, a crescent of sand fronting a calm lagoon. The beach draws shell collectors, and the clear water offers good snorkeling.

Puerto Aventuras, about 85 kilometers (53 miles) south, is a planned resort with a challenging golf course (sinkholes and Maya ruins are among the hazards incorporated into its layout). Also at Puerto Aventuras is the **Cedam Museum** *(see Playa del Carmen)*. **Xpu-ha**, about 90 kilometers (56 miles) south, is a new beachfront ecological park in a jungle setting. An information office is at Avenida Tulum #200 in Ciudad Cancún; phone (98) 84-2411.

About 105 kilometers (65 miles) south are several marked turnoffs for **Akumal** *(see separate listing)*, a diving center. Despite a spate of resorts, private homes and condominiums that have sprung up here, the atmosphere is friendly and low-key. Just north of Akumal on the access road to beachfront properties is **Yalkú**, a lagoon with clear water inhabited by tropical fish. Admission is charged to this spot increasingly thronged with tourists.

About 108 kilometers (67 miles) south is **Chemuyil** *(see Tulum)*, which advertises itself as "The Prettiest Beach in the World." Unfortunately, that claim was compromised by the deprivations of a disease known as lethal yellowing, which attacks palm trees and causes their fronds to drop off. This insect-spread blight has become endemic in the Caribbean. Chemuyil does retain its horseshoe-shaped bay, and the protection of a coral reef ensures uniformly calm water. A few kilometers farther south is the signed turnoff to **Xcacel**, yet another crescent-shaped, white-

sand beach. The sheltered water is a prime spot for swimming, snorkeling, diving and fishing; there also are camping facilities, showers and a restaurant.

About 122 kilometers (76 miles) south is the well-marked turnoff to **Xel-Há** *(see Tulum)*, a park in which interconnected freshwater lagoons form a natural aquarium. Xel-Há (shell-HAH) is a breeding ground for parrotfish and scores of other tropical species. Fish as well as coral formations can be viewed through the clear water from platforms above the rocky limestone shores of the lagoons. Snorkeling is a good reason to visit, despite the tour buses that regularly pack the parking lot (get there early). On the west side of the highway and close to the park entrance is a group of restored Maya ruins.

One look at the ruins of **Tulum**, *(see separate listing)*, about 131 kilometers (81 miles) south, and it's easy to see why the Maya chose this site: This is the only place on the low-lying Yucatán Peninsula where limestone deposits built up to create coastal cliffs. The most distinctive feature of these fortresslike ruins is their location overlooking the turquoise Caribbean. Visitors to the site can hike to the beach below and enjoy a swim in the sea. Tulum is a popular day trip from Cancún, often combined with a stop at Xel-Há.

South of Tulum Mex. 307 angles southwest into the scrubby flatlands of interior Quintana Roo. Hugging the coast directly to the south is the 1.3-million-acre **Sian Ka'an Biosphere Reserve** *(see Tulum)*, established as a protected area by the Mexican government in 1986 and designated a World Heritage Site in 1987 by the United Nations Educational, Scientific and Cultural Organization (UNESCO). This vast wilderness is a haven for numerous kinds of wildlife, some endangered, and approximately 350 species of birds.

From Mex. 307 at Tulum an unpaved road branches southeast to the **Boca Paila Peninsula**, within the far eastern edge of the Sian Ka'an Reserve. A bridge south of the Tulum ruins connects the peninsula to the mainland. This strip of land bordering the open Caribbean is dotted with lagoons, tidal pools and palm-lined beaches. A few lodges and campgrounds cater to anglers who come for the superb fishing. Dedicated birdwatchers take boats to hidden cays to observe pelicans, frigate birds and other marine species that inhabit the mangrove flats. The journey ends at the tiny lobster-fishing village of **Punta Allen**.

The route, a circuitous trail of limestone covered with packed earth and sand that is riddled with potholes during the summer rainy season, passes through dense jungle. For adventurous types who don't mind the bugs, heat and lack of civilization, the sight of colorful parrots, scuttling iguanas and the occasional curious monkey makes the trek from Tulum well worth it. A few words of caution: Top off your gas tank in Tulum, and by all means do not attempt to negotiate any part of this route at night. Insect repellent is essential, as is a supply of drinking water.

Note: Tourists are restricted to the outer buffer (coastal) zone of Sian Ka'an; the core zone on the mainland is closed to visitors. Biologist-led day trips to the Boca Paila Peninsula portion of the reserve depart from a point several miles south of the town of Tulum. For additional information, contact the nonprofit group **Amigos de Sian Ka'an** (Friends of Sian Ka'an). The office is located in downtown Ciudad Cancún at Avenida Cobá #5, Plaza Américas; phone (98) 84-9583.

SPORTS AND RECREATION

Water sports, not surprisingly, top Cancún's list of leisure activities. **Fishing** is excellent; the open Caribbean, Mujeres Bay, the channel between Cozumel and the mainland, and the waters of Nichupté Lagoon together are home to some 500 species, including all types of game fish. Bonito, dorado and sailfish run from March into July; bluefin tuna from April through June. Barracuda, grouper, mackerel and red snapper can be hooked all year.

Hotel Zone marinas offer a range of crafts and top-of-the-line equipment. Larger boats are 35-40 feet long; single-engine diesel boats average 26-28 feet. Four- and 8-hour charter excursions normally include a captain, first mate, gear, bait and soft drinks. Cost varies and the marinas compete for business, so it pays to shop around. **Aqua World** *(see attraction listing)* and **Aqua Tours**, Km 6.25 on Kukulcán, phone (98) 83-0400, both charter fishing trips; or ask at your hotel for recommendations.

In addition to the islands, fishing opportunities are plentiful all along the Caribbean coastline bordering the Cancún-Tulum Corridor and further south at **La Ascención** and **Espíritu Santo**, two large bays on the shores of the Sian Ka'an Biosphere Reserve. Shark fishing is best in **Laguna Yalahau**, at the northern tip of Quintana Roo between Isla Holbox and Cape Catoche. Boats can be hired in the port town of Chiquilá, reached via a paved road branching north off Mex. 180 just east of Nuevo Xcán.

Scuba diving and **snorkeling** also are rewarding, particularly at the southern end of Cancún Island around Nizuc Point, off Cozumel and Isla Mujeres, and in Nichupté Lagoon. Dive shops along Kukulcán rent equipment, give lessons and schedule trips; some hotels also arrange dive excursions. Check credentials, boats and equipment, and if possible get the inside scoop from a diver familiar with the area. Conditions are best from May or June through August. **Scuba Cancún**, on the lagoon side of Kukulcán at Km 5 (across from Playa Langosta), offers instruction,

Parasailing   ©John Neubauer

certification and trips to nearby reefs; phone (98) 83-1011.

Cozumel is Mexico's foremost dive destination. **Palancar Reef**, off the island's southern tip, is a wonderland of tropical fish and elaborate coral formations, all on display in water remarkable for its clarity. Diving expeditions are organized around such themes as ecology, photography and archeology, and it's an otherworldly experience indeed to explore the wreckage of a sunken ship by moonlight on a night dive.

The shallow waters of Cozumel's **Chankanaab Reef**, ideal for novice snorkelers, abound with colorful and bizarre sea creatures so tame that face-to-face viewing is the rule. Snorkeling equipment is easily rented and inexpensive. Another favored spot for snorkeling is Isla Mujeres' **El Garrafón National Park**, at the southern end of the island. Playa Garrafón, within the park, is populated by schools of fish. Changing rooms and showers are available, and the park is a short taxi ride from town.

Other activities include **water skiing, windsurfing, parasailing, swimming** and **boating**. The best place to water ski is Nichupté Lagoon; ski clubs along Kukulcán on the lagoon side rent boats and equipment. Windsurfing propels its participants across the water at exhilarating speeds; the sailboard used by windsurfers is comprised of a masted sail attached to a surfboard. The pools at the big resort hotels are masterfully designed, with the added bonus of the Caribbean as a backdrop. More watery fun is available at the **Wet 'n Wild** theme park, off Kukulcán south of Nizuc Point (southern end of the Hotel Zone).

For landlubbers there's **Pok-Ta-Pok**, a championship 18-hole **golf** course designed by Robert Trent Jones Jr. Located on an island between Laguna de Bojórquez and Laguna Nichupté (access is off Kukulcán between Km 6 and 7), it offers fine views of both lagoons and the Caribbean. Needless to say, the water hazards are challenging; duffers should stock up on balls. Another hazard to watch out for is the small Maya temple on the 12th hole. Shoes, carts and clubs are available for rent, and there are putting greens and a restaurant. Reservations are advised; phone (98) 83-0871. Another championship 18-hole course is at the **Caesar Park Beach & Golf Resort**, off Kukulcán at Km 17; phone (98) 81-8000. Greens fees vary depending on the season and are less at the Caesar Park course for guests of the hotel.

Horseback riding trips take in locations from jungle to seashore. **Rancho Loma Bonita**, off Mex. 307 at Km 49, just south of Puerto Morelos, provides transportation to and from the ranch, in addition to a guide and lunch. Phone (98) 87-5465, or make arrangements through your hotel or a local travel agency.

Bullfights are held during the winter season at Cancún's small bullring, at the intersection of avenidas Bonampak and Sayil in Ciudad Cancún. The action takes place on Wednesday afternoons at 3:30 and is preceded by a folkloric dance presentation. Tickets can be obtained from travel agencies or at major hotels and run about $45 for adults. **Note:** The bull is traditionally killed during these performances.

Tennis is offered at the big resort hotels; there are courts at the Camino Real Cancún, Cancún Sheraton Resort, Casa Maya, Fiesta Americana Condesa, Fiesta Americana Grand Coral Beach and Hotel Krystal Cancún, among others. A separate **jogging** and **bicycling** path—also used for **roller blading**—parallels the sidewalk along the northern (bay) side of Kukulcán, extending as far as Cancún Point; a path also parallels the sidewalk along most of the southern half of the Hotel Zone. Runners should make the circuit in the early morning before it gets too hot.

NIGHTLIFE

Cancún provides something for everyone after dark. The discos, needless to say, offer plenty of high-decibel action. Most of them open around 10 or 10:30 p.m., but they don't stay open all night. Most also collect a cover charge (anywhere from $5-$12 or so), which may be waived on certain nights. Inquire about the dress code;

some don't allow jeans or short shorts. **La Boom**, at Km 3.5 on Kukulcán, and **Dady'O**, at Km 9.5 on Kukulcán (near the convention center), are the most frenetic and attract the youngest crowds; **Christine**, at Km 9 on Kukulcán (in the Hotel Krystal Cancún) has theme nights.

A somewhat less frantic atmosphere prevails at **Cat's House of Reggae and Hip Hop**, in the complex of shops next to the Cancún Convention Center. **Azucar**, in the Camino Real Cancún, features dancing to live salsa bands. Most hotels also have a nightclub or lobby bar with jazz or other live music.

Two Mexican chains—**Carlos 'N Charlie's**, at Km 5.5 on the lagoon side of Kukulcán (across from the Casa Maya Hotel), and **Señor Frogs**, also at Km 5.5—are noisy but fun places for food, drinks and partying. So are the Cancún outpost of the **Hard Rock Café** chain, in the Forum by the Sea complex; **Planet Hollywood**, in Flamingo Plaza at Km 10.5 on Kukulcán (lagoon side); and the **All Star Café**, at Km 9.5 on Kukulcán. **Mango Tango**, at Km 14 on the lagoon side Kukulcán (opposite the Ritz-Carlton), features Caribbean-themed dinner shows.

Those looking for Mexican-style entertainment amid the lasers and fog machines can still find it. The **Ballet Folklórico Nacional de Cancún** performs nightly at 9 p.m. at the Cancún Convention Center. The ticket booth is just inside the center; tickets can be purchased for a Mexican buffet dinner and the show, or for the show only. The **El Mexicano** restaurant, in the Mansión Costa Blanca shopping complex in the Hotel Zone, presents folkloric dinner shows, strolling mariachis and other entertainment.

Romantics will enjoy a moonlit cruise. **Pirate's Night** begins with a sail aboard the *Crucero Tropical Cruiser* to Treasure Island, a beach on Isla Mujeres, for a buffet dinner and a floor show. Departures are Mon.-Sat. at 6:30 p.m. from the Playa Langosta Pier; the cost is around $50 per person. Reservations are required; phone (98) 83-1488. The **Columbus Lobster Dinner Cruise** sets sail from the Royal Mayan Marina dock, at Km 15.5 on Kukulcán (lagoon side, opposite the Omni Cancún), for a lagoon cruise and a lobster or steak dinner. There are daily sunset and evening departures; the cost is around $60 per person. Reservations are required; phone (98) 83-1488.

SPECIAL EVENTS

Carnaval, a fiesta in the spirit of Mardi Gras, is held the week preceding Ash Wednesday. Locals dress up in elaborate costumes and parade down the streets of Ciudad Cancún. On Mar. 21 the vernal equinox is celebrated at Chichén Itzá. *Jazz Festival Week*, takes place over the Memorial Day weekend, has in the past drawn such celebrated musicians as Carlos Santana and Ray Charles.

As in almost all of Mexico, *Independence Day* festivities take place Sept. 15-16 and include fireworks, a parade (on the 16th) and traditional food. The *ITU World Cup Triathlon*, which attracts triathletes from around the world, is held in September at Playa Langosta. The *Eve of All Souls' Day*, Oct. 31, is observed throughout the Yucatán by placing flowers and candles at gravesites. *Day of the Dead* graveside and church ceremonies take place Nov. 1-2 amid a party-like atmosphere.

Also in November is the *Caribbean Cultural Festival*, held in front of Municipal Hall in downtown Ciudad Cancún; it brings artists, dancers and singers from all over Mexico and the Caribbean. Christmas celebrations begin 9 days prior to Dec. 25 and feature *posadas* (processions) of families and friends who take part in *pastorelas* (plays) portraying Jesus' birth. The colorful nativity scenes on display are a seasonal highlight.

WHERE TO STAY

BEST WESTERN PLAZA CARIBE

▼ *Motor Inn* ((98)84-1377

12/1-4/22	$79-$88	XP $10
4/23-11/30	$55-$59	XP $10

Location: Across street from main bus terminal. Tulum Con Uxmal Lote 19 77500 (PO Box 487). Fax: 98/84-6352. **Facility:** City center. Tropical landscaping. Off-track betting. 140 units. *Bath:* shower only. 2 stories, exterior corridors. **Terms:** F12. **Amenities:** safes. **Leisure Activities:** playground. **Guest Services:** gift shop, valet laundry. *Fee:* fax. **Cards:** AE, DI, MC, VI.

CALINDA AMERICA CANCUN

▼ *Hotel* (98/84-7500

All Year	$80-$120	XP $10

Location: Off the island, in town on Ave Tulum, at jct of hwy to beaches. Aves Tulum & Calle Brisa 77500 (PO Box 600). Fax: 98/84-1953. **Facility:** Basic rooms, many with balcony. 178 units. *Bath:* combo or shower only. 5 stories, interior corridors. **Terms:** F12; 14 day cancellation notice, 7 day off season. **Amenities:** honor bars. **Leisure Activities:** wading pool. **Guest Services:** [MAP] meal plan available, gift shop, complimentary evening beverages, area transportation, valet laundry. *Fee:* fax. **Cards:** AE, DI, MC, VI.
(See color ad p 4 and p 102)

SOME UNITS

CALINDA VIVA CANCUN

▼▼▼ *Hotel* (98/83-0800

All Year	$80	XP $20

Location: Blvd Kukulkan, Km 8.5, opposite Maya Fair Plaza; on the north beach. 77500 (PO Box 673). Fax: 98/83-2087. **Facility:** Excellent views of colorful Caribbean and lagoon. Spacious beach area with a tranquil surf. All rooms have two beds, extra phone in bathroom and a balcony. In-house travel agency and car rental. 216 units, 108 with efficiency. *Bath:* combo or shower only. 8 stories, interior corridors. **Terms:** F12; 5 day cancellation notice, 7 day off season. **Leisure Activities:** wading pool, beach, swimming, scuba diving, snorkeling. *Fee:* scuba & snorkeling equipment, charter fishing, 2 lighted tennis courts. **Guest Services:** [AP] meal plan available, gift shop, valet laundry. *Fee:* fax. **Cards:** AE, CB, DI, MC, VI.
(See color ad p 4 and p 102)

SOME UNITS

FEE

⚠ CAMINO REAL CANCUN

▼▼▼▼ *Resort* ((98)48-7000

12/25-4/21	$275-$320	XP $45
12/1-12/24 & 4/22-11/30	$195-$230	XP $45

Location: On beach at Punta Cancun. Punta Cancun Lote 17 77500 (PO Box 14). Fax: 98/48-7002. **Facility:** Rooms with balcony, ocean or lagoon view. Idyllic area comprising Mayan ruins, palm tree shaded beaches and isolated coves. Camino Club rooms in town building with extra amenities. 381 units. 8 two-bedroom units and 1 unit with kitchen. Some whirlpool units ($305-$1650). 5-16 stories, interior/exterior corridors. **Parking:** valet. **Terms:** F12; 7 day cancellation notice-fee imposed. **Amenities:** voice mail, safes, honor bars, hair dryers. *Some:* CD players. **Dining:** Maria Bonita, La Brisa, see separate listing. **Leisure Activities:** steamroom, beach, swimming, paddleboats, sailboating, scuba diving, snorkeling, recreation program. *Fee:* boats, windsurfing, waterskiing, scuba & snorkeling equipment, fishing, 3 lighted tennis courts. **Guest Services:** gift shop, valet laundry. *Fee:* massage. **Business Services:** conference facilities, administrative services. *Fee:* PC, fax. **Cards:** AE, CB, DI, MC, VI.
(See color ad opposite title page & below)

FEE   SOME UNITS   FEE

CANCUN PALACE

Resort (98/85-0533

12/21-4/16	$376	XP $195
12/1-12/20 & 4/17-11/30	$150-$165	XP $100

Location: Blvd Kukulcan, at Km 14.5, on the beach; east side of island. 77500 (PO Box 1730). Fax: 98/85-1244. **Facility:** Lagoon or ocean view rooms with balcony. All inclusive resort. 557 units, 56 with efficiency (no utensils). Some whirlpool units. 9 stories, interior corridors. **Terms:** 21 day cancellation notice, in season. **Amenities:** safes. **Leisure Activities:** 3 pools, wading pool, beach, swimming, social program, exercise room. *Fee:* boats, windsurfing, waterskiing, scuba diving, snorkeling equipment, miniature golf, 2 lighted tennis courts. **Guest Services:** [AP] meal plan available, gift shop, valet laundry. **Business Services:** conference facilities. **Cards:** AE, DI, MC, VI.

CARIBBEAN VILLAGES CANCUN

Resort ((98)85-0112

All Year	$160-$180	XP $30

Location: Blvd Kukulkan, at Km 10.5. On the beach; east side of island. Blvd Kukulkan, Lote 18 77500. Fax: 98/85-0999. **Facility:** Room numbers ending in 27 (327, 427, 527, etc.) are larger corner units. In-house travel agency and car rentals. 300 units. Some suites. *Bath:* combo or shower only. 8 stories, interior corridors. **Terms:** age restrictions may apply. **Amenities:** safes (fee). **Leisure Activities:** 2 pools, whirlpool, beach, swimming, paddleboats, sailboating, windsurfing, scuba diving, snorkeling, 2 lighted tennis courts, recreation program, social program, game room. *Fee:* boats, waterskiing, scuba & snorkeling equipment, fishing. **Guest Services:** [AP] meal plan available, gift shop, valet laundry. *Fee:* massage. **Business Services:** conference facilities. *Fee:* fax. **Cards:** AE, DI, MC, VI.

SOME UNITS

CASA MAYA HOTEL

▼▼ ▼▼ *Hotel* ☏ (98)83-0555

12/23-4/15	$250	XP $30
12/1-12/22 & 4/16-11/30	$150	XP $20

Location: On the north beach at Km 5. (PO Box 656, 77500). Fax: 98/83-4414. **Facility:** Mayan pyramid style architecture. Attractive public areas. Wide beach with tranquil water. Rooms located in two towers, one newer than the other. Many rooms with Caribbean view. 356 units. 25 two-bedroom units and 200 units with kitchen. 12 stories, interior corridors. **Terms:** F11; 3 day cancellation notice, utensil extra charge. **Amenities:** safes (fee). **Leisure Activities:** 2 pools, wading pool, whirlpools, beach, swimming, scuba diving, snorkeling, children's program, social program, playground. *Fee:* boats, paddleboats, windsurfing, waterskiing, scuba & snorkeling equipment, fishing, 2 lighted tennis courts. **Guest Services:** [AP] meal plan available, gift shop, valet laundry. *Fee:* area transportation, massage. **Business Services:** meeting rooms. *Fee:* fax. **Cards:** AE, MC, VI.

SOME UNITS
🏧 🍴 🏊 ✕ 🎥 / 🖵 /
FEE

CONDO HOTEL KIN-HA CANCUN

▼▼ ▼▼ *Extended Stay Motor Inn* ☏ (98)83-2377

12/22-4/15	$170	XP $30
12/1-12/21 & 4/16-11/30	$128	XP $20

Location: On the north beach at Km 8. Paseo Kukulkan, Km 8 77500. Fax: 98/83-2147. **Facility:** Lush tropical gardens. Tranquil beach. Rooms with lagoon, pool, garden or Caribbean view. Many rooms with separate living room, dining area and kitchen. Some rooms with ceiling fan. In-house travel agency and car rental. Some units with new ceramic tile in bathroom. 150 units, 75 with efficiency. Some suites. *Bath:* shower only. 3-4 stories, interior corridors. **Terms:** F12; package plans. **Amenities:** safes (fee). **Leisure Activities:** beach, swimming, scuba diving, snorkeling, fishing. *Fee:* boats, sailboating, windsurfing, waterskiing, scuba & snorkeling equipment. **Guest Services:** [AP] meal plan available, gift shop, valet laundry. **Business Services:** meeting rooms. **Cards:** AE, MC, VI.

SOME UNITS
🍴 🏊 ✕ 🎥 / 🛢 /

CONTINENTAL PLAZA CANCUN

▼▼ ▼▼ *Resort* ☏ 98/81-5500

12/22-4/12	$266	XP $24
12/1-12/21 & 4/13-11/30	$135-$150	XP $24

Location: On the beach at Km 11.5; east side of island. Blvd Kukulcan km 11.5 77500. Fax: 98/81-5694. **Facility:** One- and two-story fourplexes on landscaped grounds and tower. High energy resort draws youthful guests. Some rooms with terrace. Most rooms facing the beach. 638 units. 40 two-bedroom units. Some whirlpool units. 2-6 stories, interior corridors. **Parking:** valet. **Terms:** F12; 7 day cancellation notice, in season, package plans. **Amenities:** voice mail, safes (fee), hair dryers. **Leisure Activities:** 3 pools, beach, swimming, children's program, social program, exercise room. *Fee:* boats, windsurfing, waterskiing, scuba & snorkeling equipment, fishing, 2 lighted tennis courts, racquetball courts. **Guest Services:** [AP] meal plan available, gift shop, valet laundry. *Fee:* massage. **Business Services:** conference facilities. *Fee:* fax. **Cards:** AE, DI, MC, VI.

SOME UNITS
🏧 🍴 🏊 ✕ 🎥 / 🛢 /
FEE

CROWN PARADISE CLUB

▼▼ ▼▼ *Resort* ☏ (98)85-1022

All Year	$250-$300	XP $100

Location: On the beach, east side of island. Blvd Kukulcan Km 18.5 77500. Fax: 98/85-1707. **Facility:** Family oriented, all inclusive resort overlooking Caribbean. Rooms in the Crown Tower are newer than rooms in the Paradise Towers. All rooms with view of Caribbean or lagoon. Extensive resort activities. 650 units. 15 stories, interior corridors. **Terms:** package plans. **Amenities:** voice mail, safes, hair dryers. *Some:* honor bars. **Leisure Activities:** 4 pools (1 heated indoor/outdoor), wading pool, whirlpools, steamroom, waterslide, beach, swimming, separate adult section with quiet rooftop pool and adult only restaurant, canoeing, paddleboats, windsurfing, scuba diving, snorkeling, miniature golf, 2 lighted tennis courts, children's program, recreation program, social program, playground, exercise room, sports court, basketball, shuffleboard, volleyball. *Fee:* scuba & snorkeling equipment, charter fishing. **Guest Services:** [AP] meal plan available, gift shop, complimentary evening beverages, afternoon tea, valet laundry. *Fee:* area transportation, massage. **Business Services:** meeting rooms, administrative services. *Fee:* PC, fax. **Cards:** AE, DI, MC, VI.

🏧 🍴 🍸 D 🏊 🏖 ✕ 🎥 🖨
FEE SOME UNITS FEE
/ ✕ 🖵 /

Ⓐ FIESTA AMERICANA CONDESA CANCUN

▼▼ ▼▼ *Resort* ☏ 98/81-4200

12/1-1/2	$345	XP $61
1/3-4/22	$239	XP $42
4/23-11/30	$126	

Location: Blvd Kukulcan Km 16.5, on the beach, east side of island. 44 Blvd Kukulcan 77500. Fax: 98/85-1800. **Facility:** Mediterranean style exterior. Lush landscaping. Refined public areas. All rooms with ocean view. Ask about rooms with both pool and ocean views. Most rooms with balcony. 502 units. 25 two-bedroom units and 1 three-bedroom unit. Some whirlpool units. 7-8 stories, exterior corridors. **Parking:** valet. **Terms:** 30 day cancellation notice. **Amenities:** voice mail, safes (fee), honor bars, hair dryers. **Dining & Entertainment:** 3 restaurants, coffee shop, 6:30 am-midnight, $12-$30, cocktails, also, Rosato Ristorante, see separate listing, entertainment. **Leisure Activities:** heated pool, wading pool, sauna, steamroom, beach, swimming, extensive beach and pool facilities, scuba diving, snorkeling, social program. *Fee:* scuba & snorkeling equipment, fishing, charter fishing, 3 lighted indoor tennis courts, exercise room. **Guest Services:** gift shop, valet laundry. *Fee:* massage. **Business Services:** conference facilities, administrative services. *Fee:* PC, fax. **Cards:** AE, DI, MC, VI.

SOME UNITS
🍴 24 🍸 🏊 ✕ 🎥 🖨 DATA PORT / ✕ 🖵 /

FIESTA AMERICANA GRAND CORAL BEACH

▼▼◈▼▼ *Resort*   (98/81-3200

12/1-4/15	$250-$330	XP $29
4/16-11/30	$200-$240	XP $29

Location: On the beach, north side of island. Blvd Kukulcan, Km 9.5 77500. Fax: 98/81-3218. **Facility:** Large rooms with balcony and view of Caribbean. Modern, spacious and sophisticated public areas. Some suites with terrace. Extensive pool and beach areas with lush landscaping, some ground floor units with direct access to pool area. 602 units. 2 two-bedroom units and 2 units with kitchen. Some suites and whirlpool units. 11 stories, interior corridors. **Parking:** valet. **Terms:** F12. **Amenities:** voice mail, safes, honor bars, irons, hair dryers. *Some:* fax. **Dining:** Coral Reef, La Joya Restaurant, see separate listing. **Leisure Activities:** 4 heated pools, wading pools, beach, swimming, pool & ocean sun decks, scuba diving, snorkeling, recreation program, social program in season, playground. *Fee:* boats, paddleboats, windsurfing, waterskiing, scuba & snorkeling equipment, fishing, charter fishing, 3 lighted indoor tennis courts. **Guest Services:** [MAP] meal plan available, gift shop, valet laundry. *Fee:* area transportation, massage. **Business Services:** conference facilities, administrative services. *Fee:* PC, fax. **Cards:** AE, DI, JC, MC, VI. *(See color ad below)*

HILTON CANCUN BEACH & GOLF RESORT

▼▼◈▼▼ *Resort*   ((98)81-8000

12/22-1/2	$350-$580	XP $30
1/3-4/22	$305-$435	XP $30
4/23-11/30	$225-$355	XP $30
12/1-12/21	$220-$350	XP $30

Location: Km 17 Blvd Kukulcan, on the beach; east side of island. Km 17 Zona Hotelera Section A 77500. Fax: 98/81-8080. **Facility:** Dramatic pyramid building with extensive pool areas. Also secluded villas on spectacular beach. Many rooms with balcony. All rooms with dramatic view of Caribbean. Occasionally vigorous surf. 426 units. 1 two-bedroom unit and 1 unit with kitchen. Some whirlpool units. 2-9 stories, interior corridors. **Parking:** valet. **Terms:** F18; 3 day cancellation notice, in season, package plans. **Amenities:** voice mail, safes, honor bars, irons, hair dryers. **Leisure Activities:** 7 heated pools, wading pools, sauna, whirlpools, beach, swimming, scuba diving, snorkeling, children's program, recreation program, social program, jogging. *Fee:* sailboating, windsurfing, scuba & snorkeling equipment, charter fishing, golf-18 holes, 2 lighted tennis courts. **Guest Services:** gift shop, valet laundry. *Fee:* area transportation, massage. **Business Services:** conference facilities, administrative services. *Fee:* PC, fax. **Cards:** AE, CB, DI, MC, VI.

HOLIDAY INN EXPRESS
Motor Inn (98/83-2200

All Year	$85	XP $15

Location: On north side of island, off Ave Kukulcan; 7 km from downtown, next to Pok-Ta-Pok Golf Club House. (Paseo Pok-Ta-Pok, Zona Hotelera, 77500). Fax: 98/83-2532. **Facility:** Quiet location with beautiful central courtyard. 119 units. 2 stories, interior corridors. **Terms:** 7 day cancellation notice. **Amenities:** irons, hair dryers. **Dining:** deli, 7 am-10 pm; in pool courtyard, $6-$18. **Leisure Activities:** wading pool, tennis privileges, beach club. *Fee:* golf-18 holes. **Guest Services:** [CP] meal plan available, gift shop, area transportation-beach & Plaza Caracol Mall, valet laundry. **Business Services:** meeting rooms. **Cards:** AE, DI, MC, VI.

SOME UNITS

HOTEL CALINDA BEACH
Resort (98/83-1600

All Year	$100-$195	XP $40

Location: On Playa Linda at north beach, Km 4. (PO Box 1034, 77500). Fax: 98/83-1857. **Facility:** Modern pyramid shaped high-rise, colorful rooms; few with balcony. Some rooms more modern and appealing than others. Wide tranquil beach. Meets AAA guest room security requirements. 470 units. *Bath:* shower only. 9 stories, interior corridors. **Terms:** F16; 3 day cancellation notice, package plans. **Amenities:** voice mail, safes, honor bars. **Leisure Activities:** 2 pools, wading pool, beach, swimming, boat dock, marina. *Fee:* boats, waterskiing, scuba & snorkeling equipment, fishing, 2 lighted tennis courts. **Guest Services:** valet laundry. *Fee:* massage. *Fee:* fax. **Cards:** AE, DI, MC, VI. *(See color ad p 4 and p 102)*

SOME UNITS

FEE

HOTEL PRESIDENTE INTER-CONTINENTAL CANCUN
Resort ((98)83-0200

12/1-1/1	$180	XP $35
1/2-4/15	$125	XP $35
4/16-11/30	$100	XP $35

Location: On the beach; north side of island. Av Kukulcan Km 7.5 77500. Fax: 98/83-2602. **Facility:** Lagoon or Caribbean views. Striking pyramid shaped pool area with five whirlpools. Superb beach area. Wide beach with palapas, hammocks and usually a tranquil surf, great for snorkeling. Meets AAA guest room security requirements. 300 units. Some suites and whirlpool units. 6-10 stories, interior corridors. **Parking:** valet. **Terms:** F18; 3 day cancellation notice-fee imposed. **Amenities:** honor bars, hair dryers. *Some:* safes. **Dining & Entertainment:** dining room, restaurant, coffee shop, deli, 7 am-11 pm, $16-$26, cocktails, entertainment. **Leisure Activities:** 2 pools, whirlpools, beach, swimming, scuba diving, snorkeling, lighted tennis court, social program, exercise room. *Fee:* boats, canoes, windsurfing, waterskiing, scuba & snorkeling equipment, charter fishing, skin diving, motor ski, kayaks. **Guest Services:** [MAP] meal plan available, gift shop, valet laundry. **Business Services:** conference facilities. *Fee:* fax. **Cards:** AE, CB, DI, MC, VI.

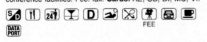

FEE

HOTEL SIERRA CANCUN
Resort ((98)83-2444

12/21-4/15	$322-$367
12/1-12/20	$309-$333
4/16-11/30	$280-$316

Location: Zona Hotelera, Km 10 on the east beach. Paseo Kukulcan Km 10 77500 (AP 138). Fax: 98/83-3486. **Facility:** Attractive lobby areas; quiet, distinguished atmosphere. All rooms with ceiling fan, balcony and view of Caribbean or lagoon. Some rooms with sleeper sofa. All inclusive resort, excluding motorized sports. Beauty shop. 260 units. 9 stories, interior corridors. **Terms:** 7 day cancellation notice. **Amenities:** hair dryers. *Some:* hair dryers. **Leisure Activities:** 2 pools, sauna, whirlpool, steamroom, beach, swimming, paddleboats, windsurfing, boat dock, snorkeling, fishing, miniature golf, 2 tennis courts, exercise room, horseshoes, shuffleboard. *Fee:* sailboating, scuba & snorkeling equipment, charter fishing. **Guest Services:** [AP] meal plan available, gift shop, complimentary evening beverages, valet laundry. *Fee:* massage. **Business Services:** meeting rooms. *Fee:* fax. **Cards:** AE, DI, MC, VI.

SOME UNITS

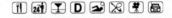

HYATT CANCUN CARIBE
Hotel (98/83-0044

12/15-4/15	$230	XP $30
12/1-12/14 & 4/16-11/30	$180	XP $30

Location: On beach, Kukulcan Blvd, Km 10.5; east side of island. 77500 (PO Box 353). Fax: 98/83-1514. **Facility:** Private balcony facing Caribbean. 226 units. 1 two-bedroom unit. Some whirlpool units. 7 stories, interior corridors. **Parking:** valet. **Terms:** F16; 3 day cancellation notice. **Amenities:** voice mail, honor bars, hair dryers. *Some:* safes. **Dining & Entertainment:** 2 restaurants, 6:30 am-11:30 pm, $18-$30, cocktails, also, Blue Bayou, see separate listing, entertainment. **Leisure Activities:** 3 pools, whirlpools, beach, swimming, boat dock, marina, 3 tennis courts (1 lighted). **Guest Services:** gift shop, valet laundry. *Fee:* massage. **Business Services:** conference facilities, fax. **Cards:** AE, DI, MC, VI.

HYATT REGENCY-CANCUN
Hotel ((98)831-234

12/1-1/2	$229-$319	XP $30
1/3-4/20	$153-$226	XP $30
4/21-11/30	$129-$174	XP $30

Location: On the beach; at Punta Cancun. (PO Box 1201, 77500). Fax: 98/83-1349. **Facility:** Attractive atrium lobby. All rooms with ceiling fan and balcony. Rooms are identical yet considered standard or deluxe based on view. Separate Regency Club room with added amenties like, data port, robes, bathroom, phone, weight scales, continental breakfast and evening treats. 300 units. Some whirlpool units. 13 stories, interior corridors. **Parking:** valet. **Terms:** F12; 15 day cancellation notice-fee imposed. **Amenities:** voice mail, safes, honor bars, hair dryers. *Some:* irons. **Leisure Activities:** 2 heated pools, wading pool, sauna, beach, swimming, snorkeling. *Fee:* waterskiing, scuba & snorkeling equipment, fishing, charter fishing, exercise room. **Guest Services:** gift shop, valet laundry. *Fee:* massage. **Business Services:** conference facilities, administrative services, fax. **Cards:** AE, CB, DI, MC, VI.

SOME UNITS

⚠️ LE MERIDIEN

◇◇◇◇ *Resort*   ((98)81-2200

12/13-1/2	$350-$400	XP $50
1/3-4/15	$290-$350	XP $50
12/1-12/12 & 4/16-11/30	$220-$250	XP $50

Location: Retorno del Rey Km 14, Zona Hotelera; on east side of island, on the beach. Km 14 Retorno del Rey 77500. Fax: 98/81-2201. **Facility:** Sophisticated French resort. All rooms with view of Caribbean. Expansive pool/beach area with occasionally strong, dramatic surf. 213 units. 6 two-bedroom units. Some suites ($390-$3000) and whirlpool units. 7 stories, interior corridors. **Parking:** valet. **Terms:** F12; 7 day cancellation notice-fee imposed, package plans. **Amenities:** safes, honor bars. **Dining & Entertainment:** dining room, coffee shop, 6:30 am-11 pm, $20-$45, entertainment. **Leisure Activities:** 3 heated pools, wading pool, sauna, whirlpool, steamroom, beach, swimming, large tri-level heated pool with 2 temperature settings, scuba diving, snorkeling & equipment, fishing, 2 lighted tennis courts, children's program, recreation program, social program, state-of-the-art spa. *Fee:* scuba equipment, charter fishing. **Guest Services:** [BP] meal plan available, gift shop, valet laundry. *Fee:* area transportation, massage. **Business Services:** conference facilities, administrative services, fax. *Fee:* PC. **Cards:** AE, DI, MC, VI.

⚠️ MARRIOTT CASAMAGNA CANCUN

◇◇◇◇ *Resort*   (98/81-2000

1/25-11/30	$234-$254	
12/21-1/24	$189-$209	
12/1-12/20	$144-$164	

Location: Blvd Kukulcan, Km 16; on the beach, east side of island. (Manzana 23, Lote 41 Section A, ZA Etapa, 77500). Fax: 98/81-2085. **Facility:** Spacious, impressive lobby. Stylish guest rooms, many with ocean view or balcony. Some garden view units. Occasionally dramatic surf. 450 units. Some whirlpool units. 6 stories, interior corridors. **Terms:** 7 day cancellation notice, in season-fee imposed. **Amenities:** voice mail, safes, honor bars, irons, hair dryers. **Dining & Entertainment:** dining room, restaurant, deli, 6:30 am-11 pm, $8-$22, cocktails, also, Mikado, see separate listing, entertainment. **Leisure Activities:** saunas, whirlpools, beach, swimming, scuba diving, snorkeling, children's program, recreation program, exercise room, volleyball. *Fee:* scuba & snorkeling equipment, charter fishing, jet ski, parasailing, scuba lessons, water skiing, 2 lighted tennis courts. **Guest Services:** [AP] meal plan available, gift shop, valet laundry. *Fee:* massage. **Business Services:** conference facilities. *Fee:* fax. **Cards:** AE, CB, DI, MC, VI.
(See color ad inside front cover)

⚠️ MIRAMAR MISION CANCUN

◇◇◇ *Hotel*   ((98)83-1755

12/23-4/14	$190-$250	XP $20
12/1-12/22 & 4/15-11/30	$144-$180	XP $20

Location: Blvd Kukulcan, Km 95 hotel zone; on the beach, east side of island. (PO Box 400, 77500). Fax: 98/83-1136. **Facility:** Extra large pool. Many units with balcony. Rates are all inclusive excluding motorized-sports activities. In-house travel agency and car rental. 266 units. 9 stories, interior corridors. **Terms:** F12; 3 day cancellation notice-fee imposed. **Amenities:** voice mail, safes, honor bars, hair dryers. **Dining & Entertainment:** dining room, 2 restaurants, 7 am-11 pm, $5-$20, cocktails, nightclub, entertainment. **Leisure Activities:** whirlpool, beach, swimming, windsurfing, snorkeling, exercise room. **Guest Services:** gift shop, valet laundry. **Business Services:** meeting rooms. *Fee:* fax. **Cards:** AE, CB, DI, MC, VI.

THE RITZ-CARLTON CANCUN

◇◇◇◇◇ *Resort*   (98/81-0808

12/19-4/12	$295-$365	XP $30
12/1-12/18 & 4/13-11/30	$220-$275	XP $30

Location: Km 17.5, on the beach, east side of island. (No. 36 Retorno del Rey Zona Hotelera, 77500). Fax: 98/81-1015. **Facility:** Elegantly furnished public areas. Refined atmosphere. Superb pool and spa facilities. Among the only 5 diamond lodging that features two 5 diamond restaurants. Poolside guests are pampered with chilled towelettes, cooling body spritzers and poolside concierge. For an extra fee, enjoy the on-the-beach cabanas and massages. Meets AAA guest room security requirements. 365 units, 1 with kitchen. Some suites ($425-$750) and whirlpool units. 9 stories, interior corridors. **Parking:** valet. **Terms:** F17; 7 day cancellation notice, package plans. **Amenities:** voice mail, safes, honor bars, hair dryers. *Some:* fax. **Dining:** The Club Grill, Fantino, see separate listing. **Leisure Activities:** 2 heated pools, wading pool, saunas, whirlpool, steamrooms, beach, swimming, scuba diving, snorkeling, children's program. *Fee:* scuba & snorkeling equipment, fishing, charter fishing, 3 lighted tennis courts. **Guest Services:** gift shop, valet laundry. *Fee:* area transportation, massage. **Business Services:** conference facilities, administrative services. *Fee:* PC, fax. **Cards:** AE, DI, MC, VI.

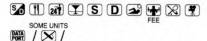

SHERATON CANCUN RESORT & TOWERS

◇◇◇ *Resort*   ((98)83-1988

12/1-12/31	$125-$299	XP $30
1/1-4/14	$214-$229	XP $30
4/15-8/15	$150-$165	XP $30
8/16-11/30	$140-$155	XP $30

Location: On the beach, Km 12.5 in hotel zone, east side of island. Blvd Kukulcan km 12.5 77500 (PO Box 834). Fax: 98/85-0204. **Facility:** Rooms with ocean or lagoon view. Well-landscaped grounds. Tower section with larger rooms than pyramid building. Many rooms with balcony. 471 units. Some whirlpool units. 6-7 stories, interior corridors. **Parking:** valet. **Terms:** F17; 3 day cancellation notice, in season-fee imposed. **Amenities:** voice mail, safes (fee), honor bars, hair dryers. **Leisure Activities:** 2 pools (1 heated), wading pool, sauna, steamroom, beach, swimming, scuba diving, snorkeling, miniature golf, 4 lighted tennis courts, children's program, recreation program, social program, playground. *Fee:* scuba & snorkeling equipment. **Guest Services:** gift shop, valet laundry. *Fee:* massage. **Business Services:** conference facilities, administrative services. *Fee:* PC, fax. **Cards:** AE, CB, DI, MC, VI.

SUNSET LAGOON HOTEL & MARINA

◇◇◇ *Resort*   (98/83-1111

All Year	$150	XP $75

Location: On north side of island; facing lagoon. Blvd Kukulcan Km 5.8 77500. Fax: 98/83-4959. **Facility:** All inclusive resort located on lagoon; reminiscent of a small whitewashed Mediterranean village. 60 units. 9 two-bedroom units. *Bath:* shower only. 2 stories, exterior corridors. **Terms:** F6; 3 day cancellation notice. **Leisure Activities:** wading pool, whirlpool, tranquil lagoon side beach, boating, paddleboats, sailboating, windsurfing, boat dock, scuba diving, snorkeling. *Fee:* marina, waterskiing, scuba & snorkeling equipment, charter fishing. **Guest Services:** [AP] meal plan available, valet laundry. **Cards:** AE, MC, VI.

WESTIN REGINA RESORT CANCUN

 Resort (98/48-7400

1/2-4/23	$230-$290	XP $30
12/1-1/1 & 4/24-11/30	$180-$250	

Location: Kukulcan Blvd, Km 20. On the beach; east side of island. (PO Box 1508, 77500). Fax: 98/85-0779. **Facility:** Ocean and lagoon views, excellent public, pool and beach areas. In-house travel agency and car rental. 293 units. Some whirlpool units. 6 stories, interior corridors. **Parking:** valet. **Amenities:** voice mail, safes, honor bars, hair dryers. **Leisure Activities:** 5 pools, wading pool, saunas, whirlpools, beach, swimming, marina, scuba diving, snorkeling, children's program, recreation program, social program. *Fee:* waterskiing, scuba & snorkeling equipment, charter fishing, 2 lighted tennis courts. **Guest Services:** [MAP] meal plan available, gift shop, valet laundry. *Fee:* massage. **Business Services:** conference facilities, administrative services. *Fee:* PC, fax. **Cards:** AE, DI, MC, VI.

SOME UNITS

/ /

The following lodging was either not evaluated or did not meet AAA rating requirements and is listed for your information only.

JW MARRIOTT CANCUN RESORT & SPA

[fyi] *Resort*

Under construction, scheduled to open February 2001. **Location:** Adjacent to Marriott CasaMagna Cancun Resort, 11 mi from Cancun International Airport, 2 mi s of Cancun Convention Center. Boulevard Kukulcan Retorno Chac 77500. Fax: 732/302-5232. **Planned Amenities:** 450 units, restaurant, coffeemakers, pool, exercise facilities, tennis.

WHERE TO DINE

BLUE BAYOU

 Regional French (98/83-0044

D $28-$42

Location: On beach, Kukulcan Blvd, Km 10.5; east side of island; in Hyatt Cancun Caribe. 77500. **Hours:** 6 pm-midnight. **Reservations:** suggested. **Features:** cocktails & lounge; entertainment; valet parking; a la carte. Unique bayou decor. Semi-formal atmosphere. Specializing in Cajun preparations. **Cards:** AE, DI, DS, MC, VI.

CARLOS 'N CHARLIE'S

 American (98/83-0846

L $5-$10   D $6-$14

Location: At the lagoon. Km 5.5 77500. **Hours:** 11 am-midnight. **Reservations:** suggested. **Features:** No A/C; casual dress; children's menu; cocktails & lounge; fee for area transportation; a la carte. Lunch served in oceanside cabana; dinner in main dining room surrounded with memorabilia. World reknown high energy mecca can provide surprisingly good food and service. Outdoor area can get very hot. **Cards:** AE, MC, VI.

CASA ROLANDI'S

 Northern Italian (98/83-1817

L $3-$8   D $5-$12

Location: On the lagoon side; in Plaza Caracol. Site 12 Plaza Caracol Shopping Mall 77500. **Hours:** 1 pm-11:30 pm. **Features:** casual dress; carryout; cocktails & lounge; a la carte. Located in heart of popular mall, this is a real local favorite. Well-known for fresh ingredients and pasta, its unique grotto walls and attentive service. **Cards:** AE, CB, DI, MC, VI.

THE CLUB GRILL

 *Continental* (98/85-0808

D $32-$40

Location: Km 17.5, on the beach, east side of island; in The Ritz-Carlton Cancun. #36 Retorno del Rey 77500. **Hours:** 7 pm-11 pm. **Features:** semi-formal attire; cocktails & lounge; entertainment; valet parking. Refined, club-like atmosphere in a lavish setting. Seafood, steak and game vividly presented and augmented by local Yucatan and Caribbean flavors. Formal service; romantic ambience; dancing in the adjoining lounge. Cuban cigars avail. **Cards:** AE, DI, MC, VI.

CORAL REEF

 Nouvelle Continental (98/83-2900

D $30-$60

Location: On the beach, north side of island; in Fiesta Americana Grand Coral Beach. 77500. **Hours:** 6 pm-1 am, Sun-midnight. **Reservations:** suggested. **Features:** semi-formal attire; cocktails & lounge; entertainment; fee for parking; valet parking; a la carte. Refined Caribbean atmosphere. Dramatic and innovative salads, soups and Continental entrees integrating fresh quality ingredients with regional influences. Fabulous desserts. Ample wine list includes 20 by-the-glass selections. **Cards:** AE, DI, MC, VI. *(See color ad p 104)*

COTE SUD

 Mediterranean (98/11-2200

L $12-$16   D $19-$22

Location: Retorno del Rey Km 14, Zona Hotelera; on east side of island, on the beach; in Le Meridien. Km 14 Retorno del Rey 77500. **Hours:** 6:30 am-11 & noon-11 pm. **Features:** children's menu; cocktails & lounge; a la carte. Mediterranean cuisine with a French twist. Bistro/casual menu at lunch; more formal dinner offerings. **Cards:** AE, DI, DS, MC, VI.

FANTINO

 Northern Italian (98/85-0808

D $40-$75

Location: Km 17.5, on the beach, east side of island; in The Ritz-Carlton Cancun. 36 Retorno del Rey 77500. **Hours:** 7 pm-11 pm. Closed: Sun. **Reservations:** required. **Features:** dressy casual; children's menu; cocktails & lounge; entertainment; valet parking; a la carte, also prix fixe. Fine dining in an elegant setting overlooking the Caribbean Sea. Varied menu mixes the flavors of Tuscany and the Mediterranean. Fine Cuban cigars available in the lounge. Features menu-de gustacion. **Cards:** AE, DI, MC, VI.

LA BRISA

Seafood (98/83-0100

D $10-$30

Location: On beach at Punta Cancun; in Camino Real Cancun. Punta Cancun 77500. **Hours:** 6 pm-11 pm. **Reservations:** suggested. **Features:** No A/C; casual dress; cocktails & lounge; entertainment; fee for parking; valet parking; a la carte. Romantic Caribbean dining with fresh seafood from around the world, enhanced through regional influences, presented artistically. File under "One to not miss". **Cards:** AE, CB, DI, MC, VI.

LA DOLCE VITA

 *Regional Italian*   (98/85-0161

D $12-$28

Location: Across from Marriott Hotel. Km 14.6 Blvd Kulkulcan 77500. **Hours:** noon-11:30 pm. Closed: 1/1. **Features:** casual dress; cocktails & lounge; a la carte. Dramatic bay side dining. Modern upbeat atmosphere, sparkling tables, fresh flowers and elegant linens. Ample wine list, good selection of by the glass choices. Artistic presentation of classic Italian fare. Among Cancun's pioneer restaurants. **Cards:** AE, MC, VI.

LA HABICHUELA

 Regional Mexican   (98/84-3158

L $4-$8   D $8-$18

Location: Downtown; 2 blks n of Ave Tulum at calle Azucenas; behind the theatre. Margaritas 25. **Hours:** 1:30 pm-midnight. **Features:** casual dress; cocktails & lounge; a la carte. Dine under the stars in a tropical Mayan setting. Flambe tableside preparations. Try the Cocobichuela. Among the city's original fine dining. Worth leaving the strip and venturing into old Cancun town. **Cards:** AE, MC, VI.

LA JOYA RESTAURANT

 Nouvelle Mexican   (98/83-2900

D $30-$50

Location: On the beach, north side of island; in Fiesta Americana Grand Coral Beach. Blvd Kukulcan, Km 8.5 77500. **Hours:** 6:30 pm-11 pm. Closed: Mon. **Reservations:** suggested. **Features:** cocktails & lounge; entertainment; valet parking; a la carte. Dine in the main plaza of a quaint Mexcian plaza and discover authentic haute cuisine Mexican food. Wide selection of unique and artistic dishes combining national and classic flavors. Splendid dining atmosphere enhanced by live mariachi music. **Cards:** AE, DI, JC, MC, VI. (See color ad p 104)

LORENZILLO'S

 Regional Seafood   (98/83-1254

L $8-$12   D $40-$50

Location: Opposite Hotel Continental Villas Plaza Cancun. Zona Hotelera Km 10.5 77600. **Hours:** noon-midnight. **Features:** casual dress; cocktails & lounge; fee for area transportation. On the pier overlooking large lagoon. Specializing in seafood and regional dishes. Casual and quiet atmosphere. A popular spot with occasionally long lines. Call ahead. **Cards:** AE, MC, VI.

MARIA BONITA

 *Regional Mexican*   (98/83-0100

D $12-$22

Location: On beach at Punta Cancun; in Camino Real Cancun. Punta Cancun Lote 17 77500. **Hours:** 6:45 pm-midnight. **Reservations:** suggested. **Features:** No A/C; casual dress; cocktails & lounge; entertainment; valet parking. Fun-filled gastronomical tour through regions of Mexico, its customs, foods and people. Among the must visit Cancun restaurants. High energy fun. Authentic Mexican food all made with fresh, quality ingredients. Colorful, artistic presentations. Excellent for families. **Cards:** AE, CB, DI, MC, VI.

MIKADO

 Ethnic   (98/81-2000

D $18-$30

Location: Blvd Kukulcan, Km 16; on the beach, east side of island; in Marriott CasaMagna Cancun. **Hours:** 6 pm-11 pm. **Reservations:** suggested. **Features:** casual dress; cocktails & lounge; a la carte. Japanese theme. Teppan style theatre grill. Thai specialties. **Cards:** AE, CB, DI, MC, VI.

RESTAURANT EL CALAMAR

Regional Mexican   (98/84-0190

L $6-$20   D $10-$20

Location: From North/South Monument; 0.5 km e to Revolution Monument, turn left to Uxmal and just e from jct; near bus terminal. **Hours:** noon-8 pm. **Features:** casual dress; cocktails; a la carte. Simple cantina style decor. Excellent local dishes featuring Tikin-Xick. Health conscience approach to food preparation. Fresh seafood. whole fish weighed table side. **Cards:** CB, DI, MC, VI.

RESTAURANT LOS PERICOS

Traditional Mexican   (98/84-3152

L $8-$12   D $10-$16

Location: In town; 5 blks w. Ave Yaxchilan 61 77500. **Hours:** 1 pm-1 am. **Features:** casual dress; cocktails & lounge; entertainment; street parking; a la carte. Open air restaurant with Mexican fiesta atmosphere. Hight energy, must see fun spot located in old Cancun town and has long lines at peak hours. **Cards:** AE, MC, VI.

ROSATO RISTORANTE

Regional Italian   (98/85-1000

D $20-$50

Location: Blvd Kukulcan Km 16.5, on the beach, east side of island; in Fiesta Americana Condesa Cancun. Km 15.5 Blvd Kukulcan 77500. **Hours:** 6 pm-midnight. **Reservations:** suggested. **Features:** semi-formal attire; cocktails & lounge; entertainment; valet parking; a la carte. Comfortable dining room with excellant variety of Italian based dishes presented with artistic flair. Wide variety of imported cheese. Focused wine list with some by-the-glass selections. **Cards:** AE, DI, MC, VI.

SAVIO'S

Italian   (98/83-2085

L $10-$14   D $18-$25

Location: On street level of Plaza Caracol. Km 8 Blvd Kulkulcan 77500. **Hours:** 11 am-midnight. Closed major holidays. **Reservations:** suggested; for dinner. **Features:** casual dress; cocktails & lounge; entertainment; a la carte. Located in heart of city mall. Popular place to see people and be seen. Bistro-style tight seating. Very fresh seafood. Light jazzy music. **Cards:** AE, DI, MC, VI.

CHETUMAL, QUINTANA ROO (H-12)

One of the oldest cities on the Yucatán Peninsula, Chetumal (cheh-too-MAHL) was a former Maya stronghold. Its strategic location, on Chetumal Bay at the mouth of the Río Hondo in the southeastern corner of the peninsula, did not go unnoticed by invading *conquistadores*. Three centuries of back-and-forth battles—some viciously barbaric—were waged as the Spanish attempted to wrest control of the region from the Maya. The city was renamed Payo Obispo in 1898 and recast as a border town dealing in jungle hardwoods, arms and smuggled goods. These profitable dealings came to an abrupt end in 1955, when a hurricane all but flattened the city.

The capital of Quintana Roo reflects the stages of its checkered history. It is at once a thriving port and a steamy backwater. The older part of town, with its rickety clapboard buildings huddled under trees ablaze with tropical blooms, has a marked Central American atmosphere (the nation of Belize, with which Chetumal shares tourist and commercial traffic, is just across the river).

There are no azure waters or talc-white sand beaches here; the bay is muddy and brackish. Boulevard Bahía, bordered by small plazas, follows the bay for several kilometers. And neither is one likely to hear the sound of traditional Mexican mariachis. The eclectic citizenry—which includes Caribbean blacks and Belizeans—is more partial to the island rhythms of reggae or calypso.

The newer sections of town, rebuilt after the hurricane, consist of wide boulevards lined with modern but architecturally uninspired government buildings. A tourist information booth is at Avenida Héroes and Aguilar, near the city market. The large, modern bus terminal is north of downtown near the intersection of avenidas Héroes and Insurgentes. "Deluxe" bus service to Cancún and Mérida is offered by ADO.

Many of Chetumal's stores line Avenida Héroes, which begins at the bay and runs west through the market area. An incongruous touch in this downtown shopping district are the numerous shops selling Dutch cheeses, Japanese stereo equipment, French perfume and other international products, all at duty-free prices. The chance to purchase such items draws crowds of Mexican and Belizean tourists (although the planned elimination of tariffs should change Chetumal's status as a shopping mecca). While it is possible to find good buys on Yucatecan hammocks, U.S. and Canadian visitors should save their pesos and purchase Mexican crafts elsewhere.

The bay on which the city sits is the largest natural harbor on the Yucatán Peninsula's eastern coast; however, it is so shallow and reefbound that barges are necessary to load or unload anchored ships. **Calderitas**, a palm-fringed bayside village 8 kilometers (5 miles) north of Chetumal, has a rocky beach and camping opportunities; it comes alive on weekends.

Day Trips

Chetumal itself is not resort-oriented and contains little to interest foreign visitors, but it's a convenient base for fishing expeditions and trips to nearby points of interest. About 40 kilometers (25 miles) northwest via Mex. 186 and Mex. 307 is **Laguna Bacalar** *(see Bacalar below)*, a freshwater lagoon also known as the "Lake of the Seven Colors" for the varying hues of its waters. Swimming is pleasant here and at nearby **Cenote Azul**.

Decidedly off the beaten path are two nearby excursions. The fishing village of **Xcalak** (shka-LAK) is at the tip of the peninsula extending across Chetumal Bay—just north of Belize's

Ambergris Cay—about 55 kilometers (34 miles) southeast of Chetumal. To reach it, however, involves driving north on Mex. 307 to the Majahual turnoff (north of Bacalar). From there a paved but unmarked road leads to coastal Majahual, from which a dirt road proceeds south to Xcalak. Adventurers will appreciate the fishing, snorkeling and birdwatching at this idyllically remote seaside spot.

Xcalak is the jumping-off point for trips to **Banco Chincorro**, a Caribbean atoll that is a natural park. About 2 hours northeast of Xcalak by boat, Banco Chincorro is studded with the remains of sunken and grounded ships and is a favored dive site. Fishing, however, is not permitted. Boats and guides to explore the area can be arranged in Chetumal.

About a mile north of Xcalak at the Costa de Cocos resort is the **Xcalak Dive Center**, which offers complete dive services, equipment rentals and trips to Banco Chincorro atoll. Local dive excursions explore the spectacular coral and sponge formations of the offshore barrier reef, which extends south to the Honduras border. The center also organizes birdwatching, snorkeling and fishing trips. For additional information phone (510) 490-5597 in the United States.

Bacalar, Quintana Roo (H-12)

Founded in 1528, Bacalar (ba-cah-LAHR) was the first Spanish colonial settlement in the region that became Quintana Roo. Although the colonists lived in relative peace for more than 100 years, Spanish-Maya hostility simmered under the surface, exploding when four local farmers were savagely murdered. The Maya community in Chetumal retaliated with equal savagery; the site was finally destroyed by pirates in 1652.

In 1726, Bacalar was resettled by Spanish expatriates from the Canary Islands. They built **Fuerte de San Felipe** (Fort San Felipe), a massive fortification encircled by a crocodile-filled moat. At the outbreak of the Castes War in 1848 the Maya, after brutal fighting, again reclaimed the settlement and the fort. Bacalar remained in Maya hands until 1901, when the Mexican government reclaimed it peacefully.

Fort San Felipe, now surrounded by landscaped gardens rather than hungry reptiles, is a museum of history and archeology containing exhibits of weapons and regional artifacts. The fort's watchtower overlooks the fishing and boating activities on Bacalar Lagoon.

Laguna de Bacalar (Bacalar Lagoon) is east of town; follow the signs from Mex. 307. This 35-mile-long body of water is a spectacular natural wonder in the midst of the otherwise unremarkable jungle scrub of southern Quintana Roo. Salt and fresh water mix in the lagoon, accentuating beautiful hues from deep turquoise to almost black (it is also known as the "Lake of the Seven Colors"). The clear water is ideal for swimming, boating, snorkeling and scuba diving. Around the southern shore are some gracious, turn-of-the-20th-century lakefront homes.

About 5 kilometers (3 miles) south of town, almost at the edge of the lagoon, is **Cenote Azul**, a freshwater sinkhole said to be the world's largest. Some 600 feet across and more than 250 feet deep, its blue water is unusually clear. The cenote, shaded by tropical trees, is popular with swimmers and divers who negotiate the underwater caves, and is crowded on weekends. There is a seafood restaurant, and camping facilities are available.

Rio Bec, Quintana Roo (H-11)

Discovered at the turn of the 20th century, the **Río Bec** (REE-oh bek) archeological zone comprises several sites that once formed a large Maya city. Scattered through the states of Quintana Roo and Campeche, the sites—which generally flourished between about A.D. 200 and 900—are believed to have served as trade routes between Maya outposts established along the Caribbean and Gulf of Mexico coasts. The most interesting of these—**Xpujil**, **Becan** and **Chicanná**—are accessible from Mex. 186 in an area about 137 kilometers (85 miles) west of Chetumal.

Architecturally the sites exhibit what is referred to as the "Río Bec" style. Features include tower-like structures more impressive than functional and temple entrances carved to look like the open jaws of a snake, dragon or other monstrous creature. The ruins are largely unexplored, and few restoration efforts have been made. What remains intact is the mystery and sense of wonder surrounding these ancient cities.

About 68 kilometers (42 miles) west of Chetumal, just before the village of Francisco Villa, and about 8 kilometers (5 miles) south of the highway are the ruins of **Kohunlich** (koh-hoon-LEECH); clumps of date palms suggest the area may once have been an oasis. The most notable structure among Kohunlich's rubble-strewn mounds is the main pyramid, or **Temple of the Masks**, which is decorated with carved faces, strongly Olmec-influenced, that resemble masks. Hints of red are still visible on these figures, which are protected by thatched coverings.

About 72 kilometers (45 miles) past Kohunlich, and just past the village of Xpujil, are the **Xpujil** (sh-pooh-HEEL) ruins. On the north side of the highway, they consist of three ornamental towers which once were extravagantly decorated. Shortly before reaching Xpujil a rough road off Mex. 186 leads to the ruins of **Río Bec**, deep in the Yucatán jungle. At present the only way to get there is with a reliable jeep and an experienced guide, although there are plans to restore the site.

Farther along Mex. 186 and about 7 kilometers (4 miles) west of Xpujil lies **Becan**, north of the highway and reached by a rutted dirt road (watch for the turnoff sign). Surrounded by a ditch that probably was meant as a fortification, it is the most developed of the Río Bec sites and has the largest structures, including temples, plazas and a ball court. About 10 kilometers (6 miles) beyond Becan another dirt road leads to **Chicanná**; these ruins are south of the highway and stand, unlike others in the area, within an enticing grove of tropical trees and other vegetation. The main temple features a fascinating doorway fashioned after a serpent's open mouth; other structures are accented by stone carvings of imaginative monster masks.

The **Calakmul Biosphere Reserve**, named for the archeological zone located in its southern half, extends south of Mex. 186 to the Guatemala border and north another 45 miles, all within the state of Campeche. Within the reserve, excavations are ongoing at the Calakmul ruins, the largest archeological site in the southern Yucatán Peninsula. The biosphere reserve was established in 1989 to preserve the natural rain forest; guided tours have yet to be developed.

A turnoff leading to the Calakmul ruins is approximately 233 kilometers (145 miles) west of the Mex. 186/307 junction. A four-wheel-drive vehicle is necessary to visit the zone; avoid the rainy-season months of May through October, when the route—difficult to negotiate at best—can become impassable.

One or more of the Río Bec sites, on the other hand, can easily be visited in the course of a day, but the only tourist-class accommodations in this remote region are in Chetumal. All sites are open daily 8-5. Admission is charged to each; there is an additional charge for use of a video camera. Water and food are not available. It's helpful to procure the services of local youths, who can act as guides. Insect repellent and sturdy shoes are essential for those who plan to do any amount of walking.

Note: Mex. 186 is a long, hot route with few services of any kind. ADO operates first-class bus service from Chetumal west to Escárcega and Villahermosa; while the buses may stop at ruins along the way, it is much more convenient to drive your own vehicle. There is a gas station shortly before reaching Xpujil, near the Quintana Roo-Campeche state line. A sign along the roadway at the state line provides information about the archeological sites. The condition of the road deteriorates once it enters Campeche. Travelers also may experience inconvenience or delays due to an ongoing dispute between the two states over the border's exact location. It is strongly recommended that Mex. 186 only be traveled during daylight hours.

CHICHEN ITZA, YUCATAN (G-11)

Chichén Itzá (chee-CHEHN eet-SAH), the Yucatán Peninsula's best known and most visited ruins, are the remains of a great Maya city and one of the archeological wonders of the world. Richly carved pyramids, temples and shrines cover a 3.75-square-mile area. Of the several hundred buildings believed to occupy the site, only about 30 have been fully restored. A few remain as they were found, and the rest are hidden under rough, underbrush-covered mounds in the thick jungle scrub of the north-central Yucatán Peninsula.

HISTORICAL OVERVIEW

It is believed that Chichén Itzá was founded sometime around A.D. 435. After being abandoned for an undetermined length of time, it was rediscovered and firmly established as an important ceremonial center by the Itzae (also known as the Putun Maya), a Maya-speaking tribe who migrated from what is now the state of Tabasco. Many archeologists believe that the gradual decline of Maya theocratic rule allowed the more warlike Toltecs from central Mexico to occupy the city around the beginning of the 11th century, and that under Toltec rule Chichén Itzá became the religious, political and cultural center of the Yucatán. An opposing school of thought suggests that Chichén Itzá, rather than being taken over, continued as a Maya site that absorbed aspects of Toltec culture.

The militaristic Toltec influence can be seen in the images—jaguars, sharp-taloned eagles, phalanxes of marching warriors, feathered serpents—employed to decorate the exteriors of pyramids and temples. A cenote (well) filled with murky water was used for sacrificial purposes; men, women and even children were hurled to their deaths. These human offerings were given in the hope that the timely arrival of rain (in a tropical climate with seasonal precipitation) would guarantee the success of the all-important corn crop.

The focus of lowland Maya civilization shifted from Chichén Itzá to Mayapán *(see description under Mérida)* around 1200; it remained there, considerably devitalized, until shortly before the Spanish arrival. Chichén Itzá was briefly the headquarters of *conquistador* Francisco de Montejo during his attempts to subjugate the peninsula in the mid-16th century. The first large-scale excavations of the site began around the turn of the 20th century.

NORTHERN ZONE

Chichén Itzá is remarkable both for its monumental scope and architectural variety. The ruins consist of two complexes connected by a dirt

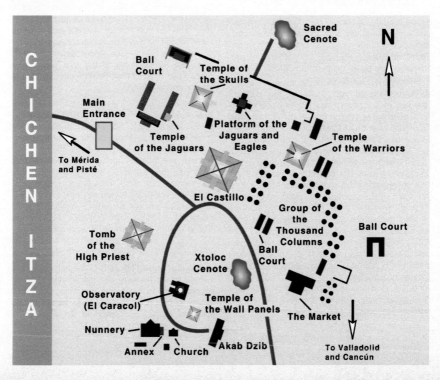

Group of the Thousand Columns   ©John Neubauer

path. Generally speaking, the older southern section contains mostly Maya ruins and the structures in the northern section combine Maya and Toltec influences, although the blending of pre-Hispanic cultures is apparent throughout.

From the visitor center at the main entrance a short, tree-shaded path leads to the northern complex of structures. And whether you're seeing Chichén Itzá for the first or the fiftieth time, the initial view of **El Castillo** (The Castle) is unforgettable. This pyramid—also called Kukulcán, the Maya name for the Toltec king Quetzalcóatl—dominates the other ruins sprinkled over a level, grassy area. Its perfectly symmetrical design incorporates the sophisticated Maya calendar. Each of the four sides is scaled by 91 steps; the total of 364 steps plus the top platform equaled the number of days in the Maya year. An additional step underneath the pyramid—the 365th—signified a trip to the underworld. Each side also has 18 terraced sections—nine on either side of a central staircase, equaling the 18 months of the Maya year—and 52 panels, corresponding to the number of years in the Maya calendrical cycle. Topping the structure are the remains of a temple that can be entered.

That El Castillo's builders were mathematically precise in their construction is borne out by a natural phenomenon that occurs at the spring and fall equinoxes (on or around Mar. 21 and Sept. 21). As the sun begins its descent, the shadows cast by the terraces on the north staircase form the body of a serpent, whose actual sculpted head rests at the base of the stairs. In the spring, the serpent appears to be slithering down the stairs; in the fall, the illusion is reversed. **Note:** Visitors from around the world attend this semiannual event, and although it is well worth seeing, expect large and boisterous crowds.

The staircases on three of the pyramid's sides can be climbed; most visitors use the one on the western side (the side you see as you first enter the site). The views from the summit are spectacular, with ruins poking above the surrounding green landscape. **Note:** The climb up is arduous but of fairly short duration (the pyramid is about 100 feet tall). It is, however, extremely steep, a fact much more apparent after you've reached the top. For those prone to vertigo or fearful of heights, the climb back down will be difficult. If you decide to brave it (and the views alone make the effort worthwhile), the easiest way to descend is backwards on hands and knees, facing the steps and proceeding slowly one step down at a time. For additional security, hold onto the link chain that extends up the middle of the staircase.

Inside El Castillo is an older temple that can be entered twice a day (double-check times at the visitor center) via a stairway at the foot of the north staircase (on the western end). Narrow steps ascend to two humid inner chambers. One contains a reclining Chac Mool figure, the other a reddish throne in the shape of a jaguar with green jade eyes. Avoid entering this temple if you're claustrophobic.

West of El Castillo is the largest pre-Hispanic **ball court** yet discovered. Two walls run parallel to the playing field. The object of this ancient game was for two teams of players to maneuver a heavy rubber ball—without using their hands—through one of two stone rings placed high on each wall. Some participants (opinion is divided on whether they were winners or losers) apparently suffered death by decapitation. Stone carvings depict this act as well as players sporting protective padding and feathered headdresses. The acoustics are startling: Two people standing on opposite sides of the field and speaking in normal voices can easily hear each other.

Temples are at both ends of the ball court. The temple at the northern end has a short stairway ascending to two columns supporting a roof. It retains only a few remnants of its former murals and sculptures. The **Temple of the Jaguars**, at the southeastern corner of the ball court, has columns carved in the shape of serpents and panels depicting jaguars and Maya warriors.

Just east of the ball court is the **Temple of the Skulls** (Tzompantli), decorated in macabre fashion with rows of human skulls. This artistic rendering reflects the gruesome act of human sacrifice that was integral to Maya religious rites, as the heads of victims were often stuck on the ends of poles. The adjacent **Platform of the Eagles and Jaguars** has carvings showing these creatures grasping human hearts. A short distance east of this structure and north of El Castillo is the **Platform of Venus**, which has depictions of a feathered serpent (a reference to the god Quetzalcóatl) holding a human head in its mouth. Serpent carvings ascend the stairways.

A short walk east of El Castillo is the **Temple of the Warriors**, with impressive rows of carved warriors; this Toltec-influenced temple is almost identical to a temple at Tula *(see separate listing under Central Mexico)*, the recognized capital of the Toltecs. The roofed structure boasts fine sculptural details of the rain god Chac, feathered serpents and mythical animals, and is guarded by a reclining Chac Mool figure. Next to it is the **Group of the Thousand Columns**, thought to have housed the residences of Chichén's ruling elite. The rows of Toltec-style pillars (in actuality, far fewer than 1,000) are covered with bas-relief. It's fascinating to wander through this geometric maze and imagine what it once supported.

Just south of the temple and the columns are the partially restored remains of what archeologists believe were steam baths and a market complex. Further to the southeast are as-yet-unrestored mounds of rubble sitting under the trees.

Two cenotes, or limestone sinkholes, served Chichén Itzá. The **Sacred Cenote**, about a 5-minute walk due north of the Platform of Venus along a dirt path (once a Maya *sacbe*, or paved causeway), is a 190-foot-wide pit that was used for human sacrifice to appease Chac. The skeletons of men, women and children have been excavated, which suggests that in addition to young maidens—the preferred sacrificial victim—the diseased and mentally ill also may have been drowned in the well.

Excavations of the cenote were sponsored by the National Geographic Society in conjunction with the Club de Exploraciones y Deportes Acuáticos de México (CEDAM, the Water Sports and Explorations Club of Mexico) and the Instituto Nacional de Arqueología e Historia (INAH, the National Institute of Archeology and History). They involved using an air lift to suck mud from under 30 feet of murky water. In addition to the bones, idols, jewelry, jade objects and other artifacts from different parts of Mexico have been unearthed, leading archeologists to believe that pilgrimages to Chichén Itzá continued long after its abandonment.

CENTRAL ZONE

The southern complex of ruins (often mistakenly referred to as Old Chichén), accessible from the northern complex via a short dirt pathway, consists of mostly Maya ruins. After passing restrooms and a refreshment stand, the first structure you come to is the **Ossuary** (High Priest's Grave), thought to be a burial ground. This partially reconstructed pyramid is topped with the remains of a temple and has distinctive serpent head carvings at the base. Its interior (not open to the public) leads to an underground cave in which human skeletons and offerings have been found.

Across the path and south of this pyramid is **El Caracol** (The Snail or Winding Stair), an astronomical observatory dating from the 10th century that may have been one of the last Maya buildings erected at this site. It received its name from the interior winding staircase (not open to the public) that led to the dome (which can be entered). The round construction is quite possibly unique in Maya architecture. Stones could be removed from slits within the dome—nine in all—enabling Maya astronomers to study different parts of the heavens. The short stairway leading to the dome can be climbed, and there are fine views from the top of the wall, particularly of the Nunnery *(see below)*. Some interesting carvings decorate the dome's exterior.

East of El Caracol a winding path leads north through dense underbrush to the **Cenote Xtoloc**. Unlike the Sacred Cenote, this well was not used for human sacrifice; it provided Chichén with its drinking water. South of El Caracol is the **Casa de las Monjas** (Nunnery), so named by the Spaniards because it reminded them of a European convent. This large complex has exquisitely carved facades of animals, flowers and designs that are reminiscent of latticework. Next to the nunnery is **La Iglesia** (The Church), also named by the Spanish. While it in no way resembles a church, this small building is lavishly decorated, primarily with beak-nosed carvings of Chac.

The exterior carvings on the **Templo de los Tableros Esculpidos** (Temple of the Carved Panels), east of the nunnery, are more difficult to discern, but may refer to Toltec warrior symbology. A rough path, also beginning east of the nunnery, runs through the scrub for several hundred feet to the **Akab-Dzib**, a classically designed Maya temple believed to be one of Chichén Itzá's oldest structures. Traces of red handprints are faintly visible in some of the interior rooms, and above one doorway are carved Maya hieroglyphics that have yet to be deciphered.

Chichén Viejo (Old Chichén) comprises the southernmost section of the ruins, about a 15-minute walk down a dirt path that begins southwest of the Nunnery. A sincere interest in archeology and a local guide are both recommended for a trek to this area of little-restored buildings, which is mosquito-infested (wear plenty of insect repellent) and overgrown with jungle scrub. Avoid exploring during the June-through-September rainy season, when the narrow pathways can become difficult to navigate.

Away from the knots of tourists viewing the better-known and fully restored landmarks are barely uncovered buildings with Classic Maya touches—masks of Chac and gargoyle-like creatures carved along cornices. The Date Group of ruins includes the **House of the Phalli**, so named for some sculptures carved into the walls of one room. The earliest date discovered in Chichén Itzá—the equivalent of A.D. 879—is carved into a lintel supported by columns; the rest of what was once a pyramid no longer remains.

PRACTICALITIES

Arrangements to join a group tour aboard a first-class bus can be made in Mérida, about 120 kilometers (75 miles) west, and Cancún, about 200 kilometers (125 miles) east. A group tour eliminates the hassle of driving but can make for a long, hectic day and requires sticking to a rigid schedule. Mérida-based Mayaland tours offers a package that includes hotel pick-up and drop-off, an escorted tour of the site and lunch at the Mayaland Hotel. A Mayaland office is next to the Hotel Fiesta Americana Mérida; phone (99) 25-0621.

If you're driving, the ruins are just a few miles south of the Chichén Itzá exit off Mex. 180-D; Yuc. 79 is the local road. One of the highway's two toll plazas is at this exit; at press time the toll was 65 pesos (about $6.50). You'll first pass through the small town of Pisté, on Mex. 180 about 2 kilometers (1.2 miles) west of the Chichén Itzá entrance. Here there are budget accommodations, restaurants and basic travel services for those who prefer to stay overnight. Taxi service also is available from Pisté to the site entrance. Several more upscale hotels are grouped east of (and within walking distance) of the southern complex of ruins. Valladolid *(see separate listing)*, about 42 kilometers (26 miles) east on Mex. 180, is another overnight alternative for those who want to spend more than a day at the site.

The ruins can be explored on your own or as part of a group led by a staff guide. A guide isn't necessary to appreciate the grandeur of the major landmarks, however, and information plaques in Spanish and English give a general architectural and historical background.

If you're visiting on your own, begin early in the morning if possible, before it gets too hot and the tour buses begin arriving. A hat or other headgear is advised for protection from the strong sun. Sturdy walking shoes with nonslip soles come in handy for clambering over rocks and especially for climbing El Castillo. Bring bottled water and/or snacks as well as insect repellent for any extended walking excursions. Three hours or so is enough to see everything, although archeology buffs could easily spend the entire day.

A sound-and-light show is presented nightly. The ruins are bathed in colored lights, and narrations in English and Spanish recount the history of and legends associated with the site. The English version begins at 8 p.m. and lasts about 45 minutes. Confirm the start time at the visitor center ticket window, as the machinery is periodically out of order.

The visitor center at the main entrance has an information desk (where admission tickets are purchased); a small museum; an air-conditioned auditorium, Chilam Balam, where an audiovisual presentation is shown; and a bookstore, restaurant and restrooms. Restrooms also are located off the path between the northern and central zone complexes. Open daily 8-6. Admission 51 pesos (about $5); free to all Sun. Parking fee 10 pesos. Sound-and-light show admission 50 pesos. There is an additional fee for using a video camera.

NEARBY DESTINATION

GRUTAS DE BALANCANCHE (Balancanché Caves) are about 5 kilometers (3 miles) east of Chichén Itzá off Mex. 180 via a very short gravel road; follow signs. A series of illuminated underground passages, discovered in the mid-1960s, extend for about half a mile past large stalactite formations. Three of the seven chambers are open to the public. In various niches along the way are offertory urns, incense burners and other artifacts. Some are carved in the likeness of Tláloc, rain god of the Toltecs; it is believed that the caves once served as an underground center for worship.

An underground stream runs to a clear lake that is home to blind fish. Outside is a small botanical garden. **Note:** The walk through the passages can be slippery. Some crawling is required; wear sturdy shoes. The caves are not recommended for those who are claustrophobic.

Guided tours in English are given daily at 11, 1 and 3 for groups of between six and 30 persons (double-check tour times at the Chichén Itzá visitor center); self-guiding tours are not permitted. A sound-and-light show accompanies the tour and recounts the cave's history. Admission is charged.

WHERE TO STAY

🔺 HOTEL HACIENDA CHICHEN

🔻🔻 *Historic Cottage* ☎ (985)1-0045

All Year	$85-$100	XP $10

Location: At entrance to archeological zone. Km 120 on Merida-Puerto Juarez Hwy 97751. Fax: 992/4-5011. **Facility:** In jungle setting. Cabins with excellent spacing nestled around large pool courtyard area. 21 units. *Bath:* shower only. 1 story, exterior corridors. **Terms:** F11; cancellation fee imposed. **Amenities:** no TVs. **Leisure Activities:** nature trails, hiking trails, jogging. *Fee:* horseback riding. **Cards:** AE, MC, VI.

SOME UNITS

🔺 HOTEL MAYALAND AND BUNGALOWS

🔻🔻 🔻🔻 *Motor Inn* ☎ (985)1-0127

All Year	$64-$188	XP $20

Location: 120.5 km e of Merida on Merida-Puerto Juarez Hwy; at archeological zone. (PO Box 407, MERIDA, YU, 97000). Fax: 985/1-0129. **Facility:** Tropical grounds. Colorful bungalows and good to very good hotel rooms, most with private balcony. Exceptionally beautiful view of the sunset over the Mayan ruins from hotel lobby and some rooms. 96 units. Some whirlpool units ($188-$224). *Bath:* some combo or shower only. 3 stories, interior/exterior corridors. **Terms:** F12; 15 day cancellation notice-fee imposed. **Amenities:** *Some:* honor bars. **Dining:** 2 restaurants, coffee shop, 7 am-10 pm, $6-$13, cocktails. **Leisure Activities:** 3 pools, nature program. *Fee:* horseback riding. **Guest Services:** gift shop. **Cards:** AE, DI, MC, VI.

SOME UNITS

COBÁ, QUINTANA ROO (G-11)

Cobá (coh-BAH), which translates roughly as "waters stirred by wind," is thought to be named for the four natural lakes situated in the vicinity. This tiny village is about 44 kilometers (27 miles) northwest of Mex. 307; the road to Cobá, which was not paved until the early 1970s, branches off Mex. 307 at a point about 2 kilometers (1.2 miles) north of the village of Tulum. From the north, Cobá is accessible via a paved road branching off Mex. 180 at Nuevo Xcán; the distance between the two points is 43 kilometers (26.5 miles). The village has very few amenities and therefore sees little in the way of profit from tourists visiting the Cobá ruins. Bringing along a simple toy or an item of clothing would be an appreciated gesture.

COBA RUINS spread out from the shores of Lake Cobá just outside of town. One of the most ambitious sites in the Maya World, this classic city/ceremonial center dates from between A.D. 600 to 900 and at its height may have supported 40,000 to 50,000 inhabitants. Never discovered by the Spaniards, it was eventually abandoned. Archeologists theorize that Cobá was an important trade link between Maya outposts on the coast and cities in the interior.

Perfectly straight Maya roads called *sacbé* (sack-BEH) led from Cobá to Chichén Itzá (*see*

separate listing) and other Maya ceremonial centers. These ancient roads were marvels of engineering, since the flatness of the land precluded the builders from benefiting from an elevated vantage point while planning the roads' construction through the almost-impenetrable jungle.

The ruins were first discovered in the late 1890s, but excavations did not begin until 1974. It is believed that as many as 15,000 structures exist; only a small fraction of that number have been restored. The sprawling site—some 80 square miles—still remains in pristine condition. Those temples, pyramids and elaborately carved stelae (vertical stone tablets) that have been excavated are surrounded by palm tree thickets, tropical hardwoods, roping vines and other vegetation.

Nohoch Mul, a 138-foot-high pyramid towering above the flat landscape, is the tallest structure of its kind in the northern Yucatán—rising even higher than the Pyramid of the Magician at Uxmal. Those who climb to the pyramid's summit will be able to see a few unexcavated structures poking through an otherwise unbroken green landscape. The descent will be more difficult than the climb up—especially for those afraid of heights, who can hold onto a guide rope for assistance. The **Cobá Group** of buildings contains another large pyramid, the **Temple of the Church**.

Broad dirt paths traverse the site and connect the main groups of ruins. Unmarked side trails—most little more than the hint of a pathway tunneling into the forest—branch off the main paths.

Guides can be hired at the entrance to the ruins, and mountain bike rentals are available. But to fully experience Cobá, visit early in the morning, when your sole companions will be vividly colored birds and butterflies and only the occasional shriek of a unseen monkey breaks the sense of profound solitude. A morning visit also allows you to avoid the worst of the jungle's formidable heat and humidity. Sturdy walking shoes, insect repellent and drinking water are necessary for those planning to spend any time exploring the site. Daily 8-5. Admission is charged.

COZUMEL, QUINTANA ROO (G-12)

Cozumel (koh-soo-MEHL) offers both an escape from Cancún's overwhelming development and an elaboration upon the small-scale maritime pleasures of tiny Isla Mujeres. Encircling coral reefs make it one of the world's top diving destinations. The wealth of feisty game and brilliantly colored tropical fish species are, respectively, an angler's and a snorkeler's delight. While the emphasis is on outdoor activity, the relaxed rhythms of a tropical island prevail, along with some real small-town atmosphere.

Cozumel was an important Maya ceremonial and trading center, and the people believed the island to be sacred. The present name descends from Cuzamil, or "the island of swallows." Cozumel's first foreign visitor was Spanish explorer Juan de Grijalva, who arrived in 1518 on a slave-hunting expedition; Hernán Cortés followed the next year, using the island as a base from which to launch attacks against mainland Indians. After the Spanish takeover Cozumel became an important port, but diseases introduced from Europe almost wiped out the local population by the late 1500s.

After a century of peaceful existence, Cozumel became a refuge for smugglers and pirates, who used the island's protected coves as hideouts. By the mid-19th century it had been all but abandoned, but Indian survivors of the racially triggered War of the Castes left mainland Yucatán and began to resettle the island. An economic boomlet then occurred when Cozumel became a port of call on the shipping route for chicle, a milky substance obtained from the trunk of the sapodilla tree that was used in making chewing gum. But as air freight became more widespread and synthetics replaced chicle in gum production, the island again lapsed into obscurity.

Growth began anew after U.S. servicemen stationed at Cozumel during World War II came back for vacations. The island's reputation as a choice dive spot was considerably enhanced in the early 1960s when undersea explorer Jacques Cousteau visited while making a television documentary. Resort development in the 1970s and '80s paralleled Cancún's, albeit at a slower pace. Although the tremendous growth of the cruise ship industry has resulted in a stream of daytripping visitors, serious divers still set the scene here, exploring the numerous offshore reefs, underwater caverns and sunken shipwrecks.

ISLAND LAYOUT

Cozumel is located about 19 kilometers (12 miles) off the coast opposite Playa del Carmen; a 3,000-foot-deep channel separates it from the mainland. Mexico's largest populated island, it has a total area of 189 square miles (about one-sixth the size of Rhode Island), is approximately 29 miles long and averages 9 miles wide.

Most of the interior comprises patches of insect-ridden jungle, expanses of thorny, uninviting scrub and scattered Maya ruins, none of them well preserved. The terrain is uniformly flat—the highest point is less than 50 feet above sea level—and inaccessible. Cozumel's soil, thin and rocky, has never been conducive to agriculture. But because so little of the island is developed, it supports an abundance of animal life. Armadillos, deer and foxes live in the jungles. Iguanas several feet long can be seen sunning on top of rocks along the eastern shore. A variety of birds—including small, multicolored parrots—inhabit the island's several swampy areas.

In contrast to this somewhat desolate landscape are the inviting beaches. Those on the western (leeward) side of the island are protected

Beach scene   ©John Neubauer

from the open Caribbean; they have calm waters and sandy shores. The eastern (windward) coast is rockier and faces the open sea. Pounding surf and powerful undertows create dangerous swimming conditions, but these beaches have a wild beauty, further underscored by the relative lack of tourist traffic.

On the western coast is Cozumel's only town, **San Miguel de Cozumel**, usually referred to as San Miguel. The island's hub, it is a conglomeration of budget hotels, businesses, shops, restaurants and nightspots. Many of them line San Miguel's main street, **Avenida Rafael Melgar**, which runs north-south along the waterfront. A cement walkway, locally referred to as the *malecón*, divides the avenue from the beach. Avenidas run north-south, calles run east-west, forming an easy-to-negotiate grid pattern. (An exception is **Avenida Benito Juárez**, which begins at the passenger ferry pier and runs due east.)

A block inland from the *malecón* is **Plaza del Sol**, the main square, bounded on the north by Juárez and on the south by Calle 1 Sur. The plaza, graced with a statue of Mexican president and hero Benito Juárez, is especially pretty in spring when royal poinciana trees are covered with orange blooms. **Note:** Many downtown streets are closed to vehicular traffic, and parking is scarce.

Hotel zones comprising Cozumel's more exclusive accommodations are to the north and to the south of San Miguel. Large-scale resort development is held in check by the island's limited supply of potable drinking water (although Cozumel actually predates Cancún as a Yucatán tourist destination). One paved road, the **Carretera Transversal** (the eastward extension of Avenida Benito Juárez, crosses the island east-west. There are no paved roads in the island's northern half, and very little development. The offshore reefs and the best beaches are toward the southern end of the island on the western (leeward) side and are accessible via the Costera Sur, the southern extension of Avenida Rafael Melgar.

THE INFORMED TRAVELER

Cozumel International Airport is about 3 kilometers (2 miles) north of San Miguel. Continental and Mexicana airlines offer direct flights from U. S. cities. The Mexicana subsidiary Aerocozumel has regular daily flights from Cancún, Isla Mujeres and Playa del Carmen; for schedule information phone (800) 531-7921. If flying to Cozumel from Cancún, you must purchase your ticket at the main terminal in the Cancún airport and then take a shuttle bus (a 5- to 7-minute ride) to a small terminal annex for the actual flight. Luggage can be checked at the main terminal. When returning to Cancún from Cozumel, request that your luggage be dropped off at the main terminal if you're catching another flight. If

your connecting flight is with a Mexican airline, alert the Cozumel ticket agent and your luggage will automatically be forwarded to the connecting flight.

There is no taxi service from the airport; instead, *colectivos* (passenger vans) drop visitors off at their hotels. *Colectivo* tickets can be purchased at the airport exit. Taxi service is available back to the airport upon departure. For additional information about airlines *see "Arriving by Air," page 53.*

Cozumel also is accessible by ferry from Playa del Carmen and Puerto Morelos *(see separate listings).* The trip on the passenger-only ferry from Playa del Carmen takes about 45 minutes. There are two types of ferries—older, open-air boats and the MV *Mexico*, an enclosed, jet-propelled, air-conditioned vessel offering refreshments and videos during the trip. Tickets can be purchased at the booths at each pier; the MV *Mexico* is the more expensive of the two services. **Note:** Those prone to seasickness should take appropriate precautions on windy days.

There are approximate hourly crossings between Playa del Carmen and Cozumel daily from around 6:30 a.m. to 8:30 p.m., but schedules are subject to frequent change; verify arrivals and/or departures in advance at the ticket booths. The passenger ferry pier is the foot of Avenida Juárez, in the center of town.

Unless you need to bring a vehicle onto the island, avoid the Puerto Morelos passenger/car ferry. The trip itself takes from 3 to 4 hours, and there can be a tedious wait before departure. It also is necessary to arrive several hours in advance in order to purchase a ticket and secure a place in line. The ferry is docked during periods of bad weather; trucks carrying fuel and other cargo take precedence over automobiles. There is one crossing daily, and the schedule is subject to change. To verify arrivals at Cozumel or departures for Puerto Morelos, check at the cruise ship pier or phone (987) 2-0950.

The passenger/car ferry arrives at the international cruise ship pier, located a couple of miles south of San Miguel near the La Ceiba Beach hotel. A number of cruise lines, among them Carnival, Holland America, Princess and Royal Caribbean, dock at Cozumel and/or Playa del Carmen.

Mopeds and motorcycles are popular ways to get around the island, but the potholed streets make them a somewhat risky means of transportation. Wearing a helmet is required. There are several moped rental establishments in San Miguel. The rate averages $25-$30 per day; insurance is not included. Open-air jeeps also can be rented but entail a similar element of risk, as they can flip over easily. There is only one gas station on the island, located 5 blocks west of Plaza del Sol at avenidas Juárez and 30. Hertz and other agencies have offices on Cozumel, but renting a car is expensive and, with the available transportation alternatives, not really necessary.

Taxis wait outside the major hotels and at the passenger ferry pier, and can be hailed on the street in San Miguel. There are normally fixed rates between downtown and the hotel zones to the north and south, or from downtown to Chankanaab Lagoon Park or Playa San Francisco. If possible, share the cost with other passengers. You also can hire a taxi driver for a tour of the island, usually for a set fee. The headquarters office is on Calle 2 Norte; phone (987) 2-0236. Most hotels will call a taxi for their guests.

The state tourist office is on the second floor of the Plaza del Sol building, which is on the eastern side of the main plaza. It is open Mon.-Fri. 8:30-3; phone (987) 2-0972 or 2-0335. The **Calling Station**, Avenida Rafael Melgar at Calle 3 Sur, is open daily and has private booths for long-distance phone calls (minus the hotel surcharge), fax service, and VCR and video rentals. The **Cruz Roja** (Red Cross) clinic is at Calle Rosada Salas and Avenida 20 Sur; phone (987) 2-1058. A 24-hour clinic and access to air ambulance service are available at the **Centro Médical de Cozumel** (Medical Specialties Center), Avenida 20 Norte #425; phone (987) 2-5370. Money can be exchanged at banks in the vicinity of Plaza del Sol during the morning. Banks have better exchange rates than the hotels and the *casa de cambio* (exchange office) at the airport. Many island shops accept U.S. dollars.

Cozumel is balmy year-round. June through October, the rainy season, is also more humid. Most of the afternoon showers during these months are brief and pose little interruption to leisure activities. The possibility of a hurricane or tropical storm is likeliest in September or October. The rest of the year is dry, warm and sunny, with an occasional cool evening December through February.

WHAT TO DO ON THE ISLAND

Cozumel is Mexico's No. 1 diving destination. From the international cruise ship pier south to Punta Celarain are miles of offshore coral reefs, including **Paraíso, Chankanaab, Yucab, Santa Rosa, Palancar** and **Colombia**. At the island's southern tip is **Maracaibo Reef**, where the coral formations are enormous and water currents make diving both exhilarating and challenging. For experienced divers only, Maracaibo is not on the regular dive boat itinerary and requires advance reservations.

The peak season is June through August, when the Caribbean waters are calm and warm and hotel rates tend to be lower. A wetsuit top is recommended for winter diving, when water temperatures are slightly lower. Night dives, underwater photography or making a customized video are all available options. A scale map of all of Cozumel's reefs, complete with water depths and other information, can be obtained from most of the local dive shops.

A variety of packaged excursions, which usually include airfare, accommodations and diving costs, can be booked in the United States. In addition, the island's dive outfits compete vigorously for both seasoned divers and beginners, offering equipment rentals, instruction, guides and organized expeditions that range from an afternoon to several days. Many hotels organize their own dive trips as well, and their facilities, while likely to be more expensive, also are more convenient. If you're not on a packaged trip or making your own arrangements, take the time to investigate credentials, boats and equipment; if possible, get the inside scoop from a diver familiar with the area.

Among the in-town outfits are **Fantasia Divers**, Avenida 25 Sur at Calle Rosado Salas (5 blocks inland from the waterfront), phone (987) 2-1007; **Blue Bubble**, Avenida 5 Sur at Calle 3 Sur, phone (987) 2-1865; and **Aqua Safari**, Avenida Rafael Melgar at Avenida 5 Sur, phone (987) 2-0101. **Note:** Make certain the instructor you choose has PADI certification and is affiliated with the island's SSS (Servicios de Seguridad Sub-Acuática) recompression chamber, located on Calle 5 Sur just off Avenida Rafael Melgar; phone (987) 2-2387.

Snorkeling is excellent in Chankanaab Bay, at Playa San Francisco, and around the offshore reefs near Colombia Lagoon, at the island's southern tip. Morning feedings from the piers of the Stouffer Presidente and La Ceiba Beach hotels attract schools of hungry fish, some of which are bold enough to break the surface of the water and take food from outstretched hands (but beware of sharp teeth). An upside-down plane, deliberately sunk for a movie production, sits on the sandy bottom a short distance from the La Ceiba pier. Those who want to view the colorful marine life but don't want to get wet can take a glass-bottom boat trip.

Snorkeling gear can be cheaply rented at Playa San Francisco, Chankanaab Lagoon Park (*see attraction listing*), or from the larger hotels. In addition, the dive shops and travel agencies provide organized snorkeling excursions to the various reefs. A representative agency is **Turismo Aviomar**, which has a central office at Avenida 5 Norte between Calles 2 and 4 Norte; phone (987) 2-0588. Other Turismo Aviomar offices are in the lobbies of the major hotels, including the Presidente Intercontinental. The **Fiesta Cozumel** agency also has offices in the major hotels.

Sport fishing is superb, and from March through June world records are sometimes set for catches of swordfish, sailfish and marlin. At other times of the year barracuda, dorado, red snapper, tarpon and wahoo can be hooked.

The major hotels organize sport-fishing expeditions. You can also hire a boat and a guide yourself at the downtown ferry dock, or through **Club Naútico de Cozumel**, at the Puerto de Abrigo Marina on Avenida Rafael Melgar, just north of downtown; phone (987) 2-1024. To arrange a fishing trip in advance write Club Naútico at Box 341, Cozumel, Quintana Roo 77600. Boats can be chartered for a half or full day. Rates (including tackle, bait and guide) vary according to the size of the vessel, the number of people and the season. To get an idea of what's available and how much it costs, visit the marina in the late afternoon when the boats are returning and talk to a couple of the captains.

Sightseeing excursions to Cancún, Playa del Carmen, Xel-Há Natural Park, Tulum and other nearby points of interest can be easily arranged; information is available at most hotels. Travel agencies also offer Cozumel tours that include such activities as sunbathing at the beach, snorkeling at Chankanaab Lagoon Park, a visit to the San Gervasio ruins or a day trip to the Xcaret ecological theme park *(see Playa del Carmen listing)*, which includes ferry transportation.

There are no golf courses on Cozumel, and tennis courts are few. You can, however go horseback riding. **Rancho Buenavista** offers a 4-hour guided trek into the interior jungle scrub, with stops at several Maya ruins; phone (987) 2-1537.

Cozumel celebrates two major annual events. *Carnaval*, the island's version of Mardi Gras, is held in February on the 3 days preceding Ash Wednesday. Colorful float parades along the *malecón*, masquerade balls, street dances and the "burning" of Juan Carnaval (a Carnaval king) take place during this exuberant fiesta. The *International Billfish Tournament* is held in May to take advantage of the narrow-jawed fishes' migrating season. Cozumel also celebrates the patron saint of San Miguel with a fiesta the last week in September.

BEACHES AND RUINS

As in the rest of Mexico, all of Cozumel's beaches are public, even those that appear to be the property of hotels. North of San Miguel are several of the more luxurious accommodations and some condominium developments. **Playa San Juan** extends to Punta Norte, where the highway ends. Beyond Punta Norte is miniscule **Isla de la Pasión**, in the middle of calm Abrigo Bay. Local boat owners can take you to this secluded spot, where there are deserted beaches and opportunities for fishing, but no facilities.

South of San Miguel, Avenida Rafael Melgar becomes the coastal highway (Costera Sur) and passes several beach and snorkeling spots. **Playa San Francisco**, south of Chankanaab Lagoon Park and off the Costera Sur (coastal highway, also known as the Carretera Sur), is one of Cozumel's most popular beaches. It has changing rooms and open-air restaurants, and beach chairs and snorkeling equipment can be rented. On weekends the beach is crowded with local families and cruise ship passengers. Just south of Playa San Francisco is **Playa del Sol**, once privately owned but now public.

The eastern (windward) coast is far less developed and thus more dramatic. The beaches, interspersed among rocky coves, are frequently empty. The open Caribbean is intensely turquoise, but the surf is often strong; swim at your own risk. A paved road follows the coast from Punta Celarain north toward **Punta Morena**, halfway up the coast; there are a few restaurants and camping spots (no facilities) along the way. **Playa Bonita, Playa Chen Río** and **Punta Chiqueros** (which is situated on a protected cove) are all good spots for beachcombing. At Punta Morena the road runs into the end of the Carretera Transversal (cross-island road), about 15 kilometers (9 miles) from San Miguel. The rocky beach here is scenic but not safe for swimming.

Several Maya ruins are scattered around the island. North of the Carretera Transversal the coastal route changes from paved to dirt and leads past waterfowl-filled lagoons and a smattering of ruins, among them **Castillo Real**, a former Maya fortification, where the few remains include a lookout tower. The snorkeling is outstanding in this little-visited area, but a four-wheel-drive vehicle is necessary to reach it. At the northern tip of Cozumel is the **Punta Molas Lighthouse**, where birdwatching is rewarding and it is possible to camp (again, no facilities).

The **San Gervasio** ruins *(see attraction listing)* are also north of and accessible from the cross-island road. At Km 17.5 on the Costera Sur, a turnoff leads about 3 kilometers (2 miles) east to the ruins of **El Cedral**. One small structure is all that remains at this site, believed to be the oldest on the island and the one first discovered by the Spanish. A tree grows from the roof, its roots snaking around the crumbled stones. Faint traces of paint and stucco are still visible. A tiny farming settlement has grown up here, dominated by a rural church painted bright green.

SHOPPING, DINING AND NIGHTLIFE

For shoppers, Avenida Rafael Melgar is the place to go. Department stores, boutiques and craft shops offer duty-free imported goods, chic sportswear and high-quality folk art reproductions, as well as T-shirts and cheap souvenirs. **La Fiesta Cozumel** caters to cruise ship passengers. Top-quality jewelry can be found at **Van Cleef & Arpels**. Bargain hunters would do well to investigate the establishments a block or two off Melgar. Another concentration of shops line the side streets in the vicinity of Plaza del Sol. The two-story **Plaza del Sol Mall** is a small complex on the east side of the plaza. A crafts market is on Calle 1 Sur across from the plaza's south side.

Those for whom shopping is more of a sidelight can try **Los Cinco Soles** on Avenida Rafael Melgar, which sells a representative selection of clothing and Mexican craft items fashioned from papier maché, wood, glass, onyx and silver. More handicrafts are on display at **Talavera**, on Avenida 5 Sur near Plaza del Sol. **Prococo**, Avenida Rafael Melgar on the waterfront, is a one-stop department store that has groceries, crafts, gifts and clothing.

Most of Cozumel's restaurants are in San Miguel. Seafood, not surprisingly, stands out. **Acuario**, half a kilometer south of downtown San Miguel on Avenida Rafael Melgar, serves fish and lobster preparations in an atmosphere accented by large saltwater aquariums lining the walls. For Mexican specialties, try **La Choza**, Calle Rosada Salas #198 at Avenida 10 Sur. The thatch-roofed, white stucco restaurant, family owned and operated, turns out hearty dishes like chicken in mole sauce, fish or shrimp in mustard sauce, pork stew and an interesting avocado pie (for dessert).

Zermatt, at the corner of Calle 4 Norte and Avenida 5 Norte, is a typical Mexican bakery where you can purchase fresh bread, rolls and pastries. For a quick pick-me-up, **Café Caribe** on Avenida 10 Sur offers ice cream, carrot cake and other sweets along with fresh-roasted coffee. When mangos are in season (during spring and summer), street vendors sell them on a stick, peeled and carved into different shapes.

After a strenuous day of diving, swimming or exploring, most visitors are content to turn in early. For after-dinner relaxation, the outdoor cafés around Plaza del Sol are pleasant places to enjoy the evening breeze. On Sunday evenings the plaza comes alive when families gather to hear Latin bands or be serenaded by mariachis. This is a good opportunity to mingle with the locals, who take tourism in stride and are friendly toward visitors.

For those with energy to burn, the ever-reliable **Carlos 'n Charlies**, on Avenida Rafael Melgar between Calles 2 and 4 Norte, is a raucous spot with beer-drinking contests and high-decibel music. Patrons also know what to expect at the Cozumel branch of the **Hard Rock Cafe**, Avenida Rafael Melgar #2A (second floor), just north of Plaza del Sol.

The **Fiesta Americana Cozumel Reef**, south of San Miguel at Km 7.5 on the Costera Sur (Avenida Rafael Melgar), sponsors a Mexican theme night on selected evenings during the high season. A buffet dinner is accompanied by folkloric dance performances, mariachis and other entertainment; phone (987) 2-2622.

WHAT TO SEE

MUSEO DE LA ISLA DE COZUMEL (Museum of the Island of Cozumel) is on Avenida Rafael Melgar north of the main square, between calles 4 and 6 Norte. Four exhibit halls chronicle the island's human history, from its reputation as a revered Maya religious destination through pre-Hispanic trade and navigation to its settlement by Maya refugees from the 19th-century War of the Castes. An overview of natural history focuses on endangered species and local plant and animal life. Guided tours in English are available. The museum also functions as a cultural center of sorts for the island. A restaurant on the second floor has expansive waterfront views. Daily 10-6. Admission is charged.

PARQUE ARQUEOLOGICO DE COZUMEL (Cozumel Archeological Park) is on Avenida 65 Sur, a 10-minute taxi ride from the main plaza. If driving, take the road across from the cruise ship pier east to Avenida 65 Sur, then turn left and follow signs. The park contains reproductions of artifacts from such Mesoamerican cultures as the Olmec, Maya, Toltec and Aztec. Familiar images—including a squat Olmec head and the reclining figure of Chac Mool—reside in a natural garden setting. An exhibit featuring a hut surrounded by medicinal plants offers insight into the rituals of daily Maya life. Guided walking tours are available (wear plenty of insect repellent). **Note:** The park suffered hurricane damage in 1995. Daily 8-6. Admission is charged.

PARQUE LAGUNA DE CHANKANAAB (Chankanaab Lagoon Park) is about 8 kilometers (5 miles) south of town off the Costera Sur (Coastal Highway), the southward extension of Avenida Rafael Melgar. Connected with **Chankanaab Bay** by a natural subterranean channel, the saltwater lagoon is part of a national park. The lagoon, sheltered bay and the offshore **Yukab Reef** all provide sanctuary for a fascinating diversity of marine life, including coral, sponges, crustaceans, turtles, moray eels and tropical fish. A sunken boat, a religious statue and encrusted anchors and cannons in the bay are popular with divers and snorkelers. The lagoon itself is protected, and swimming and snorkeling are prohibited. The beach fronting the bay, lined with thatched *palapas* (shelters), is wide and pretty.

Surrounding the lagoon is a shady botanical garden with hundreds of tropical and subtropical plant species, including those indigenous to the island. Here as elsewhere on Cozumel are bright green iguanas, ever ready to dart into the underbrush. Within the garden are reproductions of typical Maya dwellings. A small museum has exhibits about local plant, animal and marine life. The park has a dive shop, restrooms, changing areas, showers, refreshment stands and a restaurant. Snorkeling equipment can be rented. Daily 9-5. Admission is charged.

PARQUE NACIONAL SUBMARINO DE PALAN-CAR (Palancar National Submarine Park), off the western side of the island, embraces a 32-kilometer (20-mile) stretch of coral reefs. All of the exotic marine flora and fauna within this underwater national park is protected. Commercial fishing, sport fishing or the collection of any marine life is prohibited in the territory from the shoreline out to and including the El Cantil Drop-Off, and from the international cruise ship pier south to Punta Celarain.

The park's centerpiece, **Arrecife Palancar** (Palancar Reef), is about a mile offshore and accessible by boat. This is the reef most associated with Cozumel. It consists of a series of extraordinary coral formations that form archways, tunnels, twisting ravines and deep canyons, all inhabited by an unsurpassed variety of reef life. A bronze statue of Christ is submerged in the vicinity of the reef. The conditions here make Palancar a site for experienced divers rather than beginners.

PUNTA CELARAIN LIGHTHOUSE is at the island's southernmost point; where the Costera Sur (coastal highway) reaches the eastern coast, turn right onto a dirt road and proceed about 5 kilometers (3 miles) south. The journey is best made in a four-wheel-drive vehicle. Sand dunes surround the lighthouse, and there are fine, unspoiled vistas of waves crashing against the black limestone shoreline. For a tip, the lighthouse keeper will let you climb to the top (wear comfortable walking shoes); from the summit there is a 360-degree view of the island, with fishing boats suspended in the blue-green water. Locals and tourists alike gather here on Sundays, when the keeper sells fried fish and cold beer.

SAN GERVASIO RUINS are east on the Carretera Transversal (Avenida Benito Juárez) to the San Gervasio turnoff, then about 7 kilometers (4 miles) north on a dirt access road to the entrance gate. Maya women from throughout Mesoamerica traveled to this ceremonial center to worship Ixchel, the goddess of fertility and medicine. Not nearly as impressive as other archeological sites on the Yucatán Peninsula, San Gervasio was nevertheless inhabited for more than 1,000 years. The restored buildings are little more than walls of block stone with door entrances, surrounded by dense scrub vegetation. They were formerly small temples and shrines built atop platforms. The pathways connecting the groups of structures follow the raised causeways built by the Maya.

Guided tours are available, but it's just as easy to explore with the aid of a green site map, sold at most gift shops in San Miguel. Cold beverages and snacks are available at the entrance to the ruins. Daily 8-5; closed holidays. Admission is charged; there is an additional charge for using a video camera. There also is a road access fee charged per vehicle (pay at the entry gate at the San Gervasio turnoff). For a fee (usually around $30), taxi drivers will take passengers to the site entrance and wait for them.

WHERE TO STAY

DAYS INN-VILLA DEL REY

▼▼▼ *Motor Inn* (987/2-1600

12/23-4/30	$65-$75	XP $10
12/1-12/22 & 5/1-11/30	$45-$55	XP $6

Location: 1.3 km s of San Miguel town center. Ave 11, Sur 460 77600. Fax: 987/2-1692. **Facility:** Quiet residential location, very attractive pool garden area. Within walking distance of the beach. Meets AAA guest room security requirements. 43 units, 6 with efficiency. *Bath:* shower only. 2-4 stories, exterior corridors. **Terms:** F16; 7 day cancellation notice-fee imposed. **Dining:** restaurant, 7 am-noon, $5-$10, cocktails. **Cards:** AE, MC, VI.

FIESTA AMERICANA COZUMEL REEF

▼▼▼ *Motor Inn* ((987)2-2622

12/22-4/14	$130-$150	XP $30
4/15-11/30	$100-$120	XP $25
12/1-12/21	$95-$110	XP $20

Location: 7.5 km s of San Miguel, on beach road. (PO Box 207, ISLA COZUMEL, QR, 77600). Fax: 987/22-666. **Facility:** Across from the Caribbean with pedestrian foot bridge access to beach and water facilities. Large attractive rooms, some with balcony. Includes a secluded cluster of thatched roof cabanas, with separate sitting area and terrace with hammock. Meets AAA guest room security requirements. 228 units. Some whirlpool units. 3 stories, interior corridors. **Terms:** F12; 5 day cancellation notice, package plans. **Amenities:** voice mail, honor bars, hair dryers. *Some:* safes. **Dining:** dining room, restaurant, deli, 7 am-11 pm, $6-$10, cocktails. **Leisure Activities:** 2 pools, wading pool, beach access, swimming, scuba diving, snorkeling, fishing. *Fee:* windsurfing, scuba & snorkeling equipment, charter fishing, scuba instruction, lighted tennis court. **Guest Services:** [MAP] meal plan available, gift shop, valet laundry. *Fee:* area transportation. **Business Services:** conference facilities. **Cards:** AE, MC, VI.

SOME UNITS

HOTEL FONTAN COZUMEL

▼ *Motor Inn* (987/2-0300

12/1-12/15 & 5/1-11/30	$110	XP $10
12/16-4/30	$75	XP $10

Location: 1 km n of San Miguel, on beach road. (PO Box 7, ISLA COZUMEL, QR, 77600). Fax: 987/2-0105. **Facility:** On Coral Sea ledge. Many beachfront rooms with private balcony or patio facing the sea. 49 units. *Bath:* shower only. 3 stories (no elevator), interior corridors. **Terms:** F12; 15 day cancellation notice. **Leisure Activities:** wading pool, beach, boat dock, scuba diving, snorkeling, fishing. *Fee:* boats, scuba & snorkeling equipment. **Guest Services:** valet laundry. **Cards:** AE, MC, VI.

HOTEL PRESIDENTE INTER-CONTINENTAL COZUMEL

◆◆◆ ◆◆◆ *Resort*   ((987)2-0322

12/22-1/1	$280	XP $35
1/2-4/15	$175	XP $35
12/1-12/21 & 4/16-11/30	$130	XP $35

Location: 6.5 km s of San Miguel, on beach road; at La Caleta Yacht Basin. Costa Residencial S/N 77600. Fax: 987/2-1360. **Facility:** Spacious tropically landscaped grounds. Private balcony or terrace. Most rooms with ocean view. Spectacular beach areas. Architecture is reminiscent of a Mayan palace deep in the Yucatan jungle. 253 units. 2 two-bedroom units and 2 units with kitchen. Some suites. *Bath:* combo or shower only. 2-5 stories, interior/exterior corridors. **Terms:** F18; 3 day cancellation notice-fee imposed. **Amenities:** honor bars, hair dryers. *Some:* CD players, safes, irons. **Leisure Activities:** whirlpool, beach, swimming, boat dock, scuba diving, snorkeling, fishing, 2 lighted tennis courts, children's program in season, recreation program, social program, playground, exercise room. *Fee:* boats, windsurfing, scuba & snorkeling equipment, charter fishing. **Guest Services:** [AP] meal plan available, gift shop, valet laundry. *Fee:* massage. **Business Services:** conference facilities. *Fee:* PC, fax. **Cards:** AE, DI, MC, VI.

SOME UNITS

SCUBA CLUB COZUMEL

◆◆◆ *Motor Inn*   (987/2-1800

12/25-5/1	$402	XP $55
12/1-12/24 & 5/2-11/30	$250-$360	XP $40

Location: 1.5 km s of San Miguel on beach road. (PO Box 289, 77600). **Facility:** Oceanfront property with local rustic decor. Caters to divers. Individually decorated rooms, some with ceiling fans. Security guard on premises. 61 units. *Bath:* shower only. 2 stories (no elevator), exterior corridors. **Terms:** F10; 30 day cancellation notice, package plans. **Amenities:** no TVs, dual phone lines. **Leisure Activities:** beach, swimming, boat dock, scuba diving, snorkeling. *Fee:* scuba & snorkeling equipment, charter fishing, bicycles. **Guest Services:** [AP] & [BP] meal plans available. *Fee:* area transportation. **Cards:** MC, VI.

FEE

WHERE TO DINE

ARRECIFE

◆◆◆ ◆◆◆ *Continental*   (987/2-0322
D $18-$40

Location: 6.5 km s of San Miguel, on beach road; at La Caleta Yacht Basin; in Hotel Presidente InterContinental Cozumel. 6.5 km Carretera San Miguel 77600. **Hours:** 6 pm-11 pm. **Reservations:** suggested. **Features:** casual dress; cocktails & lounge; entertainment; valet parking. Overlooking colorful Caribbean. Classic selections artistically presented and enhanced with regional ingredients. Impeccable service includes tableside preparations. **Cards:** AE, DI, MC, VI.

CARLOS 'N CHARLIE'S & JIMMY KITCHEN

◆ *American*   (987/2-0191
D $8-$12

Location: On Ocean Promenade. Ave Rafael E Melgar 77600. **Hours:** 10 am-1:30 am. Closed: 1/1, 12/24. **Features:** No A/C; casual dress; cocktails & lounge; a la carte. Youthful, high-spirited, high-energy mecca usually has lines at peak hours. On second floor, overlooking Coz' main pier and promenade. **Cards:** AE, MC, VI.

RESTAURANT ACUARIO

◆◆ ◆◆ *Seafood*   (987/2-1097
L $10-$20   D $10-$20

Location: 0.5 km s of San Miguel, on beach road. Rafael Melgar Sur at Ave 77600. **Hours:** 2 pm-11:30 pm. **Features:** casual dress; cocktails & lounge; a la carte. Converted aquarium with large display of fish in the area. Beach club 10 am-6 pm, offers dining, pool and beach. A good selection of Regional dishes complimented with a focused wine list. **Cards:** AE, CB, MC, VI.

ISLA MUJERES, QUINTANA ROO (G-12)

Isla Mujeres (EES-lah moo-HEH-rehs), about 5 miles long and only half a mile wide, lies in the Caribbean Sea about 5 miles off the easternmost tip of the Yucatán Peninsula. Single male travelers anticipating their dreams to be realized on the "Island of Women" might be disappointed to find its male-female ratio rather balanced. Gold-seeking Spanish explorers led by Francisco Hernández de Córdoba accidentally discovered Isla Mujeres in 1517 after a storm blew their expedition off course. The origin of the name is attributed to two legends. One maintains that seafaring buccaneers used the island as a hideaway for their female captives; more likely, however, is that it refers to the terra-cotta female images, decorated with fruit and flower adornments, that were discovered by the Spaniards.

Pirates and smugglers took advantage of the island's isolation. After their era passed, Isla Mujeres became just another drowsy Caribbean fishing village. During the 1960s beach bums and hippies ambled over from the mainland, taken in by Isla's laid-back atmosphere and languid beaches. More recently it has experienced tourist spillover from neighboring Cancún, but Isla's small size prevents the intensive development that characterizes the bigger resort.

More typically Yucatecan than either Cancún or Cozumel, Isla Mujeres also has a greater natural beauty. Flat, sandy beaches mark the northern end; rocky bluffs and submerged coral reefs the southern. The island has a relaxed pace and a well-deserved reputation for snorkeling.

THE INFORMED TRAVELER

Isla Mujeres is accessible by ferry or boat from mainland Puerto Juárez (passengers only) or Punta Sam (passengers and/or vehicles), and from the piers at Playa Linda and Playa Langosta on Cancún Island. There are approximate hourly departures in each direction between Puerto Juárez and Isla Mujeres. Schedules are posted at the passenger ferry dock but are subject to change or delay; double check when the last ferry leaves Isla Mujeres for Puerto Juárez (usually around 6 p.m.).

Laid-back Isla Mujeres can easily be explored in an afternoon.   © John Neubauer

Enclosed, air-conditioned passenger vessels hold about 30 occupants and make the trip in about 20 minutes; one-way fare is about $2.20. The fare is paid after you board. Organized cruise excursions from Cancún usually sail once a day and cost considerably more. The car ferry from Punta Sam operates several times daily, barring bad weather; again, double check the schedule. For additional information about ferry service, *see "Sightseeing" under Cancún, page 97.*

There is no reason to bring a car onto the island for a day trip. If you're basing a vacation in Isla Mujeres and have several pieces of luggage, taxis line up by the two town docks for the short ride to the hotels concentrated in town and scattered along the beaches. The fare shouldn't be more than a dollar or two. Taxis also can be hired (at an hourly rate) for a tour of the island or to reach beaches at the southern end. A municipal bus travels from the Posada del Mar Hotel on Avenida Rueda Medina south to Playa Lancheros; the fare is inexpensive. The state tourist office *(see below)* can provide bus schedules.

Renting a "moto," the local term for mopeds, or an electric golf cart is an easy way to get around, and there are several places in town that rent both (many of the hotels also rent golf carts). Keep in mind, however, that the rental fee does not include insurance. Some hotels also rent bicycles, which cost considerably less.

The "downtown" section of Isla Mujeres occupies its northern end. Within a compact area 10 blocks long and several blocks wide are the ferry docks and most of the hotels, restaurants and shops. The waterfront street, referred to locally as the *malecón,* is **Avenida Rueda Medina**. It also runs the length of the island. In town, the principal thoroughfares are north-south avenidas Guerrero and Hidalgo, and east-west avenidas Madero and Morelos. There is little traffic on these narrow, one-way streets, and the area is pedestrian-friendly. City hall, the police station, a supermarket, a movie theater and a *farmacia* (pharmacy) are all on Avenida Hidalgo.

The state tourist office is on the second floor of Plaza Isla Mujeres, at the north end of Avenida Juárez between Lopez Mateos and Matamoros. It is open Mon.-Fri. 9-2:30 and 7-9 p.m.; phone (987) 7-0316. *Islander,* a monthly magazine available at hotels, also provides tourist information. A Cruz Roja (Red Cross) clinic is about 5 kilometers (3 miles) south of town, just north of the Hacienda Mundaca; phone (987) 7-0280. Parker International has information about island condos and villas catering to budget-minded travelers; phone (800) 400-3333 from the United States.

WHAT TO DO ON THE ISLAND

The most popular beach is **Playa Norte**, located at the northern edge of town. This stretch used to be called Playa Cocos before Hurricane Gilbert destroyed most of its namesake coconut palms in 1988. The shallow, placid waters are good for swimming or wading; there are, however, no lifeguards on duty. The wide beach is lined with thatched-roof *palapas* selling cold drinks. Umbrellas, chairs, jet-skis, sailboards, three-wheeled water "trikes" and other equipment can be rented. **Note:** Topless sunbathers are likely to be part of the landscape at this beach.

Other options are **Playa Paraíso**, **Playa Lancheros** and **Playa Garrafón**, all toward the opposite end of the island on the western (leeward) side (the surf is rougher along Isla's eastern coastline, which faces the open Caribbean). Small stalls at these beaches sell souvenirs and T-shirts. Near Playa Lancheros is a fenced-in pen containing tame sea turtles and harmless nurse sharks; the latter, unlike most of their relatives, tolerate humans swimming in their midst. Swimmers used to ride on the backs of the turtles, but they are now strictly protected and the practice is no longer permitted.

Just south of the ferry docks is a Mexican naval base (off-limits to visitors). At the island's midpoint a bridge across the lagoon leads to **Isla del Tesoro** (Treasure Island), site of a theme park with a reconstructed fort and galleon, a large *palapa* sheltering a restaurant and bar, and an open-air theater. Day and evening boat tours to Treasure Island can be arranged.

Near the southern end of **Laguna Makax**—once believed to have been an anchoring point for pirate ships—a fork off Avenida Rueda Medina leads to a turtle sanctuary dedicated to the preservation of native sea turtles. Separate pools hold several species of hatchlings and young turtles. The facility also sponsors a tag-and-release program to encourage the protection of nesting sea turtles on Isla Mujeres. Guided tours are available. Open daily 9-5. Admission is charged.

At the very southern tip of the island, on a bluff overlooking the sea, once stood the reconstructed remains of a Maya temple believed to have been built in honor of the fertility goddess Ixchel. Gilbert reduced it to a pile of stones, although restoration efforts are in progress. Archeologists believe that the Maya, en route to Cozumel on pilgrimages to worship Ixchel, stopped over at Isla Mujeres. A 30-foot-tall lighthouse nearby was left standing; if you ask (in Spanish), the keeper may let you climb to the top. A tip is appreciated.

Branching east off Rueda Medina, a paved road follows the eastern edge of the island back toward town. One justification for bringing a car to Isla Mujeres is to drive this route, stopping at one of the pull-offs for a view of the open sea.

Offshore coral reefs and **Cueva de los Tiburones Durmientes** (Cave of the Sleeping Sharks) attract scuba divers. The underwater cave, about 5 kilometers (3 miles) northeast of Isla Mujeres,

was discovered in the late 1960s. A constant flow of currents passes through the cavern, allowing sharks to remain stationary—their primitive breathing system normally requires them to move constantly in order to receive oxygen. Despite this apparent narcotized state, brave souls must descend 150 feet or more to see the sharks, and there is no guarantee they will be around. **Manchones Reef**, just off the island's southern tip, is also good for diving and snorkeling.

The summer months of June, July and August, when the water is calm, are best for diving. The **Bahía Dive Shop**, on Avenida Rueda Medina across from the car ferry dock, offers certification classes, knowledgeable instructors and a full range of dive and snorkel equipment for rent; phone (987) 7-0340. The shop also can arrange deep-sea and offshore fishing excursions. **Mexico Divers** (Buzos de México), a block from the passenger ferry dock at avenidas Rueda Medina and Madero, also offers certified instruction, organizes snorkeling and fishing trips, and rents equipment; phone (987) 7-0131.

Cooperativa Isla Mujeres (Boatmen's Cooperative), on Avenida Rueda Medina at the waterfront (next to Mexico Divers), handles island tours, sport fishing trips and excursions to Isla Contoy *(see attraction listing)*. Some outings require a minimum number of passengers; phone (987) 7-0274. Billfish (swordfish and marlin) are a good possibility in April and May; during the rest of the year catches include barracuda, grouper and red snapper.

SHOPPING, DINING AND NIGHTLIFE

As the island embraces increased tourism, more and more craft shops are opening. Although prices are decidedly lower than in Cancún, bargaining is still the best way to come out ahead. Wood carvings, ceramic and clay figurines, silver items, pottery, handmade clothing, T-shirts, and decorative objects made of sea and snail shells are among the possible purchases. Several small shops are along Rueda Medina near the passenger ferry dock. **Van Cleef & Arpels**, at avenidas Juárez and Morelos, sells jewelry.

One of the nicest restaurants on the island is **Zacil-Ha**, in the Hotel Na Balam on Calle Zazil (at Playa Norte). The seafood dishes are well-prepared, and diners have a choice of eating indoors or in an open-air garden setting. **Pizza Rolandi**, on Avenida Hidalgo between avenidas Madero and Abasolo, is a reliable chain that features pizza, calzones and pasta dishes along with fish. There are branches in Cancún and Cozumel as well. For something out of the ordinary, stop by the **Mercado Municipal** (Municipal Market), Avenida Guerrero next to the post office, and sample the fare at one of the cooking stalls.

Isla Mujeres is not known for frenetic night-life, which suits most visitors just fine. The *palapas* along Playa Norte are a great place for sunset-watching. Most of the restaurant bars have a late afternoon happy hour, and a few offer live music and dancing.

What To See

EL GARRAFON NATIONAL PARK is at the southern tip of the island off Avenida Rueda Medina. It features exceptionally clear water and schools of gaudily colored, very tame fish. Sadly, the coral reefs have largely been killed by both Hurricane Gilbert and the dropped anchors of tour boats. The park also is known for its resident turtles. Locker rooms and showers are available, and there are souvenir shops and food stands. Arrive early (before 10 a.m.) if you want to avoid the Cancún crowds. Taxis provide transportation to and from town. Open daily 8-5. Admission is charged.

HACIENDA MUNDACA is east off Avenida Rueda Medina and across from the entrance to Playa Lancheros. A stone archway is practically all that's left of the former estate built by 19th-century pirate and slave runner Fermín Mundaca. Legend has it that Mundaca chose Isla Mujeres as a hideaway and built the hacienda for La Trigueña (The Brunette), an 18-year-old girl with whom he had fallen in love. When she married a local man, Mundaca was inconsolable. His grave, in the municipal cemetery at the northern end of the island, is marked with the inscription "As you are I was, as I am you will be." A dirt footpath leads to the ruins. Insect repellent is highly advised. Free.

ISLA CONTOY is an uninhabited island about 32 kilometers (20 miles) north of Isla Mujeres and the site of **Isla Contoy National Park**, a wildlife reserve and bird sanctuary. Four miles long and only 65 feet wide at its narrowest point, the tiny islet is blanketed with lush vegetation and uninhabited except for park guards and some 70 species of birds, including pelicans, egrets, cormorants and flamingos. There are nature trails and a small museum. A sunken pirate ship graveyard is visible in the shallow waters just south of Contoy.

Note: Although Isla Contoy has been closed to visitors in the past due to the negative environmental effects of tourism, day-trip excursions to the island currently depart from Isla Mujeres. Most tour boats carry up to 15 passengers and supply life jackets, snorkeling equipment and lunch. Activities include birdwatching, snorkeling, trolling for fish and hiking on the island. For schedule and fare information contact the La Isleña travel agency, on Avenida Morelos between avenidas Medina Rueda and Juárez; phone (987) 7-0578.

Where To Stay

HOTEL NA BALAM

♦♦♦ Motor Inn   (987/7-0279

All Year $100-$134   XP $10
Location: North point of island; on the beach. Calle Zazil Ha 118 77400. Fax: 987/7-0446. **Facility:** Nestled in a palm shrouded idyllic island setting. Guest rooms located beneath thatched top dwellings with hammocks on balcony or terrace. Reminiscent of Robinson Carruso, with some creature comforts. 31 units. Some suites ($130-$154) and whirlpool units. *Bath:* shower only. 2 stories, exterior corridors. **Terms:** F12; 14 day cancellation notice. **Amenities:** no TVs, safes. **Leisure Activities:** beach, swimming, scuba diving, snorkeling, fishing. *Fee:* charter fishing. **Guest Services:** valet laundry. **Cards:** AE, MC, VI.

(icons)

HOTEL PERLA DEL CARIBE

♦♦♦ Hotel   (987/7-0444

All Year $78-$89   XP $12
Location: Just n of water taxi landing pier. Ave Francisco I Madero #10 70011. Fax: 987/70-011. **Facility:** Some balcony rooms with view of Caribbean. Short walk to public beach. All rooms with two double beds. Most rooms with ceiling fan. 91 units. *Bath:* shower only. 2 stories, interior/exterior corridors. **Amenities:** no TVs. **Cards:** AE, MC, VI.

(icons)

IZAMAL, YUCATAN (G-11)

Izamal (ee-sah-MAHL) is about 74 kilometers (46 miles) east of Mérida via two-lane Mex. 180. From Mérida, watch for the signed turnoff that says "Yuc. 53"; from Cancún, the signed turnoff from toll highway Mex. 180-D says "Izamal" and also merges into Yuc. 53. The narrow, two-lane road, which has no shoulders and occasional potholes, passes through thick green scrubland interspersed with fields of spiky, blue-green agave plants.

Between the 180-D turnoff and Izamal—a distance of about 18 kilometers (11 miles)—are three small villages: Xanaba, Sudzal and Cuauhtémoc. Cobbled *topes* (speed bumps) force vehicles to slow to a crawl when entering each one, as do the wandering dogs, chickens, turkeys and children. Xanaba has a large yellow church with white trim opposite its small central plaza. In Sudzal and Cuauhtémoc you'll see typical Maya houses—thatch-roofed huts with open doorways, dirt floors and walls constructed of upright wooden stakes—surrounded by banana trees and other tropical vegetation. This is rural life at its most basic, a world away from Cancún's glitter and Mérida's big-city bustle.

Izamal itself, although larger, is no less down to earth; dilapidated houses and commercial buildings attest to the poverty that most Yucatecans endure. Downtown clusters around the small central plaza, shaded by trees, equipped with wrought-iron benches and dominated by

Mexico's largest Franciscan monastery *(see attraction listing)*. A significant pre-Columbian political and religious center, the town developed around this church. Diego de Landa, the Spanish bishop responsible for the annihilation of most of the Maya civilization's *codices* (picture books) and documents, deliberately chose Izamal as the seat of his diocese because it was a religious center of the Maya-speaking tribe known as the Itzae.

Izamal was a center of commerce and trade during the Spanish colonial period. When Mérida took over as the Yucatán's chief city, it slipped into obscurity. One recent momentous event in this slow-paced town was a 1993 visit by Pope John Paul II. The mustard-colored government buildings surrounding the central plaza give it the nickname "Ciudad Amarillo" (Yellow City). One way to view the colonial-era architecture is by horse-drawn carriage; rides can be arranged at the plaza, where the guides congregate.

There are two ways to return to Mex. 180: Backtrack on Yuc. 53, or take the local road to the small town of Hoctún (which is on Mex. 180). The latter route, also narrow and two-lane, passes through Citilcum and Kimbila en route; all three villages are representative of the rural Yucatán countryside. If you're doing the driving, make certain you're back on Mex. 180 before dark.

Note: Because of the slow-paced driving conditions and the fact that it's easy to lose your orientation in Izamal—small as it is—take this trip with a hired taxi driver or guide. Drivers can be hired in Mérida (ask at your hotel), or check with one of the city's tour operators. Another option is to take an all-day guided rail tour. A train leaves every Sunday around 8:30 a.m. from the Mérida train station, at calles 55 and 48. A horse-drawn carriage ride, visits to the Franciscan Monastery and Kinich Kakmo pyramid, lunch and a folkloric ballet performance in Izamal are included. The cost is around $18 per person. Mérida travel agencies can provide reservation and trip information, or check with your hotel.

FRANCISCAN MONASTERY was originally dedicated to St. Anthony of Padua and was later known as the Church of Our Lady of Izamal. It was completed in 1561 atop a Maya pyramid. In 1618, monks added the monastery and an arcade. The atrium of this enormous church is reputed to be second in size to that of St. Peter's Basilica in Rome. The church's simple, mustard-colored exterior contrasts with the rough-hewn, fortresslike monastery compound; the original access ramps and stairways built by the Maya remain.

PIRAMIDE KINICH KAKMO (Kinich Kakmo Pyramid), a few blocks north of the central plaza, was once the seat of the Royal Court of the Itzae civilization. In the Maya language, its name means "Solar-Faced Macaw of Fire." Kinich Kakmo is one of Mexico's largest pyramids—some 115 feet high and almost 660 feet wide. Of its impressive bulk Spanish bishop Diego de Landa is said to have observed, "Among those pyramids, so high and amazing, there is one that frightens me." The structure also is notable for the fact that it sits in the middle of town; there are houses just across the street. A rough, cobbled exterior makes the pyramid unsafe to climb, however. One of the four sides remains unexcavated and is covered with a thick green matting of tangled underbrush.

MERIDA, YUCATAN (G-11)

Capital of the state of Yucatán and metropolis of the Yucatán Peninsula, Mérida (MEH-ree-dah) fits the description of a "colonial city" but somehow seems different from other places in Mexico. It is a peculiar mixture of the modern and the timeless, presenting the visitor with images both comfortably familiar and exotically foreign.

Mérida was founded in 1542 by Francisco de Montejo (the son of Montejo the Elder) at the site of T'ho, an ancient Maya city. The crumbling temples and palaces at the site were razed to make way for cathedrals, ornate mansions and parks, many of which survive to this day. Over time Mérida became the commercial, governmental and religious center of the Yucatán, with the Spaniards living in luxury made possible by Indian toil.

Mérida became even wealthier in the last half of the 19th century because of a tough, thorny plant. Henequén, a member of the agave family, thrived in the rocky soil and seasonally dry conditions prevalent in the northern Yucatán. The fibrous leaves were made into a variety of products, including twine, burlap sacks, furniture stuffing and hammocks. Although sophisticated machinery now processes, weaves and dyes henequén fibers, in the heyday of the large haciendas (plantations) Indian field workers manipulated this intractable plant by hand.

By World War I the city claimed more millionaires per capita than any other in the world as a result of the monopoly on sisal fiber, the valuable henequén extract. The product was named after the port town of Sisal, 50 kilometers (31 miles) northwest of Mérida, from where it was once shipped.

Although plantation barons were swimming in the revenue generated by this profitable export, they were an island unto themselves. The Yucatán Peninsula was still considered Mexico's mosquito-ridden backwater, and a lack of road and rail access isolated it as well. As a result, privileged Meridanos looked to Europe as their model for cultural sophistication. Fueled by henequén's "green gold," they built imposing, Moorish- and rococo-style mansions with arched doorways and marbled tile interiors. These buildings line **Paseo Montejo**, Mérida's wide showcase boulevard, and give the city its air of graceful elegance.

The Yucatán's commercial hub and largest city has a population estimated at more than 800,000. The henequén haciendas are long abandoned (some have been turned into museums). As in other large Mexican cities, tourism is becoming a leading industry. Mérida's tropical ambience and variety of cultural offerings make it an established destination among European travelers. It also is the most convenient base from which to explore nearby archeological ruins or the Yucatán's northern and western coasts.

PLANNING YOUR STAY

Many Yucatán travelers bypass Mérida in favor of Cancún and the Mexican Caribbean coast, but the city is a fascinating travel destination in its own right. There's plenty to do: visiting the museums and public buildings that cluster around Plaza de la Independencia; wandering through the bustling market district; taking a horse-drawn carriage ride down Paseo Montejo; sampling authentic Yucatecan cuisine at local restaurants; and attending one of the numerous free evening concerts or folkloric shows held at the downtown plazas.

Try to plan a visit around Sunday, when Mérida's charm becomes much more evident. For "Mérida en Domingo" (Mérida on Sunday), the streets surrounding Plaza de la Independencia are closed to traffic. Mexican families dressed in their Sunday best make for a great people-watching promenade as they stroll among the pushcart vendors selling *tortas* (sandwiches), corn on the cob and fruit drinks. Handicraft markets and food stalls set up shop around the plaza and also in Hidalgo Park and Santa Lucía Park.

Sunday also is the high point of Mérida's excellent public events program. In the late morning the city police orchestra performs typical Yucatecan music in **Santa Lucía Park**, on Calle 60 about 3 blocks north of Plaza de la Independencia. Groups of musicians in front of the **Palacio del Gobierno** (Government Palace), on Plaza de la Independencia, play everything from classical to jazz. A folkloric ballet interpretation of a Yucatecan wedding celebration is enacted at the **Palacio Municipal** (City Hall), on the west side of Plaza de la Independencia. Marimba music percolates at **Hidalgo Park** (also called Cepeda Peraza Park), a block northeast of the main plaza at calles 59 and 60.

By all means visit the nearby ruins of **Chichén Itzá** and **Uxmal;** and depending on your level of interest, explore the sites of **Kabah, Sayil, Labná** and **Xlapak** as well *(see Uxmal listing)*. If traveling to either Chichén Itzá or Uxmal, you may want to stay overnight in order to avoid both crowds and soaring midday temperatures, and take time to fully appreciate these fascinating legacies of Maya civilization. Other sites in this archeologically rich region—among

Traditionally dressed Meridanos perform the Belt Dance.   ©Chris Sharp

them **Mayapán** and **Dzibilchaltún**—are easy day trips from Mérida.

Progreso is the closest coastal resort to Mérida. The beaches are prettier at Cancún, Isla Mujeres, Cozumel and other spots along the Quintana Roo coast, but if you won't be visiting the Cancún area and would still like to spend a day at the beach, consider Progreso. Another day trip possibility is **Celestún**, a bird sanctuary on the gulf coast west of Mérida. A secluded estuary edged by mangrove thickets and shallow sandbars harbors many kinds of resident waterfowl, notably pale pink flamingos, and also is visited by migrating bird species.

Guided tour operators abound in Mérida, and many of them offer the same destinations with differing forms of conveyance (from economical buses to luxurious private vehicles). City tours last a couple of hours and take in the public buildings around the main plaza, Paseo Montejo, and the Museum of Anthropology and History. Popular day trips travel to Chichén Itzá or Uxmal, with admission to the ruins, lunch, a guide and often a swim at a hotel pool included in the price.

If you're unfamiliar with the area and would rather leave such details as itinerary and transportation to others, a guided tour may be well worth the expense. **Mayaland Tours** has offices in the Hotel Casa del Balam and the Hotel Fiesta Americana Mérida; phone (99) 24-6290 or 25-0621, respectively.

Weatherwise, Mérida experiences sultry heat most of the year. April through September are quite hot and humid, and in May temperatures can soar above 100 degrees. If you're visiting during one of these months, sightsee in the morning, take it easy in the afternoon and venture out again in the evening, when it cools down somewhat. December through February have the most pleasant temperatures and lower humidity. The rainy season is June through September, but precipitation isn't usually heavy or persistent enough to affect travel plans. The greatest chance for hurricanes or other stormy weather is in September and October.

The city is very crowded in July and August, when many Mexican families go on vacation; if that's when you'll be there as well, make hotel reservations in advance.

THE INFORMED TRAVELER

Mérida International Airport is off Avenida Benito Juárez, also called Avenida Itzáes (Mex. 180), about 7 kilometers (4 miles) southwest of the downtown core. Aeroméxico, phone (99) 20-1299, and Continental, phone (99) 26-3100, offer direct flights from U.S. cities. Mexicana, phone (99) 46-1332, and the Mexicana subsidiary Aerocaribe, phone (99) 28-6790, offer connecting flights from various destinations in the Yucatán, including Cancún, Cozumel and Chetu-

mal, as well as from Mexico City. For additional information about airlines see "Arriving by Air," page 53.

City bus #79 (designated "Aviación") takes airport passengers to the downtown area but is unreliable; if you're carrying any amount of luggage it's more convenient to take a taxi. Colectivo (group) minivans transport passengers from the airport to downtown hotels for around $6 per person; taxi fare should be around $10 between the airport and hotels.

The main bus terminal, **Central Camionera**, is at Calle 69 between calles 68 and 70, about 7 blocks southwest of Plaza de la Independencia. First-class buses travel frequently to and from Chichén Itzá, Uxmal, Cancún and points south along the Cancún-Tulum Corridor. "Deluxe" service between Mérida and Cancún is offered by Super Expresso. There are several departures daily from a terminal on Calle 60, across from the Hotel Fiesta Americana Mérida; phone (99) 25-0910. For additional information about buses see "Bus Service," page 63.

Sitios (taxi stands) are located in the vicinity of Plaza de la Independencia, or use a cab affiliated with your hotel. Rates to in-town destinations are usually fixed; ask what the fare is before getting in the cab. Colectivo taxis (usually white Volkswagen minivans) also take passengers to various city destinations on a first-come, first-serve basis; look for these around Plaza de la Independencia.

The state tourist information center is in the **Teatro Peón Contreras** (Péon Contreras Theater), on Calle 60 between calles 57 and 59. The office is open daily 8-8; phone (99) 24-9290 (English spoken). There also are tourist information booths at the airport and on Calle 62 next to the Palacio Municipal (City Hall). The publication Yucatán Today, available at the airport and most hotels, has detailed information about city and state attractions, as well as maps.

Mérida has a tourist police force who patrol on foot and on motorcycle in the downtown core and also in the hotel zone, the area along Avenida Colón between Paseo Montejo and Calle 60. Officers wear white-and-brown uniforms and a sleeve patch that says "Policia Turística." To register a complaint with the Consumer Protection Agency (Procuraduría del Consumidor), phone (99) 23-4927. If you lose your tourist permit, contact the Mexican Immigration Office; phone (99) 28-5823. In case of medical emergency, contact the Red Cross (Cruz Roja); phone (99) 24-9813. To contact the Green Angels, phone (99) 83-1184.

Currency exchange is most conveniently expedited at your hotel front desk, as the rates offered by hotels, banks and casas de cambio (currency exchange offices) do not differ greatly. There's an exchange office next to the Hotel Fiesta Americana Mérida.

APPROACHES

By car, the main approach from the east is Mex. 180, which becomes east-west Calle 65 within the city limits. To get to the downtown hotel zone (where such major hotels as the Hyatt and the Fiesta Americana are located), take Calle 65 west to north-south Calle 60 and turn right.

Mex. 180 also approaches Mérida from the southwest via Campeche. Mex. 261 approaches from the south, joining Mex. 180 at the town of Umán, just south of the city limits. North of downtown, the northern extension of Calle 60 continues north as Mex. 261 to Progreso on the gulf coast.

A loop road, the Anillo Periférico, encircles Mérida, offering access to regional destinations without having to negotiate the downtown area. It can be confusing, however, unless you're familiar with the exits. If you're driving, the most direct way out of the city from the Paseo Montejo/hotel zone area is to take east-west Avenida Colón west to Avenida Itzaes, a major north-south thoroughfare on the west side of town. Turn left (south); you'll pass Centenario Park and the turnoff to the airport before reaching the Anillo Periférico—a distance of about 12 kilometers (7 miles). (**Note:** Avenida Itzaes changes names twice without warning—to Avenida Internacional and then to Avenida Benito Juárez—as it proceeds south. Don't get sidetracked by the name changes; stay on the avenue.)

At the periférico junction there are signs for Cancún (Mex. 180 east), Progreso (Mex. 261 north) and Campeche (Mex. 180 southwest). To head south toward Uxmal and nearby archeological sites, continue south a mile or two on Avenida Itzaes/Internacional/Juárez to Umán. Watch for signs saying "To Campeche via Uxmal on Mex. 261," "Zona Arqueologia Uxmal" and "Ruta Puuc." Follow these signs to access Mex. 261 south.

To head east toward Cancún, turn left onto the periférico at the sign that says "Cancún/Motul." Take this four-lane divided highway about 15 kilometers (9 miles) to the Mex. 180/Cancún exit. From this point, two-lane Mex. 180 runs about 48 kilometers (30 miles) east to the town of Hoctún. At Km marker 66, Mex. 180 divides. The two-lane "libre" (free) road continues east toward the town of Kantunil, and the four-lane divided Mérida-Cancún "cuota" (toll) highway begins.

CITY LAYOUT

Mérida has long been known as the "White City." Visual evidence does not automatically bear the name out (it could be the impression created by strong sunlight reflecting off the marble and stone surfaces of white buildings), but one thing is certain: The downtown core (often called *el centro*) is compact, dense and an assault on the senses.

Downtown streets are laid out in a standard grid pattern radiating from the central plaza. They are numbered rather than named; even-numbered streets (calles) run north-south, odd-numbered streets run east-west. They are lined with many beautiful old buildings, and many more shabby ones. Most of these streets are narrow and one way. Vespa motor scooters and beat-up bikes abound, and traffic is heavy and slow. Elsewhere in the city thoroughfares are not well signed and change names without warning. They also can twist and turn confusingly, so know where you're going.

Note: In the *centro*, where buildings sit close together and sidewalks are very narrow, exhaust spewed by green city buses is a near-constant irritant. This central area is roughly bounded by Calle 49 on the north, Calle 67 on the south, Calle 52 on the east and Calle 66 on the west.

Fortunately Mérida also is a city of plazas, bursting with royal poinciana trees and other tropical greenery, that are oases of relative tranquility amid the street noise and traffic jams. **Plaza de la Independencia**, the main plaza, is bounded east and west by calles 60 and 62 and north and south by calles 61 and 63.

A social gathering place, Plaza de la Independencia is busy day and night. Men relax under the pruned branches of laurel trees in the morning; matriarchs keep an eye on groups of children at lunchtime; everyone assembles in the evening to stroll, chat or listen to music. Here and at other city plazas you'll see *confidenciales*, S-shaped white stone benches that allow two people to face each other while talking. On the streets bordering the plaza stand the cathedral and the aristocratic facades of government buildings.

A good way to experience the local atmosphere is to stroll up and down **Calle 60**, a busy street filled with restaurants, handicraft shops selling clothing, jewelry and trinkets, and several fine examples of colonial architecture. From the northeast corner of Plaza de la Independencia, walk north. In the next block is cozy little **Hidalgo Park**, where there are several outdoor restaurants. At the corner of calles 60 and 59 is the **Iglesia de Jesús**, or El Tercer Orden (Church of the Third Order), built by the Jesuits in 1618 and one of Mérida's oldest buildings. The interior contains beautiful frescoes and chandeliers. At the corner of calles 60 and 57 is the imposing, Italianate **Teatro Peón Contreras** (Peón Contreras Theater); climb the marble steps and wander around inside. Across Calle 60 is the Moorish-style **University of the Yucatán;** both the theater and the university play a major role in the city's cultural life.

Mérida's "show street" is four-lane **Paseo Montejo**, which begins at Calle 47, about 7 blocks northeast of the main plaza. This is the city's scaled-down version of Paris' Champs-Elysées. Broad and tree-lined, it also has much wider sidewalks than you'll encounter in other parts of the city, a relief from the cramped spaces of the *centro*. Montejo runs north for 10 blocks past hotels, shops, sidewalk cafés and several large, ornate 19th-century mansions. It culminates at the **Monumento a la Patria** (Monument to Patriotism), a grouping of sculptures within a traffic circle that depict various stages of Mexican history.

Mérida's streets were originally meant to accommodate *calesas* (horse-drawn carriages). Sunday is the best day to take a tour. Most of the carriages stick to regular routes, such as up and down Paseo Montejo or around Centenario Park. An hour's ride should cost from $10 to $15; determine the fare before you set out. Arrangements can usually be made in the vicinity of Plaza de la Independencia, or a *calesa* can be hailed on the street.

SHOPPING

Shopping is serious business in Mérida, where a multitude of goods are offered for sale. The city is particularly known for hammocks *(hamacas)*, clothing (especially the men's shirt called a *guayabera)*, and Panama hats, or *jipis* (HEE-pee).

The market district spreads across several blocks and encompasses hundreds of shops and open-air stalls. Roughly, the area extends from calles 63 to 69 north-south and from calles 54 to 62 east-west (the area just southeast of Plaza de la Independencia). The **Mercado Municipal** (Municipal Market), centered at calles 65 and 56, is a dizzying hodgepodge of fruit, vegetables, live chickens, tortilla stands, spices and candy, all presided over by *huipil*-clad *señoras* who have brought their wares from the small Maya villages around Mérida. Among the items for sale are baskets, pottery, gold earrings, gold and silver filigree jewelry, and pieces of amber-colored incense.

Native handicrafts from all over Mexico, but particularly the Yucatán region, are in a separate building at calles 56 and 67. Look for table mats, purses, leather goods, hammocks, piñatas, clothing, ceramics and *huaraches* (sandals with leather straps and soles made from old tires). Fixed prices prevail at many shops, but you can bargain at some of the market stalls and with street vendors. **Note:** Haggling in this crowded, noisy atmosphere is not for everyone. Although many vendors speak English, a knowledge of Spanish would be very handy for asking specific questions about merchandise. If you're uncomfortable around high-pressure sales tactics, stick to the fixed-price shops.

Hammocks—often used in the rural Yucatán in place of beds—are fashioned from various materials and come in several sizes. To judge the proper size, hold one end of the hammock even with the top of your head. Let the other end drop—if it reaches the floor and then some, it's probably big enough. Those made from cotton tend to be the most durable. Ask for a demonstration; loosely woven hammocks are an indication of poor quality.

Street vendors will assail prospective hammock purchasers, but their low prices may also indicate low quality. Shops specializing in hammocks offer a greater selection. Wherever you buy a hammock, check the workmanship carefully, since a poorly made one will wear out quickly.

The *guayabera*, a loosely worn, lightweight cotton shirt, is about as formal as men's clothing gets in sweltering Mérida. Upper-class Yucatecans in the late 19th century bought them during trips to Cuba. The garment is worn by businessmen and local politicians instead of a shirt and tie. Traditionally it is white, with a bit of colored embroidery around the front buttons, and has four pockets—two at the chest and two at the waist. **Guayaberas Jack**, on Calle 59, is one of the few city factories that still produces custom-made shirts.

Just as traditional as the *guayabera* is the *huipil*, a white cotton dress with a squared neck that often is edged with embroidered flowers. A similar but longer and more elaborate garment is the *terno*. Many women who live in rural areas still wear *huipils*. Handmade garments have largely been supplanted by machine-made ones, although the latter are usually of good quality.

A jauntily positioned *jipi* provides an effective screen against the hot Yucatán sun. The hats are made in several small towns in neighboring Campeche; residents store palm fronds in damp basements until they become soft and pliable, then weave them. Panama hats cost anywhere from about $6 to more than $60; the price is determined by the closeness of the weave and the quality of the fibers (coarse to fine). A good-quality, closely woven hat should bounce back into shape even after being folded into a suitcase or rolled up and stuck in a pocket.

Mexican markets are known for their exotica, and Mérida is no exception; here you can buy live "jeweled" beetle pins called *maquech* (ma-KETCH). The insects are displayed in glass bowls along with a few pieces of wood (their food). Bits of multicolored glass are glued to their backs, and the beetle is attached to a gold chain which hooks to a safety pin. If you do choose to indulge in a live lapel ornament, find another buyer before you leave the country; U.S. customs won't allow it across the border.

DINING AND NIGHTLIFE

Restaurants in Mérida offer Middle Eastern and Italian cuisine, fresh seafood, traditional Mexican fare and regional Yucatecan dishes, making the city a rewarding one for gastronomic adventure. Be sure to sample some of the Yucatán's culinary specialties. They include *papadzules*, tortillas stuffed with chopped hard-boiled eggs and topped with pumpkinseed or tomato sauce; *poc-chuc*, slices of pork marinated in the juice of sour oranges and served with pickled onions; *pollo pibil*, herb-infused chicken wrapped in banana leaves and baked; *sopa de lima*, a satisfying soup containing shredded chicken and strips of fried tortilla, flavored with lime juice; and *salbutes*, Yucatecan-style fast food consisting of fried tortillas topped with shredded turkey, pickled onions and slices of avocado. For stomachs unaccustomed to excessive firepower, the incendiary habanero chile is provided on the side rather than in the dish at most establishments (ask to make doubly sure).

Beverages are intriguing as well. While *licuados*—liquified fruit drinks—are sold in many parts of Mexico, they are especially refreshing in Mérida, where the vendors can draw from a variety of melons, pineapple and other tropical flavors. *Licuado* stands, marked by rows of colorful fruit, can be found throughout the city. More unusual are drinks quaffed for centuries by the Maya and their descendants. One example is *horchata*, a blend of ground rice and almonds, water and ice, sweetened with raw sugar, cinnamon, vanilla or honey.

One of the best places to sample local fare is **Los Almendros**, on Calle 50-A between calles 57 and 59 (facing Parque de Mejorada). The picture menu has descriptions in English. Their signature dish is *poc-chuc*. Order an appetizer portion of *tacos al pastor*, shredded, flame-grilled pork in a barbecue-like sauce, topped with onions and cilantro and served on freshly made corn tortillas. **La Casona**, Calle 60 #434 (between calles 47 and 49 near Parque de Santa Ana), offers Italian as well as Yucatecan dishes, served in a romantic old house with an interior courtyard garden. A good morning choice is **Sanborn's**, in the Hotel Fiesta Americana Mérida, part of the ubiquitous Mexican chain. Breakfast items at this bright, cheery, efficient restaurant come with a basket of *pan dulce* (not-too-sweet breads in a variety of shapes). The coffee is good, too.

Mérida is a friendly city, and one that's fairly safe to walk around in after dark. At dusk, Plaza de la Independencia and adjoining Hidalgo Park are alive with strollers and crowds watching street performers, listening to musicians, grabbing a bite to eat or just relaxing on benches. Sidewalk vendors set up along nearby streets, and a head-spinning array of stores and walk-in eateries sell everything from *tortas* to heavy metal CDs. To fully experience this vibrancy, hit the streets on your own two feet.

There is free evening entertainment at downtown parks and plazas several nights a week, courtesy of an active cultural arts scene. On Monday a folkloric dance troupe performs in front of the **Palacio Municipal** (City Hall), on Calle 62 across from Plaza de la Independencia. On Tuesday, dance to live big-band music at **Santiago Park**, at the corner of calles 59 and 72. The University of the Yucatán Folkloric Ballet performs Wednesday at the **Peón Contreras Theater.** On Thursday, Yucatecan serenades and regional dances are performed at **Santa Lucía Park**. On Saturday, a "Fiesta Mexicana" music and dance presentation is held at Paseo Montejo and Calle 47. For event schedule information, check with the tourist information center in the Peón Contreras Theater.

WHAT TO SEE

DOWNTOWN

CASA DE MONTEJO (Montejo House), on Calle 63 (south side of Plaza de la Independencia), was built in 1549 by the son of Francisco de Montejo, the Yucatán conqueror. It was the first Spanish house in Mérida. Montejo the Younger employed Indian labor to create the richly ornamented facade and doors, considered to be among the best examples of Plateresque decoration in Mexico. A reminder of Spanish cruelty is the carving of the *conquistador* dressed in full regalia, with feet firmly planted on top of wailing Maya heads. This restored family home now houses a Banamex Bank branch. The interior, including a huge patio lush with tropical plants, can be viewed during normal business hours (Mon.-Fri. 9-1).

CATEDRAL (Cathedral) is on the east side of Plaza de la Independencia, opposite the Palacio de Gobierno. The church stands on the site of an early temple, and much of the stone used in its construction came from the ruined buildings of T'ho, the ancient Maya city upon which Mérida was built. Begun in 1561 and completed in 1598, it has a plain, medieval-style exterior.

The interior is stark, in marked contrast to the lavish decoration of other Mexican colonial churches. One painting depicts a meeting between the Spanish and the Xiu Indians. To the left of the main altar is a chapel containing a replica of the **Cristo de las Ampollas** (Christ of the Blisters), an image of Christ carved from a tree that Indians witnessed burning sporadically. The figure drew pilgrimages to the church in the village of Ichmul until a fire destroyed the church without consuming the image. The blistered figure was brought to the cathedral in 1645.

MUSEO DE ARTE POPULAR (Museum of Popular Art) is 6 blocks east of the plaza on Calle 59,

Religious objects on display outside Mérida's cathedral   © John Neubauer

between calles 48 and 50. It is housed in one of Mérida's venerable mansions. The collection of Yucatecan handicrafts on the first floor includes regional costumes, pottery, masks, woven baskets and beautifully carved conch shells. Upstairs are exhibits of craft items from other parts of Mexico. Tues.-Sat. 9-8, Sun. 8-2. Free.

MUSEO DE LA CIUDAD (City Museum), calles 61 and 58 across the street from Plaza de la Independencia, has paintings, photographs and drawings illustrating Mérida's history. Open Tues.-Sat. 8-1 and 4-8.

MUSEO MACAY (Museum of Contemporary Yucatecan Art), Calle 60 next to the cathedral, exhibits the work of regional artists in two floors of rooms built around an interior patio. Wed.-Mon. 10-6. Admission is charged; free to all Sun.

PALACIO DE GOBIERNO (Government Palace), on the north side of Plaza de la Independencia, dates from 1892. It has a spacious, open interior. Take the wide stairway to the second floor, where the walls of one room are adorned with murals by Meridano artist Fernando Castro Pacheco depicting traditional Maya symbology as well as the violent appropriation of their culture by the Spanish. A hall of history, also on the second floor, chronicles the destruction by Spanish bishop Diego de Landa of the Maya *codices*, pictorial history books. More exhibits are on the first floor.

PALACIO MUNICIPAL (City Hall), Calle 62 on the west side of Plaza de la Independencia, is more commonly known as the Ayuntamiento. It was built atop a Maya pyramid. The exterior, yellow with white trim, shows a Moorish influence, and the clock tower is typical of Mexican government buildings. Evening concerts and performances of the *jarana*, a Yucatecan regional dance, are presented in front of the building on Mondays at 9 p.m.

TEATRO PEON CONTRERAS (Peón Contreras Theater), on Calle 60 between calles 57 and 59, just north of Cepeda Peraza Park (Hidalgo Park), was built in the early 20th century in the grand Italianate style of European opera houses. The main entrance features a staircase of Carrara marble, and the interior is typically and richly ornate. This venue for the performing arts also houses a tourist information center that is a good place to find out what's going on around town.

Elsewhere Within the City

CENTENARIO PARK AND ZOO, west of Plaza de la Independencia, runs along Avenida Itzáes between calles 59 and 65. Handsome, colonial-style yellow stone archways flank the park entrance. It is large, shady and particularly fun for children. The zoo displays a variety of animals and birds, from peacocks and flamingos to alligators, lions and jaguars, as well as species native to the Yucatán Peninsula. A miniature train offers rides through the park.

LA HERMITA DE SANTA ISABEL (Hermitage of Santa Isabel), at calles 66 and 77, was built in 1748. In colonial days it became known as the

Convent of Safe Travel, since travelers on their way to the busy port of Campeche would stop to pray for a safe journey. The restored hermitage is surrounded by a serene botanical garden accented with Maya-inspired statues and a waterfall.

MUSEO DE ANTROPOLOGIA E HISTORIA (Anthropology and History Museum) is on Paseo Montejo at Calle 43. The museum is housed in the Palacio Cantón, the former home of Mérida's prominent Cantón family. The turn-of-the-20th-century, peach-colored house, built by the architect who designed the Peón Contreras Theater, is an impressive example of their wealthy lifestyle.

The museum has an extensive collection of stone carvings, figurines and relics, including jade and gold objects retrieved from the Sacred Cenote at Chichén Itzá. Although the accompanying background information is mostly in Spanish, the displays provide a comprehensive introduction to the archeological sites of the Yucatán region. Particularly interesting are the exhibits devoted to daily Maya life, showing how babies' heads were elongated and how teeth were filed to achieve the rather bizarre standards of Maya beauty. Tues.-Sat. 9-8, Sun. 8-2. Admission is charged; free to all Sun.

NEARBY ARCHEOLOGICAL SITES

About 15 kilometers (9 miles) north of Mérida on Mex. 261 (toward Progreso) is the junction with a paved road; about 5 kilometers (3 miles) east is the entrance to the major archeological site of **Dzibilchaltún** (zeeb-eel-chal-TOON), which has been partially restored through the efforts of the National Geographic Society and the Mexican organizations CEDAM (Club de Exploraciones y Deportes Acuáticos de Mexico) and INAH (Instituto Nacional de Antropología e Historia).

Dzibilchaltún is one of the largest of Mexico's archeological discoveries. More than 8,000 structures, mostly mounds of rubble or the remains of low platforms, have been uncovered so far. The city's height of importance was between the seventh and 10th centuries, and it is estimated to be the Yucatán Peninsula's oldest continuously inhabited ceremonial center. Excavations did not begin until the 1940s.

Not much remains of Dzibilchaltún's former glory, although it is archeologically fascinating. Of interest is a Maya road, or *sacbé*, some 60 feet wide, which once connected the site's main buildings. The reconstructed Temple of the Seven Dolls was named for the seven primitive figures discovered buried under the structure's floor. Exhibiting such deformities as a hunchback and a swollen belly, they may have served as spiritual "messengers" during ceremonies to cure illness. The figures are on display at the site museum.

Nature trails wind through the site. Here the landscape is not the tropical rain forest typical of the southern parts of Campeche and Quintana Roo but a scrubbier, drier terrain characterized by palms, cactus and drought-resistant deciduous trees. Many birds nest in the vicinity of the **Xlacah** (shla-KAH) cenote, which boasts unusually clear water and a depth of more than 140 feet. It functioned both as a source of drinking water and as a sacrificial well during Maya times. Divers have recovered many artifacts, including the bones of humans and cows, from the cenote's depths. Swimming is permitted. **Pueblo Maya**, a small museum on the grounds, exhibits Maya and Spanish artifacts. The ruins are open daily 8-5. Admission is charged.

Mayapán, the Maya capital of the Yucatán Peninsula for 2 centuries, is about 56 kilometers (35 miles) southeast of Mérida. To get there, take Mex. 18, a narrow, two-lane paved road that travels southeast from Mérida through the villages of Kanasin, Acanceh and Tecoh; about 10 kilometers (6 miles) past Tecoh, watch for the signed turnoff to Mayapán. Numerous broken pyramids and buildings at this site are overgrown with dense jungle. Mayapán grew from its founding at the beginning of the 13th century to a walled city of 10,000 to 12,000 inhabitants.

Tributes to Mayapán were paid by the Itzae and Xiu Indians. It is theorized that the fierce rebellion between these two tribes resulted in the final abandonment of this Maya ceremonial center, which flourished after the heyday of Chichén Itzá and Uxmal. It was reduced to rubble in the 16th century by Spanish conqueror Francisco Montejo's forces.

Unlike other notable Maya cities, Mayapán's layout appears to have had no clear-cut plan. Paths between buildings are labyrinthine; the structures were built on a less impressive scale; and the workmanship lacks the technique and elaborate decorative motifs so evident at Chichén Itzá and Uxmal. In fact, many of Mayapán's architectural features appear to be copies of those present at Chichén Itzá.

The lack of restoration at this site also means few visitors, and those fascinated by ruins will have the crumbling temple platforms and weathered sculptures of the feathered serpent-god Quetzalcóatl (Kukulkán to the Maya) mostly to themselves. The ruins are open daily 9-5. Admission is charged.

Also historically interesting is the 1559 Temple and Convent of La Candelaria in the Maya village of **Tecoh**, about 10 kilometers (6 miles) north of Mayapán on Mex. 18. It was built in 7 months by Juan de Mérida and thousands of Indian slaves using the stone blocks of razed temples.

PROGRESO, CELESTUN, UMAN AND YAXCOPOIL

Progreso, less than an hour's drive north of Mérida, is where city dwellers go for a weekend escape to the beach. From the town center, a *malécon* (Calle 19, the waterfront drive) fronts a wide, sandy beach that extends for miles in both directions. While the warm gulf waters do not have the intense aquamarine hues or sparkling clarity of Quintana Roo's Caribbean coast, the palm-fringed, shell-strewn beach is clean, and walking along it enjoyable. Several waterfront restaurants offer a fresh fish menu and a casual outdoor atmosphere.

Progreso was founded in the mid-19th century as a port of entry for the Yucatán Peninsula and as a shipping center for henequén, which previously had been exported from the port of Sisal, about 40 kilometers (25 miles) southwest; the shallow waters there, however, could not accommodate large ships. With the rise of synthetic materials and the declining demand for henequén fiber, Progreso and Sisal both settled into the relative anonymity of beach communities. Just east of town, lining the waterfront, are rambling mansions built by the hacienda owners; many of them are now the summer homes of well-to-do Meridanos.

The town fishing pier, or *muelle*, extends for more than a mile into the shallow gulf waters and was claimed to be the longest stone wharf in the world when it was built. An extension has been added in the hope of adding Progreso to the cruise ship circuit. The pier, however, remains a salty fishing hangout, where it's said that early morning or late afternoon are the best times to cast a hook. The newer, protected harbor at **Yucalpeten**, about 6 kilometers (4 miles) west of town, now handles most of the international shipping traffic. Yucalpeten has been targeted for large-scale tourist development, although it has yet to materialize to any degree.

During the summer months and on holidays—particularly Easter—Progreso is noisy and traffic-filled, teeming with city dwellers and Mexicans on vacation. Winter, when the crowds disappear and temperatures—at least for *gringos* used to bone-chilling cold—are pleasantly warm, is a good time to visit. Accommodations are limited, and hard to come by in the high-season months of July and August, but most tourists just visit for the day and then return to Mérida.

There is daily first- and second-class service to Progreso from the bus station located at Calle 62 #524, between Calles 65 and 67. The fare is inexpensive, and the trip takes about an hour. If you have the time and don't require such travel comforts as air conditioning or express amenities, this can be a leisurely way to experience a part of the Yucatán that's off the usual tourist itineraries.

Another day trip possibility from Mérida is to the fishing village of **Celestún**, on the western Yucatán coast. To get there, take Mex. 281 (Calle 59A within the city) about 97 kilometers (60 miles) west. En route are the towns of Hunucma and Kinchil, as well as fields of henequén and old haciendas that drove this once-thriving industry.

The village sits at the tip of a strip of land separating the Celestún Estuary from the Gulf of Mexico. The atmosphere is decidedly laid-back; there are no resort amenities here. A stretch of white-sand swimming beach is at the north edge of town, although constant winds make the water choppy and silt-laden. The harbor is picturesque in a scruffy sort of way, filled with small boats and fishing nets drying in the sun.

The main reason to visit Celestún is the surrounding wildlife refuge, home to a large colony of flamingos. The flamingos are most visible from September through March, the non-breeding and nesting season. While these spindly-legged, coral-plumaged birds are the area's most spectacular residents, herons, egrets, pelicans, anhingas and ducks also can be seen. In addition, Celestún is on the flyway of many species migrating from northern climates to South America.

The best time for birdwatching is early in the morning. Boats and guides can be hired in town for expeditions into the marshes and dense mangrove thickets lining the shores of the estuary.

Just outside the Mérida city limits on Mex. 180 (south of the Anillo Periférico loop road) is **Umán**, a typical Yucatecan small town. Around the main plaza, which is dominated by a large church, are small shops, sidewalk vendors and a lineup of *triciclos* that transport local passengers as well as sightseeing visitors.

Antigua, an old hacienda, is about 34 kilometers (21 miles) south of Mérida via Mex. 180 to Umán, then south on Mex. 261 (follow the signs for Uxmal). The small village of Yaxcopoil (yawsh-koe-poe-EEL) is about 10 kilometers (6 miles) south of Umán; watch for the marked turnoff to the hacienda ("Antigua Hacienda y Museo Yaxcopoil") on your right. The Moorish-style architecture of the main buildings hints at the gracious lifestyle once enjoyed by wealthy henequén plantation owners. Hemp is still produced, although on a smaller scale than in the past; visitors are welcome to observe the processing operations. The museum is in part of the main house. Guided tours are available; there is a nominal charge.

WHERE TO STAY

BEST WESTERN MARIA DEL CARMEN

 *Hotel* ((99)30-0390
All Year $53-$65 XP $6
Location: 3 blks w of Plaza de la Independencia between Calle 68 and 70. Calle 63 No. 550 97000 (PO Box 411). Fax: 99/30-0393. **Facility:** Quiet location. Some rooms with pool view. Rooms on floors one, two and three are a bit larger than rooms on higher floors. In-house travel agency, car rental and tour operators. Clean rooms with older furnishings. 90 units. *Bath:* combo or shower only. 6 stories, interior/exterior corridors. **Terms:** F12; 3 day cancellation notice, 12/1-4/30. **Amenities:** extended cable TV. **Guest Services:** gift shop, valet laundry. **Business Services:** conference facilities. **Cards:** AE, DI, MC, VI.

DEL GOBERNADOR HOTEL

 *Hotel* (99/23-7133
1/1-11/30 $64-$70 XP $8
12/1-12/31 $53-$58 XP $7
Location: Jct Calle 59 at Calle 66. 535 Calle 59 97000. Fax: 99/28-1590. **Facility:** Quiet location. Modern rooms with many having two seperate beds. Modern and appealing restaurant. 80 units. *Bath:* shower only. 3 stories (no elevator), exterior corridors. **Terms:** F12; 3 day cancellation notice. **Leisure Activities:** small pool. **Guest Services:** valet laundry. **Business Services:** meeting rooms. **Cards:** AE, DI, MC, VI.

FIESTA AMERICANA MERIDA

Hotel ((99)42-1111
1/5-11/30 $147
12/1-12/25 $117-$140
Location: Center; Paseo de Montejo jct Ave Colon. Paseo de Montejo No. 451 97127. Fax: 99/42-1112. **Facility:** Refined atmosphere. Striking atrium lobby. 350 units. 3 two-bedroom units. Some whirlpool units. 5 stories, interior corridors. **Parking:** valet. **Terms:** open 12/1-12/25 & 1/5-11/30, 3 day cancellation notice, x, package plans. **Amenities:** safes, honor bars. **Dining & Entertainment:** dining room, restaurant, 6:45 am-midnight, Fri & Sat-midnight, $13-$18, cocktails, entertainment. **Leisure Activities:** heated pool, sauna, whirlpool, steamroom, tennis court, exercise room. **Guest Services:** gift shop, valet laundry. *Fee:* massage. **Business Services:** conference facilities, administrative services, PC, fax. **Cards:** AE, DI, MC, VI.
(See color ad below)

SOME UNITS

HOLIDAY INN

Motor Inn (99/25-6877
All Year $80-$120 XP $15
Location: Off Paseo de Montejo; behind the American Consulate at Calle 60. Ave Colon 498 97000 (PO Box 134). Fax: 98/25-7755. **Facility:** Most rooms with small balcony, some with stylish decor. Business section with added amenities and services. Meets AAA guest room security requirements. 213 units. 4 stories, interior corridors. **Terms:** F12; 3 day cancellation notice. **Amenities:** dual phone lines, voice mail, honor bars, irons, hair dryers. *Some:* safes. **Leisure Activities:** wading pool, exercise room. *Fee:* lighted tennis court. **Guest Services:** gift shop, valet laundry. **Business Services:** conference facilities, administrative services. *Fee:* PC, fax. **Cards:** AE, DI, MC, VI.

SOME UNITS

HOTEL CARIBE

Hotel ((99)24-9022
7/1-11/30 $46-$58 XP $4
12/1-6/30 $44-$55 XP $4
Location: In front of Plaza Parque Hidalgo. Calle 59 No. 500 97000. Fax: 99/ 24-8733. **Facility:** Quaint colonial atmosphere. Most rooms with ceiling fan. 53 units. *Bath:* shower only. 3 stories (no elevator), exterior corridors. **Terms:** F12. **Amenities:** dual phone lines. **Dining:** restaurant, coffee shop, 7 am-11 pm, $6-$12, wine/beer only. **Leisure Activities:** small pool. *Fee:* golf & tennis privileges. **Cards:** AE, MC, VI.

SOME UNITS

HOTEL CASA DEL BALAM

Hotel ((99)24-8844
All Year $85-$100 XP $10
Location: 2 blks n of Plaza de la Independencia. Calle 60 No. 488; corner 97000 (PO Box 708). Fax: 99/24-5011. **Facility:** Colonial atmosphere. Quiet courtyard area. 52 units. 6 stories, exterior corridors. **Parking:** extra charge. **Terms:** F11; cancellation fee imposed. **Amenities:** honor bars, hair dryers. **Leisure Activities:** small pool. **Guest Services:** [MAP] meal plan available, gift shop, valet laundry. **Cards:** AE, CB, DI, MC, VI.

▲▲▲ HOTEL EL CONQUISTADOR

▼▼▼▼▼   *Hotel*   ((99)26-2155

| 1/1-11/30 | $110 | XP $15 |
| 12/1-12/31 | $95 | XP $15 |

Location: 13 blks n of Plaza Independencia. Paseo de Montejo 458 97127. Fax: 99/26-8829. **Facility:** Private balcony. Rooftop pool with sundeck and view of city. Some corner rooms are larger and have a double balcony. 159 units. Some suites ($120-$170). 6 stories, interior corridors. **Terms:** F12; 3 day cancellation notice. **Amenities:** safes, honor bars, hair dryers. **Guest Services:** valet laundry. **Business Services:** conference facilities. **Cards:** AE, CB, DI, MC, VI.

HOTEL LOS ALUXES

▼▼ ▼▼   *Hotel*   (99/24-2199

All Year $85-$107   XP $6
Location: 5 blks n of Plaza de la Independencia. Calle 60 No. 444 97000. Fax: 99/23-3858. **Facility:** A few enclosed balconies. Rooms in rear building are newer and better furnished. In-house travel agency and tour operators. 155 units. Some whirlpool units. 3-5 stories, interior corridors. **Terms:** F12. **Amenities:** honor bars, hair dryers. **Guest Services:** gift shop, valet laundry. **Business Services:** conference facilities. **Cards:** AE, MC, VI.

HOTEL MERIDA MISION PARK INN

▼▼ ▼▼   *Hotel*   (99/23-9500

All Year $70   XP $12
Location: Calle 60, corner Calle 57. Calle 60 491 97000. Fax: 99/ 23-7665. **Facility:** Colonial ambience. Some larger corner rooms. 145 units. *Bath:* combo or shower only. Interior corridors. **Parking:** extra charge. **Amenities:** *Some:* honor bars, hair dryers. **Guest Services:** valet laundry. **Cards:** AE, DI, MC, VI.

▲▲▲ HOTEL RESIDENCIAL

▼▼▼▼▼   *Country Inn*   ((99)24-3099

All Year $63   XP $7
Location: Calle 59, No. 589 X 76. Calle 59 No. 589 97000. Fax: 99/24-0266. **Facility:** Rooftop meeting area, boutique hotel with residential location and ambience. Excellent value. Meets AAA guest room security requirements. 66 units. Some suites ($89-$99). *Bath:* shower only. 5 stories, interior/exterior corridors. **Terms:** F12; 3 day cancellation notice. **Amenities:** hair dryers. **Dining:** dining room, 7 am-11 pm, $5-$17, cocktails. **Leisure Activities:** small pool. **Guest Services:** valet laundry. **Business Services:** meeting rooms. *Fee:* fax. **Cards:** AE, MC, VI.

▲▲▲ HYATT REGENCY MERIDA

▼▼▼▼▼▼   *Hotel*   (99/42-0202

All Year $80-$160   XP $20
Location: 1 km e of historical district; jct Calle 35 at Ave Colon. Calle 60, No 344 97000. Fax: 99/25-7002. **Facility:** Striking high-rise. Elegant rooms and public areas. Meets AAA guest room security requirements. 299 units. Some whirlpool units. 17 stories, interior corridors. **Parking:** valet. **Amenities:** honor bars. *Some:* safes. **Dining & Entertainment:** restaurant, coffee shop, 7 am-2 am, $12-$24, entertainment. **Leisure Activities:** whirlpool, steamroom, exercise room. *Fee:* 2 lighted tennis courts. **Guest Services:** [ECP] meal plan available, gift shop, airport transportation-Regency Club, valet laundry. *Fee:* massage. **Business Services:** conference facilities, administrative services. *Fee:* PC, fax. **Cards:** AE, DI, MC, VI.

WHERE TO DINE

ALBERTO'S CONTINENTAL PATIO   *Historical*

▼▼▼▼   *Regional Mexican*   (99/28-5367
                              L $6-$18   D $6-$20
Location: Corner Calle 57 and 64. Calle 64 No 482 97000. **Hours:** 1   pm-11   pm.   Closed: 3/26,   8/30. **Reservations:** suggested; for dinner. **Features:** casual dress; children's menu; cocktails & lounge; a la carte. Converted 17th-century home. Open-air patio and A/C dining room serving international cuisine featuring Lebanese specialties. More like a museum, Mr. Salum has collected artifacts from Merida's rich colonial past. Try to avoid the occasional tour groups that can flood this charming restaurant. **Cards:** AE, MC, VI.

LA CASONA

▼▼ ▼▼   *Italian*   (99/23-9996
                              L $4-$10   D $7-$15
Location: 7 blks n of main plaza; on Calle 60 between Calle 49 and 47. Calle 60 No 434 97127. **Hours:** noon-2 am. **Reservations:** suggested. **Features:** No A/C; casual dress; cocktails & lounge; entertainment. Classic Italian selections made with homemade pasta and served in a turn-of-the-20th-century garden courtyard. Limited seating in air-conditioned area. Attentive staff ensures a more than pleasant dining experience. **Cards:** AE, MC, VI.

LOS ALMENDROS

▼▼ ▼▼   *Regional Mexican*   (99/28-5459
                              L $3-$9   D $5-$12
Location: 7 blks n of main plaza. Calle 50 No 493 97127. **Hours:** 11 am-11 pm. **Features:** casual dress; cocktails. Classic Yucatecan cuisine includes pibil-style dishes, fried plantains, pork and chicken marinated in citric fruits. Tender oversized tamales wrapped in banana leaves. Ask for a Leon beer. **Cards:** AE, MC, VI.

PLAYA DEL CARMEN, QUINTANA ROO (G-12)

Playa del Carmen once was the mainland departure point for Maya pilgrims visiting the sanctuaries and temples on Cozumel. Its relation to the island continued as the canoes were supplanted by ferries bearing not worshippers but tourists. "Playa" has become a tourist destination in its own right, a place where the beaches and fishing opportunities lend a "get away from it all" feeling.

The main road to town branches east off Mex. 307 about 68 kilometers (42 miles) south of Cancún. The rundown houses and small stores lining this scruffy street are typical of Mexican small towns. The older beachfront section, north of the ferry dock, has casual thatch-roofed restaurants and hammock slung between palm trees; bathing suits tend to be shed as you progress north.

South of the ferry dock is the newer hotel zone, **Playacar**. Condominiums and all-inclusive resorts frequented by Europeans are within this designated area; the cobblestoned main thoroughfare is called Paseo Xaman-Ha (sha-MAN hah). The pace here is slower than at Cancún or Cozumel, and a genuine bargain might be found during the off season (after Easter through November). Cruise ship passengers and day visitors from Cancún take advantage of **Playacar Club de Golf**, a public, 18-hole golf course designed by Robert Von Hagge that includes an outstanding clubhouse and pro shop.

Ferries carry passengers between Playa del Carmen and Cozumel *(see separate listing)*. The centrally located ferry dock is off Avenida 5, about 2 blocks south of the main square. Cars are not transported, but there is a guarded parking lot across the street from the dock. The trip to Cozumel takes about 45 minutes. There are two types of ferries—older, open-air boats and the MV *Mexico*, an enclosed, jet-propelled, air-conditioned vessel. Tickets can be purchased from the ticket booth at the dock; the MV *Mexico* is the more expensive of the two services.

There are approximate hourly crossings between Playa del Carmen and Cozumel daily from around 6:30 a.m. to 8:30 p.m. Schedules are subject to frequent change; verify arrivals and/or departures at the dock ticket office. For additional information contact Cruceros Marítimos del Caribe; phone (987) 2-1588. **Note:** Ferry schedules also are subject to change due to weather conditions, as seas can sometimes be quite rough; make sure you carry appropriate medication if you're prone to seasickness.

NEARBY DESTINATIONS

PUERTO AVENTURAS is 20 kilometers (12 miles) south of Playa del Carmen off Mex. 307. A master-planned oasis of luxury planted along the shores of a turquoise cove, Puerto Aventuras is not for those with tight pockets. Some 900 acres of landscaped grounds are adorned with imported palms and orchids, providing a suitably lush resort setting for hotels, condominiums, shops, restaurants, a 9-hole golf course and, for yacht fanciers, a 250-slip marina. Tennis, swimming, scuba diving, deep-sea fishing and a swim with a friendly dolphin are among the activities offered.

Cedam Museum (Club de Exploraciones y Deportes Acuáticos de México), at the resort, salutes Mexico's divers. It displays the tools of their trade and the treasures retrieved by CEDAM's members from 16th- and 17th-century ships that went down off Quintana Roo's coast. Boats to explore these wrecks can be hired at Akumal *(see separate listing)*, about 16 kilometers (10 miles) south of Puerto Aventuras on Mex. 307, which was the original site for the museum.

A cove offers a languid setting for swimming, snorkeling, scuba diving, windsurfing or just relaxing on the sun-drenched beach. Visitors can dive in the cove's shallow waters and explore the remains of the *Matanceros*, a Spanish galleon that sank in 1741; goblets, gold coins, medal-

lions, weapons and other items recovered from the wreck are displayed in the museum. Open Wed.-Mon.

XCARET (ISH-kah-ret) is about 6 kilometers (4 miles) south of Playa del Carmen (follow the marked turnoff off Mex. 307). The site once was an important Maya seaport called Pole, and the grounds contain the remains of Maya temples, as well as the ruins of a miniature pyramid that was once covered with animal figures and geometric carvings. Beyond the main entrance parking lot is an exact reproduction, in size and style, of the arch at the ruins of Labná *(see Uxmal listing)*. Another reproduction, the San Francisco de Asis Chapel, combines Spanish and Maya architectural influences.

Xcaret used to be a tranquil series of interlocking lagoons but has been turned into a full-scale, "eco-archeological" tourist attraction—the closest thing Mexico has to a Disneyesque theme park. Many natural attributes have been altered to accommodate the park's construction; those preferring a less commercialized experience might want to consider Xel-Há *(see Tulum listing)* instead.

Palm-lined pathways wind around secluded coves and a lagoon that is ideal for beginning snorkelers. Swimmers, snorkelers and divers also can paddle through interconnected cenotes (sinkholes) and natural pools. A highlight is the underground river that flows for 1,000 feet through a series of subterranean caves (with openings in the ceiling to let in light), ending at the park's beach (where life jackets are collected and personal belongings picked up). **Note:** Using suntan lotion is not permitted in the lagoons and underground river because of its effect on the marine habitat.

In addition to water-based recreation, Xcaret offers a butterfly pavilion, a breeding aviary with more than 30 species of birds from southeastern Mexico, a botanical garden that includes an orchid greenhouse/growing laboratory and a mushroom farm, an aquarium encompassing a natural coral reef habitat, a sea turtle nursery, an island habitat housing jaguars and cougars, horseback riding along jungle trails and on the beach, a hot-air balloon ride over the park, a dolphinarium with an observation area and a program that allows an interactive dolphin swim.

A museum has reproductions of well-known Maya archeological sites. There also are performances of the ceremonial flying pole dance, a pre-Hispanic tradition, by the Papantla Flyers. "Xcaret at Night," the park's evening show, features walks along candlelit paths, a live demonstration of the ancient and mysterious Maya ball game, a *charro* (cowboy) show and a *ballet folklórico* music and dance performance in a natural amphitheater under the stars.

Lockers and picnic facilities are available. Snack stands and several restaurants are on site (visitors are not permitted to bring food or beverages into the park). Xcaret is open daily 8:30 a.m.-9 p.m. Admission is around $40; ages 6-12, around $25 (includes use of beaches and all water areas as well as the aviary, botanical garden, butterfly pavilion, museum and archeological sites).

There are additional rental fees for snorkeling equipment, life jackets, lockers and towels. Depending upon crowds, however, the park may run out of supplies; bring your own towels and snorkeling gear. There also are separate fees for scuba diving instruction, guided diving and snorkeling excursions, horseback riding, the hot-air balloon ride and the dolphin swim (reservations for the last activity must be made in the museum building on a first-come-first-served basis and cannot be made in advance). Phone (98) 83-3143 or 83-3144.

WHERE TO STAY

HOTEL ROYAL HIDEAWAY
▼▼▼ ▼▼▼   Resort   (987/3-4500
All Year $465-$550   XP $215
Location: In Playacar Development east off Mex. 307; on the beach. Lote Hotelero No 1 Fracc Playacar 77600. Fax: 987/3-4506. **Facility:** Spectacular Caribbean all-inclusive resort with luxurious rooms, elegant dining and abundant resort activities. Guest rooms divided into 11 separate buildings, each with its own concierge, providing a high level of personalized services. Extensive pool-beach areas. Beach is leeward, occasional dramatic surf. 200 units. 1 two-bedroom unit. Some suites and whirlpool units. *Bath:* shower only. 2-3 stories (no elevator), interior corridors. **Parking:** valet. **Terms:** Variety of junior and presidential suites. **Amenities:** video games, CD players, voice mail, safes, irons, hair dryers. *Some:* fax. **Leisure Activities:** 6 pools, whirlpools, beach, swimming, poolside aerobics, state-of-the-art spa, canoeing, paddleboats, sailboating, windsurfing, boat dock, marina, scuba diving, snorkeling, 2 lighted tennis courts, recreation program, social program, bicycles. *Fee:* waterskiing, scuba & snorkeling equipment, charter fishing. **Guest Services:** [AP] meal plan available, gift shop, complimentary evening beverages, afternoon tea, valet laundry. *Fee:* area transportation, massage. **Business Services:** conference facilities, PC. *Fee:* fax. **Cards:** AE, CB, DI, MC, VI.

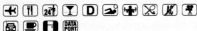

PUERTO MORELOS, QUINTANA ROO (G-12)

The fishing village of Puerto Morelos (PWEHR-toh moh-REH-los) is about 36 kilometers (22 miles) south of Cancún off Mex. 307. The atmosphere is peaceful—there are almost no phones in town—the accommodations inexpensive, the beaches palm-shaded, and the restaurants specialize in fresh seafood. The attractions are camping, deep-sea fishing and scuba diving near the large offshore coral reef.

A passenger/car ferry leaves daily from the Puerto Morelos dock for Cozumel. The ferry takes about 3 hours to reach Cozumel, but the wait can be tedious and trucks carrying fuel and other cargo take precedence over automobiles. If you're not bringing a vehicle (which is advisable, as parking on the island is limited), a quicker alternative is to board one of the passenger ferries departing from Playa del Carmen.

There is normally one departure daily from Puerto Morelos, which usually leaves in the early morning. Arrive several hours before the ferry is scheduled to depart in order to purchase a ticket and secure a place in line. In addition, double-check the return schedule to Puerto Morelos while you're on Cozumel. **Note:** This ferry has been docked for as long as a week during prolonged periods of bad weather.

CROCO CUN is just north of the Puerto Morelos turnoff on Mex. 307, at Km marker 324. Advertised as a crocodile farm, it is actually a zoological park of sorts. Crocodile specimens of all ages and sizes are on view, along with white-tailed deer, snakes, macaws, tapirs, monkeys and other regional species. Insect repellent is strongly advised. Guided tours are offered, and a restaurant is on the premises. Open daily 8:30-6. Admission is around $5.

DR. ALFREDO BARRERA MARIN BOTANICAL GARDEN is just south of the Puerto Morelos turnoff; the entrance is right off Mex. 307. This protected area features a nature trail that winds through a variety of native and regional plants, including a grove of sapodilla trees (from which the sticky substance used to make chewing gum is extracted), a mangrove swamp, and an area containing a small group of Maya ruins. Signs give plant names in Spanish and English. Wear plenty of insect repellent. Open Tues.-Sun. Admission is charged.

TULUM, QUINTANA ROO (G-12)

Once the site of four Maya cities—Solimán, Tankah, Xel-Há and Tulum—the ruins of Tulum (too-LOOM) are a legacy of Maya greatness. The ruins at Tankah *(see attraction listing below)* lie close to Mex. 307. Ruins near Xel-Há National Park *(see attraction listing below)* have been recently excavated. The village of Tulum straggles along Mex. 307 about a kilometer south of the junction with the access road to the ruins. Among the businesses are a bakery and little restaurants housed in dilapidated buildings and thatched *palapas*. Here a paved road to the Cobá ruins branches west off the highway. Past the south end of town Mex. 307 becomes a narrow, unpaved road as it heads toward the Boca Paila Peninsula.

TULUM RUINS are about half a mile east of Mex. 307 via a marked turnoff; if driving and traveling south, veer right and follow the access road that crosses Mex. 307 and leads to the parking area. One of the later Maya outposts, Tulum was constructed during the 10th century as a fortress overlooking the Caribbean Sea. While not impressive architecturally in comparison to Chichén Itzá or Uxmal, Tulum is notable for its dramatic setting—the only significant Maya site on a coast. Post-Classic Tulum flourished in the 14th century and was still inhabited when the Spanish arrived in the early 16th century.

Seven years prior to the arrival of the first *conquistadores*, a sailor who may have accompanied Christopher Columbus on one of his four trips to the New World was blown off course en route to the island of Hispañola and shipwrecked off Cozumel Island. Gonzalo Guerrero and 19 other survivors were captured by the Maya; all were sacrificed save for himself and a priest because they were too thin. Guerrero married an Indian princess, and his children were thus the first "mestizos" (people of mixed European and Indian blood) in the Americas. The priest became Hernán Cortés' *lengua* (translator), enabling the first communication between the Maya and the Spanish.

From the parking lot, a short paved walking path tunneling through thick scrub leads to the site entrance. Some 60 well-preserved buildings show the Toltec architectural influence. The most imposing building is **El Castillo** (The Castle), a clifftop pyramidal structure capped by a small temple. Below the limestone cliffs is a beach where the Maya once came ashore in their canoes. Also worth seeing is the **Temple of the Frescoes**, with interior murals that display typical Maya motifs and exterior statues bearing still-discernible traces of paint. The **Temple of the Descending God** has a winged stucco figure over the doorway that suggests a plummeting diver.

Note: Some of the buildings can be climbed; most of the building interiors are roped off. Wear nonslip walking shoes; the sandy, rocky terrain can be unexpectedly slippery. The porous limestone has created a few blowholes through which geysers of sea water can unexpectedly erupt. Weather permitting, bring a swimsuit—the beaches below, at the northeast and southeast corners of the ruins, are lovely. English-speaking guides are available, although the information you receive may or may not be historically accurate; a fee is charged. However, the site is small enough to easily tour on your own.

There are restrooms and a few souvenir shops in the visitor center next to the parking lot; craft stalls line the path at the site entrance. Open daily 8-6, late Apr.-late Oct.; 8-5, rest of year. Admission 20 pesos (about $2); free to all Sun. and national holidays. There is an additional charge to use a video camera.

NEARBY DESTINATIONS

CHEMUYIL (cheh-moo-YEEL), a sheltered cove about 21 kilometers (13 miles) north of Tulum, claims to be "La Playa Mas Bonita del Mundo" ("The Prettiest Beach in the World"). Unfortunately, its once-extravagant stand of coconut palms has been largely leveled by a disease called lethal yellowing, which causes the fronds to drop off and eventually kills the tree.

The blight has not, however, diminished Chemuyil's relaxed and friendly ambience. Facilities include camping areas, bungalows, restrooms, showers, thatched-roof pavilions and a restaurant/bar where such exotic animals as spider monkeys and baby ocelots mingle with the human patrons. A fee is charged for day use of the beach.

CHUNYAXCHE (choon-yahsh-CHEH), about 26 kilometers (16 miles) south of Tulum on the east side of Mex. 307, is the site of the Muyil ruins, a large, rarely visited Maya archeological site that contains a partially reconstructed ceremonial temple. Excavations are sporadic but ongoing; research continues to determine whether Muyil once functioned as a port, since canals join the site to the Caribbean, 15 kilometers (9 miles) east. Tours through the canals to jungle-lined lagoons along the coast can be arranged through the Cancún-based Friends of Sian Ka'an organization; phone (98) 84-9583.

CUZAN BONEFISH FLATS is within the lobster-fishing village of Punta Allen, on the Boca Paila

Carving, Tulum ruins ©Chris Sharp

Peninsula about 60 kilometers (37 miles) south of Tulum. It can be reached via the access road that branches south off Mex. 307 at the town of Tulum. Boating excursions are offered to two nearby rookery islands to observe such tropical species as frigate birds and roseate spoonbills. Visitors can snorkel or fish against a backdrop of spectacular coral reefs.

In addition, guided fishing trips explore 20 square miles of uniformly shallow water at the northern entrance to Ascención Bay. The flats of sand, marl and turtle grass are home to bonefish, tarpon, barracuda and other game fish. Fly fishing is best from November through June.

Rustic accommodations are provided on a beach with the dramatic colors of the Caribbean as a backdrop. Fees are charged for accommodations, boating excursions and fishing trips; meals are included. Credit cards are not accepted. Reservations can be made by fax transmission to the mainland town of Felipe Carrillo Puerto; fax (98) 34-0383. Waterproof sunscreen, polarized sunglasses and insect repellent all are essential for a stay at Cuzan.

Note: There is no public transportation to Punta Allen; the best way to reach Cuzan is to fly into Cancún and then rent a car. Allow up to 2 hours to reach Punta Allen from Tulum via an inferior road that passes through thick jungle. For the active outdoor or sport fishing enthusiast who does not mind roughing it, this is a beautiful and rewarding trip.

SIAN KA'AN BIOSPHERE RESERVE occupies 1.3 million acres along the Caribbean coast that includes the Boca Paila Peninsula and the mainland south of Tulum and east of Mex. 307. It was created in 1986 by the Mexican government as a protected wildlife area and designated a World Heritage Site in 1987 by the United Nations Educational, Scientific and Cultural Organization (UNESCO). The reserve, like others on the Yucatán Peninsula, was established to preserve the native environment; thousands of acres are lost each year to forestry and cultivation.

Sian Ka'an ("place where the sky is born") encompasses tropical rain forest, drier areas of tree-speckled savanna, coastal mangrove flats and some 70 miles of offshore coral reefs, all protected from encroachment or commercial development. This vast wilderness is a haven for a variety of wildlife—including some endangered species—such as deer, jaguars, ocelots, tapirs, peccaries (a form of wild pig), howler monkeys, crocodiles, manatees and sea turtles (green, loggerhead, hawksbill and leatherback).

Bird life is equally rich and diverse, and the 350 species inhabiting the reserve range from cormorants, storks, roseate spoonbills, egrets and herons to neon-colored toucans, parrots and the frigate bird, the male of which is endowed with a startlingly large and red breast pouch during the mating season. Areas of virgin jungle contain about 1,200 varieties of plants. Also within the reserve are some 30 archeological sites.

Sian Ka'an is divided into three areas. A core zone is highly protected and restricted to scientific research. A buffer zone grants visitors restricted access; families with ancestral ties to the area are allowed to live, hunt, fish and gather plants for dietary or medicinal purposes. The outer buffer zone is open to tourists; this area includes the coastal Boca Paila Peninsula. Although the reserve is huge, its only access points are the roads leading south along the coast from Tulum and from the Muyil ruins (see Chunyaxché attraction listing), off Mex. 307 on the mainland.

The **Boca Paila Peninsula**, which constitutes the far eastern edge of the reserve, is the most accessible way to experience Sian Ka'an's unspoiled beauty. Take the road that branches southeast off Mex. 307 at the southern end of the town of Tulum. Most of this route is limestone covered with packed earth and sand, studded with potholes during the summer rainy season. It travels down the peninsula some 60 kilometers (37 miles) to Punta Allen at land's end. This lobster-fishing village at the head of Bahía Ascención attracts fly-fishing enthusiasts in search of bonefish, tarpon and other game species.

Note: Sian Ka'an's core zone is closed to visitors; tourism is restricted to the outer buffer zone. Biologist-escorted day tours of the peninsula are available. For further information about the biosphere reserve, contact the **Amigos de Sian Ka'an** (Friends of Sian Ka'an), in the Plaza Américas in Ciudad Cancún; phone (98) 84-9583.

TANKAH is about 3.5 kilometers (2 miles) north of the Tulum ruins and east of Mex. 307. It was one of the satellite cities of Tulum; the others were Solimán and Xel-Há. The few ruins that remain are hidden in the underbrush and have not been fully explored.

XCACEL is about 19 kilometers (12 miles) north of the town of Tulum off Mex. 307, about a quarter mile east of the highway. Although the crescent-shaped beach is one of Caribbean Mexico's prettiest, it is bypassed by most tourists. The calm water is ideal for swimming, snorkeling, diving and fishing. There are camping facilities, changing rooms, showers and a restaurant. A wrecked tour boat, which hit offshore rocks, sank and was pushed to the shore by the waves, is at the southern tip of the beach. A fee is charged for day use of the beach.

Note: At Xcacel, Paamul and other beaches along the Mexican Caribbean coast, volunteer groups sponsored by the state of Quintana Roo periodically organize programs designed to save sea turtles from extinction. The turtles' nesting sites are being destroyed by the development occurring along much of the coast. From May through August, rare loggerhead and green turtles laboriously leave the sea to build nests on the beach and lay their eggs. The volunteer groups help ensure that the turtles complete their task, and then tag and release the hatchlings. Visitors can ask to join a night patrol; flashlights are prohibited because they drive the turtles back toward the water. Donations are appreciated.

XEL-HA NATIONAL PARK is about 16 kilometers (10 miles) north of the Tulum ruins via a well-marked turnoff on the east side of Mex. 307. It comprises a series of freshwater lagoons, fed by underwater springs, that form a large natural aquarium. Fingers of limestone jutting into the labyrinth of inlets and lagoons allow visitors to observe a variety of colorful tropical fish from above the water. Many of them gather around underwater rock formations. For landlubbers, bridges built over the lagoons are equipped with benches for easy viewing.

Snorkeling at Xel-Há (shell-HAH) can be enjoyed without the undertows or strong currents that can make the beaches dangerous, and the clarity of the water is excellent. Other activities include hiking, inner tubing and an interactive swim with dolphins. Locker rooms and showers are provided, and there are several restaurants. Open daily 8-5. To fully enjoy the park, get there early; when the tour buses arrive it can become very crowded.

Admission to the park is about $15. Snorkeling equipment (including underwater cameras) and kayaks can be rented for an additional fee; you also may bring your own equipment. There is a separate charge for the dolphin swim. Phone (98) 84-9422. Many Cancún travel agencies combine Xel-Há and Tulum as a single guided day-trip excursion.

Just south of the park turnoff on the west side of the highway is a small group of Maya ruins and a deep cenote (sinkhole) set amid a tangle of trees and vines. Seldom visited, it is a tranquil place to explore for an hour. Data gathered from the site indicates it was important to the operations of the Maya "merchant marine." Admission is charged.

UXMAL, YUCATAN (G-11)

If Chichén Itzá is considered the Yucatán Peninsula's most impressive archeological site, Uxmal (oosh-MAHL) is the most beautiful. Unlike the structures at Chichén Itzá, with their Toltec-influenced images of violent conquest, Uxmal's architecture is more purely Maya, with richly ornamented stone facades and a majestic pyramid. Don't miss it.

HISTORICAL OVERVIEW

Uxmal rose to prominence concurrently with the great civilizations at Palenque *(see separate listing under Southern Mexico)* and Tikal in Guatemala, flourishing between A.D. 600 and 1000. Little is known about its history. The name means "thrice built" in Maya, although it was actually reconstructed five times, suggesting that drought forced abandonment followed by resettlement. Uxmal gained prominence as other Maya centers in Central America and southeastern Mexico declined, and probably dominated the surrounding Puuc cities of Kabah, Labná, Sayil and Xlapak *(see attraction listings below).* The subsequent importance of Chichén Itzá and the increased intermingling of Maya cultures with those from the central Mexican highlands were likely contributors to the city's decline, which appeared to be complete by the 14th century.

Uxmal was noted by American adventurer John Lloyd Stephens and English illustrator Frederick Catherwood in 1841 on their journey by horseback through the wilds of Chiapas, the Yucatán Peninsula and Central America. The first excavations were begun in 1929 by Danish archeologist and explorer Frans Blom, who also conducted research at other Maya archeological sites. The Mexican government has since worked with a number of archeologists to reconstruct the site, and the main buildings have all been restored.

Uxmal, the focal point of a ruins-rich area called the Puuc (pook) Hills, is the defining example of the Puuc architectural style, which emphasizes elegant, horizontal proportions and intricately detailed building exteriors of cut stones assembled in geometric patterns. Cornices and entryways often feature beak-nosed representations of the rain god Chac, whose benevolence was vital for crop success (and thus survival). The detail of the stonework is even more amazing when one considers that the Maya created their buildings without benefit of metal tools. Other hallmarks of the Puuc style are pointed arches, a liberal use of columns, and buildings that are low to the ground yet also expansive.

This part of the peninsula has a hot climate with seasonal precipitation and is subject to prolonged dry spells. Unlike other Maya cities, Uxmal did not have ready availability to a source of water; there was no rain-filled cenote (sinkhole) on which the inhabitants could rely. Instead, they depended upon the *chultun* (a man-made cistern) to collect precious rainwater.

MAJOR STRUCTURES

Visitors enter the site via a short path that begins at the visitor center, and the first building is immediately evident: the **Pyramid of the Magician**, also called El Adivino (The Sorcerer). It is both taller (some 125 feet) and steeper than El

Castillo, the pyramid at Chichén Itzá, and dominates the other structures by sheer height. According to legend the pyramid was built in one night by a dwarf, hatched from an egg, who possessed mystical powers. It actually contains five superimposed layers that correspond to Uxmal's five separate periods of construction. Built on an unusual elliptical base, the pyramid's walls are rounded rather than sharply angular.

This structure probably functioned as a ceremonial building where Uxmal's rulers were crowned. Stairways ascend the eastern and western sides; the western stairway is very steep (a 60-degree angle) and leads to an earlier temple, the entire facade of which is a large Chac mask with an open mouth forming the doorway. The eastern stairway is not quite as steep. **Note:** Climbing the pyramid is very risky if you're prone to vertigo. At press time, the stairways were roped off; inquire at the visitor center whether climbing is permitted.

The western stairway faces the **Casa de las Monjas** (Nunnery), more than 70 rooms in long, low buildings that surround a large quadrangle. Named by the Spaniards, it probably was used by Uxmal's elite ruling class. Stand in the center of the courtyard to appreciate the overall harmony that prevails, even though the buildings are terraced and on different levels.

The exteriors of each wing have beautiful decorative details, including stone masks of Chac (recognized by their elongated noses), entwined serpents, mosaic patterns and latticework designs. The southern wing has an arched entryway, once the complex's main entrance. The interior rooms, dark and filled with rubble, have occasional traces of former carvings.

The ball court just south of the Nunnery is smaller and simpler than the one at Chichén Itzá. South of the ball court is the small, classically designed **Casa de las Tortugas** (House of the Turtles), named for the border of turtles carved along its upper molding. Stand on the south side of this temple and look through the central doorway (of three) for a nicely framed view of the Nunnery.

Just southeast of the House of the Turtles is the **Governor's Palace**, widely considered to be among the finest Maya architectural achievements. This low, narrow structure, more than 300 feet long, is built on three levels. Its upper facade is covered with intricately carved stone figures and geometric designs. Serpents, masks and mosaic patterns all blend into a beautifully harmonious whole. Stand back from the palace's eastern side to discern the 103 stone carvings of Chac that together form the image of an undulating serpent (dramatically illuminated during the sound-and-light show).

This complex was most likely Uxmal's administrative center and may also have served an as-

trological purpose; it faces east while the other buildings face west, perhaps to better sight the planet Venus, which the Maya associated with war. From this elevated vantage point there is an expansive view of the Nunnery and the Pyramid of the Magician.

The **Great Pyramid**, partially restored, is just southwest of the Governor's Palace. Originally terraced with nine levels, it is topped by a palace decorated with Chac masks and bird carvings that probably represent parrots. The climb to the palace level is steep but doable (be particularly careful descending if you're prone to vertigo), with sweeping views of the surrounding jungle scrub. Just west of the Great Pyramid are the remains of a building called the **Dovecote** because its lattice design somewhat resembles a bird nesting house. The view of this ruin is particularly fine from the summit of the Great Pyramid.

Other buildings at the site are only partially reconstructed, or unexcavated mounds hidden in the brush. The **Casa de la Vieja** (House of the Old Woman), an old, ruined pyramidal structure southeast of the Great Pyramid, is reached by an overgrown path. Further southeast is the **Temple of the Phalli**, another ruined structure with phallic-shaped sculptures along the cornices, presumably to divert and collect rainwater from the roof.

PRACTICALITIES

Mérida is the most convenient base from which to explore the Puuc region. ADO and other Mexican bus lines depart daily for Uxmal from Mérida's central bus station, on Calle 70 between calles 69 and 71. An easier alternative is to join a group bus tour. **Mayaland Tours** arranges all-day trips to Uxmal and nearby Kabah that include hotel pick-up and drop-off, an escorted tour of the ruins and lunch. There is a Mayaland office next to the Hotel Fiesta Americana Mérida; phone (99) 25-0621. Tour groups usually have access to a hotel restaurant and swimming pool; bring a suit and towel, as they aren't provided.

Uxmal is about 79 kilometers (49 miles) south of Mérida via Mex. 261. From downtown Mérida, take Avenida Itzaes (Mex. 180) south past the Anillo Periférico (loop road) to the town of Umán. Watch for signs saying "To Campeche via Uxmal on Mex. 261," "Zona Arqueologia Uxmal" and "Ruta Puuc"; follow these signs through Umán to access Mex. 261 south. The two-lane road (no shoulders) runs through largely undeveloped scrub country. Pass with care, as you will likely encounter an occasional slow-moving vehicle or stopped dump truck.

Note: En route to Uxmal a new bypass branches off Mex. 261, rejoining it south of Muna. Not having to drive through this small town cuts some time off the trip, which takes about an hour from Mérida. You could also take

The intricate detail characteristic of the Puuc style is evident in this section of the Nunnery complex.   ©Greg Weekes

the old road into Muna, a typical Yucatecan small town of thatch-roofed stone dwellings that also has a big Franciscan church.

For those who want to spend the night near the ruins, there are a few comfortable hotels next to the site and along Mex. 261 near the entrance. More budget-minded travelers might consider an overnight stay in the nearby town of Ticul, about a 15-minute drive from Uxmal, which offers very basic services.

Guides are available, although they aren't needed in order to appreciate the architecture. Determine the fee before agreeing to a guided tour. The information may be embellished with fanciful details, but a guide's general knowledge will be helpful to those unfamiliar with Maya history. If you'd rather explore on your own, the main buildings can all be viewed over the course of a few hours. Informational plaques at each one are in English, Spanish and Maya.

Sound-and-light shows in English and Spanish are presented nightly from a vantage point overlooking the Nunnery quadrangle. Colored lights, recorded symphonic music under the stars and melodramatic narration provide an appropriate backdrop for Maya legends. Although the "history" can be taken with a grain of salt, the artificial lighting illuminates architectural details that are missed under sharp sunlight. Contact a Mérida travel agency for information about bus excursions to see the show, or check at one of the Uxmal hotels.

Most of the site is unshaded; bring a hat or other headgear for protection from the strong sun. An early start will allow you to beat not only the heat but the tour bus crowds that begin arriving before noon. Comfortable, nonslip walking shoes are a must if you plan to do any climbing. It's also a good idea to bring bottled water and insect repellent (particularly if you're attending the sound-and-light show).

The visitor center at the entrance contains a bookstore, craft shop, ice cream parlor, casual restaurant, convenience store (where film and disposable cameras can be purchased), restrooms and an air-conditioned auditorium (Auditorio Kit Bolon Tun) that shows a film about Uxmal. Next to the visitor parking lot there are a few souvenir and T-shirt stands.

Uxmal is open daily 8-6. The English sound-and-light show begins at 8 p.m. Admission 49 pesos (about $5), under 12 free; free to all Sun. and holidays. Parking fee 10 pesos. Video camera fee 30 pesos. There is a separate fee for the sound-and-light show.

NEARBY PUUC RUINS

For true aficionados of Maya history and culture, a full day can be spent exploring the ruins along the "Puuc Trail" south and east of Uxmal, all within easy driving distance. Driving is really the only way to do it, as most tour buses don't visit these small archeological sites. Roadside services are minimal, so make sure your gas tank is full and bring food, water, insect repellent and comfortable, nonslip walking shoes. The following sites are listed in order of location from Uxmal.

KABAH is about 19 kilometers (12 miles) south on Mex. 261. Park in the small dirt lot on the east (left) side of the road. There's a small ticket booth and a one-room shack selling snacks, film and a few souvenirs. You may even have the place to yourself, as it is seldom visited.

Kabah dates to around A.D. 850. Although small—there are only two main buildings—it is well worth visiting to see the lavishly decorated **Codz-Pop** (in Maya, "rolled mat"), or Palace of the Masks. This 150-foot-long temple stands on a low escarpment overlooking the highway and is immediately visible. Its entire west exterior is emblazoned with elaborately carved stone masks of the rain god Chac, and rows of additional stone carvings sit on the grass in front of the palace awaiting placement (reconstruction efforts are ongoing). The hooked snouts of some of the carvings are large enough to function as steps that lead into the interior rooms. The busy architectural style reflects the ornate Chenes influence, which is not often seen in this region.

As amazing as the front is, make sure you walk around to the back (east) side. There are no Chac masks here, but jutting off the upper facade are the sculptures of two warriors who face the rising sun and seem to be guarding the palace. The carvings are in good condition. Below them on one of the side panels (at ground level) are bas-reliefs depicting one warrior subjugating another in classic Maya fashion—the conqueror holding the vanquished by the hair, upraised hand brandishing a spear.

Next to the Palace of the Masks is a mostly unexcavated, weed-covered pyramidal structure. The other major building on this side of the road is the well-restored **El Palacio** (The Palace), built on two levels, which features a Puuc-style colonnaded facade.

Across Mex. 261 is the the **Great Temple**, a large conical mound rising above the thick scrub. It is only partially restored. Beyond the Great Temple is a free-standing **arch** marking the spot where a Maya *sacbe* (limestone causeway) road once entered Kabah from Uxmal; compare it to the one at Labná *(see below)*. The site is open daily 8-5. Admission 14 pesos (about $1.40); free to all Sun. Video camera fee 30 pesos.

Note: About 5 km (3 miles) north of Kabah is a junction with a dirt turnoff that leads to the village of **Santa Elena** (the directional sign says "Sta. Elena"), less than a mile off Mex. 261. This quick detour offers a look at rural Maya life, where dirt paths wind past humble concrete and thatched dwellings dozing in the shade of fruit trees and vegetable gardens. The town's church, up a hill from the small, rundown main plaza, is undergoing renovations; take a peek inside. As in many Mexican villages, the **Municipal Palace** housing local government offices is the grandest building in town; here it's painted bright turquoise.

Palace of the Masks   ©John Neubauer

SAYIL is about 5 kilometers (3 miles) from Kabah; take Mex. 261 to the junction with Mex. 184 (the road to Oxkutzcab), then east about 4 kilometers (2.5 miles) to the ruins. The aptly named site, which means "place of ants," contains several hundred known structures, almost all on the south side of the road.

There is one standout: the **Palace**, a grand three-level building more than 200 feet long. The second level features rows of Grecian-style columns as well as a profusion of stone carvings. Most are of the rain god Chac, but there are additional depictions of an upside-down "diving god" (also interpreted as a descending god to the underworld); the latter appears on a temple at the later site of Tulum *(see separate listing)*. The symbolism is unclear, although the figure may have represented gods or ancestors viewing mortal events from the heavens above.

Most of the other buildings are in ruins or obscured by jungle. South of the Palace is **El Mirador**, a small temple, and beyond it a primitive stele with a carving of a prodigiously endowed phallic figure. One solitary structure stands across the road from the entrance. Also at this site are a number of man-made cisterns that were built to catch seasonal rainfall. Open daily 8-5. Admission is charged; free to all Sun. There is an additional fee for using a video camera.

XLAPAK (shla-PAHK) is about 6 kilometers (3.5 miles) east of Sayil. The notable structure at this small site ("old walls," in Maya) on the south side of the road is the partially restored **Palace of Xlapak**, which is decorated with Chac masks, some flaunting curled noses. In typical Puuc style, the lower facade is plain, and the building as a whole impressively proportioned. The restored portions are lighter in tone than the weathered, unrestored sections. Open daily 8-5. Admission is charged; free to all Sun. There is an additional fee for using a video camera.

LABNA is about 3 kilometers (2 miles) east of Xlapak. Here the best-known monument is a restored, free-standing stone arch larger and more ornately decorated than the one at Kabah. The structure to which it was once attached is now gone. Some 20 feet high and 10 feet wide, it features ornate decoration on the west side and a more geometric pattern on the east side. Above the entryway on both sides are carved representations of a thatched Maya hut. Pass through the arch to **El Mirador**, a pyramidal structure resting on a pile of rubble. Labná, like Sayil, contains the remains of many *chultunes* (cisterns) that collected rainwater for use during the dry season.

Labná's impressive **Palace** building is similar to the one at Sayil, although not in as good condition. See it for the ornamentation, which is—as on so many Maya buildings—bizarrely imaginative. One doorway is capped by a huge, toothy Chac mask with an oversized snout. Angling out from a corner is the head of a serpent, its open jaws disgorging a serene-looking human head that represents life. Open daily 8-5. Admission is charged; free to all Sun. There is an additional fee for using a video camera.

OXKUTZCAB, TICUL, MANI AND THE CAVES OF LOLTUN

Oxkutzcab (osh-koots-KAHB) is in a fertile farming region. Fields of tall corn that wouldn't look out of place in the American Midwest give way to the more tropical look of orange groves and clumps of coconut palms. In Oxkutzcab and other small Yucatán towns, a popular means of conveyance is the *triciclo*, the reverse of a tricycle—two wheels in front supporting a cargo/carrier area and one in the back, below the driver's seat. Everything from human passengers to crates of produce and chickens ride through the streets by means of this cheap transportation.

About 6 kilometers (10 miles) southwest of Oxkutzcab via the Sayil-Labná road are the **Grutas de Loltún** (Loltún Caves). The entrance to the caves is reached from a gravel path that branches off the north side of the road; the turnoff is not signed. Hieroglyphic inscriptions and carvings of flowers on the walls are estimated to be some 1,000 years old; the caves' name, loosely translated, means "one flower in the stone." The ancient Maya once lived in these subterranean chambers, which also served as a refuge for Maya rebels during the 19th-century War of the Castes.

Throughout the caves are *chultunes* (cisterns), stone troughs which were placed to collect water dripping from the roof. Other man-made artifacts include grinding tools, a jaguar sculpture and a statue of a Maya warrior. Natural formations include giant stalactites and stalagmites that hum when struck, sending echoes of sound through the caverns. Some of these bear a startling resemblance to animal forms or, in one striking case, the Virgin of Guadalupe.

The caverns can be seen by guided tour only. Tours are given daily at 9:30, 11, 12:30, 2 and 3:30; double-check this schedule at the Uxmal visitor center. (**Note:** Although the caverns are illuminated, some passages are dark and the paths may be slippery or steep; wear comfortable, nonslip walking shoes.) Most of the tours are given in Spanish; ask at the front ticket office regarding the availability of an English-speaking guide. There is a small restaurant at the cave exit. Admission to the caverns is charged.

Ticul is on the Mérida-Chetumal Highway (Mex. 184) about 19 kilometers (12 miles) northwest of Oxkutzcab. This busy regional center also specializes in the manufacture of pottery and women's shoes. It's larger than most of the other towns in this area; the streets are filled with *triciclos* (and dogs). The three-wheeled conveyances function as taxis. Street names are often posted on the sides of buildings instead of on signs.

The domed 18th-century cathedral stands next to Ticul's central plaza. An interesting exterior decoration is the facial features—two half-moon eyes and a nose—carved below the roof. Local restaurants offer Yucatecan specialties such as *poc chuc* (marinated pork and onions), bean soup and tortillas stuffed with hard-boiled eggs and topped with tomato or pumpkinseed sauce.

Many of the shops lining the downtown streets sell nothing but shoes. Small *fabricas* (factories) on the outskirts of town produce pottery and terra-cotta reproductions of classic Maya art. Craft shops offer ceramic bowls, and street vendors hawk embroidered *huipiles* and Panama hats made from woven palm fronds.

East of Ticul is the village of **Maní**; it was here that the Xius of Uxmal retired in 1451 after the destruction of the Maya capital of Mayapán. Maní also is believed to be the place where Diego de Landa, a Spanish bishop, ordered in 1562 the destruction by fire of the Maya *codices*, or hieroglyphic picture books, believing them profane. The historical loss resulting from this act was incalculable, leaving Landa's own treatise on Maya civilization, *"Relación de las Cosas de Yucatán"* ("Yucatán Before and After the Conquest"), the definitive account.

Where To Stay

HOTEL HACIENDA UXMAL

♦♦ ♦♦   *Hotel*   ☎ 99/76-2013

All Year   S98   XP $8
Location: 85 km s of Merida on Mex 261, at archeological zone. 97840 (PO Box 407, MERIDA, YU). Fax: 99/76-2011. **Facility:** Tropically landscaped grounds. 80 units. Some suites. *Bath:* combo or shower only. 3 stories, interior/exterior corridors. **Terms:** F12; 7 day cancellation notice. **Leisure Activities:** 2 pools. **Guest Services:** gift shop. **Cards:** AE, CB, DI, MC, VI.

SOME UNITS
🍴 🛥 📠 🐾 DATA/PORT / 🐾 /

THE LODGE AT UXMAL

♦♦♦♦   *Lodge*   ☎ (99)76-2102

All Year   S148
Location: 85.5 km s of Merida on Mex 261 at entrance of Uxmal archeological zone. (PO Box 407, MERIDA, YU, 97100). **Facility:** Quality deep in the Yucatan jungle. Mayan decor, architecture and service. 40 units. Some whirlpool units. 2 stories, exterior corridors. **Terms:** 3 day cancellation notice, in season, package plans. **Amenities:** honor bars. **Leisure Activities:** 2 pools, recreation program. **Guest Services:** gift shop, valet laundry. *Fee:* area transportation. **Cards:** AE, MC, VI.

SOME UNITS
✈ 🍴 🍽 🛥 📹 📺 DATA/PORT / 🐾 /
FEE

VALLADOLID, YUCATAN (G-11)

Valladolid (vah-yah-doh-LEED) was founded in 1543 by Francisco de Montejo, who established Spanish rule over much of the Yucatán Peninsula. The Spaniards constructed their churches over the site of a former Maya town, Zací. Many revolts occurred in this region during the mid-19th-century War of the Castes, when rebellious and oppressed descendants of the Maya clashed with privileged landowners. Here too was one of the first uprisings against dictator Porfirio Díaz, which foreshadowed the Mexican Revolution of 1910.

The commercial center for an agricultural district, Valladolid is on Mex. 180 and is one of the three exits off toll highway Mex. 180-D. A colonial atmosphere, somewhat gone to seed, pervades this unpretentious market town, where old buildings still bear weathered Spanish coats of arms above their doorways. The main square is bounded by calles 39, 40, 41 and 42; here visitors can browse among shops selling leather goods or sit on one of the curved stone benches and observe the local scene.

Valladolid has a number of churches. The fortifications of the convent and church of **San Bernardino de Siena**, a massive complex founded in 1552 by the Franciscan Order, were built to ward off the warring Mayas, who sacked it repeatedly. Looting during the War of the Castes has robbed the church of much of its interior ornamentation. The convent is located 3 blocks southwest of the main square. The **Church of San Roque**, a block east of the main square, houses a small museum.

The cenote **Zací** (sah-KEE), a huge sinkhole 2 blocks east of the main square, is reached by worn stone stairs that descend into a dark cavern, the upper reaches of which are populated by bats. The murky water is flecked with green scum that the locals call "lake lettuce." The cenote is spookily atmospheric but unsuitable for swimming. The **Dzitnup** cenote, about 4 kilometers (2.5 miles) southwest of town on the south side of Mex. 180 (there is a signed turnoff), is a better alternative for those who want to try swimming. The natural pool of clear, blue water is inside a cavern where a shaft of sunlight illuminates the stalactites hanging from the roof. Admission is charged for swimming; the short flight of stone steps leading down into the cavern can be slippery.

Nearby Destinations

Río Lagartos National Park, Mexico's largest flamingo sanctuary, is about 100 kilometers (62 miles) almost due north of Valladolid at the end of Mex. 295. Some 120,000 acres of protected land along the Yucatán Peninsula's northern coast comprise mangrove swamps, sand dunes and mud flats. A long inlet forms a thin peninsula of land and creates a number of shallow estuaries. In addition to the flamingos, the park is home to herons, egrets, cormorants, ducks and pelicans. It is administered by the Secretariat of Urban Development and Ecology (SEDUE), which sponsors research and provides protection for flamingos during the breeding season.

Ecotourism is slowly developing in this isolated area, which offers birdwatching, camping and hiking along deserted stretches of shoreline. The coast was once a refuge for plundering pirates, and celebrated pirate and smuggler Jean Lafitte is supposedly buried in one of the region's scattered villages. A factory near the small settlement of Las Coloradas produces salt, which is processed from numerous ponds in the surrounding marshy swamps; other mineral deposits in the water help contribute to the brilliant scarlet and pink plumage of the resident flamingos.

Boat tours can be arranged with local guides at the one hotel in the fishing village of Río Lagartos. For the best flamingo watching, it's advisable to depart by 7 a.m. Visiting the actual nesting grounds at the park's eastern end, an isolated area where the flamingos' cone-shaped mud nests rise above the flats, is prohibited during the breeding season (April through June). During these months the birds are fiercely protective of their nests and eggs. The winter months are a better—and cooler—time to observe young flamingos and other bird species. If you do go on a boat tour, bring a hat or other protection from the sun, your own water and a snack.

The village of Río Lagartos is quaint but lacks tourist facilities. Birdwatchers who want to get an early start should consider spending the night in Tizimín, on Mex. 295 about halfway between Valladolid and Río Lagartos. Boat tours also can be arranged from the coastal village of San Felipe, about 12 kilometers (7 miles) west of Río Lagartos. San Felipe has no accommodations and few facilities; visitors either come for the day or bring camping equipment for an overnight stay on the beaches along the Río Lagartos Peninsula. Another flamingo sanctuary surrounds the fishing village of **Celestún** *(see description on page 134)*, on the gulf coast west of Mérida.

Tizimín is in the middle of an agricultural and cattle-raising region. (**Note:** The *topes*—speed bumps—along Mex. 295 can significantly damage the underside of a vehicle if negotiated at too fast a speed.) An atmosphere reminiscent of the American Wild West pervades this market center, where livestock-filled trucks clatter down the streets and cowboys crowd the local *cantinas*.

Tizimín lacks the tourist-oriented souvenir and craft shops found in so many Mexican towns, but it does contain a colonial-era church and convent on the main square, named after the Three Kings (Tres Santos Reyes), the town's patron saints. In early January all Tizimín turns out for a fiesta held in their honor, which features parades, dancing, bullfights and regional food. On Jan. 6, *Three Kings Day* (Día de Reyes), gifts are exchanged and pilgrimages are made to honor the three kings.

Excavations are ongoing at **Ek-balam** (which means "black jaguar"), about 32 kilometers (20 miles) northeast of Valladolid. To get there, take Mex. 295 north about 18 kilometers (11 miles) to the junction with a winding road (watch for the sign marking the turnoff) that passes through the small village of Hunuku. Years away from complete restoration, the site is characterized by piles of carved stones waiting to be reassembled.

For archeology buffs, the lure of Ek-balam is in observing the process of reconstruction. The structures that have been fully restored are architecturally similar in style to the Puuc ruins found at sites near Uxmal. The largest pyramid is some 100 feet tall and larger than Chichén Itzá's El Castillo. Other impressive mounds have yet to be unearthed.

There is no visitor center or modern restrooms; wear comfortable walking shoes and bring drinking water. But it only takes an hour or so to view the restored portion of the site, and this makes an interesting side trip and contrast to the more "manicured" look of Chichén Itzá and Uxmal. Ek-balam is open daily 8-5. Admission is charged; there is an extra charge for use of a video camera.

BAJA CALIFORNIA

Baja California extends south from the U.S. border like a giant appendage paralleling the northwestern Mexican mainland. The peninsula broke off millions of years ago, in the process creating the Gulf of California (also known as the Sea of Cortés). Numerous fishing villages and resort lodges are scattered along the peninsula's more than 2,000 miles of coastline. Baja also is renowned for its beaches, which are for the most part uncrowded and pristine, framing the emerald-green waters of the gulf and the deep blue of the ocean. Both bodies of water are home to an amazing variety of fish, making the peninsula a sport fishing paradise. The completion in 1973 of Mex. 1, the Transpeninsular Highway, opened the more far-flung parts of Baja to visitors and ushered in economic development.

Much of the peninsula remains isolated. The state of Baja California, comprising all territory north of the 28th parallel, consists mostly of rugged mountains or harsh desert, although irrigation of the hot, arid valleys around the border city of Mexicali has turned them into a productive agricultural region. Easily accessible Tijuana—big, bustling, part trashy, part flashy—draws hordes of stay-for-a-day tourists, college-age partiers and dedicated shoppers. The port of Ensenada is a popular weekend destination offering beaches, dining and nightlife. Between the two is Rosarito Beach, a casual, rapidly growing resort area.

The state of Baja California Sur, occupying the southern portion of the peninsula, is even more barren. Occasional oases such as the village of San Ignacio, a mirage of date palms and pastel-colored buildings, pop up in the middle of the desert. At Baja's southern tip is its most popular vacation spot, the twin resorts of Cabo San Lucas and San José del Cabo, where sport fishing and surfing are augmented by an impressive string of championship golf courses.

A BAJA OVERVIEW

HISTORY

In 1535, an officer under the command of Hernán Cortés became the first European to land in Baja (Lower) California. The reports he brought back, particularly with respect to the existence of pearls in the Gulf of California, were so tantalizing that a year later Cortés himself led settlers to the present site of La Paz, near the peninsula's southern end. The poverty of the land and the fierceness of the Indians led him to abandon the area a few years later, and Spanish *conquistadores*—busy plundering other parts of Mexico—all but forgot Baja. The peninsula became the province of pirates who launched raids on Spanish galleons from the cover of Baja's protected coves.

It was not until 1697 that a permanent settlement was established—a Jesuit mission and presidio at Loreto, about 360 kilometers (220 miles) north of La Paz. Throughout the 18th century, the Indians in this barren land were ministered to

by the Jesuits, who founded the first missions and also taught them to farm. When the Jesuits were banished from Mexico in the 1760s, the Franciscans and the Dominicans followed. But along with churches, the missionaries brought disease. Smallpox had almost wiped out the indigenous population by the middle of the 19th century. Meanwhile, primitive settlements began to appear, but for many years the only means of access between them was by boat or on foot.

Loreto remained the leading town in Baja until 1829, when a storm leveled it; the capital was moved south to La Paz. In the 1840s the peninsula was occupied by U.S. forces fighting in the Mexican-American War, and efforts were made to annex Baja to the United States; the troops were later expelled. Sporadic mining operations—silver in colonial times, a French-operated copper mine established in the town of Santa Rosalía—never equaled the riches found on the mainland.

Well into the 20th century, Baja remained a lonely outpost. Except for a handful of cities and resorts that catered to the well-to-do, it was inhabited mainly by Indians and hardy fishermen. Mex. 1 opened the peninsula to mainstream travel, although subsequent headlong development poses a threat to the delicate ecological balance that exists between land and sea.

GEOGRAPHY

The Baja California Peninsula is nearly 800 miles in length and varies from about 30 to 110 miles in width. Its backbone is made up of two westward-sloping mountain ranges. Sierra de San Pedro Mártir dominates the north; Sierra de la Giganta, the south. In the former, Picacho del Diablo attains an elevation of 10,073 feet, the highest point on the peninsula. Both the gulf and Pacific coastlines are indented by an endless string of bays and coves, with many islands scattered offshore.

Geographical isolation has produced plant varieties that grow nowhere else on Earth. The giant cardón cactus is similar in appearance to the saguaro of Arizona. The cirio is a tall, columnar oddity that somewhat resembles an inverted carrot; it grows only on the peninsula and in the mainland state of Sonora. Other plants well adapted for survival in the harsh environment include a variety of cactuses. Scattered clumps of date palms are not native but were planted by Jesuit missionaries. Along both coasts are dense thickets of mangrove. The agricultural north and the tropical south support more vegetation than the rocky, desolate middle portion of the peninsula, although no part of Baja is naturally lush.

CLIMATE

Baja's weather is characterized by heat and aridity, although there are some variations. The weather along the northern Pacific coast is similar to coastal southern California: warm and dry in summer, cool and rather wet in winter. Summer highs in the 70s and 80s begin to rise rapidly a short distance inland. Fog is prevalent in late spring and early summer. Winter rains are occasionally torrential and have been known to cause mudslides and road closures; total rainfall, however, varies greatly from year to year. The inland hills and mountains even receive occasional winter snow.

The eastern side of the peninsula, including the Mexicali Valley and the Gulf of California coast, is very hot and dry from May through October and mild to warm with only small amounts of rainfall during the rest of the year. Summer temperatures are brutal in this desert region, with highs reaching 120 degrees Fahrenheit.

The central section of the peninsula receives occasional heavy rainfall from southward-moving winter storms or from late-summer tropical storms (*chubascos*) that blow up from the south.

At the other extreme, a whole year may pass with barely a drop of rain in this region. Winters are mild, with brilliant sunshine and cloudless skies; summers are uncomfortably hot, and often humid as well along the Gulf of California coast. Parts of the Pacific Coast escape the summer heat.

From La Paz to the southern tip of the peninsula the climate is semiarid, with occasional downpours from tropical storms in the late summer or fall. Winters are warm and sunny, summers hot and dry, with occasional humid spells. Conditions in this resort area are best from November through April, when lows are in the 50s and 60s and highs in the 70s and 80s.

When it comes to surviving the rigors of a Baja summer, do as the locals do: Rise early in the morning, take a *siesta* during the heat of the afternoon, then venture out again in the evening after temperatures have cooled off.

WHAT TO SEE AND DO

While tourism in Baja California is on the upswing, the peninsula remains a last frontier in some ways—isolated from the rest of Mexico, thinly populated and ruggedly scenic. **Tijuana, Ensenada, La Paz** and the **Los Cabos** area draw the majority of the tourist traffic. Much of the land is harsh. Outdoor recreation is the lure for visitors, who come to frolic on the white sand beaches, surf the Pacific breakers, fish the rich waters of the Gulf of California and contemplate the stark, inspiring scenery that unfolds away from hotel pools and souvenir shops.

The cave paintings that cover huge expanses of canyon walls in the Sierra de San Francisco Mountains of central Baja, long revered by local inhabitants, have mystified researchers. The age of these rock murals—some 10 feet tall—is unknown. Scenes depict running deer and mountain goats, warriors with elaborate headdresses and even a whale. According to one 18th-century Jesuit legend, the cave artists were a race of giants invading from the north. Rediscovered in the early 1960s, the deterioration of some paintings due to damage from wind erosion and water seepage has caused concern among scientists and conservationists.

Although difficult to reach, the Sierra de San Francisco, north of San Ignacio, harbor the most important petroglyphs yet discovered in Mexico. They are contained inside the **Cueva de la Flecha** (Arrow Cave), **Cueva de San Julio** (Cave of San Julio), **Cueva del Ratón** (Cave of the Mouse) and **Cueva Pintada** (Painted Cave), and also decorate the **Piedras Pintadas** (Painted Rocks). Access to these areas is by horse or mule; the adventurous can hire guides in Santa Rosalía *(see separate listing)*.

In other areas of central Baja, the emptiness of the surrounding landscape is brightened by the paintings of local residents; roadside rocks provide their canvas. While subjects range from family names to beer ads, a blissful painting of the Virgin Mary embellishes a granite boulder north of the town of **Cataviña** on Mex. 1.

THE INFORMED TRAVELER

Most highways in Baja California are in good condition and uncrowded outside of the cities. There are two toll highways—Mex. 1-D between Tijuana and Ensenada, and Mex. 2-D, which is complete between Tijuana and Tecate and will eventually extend to Mexicali.

Temporary vehicle importation permits are not required when visiting the Baja California Peninsula. Drivers must, however, carry acceptable proof of vehicle ownership and a valid driver's license at all times. If you plan on transporting a vehicle from Baja California to the Mexican mainland, it *is* necessary to obtain a vehicle permit. Although permits are supposed to be available at the Baja ferry offices in Santa Rosalía and La Paz, they rarely are. To avoid frustration and disrupted travel plans, obtain the permit at the border. **Note:** Because of frequent congestion at the Tijuana border crossing, it is often easier to obtain a vehicle permit or take care of any other border-crossing procedures at another point of entry.

Baja has long had a reputation as a place where anglers, campers and other outdoor recreation enthusiasts could roam at will without paying much concern to personal safety. In recent years, however, car and RV break-ins have increased, and personal attacks are not unknown. Prudent common sense will reduce the chance of becoming the victim of theft or assault. If you're on a driving or camping vacation, keep three things in mind. Find a place to stay before dark, preferably one that has a guarded parking lot. Never pull off the road to sleep in your vehicle. And never camp in a remote or deserted area, either alone or in a group; always set up at a designated campground.

AIR AND BUS SERVICE

Aero California, Aeroméxico, Alaska Airlines and Mexicana Airlines offer flights to various Baja destinations from U.S. cities. For additional information about airlines *see "Arriving by Air,"* page 53.

Regular passenger bus service between Tijuana, Ensenada, Tecate and Mexicali is offered by Autotransportes de Baja California (ABC) and Tres Estrellas de Oro. These companies operate from the **Central de Autobuses** (Central Bus Terminal) on Boulevard Lázaro Cárdenas at Calle Alamar near Tijuana International Airport in La Mesa, B.C. Phone (66) 86-9515 for information.

Autotransportes de Baja California and Tres Estrellas de Oro buses also provide service between Tijuana and La Paz. The trip takes about 24 hours and costs about $56 (U.S.) one way; for information phone (66) 26-1701.

FERRY SERVICE

A private company, **Grupo Sematur**, operates regularly scheduled ferry service between the peninsula and the Mexican mainland. Round trips connect the ports of Santa Rosalía-Guaymas, La Paz-Topolobampo (Los Mochis) and La Paz-Mazatlán.

Reservations, necessary at all times, should be made at the ferry office at least 1 week in advance and at least 1 month before the departure date for holiday periods. Although reservations can be made from the United States or within Mexico by phone, some knowledge of Spanish is necessary; it is easier to make reservations in person at one of the ferry offices. Reconfirm the rate as well as space availability before you depart.

The ferry office in La Paz is at Guillermo Prieto and 5 de Mayo, 2 blocks southeast of Plaza Constitución. It is open Mon.-Fri. 7-1 and 4-6, Sat.-Sun. 8-1; phone (112) 5-3833 or 5-4666. The ferry terminal is at Pichilingue, the deepwater port for La Paz, about 16 kilometers (10 miles) north of the city. In Santa Rosalía, the ferry office is in the terminal building on Mex. 1, just south of the main entrance into town; phone (115) 2-0013 or 2-0014. In Topolobampo, the office is at the ferry terminal; phone (681) 2-0302 or 2-0320. In Guaymas, the office is at the ferry terminal; phone (622) 2-3390 or 2-3393. In Mazatlán, the office is at the ferry terminal; phone (69) 81-7020 or 81-7021.

Expect frequent changes in schedules and rates. Additional ferry information is available through the Automobile Club of Southern California and their club publication *Baja California.*

IN CASE OF EMERGENCY

Travelers experiencing an emergency anywhere in Baja California can contact the **Binational Emergency Medical Commission**, located in Chula Vista, Calif.; phone (619) 425-5080. This voluntary organization will help those stranded due to accident, illness, legal difficulty or lack of money. The commission works with both Mexican and American authorities.

BUENAVISTA, BAJA CALIFORNIA SUR

WHERE TO STAY

HOTEL BUENA VISTA BEACH RESORT

Resort ((114)1-0033
All Year $135 XP $50
Location: On the shore of Bahia de Palmas. (APDO Postal 574, LA PAZ, BS). Fax: 114/1-0133. **Facility:** On hillside overlooking the bay. Meets AAA guest room security requirements. 60 units. *Bath:* shower only. 1 story, exterior corridors. **Terms:** D12; 15 day cancellation notice-fee imposed, package plans, 10% service charge. **Amenities:** no TVs. **Leisure Activities:** 2 pools, whirlpools, beach, swimming, swim-up bar, boat ramp, scuba diving, snorkeling, fishing, 2 tennis courts. *Fee:* boating, scuba & snorkeling equipment, charter fishing, horseback riding. **Guest Services:** [AP] meal plan available, gift shop. *Fee:* massage. **Business Services:** conference facilities. **Cards:** AE, MC, VI.

FEE

CABO SAN LUCAS, BAJA CALIFORNIA SUR (F-3)

Cabo San Lucas (KAH-boh sahn LOO-kahs), at the southern tip of Baja California, marks the convergence of the Gulf of California and the Pacific Ocean. In the 16th and 17th centuries, gulfside Bahía San Lucas was a favored hiding place for pirates who plundered Spanish galleons. Cabo drowsed away the years until the 1950s, when the private yachts of well-to-do Americans began mooring in the bay. In the process, the town metamorphosed from unassuming cannery village to international resort. Together with neighboring San José del Cabo, the region known as **Los Cabos** (the Capes) is one of Mexico's fastest growing resort areas and a Baja hotspot renowned for excellent sport fishing.

Up until a few years ago Cabo San Lucas was primarily a destination for moneyed sportsmen and those escaping the crowds at Mexico's more established seaside getaways. But Baja's tip also has become a destination of choice for suntanned, fashionably unshaven Generation Xers who—unlike '80s yuppies and their sanitized Club Med tastes—relish southern Baja's nontouristy atmosphere, nearly deserted beaches and prime surfing spots.

Some 1,050 miles from the U.S. border, the two Cabos are accessible via Mex. 1 south from La Paz or Mex. 19 south from Todos Santos. Mex. 1 is a four-lane divided highway between San José del Cabo and Cabo San Lucas. The winding stretch provides views of rugged cliffs and glimpses of steely blue gulf water edged by white-sand beaches. Luxury resort developments with lushly groomed grounds are a dramatic counterpoint to the wild, rocky landscapes that surround them. **Note:** Avoid driving on Mex. 1 at

night; as in many parts of Mexico, cattle are apt to cross the roadway unexpectedly.

Impressive proof of Cabo's popularity are the high-rise hotels, condominiums, boutiques and restaurants lining the hillsides and waterfront. They share space with trailer parks, markets, gift shops, shopping centers, auto repair shops and a marina. Glass-bottomed boats leave the marina daily for cruises to nearby rock formations, with views of a sea lion colony, pelican rookery and waters filled with brightly hued tropical fish along the way. A ferry terminal lies idle; service to Puerto Vallarta has been suspended indefinitely. The town is, however, a port of call for cruise ships.

Despite the growth, Cabo is easily negotiated. The main street, an extension of Mex. 1 (the Transpeninsular Highway) from San José del Cabo, is Lázaro Cárdenas. Branching off from it is Boulevard Marina, which follows the waterfront. Paseo Morelos (Mex. 19) enters town from the west. There is only one stoplight, in the center of town, and streets are clearly marked.

Buses also traverse the three main streets, providing inexpensive transportation to most points of interest. The Aguila bus terminal is on Avenida Zaragoza, three blocks north of Lázaro Cárdenas. Taxis can take you from downtown to the outlying hotels or to secluded beaches along Bahía San Lucas. Local maps show beaches and other points of interest in relation to Mex. 1 km markers along the 33-kilometer (20-mile) distance between Cabo San Lucas and San José del Cabo.

Solitude seekers head for idyllic **Playa del Amor** (Lovers' Beach), which is overlooked by **El Arco**, a natural arch, and the rocky pinnacles of **Los Frailes** (The Friars). This idyllic spot is accessible only by boat. At the tip of the Baja California Peninsula is **Cabo Falso**, where an old lighthouse once guided ships between the U.S. west coast and Panama.

Local tour companies or travel agencies can arrange an all-terrain vehicle excursion over enormous sand dunes to visit the lighthouse and the remains of a shipwreck. Even more offbeat is another guided ATV tour to **La Candelaria**, an isolated Indian pueblo in the mountains north of Cabo San Lucas. An underground river provides water for uncharacteristically lush growths of mango, bamboo and palms. The locals here are said to still practice witchcraft.

To the east is **Land's End** (Finisterra), where the crashing of innumerable gulf and ocean waves have sculpted striking rock formations. Isolated beaches in the vicinity can be reached by boat or on foot from the Solmar Suites Resort. (Only those in good physical condition should attempt to clamber over the rocks here, and it is advisable to travel with a partner.) Both the approach to Cabo San Lucas via Mex. 1 and elevated spots in town offer panoramic views of this area, Baja's final frontier.

The weather in Cabo San Lucas is warm all year. Daytime highs are around 80 degrees in winter but can soar to over 100 during the summer months. In October the waters of the Pacific and the Sea of Cortez have been warmed by summer's heat to between 75 and 80 degrees, making conditions for swimming and snorkeling ideal. High season is October through April; bring a sweater for occasional cool evenings if visiting in January or February. **Note:** While it hardly ever rains in this part of Baja, the ravines (called arroyos) along Mex. 1 are subject to flash floods during infrequent storms. Flooding, although rare, can make vehicle travel impossible when it occurs.

THE INFORMED TRAVELER

The tourist office is on Avenida Hidalgo near the intersection with Avenida Guerrero. It is open Mon.-Fri. 9-2 and 4-7, Sat. 9-1. Useful phone numbers include the local police, (114) 3-3977; IMSS Hospital, 3-0480; post office, 3-0989; Secretary of Fishing, 3-0564; and FONATUR (which has updates on road conditions), 3-0494 or 3-1484.

Avoid the kiosks throughout town that claim to offer visitor information. Their real purpose is to lure the unsuspecting with free lunches and drinks and then attempt to sell time-shares in a new condominium development. These sales pitches can be long and arduous for those who are just in town to relax. The booth in front of the Hotel Plaza Las Glorias (on the marina in the center of town) is an exception; it has maps and information about the entire region.

Aero California, Alaska Airlines and Mexicana Airlines offer direct flights from Los Angeles to **Los Cabos International Airport**, which is about 13 kilometers (8 miles) northwest of San José del Cabo. Transportation to and from the airport is controlled by the local taxi service. *Colectivos* (shuttle vans) transport visitors from the airport to local hotels for around $9 (U.S.). A small airstrip just outside Cabo San Lucas accommodates single- and twin-engine aircraft and small private jets. Upon arrival, local cab drivers will race to the strip to inquire if a cab is needed into town. For additional information about airlines *see "Arriving by Air," page 53, and "Air and Bus Service" under "A Baja Overview," page 150.*

"Deluxe" bus service is provided by Tres Estrellas de Oro between Cabo San Lucas and San José del Cabo at about hourly intervals during daytime and early evening hours; the trip takes about 45 minutes. *Aguila* (local) buses traveling up and down Mex. 1 between the two towns can be flagged down along the highway and for a few pesos will drop you off at the downtown bus station. For the somewhat adventurous, this is one way to beat the high taxicab rates. *Aguila* buses also travel to La Paz; the trip takes about

Fishing boats crowd the docks at the Cabo San Lucas marina.   © John Neubauer

2½ hours and costs about $4 (U.S.). Tickets should be bought in advance in order to secure a seat.

Taxis in the area are expensive. Expect to pay from $17 to $24 (U.S.) for a ride into town if staying in an outlying resort or hotel between the two Cabos. Green taxis are for local fares only; yellow taxis are for fares heading out of town. Always negotiate the fare before getting in the cab. Most of the outlying hotels provide shuttles into Cabo San Lucas that may be free at certain times of the day; however, this service does not operate during evening hours.

If you're staying in town, one way to see the sights is by moped. Several agencies offer daily rentals for about $20 to $30 (U.S.). Keep in mind that the rental fee may not include insurance.

The English-language *Baja Sun* is a widely distributed monthly with information and advertisements pertaining to the Los Cabos region as well as the rest of Baja. *El Tiempo Los Cabos Times* is a bilingual newspaper. Radio station Cabo Mil (96 FM) broadcasts a variety of music.

Cash and traveler's checks can be exchanged at the Banca Serfin on Lázaro Cárdenas in the center of town. The commercial complex in which the bank is located also contains a travel agency and a Super Mercado grocery store. The Banamex Bank at Lázaro Cárdenas and Avenida Hidalgo has an ATM machine.

OUTDOOR RECREATION

The waters of the Gulf of California and the Pacific Ocean are a breeding ground for hundreds of species of game fish, making the Los Cabos area paradise for sports anglers. Striped marlin run year-round, and the season for the majestic blue marlin is June through mid-November. Others commonly hooked include amberjack, black marlin, bonito, black sea bass, corbina, dorado (mahi mahi), roosterfish, sailfish, snapper, wahoo, yellowfin tuna and yellowtail.

Fishing charters abound, and almost any of the bigger hotels can arrange an expedition. During the season it is advisable to book fishing trips well in advance; some anglers reserve boats as much as a year in advance for the *Gold Cup Tournament* each November. A catch-and-release policy is emphasized; anglers experience the thrill of battle, and after their catch is reeled in it is tagged and set free, helping to preserve billfish species and ensure the continuation of the sport.

Pangas (small skiffs) can be rented by the hour and include fishing equipment, a license and a chest to ice the catch. Excursions can be easily arranged through one of the fleet operators at the marina sportfishing dock; inquire at your hotel's front desk. More expensive sportfishing cruisers normally rent for parties of four to six people so expenses can be shared; the cost usually includes tackle, bait, licenses, lunch, ice and a captain and mate, but not taxes or tips. Rates range from $200 to $700 per day, depending on the size of the boat. Trips depart around 7 a.m. and return by 2 or 3 in the afternoon. Most boats either travel east to the Gordo Banks or around Lover's Arch toward the Pacific.

Reputable in-town fleets include the **Hotel Cabo San Lucas Fleet**, phone (114) 3-3457; **Hotel Finisterra Fleet**, phone (114) 3-0366; **Hotel Hacienda Fleet**, phone (114) 3-0663; and **Los Dorados Fleet**, phone (114) 3-1630.

Medano Beach is the most popular local stretch of sand. Here you can rent snorkeling and water sports equipment or grab a bite at one of the outdoor restaurants. The **Pisces Watersport Center**, next to the Cascadas Resort, offers such activities as parasailing, snorkeling, water skiing, windsurfing and taking to San Lucas Bay in a catamaran sailboat. Phone (114) 3-1288. **Cabo Aquadeportes**, at the Hacienda Hotel on the bay and at Chileno Beach next to the Hotel Cabo San Lucas, can arrange diving, kayaking, sailing and snorkeling expeditions; phone (114) 3-0117. **Chileno Bay**, near the hotel and about 14 kilometers (9 miles) north of Cabo San Lucas, is a prime location for snorkeling; octopus and lobster are among the many creatures on view.

The Gulf of California coast between San José del Cabo and Cabo San Lucas is sprinkled with surfing areas, hidden beaches and secluded little coves. Dirt paths branching off Mex. 1 lead to these spots. **Playa Cementerio**, about 4 kilometers (2.5 miles) north of Cabo San Lucas, is a white-sand beach ideal for swimming. **Playa Barco Varado** (Shipwreck Beach), about 10 kilometers (6 miles) north, curves around a rocky shelf and the remains of a Japanese freighter that sunk in the 1960s.

Santa Maria Bay, about 12 kilometers (7.5 miles) north, draws divers with its excellent visibility. **Playa Palmilla**, about 27 kilometers (17 miles) north, is near the Palmilla Hotel, itself a luxurious, hacienda-style accommodation. Thatched *palapas* at this exceptionally pristine beach are sandwiched between rock formations that look like king-size sand castles.

Note: Most of the beaches are safe for swimming; others are best appreciated for the scenery. Check locally for surf conditions; the currents and undertow at some beaches can carry swimmers far out to sea. Public transportation is generally not available to these sites, although buses that run between the two Cabos may let you disembark at beach turnoffs. It's easiest to use your own car. Fly-in visitors should keep in mind that rental cars in the Los Cabos area are expensive (at least $60 per day). All beaches in Mexico belong to the government and consequently are open to the public. Parking at or camping on deserted beaches is perfectly legal; it is not legal, however, to leave behind garbage of any kind.

Whale-watching excursions to San Ignacio Lagoon and the surrounding waters are offered from December through March. Gray whales can be seen along the mid-Baja coastline as they complete their long-distance migration from the Bering Sea to the Pacific's warm waters. Day tours depart by air twice a week from Cabo San Lucas at 7 a.m., returning around 4 p.m. The cost includes the round-trip flight, four hours of whale watching, lunch and a bilingual guide. Hotels in the downtown area can provide further information, or contact the regional airline Aereo Calafia; phone (114) 3-4255.

Rivaling the popularity of sport fishing is golf. Not so long ago, golf meant one nine-hole course, the **Campo de Golf** near San José del Cabo. A process that allows reclaimed water to be used for irrigation purposes made it possible to maintain manicured greens and fairways in the midst of arid conditions. Today a half dozen courses scattered between the two Cabos are laid out against a stunning backdrop of rugged seaside vistas and desert terrain. Course designers include Roy Dye, Robert Trent Jones and Jack Nicklaus. Golfing in this resort area is by no means cheap, although greens fees normally include the use of a cart.

The signature hole at the Nicklaus-designed **Palmilla**, on the grounds of the Palmilla Hotel, is the par-4 fifth. The tee shot must carry over a cactus-filled arroyo; that same canyon wraps around in front of the green as well. The desert vegetation, which is in bloom year-round, makes this course not only challenging to play but breathtaking to view. The course is open for play to resort guests only. Phone (800) 637-2226.

The Golden Bear also designed **Cabo del Sol**, which features seven dramatic oceanfront holes, including one where the tee shot is fired from a clifftop to a green surrounded by rock outcroppings rising from the cobalt-blue Sea of Cortés. Instead of negotiating long fairways, players tee off over deep arroyos to landing pads and then chip to the green. Phone (800) 637-2226. Cabo Real is a semi-private, 18-hole course with views ranging from mountaintop to sea. Phone (800) 336-3542.

SHOPPING, DINING AND NIGHTLIFE

Cabo's small size lends itself to strolling. A pedestrian walkway wraps around the marina and can be traversed in about 30 minutes. Stop by in mid-afternoon, when local boats return from the day's fishing, for a first-hand look at the many varieties found in these waters. The Shrimp Bucket Restaurant provides a golf cart that transports visitors to points around the marina free of charge.

Most of the craft shops are on or near Lázaro Cárdenas and Boulevard Marina. They offer T-shirts and other touristy souvenirs in addition to blankets, folk art, woven goods and distinctive black coral jewelry. **Galería El Dorado**, at Boulevard Marina near Guerrero, is an arts and crafts store with a collection of paintings and ceramics executed by local artists. Open-air flea markets in the downtown area sell ceramics, pottery, silver jewelry, leather goods, blown glassware and hand-carved wooden animal figures. Bargaining is expected.

Faces of Mexico, in a bright blue building at Lázaro Cárdenas and Matamoros, is a combination art gallery-museum exhibiting a collection of religious masks dating back several hundred years. *Ex-votos* have facial writings describing why the mask was made for a particular religious ceremony; *retablos* depict emotions without the use of words. The masks manage to convey great feeling despite their simplicity; their skilled creators come from all over Mexico. Most of the works are for sale. The gallery is open Mon.-Sat. 10-1:30 and 4-7.

If shopping works up an appetite, try the taco stands and food stalls scattered around the downtown area. Use the same common sense that applies whenever sampling street food in Mexico—if there's a crowd hovering around a cart and the food looks hot and fresh, it should be fine. Tacos come in a variety of guises: *pescado* (fish), *camarones* (shrimp), *carnitas* (pork), *pollo* (chicken) and *carne asada* (beef). The open-air restaurants, many run by local families, are also good places for a hearty morning meal of *huevos rancheros* (eggs and black beans drenched in tomato salsa and sprinkled with cheese), tortillas and a cup of hot coffee.

With advance arrangements, hotel restaurants will prepare fish caught during the day for an evening meal. Seafood restaurants dot the marina area. The restaurant in the Hotel Cabo San Lucas serves fine cuisine on a patio overlooking the Sea of Cortez. Additional atmosphere is supplied by a nine-piece mariachi band playing music that is the essence of romantic Mexico. The musicians serenade diners nightly from 6 until 9 p.m. **Latitude 22**, on Lázaro Cárdenas at Calle Morelos, is a restaurant/bar popular with resident Americans.

Cabo San Lucas has a pretty active nightlife due to the preponderance of surfer types and other youthful revelers. Rather than the flashy discos common in other Mexican resorts, casual bars and rock 'n' roll are the preferred elements of a night on the town. The **Cabo Wabo Cantina**, owned by rocker Sammy Hagar, is open until the wee hours. Young crowds pack the place for occasional live shows by visiting bands; hard rock blasts from the sound system on other nights. The phallic symbol capping this rowdy watering hole is hard to miss.

The **Giggling Marlin**, overlooking the marina west off Plaza Aramburo, has frequent live music and a well-attended happy hour. The attraction here is a pulley device that dangles patrons up-side down—rather like a captured fish—to the great amusement of the masses. Also high on the see-and-be-seen circuit is **El Squid Roe**, on Boulevard Marina. The club resembles more than anything a two-story junkyard, with everything imaginable plastered on its walls. An outdoor patio accommodates those trying out the latest dance moves. Also on Boulevard Marina is the **Río Bar and Grill**, which offers free happy-hour munchies, '70s tunes, karaoke contests and live reggae bands on weekends.

The **Whale Watcher's Bar** in the Hotel Finisterra, off Boulevard Marina heading out toward Land's End, is a good place to sip a margarita and watch the sun slowly drop into the Pacific while mariachis play in the background.

WHERE TO STAY

FIESTA AMERICANA GRAND LOS CABOS
▼▼▼▼ *Resort* (114/5-6200

12/21-5/31	$344-$381	XP $20
12/1-12/20 & 6/1-11/30	$265-$352	XP $20

Location: 10 km e on Hwy 1; at Cabo del Sol. Carr Transpen Km 10.3, Lote A-1 23410. Fax: 114/5-6201. **Facility:** Large complex terraced on hillside overlooking the bay. All rooms with balcony. 278 units. 1-4 stories, exterior corridors. **Parking:** valet. **Terms:** package plans, 10% service charge. **Amenities:** extended cable TV, safes, honor bars, irons, hair dryers. **Leisure Activities:** 5 heated pools, saunas, whirlpools, steamrooms, beach, 2 lighted tennis courts. *Fee:* golf-18 holes. **Guest Services:** gift shop, valet laundry. *Fee:* massage. **Business Services:** conference facilities, administrative services. **Cards:** AE, CB, DI, DS, MC, VI. *(See color ad below)*

HOTEL FINISTERRA

 Resort ((114)3-3333

All Year	$99-$110	XP $30

Location: 1 km s of Hwy 1 and downtown on Blvd Marina. (APDO Postal No. 1, 23410). Fax: 114/3-0590. **Facility:** Spectacular location overlooking ocean. Rooms with ocean or bay view. Large lounging area surrounded by water and tropical gardens. 279 units. 2 two-bedroom units and 50 efficiencies. *Bath:* combo or shower only. 2-9 stories, interior/exterior corridors. **Parking:** valet. **Terms:** F12; 7 day cancellation notice-fee imposed, $10 service charge. **Amenities:** honor bars. **Leisure Activities:** 2 pools (1 heated), sauna, whirlpools, beach. *Fee:* 2 lighted tennis courts. **Guest Services:** gift shop. *Fee:* massage. **Business Services:** meeting rooms. **Cards:** AE, MC, VI.

MARINA FIESTA RESORT HOTEL

 Cottage (114/3-2689

12/18-1/3	$350-$450	XP $55
1/4-4/30	$200-$280	XP $45
12/1-12/17 & 5/1-11/30	$180-$250	XP $35

Location: On the east side of the marina. Lote 37 Col. La Maina 23410. Fax: 114/3-2688. **Facility:** Pueblo-style complex on the marina. 24 hour supermarket. 155 units. 60 efficiencies and 95 units with kitchen. *Bath:* combo or shower only. 7 stories, exterior corridors. **Parking:** valet. **Terms:** F12; check-in 4 pm, package plans. **Amenities:** *Some:* safes. **Leisure Activities:** 2 pools (1 heated), whirlpools, swim-up bar, marina, playground, exercise room. *Fee:* boat dock. **Guest Services:** gift shop, valet laundry. *Fee:* massage. **Business Services:** conference facilities. **Cards:** AE, MC, VI.

MELIA SAN LUCAS

 Resort (114/3-4444

1/9-4/17	$245-$295	XP $40
12/1-1/8 & 9/27-11/30	$231-$281	XP $40
4/18-9/26	$216-$266	XP $40

Location: 1 km s of Hwy 1; at El Medano Beach. Playa El Medano 23410. Fax: 114/3-0420. **Facility:** Pueblo-style architecture surrounding landscaped grounds and pool overlooking bay and Land's End. Meets AAA guest room security requirements. 187 units. 5-6 stories, exterior corridors. **Terms:** F12; 15 day cancellation notice, package plans, 10% service charge. **Amenities:** safes, honor bars. **Leisure Activities:** 2 pools, beach, swimming, scuba diving, snorkeling. *Fee:* scuba & snorkeling equipment, charter fishing. **Guest Services:** gift shop, area transportation, valet laundry. *Fee:* massage. **Business Services:** meeting rooms. **Cards:** AE, MC, VI.

PUEBLO BONITO RESORT

 Resort (114/3-2900

All Year	$180-$300	XP $30

Location: 1 km s of Hwy 1; at El Medano Beach. Playa El Medano (Apdo Postal 460, 23410). Fax: 114/3-1995. **Facility:** Beachfront location with spacious grounds and large free-form pool. 144 efficiencies. 5 stories, exterior corridors. **Terms:** F18; check-in 4 pm, 7 day cancellation notice, package plans, 10% service charge. **Leisure Activities:** heated pool, beach, swimming, scuba diving, snorkeling, exercise room. *Fee:* boating, sailboating, scuba & snorkeling equipment, charter fishing. **Guest Services:** gift shop, valet laundry. *Fee:* massage. **Cards:** MC, VI.

PUEBLO BONITO ROSE RESORT

Resort (114/3-5500

2/1-4/11	$205-$380	XP $30
12/1-1/31 & 4/12-11/30	$160-$300	XP $30

Location: 1 km s of Mex 1; at El Medano Beach. Playa El Medano (PO Box 460, 23410). Fax: 114/3-5522. **Facility:** Beachfront location with spacious grounds and gardens. Mini mart. Meets AAA guest room security requirements. 260 efficiencies. *Bath:* combo or shower only. 7 stories. **Parking:** valet. **Terms:** F18; 7 day cancellation notice, package plans, $10 service charge. **Amenities:** safes. **Leisure Activities:** heated pool, wading pool, whirlpools, steamrooms, beach, swimming, lighted tennis court. *Fee:* boating, sailboating, scuba diving/snorkeling & equipment, charter fishing. **Guest Services:** gift shop, valet laundry. *Fee:* massage. **Cards:** MC, VI.

SHERATON HACIENDA DEL MAR RESORT & SPA

Resort (114/5-8000

12/1-5/16	$240-$340	
5/17-11/30	$200-$290	

Location: 10 km e on Mex 1; at Cabo del Sol. (Corredor Turistico Km.10, Lote D, 23410). Fax: 114/5-8001. **Facility:** Expansive resort at the beach designed as a Mexican-colonial style village. 170 units. Some whirlpool units. 4-7 stories. **Parking:** valet. **Terms:** 7 day cancellation notice, package plans, $2 service charge. **Amenities:** dual phone lines, voice mail, safes, honor bars, irons, hair dryers. **Dining:** Pitahayas, see separate listing. **Leisure Activities:** 3 pools (1 heated), wading pool, beach, swim-up bar. *Fee:* charter fishing, golf-18 holes, 2 lighted tennis courts. **Guest Services:** gift shop, valet laundry. *Fee:* massage. **Business Services:** meeting rooms. **Cards:** AE, MC, VI.

SIESTA SUITES HOTEL

Motel ((114)3-2773

All Year	$50-$320	XP $10

Location: Just n of Marina Blvd and Hidalgo; downtown. Calle E Zapata (PO Box 9416, PHOENIX, AZ, 85068). Fax: 114/3-2773. **Facility:** Located in town. 20 units, 15 with kitchen. *Bath:* shower only. 4 stories (no elevator), exterior corridors. **Parking:** street only. **Terms:** F6; 15 day cancellation notice. **Leisure Activities:** fishing. *Fee:* charter fishing.

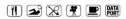

SOLMAR SUITES RESORT

Resort (114/3-3535

12/1-4/30 & 10/1-11/30	$180-$250	XP $40
5/1-9/30	$165-$225	XP $40

Location: 1.5 km s at southern most tip of Baja California peninsula via Blvd Marina. Avenida Solmar #1 23410 (Apdo Postal 8). Fax: 114/3-0410. **Facility:** On the beach at Land's End. Expansive grounds and lounging areas. Rooms and suites, each with a private patio or balcony. 125 units, 29 with kitchen. 2 stories. **Terms:** D12; 7 day cancellation notice, package plans, 10% service charge. **Amenities:** safes, honor bars. **Leisure Activities:** 3 heated pools, whirlpool, beach, swim-up bar, scuba diving, snorkeling, fishing, exercise room. *Fee:* charter fishing, tennis court. **Guest Services:** gift shop. **Business Services:** meeting rooms. **Cards:** AE, MC, VI.

Where To Dine

CASA RAFAEL'S

 Continental 📞 114/3-0739

D $22-$28

Location: 1 km s of Hwy 1, Camino al Hacienda. At El Medan 23410. **Hours:** 6 pm-10 pm. **Reservations:** suggested. **Features:** dressy casual; cocktails & lounge; street parking; a la carte. Dining room and patio service in quaint Mexican-Colonial inn, featuring International cuisine. **Cards:** AE, MC, VI.

DA GIORGIO RESTAURANT

 Italian 📞 114/3-2988

L $5-$12 **D** $9-$22

Location: 5 km e on Mex 1, then 1 km s. Km 5.5 at Misiones Del Cabo 23400. **Hours:** 8:30 am-10:30 pm. **Reservations:** required. **Features:** No A/C; casual dress; cocktails & lounge; valet parking; a la carte. An impressive, open-air, palapa covered restaurant with view of ocean and Land's End. Features pasta, seafood and pizza. **Cards:** AE, MC, VI.

GALEON ITALIAN RESTAURANT

Italian 📞 114/3-0443

D $8-$20

Location: 1 km s. Blvd Marina S/N 23410. **Hours:** 4 pm-11 pm. **Reservations:** accepted. **Features:** dressy casual; cocktails & lounge; a la carte. Dining room and balcony seating overlooking town and bay. Nice selection of seafood, pasta, veal and pizza. **Cards:** MC, VI.

MARGARITAVILLA

Mexican 📞 114/3-1740

L $5-$20 **D** $7-$22

Location: At the marina; in Plaza Bonita Shopping Center. Blvd Marina No 17 Lote 38 23410. **Hours:** 7 am-11 pm. **Features:** No A/C; casual dress; cocktails & lounge. Casual, sometimes noisy dining overlooks the marina and main street. Good food and friendly servers. **Cards:** AE, MC, VI.

MI CASA

Mexican 📞 114/3-1933

L $4-$8 **D** $10-$18

Location: Across from the town plaza between Calle Dorado and Madero. Avenida Cabo San Lucas 23410. **Hours:** noon-3 & 5:30-10 pm, Sun from 5:30 pm. **Reservations:** accepted. **Features:** No A/C; cocktail lounge; street parking; a la carte. Enchanting coutyard surrounded by colorful murals best experienced after dark. Authentic regional dishes from throughout Mexico. **Cards:** AE, MC, VI.

PEACOCKS RESTAURANT

Continental 📞 114/3-1858

D $16-$30

Location: 0.5 km s of Hwy 1. Paseo del Pescador. **Hours:** 6 pm-10 pm. **Reservations:** suggested. **Features:** No A/C; dressy casual; cocktails & lounge; street parking; a la carte. European cuisine with seafood specialties served in Palapa and patio. Duck and lamb are popular. **Cards:** MC, VI.

PITAHAYAS

Pacific Rim 📞 114/5-8010

D $14-$30

Location: 10 km e on Mex 1; at Cabo del Sol; in Sheraton Hacienda Del Mar Resort & Spa. Corredor Turistico Km 10 Lote D 23410. **Hours:** 5:30 pm-11 pm. **Reservations:** suggested. **Features:** No A/C; cocktail lounge; a la carte. "Pacific Rim" cuisine. A variety of seafood, meat and pasta dishes with an Asian influence served in an oceanfront setting. **Cards:** AE, MC, VI.

ROMEO Y JULIETA RISTORANTE

Italian 📞 114/3-0225

D $6-$20

Location: 0.5 km s; Blvd Marina at Pedregal. Blvd Marina 23410. **Hours:** 4 pm-11 pm. **Reservations:** accepted. **Features:** dressy casual; cocktails & lounge; street parking; a la carte. Pasta and seafood served in a quaint hacienda; pizza is a specialty. **Cards:** MC, VI.

THE TRAILER PARK RESTAURANT (LA GOLONDRINA) *Historical*

Mexican 📞 114/3-0542

D $16-$28

Location: Just e of Hwy 1. Paseo del Pescador S/N. **Hours:** 5 pm-10:30 pm. Closed: Mon. **Reservations:** suggested. **Features:** No A/C; casual dress; cocktails & lounge; street parking. Popular, patio setting at historic trading post. Mexican style cooking with a large selection of seafood, chicken and beef combination plates. **Cards:** AE, MC, VI.

SAN JOSÉ DEL CABO, BAJA CALIFORNIA SUR (F-4)

San José del Cabo (sahn hoh-SEH dehl KAH-boh), situated where Mex. 1 meets the Gulf of California, was founded in 1730. It serves as a marketing center for the surrounding agricultural and cattle-raising area. An abundance of mangoes, coconuts, citrus fruits and spices are produced in this tropical region. The town is the local seat of government for the *municipio* of Los Cabos. Despite its emergence as a resort area, San José del Cabo maintains a sleepy small-town charm, content to sit in the shadow of its more popular, partying neighbor 32 kilometers (20 miles) south.

Boulevard Mijares runs through the center of town, divided by a landscaped mall ending at a fountain that is attractively lit at night. The central plaza, framed by stone arches, evokes some of the atmosphere of Old Mexico. Facing this tree-shaded space are the tourism office, a monument to Gen. José Antonio Mijares and twin-steepled **San José Church**. On the church's exterior is an interesting tiled mural depicting a priest being dragged toward fire by Indians.

A block south of the plaza is the 1927 **Palacio Municipal** (City Hall), a traditionally designed structure with offices facing an interior patio. Commercial businesses and restaurants line Calle Zaragoza, where the town's two banks also are located, and Boulevard Mijares. Take time to explore the side streets, where shops and walk-in eateries are often nameless.

In San José del Cabo, phone (114) 2-0057 for the local police; 2-0180 for the General Hospital; and 2-0446 for the Municipal Tourism Office.

Most resort development occupies low hills just south of town and along the Mex. 1 corridor south to Cabo San Lucas. Palm groves and aquatic plants thrive around the freshwater estuary of the Río San José, a protected sanctuary just east of the Hotel Presidente where more than 200 bird species have been observed. Still primitive, the area is being developed for visitors;

small boats can be rented to paddle through the serene habitat.

La Playita is a pretty swimming beach about 3 kilometers (2 miles) east of town and is accessible via two dirt roads. A taxi can take you there; negotiate the fare in advance. A fleet of *pangas* sit on shore; one of the small, outboard-equipped boats can be rented for a day of surf fishing. Negotiate the rate with the local fishermen. The Los Cabos Campo de Golf, off Paseo San José just south of town, offers nine holes for the casual player (18 are planned). The surrounding land is part of a FONATUR resort development. Visitors can pick up tourist information at the FONATUR office on Mex. 1; phone (114) 2-0253 or 2-0300.

Restaurants and local eateries are concentrated along Boulevard Mijares, as are the tourist-oriented shops. You can bargain for souvenirs and handicrafts at a procession of open-air stalls. Chartered sportfishing outings can be arranged through several local hotels. Some hotels also provide horse rentals by the hour for a breezy ride along the Gulf of California shore.

About 3 kilometers (2 miles) southwest of town is the **Brisa del Mar** RV park. Full hookups, showers and a restaurant are all within a fenced-in area on a beautiful beach facing the Gulf of California. Phone (114) 2-2828. **Vagabundos Del Mar Travel and Boat Club** provides assistance to RV travelers in Baja. Services include roadside aid, RV park information, insurance needs, and medical air services and evacuation. Phone (800) 474-2252 in the United States.

WHERE TO STAY

CASA DEL MAR GOLF RESORT & SPA

▼▼▼▼	*Resort*	((114)4-0030

| 12/1-4/22 & 10/16-11/30 | $235-$325 | XP $35 |
| 4/23-10/15 | $160-$200 | XP $25 |

Location: 11.5 km w on Hwy 1; in Cabo Real. (Km 19.5 Carr Transpensinsular, 23400). Fax: 114/4-0034. **Facility:** Attractive colonial style resort at the ocean. 56 units. Some whirlpool units. 1-3 stories, exterior corridors. **Terms:** F12; 3 day cancellation notice-fee imposed, package plans, $10 service charge. **Amenities:** safes, honor bars. **Dining:** restaurant, 7 am-11 pm, $8-$25, cocktails. **Leisure Activities:** 2 pools, wading pool, saunas, whirlpools, steamrooms, beach, swim-up bar, putting green. *Fee:* golf-18 holes, 4 lighted tennis courts. **Guest Services:** gift shop, valet laundry. *Fee:* massage. **Business Services:** meeting rooms. **Cards:** AE, MC, VI.

FIESTA INN AN ALL INCLUSIVE RESORT

▼▼▼	*Motor Inn*	((114)2-0701

12/1-1/3	$266-$320	XP $96
2/1-3/31	$246	XP $74
1/4-1/31	$166-$198	XP $59
4/1-11/30	$184	XP $55

Location: 0.5 km e off Hwy 1. Blvd Malecon San Jose (APDO Postal 124, 23400). Fax: 114/2-0480. **Facility:** On the beach. Rooms with patio or balcony. Meets AAA guest room security requirements. 153 units. 3 stories, exterior corridors. **Terms:** F5; 3 day cancellation notice-fee imposed. **Leisure Activities:** heated pool, beach, swim-up bar, fishing. **Guest Services:** [AP] meal plan available, valet laundry. **Business Services:** meeting rooms. **Cards:** AE, MC, VI.

HOTEL PRESIDENTE INTER-CONTINENTAL LOS CABOS ALL INCLUSIVE EXCLUSIVE RESORT

▼▼▼▼	*Resort*	((114)2-0211

12/18-12/31	$490	XP $45
1/1-4/21	$355-$395	XP $45
4/22-11/30	$275-$375	XP $45
12/1-12/17	$270-$310	XP $45

Location: 2.5 km e of Hwy 1. Blvd Mijares S/N 23400 (APDO Postal 2). Fax: 114/2-1733. **Facility:** Spacious grounds at the beach. Many rooms with balcony or patio. Meets AAA guest room security requirements. 400 units. Some suites. *Bath:* shower only. 3 stories, exterior corridors. **Terms:** D12; 3 day cancellation notice-fee imposed. **Amenities:** hair dryers. **Leisure Activities:** 2 heated pools, wading pool, swim-up bar, 3 lighted tennis courts, children's program, bicycles, exercise room, volleyball. **Guest Services:** [AP] meal plan available, gift shop, valet laundry. **Business Services:** conference facilities. **Cards:** AE, CB, DI, MC, VI.

SOME UNITS

HOWARD JOHNSON PLAZA SUITE HOTEL & RESORT

▼▼	*Hotel*	(114/2-0999

| All Year | $90-$130 | |

Location: 0.5 km e of Hwy 1. Paseo Finisterra 1 (PO Box 152, 23400). Fax: 114/2-0806. **Facility:** Mexican colonial and Moorish-style buildings surrounding courtyard. Hotel rooms, one- and two-bedroom suites with kitchen. 172 units. 50 two-bedroom units, 5 three-bedroom units and 122 units with kitchen. 4 stories (no elevator), exterior corridors. **Terms:** 7 day cancellation notice. **Leisure Activities:** heated pool, exercise room. *Fee:* golf-9 holes, 2 tennis courts. **Guest Services:** gift shop, area transportation, valet laundry. **Business Services:** meeting rooms. **Cards:** AE, CB, DI, DS, MC, VI.

SOME UNITS

HUERTA VERDE

▼▼▼	*Bed & Breakfast*	(114/8-0511

| All Year | $115-$140 | XP $25 |

Location: 1.6 km e of Hwy 1 at Santa Rosa. Las Animas Altas 23400 (7674 Reed St, ARVADA, CO, 80003). Fax: 114/8-0511. **Facility:** Charming B & B terraced on a secluded hillside overlooking farmlands. Individually decorated suites, surrounded by tropical gardens. Meets AAA guest room security requirements. 7 units, 2 with efficiency. *Bath:* shower only. 1 story, exterior corridors. **Terms:** 30 day cancellation notice-fee imposed, 10% service charge. **Amenities:** no TVs. **Leisure Activities:** hiking trails. **Guest Services:** [BP] meal plan available. **Cards:** DS, MC, VI.

LA JOLLA DE LOS CABOS

▼▼▼ *Condominium* ((114)2-3000

| 1/5-11/30 | $143-S165 | XP $10 |
| 12/1-1/4 | $110-$120 | XP $10 |

Location: 5 km w of town on Hwy 1. Km 29 Carr Transpeninsular 23406 (Apdo Postal 127, 23400). Fax: 114/2-0546. **Facility:** On the beach. 55 units. 10 two-bedroom units and 30 units with kitchen. *Bath:* combo or shower only. 3-6 stories, exterior corridors. **Terms:** F12; 3 day cancellation notice, package plans, 10% service charge. **Leisure Activities:** 4 pools, saunas, whirlpools, steamrooms, 2 lighted tennis courts. **Guest Services:** gift shop, area transportation. *Fee:* massage. **Cards:** AE, MC, VI.

LAS VENTANAS AL PARAISO

▼▼▼ ▼▼▼ *Complex* (114/4-0300

| 12/1-5/31 & 10/16-11/30 | $525-S750 | XP $50 |
| 6/1-10/15 | $325-S550 | XP $50 |

Location: 11.5 km w on Hwy 1; at Cabo Real. Km 19.5 Carretera Transpeninsular 23400. Fax: 114/4-0301. **Facility:** Intimate oceanfront resort. All rooms with fireplace, patio and whirlpool. 60 units. Some whirlpool units. 2 stories, exterior corridors. **Parking:** valet. **Terms:** 7 day cancellation notice, package plans, $15 service charge. **Amenities:** CD players, safes, honor bars, hair dryers. **Leisure Activities:** 4 pools (1 heated), saunas, whirlpool, steamrooms, 2 lighted tennis courts. *Fee:* golf-18 holes. **Guest Services:** gift shop, valet laundry. *Fee:* massage. **Business Services:** meeting rooms. **Cards:** AE, DI, DS, MC, VI.

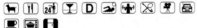

MELIA CABO REAL BEACH & GOLF RESORT

▼▼▼ *Resort* (114/4-0000

12/22-4/22	$270-S335	XP $45
4/23-11/30	$220-S275	XP $45
12/1-12/21	$215-S260	XP $45

Location: 11 km w on Hwy 1; at Cabo Real. Km 19.5 Carretera Transpeninsular 23400. Fax: 114/4-0101. **Facility:** Oceanfront resort surrounding tropical gardens and large free form pool. 309 units. 4 stories, exterior corridors. **Terms:** 15 day cancellation notice, package plans, 10% service charge. **Amenities:** safes, honor bars. **Leisure Activities:** wading pool, sauna, beach, swimming, swim-up bar, scuba diving, snorkeling, fishing. *Fee:* scuba & snorkeling equipment, charter fishing, golf-18 holes, lighted tennis court. **Guest Services:** gift shop, valet laundry. *Fee:* area transportation, massage. **Business Services:** conference facilities. **Cards:** AE, MC, VI.

MELIA LOS CABOS

▼▼▼ *Resort* (114/4-0202

| All Year | $280-S340 | XP $40 |

Location: 11.5 km w on Hwy 1; at Cabo Real. 18.5 Km Carretera Transpeninsular 23400. Fax: 114/4-0216. **Facility:** Oceanfront resort with colonial style architecture. 150 efficiencies. 4-6 stories, exterior corridors. **Terms:** 15 day cancellation notice, package plans, $10 service charge. **Amenities:** safes. **Leisure Activities:** heated pool, wading pool, whirlpool, steamrooms, swim-up bar, full service spa, exercise room. *Fee:* saunas, golf-18 holes, 2 lighted tennis courts. **Guest Services:** gift shop, valet laundry. *Fee:* area transportation, massage. **Business Services:** meeting rooms. **Cards:** AE, MC, VI.

POSADA REAL LOS CABOS

▼▼ *Motor Inn* ((114)2-0155

12/1-1/3	$79-$119	XP $15
1/4-4/14	$89-$99	XP $15
4/15-11/30	$79	XP $15

Location: 0.5 km e, off Mex 1. Malecon San Jose S/N (PO Box 51, 23400). Fax: 114/2-0460. **Facility:** On the beach; most rooms with ocean view. Meets AAA guest room security requirements. 150 units. 3 stories, interior corridors. **Terms:** F12; 3 day cancellation notice-fee imposed. **Leisure Activities:** wading pool, whirlpool, beach, swim up bar, scuba diving, snorkeling, fishing. *Fee:* bicycles. **Guest Services:** gift shop, valet laundry. **Business Services:** meeting rooms. **Cards:** AE, MC, VI.

TROPICANA INN

▼▼ ▼▼ *Motor Inn* ((114)2-0907

12/1-1/5 & 11/3-11/30	$77	XP $10
1/6-4/30	$69	XP $10
5/1-11/2	$56	XP $10

Location: In town. Blvd Mijares #30 23400. Fax: 114/2-1590. **Facility:** Convenient in town location. Attractive Mexican-style building and courtyard. Meets AAA guest room security requirements. 40 units. *Bath:* shower only. 2-3 stories (no elevator), exterior corridors. **Terms:** F12; 10 day cancellation notice. **Dining:** restaurant, see separate listing. **Leisure Activities:** swim-up bar. **Guest Services:** [CP] meal plan available. **Cards:** AE, MC, VI.

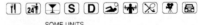

(AAA) WESTIN REGINA GOLF & BEACH RESORT, LOS CABOS

▼▼▼ ▼▼▼ *Resort* ((114)2-9000

12/1-12/31	$310-$560	XP $70
1/1-5/26 & 10/1-11/30	$310-$415	XP $45
5/27-9/30	$245-$360	XP $45

Location: 10 km w on Hwy 1. Km 22.5 Carretera Transpeninsula 23400 (Apdo Postal 145). Fax: 114/2-9011. **Facility:** Water themed landscaping blending with dramatic architecture creating a window to the sea. Large rooms with private balcony. Meets AAA guest room security requirements. 295 units. Some whirlpool units. 3-9 stories, exterior corridors. **Parking:** valet. **Terms:** F18; 7 day cancellation notice-fee imposed, package plans, $3 service charge. **Amenities:** extended cable TV, safes, honor bars, irons, hair dryers. **Dining:** 3 restaurants, 7 am-11 pm, $10-S30, cocktails, also, Arrecifes, see separate listing. **Leisure Activities:** 3 pools, saunas, whirlpools, steamrooms, beach, scuba diving, snorkeling, 2 lighted tennis courts, children's program. *Fee:* scuba & snorkeling equipment, charter fishing, golf-18 holes. **Guest Services:** gift shop, valet laundry. *Fee:* massage. **Business Services:** conference facilities, administrative services. *Fee:* PC, fax. **Cards:** AE, CB, DI, MC, VI.

WHERE TO DINE

ARRECIFES

▼▼▼ ▼▼ *Continental* (114/2-9000

D $15-S30

Location: 10 km w on Hwy 1; in Westin Regina Golf & Beach Resort, Los Cabos. **Hours:** 6 pm-11 pm. Closed: Tues. **Reservations:** suggested. **Features:** No A/C; semiformal attire; cocktail lounge; a la carte. Spectacular ocean view setting. Features creative dishes with an artful presentation. **Cards:** AE, MC, VI.

DAMIANA

 Mexican (114/2-0499

L $6-$14   **D** $10-$20

Location: Downtown; at Town Plaza. Blvd Mijares 8 23400. **Hours:** 10:30 am-10:30 pm. Closed: 12/25. **Reservations:** accepted. **Features:** No A/C; casual dress; cocktails & lounge; street parking; a la carte. Patio and inside dining in quaint atmosphere. Traditional Mexican seafood and regional dishes. **Cards:** MC, VI.

LA CONCHA BEACH CLUB SEAFOOD RESTAURANT

 Seafood (114/4-0102

L $5-$22   **D** $9-$32

Location: 11 km w on Mex 1. At Cabo Real on the beach 23400. **Hours:** 10 am-10 pm. **Features:** No A/C; casual dress; cocktails & lounge; a la carte. Dining under palapa at beach side. Specializing in fresh seafood with limited beef and chicken entrees. **Cards:** AE, MC, VI.

LA PROVENCE GARDEN RESTAURANT

 Continental (114/2-3373

D $14-$20

Location: Downtown, just n of Zaragoza. Esq Morelos YA Obregon Centro 23400. **Hours:** 5:30 pm-10 pm. **Reservations:** accepted. **Features:** No A/C; dressy casual; cocktails & lounge; street parking; a la carte. Mediterranean cuisine with upscale service in a colorful bistro and patio setting. **Cards:** AE, MC, VI.

MORGAN'S RESTAURANT & CELLAR

 International (114/2-3825

L $10-$20   **D** $15-$25

Location: Manuel Doblado No 107 23400. **Hours:** Open 12/1-6/30 & 10/1-11/30; 8 am-10 pm. **Reservations:** suggested. **Features:** No A/C; casual dress; street parking; a la carte. Charming creative dining with highly trained staff. Mediterranean/International dishes with Mexican influence. Entrees with choice of sauce and accompaniments. Rice with raisins and curry very good. Fresh pastries made daily. **Cards:** AE.

TEQUILA RESTAURANTE

 Mexican (114/2-1155

D $12-$30

Location: In town, just w of Blvd Mijares. Manuel Doblado 5/N 23400. **Hours:** 5:30 pm-10:30 pm. **Reservations:** accepted. **Features:** No A/C; dressy casual; cocktails; street parking; a la carte. Mediterranean influenced cuisine with Mexican and Asian flavors served in a pleasant garden. Limited menu. Busy at times with groups. **Cards:** AE.

TROPICANA BAR & GRILL

 Mexican (114/2-0907

L $5-$20   **D** $10-$24

Location: In town; in Tropicana Inn. Blvd Mijares No 30. **Hours:** 8 am-11 pm. **Features:** No A/C; casual dress; cocktails & lounge; street parking. Hacienda and street side patio dining featuring Mexican and European entrees. **Cards:** AE, MC, VI.

TODOS SANTOS, BAJA CALIFORNIA SUR (F-3)

An old farming and fishing community about 72 kilometers (45 miles) north of Cabo San Lucas, Todos Santos (TOH-dos SAHN-tos) was long isolated from visitors. That changed in 1986 with the completion of Mex. 19 from La Paz south to Cabo San Lucas. Even as rumors of large-scale resort development are passed along by the locals, Todos Santos retains a relaxed air and the charms of a traditional Mexican town—in distinct contrast to the crowds of its more hectic southern neighbor.

Located just south of the Tropic of Cancer, Todos Santos is tropical but not quite as torrid as the towns lying next to the warm Gulf of California waters. Underground water from the Sierra de la Laguna range, which rises to the east, provides irrigation for orchards of mangoes, papayas and vegetables. Most of the streets are unpaved, and many of the roofs are thatched. The town's 19th-century status as a sugar cane producer is evidenced by the ruins of a few sugar mills, which crumble amid scattered farms, palm trees and cactus groves on the outskirts of town.

The peak tourist season is from October through February; many businesses are closed or open irregular hours from July through September, when the weather is hotter and more humid and the beaches are plagued by mosquitos. On Oct. 12 Todos Santos celebrates the *Festival of the Virgin of Pilar.*

Facing the central plaza is the **Iglesia Nuestra Señora del Pilar** (Church of Our Lady of Pilar), a successor to an early mission from which the town received its name (Todos Santos means "All Saints"). On Calle Juárez, the main street, is the **Hotel California**, which dates to 1928 and is said to be the lodging referred to in the same-named song by the Eagles (an unsubstantiated claim). **Caffe Todos Santos**, on Calle Centenario at Calle Topete, is where English-speaking visitors head for breakfast; **Café Santa Fe**, an Italian restaurant that faces the plaza, invites lingering over dinner (the restaurant is closed Tuesday). Todos Santos also has a reputation as a bohemian enclave of sorts. Local galleries include **Galería de Todos Santos** on Calle Topete, where works by Mexican and American artists are on display.

About 3 kilometers (2 miles) west of town on a dirt road is **Playa Punta Lobos**. Here local fishermen embark in their *pangas* for the day's catch; visitors can enjoy the dramatic Pacific surf. South of town via Mex. 19, dirt-road turnoffs offer access to unspoiled, unpopulated beaches—good for surfing—along the rocky coastline. Just 23 kilometers (14 miles) east the Sierra de la Laguna Mountains rise to 6,000 feet; pack trips to explore the area can be arranged in town.

WHERE TO DINE

CAFE SANTA FE

 Italian (114/5-0340

L $7-$12   **D** $10-$21

Location: In town center. Calle Centenario No 4. **Hours:** noon-9 pm. Closed: Tues & 10/1-10/31. **Reservations:** suggested. **Features:** No A/C; casual dress; cocktails; street parking; a la carte. Refined Italian dishes served in an attractively decorated dining room and lush tropical patio.

CATAVINA, BAJA CALIFORNIA

WHERE TO STAY

The following lodging was either not evaluated or did not meet AAA rating requirements and is listed for your information only.

HOTEL LA PINTA
[fyi] *Motor Inn*
Does not meet all AAA rating requirements for bathrooms; previously evaluated on 11/20/99. **Location:** On Hwy 1. (APDO Postal 179, SAN QUINTIN, BA). Facilities, services, and decor characterize a basic property.

EL ROSARIO, BAJA CALIFORNIA

WHERE TO DINE

MAMA ESPINOSA'S
▼ *Mexican* (616/5-8770
L $3-$10 D $5-$10
Location: On Hwy 1 in town center. KM 55 Carretera Transpeninsular. **Hours:** 6 am-9 pm. **Features:** No A/C; casual dress; beer & wine only. Historic restaurant and home of Dona Anita. Serves lobster, fish and beef dishes in the Baja tradition.

ENSENADA, BAJA CALIFORNIA (B-1)

One of Baja California's foremost summer resorts and its third largest city, Ensenada (ehn-seh-NAH-dah) spreads over scrub-covered hills that slope down to the shores of large, lovely **Bahía de Todos Santos** (Todos Santos Bay). The city (its name, not surprisingly, means "bay") boasts a scenic setting, attractive beaches, pleasant weather, duty-free shopping, fine sport fishing and close proximity to the United States; for many weekend visitors, Ensenada is the farthest they ever get into Mexico.

The area was relatively isolated before the completion of Mex. 1 from Tijuana and the development of port facilities in the mid-1930s. More than 300 years earlier, Spanish explorer Sebastián Vizcaíno sailed into the bay and, entranced by its beauty, named it Ensenada de Todos Santos—"All Saints' Bay." A lack of fresh water prevented any permanent settlement from taking hold, although the bay often sheltered whaling ships, treasure-laden galleons and the privateers who preyed upon them.

Ranchers securing a foothold in Mexico's northern frontier began to settle the area early in the 19th century. Ensenada temporarily boomed in 1870 with the discovery of gold at nearby Real del Castillo. The town became a supply depot for miners and was designated the capital of the Baja California Territory in 1882. By the early 20th century, however, the mines had given out, the capital was relocated to Mexicali and Ensenada lapsed back into obscurity.

After U.S. Prohibition went into effect in the late 1920s, Ensenada—along with Tijuana—became a favored drinking and gambling destination for Hollywood types. Real revitalization came with agricultural reform and development in the Mexicali Valley. A nearby port was needed to handle the export of farm produce to the United States and mainland Mexico, and Ensenada's harbor facilities made it an obvious choice for development. Tuna fishing provided further economic incentive. But it was the completion of paved highway Mex. 1 from Tijuana that opened up Ensenada to American vacationers and sport fishing enthusiasts.

Connected to Tijuana by the four-lane Mex. 1-D toll highway, Ensenada has continued to grow, with an estimated population of 230,000. It is the governmental seat of the *municipio* of Ensenada, which extends south to the Baja California Sur state line and includes shoreline on both the east and west coasts of the peninsula. The local economy has long relied on the cultivation of olives and grapes and the harvesting of halibut and yellowtail. A decline in commercial shipping activity and recent cutbacks in cruise ship schedules, however, have made tourism more important to the city than ever before.

PLANNING YOUR STAY

While Ensenada is a little far for a day trip from the United States, it makes a great weekend getaway. For a time most visitors were sports anglers, or college students who came to frolic on the beaches by day and carouse by night. In recent years city boosters have attempted to woo business travelers as well. Upscale waterfront developments are springing up, replacing some of the laid-back charm. Even so, Ensenada remains a good choice for dining, strolling, perhaps a little shopping, and relaxing on the beach or on a boat. Summer is the high season; to avoid crowds, visit April-May or October-November.

The waters of Todos Santos Bay provide opportunities for swimming, scuba diving, kayaking, jet skiing and surfing. To the north, the Guadalupe Valley encompasses miles of vineyards, and several wineries offer tours and tastings. The adventurous can head inland, where mountainous terrain and pine forests form a backdrop for exploring, hiking, backpacking, camping and fishing.

THE INFORMED TRAVELER

Ensenada is about 109 kilometers (68 miles) south of Tijuana. The city's small airstrip currently accommodates only private planes, although regular service from Los Angeles via Air L.A. may eventually be initiated. A tourist card is required, even for stays of less than 72 hours. For additional information about border crossing regulations *see "Arriving in Mexico," page 52.*

Four-lane toll highway Mex. 1-D is a quick, convenient route south from Tijuana. There are three toll booths between the two cities; restrooms are available near the booths. Although towing and Green Angels assistance are free, motorists who run out of gas on this stretch are required to pay for it. Emergency telephones also appear along Mex. 1-D approximately every 3 kilometers (2 miles). There are frequent panoramic views of the scenic Baja coastline, particularly around **Punta Salsipuedes**, just south of El Mirador and about 32 kilometers (20 miles) north of Ensenada. Some of the highway's curves can be daunting to drivers not used to them.

Free Mex. 1 (look for signs that say *Libre*) parallels Mex. 1-D most of the way, although it turns inland south of La Misión, out of sight of the ocean. The driving time is longer, and the road has some rough spots. Night driving along this and other two-lane secondary roads in northern Baja should be avoided; both cattle and pedestrians frequently cross them, usually with little or no warning.

The bus station is in the northern section of town at Calle 11 and Avenida Riveroll. Bus service is inexpensive, and taking the bus is a good way for visitors who want to mix with the locals. Local bus routes are designated by street name, usually painted on the windshield. Intercity buses travel frequently between Ensenada along both Mex. 1 and Mex. 1-D; the ABC line offers "deluxe" service to Tijuana and Mexicali. For additional information about buses *see "Bus Service," page 63.*

Taxicabs congregate near the bus station and at the hotels along Avenida López Mateos. Although their ubiquitous solicitations can be annoying, drivers are normally courteous and knowledgeable. Make sure, however, that the fare is set before you get in the cab. Taxis can be hired for trips to such outlying destinations as La Bufadora.

One of Ensenada's best features is its mild climate, similar to coastal southern California but with fewer extremes of heat than almost any other Baja city. Winter evenings can be chilly, but the temperature seldom drops much below 40 F. Summers are warm and dry, with occasional hot spells caused by Santa Ana winds blowing in from the desert. Precipitation averages only 10 inches annually, with almost all of it falling between December and March. Fierce Pacific storms sometimes bring torrential winter rains.

Personal safety in Ensenada is a matter of common sense. Although it has experienced tremendous growth, the city still has a relaxed, laid-back atmosphere. Tourists are invariably welcomed, as it is their dollars that sustain many Mexican businesses. If traveling by car, the best advice is to drive safely; traffic accidents are often the biggest source of vacation headaches in Mexico. One way to minimize risk is to stop at every intersection, even those that don't have stop signs.

For local visitor information, including ecotours into the surrounding countryside, contact the State Tourism Office, across from the Corona Hotel in a one-story yellow building on Boulevard Lázaro Cárdenas (Boulevard Costero) and Calle Las Rocas. The office is open Mon.-Sat. 9-7, Sun. 9-2; phone (61) 72-3022 (English spoken). In the same building is Asistencia al Turista (Tourist Protection), which provides legal assistance to tourists; the hours and phone number are the same. The Convention and Visitors Bureau operates a booth on Boulevard Lázaro Cárdenas near the western entrance to the city. It is open Mon.-Fri. 9-7, Sat. 10-4, Sun. 10-3; phone (61) 78-2411 (English spoken).

The English-language *Baja Sun* is a tourist-oriented newspaper containing travel information, articles about Baja cities and lots of local advertising. Radio Bahía Ensenada (1590 AM) has an English/Spanish program Saturdays from 4-6 p.m. ATM machines are located in the Serfin Bank, Avenida Ruíz #290, and the Banamex Bank, Avenida Reyerson and Calle 3. *Casas de cambio* (exchange booths), such as the one located at avenidas Juárez and Reforma on the east side of town, offer the best foreign exchange rates.

Baja Lodging offers pre-arrival travel services for tourists; phone (619) 491-0682 in the United States. In the event of emergency, the Hospital Las Americas is located at Avenida Arenas #151, between Calle Agustín Sangines and Calle Diamante southeast of downtown. Phone (61) 76-0301 (English spoken).

City Layout

Ensenada has two separate business districts that serve its commercial and resort interests. Local businesses, stores, banks, offices and *cantinas* line avenidas Ruíz and Juárez, which are extensions of Mex. 1 through the city. Closer to the waterfront, toll highway Mex. 1-D enters the city from the west. (**Note:** Negotiate the three metal speed bumps just west of downtown very carefully, as they can damage the underside of a vehicle.)

Along Avenida López Mateos and Boulevard Lázaro Cárdenas (also called Boulevard Costero) are hotels, restaurants, nightspots, sportfishing outfits and shops that cater primarily to tourists. The Costero, which follows the bay, ends at Calle Agustín Sangines (also called Calle Delante), which proceeds east to Mex. 1; Mex. 1, the Transpeninsular Highway, then heads south down the length of the peninsula.

Away from the major arterials, Ensenada is easy to negotiate. The terrain is flat, and the layout is a basic grid. Avenues (avenidas) are named and run north-south; streets (calles) are numbered and run east-west. Streets and avenues are often unmarked, however. To orient yourself, count off city blocks inland from Avenida López Mateos, which is also known as Calle 1 (First Street); successive streets are Calle 2, Calle 3, etc. The prominent clock tower at the **Historical and Cultural Center**, Boulevard Lázaro Cárdenas and Avenida Club Rotario, can function as a downtown orientation landmark.

Driving tips to keep in mind: As in other Baja cities, traffic lights are small and often hard to spot from a distance. *Alto* (stop) signs placed at intersections can be obscure, so always proceed slowly and with caution. Some downtown streets are one way. On-street parking is usually available. The pay lot at the Plaza Marina shopping center, on Boulevard Costero just north of the sportfishing piers, is convenient for nearby waterfront wandering.

The city's low skyline is distinguished by the twin spires of **Nuestra Señora de Guadalupe** (Our Lady of Guadalupe), Calle 6 and Avenida Florestra. The church, built in typical Spanish colonial style, is one of Ensenada's most prominent structures. West of downtown, Avenida Alemán (accessible via Avenida Hidalgo Reyerson) encircles **Chapultepec Hills**, an attractive residential area. From this vantage point there is a bird's eye view of the entire city and Todos Santos Bay.

SPECIAL EVENTS

Something always seems to be going on in Ensenada. *Carnaval* (Mardi Gras) is usually celebrated in mid-February on the 6 days prior to Ash Wednesday. A downtown street fair takes place each night, with rides, live music, food vendors, parades of flower-covered floats and other merriment. The festivities climax with a masquerade ball; prizes are awarded for the best costume.

The popular *Hobie Cat Regatta* from Newport Beach, Calif., to Ensenada is held each year in late April. Approximately 400 boats in different classes race to the finish line; most remain in the city for a day or two, and a huge party ensues. For information contact the Newport Ocean Sailing Association in California; phone (714) 771-0691.

The *Estero Beach Volleyball Tournament* takes place in late June on the sands in front of the Estero Beach Hotel. The tournament attracts some of the best volleyball players in North America. For 10 days in mid-August the *Fiesta de le Vendimia* (Wine Harvest Festival) celebrates the grape. Several Guadalupe Valley wineries, including Bodegas de Santo Tomás, San Antonio and Monte Xanic (sha-NEEK), offer fine cuisine to accompany the first-rate, locally produced wines. Contact the State Tourism Office for information.

Local restaurants participate in the *Seafood Fair*, which takes place in late September. The *Juan Hussong International Chili Cookoff*, normally the second weekend in October, brings together chili cooks from around the region. Popular Mexican beers and a selection of local wines help their fiery concoctions go down more smoothly. Admission is charged.

Ensenada, like most of Mexico, honors the deceased during *Day of the Dead* celebrations Nov. 1-2. Also beginning in early November is the *SCORE Baja 1000 Off-Road Race* (commonly known as the Baja Mil), one of the world's most prestigious off-road races. There are separate categories for cars, trucks, motorcycles and ATVs. The course alternates each year between a straight, 1,050-mile run from Ensenada to La Paz and a shorter 620-mile loop that begins and ends in Ensenada. For information contact SCORE International in the United States; phone (626) 583-8068.

Another major festival is *Día de Nuestra Señora de Guadalupe* (Our Lady of Guadalupe Day), celebrated Dec. 12. It honors the nation's patron saint, the Guadalupe Virgin. All manner of amusement rides are set up in front of Our Lady of Guadalupe Church, and another attraction is the array of culinary specialties from all over Mexico.

SHOPPING

Some visitors prefer Ensenada's low-pressure shopping environment to Tijuana's more raucous atmosphere. Like that city, Ensenada is a duty-free zone, and savvy shoppers can purchase imported items at significant savings over U.S. prices.

The main tourist shopping area is along Avenida López Mateos. Gift shops carry such imported merchandise as silver and gold jewelry, onyx chess sets, leather boots and fine liquor. Some of the shops have fixed prices; English is usually spoken and credit cards are welcomed. **Artesanias Castillo**, Avenida López Mateos #656, and **Los Castillo**, Avenida López Mateos #815, carry Taxco silver jewelry guaranteed to be at least 92.5 percent pure (designated by the numerals ".925"). **La Cucaracha**, another gold and silver jewelry shop on Avenida Blancarte just off López Mateos, offers senior citizen discounts.

La Mina de Solomon, Avenida López Mateos #1000, sells jewelry by renowned designer Sergio Bustamante of Tlaquepaque, Jalisco. **La Esquina de Bodegas**, on Avenida Miramar and Calle 6 near the Santo Tomás winery, has a bookstore and gift shop and sells locally produced Baja wines.

Quality imported items can also be found in shops at the Estero Beach Resort south of Ensenada off Mex. 1. **Importaciones** carries

Rolex watches, while **Bazar Mexicano** has sterling silver jewelry, onyx sculptures and decorative objects in copper, brass and glass. Also at the resort is a museum displaying a seashell collection and replicas of statues and ceramic figurines from various pre-Columbian cultures.

Curio shops up and down López Mateos stock traditional Mexican craft and clothing items like baskets, ceramics, guitars, jewelry, wrought-iron furniture, and leather jackets, purses and sandals. On Boulevard Lázaro Cárdenas (Costero) at Avenida Castillo is **Centro Artesenal**, a cluster of privately owned craft shops. One shop, **Galería de Pérez Meillon**, sells Casas Grandes pottery, Kumiai baskets and other handmade items fashioned by native artisans using age-old techniques.

Outdoor flea markets offer a chance to find the odd treasure amid piles of merchandise. **Los Globos**, at Los Globos and Calle 9 (three blocks east of Avenida Reforma), is especially busy on weekends. In one area there are foodstuffs—fruit, vegetables, nuts, grains, freshly made tacos and *churros*, a sweet fritter similar to a doughnut. Browse among the new and used tools, electrical appliances, clothing, toys and innumerable other items for sale.

For local shopping, try **Dorian's**, a branch of the Baja department store chain, at Avenida Ruíz #328. Among the everyday goods are imported perfumes and clothing. **Calimax**, Calle 3 and Avenida Gastelum, carries grocery staples as well as Mexican liquors and wines.

Outdoor Recreation

Ensenada still proclaims itself "the yellowtail capital of the world," although catches have dwindled in recent years. The protected harbor and nearby waters yield barracuda, bonito and rockfish. The game season is roughly June through mid-September, although such bottom-feeding species as sea bass, rock cod, halibut and whitefish can be caught all year.

Charter arrangements can be made at the piers off Boulevard Costero and at some shops along Avenida López Mateos. Rates for private groups range upward from about $550 per day, depending on the size of the craft and the number of passengers. These excursions usually leave at the crack of dawn and last until early afternoon. For those who would rather go it alone, surf fishing can be enjoyed along sandy stretches south of the city.

Gordo's Sport Fishing offers daily yellowtail excursions that leave around 7 a.m. The cost is about $35 (U.S.) per person; rod rental is extra. A fishing license costs $6.50. Night fishing for albacore also is available. For information phone (61) 78-3515. The **Ensenada Clipper Fleet** offers fishing trips, whale-watching excursions (December to March) and party cruises aboard the *Clipper Deluxe*. For information phone (61) 78-2185.

Boat rides around the bay can be arranged; look for the small fishing boats *(pangas)* at the end of the fish market pier. This is also a good spot to watch local fishermen bringing in the daily catch.

There are no beaches within the city proper. Most visitors head for **Estero Beach**, about 12 kilometers (7 miles) south of downtown Ensenada via Mex. 1; the turnoff, about 7.5 kilometers (4.5 miles) south, is well marked. Here, along the shores of Estero Bay, there are gentle waves and a long stretch of sand. The rocky beach near the village of **San Miguel**, north of Ensenada, is a favorite destination for surfers.

Punta Banda, the rocky peninsula forming the southern end of Todos Santos Bay, is popular with scuba and skin divers. This area also has an abundance of hot springs; at spots along the beaches here, it is possible to dig into the sand and create your own hole from which soothing hot waters bubble. There are a couple of RV parks along BCN 23, the paved road that traverses the peninsula. Several unmarked hiking trails also lead off this road.

Dining and Nightlife

While Ensenada has a wide variety of restaurant choices, from Chinese to French to prime rib to American fast food, visitors would do well to concentrate on the local seafood. For fresh fish, try **Haliotis**, on Calle Delante a short distance southeast of the city (off Mex. 1). The name stands for abalone, the house specialty. Fishy delights also await at Ensenada's open-air fish market, on Boulevard Costero at Avenida Miramar, just north of the sportfishing piers. Known to locals as the **Mercado de Mariscos**, or Seafood Market, the covered sheds displaying freshly caught fish and shellfish have a suitably salty ambience. Handcart vendors hawk fresh clams, oysters shucked on the spot and ceviche, a mixture of salsa and marinated raw fish that is likely just hours out of the ocean.

Fish tacos are an Ensenada staple. Stands opposite the market offer strips of savory fried fish wrapped in a folded tortilla along with sour cream, guacamole, salsa (both *verde* and *rosa*, green and red), cabbage, onions and cilantro; avoid the mayonnaise that is left out on the tables. Other stands sell spicy shellfish cocktails *(cocteles)* made with clams or shrimp. Stumbling into a small, out-of-the-way seafood restaurant hidden on a side street is one of the joys of exploring the downtown area. Check the customers; if a place is full of locals, it's likely to be good. To be on the safe side, patronize only those places that use purified water in their preparations.

Although Ensenada is very quiet during the week—particularly in winter—it becomes a party town on weekends. Most of the nightspots catering to tourists are in the vicinity of avenidas Ruíz and López Mateos at the western end of downtown. **Hussong's Cantina**, on Ruíz just east of Mateos, revels in its reputation as one of Baja's rowdiest cantinas, although the designated driver in a group is treated to free soft drinks while his or her companions indulge in margaritas and Mexican beer. Discos roar with loud music as whistle-blowing waiters pour shots of tequila from their holstered pouches.

An offbeat alternative to all this raucousness can be found at **Café Café**, near the corner of avenidas Gastelum and López Mateos. This bohemian-style hangout offers local musicians, poetry readings, weekend jazz and arthouse film fare on Thursday evenings.

Behind Plaza Civica on Boulevard Costero is a Caliente sports betting facility, similar to those found in Tijuana, where wagers can be placed for just about every sporting event going on in Mexico and the United States. The complex, which has a bar and snack bar, is open daily.

Mexican dance, ballet and theatrical productions take place at the **Teatro de la Ciudad** (City Theater), on Calle Diamante between avenidas Pedro Loyola and Reforma. Chamber music concerts are given Thurs.-Sat. evenings at 8 p.m. (except mid-December through mid-January) by Pro Musica Ensenada. Performances are given in the **Sala de Barricas**, an old winery warehouse at Avenida Miramar #666, across the street from the Bodegas de Santo Tomás winery.

WHAT TO SEE

DOWNTOWN ATTRACTIONS

BODEGAS DE SANTO TOMAS, Avenida Miramar at Calle 7, is Baja California's oldest winery and also is said to be Mexico's largest. Dominican monks of the St. Thomas Aquinas Mission began cultivating the vineyards of the broad, lush Santo Tomás Valley, about 30 miles south of Ensenada, in 1791. Winery operations began in 1888; the present location was established in the 1920s. Forty-five-minute guided tours in English begin daily at 11, 1 and 3 and include a sampling of the winery's award-winning vintages. Fee for the guided tour is $2 (U.S.); a tip is expected. Live jazz and classical performances take place on Friday evenings during the summer. Phone (61) 78-3333.

CENTRO SOCIAL, CIVICO Y CULTURAL DE ENSENADA (Social, Civic and Cultural Center of Ensenada), Boulevard Lázaro Cárdenas (Costero) at Avenida Riviera, occupies the former Riviera del Pacífico, a gambling casino and hotel. The mansion, with its elegant Moorish-style architecture, detailed mosaics, intricate ironwork and extravagant chandeliers, was a favored gathering place for wealthy Americans and Mexicans during the Prohibition era. The glamorous clientele included Bing Crosby, Rita Hayworth, Johnny Weissmuller and the Ali Khan; Jack Dempsey managed the casino. The building fell into disuse after the Mexican government outlawed gambling in the late 1930s, and it was nearly 40 years later before refurbishment began.

The center now hosts conventions, civic and social events, and occasional art shows. Visitors can view the murals in the entry hall, explore the restored ballroom and gambling rooms, and relax in the patio gardens with a drink from the impressive wooden Andaluz Bar. Historical monuments and plaques are scattered about the landscaped grounds. Open Tues.-Sun. 10-4 (but can close up to 2 hours for lunch). Donations.

MUSEO DE HISTORIA Y ANTROPOLOGIA (Museum of History and Anthropology) is at Avenida Reyerson and Calle Virgilio Uribe. The oldest public building in the state of Baja California, it was built in 1887 by the International Co. of Mexico, an American firm established to promote the urban colonization of Baja. Over the years it has housed both government agencies and private enterprises, including gold mining and railroad ventures and the offices of Mexican Maritime Customs.

Since 1992 the two-story structure has been the regional headquarters for the National Institute of Anthropology and History (INAH). Changing exhibits (with Spanish descriptions) mounted by the **Historical Society of Baja California** chronicle the area's past. It is also said that a ghost inhabits the building. Tues.-Fri. 8-3, Sat.-Sun. 10-5. Donations.

MUSEO DE CIENCIAS DE ENSENADA (Science Museum of Ensenada) is at Avenida Obregón #1463 between calles 14 and 15. Oceanographic and marine life exhibits pertaining to the area stress endangered species and environmental preservation. Information about the displays is in Spanish. The main museum is in a two-story house; on a lower level, the **Ark** presents changing exhibits geared to children. Mon.-Fri. 9-5, Sat.-Sun. noon-5. Admission is charged.

The museum also sponsors boat tours to observe gray whales. From late December through March an estimated 15,000 whales pass by Todos Santos Island in Ensenada Bay, little more than a mile offshore, on a migration journey that begins in the Bering Sea and ends at Scammons Lagoon, midway down Baja's Pacific coast. Some of the whales come close enough to the shoreline to scratch their backs along the bay floor, removing barnacles and parasites. In addition to the possibility of whale sightings, the bilingual guided tours offer information about the bay's history, geography and wildlife, which includes dolphins, sea lions, gulls, pelicans and jellyfish.

For information about whale-watching tours contact **Baja California Tours** in San Diego; phone (800) 336-5454.

PLAZA CIVICA (Civic Plaza) is at Boulevard Lázaro Cárdenas (Costero) and Avenida Macheros. Also known as **Three Heads Park**, this small landscaped court has 12-foot-high busts of Mexican freedom fighter Father Miguel Hidalgo and former presidents Benito Juárez and Venustiano Carranza. Horse-drawn sightseeing carriages, or *calandrias*, depart the plaza, and cruise ships dock offshore. There also are public restrooms. A block south at Avenida Alvarado is the **Naval Base**, where flag ceremonies with a drum and bugle corps take place at sunrise and sunset.

NEARBY DESTINATIONS

An easy and popular side trip from Ensenada is to **Punta Banda**. A paved road, BCN 23, splits west off Mex. 1 just north of Maneadero, passing olive orchards, cultivated fields, trailer parks and the private Baja Beach and Tennis Club before ending at a parking lot (fee charged) at the tip of the peninsula. Climb the steps to observe **La Bufadora** (the Snort), a hollow rock formation that acts as a sea spout. During incoming tides, water rushes into an underground cavern, sending spray shooting into the air like a geyser. Snack vendors congregate along the path to the blowhole, many of them selling doughnut-like *churros*.

About 42 kilometers (26 miles) north of Ensenada is the quiet village of **La Misión**, situated in a valley ringed with steep volcanic walls. The exit off Mex. 1 is not signed; watch carefully for it. On the valley's south side are the ruins of Mission San Miguel, founded in 1787 by Dominican friars.

Also north of Ensenada is the **Guadalupe Valley**, where there are miles of vineyards and olive orchards and several wineries. To reach the valley, take Mex. 1-D north about 10 kilometers (6 miles) to the junction with Mex. 3, then proceed north toward Tecate. The two-lane road passes through scenic, level countryside bordered by low hills. About 18 miles (29 km) north and a mile or so west off Mex. 3 via a paved road is the village of **Guadalupe**, which was settled early in the 20th century by Russian immigrants.

The largest winery in the area is **Casa Pedro Domecq**, a few miles north of Guadalupe on Mex. 3. Tours and tastings are offered Mon.-Fri. 10-2. **L.A. Cetto Winery** conducts tours Tues.-Sun. 10-5. For information phone (66) 85-4450 or 85-3031.

Parque Nacional Constitución de 1857 (Constitution of 1857 National Park), in the high plateau country of the Sierra de Juárez range, offers a contrast to Ensenada's seaside air. The rugged terrain, highlighted by unusual rock formations, is blanketed with thick forests of ponderosa pine. In the middle of the park is **Laguna Hanson**, a small lake surrounded by primitive campsites. Fishing is permitted (bass and catfish inhabit the lake when rainfall is adequate); hunting is prohibited.

To get to the park, take Mex. 3 to Ojos Negros, a small farming community about 40 kilometers (25 miles) east of Ensenada. At Km 55, a dirt road branches northeast and steadily ascends for about 35 kilometers (22 miles) to the park entrance. Although ungraded, the road is normally negotiable in a passenger vehicle. An entrance fee is charged. For information phone (61) 76-3120.

Ensenada also is the most convenient base in the state of Baja California from which to visit **Sierra San Pedro Mártir National Park**, an alpine preserve of rocky peaks, pine and fir forests, freshwater streams and mountain meadows—all in distinct contrast to the blazing heat and barren landscapes that characterize most of Baja. Snow falls regularly during the winter. Experienced hikers searching for solitude will find it here, as the park is one of Mexico's least visited.

Because of the remarkably clear air and absence of pollution at this high altitude, the Mexican government built an astronomical observatory within the park. The observatory is closed to the general public but may be open some Saturdays; for information phone (61) 74-4580 or 74-4593 (English spoken). A nearby viewpoint offers a striking panorama of Picacho del Diablo, the Baja Peninsula's highest peak, the desert far below and the Gulf of California in the distance. **Note:** Visitors must walk about a mile from the parking area to reach the observatory and viewpoint.

Sierra San Pedro Mártir is accessible via a graded dirt road that begins at the village of San Telmo de Abajo, on Mex. 1 about 121 kilometers (75 miles) south of Ensenada and 13 kilometers (8 miles) south of Colonet. The park entrance is about 78 kilometers (48 miles) east of Mex. 1; follow signs marked "Observatorio." A high-clearance vehicle is recommended to negotiate the somewhat rough and steep road. Fishing, hiking, camping and backpacking are all possible, but established campsites and trails are only minimally maintained. Hunting is prohibited. Visitors should bring drinking water and a compass. A fee is charged at the entrance station for day use or overnight stays. For park information phone (61) 76-3120.

WHERE TO STAY

BEST WESTERN CASA DEL SOL MOTEL

Motel   ℂ 617/8-1570

| All Year | $65-$99 | XP $10 |

Location: At Ave Blancarte. Ave Lopez Mateos No 1001 22800 (PO Box 557). Fax: 617/8-2025. **Facility:** Located in the tourist area with many shops and restaurants. Meets AAA guest room security requirements. 48 units, 1 with kitchen. *Bath:* shower only. 2 stories, exterior corridors. **Parking:** limited. **Terms:** F12; 14 day cancellation notice, small pets only. **Cards:** AE, MC, VI.

SOME UNITS

BEST WESTERN EL CID

Motor Inn   ℂ (617)8-2401

| All Year | $47-$99 |

Location: At Ave Blancarte. Ave Lopez Mateos No 993 22800 (PO Box 786, CHULA VISTA, CA, 91910). Fax: 617/8-3671. **Facility:** In the tourist area with shops and restaurants. Meets AAA guest room security requirements. 52 units. Some whirlpool units ($89-$120). *Bath:* combo or shower only. 3 stories (no elevator), interior corridors. **Cards:** AE, MC, VI.

SOME UNITS

CORONA HOTEL

Motor Inn   ℂ 617/6-0901

6/1-8/31	$65-$95	XP $10
9/1-11/30	$52-$65	XP $8
12/1-5/31	$52-$65	XP $10

Location: 1 km s. Blvd Lazaro Cardenas No. 1442 22800 (482 W San Ysidro Blvd #303, SAN YSIDRO, CA, 92173). Fax: 617/6-4023. **Facility:** Meets AAA guest room security requirements. 92 units. 4 stories, interior corridors. **Terms:** F13; 3 day cancellation notice. **Leisure Activities:** heated pool. **Cards:** AE, MC, VI.

DAYS INN-VILLA FONTANA HOTEL

Motel   ℂ (617)8-3434

| 4/1-9/30 | $46-$60 | XP $10 |
| 12/1-3/31 & 10/1-11/30 | $46-$50 | XP $10 |

Location: Just w of Ave Blancarte. Ave Lopez Mateos 1050 22800. Fax: 617/8-3434. **Facility:** In the tourist area with many shops and restaurants. Meets AAA guest room security requirements. 65 units. Some suites ($98-$116) and whirlpool units ($98-$116). *Bath:* combo or shower only. 2 stories, exterior corridors. **Terms:** F12; cancellation fee imposed. **Leisure Activities:** whirlpool. **Business Services:** meeting rooms. **Cards:** AE, MC, VI.

SOME UNITS

ESTERO BEACH RESORT HOTEL

Resort   ℂ 617/6-6230

| 4/1-9/30 | $75-$130 | XP $10 |
| 12/1-3/31 & 10/1-11/30 | $55-$95 | XP $5 |

Location: 10.5 km s of town on Mex 1, then 1.5 km w on aves Jose Ma Moreles and Lupita Novelo O. 22800 (PMB 1186, 482 W San Ysidro Blvd, SAN YSIDRO, CA, 92173). Fax: 617/6-6925. **Facility:** On several acres of nicely landscaped, oceanfront grounds. Many large rooms with balcony or patio, some smaller rooms in cottage type units. Laundry facility available in season. 96 units. 2 two-bedroom units and 5 units with kitchen. Some suites ($400). *Bath:* combo or shower only. 2 stories, exterior corridors. **Terms:** F5; 3 day cancellation notice-fee imposed. **Leisure Activities:** heated pool, whirlpools, beach, swimming, boat ramp, waterskiing, playground, volleyball. *Fee:* boats, fishing, 3 lighted tennis courts, bicycles, horseback riding. **Guest Services:** gift shop. **Cards:** MC, VI.

SOME UNITS

HACIENDA BAJAMAR

Resort   ℂ 615/5-0151

| All Year | $220 | XP $35 |

Location: On Hwy 1-D (toll road), exit Baja Mar, 33 km n of town. Carr Escenica Tijuana Km 77.5 22760 (416 W San Ysidro Blvd #L-732, SAN YSIDRO, CA, 92173). Fax: 615/5-0150. **Facility:** A golf resort. Mexican colonial-style hacienda surrounded by golf course. Rooms with patio or balcony. 81 units, 10 with kitchen. 2 stories, interior/exterior corridors. **Terms:** F12; 8 day cancellation notice-fee imposed. **Amenities:** safes, hair dryers. **Leisure Activities:** heated pool, whirlpool, golf-27 holes, 2 tennis courts, playground. **Guest Services:** gift shop, valet laundry. *Fee:* massage. **Business Services:** meeting rooms. **Cards:** AE, MC, VI.

SOME UNITS

HOTEL CORAL & MARINA RESORT

Hotel   ℂ 617/5-0000

| All Year | $135-$220 |

Location: On Hwy 1-D, 3 km n of town at km 103. Carr Tijuana-Ensenada No. 3421 22860. Fax: 617/5-0005. **Facility:** Overlooking the bay and marina. Most rooms are suites, some with full cooking efficiency, all with balcony or patio. Meets AAA guest room security requirements. 147 units. 5 two-bedroom units, 1 three-bedroom unit and 11 efficiencies. 6 stories, exterior corridors. **Parking:** valet. **Terms:** package plans. **Amenities:** hair dryers. **Leisure Activities:** 2 pools (1 heated, 1 indoor), wading pool, saunas, whirlpools, steamrooms, 2 lighted tennis courts. *Fee:* boating, sailboating, marina, charter fishing. **Guest Services:** gift shop, valet laundry. *Fee:* massage. **Business Services:** meeting rooms. **Cards:** AE, MC, VI.

SOME UNITS

FEE

HOTEL CORTEZ

 *Motor Inn*   ((617)8-2307

All Year $60   XP $7

Location: At Ave Castillo; downtown. Ave Lopez Mateos No. 1089 22800 (PO Box 5356, CHULA VISTA, CA, 91912). Fax: 617/8-3904. **Facility:** Meets AAA guest room security requirements. 82 units. Some suites ($90-$110). *Bath:* combo or shower only. 2 stories, interior/exterior corridors. **Parking:** valet. **Terms:** F12; 30 day cancellation notice-fee imposed. **Leisure Activities:** heated pool. **Guest Services:** gift shop. **Business Services:** meeting rooms. *Fee:* fax. **Cards:** AE, MC, VI.

SOME UNITS

HOTEL MISION SANTA ISABEL

 Motor Inn   (617/8-3616

All Year $55-$70   XP $10

Location: At Blvd Lazaro Cardenas. Ave Castillo No. 1100 22800 (Box 120818, CHULA VISTA, CA, 91912). Fax: 617/8-3345. **Facility:** 57 units. *Bath:* combo or shower only. 3 stories, exterior corridors. **Terms:** F11; 3 day cancellation notice. **Amenities:** safes. **Business Services:** meeting rooms. **Cards:** AE, MC, VI.

SOME UNITS

HOTEL PARAISO LAS PALMAS

 Motor Inn   (617/7-1701

All Year $58-$71   XP $5

Location: 2 km s of town via Ave Castillo. Calle Augustin Sangines 206 92173 (445 W San Ysidro Blvd #2507, SAN YSIDRO, CA). Fax: 617/7-1701. **Facility:** 67 units. Some whirlpool units ($111-$120). *Bath:* shower only. 3 stories, exterior corridors. **Terms:** F12; 3 day cancellation notice, pets (in limited rooms). **Leisure Activities:** whirlpool, playground. **Guest Services:** [AP] meal plan available. **Business Services:** conference facilities. **Cards:** AE, MC, VI.

SOME UNITS

HOTEL SANTO TOMAS

Motor Inn   ((617)8-1503

All Year $60   XP $7

Location: At Ave Miramar. Blvd Costero No. 609 22800 (PO Box 5356, CHULA VISTA, CA, 91912). Fax: 617/8-1504. **Facility:** Across from the port. Meets AAA guest room security requirements. 80 units. Some suites ($90-$110). *Bath:* shower only. 3 stories, interior corridors. **Terms:** 30 day cancellation notice-fee imposed. **Guest Services:** [CP] meal plan available, gift shop, valet laundry. **Business Services:** meeting rooms. *Fee:* fax. **Cards:** AE, MC, VI.

SOME UNITS

LAS ROSAS HOTEL

Motor Inn   (617/4-4310

All Year $126-$154   XP $22

Location: On Hwy 1, 7 km n of town. Hwy 1-D 22800 (Box 316). Fax: 617/4-4595. **Facility:** Located on a bluff, all rooms have balcony with spectacular oceanfront view. Ocean access and full service spa. 48 units. 4 two-bedroom units. Some whirlpool units. *Bath:* combo or shower only. 5 stories, exterior corridors. **Terms:** D12; 3 day cancellation notice-fee imposed. **Leisure Activities:** heated pool, sauna, whirlpool. *Fee:* lighted tennis court, exercise room. **Guest Services:** gift shop, valet laundry. *Fee:* massage. **Business Services:** meeting rooms, administrative services, PC, fax. **Cards:** MC, VI.

POSADA EL REY SOL

Motor Inn   ((617)8-1601

All Year $64-$110   XP $12

Location: Just off Ave Lopez Mateos. Ave Blancarte No 130 22800 (4492 Camino De La Plaza, Suite ESE-118, SAN YSIDRO, CA, 92173-3097). Fax: 617/4-0005. **Facility:** In the tourist area with many shops and restaurants. Meets AAA guest room security requirements. 52 units. Some whirlpool units. *Bath:* shower only. 3 stories, exterior corridors. **Terms:** F12; 8 day cancellation notice. **Amenities:** safes, honor bars, hair dryers. **Leisure Activities:** whirlpool. **Guest Services:** valet laundry. **Business Services:** meeting rooms. **Cards:** AE, MC, VI.

SOME UNITS

PUNTA MORRO HOTEL SUITES

Suite Motor Inn   (617/8-3507

All Year $98-$260   XP $25

Location: 5 km n of town on Hwy 1, 0.5 km w. Km 106 Carr Tijuana-Ensenada (PO Box 434263, SAN DIEGO, CA, 92143). Fax: 617/4-4490. **Facility:** All rooms with fireplace, private patio or balcony and ocean view. Three studio units. 24 units. 9 two-bedroom units and 3 three-bedroom units. *Bath:* shower only. 3 stories, exterior corridors. **Terms:** F12; 7 day cancellation notice-fee imposed. **Amenities:** extended cable TV, hair dryers. **Leisure Activities:** whirlpool. **Guest Services:** [CP] meal plan available. **Cards:** AE, MC, VI.

WHERE TO DINE

ANGELO'S RISTORANTE

Italian

L $5-$13   D $7-$13

Location: Northeast end of town between 1st and 2nd sts. Ave Ruiz No. 153-1 22800. **Hours:** 1 pm-10 pm. Closed: Mon. **Features:** No A/C; casual dress; cocktails; street parking; a la carte. Pasta, pizza and traditional Italian entrees with fresh baked bread. Made on premises, the soup is well prepared; the Duck Suppema and Marcella Beef are special choices. **Cards:** MC, VI.

EL REY SOL RESTAURANT

French   (617/8-1733

L $9-$22   D $9-$28

Location: 1 km s. Ave Lopez Mateos 1000. **Hours:** 7:30 am-11 pm. **Features:** casual dress; cocktails; street parking; a la carte. Formal decor and service provided since 1947. Poultry, seafood and beef dishes prepared in French style, and there are a few traditional Mexican entrees. **Cards:** AE, MC, VI.

HALIOTIS

Seafood   (617/6-3720

L $7-$33   D $7-$33

Location: From Hwy 1 (Ave Reforma), 1 km e at south end of town. Calle Delante 179. **Hours:** 12:30 pm-10 pm. Closed: 1/1, 12/25; also 5/1. **Features:** casual dress; cocktails & lounge. Popular with the local community. A variety of seafood dishes are offered, specializing in lobster and abalone. **Cards:** AE, MC, VI.

LA EMBOTELLADORA VIEJA RESTAURANTE

 Continental (617/4-0807

D $8-$15

Location: Just n of downtown area. Ave Miramar No. 666.
Hours: noon-10 pm, Thurs-Sat to 11 pm. Closed: Tues.
Features: casual dress; wine only; street parking; a la carte.
At the Bodegas de Santo Tomas Winery. Fine dining in a
large room that once was used to age the wines, with a selection of international dishes. Each entree has a recommended wine selection from the extensive wine list. Dining
includes admission to the winery tour. **Cards:** AE, MC, VI.

LAS CAZUELAS RESTAURANT

 Mexican (617/6-1044

L $6-$20 D $6-$20

Location: South end of town at Blvd Lazaro Cardenas. Av
Sangines No. 6 22800. **Hours:** 7 am-11 pm. **Features:** casual dress; cocktails. Busy dining room with comfortable
food. Full menu of traditional Mexican dishes with many lobster and other seafood specialties. Breakfast is the special
draw here. Fast, friendly service and generous portions.
Cards: MC, VI.

RESTAURANTE LA MANSION DE ENSENADA

 International (617/8-3271

L $7-$25 D $7-$25

Location: Northeast end of town between 1st and 2nd sts.
Av Ruiz No. 149 22800. **Hours:** 8 am-10 pm. **Features:** No
A/C; casual dress; cocktails; street parking; a la carte.
Downtown near shopping area. Beef, poultry and seafood
prepared in International and Mexican styles. Steak is a
popular choice. **Cards:** MC, VI.

GUERRERO NEGRO,
BAJA CALIFORNIA SUR (D-2)

Guerrero Negro (geh-REH-roh NEH-groh) is
located within the barren Desierto Vizcaíno
(Vizcaíno Desert), just south of the Baja California Sur state border. The name, which means
"black warrior" in Spanish, was the moniker of
an American whaling ship wrecked at the entrance to nearby **Laguna Ojo de Liebre** (Scammon's Lagoon). Summer temperatures here are
much cooler than in the interior of the peninsula
due to the cold California Current, which extends
north off the Pacific coast.

Founded in 1955, Guerrero Negro is much
younger than other southern Baja communities. It
also plays a significant role in the peninsula's
economy: The area is one of the world's largest
producers of salt for industrial use. Thousands of
evaporating ponds south of town are routinely
flooded with salt water from the lagoon. The water evaporates quickly in the baking desert sun,
leaving behind deposits of pure white salt. The
conditions needed for successful salt harvesting,
rare in nature, are ideal in this remote section of
the peninsula.

A barren, rugged island about 89 kilometers
(55 miles) off the coast, **Isla Cedros** is the shipping point for salt mined on the mainland. Accessible via local flights from Guerrero Negro
and Ensenada, the island is virtually unspoiled

and seldom visited. Beaches, fishing and hiking
all are available, and despite its remoteness, there
are several restaurants and low-priced inns.

While this company town and highway stop
offers little in the way of tourist diversions, it is
a departure point for excursions to view California gray whales (locally called Mexican gray
whales). They migrate south some 6,000 miles
each year from the Bering Sea off Alaska. Their
journey ends at several lagoons along the central
Baja coast: Scammon's Lagoon, **Bahía
Magdalena** (Magdalena Bay) and **Laguna de
San Ignacio** (San Ignacio Lagoon), which is
about 100 miles south. The whales mate, return
to Alaska and come back the following year; fe-
males bear their young in these warm, shallow
waters from January through March.

Scammon's Lagoon was discovered by enterprising American whaler Charles Scammon in
the mid-19th century, and the whales were nearly
exterminated for their valuable oil. International
laws granting the whales protected status were
not enacted until the 1940s. Gray whales were
designated an endangered species in 1973 but removed from the list in 1994.

To reach the lagoon by car, take Mex. 1 south
about 9 kilometers (5.5 miles) to the graded dirt
turnoff (sandy but passable) that branches southwest; signs at this junction read "Laguna Ojo de
Libre" and "Parque Natural de la Ballena Gris/
Gray Whale Natural Park." There is a salt company checkpoint about 6 kilometers (4 miles)
west. About 16 kilometers (10 miles) farther is a
shack where admission to the natural park is
charged. Just beyond the shack is a fork; the
road to the left leads to the beach offering the
best views. Since the whales are usually some
distance offshore, bring a pair of binoculars.

From late December through March, group
tours in small boats *(pangas)* are offered by local
fishermen, who charge about $20 per person. Pri-
vate boats are not permitted anywhere in the lagoon during the season; local operators receive
special permits. Morning is the best time to spot
whales, as afternoon fog frequently obscures visibility. Group whale-watching excursions, including transportation and a boat trip led by a local
guide, also can be arranged through the Malarrimo restaurant, motel and campground complex
just outside of Guerrero Negro; phone (115)
7-0250.

Significantly more expensive, but worth it if
you want convenience and a complete experience, is an all-inclusive package excursion under
the guidance of an experienced naturalist. Most
of these trips depart from San Diego and include
transportation and accommodations. A representative package tour company is the environmentally oriented, San Diego-based **Baja
Expeditions**; phone (800) 843-6967.

Whale-watching excursions to San Ignacio Lagoon and Magdalena Bay depart from the desert oasis of **San Ignacio**, southeast of Guerrero Negro on Mex. 1. San Ignacio Lagoon is about 48 kilometers (30 miles) southwest of town via a dirt road. Information about these trips can be obtained in town. San Ignacio's role as a whale-watching departure point is evidenced by the whale skeleton on display at the junction of Mex. 1 and the paved road leading into town.

Local fishermen in the coastal village of Punta Abreojos, west of the lagoon, also act as guides for boat trips to observe the whales. The pristine lagoon has recently become the focus of conflict between environmentalists and the company, co-owned by the Mitsubishi Corp. and the Mexican government, that operates Guerrero Negro's salt-harvesting operation and is trying to establish a similar operation here.

About 81 kilometers (50 miles) north of Guerrero Negro via Mex. 1, through the desolate, windy Vizcaíno Desert, is the hamlet of Rosarito, B.C. Just east of the highway, Rosarito (not to be confused with the popular seaside tourist town of the same name in northern Baja California state) marks the beginning of a side road to the **Mission San Borja**. This is one of Baja's most interesting missions, partly because of its very remoteness. Although there are no steep grades, numerous rough and rocky spots require that the trip be made in a high-clearance vehicle only.

The single-track, open-desert dirt road winds northeast through scrubby desert, passing several flat-topped buttes along the way. Vegetation that has adapted to this inhospitable environment includes various species of cactus and the tall, columnar cirio tree, which grows only in the central part of the peninsula and in the mainland state of Sonora. At about 22 kilometers (13.5 miles) is a junction; bear left. After passing a large cattle ranch the road begins a gradual descent to the mission, which lies in a broad valley at the base of barren mountains.

Founded in 1759 by the Jesuits shortly before they were expelled from the New World, San Borja once served more than 3,000 Indians but was abandoned in 1818 after introduced diseases devastated the native population. The restored structure is largely intact; nearby are several adobe ruins and the remains of an irrigation system built by the mission friars.

WHERE TO STAY

The following lodging was either not evaluated or did not meet AAA rating requirements and is listed for your information only.

HOTEL LA PINTA

[fyi] *Motor Inn*   (115/7-1301

Does not meet all AAA rating requirements; previously evaluated on 11/20/99. **Location:** 7.5 km ne on Hwy 1; at 28th parallel. Facilities, services, and decor characterize a basic property.

WHERE TO DINE

MALARRIMO RESTAURANT

▼▼▼ *Seafood*   (115/7-0250
                                      L $3-$5   D $4-$12
Location: 1 km w of Mex 1; at east edge of town. Hwy 1. **Hours:** 7:30 am-10:30 pm. Closed: 12/25. **Features:** No A/C; casual dress; cocktails. Long established, serving local seafood and beef specialties.

LA PAZ,
BAJA CALIFORNIA SUR (F-3)

La Paz (lah PAHS) is the commercial as well as the governmental capital of the state of Baja California Sur. Its name means "peace," and the **Dove of Peace Monument**, a large contemporary sculpture that acts as a gateway to the city, bears the following (translated) inscription: "And if you want peace, I offer it to you in the sunny peace of my bay." Today's city spreads out from the curving shore of beautiful **Bahía de la Paz**, the largest bay along Baja's eastern coastline.

Ironically, La Paz's history is one of the most turbulent of any community on the entire Baja California Peninsula. Two years after the bay was discovered by a Spanish expedition in 1533, supply problems doomed a colonization attempt by Hernán Cortés. Nearly 300 years of isolation and hardship prevented a permanent settlement from taking hold. The most persistent inhabitants were the privateers who sought haven in the bay. The name of one—Cromwell—lives on (Hispanicized) in the *coromueles*, or offshore breezes, and in such local place names as Playa Coromuel.

Rich oyster beds below the surface of the Gulf of California attracted a handful of fortune seekers throughout the 17th century. The Jesuits founded a mission at La Paz in 1720 and kept it going despite a series of Indian uprisings. It was abandoned nearly 30 years later after disease had virtually wiped out the area's indigenous population; the city's cathedral stands on the site today.

A group of determined Spaniards finally established a settlement in 1811. Continued pearl diving and some mining provided impetus for growth, and when Loreto *(see separate listing)* was destroyed by a hurricane in 1829, La Paz was named the territorial capital. Beautiful black and pink pearls from gulf waters filled the coffers of the Spanish royal treasury. But conflict broke out again, this time in the form of the Mexican-American War. Battles were fought in the city's streets, but American soldiers departed after the Treaty of Guadalupe Hidalgo was signed in 1848.

Southern Baja's remoteness continued to hinder any large-scale development. After the pearl and mining industries gave out toward the end of the 1930s, La Paz languished. But as was the case with Ensenada and Cabo San Lucas, sportsmen and tourists slowly rediscovered the area's balmy winter climate and fine fishing. After years of existence as a neglected territory, Baja California Sur—along with Quintana Roo, one of Mexico's two newest states—suddenly exploded with economic and population growth, and La Paz evolved from a sleepy port into a modern state capital.

This jolt into the Mexican mainstream has not come without a few rude awakenings—the traffic congestion on downtown's cramped, narrow streets being but one example. La Paz's population, about 138,000 according to the 1990 Census, has expanded to an estimated 176,000. Still, the shady plazas and palm-fringed *malecón* (waterside Paseo Alvaro Obregón) retain some of the colonial grace of old. For every contemporary structure and each car blaring the latest pop hits, there is a quaintly arched doorway or an old cobblestone sidewalk.

The city sports a growing number of resorts and fleets of pleasure craft. La Paz also is a busy commercial port, and downtown streets are lined with small shops full of foreign goods. Some of these businesses still observe the traditional *siesta*, closing their doors in the early afternoon.

Despite its commercial bustle, La Paz is a laid-back city. Residents carry themselves with pride and respect; drivers actually stop for pedestrians crossing the street. While tourism is accommodated willingly, a thoroughly Mexican atmosphere prevails. This old-fashioned charm is most fully evident on Sunday evenings, when throngs of couples and families customarily promenade along the *malecón*, often against the backdrop of a spectacular sunset.

THE INFORMED TRAVELER

The most reliable source for visitor information is the State Tourism Office. It is located on Mex. 1 at Km marker 5.5, at the north end of town in the Fidepaz Building (near the marina). It is open Mon.-Fri. 8-8; phone (112) 4-0199 or 4-0103. The staff is helpful and bilingual. Another office is on the *malecón* at the intersection of Paseo Alvaro Obregón and 16 de Septiembre; here visitors can obtain information about various city tour packages. It is open Mon.-Fri. 8-3 and 3:30-7; phone (112) 2-5939. In the same building is **Turismo Express**, a travel agency that has additional information and can arrange for boat tours or other travel needs; phone (112) 5-6310 or 5-6311 (English spoken).

The airport is located 18 kilometers (11 miles) southwest of the city off Mex. 1 (north toward Ciudad Constitución). Aero California and Aeroméxico have daily flights from Los Angeles and Tijuana to La Paz. These two companies also fly to and from several Mexican mainland cities, including Guadalajara, Los Mochis and Mexico City. Alaska Airlines flies from Los Angeles, Portland, San Diego, San Francisco and Seattle Tuesday, Thursday and Saturday during the winter season. *Colectivos* (shuttle vans) transport passengers from the airport into the city but not the other way around; you'll need to take a taxi when departing. *Also see "Arriving by Air," page 53, and "Air and Bus Service" under "A Baja Overview," page 150.*

Buses to the beaches and the deep-water port of Pichilingue depart from the station at Paseo Alvaro Obregón #125 (the *malecón* terminal). Long-distance travel to other Baja cities is provided by Autotransportes de Baja California and Tres Estrellas de Oro; these buses arrive and depart from the terminal at Jalisco and Héroes de Independencia, a couple of miles southwest of downtown. Both lines provide regular passenger service between La Paz and Tijuana—a 24-hour trip. Also arriving at this terminal are *Aguila* (local) buses from Cabo San Lucas, about 209 kilometers (130 miles) south of La Paz. A taxi can take you from the terminal to the *malecón* area.

In-town routes cover the city. The fare is inexpensive, but a knowledge of Spanish is helpful and riders should be familiar with the city layout. The central depot is located at avenidas Revolución de 1910 and Degollado, next to the public market.

Taxis are plentiful, especially along the *malecón* and near the bigger hotels. Rates average about $4 for 2 miles, or about $11 from downtown to the airport. Make sure the fare is set before you get in the cab.

If you've arrived by air, a car will come in handy for exploring outlying beaches, but keep in mind that rental cars can be much more expensive in Mexico than in the United States. The city has several rental car agencies; unless otherwise specified, the vehicles tend to be Volkswagen Beetles.

Air-conditioned, automobile-passenger ferries operated by **Grupo Sematur** link La Paz with the mainland cities of Mazatlán (sailings Sun.-Fri. at 3, with Sat. sailings during holiday periods) and Topolobampo, near Los Mochis (sailings Wed.-Mon. at 8 p.m.). The Pichilingue ferry terminal is about 19 kilometers (12 miles) north of La Paz via Mex. 11. The trip to Topolobampo takes about 9 hours; the trip to Mazatlán takes about 19 hours. Although boats usually are equipped with a cafeteria or restaurant, travelers may want to bring their own food and beverages.

The Grupo Sematur ferry office in La Paz is on Guillermo Prieto at 5 de Mayo, 2 blocks inland from Plaza Constitución. It is open Mon.-Fri. 7-1 and 4-6, Sat.-Sun. 8-1; phone (112) 5-3833 or 5-4666. Phone (112) 2-9485 for the Pichilingue ferry terminal. For passengers not transporting a vehicle, reservations can be made at the ferry office in advance; however, tickets cannot be purchased until between 4 and 6 p.m.

of the day before departure. While local tourist agencies book reservations for the ferry, it is best to make reservations and obtain tickets in person at the ferry office. A knowledge of Spanish will prove very helpful.

There are four accommodation classes for passengers: salon, tourist, cabin and special cabin. Salon class is a padded seat. *Turista* is a cabin with a washbasin and four bunks that are shared, often with strangers. Cabins offer bunks and a bath for two persons, and a special cabin is an upgraded, private cabin. All four classes are available on the La Paz-Mazatlán crossing; only salon accommodations are available on the La Paz-Topolobampo crossing.

Separate fares are charged for passengers and for vehicles; the rate for vehicles is determined by the length of the vehicle in meters. **Note:** Fares are subject to frequent change.

Public passengers may not be permitted on the ferry to Mazatlán on Tuesdays; inquire as to whether this restriction is still in effect when making your reservations. If you plan to transport a vehicle on the ferry, contact a Mexican consulate office prior to your trip for the latest updates regarding laws and regulations. Random but thorough searches may occur before vehicles are boarded. Owners are not permitted to retrieve articles from their vehicles after they have been boarded. For additional information about the ferry, *see "Ferry Service," page 64, and "Ferry Service" under "A Baja Overview," page 150.*

The English-language *Baja Sun* carries recreational articles and advertisements pertaining to La Paz and other Baja California cities. The **Librería Contempo** bookstore, on Agustín Arreola near Paseo Alvaro Obregón, sells several English publications. Radio station XERT, 800 AM, plays a variety of music; more traditional Mexican sounds can be heard on Radio Alegría, 90.1 FM. The satellite dish antennas at the large hotels bring in TV stations from Mexico City as well as the United States.

Currency can be exchanged at Banco Internacional, 5 de Mayo and Avenida Revolución de 1910 across from Our Lady of La Paz Cathedral. Clinica La Paz, a hospital at Avenida Revolución de 1910 #461, has English-speaking staff; phone (112) 2-2800.

Accommodations in La Paz range from budget hotels lining the *malecón* to more luxurious properties scattered along the road to Pichilingue. For adventurers or those traveling on shoestring budgets, there are several *pensións*, or boardinghouses, in the downtown area. These are no-frills places and frequently rundown-looking, although they tend to have a friendly, communal feeling. The Hostería del Convento, Avenida Francisco Madero #85, has a lush tropical courtyard; the colonial building was once a Spanish mission.

November through April or May is the best time to visit La Paz, when days are warm and nights can be refreshingly cool. Summer's sticky heat and humidity is uncomfortable, to say the least, despite the presence of afternoon breezes coming off the bay. Rainfall in this desert region is scant and varies from year to year, although violent tropical storms called *chubascos* bring occasional downpours in late summer or fall.

City Layout

La Paz appears as somewhat of a mirage among the barren, cactus-covered foothills of southern Baja. Clearly marked signs indicate two routes. Following "Centro" will take you straight into downtown; the Mex. 1 fork proceeds south to San José del Cabo and Cabo San Lucas. Situated at Bahía de la Paz's southeastern end, the city faces northwest, an ideal location from which to appreciate the sunsets that turn the Gulf of California ablaze with color. A long, narrow sandbar, **El Mogote**, protects La Paz from the gulf's open waters.

The city is laid out in a simple grid pattern, with long, straight streets oriented northwest-southeast and southwest-northeast. The "tourist zone" runs along the *malecón* between avenidas Sinaloa and Colegio Militar. Adjoining the bayfront is old downtown, a congested section of irregular streets that is more easily navigated on foot than by car. Many streets in La Paz are one way, although clearly marked. The major thoroughfares are Paseo Alvaro Obregón, Avenida 16 de Septiembre and Avenida 5 de Mayo. Streets running inland from the waterfront are uphill, becoming primarily residential within 10 blocks. **City Hall**, at avenidas 16 de Septiembre and Francisco Madero, is housed in a 150-year-old building that was formerly a jail.

What To Do

La Paz, like Cabo San Lucas and Ensenada, is famed for its sport fishing. Blue marlin weighing up to 1,000 pounds are found in offshore waters from mid-March through October; sailfish can be hooked from the end of May through October. Bonito, roosterfish and yellowtail are available all year. Other game species include black marlin, dorado, grouper, red snapper, triggerfish and yellowfin tuna.

Boats for a day of deep-sea fishing—either a *panga* (skiff) or a more expensive cruiser for four or more people—can be arranged through travel agencies along the *malecón* and at the fishing desk in the Los Arcos Hotel, on Paseo Alvaro Obregón between Allende and Rosales. Rental rates usually include tackle, bait and crew. Most boats depart from the Pichilingue docks. Reservations are advised from April to early July, when the big marlin are running.

One well-known outfit is the **Dorado Velez Fleet**, which operates out of the Los Arcos Hotel; for reservations information phone (112) 2-2744, ext. 637. At the **Viajes Palmira Travel Agency**, on Paseo Alvaro Obregón across from the Los Arcos Hotel, visitors can make arrangements for accommodations, car rentals, fishing trips and guided tours; phone (112) 2-4030 or 5-7278. If you're visiting on your own boat, **Marina de La Paz**, avenidas Topete and Legaspy near the western end of the *malecón*, has slips ranging from 30 to 70 feet and also provides a variety of shoreside services.

The nicest beaches are north of the city via Mex. 11 (known locally as the Pichilingue Highway) toward Pichilingue. The highway is not marked, although signs indicate that you are heading in the direction of Pichilingue and the ferry docks. Mex. 11 continues north all the way to Playa Tecolote.

A short distance north of the tourist wharf in town is **Playa Coromuel**, which has thatched-roofed bars and restaurants. About 10 kilometers (6 miles) north of downtown is **Playa Comancito**, located at La Concha (Km 5.5 on the Pichilingue Highway), the area's most exclusive resort. The beach, however—as are all beaches in Mexico—is open to the public. Here equipment for snorkeling, scuba diving and water skiing can be rented.

Pichilingue itself was once a haven for pirates plundering the bounty of black pearls harvested from oysters residing in the bay. By about 1940, however, the mollusks had mysteriously disappeared, presumably wiped out by disease. Today the town functions as the deep-water port for La Paz and a recreational getaway where sportfishing boats bring in the day's catch.

The beaches become more secluded the farther you go. **Playa Pichilingue** is north of the ferry dock; stop here for a dip in the clear blue water followed by a cold beer and some freshly grilled fish at one of the beachside *palapas*. Next is **Punta Balandra**, a lovely series of quiet coves framed by dramatic rock formations. At the tip of the point is **Playa Tecolote**, where conditions for diving and snorkeling are just about ideal. There are few facilities other than outhouses and a few barbecue pits here, but camping and RV parking is currently free and the water is crystal clear.

GUIDED TOURS

San Diego-based **Baja Expeditions** offers an array of exciting excursions, with a focus on environment, education and adventure. Sea kayaking, whale watching and scuba diving are among the trips offered. Serious naturalists or divers will relish scuba excursions of up to 7 days' duration, exploring some of the peninsula's most beautiful spots. Most trips include accommodations, equipment, meals and a knowledgeable trip leader. Operations are based in La Paz; many trip organizers live in the city and are well acquainted with the area. For additional information, write Baja Expeditions at 2625 Garnet Ave., San Diego, Calif. 92109; phone (800) 843-6967.

Baja Diving, Paseo Alvaro Obregón #1665-2, Plaza Cerracvo, offers scuba and snorkeling expeditions to various offshore locations, including Isla Espíritu Santo, site of the sunken vessel the *Salvatierra*; **Isla La Partida**, home to a large colony of friendly sea lions; the remote beaches on **Isla Cerralvo**; and underwater mountains, or seamounts. For further information phone (112) 2-1826, daily 8-3:30, or write the outfitter at P.O. Box 782, La Paz, B.C.S. Another Baja Diving office is located at the La Concha resort; phone (112) 2-6544.

Trips to **Magdalena Bay** to view gray whales depart from the La Concha Beach Resort on Pichilingue Road (Mex. 11). After a 3½-hour drive to this bay on Baja's western coast, tour guests board a 16-foot *panga* for 2 hours of observation. The tour includes a seafood lunch in the small coastal village of Puerto López-Mateos. The all-day trip is offered from December to March, depending on the whales' cycle of arrival and departure, and costs $90 per person. For information phone the resort at (619) 275-7050 (from the United States) or (112) 2-6240 (in La Paz).

SHOPPING, DINING AND NIGHTLIFE

As a free port, La Paz offers the savvy shopper good buys on imported merchandise as well as such handicrafts as coral jewelry, seashell knickknacks, leather goods and woven baskets. Tourist-oriented shops cluster along Paseo Alvaro Obregón. **Curios La Carretera**, on Morelos near the corner of Revolución de 1910, is a shopping complex featuring carved wood furniture, clothing and folk art from various parts of mainland Mexico.

A wide assortment of utilitarian goods fill the stalls of La Paz's **Mercado** (public market), in the center of town on Avenida Revolución de 1910 at Degollado. Produce, meats, fish and cheeses spill from the open-air stalls, and a juice bar offers orange, papaya, mango, grapefruit and strawberry liquid refreshment. Next to the market are several outdoor cafés that dish up freshly prepared tacos and locally caught fish prepared in a variety of ways.

La Perla de La Paz, in the thick of downtown on Mutualismo at Agustín Arreola, carries an impressive spectrum of upscale merchandise, while **Dorian's**, at avenidas 16 de Septiembre and 21 de Agosto, stocks typical department store items. Avenida 16 de Septiembre is chock-ablock with small storefronts selling name-brand stereos, car phones, word processors, TVs and Sony Walkmans. Clothing boutiques offer everything from high fashion to Levi 501's. You'll find clothing from Guatemala as well as Guadalajaran shoes, boots and hats.

In addition to mass-produced merchandise, the local artisans are worth searching out. At **Artesanía Cuauhtémoc** (The Weaver), southwest of downtown on Abasolo (Mex. 1) between calles Jalisco and Nayarit, Fortunato Silva makes and sells handwoven cotton and woolen articles—rugs, tablecloths, placemats and the like. At **Cerámica Acuario**, Guillermo Prieto #625 near the Sematur ferry office, the Ibarra family fires pottery the old-fashioned way. Exquisite floral designs are carefully hand-painted on plates, pitchers, mugs and vases. Look for the various plates hanging on the shop's outside wall.

Steak and seafood head the bill of fare at local restaurants. One popular eatery is **La Paz-Lapa**, on Paseo Alvaro Obregón at León, part of the Carlos Anderson chain. The noise level is deafening, but the beef and fish are tasty and the atmosphere convivial. There are a number of fast-food restaurants in the downtown area, but rather than burgers and fries these takeout cafés offer such Mexican basics as burritos, roasted *pollo* (chicken) and fish tacos.

Although nightlife in La Paz pales when compared to the surf and sport set down in Los Cabos, there are still options. Much of the activity takes place along the *malecón* at the water's edge. Discos at the Hotel Palmira and the Hotel Gran Baja offer dancing, live entertainment or both. The nightclub **La Cabaña** is on the lobby floor of the Hotel Perla. At other clubs, such as the **Grill Xtasis and Video Bar**, downtown at calles Zaragoza and Arreola, dancers shimmy to pulsating laser lights and the latest music videos.

Local and visiting performing arts groups take to the stage at the **Teatro de la Ciudad** (City Theater), at Miguel Legaspy and Héroes de Independencia. The most enjoyable activity, though, might be to simply take a seat at an outdoor café along the *malecón* at sunset and watch as the waters of the bay turn to spectacular hues of red and gold.

WHAT TO SEE IN TOWN

BIBLIOTECA DE HISTORIA DE LAS CALIFORNIAS (Historical Library of the Californias), north side of Plaza Constitución, occupies the Casa de Gobierno, a former government building. Vivid paintings depict Baja California Sur's early days, and the library maintains a collection of books and historical documents—in both English and Spanish—recounting the history of the Baja California Peninsula and California. Mon.-Sat. 8-6. Free. Phone (112) 2-0162.

MUSEO DE ANTROPOLOGIA E HISTORIA DE BAJA CALIFORNIA SUR (Anthropological and Historical Museum of Baja California Sur) is at Ignacio Altamirano and 5 de Mayo. The museum features exhibits on the geology, geography, flora and fauna of the state. Dioramas and photographs of cave paintings depict the region's Indian cultures, and an actual excavation site shows human bones being painstakingly extracted. Spanish mission settlement and Mexican ranch life are among the historical subjects covered. Most of the exhibit descriptions are in Spanish, although museum staff can help translate them. Mon.-Fri. 9-6, Sat. 9-2. Donations. Phone (112) 5-6424.

NUESTRA SENORA DE LA PAZ, south side of Plaza Constitución, was originally a Jesuit mission. Large bilingual plaques relate the church's history as well as La Paz's beginnings. The plaza itself—also called Jardín Velazco—has tiled, tree-shaded paths and is landscaped with colorful hibiscus shrubs. It's a peaceful place to relax and watch city life go by.

WHERE TO STAY

ARAIZA INN PALMIRA
▼▼▼
Motor Inn   (112/1-6200
All Year $90   XP $7
Location: 2.5 km n on Carretera a Pichilingue. Blvd Alberto Aramburu S/N (Apdo Postal 442, 23010). Fax: 112/1-6227. **Facility:** Across from bay, with tropical grounds. Large convention center. Meets AAA guest room security requirements. 120 units. *Bath:* shower only. 3 stories, interior corridors. **Terms:** package plans. **Leisure Activities:** wading pool, playground. *Fee:* lighted tennis court. **Guest Services:** gift shop, valet laundry. **Business Services:** conference facilities. **Cards:** AE, MC, VI.

⊞ ⊤ ⊠ ⊛

CABANAS DE LOS ARCOS
▼▼ ▼▼
Motel   ((112)2-2744
All Year $75   XP $10
Location: Center; just off Paseo Alvaro Obregon opposite the Malecon, adjacent to Hotel Los Arcos. (PO Box 112, 23000). Fax: 112/5-4313. **Facility:** 1/2 block from bay. Tropical garden setting. Rooms and bungalows. Meets AAA guest room security requirements. 52 units. *Bath:* shower only. 1-4 stories, interior/exterior corridors. **Parking:** street only. **Terms:** F12; 30 day cancellation notice-fee imposed. **Amenities:** honor bars. **Leisure Activities:** heated pool. *Fee:* charter fishing. **Guest Services:** valet laundry. **Cards:** AE, MC, VI.

⊞⁺ ⊠ ⊛ ⊟ 🔲

CLUB EL MORO
▼▼ ▼▼
Suite Motor Inn   ((112)2-4084
All Year $60
Location: 2 km n on Carretera a Pichilingue. Km 2 Carr. a Pichilingue (Apdo Postal 357, 23010). Fax: 112/5-2828. **Facility:** Moorish style buildings across from the bay. 21 units. 3 two-bedroom units, 2 efficiencies and 18 units with kitchen. *Bath:* shower only. 2 stories, exterior corridors. **Terms:** 15 day cancellation notice, pets (in designated rooms). **Leisure Activities:** whirlpool, swim-up bar. **Guest Services:** coin laundry. **Cards:** AE, MC, VI.

CROWNE PLAZA RESORT

▼▼▼▼ *Suite Hotel* 〖 112/4-0830

All Year $120-$150 XP $10
Location: 5.5 km w on Hwy 1. Lote A Marina Norte Fidepaz 23090 (Apdo Postal 482). Fax: 112/4-0837. **Facility:** Meets AAA guest room security requirements. 54 units. 9 two-bedroom units. 2 stories, exterior corridors. **Terms:** F12; 3 day cancellation notice, package plans. **Amenities:** safes, irons, hair dryers. **Leisure Activities:** 3 pools, whirlpool, beach, playground, exercise room, sports court. *Fee:* charter fishing. **Guest Services:** gift shop, area transportation, valet laundry. **Business Services:** conference facilities. **Cards:** AE, MC, VI.

SOME UNITS
/ ⊠ /

HOTEL LAS ARENAS

▼▼▼ *Resort* 〖 112/2-3146

All Year $160 XP $35
Location: 70 km se, Hwy 286 to Los Planes, 18.5 km on gravel and dirt road. Bahia de la Ventura 23000 (PO Box 182). **Facility:** Oceanfront fishing. 40 units. *Bath:* shower only. 2 stories, exterior corridors. **Terms:** package plans, 10% service charge. **Amenities:** no TVs. **Leisure Activities:** beach, windsurfing, snorkeling, fishing. *Fee:* charter fishing. **Guest Services:** [AP] meal plan available. **Cards:** AE, MC, VI.

HOTEL LOS ARCOS

▼▼▼ *Hotel* 〖 (112)2-2744

All Year $75 XP $10
Location: Center of town. Alvaro Obregon 498 (PO Box 112, 23000). Fax: 112/5-4313. **Facility:** Across from bay. Central courtyard with large pool. All rooms with balcony. Meets AAA guest room security requirements. 130 units. *Bath:* shower only. 3 stories, interior corridors. **Terms:** F12; 30 day cancellation notice-fee imposed, package plans. **Amenities:** honor bars. **Leisure Activities:** heated pool. *Fee:* sauna, charter fishing. **Guest Services:** gift shop, valet laundry. *Fee:* massage. **Business Services:** meeting rooms. **Cards:** AE, MC, VI.

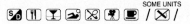

HOTEL MARINA

▼▼▼ *Hotel* 〖 (112)1-6254

12/16-11/30 $95 XP $20
12/1-12/15 $94 XP $16
Location: Km 2.5 Carretera a Pichilingue 23010 (Apdo Postal 194). Fax: 112/1-6177. **Facility:** On the bay and marina. Tropical courtyard with birds and colorful plants. Meets AAA guest room security requirements. 92 units. 17 efficiencies and 5 units with kitchen. *Bath:* combo or shower only. 5 stories, exterior corridors. **Terms:** F12; 15 day cancellation notice-fee imposed. **Amenities:** hair dryers. **Leisure Activities:** wading pool, whirlpool, snorkeling, fishing, lighted tennis court. *Fee:* boats, boat dock, marina. **Guest Services:** gift shop, valet laundry. **Cards:** AE, JC, MC, VI.

SOME UNITS

▣ 🍽 🍷 🏊 ⊠ 📷 💻 / ⊠ /

LA CONCHA BEACH RESORT

▼▼▼ *Resort* 〖 (112)1-6161

All Year $95 XP $20
Location: 5 km ne on Carretera a Pichilinque. (Apdo Postal 607, 23010). Fax: 112/1-6218. **Facility:** Tree-shaded grounds at the beach. All rooms with balcony. 119 units. 1 two-bedroom unit and 1 three-bedroom unit. *Bath:* shower only. 3-6 stories, exterior corridors. **Terms:** F12; age restrictions may apply, 3 day cancellation notice, package plans. **Leisure Activities:** heated pool, whirlpool, beach, swimming, fishing, exercise room. *Fee:* boating, windsurfing, scuba diving/snorkeling & equipment, charter fishing. **Guest Services:** gift shop, area transportation. *Fee:* massage. **Business Services:** conference facilities. **Cards:** AE, MC, VI.

▣ 🍽 🍷 🏊 ⊠ 📷 🅑

WHERE TO DINE

EL TASTE

▼▼▼ *Mexican* 〖 112/2-8121

L $4-$18 D $7-$18
Location: Paseo Alvaro Obregon 23000. **Hours:** 8 am-midnight. **Features:** No A/C; casual dress; cocktails; street parking. Overlooking the Malecon and Bay. Featuring seafood and beef. **Cards:** MC, VI.

LA PAZ-LAPA DE CARLOS 'N CHARLIES

▼▼▼ *Mexican* 〖 112/2-9290

L $4-$13 D $5-$13
Location: On Malecon at Calle 16 de Septiembre. Paseo Alvaro Obregon 23010. **Hours:** noon-1 am. **Features:** No A/C; casual dress; children's menu; cocktails & lounge; street parking; a la carte. Fun and friendly atmosphere with energetic staff and colorful patio dining across from the bay. **Cards:** MC, VI.

RESTAURANT TRATTORIA LA PAZTA

▼▼▼ *Continental* 〖 112/5-1195

L $3-$5 D $5-$9
Location: 1/2 blk from Malecon. Allende 36 23000. **Hours:** 7 am-10 pm. Closed: Tues. **Features:** No A/C; casual dress; cocktails & lounge; street parking; a la carte. Charming trattoria featuring fresh pasta and pizza made to order; also authentic Swiss dishes and fondue. Bistro open for breakfast and lunch daily to 4 pm. **Cards:** AE, MC, VI.

LORETO,
BAJA CALIFORNIA SUR (E-3)

Loreto (loh-REH-toh) dates from 1697, when a mission was founded by Jesuit padre Juan María Salvatierra. It became the first capital of both Alta (the present state of California) and Baja California and is the peninsula's oldest permanent settlement. The base from which exploration and colonization efforts of the Californias began, Loreto also was the departure point from which Junípero Serra launched his northward quest in 1769 to establish a chain of missions in Alta California.

After Mexico won its independence from Spain in 1821, the missions began to decline. When a devastating hurricane struck in 1829, the capital was moved south to La Paz. Loreto fell into near oblivion until its impressive natural attributes—craggy mountains, the cobalt-blue Gulf of California, year-round sunny weather—began attracting U.S. sportsmen, who discovered that the fishing was outstanding even by the gulf's high standards.

Like Baja California Sur's other desert oases, Loreto lies within a grove of date palms, and other touches of green are provided by vineyards and orchards of fig and olive trees. The town is overshadowed by the jagged peaks of the Sierra de la Giganta to the west. Many of its streets remain unpaved, exuding a relaxed though dusty ambience. Loreto is easily reached from points north via the transpeninsular highway (Mex. 1). The airport, about 7 kilometers (4 miles) southwest of town, receives regular flights from southern California. Direct flights are offered from Los Angeles by Aero California; for schedule and fare information phone (800) 237-6225.

Fondo Nacional de Fomento al Turismo (FONATUR), a government-funded agency responsible for turning deserted sections of Mexican shoreline into planned resort centers, has attempted to create at Loreto the same megaresort status already accomplished spectacularly on the Caribbean at Cancún and in progress along the southern Pacific coast at Bahías de Huatulco. The town's *malecón* (waterfront promenade, or boardwalk) was recently renovated and benches were added.

Tasked with establishing the infrastructure necessary for the creation of a tourist-oriented city, FONATUR built the Loreto Tennis Center and created an 18-hole golf course (nine holes were open at press time) at **Nopoló Bay**, about 8 kilometers (5 miles) south of Loreto. Miles of streets were laid out, installed with lights and telephone poles, and planted with palms. At **Puerto Escondido**, a deep water port about 15 kilometers (9 miles) south via a short paved road off Mex. 1, a large concrete marina was constructed.

So far, these enterprises have failed to generate much in the way of a hoped-for tourist influx. The maze of streets, without houses or other buildings, resembles more than anything a weedy ghost town of concrete foundations. Some planned hotel construction is still on hold, and it remains to be seen whether FONATUR's ambitious plans for the area will be realized. The town of Loreto remains a relatively unspoiled haven for sports fishermen. Beach lovers should skip the rocky public stretches in town and head for the indented shores of **Bahía Concepción**, about an hour's drive north up the Gulf of California coast toward Mulegé.

Near the central plaza is the **Mission of Nuestra Señora de Loreto** (Our Lady of Loreto). Severely damaged by earthquakes, the 1752 mission—including the tower with its modern clock—has been almost completely rebuilt and still functions as an active church. It features baroque stone ornamentation and a gilded group of altar paintings.

Loreto continues to attract fly-in anglers in search of yellowtail, roosterfish, marlin, sailfish and almost every other major game species. Spring is the season for yellowtail, sailfish and marlin run in the summer months, and cabrillo (sea bass) and red snapper are available all year. One of the waterfront hotels should be able to arrange a fishing expedition. **Alfredo's Sport Fishing**, on Benito Juárez near the *malecón*, has knowledgeable guides.

There are two opportunities for interesting day trips. A boat excursion can be taken to **Isla Coronado**, about a mile and a half offshore, where the only residents are a colony of sea lions. Snorkeling and scuba diving are possible; the best diving conditions are from June through October, when the water is warmest. Trip arrangements can be made through local hotels.

Mission San Javier is a beautifully restored structure of dark volcanic rock in the *mudéjar* (Moorish) style. Every bit as impressive as the mission is the journey to reach it, which passes through stunning mountain and canyon scenery. From a signed junction about 2 kilometers (1 mile) south of the Loreto turnoff, a fairly good graded dirt road proceeds southwest for about 37 kilometers (23 miles), with the landscape evolving from flat desert to rounded hills to the rugged Sierra de la Giganta. The 2-hour-plus trip from Loreto should be made in a high-clearance vehicle only. Local hotels sometimes will put together a guided tour, although a minimum number of people may be required.

The mission itself sits at the bottom of a deep valley, surrounded by the small village of San Javier. The second oldest of the Jesuit missions established on the peninsula, it was founded in 1699 but not completed until 1758. The towering walls feature exemplary stonework, and the gilded altar was brought from Mexico City. It's possible to climb the winding stairs to the roof and bell tower, which offers a panoramic view of the valley below. The mission is still active as a parish church, and contributions are appreciated.

Note: Few merchants in town take credit cards or traveler's checks for payment, although both pesos and U.S. dollars are readily accepted. Currency can be exchanged at the Bancomer bank, on the main plaza, Mon.-Fri. during the morning.

MUSEO DE LAS MISIONES (Mission Museum) is next to the Nuestra Señora de Loreto Mission. The artifacts and manuscripts on display relate to Baja California's historic missions. Other exhibits include religious art and saddles used in colonial times. Admission is charged.

WHERE TO STAY

EDEN LORETO RESORT-ALL INCLUSIVE

▼▼◆◇▼ *Resort* ℂ 113/3-0700

All Year $240-$310 XP $80
Location: 8 km s on Hwy 1, 1 km e in Nopolo. Blvd Mision de Loreto S/N 23880. Fax: 113/3-0377. **Facility:** Spacious oceanfront grounds. Rooms with patio or balcony. Rate includes all meals, beverages, taxes, gratuity and most recreational services. 236 units. *Bath:* shower only. 3 stories. **Terms:** age restrictions may apply, 14 day cancellation notice, package plans. **Amenities:** safes. **Leisure Activities:** 2 heated pools, whirlpool, beach, sailboating, windsurfing, snorkeling, fishing, golf-18 holes, lighted tennis court, bicycles, exercise room. *Fee:* scuba diving & equipment, charter fishing. **Guest Services:** [AP] meal plan available, gift shop, valet laundry. **Cards:** AE, MC, VI.

The following lodging was either not evaluated or did not meet AAA rating requirements and is listed for your information only.

HOTEL LA PINTA
[fyi] *Motor Inn* ℂ 113/5-0025

Does not meet all AAA rating requirements for room decor/ambiance; previously evaluated on 11/10/99. **Location:** From Hwy 1, 1 km e into town, then 1 km n. (Apdo Postal 28, 23880). Facilities, services, and decor characterize a basic property.

WHERE TO DINE

EL NIDO RESTAURANT
▼▼ ◆▼ *Steak & Seafood* ℂ 113/5-0284
D $6-$20

Location: 1 km e of Hwy 1; at town entrance. Salvatierra No 154. **Hours:** 2 pm-10:30 pm. Closed: 12/25. **Features:** cocktails & lounge. Ranch atmosphere; featuring mesquite broiled steak and seafood.

LOS BARRILES, BAJA CALIFORNIA SUR

WHERE TO DINE

TIO PABLO'S BAR & GRILL
▼ *American* ℂ 114/2-1214
L $4-$14 D $5-$14

Location: 1 km e of Hwy 1 in town. Camino al Cardonal S/N 23501. **Hours:** 11 am-10 pm. **Features:** No A/C; casual dress; Sunday brunch; children's menu; cocktails & lounge. Casual setting with palapa and patio dining. Hamburgers, sandwiches, pizzas and full dinners. **Cards:** MC, VI.

MEXICALI, BAJA CALIFORNIA (B-2)

Capital of the state of Baja California, Mexicali (meh-hee-CAH-lih) is a border city and duty-free port opposite Calexico, Calif. Mexican and U.S. customs offices are open 24 hours daily. Tourists in need of assistance can contact the Secretaría de Turismo del Estado; phone (65)

56-1172 or 56-1072 Mon.-Fri. 8-7, Sat. 9-1 (English spoken).

Mexicali developed as a market center for surrounding farms in the early 20th century. It became the capital of the territory of Baja California Norte in 1915. Visitors from across the border were attracted by legalized alcohol and gambling as well as by land speculation. In the late 1930s, however, the fertile land of the Mexicali Valley was distributed, under the leadership of President Lazaro Cárdenas, among Mexican farmers and *ejidos* (collective agricultural colonies).

Water has been integral to the city's subsequent growth. The aridity of the valley—it receives on average only 2 inches of rain yearly—prevented the silt-laden soil from being exploited. When the flow of irrigation water from the Colorado River was guaranteed by international treaty, Mexicali bloomed both agriculturally and industrially.

This extension of the Imperial Valley of California now contributes mightily to Mexico's economy. Wheat, cotton, cantaloupes and many other truck crops are grown in abundance. A brewery, large cotton gins and its status as the terminus of a major Mexican railroad contribute to the city's livelihood. *Maquiladoras,* foreign-owned businesses established in Mexican border areas because of low production costs, have further bolstered the economy. **Parque Industrial** (Industrial Park), Avenida Brasil and Boulevard de las Americas near the airport, contains electronic and other industrial plants.

Indicative of Mexicali's prosperity is the **Centro Cívico-Comercial** (Civic-Commercial Center) along Calzada Independencia on the southern edge of the city. The extensive urban project includes state and federal government offices, hospitals, a bullring, shopping and restaurants.

Most of Mexicali's shops, restaurants and nightclubs are near the international border in an irregular rectangle bounded by avenidas Cristóbal Colón and Alvaro Obregón, the Río Nuevo and Calle C. In the former state governor's residence at Avenida Alvaro Obregón #1209, between calles D and E, is **Galería de la Ciudad**, an art gallery displaying works by Mexican artists.

Bullfights are held in September and October at **Plaza de Toros Calafia**, in the Civic-Commercial Center on Calle Calafia. *Charreadas*, the Mexican forerunner of Western-style rodeos, are usually held one Sunday each month during the winter and on Mexican holidays. These equestrian events occur approximately 5 kilometers (3 miles) east of Calzada Justo Sierra on Calle Compuertas.

MUSEO REGIONAL, UNIVERSIDAD DE BAJA CALIFORNIA (Regional Museum, University of Baja California), Avenida Reforma and Calle L, offers a cultural perspective of the city. Its exhibits focus on paleontology, archeology, ethnography, landscape photography and the missions of Baja California. Mexicali

WHERE TO STAY

ARAIZA INN CALAFIA

Motor Inn 〔 656/8-3311

All Year $72 XP $8
Location: From the border, 4.5 km e on Ave Cristobal Colon, then 2.4 km s. Calzada Justo Sierra #1495 21230. Fax: 656/8-2010. **Facility:** 171 units. *Bath:* shower only. 2-4 stories, exterior corridors. **Guest Services:** valet laundry. **Business Services:** meeting rooms. **Cards:** AE, MC, VI.

SOME UNITS

ARAIZA INN MEXICALI

Motor Inn 〔 656/4-1100

All Year $104 XP $10
Location: From the border, 4.5 km e on Ave Cristobal Colon, then 3 km s on Calzada Justo Sierra and Benito Juarez. Blvd Benito Juarez 2220 21270 (233 Pauline Ave, Suite 947, CALEXICO, CA, 92231). Fax: 656/4-1113. **Facility:** 172 units. 6 stories, interior corridors. **Terms:** F18. **Amenities:** hair dryers. **Leisure Activities:** wading pool, exercise room. *Fee:* lighted tennis court. **Guest Services:** gift shop. **Business Services:** meeting rooms. **Cards:** AE, MC, VI.

SOME UNITS

CROWNE PLAZA HOTEL

Hotel 〔 (655)7-3600

7/1-11/30 $140-$155 XP $40
12/1-6/30 $135-$150 XP $40
Location: 7 km s of border via Blvd Lopez Mateos. Ave de los Heroes No 201 21200. Fax: 655/7-0555. **Facility:** Highrise with underground parking. 158 units. 8 stories, interior corridors. **Terms:** F16; 3 day cancellation notice-fee imposed. **Amenities:** irons, hair dryers. **Dining:** The Premiere, see separate listing. **Leisure Activities:** exercise room. **Guest Services:** gift shop. **Business Services:** meeting rooms, administrative services. **Cards:** AE, MC, VI.

SOME UNITS

HOTEL LUCERNA

Hotel 〔 (656)4-7000

All Year $130 XP $15
Location: From the border, 4.5 km e on Ave Cristobal Colon, then 3.8 km s on Calzads to Sierra and Benito Juarez. Blvd Benito Juarez No. 2151 21270 (PO Box 2300, CALEXICO, CA, 92232). Fax: 656/6-4706. **Facility:** Landscaped grounds. Rooms in bungalows, three and six story buildings, many with balcony or patio. 175 units. *Bath:* combo or shower only. 1-6 stories, interior/exterior corridors. **Terms:** F12. **Amenities:** hair dryers. **Dining:** Mezzosole Restaurante Italiano, see separate listing. **Leisure Activities:** 2 pools, sauna, exercise room. **Guest Services:** gift shop, valet laundry. **Business Services:** meeting rooms, administrative services. *Fee:* PC, fax. **Cards:** AE, CB, DI, MC, VI.

SOME UNITS

MOTEL COLONIAL LAS FUENTES

Motel 〔 655/6-1312

All Year $94-$104 XP $10
Location: 7 km se of border; at Calle Calafia. Blvd Lopez Mateo No 1048 92231 (PO Box 772, Suite 9, CALEXICO, CA, 92232). Fax: 655/6-1141. **Facility:** 144 units. Some suites ($150). 2 stories (no elevator), exterior corridors. **Terms:** F18. **Leisure Activities:** wading pool. **Guest Services:** valet laundry. **Business Services:** meeting rooms. **Cards:** AE, MC, VI.

WHERE TO DINE

MEZZOSOLE RESTAURANTE ITALIANO

Italian 〔 656/4-7000

L $7-$14 D $7-$14
Location: From the border, 3.8 km s on Calzads to Sierra and Benito Juarez; in Hotel Lucerna. 2151 Blvd Benito Juarez 21270. **Hours:** noon-midnight. Closed: Mon. **Reservations:** suggested. **Features:** dressy casual; cocktail lounge; a la carte. Intimate theme and dining room with wall and ceiling murals overlooking a swimming pool creating a cool/relaxing feeling. Fresh pasta, pizza, seafood, poultry and beef. The seafood linguini and gorgonzola steak are popular dishes. **Cards:** AE, CB, DI, MC, VI.

THE PREMIERE

International 〔 655/7-3600

D $8-$22
Location: 7 km s of border via Blvd Lopez Mateos; in Crowne Plaza Hotel. Av de Los Heroes #201 21200. **Hours:** 2 pm-10:30 pm. **Reservations:** suggested. **Features:** semi-formal attire; cocktails; a la carte. An elegant dining room with formal service offering a variety of seafood, pasta and steak entrees. Tableside salad preparation. Pressed coffee. **Cards:** AE, MC, VI.

MULEGÉ,
BAJA CALIFORNIA SUR (E-2)

Mulegé (moo-leh-HEH) is an old, traditional Mexican town and an oasis in the middle of the inhospitable Baja California desert. Perched on a terrace above the Río Mulegé—one of the peninsula's few rivers—it has dirt streets and a laid-back air. Mulegé also offers easy accessibility to the stunning beaches and tucked-away coves of **Bahía Concepción**, which begins 19 kilometers (12 miles) south of town.

Mulegé's history dates back to 1705 with the founding of the Mission Santa Rosalía de Mulegé (Mulegé means "large creek"). Mulegé thrived as a producer of subtropical fruits and as a regional market center long before the completion of Mex. 1 brought tourists from the United States.

The **Mission Santa Rosalía de Mulegé**, just upstream from the Mex. 1 bridge over the river, is reached by a pathway shaded by broad-leafed banana plants. Sunday services are still held in the solid stone structure. A hilltop view takes in the town, the green-tinged, mangrove-edged waters of the river and date palm groves spreading toward the mountains.

About 3 kilometers (2 miles) northeast of town is the public beach, at the end of a dirt road where the Río Mulegé empties into the Sea of Cortés. The beach has dark sand, a few waves and, in summer, jellyfish. Nearby **El Sombrerito**, at the mouth of the river, is a hat-shaped monolith with stone steps leading to a lighthouse at the summit.

Mulegé offers outstanding fishing and boating opportunities at the mouth of the river and on the bay. Game species include grouper, sea bass, red snapper and occasional billfish. Fishing arrangements can be made through most hotels or at one of the many RV parks along the river south of town. The area also attracts scuba divers and snorkelers; the underwater life in Bahía Concepción includes impressively large sea turtles. **Mulegé Divers**, in town at Madero #45, can arrange scuba and snorkeling expeditions and rents equipment; phone (115) 3-0134.

The beaches south off Mex. 1 along the shores of the bay are lauded by aficionados, and with good reason. The water is warm, clear and gloriously blue, and the beaches of coarse white sand are studded with shells. For a backdrop, there are mountains tinted shades of rose by the sun. All of the beaches are accessible from Mex. 1, with signs posted at each turnoff; however, the access roads are likely to be sandy, rutted or both. For those who wish to hike from the highway (wear sturdy shoes), bus drivers will make drop-offs at the access roads; double-check the time the last northbound bus heads back to town. Expect to share these beaches with an army of RVers and campers.

The first beach south of Mulegé is **Playa Punta Arena**, about 16 kilometers (9 miles) south. Palm-thatched *palapas* line the sand, and hillside caves south of the beach are littered with shells discarded by ancient inhabitants. **Playa Santispac**, crowded with campers, is the most active; craft from sailboats to yachts cruise on the bay. **Playa El Coyote** is especially beautiful, although extensive use has made cleanup efforts necessary. It fronts a sparkling cove and has several trees, rare on Baja's desert beaches. **Playa El Requesón**, a narrow point of land connected to an offshore island that can be reached by vehicle at low tide, is a prime windsurfing location. Don't expect much in the way of tourist facilities at any of the bay beaches, aside from some *palapa* shelters and a few toilets.

WHERE TO DINE

LAS CASITAS RESTAURANT

 Mexican   (115/3-0019
                                     L $3-$8   **D** $5-$12
Location: In Town Center Callejon de los Estudiantes and Ave Independencia. **Hours:** 7 am-10 pm. Closed: 12/25. **Features:** No A/C; cocktails & lounge. Casual setting and service with attractive patio that is popular for breakfast and lunch. Friday night fiesta.

ROSARITO, BAJA CALIFORNIA (B-1)

This rapidly growing resort town, easily reached from the United States, is about 29 kilometers (18 miles) south of Tijuana. Also known as Rosarito (roh-sah-REE-toh) Beach and Playas de Rosarito, it is located at the junction of free Mex. 1 and toll Mex. 1-D, both four lanes from Tijuana. Mex. 1 passes directly through town. Commanding a favored ocean site fronting several miles of gray-sand beach, Rosarito is one of Baja's fastest growing communities.

The opening of the Rosarito Beach Hotel in 1927 launched the town's vacation reputation, and it soon won favor as a secluded fly-in spot for movie stars. Still a village in 1960, it has since expanded in each succeeding decade—particularly the 1980s—mirroring the growth of tourism in general in Baja California. Numerous hotels now line the waterfront.

Mex. 1 (the Old Ensenada Highway) through town is called Avenida Benito Juárez and swarms with restaurants, bars and businesses. **Quinta Plaza**, at the avenue's northern end, has a discount department store, Comercial Mexicana, and also contains restaurants and a convention center. A Protección al Turista (tourist assistance) office is at Avenida Benito Juárez #100; phone (661) 2-0200. The bigger hotels have shopping arcades where visitors can poke around for Mexican handicrafts, although the selection is nowhere near as varied as in Tijuana.

The far northern end of town is anchored by a power plant that supplies electricity to both Rosarito and Tijuana. South of town Mex. 1 and Mex. 1-D run parallel along the rocky Pacific shoreline for some 39 kilometers (24 miles). Mex. 1, here called Ensenada Libre (Old Ensenada Highway), follows the coast past ever-sprouting time-share condominiums, resorts and private homes, all hugging scenic oceanfront cliffs.

Note: Due to extensive construction along Mex. 1 south of town, slowdowns may occur unexpectedly. Watch carefully for rocks positioned in the roadway, which sometimes are the only warning that repairs are taking place.

Rosarito has no airport, but regular bus service from Tijuana to Ensenada is provided by Tres

Estrellas de Oro. Buses stop at the Rosarito bus terminal, on Avenida Benito Juárez across from the Rosarito Beach Hotel. Taxis make regular trips to Rosarito from Tijuana and also travel the stretch of Mex. 1 south of town. Rates are negotiable; decide on the fare in advance.

Local authorities are trying to preserve a measure of the laid-back charm that once characterized the town. Although a relaxed pace holds forth during the week, on weekends there is bumper-to-bumper traffic as visitors—including no small number of border-hopping southern Californians—converge on the beaches.

Rosarito's stretch of sand runs uninterrupted for more than 5 miles. Swimming and surfing should be done at your own risk, for the ocean waters off northern Baja are often polluted. Rocks jutting from the ocean are used as sunning spots by the local sea lion population. Horses can be rented for rides up and down the beach or into the surrounding hills. Bicycle and motorcycle races are held in and around Rosarito as well, including the popular *Rosarito-Ensenada 50-Mile Fun Bike Ride* each April and September.

At the corner of Avenida Benito Juárez and Calle del Nogal on the south end of town is **Festival Plaza**, a phantasmagoria of watermelon sculptures, metallic streamers, tiled waterfalls and a giant concrete sombrero, all contained within an eight-story structure that resembles a wildly colorful roller coaster. This beachside resort has restaurants, shops and bars within a village-style complex.

About 21 kilometers (13 miles) south of Rosarito via the Old Ensenada Highway (Mex. 1) is **Puerto Nuevo** (Newport), a fishing village distinguished by the number of restaurants specializing in lobster. Some have an ocean view and an air of elegance; others are down-home places operated by local families. Regardless of the establishment, the menu is similar—grilled lobster (ordered by size), rice, beans and freshly made tortillas, with butter, lime and hot sauce on the side. Ironically, most of the seafood is imported. After dinner, browse among the stands set up around the restaurants and along the road into town for pottery, T-shirts and an amusingly kitschy array of souvenirs.

WHERE TO STAY

LAS ROCAS RESORT & SPA

▼▼ ▼▼ *Motor Inn* (661/2-2140

7/1-8/31	$89-$169	XP $10
5/1-6/30 & 9/1-11/30	$85-$159	XP $10
12/1-4/30	$65-$119	XP $10

Location: On Hwy 1, 10 km s of town. Km 38.5 Carretera Libre Tijuana-Ensenada 22710 (PO Box 189003 HLR, CORONADO, CA, 92178-9003). Fax: 661/2-2140. **Facility:** On a bluff overlooking ocean. All rooms with ocean view. Many spacious rooms with microwave, refrigerator and fireplace. Standard rooms in north building. Full service spa. Meets AAA guest room security requirements. 74 units. Some whirlpool units. 4 stories (no elevator), exterior corridors. **Terms:** F10; 3 day cancellation notice. **Leisure Activities:** 2 pools (1 heated), whirlpools, tennis court, sports court. *Fee:* exercise room. **Guest Services:** *Fee:* massage. **Cards:** MC, VI.

SOME UNITS

🅢🅓 🍴 🍸 ⊠ 🐾 🎥 / 💻 📻 🛢 /

OASIS RESORT & CONVENTION CENTER

▼▼ ▼▼ *Suite Motor Inn* ((663)1-3250

All Year	$149-$379	XP $15

Location: On Hwy 1-D (toll road), southbound exit E1 Oasis; northbound exit Rancho Del Mar, s on Mex 1-D, 8 km n of town. Km 25 Carr. Escenica Tijuana-Ensenada (Box 158, IMPERIAL BEACH, CA, 91933). Fax: 663/1-3252. **Facility:** All suite resort and RV park on the beach. 100 units. 2-3 stories, exterior corridors. **Terms:** F12; 3 day cancellation notice. **Amenities:** hair dryers. **Leisure Activities:** 2 pools, wading pool, sauna, whirlpools, beach, putting green, tennis court, playground. **Guest Services:** coin laundry. **Business Services:** conference facilities. **Cards:** AE, MC, VI.

SOME UNITS

🅢🅓 🍴 🍸 🄳 🐾 ⊠ 🐾 🛢 / 🄰🄲 /

ROSARITO BEACH HOTEL & SPA

▼▼ ▼▼ *Resort* ((661)2-0144

4/16-9/3	$109-$189	XP $40
3/9-4/15	$99-$189	XP $40
12/1-3/8 & 9/4-11/30	$89-$159	XP $20

Location: From Hwy 1-D (toll road), exit south end of town, just prior to the toll station. Blvd Bonito Juarez No. 31 22710 (PO Box 430145, SAN DIEGO, CA, 92143-0145). Fax: 661/2-1125. **Facility:** Long established beachfront resort. Full service spa. 276 units. 14 two-bedroom units and 60 efficiencies. *Bath:* some combo or shower only. 1-7 stories, interior/exterior corridors. **Terms:** F12; check-in 4 pm, 4 day cancellation notice. **Dining:** Chabert's Restaurant, see separate listing. **Leisure Activities:** 2 heated pools, whirlpools, beach, lighted tennis court, sports court. **Guest Services:** gift shop. *Fee:* massage. **Business Services:** meeting rooms. **Cards:** MC, VI.

🅢🅓 🍴 🍸 🄳 🐾 🕴 🐾
FEE

SOME UNITS

/ ⊠ 🄰🄲 VCR 🛢 /
FEE

WHERE TO DINE

CHABERT'S RESTAURANT

 International   (661/2-0144
                                    D $11-$21
Location: From Hwy 1-D (toll road), exit south end of town, just prior to the toll station; in Rosarito Beach Hotel & Spa. **Hours:** 5 pm-midnight. Closed: Tues, also Mon in winter. **Features:** dressy casual; cocktails & lounge; a la carte. An elegant dining room in the stately mansion of the founder of the resort. The attentive staff serves steak, seafood and poultry dishes prepared in traditional European and Mexican style. Tableside preparation of Ceasar and spinach salads. **Cards:** MC, VI.

EL NIDO STEAKHOUSE

 Steak House   (661/2-1431
                    L $4-$18   **D** $4-$18
Location: In center of town. Blvd Benito Juarez 67. **Hours:** 8 am-11:30 pm. Closed: 9/16. **Features:** No A/C; casual dress; cocktails; street parking. Ranch atmosphere featuring mesquite broiled meats. Steaks are very tender; venison and quail raised on their own farm. Pleasant patio with aviary.

LOS PELICANOS

 Steak House   (661/2-1757
                    L $6-$18   **D** $6-$18
Location: On the beach, just w of Blvd Benito Juarez. Calle Ebano 113. **Hours:** 8 am-midnight. Closed: 9/16. **Features:** No A/C; casual dress; cocktails & lounge. Mesquite broiled steak and seafood. Dining room and patio overlook the ocean. **Cards:** AE, MC, VI.

SAN FELIPE, BAJA CALIFORNIA (C-2)

Although nomadic fishermen first gravitated to the area around San Felipe (sahn feh-LEE-peh) in the mid-19th century, the town was not permanently settled until the 1920s. The completion of Mex. 5 from Mexicali in 1951 brought a steady stream of American sportsmen who have helped transform San Felipe into a major winter vacation destination. Rapid expansion that began in the 1980s has produced a slew of waterfront trailer parks, condominiums and hotels. Even so, do not expect a luxury-style resort: San Felipe's style is distinctly no-frills.

About 193 kilometers (120 miles) south of Mexicali, the town's location combines the inviting—the Gulf of California's shimmering blue waters—with the forbidding—an extremely arid desert environment. Mex. 5 south from Mexicali is in excellent condition, including an initial stretch of four-lane divided highway. **Note:** There are only two gas stations between the village of La Puerta and San Felipe—a distance of some 100 miles—and only one selling unleaded fuel. Make sure your tank is full before starting out.

After traversing open desert, an archway heralds the arrival into town. The steep eastern flank of the Sierra San Pedro Mártir range—which includes Baja California's tallest mountain, Pica-

cho del Diablo—is clearly visible to the west. The town spreads out under 940-foot-tall Punta San Felipe, a promontory that forms the northern end of Bahía San Felipe. Yellow-sand beaches line the coast southeastward from the crescent-shaped bayfront to Punta Estrella, about 19 kilometers (12 miles) distant. A splendid view of the town and coastline is available from the **Virgin of Guadalupe Shrine**, atop a hill just north of San Felipe.

The bay, along with the entire northern Gulf of California, has an extreme tidal range that often reaches more than 20 feet, requiring an experienced boater to successfully navigate the waters. At high tide waves break against the shore; at low tide it is possible to wade far out over sand and mud flats.

South of town, an unnumbered, very rough road passes the airport and continues 85 kilometers (53 miles) to Puertecitos. Along the way are turnoffs leading to vacation home communities and trailer camps, but very few motorist facilities.

About 21 kilometers (13 miles) south of San Felipe via the Gulf of California coast road is **El Valle de los Gigantes** (Valley of the Giants). Watch for the sign for Colonia Gutierrez Polanco, then take the sandy road going in the opposite direction—southwest—about 5 kilometers (3 miles). The cluster of very large, very old cardón cactuses and other desert vegetation makes for an intriguing sight. It is recommended that this excursion be made only in a sturdy, high-clearance vehicle.

San Felipe attracts campers, anglers, road racers and beachcombers. Dwellings are modest, vegetation scarce, and litter sometimes an eyesore. The town attracts a rowdy crowd of motorcyclists and dune buggy fanciers on holiday weekends and the 2 weeks around Easter. At these times noise and congestion reign. Also avoid the blistering summer months, when temperatures can soar to 120 degrees under cloudless skies. November through April is much more pleasant weatherwise, although still crowded on such holiday weekends as Washington's Birthday and Thanksgiving. A tourist information office is on the south side of town at Manzanillo and Mar de Cortés, the waterfront drive (*malecón*); phone (657) 7-1155.

At this major fishing center shrimp are caught commercially, and surf fishing and package or chartered fishing trips are available. Cabrilla, white sea bass, yellowtail, dorado and other game species are found in the gulf waters. Boat rentals range from oar-propelled *pangas* to large craft that can accommodate a party for several days. Local boating outfits are concentrated along Mar de Cortés, as are San Felipe's restaurants, bars and nightspots.

WHERE TO STAY

SAN FELIPE MARINA RESORT
  Motor Inn ((657)7-1568

3/16-9/30 & 10/1-11/30 $105-$145   XP $15
Location: 4.5 km s on road to airport. Km 4.5 Carr San Felipe Aero Puerto 21850 (233 Pauline Ave; PMB 8518, CALEXICO, CA, 92231). Fax: 657/7-1566. **Facility:** On the beach overlooking the bay. 11 smaller studio units. Meets AAA guest room security requirements. 59 units, 47 with efficiency. *Bath:* shower only. 2 stories, exterior corridors. **Terms:** F12; open 3/16-9/30 & 10/1-11/30, 8 day cancellation notice, package plans. **Leisure Activities:** 2 pools (1 heated, 1 indoor), beach, 2 lighted tennis courts. *Fee:* saunas, steambath. **Guest Services:** gift shop, valet laundry. **Business Services:** meeting rooms. **Cards:** AE, MC, VI.

SOME UNITS

WHERE TO DINE

EL NIDO STEAKHOUSE
 Steak House (657/7-1660
                                    L $5-$20   D $5-$20
Location: 0.5 km s of town center. Mar de Cortez Sur No. 348 21850. **Hours:** 2 pm-10 pm. Closed: Wed. **Features:** casual dress; cocktails. The mesquite wood aroma wets your appetite as you enter the ranch-style dining room. Steak, shrimp and seafood fills the menu. The mesquite grilled steak or seafood Mexican plate are great choices for dinner; the hamburger for lunch.

GEORGE'S STEAKHOUSE
 Mexican (657/7-1057
                                    L $4-$12   D $5-$12
Location: Ave Mar De Cortez Sur #336 21850. **Hours:** 6:30 am-9:30 pm. **Features:** casual dress; carryout; cocktails. Family dining, pleasant atmosphere, Mexican food, steak, seafood and sandwiches. The American style breakfast is popular for locals to meet and exchange stories.

ROSITA RESTAURANT
 Mexican (657/7-1770
                                    L $4-$11   D $4-$11
Location: At the north end of the Malecon. Paseo de Cortez No. 381 21850. **Hours:** 7 am-10 pm. **Features:** No A/C; casual dress; street parking. Casual, open air dining with great view of the bay fishermen. Consistently good food. Soup, steak and the daily fresh fish are popular choices. **Cards:** MC, VI.

SAN IGNACIO,
BAJA CALIFORNIA SUR

WHERE TO STAY

The following lodging was either not evaluated or did not meet AAA rating requirements and is listed for your information only.

HOTEL LA PINTA
[fyi] *Motor Inn* (115/4-0300

Does not meet all AAA rating requirements; previously evaluated on 11/20/99. **Location:** 2.5 km w of jct Hwy 1, towards town plaza. Apartado Postal 37 23930. Facilities, services, and decor characterize a basic property.

SAN QUINTIN,
BAJA CALIFORNIA

WHERE TO STAY

The following lodging was either not evaluated or did not meet AAA rating requirements and is listed for your information only.

HOTEL LA PINTA
[fyi] *Motor Inn* (616/5-2878

Does not meet all AAA rating requirements; previously evaluated on 11/20/99. **Location:** 16 km s on Hwy 1, 4.5 km w to outer San Quintin Bay. (Apartado Postal 168, 22930). Facilities, services, and decor characterize a basic property.

SANTA ROSALIA,
BAJA CALIFORNIA SUR (D-3)

A mining town that has been designated a national historic monument, Santa Rosalía (SAHN-tah roh-sah-LEE-ah) was established by the French-owned El Boleo Copper Co. during the 1880s. Prosperity reigned until the mines gave out in 1953. Mining operations were later reactivated with the discovery of new copper and manganese deposits, but these too failed. Commercial fishing and boat building contribute to today's economy.

The French left their mark on Santa Rosalía's narrow, bustling streets. Instead of Mexican-style stucco walls and tiled roofs, many houses are built of wood painted in pastel shades, and gardens are enclosed by picket fences. One of these residential neighborhoods sits on a plateau north of town and offers a panoramic view of the old copper smelter. Another European touch shows up on some of downtown's 19th-century buildings, which are topped with square clock towers.

In keeping with its mineral assets, Santa Rosalía's most interesting feature is the **Iglesia Santa Barbara**, a prefabricated, galvanized-iron church at Avenida Obregón and Calle 1. Designed by A.G. Eiffel for the 1898 Paris World's Fair, the metal structure was shipped in pieces from France. The **Biblioteca Mahatma Gandhi** (Mahatma Gandhi Library), Calle Playa and Avenida Constitución, displays original account ledgers and photographs of past mining operations.

Santa Rosalía also is known—somewhat incongruously—for bread. The **El Boleo** bakery, Avenida Obregón and Calle 4, has earned a regional reputation for its fresh-baked specialties.

Santa Rosalía's small harbor serves as the terminal for ferry service to Guaymas (*see separate listing under Northwestern Mexico*) on the Mexican mainland. Ferries operate on Wednesday and Sunday and depart Santa Rosalía at 8 a.m.; sailing time is about 8 hours. The ferry leaves Guaymas on Tuesday and Friday at 8 a.m. Each vessel is equipped with a cafeteria, although passengers may want to bring their own food and water. Make reservations well in advance, and double-check rates and schedules prior to departure. The ferry office is in the terminal building just south of town on Mex. 1; phone (115) 2-0013 or 2-0014. *Also see "Ferry Service," page 64, and "Ferry Service" under "A Baja Overview," page 150.*

Also of interest are the nearby caves of **San Borjita**, which contain possibly the oldest cave paintings yet discovered in Baja California. Reached by an inferior side road off Mex. 1 south of Santa Rosalía, the caves are best visited in the afternoon when the sun illuminates their vibrantly executed designs. A local guide can be hired in town; check at the **Palacio Municipal** (City Hall) on the main square. The fee is usually negotiable (determine it in advance), and a tip is customary. The trip via pack mule is most comfortable during the winter months.

A pleasant side trip is the farming community of **San José de Magdalena**, reached via a well-marked turnoff that branches west off Mex. 1, about 27 kilometers (17 miles) south of Santa Rosalía. The road is graded dirt and can be negotiated by a high-clearance vehicle, but it becomes rough past the village. An oasis sheltered by palm groves, the village dates from Baja California's Spanish colonial period, when it served as a visiting station of the Mission Santa Rosalía de Mulegé *(see Mulegé listing)*. In the vicinity are the ruins of a chapel built by the Dominicans in 1774.

TECATE, BAJA CALIFORNIA (B-1)

A port of entry about 51 kilometers (32 miles) southeast of San Diego, Calif., Tecate (teh-KAH-teh) has managed to maintain a Mexican small-town atmosphere. Daily life centers on the tranquil, tree-shaded main plaza. The town lies in a bowl-shaped valley below 5,884-foot Tecate Peak. Mexican customs offices are open daily 8-4; U.S. customs offices are open daily 6 a.m.-midnight.

Tecate was first settled in the 19th century by farmers and ranchers attracted by its abundant water and fertile soil. Although industry—beer and instant coffee production—and tourism continue to grow in importance, the town remains a commercial center for the surrounding grape-, olive- and grain-growing area.

The **Tecate Brewery** on the outskirts of town offers tours; phone (665) 4-1709 for a schedule. Visitor information also can be obtained at the State Tourism Office, at Callejón Libertad #1305 on the south side of the main plaza. The office is open Mon.-Fri. 8-7, Sat.-Sun. 10-3; phone (665) 4-1095. Tourist Assistance, which provides legal assistance to visitors experiencing difficulties

with local merchants or police, is located in the same office and has the same phone number.

TIJUANA, BAJA CALIFORNIA (B-1)

Tijuana (tee-HWAH-nah), some 29 kilometers (18 miles) south of San Diego, is the main U.S. point of entry to Baja California. A booming tourism industry has helped transform this former tawdry border town into a bustling metropolis of high-rise buildings, broad boulevards and an extraordinary assortment of shops, restaurants and bars aimed squarely at the thundering hordes of incoming visitors. "The World's Most Visited City" (as its boosters optimistically proclaim) extends for more than a dozen miles along the international border; its downtown core is less than a mile from the United States and about 6 miles inland from the Pacific Coast.

Tijuana is a window to Mexico, although it's not necessarily typical of how the rest of the country lives. It benefits from geographical location. To the north is San Diego, linked to the city via two border crossings. The bustling port city of Ensenada lies an hour south. To the east via Mex. 2 is the Baja California state capital, Mexicali.

Tijuana, often referred to as "TJ," is the farthest point in the country from Mexico City and does indeed seem apart. The area was settled relatively recently in comparison to other areas of Mexico—the 1860s—although the region has been inhabited by indigenous peoples for centuries. The city's name is derived from "Tia Juana," a former 10,000-hectare working ranch. When Mexico lost Upper California to the United States as a result of the Mexican-American War in 1848, the area around the ranch became the new border between the two countries. Along the way Tia Juana progressed from grazing grounds to customs house to genuine, albeit rickety, town.

The city's urban beginnings date from 1889, when the streets of the central downtown area were laid out. Californians first filtered across the border to watch horse races and boxing matches, shop around for souvenirs and enjoy hot springs bathing. Northwestern Baja has welcomed Golden State residents seeking an easily accessible weekend retreat ever since.

The 1920s brought important changes. Prohibition fueled tremendous growth as well as Tijuana's sinful reputation for drinking, gambling and worse. Hollywood movie stars and the indolently rich jetted into the city, congregating at the Agua Caliente Racetrack and its neighboring resort. Upon Prohibition's repeal and the Great Depression's onset, the resort folded, the jetsetters moved on and Tijuana slumped. President Lázaro Cárdenas' administration closed down the casinos in the 1930s, furthering the city's decline. The government did, however, designate all of

Baja California a duty-free port, and shoppers began flocking to Tijuana in search of bargains.

U.S. servicemen kept alive the city's reputation as a bawdy center for illicit fun. Reform laws instituted in the 1930s began curbing some of the more undesirable aspects, but it was not until the 1960s that city leaders took steps to create a more family-friendly image for Tijuana.

Meanwhile, industrial expansion in the post-World War II era contributed to renewed growth. Mexican immigrants from all over the country came to Tijuana in search of jobs, higher wages, a better standard of living and perhaps the opportunities waiting beyond the border in California's rich agricultural industry. The population tripled between 1940 and 1950. According to the 1990 Mexican Census the city's official population was just under 700,000; it is estimated, however, that some 1,500,000 people crowd the metropolitan region, making Tijuana Mexico's fourth largest urban area. Millions more pour back and forth across the San Ysidro border crossing—said to be the world's busiest—each year, and the resulting combination of tourism, manufacturing and commerce places Tijuana among the top visitor attractions on the West Coast.

In the decades since 1970 the city really began reaping the rewards of a vast, money-spending *gringo* population just across the border. College students and weekend tourists flock to Tijuana to shop, play golf, have dinner, bet on sports and party the night away, although not all at once. International visitors are attracted by the opportunity to purchase expensive foreign goods at discounted prices. City boosters have so far failed, however, to move Tijuana beyond its image as a day-trip destination. While the city receives 10 times as many annual visitors as Cancún, its challenge is to keep them for more than an afternoon.

Tijuana is a hybrid—it's an Americanized place where English is widely spoken, yet has the curiosity appeal of a foreign country. It is also a city of contrasts. When viewed from the United States side, Tijuana looks decidedly ramshackle. Much of the central downtown area, however, is booming, vibrant and newly constructed. In the fashionable Zona Río district, **Paseo de los Héroes** (roughly, "avenue of heroes") is lined with substantial hotels and office buildings, testaments to the city's prosperity. The name refers to the statues of historical figures—among them Aztec ruler Cuauhtémoc and U.S. President Abraham Lincoln—standing in the center of several traffic circles.

The passage of the North American Free Trade Agreement (NAFTA) furthered the proliferation of foreign-owned businesses, the majority of them attracted by Tijuana's low production costs; an educated, relatively cheap labor force; and a prime location. *Maquiladoras*—the term for foreign-owned manufacturing operations—have

sprung up here and at other Mexican border areas over the last several decades. One example is the **Otay Mesa Industrial District**, a sprawling conglomeration of plants southeast of the same-named border crossing. Goods of all kinds are churned out of Tijuana factories, including several million TV sets each year; the big electronics manufacturers have all set up shop in the city.

Not all is rosy. Away from the familiar tourist areas are grimy warehouses. Uncontrolled growth without an underlying infrastructure has resulted in the rise of glum shantytowns, or *colonias*, which spread across the low hills east, west and south of downtown. Political violence has visited the city as well. The 1994 assassination of Luis Donaldo Colosio, the handpicked presidential candidate of Mexico's ruling governmental party, occurred at a Tijuana political rally and underscored the economic pressures being felt by many Mexicans.

Although industry has dramatically changed the city's face, tourism still bolsters the local economy, and Tijuana has shed some of the tackier aspects of its enduring appeal as a Mexican vacation spot. **Avenida Revolución**, the main street and traditional tourist zone, once was lined with cheap souvenir stands, rowdy bars and sleazy strip joints. While many endearingly kitschy curio shops remain, much of the street has been extensively cleaned up. Benches along tree-shaded brick walkways invite idling—if only for a moment.

PLANNING YOUR STAY

For most visitors, Tijuana is a day city; you won't find outstanding museums, historical monuments or venerable architecture. Perhaps its greatest appeal is to souvenir hounds and shopaholics, who will feel like they're in paradise.

Recreational diversions in Tijuana have changed little over the years. Some of the world's top matadors perform at two bullrings in town. Bullfights are held on selected Sunday afternoons from May through September; July and August are the busiest months. During the season sites alternate between **El Toreo de Tijuana**, about 3 kilometers (2 miles) east of downtown on Boulevard Agua Caliente, and the larger **Plaza de Toros Monumental** (Bullring-by-the-Sea), 10 kilometers (6 miles) west of downtown via Mex. 1-D. Reserved and general admission seating is available. Ticket prices start at around $7 (U.S.); seats on the shady side of each arena are more expensive. Tickets can be obtained at the bullrings and from Five Star Tours/Mexicoach; phone (619) 232-5049. A small kiosk on Avenida Revolución between calles 4 and 5 also sells tickets.

Charreadas, the colorful equestrian spectacles held in many parts of Mexico, take place most Sunday afternoons from May through September.

The rodeos alternate among several sites; for details contact the Asociación de Charros, phone (66) 81-3401. They're usually free.

The fast and furious action of jai alai takes place at the **Frontón Palacio** (Jai Alai Palace), Avenida Revolución at Calle 7. The game is something of a cross between tennis and handball. Players endeavor to prevent a ball about the size of a golf ball from bouncing more than once as it is hurled against 30-foot front and rear walls. The first team to score six points wins. Matches begin Monday and Tuesday afternoons at noon and Thursday through Sunday evenings at 8 p.m.; doors open about an hour prior to game time. General admission tickets are $2; reserved seats $5 (U.S.). Betting is spirited, and fronton staff are on hand to explain the rules and betting procedure to jai alai neophytes. For information phone (619) 231-1910 or (66) 85-2524.

The building itself is a Tijuana landmark, a Moorish-inspired structure with tile mosaics adorning its front. Adjoining it is an LF Caliente sports betting facility, where wagers can be placed for just about any event. Multiple giant-screen TVs broadcast the action. Visitors must purchase a $20 voucher good for betting. If it is used for bets totaling less than $20, change is returned in cash. While it is easy to spend an entire day here, big spenders (or losers) may find themselves heading back across the border earlier than they had planned.

The **Agua Caliente Racetrack**, about 5 kilometers (3 miles) east of downtown off Boulevard Agua Caliente, presents greyhound racing nightly at 7:45 and also on Saturdays and Sundays at 2; closed Dec. 25. The track no longer has horse racing, but another LF Caliente betting facility here is popular for wagering on U.S. horse races and professional sports teams. General admission is free. A third LF Caliente facility is located at the Pueblo Amigo complex, a 5-minute walk from the international border. For general information phone (619) 231-1910 in the United States.

The **Social Campestre** (Tijuana Country Club), also east of downtown via Boulevard Agua Caliente, boasts an 18-hole golf course designed by Alister MacKenzie, the man responsible for the Pebble Beach and Augusta National courses in the United States. The course is surrounded by resort hotels. Some tee times are reserved for members; nonmembers may play Wed. and Sat.-Sun. after noon, all day Mon.-Tues. and Thurs.-Fri. Reservations are accepted up to a month in advance; phone (66) 81-7855 and ask for the pro shop.

The nearby Pacific Ocean beckons most visitors to Baja, although beach access is primarily south of Tijuana. **Playas de Tijuana**, 10 kilometers (6 miles) west via Mex. 1-D, is a seaside community visited mainly by locals. At the fence separating it from Imperial Beach, Calif., stands the **Monumento de la Frontera** (Boundary Monument), denoting the western terminus of the U.S.-Mexico border. Border history is recounted on bilingual plaques. **Rosarito** *(see separate listing)*, about 21 kilometers (13 miles) south via Mex. 1 or Mex. 1-D, is a growing resort town with facilities catering mainly to tourists. Diversions include ocean swimming and surfing and horseback riding along several miles of wide, sandy beach.

Several diversions cater to families. Youngsters will enjoy the **Museo de Cera de Tijuana** (Tijuana's Wax Museum), at Calle 1 near Avenida Revolución. Figures depict both the famous and infamous from Mexico, the United States and around the world. While some of them bear little resemblance to the actual personage—John F. Kennedy, for example—Michael Jackson is suitably lifelike, and the Ayatollah Khomeini looks as menacing in wax as he did in person. Open Mon.-Fri. 10-7, Sat.-Sun. 10-8. Admission is charged. Phone (66) 88-2478.

Q-Zar, in the Pueblo Amigo shopping center at Via Oriente and Paseo de Tijuana near the border, is a state-of-the-art live action laser game. Participants don chest and back packs and carry phasars that fire red and green laser beams; they do battle in a specially designed, mazelike arena filled with smoke, fluorescent lighting and pumping music. There are video games and pinball machines as well. Open Sun.-Thurs. 10-10, Fri.-Sat. 7 a.m.-1 a.m. Phone (66) 83-6183 or 83-6184.

Mundo Divertido (Fun World), at the corner of Paseo de los Héroes and José Ma. Velasco in the Zona Río, is a family oriented theme park with rides for all ages. Park admission free; cost of ride tickets varies. Phone (66) 34-3234.

Many of the fiestas and holidays celebrated with much fanfare in other parts of Mexico pass with little notice in Tijuana. *Independence Day* is one exception, and large crowds gather for observances on Sept. 15 and 16. Restaurants and public places are festooned with flags, beautiful patriotic decorations, and red, white and green streamers. Adding to the festivities are live bands playing traditional music.

THE INFORMED TRAVELER

Tijuana International Airport is on the eastern edge of the city near the Otay Mesa border crossing. Aero California flies from Tijuana to La Paz, B.C.S. *Combis* (shuttle vans) run between the airport, the border crossings and downtown. For additional information about airlines *see "Arriving by Air," page 53, and "Air and Bus Service" under "The Baja Peninsula," page 150.*

Local bus lines cover all parts of the city and run along the major thoroughfares. Most fares are inexpensive, usually about 25c. Familiarity with the city layout and proficiency in basic

Spanish both come in handy, as does a tolerance for old vehicles that don't offer the highest degree of comfort. The **Central de Autobuses** (Central Bus Terminal) is on Boulevard Lázaro Cárdenas at Calle Alamar in the eastern section of the city, near the airport. Regular passenger service is offered from Tijuana to the nearby cities of Ensenada, Mexicali and San Felipe. "Deluxe" bus service is provided by Tres Estrellas de Oro, Autobuses de Baja California, Elite and Transportes del Pacífico. All of these lines operate out of the Central Bus Terminal; phone (66) 21-2911. For additional information about buses *see "Bus Service," page 63.*

Five Star Tours provides service from San Diego to Tijuana. Buses depart daily from San Diego's Amtrak depot, Broadway at Kettner Boulevard, and drop passengers off at the Mexicoach Terminal, near the Jai Alai Palace on Avenida Revolución between calles 6 and 7. The round-trip fare is $8. Five Star Tours also offers bullfight trips. For information phone (619) 232-5049. Another outfit, **Mexicoach**, runs numerous buses daily from the trolley station in San Ysidro, Calif., to the Mexicoach Terminal. A round-trip ticket is $2.

On-street parking is available, and most shopping centers have free parking lots. A number of pay lots, some of them guarded, are located downtown. Many day visitors prefer to park on the California side and enter the city on foot via an elevated pedestrian promenade. Taxicabs congregate around the tourist information booth just south of the border. Tijuana cabs have colors—yellow, red, green, black—correlating to different city zones. The yellow cabs take tourists to the central downtown area. Cabs are not metered; make sure you negotiate the fare before setting off.

There are no RV park facilities in Tijuana. The **Oasis Resort**, off Mex. 1-D just north of Rosarito (southbound, Oasis exit; northbound, San Antonio exit), has 55 RV sites. Phone (800) 462-7472. Another facility between Tijuana and Rosarito is the **KOA Rosarito**, about 11 kilometers (7 miles) north of Rosarito via Mex. 1-D (San Antonio exit). Sixty-five RV and tent sites are located on a bluff overlooking the ocean. Phone (66) 13-3305.

Note: Keep in mind that facilities, maintenance and services at trailer parks in Baja California may not be up to U.S. standards. Tap water is not fit for drinking, and bathroom facilities can be rustic. Campgrounds in the southern part of the peninsula may not have English-speaking employees; a knowledge of basic Spanish comes in handy.

A visitor information booth just south of the San Ysidro border crossing has information and maps; phone (66) 83-1405. A kiosk serves those walking across the border. The Tijuana Chamber of Commerce, on Calle 1 at Avenida Revolución,

also has a booth; phone (66) 82-8488. At the southeastern end of town is the State Tourism Department, on the third level of the Plaza Patria on Boulevard Díaz Ordaz. It is open Mon.-Fri. 9-3 and 5-7; phone (66) 81-9492, 81-9493 or 81-9494. Easier for tourists to locate is a branch office of the department at Calle 1 and Avenida Revolución. The Tijuana Convention & Visitors Bureau provides information as well; phone (66) 84-0481. **Note:** Good English is spoken at just about every tourism office in Tijuana.

Protección al Turista (Tourist Assistance) provides legal assistance to visitors who experience difficulties with local merchants or police while in Tijuana. It is located in the State Tourism Department offices at the Plaza Patria; the hours and phone number are the same. The U.S. consulate office is on Calle Tapachula near the Agua Caliente Racetrack. Assistance is offered to U.S. citizens who receive inappropriate treatment by Mexican police while traveling in northern Baja California. The office will furnish a questionnaire pertaining to incidents of mistreatment. In case of an after-hours emergency, phone (619) 585-2000, or write to P.O. Box 439039, San Ysidro, CA 92143.

Baja Sun and *Baja Shopper* are two English-language newspapers distributed free at tourist information centers, hotels and some stores. In addition to advertisements, they contain information about tourist attractions in Tijuana and other parts of Baja California. A number of California radio stations can be picked up in Tijuana and all over northern Baja. Tijuana stations feature Mexican music. The TV dial includes San Diego, Tijuana and Mexico City channels.

The weather in Tijuana is similar to that in southern California—mild, overcast and rather wet in winter, warm and dry in summer. Daily maximums are usually in the 60s during the winter months, rising to the low 80s in summer. While there are occasional hot spells, the moderating influence of the Pacific Ocean largely spares the city from the blazing temperatures common in many other parts of Baja. Precipitation averages only about 10 inches a year, with almost all of it falling during the winter; the months of May through September are essentially rainless.

Personal safety involves mostly common-sense precautions. Gang activity has increased, so stick to the established tourist zone—roughly Avenida Revolución east to Paseo de los Héroes and Revolución southeast as it turns into Boulevard Agua Caliente. Avoid side streets and unlighted areas at night. And despite an emphasis on family entertainment, Tijuana still attracts a large contingent of partying revelers. Those who end an evening overindulging on margaritas or Tecate beer should take the appropriate measures to get back to their hotel room (or car) safely. It's a good idea to take a taxi after dark; rides within the city average about $6.

BORDER TIPS

There are two border crossings—at Tijuana-San Ysidro and at Otay Mesa, just east of Tijuana International Airport and south of SR 117 (Otay Mesa Road). U.S. customs offices are open 24 hours daily. Mexican customs offices are open Mon.-Fri. 8 a.m.-9 p.m., Sat. 8-5. The San Ysidro border crossing is open daily 24 hours. The Otay Mesa border crossing is open daily 6 a.m.-10 p.m. and is particularly useful for travelers returning from weekend excursions to such Gulf of California spots as San Felipe. For additional information *see "Arriving in Mexico," page 52.*

Crossing the border into Tijuana can usually be accomplished without delay, but the same thing cannot always be said about returning to the United States. The best times to cross are before 10 a.m. and after 10 p.m. spring through fall, and before 2 p.m. and after 8 p.m. during the winter (except holidays). Occasional cloudy summer days—locally referred to as "June gloom"—often prompt weekend visitors to leave earlier on Sunday afternoons.

Crossing on or around major holidays—Memorial Day, July 4, Labor Day, Thanksgiving and Christmas—can entail waits of up to 3 hours. The 2-week college spring break and the first 2 weeks of December, when citizens of both countries are traveling back and forth doing their Christmas shopping, are other times when significant delays can be expected, as are Mexican holidays.

For those who choose to leave their vehicle on the U.S. side, **San Diego Trolleys** provides transport to the border from three downtown stops—Americas Plaza, Civic Center and Fifth Avenue. Parking is not provided. There are public lots at each stop; daily rates range from $5 to $7. One-way fare $1.75; over 59, 75¢. For information and schedules phone (619) 233-3004 or 685-4900 (recording). From the border, shuttles take passengers to the downtown tourist zone along Avenida Revolución; the fare is $5.

CITY LAYOUT

The intermittently flowing Tijuana River passes through the heart of Tijuana on its way northwest across the U.S. frontier, where it empties into the Pacific Ocean. The old downtown (referred to as El Centro) is just south of the river and less than a mile south of the San Ysidro border crossing. The traditional tourist zone is along Avenida Revolución. This busy thoroughfare is lined with restaurants, nightclubs and souvenir shops. About a mile to the southeast rise Tijuana's newer, modern office buildings and shopping centers.

To reach the tourist zone after crossing the border, follow the signs that say "Downtown Centro"; they will lead you to Calle 3, which runs west to Avenida Revolución. Although a car is the most convenient means of transportation, city traffic is daunting. North-south avenidas Revolución and Constitución and east-west calles 2 and 3, which traverse the downtown core, are very congested. The old-fashioned traffic signals are not readily visible; watch carefully for them.

Traffic circles, or *glorietas*, along northwest-southeast Paseo de los Héroes and Paseo de Tijuana can be confusing; always bear right when entering a traffic circle, following the flow of traffic counterclockwise. There are many one-way street signs. Side streets away from the main business districts are often unpaved, rutted or potholed. Fortunately, several wide through streets facilitate traffic flow through central Tijuana.

Mex 1-D, a divided, fully access-controlled toll highway, provides a quick and safe route south to Ensenada and is preferable to old, free Mex. 1. From the international border, it proceeds west, paralleling the border fence and bypassing much of Tijuana's congestion (follow the "Ensenada Cuota" signs along Calle Internacional). You may, however, encounter detours that route traffic along downtown streets. Mex. 1-D runs west to Playas de Tijuana, then turns south, with the ocean in view along most of the scenic route. There are three toll plazas between the two cities; the total charge is about $7. There also are emergency telephones along the highway at 3-kilometer (2-mile) intervals.

When toll highway Mex. 2-D is completed it will link Tijuana and Mexicali. The sections from Tijuana to Tecate and from the Mexicali Valley to the town of Rumorosa are complete; expect to pay about $20 in tolls. Work is still in progress on sections from Tecate to Mexicali.

SHOPPING

Shopping is the No. 1 tourist activity in a city where the options range from French perfume to false teeth. Although the cheap souvenirs manufactured locally for the tourist trade are inescapable (yet somehow irresistible), there is much more to tempt the eyes and wallets of dedicated shoppers. Good buys can be found on Mexican-made articles—blankets, blown glass, ceramics, guitars, jewelry, leather goods, piñatas, pottery, silver and tin objects, stoneware, straw baskets, sweaters, wrought-iron furniture, hand-tooled saddles and decorative objects.

Because of its status as a duty-free port of entry, Tijuana offers head-turning displays of Rolex watches, Russian caviar, Italian shoes, French cosmetics, European designer fashions, Scottish cashmere sweaters, Oriental rugs, fine crystal, gold jewelry and other international goods, as well as fine-quality Mexican crafts. Merchants go out of their way to make the shopping experience as pleasant as possible. But although there are certainly bargains to be had, don't assume that prices will automatically be lower than back home; compare before you buy.

Some 10 blocks of Avenida Revolución downtown form the traditional tourist row, where curio shops still line the sidewalks and spill out of numerous arcades. Haggling is expected if you're buying from street vendors or open-air stalls; in more established shops, ask if bargaining is accepted. The only ground rule in this culturally rewarding experience is to maintain a serious yet light-hearted approach, for a merchant's initial offering price will usually be about twice what the item is worth. Avenida Constitución, a block to the west, is favored by local shoppers. Booths selling crafts and clothing crowd the **Mercado de Artesanías** (Arts and Crafts Market), on Calle 2 between avenidas Negrete and Ocampo.

In this swirl of buying and selling, keep expectations in mind. For example, if you're looking for quality and authenticity in silver jewelry instead of a simple trinket, avoid the street vendors whose arms are garlanded with necklaces. Tijuana is considered the leather capital of Baja, and boots, shoes, sandals, luggage, purses, wallets, briefcases, belts and coats can all be bargained for—but again, check for quality before committing your dollars.

Tijuana has great bargains on such Mexican liquors as Kahlua, tequila, run, brandy and local Baja wines. The best buys are found not in the smaller liquor stores but in the Mexican grocery stores called *super mercados*. Calimax is one of several chains in the city. Nondrinkers can stock up on gourmet coffees. The supermarkets are also a good place to pick up breads, pastries, sugar, aloe vera lotion and other items.

For those who would rather browse in a more concentrated area, Tijuana has at least half a dozen modern malls. **Plaza Río Tijuana**, along Avenida Paseo de los Héroes next to the Tijuana Cultural Center, has more than a hundred stores and restaurants, including Sears, Comercial Mexicana and Dorian's, a Baja department store chain. For kids, there is a carrousel in front of Sears. Directly across the street is **Plaza Fiesta**, a collection of small shops and eateries in a traditional colonial-style complex. Next door is **Plaza del Zapata**, where the focus is on footwear. **Pueblo Amigo**, a 5-minute walk from the border, has shops, restaurants, nightspots and a sports book betting facility.

Across from the cultural center at Paseo de los Héroes and Avenida Independencia is the **Mercado M. Hidalgo** (public market), typically lively and filled with fresh produce stalls, art and craft shops and liquor stores. Stores and businesses line Boulevard Agua Caliente for several miles. **Plaza Patria**, a three-level mall in the La Mesa District, is on Boulevard Díaz Ordaz, Agua Caliente's southeast extension. One of the newest and largest malls is **Plaza Viva Tijuana**, just south of the San Ysidro border crossing near the tourist information booth.

In addition to merchandise, city businesses offer a wide variety of services at reasonable prices. In the area bounded by avenidas Ocampo and Pío Pico and calles 2 and 9 are a bevy of auto shops offering paint jobs, upholstering and body work for up to half the cost of similar repairs stateside. Most have English-speaking managers and will provide a written estimate of the cost and time involved to do the work.

Shoe and watch repair and clothing alterations are other services of which visitors may avail themselves. Optical and dental services can be a bargain, but seek out established businesses with professional, English-speaking staffs. Pharmaceuticals for personal use can be purchased at *farmacias* near the border, where the cost for some prescription drugs can be much less expensive than at pharmacies in the United States.

The Mexican peso and the American dollar are practically interchangeable in Tijuana. This is the one Mexican city where visitors rarely have to worry about currency exchange. Prices are fixed in department stores and the finer shops selling imported items; elsewhere, bargaining is expected. Some stores accept U.S. credit cards.

English is spoken in the main shopping centers and the shops along Avenida Revolución; for street haggling, some knowledge of Spanish is helpful. Most stores are open daily 10-9. U.S. Customs allows up to $400 in duty-free merchandise and one liter of spirits per adult to be brought back into the United States. For additional information *see "What U.S. Citizens May Bring Back," page 75.*

DINING AND NIGHTLIFE

One of the more common misconceptions about Tijuana is that dining options are limited to tacos, burritos and enchiladas. While these are certainly in abundant supply, the city offers a variety of international cuisines as well, including American, Chinese, Continental, French, Italian, Japanese and Spanish.

Gastronomic lore names Tijuana as the birthplace of the Caesar salad, originally intended to serve a crowd of late diners from a restaurant's depleted food supply. The greens go well with steak or seafood, and there are plenty of restaurants specializing in one or the other. Tijuana also abounds in local establishments that offer traditional Mexican fare. Meals of charbroiled chicken in a *mole* sauce with rice and beans, or *carnitas* (marinated pork) served with salsa, guacamole and onions, all wrapped in warm flour tortillas and washed down with a frosty *cerveza* (beer), can be enjoyed for around $10 (U.S.).

For those in search of quick, inexpensive street food, taco vendors line Calle 1 near Avenida Revolución downtown. These snacks are filling but can play bacterial havoc with stomachs not made of steel. If you indulge, look for food that is hot, freshly prepared and cooked using purified water. For the gastronomically unadventurous, Tijuana has a full complement of familiar franchises such as Dennys, Jack in the Box and McDonalds, along with local versions of such American staples as Southern fried chicken.

Do not include the 15 percent I.V.A. tax that is automatically added to the check in restaurants when deciding what to tip. A 20 percent tip is not expected in Mexico; 10 percent is acceptable, unless you feel the service has been truly outstanding.

The '60s sexual revolution effectively ended Tijuana's reputation as a center of sin. These days nightlife revolves around discos that are popular with locals and visitors alike. Music—both recorded and live—pouring out of the clubs along Avenida Revolución can be ear-splitting, and shills are stationed at every door luring potential customers with free drink cards. If you do go in, don't look for bargains, as cover charges and drink prices are frequently equal to if not more than similar prices in the states. Most discos are open Thursday through Sunday evenings. The Tijuana branch of the **Hard Rock Café**, Avenida Revolución #520 (between calles 1 and 2), is a popular hangout.

More sedate are the lobby bars and lounges in such hotels as the Lucerna, in the Zona Rio district along Paseo de los Héroes. This area, which caters to the wealthy, also has discos. Two popular ones are **Baby Rock**, across the street from the Hotel Lucerna, and **Oh!**, on Paseo de los Héroes near Alcazar del Río. The Zona Rio discos are sophisticated and discriminating; those in jeans and T-shirts won't get in.

If thumping beats and flashing lights aren't your cup of tea, **Jazz Alley**, Boulevard Agua Caliente #3410, Colonia Chapultepec, offers an evening of mellow jazz sounds. Attracting the sports crowd is **Tia Juana Tilly's**, next to the Jai Alai Palace on Avenida Revolución at Calle 7. This combination bar, restaurant and dance spot that is a local institution of sorts.

Note: While Tijuana promotes fun, remember that you are in a foreign country where a different set of rules and laws are in effect. The police invariably arrest those who are inebriated and causing a disturbance in public, and nothing will ruin a vacation like a night in a Mexican jail and the ensuing bureaucratic hassle to get out.

WHAT TO SEE

CENTRO CULTURAL TIJUANA (Tijuana Cultural Center) is at Paseo de los Héroes and Avenida Independencia. The ultramodern complex was built by the Mexican government in 1982 and includes a museum, exhibit halls, a spherical om-

nitheater, a 1,000-seat performing arts theater, art gallery, bookstore, restaurant and shopping arcade. The museum contains archeological displays and permanent exhibits chronicling pre-Hispanic, colonial and modern Mexico as well as the history of Tijuana. Temporary exhibitions spotlight contemporary Mexican artists and various cultural traditions.

During the summer months the **Papantla Flyers**, a troupe of Totonac Indians, perform the ancient "Flying Pole" dance in a park in front of the museum. From the border, "Baja P" buses take passengers to the cultural center. Admission is charged to the museum. Phone (66) 84-1111.

MEXITLAN, Calle 2 and Avenida Ocampo, features an outdoor display of some 150 scale models. A remarkable feat of miniature engineering, the representations include some of the nation's outstanding monuments, colonial churches and architectural treasures, including ancient Maya ruins. One highlight is the replication of Mexico City's Olympic Stadium, built for the 1968 summer games, in which literally 100,000 miniature figures are watching the opening ceremonies. On the field are players representing all of the participating countries. The display spans hundreds of years of history and focuses on Mexico's south-central plateau region. Music characteristic of each area plays at the different exhibits.

Rock concerts take place on weekends beginning at 9 p.m. Open Wed.-Sun. 10-7, May-Sept.; 10-5, rest of year. (**Note:** Although Mexitlan was open at press time, call ahead to confirm schedule.) Admission is charged. Phone (66) 38-4101.

WHERE TO STAY

CAMINO REAL TIJUANA

▼▼▼ *Hotel*   ☎ (66)33-4000

1/1-11/30	$140 XP $50
12/1-12/31	$120 XP $40

Location: 3.3 km se of border; in Rio Tijuana. Paseo de Los Heroes No 10305 22320. Fax: 66/33-4001. **Facility:** Meets AAA guest room security requirements. 241 units. 7 stories. **Terms:** F10; cancellation fee imposed. **Amenities:** hair dryers. *Some:* honor bars. **Guest Services:** gift shop, valet laundry. **Business Services:** conference facilities, administrative services, fax. **Cards:** AE, DI, MC, VI.

EL CONQUISTADOR HOTEL

▼▼ *Motel*   ☎ 66/81-7955

All Year	$50 XP $5

Location: 0.5 km e of Ave Rodriguez; near Tijuana Country Club. Blvd Agua Caliente 10750 22320 (Box 5355, CHULA VISTA, CA). Fax: 66/86-1340. **Facility:** 105 units. *Bath:* shower only. 2 stories, exterior corridors. **Terms:** F11. **Leisure Activities:** sauna, whirlpool. **Guest Services:** valet laundry. **Business Services:** meeting rooms. **Cards:** AE, MC, VI.

FIESTA INN

▼▼ ▼▼ *Motel* (66/34-6901

All Year $94 XP $14
Location: 4 km se of border on Via Rapida Poniente. Paseo de Los Heroes No 18818 22320. Fax: 66/34-6912. **Facility:** Natural hot springs whirlpool. Full service spa. 127 units. *Bath:* combo or shower only. 3 stories, interior corridors. **Terms:** F19. **Leisure Activities:** heated pool, whirlpool. **Guest Services:** gift shop, valet laundry. *Fee:* massage. **Business Services:** meeting rooms. **Cards:** AE, MC, VI.

SOME UNITS

[icons]

GRAND HOTEL TIJUANA

▼▼▼▼ *Hotel* ((66)81-7000

All Year $100-$135 XP $10
Location: 0.6 km e of Ave Rodriquez. Blvd Agua Caliente No. 4500 22420 (PO Box BC, CHULA VISTA, CA, 91912). Fax: 66/81-7016. **Facility:** 422 units. 25 stories, interior corridors. **Parking:** extra charge. **Terms:** F12. **Amenities:** honor bars. **Leisure Activities:** heated pool, whirlpool, 2 tennis courts. *Fee:* exercise room. **Guest Services:** gift shop, valet laundry. **Business Services:** conference facilities, administrative services, PC, fax. **Cards:** AE, CB, DI, DS, MC, VI.

SOME UNITS

[icons]

HOTEL COUNTRY CLUB

▼▼ *Motor Inn* ((66)81-7733

All Year $57 XP $8
Location: 4.8 km e of border via Blvd Agua Caliente; between Tijuana Country Club and Caliente Race Track. Calle Tapachula No. 1 22420 (PO Box 5356, CHULA VISTA, CA, 91912). Fax: 66/81-7692. **Facility:** 135 units. *Bath:* shower only. 2-4 stories, exterior corridors. **Terms:** F12; 30 day cancellation notice-fee imposed. **Leisure Activities:** heated pool, whirlpool. **Guest Services:** gift shop. **Business Services:** meeting rooms. **Cards:** AE, MC, VI.

SOME UNITS

[icons]

HOTEL HACIENDA DEL RIO

▼▼ ▼▼ *Motor Inn* ((66)84-8644

All Year $71 XP $9
Location: 3 km se of the border. Blvd Rodolfo Sanchez Taboada No. 10606 22320 (PO Box 5356, CHULA VISTA, CA, 91912). Fax: 66/84-8620. **Facility:** 131 units. Some suites ($84-$149). *Bath:* shower only. 3 stories, exterior corridors. **Terms:** F12; 30 day cancellation notice-fee imposed. **Amenities:** hair dryers. **Leisure Activities:** heated pool, exercise room. **Guest Services:** gift shop, valet laundry. **Business Services:** meeting rooms, fax. **Cards:** AE, MC, VI.

SOME UNITS

[icons]

HOTEL LA MESA INN

▼▼ *Motor Inn* ((66)81-6522

All Year $57 XP $8
Location: 5 km e of border via Blvd Agua Caliente; in La Mesa area. Blvd Diaz Ordaz Esq. con Cardenias No. 50 22440 (PO Box 5356, CHULA VISTA, CA, 91912). Fax: 66/81-2871. **Facility:** 122 units. *Bath:* combo or shower only. 1-3 stories. **Terms:** F12; 30 day cancellation notice-fee imposed. **Amenities:** extended cable TV. **Leisure Activities:** heated pool. **Guest Services:** gift shop. **Business Services:** meeting rooms. **Cards:** AE, MC, VI.

SOME UNITS

HOTEL LUCERNA

▼▼▼ *Hotel* (66/33-3900

All Year $146-$164 XP $15
Location: 3.5 km se of border; in Rio Tijuana area. Paseo de Los Heroes No. 10902 22320. Fax: 66/34-2400. **Facility:** Central pool area. Meets AAA guest room security requirements. 167 units. 2-6 stories, interior/exterior corridors. **Parking:** valet. **Terms:** F12. **Amenities:** extended cable TV, hair dryers. **Dining:** Rivoli's, Rivoli's, see separate listing. **Leisure Activities:** heated pool, exercise room. **Guest Services:** gift shop, valet laundry. **Business Services:** meeting rooms, administrative services, PC, fax. **Cards:** AE, DI, MC, VI.

SOME UNITS

[icons]

HOTEL REAL DEL RIO

▼▼ ▼▼ *Motor Inn* (66/34-3100

All Year $83-$90 XP $13
Location: 3 km se of border; in Rio Tijuana area, just n of Paseo de Los Heroes. Jose Ma Velasco 1409-A 22320. Fax: 66/34-3053. **Facility:** Meets AAA guest room security requirements. 105 units. 5 stories, interior/exterior corridors. **Terms:** F11. **Amenities:** safes, hair dryers. **Business Services:** meeting rooms. **Cards:** AE, MC, VI.

SOME UNITS

[icons]

PALACIO AZTECA HOTEL

▼▼ *Hotel* (66/81-8100

All Year $55-$73 XP $10
Location: 0.5 km s of Paseo de Los Heroes. Blvd Cuauhtemoc Sur No. 213. Fax: 66/81-8100. **Facility:** 175 units. Some suites. 7 stories. **Leisure Activities:** exercise room. **Guest Services:** [BP] meal plan available, gift shop. **Business Services:** meeting rooms. **Cards:** AE, MC, VI.

[icons]

PLAZA LAS GLORIAS

▼▼ ▼▼ *Hotel* (66/22-6600

All Year $92 XP $10
Location: Adjacent to Tijuana Country Club golf course. Blvd Agua Caliente No. 11553 22420 (PO Box 43-1588, SAN YSIDRO, CA, 92173). Fax: 66/22-6602. **Facility:** 187 units. 10 stories, interior corridors. **Terms:** F12. **Leisure Activities:** heated pool, whirlpool, exercise room. **Guest Services:** gift shop, valet laundry. **Business Services:** meeting rooms. **Cards:** AE, MC, VI.

SOME UNITS

[icons]

PUEBLO AMIGO HOTEL

▼▼ ▼▼ *Hotel* (66/83-5030

All Year $150-$172 XP $25
Location: 0.8 km se of border, 1st right after border, veer left under bridge to Paseo de Tijuana. Via Oriente 9211 22320. Fax: 66/83-5032. **Facility:** Atrium lobby. Meets AAA guest room security requirements. 108 units. 7 stories, interior corridors. **Parking:** valet. **Terms:** F12; package plans. **Amenities:** safes, hair dryers. **Leisure Activities:** heated pool, exercise room. **Guest Services:** [BP] meal plan available, gift shop, valet laundry. **Business Services:** meeting rooms, administrative services, PC, fax. **Cards:** AE, MC, VI.

SOME UNITS

[icons]

RESIDENCE INN BY MARRIOTT-REAL DEL MAR

 Suite Motor Inn (66/31-3670

All Year $79-$149 XP $10

Location: From Hwy 1-D, exit Real Del Mar, then just e; 19.5 km s of the border. Km 19.5 Carretera Custa 22605 (4492 Camino de la Plaza, #1246, SAN YSIDRO, CA, 92173-3097). Fax: 66/31-3677. **Facility:** Hillside location. Studio and one-bedroom suites. Many units with golf course or ocean view. Suites with electric fireplace and patio. Meets AAA guest room security requirements. 75 units with kitchen. 2 stories, exterior corridors. **Terms:** F12; 3 day cancellation notice. **Amenities:** extended cable TV, irons, hair dryers. **Leisure Activities:** heated pool, sauna, whirlpool, steamroom, 2 lighted tennis courts, exercise room, basketball. *Fee:* golf-18 holes. **Guest Services:** [CP] meal plan available, gift shop, complimentary evening beverages, valet laundry. **Business Services:** meeting rooms. **Cards:** AE, MC, VI.

SOME UNITS

WHERE TO DINE

RESTAURANTE LA COSTA

 Seafood (66/85-8494

L $8-$10 D $10-$29

Location: Just w of Ave Revolucion; in the downtown tourist area. Calle 7A. **Hours:** 10 am-11 pm, Fri & Sat-midnight. **Features:** casual dress; cocktails & lounge. Large seafood selection including lobster, shrimp, oysters, filet and whole fish. **Cards:** AE, MC, VI.

RIVOLI'S

 International (66/33-3900

L $7-$14 D $7-$14

Location: 3.5 km se of border; in Rio Tijuana area; in Hotel Lucerna. Paseo de Los Heroes No. 10902 22320. **Hours:** 7 am-11 pm. **Features:** dressy casual; cocktails; valet parking; a la carte. Colorful murals complement the glass wall view of the pool, creating a pleasant and relaxing setting. Attentive servers present duck, chicken, beef and pasta entrees with unique sauces. **Cards:** AE, CB, DI, MC, VI.

SAN ANGEL STEAK HOUSE

Steak House (66/81-7542

L $9-$18 D $9-$18

Location: 0.6 km s of Agua Caliente Blvd, on Mex 1 northbound. Gobernador Ibarra 252. **Hours:** 7:30 am-10:30 pm, Fri & Sat-11:30 pm. Closed: Sun & last week of Dec. **Reservations:** suggested. **Features:** No A/C; dressy casual; cocktails; valet parking. Converted cottage with many small dining areas and outdoor patio. Numerous cuts of high quality beef. Several fish and chicken dishes, plus quail and duck. **Cards:** AE, MC, VI.

NORTHWESTERN MEXICO

Northwestern Mexico encompasses three of the country's four largest states—Chihuahua, Durango and Sonora—and vast expanses of insurmountable territory. Desolate plateaus stretch for miles, and the sun sets over panoramic mountain and desert vistas. One of the most rewarding ways to view this rugged scenery is from the window of a passenger train traversing the Copper Canyon region, a complex of interconnected canyons almost four times larger and some 280 feet deeper than the Grand Canyon. Similarly spectacular are the views along El Espinazo del Diablo (The Devil's Backbone), a winding, 6-mile stretch of Mex. 40 about midway between the cities of Durango and Mazatlán.

Despite the inhospitable conditions, this part of Mexico is economically rich. Irrigated river valleys produce flourishing crops of cotton, peanuts, sugar cane, tobacco, fruits and vegetables. Extensive ranchlands in Sonora yield what is considered to be the country's best beef cattle. And mining remains important; looming over the city of Durango is one of the world's largest single iron deposits, Cerro de Mercado (Mercado Hill).

A harsh climate and landscape long impeded large-scale settlement of the region, and there are few ancient ruins or cultural reminders of past greatness. The big cities—Chihuahua, Ciudad Obregón, Culiacán, Durango, Hermosillo—are mostly industrialized and therefore lacking in sightseeing opportunities. Two small but growing resorts are in Sonora. San Carlos, just outside the port city of Guaymas, is in an area known for deep-sea fishing, while Puerto Peñasco, on the state's northwestern Gulf of California coast, attracts weekenders from California and Arizona. Another day-trip destination is the hustling border city of Ciudad Juárez, opposite El Paso.

ALAMOS, SONORA (E-4)

Alamos (AH-lah-mohs), situated in the foothills of the Sierra Madre Occidental in Sonora's southeastern corner, began as an early Spanish stronghold in the vastness of northwestern Mexico. Explorer Francisco Vásquez de Coronado camped in the area as early as 1540, unaware that the ground beneath him held rich deposits of silver. By the end of the 17th century, however, a settlement had sprung up to service regional mining operations.

Spanish expeditions to the north were funded with wealth from the mines, the northernmost in Mexico, and their exploitation had boosted the town's population to 30,000 by 1781. But although Alamos had its own mint in the 1860s, the mines became depleted over the years, and were all but abandoned by the turn of the 20th century. Successive Indian attacks, droughts and the turmoil of the 1910 Revolution all took their toll. Many of the wealthier citizens pulled up stakes, and the colonial-style mansions they had built were left to deteriorate.

A turnaround took place following World War II, when U.S. artists and retirees began to arrive and restore some of the old homes to their former glory. Today Alamos is a designated national historic monument, the site of an established expatriate community and is considered the state's most authentically "Mexican" destination. Some 52 kilometers (32 miles) east of Navojoa via Mex. 10, it's about a 5-hour drive from the U.S. border at Nogales. The presence of cottonwood trees and blooming flowers suggests an oasis of sorts in the otherwise barren landscape of coastal Sonora.

Arcaded **Plaza de Armas** marks the center of town. On the plaza are the **Iglesia de la Inmaculada Concepción** (Church of the Immaculate Conception), completed in the early 19th century, and the **Palacio Municipal** (City Hall). A popular morning gathering place is the **Casa de Café**, Calle Obregón #10, a coffeehouse located at the entrance to the Hotel de Los Tesoras. Many visitors take a guided tour of Alamos' restored colonial-era homes. For information about tour schedules and fees, contact the tourist office, Calle Juárez #6 at Plaza de Armas; phone (642) 8-0450.

One of the area's best known exports is the Mexican jumping bean. Powered by a hyperactive larva, it is collected from leguminous plants growing in the region. Nearby **Presa Mocuzari** (Mocuzari Dam), reached by a gravel road branching north off Mex. 10, offers fishing and other recreational opportunities.

MUSEO COSTUMBRISTA DE SONORA (Museum of Social Customs of Sonora), Guadalupe Victoria #1 on Plaza de Armas, occupies a 19th-century colonial house with three patios. The state's past is preserved through displays of furniture, photographs, machinery and work tools, clothing, documents and ethnographic displays. There also is a reproduction of a typical 19th-century Mexican kitchen and a collection of coins from the former mints in Alamos and Hermosillo. Exhibit information is in Spanish. Open Wed.-Sat. 9-1 and 3-6, Sun. 9-6. Donations.

WHERE TO STAY

CASA DE LOS TESOROS
◈◈◈◈ *Historic Motor Inn* ☎ (642)8-0010

12/1-6/1 & 10/29-11/30	$75-$95	XP $15
6/2-10/28	$55-$65	XP $15

Location: Just se of Plaza de Armas. Calle A Obregon 10 85763 (PO Box 12). Fax: 642/8-0400. **Facility:** Unique 18th-century converted convent. Period furniture; fireplaces. Indian dances every Saturday night. Strolling musicians in the evening. 15 units. 3 two-bedroom units. *Bath:* shower only. 1 story, exterior corridors. **Terms:** F12; 14 day cancellation notice, pets ($5 extra charge). **Amenities:** no TVs. **Leisure Activities:** small pool. **Guest Services:** [BP] meal plan available. **Cards:** MC, VI.

SOME UNITS

CASA ENCANTADA DE LOS TESOROS
◈◈◈ *Historic Bed & Breakfast* ☎ 642/8-0482

12/1-6/1	$70	XP $15

Location: Next to Palacio Municipal. Ave Juarez 20 85763. Fax: 642/8-0400. **Facility:** This is a converted 250-year-old hacienda, large rooms, high ceilings and attractive inner courtyard. Smoke free premises. 10 units. *Bath:* shower only. 1 story, exterior corridors. **Terms:**open 12/1-6/1, 14 day cancellation notice. **Amenities:** no TVs. **Leisure Activities:** small pool. **Guest Services:** [BP] meal plan available. **Cards:** MC, VI.

HOTEL LA POSADA DE ALAMOS
◈◈◈ *Motor Inn* ☎ 642/8-0045

All Year	$59-$74	XP $10

Location: 1 km e of the Palacio. 2 De Abril Sur 85760. Fax: 642/80-045. **Facility:** Attractive inner courtyard. Secured parking. All rooms with fireplace. Unique historical property is over 200 years old. Smoke free premises. 9 units, 4 with efficiency (no utensils). *Bath:* combo or shower only. 1 story, exterior corridors. **Amenities:** no TVs. **Cards:** MC, VI.

SOME UNITS

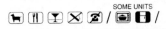

CEROCAHUI, CHIHUAHUA

WHERE TO STAY

HOTEL MISION
◈ *Lodge* ☎ 681/8-7046

All Year	$195

Location: 18 km from Bahuichivo Station; accessible only by train. Bahuichivo Station. Fax: 681/2-0046. **Facility:** In a remote area. Some fireplaces and woodburning stoves. 38 units. *Bath:* shower only. 1 story, interior/exterior corridors. **Terms:**20 day cancellation notice-fee imposed. **Amenities:** no TVs. **Leisure Activities:** *Fee:* horseback riding. **Guest Services:** [AP] meal plan available, gift shop. **Business Services:** meeting rooms. **Cards:** AE, DI, MC, VI.

CHIHUAHUA, CHIHUAHUA (D-5) elev. 4,690'

Founded in 1709, Chihuahua (chee-WAH-wah) is capital of the state of Chihuahua and one of the major cities of northern Mexico. The center of a rich silver-mining, lumbering and cattle-raising district, the city's familiar name is shared by *perritos chihuahueños*, the very small Mexican dog breed that were actually considered pests at the turn of the 20th century because they were so common.

Tarahumara Indians who dwell in the surrounding area are Mexico's largest surviving tribe. Accomplished hunters and gatherers, they wrest sustenance from the land in a surprising variety of ways—corn, beans, squash, apples and peaches; fish, insects, grubs, snakes and lizards; berries, cactuses and roots; and cattle, sheep and pigs. The Tarahumara refer to themselves as *rarámuri*, or "foot runners," and it is said that they can run wild turkeys or deer to exhaustion. Both men and women compete in races called *rarajípari*, which can last several days and cover hundreds of miles. A museum-craft shop devoted to the Tarahumara culture is located at Avenida Leyes de Reforma #5.

Chihuahua, despite its geographical isolation, has figured prominently in Mexico's history. Miguel Hidalgo y Costilla, champion of Mexico's independence, was executed in the city in

1811. It served as headquarters for Benito Juárez when French troops invaded Mexico between 1862 and 1867. Outlaw Pancho Villa frequented Chihuahua's countryside and once captured the city by disguising his men as peasants going to market.

Chihuahua's colonial aqueduct was completed in 1864. Many of the arches, some 50 feet high, are in ruins, but others still carry water from Chuvíscar Dam, 4 kilometers (2.5 miles) west of the city.

Lerdo Park on Paseo Bolívar is the scene of Sunday concerts. There are seasonal Sunday afternoon bullfights in the 8,000-seat Plaza La Esperanza. The *Fiesta de Santa Rita*, May 19-22, is a major local fair with commercial exhibits, cultural events, food and Indian dances. For tourist information phone (14) 15-8501 or 17-8972 (information module). The Departmento de Comercio y Turismo (State Tourism Office), Libertad and Calle 13, also has information; phone (14) 15-9879 or 16-2436.

Many roads out of the city are four-lane and divided for a considerable distance, traversing open, desert-like areas; driving at night is not recommended. Interesting day trips can be made to Aquiles Serdán (also known as Santa Eulalia), the oldest mining town in northern Mexico, and to Aldama, in the center of an important fruit-producing area. Near Aldama are the ruins of the **Santa Ana de Chinarras Mission**, founded by Jesuits in 1717.

CATHEDRAL, facing Plaza de la Constitución, is considered to be the finest example of colonial architecture in the state. Although it was begun in 1724, Indian wars delayed its completion until 1826.

MUSEO DE LA REVOLUCION (Museum of the Revolution), Calle 10 Norte #3014, was the home of Pancho Villa, outlaw and hero of the Mexican Revolution. Also known as Quinta Luz in honor of Señora Luz, Pancho Villa's only legal wife (although others claimed the distinction), the 50-room mansion is a museum. On display are the bullet-riddled car in which Villa was ambushed and killed, his firearms, cartridge belts, uniforms and archives. Secret passageways connect the center of the building with various entrances and exits. An equestrian statue of Villa stands at avenidas Universidad and División del Norte.

MUSEO REGIONAL DE CHIHUAHUA (Regional Museum of Chihuahua), Paseo Bolívar #401, is a restored turn-of-the-20th-century mansion. Completed in 1910, it is furnished in the art nouveau style with stained-glass windows and skylights; several Louis XV pieces decorate the main dining room. Exhibits on the second floor are devoted primarily to memorabilia, photographs and farming tools of the Mormons and Mennonites who established communities in and around Chihuahua beginning in the late 19th century. Admission is charged.

PALACIO DE GOBIERNO (Government Palace), the state capitol, stands on the north side of Plaza Hidalgo. In this building Miguel Hidalgo y Costilla was executed in 1811 during the War of Independence.

PALACIO FEDERAL (Federal Palace), at Avenida Juárez and Vicente Guerrero, dates from 1910 and preserves the cell in which Hidalgo was held prisoner while awaiting execution. His former prison quarters now contain museum exhibits.

SAN FRANCISCO CHURCH, on Calle Libertad, was begun by Franciscan missionaries in 1721 and completed 20 years later. Underground passages are said to connect this church with the cathedral.

WHERE TO STAY

BEST WESTERN MIRADOR MOTOR INN
▼▼▼ *Motor Inn* ((14)13-2205
All Year $90 XP $8
Location: On Mex 45; 6 blks s of Pancho Villa Monument. Ave Universidad 1309 31240. Fax: 14/13-8906. **Facility:** 90 units. *Bath:* shower only. 2 stories, exterior corridors. **Terms:** F9; 3 day cancellation notice. **Leisure Activities:** wading pool. **Guest Services:** valet laundry. **Business Services:** meeting rooms, administrative services, fax. **Cards:** AE, MC, VI.

FIESTA INN
▼▼▼ *Hotel* ((14)29-0100
7/1-11/30 $139-$150 XP $10
1/1-6/30 $135-$146 XP $9
12/1-12/31 $120-$129 XP $8
Location: 2 km w on Ortiz Mena at the intersection with Minnesota St. 2801 Ortiz Mena 31250. Fax: 14/29-0110. **Facility:** In a commercial area. Well appointed rooms. 152 units. 7 stories, interior corridors. **Terms:** F12; 7 day cancellation notice. **Leisure Activities:** heated pool, exercise room. **Guest Services:** gift shop. **Business Services:** meeting rooms, administrative services. **Cards:** AE, DI, MC, VI.

SOME UNITS

HOLIDAY INN EXPRESS
▼▼▼ *Motel* ((14)42-2200
All Year $140 XP $15
Location: 8 km n Mex 45. Ave Cristobal Colon 11390 31109. Fax: 14/42-2211. **Facility:** Newly constructed facility, ample secured parking and well appointed rooms. Meets AAA guest room security requirements. 96 units. 2 stories, interior corridors. **Terms:** F18; 3 day cancellation notice-fee imposed. **Amenities:** voice mail, safes, irons, hair dryers. **Leisure Activities:** heated pool, whirlpool, exercise room. **Guest Services:** [CP] meal plan available, gift shop, coin laundry. **Business Services:** conference facilities, administrative services, PC. **Cards:** AE, MC, VI.

SOME UNITS

HOLIDAY INN HOTEL & SUITES CHIHUAHUA

▼▼▼▼ *Apartment* ((14)39-0000

All Year $120 XP $15
Location: On Mex 45; 6 blks s of Pancho Villa Monument. Escudero 702 31000. Fax: 14/14-3313. **Facility:** Well-appointed rooms. Ample paved parking with security. Meets AAA guest room security requirements. 74 units with kitchen. 14 two-bedroom units. 2 stories, exterior corridors. **Terms:** F19. **Amenities:** voice mail, safes, irons, hair dryers. **Dining:** restaurant, noon-11 pm, $7-$12, cocktails. **Leisure Activities:** 2 heated pools, sauna, whirlpool, exercise room, sports court. **Guest Services:** [CP] meal plan available, coin laundry. **Business Services:** meeting rooms. **Cards:** AE, DI, MC, VI.

SOME UNITS

HOTEL CASA GRANDE

▼▼▼▼ *Motor Inn* ((14)39-4444

All Year $70 XP $5
Location: 7 km n on Mex 45. Ave Tecnologico 4702 31160. Fax: 14/39-4401. **Facility:** 115 units, 3 with efficiency. 2 stories, interior corridors. **Terms:** F12. **Amenities:** hair dryers. **Leisure Activities:** tennis court, exercise room, sports court. **Guest Services:** gift shop, valet laundry. **Business Services:** meeting rooms, administrative services. **Cards:** AE, DI, MC, VI.

SOME UNITS

HOTEL PALACIO DEL SOL

▼▼▼ *Hotel* ((14)16-6000

All Year $96-$128
Location: Just n of Plaza de Armas. Ave Independencia 116 31000. Fax: 14/15-9947. **Facility:** Located downtown. Traditional room decor. Ample parking facilities. Extensive meeting facilities. 182 units. 17 stories, interior corridors. **Dining:** Las Truffas Restaurante, see separate listing. **Leisure Activities:** exercise room. **Guest Services:** gift shop, valet laundry. **Business Services:** meeting rooms. **Cards:** AE, MC, VI.

SOME UNITS

HOTEL SAN FRANCISCO PARK PLAZA

▼▼▼ *Hotel* ((14)16-7770

All Year $81-$142 XP $8
Location: Center. Calle Victoria 409 31000. Fax: 14/15-3538. **Facility:** Located downtown just off Main Plaza. 131 units. 4 stories, interior corridors. **Terms:** F12; 3 day cancellation notice. **Amenities:** hair dryers. **Dining:** Restaurante Dega, see separate listing. **Leisure Activities:** exercise room. **Guest Services:** valet laundry. **Business Services:** meeting rooms, administrative services, PC, fax. **Cards:** AE, MC, VI.

SOME UNITS

HOTEL SICOMORO

▼▼▼ *Motor Inn* ((14)13-5445

All Year $79 XP $10
Location: 3.2 km nw on Ave Universidad to VW dealer, 0.3 km sw on Americas to Pemex Station, then 1.6 km s. Blvd Ortiz Mena 411 31230 (Apartado Postal 1121). Fax: 14/13-1411. **Facility:** Ample paved parking with security. 128 units. *Bath:* shower only. 2 stories, interior corridors. **Amenities:** extended cable TV. *Some:* safes. **Dining:** Restaurant El Trigal, see separate listing. **Guest Services:** valet laundry. **Business Services:** meeting rooms. **Cards:** AE, DI, MC, VI.

SOME UNITS

HOTEL WESTIN SOBERANO

▼▼▼▼ *Hotel* ((14)29-2929

7/1-11/30 $168-$179 XP $20
1/1-6/30 $164-$175 XP $20
12/1-12/31 $160-$170 XP $20
Location: 8 km nw on the Cuauhtemoc Bypass. Barranco Del Cobre S/N 3211 31125. Fax: 14/29-2900. **Facility:** On a hillside overlooking the city. Attractive public areas, very well-appointed guest rooms. Meets AAA guest room security requirements. 204 units. 5 stories, interior corridors. **Parking:** valet. **Terms:** F17; 4 day cancellation notice-fee imposed. **Amenities:** voice mail, safes, honor bars, hair dryers. **Leisure Activities:** heated pool, whirlpool. **Guest Services:** gift shop, valet laundry. *Fee:* massage. **Business Services:** meeting rooms, administrative services, fax. **Cards:** AE, DI, MC, VI.

SOME UNITS

POSADA TIERRA BLANCA

▼▼▼ *Motor Inn* ((14)15-0000

All Year $56 XP $4
Location: Just n of Plaza de Armas. (Ave Independencia & Ninos Heroes, 31000). Fax: 14/16-0063. **Facility:** 103 units. *Bath:* shower only. 3 stories, interior/exterior corridors. **Terms:** F12; 3 day cancellation notice. **Leisure Activities:** whirlpool, exercise room. **Cards:** AE, DI, MC, VI.

SOME UNITS

WHERE TO DINE

EL BIGOTE ITALIANO

▼▼▼ *Italian* (14/16-8399

L $5-$12 D $7-$20
Location: Blvd Ortiz Mena 1800 59214. **Hours:** noon-11 pm, Fri & Sat-midnight. **Reservations:** suggested. **Features:** casual dress; children's menu; cocktails. Unpretentious dining, offering well prepared Italian entrees. **Cards:** AE, MC, VI.

EL RETABLO

▼▼▼ *Mexican* (14/15-5545

L $8-$16 D $8-$16
Location: 3.2 km nw. Blvd Ortiz Mena 1810 59214. **Hours:** 1 pm-11 pm, Fri & Sat-midnight. **Reservations:** suggested. **Features:** casual dress; children's menu; cocktails. Well prepared regional Mexican specialties. **Cards:** MC, VI.

LA CALESA

Continental   (14/16-0222

L $9-$24   D $9-$24

Location: 1.8 km e on Mex 45. Ave Juarez y Colon 3300 31000. **Hours:** 1 pm-midnight. **Features:** cocktails; entertainment; fee for parking. Casual. Well prepared Mexican specialties. **Cards:** AE, MC, VI.

LA OLLA DE CHIHUAHUA

Continental   (14/16-2220

L $7-$18   D $7-$18

Location: 1.8 km e on Mex 45, just n of Juarez and Colon. Ave Juarez 3331. **Hours:** 1 pm-1 am. **Features:** cocktail lounge; entertainment; a la carte. Interesting restaurant in a converted brewery built in late 1800s. Serves well-prepared food, with good selections of steak and seafood. **Cards:** AE, MC, VI.

LAS TRUFFAS RESTAURANTE

Continental   (14/16-6000

L $5-$12   D $5-$12

Location: Just n of Plaza de Armas; in Hotel Palacio del Sol. Ave Independencia 500 31000. **Hours:** 7 am-4 & 6-2 am. **Features:** casual dress; children's menu; cocktails; valet parking. Well-prepared international specialties. **Cards:** AE, MC, VI.

RESTAURANTE DEGA

Continental   (14/16-7550

L $7-$15   D $7-$15

Location: Center; in Hotel San Francisco Park Plaza. Calle Victoria 409 31000. **Hours:** 7 am-10:30 pm. **Features:** casual dress; cocktails. **Cards:** AE, MC, VI.

RESTAURANT EL TRIGAL

Continental   (14/13-5445

L $11-$19   D $11-$19

Location: 3.2 km nw on Ave Universidad to VW dealer, 0.3 km sw on Americas to Pemex Station, then 1.6 km s; in Hotel Sicomoro. Ortiz Mena 411 31230. **Hours:** 6:30 am-midnight. **Features:** casual dress; cocktails; a la carte. Informal dining. **Cards:** AE, DI, MC, VI.

RESTAURANTE ORLEANS Y BAR REGGE

Continental   (14/15-4755

L $6-$12   D $6-$12

Location: 3.5 km nw. Blvd Ortiz Mena 1832 59214. **Hours:** 1 pm-11 pm, Fri & Sat-midnight. **Reservations:** suggested. **Features:** casual dress; cocktails; valet parking. Some Cajun style entrees. **Cards:** AE, MC, VI.

RINCON MEXICANO RESTAURANT

Mexican   (14/11-1510

L $12-$22   D $12-$22

Location: 2 km sw on Calle Victoria. Ave Cuauhtemco 2224 31020. **Hours:** 1 pm-midnight. **Reservations:** suggested. **Features:** casual dress; cocktails. Well-prepared steak and seafood specialties. **Cards:** AE, MC, VI.

CIUDAD JUAREZ,
CHIHUAHUA (C-5) elev. 5,000'

On the Río Grande opposite El Paso, Tex., Ciudad Juárez (HWAH-res) once served as a stop on the Santa Fe Trail. It was linked to El Paso first by mule-drawn trolley and later by electric trolleys. Juárez can be reached by several bridges. The **Zaragoza Bridge** (toll) on Zaragoza Avenue enters Mexico east of Ciudad Juárez; the **Cordoba Bridge** (Bridge of the Americas, or the "free bridge") enters the suburb of San Lorenzo, just east of the city; and the **Stanton Street Bridge** (toll) is one way into downtown Ciudad Juárez. Toll fees are $2 per vehicle; pedestrians 30c. **Note:** The Cordoba Bridge is the only city crossing that processes the paperwork necessary for vehicle travel beyond the border area.

A newer border crossing at Santa Teresa in New Mexico, just west of the El Paso/Ciudad Juárez area, can be used to bypass the cities. This port of entry also can process the paperwork necessary for travel into the interior.

Motorists returning to the United States from downtown Juárez must use the northbound-only **Paseo del Norte Bridge** (toll) via Avenida Juárez or the free Bridge of the Americas via Avenida Lincoln. Toll fees are $2 per vehicle; pedestrians 70c. Dollars or pesos are accepted when entering or departing Mexico or the United States. Baggage may be inspected at the customs offices. Both Mexican and U.S. customs and immigration offices are open 24 hours daily.

Juárez is an interesting blend of both countries, where markets offer local products ranging from pottery to fruit. The traditional downtown shopping area is close to the border, along Avenida Juárez. English is as widely spoken as Spanish. AAA/CAA members can obtain auto insurance and make arrangements for bus tours of the city through the El Paso office of AAA Texas.

Just across the Bridge of the Americas on Avenida de las Américas is **El Chamizal National Park**. Mexico claimed El Chamizal after the Mexican-American War established the Río Grande as the international border in 1848. However, the park fell into U.S. possession when the river changed its course 16 years later. In 1964 U.S. President Lyndon Johnson returned approximately 640 acres to Mexico, a goodwill gesture initiated by John F. Kennedy. The land, reduced in size since then, is now used in reforestation efforts. The park offers several recreational facilities, including a wave pool and another pool with a toboggan run.

Bullfights are staged in the **Plaza de Toros Monumental**, Avenida 16 de Septiembre near the junction of Boulevard López Mateos and Mex. 45. Traditionally, the first *corrida de toros* of the season begins in spring, often on or near Easter Sunday. Thereafter, *corridas* are held on occasional Sundays (often in conjunction with long U.S. holiday weekends) through Labor Day, although scheduling decisions are often made on short notice.

From April through October *charreadas*, Mexican-style rodeos, take place on Sundays at the **Lienzo Charro Adolfo López Mateos**, on the Pan American Highway at Avenida del Charro. Horse racing is offered on some Sundays from mid-May to late September. During the rest of the year, greyhounds race at the *galgódromo* (dog track), north of the country club in Colonia Manuel Doblado.

Expo-Juárez, usually held in June, is a large fair with commercial, industrial, agricultural, livestock and crafts exhibits.

Note: In recent years Ciudad Juárez has become a center of narcotics smuggling along the border. Exercise caution if visiting the nightspots in the entertainment district west of Avenida Juárez.

CENTRO ARTESANAL (Arts and Crafts Center) displays and sells handicrafts from throughout Mexico. Glass, jewelry, pottery, textiles and leather goods range in style from pre-Columbian to contemporary. Free.

MUSEO DE ARTE E HISTORIA (Museum of Art and History) depicts the archeology, arts and crafts of Mexico through lectures and movies. Admission is charged; students with ID and under 12 free.

WHERE TO STAY

FIESTA INN
▼▼▼▼ *Motor Inn* ((16)86-0700

1/1-11/30	$85	XP $7
12/1-12/31	$80	XP $6

Location: 3.7 km e on Mex 45. Paseo Triunfo de la Republica 3451 32315. Fax: 16/86-0701. **Facility:** Large modern facility with well appointed rooms and attractive public areas. Near the border, International Bridge and the northern part of the city. Secure, underground parking. 166 units, 8 with efficiency. 9 stories, interior corridors. **Parking:** valet. **Terms:** F12. **Amenities:** voice mail. *Some:* hair dryers. **Leisure Activities:** heated pool, whirlpool, exercise room. **Guest Services:** gift shop, valet laundry. **Business Services:** conference facilities, administrative services, PC, fax. **Cards:** AE, DI, MC, VI.

SOME UNITS

HILTON GARDEN INN
▼▼▼▼ *Hotel* ((16)29-0994

All Year	$95	XP $10

Location: 10 km e on Mex 45. Avenida Tecnologico 3750 32612. Fax: 16/18-5827. **Facility:** Near major industrial parks. Well appointed rooms and public areas. 120 units. 5 stories, interior corridors. **Terms:** F12; cancellation fee imposed. **Amenities:** voice mail, irons, hair dryers. **Leisure Activities:** heated pool, whirlpool, exercise room. **Guest Services:** area transportation, valet laundry. **Business Services:** meeting rooms, administrative services. **Cards:** AE, DI, MC, VI.

FEE

SOME UNITS

HOLIDAY INN EXPRESS
▼▼▼▼ *Motel* ((16)29-6000

12/1-12/31 & 7/1-11/30	$87	XP $8
1/1-6/30	$83	XP $8

Location: 4 km e. 3745 Triunfo de La Republica 32310. Fax: 16/29-6020. **Facility:** Located near large shopping mall. Ample paved parking. Connected to Sanborn's which has restaurant and lounge service. 148 units. 4 stories, interior corridors. **Terms:** F12; 3 day cancellation notice. **Amenities:** extended cable TV, voice mail, irons, hair dryers. **Leisure Activities:** exercise room. **Guest Services:** [CP] meal plan available. **Business Services:** meeting rooms. **Cards:** AE, MC, VI.

SOME UNITS

ⓐ HOLIDAY INN-LINCOLN
▼▼▼▼ *Motor Inn* ((16)13-1310

All Year	$118-$124

Location: 3.5 km s of Bridge of the Americas. Ave Lincoln & Coyoacan 32310. Fax: 16/13-0084. **Facility:** Ample paved parking with security. Attractive grounds. Traditional room decor. 174 units. 5 two-bedroom units. 2 stories, exterior corridors. **Terms:** 7 day cancellation notice. **Amenities:** extended cable TV, voice mail, irons, hair dryers. **Dining:** dining room, 7 am-11 pm, $4-$12, cocktails. **Leisure Activities:** heated pool, exercise room. **Guest Services:** complimentary laundry. **Business Services:** meeting rooms. **Cards:** AE, MC, VI.

SOME UNITS

HOTEL COLONIAL
▼▼ *Motor Inn* (16/13-5161

All Year	$74	XP $5

Location: 3 km s of Bridge of the Americas. Lincoln & Ave de Las Americas 32310. Fax: 16/13-4081. **Facility:** Conveniently located near malls and International Bridge. This hotel has a traditional local flavor. 229 units, 9 with efficiency. Some whirlpool units. 3 stories, exterior corridors. **Terms:** F12. **Leisure Activities:** 2 heated pools, wading pool. **Guest Services:** [CP] meal plan available. **Cards:** AE, MC, VI.

HOTEL LUCERNA
▼▼▼▼ *Hotel* ((16)29-9900

All Year	$71-$102	XP $17

Location: P T de la Rep 3976 32310. Fax: 16/13-3778. **Facility:** Attractive lobby and courtyard. Traditional decor. 138 units. 8 stories, interior corridors. **Terms:** F12. **Amenities:** voice mail, hair dryers. **Leisure Activities:** wading pool, whirlpool, exercise room. **Guest Services:** gift shop, valet laundry. **Business Services:** meeting rooms. **Cards:** AE, DI, MC, VI.

SOME UNITS

RADISSON HOTEL CASA GRANDE CD JUAREZ

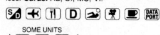 *Motor Inn* (16/29-4000

All Year $70 XP $15
Location: 10 km e on Chihuahua Hwy (Mex 45). Ave Tec-nologico 3620 32617. Fax: 16/29-4033. **Facility:** Modern, well-appointed rooms and public areas. 145 units. 4 stories, interior corridors. **Terms:** F12. **Amenities:** extended cable TV, voice mail, irons, hair dryers. **Leisure Activities:** heated pool, exercise room. **Guest Services:** gift shop, valet laun-dry. **Business Services:** meeting rooms, administrative serv-ices. **Cards:** AE, DI, MC, VI.

SOME UNITS

WHERE TO DINE

SHANGRI-LA RESTAURANT

Continental (16/13-0033
L $8-$20   D $8-$20
Location: 4.5 km sw of Bridge of the Americas. Ave de Las Americas 133 32310. **Hours:** 11 am-1 am. **Reservations:** suggested. **Features:** casual dress; cock-tails & lounge; valet parking; a la carte. Oriental decor. **Cards:** AE, MC, VI.

CIUDAD OBREGON, SONORA

WHERE TO STAY

HOLIDAY INN CD OBREGON

Motor Inn (641/4-0940

All Year $68 XP $10
Location: 1.2 km n on Mex 15. Ave Aleman & Tetabiate 85000 (PO Box 39, OBREGON, SO). Fax: 641/3-4194. **Facility:** At-door parking with security. 135 units. *Bath:* combo or shower only. 2 stories, exterior corridors. **Terms:** F12. **Amenities:** safes, irons, hair dryers. *Some:* honor bars. **Leisure Activities:** wading pool. **Business Services:** meeting rooms, administrative services. **Cards:** AE, MC, VI.

SOME UNITS

OBREGON PLAZA HOTEL

Motor Inn (641/4-3830

All Year $53-$68 XP $5
Location: Center. Miguel Aleman 200 N y Allende 85000. Fax: 641/4-3830. **Facility:** Located in a commercial area, near center of town. 89 units. *Bath:* shower only. 3 stories (no elevator), exterior corridors. **Terms:** F12. **Amenities:** *Some:* hair dryers. **Leisure Activities:** wading pool. **Business Services:** meeting rooms. **Cards:** AE, MC, VI.

SOME UNITS

COPPER CANYON, CHIHUAHUA (D-4)

The **Barranca del Cobre** (Copper Canyon) area of northwestern Mexico was created by more than 60 million years of erosion, volcanic eruptions and faults. Elevations in this region vary from 7,500 to 9,500 feet, with a few peaks reaching 12,000 feet.

The Copper Canyon is the domain of the Tarahumara Indians. Of all Mexico's native peoples, they have perhaps been the most suc-cessful in preserving their centuries-old culture by dwelling in the shadow of vast mountains and in the isolation of caves set in deep canyons. The Tarahumara are renowned for running feats, per-formed by both men and women. These mara-thons of stamina last as long as 3 days and nights.

Traveling across the rugged Sierra Madre Mountains, the **Chihuahua al Pacífico** railway offers rail excursions from Chihuahua to Los Mochis and Topolobampo through the spectacu-larly rugged scenery of this outstanding natural area. The rail line was begun in the late 19th century, envisioned as the shortest trade route linking Kansas City with Mexico's Pacific coast. Finally finished in 1961, it made engineering his-tory after intermittent work was delayed by lack of funds, the 1910 Revolution and what seemed like insurmountable terrain and engineering prob-lems associated with crossing the Sierra Madre. Years of construction, 39 bridges and 87 tunnels were required to move a train from sea level to a maximum altitude of 8,056 feet.

Travel to this remote region, which has in-creased markedly in recent years, is seen as one way of stemming the uncontrolled logging that continues to take place. Copper Canyon travel packages—many emphasizing an ecotourism angle—feature coach tours and might also in-clude guided hiking or horseback riding expedi-tions or overnight camping trips to canyon-bottom locations. Chihuahua al Pacífico was privatized in 1998; the owner, FerroMex, has re-furbished the first-class passenger train service popular with tourists and tightened security mea-sures. Second-class passenger trains, used as transportation by locals, are not recommended for touring unless you want an authentic Mexi-can experience (complete with livestock). Also sharing the rails are deluxe private cars operated by U.S.-based tour companies.

Ferromex's first-class service features air-conditioned cars, reclining seats and picture win-dows. Although most first-class trains have dining car service, and vendors at stops hawk homemade burritos and other items, passengers may want to pack their own food. It's also a good idea to bring water and toilet paper, both of which may not be replenished on the train.

Allow plenty of time for the journey: First-class trains departing Chihuahua or Los Mochis in the early morning take anywhere from 14 to 17 hours (depending on whether there are weather-related delays) to cover the 654-kilometer (406-mile) distance. You may also want to spend at least one night en route to better experience what the region has to offer. During the winter months, leaving from Los Mochis guarantees seeing the most spectacular scenery in full daylight; coming from the opposite direction, towering canyon walls can block the last rays of the sun and magnify the gathering gloom of evening. Summer's extended daylight hours, however, make this decision less crucial.

The most convenient way to tour the Copper Canyon is to take one of the all-inclusive trip packages offered by U.S. tour companies. Rail Travel Center offers an 8-day excursion aboard the "Sierra Madre Express," with domed cars recalling the early days of leisurely train travel. The trip departs from Tucson, Ariz. For additional information, contact Rail Travel Center, 2 Federal St., Suite 101A, St. Albans, VT 05478; phone (800) 458-5394 in the United States or Canada.

The best time of year to take the train trip is in October or November, when the weather is still warm, the June-September rainy season is over and the leaves are at their most colorful. Those planning to visit villages deep in the canyons should keep in mind that temperatures rise with the descent in altitude.

Creel (see separate listing) is the approximate midway point and center of the region inhabited by the Tarahumara. The most spectacular scenery, ranging from dense forest and lush plantations below to craggy peaks and twisted rock formations above, lies between El Divisadero and Témoris.

From subtropical lowlands near the Pacific Coast, the train ascends—by means of a spectacular series of loops and reverse turns—to pine-forested uplands. At **El Divisadero**, it stops for about 15 minutes so passengers—somewhat hurriedly—can view the steep sides and pine-clad ridges of the canyon complex and, using gestures, bargain for woven baskets and other handcrafted souvenirs sold by the Tarahumara. Here, at about 7,400 feet, the canyon cliffs are a vast, overlapping series of rust-colored walls. Prominent overhangs offer canyon vistas that can truly be described as magnificent.

Hotels in Creel can arrange for guided day or overnight trips to towns on the canyon floor. Rough paved or dirt-gravel roads descend from Creel to the towns of **Cusárare**, **Basíhuare** and **Batopilas**; from Bahuichivo to Cerocahui; and from Témoris to Chínipas. Rusticity is the keynote characteristic of any Copper Canyon exploring excursion. Most lodgings, while comfortable, lack electricity and telephones. The ride to canyon-bottom towns—usually in a school bus—is dusty and can be bone-jarring. Sturdy walking shoes are absolutely essential for exploring; even guided hikes may involve anything from fording a brook to clambering over fallen logs. Also make certain that a hired guide is

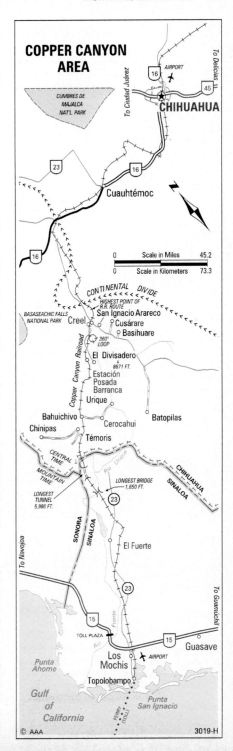

COPPER CANYON AREA

thoroughly familiar with your destination, for much of this area still is authentic wilderness.

From the train station at Bahuichivo, a trip can be arranged to the mountain village of **Cerocahui**. The town has a Jesuit mission established in the late 17th century; Jesuit priests proselytized widely among the Tarahumara Indians. From Cerocahui it is possible to visit a vantage point that overlooks Urique Canyon, one of the main gorges in the Copper Canyon region. Hiking to nearby waterfalls is an exhilarating way to enjoy the scenery. In addition, local hotels can arrange round-trip excursions from Bahuichivo to the canyon-bottom village of Urique. Cusárare, about 19 kilometers (12 miles) from Creel, also has a Jesuit mission built for the Tarahumara. In the vicinity is **Lake Arareco** *(see Creel)* and an area of volcanic rock formations that resemble mushrooms.

A trip to Batopilas, in the depths of a canyon about 129 kilometers (80 miles) southwest of Creel, is an 8-hour adventure if taken by local bus. The narrow, dusty dirt road to the bottom passes **Cerro El Pastel** ("Cake Mountain"), aptly named for its alternating layers of pink and white volcanic rock. The Urique and Basíhuare rivers trace tight, meandering paths before their headwaters lose themselves in unnamed chasms. As the route descends, temperatures rise, and forests of cactus replace stands of pine.

Batopilas itself is a former silver-mining town. It began to boom in the 1740s, although mining operations had been in existence for more than 100 years before that. According to local legend, the town's cobblestone streets were once paved with silver. Distinctly different from the canyon-top villages, Batopilas has whitewashed houses, swaying palm trees and gardens of subtropical flowers—temperatures here are some 30 degrees warmer than at the top of the canyon. Local ranchers ride into town on horseback, and it's not unusual to see such livestock as goats and pigs wandering the streets. Accommodations for overnight stays are modest.

Noteworthy fiestas focusing on Indian rituals are held during *Holy Week* (Palm Sunday to Easter Sunday) and during Christmas in Cusárare, Chínipas, San Ignacio Arareco and other Tarahumara towns.

CREEL, CHIHUAHUA (D-5) elev. 7,650'

The logging village of Creel (creh-EHL) was once the western terminus of the Chihuahua al Pacífico Railway; it is now the approximate midway point. Although the quantity of pine shipped from the vicinity has diminished over the years, active lumber camps still operate.

Creel retains much of its raw charm despite an ever-developing tourist industry. Almost every lodging, restaurant and service is on or within walking distance of the main street, López Mateos. Men ride by on horseback, and brightly dressed Tarahumara Indian women sell pottery and baskets from the curbsides. Several shops also sell Tarahumara arts and crafts, which include rugs, wood carvings, necklaces, dolls and violins. A concrete statue of Christ gazes down from the cliffs north of town, testimony to the Jesuit priests who have ministered to the Tarahumara since the early 17th century.

This is the largest settlement in the Copper Canyon area and makes a good base for exploration of the region. Dirt-gravel roads lead to Tarahumara villages at the edges of scenic canyons. **Basaseáchic Falls National Park** *(see the "Mexico's National Parks" box on page 31)* is about 5 hours away via a paved road running from Creel north to the Mex. 16 junction, then west on Mex. 16 to the park. **Note:** If you're planning to drive to the Copper Canyon area, fill the gas tank in Chihuahua or the town of La Junta, on Mex. 16. Driving time from Chihuahua to Creel is about 3 1/2 hours; a sturdy vehicle is recommended.

LAGO ARARECO (Lake Arareco), 7 kilometers (4 miles) south on a paved road, is a horseshoe-shaped, man-made lake surrounded by diversified forest and oddly-shaped rock formations. Lodging, horseback riding, boat rental and food service facilities are available. Fishing and camping are permitted.

WHERE TO STAY

BEST WESTERN THE LODGE AT CREEL
▼▼▼   *Motor Inn*   ((141)3-9020
12/1-4/30 & 9/1-11/30	$85-$93	XP $10
5/1-8/31	$65-$85	

Location: Center. Lopez Mateos 61 33200. Fax: 141/4-6690. **Facility:** 27 units. 1 story, exterior corridors. **Terms:** 3 day cancellation notice. **Guest Services:** gift shop. **Business Services:** meeting rooms. **Cards:** AE, MC, VI.

🍽 🍸 ✕ 🏋 ⚐ 🖵 DATA PORT

CREEL COPPER CANYON HOTEL
▼   *Motor Inn*   ((145)6-0666
All Year	$55-$65	XP $15

Location: Center. Lopez Mateos S/N 33200. **Facility:** Rustic log cabins. Adjacent to KOA. 20 units, 2 with kitchen. *Bath:* shower only. 1 story, exterior corridors. **Terms:** F12; 3 day cancellation notice. **Amenities:** no TVs. **Leisure Activities:** playground. **Cards:** AE, MC, VI.

SOME UNITS
$⓪ 🍽 🍸 ✕ ☎ / 🛏 /

MARGARITA'S PLAZA MEXICANA
▼   *Motel*   ((145)6-0245
All Year	$50	XP $3

Location: Elefido Batista S/N 33200. Fax: 145/6-0245. **Facility:** Enclosed courtyard. 26 units. *Bath:* combo or shower only. 2 stories, exterior corridors. **Parking:** extra charge. **Guest Services:** [MAP] meal plan available.

🛏 🍽 🏋 ☎

MOTEL PARADOR DE LA MONTANA

▼▼▼ *Motel* ☏ 145/6-0075

All Year $54 XP $3
Location: Center. Calle Lopez Mateos 41 (Apartado Postal 15). Fax: 145/6-0085. **Facility:** 24 hour phone service. 50 units. *Bath:* shower only. 2 stories, exterior corridors. **Terms:** F12. **Leisure Activities:** Fee: horseback riding. **Guest Services:** valet laundry. **Business Services:** meeting rooms. **Cards:** AE, MC, VI.

CULIACAN, SINALOA (F-4)

Culiacán (coo-lee-ah-CAN), founded by *conquistador* Nuño de Guzmán in 1533, is located in the hot, humid lowlands near the southern end of the Gulf of California. The capital of the state of Sinaloa is a prosperous but sprawling and not particularly attractive city. It offers little for tourists other than a brief stopping place to refuel or refresh if you're driving the length of Mex. 15/15-D. Those just passing through will find traffic patterns confusing. A complicated interchange just south of Culiacán links Sinaloa Hwy. 1 (SIN-1), Mex. 15 and Mex. 15-D. Poor signage greets motorists who are heading north and attempting to access SIN-1.

Note: SIN-1, a four-lane, divided toll highway, runs parallel to and west of free Mex. 15 from Guamúchil to south of Culiacán. The condition of alternate Mex. 15 between these two cities is substandard. Another four-lane, divided toll highway, Mex. 15-D, extends from Culiacán south to Mazatlán, allowing for quicker travel than alternate Mex. 15. The condition of nontoll Mex. 15 from Culiacán south to Tepic, the Nayarit state capital, also tends to be substandard. Said to be particularly rough are the 64 kilometers (40 miles) between the town of Acaponeta, south of Mazatlán, and the Río San Pedro bridge, a stretch marked by broken pavement and narrow shoulders.

WHERE TO STAY

🔺🔺🔺 **HOTEL EXECUTIVO**

▼▼ *Hotel* ☏ (67)13-9300

12/23-2/5 $130-$140 XP $30
12/1-12/22 & 9/19-11/30 $80-$85 XP $30
2/6-9/18 $75-$80 XP $30
Location: Center of town; just n of jct Francisco I Madero and Obregon. (Blvd Fransisco I Madero & Obregon, 80000). Fax: 67/13-9300. **Facility:** 230 units. 6 stories, interior corridors. **Terms:** F12; cancellation fee imposed. **Amenities:** voice mail. *Some:* honor bars. **Dining & Entertainment:** 2 restaurants, coffee shop, 7 am-1 am, $7-$20, cocktails, entertainment. **Leisure Activities:** gift shop, exercise room. **Guest Services:** gift shop, valet laundry. **Business Services:** meeting rooms, administrative services, fax. **Cards:** AE, DI, MC, VI.

SOME UNITS

HOTEL SAN LUIS LINDA VISTA

▼▼▼▼ *Hotel* ☏ 67/16-7010

All Year $65-$95
Location: 1.8 km s on Ave Alvaro Obregon. Ave Las Palmas 1 80220 (PO Box 312). Fax: 67/15-0815. **Facility:** On a hill, offering a panoramic view of the city. 16 units with balcony. Very good to excellent rooms. 90 units. 5 two-bedroom units. Some whirlpool units ($195). *Bath:* combo or shower only. 2-5 stories, interior corridors. **Amenities:** hair dryers. **Dining:** El Mirador, see separate listing. **Leisure Activities:** small pool. **Guest Services:** valet laundry. **Business Services:** meeting rooms. **Cards:** AE, MC, VI.

SOME UNITS

WHERE TO DINE

EL MIRADOR

▼▼ ▼▼ *Steak & Seafood* ☏ 67/16-7010

L $10-$18 D $10-$18
Location: 1.8 km s on Ave Alvaro Obregon; in Hotel San Luis Linda Vista. Ave Las Palmas 80220. **Hours:** 7 am-11 pm. **Reservations:** suggested. **Features:** casual dress; cocktails; a la carte. Excellent panoramic views of the city. **Cards:** AE, MC, VI.

DELICIAS, CHIHUAHUA
WHERE TO STAY

HOTEL CASA GRANDE

▼▼▼ *Motor Inn* ☏ (14)74-0404

All Year $70 XP $14
Location: 6 blks e of center, just w of Mex 45. Ave 6 Oriente 601 33000. Fax: 14/74-0404. **Facility:** Modern structure with spacious atrium lobby and stylish guest rooms. 89 units. 3 stories, interior corridors. **Terms:** F12. **Amenities:** voice mail. **Leisure Activities:** heated pool, wading pool. **Guest Services:** gift shop, valet laundry. **Business Services:** meeting rooms. **Cards:** AE, DI, MC, VI.

SOME UNITS

WHERE TO DINE

LOS NOGALES RESTAURANTE

▼▼ ▼▼ *Mexican* ☏ 14/74-0404

L $8-$15 D $8-$15
Location: 6 blks e of center, just w of Mex 45; in Hotel Casa Grande. Ave 6 Oriente 601 33000. **Hours:** 7 am-11 pm. **Features:** casual dress; cocktails & lounge. Well prepared Mexican specialties, also good selection of meat, poultry and seafood selections. Well appointed dining room in covered atrium. **Cards:** AE, DI, MC, VI.

DURANGO, DURANGO (F-5) elev. 6,196'

Durango (doo-RAHN-goh) was founded in 1563 by Francisco de Ibarra and presumably named for Durango, Spain, the home of his parents. The settlement was an early Spanish outpost, and at one time the province known as

Nueva Vizcaya covered a huge area equal to the present-day states of Chihuahua, Durango, Sinaloa and Sonora. Conflict between Spaniards and Indians was particularly turbulent in this rough region; from the late 17th to early 18th centuries, provincial governors carried out their terms in the city of Parral, some 250 miles to the north.

A lumber and mining camp established at El Salto around the turn of the 20th century spurred growth. After a railway was constructed between El Salto and Mexico City, Durango became an important shipping point for lumber and minerals taken from the surrounding mountains. Today the city has a population of around 600,000 and is a major crossroads, sitting at the junction of Mex. 40, which connects Monterrey and Mazatlán, and Mex. 45, which leads to Mexico City.

The city, officially known as Victoria de Durango, rises from the level Guadiana Valley, which is bordered by the foothills of the Sierra Madre Occidental. Much of Durango's charm lies in a 17th- and 18th-century architectural legacy, for which it has been designated a national historic monument. Visitors passing through on the main roadways linking Mex. 40 and 45 will see few of the city's attractions; fortunately, the mild climate (due to elevation) makes it pleasant to explore Durango on foot.

The main plaza, between avenidas 20 de Noviembre and 5 de Febrero and calles Constitución and Juárez, has pretty gardens and a circular bandstand, and is the scene of Sunday concerts. Two blocks west of the plaza on Avenida 5 de Febrero is the **Palacio de Gobierno** (Government Palace), an 18th-century baroque building distinguished by its arcades. A block north is the **Teatro Ricardo Castro**, originally called the Teatro Principal but renamed for a Durangueño pianist and composer when it was renovated in 1990. Visiting music, theater and dance troupes use the theater, which has beautiful marble and tile flooring.

The **Mercado Municipal**, about 4 blocks east of the plaza between avenidas 20 de Noviembre and 5 de Febrero, is a typical Mexican market that stocks wool *sarapes,* leather goods and handicrafts, among many other items. Smaller shops cluster around the plaza itself. *Charreadas* (Mexican rodeos) are very popular, and there are several *charro* rings around town. Check with the State Tourism Office (*see next paragraph*) for schedule information. Two fairs held consecutively during the first half of July—one revolving around the founding of the city and the other an agricultural and ranching exposition—are Durango's biggest annual events. The festivities at both include live music, folkloric dance performances and exhibits of all types.

For information about the city and state visit the State Tourism Office (Dirección Estatal de Turismo), Calle Hidalgo Sur #408 (3 blocks west of the main plaza); phone (181) 1-2139. The Durango airport is northeast of the city. There are no direct flights from the United States; Aeroméxico and Aero California fly to Durango from Guadalajara, Mexico City and Torreón. The central bus station is northeast of downtown near the junction of avenidas Felipe Pescador and Colegio Militar (Mex. 40). Transportes del Norte offers "deluxe" bus service from Chihuahua, Ciudad Juárez, Mexico City, Monterrey and other Mexican cities. In town, the line running west from the station along Avenida 20 de Noviembre (the city's main east-west thoroughfare) is closest to downtown points of interest.

Local legend maintains that it was in a cave in one of the buttes punctuating the countryside north of Durango that Pancho Villa traded his soul to the Devil in return for mastery over other men. Villa was born Doroteo Arango in 1877 on a hacienda near the village of San Juan del Río, 110 kilometers (68 miles) north of Durango on Mex. 45.

The 320-kilometer (200-mile) journey west from Durango to Mazatlán via two-lane Mex. 40 passes some of Mexico's most spectacular scenery. The views of the Sierra Madre Occidental in this region are truly impressive, and the condition of the roadway is good. Make certain, however, that your vehicle is in tip-top shape; repair facilities between the two cities are nonexistent.

About 57 kilometers (35 miles) west of Durango is **Parque Nacional El Tecuán**, where cabins, campsites and picnic facilities are set in the midst of a pine forest. About 100 kilometers (62 miles) west is the rustic timber town of El Salto; south of El Salto is **Parque Nacional Puerta de los Angeles**, characterized by interesting geological formations, waterfalls and thick forests at elevations of up to 8,500 feet.

Beginning about 46 kilometers (29 miles) west of El Salto is **El Espinazo del Diablo** (The Devil's Backbone), a narrow, 5-mile-long mountain ridge with steep cliffs slanting down from the edges of the highway. Views of Mazatlán and the Pacific, more than 90 kilometers (55 miles) southwest, are possible on clear days. Mex. 40 through this region is a triumph of man's ingenuity over a challenging environment. The town of La Ciudad offers basic services for those continuing the trek southwestward to the coast.

WHAT TO SEE

CASA DEL CONDE DE SUCHIL (House of the Count of Suchil), 2 blocks east of the main plaza at Avenida 5 de Febrero and Calle Madero, is a fine example of mid-18th-century Spanish colonial architecture. Built for a wealthy landowner, the restored mansion's former grandeur is evident in such features as the tile accenting the floors and wooden wall paneling. The building is now occupied by a bank and several shops.

CATHEDRAL, is on Avenida 20 de Noviembre facing the north side of the main plaza. Construction was begun in 1695 and completed in 1750. This massive structure is surmounted by two square towers. The exterior is a mixture of styles, with baroque predominating. The entrance is richly decorated. Inside are choir stalls adorned with finely carved wooden figures of saints and apostles. Bell ringers in the towers are visible from the plaza.

EL CERRO DE MERCADO (Mercado Hill) is a hill of high-content iron ore just north of the city. Said to be one of the largest single iron deposits in existence, it rises some 700 feet above the surrounding plain and is still producing. The hill was named for the man who discovered it in 1552, Ginés Vázquez del Mercado.

MOVIE SETS, or *escenarios,* are permanent fixtures in this area. Durango's heyday as a moviemaking center began in the 1950s and continued through the '70s, as actors like John Wayne, Burt Lancaster and Robert Ryan came here to make Hollywood westerns. Among the classics shot in the vicinity was Sam Peckinpah's "The Wild Bunch." The trend slowed in the '80s as the western genre declined, although location filming still takes place occasionally. Many Mexican productions also have used Durango as a backdrop. Filmmakers favor the state for its consistently sunny weather, inexpensive labor pool and relative lack of power lines and other telltale signs of modern life.

Group tours of local movie sets can be taken on weekends. Make arrangements at the State Cinematography Office (Dirección Estatal de Cinematografía), located in the same building as the State Tourism Office.

Chupaderos is about 14 kilometers (9 miles) north of Durango on Mex. 45. An actual Mexican village, it has been used for filming more than any other area location. The town's original buildings have been augmented over the years by Old West-style structures. A few kilometers south on Mex. 45 is **Villa del Oeste,** a village that first came into being as a constructed "western" town.

Los Alamos is about 29 kilometers (18 miles) south of Durango on the paved road to the village of La Flor; take Boulevard Domingo Arrieta (about 7 blocks east of the main plaza) south out of town. This set was built to re-create the town of Los Alamos, New Mexico, for the 1989 film "Fat Man and Little Boy," about the development of the atomic bomb. The canyon scenery en route is impressive.

EL FUERTE, SINALOA
WHERE TO STAY

HOTEL POSADA DEL HIDALGO
▼▼ ▼▼   *Historic Motor Inn*   ☏ 689/3-0242
All Year $80
Location: From Hwy 15, just s of km 55, 55 km e on rural paved road; just ne of main plaza. Hidalgo 101 818200 (PO Box 24, 81200). Fax: 681/2-0046. **Facility:** Some guest rooms and public areas constructed in 1890. Attractive gardens. Historic building located in center of town. Convenient for train tour of Copper Canyon. Automobiles may be left here while on the tour. Tour tickets available here. 50 units. 2 two-bedroom units. *Bath:* shower only. 2 stories, exterior corridors. **Terms:** 14 day cancellation notice, 12/15-4/30. **Amenities:** no TVs. **Leisure Activities:** small pool. **Business Services:** meeting rooms. **Cards:** AE, MC, VI.

ESTACION POSADA BARRANCA, CHIHUAHUA
WHERE TO STAY

HOTEL POSADA BARRANCA AT THE RIM
▼▼ ▼▼   *Hotel*   ☏ (681)8-7046
All Year $190   XP $60
Location: 3 km se of El Divisadero Station; accessible only by train. Estacion Posada Barranca. Fax: 681/2-0046. **Facility:** In remote area at canyon's edge. All rooms with private balcony overlooking canyon. 45 units. *Bath:* shower only. 2 stories, exterior corridors. **Terms:** 5 day cancellation notice. **Amenities:** no TVs. **Guest Services:** [AP] meal plan available, gift shop. **Business Services:** meeting rooms. **Cards:** AE, DI, MC, VI.

HOTEL POSADA RANCHO
▼▼   *Lodge*   ☏ 681/8-7046
All Year $195
Location: 3 km se of El Divisadero Station; accessible only by train. Estacion Posada Barranca. Fax: 681/2-0046. **Facility:** In a remote area. All rooms with fireplace. Interesting garden. 35 units. *Bath:* shower only. 1 story, exterior corridors. **Terms:** 15 day cancellation notice-fee imposed. **Amenities:** no TVs. **Guest Services:** [AP] meal plan available, gift shop. **Business Services:** meeting rooms. **Cards:** AE, MC, VI.

GOMEZ PALACIO, DURANGO
WHERE TO STAY

HOTEL POSADA DEL RIO BEST WESTERN
▼▼▼▼   *Motor Inn*   ☏ 17/14-3399
All Year $75   XP $7
Location: 4 km s on Mex 49, which becomes Fco Madero, to Ave Juarez. Fco Madero y Ave Juarez 35000. Fax: 17/14-7483. **Facility:** Downtown. Ample parking with security. 100 units. *Bath:* shower only. 2 stories, interior/exterior corridors. **Terms:** F12. **Amenities:** *Some:* honor bars. **Dining:** El Parador, see separate listing. **Leisure Activities:** heated pool. **Guest Services:** gift shop. **Business Services:** meeting rooms. **Cards:** AE, MC, VI.

SOME UNITS

WHERE TO DINE

EL PARADOR

 Continental   (17/14-3399
                                    L $4-$6   **D** $4-$8
Location: 4 km s on Mex 49, which becomes Fco Madero, to Ave Juarez; in Hotel Posada del Rio Best Western. FCO Madero y Ave Juarez 35000. **Hours:** 7 am-11 pm. **Features:** casual dress; cocktails. Well prepared meat, poultry and seafood specialties. Also soup, sandwiches and some Mexican specialties. **Cards:** AE, MC, VI.

MARTIN'S RESTAURANT

 Mexican   (17/14-7541
                                    L $4-$16   **D** $4-$16
Location: 4 km s on Mex 40. Blvd Aleman y Victoria 27000. **Hours:** 7 am-midnight. **Features:** beer only. Mexican specialties, also a good selection of soup and sandwiches. **Cards:** AE, MC, VI.

GUAMUCHIL, SINALOA

WHERE TO STAY

MOTEL YORK

Motor Inn   (673/2-5777
All Year $40
Location: 1.5 km n on Mex 15. 81400 (PO Box 152). Fax: 673/2-5777. **Facility:** 80 units. 1 two-bedroom unit. Some whirlpool units ($40). *Bath:* shower only. 2 stories, exterior corridors. **Amenities:** extended cable TV. **Dining & Entertainment:** restaurant, 7 am-11 pm, $5-$10, cocktails, entertainment. **Leisure Activities:** playground. **Guest Services:** gift shop, valet laundry. **Business Services:** meeting rooms. **Cards:** AE, MC, VI.

SOME UNITS

GUAYMAS, SONORA (D-3)

Backed by bare mountains that advance almost to the coast, Guaymas (GWAY-mahs) is one of Mexico's principal seaports. The surrounding area was originally occupied by Indians known as Guaymenas, thought to be an offshoot of the Seri tribe. Spanish explorers discovered the region in the 1530s, but it wasn't until 1701 that a nearby mission was established jointly by Fathers Eusebio Francisco Kino and Juan María Salvatierra. The settlement of Guaymas was founded in 1769, and in 1814 it was opened to general trade as a Spanish-Mexican free port.

The next 100 years were turbulent. In 1847, during the Mexican-American War, the city was occupied by the U.S. Navy. In 1854 William Walker, the American filibuster known for his later exploits in Central America, landed in Guaymas with a band of adventurer "colonists" and unsuccessfully attempted to annex the state of Sonora. Walker also invaded Baja California, declaring it an independent republic and himself president; he was later forced out of Mexico. Around that same time the city was the scene of

more conflict when Count Gaston Raousset de Bourbon, a Frenchman, and 400 of his pirate followers tried to seize it, but they too were foiled.

Under Archduke Maximilian, the French finally did succeed in taking the port for a short time in 1865. During the U.S. Civil War, supplies destined for troops in Arizona were shipped to Guaymas from San Francisco, then transported overland. And in 1913, what is believed to be the world's first bombardment from an airplane took place when General Alvaro Obregón ordered an aerial attack against Mexico's federal army in the midst of the 1910 Revolution.

The old city sits along the shore of a fine natural harbor crowded with freighters, tankers and shrimp boats. This part of Guaymas is divided by a mountainous peninsula from the newer resort area, which spreads out to the northwest along Bacochibampo and San Carlos bays. The mountain backdrop, brilliant blue sky and equally blue gulf waters are best appreciated by strolling along the waterfront section of **Avenida Serdán**, the main east-west thoroughfare.

Two blocks to the north is the 19th-century **Iglesia de San Fernando** (Church of San Fernando). In front of the church is a small park complete with white wrought-iron bandstand and benches set under trees that provide welcome shade. Nearby, at Avenida Serdán and Calle 23, is the **Plaza de los Tres Presidentes**. In front of the Palacio Municipal (City Hall) on the plaza are statues honoring Plutarco Elías Calles, Adolfo de la Huerta and Abelardo Rodríguez, political leaders born in Sonora; Calles was president of Mexico 1924-28.

Native heritage is evident in the celebrations and ritual dances of the Yaqui Indians, who still inhabit the villages in the Yaqui River valley southeast of Guaymas. One of Mexico's most fiercely independent ethnic peoples, the Yaqui staged frequent rebellions against ruling governments during the 18th and 19th centuries. Politically assimilated into modern Mexico, the Yaqui have nevertheless maintained certain aspects of their culture, most notably the *Danza del Venado* (Stag Dance), which is performed both locally and at folkloric festivals throughout the country. The main participant wears a deer's head to enact the dance's symbolic representation of the battle between good and evil.

The beaches and resort areas west of the port city are distinctly separate entities. Closest to Guaymas is **Playa Miramar**, a residential area on Bacochibampo Bay, a few miles to the north. More developed is **San Carlos**, about 8 kilometers (5 miles) north on Mex. 15, then 24 kilometers (15 miles) west on a recently completed four-lane highway. Upscale condominiums, a marina and the most luxurious accommodations in Sonora attract well-to-do Mexicans and foreign tourists, but there also are inexpensive motels and RV parks catering to budget travelers. The San Carlos Country Club has an 18-hole golf course, among other amenities (non-members must pay fees). West of San Carlos is **Playa Algodones**, where the movie "Catch 22" was filmed in the late 1960s.

The Guaymas area is well known to deep-sea fishing enthusiasts. The warm gulf waters teem with fish—literally hundreds of different species can be found here. Prized catches include marlin, sailfish, yellowtail, corbina, sea bass and red snapper. Even the local oysters are celebrated for their flavor. Fishing excursions and sunset cruises can be arranged in San Carlos.

THE INFORMED TRAVELER

Aeroméxico offers direct flights to Guaymas from Tucson; for additional information about airlines see *"Arriving by Air," page 53*. Taxis provide service to and from the airport, which is located west of town. "Deluxe" bus service to border cities and other Mexican destinations is provided by Transportes del Pacífico. Schedule and fare information can be obtained at one of the city's three bus stations, all located at the intersection of Avenida Rodríguez and Calle 14, 2 blocks south of Avenida Serdán. In addition, local buses to Playa Miramar and San Carlos make stops at various points along Serdán.

Despite breezes coming off the water, Guaymas is uncomfortably hot (and often humid) during the summer months. The winter season, roughly November through March, is much more pleasant—warm days, rather cool nights and mostly sunny skies.

A tourist information office is at Avenida Serdán #441, between Calles 12 and 13 (2nd floor); phone (622) 4-2932 or 2-5667. The Sonora Department of Tourism operates an Arizona office that will send travel information by mail. Phone (602) 930-4871; for a recorded information menu from a fax phone, dial (602) 930-4815.

A private company, **Grupo Sematur**, offers round-trip, automobile-passenger ferry service between Guaymas and Santa Rosalía *(see separate listing under Baja California)* on the Baja California Peninsula. The ferry terminal is about a mile east of downtown on Avenida Serdán. Normal departures from Guaymas are on Tuesday and Friday at 8 a.m.; sailing time is about 9 hours. Schedules and rates are subject to change, however, and should be double-checked in advance. Phone (622) 2-3390 or 2-3393, or check with the Guaymas tourist office. For additional information about ferries see *"Ferry Service," page 64.*

HERMOSILLO, SONORA (D-3)

Capital of the state of Sonora, Hermosillo (ehr-moh-SEE-yo) rises abruptly from the sparsely settled terrain of northwestern Mexico. It was named after Jaliscan general José María González Hermosillo, a patriot in the Mexican War of Independence from Spain. Irrigation has turned the surrounding land into a productive agricultural area producing citrus fruits, melons, vegetables and cotton. A huge Ford assembly plant is representative of the region's industrial expansion. The most distinctive landmark is the rocky outcrop, right in the center of town, that is covered with a web of radio antennas.

Aside from the colonial-era architecture of the 18th-century **Catedral de la Asunción** (Cathedral of the Assumption), the **Palacio de Gobierno** (Government Palace) and the pink-hued **Palacio Municipal** (City Hall), most of Hermosillo looks blandly modern. **Plaza Zaragoza**, near the cathedral, provides welcome shade trees and an oasis from the crowded and frequently dusty downtown streets. Those willing to brave the heat, however, will find good buys on blankets, cowboy hats and boots, and other items in the shops that line avenidas Serdán and Monterrey. Several colorful murals decorate the Government Palace's tree-shaded inner courtyard.

Big and spread out, the city is not conducive to sightseeing but is a popular stop for motorists proceeding south to Pacific coast resorts. Aeroméxico flies direct from Tucson and from Los Angeles via Tijuana, and has direct flights to Hermosillo from Mexico City, Guadalajara and other Mexican cities. Aero California flies direct from Los Angeles and Tucson. "Deluxe" bus service from Nogales is provided by the Elite line. For visitor information from the Sonora Department of Tourism, phone (800) 476-6672 (from the United States).

Mex. 15, also called the Pacific Coast Highway, extends from the U.S. border at Nogales south and east to Mexico City. From the border to just north of Guamúchil in the state of Sinaloa, Mex. 15 is a four-lane highway, divided except for the stretch through Hermosillo and where it passes through some small towns and villages. Watch for occasional potholes and rocks, especially in the vicinity of hills or low mountains. As in much of Mexico, highway repair work is frequent, and traffic may be diverted to the two-lane stretch that is open. Periodic agricultural checkpoints and gun/drug checks may be encountered in each direction. These stops involve no monetary transactions and are normally routine; English is spoken, although a knowledge of Spanish is helpful.

Tollbooths are presently located just south of Magdalena; just north of the junction with Mex. 21, north of Hermosillo; on the Guaymas bypass road; at the Río Yaqui northwest of Ciudad Obregón; between Ciudad Obregón and Navojoa; south of Bacabachi; north of Los Mochis; southeast of Guasave; outside Culiacán; and north of Tepic. **Note:** Toll charges can go up without warning, and rates for different types of vehicles aren't always posted.

There also are sections of Mex. 15 that bypass Hermosillo and Guaymas. SIN-1 (Sinaloa Highway 1) is a toll alternative from Guamúchil south to Culiacán. Toll highway Mex. 15-D connects Culiacán and Mazatlán *(see Culiacán listing).*

Mex. 16 connects Hermosillo with Chihuahua and cuts through the Sierra Madre range. Before it opened, the only paved road running east-west through the Sierra Madres was Mex. 2, roughly paralleling the U.S. border between Agua Prieta and Janos in the state of Chihuahua. Mex. 16 is a narrow, two-lane blacktop without shoulders. There are many turns and steep grades, and horses, burros or grazing cattle may be encountered at almost any point. For the adventurous traveler with a reliable vehicle, the route offers breathtaking mountain scenery of canyons, cliffs, rivers and masses of vegetation.

Mex. 16 also can be used to access the Copper Canyon area *(see Copper Canyon listing).* Those who do decide to travel on Mex. 16 should keep in mind that viewing scenic areas or dealing with a flat tire will require stopping on the roadway. There are no guardrails, and rock falls from the cliffs above may require sudden stops or veering into the opposite lane. Due to a lack of service stations, make sure your gas tank is full before starting out.

Saltwater fishing is the main attraction at the Gulf of California resort town of **Bahía Kino**, some 105 kilometers (65 miles) southwest of Hermosillo via Mex. 16. Named for Jesuit missionary Francisco Eusebio Kino, this was long a hideaway known only to a few intrepid RV owners. Lately condominiums and secluded vacation homes have been springing up, although the mountain-backed beaches of golden sand for the most part remain unspoiled. Tourist facilities are concentrated in **Kino Nuevo** (New Kino), which is separated by some 4 kilometers (2.5 miles) of open beach from **Kino Viejo**, the Mexican village. The beaches are practically deserted during the summer months, but they also are blazingly hot.

Across a narrow channel is **Isla Tiburón** (Shark Island), currently being developed into a game and wildlife refuge. A special permit is necessary to visit the island; check with one of the hotels or RV parks in town regarding guide service. About 24 kilometers (15 miles) north of Bahía Kino via a winding gravel road is the fishing village of **Punta Chueca**, where Seri Indians offer wood carvings and shell necklaces for sale.

WHAT TO SEE

CENTRO ECOLOGICO DE SONORA (Sonora Ecological Center) is about 3 kilometers (2 miles) south of the city on Mex. 15. This zoological park exhibits flora and fauna native to the region's varied ecosystems, from arid desert to the rich marine environment of the Gulf of California. Snakes, tortoises, sea lions and the Mexican gray wolf can all be seen. A highlight are the more than 300 species of cacti, many of them labeled. The zoo covers a large area and thus is more pleasant to walk during the cooler winter months. Bottled water is available. Open Wed.-Sun. Admission is charged.

MUSEO REGIONAL DE LA UNIVERSIDAD DE SONORA (Regional Museum of the University of Sonora), calles Luis Encinas and Rosales, has exhibits relating to the Yaqui, Mayo, Pima, Pápago and Seri Indian groups. Also on view are photographs of Mexican Revolution activities in Sonora, exhibits pertaining to the local history of the area and the university, and numismatic collections. Open Wed.-Sun. Admission is charged.

MUSEO REGIONAL DE SONORA (Regional Museum of Sonora) sits on the eastern slope of Cerra de la Campana (Hill of the Bells), which overlooks the city. It is housed in a former penitentiary dating from the beginning of the 20th century. Some of the underground dungeons and wards have been preserved. The museum's archeological, ethnological and historical exhibits emphasize northwestern Mexico. Open Wed.-Sun. Admission is charged.

WHERE TO STAY

ARAIZA INN

 *Hotel* ☎ (62)10-2717

All Year $80   XP $5
Location: 4 km ne on Mex 15. Blvd Eusebio Kino 353 83010. Fax: 62/10-4541. **Facility:** Located in a commercial area near other hotels. Attractive rooms; secured parking lot. 157 units. 4 stories, interior/exterior corridors. **Terms:** F12. **Leisure Activities:** lighted tennis court, exercise room. **Guest Services:** gift shop, valet laundry. **Business Services:** meeting rooms, administrative services. **Cards:** AE, MC, VI.

SOME UNITS

BEST WESTERN SENORIAL HOTEL

Hotel ☎ 62/15-5958

All Year $60   XP $6
Location: 3.6 km ne on Mex 15. Guillermo Carpena 203 83010. Fax: 62/15-5093. **Facility:** Modern exterior. Located in a commercial area near other hotels. 68 units. Some whirlpool units. 5 stories, interior corridors. **Terms:** F12. **Leisure Activities:** small heated pool. **Business Services:** meeting rooms. **Cards:** AE, MC, VI.

SOME UNITS

HOLIDAY INN HERMOSILLO

 *Motor Inn* ((62)14-4570

7/1-11/30	$135	XP $30
1/1-6/30	$123	XP $30
12/1-12/31	$112	XP $20

Location: 3.8 km ne on Mex 15. Blvd Kino y Ramon Corral 83010 (PO Box 988). Fax: 62/14-6473. **Facility:** Balcony or patio. Secured parking. 132 units. *Bath:* combo or shower only. 3 stories, interior/exterior corridors. **Amenities:** voice mail, safes, irons, hair dryers. **Leisure Activities:** wading pool. **Guest Services:** gift shop. **Business Services:** meeting rooms. **Cards:** AE, MC, VI.

SOME UNITS

HOTEL BUGAMBILIA

 *Motor Inn* (62/14-5050

All Year $65

Location: 3.8 km ne on Mex 15. Blvd Kino 712 83010. Fax: 62/14-5252. **Facility:** Located in a commercial area on east side of town. At-door parking with security. 104 units. *Bath:* shower only. 1-3 stories (no elevator), exterior corridors. **Terms:** 3 day cancellation notice. **Guest Services:** [BP] meal plan available. **Cards:** AE, MC, VI.

AAA HOTEL FIESTA AMERICANA HERMOSILLO

 Hotel ((62)59-6000

All Year $159-$173 XP $14

Location: 4.5 km n on Mex 15. Blvd Kino 83010. Fax: 62/59-6060. **Facility:** Attractive public areas and guest rooms. Ample parking with security. 225 units. Some whirlpool units. 11 stories, interior corridors. **Parking:** valet. **Terms:** F12; 3 day cancellation notice-fee imposed. **Amenities:** voice mail, honor bars, irons, hair dryers. *Some:* safes. **Dining & Entertainment:** restaurant, coffee shop, 6 am-midnight, $7-$25, cocktails, also, La Hacienda Restaurant, see separate listing, nightclub, entertainment. **Leisure Activities:** wading pool, lighted tennis court, exercise room. **Guest Services:** gift shop, complimentary evening beverages, airport transportation-hotel, valet laundry. **Business Services:** conference facilities, administrative services, PC, fax. **Cards:** AE, DI, MC, VI. *(See color ad p 36)*

SOME UNITS

WHERE TO DINE

LA HACIENDA RESTAURANT

 Mexican (62/59-6000

D $7-$25

Location: 4.5 km n on Mex 15; in Hotel Fiesta Americana Hermosillo. Blvd Kino 369 83010. **Hours:** 6 am-midnight. Closed: Sun. **Reservations:** suggested. **Features:** casual dress; children's menu; cocktails; valet parking. Regional Mexican specialties including an extensive variety of steak. **Cards:** AE, DI, MC, VI. *(See color ad below)*

SANBORNS RESTAURANT

Mexican (62/14-7966

L $5-$12 D $5-$12

Location: 2 km sw on Bahia Kino Hwy. Blvds Navarrete y Luis Encinas 83010. **Hours:** 7 am-1 am. **Features:** casual dress; cocktails; a la carte, buffet. Casual. Good selection of soup and sandwiches. Well-prepared Mexican specialties. **Cards:** AE, MC, VI.

The following restaurant has not been evaluated by AAA and is listed for your information only.

VILLA CENTARIO

[fyi] (62/17-5040

Not evaluated. **Location:** Just w of the Cathedral. Dr Paliza y Campodonico 83000. Casual restaurant with local flavor located in a quiet residential neighborhood.

LOS MOCHIS, SINALOA (E-4)

Los Mochis (los MO-chees) was founded in 1893 by Benjamin Johnston, who arrived from Pennsylvania to grow sugar cane. Johnston also founded the **Ingenio Azucarero**, an enormous sugar refinery around which the city developed; visitors can tour the building.

Los Mochis is the major coastal terminus of the **Chihuahua al Pacífico Railway**, which travels across the rugged Sierra Madre Occidental to Chihuahua via the spectacular **Barranca del Cobre** (Copper Canyon) region *(see Copper Canyon listing).*

Technically the end of the rail line is 24 kilometers (15 miles) south at Topolobampo. This

deep sea port, known for its shrimp fleet and fishing, is connected by ferry to La Paz, B.C.S. Topolobampo's name, meaning "lion's watering place," is derived from the sea lion population occupying offshore **Isla Farallón**.

Topolobampo is the site of a colony developed in the late 19th century by a group of Americans headed by Alfred K. Owens, who originally conceived the Chihuahua-Pacífico Railway as part of a trade route linking Kansas City with Mexico's Pacific coast. Owens was an idealistic socialist intent on establishing a utopian community that would rival San Francisco in importance. Disillusioned followers and the ravages of typhoid eventually caused the colony to fail, and construction of the rail line faced a formidable obstacle burrowing through the Sierra Madre. Nevertheless, Owens' dream of success was realized in part; the completion of the line in 1961 brought new opportunities to the area.

Los Mochis is an agricultural boomtown and the export center of the state of Sinaloa. A dam on the Río Fuerte, part of a tri-river federal irrigation program in northern Sinaloa and southern Sonora, has increased the productivity of this semiarid region. The city is surrounded by mango trees and fields of cotton, wheat, rice, corn, tomatoes and sugar cane. What looks like acres of bright yellow carpet are actually marigolds, grown for the natural dye substance in their petals. When added to chicken feed, it enhances the yellow color so desirable in egg yolk.

Cártamo, or safflower, also is grown. Its seeds yield a dye, a drug and an edible oil that is a popular ingredient in fat-restricted diets as well as a paint-drying agent.

Direct U.S. flights to Los Mochis are offered by Aeroméxico. Aero California has daily flights to Los Mochis from Los Angeles.

A ferry operated by **Grupo Sematur** links Topolobampo with La Paz. There is no service from Topolobampo on Sunday. The trip departs in the morning and takes about 9 hours. Although there normally is a cafeteria or restaurant, it is advisable to bring your own food and beverages. Schedules and rates are subject to change and should be double-checked in advance; phone (68) 62-0141. "Baja Express" speedboat service makes a run from Topolobampo to La Paz in about 5 hours (no service on Wednesday), but it is more expensive than the Sematur ferry. For additional ferry information *see "Ferry Service," page 64*.

The Chihuahua-Pacífico Railway runs two first-class tourist trains daily between Los Mochis and Chihuahua. The train leaving Los Mochis eastbound for Chihuahua departs around 6 a.m. The journey takes about 12 hours; tickets can be purchased at the downtown hotels.

The Hotel Santa Anita, downtown on Avenida Gabriel Leyva, is a good orientation landmark.

The first-class bus station is nearby on Avenida Degollado. The local tourist information office is in the back of the Gobierno del Estado (State Government) building on Calle Allende; phone (68) 12-6640.

WHERE TO STAY

EL DORADO HOTEL Y MOTEL

Motor Inn ((68)15-1111

| All Year | $57 | XP $4 |

Location: 3.5 km w of Mex 15. Ave Gabriel Leyva & H Valdez 81200 (PO Box 412). Fax: 68/12-0179. **Facility:** 93 units. *Bath:* shower only. 2-3 stories, interior/exterior corridors. **Terms:** F12. **Leisure Activities:** playground. **Guest Services:** valet laundry. **Business Services:** meeting rooms. **Cards:** AE, MC, VI.

HOTEL SANTA ANITA

Hotel (68/18-7046

| All Year | $110 | XP $10 |

Location: Downtown. Gabriel Leyva & Hidalgo 81200 (PO Box 159). Fax: 68/18-0046. **Facility:** 122 units. *Bath:* shower only. 5 stories, interior corridors. **Terms:** F12; 7 day cancellation notice-fee imposed. **Dining:** restaurant, see separate listing. **Guest Services:** gift shop, valet laundry. **Business Services:** meeting rooms. **Cards:** AE, DI, MC, VI.

PLAZA INN

Motor Inn ((68)18-1043

| All Year | $110 | XP $12 |

Location: 0.5 km e. Ave Gabriel Leyva & Cardenas 81200 (PO Box 159). Fax: 68/18-1590. **Facility:** Ample at-door parking. Meets AAA guest room security requirements. 122 units. Some suites ($120-$135). *Bath:* combo or shower only. 5 stories, interior/exterior corridors. **Terms:** F12. **Amenities:** extended cable TV, voice mail, hair dryers. *Some:* safes. **Dining & Entertainment:** 2 restaurants, coffee shop, 6 am-1 am, $10-$18, cocktails, also, Mr Owen's, see separate listing, nightclub, entertainment. **Guest Services:** valet laundry. **Business Services:** meeting rooms. **Cards:** AE, MC, VI.

SOME UNITS

WHERE TO DINE

MR OWEN'S

Continental (68/18-1043

| | L $8-$18 | D $8-$18 |

Location: 0.5 km e; in Plaza Inn. Ave Gabriel Leyva & Cardenas. **Hours:** 6 am-1 am. **Features:** casual dress; cocktails. American style operation. **Cards:** AE, MC, VI.

RESTAURANTE SANTA ANITA

Continental (68/18-7046

| | L $8-$18 | D $10-$25 |

Location: Downtown; in Hotel Santa Anita. Gabriel Leyva & Hidalgo 81200. **Hours:** 7 am-11 pm. **Features:** casual dress; cocktails & lounge; entertainment; fee for parking. Mexican charm prevails. Good selection of International specialties. Casual. **Cards:** AE, DI, MC, VI.

NAVOJOA, SONORA

WHERE TO STAY

BEST WESTERN HOTEL DEL RIO

▼▼▼ *Motor Inn*   ((642)2-0331

All Year $65-$80   XP $10
Location: On Mex 15 at south end of bridge over Rio Mayo. Pesqueira Norte, APDO 228 85800. Fax: 642/2-0331. **Facility:** Located on north end of town. 77 units, 4 with efficiency. *Bath:* shower only. 2 stories, exterior corridors. **Terms:** F12. **Amenities:** extended cable TV. **Leisure Activities:** wading pool. **Guest Services:** gift shop, valet laundry. **Business Services:** meeting rooms, administrative services. **Cards:** AE, CB, MC, VI.

SOME UNITS

MOTEL EL MAYO

▼▼▼ *Motel*   (642/2-6828

All Year $45-$80
Location: Just s of jct Mex 15 and SR 162/10 to Otero y Jimenez, just e. Otero y Jimenez 85870 (PO Box 234). Fax: 642/2-6515. **Facility:** 48 units, 10 with efficiency. Some whirlpool units ($80-$90). *Bath:* combo or shower only. 2 stories, exterior corridors. **Terms:** 7 day cancellation notice, small pets only. **Amenities:** extended cable TV. **Guest Services:** [CP] meal plan available, valet laundry. *Fee:* area transportation. **Business Services:** meeting rooms. **Cards:** AE, MC, VI.

SOME UNITS

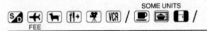
FEE

NOGALES, SONORA (C-3)   elev. 3,674'

The border town of Nogales (noh-GAH-lehs) is separated by the international boundary fence from Nogales, Ariz. Following the ceding in 1848 of present-day New Mexico, Arizona and California to the United States as a result of the Mexican-American War, settlement on both sides of the new border was encouraged to help thwart across-the-border raids. With fewer defense resources at hand, Nogales became—and continues to be—larger than its U.S. counterpart, and also has maintained a stronger Mexican identity than other border towns. It is a major shipping point for Sonoran fruits and vegetables making their way to American grocery stores.

Nogales also is the gateway into northwestern mainland Mexico and points south, although many visitors just come for the day. Things heat up on weekends, when the underage crowd makes the 1-hour pilgrimage south from Tucson to patronize the local bars and nightspots.

Mexican and U.S. customs offices are open 24 hours daily. A tourist card is not needed for in-town stays of less than 72 hours, but proof of citizenship is required. For motorists traveling into the interior, the official checkpoint (where your temporary vehicle importation permit must be presented, the $11 administrative fee paid and

a windshield sticker obtained) is located 21 kilometers (13 miles) south of Nogales.

Note: Four-lane, divided Mex. 15 begins in Nogales. I-19 south from Tucson ends at Nogales, Ariz.; signs then point the way to the border crossing. This route, however, passes through the most congested part of town. Motorists intending to drive into the interior or to other points within Sonora can take the Mariposa exit west off I-19 and use the international truck crossing; the toll road bypasses downtown Nogales and connects with Mex. 15 to the south, at the 21-kilometer (13-mile) immigration checkpoint. At press time, the toll was about $2 (U.S.).

If you're driving through downtown Nogales back to the United States, watch for the sign that says "Linea International"; follow the directions for the road that leads to the border crossing.

With several good restaurants and an array of shops selling everything from cheap curios to high-quality handicrafts, Nogales is a popular day-trip destination. Since almost all of the tourist-oriented shopping is within easy walking distance of the border, it's easiest to park on the Arizona side, where guarded lots are available, and head into Mexico on foot.

The shops and markets catering to tourists are concentrated near the border along **Avenida Obregón**. They offer pottery, baskets, leather goods, glassware, furniture, rugs, jewelry and more. Where prices are not fixed, bargaining is acceptable and even expected. The more exclusive establishments carry crafts and gift items from all over Mexico. When buying at stalls or from street vendors, always check for quality (*see the tips under "Best Buys," page 72*).

The *Cinco de Mayo Festival*, held in early May, commemorates Mexico's defeat of Napoleon III's French army in 1862.

PUERTO PENASCO, SONORA (C-2)

Puerto Peñasco (PWEHR-toh peh-NYAHS-coh) is situated in the midst of some of Mexico's most inhospitable territory: blazingly hot, extremely arid and absolutely desolate. No matter. About 97 kilometers (60 miles) from the international border at Lukeville, Ariz., and just 3 hours from Tucson, Puerto Peñasco—like much of northern Baja California—attracts legions of weekenders.

This shrimping village—known as Rocky Point to many U.S. visitors, even though the Spanish translation is "rocky port"—might today be an Arizona seaport had it not been for the negotiating skills of the Mexican government. Following the 1846-48 territorial war between Mexico and the United States, ongoing negotiations were conducted to determine the new border. President Antonio López de Santa Anna did not want to give up territory that would separate mainland Mexico from the Baja California Peninsula; James Gadsden, a South Carolina railroad promoter, lobbied for a settlement that would give the United States a southern railroad route to the Pacific and a port on the gulf. In 1854, the Gadsden Purchase acquired what is now the southern portions of Arizona and New Mexico for $10 million, but Mexico retained the land bridge to Baja.

The discovery of blue shrimp in the waters off Cerro de Peñasco (Rocky Point) in the 1920s established the village. For a time, fresh water had to be hauled from the border town of Sonoita, 60 miles away over a sandy trail (now Mex. 8). The route was paved during World War II to provide a potential backup for U.S. West Coast shipping interests, then feared under attack by the Japanese. Puerto Peñasco's shrimping industry took off in the 1950s, although overharvesting has depleted natural resources.

The town now benefits from its easy access for North American visitors. It remains a leisurely destination for California and Arizona RVers and campers, and is a popular beach getaway for college students on spring break. But a development program already under way—to include luxury hotels, a marina, a country club, two championship golf courses, an aquatic theme park, and upscale condominiums and beachfront homes—will likely change the character of this coast.

An extreme range between low and high tide, which can be more than 20 feet, characterizes the local waters. This phenomenon also occurs at San Felipe (see separate listing under Baja California), on the Baja side of the gulf. During low tide, marine life inhabiting the shallow tide pools can be explored. Tide calendars are available at the **Desert and Ocean Studies Center (CEDO)**, on the eastern edge of town at Playa Las Conchas; the facility also can be toured.

Puerto Peñasco's beaches stretch for miles. They tend to be rocky, but the gulf waters are clear and warm. Summer temperatures in this region are among the hottest in all Mexico; the weather is much cooler November through March. **Note:** A temporary vehicle importation permit is not needed if visiting Puerto Peñasco from the United States. Motorists must, however, carry Mexican automobile insurance.

About 48 kilometers (30 miles) north of Puerto Peñasco Mex. 8 passes near the crater-strewn landscape of **Pinacate Desert National Park**, which was designated a biosphere reserve in the early 1990s to preserve the volcanic rock formations and protect endangered species. One of the world's most unique environments, it consists almost entirely of lava fields interspersed with sand dunes and moonlike craters. The park entrance is off Mex. 2, west of Sonoita. There are no facilities, although camping is permitted in designated areas (a permit is required). The tourist office in Puerto Peñasco can provide information about guided tours; phone (638) 3-4129.

San Carlos, Sonora

Where To Stay

SAN CARLOS PLAZA

 *Motor Inn* ((622)7-0077

All Year .... S173 .... XP $20
Location: 5.5 km nw on Paseo Mar Bermejo; Hwy 124 to Los Algodones. Paseo Mar Bermejo Nte #4 85506 (PO Box 441). Fax: 622/7-0098. **Facility:** Semi-secluded location. Ample parking with security. 173 units. 1 two-bedroom unit. Some whirlpool units. 4 stories, interior/exterior corridors. **Terms:** F12. **Amenities:** safes, honor bars, hair dryers. **Leisure Activities:** wading pool, whirlpool, beach, swimming, 2 lighted tennis courts, exercise room. **Guest Services:** gift shop. **Business Services:** meeting rooms. **Cards:** AE, MC, VI.

NORTHEASTERN MEXICO

Northeastern Mexico is not the Mexican vacation paradise touted in glossy travel brochures. The gulf beaches along the low-lying, marshy, lagoon-fringed coastal strip of Tamaulipas, for example, are muddy, rife with mosquitoes and patronized mainly by locals. Sprawling Coahuila is arid, largely undeveloped and sparsely populated, with tourist facilities few and far between. The clang of machinery is the pulsebeat of Nuevo León, where Latin America's first heavy industries—ironworks, steelworks, smelting plants—were developed.

Still, northeastern Mexico does have diversions for the visitor. Matamoros, Nuevo Laredo and Reynosa, all just across the southeastern Texas border, are easy day-trip destinations for shopping expeditions and a Mexican dinner. Industrial powerhouse Monterrey, known locally as the "Sultana del Norte," or Sultan of the North, is a favored weekend getaway for nearby Texans. Sheer size (more than 2 million residents) and urban sprawl can make it a daunting choice for the casual tourist. But Monterrey's old city center—with its flower-filled plazas, narrow streets, centuries-old buildings and colorful patios—retains the flavor of Spanish colonial days.

MATAMOROS, TAMAULIPAS (E-8)

Main port of entry to Mexico from the lower Río Grande Valley, Matamoros (mah-tah-MOH-rohs) is connected with Brownsville, Tex. The city is the commercial center for the surrounding cotton-producing and cattle-raising region, and also serves as a crafts and housewares emporium for border-hopping tourists. U.S. customs offices as well as Mexican customs and immigration offices at the **B & M** and **Gateway** bridges are open daily 24 hours; the office at **Veterans Bridge** is open daily 6 a.m.-midnight. Baggage must be inspected if you plan to go beyond Matamoros.

This is the most historically significant of the Río Grande border towns. Settled around 1700, burned twice and pillaged several times, Matamoros is known as the "Thrice Heroic" city. It derived much of its wealth during the U.S. Civil War, when the Confederates smuggled contraband cotton across the border for shipment to European markets.

The center of this trade was the short-lived Mexican town of Bagdad, about 12 kilometers (8 miles) north of Playa Lauro Villar at the mouth of the Río Grande, where weapons were channeled to the Confederate Army in exchange for cotton. The city, which once boasted 6,000 residents, died out after suffering floods, hurricanes and military attacks; old artifacts can often be found by digging into the sand that now buries much of the site.

While Bagdad crumbled into the Río Grande, Matamoros began to lure tourists with bargains on housewares, glass items, basketry, pottery, papier-maché items and table linens. The most popular shopping districts include the **Mercado Juárez**, an enclosed marketplace that covers several blocks; the shops along Avenida Obregón; and the **Centro Artesanal**, the government-run crafts center. Also of interest is the **Casamata Museum**, which is housed in a small fort. A local escape outside the city is **Playa Lauro Villar**, 38 kilometers (24 miles) east.

The most complete visitor information is available at the Brownsville Chamber of Commerce, a block from the international bridge at 1600 E. Elizabeth in Brownsville, Tex. The office is open daily 9-5; phone (956) 542-4341.

MONTERREY, NUEVO LEON (E-7)

Founded in 1596 by Don Diego de Montemayor, Monterrey (mohn-teh-REY) was named for the Viceroy of New Spain, Don Gaspar de Zúñiga y Acevedo, Count of Monterrey. Real development began in the 18th century, when El Obispado, or the Bishop's Palace *(see attraction listing below)*—initially built as a place of retirement for Catholic bishops—became the seat of the religious diocese.

Capital of the state of Nuevo León, this is Mexico's third largest metropolis and its most dynamic industrial powerhouse. Numerous factories produce transportation equipment, electrical appliances, cement, steel, chemicals, clothing, beer, cut glass and many other products. Industrialization also has made the city a major Mexican rail center and an important point of commerce with the United States. Monterrey's business muscle is exemplified by the Centro Internacional de Negocios (CINTERMEX), said to be the largest trade and convention center in Latin America.

Passage of the North American Free Trade Agreement (NAFTA) in the early 1990s added further economic impetus to an already-healthy industrial environment. Multinational corporations drawn by the availability of cheap Mexican labor meant jobs for Mexican workers, and *maquiladoras*—assembly plants—sprang up here and in the border cities. Real prosperity, however, is a fact of life for only a small—although growing—percentage of the population.

The city lies in a valley ringed with craggy mountains, including 5,700-foot **Cerro de la Silla** (Hill of the Saddle) and 7,800-foot **Cerro de la Mitra** (Hill of the Miter). The former is saddle-shaped; the latter resembles a bishop's headdress. The mountains trap smog created by the dense concentration of industry, and Monterrey is fast catching up to Mexico City in terms of pollution and congestion. These urban pains are compensated for, however, by some impressive natural attractions outside the metropolitan area. And despite the lack of touristic charm, there is a palpable sense of progress.

THE INFORMED TRAVELER

Monterrey's **Mariano Escobedo International Airport** is about 6 kilometers (4 miles) northeast of the downtown area. Taxis shuttle passengers between the airport and the central city. Aeroméxico, American, Continental and Mexicana airlines offer direct or connecting flights from U.S. cities. The Aeroméxico subsidiary Aerolitoral flies from San Antonio and McAllen, Tex.; reservations can be made through Aeroméxico. For additional information about airlines *see "Arriving by Air," page 53.*

Motorists can access the city via two major toll highways—Mex. 85-D from Laredo/Nuevo Laredo or Mex. 40-D from McAllen/Reynosa. These highways more or less parallel free Mex. 85 (the Pan-American Highway) and Mex. 40. Although the less scenic of the two, Mex. 40-D is convenient to downtown Monterrey.

Metro, the city's subway system, consists of two elevated lines, one running east-west along Avenida Colón and another originating at Gran Plaza and running north-south along avenidas Pino Suárez and Cuauhtémoc. A third line is under construction. Metro is used primarily by office workers and is not particularly helpful for the visitor interested in sightseeing, although the north-south line does provide access to the Zona Rosa, downtown's upscale shopping/dining area. Inexpensive magnetic ticket cards can be purchased from vending machines at the subway stations. Trains run daily from 6 a.m.-midnight. Check with the tourist information office *(see below)* for further information.

The downtown streets, wedged within a ring of expressways, tend to be narrow, one way and congested. Street parking in this area is difficult, and overnight parking is prohibited. The best way to see the sights is by taxi or bus tour. Taxis are plentiful and can be hailed on the street; always determine the fare in advance. "Deluxe" bus service to Monterrey from Dallas, Houston and San Antonio is offered by Transportes del Norte. Valley Transit in Laredo, Tex., provides information about bus lines serving northeastern Mexico; phone (956) 723-4324.

For tourist information contact **Monterrey Infotur**, on Calle Hidalgo in the Gran Plaza. The staff speaks English, and brochures and maps are available. The office is open Tues.-Sun. 10-5. In Monterrey, phone (8) 345-0870 or 345-0902; elsewhere in Mexico, phone 01 (800) 832-2200; in the United States, phone (800) 235-2438. A better bet, however, is to check in Laredo, McAllen or other Texas border towns, particularly at places that sell Mexican automobile insurance.

CITY LAYOUT

At first glance, Monterrey seems to be all factories, grimy housing projects and noisy traffic congestion. But the city center is a haven of sorts from industrial sprawl, where modern hotels and office buildings stand next to venerable flat-roofed houses. One landmark symbolizes Mexico's break from Spain—the figure of "Patria" (Fatherland) holding a broken chain, which sits atop the **Arco de la Independencia** (Independence Arch) at Avenida Pino Suárez and Calzada Francisco Madero.

Gran Plaza, the central plaza, is one of the world's largest city squares. Also known as the Macro Plaza, its construction during the 1980s helped revitalize the downtown area. Graced by fountains, statuary, gardens and boldly modern buildings, the 100-acre expanse stretches from the **Palacio Municipal** (City Hall) north to the **Palacio de Gobierno** (Government Palace). Several streets pass under the raised plaza.

This huge paved space is dominated by a 230-foot-tall, bright-orange laser beam tower, the **Faro de Comercio** (Trade Beacon), which bathes the plaza with green light in the evenings. Another contemporary structure is the **Teatro de la Ciudad** (City Theater). The impressive **Fuente de la Vida** (Fountain of Life) boasts a

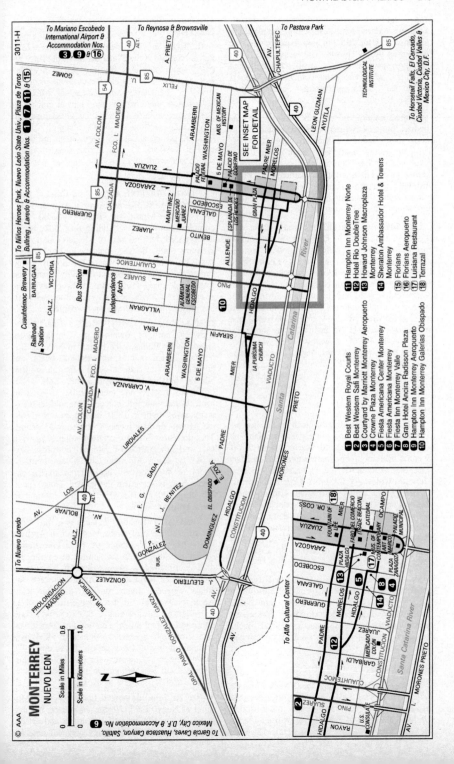

MONTERREY
NUEVO LEON

© AAA

Scale in Miles
0   0.6
Scale in Kilometers
0   1.0

To Mariano Escobedo
International Airport &
Accommodation Nos.
3, **9** & **16**

To Niños Heroes Park, Nuevo León State Univ., Plaza de Toros
Bullring, Laredo & Accommodation Nos. **1** **7** **11** & **15**

To Reynosa & Brownsville

To Pastora Park

To Horsetail Falls, El Cercado,
Ciudad Victoria, Ciudad Valles &
Mexico City, D.F.

SEE INSET MAP
FOR DETAIL

Cuauhtémoc Brewery ■
Railroad
■ Station

Bus Station ■

Independence
Arch

To Nuevo Laredo

To Alfa Cultural Center

To Garcia Caves, Huasteca Canyon, Saltillo,
Mexico City, D.F. & Accommodation No. **6**

1 Best Western Royal Courts
2 Best Western Safi Monterrey
3 Courtyard by Marriott Monterrey Aeropuerto
4 Crowne Plaza Monterrey
5 Fiesta Americana Center Monterrey
6 Fiesta Americana Monterrey
7 Fiesta Inn Monterrey Valle
8 Gran Hotel Ancira Radisson Plaza
9 Hampton Inn Monterrey Aeropuerto
10 Hampton Inn Monterrey Galerías Obispado
11 Hampton Inn Monterrey Norte
12 Hotel Rio DoubleTree
13 Howard Johnson Macroplaza Monterrey
14 Sheraton Ambassador Hotel & Towers Monterrey
15 Florians
16 Florians Aeropuerto
17 Luisiana Restaurant
18 Terrazal

bronze statue of Neptune surrounded by cavorting steeds and nymphs. Also within the plaza are the **Bosque Hundido** (Hidden Garden) and the **Esplanada de los Héroes**. The former is a relaxing green space with trees, smaller fountains and sculptures, while the latter contains monuments to Mexican historical figures Father Miguel Hidalgo, Benito Juárez and José María Morelos.

At the southern end of Gran Plaza is the **Cathedral**, built over a period of more than 2 centuries and reflecting several architectural styles. The pale yellow facade is baroque, while Platteresque decoration adorns the entrance door. Across Gran Plaza from the cathedral is **Plaza Hidalgo**, a more traditional Mexican square framed with colonial-style buildings and dotted with shops and little outdoor cafes.

La Purísima Church, at Serafín Peña and Hidalgo on the way to El Obispado, is considered an outstanding example of modern ecclesiastical architecture. The **Nuevo León State University** campus is in the northern section of the city. An interesting combination of contemporary and age-old building designs distinguishes the campus of Monterrey's **Technological Institute**. Considered by many to be Mexico's best engineering school, the institute is a short distance southeast of downtown on Mex. 85. **Parque la Pastora** (Pastora Park), east of downtown off Avenida Chapultepec, is a naturally landscaped recreation area featuring a lake and a zoo.

SHOPPING

Folk arts and handicrafts such as leather articles, blown glass and pottery are available at two downtown markets. **Mercado Juárez** is off Avenida Benito Juárez between avenidas Martinez and Aramberri; the more tourist-oriented **Mercado Colón** is on Avenida Constitución west of Gran Plaza. Other craft shops can be found around Plaza Hidalgo near the big downtown hotels; **Carapan**, Avenida Hidalgo #305 Oriente, offers a variety of high-quality merchandise. The **Casa de las Artesanías** (House of Crafts) is just east of Gran Plaza at avenidas Dr. Coss and Allende.

Monterrey also has its own **Zona Rosa**, not unlike the one in Mexico City, which runs along Calle Morelos in the vicinity of Gran Plaza. Craft shops, fashionable boutiques, restaurants and nightclubs line an open mall several blocks long and 2 blocks wide, reserved for pedestrians only.

SPECIAL EVENTS

Starting on Palm Sunday, the 2-week *Feria de Primavera* (Spring Fair) festivities offer parades, art expositions, auto races and other sports events. The *Feria del Norte de Mexico* (North Mexican Fair) and the *Festival of the Virgin of Guadalupe* take place during the first half of December.

Bullfights are held periodically between May and December at the **Plaza de Toros** bullring, located south of Niños Heroes Park at avenidas Ruíz Cortines and Alfonso Reyes. Feats of horsemanship characterize *charreadas*, or Mexican-style rodeos, held Sunday mornings at ranches in the eastern suburb of Villa de Guadalupe. To reach them, follow the signs reading "Lienzo Charro" posted along free Mex. 40 in the direction of Reynosa. Contact Infotur Centro regarding schedule information.

WHAT TO SEE IN TOWN

CENTRO CULTURAL ALFA (Alfa Cultural Center) is southwest of downtown on Avenida Manuel Gómez Morín (at Roberto Sada). The complex, housed in a building that looks like a leaning cylinder, has one of Mexico's best planetariums, an IMAX theater and numerous hands-on exhibits. Free buses run hourly to the center from the Alameda, a downtown park just west of Avenida Pino Suárez between avenidas Aramberri and Washington. Tues.-Sun. 3-9 (also Sat.-Sun. noon-3). Admission is charged.

CERVECERIA CUAUHTEMOC (Cuauhtémoc Brewery), north of downtown at Avenida Universidad #2002 Norte, is the largest in Mexico. Bohemia, Tecate and Carta Blanca beers are produced at the rate of more than a million bottles a day. A **Salón de la Fama** (Sports Hall of Fame) displays the memorabilia of Mexican professional baseball players. The old brewery warehouses, built in 1890, have been turned into the **Museo de Monterrey** (Monterrey Museum). The museum displays original copper brewing vats and other artifacts, regional costumes, and works by Latin American and Mexican artists. Tours of the brewery are offered during the week; beer is served in the garden. Open Tues.-Sun. Free. Phone (8) 375-2200 for information about brewery tours.

EL OBISPADO (Bishop's Palace) is in the western part of the city at the west end of Avenida Padre Mier. It was built by Fray José Rafael Verger in 1787, a year of famine, to employ Indian victims of a severe drought. The pre-independence home of the Catholic diocese, the palace gained fame during the Mexican-American War. Fortified for battle, it resisted an onslaught by the invading U.S. Army for 2 days after the city had fallen. The building also served as a stronghold against the French in 1864, as a hospital during a 1903 yellow fever epidemic, and as temporary quarters for Pancho Villa during the 1910 Revolution. On smog-free days, it offers a wonderful view of the city.

Museo Regional de Nuevo León (Regional Museum of Nuevo León), inside the palace, has displays tracing the industrial, cultural and artistic development of the Monterrey area. Of note are the guns that were used to execute emperor Archduke Maximilian. Open Tues.-Sun. 10-5. Admission is charged.

MUSEO DE ARTE CONTEMPORANEO (Museum of Contemporary Art, or MARCO), calles General Zuazua and Ocampo at Gran Plaza, is one of the city's architectural highlights. Exhibits in the 14 halls change every few months and emphasize Mexican and Latin American artists. A gigantic bronze sculpture of a dove, "La Paloma," stands at the front entrance. Live music can be heard Wed. and Sun. afternoons. Tues.-Sun. 11-7 (also Tues.-Wed. and Sun. 7-9 p.m.). Admission is charged; free to all Wed. Phone (8) 342-4820.

MUSEO DE HISTORIA MEXICANA (Museum of Mexican History) is at Dr. Coss #445, a few blocks east of the Government Palace. Monterrey's newest museum focuses on the Revolution of 1910. Multimedia exhibits, including a railroad car that transported rebels under guerrilla leader Pancho Villa, chronicle the political turmoil of that era. Also on display is a collection of Huastec Indian artifacts. Guided tours in English are available. Daily 11-6:30 (also Fri.-Sun. 6:30-7:30 p.m.). Donations.

PALACIO DE GOBIERNO (Government Palace), the Nuevo León state capitol, is at the north end of Gran Plaza. The Spanish colonial-style building was built in 1908 of pink stone quarried from around San Luis Potosí; it has a typically Spanish patio.

PARQUE NIÑOS HEROES (Heroic Children's Park) is on Avenida Alfonso Reyes, just south of Nuevo León State University. It was named in honor of the young cadets who defended Mexico City's Chapultepec Castle from U.S. forces during the Mexican-American War. Within the park is the **Museo de la Fauna y Ciencias Naturales** (Museum of Fauna and Natural Sciences); the **Pinacoteca de Nuevo León** (Nuevo León Art Gallery), which surveys the state's artistic heritage; a baseball stadium; gardens; and an artificial lake. Open Tues.-Sun. 10-7. Admission is charged. Phone (8) 331-3890.

NEARBY DESTINATIONS

GRUTAS DE GARCIA (García Caves) are northwest of downtown Monterrey via Mex. 40. A paved road runs to the caves, which are about 8 kilometers (5 miles) east of the village of Villa de García. A swimming pool, restaurants, and picnic and recreational areas cluster at the foot of the mountain where the caves are located. From the parking area, a cable car transports visitors past rugged scenery to the cavern entrance, tucked high on a cliffside.

Discovered about 1843 by parish priest Juan Antonio Sobrevilla, the caves are among the largest and most beautiful in Mexico. Their estimated age is 50 to 60 million years; it is presumed the caves were once submerged due to the shellfish fossils scattered over the walls and ceilings. Ten "rooms" contain stalagmite and stalactite formations with such names as "The Eagle's Nest," "The Hall of Clouds" and "The Chapel." The cement passageways connecting the caves are well lighted. Open daily. Admission includes the cable car ride and a guided tour.

HUASTECA CANYON (wahs-TEH-kah) is about 32 kilometers (20 miles) west of Monterrey on Mex. 40 to the village of Santa Catarina, then 3 kilometers (2 miles) south. This magnificent rock gorge is located in **Parque Nacional Cumbres de Monterrey** (Monterrey Heights National Park). The sheer walls reach heights of 750 to 1,000 feet. In places the softer rock has been eroded into curious formations. Restrooms, a snack bar and picnic areas are available.

EL CERCADO, NUEVO LEON (E-7)

About 36 kilometers (22 miles) south of Monterrey on Mex. 85, El Cercado (el sehr-KAH-doh) sits in the Río Escamillas Valley. This boat-launching site is on the lake impounded by **Presa Rodrigo Gómez** (Rodrigo Gómez Dam). The man-made lake, about 3.25 kilometers (2 miles) north of town, functions as a reservoir for the city of Monterrey. This is a popular spot for fishing, boating, swimming and water skiing. A rough road leads from the dam through Cañón Garrapatas (Tick Canyon) to the hamlet of **Los Canelos**, known locally for a warm spring and "El Bañito," a huge "bathtub" carved from solid rock.

Cascada Cola de Caballo (Horsetail Falls) is about 6 kilometers (4 miles) northwest in the village of Santiago. A paved road off Mex. 85 winds to the parking area; from there a pathway climbs three-quarters of a mile to the base of the falls. You can walk it yourself or hire burros, horses or horse-drawn carts for the round trip; jeeps with drivers are sometimes available. The crystalline 75-foot waterfall is surrounded by lush natural vegetation, unusual in mostly arid northeastern Mexico. Steps carved into the pathway allow the falls to be observed from different angles. A parking fee is charged.

The village of **Santiago** is known as "the Garden of Nuevo León" for its picturesque mountain setting. Notable examples of colonial-style architecture include the 19th-century **Templo de Santiago Apóstol** (Church of St. James the Apostle), which has a baroque facade and twin bell towers.

WHERE TO STAY

BEST WESTERN ROYAL COURTS

Motor Inn ((8)305-1900

| 5/1-8/31 | $85-$95 | XP $5 |
| 12/1-4/30 & 9/1-11/30 | $80-$90 | XP $5 |

Location: On Mex 85, 8.5 km of toll road to Nuevo Laredo. Ave Universidad 314 66450. Fax: 8/305-1919. **Facility:** Walled parking with 24 hour security. Located in northern section of city. Attractive center courtyard. Colonial style rooms. 82 units. *Bath:* shower only. 2-3 stories (no elevator), exterior corridors. **Terms:** F17; 3 day cancellation notice. **Amenities:** safes, hair dryers. **Dining:** restaurant, 6:45 am-10 pm, $6-$18, cocktails. **Leisure Activities:** heated pool. **Guest Services:** [CP] meal plan available, valet laundry. **Business Services:** conference facilities. **Cards:** AE, DI, MC, VI. *(See color ad below)*

SOME UNITS

BEST WESTERN SAFI MONTERREY
Hotel ((8)399-7000

| All Year | $60-$68 | XP $8 |

Location: From Laredo toll road, s on Ave Universidad to Pino Suarez, s to northern edge of downtown. Pino Suarez 444 Sur 66450. Fax: 8/399-7020. **Facility:** Striking marble lobby. Large tastefully appointed rooms. Meets AAA guest room security requirements. 116 units. 7 stories, interior/exterior corridors. **Terms:** F12. **Amenities:** hair dryers. **Leisure Activities:** heated pool, whirlpool, exercise room. **Guest Services:** gift shop, valet laundry. **Business Services:** meeting rooms, fax. **Cards:** AE, MC, VI.

SOME UNITS

COURTYARD BY MARRIOTT MONTERREY AEROPUERTO
Motor Inn ((8)156-9090

7/1-11/30	$157-$170
1/1-6/30	$143-$154
12/1-12/31	$130-$140

Location: 15 km ne; at entrance to International Airport. Carr Miguel Aleman km 24.5 66600. Fax: 8/156-9080. **Facility:** 130 units. Some suites. *Bath:* combo or shower only. 5 stories, interior corridors. **Amenities:** voice mail, irons, hair dryers. **Leisure Activities:** exercise room. **Guest Services:** area transportation, valet and coin laundry. **Business Services:** meeting rooms, administrative services. *Fee:* PC, fax. **Cards:** AE, DI, MC, VI. *(See color ad opposite inside front cover & p 217)*

FEE

SOME UNITS

CROWNE PLAZA MONTERREY

▼▼▼ Hotel (8/319-6000

All Year $200 XP $20
Location: Just w of Plaza Hidalgo. Constitution 300 Ote 64000 (PO Box 1619). Fax: 8/344-6060. **Facility:** Tastefully decorated atrium lobby. Meets AAA guest room security requirements. 403 units. Some whirlpool units. 10 stories, interior corridors. **Parking:** valet. **Terms:** F18. **Amenities:** honor bars, irons. **Leisure Activities:** heated pool, sauna, whirlpool, exercise room. *Fee:* lighted tennis court. **Guest Services:** gift shop, valet laundry. *Fee:* area transportation, massage. **Business Services:** conference facilities, administrative services, fax. **Cards:** AE, DI, MC, VI.

[icons]
FEE
SOME UNITS
/ [icon] /

FIESTA AMERICANA CENTER MONTERREY

▼▼▼ Suite Hotel (8/319-0900

8/1-11/30 $110 XP $17
12/1-7/31 $100 XP $15
Location: In downtown Historic Zona Rosa district. 519 Corregidora Zona Rosa 64000. Fax: 8/319-0980. **Facility:** Striking high-rise with elegant public areas. Meets AAA guest room security requirements. Meets AAA guest room security requirements. 207 units. 11 stories, interior corridors. **Parking:** valet. **Terms:** F12; cancellation fee imposed. **Amenities:** voice mail, honor bars, hair dryers. **Leisure Activities:** heated pool, exercise room. **Guest Services:** gift shop, valet laundry. **Business Services:** meeting rooms, administrative services. **Cards:** AE, DI, MC, VI.

[icons]
FEE

⚠ FIESTA AMERICANA MONTERREY

▼▼▼▼ Hotel (8/363-3030

All Year $200 XP $40
Location: 3 km sw on Mex 85. Ave Vasconcelos 300 Ote 66260. Fax: 8/363-4322. **Facility:** Expansive public areas. Outdoor courtyard area with waterfalls. Tastefully decorated guest rooms. Meets AAA guest room security requirements. 305 units. 2 two-bedroom units. Some suites and whirlpool units. 9 stories, interior corridors. **Terms:** F12. **Amenities:** voice mail, safes, honor bars, hair dryers. **Dining & Entertainment:** dining room, restaurant, 24 hours, $10-$20, cocktails, nightclub, entertainment. **Leisure Activities:** heated pool, wading pool, whirlpool. *Fee:* lighted tennis court, tennis pro. **Guest Services:** gift shop, valet laundry. *Fee:* area transportation, massage. **Business Services:** conference facilities, administrative services, fax. **Cards:** AE, CB, DI, MC, VI.

[icons]
FEE FEE FEE
SOME UNITS
/ [icon] /

FIESTA INN MONTERREY VALLE

▼▼▼ Motor Inn ((8)399-1500

All Year $120-$160 XP $8
Location: 1 km e of Vasconcelos. Ave Lazro Cardenas #327 66269. Fax: 8/339-1501. **Facility:** Caters to the Valle financial district. Meets AAA guest room security requirements. 176 units. 6 stories, interior corridors. **Terms:** F14. **Amenities:** voice mail. **Leisure Activities:** whirlpool, exercise room. **Guest Services:** [CP] meal plan available, valet laundry. **Business Services:** meeting rooms, administrative services. **Cards:** AE, CB, DI, MC, VI.

[icons]
SOME UNITS
FEE FEE / [icon] /

⚠ GRAN HOTEL ANCIRA RADISSON PLAZA

▼▼▼▼ Historic Hotel ((8)150-7000

All Year $95-$145 XP $15
Location: Sw corner of Plaza Hidalgo, entrance only by one-way eastbound Hidalgo. (PO Box 697, 64000). Fax: 8/345-1121. **Facility:** Neoclassic landmark boasting a grand marbled lobby combined with contemporary amenities and service. 241 units. *Bath:* combo or shower only. 5 stories, interior corridors. **Terms:** F12; small pets only. **Amenities:** honor bars, hair dryers. **Dining:** 2 dining rooms, coffee shop, 7 am-11:30 pm, $8-$15. **Leisure Activities:** small heated pool, sauna, exercise room. **Guest Services:** gift shop, valet laundry. **Business Services:** conference facilities, administrative services. **Cards:** AE, DI, MC, VI.

[icons]
SOME UNITS
FEE
[icon] / [icon] /

HAMPTON INN MONTERREY AEROPUERTO

▼▼▼ Motel ((8)386-3800

All Year $115
Location: 15 km ne; at entrance to International Airport. Km 23.7 Carr Miguel Aleman 66600. Fax: 8/386-3435. **Facility:** Remote location. Modern, well-furnished public areas. 181 units. *Bath:* combo or shower only. 5 stories, interior corridors. **Terms:** cancellation fee imposed. **Amenities:** dual phone lines, voice mail, irons. **Dining:** Florians Aeropuerto, see separate listing. **Leisure Activities:** exercise room, sports court. **Guest Services:** [CP] meal plan available, area transportation, valet and coin laundry. **Business Services:** meeting rooms, PC. **Cards:** AE, DI, MC, VI. *(See color ad p 218)*

[icons]
SOME UNITS
/ [icon] /

HAMPTON INN MONTERREY GALERIAS OBISPADO

▼▼▼▼▼   *Motel*   ((8)348-1515

1/16-11/30	$135-$150	XP $10
12/1-1/15	$115-$135	XP $10

Location: Adjacent to Galerias Mall. Ave Gonzalitos 415 S 64060. Fax: 8/333-4490. **Facility:** In upscale Galerias district. Meets AAA guest room security requirements. 146 units. 7 stories, interior corridors. **Terms:** F18; 3 day cancellation notice. **Amenities:** dual phone lines. **Leisure Activities:** exercise room. **Guest Services:** [CP] meal plan available, area transportation, valet laundry. **Business Services:** meeting rooms, administrative services, PC, fax. **Cards:** AE, DI, MC, VI. *(See color ad below)*

FEE
SOME UNITS
/ ⊠ /

HAMPTON INN MONTERREY NORTE

▼▼▼▼   *Motor Inn*   (8/376-5000

All Year $95-$120
Location: On northern outskirts. 8 km s of Mex 85 & toll road. Ave Universidad 501 Nte 66450. Fax: 8/352-0747. **Facility:** Secured parking lot. Meets AAA guest room security requirements. 170 units. *Bath:* combo or shower only. 6 stories, interior corridors. **Parking:** valet. **Amenities:** voice mail, irons. **Leisure Activities:** exercise room, basketball. **Guest Services:** [CP] meal plan available, area transportation, valet laundry. **Business Services:** meeting rooms, administrative services. **Cards:** AE, DI, MC, VI. *(See color ad below)*

SOME UNITS
DATA/PORT / ⊠ /

⟲⟲⟲ HOTEL RIO DOUBLETREE

▼▼▼▼   *Hotel*   (8/344-9040

All Year $130   XP $10
Location: 0.7 km w of Grand Plaza. Padre Mier 194 Pte 64000 (PO Box 35). Fax: 8/345-7119. **Facility:** Large twin-tower hotel with expansive public areas. Very well furnished rooms of varying sizes. Meets AAA guest room security requirements. 395 units. Some whirlpool units. *Bath:* combo or shower only. 9-14 stories, interior corridors. **Parking:** extra charge. **Terms:** F12; package plans. **Amenities:** voice mail, irons. *Some:* honor bars. **Dining & Entertainment:** dining room, 6 am-1 am, $7-$12, cocktails, entertainment. **Leisure Activities:** heated pool, wading pool, tennis court, playground, exercise room, sports court. **Guest Services:** gift shop, valet laundry. *Fee:* area transportation. **Business Services:** conference facilities, administrative services. **Cards:** AE, DI, MC, VI. *(See color ad below)*

FEE
SOME UNITS
DATA/PORT / ⊠ /

HOWARD JOHNSON MACROPLAZA MONTERREY

 *Hotel* (8/380-6000

All Year $72-$110 XP $12
Location: In front of Plaza Zaragoza. Morelos 574 Ote 64000 (PO Box 349). Fax: 8/344-7378. **Facility:** Overlooks Marco Plaza. Modern public areas. Tastefully appointed rooms. Featuring home office rooms. Meets AAA guest room security requirements. 198 units. Some suites and whirlpool units. *Bath:* combo or shower only. 9 stories, interior corridors. **Terms:** F12. **Amenities:** voice mail, irons, hair dryers. *Some:* safes. **Dining & Entertainment:** dining room, coffee shop, 7 am-10 pm, $6-$12, cocktails, nightclub, entertainment. **Guest Services:** [BP] meal plan available, gift shop, valet laundry. *Fee:* area transportation. **Business Services:** conference facilities, administrative services. **Cards:** AE, DI, MC, VI.

FEE FEE
SOME UNITS
/ ⊠ /

SHERATON AMBASSADOR HOTEL & TOWERS MONTERREY

 Hotel ((8)380-7000

All Year $190 XP $15
Location: Just w of Plaza Hidalgo at Hidalgo and E Carranza. 64000 (PO Box 1733). Fax: 8/345-1984. **Facility:** Turn-of-the-20th-century ambience. Elegant public areas. Spacious units. Meets AAA guest room security requirements. 239 units. Some whirlpool units. 12 stories, interior corridors. **Parking:** valet. **Terms:** F17. **Amenities:** voice mail, safes, hair dryers. **Leisure Activities:** heated pool, wading pool, whirlpool, indoor tennis court. **Guest Services:** gift shop, valet laundry. *Fee:* massage. **Business Services:** conference facilities, administrative services, fax. **Cards:** AE, DI, MC, VI.

FEE
SOME UNITS
DATA PORT / ⊠ ▣ /

WHERE TO DINE

FLORIANS

 Mexican (8/352-8930
L $6-$10 D $10-$24
Location: On northern outskirts; 8 km s of Mex 85 & toll road; at Hampton Inn Monterrey Norte. Ave Universidad 501 Nte 66450. **Hours:** 7 am-1 am. **Reservations:** suggested; for dinner. **Features:** casual dress; children's menu; carryout; cocktail lounge. Strong selection of Mexican and American dishes. Refined, yet casual atmosphere. **Cards:** AE, DI, MC, VI.

⊠

FLORIANS AEROPUERTO

 Mexican (8/386-0020
L $6-$10 D $10-$24
Location: 15 km ne; at entrance to International Airport; in Hampton Inn Monterrey Aeropuerto. Km 23.7 Carr Miguel Aleman 66000. **Hours:** 7 am-midnight, Sat & Sun-11 pm. **Features:** casual dress; children's menu; carryout; cocktails & lounge. Strong selection of Mexican dishes. Refined yet casual atmosphere. Wide assortment of traditional American favorites including burgers, sandwiches and fountain drinks. **Cards:** AE, DI, MC, VI.

⊠

LUISIANA RESTAURANT

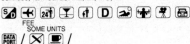 *Continental* (8/343-1561
L $10-$17 D $18-$30
Location: In downtown historic center. Plaza Hidalgo 530 64000. **Hours:** noon-midnight. Closed major holidays. **Reservations:** suggested. **Features:** semi-formal attire; children's menu; cocktails & lounge; entertainment; a la carte. Classic fine dining. Large, quiet dining room with soft piano music. Formally attired staff with clean, crisp, white napkin draped perfectly over the forearm. Very European. True meaning of the word restaurant: To restore. **Cards:** AE, DI, MC, VI.

TERRAZAL

Regional Mexican (8/340-0840
L $5-$10 D $8-$18
Location: Downtown; in historic district. Dr Coss Esq con Matamoros 64000. **Hours:** 1 pm-1 am, Sun & Mon-6 pm. **Reservations:** suggested. **Features:** casual dress; cocktails & lounge; a la carte. Cantina style decor. Creative Mexican approach to steak, veal, chicken and seafood. Picadillo tacos, dark mole (pronounced mo-lay) and enchiladas make it worth the trip. **Cards:** AE, MC, VI.

NUEVO LAREDO, TAMAULIPAS (D-7)

Nuevo Laredo (noo-EH-voh lah-REH-doh) is a major point of entry to the Mexican mainland from the United States. It is connected to Laredo, Tex., by four international toll bridges across the Río Grande. **International Bridge 1** is open to vehicular and pedestrian traffic; **International Bridge 2 (Juárez Lincoln)** is open to vehiclar traffic only. Both can be used by vehicles entering the interior. Bridge 3 (Columbia) primarily serves commercial vehicles, and Bridge 4 (World Trade Bridge) is reserved for commercial vehicles only. For day trips to shop or dine, consider leaving your car in Laredo and walking across the border, which eliminates time-consuming crossing procedures. The Mexican customs and immigration office is open 24 hours daily. U.S. customs offices at Bridge 1 and Bridge 2 are open 24 hours daily; the office at Columbia is open daily 8 a.m.-midnight.

Nuevo Laredo is a center for *maquiladora* (foreign-owned) manufacturing plants utilizing inexpensive Mexican labor, and as a result the atmosphere is more industrial than picturesque. It does, however, offer an enormous variety of shops and souvenir stalls for those seeking bargains on Mexican crafts, and there are several good restaurants. While occasional Sunday bullfights are held, the city's racetrack, formerly a big attraction, is long gone.

The **Falcon Dam**, a joint Mexico/United States project on the Río Bravo (Rio Grande) River, can be reached on the Mexican side by taking Mex. 85 south to Mex. 2, then Mex. 2 about 101 kilometers (63 miles) southeast to the town of Nueva Ciudad Guerrero. Local outfits offer boat rentals for fishing, water skiing and cruising the dam's lake.

PIEDRAS NEGRAS,
COAHUILA (D-7)

Piedras Negras (pee-EH-drahs NEH-grahs) faces Eagle Pass, Tex., across the Rio Grande. A toll bridge connects the two towns. The U.S. customs office is open 24 hours daily; the Mexican customs office is open Mon.-Fri. 8-8, Sat. 10-2. This typical border town is notable chiefly as the beginning of Mex. 57—the Constitution Highway, which runs south to Mexico City—and as the setting for the popular book "Like Water for Chocolate."

REYNOSA, TAMAULIPAS (E-8)

On the Rio Grande just south of McAllen, Tex., Reynosa (reh-NOH-sah) is reached via the **McAllen International Toll Bridge**. The toll to enter Mexico is $1.25 per vehicle; to return the toll is $1.50 per vehicle. Both Mexican and U.S. customs and immigration offices are open 24 hours daily.

A major gas-processing and oil-refining center, Reynosa is decidedly short on charm but does have a small tourist district, the **Zona Rosa**, where there are a few shops and restaurants. More shopping can be found in the vicinity of **Plaza Principal**, the main plaza (some 20 blocks in from the toll bridge), a typical Mexican square with a colonial-style cathedral upon which has been grafted an ultramodern addition. The city provides access to fishing camps around **El Azucar (Sugar) Dam**, some 81 kilometers (50 miles) to the west, which teems with bass and other freshwater game species.

SALTILLO,
COAHUILA (E-7)   elev. 5,245'

Saltillo (sahl-TEE-yoh), in a broad valley surrounded by the imposing peaks of the Sierra Madre Oriental, was founded as a Spanish outpost in 1577 by Alberto del Canto. In 1591, Francisco de Urdiñola established a mining settlement populated by relocated Tlaxcaltec Indians. By the early 17th century, the town was a strategic center for Spanish expeditions embarking on explorations to the north. From 1835 to 1847 Saltillo was capital of a territory that included Texas and extended as far northward as present-day Colorado.

About 85 kilometers (53 miles) southwest of Monterrey on Mex. 40, Saltillo is the capital of and leading industrial city in Coahuila. Its outskirts are a sprawl of manufacturing plants producing automobiles, engine parts and textiles. Saltillo's wool, silk and cotton mills are the source of brightly colored *sarapes*, the familiar woolen blanket worn as an outer garment. Although artificial fibers and chemical dyes are steadily replacing the old methods, *sarapes* and

small throw rugs are still made by hand in shops clustered along Calle Victoria downtown; visitors are welcome to watch the weaving process. Unglazed terra-cotta tiles are another local product.

There are two downtown plazas. Dignified monuments and well-preserved colonial buildings line the streets around **Plaza de Armas**. The feeling of formality is reinforced by its paved surface, a central fountain overlooked by four female statues, and the lack of trees and benches. The plaza is flanked by the city's grand 18th-century cathedral and the **Palacio de Gobierno** (Government Palace), which contains murals illustrating regional history.

Much livelier is **Plaza Acuña**, 2 blocks northwest. Here there are an abundance of shops, and the square is ringed with little cafes and bars. Occupying one corner of the plaza is **Mercado Juárez**, which is a good place to browse for handicrafts, *sarapes*, rugs, pottery, silverwork and bizarre-looking tin masks. Families and wandering musicians fill the plaza, which is a good spot to soak up the local atmosphere.

A monument to Emilio Carranza, who made the first nonstop flight from Mexico City to New York, stands along Calle Victoria. The street begins at the **Alameda**, a shady park just west of Plaza de Armas that is frequented by students and joggers. Here stands an equestrian statue of General Ignacio Zaragoza, hero of the 1862 Battle of Puebla. Zaragoza was born in 1829 in Bahía del Espíritu Santo, near what is now Goliad, Tex.

Because of its altitude and dry, mild climate, Saltillo is a popular summer resort. Golf, tennis, polo and swimming are popular recreational pursuits. The city's annual *feria* (fair) takes place the first half of August.

The central bus station is southwest of downtown on Boulevard Luis Echeverría. For tourist information contact the Secretaría de Fomento Turístico Estatal; phone (84) 14-0510. To contact the Green Angels, phone (84) 12-4050 (English spoken).

ATENEO FUENTE (Fuente Atheneum), Boulevard Venustiano Carranza on the University of Coahuila campus, is an art deco-style building that contains an art gallery with works by well-known European and Mexican painters.

CATEDRAL DE SANTIAGO, calles Hidalgo and Juárez facing Plaza de Armas, was built 1746-1801 and exhibits a mix of architectural styles, most notably the Mexican Churrigueresque. Decorative baroque carvings representing plants and shells adorn its facade and doors. The relatively restrained interior features a gilded altarpiece and a pulpit covered in gold leaf. The 1762 chapel contains a Spanish image of Christ associated with numerous legends. A 200-foot tower dominates the church and offers a panoramic view of the city.

MUSEO HERRERA (Herrera Museum), Bravo Norte #342, is the former home and studio of early 20th-century Mexican painter Rubén Herrera. The 18th-century residence contains more than 400 of his paintings, mostly Italian landscapes and pastoral scenes representing the artist's apprenticeship in Rome.

NEARBY DESTINATION

LA ANGOSTURA BATTLEGROUND, about a half-hour drive south of the city off Mex. 54, was the scene of a bloody Mexican-American War battle on Feb. 22-23, 1847. A monument on the east side of Mex. 54 marks the site.

WHERE TO STAY

(AAA) CAMINO REAL SALTILLO
▼▼▼ ▼▼▼ *Motor Inn* (84/30-0000
All Year $110 XP $20
Location: 6 km se on Mex 57. No 2000 Blvd Las Fundadores 26000 (PO Box 55, 25000). Fax: 84/30-1030. **Facility:** On mountain slope above Saltillo Valley. Extensive landscaped gardens. 140 units. Some whirlpool units. *Bath:* combo or shower only. 2 stories, exterior corridors. **Terms:** F18; 10 day cancellation notice. **Amenities:** honor bars. **Dining:** Buena Vista, see separate listing. **Leisure Activities:** heated pool, putting green, miniature golf, 2 lighted tennis courts, playground. **Guest Services:** valet laundry. *Fee:* area transportation. **Business Services:** conference facilities, fax. **Cards:** AE, DI, MC, VI.
(See color ad opposite title page)

SOME UNITS

FEE

(AAA) HOLIDAY INN EUROTEL
▼▼▼ *Motor Inn* ((84)15-1000
All Year $100-$135 XP $20
Location: 0.5 mi s on V Carranza Blvd from Glorieta at N Ortiz G and V Carranza. V Carranza Blvd #4100 25230. Fax: 84/15-3353. **Facility:** Parking area with security guard. 154 units. 3 stories, interior corridors. **Terms:** F12. **Amenities:** voice mail, honor bars, irons, hair dryers. **Dining & Entertainment:** dining room, coffee shop, 6:30 am-midnight, $6-$15, cocktails, entertainment. **Leisure Activities:** heated pool, sauna, whirlpool, playground, exercise room. **Guest Services:** [CP] meal plan available, gift shop, valet laundry. **Business Services:** conference facilities, administrative services. **Cards:** AE, DI, MC, VI.

SOME UNITS

HOLIDAY INN RAMOS ARIZPE
▼▼▼ *Motor Inn* (84/32-2626
All Year $100-$135 XP $20
Location: 18 km n on Carretera Monterrey-Saltillo. Carr Mty Salt #9000 25015. Fax: 84/32-2150. **Facility:** 127 units. 2 stories, interior corridors. **Terms:** F12. **Amenities:** voice mail. *Some:* honor bars, irons, hair dryers. **Leisure Activities:** heated pool, wading pool, whirlpool, exercise room. **Guest Services:** [CP] meal plan available, valet and coin laundry. **Business Services:** meeting rooms, administrative services. **Cards:** AE, DI, MC, VI.

SOME UNITS

HOTEL SAN JORGE
▼▼ *Hotel* (84/12-2222
All Year $35-$55 XP $8
Location: Downtown. Manuel Acuna 240 Nte 25000. Fax: 84/12-2222. **Facility:** 120 units. *Bath:* combo or shower only. 8 stories, interior corridors. **Terms:** F12. **Leisure Activities:** rooftop pool. **Guest Services:** valet laundry. **Business Services:** meeting rooms. **Cards:** AE, DI, MC, VI.

SOME UNITS

QUINTA DORADO HOTEL & SUITES
▼▼▼ *Motor Inn* ((84)16-4949
12/1-12/31 & 9/1-11/30 $89 XP $9
5/1-8/31 $82 XP $8
1/1-4/30 $76 XP $7
Location: 0.5 km e jct Mex 40 (Venustiano Carrana). (1416 Pte Periferico Luis Echeverria, 25280). Fax: 84/16-6787. **Facility:** Meets AAA guest room security requirements. 148 units. 2-3 stories (no elevator), exterior corridors. **Terms:** F12. **Leisure Activities:** heated pool, exercise room. **Guest Services:** [CP] meal plan available, valet laundry. **Business Services:** conference facilities. **Cards:** AE, MC, VI.

SOME UNITS

WHERE TO DINE

BUENA VISTA
▼▼▼ *Regional Mexican* (84/30-0000
L $8-$12 D $10-$20
Location: 6 km se on Mex 57; in Camino Real Saltillo. **Hours:** noon-midnight. **Reservations:** suggested. **Features:** semi-formal attire; Sunday brunch; children's menu; cocktails; fee for area transportation; a la carte. Upscale western decor. View of surrounding mountains. **Cards:** AE, DI, MC, VI.

RESTAURANT LA CANASTA
▼▼▼ *Continental* (84/15-8050
L $4-$7 D $5-$9
Location: 0.8 mi on V Carranza from Glorieta at N Ortiz G and V Carranza. Blvd V Carranza 2485 25280. **Hours:** noon-midnight. **Reservations:** suggested. **Features:** casual dress; cocktails; a la carte. Elegant, informal country style decor with fireplaces. Located north of downtown. Ample parking in rear. Wide selection of popular regional Mexico dishes. Try the Yucatecan cochinita pibil. **Cards:** AE, MC, VI.
⊠

TORREON, COAHUILA

WHERE TO STAY

HOLIDAY INN EXPRESS

 Motel   ((17)29-6000

9/1-11/30	$131	XP $15
5/1-8/31	$124	XP $15
12/1-4/30	$118	XP $15

Location: Just ne on Mex 30. (Blvd Independencia 1133 Ote Cd Granjas, 27000). Fax: 17/29-6020. **Facility:** Attractive hacienda style breakfast atrium. Close to airport. Located in financial district. Parking garage. 166 units. Some whirlpool units. 5 stories, interior corridors. **Terms:** F18; cancellation fee imposed. **Amenities:** extended cable TV, voice mail, irons, hair dryers. **Leisure Activities:** small heated pool, exercise room. **Guest Services:** [BP] meal plan available, gift shop, valet laundry. **Business Services:** meeting rooms. **Cards:** AE, MC, VI.

SOME UNITS
/ ☒ /

PARAISO DEL DESIERTO GRAND HOTEL

 Motor Inn   (17/16-1122

All Year	$101	XP $4

Location: 2 km ne on Mex 30. Blvd Independencia 100 Pte 27000. Fax: 17/16-1122. **Facility:** Adequate parking with security. 153 units. 1 two-bedroom unit. Some whirlpool units. *Bath:* combo or shower only. 4-6 stories, interior/exterior corridors. **Terms:** F12. **Amenities:** hair dryers. **Leisure Activities:** wading pool, exercise room. **Guest Services:** [CP] meal plan available, valet laundry. **Business Services:** meeting rooms, administrative services. **Cards:** AE, MC, VI.

SOME UNITS
/ VCR /

THE PACIFIC COAST

Also known as the Mexican Riviera, Mexico's Pacific coast boasts hundreds of miles of surf-pounded shoreline and a string of destinations stretching from Mazatlán south to Bahías de Huatulco. They range from funky beach communities—traditional getaways for budget-conscious backpackers and Mexican families of modest means—to luxurious oceanside retreats catering to the well-heeled international set.

The Mexican Riviera unofficially begins at Mazatlán, a shrimping center, commercial port and burgeoning beach resort that has long attracted sport fishing enthusiasts. Puerto Vallarta was for centuries a tiny fishing village blessed with a stunning natural backdrop. Then a larger-than-life movie star romance in the early 1960s brought worldwide attention, setting the stage for the development of a world-class destination. Those who opt for a more laid-back beach vacation head for Manzanillo, where the elemental combination of sun, sea and sand mixes with the matter-of-fact grime of a real working city.

Ixtapa and Zihuatanejo are twin resorts, only 4 miles apart but decidedly different in atmosphere. Ixtapa, planned by the Mexican government and inaugurated in 1972, indulges visitors with expensive pampering; Zihuatanejo, founded by Spanish conquistadores in the early 16th century, has more of a quaint village feel. Perennially popular Acapulco may now play second fiddle to Cancún as Mexico's beach of choice, but its glittery atmosphere and boisterous nightlife remain in a class of their own. Rounding out the Riviera is Bahías de Huatulco, another government-planned resort set along a series of nine bays that scallop the Pacific coast like a necklace of aquamarine jewels.

ACAPULCO, GUERRERO

This Pacific playground instantly conjures images of idle days spent soaking up the sun and evenings of dining, dancing and revelry. Certainly Acapulco fulfills the scenic requirements for a tropical resort. Lofty mountains and green foothills extend to the sparkling blue of bay and ocean waters. Tall palm trees stand silhouetted against picturesque sunsets. And the view of Acapulco Bay at night, set off by thousands of city lights, is breathtaking.

As early as the 1530s, ships for exploration purposes were built at a Spanish settlement occupying the city's present site. Due to its excellent natural harbor, Acapulco (the name is an Indian word meaning "place where the reeds were destroyed") became the main west coast seaport for the Manila galleons and their treasures from the Orient. It was designated a city in 1599 and established as the only authorized trading port between the Americas and the Orient. From here silks, spices and other exotic goods were carried

overland on mules to Mexico City and then Veracruz for shipment to Spain, while galleons

Fast Facts

LOCATION: On the southwestern Pacific coast.

POPULATION: 516,300 (1990 Census).

AREA CODE: 74.

HIGHLIGHTS: Dramatic Acapulco Bay, fringed with beaches and backed by jungle-covered mountain slopes; Mexico's liveliest nightlife, from torchlit cliff diving to pulsating discos to folkloric dance shows; a galaxy of options for dining out; accommodations from budget style to ultra luxurious; deep-sea fishing on the bay, water skiing on Coyuca Lagoon, horseback riding along the beach.

moored in Acapulco Bay refilled their holds with silver and other Mexican products. That mercantile tradition continues, as the city remains a major export point for coffee, sugar and other products.

This rich trade with the Orient brought Mexico City merchants to annual unloading fairs. It also attracted Dutch and English pirates. Sir Francis Drake supposedly lay in wait for laden galleons near Puerto Marqués, just south of the present city, and pounced upon them as they left the sheltered harbor. To protect the ships from such raiders, the Spanish built the fort El Castillo de San Diego in 1616.

Commerce between Acapulco and Manila lasted some 250 years but came to a close in 1815 with the Mexican War of Independence. This conflict and the continued discovery and settlement of North and South America contributed to the rerouting of the China trade. As a result, Acapulco lapsed into the lethargy of an almost forgotten fishing village, punctuated by the excitement that accompanied a brief boom period during the California gold rush.

Not until 1927 was a road cut through the mountains to form an overland connection with the progressive cities to the north, particularly Mexico City. Acapulco's beaches are the country's closest to Mexico City by road, and although the trip took more than a week, the sleepy port was roused into a fever of development. When a new highway from Mexico City was completed in 1955, Acapulco was on its way to becoming Mexico's most notorious party spot.

Direct international air service began in 1964, ushering in the city's '60s and '70s heyday of glorious excess as it became a luxurious haven for the international and Hollywood jet sets, as well as one of the world's top resort destinations. The shore along Acapulco Bay was transformed into a 9-mile swath of glitter and indulgence patronized by *la gente bonita* (the beautiful people). Three decades of unmonitored growth, however, eventually tarnished Acapulco's image. Slums multiplied in the foothills behind the gleaming, high-rise bayfront buildings; traffic clogged the streets; some of the hotels became worn around the edges.

To maintain the city's standing as a world-class vacation destination—and to ward off the challenge of rapidly developing Cancún—the Mexican government spent more than $500 million during the 1980s on redevelopment projects and planning for future improvements. **Costera Miguel Alemán**, the city's main thoroughfare, and other streets were cleared of rubbish, and a mostly successful campaign rid the beaches of ever-present and aggressively persistent souvenir vendors.

A program called Aca-Limpia, or "Clean Acapulco," has devoted effort to cleaning up the water in the bay (which, despite its deep blue color, had become polluted). Boat sweepers clean the bay daily (the beaches are swept daily as well). Pollution is still evident in some locations, notably the area around **La Quebrada**, where Acapulco's famous cliff divers plunge into the surf.

Despite the fact that Cancún is now Mexico's beach of choice for foreign visitors, Acapulco seems back on track. There is expansion eastward toward the airport, and a new condominium development or resort hotel project is always sprouting up. Another factor contributing to the renaissance is the rise in domestic tourism. Many Mexicans love the city, and those who do often dismiss its Caribbean rival as pretty but characterless.

Acapulco contains neither sober historical monuments nor venerable colonial architecture. Although it is a real city and important commercial center, the economy depends most heavily on the tourist trade. Visitors—some 1.5 million annually—come not so much to sightsee but to relax. In addition to letting life's cares melt away at the beach, water recreation—from motorboat tours and fishing excursions to water skiing and parasailing—shopping and nightlife are favorite diversions.

For those with money to burn, the fun and flash are indeed heady. Big hotels—some of the finest in Mexico—pamper guests with private villas and every convenience. Dining here is an event, where al fresco tables at intimate restaurants overlook the bay. Night owls relish the city's 24-hour fun and flamboyant discos, which often don't wind down until the sun comes up. But Acapulco also has budget-friendly alternatives, and its beaches, fish shacks and fun-filled atmosphere draw hordes of Mexican families. Those who keep coming back are drawn by those ever-reliable basics—sun, sand and water.

APPROACHES

BY AIR

Acapulco International Airport is about 23 kilometers (14 miles) southeast of the city and the hotel zone, near Puerto Marqués. Major carriers frequently fly into Mexico City, where connections can be made to Acapulco.

American, Continental, Delta and Mexicana airlines offer direct flights from U.S. cities. Within Mexico, Aeroméxico and Taesa airlines offer direct flights from Mexico City and other major cities. For additional information about airlines see "Arriving by Air," page 53.

Transportes Terrestres is an airport taxi service that transports visitors to and from the airport and the city's hotel zone along Costera Miguel Alemán. The 30-minute ride costs about $6; phone (74) 83-6500.

By Car

From Mexico City, toll highway Mex. 95-D, the **Autopista del Sol** (Sun Highway), is by far the quickest and best option. Between Mexico City and Cuernavaca the nontoll funnel road (also called Mex. 95-D) is still the main route. Called the Super Highway, it splits off from the old road south of Cuernavaca near Puente de Ixtla, proceeds south to Chilpancingo and then to the international airport. Total driving time is about 3½ hours.

The four-lane, largely traffic-free highway twists and turns through beautiful valleys and around mountainous curves. Signs denote scenic stops. About halfway to Acapulco a suspension bridge 600 feet above a river affords a spectacular view; acrophobes will probably want to keep their eyes shut.

The one drawback to traveling this well-maintained, 416-kilometer (260-mile) route is the cost: Tolls are some of the most expensive in the world, at press time averaging about $85 (U.S.) between the two cities. Tolls must be paid for and gas must be purchased in pesos. The highway is economically out of the question for the average Mexican driver; most of the traffic is luxury buses, long-distance trucks and tourists willing to pay for convenience.

Mex. 95, an older, free highway, begins at Mexico City and proceeds south through Cuernavaca, Taxco, Iguala and Chilpancingo to Acapulco, roughly paralleling toll Mex. 95-D. It's scenic, but also very winding. Coastal Mex. 200 links Acapulco with Bahías de Huatulco to the southeast and with Ixtapa/Zihuatanejo to the northwest.

Acapulco is a long way from the United States; from McAllen, Tex., one of the closest U.S. border points, the distance is nearly 900 miles. From points north or south along the Pacific coast, Mex. 200 is the only route. Portions of this roadway within the state of Guerrero, however, can be potholed or marked with detours that slow driving time. As a result, most visitors fly directly to the city or drive from Mexico City.

By Bus

"Deluxe" *(ejecutivo)* buses operated by Tres Estrellas de Oro make daily runs on the Autopista del Sol between Mexico City's southern bus terminal and Acapulco; the trip takes 5 to 6 hours and costs about $30 one way. This bus line also has service to Taxco, Ixtapa and Zihuatanejo. Buses coming from Mexico City on Friday and departing Acapulco on Monday are often very crowded. **Note:** This highway is very steep and winding in places. For additional information about buses *see "Bus Service," page 63.*

By Cruise Ship

Acapulco is a major port of call for cruise ships, most of which originate from Los Angeles. Ships dock at **Puerto Acapulco**, near the old downtown area. Lines that visit the city include Cunard, Holland America, Norwegian, Princess

Plaza Alvarez   ©John Neubauer

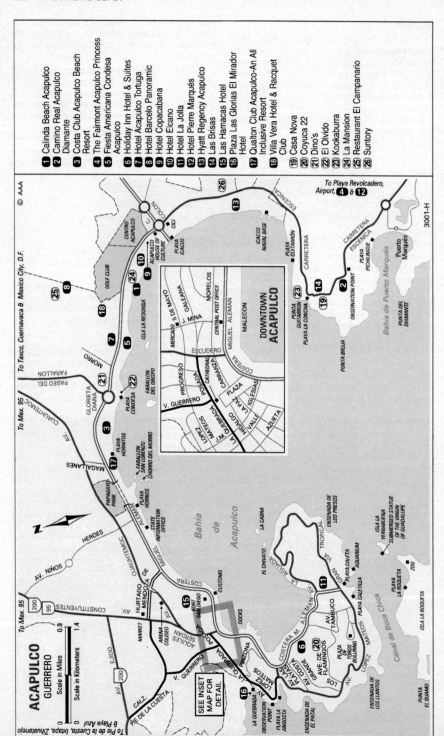

1 Calinda Beach Acapulco
2 Camino Real Acapulco Diamante
3 Costa Club Acapulco Beach Resort
4 The Fairmont Acapulco Princess
5 Fiesta Americana Condesa Acapulco
6 Holiday Inn Hotel & Suites
7 Hotel Acapulco Tortuga
8 Hotel Barcelo Panoramic
9 Hotel Copacabana
10 Hotel Elcano
11 Hotel La Jolla
12 Hotel Pierre Marqués
13 Hyatt Regency Acapulco
14 Las Brisas
15 Las Hamacas Hotel
16 Plaza Las Glorias El Mirador Hotel
17 Quatlon Club Acapulco-An All Inclusive Resort
18 Villa Vera Hotel & Racquet Club
19 Casa Nova
20 Coyuca 22
21 Dino's
22 El Olvido
23 Kookaburra
24 La Mansion
25 Restaurant El Campanario
26 Suntory

ACAPULCO
GUERRERO

Scale in Miles

Scale in Kilometers

To Pie de la Cuesta, Ixtapa, Zihuatanejo & Playa Azul

To Mex. 95

To Taxco, Cuernavaca & Mexico City, D.F.

© AAA

3001-H

DOWNTOWN ACAPULCO

SEE INSET MAP FOR DETAIL

To Playa Revolcadero, Airport, 4 & 12

Bahia de Acapulco

Bahia de Puerto Marqués

Canal de Boca Chica

The Informed Traveler

Media

Small newsstands and the Super-Super grocery store carry *The News*, Mexico City's English-language daily. Sanborn's, a restaurant chain, has English-language books and periodicals. In Acapulco, Sanborn's can be found near Playa Condesa and in the old downtown area; both are on Costera Miguel Alemán.

The bigger hotels carry *USA Today*, the *New York Times* and the *Los Angeles Times*. *Adventure in Acapulco* is a monthly publication in English that offers information on what's happening around town.

Weather

Acapulco is always balmy: highs average in the upper 80s or low 90s, lows in the 70s. It's said that the sun shines 360 days a year, and the ocean and bay are warm enough for swimming year-round. June through October is humid as well as hot, and these months also produce brief but torrential rains. Occasional hurricanes affect Mexico's Pacific coast. November is one of the nicest months, as high-season prices haven't yet kicked in.

Formality can be left at home with your coat; this is primarily a city of scandalous bathing suits and body-flaunting attire designed to turn heads at the discos.

Staying Safe

Areas frequented by tourists are generally safe, even after dark. Tourists, however, often are the target of petty theft; stay alert in such crowded public places as markets or buses. Don't take large sums of money or other valuables to the beach, and always keep your hotel key with you.

In Case of Emergency

If you need police assistance phone (74) 85-0650 or 85-0862. English-speaking tourist police on the streets wear white uniforms and safari hats and are very helpful to tourists. The Policía Federal de Caminos (Highway Patrol) can be reached by phoning (74) 85-0647 or 85-0439. LOCATEL, phone (74) 81-1111, can help locate missing persons or vehicles and gives assistance to those in need of public services. To contact the Green Angels, phone (74) 85-1178.

In case of medical emergency contact the IMSS (Mexican Social Security Hospital), downtown at Avenida Cuauhtémoc #95; phone (74) 83-5550. The Cruz Roja (Red Cross) is at Avenida Ruíz Cortines #126; phone (74) 85-4100 or 85-4101. Hospital Privado Magallanes, Wilfrido Massieu #2, provides medical services; phone (74) 85-6544. Most hotels have an in-house doctor or a doctor on 24-hour call.

Local phone calls in Acapulco cost 15c for 3 minutes. Many public phones take Ladatel credit cards only; these can be purchased in stores and other locations that display the Ladatel logo.

Cruises and Royal Caribbean. The ship's excursion manager plans tours of the city; on-shore visits include Fort San Diego (across the street from where the cruise ships are moored); La Quebrada, where the cliff divers perform; the city market; and the Mercado de Artesanías (flea market). The fine harbor and 4-mile-long bay also teem with smaller pleasure and commercial vessels.

GETTING AROUND

CITY LAYOUT

The oldest part of Acapulco fills a peninsula that forms the western side of the bay. This is where residents attend to such daily errands as grocery shopping and stopping at the post office. **Plaza de Toros**, where occasional bullfights are held, is south of the central downtown area. On the western side of the peninsula is **La Quebrada**.

Besides the **Mercado Municipal** (city market), Old Acapulco features a Moorish-looking cathedral—complete with onion-shaped blue bulb and yellow spires—that dominates **Plaza Alva-** **rez**, the city's main square. The cathedral's appearance can be misleading: It was actually constructed from parts of an uncompleted movie theater. The main square, shaded by large trees, is a meeting place in which to stop and socialize, or peruse the newspaper over a cup of coffee. Band concerts are held here on Sunday evenings.

The waterfront contains the docks and fishermen's wharves, reminders of Acapulco's continuing importance as a commercial port. This is where both cruise ships and smaller fishing boats dock. Historic **Fort San Diego** is in this section.

Along the bay runs **Costera Miguel Alemán**, the scenic boulevard named for the former Mexican president who was responsible for much of Acapulco's resort development. Most of the luxury hotels, along with many restaurants and shops and the major beaches, are in the central bay area lining the "Costera," as the thoroughfare is commonly known. Beyond the junction with Mex. 95, the coastal drive follows Acapulco Bay toward Puerto Marqués and the airport, where another group of newer luxury hotels are clustered. Inland, the major route is **Avenida Cuauhtémoc**, which roughly parallels the Costera.

As in many other parts of Mexico, streets are bewilderingly named and frequently change names as well. Street signs are difficult to locate. Orient yourself by using the Costera as a reference point—the great majority of Acapulco's accommodations, restaurants, nightspots and attractions are on or a short distance off it.

RENTAL CARS

Hertz is one of several rental car agencies with offices in Acapulco. Be sure you fully understand the terms of any rental contract. Some luxury hotels provide jeeps for their guests.

Note: AAA/CAA members enjoy exceptional discounts through Hertz for vehicles booked in the United States. Consult your local AAA/CAA club or phone Hertz, (800) 654-3080.

BUSES

Local buses connect the city with the beaches and various points of interest; fares are inexpensive, and the newer tourist buses are air-conditioned. If you are taking a bus to one of the outlying areas, such as Pie de la Cuesta or Puerto Marqués, find out when and where to board the last bus going back into town. Buses run regularly all along the Costera, and maps at covered bus stops illustrate routes to major hotels and tourist attractions. Stay alert while on the bus and beware of pickpockets, who sometimes target foreign tourists.

TAXIS

Hotel taxis are the most expensive, but they also are the most comfortable. A list showing the rates to which drivers must adhere is posted in most hotel lobbies. Rates usually go up at night. Taxis not affiliated with the hotels are usually white or blue-and-white Volkswagen Beetles. They usually charge by zone, destination or the distance traveled. Make certain that you come to an agreement on a rate before getting in the cab.

PARKING

Old Acapulco has narrow streets and is better suited to walking than driving. It is illegal to park anywhere along Miguel Costera Alemán. An easier alternative is to use city buses or take a taxi where you want to go.

WHAT TO SEE

CASA DE LA CULTURA DE ACAPULCO (Acapulco House of Culture), 1 block east of CICI near the Acapulco Cultural & Convention Center, displays pre-Columbian artifacts. Other exhibits in this small complex of buildings include well-made reproductions of Mexican art and handicrafts, many of which are for sale.

CICI (Children's International Center), on Costera Miguel Alemán at Calle Cristóbal Colón, contains a wave pool, waterslides, swimming pools with water pistols and boats, and an aquarium. There also are shows featuring performing dolphins and sea lions. Admission is charged.

FUERTE DE SAN DIEGO (Fort San Diego) stands on a hill east of the main square in Old Acapulco, overlooking the harbor and the oldest section of the city's port. Originally built in 1616 as a series of ramparts to ward off Sir Francis Drake and other marauding pirates, the fort was extensively damaged by an earthquake and rebuilt in 1776 as a stout, star-shaped fortress. In 1813, during the War of Independence, Gen. José María Morelos attacked the fort; after a 4-month siege, the Spanish capitulated, giving up their lucrative trading base. On Jan. 10, 1863, a French fleet bombarded the fortress. During the 1910 Revolution Fort San Diego was instrumental in preventing revolutionaries from taking Acapulco.

Museo Histórico de Acapulco (Acapulco Historical Museum), within the fort, documents Acapulco's role in Mexican history from pre-Hispanic times through Mexican independence. Other exhibits include artifacts from the city's former lucrative trade with the Orient, including furniture and vases. Open Tues.-Sun. Admission is charged.

PARQUE PAPAGAYO (Papagayo Park), along the Costera between Hornos and Hornitos beaches, occupies the site of the old Hotel Papagayo. The park features a children's amusement center offering a roller-skating rink, go-cart racing, a man-made lagoon with boats and a toboggan run down a hill whose summit is reached by cable car. Also in the park is an aviary where various exotic birds can be seen on a stroll along shaded paths. Admission is charged for rides.

PUERTO MARQUES, on a narrow neck of the bay east of Acapulco, is accessible by car or bus. While this fishing village is in itself unremarkable, the water is calm and suitable for swimming or water skiing, and the beach is lined with seafood restaurants. The real attraction is the 18-kilometer (11-mile) drive east from Old Acapulco's Plaza Alvarez via the naval base at **Icacos,** which offers magnificent views of the city, Acapulco Bay and smaller Puerto Marqués Bay.

In the vicinity of Punta Diamante (Diamond Point) is **Acapulco Diamante,** an exclusive area of luxury hotels, expensive condominiums and private homes that will eventually include shopping complexes, a country club, 18-hole golf course, a floating marina and a hospital. Tour boats leave Acapulco's *malecón* (waterfront) and enter Puerto Marqués Bay, although passengers are not allowed to disembark. This trip is particularly rewarding at sunset.

WHAT TO DO

DINING

Dining out is one of Acapulco's principal pleasures. Although the city has its share of local hangouts dishing out regional Mexican fare, get casually dressed up (no tie or jacket, but no shorts or jeans either) and splurge at one of the gourmet hotel restaurants. The view of the bay from a rooftop establishment at dusk is invariably glorious.

The bigger hotel restaurants offer a wide selection of international cuisine as well as local specialties. Prices tend toward the expensive side (dinner for two without drinks, wine or tip can cost upwards of $40), but the quality of the food and luxury of the setting help compensate. Atmosphere and entertainment vary with the establishment. Dinner rarely begins before 9 p.m., although some hotel restaurants begin serving around 6 or 7.

Along Costera Miguel Alemán there are numerous *palapa* (palm frond-roofed) places with a seafood menu and a funky air. Look for those where people are eating and not just having a drink. The Costera also has no shortage of rib and hamburger joints, where big portions, potent libations, wild decorations and a wilder crowd are the rule. Those homesick for fast food will find the usual American outlets lining the Costera, although prices are not cheap.

The area around the main square has many small, traditional restaurants where you can get a good Mexican meal. As elsewhere in the country, the *comida corrida* (lunch special) can be a good bargain, with soup, rice or noodles, an entree and dessert or coffee for a very reasonable price. Neighborhood street stands sell fresh seafood, but use caution when buying any food item from street vendors—if it's *not* fresh, your stomach could regret it.

In most restaurants it is customary to leave a tip (*propina*) of 10 to 15 percent. Establishments catering to tourists normally use purified water to cook vegetables and wash produce. At smaller places or if in doubt, ask for or order bottled water, juice, soda or beer. It's best to avoid ice cubes in drinks. For a list of AAA-RATED establishments in Acapulco, *see the Lodgings & Restaurants section.*

SHOPPING

Acapulco offers a wide variety of men's and women's clothing—both designer and casual—as well as Taxco silver items. The chief shopping districts are the air-conditioned complexes along the Costera and in the downtown area of **Old Acapulco.** Boutiques along the Costera are stocked with the usual resort wear, shoes and trendy fashions.

The **Plaza Bahía,** on Costera Miguel Alemán next to the Acapulco Plaza Hotel, is an enclosed mall with stores and small restaurants on two levels. Most hotels have their own specialty shops as well; the plush shopping arcade at the **Acapulco Princess** is worth stopping by. Some establishments still shut down in the early afternoon for the traditional long lunch break from about 2-4 p.m.

The **Artesanías Finas de Acapulco,** better known as AFA, is a huge, air-conditioned store 1 block off the Costera at Avenida Horatio Nelson, behind the Baby-O disco. This is the place to search for handicrafts, jewelry, luggage, handblown glassware, pottery and leather goods at fixed prices. The government-run **FONART** store on the Costera has crafts from all over the country.

For a more down-to-earth shopping experience, visit the **Mercado de Artesanías** (also called El Parazal), near Calle 5 de Mayo in the downtown area. About a 20-minute walk from the main plaza, this flea market is a melange of stalls with shopkeepers hawking replicas of archeological artifacts, rugs, papier-mâché souvenirs, ceramics and other assorted curios. Here the time-honored custom of bargaining prevails. The selling price is apt to be outrageous. If you don't have the time or patience to stand and haggle, pretending to walk away often brings the price down quickly. Go early in the morning, before it gets too hot or crowded.

The **Mercado Municipal** (Municipal Market), a few blocks off the Costera at avenidas Cuesta Hurtado de Mendoza and Constituyentes, offers a distinct change from the upscale stores of the tourist strip. This is where the locals do their shopping, and stall after stall displays everything from fresh produce to good luck charms. Souvenirs abound, and fans of kitsch will appreciate the gaudy ashtrays and shell ornaments.

BEACHES

Noisy band concerts and frivolous teeny-bikini contests notwithstanding, Acapulco's shoreline does have its business side. The bay is anchored by a commercial port at one end and a naval base at the other. Still, there is plenty of room in between for a swath of sand that is broken only by a few rock outcroppings, and more secluded beaches stretch northwest of the bay along the Pacific coastline. Keep in mind that all beaches in Mexico are federally owned property and therefore public, even stretches that may seem private because they are in front of one of the big hotels.

For safety's sake, avoid completely isolated beaches. Chairs, umbrellas, showers, hammocks and refreshments are available at most locations. Due to unpredictable or rough surf conditions, the beaches facing the open Pacific—northwest of more protected Acapulco Bay—are better suited for watching the sky turn a pretty pink at sunset or taking a romantic stroll along the shore than for swimming. The following beaches are listed alphabetically.

PIE DE LA CUESTA (Foot of the Hill) is about 16 kilometers (10 miles) northwest of Acapulco. This uncrowded, golden-sand beach offers a laid-back alternative to the city's glitz and neon and makes a good day trip. Thatched *palapa* restaurants shaded by graceful coconut palms are a perfect place to savor the local fish, caught fresh in the morning and broiled over charcoal fires. Crashing breakers and treacherous currents make swimming or bodysurfing at this beach very risky; there are no lifeguards.

Watching the sun go down over the water is a daily ritual. Families line up rows of chairs pointed toward the descending sun. Vendors mill around selling snacks and trinkets. All heads turn at sunset. If there are clouds in the sky, the patterns of color will be magnificent; even if the weather is perfect, the Pacific turns into pale gold as the sun drops.

Separated from the ocean is **Laguna de Coyuca** (Coyuca Lagoon), a bird sanctuary. Lined with mangroves, this huge freshwater lagoon is festooned with water hyacinths, filled with catfish and mullet, and populated by colorful tropical birds. Water skiing is popular, and boat and equipment rentals are available. Boat rides also can be taken to visit a coconut, pineapple or banana plantation, or simply to enjoy the solitude and water views.

PLAYA CALETA (Caleta Beach) and twin beach **Playa Caletilla** used to be known as the "morning beaches." On the peninsula that contains Old Acapulco, they formerly attracted the city's chic elite. Not quite so elegant today, the beaches cater more to families. The ocean water is very calm here. Inner tubes and other water sports equipment can be rented.

Magico Mundo Marino (Magic Marine World Aquarium) occupies a small island between Caleta and Caletilla beaches. The complex has indoor and outdoor marine life exhibits, as well as enclosures housing alligators, sea lions and turtles. Other facilities include a pool, waterslides and a scuba diving school. Rock platforms allow access into the ocean; snorkeling equipment and water skis can be rented.

Across from Caleta Beach is the secluded island of **La Roqueta**, reached by a 15-minute trip aboard a motorboat or glass-bottom boat. A lighthouse stands on the island. It's a peaceful place to sunbathe, snorkel or windsurf; boards, beach chairs, inner tubes and canoes all can be rented at Caletilla Beach.

Standing submerged in the harbor near the island is a bronze statue of the Virgin of Guadalupe. It is best seen on a glass-bottom boat ride, as the shrine is not easily visible from the surface.

PLAYA HORNOS (Hornos Beach) and twin beach Hornitos are just off Costera Miguel Alemán. The once-fashionable spot for afternoon bathers, both are now packed with Mexican tourists. Here the water of Acapulco Bay is calm, though not particularly clean. However, palm trees shade the sand, and there are numerous casual, thatched-roof restaurants lining the beach.

PLAYA LA CONDESA (La Condesa Beach) faces the middle of Acapulco Bay. Crowded with singles, this is the place to see and be seen, view Acapulco's most daring swimwear (on both sexes) and watch the parasailers. Along Costera Miguel Alemán there are many lunch spots.

PLAYA REVOLCADERO (Revolcadero Beach), approximately three-quarters of a kilometer (half a mile) beyond Puerto Marqués, is popular for swimming and surfing, although the waves can be rough and there is a powerful undertow; stay close to shore. The wide strip of sand is well suited for those who enjoy horseback riding along the beach. **Puerto Marqués**, which is lined with restaurants that are literally at the water's edge, is popular with Mexican tourists and is crowded on weekends.

A view of the bay ©John Neubauer

Visitor Services

Guides/Tours

With the focus on sunning, shopping and eating out, a guide is not really necessary in Acapulco. If you do hire one, make certain he or she is a reputable, bonded guide licensed by the State Department of Tourism. Guides can usually be found in the lobbies or at the entrances of the more expensive hotels.

Better yet, take one of the city's many organized tours. Excursions to the Old Acapulco market or to a nighttime Mexican fiesta are easily arranged. Tour operators often have offices at the large hotels. The Acapulco Tourism Board and Convention Bureau offers various guided tours of the city and environs; phone (74) 84-7819 (English spoken).

Information Sources

The state information office in Acapulco is at Costera Miguel Alemán #187 in the vicinity of Playa Hornos; phone (74) 86-6268, 86-9171 or 86-9164 (English spoken); fax (74) 86-9168. The building also houses the local Green Angels office. It is open Mon.-Fri. 8-8, Sat.-Sun. 10-6. For English answers to questions about hotels, restaurants, attractions, public facilities and sports, contact the Secretaría de Fomento Turístico (Secretary of Tourism Promotion). The office is in the Acapulco Cultural & Convention Center, on Costera Miguel Alemán next to the city golf course. It is open Mon.-Fri. 9-3 and 6-9 p.m.; phone (74) 84-7050 or 84-7152.

CANACO (Acapulco Chamber of Commerce) also provides tourist information; it is at Quebrada #31 (second floor) at the corner with Hidalgo and is open Mon.-Sat. 9-2 and 4:30-8. Phone (74) 83-5939 or 83-1711 (English spoken). City Hall Public Relations is open Mon.-Fri. 8-2; phone (74) 86-2676 or 86-2666.

The post office building (Correo) is on Costera Miguel Alemán near Plaza Juan Alvarez. A branch office is on the Costera near Playa Caleta.

Currency Exchange

Most banks along the Costera, both in the downtown area and the hotel zone, are open Mon.-Fri. 9-1:30 (some stay open until 5 or 6) and may have better currency exchange rates than the hotels. Casas de cambio (currency exchange offices) line the Costera in the vicinity of the big hotels; these are open daily and often until 8 p.m.

SIGHTSEEING

The sights here are scenic, not historic. Brightly decorated *calandrias* (horse-drawn carriages) regularly parade along Costera Miguel Alemán, a leisurely way to tour the city. They also can be hired as taxis. In Fraccionamiento Las Brisas, an upscale subdivision of homes, is **La Capilla de la Paz**, a simple, modern chapel. From this mountainside location a large white cross overlooks the east side of the bay. The attractive grounds offer a peaceful retreat from Acapulco's hectic pace.

Rental cars and jeeps are available for drives along the outlying coastal roads. An interesting side trip is through the **Costa Chica** (Little Coast), a 240-kilometer (150-mile) stretch of coastline that stretches southeast of Acapulco to the Guerrero-Oaxaca border. Mex. 200, in poor paved condition in some areas of this coastal route, runs past the town of San Marcos through a deserted terrain of lagoons and rocky cliffs in the shadow of the Sierra Madre mountains.

Costa Chica is inhabited by descendants of two boatloads of slaves who managed to evade their intended Acapulco destination. Many African customs have been preserved among the Costa Chicans, who are descendants of the Bantu tribe. This cultural enclave is most evident in and around the small mining village of **Ometepec**.

Driving northwest from Acapulco on Mex. 200 (the **Costa Grande**, or Big Coast) is another scenic excursion encompassing palm-lined lagoons and secluded beaches. Jungle-covered hills and high rock promontories finally yield to the high-rise hotels of Ixtapa.

Yachts that depart daily from the *malecón* offer morning, afternoon and moonlight cruises around **Acapulco Bay**. Tickets can be purchased at the boat or from any hotel travel agent. Lunch or dinner, music and dancing are frequently part of the package. The water also is a prime vantage point from which to view Acapulco's sunsets or the La Quebrada cliff divers. Glass-bottom boat tours of the bay are available at Caleta Beach and several other waterfront locations.

SPORTS AND RECREATION

All forms of water recreation are natural choices for leisure activity. Big-game **fishing** for marlin, sailfish, dolphin, barracuda, yellowtail, shark, red snapper and pompano is excellent all year. An international sailfish tournament is held in late November or early December. Besides deep-sea fishing, there's fresh-water fishing in Tres Palos Lagoon and Coyuca Lagoon, near Pie de la Cuesta. Small boats can be rented, with catfish the frequent catch. Favored spots for inland river fishing are along the Río Papagayo, east of Acapulco just beyond Tres Palos Lagoon, and the Río Coyuca, just beyond Coyuca Lagoon and west of Pie de la Cuesta.

Guides are available for hire, and fishing trips also can be arranged through your hotel or the **Pesca Deportiva**, near the dock across from the main square. Rates at the dock are negotiable; select a reliable outfit whose equipment is in good, safe condition. Deep-sea boats with experienced crews can be rented by the day; these excursions usually leave in the early morning and return in the early afternoon. Make arrangements ahead of time. A fishing license is required, but local companies frequently will take care of this for you.

Almost every type of **boating** can be enjoyed. Sailboats, speedboats, catamarans and other pleasure craft prevail on the bay. Yachts and deep-sea fishing vessels are available as well; some host sunset and moonlight cruises complete with champagne. Arrange boat rentals through hotels or travel agents. For larger vessels with fully-equipped crews, make reservations in advance. An information booth at Caletilla Beach rents canoes, paddleboats and other small craft and can arrange water skiing and scuba diving excursions.

Swimming in certain areas of Acapulco Bay is not recommended, despite the enticing hue of its waters. Although cleanup efforts are ongoing, pollution is still evident. The beaches tend to have rough surf and strong undertows; pay particular heed to any warning flags posted. There also are periodic shark sightings. Fortunately, almost every hotel has a pool, if not several. Some of them are huge, set against a backdrop of rustling palms and tropical plantings, and have swim-up bars for the truly indolent. Luxury hotels feature private or semi-private pools.

All of the major hotels offer **scuba diving** lessons and equipment. The waters off Roqueta Island are especially suited to diving. **Divers de México** provides dive packages with English-speaking instructors, plus lessons beginning in a swimming pool; phone (74) 82-1398. Boats for **water skiing** can be booked at hotels as well. The gentler waters at Puerto Marqués and Caleta Beach are good for beginners. Exhibitions of barefoot skiing can be viewed at Coyuca Lagoon. **Surfing** is not permitted in Acapulco Bay; the best place to surf is Revolcadero Beach, near Puerto Marqués.

Another popular sport is **parasailing**, although it is not without risks. From a standing position, a speedboat hauls a "sailor" to an altitude of more than 325 feet. This thrill can be had at almost any beach, although many parachute operators set up at La Condesa. **Windsurfing** is good at Puerto Marqués and also can be arranged at Caleta Beach. **Horseback riding** is best at Playa Revolcadero and Pie de la Cuesta.

Bullfights are held on Sundays and some holidays from November through mid-April at the **Plaza de Toros** bullring, off Avenida López Mateos in Old Acapulco. Tickets are available through travel agencies or hotels; tickets purchased through agencies include transportation to and from the hotel. The *corrida* begins promptly at 5:30, so arrive early, particularly if you plan to buy a ticket at the window. Prices average about $20 but vary with the location of the seat. *Sombra* (in the shade) seats are more expensive but more desirable than *sol* (in the sun). If it's your first bullfight, try to obtain seats near the top of the arena. They are less expensive than seats closer to the action but provide a sweeping view of the spectacle.

Fans of **jai alai** can watch this fast-paced sport at the Jai-Alai Stadium, which also is in Old Acapulco, near the bullring. This state-of-the-art complex contains restaurants, specialty shops and an art gallery, in addition to a Racing & Sports Book betting facility where wagers can be placed.

Most accommodations provide **tennis** courts for their guests; non-guests can use the facilities but will pay more per hour for court fees. There are both indoor and outdoor courts; some are lighted for night play. Lessons with English-speaking instructors are available. A tennis center at the new Vidafel Mayan Palace hotel, in the Punta Diamante area at the eastern end of Acapulco Bay, has 12 clay and synthetic-floor courts surrounded by nylon netting that screens the sun but allows cooling breezes in.

Championship **golf** courses include the 18-hole course at the Acapulco Princess Hotel and the 18-hole course at the Pierre Marqués Hotel, both along Revolcadero Beach, and the Tres Vidas Golf & Country Club at Punta Diamante, designed by renowned golf course architect Robert von Hagge. There also is a nine-hole public course off Costera Miguel Alemán, next to the Acapulco Cultural & Convention Center. All four charge greens fees, although reduced fees are offered to Acapulco Princess and Pierre Marqués hotel guests. Advance reservations are suggested during the winter season. Try to schedule a weekday round, when courses are generally less crowded.

Opportunities for **jogging** are not plentiful. A morning run is possible along the sidewalk on the beach side of Costera Miguel Alemán; do it before traffic gets too heavy. The truly dedicated can run on the shifting sands of the beaches. For those unwilling to sacrifice regular workouts just because they're on vacation, the Villa Vera Hotel & Racquet Club has a **fitness center** with step aerobic machines and free weights. The center is open to nonguests.

NIGHTLIFE

Acapulco's reputation for wild nightlife is renowned: The fun usually begins after a long dinner and can last until dawn. Most activity centers on discos, nightclubs and hotel bars; for a full night on the town, try several establishments for dinner, dancing and drinks. Other options, such as flamenco dancers, drag shows, stand-up comedy or live salsa music, are plentiful.

The city's glitzy discos still recall the legendary excess of that 1970s music/dance craze. They feature elaborate strobe lights, mirrored walls, video screens and dance beats pounding from state-of-the-art sound systems. Some have breathtaking views of Acapulco Bay. Discos start hopping after 10:30 p.m. and stay open until the wee hours. While always crowded, most are conveniently located along Costera Miguel Alemán and are grouped in clusters; if there's a line at one place, try another. A dress code is standard (jeans and T-shirts are usually frowned on). Cover charges are steep, although they are sometimes waived to draw customers, and you can run up a hefty drink tab as well if you're not careful. Present hot spots include **Baby'O, Extravaganzza, Fantasy, Le Dome, News** and **Palladium**. Another popular watering hole is the Acapulco branch of the **Hard Rock Cafe**, at Costera Miguel Alemán #37.

The city's most celebrated nighttime attraction, however, is the diving from **La Quebrada** cliff. From a torchlit spot atop a natural rock wall, men ranging in age from mid-teens to mid-40s plunge 135 feet into a narrow cove bordered by treacherous rocks. A diver hits the water at a speed of about 60 miles per hour.

The success of the spectacular dive depends not only on skill but also on split-second timing, since the tide fills the cove with swirling surf and then recedes quickly, leaving the water level as low as 12 feet during a brief period. Getting to the top of the cliff is risky as well—the divers scale the steep, vertical cliffside by grasping at rocky outcrops that occasionally snap off.

The cliff diving dates back to 1934, when La Quebrada first became a popular spot for local divers to display their talent. It is now presented with blazing torches each evening; dives can be viewed from a public platform where a small admission is charged or from the expensive nightclub of an adjacent hotel. There is a daily daytime dive as well, usually around 1 p.m.

In keeping with the local love for feats of daring, the celebrated **Voladores de Papantla** (Papantla Flyers) perform a flying pole act Monday, Wednesday and Saturday evenings as part of the Fiesta Mexicana at the Acapulco Cultural & Convention Center, Costera Miguel Alemán #2332. With poles far higher than those traditionally used, the Indians' act is very hazardous and dramatic. For those who prefer less life-threatening drama, there are the native dance performances of the **Acapulco Ballet Folklórico**, held in the plaza of the Convention Center. General admission or dinner show tickets can be purchased; phone (74) 84-7050 for reservations, or consult your hotel tour desk or a local travel agency.

The high-rise hotels frequently offer nightly entertainment, such as Mexican-style fiestas or theme parties. Live music accompanies the happy hour at these establishments, which also have the usual poolside cocktail bars and evening floor shows. The Convention Center, in addition to hosting the flying pole dancers, has several entertainment facilities, including mariachi and piano bars and outdoor performance areas.

SPECIAL EVENTS

The year's greatest influx of visitors is during *Holy Week* and the week after, marked by several religious observances. Many local businesses close, and the city becomes so crowded that some people sleep on the beach. Those wishing to visit during this time should make reservations far in advance.

For music lovers the *Acapulco International Music Festival*, which takes place in May, draws participants from many countries. The offerings encompass everything from top-of-the-charts pop to traditional boleros, and are performed by orchestras, bands, trios and individual artists. Concerts are given at the Acapulco Cultural & Convention Center, the Plaza de Toros bullring and at beaches, hotels and other open-air spots around the city.

The Virgin of Guadalupe is the focus of a nationwide pilgrimage on Dec. 12 to the Basilica of Our Lady of Guadalupe, in a northern suburb of Mexico City *(see the Mexico City attraction listing, page 312)*. The event, celebrated with dancing and other forms of merriment, is observed with special exuberance in Acapulco. Also in December are the *Cliff Diving Championships*. Acapulco closes out the year with a huge party on New Year's Eve.

WHERE TO STAY

CAMINO REAL ACAPULCO DIAMANTE

▼▼▼▼▼ *Hotel* ((74)35-1010

12/17-4/22	$270	XP $40
4/23-11/30	$230	XP $40
12/1-12/16	$220	XP $40

Location: 13 km se on Mex 200 overlooking Bahia de Puerto Marques. Carretera Escenica Km 14 39867 (Calle Baja Catita S/N). Fax: 74/35-1020. **Facility:** Comfortable, spacious rooms; all with balcony. Most with view of Puerto Marques Bay. Picturesque bayside setting in secluded area. 156 units. Some suites and whirlpool units. 5 stories, interior corridors. **Parking:** valet. **Terms:** F12; 7 day cancellation notice-fee imposed, package plans. **Amenities:** safes, honor bars, hair dryers. **Leisure Activities:** 3 pools, steamroom, beach, lighted tennis court, children's program. *Fee:* sailboating, windsurfing, waterskiing, scuba diving, exercise room. **Guest Services:** [BP] & [MAP] meal plans available, gift shop, valet laundry. *Fee:* massage. **Business Services:** meeting rooms, PC. *Fee:* fax. **Cards:** AE, DI, MC, VI. *(See color ad opposite title page)*

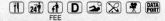
FEE

COSTA CLUB ACAPULCO BEACH RESORT

▼▼▼▼ *Hotel* ((74)85-9050

12/24-4/14	$155	XP $28
4/15-11/30	$135	XP $26
12/1-12/23	$125	XP $25

Location: 4.5 km w. Costera M Aleman 123 39670. Fax: 74/85-5493. **Facility:** Modern, high-rise central tower. All rooms with balcony. Some renovated units. 506 units. Some whirlpool units. 28 stories, interior corridors. **Parking:** extra charge or valet. **Terms:** F11; 3 day cancellation notice. **Amenities:** voice mail, safes, honor bars. **Leisure Activities:** 3 pools, beach, children's program, exercise room, game room. Fee: sauna, whirlpool, 3 lighted tennis courts. **Guest Services:** [AP], [BP] & [MAP] meal plans available, gift shop, valet laundry. Fee: massage. Fee: fax. **Cards:** AE, DI, MC, VI.

FEE

THE FAIRMONT ACAPULCO PRINCESS

▼▼▼ ▼▼▼ *Resort* (74/69-1000

All Year $259
Location: 19.3 km se, off Mex 200, Airport Hwy. Playa Revolcadero 39300 (PO Box 1351). Fax: 74/69-1015. **Facility:** Beautiful, sprawling, tropical grounds on the ocean, away from the hustle and bustle of downtown. A wonderful getaway. 1017 units. 14 stories, interior corridors. **Parking:** valet. **Terms:** 14 day cancellation notice, 7 day off season, package plans. **Amenities:** voice mail, safes, hair dryers. **Leisure Activities:** 5 pools, wading pool, beach, 1 saltwater pool, fishing, putting green, playground. Fee: sauna, golf-18 holes, 11 tennis courts (2 indoor, 9 lighted). **Guest Services:** [AP], [BP] & [MAP] meal plans available, gift shop, valet laundry. **Business Services:** conference facilities, PC, fax. **Cards:** AE, CB, DI, MC, VI.

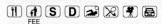
FEE

FIESTA AMERICANA CONDESA ACAPULCO

▼▼ ▼▼ *Hotel* (74/84-2828

All Year $115-$150   XP $25
Location: 5.3 km e. Costera M Aleman 97 39690 (PO Box 934). Fax: 74/84-1828. **Facility:** Attractive public areas. Large terrace pool area directly over Acapulco Bay. 500 units. 18 stories, interior corridors. **Parking:** valet. **Terms:** F12; 3 day cancellation notice, package plans. **Amenities:** voice mail, honor bars. Some: safes, hair dryers. **Leisure Activities:** 2 pools, wading pool, beach, children's program. Fee: boats, sailboating, windsurfing, waterskiing, scuba diving/snorkeling & equipment, fishing, charter fishing. **Guest Services:** gift shop, valet laundry. Fee: massage. **Business Services:** meeting rooms, administrative services, fax. Fee: PC. **Cards:** AE, DI, MC, VI.

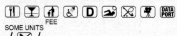
FEE
SOME UNITS
/ ⊠ /

HOTEL ACAPULCO TORTUGA

▼ *Hotel* ((74)84-8889

12/21-4/30	$100-$125	XP $15
12/1-12/20 & 5/1-11/30	$65-$75	XP $15

Location: 5 km e. Costera M Aleman 132 39690. Fax: 74/84-7385. **Facility:** Across from beach. Atrium lobby area. Rooms with balcony. 252 units. Bath: combo or shower only. 7 stories, interior corridors. **Parking:** valet. **Terms:** F10; 7 day cancellation notice. **Leisure Activities:** wading pool, exercise room. **Guest Services:** [AP] & [BP] meal plans available, valet laundry. **Business Services:** meeting rooms. Fee: fax. **Cards:** AE, DI, DS, MC, VI.

HOTEL BARCELO PANORAMIC

▼▼ *Hotel* ((74)84-0724

All Year $70-$100   XP $10
Location: 2 km n of Costera M Aleman; in Condesa sector. Ave Condesa 1 39690. Fax: 74/84-8639. **Facility:** Attractive gardens; on a hill with bay view. 200 units. Some whirlpool units. Bath: shower only. 9 stories, exterior corridors. **Terms:** F12; 7 day cancellation notice-fee imposed. **Amenities:** safes. Some: honor bars, hair dryers. **Leisure Activities:** 2 pools, wading pool, sports court. Fee: 2 lighted tennis courts. **Guest Services:** [AP] & [BP] meal plans available, gift shop, area transportation, coin laundry. **Business Services:** meeting rooms. Fee: fax. **Cards:** AE, DI, MC, VI.

FEE

(AAA) HOTEL COPACABANA

▼▼ ▼▼ *Hotel* ((74)84-3260

12/1-12/31	$100-$120	XP $15
1/1-11/30	$70-$100	XP $10

Location: 6 km e, off Costera M Aleman on the bay. Tabachines 2 39690. Fax: 74/84-6268. **Facility:** Most rooms with oceanview. 432 units. Bath: shower only. 18 stories, interior corridors. **Terms:** F12. **Amenities:** extended cable TV, voice mail, honor bars. Some: safes. **Leisure Activities:** wading pool, whirlpools, beach, scuba diving, snorkeling. Fee: boats, waterskiing, scuba & snorkeling equipment. **Guest Services:** [AP], [BP] & [MAP] meal plans available, gift shop, complimentary evening beverages, valet laundry. **Business Services:** conference facilities. Fee: fax. **Cards:** AE, DI, MC, VI.

FEE

(AAA) HOTEL ELCANO

▼▼▼ *Hotel* (74/84-1950

12/18-4/15	$190-$215	XP $25
4/16-11/30	$130-$170	XP $25

Location: 6 km e, on the bay. Ave Costera Miguel Aleman 75 39690 (PO Box 430). Fax: 74/84-2230. **Facility:** Open breezeway, lobby and public areas. All rooms with oceanview and ceiling fan; some with balcony. 180 units. 1 two-bedroom unit. Some whirlpool units. 9 stories, interior corridors. **Parking:** valet. **Terms:** F12; 7 day cancellation notice, winter, package plans. **Amenities:** voice mail, safes, honor bars, hair dryers. **Dining & Entertainment:** 2 restaurants, 7 am-11 pm, $15-$25, cocktails, entertainment. **Leisure Activities:** sauna, whirlpool, beach, exercise room. Fee: boats, waterskiing, scuba diving & equipment, charter fishing, golf & tennis privileges. **Guest Services:** [AP], [CP] & [MAP] meal plans available, gift shop, valet laundry. Fee: massage. **Business Services:** meeting rooms. Fee: fax. **Cards:** AE, DI, MC, VI.

SOME UNITS
 / ⊠ /
FEE

HOTEL LA JOLLA

▼ *Motel* (74/82-5862

All Year $35   XP $5
Location: 1 km s at Caletilla Beach. Costera M Aleman 506 39390. Fax: 74/82-5862. **Facility:** All rooms with balcony, garden and pool view. 73 units. Bath: shower only. 3 stories, exterior corridors. **Terms:** F10; monthly rates available. **Amenities:** no TVs. **Leisure Activities:** wading pool. **Business Services:** fax. **Cards:** MC, VI.

HOTEL PIERRE MARQUES

▼▼▼ *Resort* (74/66-1000

12/20-1/5	$185-$250	XP $45
12/1-12/19, 1/6-5/2 & 11/1-11/30	$95-$115	XP $25

Location: 17.5 km se, off Airport Hwy. Revolcadero Beach S/N 39300 (PO Box 474). Fax: 74/66-1016. **Facility:** Quiet location, sprawling grounds; some rooms with ocean view. Variety of room types including bungalows and villas. 343 units. 36 two-bedroom units. 1-5 stories, interior/exterior corridors. **Parking:** valet. **Terms:** F16; open 12/1-5/2 & 11/1-11/30, 14 day cancellation notice, package plans. **Amenities:** voice mail, safes. **Leisure Activities:** 3 pools, wading pools, beach, putting green, playground, exercise room. *Fee:* sauna, golf-18 holes, 5 lighted tennis courts. **Guest Services:** [AP], [BP] & [MAP] meal plans available, gift shop, valet laundry. **Business Services:** meeting rooms. *Fee:* fax. **Cards:** AE, CB, DI, MC, VI.

SOME UNITS

⏺ HYATT REGENCY ACAPULCO

▼▼▼ *Hotel* ((74)69-1234

12/24-4/20	$185-$200	XP $25
4/21-11/30	$155-$170	XP $25
12/1-12/23	$150-$165	XP $25

Location: 8 km e; next to Icacos Naval Base. Costera Aleman 1 39869. Fax: 74/84-3087. **Facility:** Most rooms with private balcony. Attractive public areas displaying regional artwork. 645 units. 2 two-bedroom units. Some whirlpool units. 22 stories, interior corridors. **Parking:** valet. **Terms:** F12; 7 day cancellation notice, package plans. **Amenities:** extended cable TV, voice mail, hair dryers. *Some:* safes, honor bars. **Dining & Entertainment:** dining room, 2 restaurants, coffee shop, 7 am-2 am, $9-$25, cocktails, entertainment. **Leisure Activities:** 2 pools, wading pool, beach. *Fee:* boats, waterskiing, scuba diving, snorkeling, fishing, charter fishing, 3 lighted tennis courts. **Guest Services:** [AP], [BP] & [MAP] meal plans available, gift shop, valet laundry. **Business Services:** meeting rooms, administrative services. *Fee:* PC, fax. **Cards:** AE, DI, MC, VI.

SOME UNITS

"LA MARINA" HOTEL, SUITES & SPA

▼▼▼ *Motor Inn* (74/82-8556

All Year $110 XP $18

Location: 1.7 km sw of Zocalo. Av Costera Miguel Aleman 222 39390. Fax: 74/82-8595. **Facility:** Mexican villas in beautifully landscaped tropical setting. All rooms with ceiling fan. 44 units, 5 with efficiency. 1-2 stories, exterior corridors. **Terms:** F12; weekly & monthly rates available. **Amenities:** extended cable TV, voice mail, safes, irons, hair dryers. **Leisure Activities:** wading pools. **Guest Services:** [BP] meal plan available, area transportation, valet laundry. **Business Services:** meeting rooms, PC. *Fee:* fax. **Cards:** AE, MC, VI.

LAS BRISAS

▼▼▼ *Resort* (74/69-6900

12/20-3/31	$200-$345	XP $35
12/1-12/19 & 4/1-11/30	$150-$210	XP $35

Location: 11.3 km se on Mex 200. Carretera Escenica 5255 39868 (PO Box 281). Fax: 74/46-5328. **Facility:** Picturesque mountainside location with commanding view. Duplex cottages with private or semi-private swimming pools. 300 units. 3 two-bedroom units and 1 three-bedroom unit. Some whirlpool units. 1 story, exterior corridors. **Parking:** valet. **Terms:** age restrictions may apply, 7 day cancellation notice, 3 day off season, package plans, $20 service charge. **Amenities:** no TVs, voice mail, safes, honor bars, irons, hair dryers. **Leisure Activities:** 2 saltwater pools, boat dock. *Fee:* boats, waterskiing, scuba diving/snorkeling & equipment, fishing, charter fishing, 5 lighted tennis courts. **Guest Services:** [CP] meal plan available, gift shop, valet laundry. **Business Services:** meeting rooms, PC. *Fee:* fax. **Cards:** AE, DI, JC, MC, VI. Affiliated with Westin Hotels.

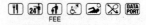

LAS HAMACAS HOTEL

▼▼▼ *Hotel* (74/83-7006

12/16-4/30	$90-$100	XP $12
12/1-12/15 & 5/1-11/30	$60-$70	XP $12

Location: 1 km e. Costera M Aleman 239 39360 (PO Box 399). Fax: 74/83-0575. **Facility:** In coconut grove. Modestly furnished guest rooms, all with balcony. 127 units. Some suites. *Bath:* shower only. 5 stories, exterior corridors. **Terms:** F12; 15 day cancellation notice, 7 day off season. **Amenities:** extended cable TV. **Leisure Activities:** wading pool, playground, exercise room. **Guest Services:** [AP], [CP] & [MAP] meal plans available, valet laundry. **Business Services:** meeting rooms. *Fee:* fax. **Cards:** AE, DI, MC, VI.

PLAZA LAS GLORIAS EL MIRADOR HOTEL

▼▼▼ *Hotel* (74/83-1155

12/16-4/30	$75-$80	XP $18
12/1-12/15 & 5/1-11/30	$55-$70	XP $18

Location: 1 km w, on La Quebrada Cliffs. Plazoleta De La Quebraoa #74 39300 (PO Box 32). Fax: 74/82-4564. **Facility:** Picturesquely situated on cliffs overlooking ocean. Some rooms with terrace views of cliff diver performances. 130 units, 128 with efficiency. Some whirlpool units. *Bath:* combo or shower only. 1-3 stories, exterior corridors. **Terms:** F12; 7 day cancellation notice, 3 day off season, monthly rates available, package plans. **Amenities:** voice mail. **Leisure Activities:** 3 pools, saltwater pool. **Guest Services:** [AP], [BP] & [CP] meal plans available, gift shop, valet laundry. *Fee:* fax. **Cards:** AE, CB, DI, MC, VI.

SOME UNITS

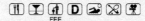

QUALTON CLUB ACAPULCO-AN ALL INCLUSIVE RESORT

▼▼▼ *Hotel* (74/86-8210

12/19-1/2	$200	XP $65
1/3-11/30	$150-$170	XP $50
12/1-12/18	$150	XP $40

Location: 4.2 km e. Costera Miguel Aleman 159 39670 (PO Box 259). Fax: 74/86-8324. **Facility:** High-rise towers on beachfront. Average sized rooms with contemporary decor. Most with balcony and ocean view. 240 units. *Bath:* combo or shower only. 11-14 stories, interior corridors. **Parking:** extra charge or valet. **Terms:** F6; 3 day cancellation notice. **Amenities:** safes (fee). **Leisure Activities:** wading pool, beach, boogie boards, windsurfing, snorkeling, children's program, social program, exercise room. **Guest Services:** [AP] meal plan available, gift shop, valet laundry. **Business Services:** meeting rooms. *Fee:* fax. **Cards:** AE, DI, MC, VI.

VILLA VERA HOTEL & RACQUET CLUB

▼▼▼▼ *Hotel* (74/84-0333

12/24-4/3	$190-$280	XP $50
12/1-12/23 & 4/4-11/30	$165-$255	XP $50

Location: 6 km e, 5 blks opposite from Beach Blvd. Lomas del Mar 35 39690 (PO Box 560-488). Fax: 74/84-7479. **Facility:** Tropical gardens throughout property. Many rooms with balcony. Meets AAA guest room security requirements. 69 units. 2 two-bedroom units and 2 efficiencies. 2 stories, exterior corridors. **Terms:** age restrictions may apply, 3 day cancellation notice, package plans. **Amenities:** safes, honor bars, irons, hair dryers. *Some:* CD players. **Leisure Activities:** sauna, whirlpool, 16 additional private or shared pools, 2 lighted tennis courts, racquetball courts, exercise room. **Guest Services:** gift shop, valet laundry. *Fee:* massage. **Business Services:** meeting rooms, fax. Cards: AE, DI, MC, VI.

SOME UNITS

The following lodging was either not evaluated or did not meet AAA rating requirements and is listed for your information only.

CALINDA BEACH ACAPULCO

[fyi] *Hotel* (74/84-0410

12/21-4/19	$130	XP $10
4/20-11/30	$120	XP $10

Under major renovation, scheduled to be completed December 2000. **Last rated:** 2 Diamond. **Location:** 6 km e, on the bay. Costera Miguel Aleman 1260 39690. Fax: 74/84-4676. **Facility:** All rooms with balcony, many with view of Acapulco Bay. 357 units. 1 two-bedroom unit. 26 stories, interior corridors. **Parking:** valet. **Terms:** F12; 7 day cancellation notice, package plans. **Amenities:** voice mail, honor bars, hair dryers. *Some:* safes. **Leisure Activities:** 2 pools, beach. *Fee:* boats, waterskiing, scuba diving & equipment, fishing. **Guest Services:** gift shop, valet laundry. **Business Services:** meeting rooms. *Fee:* PC, fax. Cards: AE, DI, MC, VI. *(See color ad p 4 and p 36)*

SOME UNITS

WHERE TO DINE

CASA NOVA

▼▼▼ ▼▼▼ *Italian* (74/46-6237

D $30-$50

Location: 12 km se on Mex 200. Escenica Las Brisas 5256 39868. **Hours:** 7 pm-11 pm, Fri & Sat-midnight. **Reservations:** suggested. **Features:** dressy casual; cocktails; entertainment; valet parking; a la carte. Elegant atmosphere. Indoor-outdoor dining on hilltop with stunning view of Acapulco Bay. Attentive service staff in semi-formal attire. Menu features varieties of veal, shrimp, fresh fish, beef, lamb and pastas, as well as traditional antipastas and desserts. Cards: AE, CB, DI, MC, VI.

COYUCA 22

▼▼▼ ▼▼▼ *Steak & Seafood* (74/82-3468

D $25-$38

Location: Coyuca 22 39390. **Hours:** Open 12/1-4/30 & 11/1-11/30; 7 pm-11 pm. **Reservations:** suggested. **Features:** No A/C; dressy casual; cocktails; valet parking; a la carte, also prix fixe. Very attractive open-air restaurant on mountainside with panoramic view of Acapulco Bay. Features lobster and prime rib. Cards: AE, DI, DS, MC, VI.

DINO'S

▼▼▼ ▼▼ *Italian* (74/84-0037

D $7-$15

Location: 4.7 km e; opposite Condesa Beach. Costera M Aleman 136 39690. **Hours:** Open 12/1-4/30 & 11/1-11/30; 4 pm-midnight. **Features:** No A/C; casual dress; cocktails & lounge; street parking; a la carte. Attractive 2nd story open-air patio-terrace dining room with bay view. Informal restaurant. Cards: AE, DI, MC, VI.

EL OLVIDO

▼▼▼ *Continental* (74/81-0214

D $10-$19

Location: 5 km e of Zocalo; adjacent to Diana Glorieta traffic circle. Costera Miguel Aleman S/N 39690. **Hours:** 6 pm-midnight. **Reservations:** accepted. **Features:** No A/C; dressy casual; cocktails; a la carte, also prix fixe. Fusion of French and Mexican cuisine. Open breezeway restaurant located right on Acapulco Bay. Multi-tiered dining terraces among palm trees with mood lighting. Tabletop candles flicker to the soothing sound of crashing waves. Cards: AE, DI, MC, VI.

KOOKABURRA

 Seafood (74/46-6039
D $10-$19

Location: 10 km e, 3 km s of Costera M Aleman. Carretera Escenica S/N 39359. **Hours:** 6:30 pm-midnight. **Reservations:** suggested. **Features:** No A/C; casual dress; cocktails; valet parking; a la carte. Open air restaurant on a hill with creatively presented entrees include quail, duck, local red snapper and beef filets. Fun desserts. Dishes with citrus flavorings. Gracious, friendly wait staff. Breathtaking panoramic view of Acapulco Bay. **Cards:** AE, DI, MC, VI.

LA MANSION

▼▼ *Steak & Seafood* (74/81-0796
L $10-$28   D $10-$28

Location: 5.8 km e. Av Costera Miguel Aleman 81 B 39690. **Hours:** 2 pm-midnight. **Reservations:** accepted. **Features:** casual dress; cocktails & lounge; a la carte. Part of a small chain of restaurants in Mexico. Specializing in steaks of various cuts, qualities and sizes, some for the hearty appetite. Also a few seafood and poultry dishes grilled tableside. **Cards:** AE, DI, MC, VI.

RESTAURANT EL CAMPANARIO

▼▼▼ *Continental* (74/84-8830
D $31

Location: 2.5 km n of Costera M Aleman. Calle Paraiso S/N 39690. **Hours:** 6 pm-11:30 pm. **Reservations:** suggested. **Features:** No A/C; dressy casual; cocktails & lounge; valet parking; prix fixe. Colonial decor in a bell tower dining room. The draw here is the mountainside setting and magnificent views of the city, entire Acapulco Bay and out into the Pacific Ocean. Menu selection consists of simple seafood, beef, poultry and pasta dishes. **Cards:** AE, DI, MC, VI.

SUNTORY

▼▼ *Ethnic* (74/84-8088
L $11-$24   D $11-$24

Location: 7.5 km e. Costera M Aleman 36 39850. **Hours:** 2 pm-midnight. **Reservations:** accepted. **Features:** casual dress; cocktails & lounge; valet parking; a la carte, also prix fixe. A Japanese restaurant where dishes are prepared tableside. Featuring combinations of fresh seafoods, poultry and beef, as well as sushi and rices. Dining room windows look over manicured garden. Nice spot for groups and conversation. **Cards:** AE, DI, MC, VI.

BAHÍAS DE HUATULCO, OAXACA (I-9)

At some point in the future, Bahías de Huatulco (wah-TOOL-co) is likely to rival such hotspots as Acapulco, Cancún and Puerto Vallarta as one of Mexico's most desirable beach getaways. It will boast a full range of accommodations, from budget-minded to first class; topflight restaurants, nightclubs and recreational facilities; and upscale condominiums and handsome homes. The graduation of the resort to major-league status, however, is not yete a reality.

While its resort aspects are a recent development, the settlement of Huatulco has been around for quite awhile. Zapotec, Mixtec and Aztec merchants established a trade route through this region during pre-Hispanic times, and the coastal settlement of Santa Cruz Huatulco became a thriving port and shipyard. By the late

16th century, however, Acapulco had absorbed the galleon trade, and pirate attacks brought about a further decline. Until recently, Huatulco and other small villages along this stretch of coast remained forgotten outposts.

Then FONATUR, Mexico's government-funded tourist development agency, stepped in. As part of a long-range tourism development plan, it selected a 22-mile stretch of bays, coves and inlets surrounding Huatulco as the site for an integrated, master-planned resort. Bahías de Huatulco was officially inaugurated in 1988. Other resort projects masterminded by FONATUR and created more or less from scratch—with varying degrees of success—are Cabo San Lucas, Cancún, Ixtapa and Loreto.

Jagged boulders and small islands characterize this section of Mexico's Pacific coastline, much of which is backed by dense tropical forest. The resort area comprises nine bays in all. From east to west, they are **Bahía Conejos, Bahía Tangolunda, Bahía Chahue, Bahía Santa Cruz, Bahía El Organo, Bahía El Maguey, Bahía Cacaluta, Bahía Chachacual** and **Bahía San Agustín.** Currently, only two are equipped with standard tourist amenities. Conejos, Tangolunda, Chahue and Santa Cruz are accessible by car; others can be reached only by boat. At Bahía Maguey, there are a few open-air *palapa* restaurants; Bahía El Organo, on the other hand, is empty. All of the bays, however, share lovely white-sand beaches and pristine waters, the result of a sewage system that permits nothing to be dumped into the ocean.

Thanks to the natural layout of the bays, large-scale development will be broken into a series of resort areas targeting budget, mid-range and upper-end travelers. Planners have vowed to set aside the majority of the resort's approximately 52,000 acres as ecological preserves in order to protect the area's natural environment. When projected development is complete (scheduled for 2018), the resort is expected to have some 30,000 hotel rooms, bring in 2 million visitors annually, and generate nearly 25 percent of the state's total revenue.

The Mexican peso devaluation and related economic troubles have slowed the pace of construction over the last few years, giving Huatulco the feel of a vacation paradise still waiting to happen. Presently, most of the visitors are diving enthusiasts, European vacationers and Mexico City families escaping that city's hectic pace. The scenery is spectacular, with dark, jagged peaks offset by white sand and the deep blue bays. The year-round warm waters are excellent for snorkeling. Sport fishing also is good, with sailfish the catch of choice.

THE INFORMED TRAVELER

Huatulco International Airport is off Mex. 200, about 19 kilometers (12 miles) north of the town of Santa Cruz and 28 kilometers (17 miles) north of the Tangolunda resort area. To those travelers arriving by air, Huatulco from above resembles more than anything a vast green carpet of jungle descending from the foothills of the Sierra Madre del Sur to the ocean shore. The tropical feeling is reinforced by the airport's aesthetically pleasing appearance. The two terminals—one for international flights, one for domestic flights—are large, *palapa*-style hardwood structures with high ceilings and thatched roofs.

Mexicana Airlines flies direct from Los Angeles to Huatulco; Continental flies direct from Houston. Aeroméxico, Aeromorelos and Mexicana offer domestic flights to Huatulco from Acapulco, Guadalajara, Mexico City, Monterrey and Oaxaca. For additional information about airlines *see "Arriving by Air," page 53.*

Visitors are shuttled from the airport to hotels in the resort area via private taxi (usually a Chevrolet Suburban) or shared minivan *(colectivo)*. Colectivo fares average about $7 per individual, taxi fares $19 (both U.S.). Taxi service also links Tangolunda, Santa Cruz and La Crucecita, which together comprise Huatulco's present core. **Boulevard Benito Juárez**, the main thoroughfare, runs through these areas, and white taxicabs are the main form of transportation connecting them. Cabs wait in front of the hotels and also congregate around the plazas in Santa Cruz and La Crucecita. Bus service connects Tangolunda, Santa Cruz and Chahue bays. The fare is inexpensive (50c or less); buses operate daily 9-7.

Reliable tourist information is not yet very plentiful. Travel agents in the bigger hotels are probably the best sources. The Huatulco Hotel and Motel Association office is located near the bank buildings at Plaza San Miguel, in the village of Santa Cruz. They can arrange a variety of excursions, including day trips to Puerto Escondido, Puerto Angel and Tehuantepec. The office is open Mon.-Fri. 9-6, Sat. 9-1; phone (958) 7-0848.

The climate is tropical, with an average annual temperature of 82 degrees. Temperatures in May, the hottest month, can reach 100. January through May is practically rainless; heavy rains fall July through September. As in Mexico's other Pacific coast resorts, the "winter" months, December through March, are the sunniest, driest and least oppressive. **Note:** Mosquitos can be fierce all along the coast. Pack an effective insect repellent or pick up Autan Classic, a widely available Mexican brand.

TANGOLUNDA

Luxury hotel development in Huatulco is focused along Bahía Tangolunda. In the Zapotec dialect the name means "place where the gods live." Tangolunda's look differs in certain respects from that of other FONATUR resort projects. High-rise buildings are absent—no structure here is more than six stories tall. As a result, there are unobstructed views from many different vantage points. Six resorts hug the bay, and no additional development is planned. Careful attention has been given to paving and landscaping, with sculptured rocks separating the roads running to and from the resort properties. Tangolunda also is kept meticulously clean; you're not likely to see even a cigarette butt on the streets.

Several beaches line this bay, including **Playa La Hierbabuena**, **Playa del Amor** (Love Beach), **Punta Paraiso** and **Playa La Entrega**, where a coral reef lies just a few feet offshore. Most of the resorts are all-inclusive, with shuttle service to the beach and such diversions as themed evening shows and Mexican Fiesta nights.

SANTA CRUZ

Bahía Santa Cruz, the site of the original fishing settlement, is the second developed area. Day cruises to the other eight bays depart from the marina here; arrangements can be made at your hotel or through local travel agents.

The village of Santa Cruz, which developed in the wake of Huatulco's resort inauguration, has a shady main square surrounded by shops, restaurants, bars and a few Mexican-style, middle-class hotels. **Playa Santa Cruz**, the main beach, is a short distance from the marina. It has clear, calm water and is a pleasant spot to snorkel or simply lay around after lunch. Nearby **Playa Yerbabuena** and Playa La Entrega are accessible by boat, either an outboard motor-propelled *panga* (skiff) or a deluxe cruise vessel.

LA CRUCECITA

La Crucecita is a town and planned housing development a mile or so inland from Bahía Chahue (CHAH-way). Located between Tangolunda and Santa Cruz bays, Chahue is the largest of the nine, with three separate stretches of sandy beach that are slated for new development. A marina that will receive cruise ships is in the planning stages. Many hotel employees and construction workers live in La Crucecita, which was built in 1986. Its main square, while not particularly authentic, is attractive, graced with a central bandstand, brick walkways, green lawns, shade trees and white stone benches.

Surrounding this plaza are restaurants and hotels, as well as a handful of shops specializing in Oaxacan handicrafts. Horse-drawn carriages depart from the plaza for leisurely tours. The central part of town is very lively in the evening, when locals and visitors mingle at the restaurants and in the square. For dancing and other nightlife options, Santa Cruz is a short cab ride away.

What To Do

Huatulco's cove-pocked coastline is its major attraction, and the best way to experience it is to take a cruise. Boat tours visit the more pristine of the nine bays, such as El Maguey or Chachacual, with time out for swimming or snorkeling in the crystal-clear water and lunch on the beach. Guided kayaking trips also are available up the Copalita River, which winds into the nearby mountains. The easiest way to arrange such excursions is through a travel agency. A representative local company is **Huatulco Tours**; phone (958) 7-0778.

Each of the bays has its own character. **Isla La Blanquita**, off Bahía Santa Cruz, looks white from a distance, crowded as it is with seagulls, ducks, pelicans and albatrosses. Bahía El Organo's U-shaped **Playa Violín** has very fine sand and gentle waves that form a sort of natural swimming pool. Here also are two natural phenomena: **El Bufadero**, a blowhole in a shoreline cliff from which spouts of water occasionally erupt, and the "**Mixtecan Face**," a rock formation just above the water that resembles the visage of an old man. Offshore coral reefs at heart-shaped Bahía Cacaluta reach almost to the surface of the water. Bahía Chachacual is a designated ecological preserve, its shores lined with acacia, ficus and mangrove trees.

Calm water is a prevailing characteristic of these bays, making them ideal for swimming, sailing and snorkeling. The warmth and clarity of the water makes snorkeling and scuba diving rewarding as well, and there are numerous coral reefs and shoreline coves to explore. Tangolunda and Santa Cruz bays have the most extensive equipment rental facilities. Among the prettiest beaches are Bahía Chahue's **Playa Esperanza** and **Playa Tejón**, and Bahía Chachacual's **Playa La India**. Swimming is best at Conejos, Tangolunda, Santa Cruz, El Organo and El Maguey bays. The offshore island and abundant reefs at Bahía San Agustín beckon divers.

In the mountains above Huatulco are coffee plantations begun by German immigrants more than 200 years ago. The tropical highlands in the vicinity of Huatulco offer ideal conditions for growing coffee, an evergreen shrub native to East Africa. Methods of harvesting and processing the plant's seeds, or beans, have changed little over time.

The trek up into this mountainous area is not for the faint of heart. Roads leading to the plantations must be traversed by four-wheel-drive vehicle. As the route ascends the vegetation changes, becoming more lush. Particularly beautiful are the intertwined limbs of saba trees, which are considered sacred. Scattered waterfalls and numerous streams in the vicinity feed into the Copalita River. Some of the plantations are only accessible via horseback.

For those in good physical condition, this is an opportunity to explore southern Mexico's rugged back country. Contact a Huatulco or Oaxaca travel agency for information about guided coffee plantation tours, or ask at your hotel.

Motor Tours organizes guided 3-hour excursions through the jungle on four-track, all-terrain motorcycles. The trip includes a stop at Bahía El Maguey and time out for lunch (not included in the cost). The jaunt is recommended for those in good shape; expect to get rather dusty. Tours depart from the Hotel Club Plaza, on Boulevard Benito Juárez in Tangolunda; for reservation information phone (958) 1-0024.

The **Campo de Golf Tangolunda** is an 18-hole course built along Tangolunda Bay. Tennis also is available. **Rancho Caballo del Mar**, at Bahía Conejos, offers horseback rides along the beach. Phone (958) 7-0366, or check with your hotel desk for information about riding excursions.

Dining and Nightlife

Huatulco is by no means a hotbed of authentic Mexican cuisine, although dining choices are not necessarily limited to the hotel restaurants. One of the house specialties at Santa Clara, on Avenida Carrizal in La Crucecita, is *pollo al barro*, a whole chicken slowly baked inside a clay pot. Also in La Crucecita is **1/2 Carlos'n Charlies**, a small (hence the name) branch of the popular Mexican chain. **El Sabor de Oaxaca**, in La Crucecita at the Hotel Las Palmas, features chicken in *mole* sauce, Oaxacan cheeses and other regional fare. **Café Huatulco**, Plaza San Miguel in Santa Cruz, has good coffee.

Nightlife has a long way to go before catching up with Acapulco or Cancún. Most of the hotels have their own bars, and the bigger ones stage Mexican Fiesta nights. **Boom Boom**, at the Royal Maeva Hotel, and **Savage**, across from the Maeva, offer music and dancing. **Magic Circus**, in Santa Cruz near the marina, is another rollicking disco. There is a cover charge at all three establishments. **Note:** Although these and other nightspots may stay open into the wee hours, finding a cab late at night can be difficult. Make any necessary arrangements for transportation back to your hotel before stepping out.

Nearby Destinations

Northwest of the airport off Mex. 200, sitting at the foot of the jungle-carpeted Sierra Madre del Sur, is **Santa María Huatulco**, which functioned as a trade center for the coastal region during pre-Hispanic times. Today the town serves as the governmental center for the different districts that make up Huatulco. It is about 10 kilometers (6 miles) from the airport and west of the developed bays; watch for the marked turnoff on Mex. 200. Unlike the resort area, Santa María Huatulco has the look of a typical

Mexican small town. Activity centers on the main square, where there is a museum housing an interesting collection of masks. Also on the square is the 18th-century, red-and-white cathedral; inside is a fragment of wood that is said to be part of Jesus' cross.

A day trip can be made to the coastal town of **Puerto Angel**, about 49 kilometers (30 miles) west of Huatulco via Mex. 200 to the town of Pochutla, then about 12 kilometers (7 miles) south. Buses travel from Huatulco to Pochutla, from which a taxi can be taken to Puerto Angel. This small fishing village was severely damaged by a hurricane in 1997 but has been rebuilt. It offers a distinct contrast to Huatulco's planned environment. The beaches are rocky but pretty, and the bay is dotted with *pangas*—small, motor-propelled skiffs. The town itself consists of little more than a naval base, a post office, and a few modest hotels and restaurants.

The most popular in-town swimming and sunning beach is **Playa del Panteón**, where there are sandy-floored *palapa* eateries and an oceanfront graveyard filled with colorful tombstones. **Playa Zipolite**, about 5 kilometers (3 miles) west of Puerto Angel via the paved road toward Mazunte, is one of the few beaches in Mexico where nudity is tolerated. In addition to *au naturel* sunbathers (who congregate at one end of the beach), Zipolite attracts a young crowd of surfers and backpackers. Strung along the sand are huts where one can eat, drink or just lounge in a hammock. Camping is permitted at the beach's trailer park. If you do venture here, don't bring anything valuable, as petty theft is common. **Note:** Zipolite faces the open ocean, and the undertow is very strong; swim at your own risk. Avoid walking on the beach after dark.

About 10 kilometers (6 miles) west of Puerto Angel (past Zipolite), in the small seaside village of Mazunte, is the **National Mexican Turtle Center**, operated by the Mexican National Fisheries Institute. This museum is dedicated to the ongoing preservation of endangered sea turtle species inhabiting Mexican coastal waters. Prior to 1990, when the government imposed a ban on turtle hunting, the local economy depended upon the slaughter of turtles for their meat and leathery hides; the opening of the center refocused efforts toward conservation.

The adventurous can hike from Mazunte to Punta Cometa, a rocky point, and from there negotiate a winding jungle path to **Mermejita**, a deserted and scenic stretch of undeveloped beach.

Oaxaca, with its colonial architecture, major archeological ruins and bustling native markets, is a 40-minute plane ride away. Your travel agent can book a sightseeing trip to the city through Chicago-based Zapotec Tours; phone (800) 446-2922. Oaxaca-based **Cantera Tours** arranges a variety of special interest excursions in and around the city. The agency has offices in Huatulco and Puerto Escondido; phone (951) 6-0512.

Where To Stay

BARCELO HUATULCO BEACH RESORT

▽▽▽▽   *Resort*   (958/1-0055

All Year $130-$190   XP $20
Location: In Tangolunda Hotel Zone. Paseo Benito Juarez 70989. Fax: 958/1-0113. **Facility:** Wide sandy beach. All rooms with balcony view of Pacific Ocean. In-season entertainment and social activities. 347 units. 1 two-bedroom unit. Some whirlpool units. 4-6 stories, interior corridors. **Terms:** F12; 3 day cancellation notice, package plans. **Amenities:** safes, honor bars. **Dining:** Casa Real, see separate listing. **Leisure Activities:** 2 pools, wading pool, 4 lighted tennis courts, social program, playground, exercise room, volleyball. *Fee:* boats, sailboating, windsurfing, waterskiing, scuba diving, fishing, golf-18 holes. **Guest Services:** [AP], [BP] & [MAP] meal plans available, gift shop, valet laundry. *Fee:* massage. **Business Services:** conference facilities. **Cards:** AE, DI, MC, VI.

🍴 24 ▼ 📶 S D 🏊 ✕ 🎥
SOME UNITS   FEE
/ ✕ /

HOTEL MEIGAS BINNIGUENDA

▽▽▽   *Hotel*   (958/7-0077

All Year $45-$88   XP $10
Location: In Santa Cruz Bay area. 70989 (Blvd Benito Juarez 5, Bahi de Santa Cruz). Fax: 958/7-0284. **Facility:** Luxuriant landscaped courtyard. Tile floors, pottery decorations. All rooms with two beds, sofa, balcony and bottled water. In-house travel agency and tour operators. 74 units. *Bath:* shower only. 2 stories, interior corridors. **Terms:** F12. **Leisure Activities:** wading pool. **Guest Services:** gift shop, area transportation. **Cards:** AE, MC, VI.

🍴 🏊 📶

MAGNIHOTEL HUATULCO SUITES RESORT

▽▽▽▽   *Resort*   (958/1-0044

All Year $240   XP $120
Location: In Tangolunda Hotel Area. Blvd Benito Juarez No 8 70989. Fax: 958/1-0221. **Facility:** Lavish, built on terraced hillside overlooking ocean. Flamboyant design. Some rooms reached by funicular. Large, attractive suites. Meets AAA guest room security requirements. 135 units. Some whirlpool units. 2-4 stories, exterior corridors. **Parking:** valet. **Terms:** F12; 20 day cancellation notice-fee imposed. **Amenities:** safes. **Leisure Activities:** 2 pools, wading pool, beach, swimming, steam room, paddleboats, sailboating, scuba diving/snorkeling & equipment, lighted tennis court, children's program, playground, exercise room. **Guest Services:** [AP] meal plan available, gift shop, area transportation, valet laundry. **Business Services:** conference facilities, fax. **Cards:** AE, DI, MC, VI.

🍴 ▼ 📶 D 🏊 ✕ 🎥 📶 DATA PORT
SOME UNITS   FEE
/ ✕ /

WHERE TO DINE

CASA REAL

  Latino (958/1-0055

D $11-$18

Location: In Tangolunda Hotel Zone; in Barcelo Huatulco Beach Resort. Paseo Benito Juarez 70989. **Hours:** 7 pm-11:30 pm. **Reservations:** suggested; in season. **Features:** semi-formal attire; cocktails & lounge; valet parking; a la carte. Imposing split-level dining room looking out into landscaped grounds. Accomplished food preparation with nouvelle presentation. Informal resort attire. **Cards:** AE, DI, MC, VI.

COLIMA, COLIMA (I-3)

Although the city of Colima (koh-LEE-mah) is little visited, it makes it a very pleasant day trip from Manzanillo and a nice break from the beach. The 70-minute drive—via the Manzanillo-Colima toll highway to the town of Tecomán, then north on Mex. 110—passes beautifully unspoiled tropical and mountain scenery. If you don't have a car, trips to Colima can be arranged through travel agencies at Manzanillo resorts *(see "What To Do" under the Manzanillo listing)*. **Note:** The toll charge is about $6.75 (U.S.) each way.

South of Manzanillo is **Laguna de Cuyutlán**, rimmed with forest-covered hills. Dense growths of mangrove frame this large lagoon, and water lilies float on the calm, clear surface. Wildlife is abundant, particularly herons, flamingos and other shore birds. Cuyutlán also is surrounded by what seems like endless groves of mango trees, coconut palms and banana plants that paint the landscape rich shades of green.

Colima itself lies in a fertile valley. Although tropical in appearance, it is cooler than the lowlands along the coast. The Río Colima divides the city in two, running through tropical fruit orchards and clusters of coconut palms (the region is an important producer of coconuts, bananas and lemons). Entering the city via Mex. 110 from Manzanillo, the first landmark visitors see is the **King Colima Monument**, a sculpture erected in 1955.

What makes Colima especially enticing to visitors—besides the remarkable cleanliness of its streets and parks—is the carefully preserved colonial atmosphere of the town center. **Plaza Principal**, the main square, is located between avenidas Madero and Hidalgo. The plaza is surrounded by the **Jardín Libertad** (Liberty Garden), where there are white benches and huge, sculpted iron fountains shooting streams of water 20 feet into the air. Arcades around the plaza shelter shops and commercial businesses.

On the plaza's east side are the city's cathedral and the **Palacio de Gobierno** (Government Palace), which has a cool inner courtyard. Covering four walls around an interior staircase is a mural by Jorge Chavez Carrillo illustrating scenes from Mexican history, beginning with the Conquest and ending with the 1910 Revolution. Many of the downtown buildings were constructed in the neoclassic style during the later years of dictator Porfirio Díaz's regime. Earthquakes in 1932 and 1944 leveled some of the structures, which were later rebuilt. The **Teatro Hidalgo** (Hidalgo Theater), a block southwest of Plaza Principal, was completed in 1883. Its interior has a 19th-century elegance. Check with the tourism office for information about scheduled performances.

A block or so east of the main plaza is **Jardín Quintero**, which has a fountain in its center. About 3 blocks further east is larger **Jardín Nuñez**, with lush greenery that makes it a good spot for relaxing. Just south of the Casa de la Cultura *(see attraction listing)* and east of Calzada Galván is **Parque Piedra Lisa**. The name means "sliding stone," and those who do slide on the namesake rock will supposedly return to Colima one day. For lunch, try **Samadhi**, about 3 blocks north of Jardín Nuñez on Avenida Filomeno Medina (where it branches off Avenida Juárez). This vegetarian restaurant has a shady courtyard and serves a tasty, inexpensive *comida corrida*. Have a *licuado* (fruit shake) or juice rather than taking a chance on the water.

Crammed into a huge warehouse at Avenida Belisario Domínguez #80, near the central downtown area, is a collection of some 350 antique automobiles ranging from late 19th-century carriages and coaches to 1950 models.

Recent, ongoing archeological excavations just north of the capital have begun to uncover a much older city. The site, **La Campana**, is in the village of Villa de Alvarez, next to the Plaza Diamante shopping mall on Avenida Tecnológico. The earliest remains are believed to date from around 1500 B.C. Seven buildings have been excavated; structure No. 2 is the most impressive, with Volcán de Fuego as a backdrop. The site is open Tues.-Sun. 9-5. Admission is charged; free to all Sun.

Colima's tourism office is located on the west side of Plaza Principal, across from the Government Palace on Portal Hidalgo. It is open Mon.-Fri. 9-3 and 6-9 p.m., Sat. 9-1; phone (331) 2-4360 or 2-8360 (English spoken). The **Central de Autobuses** (Main Bus Terminal) is a mile or so east of town via Avenida Niños Heroes.

Twin volcanoes just 3 miles apart are the focus of **Volcán de Colima National Park**, about 40 kilometers (25 miles) north of the city via Highway 16. Dormant **Volcán Nevado de Colima**, 14,365 feet tall, has flanks cloaked with forests of green conifers. Its neighbor, 12,989-foot **Volcán de Fuego de Colima**, has acted up numerous times since a disastrous eruption in 1941. The most recent outburst occurred in May 1999, spewing rocks and lava, necessitating the evacuation of nearby villages and creating spectacular night scenes for intrepid photographers.

From May through July, orchids line the paved, winding road that ascends Fuego's slope to the town of San Antonio, just outside the national park. The clear, dry winter months, when the volcanoes are snowcapped, is the best time for viewing them. Experienced mountaineers often hike or climb to the summit of Nevado de Colima.

A short distance north of the volcanoes is **Laguna la María**, a lake with calm, green-hued waters surrounded by thick vegetation. The entire area is a deer sanctuary and a haven for numerous bird species. Local buses make the slow, bumpy trek to La María; check with the Colima tourism office for additional information.

About 7 kilometers (4 miles) north of Colima (via Avenida Manuel Alvarez out of town) is the village of **Comala** ("the place of the griddles"). It's a quick trip by car or bus; "suburban" buses leave from the Terminal de Autobuses Suburbana at Plaza Colimán, on the western outskirts of town. Comala was once known as El Pueblo Blanco ("The White Town") for its all-white buildings with red-tiled roofs.

Passing time in the central plaza, with its shade trees and white benches, makes for a pleasant afternoon outing. A group of small restaurants on the plaza's south side (including local favorite **Comala Bucaramanga**) serve a variety of *botanas*, or appetizers, for the price of potent Mexican libations. As the afternoon wears on, the square fills with the sound of music as mariachi bands try to outdo each other for customers' business.

The **Artesanías Cooperativa Comala**, a short walk from the town center, is a cooperative factory and crafts school. Local artisans create wood furniture, leather goods and art objects using traditional methods. Good buys are possible.

WHAT TO SEE IN TOWN

CASA DE LA CULTURA (House of Culture) is on Calzada Galván at Ejército Nacional, about half a mile northeast of Plaza Principal; it is most easily reached by bus. The modern buildings of this extensive complex, the University of Colima's arts center, contain theaters, art schools and the Museum of the Western Cultures, all set among landscaped grounds. Art exhibits and traditional music, dance and dramatic performances are regularly given; consult the tourism office for schedule information.

Museo de las Culturas del Occidente (Museum of the Western Cultures) has a wonderful collection of pre-Columbian pottery and artifacts. Statues of both men and women depict many aspects of daily life in pre-Hispanic western Mexico. Noteworthy are the Izcuintli, or "Colima dog" figurines, playful representations of dancing canines that originated in this state. Deposited in the tombs of the departed, they were said to guide the dead in the journey toward *tlalocan*

(paradise). Other animal and human figures are on display, as well as jewelry fashioned from shells and bones. The museum's café has a smoky ambience accentuated by Salvador Dalí posters hanging on the walls. Open Tues.-Sun. 9-7. Free. Phone (331) 2-3155.

MUSEO DE HISTORIA (History Museum), is on Calle 16 de Septiembre and Avenida Reforma, on the south side of Plaza Principal. It exhibits archeological and craft displays and a group of pre-Hispanic ceramics, smaller than the collection at the Museum of the Western Cultures but just as fascinating. Next door is an art gallery that features traveling exhibits. Tues.-Sun. 9-2 and 4-8. Free. Phone (331) 2-9228.

MUSEO UNIVERSITARIO DE CULTURAS POPULARES (University Museum of Popular Cultures) is about 8 blocks north of the main plaza at calles 27 de Septiembre and Manuel Gallardo. The emphasis is on traditional masks; there is also a small display of musical instruments. Information is presented in Spanish. Mon.-Sat. 9-2 and 4-7. Free.

WHERE TO STAY

MOTEL LOS CANDILES

 Motor Inn ☏ (331)2-3212
All Year $30-$45 XP $5
Location: 1.5 km ne on Mex 54. Blvd Camino Real #399. Fax: 331/3-1707. **Facility:** Convenient location on Guadalajara Highway. Clean, well-maintained rooms. 75 units. *Bath:* shower only. 3 stories, interior/exterior corridors. **Guest Services:** gift shop. **Business Services:** meeting rooms. **Cards:** AE, MC, VI.

COSTA ALEGRE, JALISCO (I-1)

Travelers who want to experience a bit of seaside old Mexico should explore the **Costa Alegre** (Happy Coast)—also known as the Costa Careyes, or Turtle Coast—which extends from Chamela south to Barra de Navidad. A few expensive, exclusive, secluded resorts catering to celebrities and the wealthy are tucked among a string of modest beach towns that are popular weekend getaways for Guadalajarans.

To reach the area by car, simply take Mex. 200 south from Puerto Vallarta. (Buses traveling between Puerto Vallarta and Manzanillo also make stops along the coast.) At Boca de Tomatlán, south of Puerto Vallarta, the road swings inland, bypassing Cabo Corrientes (the southern tip of Banderas Bay) before nearing the Pacific again in the vicinity of Chamela. Although not strictly a coastal route, the highway does offer occasional views of the ocean. The scenery is varied—hills spiked with cactus give way to palm groves as the route winds south, and views shift from craggy mountains to waterfowl-filled lagoons. Many of the villages, beaches and private resorts along the Costa Alegre are accessed from dirt roads branching off Mex. 200.

Along the shoreline, protected coves and bays alternate with stretches of sand pounded by breakers and subject to strong currents. Just north of Chamela is the resort property of **Las Alamandas**, hidden off Mex. 200. A dirt road passing through the humble agricultural village of Quemaro leads to the guarded entrance of this small (six villas) but extravagantly appointed resort hideaway, one of Mexico's most exclusive (and expensive). Bolivian tin baron Antenor Patiño, who built Manzanillo's Las Hadas, initially planned Las Alamandas as a similar high-volume venture; his granddaughter opened it in 1990 as a scaled-down but even more luxurious property. Don't expect to just drop in and take a look around; guests must be expected or have a reservation.

The village of **Chamela** sits on bluffs overlooking Bahía Chamela. First settled in 1525, it served as a fortified anchoring ground for Spanish galleons returning from the Orient. Sea turtles and good-sized oysters inhabit the local beaches. During February and March, huge flocks of migrating sea birds settle on the small islands in the bay. A few rustic bungalows, restaurants and campsites accommodate travelers.

The next major development is **Costa Careyes**, where two luxury, all-inclusive resort developments—one of them a Club Med—are situated along a series of rocky, jungle-edged coves protected from the open ocean. Further south is the palm-lined beach at **Tenacatita**, which is reached by a 8-kilometer (5-mile) dirt road turnoff.

The most popular stretch of the Costa Alegre is anchored by the towns of **Barra de Navidad** and **San Patricio Melaque** (meh-LAH-keh), just north of the Colima state border. They lie about 3 miles apart along the shore of crescent-shaped **Bahía de Navidad**, which is edged with sandy beaches. Small, inexpensive hotels and thatch-roofed restaurants line the beach, which is known for its blazing sunsets. Try to visit during the week; on weekends, and particularly on Mexican holidays, this stretch is jampacked with people and much less pleasant.

Barra de Navidad, on a sandbar lying between the bay and a lagoon, is the more picturesque of the two towns and the one most dependent on tourism. It has more upscale accommodations than San Patricio Melaque, although they are not luxurious. Several hotels line Avenida Legazpi, the beachfront street. Simple, casual eateries such as **Restaurant Patty**, in the center of town at the corner of avenidas Veracruz and Jalisco, dish up standard Mexican dishes. On the opposite corner, **Café Ambar** specializes in crêpes.

An established group of American expatriates lives in Barra de Navidad; one of them runs **Beer Bob's**, a paperback book exchange located at Avenida Mazatlán #61, a few blocks inland from the beach. The local *cooperativa*—an association of individual boat operators—can arrange fishing and water skiing excursions, a tour of the lagoon, or a trip across it in a small *lancha* (outboard launch) to the seafood restaurants in the little village of **Colimilla**.

Local buses connect Barra de Navidad with San Patricio Melaque, toward the northern end of Bahía de Navidad. Melaque is more like a typical Mexican town with its main plaza, church, municipal market and bus station. It has a greater number of hotels in the budget range. For RV owners, a designated camping area is located along the rather unattractive stretch of beach just west of town, as well as the Playa Trailer Park, closer to the main beach area.

A short boat ride south from Barra de Navidad's town pier is **Isla Navidad**, a resort complex featuring a luxury hotel, the Grand Bay; a 27-hole golf course designed by Robert Von Hagge; and a sprinkling of upscale condominiums and residential villas.

IXTAPA/ZIHUATANEJO, GUERRERO (H-6)

Twin resorts on Guerrero's Pacific Coast, Ixtapa (eeks-TAH-pa) and Zihuatanejo (see-wah-tah-NEH-ho) are geographically close but different in character. Ixtapa materialized just under 3 decades ago, largely through the efforts of FONATUR, the Mexican government's tourism development agency. Zihuatanejo, in contrast, was a quaint little fishing town long before its northern neighbor's first lofty hotel rose from the sand. While Ixtapa indulges visitors with luxurious amenities at world-class hotels, Zihuatanejo beguiles them with centuries-old traditions and—despite its own increased growth—a relaxed village feel.

Artifacts, stone carvings and stelae found in the vicinity of Zihuatanejo offer evidence that the region has been inhabited as far back as 3,000 B.C. Spanish *conquistadores* began sailing from **Bahía de Zihuatanejo** in 1527; their galleons returned laden not only with silks and spices but with coconut palms brought from the Philippines. The graceful fronds of this palm are now a common sight at seaside resorts up and down the Mexican Pacific coast. For awhile Zihuatanejo vied with Acapulco for the Orient trade, but when that early era of maritime commerce faded, the settlement lapsed into obscurity.

During an early Spanish exploration of the area, an officer under Hernán Cortés is said to have asked his guide the name of the place. In the Náhuatl language, the guide replied "Cihuat-lán," meaning "place of women"—a reference to the existing matriarchal society, in which weaving was the chief occupation. Along the way, Cihuatlán was mispronounced and the somewhat dismissive Spanish suffix "nejo" was tacked on at the end, resulting in the present name.

Ixtapa, on the other hand, blossomed almost overnight after FONATUR determined the stretch of sand a few miles northwest of Zihuatanejo Bay to be ripe for resort development. The construction of hotels, restaurants, shopping plazas and a marina created employment opportunities in a largely impoverished state. As Ixtapa grew, Zihuatanejo followed suit, albeit at a slower pace. For starters, many of the dirt streets were paved. Although restaurants and boutiques give the *malecón* (waterfront promenade) a touristy look, Zihuatanejo to a large degree has managed to hold on to its charm.

Those who decry Cancún level the same criticisms at Ixtapa—too big, too expensive, soulless, manufactured. But like Cancún, Ixtapa appeals to the traveler who craves an extravagant vacation, a getaway from any and all daily concerns. Beauty and pampering come with a price, of course, but for those willing to pay it, the big-league resort trappings of Ixtapa definitely satisfy. Here, however, vacationers can have the best of both worlds—sampling Ixtapa's air-conditioned luxury as well as Zihuatanejo's funkier informality.

THE INFORMED TRAVELER

Ixtapa/Zihuatanejo International Airport is off Mex. 200 (referred to as the Carretera Costera, or Coastal Highway), about 10 kilometers (6 miles) east of Zihuatanejo and 17 kilometers (10.5 miles) southeast of Ixtapa. Continental flies direct from Houston, with connecting flights linking other U.S. cities. Mexicana offers flights from U.S. cities to Guadalajara and Mexico City, where connections can be made to Zihuatanejo. TWA offers seasonal service (Dec.-May). For schedule and reservation information, contact the individual airline. For information about Continental vacation packages to Ixtapa/Zihuatanejo, phone (800) 634-5555.

Aeroméxico offers flights to Mexico City, where connections can be made to Zihuatanejo. Aerolitoral, an Aeroméxico subsidiary, has daily nonstop flights from Guadalajara. For Aeroméxico schedule information, phone the airport ticket office at (755) 4-2237 or 4-2634. For additional information about airlines *see "Arriving by Air," page 53.*

Fixed-price *colectivos* (minivans) shuttle groups of passengers from the airport to hotels in either Ixtapa or Zihuatanejo. Tickets are purchased at the transportation desk in the arrival

area. It will cost slightly more for a ride to Ixtapa. Private taxis from the airport are more than twice as expensive. Arrange transportation back to the airport through your hotel.

By car, the main—really the only—route is Mex. 200. Acapulco is about 256 kilometers (160 miles) to the southeast (a 3½-hour drive); Manzanillo is 560 kilometers (350 miles) to the northwest. The condition of the roadway is generally good, although heavy summer rainstorms can create potholes or trigger mudslides. Most of the *topes* (speed bumps) scattered along Mex. 200 between Zihuatanejo and Acapulco have been removed.

Mexico City is 576 kilometers (360 miles) to the northeast via Mex. 134, the most direct route. **Note:** Avoid Mex. 134 unless you have a four-wheel-drive vehicle. From Ciudad Altamirano to the junction with Mex. 200, Mex. 134 is filled with potholes, and portions of the roadway are likely to be washed out or blocked by rock slides. Regardless of the highway, do not drive after dark.

Taxis are a convenient and relatively inexpensive means of shuttling between Zihuatanejo and Ixtapa's Hotel Zone (about a 10-minute ride). Fares go up after midnight. Current rates are posted in hotel lobbies, but it shouldn't cost more than $5 (U.S.) to get from one place to the other. Taxi fares within either town are usually under $2, although Ixtapa's Hotel Zone and downtown Zihuatanejo are both easily negotiated on foot. Regardless of where you're going, agree to a fare before getting in the cab.

City buses run frequently between Ixtapa and Zihuatanejo. The fare is inexpensive, about 50c one way. Buses make numerous stops along Boulevard Ixtapa; in Zihuatanejo, they stop near the intersection of avenidas Morelos and Benito Juárez, some 3 blocks north of the city market. If you're driving from one town to the other, use caution; the road narrows and widens unexpectedly, and there are several speed bumps. **Moto Rent**, located in the Los Patios shopping center on Boulevard Ixtapa, rents mopeds, mountain bikes and rollerblades; phone (755) 3-1630. **Note:** While a moped is a convenient way to get around, keep in mind that the rental fee may not include insurance.

A Guerrero state tourism office is in the La Puerta shopping center on Boulevard Ixtapa (across the street from the Presidente Forum Resort). The office is open Mon.-Fri. 9-2 and 4-7; phone (755) 3-1968. The Ixtapa/Zihuatanejo Hotel Association also can provide general information about the area; phone (755) 3-1566. Avoid booths with "Tourist Information" signs (found mostly at the airport), which are essentially pushing time-share sales.

Currency can be exchanged at hotels, banks and *casas de cambio* (exchange offices). Banks usually have the best rates and are open Mon.-Fri. 9-1. There are 24-hour Banamex automatic teller machines (designated *Caja Permanente*) on Boulevard Ixtapa next to the Hotel Fontan, and on Calle Cuauhtémoc in downtown Zihuatanejo (next to the Banamex bank). Each ATM accepts MasterCard or VISA and dispenses pesos.

For assistance or in case of an emergency, contact the Ixtapa tourist police; phone (755) 4-5360. The Cruz Roja (Red Cross), in Zihuatanejo, provides 24-hour ambulance service; phone (755) 4-2009. Major hotels should be able to provide the names and phone numbers of English-speaking doctors.

The average annual temperature at this tropical location is a balmy 79 degrees. Summers are hot, with temperatures ranging from the upper 70s to the low 90s. The winter months—high tourist season—are slightly cooler, with lows in the low 70s, highs in the upper 80s. The rainy season, from July through September, turns the normally brown countryside a brilliant green. Showers frequently fall at night, guaranteeing sunny days almost all year. Pacific hurricanes occasionally strike; two storms hit this section of the coast within a week in June 1996.

LAYOUT

The coastal strips of both Guerrero and Michoacán states are essentially undeveloped and remote, giving Ixtapa/Zihuatanejo somewhat the feel of an oasis. This twin resort area encompasses some 16 miles of sandy beaches, tiny offshore islets, scalloped coves and placid lagoons, all backed by the Sierra Madre del Sur.

An impressive string of high-rise hotels, surrounded by clusters of palm trees, make up the 2-mile stretch of Ixtapa's **Hotel Zone**, which fronts broad Palmar Bay. **Boulevard Ixtapa** is the main street and runs behind the hotels. On the other side of this thoroughfare are a number of small shopping malls. At the Hotel Zone's eastern end is the **Ixtapa Golf Club**. Almost anything of interest to visitors will be on either side of Boulevard Ixtapa.

About a mile before the end of the Hotel Zone (if you're heading north), a road branching to the right off Boulevard Ixtapa leads to Mex. 200, and is also the way to get to Playa Quieta, Playa Linda and other beaches north of Ixtapa proper (watch for signs indicating the destination). Boulevard Ixtapa itself ends in a traffic circle at the 450-acre **Marina Ixtapa** complex, where luxury villas and condominiums share space with a 622-slip yacht marina, the **Marina Golf Course** and a dockside promenade lined with restaurants. Overlooking the marina is **El Faro**, an 85-foot-tall tower that offers a 360-degree view of the surrounding area.

Ixtapa is connected with Zihuatanejo, about 7 kilometers (4 miles) to the southeast, by Mex. 200 (which is called Boulevard Leonardo D

Vinci between the two towns). Zihuatanejo (affectionately referred to by locals as "Zihua") spreads along the shores of oyster-shaped Bahía de Zihuatanejo, a naturally protected harbor. Less than 2 miles wide, this is one of the more picturesque bays along Mexico's Pacific coast.

Zihuatanejo's small downtown lies north of the bay; to the east are unobstructed beaches and the foothills of the Sierra Madre del Sur. Locals and tourists alike congregate along the *malecón* (waterfront promenade), officially called **Paseo del Pescador**. In Zihuatanejo, the basketball court fronting the beach right in the center of town takes the place of the traditional Mexican main square. East-west Avenida Juan Alvarez, a block north of and paralleling the *malecón*, is the principal traffic artery, but there are several pedestrian-only streets just off the waterfront. The main north-south thoroughfares are 5 de Mayo, Cuauhtémoc, Vicente Guerrero and Benito Juárez.

Hotels perch atop the cliffs surrounding the bay. A clifftop *mirador* (lookout point) along Camino a la Playa la Ropa, the road that connects Zihuatanejo and La Ropa Beach (*see "The Beaches" below*), offers a spectacular view of the town and the bay. A bronze plaque (in Spanish) commemorates the first commercial maritime expedition that left the port in 1527, bound for the Philippines.

The area's history is recounted at the small **Museo Arqueológico de la Costa Grande** (Archeological Museum of the Costa Grande), on the waterfront at the eastern end of Paseo del Pescador (near Calle Vicente Guerrero). Maps and murals chart pre-Hispanic migrations to the Costa Grande, the section of coastline between Zihuatanejo and Acapulco. Pottery and other artifacts bear evidence of extensive trade relations with cultures as far-flung as the Olmecs of the lower Gulf of Mexico coast. Information is presented in Spanish. Open Tues.-Sun. 10-6. Donations are accepted.

THE BEACHES

The coastline between Ixtapa/Zihuatanejo and Acapulco is known as "La Costa Grande" because of its broad, open beaches. The swath fronting the Ixtapa Hotel Zone is called **Playa del Palmar**. The dramatic arc of white sand forms a wide curve, with clusters of rock formations rising out of the offshore waters. This beach faces the ocean, and the surf is rough at times. At the eastern end of the Hotel Zone, near the Ixtapa Golf Club, is **Playa Vista Hermosa**. Between Ixtapa and Zihuatanejo is **Playa Majahua**, a secluded, little-visited beach where resort development is under way.

At the northwest end of Palmar Bay is **Punta Ixtapa** (Ixtapa Point). A residential and recreational complex is being constructed on this peninsula. Just off the tip of the point is **Isla de a**

Pie ("island on foot"), so named because it can be reached at low tide by traversing the rocks. Marine birds, especially pelicans and seagulls, congregate on the islet. Along the west side of the peninsula is **Playa Quieta** (Quiet Beach), which is now largely devoted to the water sports facilities of Club Med and is closed to the public.

Playa Linda, about a mile up the coast from Playa Quieta, has a jungly backdrop of coconut plantations. Open-air restaurants along the beach serve fresh seafood. Outboard motor-powered skiffs *(pangas)* depart from the small jetty for the 10-minute boat ride to **Isla Ixtapa**, a short distance offshore. The wooded island is a pleasant place to spend a day sunning, snorkeling or diving. **Playa Cuachalalate**, the main beach, is lined with *palapa* restaurants. On the other side of the island, behind the El Marlin Restaurant, is tiny **Playa Coral**, with calm, crystal-clear water ideal for snorkeling. Basic gear is available for rent on the island.

Round-trip tickets for the boat ride to Isla Ixtapa can be purchased at the Playa Linda pier landing for about $2.25 (U.S.). The last boats leave for the mainland around 5 p.m.; keep your ticket stub for the return trip. **Note:** Only take a boat displaying the local *Cooperativa* emblem.

Zihuatanejo's main beach is **Playa Principal**, a sandy stretch in front of the *malecón* (Paseo del Pescador). At the *malecón's* western end is the town pier *(muelle)*. Local fishermen store their boats and gear on the sand after returning with the morning's catch. At the western end of the *malecón*, a rickety wooden bridge (locals call it the "Popeye Bridge") crosses a small canal; to the south is the Puerto Mío resort and marina.

Just east of Playa Principal and the main part of town is **Playa la Madera** (Wood Beach). The name comes from colonial days, when pine, oak, cedar and mahogany cut from the mountain forests were shipped back to Spain. Small hotels, private bungalows and restaurants crowd **Cerro la Madera** (Madera Hill), which rises behind the narrow beach. A bayside footpath (known as *Continuación del Paseo del Pescador*) cuts through the rocks that once separated the two beaches. It's a pleasant walk if not attempted at high tide, when you're bound to get wet. Also avoid the footpath after dark.

Particularly pretty is **Playa la Ropa** (Clothes Beach), on the protected eastern side of the bay and a 5-minute taxi ride from downtown Zihuatanejo. The name refers to the cargo of silks that were strewn all over the beach when a Spanish galleon shipwrecked here. Palm trees fringe the mile of soft white sand, and several sand-floored, open-air *palapa* eateries offer both seafood and Mexican cooking. Playa la Ropa is good for swimming, water skiing, jet skiing, parasailing and windsurfing. A steep rock bluff separates this beach from Playa la Madera.

Divers and snorkelers head for the crystalline waters of **Playa las Gatas**, which is reached by boat. Harmless nurse sharks once populated the shallow, rocky bay bottom, hence the name. Legend has it that the long row of rocks that functions as a breakwater were deposited by a pre-Hispanic ruler as a shelter for his daughter's private beach, although it is possible they could also be ballast dumped from Spanish galleons. There are more *palapa* restaurants here.

Small, canopied *pangas* depart from the Zihuatanejo town pier for a scenic 10-minute ride across the bay to the small dock at Las Gatas. Round-trip tickets cost about $2.50 (U.S.) and can be purchased at the *Cooperativa* office at the head of the pier. The boats, often called "water taxis," run frequently; keep your ticket stub for the return trip.

Playa Blanca is about 10 kilometers (6 miles) east of Zihuatanejo; it is accessible via a dirt road that branches off Mex. 200. The scenic stretch of sand curves southeast to **Barra de Potosí**; off the tip of this hook-shaped peninsula is a group of rock islets, called *morros*, that are characteristic of this section of coastline. One of them, "The Iceberg," gets its name from the shower of white guano left behind by innumerable marine birds.

OUTDOOR RECREATION

Although Mazatlán and Baja California are better-known Pacific coast sport fishing destinations, anglers are discovering the offshore waters here. Sailfish is the pre-eminent big-game catch, along with blue and black marlin, dorado (mahimahi) and yellowfin tuna; smaller species like barracuda, grouper, roosterfish, Spanish mackerel and wahoo also put up a spirited fight. An environmentally friendly tag-and-release policy is promoted.

The **Boat Cooperative** *(Cooperativa de Lanchas de Recreo)* at the Zihuatanejo town pier can arrange an excursion; phone (755) 4-2056. Prices vary based on the size of the boat and the number of people and can be negotiated with the boat owners. Most of the boats depart the bay by 7 a.m. and return around 3. Your hotel may be able to arrange a fishing trip, although it will cost more.

Aeroméxico Vacations, an affiliate of the airline, offers Ixtapa/Zihuatanejo sportfishing packages that include airfare, accommodations, licenses, a boat and all gear. Travel agencies can book a package; for general information and a brochure, phone (800) 245-8585 in the United States. **Baja Fishing Adventures** puts together similar package excursions departing from Los Angeles; for information phone (310) 594-9441 or (800) 458-3688.

The **Zihuatanejo Scuba Center** arranges scuba and snorkeling trips and also organizes night dives and excursions for underwater still and video photography. Visibility is best from May through December, although diving is possible year-round. Juan Bernard, a marine biologist and the center's dive instructor, is very knowledgeable about the area's scuba sites, which range from shallow reefs to submerged shipwrecks to canyons 100 feet below the surface. One of the most recent discoveries was made by divers exploring the rock islets off Barra de Potosí; they found a series of caverns leading to a large dome rising above the water's surface. Snorkelers favor **Playa Manzanillo**, just south of Zihuatanejo Bay and accessible only by boat. Here, offshore in 15 to 20 feet of water, dwell an impressive variety of coral reef fish.

The scuba center operates two full-service dive shops. One is in downtown Zihuatanejo at Calle Cuauhtémoc #3 (across from the Banamex bank). The other is at the main dive facility within the private marina at the Puerto Mío resort, just inside the mouth of Zihuatanejo Bay. Full-day packages include separate morning and afternoon dives, all equipment, instructors and soft drinks on board. Morning, afternoon and night dives also are available. For information and reservations phone (755) 4-2147.

Yates del Sol's trimaran *Tristar* departs from the marina at the Puerto Mío resort for "sunshine" cruises to Ixtapa Island and a stop for lunch, snorkeling and swimming. A snorkeling cruise casts off for Playa Manzanillo, and a "magical sunset" cruise sails from the bay into the open Pacific for sunset watching and a view of Ixtapa's Hotel Zone. Reservations are required. Cruises can be arranged through a local travel agency, or phone Yates del Sol at (755) 4-3589.

The usual water sports—water and jet skiing, windsurfing, parasailing—can be enjoyed at both Ixtapa and Zihuatanejo. Facilities and equipment rentals are usually available at Playa del Palmar, Playa la Ropa and Playa las Gatas. Surfers favor **Playa Troncones**, which faces the open ocean northwest of Ixtapa. **Note:** Make certain that parasailing is arranged only through a reputable outfit. Not all boat operators have the required level of experience, and accidents have occurred.

There are two 18-hole golf courses in the area. The **Ixtapa Golf Club**, a Robert Trent Jones, Jr.-designed course at the eastern end of the Hotel Zone, extends to the ocean's edge. The grounds, considered a wildlife preserve, are lush with tropical vegetation and home to numerous exotic birds. Crocodiles inhabit some of the water hazards, discouraging any attempts to search for balls lost in the drink; zoologists from Mexico City visit once a year and retrieve the largest specimens for relocation to Mexican zoos. Clubhouse facilities include a pro shop, restaurant and pool with a lounge deck. For reservations information phone (755) 3-1062.

The **Marina Golf Course**, within the Marina Ixtapa complex just past the western end of the Hotel Zone, was designed by Robert von Hagge. Recreational boaters take advantage of the course's crisscrossing canals, and water hazards come into play on 14 holes. The challenging 600-yard, par-5 18th is known locally as *"el hoyo del diablo"* (the devil's hole). Golfers have the use of a clubhouse, restaurant, pro shop, pool and tennis courts, and the marina's dockside promenade is close by. For reservations information phone (755) 3-1410.

Tennis courts are located at the Ixtapa Golf Club, the clubhouse at Marina Ixtapa, at the major Ixtapa hotels, and at the Hotel Villa del Sol at Playa la Ropa in Zihuatanejo. Most courts are illuminated for night play; nonguests can usually play at the hotel courts for a fee.

At Playa Linda and **Playa Larga**, both northwest of Ixtapa's Hotel Zone, horses can be rented by the hour for rides along the beach or through one of the nearby coconut plantations. Sunset rides are especially nice (wear insect repellent). Local travel agencies can arrange a trip, or make reservations through Rancho Playa Linda; phone (755) 4-3085.

SHOPPING

There are no malls in the traditionally sprawling sense in either Ixtapa or Zihuatanejo. Instead, small, air-conditioned complexes line Boulevard Ixtapa, across the street from the big hotels. Fashionable resort wear, sportswear, jewelry, art and handicrafts fill the boutiques at **Ixpamar, La Puerta, Las Fuentes** and **Los Patios**, among other shopping plazas. **Laddi Guichi**, in the Los Patios shopping center, specializes in woven goods made in the state of Oaxaca. **La Fuente**, also in the Los Patios center, has a fine selection of talavera pottery, hand-blown glass, ceramics and papier-maché figures. **Mic-Mac**, in the La Puerta center, offers native handicrafts, embroidered clothing and wall hangings. All of the shopping centers contain restaurants and snack shops for those in need of refueling. Most of the stores are open daily; many of them close from 2-4.

Downtown Zihuatanejo has its share of souvenir stands and T-shirt emporiums, but it's also a good place to search out Mexican crafts. Shops and stalls line Paseo del Pescador and the adjacent streets. **Mario's Leather Shop**, Calle Vicente Guerrero #12, features custom-made saddles, hats, vests, purses and belts. **Galería Maya**, Avenida Nicolas Bravo #31, and **Arte Mexicano Nopal**, Avenida Juan Alvarez #13B (at Calle Agustín Ramírez), display such items as pewter frames, straw baskets, wooden sculptures and handmade leather bags. **Coco Cabaña**, at Avenida Juan Alvarez and Calle Vicente Guerrero, also has a high-quality collection of handicrafts.

Casa Marina, Paseo del Pescador #9 (near Calle 5 de Mayo), consists of five family-owned folk art and handicraft shops under one roof. There are displays of pottery, rugs, pillows, regional costumes, silver jewelry, hammocks, hand-painted lacquer boxes and masks created by Guerrero artisans. Visitors can observe weaving demonstrations at **La Zapoteca**, one of the stores. Within the complex is **Café la Marina**, where you can have a pizza and a beer and then browse through the large collection of used books for sale and trade.

Vendors, formerly a persistent presence at the beaches, now hawk their wares at specially designated handicrafts markets. At the **Mercado de Artesanía Turístico**, on Boulevard Ixtapa across from the Ixtapa Sheraton, there are numerous souvenir and handicraft stands. In Zihuatanejo, a similar tourist-oriented market is located along Calle 5 de Mayo across from the church. Families occupy many of the stalls at these markets, producing hand-painted ceramics, seashell knick-knacks and embroidered goods. Zihuatanejo's **Mercado Central** (Central Market) spreads along Avenida Benito Juárez several blocks inland from the waterfront. Here the emphasis is on foodstuffs—tropical fruits, vegetables, seafood and medicinal herbs. Good buys at the market include Guerrero coffee and leather *huaraches* (sandals).

DINING AND NIGHTLIFE

For an expensive but reliably good dining experience, the Ixtapa Hotel Zone is an obvious choice. The view matches the richly prepared food at **Villa de la Selva**, next to the Westin Brisas Resort on Playa Vista Hermosa. This open-air restaurant has three tiers of tables overlooking the ocean; the lower terrace has the most spectacular views. It's a romantic spot for sunset watching. Reservations are suggested, especially during the high season. Three upscale restaurants—**Beccofino**, **Bucanero's** and **El Galeón**—front the dockside promenade at Marina Ixtapa.

Zihuatanejo has a lower price range and a greater variety of eateries. **Villa del Sol**, in the Hotel Villa del Sol at Playa la Ropa, matches Ixtapa's expense with its elegant Continental cuisine and excellent service. For typical Mexican fare at more affordable prices, try **Casa Elvira**, on Paseo del Pescador between the town pier and the basketball court. One of Zihuatanejo's oldest restaurants, it offers the likes of fresh crayfish and chicken in *mole* sauce. **Nueva Zelanda**, Calle Cuauhtémoc #23 (at Avenida Ejido), is casual and family-oriented, specializing in *tortas* (Mexican sandwiches), enchiladas and *licuados* (fruit shakes). There is a branch in Ixtapa as well.

Imported fast-food chains are conspicuously absent here. Seafood—lobster, clams, squid, *huachinango* (red snapper) and a local specialty, *ca-*

marones al ajo (shrimp encrusted with garlic)—is emphasized on most menus. Sample the local bounty at **Chez Arnoldo**, the only tile-roofed structure among the thatched, open-air restaurants dotting Playa las Gatas. Here you can feast on expertly prepared seafood dishes in your bathing suit. **La Perla**, an open-air eatery at Playa la Ropa, has fish soup, whole red snapper and fried oysters, which the owner is likely to be shucking as you are seated.

La Sirena Gorda, on the *malecón* next to the town pier, is known for its fresh seafood tacos—fish, shrimp, octopus and conch—and is also a pleasant spot for breakfast. **Coconuts** is a local gathering place on Calle Agustín Ramirez; Igorian Hacienda, the site's original building, served as a weigh-in station for the coconut plantations that once surrounded Zihuatanejo. **J.J's Grill**, Calle Vicente Guerrero #6 (a few blocks inland from the waterfront), prepares tempting seafood platters and lobster salad served in the shell. The piano bar makes it one of the few places in Zihuatanejo with live entertainment.

One thoroughly Mexican dish should not be overlooked. *Pozole* is a hearty, hominy-thickened stew containing chicken or pork. Toppings include chopped onion, lettuce or cabbage; herbs and spices vary depending on who is making the *pozole*. Less adventurous diners will appreciate the fact that pickled pig knuckles are normally served on the side. The addition of chilies gives *pozole* three different colors—red, green or white. Thursday is the traditional day to eat *pozole*, and perhaps the favorite local *pozolería* is **El Profe** (The Professor), between Zihuatanejo and the airport in the village of Coacoyul (most easily reached by taxi). Fittingly enough, it is open only for lunch on Thursdays.

Mexican "Fiesta Nights" are popular evening entertainment in Ixtapa during peak tourist season (November to April). They start around 7 p.m. with a lavish buffet spread, after which live music and folkloric dance performances are presented. The cost, around $30-$40 per person, normally includes dinner, drinks and the show. The Westin Brisas Ixtapa offers its Fiesta Night on Sunday; the Hotel Krystal in Ixtapa on Monday; the Hotel Villa del Sol in Zihuatanejo on Friday. The Sheraton Ixtapa presents a Wednesday Fiesta Night all year. Reservations or advance tickets are necessary; call the hotel or make arrangements through a local travel agency.

Casual is the standard attire in both Ixtapa and Zihuatanejo, although shorts and sandals are frowned on for an evening out at an expensive restaurant or fashionable nightspot. For a list of AAA-RATED establishments in Ixtapa and Zihuatanejo, *see the Lodgings & Restaurants section*. Most restaurants use purified water to make the ice in drinks (check to see if the cubes have holes). If in doubt, order bottled mineral water (the brands Agua de Taxco or Tehuacán are good), beer or a soft drink; the *limón* flavor of Yoli, a soft-drink brand sold only in the state of Guerrero, is similar to 7-Up.

Nightlife is concentrated in Ixtapa. **Christine**, in the Hotel Krystal, is the splashiest of several discos. A laser light show set to music takes place at midnight; after that dancing takes over. Tiers of tables overlook the dance floor. The doors open nightly around 10:30 p.m. (the off-season schedule varies); there is a cover charge. Shorts, jeans and tennis shoes are not allowed. Other discos are **Euforia**, on Boulevard Ixtapa in front of the Best Western Posada Real, and **Visage**. Also on Boulevard Ixtapa (near the Best Western) is an outpost of **Carlos'n Charlie's**, which offers food, drinks and dancing to rowdy rock on an elevated platform by the beach. **Señor Frog's**, in the La Puerta shopping center, also serves food to the accompaniment of loud rock 'n' roll. There is a cover charge here for dancing.

SPECIAL EVENTS

Two major tournaments draw serious sportfishing enthusiasts to Ixtapa/Zihuatanejo: the *Billfish Classic* in January and the *International Sailfish Tournament* in May. Other sporting events include a Pro-Am tournament held at the Ixtapa Golf Club in June or July, a national triathlon in Ixtapa during September, and a high-powered boat race in Zihuatanejo in November. Amateur golf and tennis tournaments and a marathon are organized annually in Ixtapa as well; check with the tourism office for dates, which tend to be erratic.

Every Sunday at the basketball court in downtown Zihuatanejo, *Cultural Sunday* takes place. Young children are in the spotlight at this delightful event, performing regional dances from all over Mexico in full, colorful costume. The festivities begin around 6 p.m.

NEARBY DESTINATIONS

Local travel agencies maintain offices in Ixtapa and Zihuatanejo hotel lobbies and can organize a variety of sightseeing excursions. Yachts and trimarans cruise Zihuatanejo Bay or sail to Isla Ixtapa. Also available are sightseeing tours of coconut, mango and papaya plantations or trips to inland villages. **Barra de Potosí**, a fishing settlement down the coast from Zihuatanejo, is situated near a lagoon that provides good opportunities for birdwatching.

Playa Troncones is an idyllic getaway about 16 kilometers (10 miles) north of Ixtapa. To get there, proceed north on Mex. 200 and watch for the turnoff marked by a sign that says *Burro Borracho* ("Drunken Donkey"). The sporadically paved road leads to a small village and a 3-mile stretch of beautifully unspoiled beach. (Note: A taxi driver can be hired for the 30-minute drive from Ixtapa—45 minutes from Zihuatanejo—and then come back to pick you up at a prearranged time.) There are several bed-and-breakfast properties here, and a couple of tiny beachside restaurants serve up briny-fresh seafood. Activities include surfing, sea kayaking and hiking through the jungle, but for some, the solitude of the all-but-deserted beach is the real attraction.

The small town of **Petatlán** is about 35 kilometers (22 miles) south of Zihuatanejo on Mex. 200 (watch for the marked turnoff just past the Petatlán Bridge). The town church has an intriguing history. It is said that a wealthy Mexican landowner turned in desperation to a padre of the church for help in finding a cure for his daughter's blindness, promising in return to completely remodel the building. Several months later the girl regained her eyesight, and the church was meticulously restored. On a more secular note, *Expo Petatlán* is held in town the first week of April. Cockfights and folkloric dance performances are among the events that take place at this typical Mexican fair.

IXTAPA, GUERRERO

WHERE TO STAY

BARCELO-IXTAPA BEACH RESORT

▼▼▼▼ *Hotel* ((755)3-1858

12/23-4/15	$190	XP $30
4/16-11/30	$175	XP $30
12/1-12/22	$170	XP $30

Location: South end of hotel zone. Blvd Ixtapa S/N 40880 (PO Box 201). Fax: 755/3-2438. **Facility:** Atrium lobby with panoramic elevators. Attractive guest rooms with colorful, contemporary decor. Oceanview with balcony. 331 units. 12 stories, interior corridors. **Terms:** F17; 3 day cancellation notice-fee imposed. **Amenities:** safes (fee), honor bars. **Dining:** Sunset Terrace, see separate listing. **Leisure Activities:** wading pool, beach, 4 lighted tennis courts, social program, playground, exercise room. *Fee:* fishing. **Guest Services:** gift shop, valet laundry. *Fee:* massage. **Business Services:** meeting rooms. **Cards:** AE, DI, MC, VI.

SOME UNITS
/ ⊠ /

CONTINENTAL PLAZA IXTAPA

▼▼▼▼ *Hotel* ((755)3-1175

12/1-3/31	$180-$200	XP $24
7/1-8/31	$114-$142	XP $26
4/1-6/30 & 9/1-11/30	$103-$128	XP $24

Location: North end of hotel zone. Blvd Ixtapa S/N Lote 5 40880. Fax: 755/3-0790. **Facility:** Well equipped, contemporary looking guest rooms. Most with balcony. 152 units. 9 stories, interior corridors. **Terms:** F12; check-in 4 pm, cancellation fee imposed, package plans. **Amenities:** safes, honor bars. **Leisure Activities:** wading pool, beach, social program, playground, exercise room. **Guest Services:** [AP] meal plan available, gift shop, valet laundry. *Fee:* massage. **Business Services:** meeting rooms. **Cards:** AE, MC, VI.

SOME UNITS

HOTEL FONTAN IXTAPA BEACH RESORT

 *Hotel*   ((755)3-1666

12/26-2/5	$187	XP $28
12/1-12/25	$147	XP $40
5/12-11/30	$133	XP $25

Location: Center of hotel zone. Blvd Ixtapa S/N 40880. Fax: 755/3-2126. **Facility:** Guest units with garden or ocean view. Closed 12/26-1/2. 473 units, 12 with efficiency. *Bath:* shower only. 8 stories, interior corridors. **Terms:** F12; open 12/1-2/5 & 5/12-11/30, check-in 4 pm, 14 day cancellation notice-fee imposed. **Amenities:** voice mail. **Leisure Activities:** 2 pools, wading pool, beach, lighted tennis court, social program, bicycles, exercise room. **Guest Services:** [AP] meal plan available, gift shop, valet laundry. **Business Services:** meeting rooms. **Cards:** AE, DI, MC, VI.

SOME UNITS

FEE

HOTEL KRYSTAL IXTAPA

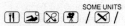 *Hotel*   ((755)3-0333

12/20-4/15	$150	XP $15
12/1-12/19 & 4/16-11/30	$115	XP $15

Location: North end of hotel zone. Blvd Ixtapa S/N 40880 (PO Box 68). Fax: 755/3-0216. **Facility:** Attractive gardens. Modern facility with nice beach and secure parking. 255 units. 11 stories, interior corridors. **Terms:** F12; 3 day cancellation notice, package plans. **Amenities:** *Some:* safes, honor bars. **Dining:** Bogarts, see separate listing. **Leisure Activities:** wading pool, beach, fishing, children's program, social program, playground, exercise room. *Fee:* 2 lighted tennis courts, racquetball court. **Guest Services:** gift shop, valet laundry. **Business Services:** meeting rooms. **Cards:** AE, DI, MC, VI.

SOME UNITS

FEE

PRESIDENTE INTER-CONTINENTAL-IXTAPA, AN ALL INCLUSIVE RESORT

Hotel   (755/3-0018

12/20-4/21	$275	XP $40
4/22-11/30	$255	XP $40
12/1-12/19	$235	XP $35

Location: Center of hotel zone. Blvd, Ixtapa S/N 40880 (PO Box 95). Fax: 755/3-2312. **Facility:** Few rooms with balcony facing bay. 420 units. Some whirlpool units. 3-11 stories, interior/exterior corridors. **Terms:** 7 day cancellation notice-fee imposed. **Leisure Activities:** 2 pools, wading pool, sauna, steamroom, beach, 2 lighted tennis courts, children's program, social program, exercise room. **Guest Services:** [AP] meal plan available, gift shop, valet laundry. *Fee:* massage. **Business Services:** meeting rooms. **Cards:** AE, MC, VI.

QUALTON CLUB IXTAPA ALL INCLUSIVE

Hotel   ((755)2-0080

12/1-4/15	$180	XP $45
4/16-11/30	$120	XP $45

Location: 2 km n on Mex 200 at Playa Linda. Carretera Escenica S/N 40880. Fax: 755/2-0070. **Facility:** All rooms have balcony or terrace. 152 units. *Bath:* shower only. 2 stories, exterior corridors. **Parking:** valet. **Terms:**3 day cancellation notice. **Amenities:** safes. **Leisure Activities:** 2 pools, beach, 2 tennis courts, bicycles. **Guest Services:** [AP] meal plan available. **Cards:** AE, MC, VI.

RADISSON RESORT-IXTAPA

Hotel   ((755)3-0003

12/19-3/31	$185	XP $20
12/1-12/18 & 4/1-11/30	$120	XP $15

Location: North end of hotel zone. Blvd Ixtapa S/N 40880. Fax: 755/3-1555. **Facility:** Colonial decor with ocean view rooms. Large swimming pool, secured parking and very nice beach. 275 units. Some whirlpool units. *Bath:* combo or shower only. 13 stories, interior corridors. **Parking:** valet. **Terms:** F12; 7 day cancellation notice. **Amenities:** honor bars. **Leisure Activities:** wading pool, sauna, beach, social program, playground, exercise room. **Guest Services:** gift shop, valet laundry. **Business Services:** meeting rooms. **Cards:** AE, DI, MC, VI.

RIVIERA BEACH RESORT & SPA

Hotel   (753/3-1066

12/22-4/14	$90-$100	XP $30
4/15-11/30	$75-$85	XP $25
12/1-12/21	$65-$75	XP $20

Location: Center of hotel zone. Blvd Ixtapa S/N (PO Box 50). Fax: 753/3-0400. **Facility:** Many rooms with ocean view. Meets AAA guest room security requirements. 197 units. *Bath:* combo or shower only. 11 stories, interior corridors. **Parking:** valet. **Terms:** F12; 3 day cancellation notice. **Amenities:** safes, honor bars, hair dryers. **Leisure Activities:** wading pool, sauna, whirlpool, beach, 2 tennis courts (Fee: 2 lighted), children's program, exercise room. **Guest Services:** [AP], [BP] & [MAP] meal plans available, gift shop, afternoon tea, valet laundry. *Fee:* massage. **Business Services:** meeting rooms. **Cards:** AE, MC, VI.

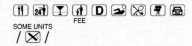
FEE
SOME UNITS

THE WESTIN BRISAS RESORT IXTAPA

Hotel   ((755)3-2121

1/3-4/15	$278	XP $40
4/16-11/30	$194	XP $40
12/1-1/2	$185	XP $40

Location: On beach at Playa Vistahermosa. Playa Vistahermosa S/N 40880 (PO Box 97). Fax: 755/3-1091. **Facility:** All units with private balcony overlooking ocean. 423 units. Some whirlpool units ($362-$488). 12 stories, interior corridors. **Parking:** valet. **Terms:** F12; 3 day cancellation notice-fee imposed. **Amenities:** extended cable TV, voice mail, safes, honor bars. **Dining:** Portofino, El Mexicano Restaurant, see separate listing. **Leisure Activities:** 3 pools, wading pool, beach, fishing, children's program, social program, exercise room. *Fee:* 4 lighted tennis courts. **Guest Services:** gift shop, valet laundry. *Fee:* massage. **Business Services:** meeting rooms. **Cards:** AE, DI, MC, VI.

FEE   FEE
SOME UNITS

WHERE TO DINE

BECCOFINO RESTAURANT AND BAR

Northern Italian   (755/3-1770
L $15-$25   D $15-$25

Location: 1.5 km n of hotel zone, via Blvd Ixtapa; at Ixtapa Marina. **Hours:** 8 am-midnight. **Reservations:** suggested. **Features:** No A/C; casual dress; cocktails; a la carte. Beautiful teak wood deck right on the water. Mediterranean atmosphere. **Cards:** AE, MC, VI.

BOGARTS

▼▼▲▼▲▼▼ *Continental* (755/3-0333

D $15-$20

Location: North end of hotel zone; in Hotel Krystal Ixtapa. Blvd Ixtapa S/N 40880. **Hours:** 6 pm-11 pm. **Reservations:** suggested. **Features:** semi-formal attire; cocktails; entertainment; a la carte. Elegant atmosphere themed after the movie "Casablanca." Creative menu selection featuring many flambe selections. **Cards:** AE, DI, MC, VI.

BUCANERO'S RESTAURANT

▼▼▲▼▲▼▼ *Continental* (755/3-0916

L $6-$15   D $10-$20

Location: 1.5 km n of hotel zone via Blvd Ixtapa; at marina. 40880. **Hours:** 8 am-midnight. **Features:** No A/C; cocktails; a la carte. Outdoor dining overlooking the marina. Creative menu selection. Light luncheon menu also available. **Cards:** AE, MC, VI.

CARLOS 'N CHARLIE'S

▼▲▼▲▼▼ *Continental* (755/3-0085

L $8-$14   D $8-$14

Location: North end of hotel zone; next to Best Western Posada Real. Blvd Ixtapa S/N 40880. **Hours:** 10 am-midnight. **Features:** No A/C; casual dress; cocktails & lounge; a la carte. Open air, fun-type atmosphere. Beach club open 10 am-5 pm. Loud, lively and casual. **Cards:** AE, MC, VI.

EL GALEON

▼▲▼▲▼ *Seafood* (755/3-2150

L $7-$14   D $7-$14

Location: 1.5 km n of hotel zone via Blvd Ixtapa; at marina. **Hours:** 10 am-midnight. **Reservations:** suggested. **Features:** No A/C; cocktails & lounge; a la carte. Open-air dining. Menu also includes pasta, chicken and beef selections. **Cards:** AE, MC, VI.

EL MEXICANO RESTAURANT

▼▼▲▼▲▼ *Mexican* (755/3-2121

D $13-$28

Location: On beach at Playa Vistahermosa; in The Westin Brisas Resort Ixtapa. 40880. **Hours:** 7 pm-midnight; open every other night 4/15-12/15. **Reservations:** suggested. **Features:** casual dress; cocktails; valet parking. Gourmet specialties. **Cards:** AE, DI, MC, VI.

PORTOFINO

▼▼▲▼▲▼▼ *Italian* (755/3-2121

D $10-$28

Location: On beach at Playa Vistahermosa; in The Westin Brisas Resort Ixtapa. **Hours:** 6 pm-midnight; open every other night 4/15-12/15. **Reservations:** suggested. **Features:** cocktails; valet parking. Casual; contemporary decor. **Cards:** AE, DI, MC, VI.

SUNSET TERRACE

▼▼▲▼▲▼▼ *Continental* (755/3-1858

D $18-$33

Location: South end of hotel zone; in Barcelo-Ixtapa Beach Resort. Blvd Ixtapa 40800. **Hours:** 7 pm-11 pm. **Closed:** Wed. **Features:** No A/C; cocktails & lounge; a la carte. Romantic seaside restaurant. **Cards:** AE, DI, MC, VI.

VILLA DE LA SELVA

▼▼▲▼▲▼ *Continental* (755/3-0362

D $25-$30

Location: On the beach at Playa Vistahermosa, next to The Westin Brisas Resort Ixtapa. Paseo de Las Rocas Lote D 40880. **Hours:** 6 pm-11:30 pm. **Closed:** 9/1-9/30. **Reservations:** suggested. **Features:** No A/C; cocktails & lounge; a la carte. Cliffside restaurant with breathtaking bay view. **Cards:** AE, MC, VI.

ZIHUATANEJO, GUERRERO

WHERE TO STAY

HOTEL VILLA DEL SOL

▼▼▲ ▼▼▲▼ *Country Inn* ((755)4-2239

12/1-3/31 & 11/1-11/30	$275-$300	XP $40
4/1-5/31	$250-$278	XP $40
6/1-10/31	$230-$260	XP $40

Location: 10 km n of airport. Playa La Ropa S/N 40880 (PO Box 84). Fax: 755/4-2758. **Facility:** Charming and personable. 26 rooms with private plunge pool. Surrounded by palms and tropical gardens. 55 units. 7 two-bedroom units. *Bath:* shower only. 2 stories, exterior corridors. **Terms:** F6; age restrictions may apply, 15 day cancellation notice-fee imposed, small pets only. **Amenities:** safes, honor bars, hair dryers. *Some:* CD players. **Dining:** dining room, see separate listing. **Leisure Activities:** 4 pools, beach, lap pool. *Fee:* 2 lighted tennis courts. **Guest Services:** [MAP] meal plan available, gift shop, valet laundry. *Fee:* massage. **Business Services:** meeting rooms. **Cards:** AE, MC, VI.

SOME UNITS

FEE

LA CASA CUITLATECA

▼▼▲▼▲▼ *Bed & Breakfast* (755/4-2448

All Year $350-$425   XP $50

Location: Playa La Popa, 9 km n of airport. Calle Playa La Ropa S/N 40880. Fax: 755/4-7394. **Facility:** Cliff top location offering spectacular views. 4 units. *Bath:* combo or shower only. 3 stories (no elevator), interior/exterior corridors. **Terms:** age restrictions may apply, 30 day cancellation notice. **Amenities:** no TVs. **Leisure Activities:** whirlpool. **Guest Services:** [BP] meal plan available, gift shop, valet laundry. **Business Services:** meeting rooms. **Cards:** AE, DS, MC, VI.

LA CASA QUE CANTA

▼▼▲▼▲▼ *Country Inn* ((755)5-7030

All Year $330-$685

Location: Playa La Ropa; Mirador sector; 9 km n of airport. Camino Escenico A Playa La Ropa S/N 40880. Fax: 755/4-7900. **Facility:** On a cliff with bay view. Elegance with Mexican folk art. Requires stair climbing to reach most areas of hotel. Only a few rooms with elevator access. 24 units. *Bath:* shower only. 3 stories, exterior corridors. **Terms:** age restrictions may apply, 30 day cancellation notice-fee imposed. **Amenities:** no TVs, safes, honor bars. **Leisure Activities:** 2 pools, whirlpool, swimming, exercise room. **Guest Services:** gift shop, valet laundry. *Fee:* massage. **Business Services:** meeting rooms. **Cards:** AE, MC, VI.

PUERTO MIO HOTEL MARINA RESORT

▼▼▼ *Motor Inn* ((755)4-3344

12/1-4/30	$225-$750	XP $30
5/1-11/30	$200-$750	XP $30

Location: 3 km w of Hwy 200 interchange; follow Morelos. Playa del Almacen 5 40880 (PO Box 84). Fax: 75/54-3535. **Facility:** Converted mansion on hillside overlooking Zihuatanejo Bay. Bright and cheerful guest rooms with classic Mexican decor. A few rooms with balcony. 25 units. 5 two-bedroom units. Some whirlpool units ($300-$425). *Bath:* combo or shower only. 4 stories (no elevator). **Terms:** 46 day cancellation notice. **Amenities:** safes, honor bars. **Dining:** La Cala, see separate listing. **Leisure Activities:** 2 pools. **Guest Services:** gift shop, valet laundry. **Business Services:** meeting rooms. **Cards:** AE, MC, VI.

SOME UNITS

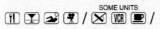

SOTAVENTO CATALINA BEACH RESORTS

▼▼ *Hotel* ((755)4-2032

12/16-4/24	$95-$120	XP $25
12/1-12/15 & 4/25-11/30	$65-$75	XP $15

Location: Playa La Ropa, 9 km n of airport. Camino escenico S/N Playa La Ropa 40880 (APDO Postal No 2). Fax: 755/429-75. **Facility:** On a hillside overlooking the bay. Requires stair climbing. 126 units. 5 two-bedroom units and 2 efficiencies. Some whirlpool units. *Bath:* shower only. 5-8 stories (no elevator), exterior corridors. **Terms:** F11; 30 day cancellation notice. **Amenities:** no TVs. *Some:* safes. **Leisure Activities:** wading pool, beach. **Guest Services:** gift shop, valet laundry. **Cards:** AE, DI, MC, VI.

SOME UNITS

WHERE TO DINE

LA CALA

▼▼▼ *Continental* (755/4-3344

L $7-$20　D $10-$30

Location: 3 km w of Hwy 200 interchange; follow Morelos; in Puerto Mio Hotel Marina Resort. Playa Del Almacen 5 40880. **Hours:** 7 am-11 pm. **Reservations:** suggested. **Features:** No A/C; cocktails & lounge; a la carte. Spectacular view overlooking private cove. Mexican inspired cuisine. **Cards:** AE, MC, VI.

VILLA DEL SOL RESTAURANT

▼▼▼ *Continental* (755/4-2239

L $8-$18　D $10-$30

Location: 10 km n of airport; in Hotel Villa Del Sol. Playa La Ropa S/N 40880. **Hours:** 8 am-10:30 pm. **Reservations:** suggested. **Features:** No A/C; cocktails. Mexican buffet with live music Friday from 8:30 pm. **Cards:** AE, MC, VI.

MANZANILLO, COLIMA (I-2)

Manzanillo (mahn-sah-NEE-yoh) may have participated in trade with the Orient before the arrival of the Spanish. Settled by Europeans shortly after the Conquest, it became an important departure point for Spanish expeditions, not only to other parts of Mexico but to such far-flung locations as the Philippines and Alta California (the present state of California). Hernán Cortés established what is believed to be Latin America's first shipyard at Manzanillo in 1531. This maritime legacy thrives today, and tour-

ism—although well developed—takes a back seat to commerce.

Manzanillo began attracting foreigners in the 1970s, along with new seaside playgrounds like Cancún and Ixtapa. As with Puerto Vallarta, its neighbor some 259 kilometers (160 miles) to the north, Manzanillo was blessed with natural attributes. Twin bays, golden-sand beaches and a lush tropical backdrop of jungle and banana plantations drew U.S. and Canadian vacationers searching for something a little off the beaten track.

What put the city on the tourist map for good was the 1974 opening of **Las Hadas**, a luxurious beach retreat conceived by Bolivian tin magnate Antenor Patiño. The opulent hotel began attracting an international set of moneyed pleasure seekers. Manzanillo gained further exposure when the hotel was chosen as the setting for the 1979 film "10," although for many the movie's most striking image was a cornrowed Bo Derek jogging down the beach.

The city (Las Hadas' pampering excepted) doesn't go out of its way to lay out the welcome mat for visitors, which gives it an unpretentious air. Sportfishing is one of the big draws. And Manzanillo all but shuts down on Sunday, when practically everyone heads for—where else—the beach.

THE INFORMED TRAVELER

Playa de Oro International Airport is located about 47 kilometers (29 miles) northwest of Manzanillo, on the way to Barra de Navidad. Inside the small terminal building are rental car counters, several shops, a restaurant and a lovely mural. International flights are limited. Aeroméxico and Mexicana both offer flights from Los Angeles, with connections en route. America West flies from Phoenix; Aero California, from Los Angeles. Most flights to Manzanillo arrive via Mexico City. The commuter airlines Aeromar and Aerolitoral both offer flights to Manzanillo from Mexico City, as well as from other Mexican destinations; phone (333) 3-0151 and (333) 3-2424, respectively. Charter packages to Manzanillo from various U.S. cities are available during the winter months; consult a travel agency for details. For additional information about airlines *see "Arriving by Air," page 53.*

Colectivos (usually orange Volkswagen vans) shuttle passengers from the airport to the major hotels. Fares are based on a zone system but average around $9 (U.S.) per person. Make advance arrangements for a ride back to the airport upon your departure. Taxis are another, more expensive, transportation option.

"Deluxe" bus service is provided by Primera Plus from Manzanillo to Puerto Vallarta and to Guadalajara; phone (333) 2-0210. Transportes Cihuatlán also offers service to Puerto Vallarta and the closer beaches around Barra de Navidad, about 1½ hours up the coast; phone (333) 2-0515. (**Note:** Despite the amenities provided on first-class buses, the trip from Puerto Vallarta to Manzanillo along winding Mex. 200 can seem like an amusement park thrill ride for those unaccustomed to mountainous terrain.) The **Central Camionera** (main bus station) is on Avenida Hidalgo, on the eastern outskirts of town. For additional information about buses see "Bus Service," page 63.

From Guadalajara, Manzanillo can be reached by car via two-lane Mex. 80, which runs into coastal Mex. 200 at Barra de Navidad, or by the toll highway Mex. 54-D, which passes through Colima. Driving Mex. 200 southeast from Puerto Vallarta or northwest from Ixtapa/Zihuatanejo can be an adventure, particularly during the July-through-September rainy season, when downpours can create hazardous potholes and unexpected detours.

The tourism office is at Boulevard Miguel de la Madrid #4960 (Mex. 200), a short distance east of the Las Hadas resort. The yellow, one-story building is on the beach side of the highway. It is open Mon.-Fri. 9-3 and 4-6, Sat. 9-1; phone (333) 3-2277 (English spoken).

LAYOUT

Manzanillo is first and foremost a commercial port. With a fine natural harbor and rail connections to the interior, it handles an enormous amount of Mexican industrial and agricultural output. The downtown district occupies a narrow isthmus at the southern end of Manzanillo Bay. It's a noisy, bustling jumble of shipyard activity and railroad tracks. Few tourist amenities will be found among the businesses, cheap hotels and no-frills restaurants, although an ongoing port beautification project—undertaken to help establish Manzanillo as a port of call for cruise ships—has resulted in a landscaped promenade.

Jardín de Obregón, the main plaza, is at the north end of downtown overlooking the harbor, which is studded with Mexican military vessels. This small square has an elaborate bandstand and a gazebo. Near the plaza are courts where pickup basketball and *fútbol* games attract lively crowds of spectators. Avenida México, the city's main commercial thoroughfare, runs south from the plaza.

The resort area spreads out north and then west of downtown along the shores of twin bays, **Bahía de Manzanillo** and **Bahía de Santiago**. Manzanillo Bay encompasses the harbor and some of the more reasonably priced hotels. The **Santiago Peninsula**, on which Las Hadas and the Hotel Sierra Plaza are located, separates the bays. This tourist-oriented area includes the Santiago and Salahua developments, where there are homes, restaurants and shopping centers. On the other side of the peninsula is Santiago Bay, where luxury homes and condominiums have begun springing up.

Note: In the Manzanillo area, Mex. 200 is referred to variously as the Santiago-Manzanillo Highway or the Costera Highway; the official name is **Boulevard Miguel de la Madrid**. Between the Santiago area and downtown, there are three major junctions along this highway: with the road to the Santiago Peninsula and Las Hadas; with the road to the Las Brisas Peninsula, the resort area closest to town (known as the *crucero*, or crossroads); and with the highway leading into downtown Manzanillo. At the last junction, Mex. 200 continues southeast down the coast toward Colima and Ixtapa/Zihuatanejo, while the Santiago-Manzanillo Highway bears south toward downtown, running into Calzada Niños Heroes.

Roads, many of them dirt, branch off Mex. 200, leading to resort and condominium developments. While Mex. 200 and other major roadways are in good condition, streets within the city can be potholed. City buses (the newer ones are blue and white) make a circuit from downtown north along Mex. 200 and the shores of the two bays. Destinations are marked on the left side of the windshield; for example, "Centro" (downtown), "Las Brisas," "Las Hadas" or "Santiago." The fare is inexpensive—just 25c from the main resort areas to downtown—and is an easy way to get a look at the coastline and some of the hotels without driving.

THE BEACHES

There are several beaches to choose from along the wide curve of Manzanillo's two bays. **Playa las Brisas** is the closest to town, although to reach it by road requires detouring around Laguna de San Pedrito to the narrow strip of land fronting Manzanillo Bay. Older hotels and restaurants line both sides of the bayfront drive, a popular destination for weekenders from Guadalajara. Beyond Playa las Brisas is the long curve of golden-brown sand called **Playa Azul**. The water gets rougher heading north toward the Santiago Peninsula, and the bottom drops off sharply along much of this stretch, making it problematic for wading or swimming.

The water in Santiago Bay, which is not used for shipping, tends to be cleaner than at the beaches fronting Manzanillo Bay closer to town. One of the area's best swimming beaches is **Playa la Audiencia**, which occupies a pretty, sheltered cove below jungle-covered hills on the north side of the Santiago Peninsula. The rocky outcroppings here are one of Manzanillo's few good snorkeling spots. Farther around Santiago Bay is **Playa Miramar**, another nice beach popular with windsurfers and boogie boarders. Beyond Playa Miramar, the shoreline curves to form the **Juluapan Peninsula**. Here the water becomes tranquil and the beach is dotted with thatch-roofed souvenir shops. Locals crowd this area on Sundays.

Swimmers should exercise care due to occasional rough surf; flags are posted at most beaches to indicate conditions. Red flags mean potentially dangerous conditions; white flags mean safe conditions.

About 49 kilometers (30 miles) southeast of Manzanillo and accessible by bus is **Playa Cuyutlán**, a beach known for the *Ola Verde*, or "Green Wave." This mountainous wave—with crests that are said to reach 30 feet or more from March through May—seems to be more talked about than actually seen. The greenish hue is due to the glow of phosphorescent marine organisms. Despite their color, the waves pounding this beach are impressive at any time. The black sand is the result of crushed volcanic rock. The long, open beach, backed by coconut palms, is all but deserted during the summer; lifeguards are normally present during the high season (December to May). Swimmers should beware of rough seas and strong undertows.

The tiny village of Cuyutlán, which consists of a few budget hotels and small seafood restaurants, drowses away most days, although *Semana Santa* (Holy Week) brings an influx of Mexican families. Facilities are spartan, but it's an appealing day trip for those seeking solitude. To get there, take a local bus to the town of Armería, south of Manzanillo on Mex. 200; buses leave frequently from Armería for Cuyutlán. If you're driving, there is a signed turnoff for Cuyutlán on Mex. 200 about 5 kilometers (3 miles) before Armería, or take the Manzanillo-Colima toll highway that parallels the railroad line.

What To Do

Several of the major resort properties in Manzanillo are all-inclusive, providing guests with an array of entertainment and recreational options in addition to lodging and meals. It therefore tends to be easier to arrange such activities as tennis, horseback riding, scuba trips, sunset cruises, or fishing and golf packages if you are staying at a hotel that provides them. If you're not, try one of the local travel agencies, which have offices along Boulevard Miguel de la Madrid. These agencies can arrange tours of the city and trips to such nearby destinations as Colima, the state capital, and Barra de Navidad.

Like other resorts along Mexico's Pacific coast, Manzanillo claims to be the sport fishing capital of the world, particularly with regard to sailfish. Marlin, dorado, tuna and wahoo are also hooked. The peak season is November through March. There are two annual fishing tournaments, one in early November and one in early February. Reservations for fishing excursions can be arranged through any of the resorts; booking as part of a group will lower costs.

Baja Fishing Adventures puts together Manzanillo package excursions that include round-trip airfare, lodging, a boat and licenses. All trips depart from Los Angeles. For information, write 2221 Palo Verde Ave., Ste. 1-D, Long Beach, CA 90815; phone (800) 458-3688. In Manzanillo, the *Albatros I* and *II* normally depart from the naval station pier downtown. Bait and tackle are included; phone (333) 6-6155. Again, going with a group will lower the cost. Less expensive are the *pangas* (outboard motor-powered launches) operated by individual owners; determined haggling can lower the fee.

Honeycombed with lagoons, the coastal region offers good birdwatching. **Laguna de Cuyutlán**, just south of Manzanillo, is populated by different species depending on the season. Herons, pelicans and flamingos can be seen at **Laguna de las Garzas** (Lagoon of the Herons), the waterway separating the Las Brisas Peninsula from the mainland. The views here are especially nice at sunset.

There are three area golf courses. The Club Santiago Resort has a nine-hole course. The 18-hole **La Mantarraya**, at the Las Hadas resort, offers plenty of water hazards, notably the water-encircled tee-off at the finishing hole. The course is open to the public, although hotel guests receive preferred tee times. To make reservations phone (333) 4-0000.

A 27-hole course designed by Robert von Hagge is the centerpiece at **Isla Navidad**, about 30 kilometers (19 miles) north of the airport and a 45-minute trip from Manzanillo. Laid out along the ocean, with breathtaking views at the 13th and 14th holes, the course is lushly landscaped and immaculately maintained.

Tennis courts, all lighted for night play, are located at the following resorts: Club Maeva, on Boulevard Miguel de la Madrid at Playa Miramar; Las Hadas Resort, on the Santiago Peninsula off Boulevard Miguel de la Madrid; and the Hotel Sierra Manzanillo, on the Santiago Peninsula at Avenida de la Audiencia #1.

Although Manzanillo is geared more toward relaxing at the beach than to sightseeing, its premier resort, **Las Hadas**, is an attraction in itself. Set against the eastern side of the Santiago Peninsula, this blindingly white hotel is a dazzling spectacle. With its minarets, cupolas and turrets, Las Hadas resembles a Moorish village. If you're not a guest, stop in and stroll the luxuriously landscaped grounds (although restaurant reservations are needed to enter the property through the guarded gate). The marina here accommodates up to 45 vessels; a fee is charged. Adjacent to the marina is a calm bay where boats can be moored without a fee.

One cultural bright spot stands out: the **Museo Universitario de Arqueologia** (University Museum of Archeology), off Boulevard Miguel de la

Madrid a few minutes north of downtown Manzanillo (on the San Pedrito campus of the University of Colima). Here are numerous metal and shell artifacts from western Mexico and a display of fabrics, looms and fabric-making implements. Open Tues.-Sun. Free.

SHOPPING, DINING AND NIGHTLIFE

Simply put, Manzanillo is not a shopper's paradise. A couple of shops on and around the main downtown plaza offer shell jewelry and a few handicrafts, but they're not worth a special trip. Pricey boutiques appear here and there along Boulevard Miguel de la Madrid and at the shopping arcade at the Las Hadas resort. **Galería de Arte**, at Las Hadas, displays a selection of works by Sergio Bustamante. **Plaza Manzanillo**, on Boulevard Miguel de la Madrid in the Salahua neighborhood, is an air-conditioned mall with a Comercial Mexicana department store, specialty boutiques and a food court.

The No. 1 choice for a dining splurge is **Legazpi**, at Las Hadas. The ambience, food and service exude elegance, and windows in the candlelit room have a view of Manzanillo Bay. It is open for dinner only during the high tourist season, and is closed 3 days a week. For reservations phone (333) 4-0000. **L'Recife**, off Boulevard Miguel de la Madrid about a 10-minute drive north of Las Hadas, has a spectacular clifftop setting and a local reputation for Sunday brunch (available only during the winter tourist season). Easier on the wallet is **Moustache's Bigotes**, overlooking the bay off Boulevard Miguel de la Madrid (next to the tourist office). Fresh seafood is the specialty. **Willy's** is at the end of Calle Benito Rincón Lopez, near the Las Brisas crossroads (the intersection of Boulevard Miguel de la Madrid and the road to the Las Brisas Peninsula). This small, casual beachside eatery serves seafood with a French flair. Reservations are required; phone (333) 3-1794.

Casual dress is appropriate at all Manzanillo restaurants (resort wear at the more expensive places). Keep in mind that a service charge may automatically be added to the bill (in addition to the 15 percent I.V.A. tax). While purified water is used at the well-known restaurants, for gastrointestinal reasons it's best to steer clear of the *enramadas* (beach shack restaurants) and outdoor taco stands.

Nightlife centers around the resorts. A Mexican "Fiesta Night" is offered at the Club Maeva resort during the high tourist season. Discos include **Boom Boom**, at Club Maeva, and **Cartouche**, at Las Hadas. There is a cover charge at both, and shorts and sandals are not permitted (this dress code is more likely to apply to men than to women). **Disco Voque** is on Boulevard de la Madrid between the Las Brisas crossroads and the Salahua neighborhood. Hours at all discos may vary outside of the high season.

Carlos'n Charlies, on Boulevard Miguel de la Madrid near Km 7, offers dinner and dancing in a typical rowdy atmosphere. Reservations are a good idea in the evening, and during high season there may be a cover or order charge.

WHERE TO STAY

CAMINO REAL LAS HADAS

▼▼▼▼ *Resort* ☎ 333/10101

All Year	$215-$310	XP $40

Location: 11.5 km nw on Mex 200, 2.5 km s on Peninsula Santiago. 28860 (Apartado Postal 158). Fax: 333/10-125. **Facility:** Spectacularly situated on private cove, at base of rugged hills. Arabesque architecture. All rooms with patio or balcony. 233 units. Some whirlpool units ($385-$440). 2-5 stories, interior/exterior corridors. **Parking:** valet. **Terms:** F12; 7 day cancellation notice-fee imposed. **Amenities:** voice mail, safes, honor bars. **Leisure Activities:** 2 pools, wading pool, beach, boat ramp, social program, exercise room. *Fee:* sailboating, marina, waterskiing, scuba diving & equipment, snorkeling, fishing, golf-39 holes, 10 lighted tennis courts. **Guest Services:** gift shop, valet laundry. *Fee:* massage. **Business Services:** meeting rooms. **Cards:** AE, DI, MC, VI. (See color ad opposite title page)

SD ❒ 24 ❒ ❒ ❒ ❒ DATA PORT

HOTEL LA POSADA

▼▼ *Lodge* ☎ (333)3-1899

12/1-5/14	$72-$80	XP $22
5/15-11/30	$54-$60	XP $22

Location: 3 km off Mex 200, in Las Brisas; on Playa Azul. Lazaro Cardenas 201 28210 (Apartado Postal 135, 28200). Fax: 333/3-1899. **Facility:** Unique seaside inn with rustic charm. Meets AAA guest room security requirements. 23 units. *Bath:* shower only. 1-2 stories, exterior corridors. **Terms:** 10 day cancellation notice. **Amenities:** no TVs. **Leisure Activities:** beach. **Guest Services:** [BP] meal plan available, valet laundry. **Cards:** AE, MC, VI.

SOME UNITS

❒ ❒ ❒ / ❒ /

SIERRA HOTEL MANZANILLO

▼▼▼ *Resort* ☎ (333)3-2000

12/20-4/17	$190	XP $75
12/1-12/19 & 4/18-11/30	$150	XP $75

Location: 11.5 km nw on Mex 200, 2.5 km s on Peninsula Santiago. Ave de La Audencia #1 28200 (PO Box 777). Fax: 333/3-2272. **Facility:** Very attractive facilities and guest rooms. Fine location on pretty cove. 350 units. Some whirlpool units. 19 stories, interior corridors. **Parking:** valet. **Terms:** F12; 3 day cancellation notice. **Leisure Activities:** wading pool, sauna, whirlpool, beach, waterskiing, fishing, 4 lighted tennis courts, exercise room. *Fee:* steam room, golf-18 holes. **Guest Services:** [AP] meal plan available, gift shop, valet laundry. *Fee:* massage. **Business Services:** meeting rooms. **Cards:** AE, MC, VI.

❒ 24 ❒ ❒ S D ❒ ❒ ❒ ❒ DATA PORT

SOME UNITS

/ ❒ /

MAZATLAN, SINALOA (F-4)

Mazatlán (mah-saht-LAHN), "The Pearl of the Pacific," is both an important commercial port and a major international resort destination. The name is derived from the Náhuatl Indian word *mazatl*, meaning "place of deer"—a reference to former inhabitants, as these fleet creatures are nowhere to be seen in the midst of today's oceanfront bustle.

Mazatlán is a fairly young city by Mexican standards. Its earliest history predates the Spanish conquest, when itinerant sailors passing through the region dubbed it the "islands of Mazatlán" due to the many hills, lagoons and estuaries in the vicinity. It was officially founded on Easter Sunday in 1531 by a group of 25 Spaniards under the command of Nuño de Guzmán, but for many years thereafter remained a dormant settlement. Spanish galleons periodically departed the natural harbor laden with gold from inland mines, and legend has it that pirates buried their treasures in secret coves up and down the coast.

It wasn't until the early 1820s that a permanent colony took root. After years of virtual anarchy, municipal government was finally established by a group of enterprising German settlers who developed Mazatlán's port facilities in order to facilitate the import of agricultural equipment. Flourishing international trade followed.

The port was besieged several times over the years—first in 1847 by U.S. troops during the Mexican-American War, and again in 1864 during the French occupation of Mexico. At one point the city was even overrun by Southerners from the United States attempting to perpetuate Confederate ideals south of the border.

The Sierra Madre range retreats out of sight along this section of the coast, depriving Mazatlán of the scenic backdrop of mountains that frame other resorts along the "Mexican Riviera." The original lures were hunting and sport fishing. But other natural attributes, such as year-round warm weather and noteworthy sunsets, attracted sun worshippers and beachcombers beginning in the 1930s. The abundance of billfish in the Pacific's blue waters remains a major draw, although Mexico's continuing efforts to conserve natural wildlife mean that hunters must search farther and farther afield. Duck hunting is the chief sport today.

Now a year-round resort, Mazatlán blends colonial charm with the modern allure of high-rise hotels. Strung along miles of scenic Pacific shoreline and with some 10,000 hotel rooms and condominium units covering all categories and rates, the city is northwest Mexico's major beach destination. The seaside boulevard, or *malecón*, stretches for more than 10 miles past golden sands and crashing waves. The combination of sun, sea and sand draws more than half a million visitors each year, augmenting a resident population estimated at about 600,000.

While affordability has always been part of Mazatlán's appeal, ambitious new construction to accommodate the tourist influx is becoming increasingly evident, particularly on the north side of town. One large-scale development is **Marina Mazatlán**, which when completed will be one of Mexico's largest boating facilities. Plans include moorings for more than 2,000 yachts, hotel accommodations, golf and tennis facilities, and a man-made island with a resort featuring cabanas equipped with their own slips for private docking. Already in operation is the deep-water access marina at the **El Cid Mega Resort**, with upscale recreational boating facilities tucked inside a protected ocean inlet.

Balancing the tourist atmosphere are the activities of a busy commercial port. Minerals and agricultural products—tomatoes, cantaloupes, cotton—from throughout the fertile state of Sinaloa are brought to the city's harbor for export. Mazatlán maintains the largest fleet of shrimp boats in Mexico, and thousands of tons of the frozen crustaceans find their way to the United States and Japan, the two main foreign markets.

PLANNING YOUR STAY

Mazatlán offers little in the way of historical attractions or cultural enlightenment. And unlike Acapulco or Puerto Vallarta, glitz is in fairly short supply. The Pearl of the Pacific caters unabashedly to tourists with its glut of vacation-oriented businesses. What keeps visitors coming back are the natural environment's beauty, the wide range of water recreation and superb sport fishing. Add to these enticements such spectator sports as baseball and bullfights, leisurely explorations of **Old Mazatlán**, day trips to nearby towns or tropical jungles, shopping in the **Golden Zone** and major celebrations like *Carnaval*, and travelers could easily spend a full week in the city.

The fishing, in fact, ranks among the best anywhere. Striped marlin are hooked between November and April; sailfish and black marlin are caught between May and October. Other game species taken from the Pacific waters include blue marlin, bonito, dolphin and yellowfin tuna.

Outdoor recreation—for both spectators and participants—is plentiful. Baseball in Mazatlán is considered something of a tradition. Loyal fans fervently support the local Pacific Coast League team, which has produced players who have gone on to the American majors. Games are played at **Teodoro Mariscal Stadium**, off Avenida del Mar and convenient to the tourist zone. Check at the front desk of your hotel for game schedules.

Bullfights take place on Sundays at 4 p.m. from December to April at the bullring on Boulevard Rafael Buelna. Tickets can be purchased at the bullring, through most hotels or in front of Valentino's Disco. Prices depend on where you sit; seats in the shade are more expensive.

Kayaking is fast becoming a popular activity in and around Mazatlán, offering a way to stay fit and the chance to observe secluded ecological

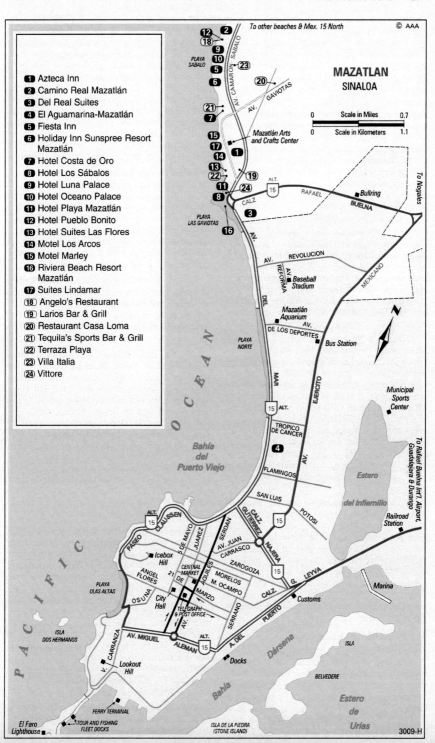

MAZATLAN
SINALOA

Scale in Miles   0   0.7
Scale in Kilometers   0   1.1

1 Azteca Inn
2 Camino Real Mazatlán
3 Del Real Suites
4 El Aguamarina-Mazatlán
5 Fiesta Inn
6 Holiday Inn Sunspree Resort Mazatlán
7 Hotel Costa de Oro
8 Hotel Los Sábalos
9 Hotel Luna Palace
10 Hotel Oceano Palace
11 Hotel Playa Mazatlán
12 Hotel Pueblo Bonito
13 Hotel Suites Las Flores
14 Motel Los Arcos
15 Motel Marley
16 Riviera Beach Resort Mazatlán
17 Suites Lindamar
18 Angelo's Restaurant
19 Larios Bar & Grill
20 Restaurant Casa Loma
21 Tequila's Sports Bar & Grill
22 Terraza Playa
23 Villa Italia
24 Vittore

© AAA

To other beaches & Mex. 15 North

3009-H

sanctuaries at close range. Excursions travel to area rivers, streams and estuaries that abound with wildlife. The eco-friendly **Mazatleco Sport Center** offers 4-hour guided trips that include state-of-the-art kayaks, instruction, snacks and transportation. Trips can be arranged through the tour desk at the Hotel Suites Las Flores; phone (69) 81-0302 or 16-3700.

Another popular activity is parasailing, which provides 15 minutes of sheer thrills for those not prone to vertigo. Arrangements can be made in front of the Playa Mazatlán and Las Flores hotels in the Golden Zone. Other Golden Zone hotels rent jet skis, Hobie Cats and windsurfing equipment. Back on land, a 27-hole golf course designed by Robert Trent Jones is at the El Cid Mega Resort; play is reserved for those staying at the hotel and their guests.

Stroll the *malecón* for a look at some of Mazatlán's sculptural monuments. The **Monumento al Pescador** (Fisherman's Monument), on Avenida del Mar north of Playa Olas Altas, is a local landmark. A woman and a fisherman dragging his net—both of them nude—present a curious sight. The **Venado, La Mujer Mazatleca** and **La Continuidad de la Vida** monuments honor a deer, a nymph and life, respectively.

Cerro de la Nevería (Icebox Hill), in the Olas Altas area, is a residential zone. A gradually ascending road reaches its summit, from which are views of a great part of the city, the immense blue bay and awe-inspiring sunsets that tint the sea and clouds a brilliant orange-red. Nearby **El Mirador**, off Paseo Claussen, is where daring locals plunge from a platform 45 feet above turbulent water surrounded by dangerous rocks. The feat requires expert timing; without the cushioning effect of a wave, a diver meets just 6 feet of water. In the evening these young daredevils carry torches for flamingly theatrical effect. Tips are expected.

Also exhibiting derring-do are the **Papantla Flyers**, a folkloric group, who perform their death-defying "Flying Pole" dance suspended from poles 50 feet tall. The dance originated in the state of Veracruz as part of pre-Hispanic agricultural ceremonies designed to ensure a bountiful harvest. The spectacle takes place in an open-air theater at the Mazatlán Arts and Crafts Center on Avenida Rodolfo Loiaza. Check at your hotel desk regarding schedule and admission information.

THE INFORMED TRAVELER

One of Mazatlán's attractions is its relative closeness to the U.S. border. As a result, a greater percentage of the city's tourist traffic arrives by motor vehicle, at least when compared to beach resorts further south and the colonial cities of the southern interior. Mazatlán is about 750 miles from the border at Nogales via Mex. 15, Sinaloa Hwy. 1 (SIN-1) and Mex. 15-D.

All three routes are four-lane, divided highways. Mex. 15 runs from the border to Guamúchil, Sin. There are presently eight tollbooths along this stretch, beginning at Magdalena, Son., and ending just south of Guasave. Toll road SIN-1 runs from Guamúchil to just south of Culiacán, paralleling free Mex. 15; toll road Mex. 15-D continues to Mazatlán, also paralleling Mex. 15. There are three toll plazas between Culiacán and Mazatlán. The condition of nontoll Mex. 15 between Guamúchil and Mazatlán is substandard. Night driving is not recommended; plan on a 2-day journey from the United States.

Rafael Buelna International Airport is about 40 kilometers (25 miles) south of downtown via Mex. 15 and is a good 45-minute drive to the major resort areas. Aero California, Alaska, America West, Continental, Delta and Mexicana airlines offer direct flights from U.S. cities. Aeroméxico and Mexicana airlines fly in from other Mexican cities. For additional information about airlines *see "Arriving by Air," page 53.*

Shuttle van service costs about $7 (U.S.) into town. Taxis also take visitors into Mazatlán or to the beachfront hotels. Costs can be cut by sharing the ride; the driver usually will carry up to four people. Establish the fare before the cab sets off.

Elite provides "deluxe" bus service to many inland Mexican cities, including hourly departures for Mexico City. Elite also offers service north to the border at Nogales, Ariz. The buses are clean and often have on-board television and a stewardess serving beverages and snacks. Another company, Transportes Norte de Sonora, offers service from Nogales to Mazatlán. Other lines offering "deluxe" service are Futura, Transportes del Pacifico and Tres Estrellas de Oro. The Central de Autobuses (Central Bus Station) is downtown on Carretera Internacional (International Highway), 3 blocks inland from the *malecón* at Playa Norte. For additional information about buses *see "Bus Service," page 63.*

Automobile-passenger ferry service links Mazatlán with La Paz *(see separate listing under Baja California)* on the Baja California Peninsula; for information phone **Grupo Sematur** at (69) 81-7020 or 81-7021. Departures from the Playa Sur terminal, at the southern end of town near the sport fishing docks, are Sun.-Fri. at 3 p.m.; sailing time is about 19 hours. Schedules and rates are subject to change; double-check both prior to departure and purchase tickets in advance. Within Mexico, current schedule and fare information may be obtained by calling 01 (800) 696-9600 (toll-free long distance within Mexico). For additional information *see "Ferry Service," page 64.*

The city is a port of call for cruise ships as well. The Carnival and Princess lines arrive regularly during the winter season.

The tourism office is at Paseo Olas Altas #1300, on the first floor of the sand-colored Bank of Mexico Building. The staff is friendly and speaks English. The office is open Mon.-Fri. 8-8, Sat. 9-1; phone (69) 85-1220, 85-1221 or 85-1847.

Banks are generally open Mon.-Fri. 8-5 and set aside morning hours—8:30 to 11 a.m.—to cash traveler's checks. Banamex is the only bank authorized for ATM transactions; you must have a personal pin number to access your account. Most other banks will provide a cash advance on credit cards. *Casas de cambio* (currency exchange offices) stay open longer than banks, although their rates are usually not as good; you pay for the convenience. The American Express office, on Avenida Camarón Sábalo in the Balboa shopping center (near the traffic circle), exchanges traveler's checks and accepts wire transfers of funds; it is open Mon.-Fri. 9-5, Sat. 9-2.

A variety of pay phones throughout the city serve different purposes. Beige plastic phones accept Mexican bank cards only. Small black street phones accept peso coins and buy 3 minutes of local calling time. Stainless steel Ladatel phones are the easiest to use for international calling.

The post office is downtown on Avenida Benito Juárez, in front of the cathedral and across the street from the main plaza.

Mazatlán's weather can be characterized as tropical, although not as hot as points farther down the coast. From November through May, daytime temperatures are in the 70s, nighttime temperatures in the 60s. It's hotter and more humid during the summer months, but afternoon highs are usually in the 80s rather than the sultry 90s. The ocean water is warmest in late summer and fall. Leave your heavy coat at home; the temperature at this seaside location has never dropped below 50 F. July, August and September are the rainiest months; the rest of the year rain is infrequent and seldom a threat to vacation plans. Clothing is decidedly informal—bathing suits, shorts, jeans and T-shirts—unless you wish to "dress up" in casual resort wear for an evening out to dinner or a disco.

City Layout

Mazatlán occupies a peninsula that juts into the Pacific Ocean, forming Bahía del Puerto Viejo, a natural bay and protected harbor. The main approach into the city is via Mex. 15, which becomes the **Carretera Internacional** (International Highway). Mex. 15 essentially loops around the city, changing names in the process. As **Avenida Rafael Buelna**, it veers west off Carretera Internacional, passing the bullring and ending at the Sábalo traffic circle at the waterfront. It then proceeds south as **Avenida del Mar** and **Paseo Claussen**. It skirts the southern edge of downtown as **Avenida Miguel Alemán**, running east to Avenida del Puerto (Port Av-

enue). At the customs office it becomes **Avenida Gabriel Leyva** and continues east toward the airport. Once out of town, Mex. 15 heads south to Tepic and Guadalajara.

The *malecón*, or waterfront boulevard, runs along the coast for some 17 kilometers (11 miles). In Mazatlán this thoroughfare also changes names—four times. At the southern end of the city (the old downtown area), it is called **Paseo Claussen**. North of downtown it becomes **Avenida del Mar**. At Punta Camarón (Shrimp Point, on which Valentino's Disco is perched), the name changes to **Avenida Camarón Sábalo**. At this point it runs inland and is paralleled by Avenida Rodolfo Loaiza, along which several of the city's luxury hotels sit. After a mile or so the two streets rejoin. Further north the name changes again to **Avenida Sábalo Cerritos**, which runs north toward the marinas.

The section of the *malecón* along Avenida Camarón Sábalo is known as the **Zona Dorado** (Golden Zone), which is the main tourist area. Here are hotels, restaurants, shops and nightspots, all within a compact area, and the nicest beaches.

South of the Golden Zone is the colonial-style central city, also called **Old Mazatlán**. Although it remains unseen by many tourists staying at the substantial hotels to the north, Old Mazatlán is worth a look. This is where the city's daily business is conducted amid the rushing of people and vehicles. **Plaza Revolución**, the main plaza, has the usual vendors and shoeshine stands as well as an ornate, wrought-iron bandstand beneath which is a rather incongruous fast-food diner. At calles Ocampo and Juárez is Mazatlán's twin-steepled cathedral, which has a partially yellow-tiled facade and a lavishly gilded altar.

At the southern end of town are the ferry terminal, tour boat operators, sport fishing fleets and commercial port activities. Standing guard over the harbor's entrance is **El Faro**, said to be the tallest lighthouse in the Western Hemisphere and second only to Gibraltar in the world, with a range of some 35 nautical miles. Those undertaking the strenuous half-hour hike up the rocky pinnacle will be rewarded with an expansive view of the harbor and ocean. Another great view of the city and its watery surroundings—particularly in the evening—can be seen from the top of **Cerro de Vigía** (Lookout Hill), a short distance north of El Faro. This climb, also steep, is better made via taxi.

Because of Mazatlán's waterfront sprawl, walking is an ill-advised choice for exploration. Fortunately, there are several public transportation options. A common sight are *pulmonías*, which are essentially open-air Volkswagen jeeps seating up to three people. They make the beach circuit and travel up and down the *malecón*. Unless money is no object, never hop in one of these vehicles and say, "Let's go." Always negotiate the fare in advance; it's expected. A word of caution: Those sensitive to exhaust fumes should avoid riding in a *pulmonía*.

The transit system is excellent and cheap: For about 20¢ (U.S.), one can get to just about any place in the city via local buses. The air-conditioned Sábalo Centro bus travels from the hotel zone to downtown; buses run every 10 to 15 minutes from 5:30 a.m. to 10 p.m. **Note:** During rush hour, about 5 to 7 p.m., buses that are full may pass waiting passengers. The Cerritos Juárez bus stops at the Gran Plaza shopping mall and the baseball stadium. The Sábalo Cocos bus stops at the Gigante supermarket.

Mazatlán is a favorite destination for RV travelers due to its access from the United States via Mex. 15. Most of the RV parks are at the north end of the city, along avenidas Camarón Sábalo/Sábalo Cerritos (the *malecón*). Two of the largest are Holiday, phone (69) 88-0077, and La Posta, phone (69) 83-5310.

BEACHES AND FISHING

Mazatlán's beaches offer something for everyone and accordingly attract different groups of sunseekers. Some are patronized mainly by Mazatlecos; others draw tourists. The following beaches are described as they appear from south to north along the coast.

Playa Norte   ©John Neubauer

Isla de la Piedra (Stone Island), at the southern end of the city, is actually a peninsula offering miles of mostly undeveloped oceanside beaches that can be explored on horseback. Small motorboats carry passengers to and from the island (about a 5-minute ride), departing from a launch along the harbor channel north of the ferry terminal. On weekends—and particularly Sunday—entire families spread out along the sand or under the coconut palm groves. Open-air restaurants offer smoked fish, shrimp and beer along with music and dancing.

Playa Olas Altas, off Old Mazatlán, was the city's first tourist beach and is where the *malecón* begins. The name means "high waves," and surfers congregate here during the summer. This is not the best beach for swimming; instead, enjoy the tremendous views of the surf from one of the many outdoor cafés that line the seaside walkway.

Playa Los Piños, located between the Marine House and the Fisherman's Monument, is where local fishermen sell their catch. If you're interested in purchasing fresh fish without angling for it, arrive early; the catch disappears quickly. Just north of Playa Los Piños is **Playa Norte**, which stretches between the Fisherman's Monument and Punta Camarón. This beach is popular with locals who play impromptu baseball and soccer games in the sand or take to the water on a three-wheeled floating trike.

Playa Martín fronts the seaside promenade along Avenida del Mar. A tunnel connects the beach with the Hotel Hacienda. Big Pacific rollers crash against the rocks at Punta Camarón. On the north side of this outcrop jutting into the water is **Playa Las Gaviotas**, popular with tourists who want to soak up some sun or play a game of beach volleyball. Further up is **Playa Sábalo**, where the wide, white sands attract droves of tourists and what seems like equal numbers of Mexican vendors. Parasailers and windsurfers utilize these beaches fronting the Golden Zone. They are protected from the open surf by Bird, Deer and Goat islands, which rise out of the water a short distance offshore.

Beyond Playa Sábalo, at the north end of Mazatlán, are **Playa Brujas** and **Playa Los Cerritos**, which stretch north to Punta Cerritos (Cerritos Point). These beaches are the least crowded, although more and more condominiums are beginning to poke skyward. The more isolated Brujas is frequented by local surfers. Open-air restaurants offer delicious seafood and a relaxed atmosphere.

Because the migratory path of billfish includes the waters off Mazatlán, the city proclaims itself "The Sailfish Capital of the World." Well-equipped fleets are headquartered at the docks at the southern end of town, where the ferry and charter tour boats are moored. Charter fishing boat rates start at around $270 for the day and include lunch, bait, tackle and crew. Tipping the captain and first mate is customary, particularly if the day's catch has been bountiful. Many outfits promote a catch-and-release policy. Make fishing arrangements in advance of your arrival with either the fleet itself or through your hotel.

The marina and yacht club at the El Cid Mega Resort offers a variety of fishing packages utilizing its own fleet of boats. Sightseeing trips include tours of Mazatlán's commercial fishing port, sunset cruises, and trips to Stone Island and the trio of islands off the Golden Zone. For information and reservations phone (800) 633-3085 in the United States, (69) 16-3468 (the harbormaster) or 13-3333 (the resort) in Mazatlán, or contact a travel agency. Local charter companies include Star Fleet, phone (69) 82-2665, and **Flota Faro** (Mike's Sportfishing Fleet), phone (69) 81-2824 or 82-4977. Hotels will usually try to arrange group excursions, thereby sharing the cost of boats.

SHOPPING

Shopping in Mazatlán is centered primarily around the Golden Zone running along avenidas Rodolfo Loaiza and Camarón Sábalo. The shops and galleries here feature the usual assortment of clothing, sportswear, resort wear, jewelry, handicrafts and leather goods. Many shops observe the traditional *siesta* from 2-4 p.m., and some do not accept credit cards.

Be sure to stop by **Sea Shell City**, a combination museum and shop on Avenida Loaiza across from the Playa Mazatlán Hotel. A kaleidoscopic variety of shells from around the world are on display, and there are many shell craft items as well as Mexican handicrafts for sale. Upstairs is an amazing fountain covered in shells that holds living sea turtles.

Just north of Sea Shell City on Avenida Loaiza is **Maya del Pacífico**, an upscale shop selling high-quality arts and crafts, jewelry, pottery, leather boots, wallets and tableware. Prices are correspondingly high. For better bargains, visit the nearby **Mazatlán Arts and Crafts Center**, which stocks everything from tablecloths and rugs to pottery, *guayabera* shirts, embroidered dresses and footwear. Artisans can sometimes be seen creating both artwork and jewelry designs. Within the complex is the **No-Name Café**, where shoppers can cool their heels and get a bite to eat. Be careful, however, not to pet the parrots in the courtyard—they'll bite.

For a more authentic Mexican shopping experience, head downtown. In the municipal market *(mercado)* are piles of fresh shrimp, fish and produce, as well as open-air stalls packed with Mexican-made shoes, hats, belts, pottery and handicrafts. Good quality is harder to find, but for dedicated browsers the opportunity to haggle with local merchants is the real fun. **Midart** is in Old Mazatlán, in a bright blue building next to

the Angela Peralta Theater. This gallery features superbly crafted leather masks, sculptures, burlap dolls and clay figurines. South of Avenida Rafael Buelna and about a quarter of a mile inland from the *malecón* (Avenida del Mar) is the **Grand Plaza Mall**, which offers American-style shopping with an appropriately Mexican flair. The mall is easily reached by taxi or the Sábalo Cocos bus.

DINING AND NIGHTLIFE

Everything from American fast food to spicy creole fare is available in Mazatlán. But for a city that touts itself as "the shrimp capital of Mexico," seafood understandably is the star on many local menus. Shrimp dishes are prepared in every way imaginable, and almost nowhere else is the crustacean fresher or more tempting.

Mamucas, on Boulevard Simon Bolivar in Old Mazatlán, has been in business for more than 30 years. This is where the locals go for authentically prepared Mexican seafood. Go with a group and order a bit of everything from the extensive menu; the options range from smoked marlin, fried fish and broiled shrimp to such exotica as octopus in its own ink. Reservations are a good idea; phone (69) 81-3490. Any cab driver in town will know how to get there. Another longtime institution is **El Shrimp Bucket**, at Avenida Olas Altas #11, which has a center courtyard.

For sophistication, elegance and perhaps the best steak in town, try **Señor Pepper**, on Avenida Camarón Sábalo at the northern end of the Golden Zone across from the Camino Real Hotel. A jazz piano bar adds to the ambience. Reservations are suggested; phone (69) 14-0101.

The Hotel Playa Mazatlán on Avenida Rodolfo Loaiza in the Golden Zone presents "Fiesta Mexicana" on Tuesday, Thursday, Friday and Saturday evenings beginning at 6:45 p.m. An all-you-can-eat buffet of char-broiled steaks and chicken, tacos, burritos, guacamole, salsa and fresh fruit is followed by folkloric dance and music performances from various regions of Mexico. The entertainment includes an amazing display of rope twirling by a *charro*, or Mexican cowboy, and a flamboyantly costumed troupe who re-enact a bit of Carnaval, Mazatlán's version of Mardi Gras. Admittance to the shows is first-come-first served. Dress is casual, but shorts are not permitted. For information phone (800) 222-4466 in the United States, or contact the hotel at (69) 13-4444.

In addition to the big hotel restaurants and fine dining spots, there are numerous establishments along the *malecón* serving fish filets, various shrimp concoctions or such Yucatecan specialties as *pollo pibil*, chicken slowly baked in a banana leaf wrapper.

Most of the restaurants and hotels in Mazatlán offer purified water and ice. There should be no cause for concern about drinking the water in these establishments, but double check if in doubt. Purified water can be bought in any of the *mercados* (markets) around town. For a list of AAA-RATED establishments in Mazatlán, *see the Lodgings & Restaurants section.* **Note:** Some restaurants tack on a standard 10 to 15 percent gratuity to the bill. Be sure to differentiate between this charge and the I.V.A. tax that is added to every check, and tip accordingly.

The disco scene, '70s style, is still big in Mazatlán (although the pounding music is up to the minute). Many of the big hotels in the Golden Zone have discos, bars or lounges, with plenty of evening happy hours featuring two-for-one drink prices. **Valentino's,** an all-white structure perched atop Punta Camarón, the rocky outcrop near the Sábalo traffic circle, attracts a glamorous crowd into the wee hours. There are several discos within this complex, including one with a blown-up photograph of Rudolph Valentino above the dance floor; the Bora Bora Bar has a great view of the surf below. **Joe's Oyster Bar** in the Los Sábalos Hotel along the Golden Zone beachfront is a loud, rollicking nightspot where patrons are likely as not to gyrate on top of the bar.

Mellower options also exist. A romantic atmosphere prevails at the **Mikinos Piano Bar,** on Avenida Camarón Sábalo in the Golden Zone. **Café Pacífico,** in Old Mazatlán at the corner of calles Constitución and Heriberto Frias (on Plaza Machado), has a pool table, walls hung with old photographs and a relaxed air.

EVENTS

The year's biggest party is the pre-Lenten *Carnaval,* or Mardi Gras, held in late February or early March. All Mazatlán—not to mention revelers from around the world—gathers for 5 days and nights of fireworks, parades with elaborate floats, the coronation of a festival queen and of course, plenty of music and dancing. If you'll be visiting around this time, make hotel reservations several months in advance and inquire regarding exactly when *Carnaval* begins. Expect prices to climb as well.

Historical records of the event date to 1827, when military men demanding salaries staged a protest by masquerading. Over the years the tradition grew, with mask wearing becoming part of the festivities at both public assemblies and private parties. By the end of the 19th century, French, German and Italian immigrants were adding facets of their own culture to *Carnaval,* and today the city claims that its celebration is the world's third largest after those in Rio de Janeiro and New Orleans.

Like much of Mexico, Mazatlán celebrates *Day of the Dead* celebrations Nov. 1 and 2 with a combination of feasting and somber remembrances. Several sport fishing tournaments also occur in November.

WHAT TO SEE

ACUARIO MAZATLAN (Mazatlán Aquarium), half a block east of Avenida del Mar at Avenida de los Deportes #111, displays 150 species of fresh and saltwater marine life, from colorful reef fish to moray eels to sea turtles, in some 50 tanks. A 33,000-gallon tank just inside the aquarium entrance features a bull shark that swims in constant lazy circles. Tanks are labeled in Spanish, although English-language signage is planned. A focal point of the freshwater section is the piranha tank, where feeding time for these Amazon River natives is frenzied to say the least. Also inside the aquarium is a small museum that displays shells, miniature fishing nets and displays depicting Gulf of California marine life.

A sea lion show is presented several times daily in an open-air amphitheater. There also is an exotic bird show utilizing birds confiscated from vendors who captured them illegally. Hand fish feedings by a diver take place three times daily. Marine-related films are shown in the aquarium's auditorium. On the grounds is a botanical garden with various tropical ornamentals and a crocodile exhibit. Tues.-Sun. 9:30-6:30; 9-7, summer months and holidays. Admission is charged. Phone (69) 81-7815 or 81-7817.

MAZATLAN JUNGLE TOUR is not really a jungle excursion but a tour of the bay. The tour boat passes shrimp fleets and cruise ship docks, proceeds through inlets and waterways lined with mangroves, and ends up at Isla de la Piedra (Stone Island). A bus takes visitors to the island's beach. A charcoal-grilled fish lunch, prepared beachside, is included; horseback rides along the beach are extra. The boat departs at 9:30 a.m. and returns at 3; the schedule varies according to season. A fare is charged. Phone (69) 14-2400.

EXPLORING OLD MAZATLAN

A world away from the sparkle and glitter of the tourist zone is **Old Mazatlán,** the oldest part of the city just inland from Playa Olas Altas. Here ongoing restoration efforts are preserving a number of historical structures. Blocks of buildings and private residences—including rows of town houses with wrought-iron and stone trim—line the narrow streets, especially along avenidas Heriberto Frias, Venus and Niños Héroes.

Old Mazatlán is the site of the lovingly restored **Teatro Angela Peralta** (Angela Peralta Theater), which first opened in 1874 as Teatro Rubio. Renowned diva Angela Peralta, dubbed "the Mexican Nightingale," arrived for an engagement in 1883 but tragically died (in addition to most of her company) of bubonic plague before uttering a single note.

After stints as a Mardi Gras ballroom, boxing arena and movie palace, the theater finally closed in 1964. A 1975 hurricane severely damaged the building, and it was nearly enveloped by jungle in the succeeding decade. Renovations began in 1987 and were completed in 1992, when the theater was renamed in honor of Peralta. Its wide range of cultural offerings has given the city a welcome touch of class, and the opulent interior is well worth touring.

On the north side of **Plaza Revolución** (the main plaza, between avenidas Flores and 21 de Marzo), is the late 19th-century **Basílica de la Inmaculada Concepción**, the city's cathedral. Easily recognized by its gold-colored twin spires, the cathedral has a rather plain exterior but boasts a lavishly gilded altar. A wrought-iron gazebo sits at the center of the plaza, which is filled with shoeshine vendors.

Outdoor art shows and music concerts take place on Sundays at **Plaza Machado**, at avenidas Constitución and Carnaval a few blocks southwest of Plaza Revolución. Just off Plaza Machado at Sixto Osuna #76, a block east of Olas Altas, is the **Museo Arqueología de Mazatlán** (Archeological Museum of Mazatlán), where exhibits focus on the cultural legacy of the state of Sinaloa. Painting, sculpture and photography exhibitions are presented regularly. The museum is open Tues.-Sun. 10-1 and 4-7. Admission is charged.

Guided Tours

A guided tour is a good way to see both the city and several interesting towns in the surrounding area. Within a short distance of Mazatlán visitors can experience venerable history, cultural charm, and varied flora and fauna at several protected ecological preserves. Information about city and vicinity tours can be obtained through all of the major hotels or at any local travel agency.

A standard city tour hits Mazatlán's highlights, including Old Mazatlán, the central market and the waterfront. **Mazatlán Cruises and Tours** offers a selection of excursion packages both in and around the city; phone (69) 14-3009. **Marlin Tours** provides city excursions and tours to Concordia/Copala, Rosario and Teacapán; phone (69) 13-5301 or 14-2690. **Note:** Beware the numerous sidewalk entrepreneurs who offer free tours; their real goal is to pitch the sale of time-share units.

A 3-hour cruise of the harbor and bay aboard the double-deck *Fiesta* passes by El Faro Lighthouse, various cave rock formations and the 17-kilometer (11-mile) stretch of the *malecón* and its string of luxury hotels. Beverages are available for purchase, and there is dancing (to taped music) on board. The boat departs at 11 a.m. from the dock near the sport fishing fleets and returns at 2. Reservations can be made directly

through your hotel or by calling Yate Fiesta Mazatlán; phone (69) 85-2237 or 85-2238.

Day excursions also can be arranged to several of the islands off the Golden Zone section of the coast, including **Palmito de la Virgen**, a haven for birdwatchers, and **Isla del Venado** (Deer Island), where little coves offer up a bounty of seashells and schools of multicolored fish draw snorkeling enthusiasts. The El Cid Mega Resort offers a tour of the bay via trimaran, which includes drinks, lunch on Deer Island and the use of kayaks and snorkeling gear. The boat departs from the El Cid marina at 10 a.m. and returns at 3; for information contact the hotel at (69) 13-3333.

A popular tour takes in the colonial town of **Concordia**, located east on Mex. 40 toward Durango. Founded in 1565, it is still a furniture and pottery making center. The main plaza contains a gazebo and an enormous wooden chair that provides an amusing photo opportunity. Across the street is the **Church of San Sebastian**, with an ornate stone facade.

A few kilometers east of Concordia is **Copala**. A walk down the town's cobblestone streets and past such landmarks as the **Church of Saint Joseph** is like a journey back in time. Tons of silver were once extracted from the surrounding mountains, and many homes here cling precariously to the hillsides. Charles Butter, an American entrepreneur, was responsible for much of the mining effort in this region, and a restaurant and small hotel in the center of town are named after him. The tour includes lunch at the restaurant, where one of the mouth-watering specialties is banana pie. Also on the premises is a small museum with exhibits depicting the process of melting down silver.

South of Mazatlán via Mex. 15 is **Rosario**, another old mining community. At the end of the 18th century it had a population of 7,000 and was one of the richest towns in northwest Mexico. Mining activities ceased in the 1940s. Of particular interest is **Our Lady of the Rosary**, the town's beautiful colonial church; its marvelous altarpiece is completely covered with intricate gold-leaf designs. Some 70 kilometers (43 miles) of underground tunnels, dug over a 300-year period to aid in extracting gold and silver, remain behind; locals attest that they outnumber the surface streets.

Further south are the towns of **Escuinapa** and **Teacapán**, the latter at the tip of a peninsula reached by a paved side road that branches west off Mex. 15 just north of Escuinapa. The countryside becomes notably lusher here, with extensive groves of coconut palms and mango trees (this is an important mango-producing area). The region around Teacapán is crisscrossed by saltwater canals meandering through tall thickets of mangrove—a natural breeding area for shrimp as well as a wide variety of bird species. Snook, red and bay snapper, bonito and mackerel inhabit the brackish waters. **Rancho Los Angeles**, in the middle of this ecological preserve, offers trips via *panga* (open boat) to fish, observe bird-filled estuaries or visit pristine beaches. For information phone (69) 81-7867 in Mazatlán.

WHERE TO STAY

AZTECA INN

▼▼ *Motor Inn*   ((69)13-4477

12/18-4/30	$70	XP $5
5/1-11/30	$40-$50	XP $5
12/1-12/17	$40	XP $5

Location: 7.3 km nw on Sabalo Beach Rd. Rodolfo T Loaiza 307 82110 (Apartado Postal 841). Fax: 69/13-7476. **Facility:** Across street from beach. 74 units. *Bath:* shower only. 3 stories (no elevator), exterior corridors. **Terms:** F12; 5 day cancellation notice. **Leisure Activities:** heated pool, whirlpool. **Guest Services:** valet laundry. **Cards:** AE, MC, VI.

CAMINO REAL MAZATLAN

▼▼▼ *Resort*   ((69)13-1111

12/27-11/30	$137-$157	XP $35
12/1-12/26	$130-$150	XP $31

Location: 11.5 km nw on Sabalo Beach Rd. On Punta del Sabalo S/N 82100 (Apartado Postal 538). Fax: 69/14-0311. **Facility:** On promontory. Some rooms with oceanview. 165 units. Some whirlpool units. 4 stories, interior corridors. **Terms:** F12; 7 day cancellation notice. **Amenities:** honor bars. **Leisure Activities:** wading pool, beach, social program. *Fee:* 5 lighted tennis courts. **Guest Services:** gift shop, valet laundry. **Business Services:** meeting rooms. **Cards:** AE, DI, MC, VI.

SOME UNITS

DEL REAL SUITES

▼▼ *Motel*   ((69)83-1955

All Year $28-$40   XP $10

Location: Just s of Zona Dorada. Ave del Mar 1020 82140 (APDO Postal 1003). Fax: 69/86-4110. **Facility:** 42 units, 36 with efficiency. *Bath:* shower only. 7 stories, exterior corridors. **Terms:** F12; 3 day cancellation notice. **Guest Services:** gift shop, valet laundry. **Cards:** AE, DI, MC, VI.

EL AGUAMARINA-MAZATLAN

▼▼ *Motor Inn*   ((69)81-7080

12/1-6/30	$51-$77	XP $6
7/1-8/21	$68	XP $6
8/22-11/30	$51	XP $6

Location: 3.3 km nw. Ave del Mar 110 82000. Fax: 69/82-4624. **Facility:** Across from beach. Some rooms with balcony. 125 units, 2 with efficiency. *Bath:* combo or shower only. 3 stories (no elevator), interior/exterior corridors. **Terms:** F12; 3 day cancellation notice-fee imposed. **Leisure Activities:** wading pool, beach. **Guest Services:** valet laundry. **Business Services:** meeting rooms. **Cards:** AE, MC, VI.

FIESTA INN

▼▼▼ *Motel*   ((69)89-0100

12/20-4/20	$90-$134	XP $15
12/1-12/19 & 4/21-11/30	$90	XP $15

Location: 10 km nw. Ave Camaron Sabalo 1927 82110. Fax: 69/89-0130. **Facility:** Attractive public areas. 117 units. 2-9 stories, interior corridors. **Parking:** valet. **Terms:** F12. **Amenities:** *Some:* safes. **Leisure Activities:** heated pool, wading pool, beach, exercise room. **Guest Services:** gift shop, valet laundry. **Business Services:** meeting rooms, administrative services. **Cards:** AE, DI, MC, VI.

SOME UNITS

HOLIDAY INN SUNSPREE RESORT MAZATLAN

▼▼ *Hotel*   ((69)13-2222

All Year $120-$140   XP $20

Location: 9.2 km nw. Ave Camaron Sabalo 696 82100. Fax: 69/14-1287. **Facility:** Attractive grounds and public areas. 183 units. 6 stories, interior corridors. **Terms:** F12; 4 day cancellation notice. **Amenities:** irons, hair dryers. **Leisure Activities:** wading pool, beach, tennis court, exercise room. **Guest Services:** gift shop, valet laundry. **Business Services:** meeting rooms. **Cards:** AE, MC, VI.

SOME UNITS

◍◍◍ HOTEL COSTA DE ORO

▼▼▼ *Resort*   ((69)13-5344

All Year $75   XP $13

Location: 8.8 km nw on Sabalo Beach Rd. Calz Camaron Sabalo S-N 82110 (PO Box 130). Fax: 69/14-4209. **Facility:** On beach; some rooms with balcony. 290 units. 6 two-bedroom units and 110 units with kitchen. *Bath:* shower only. 3-10 stories, exterior corridors. **Terms:** F12; 7 day cancellation notice-fee imposed. **Dining & Entertainment:** 2 restaurants, deli, 6:30 am-10 pm, $5-$12, cocktails, entertainment. **Leisure Activities:** wading pool, beach, 3 tennis courts. **Guest Services:** gift shop, valet laundry. **Business Services:** meeting rooms. **Cards:** AE, MC, VI.

(See color ad p 265)

SOME UNITS

HOTEL LOS SABALOS

▼▼▼ *Hotel*   ((69)83-5333

All Year $85-$100   XP $10

Location: 7 km nw on Sabalo Beach Rd. Rodolfo T Loaiza 100 82110 (Apartado Postal 944). Fax: 69/83-8156. **Facility:** Some rooms with ocean view. Some balconies. 185 units. 19 two-bedroom units. *Bath:* combo or shower only. 8 stories, exterior corridors. **Terms:** F12; 4 day cancellation notice. **Amenities:** safes, hair dryers. **Leisure Activities:** beach, 2 lighted tennis courts. *Fee:* sauna, whirlpool. **Guest Services:** gift shop, valet laundry. **Business Services:** meeting rooms. **Cards:** AE, MC, VI.

SOME UNITS

HOTEL LUNA PALACE

▼▼▼▼ *Hotel* ((69)14-6366

12/20-4/20	$88-$125	XP $15
12/1-12/19 & 4/21-11/30	$69-$95	XP $15

Location: 12 km nw. Ave Camaron Sabalo S/N 82100. Fax: 69/14-6366. **Facility:** Attractive grounds. Ample parking with security. Well-appointed rooms. 71 efficiencies. 1 two-bedroom unit. 8 stories, exterior corridors. **Amenities:** safes, hair dryers. **Leisure Activities:** heated pool, wading pool, beach. **Guest Services:** valet laundry. **Business Services:** meeting rooms. **Cards:** AE, DI, MC, VI.

HOTEL OCEANO PALACE

▼▼ ▼▼ *Hotel* ((69)13-0666

All Year	$59-$69	XP $7

Location: 12 km nw. Ave Camaron Sabalos S/N 82100 (PO Box 411). Fax: 69/13-9666. **Facility:** Many rooms with ocean view and balcony. 200 units, 38 with efficiency. *Bath:* combo or shower only. 6 stories, interior corridors. **Leisure Activities:** wading pool, beach. **Guest Services:** gift shop, valet laundry. **Business Services:** meeting rooms. **Cards:** AE, DI, MC, VI.

SOME UNITS

⏣ HOTEL PLAYA MAZATLAN

▼▼▼▼ *Resort* ((69)89-0555

12/1-4/21	$90-$116	XP $10
4/22-11/30	$81-$91	XP $10

Location: 7.3 km nw on Las Gaviotas Beach. Rodolfo T Loaiza 202 82110 (Apartado Postal 207). Fax: 69/16-5125. **Facility:** Well-appointed rooms with ocean view. Balcony or patio. Very attractive grounds, beach and restaurant facilities. 413 units. 13 two-bedroom units. *Bath:* shower only. 3-5 stories, interior/exterior corridors. **Terms:** F13; 7 day cancellation notice. **Amenities:** irons, hair dryers. **Dining & Entertainment:** deli, also, Terraza Playa, see separate listing, nightclub, entertainment. **Leisure Activities:** 4 heated pools, wading pool, whirlpool, beach, social program, exercise room. *Fee:* sailboating, skin diving equipment, surfboards. **Guest Services:** gift shop, valet laundry. **Business Services:** meeting rooms. **Cards:** AE, MC, VI.
(See color ad below)

SOME UNITS

HOTEL PUEBLO BONITO

▼▼▼▼ *Cottage* ((69)14-3700

12/21-4/24	$120-$140	XP $15
12/1-12/20 & 4/25-11/30	$105-$125	XP $15

Location: 12.5 km nw. Ave Camaron Sabalo 2121 82110. Fax: 69/14-1723. **Facility:** All rooms have balcony or patio. 250 efficiencies. Some whirlpool units. 4-5 stories, exterior corridors. **Terms:** F18; check-in 4 pm. **Amenities:** extended cable TV, voice mail. **Dining:** Angelo's Restaurant, see separate listing. **Leisure Activities:** 2 heated pools, wading pools, whirlpool, beach, exercise room. **Guest Services:** gift shop, valet laundry. *Fee:* massage. **Business Services:** meeting rooms. **Cards:** AE, MC, VI.

SOME UNITS

⊕ HOTEL SUITES LAS FLORES

▼▼ ▼▼ *Hotel*   (69/13-5100

12/24-4/15	$75-$115	XP $10
4/16-11/30	$55-$105	XP $10
12/1-12/23	$50-$90	XP $8

Location: 7.3 km n on Las Gaviotas Beach. Rodolfo T Loaiza 212 82110 (Apartado Postal 583). Fax: 69/ 14-3422. **Facility:** Most rooms with balcony and ocean view. 119 units, 104 with efficiency. *Bath:* combo or shower only. 12 stories, interior/exterior corridors. **Terms:** F12; check-in 4 pm, 3 day cancellation notice-fee imposed. **Dining & Entertainment:** restaurant, coffee shop, 7:30 am-11 pm, $6-$12, cocktails, entertainment. **Leisure Activities:** beach. **Guest Services:** valet laundry. **Business Services:** meeting rooms. **Cards:** AE, MC, VI. *(See color ad below)*

SOME UNITS

MOTEL LOS ARCOS

▼▼ ▼▼ *Apartment*   (69/13-5066

All Year $60-$90   XP $8
Location: 7.5 km nw on Las Gaviotas Beach. Rodolfo T Loaiza 214 82110 (Apartado Postal 132). Fax: 69/13-5066. **Facility:** Located on the beach near shops and restaurants. 20 efficiencies. 8 two-bedroom units. *Bath:* shower only. 2 stories, exterior corridors. **Terms:** F10; small pets only. **Amenities:** no TVs. **Leisure Activities:** beach. **Cards:** MC, VI.

MOTEL MARLEY

▼▼ ▼▼ *Apartment*   (69/13-5533

All Year $57-$69   XP $8
Location: 7.5 km nw on Las Gaviotas Beach. Rodolfo T Loaiza 226 82110 (Apartado Postal 214). Fax: 69/13-5533. **Facility:** One- and two-bedroom efficiencies. Balcony or patio. 16 efficiencies. 4 two-bedroom units. *Bath:* shower only. 2 stories, exterior corridors. **Terms:** 7 day cancellation notice. **Amenities:** no TVs. **Leisure Activities:** beach. **Cards:** MC, VI.

⊕ RIVIERA BEACH RESORT MAZATLAN

▼▼▼▼▼▼ *Hotel*   ((69)83-4344

12/20-4/15	$82	XP $10
12/1-12/19 & 4/16-11/30	$67	XP $10

Location: 6.5 km nw on Sabalo Beach Rd. Ave Camaron Sabalo 51 82110. Fax: 69/84-4532. **Facility:** Attractive rooms and grounds private beach. 170 units. 36 two-bedroom units and 36 efficiencies. *Bath:* combo or shower only. 4 stories, exterior corridors. **Terms:** F12. **Amenities:** hair dryers. *Some:* safes. **Dining & Entertainment:** restaurant, 7 am-11 pm, $8-$15, entertainment. **Leisure Activities:** 2 heated pools, whirlpool, beach. **Guest Services:** valet laundry. **Cards:** AE, MC, VI.

SUITES LINDAMAR

▼▼▼▼ *Apartment*   (69/13-5533

All Year $57-$69   XP $8
Location: 7.5 km nw on Las Gaviotas Beach. Rodolfo T Loaiza 222 82110 (Apartado Postal 214). Fax: 69/13-5533. **Facility:** Balcony or patio. 12 units with kitchen. *Bath:* shower only. 3 stories (no elevator), exterior corridors. **Terms:** 7 day cancellation notice. **Leisure Activities:** beach. **Guest Services:** valet laundry. **Cards:** MC, VI.

WHERE TO DINE

ANGELO'S RESTAURANT

▼▼▼▼▼▼ *Italian*   (69/14-3700
                                    D $20-$35
Location: 12.5 km nw; in Hotel Pueblo Bonito. Ave Camaron Sabalo 2121 82110. **Hours:** 6 pm-midnight. **Reservations:** suggested. **Features:** casual dress; cocktails; entertainment; valet parking; a la carte. Casual, elegant. **Cards:** AE, MC, VI.

LARIOS BAR & GRILL

▼▼ ▼▼ *Continental*   (69/14-1767
                          L $4-$16   D $4-$16
Location: 7.3 km nw on Ave Gaviotas. Bugamvilias 18 82110. **Hours:** 7 am-11 pm. **Reservations:** suggested; 10/1-4/30. **Features:** No A/C; cocktails; street parking. Casual. **Cards:** AE, MC, VI.

RESTAURANT CASA LOMA

▼▼ ▼▼ *Continental*   (69/13-5398
                          L $10-$18   D $10-$18
Location: 7.8 km nw. Ave Las Gaviotas 104 82110. **Hours:** 1:30 pm-10:30 pm. **Reservations:** suggested. **Features:** cocktails; a la carte. Converted home with patio and formal dining. **Cards:** MC, VI.

TEQUILA'S SPORTS BAR & GRILL

▼▼ ▼▼   *Mexican*   (69/13-5344

L $5-$12   **D** $5-$12

Location: 8.8 km nw on Sabalo Beach Rd; in Hotel Costa de Oro. Calz Camaron Sabalo S/N 82110. **Hours:** noon-midnight. **Features:** cocktails. Good place for viewing major sporting events. **Cards:** AE, DI, MC, VI.

TERRAZA PLAYA

▼▼ ▼▼   *Continental*   (69/13-4444

D $8-$17

Location: 7.3 km nw on Las Gaviotas Beach; in Hotel Playa Mazatlan. **Hours:** 6 am-11, noon-4 & 6-11 pm, Sun 6 am-11 pm. **Features:** No A/C; cocktails; entertainment; a la carte. On beachside terrace; casual. **Cards:** AE, MC, VI.

VILLA ITALIA

▼▼ ▼▼   *Italian*   (69/13-0311

L $11-$16   **D** $11-$16

Location: 8 km nw; in front of Hotel El Cid. Av Camaron Sabalo S/N 82100. **Hours:** 1 pm-11 pm. Closed: 9/1-10/1. **Reservations:** suggested. **Features:** cocktails; a la carte. Casual, well-prepared Italian specialties. Patio and indoor dining. Outdoor brick oven used to prepare bread and pizza. **Cards:** AE, MC, VI.

VITTORE

▼▼ ▼▼▼   *Italian*   (69/83-5333

L $10-$20   **D** $10-$20

Location: 7 km nw on Sabalo Beach Rd; in Hotel Los Sabalos. Rodolfo T Loaiza 100 82110. **Hours:** 1 pm-1 am. **Reservations:** suggested. **Features:** casual dress; cocktails & lounge. Wood burning pizza oven. Trattoria ambience. **Cards:** AE, DI, MC, VI.

Nuevo Vallarta, Nayarit
Where To Stay

ALLEGRO RESORT NUEVO VALLARTA ALL INCLUSIVE

▼▼▼▼   *Resort*   (329/7-0400

All Year $120-$173   XP $60

Location: 2 km n on Nuevo Vallarta, exit Mex 200. Paseo Los Cocoteros No 18 63732. Fax: 329/7-0082. **Facility:** Large modern facility, very good beach, pools. Well-appointed rooms, lots of activities and opportunities to enjoy the sun, sand and water. 294 units. *Bath:* shower only. 7 stories, interior corridors. **Amenities:** safes, irons, hair dryers. **Leisure Activities:** heated pool, wading pool, beach, boating, sailboating, scuba diving, 2 lighted tennis courts, children's program, bicycles, playground, exercise room. *Fee:* fishing. **Guest Services:** [AP] meal plan available, gift shop, afternoon tea, valet laundry. *Fee:* massage. **Business Services:** meeting rooms. **Cards:** AE, MC, VI.

   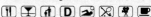

Puerto Escondido,
Oaxaca (I-8)

Puerto Escondido (PWEHR-to ehs-cohn-DEE-doh) means "hidden port," and until fairly recently the translation was quite appropriate. The town was named for Punta Escondida, the rocky outcrop that protects a half-moon bay. A port was established here in 1928 as a shipping point for coffee grown on the forested seaward slopes of the Sierra Madre del Sur. Coastal Mex. 200 came through in the 1960s, opening up the area to tourism. Among the first visitors were surfers, who were drawn by the big waves and dirt-cheap lodgings. Today they're still here, but Puerto Escondido is no longer a hideaway and not quite as cheap. Instead, it's an established destination, frequented by an international group of travelers preferring a more laid-back alternative to the shiny expense of Bahías de Huatulco and other carefully planned seaside resorts.

The Informed Traveler

Puerto Escondido is about 113 kilometers (70 miles) west of Huatulco via Mex. 200. This highway, often referred to as the Carretera Costera (Coastal Highway), divides the town roughly in half. The older, upper section, above the highway, is where most of Puerto Escondido's 40,000 or so residents live and conduct their daily business. Below the highway is the newer, tourist-geared waterfront, where hotels, restaurants and shops spread for about a mile along the main thoroughfare, **Avenida Peréz Gasga.** At noon each day, chains are raised at the eastern and western ends of the beachfront strip, closing the street to vehicular traffic. At the western end of this pedestrian zone, Gasga begins winding uphill and crosses Mex. 200, where its name changes to Avenida Oaxaca (Mex. 131). The junction, marked by a traffic signal, is known as **El Crucero.**

The local bus stations are all within a block or so of the El Crucero intersection. Estrella Blanca provides first-class service along Mex. 200 between Acapulco and Bahías de Huatulco (be sure to specify the La Crucecita terminal as your destination if you're taking a bus to Huatulco from Puerto Escondido). The station is on Avenida Oaxaca, just north of the El Crucero junction.

By car, Puerto Escondido can be reached from Oaxaca by taking Mex. 175—a winding 6- to 8-hour drive over mountainous terrain—to the junction with coastal Mex. 200 (just south of Pochutla), then west about 81 kilometers (50 miles). Avoid Mex. 131, a direct route between Oaxaca and Puerto Escondido but one that has long unpaved stretches. Coastal Mex. 200 southeast from Acapulco or west from Bahías de Huatulco is generally negotiable, although the route winds between Acapulco and Puerto Escondido and is likely to be potholed in spots during the summer rainy season (roughly July through September). A word of caution: Do not drive after dark.

The airport is about 3 kilometers (2 miles) west of town off Mex. 200, near the newer hotel and resort development around Playa Bacocho. The single terminal receives flights from Mexico City (via Mexicana) and Oaxaca (via Aeromorelos). Taxis and less expensive *colectivos* (minibuses) operated by Transportes Terrestres shuttle airport passengers to and from hotels. For additional information about airlines *see "Arriving by Air," page 53*.

A tourist information office is near the airport, at the intersection of Mex. 200 (Carretera Costera) and Avenida Benito Juárez. It is open Mon.-Fri. 9-2 and 5-8, Sat. 9-1; phone (958) 2-0175. An information booth located near the western end of beachside Peréz Gasga is normally open the same hours. There is a *casa de cambio* (currency exchange) office on each side of Peréz Gasga near the Rincón Pacífico Hotel.

THE BEACHES

A lighthouse atop Punta Escondida at the western end of the bayfront affords a panoramic view of town. Running east from the rocky cove beneath the lighthouse is **Playa Principal**, the in-town beach. Here the stretch of sand is narrow, the water calm and the beach backed by rustling palms. It can be crowded: Mexican families flock here on Sundays and holidays to wade and paddle in the shallows, and local fishermen cast their nets at the sheltered west side of the bay or launch small, colorfully painted boats. **Note:** Avoid walking along any of Puerto Escondido's beaches at night, as robberies and muggings have occurred.

To the east of Playa Principal is **Playa Marineros**, which begins at the jutting rocks below the Hotel Santa Fe. Here the shoreline begins curving toward the south and increasingly faces the open ocean. The surf gets rougher, and swimmers should exercise caution. Further to the southeast is **Playa Zicatela**, considered to be one of the world's best surfing beaches. The wide expanse of golden-colored sand stretches for miles, and the thundering Pacific breakers crashing onto it are impressive indeed. The biggest waves occur between August and November. Surfers from all over the world congregate at Zicatela, especially for the international tournament held annually in November. Spectators line the beach to watch these daredevils finesse the "pipeline," a long tubular swell of water. Needless to say, swim here at your own risk.

West of town are the coves of **Puerto Angelito** and **Carrizalillo**. With small beaches, submerged rock formations and close-in shelves of coral, these sheltered spots are ideal for snorkeling and scuba diving (bring your own gear, as facilities are limited at best). Both coves can be reached either by taxi, a boat launched from Playa Principal or a circuitous concrete footpath (wear a hat and bring water if you decide to walk). Farther west is **Playa Bacocho**, another open strip of sand; the waves and undertow make it better for sunning and hiking than swimming. Most of the more expensive hotels cluster around this beach.

WHAT TO DO

The main reason to visit Puerto Escondido is to relax at the beach; shopping and entertainment are not high on its list of diversions. The local *mercado* (municipal market) is in the upper section of town on Avenida 10 Norte, several blocks west of Avenida Oaxaca. It sells mostly produce, but one group of stalls offers a selection of regional handicrafts that includes the black pottery made in the village of San Bartolo Coyotepec *(see "Village Day Trips" under Oaxaca)*. Along the tourist strip, there are a few clothing shops and the usual hodgepodge of T-shirts, postcards and souvenirs.

Several restaurants line beachside Avenida Peréz Gasga, with fish and seafood—from sushi to octopus—the main menu items. Most places provide a view of the beach and the activity along it. The restaurant in the Hotel Santa Fe, on Avenida del Morro at the eastern end of the bay (about half a mile southeast of the town center), has good food and a breezy atmosphere, with tables overlooking the Playa Zicatela surf. **Art and Harry's Surf Inn**, as the name suggests, attracts the local surfer contingent. The fresh fish, salads and unobstructed sunset views are a good way to cap off a day at the beach. The restaurant is on Avenida del Morro, at the southern end of Zicatela.

The best places to watch the sun sink into the Pacific are along Playa Zicatela, where there is an unobscured view of the western horizon. The clifftop lawn on the grounds of the Posada Real Hotel, west of town overlooking Playa Bacocho, is an ideal perch for sunset watching. A taxi can get you there. There are a couple of noisy bars and discos in the tourist zone along Avenida Peréz Gasga and in the hotels around Playa Bacocho.

The surrounding coastal region is a natural paradise, and because most locations are inaccessible except by boat, ecotourism is actively promoted. **Hidden Voyages Ecotours** offers seasonal guided birdwatching and nature trips to some of the lagoons that indent the Oaxacan coast. Early morning trips visit **Manialtepec Lagoon**, about 15 kilometers (9 miles) west of Puerto Escondido, which is encircled by mangroves and home to a rich variety of wetland bird species and tropical vegetation. An all-day excursion to **Lagunas de Chacahua National Park**, a larger series of lagoons west of Manialtepec, includes a midday swim and a visit to a crocodile hatchery. Sunset cruises also are available.

Round-trip transportation is provided from Puerto Escondido hotels. Food is not included; the Chacahua tour stops at a restaurant for lunch. The restaurant at the departure dock sells beverages to go. Bring a hat, sunblock and a dollar or two to tip the boatman. Binoculars are provided.

There is a four-person minimum for tours. Fees range from $30 to $40 per person. Reservations must be made through the Turismo Rodimar Travel Agency, Avenida Peréz Gasga #905 on the beachfront. It is usually open daily 7:30 a.m.-10 p.m.; phone (958) 2-0734. This agency also can arrange three- or four-person fishing trips to the waters off Puerto Escondido for mackerel, sea bass, snook or tuna. Boats depart from Playa Principal.

WHERE TO STAY

HOTEL POSADA REAL BEST WESTERN

♥♥ ♥♥   *Motor Inn*   ((958)2-0133

12/1-1/3	$69-$109	XP $10
1/4-4/14	$69-$89	XP $10
4/15-11/30	$69-$75	XP $10

Location: 2.2 km n of jct Hwy 200 and 131, just w of tourist info booth. Blvd Benito Juarez S/N 11980. Fax: 958/2-0192. **Facility:** Spacious landscaped gardens overlooking ocean. Beach club reached by shuttle or by short walk down hill. Welcome cocktail. All inclusive meal plan available. Meets AAA guest room security requirements. 100 units. *Bath:* shower only. 4 stories, interior/exterior corridors. **Terms:** F12; 3 day cancellation notice-fee imposed. **Amenities:** voice mail. **Leisure Activities:** 2 pools, wading pools, putting green, recreation program, sports court, game room. *Fee:* tennis court. **Guest Services:** [AP] & [BP] meal plans available, gift shop, valet laundry. *Fee:* fax. **Cards:** AE, DI, MC, VI.

🆘 🍴 🍸 🏊 ✂ 🐾 📠

HOTEL SANTA FE

♥♥ ♥♥   *Country Inn*   ((958)2-0170

All Year	$50-$80	XP $11

Location: At Playa Zicatela, off Mex 200 at south end of town. Calle del Morro S/N 71980 (PO Box 96). Fax: 958/2-0260. **Facility:** Across road from beach. Beautifully rustic architecture resembles a small hamlet. Large rooms with clay tile floors and hand painted tiles. 61 units. *Bath:* shower only. 3 stories (no elevator), exterior corridors. **Terms:** F11; 30 day cancellation notice. **Leisure Activities:** 3 pools, wading pool. **Guest Services:** gift shop, valet laundry. *Fee:* fax. **Cards:** AE, MC, VI.

SOME UNITS

🍴 🍸 🏊 ✂ / 💻 🛗 /

PUERTO VALLARTA, JALISCO

One of Mexico's top resorts, Puerto Vallarta is situated roughly at the midpoint of **Bahía de Banderas** (Banderas Bay). Spanish soldiers engaged in expeditions to Lower (Baja) California discovered the bay's shores in the early 16th century, stopping for supplies of water, firewood and food. Written chronicles of the time extolled the land's beauty and fertility, as well as the refuge the bay offered ships from marauding pirates.

A shipyard was built in 1644 to aid in the colonization efforts of Lower California. Entries in 17th-century ship logs made reference to whaling ships and fishing boats anchored in the bay, which at that time was also known as Bahía

de los Jorobados (Humpback Bay) because of the number of humpback whale sightings. The first known settlement, called Las Peñas, was established in 1851. It consisted of families who farmed, raised cattle or brought in salt that was used in the refining process for silver-mining operations in the surrounding area.

Las Peñas was opened to national maritime traffic in 1885. There were both highs and lows over the next 50 years. A fire in 1888 destroyed more than half the town's homes (local legend maintains that the damage would have been far less severe if more of the male population had not been attending a cockfight at the time). In 1918, the town's name was changed to Puerto Vallarta, in honor of Jaliscan lawyer and state governor Don Ignacio L. Vallarta, who helped draft the Mexican Constitution. A yellow fever epidemic hit in 1922, but the town began to boom 3 years later with jobs created by the opening of banana plantations. And the first airplane landed in 1931.

Tourists began to arrive around 1930, and Mexican warships fired a 21-gun salute when the town celebrated its centennial in 1951. The event that really put Puerto Vallarta on the tourist map, however, was the 1964 filming of "Night of the Iguana." John Huston's film showcased the tropical beauty of Mismaloya Beach, and the torrid romance of star Richard Burton and tagalong Elizabeth Taylor—both of whom were married to others—titillated millions and generated an avalanche of publicity. Visitors came pouring in, hoping to glimpse a movie star. Improved road and air accessibility led to the construction of first-class hotels, and soon agriculture—previously the area's principal source of income—took a back seat to tourism.

Growth since then has been swift and steady, fueled by the annual invasion of sun-seeking visitors. Resort development, which has spread

Fast Facts

LOCATION: On the Bay of Banderas along Jalisco's Pacific shoreline.

POPULATION: 250,000 (estimated).

AREA CODE: 322.

WHAT'S THERE: A magnificent natural setting, with a backdrop of jagged mountains and graceful stands of coconut palms overlooking blue water; Viejo Vallarta (Old Town), an enclave that evokes Mexico's colonial atmosphere to a greater degree than any other beach resort in the country; restaurants offering fresh seafood and views of the sun setting over Banderas Bay; organized day trips to secluded coastal villages or into the surrounding jungle.

both north and south of the original village, is extensive but somehow does not overshadow the prevailing sense of charm that makes Puerto Vallarta (or "PV," as it is often called) so appealing. The city is simultaneously sophisticated, laid-back, very modern and timelessly Mexican.

The tourist influx peaks between mid-December and mid-April; if you plan on visiting during this period, reservations will need to be booked several months in advance. With all the activities at hand—sun, sand, strolling, shopping, swimming, fishing, boat trips or just kicking back and doing nothing—it's easy to spend a week or two.

Puerto Vallarta is basically a one-stop vacation destination, where an idyllic locale is complemented by a full spectrum of luxury amenities. It combines a leisurely, slow-paced ambience with such expected big-resort features as fine dining and flashy nightlife. Accommodations range from small and unpretentious to decidedly upscale. Most of the city's older section is postcard pretty and pleasant to stroll.

The surrounding region is rich in natural beauty as well, and ecotourism is in full swing here. Many day trips revolve around the inviting beaches lining Banderas Bay. **Mismaloya, Quimixto** and **Yelapa**, all south of Puerto Vallarta, are secluded spots (the latter two accessible only by boat) made to order for a relaxed outing away from the tourist hustle. More strenuous but equally rewarding options include taking in the jungle scenery by bike or on foot, or perhaps exploring coastal lagoons by kayak.

Approaches

By Air

Gustavo Díaz Ordaz International Airport is on the main highway about 7 kilometers (4 miles) north of downtown. Aeroméxico, Alaska Airlines, American, America West, Continental, Delta and Mexicana all provide service to Puerto Vallarta. Connections for flights from the United States are normally via Mexico City. The regional carriers Aero Guadalajara and Taesa provide service to Puerto Vallarta from other cities within the country, including Mexico City, Guadalajara, Mazatlán and San José del Cabo. For additional information about airlines see "Arriving by Air," page 53.

Colectivos (minivans) operated by Transportes Terrestres provide shared transportation from the airport to hotels. More expensive airport taxis operated by Aeromovil also take passengers to hotels. In both cases, fares are based on a zone system. Zones are posted at the minivan and taxi ticket booths; ask if you don't know the zone in which your hotel is located. The *colectivos* depart as soon as they're full, so try to flag one as soon as possible after landing.

By Car

Reaching Puerto Vallarta by car involves a lengthy journey; the city lies some 1,200 miles south of the border at Nogales, Ariz., via Mex. 15/15-D and Mex. 200. From Tepic, the Nayarit state capital, the latter highway is a slow, winding route through mountains that reach to the coast. A toll highway that will link Puerto Vallarta and Guadalajara is in the works.

By Bus

Puerto Vallarta has a new, modern central bus station *(camionera)* located just off the Tepic Highway, about a kilometer north of the airport. Consolidating the small stations along Avenida Insurgentes that served different bus lines has considerably reduced the noise and pollution on downtown streets. The Elite line offers "deluxe" bus service to and from Aguascalientes, Guadalajara and Mexico City. Transportes del Pacífico is another major bus line operating out of the station. Travel agencies around town can sometimes provide bus routes and schedules. For additional information about buses see "Bus Service," page 63.

By Cruise Ship

Puerto Vallarta is a major port of call for cruise ships, most arriving from Los Angeles during the peak tourist season. Cruise lines dock at the Terminal Marítima (Maritime Terminal), north of downtown at the Marina Vallarta complex, and include Carnival, Holland-America, Norwegian, Princess and Royal Caribbean.

Getting Around

Layout

The downtown area is small and compact, hemmed in as it is between the mountains and the bay. The **Río Cuale** divides it into two sections. North of the river is the *malecón* (seaside promenade); the street along this waterfront stretch is known as Paseo Díaz Ordaz. White wrought-iron benches offer an opportunity to sit and contemplate the bay views. Along the *malecón* are three nautically themed bronze statues: **La Fuente de los Delfines** (Fountain of the Dolphins), **Neptune y Serena** (Neptune and the Mermaid) and **Caballito de Mar** (The Seahorse), which is the city's trademark. Across from the seawall are shops, nightspots, open-air cafés and fast-food outlets. The view is particularly nice from the second-story restaurant balconies.

Tree-shaded **Plaza de Armas** is just off the *malecón* between avenidas Morelos and Juárez. This traditional-looking square has a bandstand in the middle. On the east side of the plaza is **La Iglesia de Nuestra Señora de Guadalupe** (Church of Our Lady of Guadalupe), which is notable for the large crown atop its steeple, modeled after one worn by Carlota, wife of Archduke

Maximilian, Mexico's ruler for 3 years in the 1860s. Angels clasping hands decorate the exterior. (**Note:** Do not wear shorts or T-shirts if you wish to enter the church.)

Whitewashed stucco walls and red-tiled roofs characterize **Viejo Vallarta** (Old Town), PV's heart. An irregular grid of narrow streets extends some 6 blocks up into the hills above the bay, forming the oldest section of Puerto Vallarta. Street names are denoted on Mexican tiles on the sides of buildings. Viejo Vallarta exudes charm, although dusty cobblestones, street construction, sputtering taxicabs and even an occasional burro are all reminders of a more prosaic Mexico.

Overlooking the river is the hillside dubbed **Gringo Gulch**, named for the well-connected Americans who settled in Puerto Vallarta during the 1950s and '60s. Among the beautiful homes is Elizabeth Taylor's former residence, Casa Kimberly, which is now a bed-and-breakfast. On Avenida Miramar, just north of the Río Cuale's north bank (near the Municipal Market) is a statue of Burton and Taylor.

Two stone bridges (as well as a couple of rickety suspension foot bridges) connect the river with **Río Cuale Island**. The benches at this elongated sandbar's western end, overlooking the bay, are a prime spot for sunset watching. Between the bridges are souvenir stalls and casual little eateries in a parklike setting. Strolling the island is pleasant, although the river water in the canals is polluted. Just east of the Avenida Insurgentes bridge in a shady plaza is a life-size statue of actor/director John Huston.

The area south of the Río Cuale used to consist only of tucked-away coves and sandy beaches. Just below the river are more shops and restaurants, Plaza Lázaro Cárdenas Park, and motels catering to budget-minded travelers. Like Viejo Vallarta, this area is easily traversed on foot. **Basilio Badillo**, which runs east-west about five blocks south of the river, is appropriately known as "Calle de las Cafés." Further south, heading toward Mismaloya Beach, are hotels and expensive villas wedged into the rocky cliffs overlooking the shore.

More luxury properties form a glittering **Hotel Zone** north of old Puerto Vallarta. Landscaped, four-lane Avenida de las Palmas (formerly called the Airport Highway) passes through this area. Approaching the city from the airport, this highway divides; downtown is to the right. **Note:** The 60 km/h (35 mph) speed limit is strictly enforced.

Marina Vallarta, at the northern edge of the Hotel Zone, is practically a city unto itself. It encompasses major hotels, a flurry of upscale condominium developments, an enormous yacht club, an 18-hole golf course, restaurants, shopping centers and the Maritime Terminal, the point of departure for fishing trips and day cruises to Yelapa, Las Animas and other points south of town. This is the resort development closest to the airport, and as a result can be affected by noise from landing and departing aircraft.

Nuevo Vallarta, about 13 kilometers (8 miles) north of the city, is just over the Nayarit state

The Informed Traveler

Media

Vallarta Today is an English-language daily newspaper geared toward tourists; it has information on everything from restaurants to currency exchange rates.

Weather

The weather in Puerto Vallarta is balmy year-round, with an average annual temperature of 80 degrees. Daily highs range from the 80s to the low 90s, nightly lows from the low 60s to low 70s. The temperature rarely drops below 60 degrees, making coats or jackets unnecessary.

The nicest weather is during the high season, from December through April. July to October is hot, humid and characterized by afternoon showers and thunderstorms. Bring along an effective insect repellent, as mosquitos can be a nuisance at any time of year; Autan Classic is a widely available Mexican brand.

Earthquakes, a possibility in many parts of Mexico, are rare but not out of the question. A 1995 quake damaged the crown atop the Church of Our Lady of Guadalupe.

Staying Safe

Tourist crime is uncommon, although visitors would do well not to carry large amounts of cash in public. If your hotel provides safety deposit boxes, they are a good place to keep money, airline tickets, tourist cards and so forth. Bilingual "tourist police" wearing white safari outfits and white (tourist) or blue (traffic) pith helmets patrol the downtown area and are generally friendly and helpful.

In Case of Emergency

In the event of medical emergency, the C.M.Q. Hospital, Basilio Badillo #365, is conveniently located and open 24 hours; phone (322) 2-3572. The Red Cross also is open 24 hours; phone (322) 2-1533.

Blue-and-white telephone booths in the bus stations and at the airport can be used to secure an English-speaking U.S. operator and are much less expensive than making the same call from your hotel.

line at the mouth of the Río Ameca. This planned resort area, which seems removed from the rest of PV, has condominiums, time-share units, bayfront homes, a yacht marina and a sprinkling of all-inclusive accommodations. Water taxis make daily trips from the marina to downtown Puerto Vallarta.

A bit farther north is the village of **Bucerías**, an enclave of cobblestone streets, walled villas and tidy little hotels. Some travelers prefer this lower-cost alternative to Puerto Vallarta for its uncrowded beaches, casual seafood restaurants and decidedly relaxed pace. Bucerías is most easily reached by bus; minivans also shuttle passengers from the airport to the village and back.

RENTAL CARS

If you've driven your own vehicle or rented one for exploring north or south of the city, keep in mind that there are only three gas stations in town. Also avoid driving anywhere out of the city after dark; cows wandering onto the roadway are a very real hazard. For sightseeing purposes, take advantage of the green-and-white tourist buses that cover the area from Marina Vallarta south to Mismaloya Beach.

Note: AAA/CAA members enjoy exceptional discounts through Hertz for vehicles booked in the United States. Consult your local AAA/CAA club or phone Hertz, (800) 654-3080.

BUSES

City buses take passengers to almost all points along Banderas Bay, from the airport south through the Hotel Zone, into downtown via the Ignacio Vallarta Bridge, and points south to Mismaloya Beach. In addition to the newer minibuses (*combis* or *colectivos*) that are equipped with emission controls, there are still old public buses on the streets spewing clouds of exhaust. Stops are designated by a white bus outlined on a dark blue sign. Destinations and routes (for example, "Olas Altas," "Ixtapa," "Hoteles" or "Aeropuerto") are painted on the front of the bus or posted in the window. Local routes are normally covered from 6 a.m. to 11 p.m. Fares are inexpensive, normally less than 50c within town.

The local bus station is on Avenida Olas Altas at Plaza Lázaro Cárdenas, south of the Río Cuale and just inland from the beach. City buses also depart from Plaza de Armas, the main square.

TAXIS

Taxis cover the same routes as buses, but are more expensive. Although there are supposed to be established rates based on a zone system, always decide on a fare before you get in the cab. Many hotels post a list of rates to specific destinations, which can come in handy for those unfamiliar with the city. It is customary not to tip drivers.

PARKING

Parking in the compact downtown area is scarce, and driving around Puerto Vallarta in general presents a challenge. During the winter tourist season the narrow streets are jammed; in the summer they can be flooded by heavy rain.

WHAT TO DO

DINING

PV offers many options for dining well, if not particularly cheaply. A plus for foreign visitors is the purified water—including ice—that is universally used by licensed food and beverage establishments. (If in doubt, ask for bottled water, juice, beer or a soft drink.) While food quality is dependable, it is the striking water views that distinguish many restaurants. Most hotel establishments offer a standard steak and seafood menu, although **La Perla**, in the Camino Real, is worth a splurge for its Mexican specialties and excellent service.

For a break from the hotel dining scene, try **Le Bistro Jazz Café**, on Río Cuale Island just east of Avenida Insurgentes, or **Café des Artistes**, 3 blocks inland from the *malecón* at Calle Guadalupe Sánchez #740. Also worth checking out is Calle Basilio Badillo, somewhat of a "restaurant row." Seafood, Mexican and Argentinian are some of the choices at eateries along the 3 blocks between Pino Suárez and Insurgentes. **Memo's Pancake House**, Basilio Badillo #289, just might be the city's favorite breakfast place. Here you can get pancakes, waffles, omelets and other familiar yet well-prepared fare, plus good coffee. Coffee—plus fresh fruit, sandwiches and desserts—can be sampled at **Café San Cristóbal**, Calle Corona #172, a couple of blocks north of the main plaza.

Two large, tourist-oriented restaurants in the vicinity of Mismaloya Beach—most easily reached by taxi—offer open-air dining amid beautiful tropical surroundings. **Chino's Paraiso** is located in an area known as El Edén, along a stream that flows down from the hills to the beach. About 5 kilometers (3 miles) inland from the village of Boca de Tomatlán is the similarly named **Chico's Paradise**, in a similarly idyllic hillside setting among rocks and waterfalls. If they wish, guests can swing Tarzan-style via rope and splash into a protected natural pool. Less active diners handpick their lunch from a fish-filled adobe water tank in the middle of the restaurant. Chico's Paradise has no electricity and is open during daylight hours only; confirm the hours for both restaurants at your hotel desk or with the Tourism Information Office.

A casual dress code applies at almost all Puerto Vallarta restaurants, although wearing shorts to dinner may be frowned on. Some places shut down for a month during the summer. For a

Visitor Services

Guides/Tours

The standard city tour provides an all-purpose Puerto Vallarta orientation. A short version of the tour covers the local sights by air-conditioned minibus, including the main plaza and its crown-topped cathedral, the exclusive neighborhood of Conchas Chinas, Gringo Gulch, and the former homes of Elizabeth Taylor and Richard Burton.

The tropical tour is a longer version that throws in a trip to Mismaloya Beach and lunch in a jungle setting at Chino's Paradise. Hotel pickup and drop-off is included in the fee; lunch is not. City tours are given Mon.-Sat. 10-1, tropical tours Mon.-Sat. 10-3. Make arrangements through your hotel.

Information Sources

The Tourism Information Office is on the first floor of the Palacio Municipal (City Hall), on the north side of Plaza de Armas, the main square. The office is open Mon.-Fri. 9-8, Sat. 9-1; phone (322) 2-0242. On the building's second floor, within the courtyard, is a lovely mural by the late local artist Mañuel Lepe.

Avoid the many "information" booths along the *malecón*; their main purpose is to sell time-share properties to the unsuspecting, and the promise of a "free" breakfast is not worth enduring a high-powered sales pitch.

Currency Exchange

Banks and currency exchange offices *(casas de cambio)* are concentrated in the downtown area. Banks are usually open Mon.-Fri. 9-1:30, although hours for exchanging foreign currency may be restricted. Currency exchange offices are open longer hours and may offer better rates. Stores, restaurants and even street vendors often will accept U.S. dollars, however.

---

list of AAA-RATED establishments in Puerto Vallarta, *see the Lodgings & Restaurants section.*

SHOPPING

Shopping is a major pastime in Puerto Vallarta. Merchandise from all over Mexico turns up, although prices tend to be higher than in the cities where the items originate. You'll find jewelry, especially silver; clothing ranging from beach T-shirts to designer fashions; colonial-style furniture; pottery and ceramics; hand-tooled leather goods, including *huaraches* (sandals); shoes (keep in mind that sizes are measured in centimeters); and sombreros and other hats. Fine handicrafts include beaded tapestries from Nayarit, lacquered boxes and ceremonial masks from Michoacán, and handwoven baskets, rugs and shawls from Central America.

A typical Mexican shopping experience can be had at the open-air **Mercado Río Cuale**, (Municipal Market), which spreads out under the trees below the steps leading down from the northern end of the Avenida Insurgentes Bridge. Clothes, crafts and trinkets fill the maze of stalls—everything from piñatas to whips. Bargain hunters should be ready to haggle, as vendors are always willing to lower their prices *un poquito* (just a little bit). Here you're also apt to find young boys roaming around with their pet iguanas; for about a dollar (U.S.) they will place the lizard on your shoulder and take a picture with your camera.

Those interested in more than a souvenir should head for **Viejo Vallarta** and its assortment of galleries. The **Sergio Bustamante Gallery**, Avenida Juárez #275, is devoted to the works of the acclaimed artist, who specializes in whimsical bronze, ceramic and papier maché animals. Other galleries display the wares of a resident community of painters, sculptors and artisans. Many of the merchants accept American dollars or credit cards, and store prices are usually fixed. **Galería Uno**, downtown at Calle Morelos #561 (at Calle Zaragoza), exhibits a range of contemporary and abstract works. It is open Mon.-Sat. 10-8; phone (322) 2-0908. **Galería Pacífico**, Avenida Insurgentes #109 (just south of Río Cuale Island), specializes in contemporary works by Mexican and Latin American artists.

Downtown shops carry an excellent selection of Mexican folk art. Prices tend to be high, but so does quality. **Olinalá**, south of the river at Lázaro Cárdenas #274, has two floors of crafts and a particularly wide selection of masks. It is open Mon.-Sat. 10-2 and 5-9; phone (322) 2-4995. **La Rosa de Cristal**, also south of the river at Insurgentes #272 (between calles Lázaro Cárdenas and Madero) is the place to go for blown-glass items, which are made in the Guadalajara suburb of Tlaquepaque. On display at **Tlaquepaque**, Avenida México #1100, are baskets, woodcarvings, glassware and ceramics.

Puerto Vallarta's shopping centers feature boutiques offering sportswear and casual yet fashionable evening wear. They are located primarily along the *malecón* and north into the Hotel Zone. Most stores are open until at least 8 p.m., and some may close from 2-4 for *siesta*. Many stores are closed on Sunday. Among the arcades with browsing potential are **Plaza Malecón**, on the oceanfront at Paseo Díaz Ordaz and Calle Allende; **Plaza Marina**, within the Marina Vallarta complex; and **Villa Vallarta**, on Avenida de las Palmas in the Hotel Zone.

A flea market offering the usual T-shirts and souvenirs sets up at the Marina Vallarta docks where the cruise ships anchor. Gaggles of vendors also peddle their wares at the beaches, especially Playa de los Muertos. Their persistence can be annoying, so be very firm if you're not interested in purchasing anything.

BEACHES

Puerto Vallarta's beaches are divided into three zones: north of town, in town and south of town. Perhaps the most popular is **Playa de los Muertos** (Beach of the Dead), which city officials have long tried to rename Playa del Sol. It stretches south from the river and can be accessed from Calle Olas Altas. Better for sunning than for swimming (the water is somewhat polluted), it attracts locals, European tourists and budget travelers. Sunbathers crowd the sand (particularly on Sundays and holidays), parasailers soar above it and roaming vendors hawk barbecued fish on a stick—the PV equivalent of a Coney Island hot dog. At the southern end of the beach is **El Púlpito**, a rock formation shaped like a pulpit.

About 10 kilometers (6 miles) south of town off Mex. 200 (the southward extension of Avenida Insurgentes) is **Playa Mismaloya**, protected by a pretty cove. This is where "Night of the Iguana" was filmed, and it is still possible to hike to the ruins of the movie set, at the southern end of the cove. Although the spot's tranquil beauty has been compromised by such sprawling developments as the La Jolla de Mismaloya hotel complex, the water is clear, the sand white and the beach backed by jungle-cloaked hills. A string of *palapa* restaurants sell beer and seafood, and also rent out tables and beach chairs. In the rugged country above Mismaloya another movie was made—Arnold Schwarzenegger's 1987 science-fiction opus "Predator."

On the north side of town is **Playa de Oro**, which is backed by the Hotel Zone. Although it may seem like the stretches of golden-brown sand in front of the big hotels are private, they are not; all beaches in Mexico are federal property and thus open to the public. The wide, flat expanse of sand, divided into sections by iron jetties and rocky in spots, faces the open bay; waves can be surprisingly rough.

At all of the beaches there are efforts to protect the eggs of endangered sea turtles, evidence of an increased ecological awareness throughout the country. Puerto Vallarta's program, known as "Vallarta-Tortuga 2000," involves regular patrols of turtle nesting grounds. Eggs are taken to protected nurseries, and hatchlings are released in the open water.

SIGHTSEEING

Nearby beaches and islands make easy day trip destinations from Puerto Vallarta. More and more ecotouristic activities allow participants to explore or learn about the local environment without disturbing it. Local travel agencies maintain offices at hotels and in town. **Intermar Caribe** organizes a variety of tours; phone (322) 1-0734.

Several companies in town organize guided trips into the surrounding region. **Open Air Expeditions** specializes in adventure travel, taking small groups on hiking, kayaking, birdwatching and wildlife observation excursions; phone (800) 484-5506 in the United States. **Terra Noble** is an arts center situated on a high plateau at the north end of town, surrounded by mountains and jungle. Visitors attend a hands-on clay and art workshop utilizing pre-Hispanic techniques. Lunch is provided, and nature walks are available. Tours depart downtown at 10 a.m. and return at 2. Reservations can be made through local travel agencies, or phone (322) 3-0308.

About 16 kilometers (10 miles) south of the city, just before Mex. 200 veers inland, is the village of **Boca de Tomatlán**, at the mouth of the Río Tomatlán. It is easily reached by taxi or bus (buses post their destination in the window or above the windshield). A relaxed tropical atmosphere prevails here amid lush hillsides, freshwater pools and water burbling past huge rocks. The small but enticing beach is sheltered by a narrow cove. For about $9 (U.S.) you can hire a *panga* (skiff) for a trip to the secluded beach at **Las Animas**, a bit farther southwest.

Separate daily cruises set sail for the coastal villages of **Yelapa** and **Quimixto** (key-MISH-toh). Cruises depart Marina Vallarta's Maritime Terminal at 9 a.m., returning around 4. The coastline here is punctuated by small coves set against a jungle backdrop. At Yelapa, passengers can swim, snorkel or just stretch out in the sun; a short hike or horseback ride from Quimixto leads to a jungle waterfall. Lunch and snorkeling gear are normally provided. The trimaran *Bora Bora* sails to the beach at Las Animas, with snorkeling and lunch included on the all-day agenda. Many of these excursions provide music on board. Dinner and sunset cruises also are available. Make cruise reservations with one of the local travel agencies. For those who wish to tarry, rustic overnight accommodations are available in Yelapa.

About 36 kilometers (22 miles) north of Puerto Vallarta via Mex. 200 is the fishing village of **Sayulita**. The location boasts beautiful views of Banderas Bay and the rich tropical forest environment of the coastal Sierra Madre mountains. Within the village is **Papa's Palapas**, a collection of beachfront bungalows constructed in rustic Mexican *palapa* style but equipped with modern conveniences. A variety of eco-oriented activities can be arranged, including kayaking on the bay, nature hikes through an ecological reserve, bird and whale-watching expeditions, and organized mountain bike rides (more comfortably undertaken during the dry winter season) through the jungles surrounding Puerto Vallarta.

Transportation, guides and equipment are provided; wear a hat or cap and comfortable walking shoes, and bring insect repellent. For schedule and reservation information contact Papa's Palapas, P.O. Box 666, Pismo Beach, CA 93449; phone (805) 473-5300 in the United States, (327) 5-0082 in Mexico.

Sports and Recreation

Water sports are a given in an environment where boaters have access to modern marine facilities within a protected bay. The **Bay of Banderas** extends north to Punta de Mita (Mita Point) and south to Cabo Corrientes (Corrientes Cape), where the foothills of the Sierra de Cuale range begin. It forms a natural barrier against most serious storms; the region's only hurricane was recorded in 1911. Water depths of up to 1,500 feet give the bay characteristics normally associated with oceans, but it is also protected due to its shape and the surrounding geography. The result is generally calm water and clear visibility. Favored by experienced divers are the Marietas Islands, off Punta de Mita at the bay's northern end. These islets were once used as a hiding place by pirates who plundered galleons loaded with silver from Sierra Madre mines.

For snorkelers, the bay teems with tropical fish. Dolphins, sea turtles, giant manta rays and migrating humpback whales also can be seen. A favorite snorkeling destination is the underwater park at **Los Arcos** (also called Las Peñas), a short distance offshore from Mismaloya Beach. The oddly eroded formations jutting out of the bay served as an early landmark for ships. Colorful marine life is particularly evident around these rocks. **Chico's Dive Shop**, Paseo Díaz Ordaz #770 at the northern end of the *malecón*, rents equipment and organizes dive trips; phone (322) 2-1895. Scuba and snorkeling trips also can be arranged at Marina Vallarta.

Boats for sport fishing can be hired through the **Cooperativo de Pescadores** (Fishing Cooperative), at the northern end of the *malecón*. Rates for fishing vessels depend on the size of the boat, where you fish, and whether bait and tackle are supplied. Bring your own refreshments, since most trips don't include them. Sailfish and blue marlin are hooked November through February; smaller game species such as dorado, roosterfish and tuna can be caught seasonally most of the year. A catch-and-release policy is stressed if the fish is not going to be eaten.

Marina Vallarta has more than 500 slips and offers boaters fresh water, as well as cable TV and telephone hookups. Hardware and boating supply outlets are located along the boardwalk of this sprawling complex, which also has an 18-hole golf course, luxury hotels and condomin-

iums. Tour boats and fishing excursions depart from the marina's Maritime Terminal. Boaters can explore a variety of tiny coves and hidden beaches along the shore of Banderas Bay, or drop anchor for awhile at **Bahía de Banderas Yacht Club** in Nuevo Vallarta.

Swimming, water skiing, parasailing and other watery pursuits can be enjoyed at many spots along the bay. Surfers head for the open waters and bigger waves around Punta de Mita. For those who would rather view the bay than venture into it, saddle horses for shoreline rides can be rented through a travel agency or the beachfront hotels. **Rancho El Charro** and **Rancho Ojo de Agua** organize guided 2- to 3-hour rides into the foothills of the Sierra Madre, past jungle plantations and rural villages. Transportation is included and reservations are necessary; phone (322) 4-0114 for Rancho El Charro, (322) 4-8240 for Rancho Ojo de Agua.

There are two 18-hole golf courses in the area. Water comes into play on 11 holes at the **Marina Vallarta Country Club** course. A cart or caddy is mandatory, and member privileges are extended to guests staying at certain hotels. Golfers wishing to play outside peak tourist season should check with the club; phone (322) 1-0171. The **Los Flamingos Golf Club** is about 13 kilometers (8 miles) north of the airport off Mex. 200, in the state of Nayarit. The greens fee at this older, par-71 course is about $35 (U.S.); caddies and motorized carts are available. (**Note:** Nayarit observes Mountain Standard Time, which is an hour earlier than Puerto Vallarta and the rest of Jalisco.) Reservations and transportation can be arranged through your hotel, or phone (329) 8-0606.

Most of the resorts provide clay tennis courts for their guests. PV also has two tennis centers: the **John Newcombe Tennis Center**, at the Continental Plaza Puerto Vallarta in the Hotel Zone, and the **Los Tules Tennis Center**, near the Fiesta Americana Hotel. For bullfight fans, the **La Paloma Bullring** is across Avenida de las Palmas from Marina Vallarta. Bullfights begin Wed. afternoons at 5, November through April; tickets can be obtained through travel agencies.

Nightlife

After-dark options are plentiful. The cheapest is strolling along the *malecón* (Paseo Díaz Ordaz). Sunday evenings in particular bring out local families, mariachi bands, street performers and the ubiquitous vendors. Three popular watering holes along the *malecón* are **The Zoo**, **Carlos O'Brien's** and the PV branch of the **Hard Rock Café**, all of which tend to attract a younger crowd. **Andale**, Calle Olas Altas #425 at Avenida Rodriguez (near the Los Muertos Pier), caters to all ages with a video bar and upstairs restaurant.

Puerto Vallarta's discos are loud, flashy and stay open until the early hours of the morning. There is normally a cover charge, and drink prices can be steep; look for free passes that are available at tourist-frequented hotels and restaurants. Many hot spots are in the hotels. **Christine's**, in the Krystal Vallarta Hotel, features a nightly laser light show set to music that begins around 11 p.m. Afterwards the dance music heats up. (**Note:** The dress code prohibits shorts for men.) **Friday López**, in the Fiesta Americana Puerto Vallarta, has karaoke and live bands playing good old rock 'n' roll.

In addition to the discos, there are nightclubs with live floor shows. **La Pachanga**, Avenida México #918, offers folkloric dance performances and mariachi bands. Mexican-style fiestas are another popular diversion and include dinner buffets, folk dancing, live music and even fireworks. One of the oldest is **La Iguana**, south of the river at Calle Lázaro Cárdenas #311 (at Constitución). A Mexican buffet dinner is accompanied by live music, mariachis, rope twirling, colorfully costumed folk dancers and breaking open a piñata. Shows begin Thurs. and Sun. at 7 p.m.; phone (322) 2-0105. Other fiestas take place at big hotels like the Krystal Vallarta and the Westin Regina. For schedule and reservation information, check with the hotels or a local travel agency.

SPECIAL EVENTS

Luckily for visitors, Puerto Vallarta's biggest events occur during the peak tourist season. The *International Sailfish Tournament*, held the first week of November, attracts anglers from all over Mexico and the United States. The yachting season kicks off in late fall with the *San Diego to Puerto Vallarta Annual Regatta*, which heralds the arrival of some impressive craft. Parades and other doings mark *Fiesta de Puerto Vallarta*, held in December.

Perhaps the year's biggest celebration is the *Tribute to the Virgin of Guadalupe*, honoring Mexico's patron saint. Daily evening processions to the Church of Our Lady of Guadalupe from various *colonias*, or residential sections of town, take place the 2 weeks prior to Dec. 12. Young and old alike participate in the celebration, all dressed in their best outfits and many carrying candles or offerings of food and flowers. Mass is held in front of the cathedral, accompanied by dancing and singing. The festivities culminate on Dec. 12 with a grand fireworks display.

WHERE TO STAY

BUENAVENTURA HOTEL & BEACH CLUB

 Motor Inn ((322)2-3737

12/1-4/15	$150	XP $25
4/16-11/30	$115	XP $25

Location: 1 km n on Airport Hwy, Mex 200. Ave Mexico 1301 48350 (Apartado Postal 8-B, PUERTA VALLARTA, JA). Fax: 322/2-3546. **Facility:** Near downtown. Traditional room decor. 236 units. Some whirlpool units. *Bath:* shower only. 5 stories, interior corridors. **Parking:** street only. **Terms:** 20 day cancellation notice-fee imposed. **Leisure Activities:** 3 heated pools, wading pool, whirlpool, beach, children's program, social program. **Guest Services:** gift shop, valet laundry. *Fee:* massage. **Cards:** AE, DI, MC, VI.

CAMINO REAL PUERTO VALLARTA

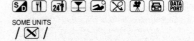 *Resort* ((322)1-5000

12/18-1/2	$275-$405	XP $40
1/3-4/21	$210-$299	XP $40
4/22-11/30	$163-$252	XP $30
12/1-12/17	$135-$180	XP $30

Location: 3.5 km s on Mismaloya Hwy, Mex 200. Playa Las Estacas S/N, Km 3.5 48300 (Apartado Postal 95). Fax: 322/1-6000. **Facility:** Private cove and beach. Fine public facilities. All rooms with ocean view. Some with balcony. Excellent staff. 337 units, 2 with kitchen. Some suites and whirlpool units. 11 stories, interior/exterior corridors. **Parking:** valet. **Terms:** F30; 3 day cancellation notice. **Amenities:** safes, honor bars. *Some:* hair dryers. **Dining:** La Perla Restaurant, see separate listing. **Leisure Activities:** 2 pools, wading pool, beach, social program, playground, exercise room. *Fee:* boats, waterskiing, fishing, 2 lighted tennis courts. **Guest Services:** [MAP] meal plan available, gift shop, valet laundry. *Fee:* massage. **Business Services:** meeting rooms. **Cards:** AE, DI, MC, VI.
(See color ad opposite title page & p 277)

SOME UNITS

CASA MIRADOR BED & BREAKFAST

 *Bed & Breakfast* ((322)1-5597

12/1-4/30	$115-$145	XP $15
5/1-11/30	$60-$76	XP $15

Location: 2 km s. 1200 Carr a Barra de Navidad Hwy 48399. Fax: 322/1-5597. **Facility:** Requires extensive stair climbing. Small, beach area. 5 units with kitchen. 2 two-bedroom units. *Bath:* combo or shower only. 5 stories (no elevator), exterior corridors. **Terms:** 60 day cancellation notice. **Amenities:** no TVs, hair dryers. **Leisure Activities:** small pool, beach. **Guest Services:** [BP] meal plan available, valet laundry.

SOME UNITS

CLUB MEZA DEL MAR AN ALL INCLUSIVE HOTEL

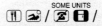 *Hotel* ((322)2-4888

All Year	$82-$144	XP $25

Location: 1 km s, on Playa de Los Muertos. Amapas 380 48380. Fax: 322/2-2308. **Facility:** Many rooms with ocean view and balcony. 128 units. 30 two-bedroom units, 13 three-bedroom units and 53 units with kitchen. *Bath:* shower only. 4-8 stories, interior/exterior corridors. **Parking:** street only. **Terms:** 3 day cancellation notice. **Amenities:** no TVs. *Some:* safes (fee). **Leisure Activities:** 2 pools, wading pool, beach, tennis court. **Guest Services:** [AP] meal plan available, gift shop, valet laundry. **Cards:** AE, DI, MC, VI.

SOME UNITS

FIESTA AMERICANA PUERTO VALLARTA

Hotel ((322)4-2010

12/21-1/3	$318	XP $40
1/4-4/2	$205	XP $26
12/1-12/20 & 4/3-11/30	$134	XP $17

Location: 4 km n on Paseo de Las Palmas off Airport Hwy Mex 200. Ave Fco Medina Ascencio Km 2.5 48300. (Apartado Postal 270, PUERTA VALLARTA, JA, 48300). Fax: 322/4-2108. **Facility:** All rooms with ocean view from balcony. 291 units. 9 stories, interior corridors. **Terms:** F12; 3 day cancellation notice, package plans. **Amenities:** voice mail, safes, honor bars, hair dryers. **Dining & Entertainment:** 2 dining rooms, coffee shop, 7 am-midnight, $14-$23, cocktails, entertainment. **Leisure Activities:** heated pool, wading pool, beach. **Guest Services:** gift shop, valet laundry. *Fee:* massage. **Business Services:** conference facilities, administrative services. **Cards:** AE, DI, MC, VI. *(See color ad below)*

SOME UNITS

HACIENDA BUENAVENTURA

Hotel ((322)4-6667

2/9-4/15	$85	XP $20
12/21-2/8	$80	XP $20
12/1-12/20 & 4/16-11/30	$65	XP $20

Location: 4.8 km n just off Airport Hwy, Mex 200. Francisco Medina Ascencio 2699 38310 (Apartado Postal 95-B, PUERTA VALLARTA, JA). Fax: 322/5-2023. **Facility:** One block from beach and close to cruise ship terminal. Converted original hacienda, traditional colonial architecture and decor. 155 units. *Bath:* combo or shower only. 2-4 stories (no elevator), interior corridors. **Parking:** street only. **Terms:** F12. **Leisure Activities:** wading pool, beach. **Guest Services:** gift shop, valet laundry. **Business Services:** meeting rooms. **Cards:** AE, DI, MC, VI.

HOLIDAY INN PUERTO VALLARTA

Hotel ((322)6-1700

12/21-4/15	$100-$120	XP $20
12/1-12/20 & 4/16-11/30	$70-$85	XP $15

Location: 4 km n on Airport Hwy, Mex 200. Blvd FCO Medina Ascencio S/N Km 3.5 48300 (Apartado Postal 555, PUERTA VALLARTA, JA). Fax: 322/4-5683. **Facility:** 231 units. 9 stories, interior corridors. **Parking:** valet. **Terms:** F12. **Amenities:** safes, irons, hair dryers. **Dining & Entertainment:** dining room, 2 restaurants, 7 am-midnight, $12-$18, cocktails, entertainment. **Leisure Activities:** 2 pools, wading pool, whirlpools, steamrooms, beach, fishing, 2 lighted tennis courts, exercise room. *Fee:* boats, waterskiing, horseback riding. **Guest Services:** gift shop, valet laundry. *Fee:* massage. **Business Services:** meeting rooms, administrative services. **Cards:** AE, DI, MC, VI.

SOME UNITS

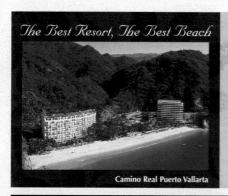

LAS PALMAS ALL INCLUSIVE BEACH RESORT

▼▼▼▼   *Motor Inn*   ☎ (322)4-0650

12/20-4/15	$120	XP $95
12/1-12/19 & 4/16-11/30	$95	XP $75

Location: 2.5 km n off Airport Hwy, Mex 200. Blvd Francisco Medina Ascencio S/N 48300. Fax: 322/4-0543. **Facility:** Balconies and patios. Beachfront dining. 180 units. *Bath:* shower only. 4 stories, interior/exterior corridors. **Terms:** F12. **Amenities:** safes (fee). **Leisure Activities:** 2 pools, wading pools, beach, snorkeling, social program. *Fee:* sailboating, waterskiing, scuba diving & equipment, fishing. **Guest Services:** [AP] meal plan available, gift shop, valet laundry. **Cards:** AE, MC, VI.

SOME UNITS

🔷 MARRIOTT CASA MAGNA

▼◆▼◆▼   *Hotel*   ☎ (322)1-0004

12/15-4/15	$199-$220	XP $10
12/1-12/14 & 4/16-11/30	$114-$134	XP $10

Location: 5 km n on Mex 200; at Marina Vallarta. Av Paseo de La Marina 5 48354. Fax: 322/1-0760. **Facility:** Fine location, very attractive grounds and public facilities. Pleasant, well appointed rooms. 433 units. Some whirlpool units. 9 stories, interior corridors. **Terms:** F12; check-in 4 pm. **Amenities:** voice mail, safes, honor bars, irons, hair dryers. **Dining & Entertainment:** 3 restaurants, 7 am-2 am, $8-$20, cocktails, also, Mikado, see separate listing, entertainment. **Leisure Activities:** wading pool, saunas, whirlpool, beach, exercise room. *Fee:* 3 lighted tennis courts. **Guest Services:** gift shop, valet laundry. **Business Services:** meeting rooms. **Cards:** AE, DI, MC, VI.
(See color ad inside front cover & p 198)

SOME UNITS

MELIA PUERTO VALLARTA ALL INCLUSIVE BEACH RESORT

▼◆▼◆▼   *Hotel*   ☎ (322)1-0200

12/1-12/31 & 4/4-11/30	$168-$190	XP $48
1/1-4/3	$190	XP $67

Location: In Marina District, 5 km n off Mex 200. Paseo de la Marina Sur Lote #7 48354. Fax: 322/1-0118. **Facility:** Very good recreational facilities. Modern, well-appointed rooms, attractive grounds. 370 units. 5-9 stories, interior corridors. **Parking:** valet. **Terms:** F7; 7 day cancellation notice, package plans. **Amenities:** safes, honor bars. **Leisure Activities:** beach, children's program, recreation program, social program, playground, exercise room. *Fee:* sailboating, waterskiing, 2 lighted tennis courts. **Guest Services:** [AP] meal plan available, gift shop, valet laundry. **Business Services:** meeting rooms. **Cards:** AE, MC, VI.

SOME UNITS

MOLINO DE AGUA HOTEL

▼◆▼◆   *Motor Inn*   ☎ (322)2-1907

12/1-4/15	$92-$150	XP $15
4/16-11/30	$67-$109	XP $15

Location: Just s of Puente Cuale bordering Rio Cuale and Playa Ozas Altas. Ignacio L. Vallarta, 130 48380 (Apartado Postal 54, PUERTA VALLARTA, JA). Fax: 322/2-6056. **Facility:** Restful, well landscaped grounds. Attractive rooms and cottages; terraces. Very clean and well maintained. Modern, immaculate kitchen. 52 units. *Bath:* shower only. 1-3 stories (no elevator), exterior corridors. **Terms:** F12; 15 day cancellation notice-fee imposed. **Amenities:** no TVs. **Leisure Activities:** 2 pools, whirlpool, beach. **Cards:** AE, MC, VI.

PLAYA LOS ARCOS HOTEL

▼◆▼◆   *Hotel*   ☎ (322)2-1583

12/21-4/21	$65-$85	XP $10
12/1-12/20 & 4/22-11/30	$53-$67	XP $10

Location: Center; in the "romantic zone" of the older part of Puerto Vallarta. Olas Altas 380 48380. Fax: 322/2-2418. **Facility:** A traditional Mexican hotel. 175 units, 13 with efficiency. Some suites ($95-$110). *Bath:* shower only. 4 stories, interior/exterior corridors. **Parking:** street only. **Terms:** F15; 7 day cancellation notice-fee imposed. **Leisure Activities:** heated pool, beach. **Guest Services:** gift shop, valet laundry. **Cards:** AE, MC, VI.

PRESIDENTE INTER-CONTINENTAL PUERTO VALLARTA

▼◆▼◆▼   *Hotel*   ☎ (322)8-0507

12/1-12/31	$300-$330	XP $50
1/1-4/30	$246-$310	XP $50
5/1-11/30	$210-$252	XP $50

Location: 8.5 km s on Mex 200. Km 8.5 Mexico 200 48300 (PO Box 448, PUERTA VALLARTA, JA). Fax: 322/8-0609. **Facility:** Fine location on pretty beach. Beautiful landscaping. All guest rooms have balcony overlooking the ocean. 120 units. 4 two-bedroom units. Some whirlpool units ($342-$410). 10 stories, exterior corridors. **Terms:** F6; 3 day cancellation notice. **Amenities:** *Some:* honor bars. **Leisure Activities:** heated pool, beach, lighted tennis court. *Fee:* waterskiing, scuba diving, fishing. **Guest Services:** [AP] meal plan available, gift shop, valet laundry. *Fee:* massage. **Business Services:** meeting rooms. **Cards:** AE, DI, MC, VI.

SOME UNITS

QUALTON CLUB & SPA AN ALL INCLUSIVE RESORT

▼◆▼◆▼   *Resort*   ☎ (322)4-4446

12/1-4/15	$180	XP $45
4/16-11/30	$120	XP $45

Location: 4 km n on Ave de las Palmas off Airport Hwy, Mex 200. Blvd FCO Medina Ascencio S/N, Km 2.5 48300 (PO Box 308, PUERTA VALLARTA, JA). Fax: 322/4-4445. **Facility:** Extensive spa facilities. 218 units. 2 two-bedroom units. Some whirlpool units. 4-14 stories, interior corridors. **Terms:** 3 day cancellation notice. **Amenities:** safes (fee). **Leisure Activities:** saunas, whirlpools, steamrooms, beach, lighted tennis court, recreation program, social program. **Guest Services:** [AP] meal plan available, gift shop, afternoon tea, valet laundry. *Fee:* massage. **Business Services:** meeting rooms. **Cards:** AE, DI, MC, VI.

🔷 VISTA CLUB HOTEL PLAYA DE ORO-ALL INCLUSIVE

▼◆▼◆▼   *Resort*   ☎ (322)6-6868

12/25-4/15	$218	XP $99
12/1-12/24 & 4/16-11/30	$138	XP $62

Location: 4.8 km n, off Airport Hwy, Mex 200. Ave Las Garzas #1 48333 (Apartado Postal 78, PUERTA VALLARTA, JA, 48300). Fax: 322/6-6810. **Facility:** Attractive grounds. Pleasant rooms, some with ocean view; balcony. 330 units. *Bath:* shower only. 4-7 stories (no elevator), exterior corridors. **Terms:** F5; check-in 4 pm. **Amenities:** *Some:* safes. **Dining & Entertainment:** 4 restaurants, 7 am-1 am, $6-$15, cocktails, entertainment. **Leisure Activities:** 2 pools, beach. *Fee:* boats, waterskiing, scuba equipment, fishing, 2 lighted tennis courts, horseback riding. **Guest Services:** [AP] meal plan available, gift shop, valet laundry. **Business Services:** meeting rooms. **Cards:** AE, MC, VI.

WESTIN REGINA RESORT PUERTO VALLARTA

▼▼▼ ▼▼▼   *Resort*   ☎ (322)6-1100

12/24-4/14	$205-$215	XP $40
4/15-11/30	$170-$180	XP $40
12/1-12/23	$160-$170	XP $35

Location: In Marina Vallarta, 5 km n on Mex 200. Paseo de la Marina Sur 205 48354 (AP Postal 4-100). Fax: 322/1-1121. **Facility:** Handsome beachfront hotel with excellent facilities and very attractive rooms. 280 units. Some whirlpool units. *Bath:* some shower or tub only. 8-14 stories, interior corridors. **Terms:** F18; 7 day cancellation notice-fee imposed. **Amenities:** voice mail, safes, honor bars, hair dryers. **Leisure Activities:** 4 heated pools, sauna, whirlpools, steamroom, beach, children's program, playground. *Fee:* 3 lighted tennis courts. **Guest Services:** gift shop, valet laundry. *Fee:* massage. **Business Services:** meeting rooms, administrative services, PC, fax. **Cards:** AE, DI, MC, VI.

FEE

WHERE TO DINE

CAFE DES ARTISTES

▼▼▼ ▼▼▼   *French*   ☎ 322/2-3228
D $20-$25

Location: Center. Guadalupe Sanchez 740 48300. **Hours:** 6 pm-11:30 pm. **Reservations:** required. **Features:** No A/C; casual dress; cocktails & lounge; entertainment. Innovative cuisine combining French and Mexican-style preparation. Offers a custom prepared menu de degustacion. **Cards:** AE, DI, MC, VI.

CAFE' MAXIMILIAN

▼▼▼ ▼▼▼   *Continental*   ☎ 322/3-0760
D $12-$20

Location: In the older part of town. Olas Altas 380 B 48380. **Hours:** 6 pm-11 pm. Closed: Sun. **Reservations:** suggested. **Features:** casual dress; cocktails. European decor and ambience. Indoor dining room, also sidewalk dining. Offers a few Austrian specialties. Separate coffee bar with very good coffee and pastry selection. **Cards:** AE, MC, VI.

CHEF ROGER RESTAURANT

▼▼▼ ▼▼▼   *Continental*   ☎ 322/2-5900
D $10-$25

Location: Center. 267 Agustin Rodriguez 48300. **Hours:** 6:30 pm-11 pm. Closed: 7/27-10/1. **Reservations:** suggested. **Features:** No A/C; casual dress; cocktails. Innovative menu. European style bakery on premises. **Cards:** MC, VI.

LA PERLA RESTAURANT

▼▼▼ ▼▼▼   *Continental*   ☎ 322/1-5000
D $12-$24

Location: 2.5 km s on Mismaloya Hwy, Mex 200; in Camino Real Puerto Vallarta. Playa Las Estacas 48300. **Hours:** 7 pm-11:30 pm. **Reservations:** suggested. **Features:** casual dress; cocktails & lounge; entertainment; valet parking; a la carte. Elegant dining room. Well-prepared cuisine. Excellent service. **Cards:** AE, DI, MC, VI.

LE BISTRO JAZZ CAFE

▼▼▼ ▼▼▼   *Continental*   ☎ 322/2-0283
L $8-$15   D $8-$15

Location: On Rio Cuale Island, center of city. Rio Cuale Island 16A 48300. **Hours:** 9 am-midnight. Closed: Sun. **Features:** No A/C; cocktails. Casual. Outdoor and covered dining. **Cards:** AE, MC, VI.

MIKADO

▼▼▼ ▼▼▼   *Ethnic*   ☎ 322/1-0004
D $15-$30

Location: 5 km n on Mex 200; at Marina Vallarta; in Marriott Casa Magna. Ave Paseo De La Marina 5 48354. **Hours:** 6 pm-11 pm. **Reservations:** suggested. **Features:** casual dress; cocktails & lounge; a la carte. Japanese sushi bar and teppan-yaki tableside cooking. Entertaining chefs. **Cards:** AE, DI, MC, VI.

MOGAMBO RESTAURANT

▼▼▼ ▼▼▼   *Continental*   ☎ 322/2-3476
L $8-$25   D $8-$25

Location: Center. Paseo Diaz Ordaz 646 48300. **Hours:** noon-1 am. **Features:** No A/C; cocktails. Casual attire. Good place to watch sunsets. **Cards:** AE.

PANCAKE HOUSE

▼▼ ▼▼   *American*   ☎ 322/2-6272
L $3-$6

Location: 4 blks s of Rio Cuale. 289 Basilio Badillo 48380. **Hours:** 8 am-2 pm. Closed major holidays. **Features:** No A/C; cocktails. Casual attire. Very good selection of American style breakfast dishes; waffles, pancakes and blintzes. Cooking classes covering basic preparation of Mexican cuisine 11/1-4/30.

SAN BLAS, NAYARIT (G-5)

Although present evidence refutes it, this bedraggled fishing village was a major port from the late 16th into the 19th centuries. Galleons involved in the Manila trade routinely stopped at San Blas (sahn BLAHS). During the mid-18th century it also became a shipbuilding center and was a garrison for the Spanish armada, which fought French, Dutch and British pirates; the ruins of a Spanish fortress occupy a hill looming above the town. In 1768, Jesuit missionary Fray Junípero Serra departed this region on his northward trek to establish missions in the wilderness of northern Mexico and Baja California.

History then bypassed San Blas. Today, shaded by the fronds of myriad coconut palms, it mostly dozes in the tropical heat. The worn main plaza is likely to be inhabited by California surfers and other laid-back types. Battered old bicycles are a more frequent means of transportation for the locals than cars. The town shakes off its torpor after the sun goes down, when benches around the plaza fill with chatting couples and the front door of the church across from the plaza is likely to be open, letting the sounds of evening Mass filter out into the warm air.

Adventurous travelers who want to avoid the hubbub of Mazatlán to the north or Puerto Vallarta to the south might consider San Blas, which is accessible via Mex. 11 branching off Mex. 15-D. (**Note:** Mex. 11 is isolated and jungle-lined; make sure the gas tank is full and your vehicle is in tip-top shape.) The main draw for tourists are the tan-colored beaches, which encircle nearby Matanchen Bay. **Playa Borrego** is the most convenient to town. This typical

Mexican beach has few amenities other than the open-air shacks serving cold beer and whole smoked fish. **Playa Los Cocos**, reachable by taxi, has a backdrop of palm trees. The rainy summer season is plagued by mosquitos; *jejenes* (hey-HAY-nays), or "no-see-ums," are bothersome biting gnats that materialize at dawn and dusk year-round. Needless to say, insect repellent is a necessity.

Another tourist attraction, and a favorite of birdwatchers, is the jungle trip to the springs of **La Tovara** via motorized dugout *(lancha)*. An excursion can be arranged through the tourist office on Calle Juárez, the main street in town, or with the boat owners themselves at the docking area, at the eastern end of Juárez. The boats pass through swampy lagoons and dense mangrove forests inhabited by herons, egrets, turtles, lizards and fish. Some 300 bird species have been identified in this area. The spring itself forms a cool, freshwater pool where swimming is possible. For the best wildlife views, go early in the morning. Most trips last about 3 hours. A fee is charged; lunch at the *palapa* restaurant at the springs is not included.

TEPIC, NAYARIT (G-5)

Tepic (teh-PEEK), the state capital, lies at the foot of the extinct Sangangüey (sahn-gahn-GWAY) volcano. The city dates from the 16th century, but grew slowly at first because of its isolated location. Today Tepic (a Náhuatl Indian word meaning "hard stone") functions mainly as a stopover for travelers en route to Guadalajara or Puerto Vallarta, although there are a few places of interest. The cathedral bordering **Plaza Principal** has twin towers and a yellow exterior. At the summit of a hill south of the town center is the 18th-century **Convento de la Santa Cruz** (Convent of the Holy Cross). The restored former convent was built around a growth of grass in the shape of a cross, said to be a miraculous site.

The surrounding countryside is mountainous and isolated, although it has a wild beauty. Here live the Huichol and Cora Indians, among the least affected of Mexico's indigenous peoples by the intrusions of modern life. Appropriately, religion and ritual are an integral part of daily life. Huichol art, particularly the brightly colored wall hangings, incorporates symbols relating to fertility, nature and the heavens. Shops bordering Plaza Principal sometimes offer beads and other handicrafts made by local Huichol and Cora artisans.

The **Museo Regional de Antropología** (Regional Museum of Anthropology), south of Plaza Principal at Avenida México #91 Norte (at Avenida Zapata), is housed in an 18th-century mansion, the former House of the Counts of Miraville. On view are a collection of Huichol artifacts, including animal-shaped pottery, and an exhibit pertaining to the archeological site surrounding the town of Ixtlan del Río, which is distinguished by a circular pyramid. Open Tues.-Sun.

WHERE TO STAY

HOTEL BUGAMVILLAS
♦♦ ♦♦   *Motor Inn*   (321/8-0227

All Year $49   XP $6
Location: 3 km n on Mex 15. Ave Insurgentes Y Libramiento Pte 63117. Fax: 321/8-0225. **Facility:** High wall surrounds property. Ample at-door parking. Extensive grounds. 50 units. *Bath:* combo or shower only. 2 stories, exterior corridors. **Terms:** F12; 8 day cancellation notice. **Leisure Activities:** heated pool. **Guest Services:** valet laundry. **Cards:** AE, MC, VI.

SOME UNITS
🆂🅓 🍽 🍸 🐾 🎥 / 🖥 /

HOTEL LAS PALOMAS
♦♦♦   *Motor Inn*   ((321)4-0953

All Year $40   XP $8
Location: 3 km w on Mex 15. Insurgentes 2100 ote 63170. Fax: 321/4-0948. **Facility:** 67 units. *Bath:* combo or shower only. 2 stories, exterior corridors. **Leisure Activities:** whirlpool. **Guest Services:** valet laundry. **Cards:** AE, MC, VI.

SOME UNITS
🍽 🐾 🎥 / 🔒 /

HOTEL MELANIE
♦♦   *Motor Inn*   ((321)4-2310

All Year $35
Location: 2 km se on the Tepic-Puerto Vallarta Hwy. Blvd Tepic-Xalixco #109 63168. Fax: 321/3-9846. **Facility:** 56 units. *Bath:* shower only. 4 stories, interior corridors. **Guest Services:** gift shop, valet laundry. **Business Services:** meeting rooms. **Cards:** AE, MC, VI.

🍽 🎥

MOTEL LA LOMA
♦♦   *Motor Inn*   ((321)3-2222

All Year $25   XP $5
Location: Just w of Mex 15; opposite Loma Park. Paseo de La Loma 301 63000. Fax: 321/3-2222. **Facility:** 47 units. *Bath:* shower or tub only. 2 stories, exterior corridors. **Terms:** 4 day cancellation notice. **Leisure Activities:** wading pool. **Business Services:** meeting rooms. **Cards:** AE, MC, VI.

SOME UNITS
🍽 🐾 / 🎞 🔒 /

MEXICO CITY AND VICINITY

Mexico City is the country's all-encompassing, vitally beating heart. Within the 571 square miles of the Federal District, politically separate from Mexico's 31 municipally governed states, sprawls the nation's industrial, financial and cultural nerve center. Historically significant for nearly 700 years, the city and its environs is the Western Hemisphere's largest metropolis, the place of residence for more than one in five Mexican citizens.

It's unfortunate that perhaps the most widely held perception about Mexico City is the fact that it has polluted air, for there is much more to the national capital than meets the eye (or nose). Magnificent colonial buildings fill its historic center. A wealth of museums exhibit priceless historical artifacts. The world-famous Ballet Folklórico celebrates the history of Mexican folk music and dance. Leaving without a shopping bag full of treasures is, in a word, unthinkable. Although Mexico City's size and unfamiliarity can seem overwhelming to the first-time visitor, it nevertheless is a major leisure and business travel destination.

Several noteworthy side trips are a short hop away. Perhaps the most impressive is the archeological zone of Teotihuacán, easily reached from Mexico City and the site of two awe-inspiring pyramids. Cuernavaca is an attractive city south of the metropolitan area that has long been a weekend playground for well-to-do Mexico City families. Several national parks also ring the Federal District, cool retreats where fresh air, sparkling lakes and green pine forests replace urban grit and grime.

ACOLMAN, MEXICO (C-10) elev. 7,511'

Acolman is a small village off Mex. 132-D on the way to the ruins of Teotihuacán. From downtown Mexico City, take Avenida Insurgentes Norte (Mex. 85-D) northeast to the Mex. 132-D turnoff. The route is pleasantly scenic, although slow going because of heavy bus and truck traffic.

CONVENTO DE SAN AGUSTIN ACOLMAN (Convent of San Agustín Acolman) is a fortresslike structure that displays Mexico's first plateresque ecclesiastic facade. Completed in 1560, the convent was restored after falling into disuse. Two sets of columns, with the statue of a saint between each, flank the elaborate entrance. The immense building, with its beautiful frescoes, sculptures and cloister, has some of Mexico's best examples of Renaissance art. It also contains a small state museum. At Christmas the convent's chapel provides the setting for nativity plays, or *pastorelas*. Open daily. Admission is charged.

CUAUTLA, MORELOS (D-10) elev. 4,198'

Cuautla (coo-WOW-tlah), popular with the Aztecs for its mineral springs, became a fashionable Spanish spa early in the 17th century. The city witnessed one of the most dramatic battles of Mexico's War of Independence when patriot José María Morelos and 3,000 rebels managed to withstand a 58-day siege by Royalist troops.

Cuautla lies in a fertile valley that produces rice, sugar cane and tropical fruits. Next to the Río Cuautla in town is **El Almeal Spring**, a cool oasis with a large swimming pool, landscaped grounds and pavilions. The older, southern part of town comprises an Indian settlement called **San José**; the market here sprawls over several blocks. Pottery is one of the major handicrafts.

Some 31 kilometers (19 miles) south of Cuautla is **Chinameca**, the hacienda where Emiliano Zapata was assassinated; the site has been designated a national historic monument. Another historical site is **Ayala**, about 6 kilometers (4 miles) south of Cuautla. In 1910, Zapata issued a declaration of land reform here; later the townsite was a battlefield during the Revolution of 1910.

AGUA HEDIONDAS ("stinking waters"), a series of connected thermal pools, are about 3 kilometers (1.9 miles) east of town. Aztec emperor Moctezuma is said to have spent time improving his health in the spa's sulphurous waters. Facilities include swimming pools, bathhouses, dressing rooms, a pavilion and gardens.

LAS ESTACAS, a popular swimming resort southwest off Mex. 115, is built over several deep and powerful springs. **Blue Wells Spring** is a popular skin diving and snorkeling spot. The resort also contains three swimming pools, a wading pool, a restaurant, sports facilities and camping and picnicking areas. **Note:** Pools are normally drained on Monday for weekly cleanings.

At the entrance road to Las Estacas is the town of Tlaltizapán, which was the site of Emiliano Zapata's headquarters during the Revolution of 1910. The town's **Museo Cuartel General de Zapata** (Zapata Headquarters Museum) displays photographs, weapons and clothing, including the clothes Zapata had on when he was assassinated.

CUERNAVACA,
MORELOS (C-9)   elev. 5,058'

Capital of the state of Morelos, Cuernavaca (kwehr-nah-VAH-cah) is one of the most attractive spots in Mexico. Pink, blue and yellow houses with red-tiled roofs, luxuriant vegetation and brilliant flowers add to its charm. Many affluent Mexico City residents have second homes here, with swimming pools and extravagant gardens hidden behind high walls. Some of the homes are opened to the public on Thursdays during the first 3 months of the year.

At Mex. 95 and Avenida Fundadores a grand equestrian statue pays tribute to Emiliano Zapata, the popular leader of the Revolution of 1910. Zapata's battle cry of "Land and liberty, and death to the haciendados" struck at the great hacienda owners throughout the state. His Plan de Ayala, the beginning of a program toward agrarian reform, was signed near Cuautla on Nov. 28, 1911. In 1914 Zapata briefly joined Pancho Villa in occupying Mexico City before returning to Cuernavaca to prevent its seizure by federal troops.

Those maintaining summer homes in Cuernavaca over the centuries have included Aztec emperors, Hernán Cortés, Archduke Maximilian and his wife Carlota, various Mexican rulers and José de la Borda, the "silver king" (*see Taxco listing under Southern Mexico*). On the outskirts of town in the suburb of Acapantzingo is the **Olvido House,** Maximilian and Carlota's summer home. The restored structure is now known as **El Museo de Herbolaria** (Municipal Herb Museum).

Cuernavaca is a favored resort for Mexican officials and foreign diplomats. Several spas with mineral and thermal waters, landscaped grounds and camping areas are nearby, including **Cuautla, Atotonilco, La Fundición, Las Estacas, Oaxtepec** and **Temixco**. Golf, horseback riding, tennis, water skiing and sailing are some of the activities that can be enjoyed throughout this area. Reservations are advisable for weekend stays.

Quaint furniture, fine silver and leather articles, colorfully woven *huaraches* and straw hats can all be purchased in Cuernavaca; on market day wares are sold in the streets and plazas as well as at the market. The main plaza teems with vendors and also has restaurants and cozy cafés. Distinctive silver religious items are hand wrought by monks at the **Emaus Monastery**, Calle Laurel off Boulevard Zapata, and sold there on Sundays or in the atrium of the cathedral daily.

A colorful local fiesta is the *Flower Fair*, held the first week in April. It features exhibits and competitions in floriculture and gardening as well as a sound-and-light show and performances by popular entertainers. For visitor information contact the Morelos State Tourism Office, Avenida Morelos Sur #802 (south of the cathedral). It is open Mon.-Fri. 9-8, Sat.-Sun. 10-4; phone (73) 14-3872 (English spoken). There also is a visitor kiosk on the cathedral grounds that is open Mon.-Sat.

Southeast of the city, toward Jiutepec, is **Hacienda de Atlacomulco**, believed to be the first sugar mill in the continental Americas. Built around 1564 by Martín Cortés, son of Hernán, the structure is now a hotel.

WHAT TO SEE IN TOWN

CATEDRAL DE LA ASUNCION is at avenidas Hidalgo and Morelos, a block or so from the Borda Gardens. It was founded by Hernán Cortés in 1529 and is one of the oldest churches in Mexico. The fortresslike construction is similar to others built by the Franciscans during the same period. The cathedral was the focal point of missionary activities by the Franciscans in Japan, the Philippines and other countries of the Far East during the colonial era. The interior was renovated in the 1960s in a spare, modern style, but remains of early frescoes can still be seen. At the rear of the cathedral is the **Capilla de la Tercer Orden** (Chapel of the Third Order). Sculptures by Indian artists flank the atrium.

JARDINES BORDA (Borda Gardens), near the cathedral, are part of the magnificent mansion, landscaped grounds and botanical gardens built by José de la Borda. A Frenchman, Borda came to Mexico in 1716 and made a fortune in mining. He is said to have spent a million pesos on the gardens that surround the house. Borda is buried in the 1760 **Church of Guadalupe** next to the

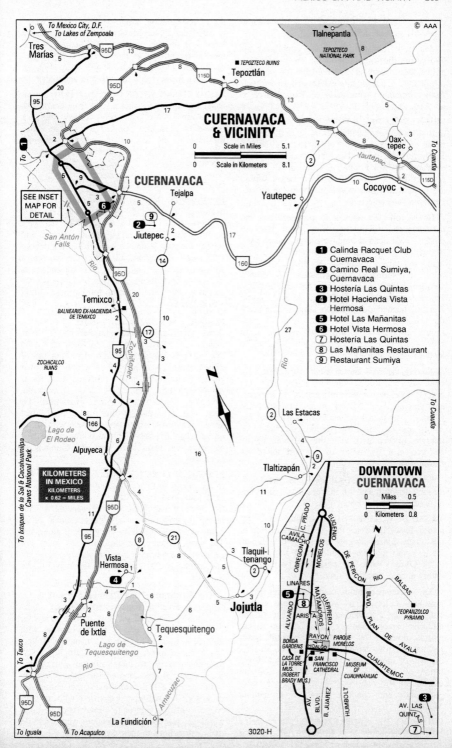

To Mexico City, D.F.
To Lakes of Zempoala

Tres Marías
5

13

© AAA

Tlalnepantla

TEPOZTECO NATIONAL PARK

8

20

95

95D

2

10

115D

TEPOZTECO RUINS

Tepoztlán

17

13

CUERNAVACA & VICINITY

Scale in Miles 0 — 5.1
Scale in Kilometers 0 — 8.1

7

8

7

Oax-tepec

3

To Cuautla

2

Yautepec

To Cuautla

SEE INSET MAP FOR DETAIL

CUERNAVACA

Tejalpa

5

3

5

2

9

Jiutepec

5

Yautepec

10

Cocoyoc

2

115D

San Antón Falls

Río

95D

5

20

14

17

160

27

Río

Temixco

BALNEARIO EX-HACIENDA DE TEMIXCO

2

Zochitepec

10

17

3

95

4

3

ZOCHICALCO RUINS

4

4

Las Estacas

2

To Cuautla

4

To Ixtapan de la Sal & Cacahuamilpa Caves National Park

8

166

Lago de El Rodeo

6

Alpuyeca

16

9

2

Tlaltizapán

11

10

KILOMETERS IN MEXICO
KILOMETERS × 0.62 = MILES

95D

11

15

8

21

3

Tlaquil-tenango

2

95

4

8

5

Vista Hermosa

4

3

3

Jojutla

5

6

6

3

2

To Taxco

8

8

Puente de Ixtla

2

Tequesquitengo

7

Lago de Tequesquitengo

Río

95D

95D

To Iguala   To Acapulco

La Fundición

Amacuzac

3020-H

Hotels/Restaurants

1 Calinda Racquet Club Cuernavaca
2 Camino Real Sumiya, Cuernavaca
3 Hostería Las Quintas
4 Hotel Hacienda Vista Hermosa
5 Hotel Las Mañanitas
6 Hotel Vista Hermosa
7 Hostería Las Quintas
8 Las Mañanitas Restaurant
9 Restaurant Sumiya

DOWNTOWN CUERNAVACA

Miles 0 — 0.5
Kilómetros 0 — 0.8

C. PRADO

AVILA CAMACHO

OBREGON

EUGENIO

MORELOS

DE PERICON

RIO

BALSAS

LINARES

5

8

ALVARADO

ARISTA

GUERRERO

MATAMOROS

BLVD.

PLAN

DE

AYALA

TEOPANZOLCO PYRAMID

BORDA GARDENS

RAYON

HIDALGO

PARQUE MORELOS

CASA DE LA TORRE MUS. (ROBERT BRADY MUS.)

SAN FRANCISCO CATHEDRAL

MUSEUM OF CUAUHNÁHUAC

CUAUHTEMOC

AV. BLVD.

B. JUAREZ

HUMBOLT

AV. LAS QUINTAS

3

7

gardens. Archduke Maximilian made the palatial estate his summer retreat in 1864.

The front rooms of the house contain an art gallery; on the south side of the inner court is a coffee shop. Rowboats are available for rent. The refurbished gardens still evoke images of their former grandeur. Admission is charged; free to all Wed. Phone (73) 18-6372.

MUSEO CASA DE LA TORRE, next to the cathedral at Calle Netzahualcóyotl #4, is in the former home of American artist Robert Brady (1928-86). Brady restored the 16th-century stone and adobe mansion, once a Franciscan convent; it is now operated by the Robert Brady Foundation. Within are more than 1,000 works of arts and crafts notable for their eclecticism.

Brady collected as well as produced art, and the museum offers everything from Balinese masks to Mexican colonial carvings. Pieces from throughout the world are displayed on shelves, walls and tables essentially as Brady left them, often in whimsical juxtapositions. A French wooden puppet of American dancer Josephine Baker sits next to an African female figure; Huichol beaded doves perch atop a table from the Federal Republic of Cameroon. Various rooms are painted in bright yellows and deep reds, which combine with the colorful artwork to lend a surreal appearance.

Among the well-known artists represented are Diego Rivera, Rufino Tamayo, Frida Kahlo and several foreign painters influenced by Mexican art, among them Milton Avery and Marsden Hartley. Two patios are landscaped with tropical plants and accented by sculptures. **Note:** Although children may visit the museum, unruly children will be asked to wait in the foyer entrance.

Guided tours in several languages are available by appointment. Open Tues.-Sun. 10-5. Admission is charged. Phone (73) 18-8554.

MUSEO DE CUAUHNAHUAC (Cuauhnáhuac Museum), formerly Cortés Palace, flanks one side of the main plaza. Begun in 1530 by Hernán Cortés, who mistakenly anticipated gaining title to the Oaxaca Valley, the palace has been considerably altered since that time.

The museum contains many interesting paintings and sculptures, as well as exhibits chronicling Mexico's evolution from the age of the dinosaur to contemporary Indians. Diego Rivera murals donated by former U.S. Ambassador Dwight Morrow depict the conquest of Mexico, the War of Independence and the Mexican Revolution of 1910. Four murals are by Roberto Cueva del Río, who contributed others to governmental and public buildings throughout Mexico.

PIRAMIDE DE TEOPANZOLCO (Teopanzolco Pyramid), probably built by the Aztecs, is near the railroad station. The pyramid was discovered in 1910 during the Mexican Revolution, when a large hill on the outskirts of Cuernavaca was used as a platform for attacks on the city. Tremors resulting from gunfire shook away some of the earth and revealed the pyramid underneath.

SALTO DE SAN ANTON (San Antón Falls) are located less than less than a mile from downtown Cuernavaca. A walk has been cut into the rock behind the cascade. Clinging to a ledge above the falls is the tiny village of **San Antonio**, where celebrated Cuernavaca pottery is produced.

NEARBY DESTINATIONS

BALNEARIO EX-HACIENDA DE TEMIXCO (Bathing Resort of the Ex-Hacienda of Temixco), 8 kilometers (5 miles) south off Mex. 95, is a complex of 15 swimming pools, 10 wading pools, toboggan runs, sports fields and about 12.5 acres of gardens, all within the ruins of a 17th-century sugar hacienda. The hacienda was used as a fort during the War of Independence and as a concentration camp for Japanese during World War II.

PARQUE NACIONAL LAGUNAS DE ZEMPOALA (Lakes of Zempoala National Park) is 22 kilometers (14 miles) north on old Mex. 95 to the town of Tres Marías, then some 15 kilometers (9 miles) west on a narrow, winding road that passes Huitzilac. A toll is charged at a forest ranger station. The seven lakes—Zempoala, Compela, Tonatihagua, Quila, Hueyapan, La Seca and Ocoyotongo—lie about 9,500 feet above sea level. Three are stocked with trout, golden carp and bass. Several hiking paths radiate from the main open meadow. Camping is permitted.

ZOCHICALCO RUINS, about 37 kilometers (23 miles) southwest, are reached by turning west onto Mex. 421 from Mex. 95 or Mex. 95-D at the town of Alpuyeca, then proceeding 8 kilometers (5 miles) beyond Alpuyeca on a paved road that winds north to the top of a mountain. The ruins, which cover about 6 square miles, are believed to have been a major ceremonial center approximately 500 years before the arrival of the Spanish.

The **Pyramid of the Plumed Serpent** is the dominant structure, ornamented with rock reliefs of spiraling, feathered serpents, precise geometric designs and cross-legged, seated humans with plumed headdresses. It bears evidence of Toltec, Maya and Zapotec influence. Hieroglyphs still retaining traces of their original polychrome paint represent dates and eclipse signs. Close by is the entrance to a tunnel/maze that culminates in a stone-hewn, stepped chamber with a "telescope" orifice; through this aperture the astrologer-priests of Zochicalco were able to make corrections to their calendar.

Continuing excavations have unearthed a well-preserved ball court, perhaps the oldest in Mexico. Aside from its fortresslike position commanding views of the Valley of Cuernavaca and Laguna del Rodeo (which offers swimming and fishing), Zochicalco (so-chee-KAHL-coh, which means "house of flowers" in the Náhuatl Indian language) was possibly a communications center for drummed messages to and from the hinterlands. Admission is charged.

WHERE TO STAY

CALINDA RACQUET CLUB CUERNAVACA

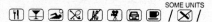 *Hotel* (73/11-2400
All Year $80-$110 XP $10
Location: 0.8 km n from Zapata's monument, follow the hotel's signs. Francisco Villa 100 62120. Fax: 73/17-5483. **Facility:** One-bedroom suites with living room and fireplace. Tranquil country club atmosphere. 16th-century hacienda. Lush tropical setting. Extensive landscaping. 52 units. Some suites. 4 stories, interior/exterior corridors. **Terms:** F12; 3 day cancellation notice. **Amenities:** safes, honor bars, hair dryers. **Leisure Activities:** heated pool, wading pool, 9 tennis courts (4 lighted), exercise room, game room. **Guest Services:** valet laundry. **Business Services:** conference facilities. **Cards:** AE, DI, MC, VI.
(See color ad p 4 and below)

SOME UNITS

CAMINO REAL SUMIYA, CUERNAVACA

 Motor Inn (73/20-9199
All Year $160 XP $20
Location: 3 km se from Mex 95D, exit Mex 160 Cuernavaca-Cuautla Rd; follow the signs. Interior de Fracc Sumiya 62550. Fax: 73/20-9142. **Facility:** Authentic Japanese architecture, gardens and artwork. 163 units. Some suites. 4 stories, exterior corridors. **Terms:** F12; package plans. **Amenities:** safes, honor bars. *Some:* hair dryers. **Dining:** Restaurant Sumiya, see separate listing. **Leisure Activities:** 2 heated pools, wading pool, sauna, whirlpool, steamroom, playground. *Fee:* 8 tennis courts (6 lighted). **Guest Services:** gift shop, valet laundry. *Fee:* massage. **Business Services:** conference facilities, administrative services. *Fee:* fax. **Cards:** AE, CB, DI, MC, VI.

HOSTERIA LAS QUINTAS

 Motor Inn (73/18-3949
All Year $80-$100 XP $15
Location: 3 km e of Cortez Palace, off Ave Cuauhtemoc at Ave Las Quintas 107. Diaz Ordaz 9 62440 (PO Box 427). Fax: 73/18-3895. **Facility:** Spacious tropical grounds. Colonial-style inn. Some rooms with fireplace. All rooms with ceiling fans. Variety of suites and junior suites available. 60 units. *Bath:* combo or shower only. 2 stories, interior/exterior corridors. **Parking:** valet. **Amenities:** safes, honor bars. **Dining:** dining room, see separate listing. **Leisure Activities:** 2 heated pools, saunas, whirlpool, steamrooms, exercise room. *Fee:* spa. **Guest Services:** gift shop, valet laundry. *Fee:* massage. **Business Services:** conference facilities. **Cards:** AE, MC, VI.

HOTEL LAS MANANITAS

 Country Inn (73/14-1466
All Year $118
Location: Just e of Mex 95. Ricardo Linares 107 62000. Fax: 73/18-3672. **Facility:** Colonial-style inn. Tropical gardens. Few fireplaces. Large meeting facility adjacent to the inn with extensive landscaping including a waterfall. 22 units. Some suites. 2 stories, interior/exterior corridors. **Parking:** valet. **Terms:** 7 day cancellation notice, $5 service charge. **Amenities:** no TVs, safes. **Dining:** restaurant, see separate listing. **Leisure Activities:** heated pool. **Guest Services:** valet laundry. **Business Services:** meeting rooms. **Cards:** AE.

HOTEL VISTA HERMOSA

Country Inn (73/15-2374
All Year $100-$130 XP $10
Location: From Hwy 95D, southbound exit Calle Diana; northbound exit Unidad. 1 km sw on Calle Diana, 0.4 km sw on Rio Mayo, then 1.2 km s on Rio Panuco. (Rio Papaloapan, Corner Rio Panuco, 62290). Fax: 73/15-2374. **Facility:** Colonial inn located in quiet residential area with tranquil inner garden; some rooms with small private garden terrace. 40 units. *Bath:* shower only. 2 stories, interior/exterior corridors. **Parking:** valet. **Terms:** F12; 5 day cancellation notice. **Leisure Activities:** heated pool, wading pool, playground. **Guest Services:** valet laundry. **Cards:** AE, MC, VI.

WHERE TO DINE

HOSTERIA LAS QUINTAS

 Regional Continental (73/18-3949

L $10-$16   **D** $10-$19

Location: 3 km e of Cortez Palace, off Ave Cuauhtemos at Ave Las Quintas 107; in Hosteria Las Quintas. 62440. **Hours:** 7 am-11 pm, Sun-10 pm. **Reservations:** suggested. **Features:** No A/C; dressy casual; cocktails & lounge; fee for valet parking; a la carte. Hosteria Las Quintas is renown for its lush tropical gardens in the city of "Eternal Spring". Dine in a colonial setting, select from authentic regional and continental dishes. Worth the trip. **Cards:** AE, MC, VI.

LAS MANANITAS RESTAURANT

 Regional Continental (73/14-1466

L $15-$25   **D** $20-$30

Location: Just e of Mex 95; in Hotel Las Mananitas. Ricardo Linares 107 62000. **Hours:** 1 pm-5 & 7-10:30 pm, Fri & Sat-11 pm. **Reservations:** suggested. **Features:** No A/C; semi-formal attire; cocktails & lounge; valet parking; a la carte. Located in a colonial country inn, overlooking manicured lawns and gardens. Daily changing menu with extensive selections. Dine on the terrace or in the garden. **Cards:** AE.

RESTAURANT SUMIYA

 Continental (73/20-9199

L $8-$15   **D** $8-$15

Location: 3 km se from Mex 95D, exit Mex 160 Cuernavaca-Cuautla Rd; follow the signs; in Camino Real Sumiya, Cuernavaca. **Hours:** 12:30 pm-11 pm, Fri-midnight, Sat-12:30 am. Closed: Mon & Tues. **Reservations:** required. **Features:** casual dress; cocktails & lounge; valet parking; a la carte. Replica of the Japanese Imperial Palace. Overlooking expansive Japanese gardens. Taking this detour to Japan is well worth the trip. Transportation by taxi to restaurant is suggested. Also features regional Mexican cuisine. **Cards:** AE, DI, MC, VI.

IXTAPAN DE LA SAL, MEXICO (D-9) elev. 6,311'

Ixtapán de la Sal (ees-tah-PAHN deh lah SAHL) is a *balneario* (spa) known for its warm mineral waters; bathing in them is certainly soothing, and reputed to aid arthritis and rheumatism as well. While the outdoor springs may not be crystal clear due to the mineral content of the water, many people vouch for their curative properties. Public pools, flowing fountains, flowers and lush landscaping lend a cool, refreshing appearance to this popular resort. In addition to bathing, tennis and horseback riding are available. Although Ixtapán de la Sal makes a nice day trip from either Taxco or Cuernavaca, weekends and holidays can be quite crowded. **Tonatico**, a town just south, also has swimming facilities.

GRUTAS DE LA ESTRELLA (Star Grottoes), 19 kilometers (12 miles) south off Mex. 55, are most dramatic during the July-September rainy season, when waterfalls cascade among such spectacular rock formations as "The Holy Family" and "The Human Ear." Ancient Matlaltzinca Indians may have conducted religious ceremonies in the grottoes. Guided tours are possible along a lighted, protected footpath.

WHERE TO STAY

HOTEL AVENIDA

Motor Inn (714/3-1039

All Year $23   XP $10

Location: Center. Ave Benito Juarez 614 51900. Fax: 714/3-1039. **Facility:** 39 units. 4 two-bedroom units. Some suites and whirlpool units. *Bath:* combo or shower only. 3 stories, exterior corridors. **Leisure Activities:** wading pool, whirlpool, playground. **Guest Services:** valet laundry. **Business Services:** meeting rooms. **Cards:** MC, VI.

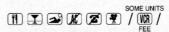

HOTEL BUNGALOWS LOLITA

Hotel (714/3-0169

All Year $38   XP $33

Location: 1.5 km n on Mex 55. Blvd Arturo San Roman 33 51900. Fax: 714/3-0230. **Facility:** Colonial style bungalows. 38 units. 2 two-bedroom units. *Bath:* shower only. 1-2 stories, interior/exterior corridors. **Leisure Activities:** heated pool, wading pool, playground. **Guest Services:** [AP] meal plan available, gift shop, valet laundry. *Fee:* massage. **Cards:** AE, MC, VI.

SOME UNITS

  / VCR / FEE

HOTEL CASA BLANCA

Motor Inn (714/3-0036

All Year $24   XP $19

Location: Center. Ave Benito Juarez 615 51900. Fax: 714/3-1031. **Facility:** 25 units. *Bath:* shower only. 1 story, exterior corridors. **Leisure Activities:** wading pool. **Guest Services:** [AP] meal plan available, valet laundry. **Business Services:** meeting rooms. **Cards:** MC, VI.

HOTEL SPA IXTAPAN

Motor Inn (714/3-0021

All Year $135   XP $32

Location: Just off Mex 55, from jct of Mex 55 and Blvd San Roman, just w via signs. Blvd San Roman S/N 51900. Fax: 714/3-0856. **Facility:** Beautiful grounds and extensive spa facilities. Clean, comfortable rooms and villas. 217 units. *Bath:* some combo or shower only. 6 stories, interior/exterior corridors. **Parking:** valet. **Terms:** F12; 7 day cancellation notice, package plans. **Leisure Activities:** 2 pools (1 heated), miniature golf, 2 tennis courts. *Fee:* golf-9 holes, horseback riding, exercise room. **Guest Services:** [AP] meal plan available, valet laundry. *Fee:* area transportation, massage. **Business Services:** conference facilities. **Cards:** AE, MC, VI.

HOTEL VILLA VERJEL

Motor Inn ((714)3-0349

All Year $120-$180   XP $50

Location: 1.5 km n on Mex 55. Blvd San Roman y Ave Juarez 51900. Fax: 714/3-0842. **Facility:** Centrally located in town, convenient to highway. Clean well maintained rooms and public areas. 64 units. *Bath:* combo, shower or tub only. 2-3 stories, interior corridors. **Terms:** F10; 15 day cancellation notice-fee imposed. **Amenities:** *Some:* honor bars. **Leisure Activities:** heated pool, wading pool, sauna. *Fee:* whirlpool. **Guest Services:** [AP] meal plan available, gift shop, valet laundry. *Fee:* massage. **Business Services:** meeting rooms. **Cards:** AE, MC, VI.

Izta-Popo National Park, Mexico (C-11)

Embracing the pass between Mexico's two most famous volcanoes, Iztaccíhuatl-Popocatépetl National Park is reached by a paved road branching east off Mex. 115 south of Amecameca. The last eruption of 17,887-foot Popocatépetl—the Smoking Mountain—occurred in 1802. Iztaccíhuatl, The White Lady, rises 17,343 feet. The volcanoes are Mexico's second and third highest mountains, and although located in the tropical zone, both are high enough to be perpetually snowcapped.

Immense quantities of sulphur have been taken from the crater of Popo; Hernán Cortés' soldiers used it to make gunpowder. Aztec runners made daily trips to fetch ice for Emperor Moctezuma's drinks and to preserve fish. A climb to the summit of either mountain requires 2 days; mountain-climbing experience is a prerequisite. Horses and guides are available in Amecameca. **Tlamacas**, the tourist area between the two volcanoes, is crowded on weekends and holidays.

One of Mexico's most inspiring vistas unfolds for those flying into Benito Juárez International Airport. The nation's five highest mountain peaks—Citlaltépetl, Popocatépetl, Iztaccíhuatl, Xinantécatl and Matlalcuéyetl—stand like monolithic sentries ringing in the Valley of Mexico. Even on a gray day, the peaks are usually visible above the clouds.

Mexico City, Distrito Federal

Mexico City, which celebrated its 675th anniversary in 2000, is the North American continent's oldest capital. High-rise buildings flank its broad, tree-lined boulevards, yet the city is permeated by the past. And nothing seems to be able to slow down inexorable growth. Despite choking air pollution—the result of daily exhaust fumes from several million vehicles—and devastating natural disaster—the 1985 earthquake—it continues to persevere.

Mexico City lies in the **Valley of Mexico**, or Anáhuac, a great basin about 60 miles long and 30 miles wide, bounded by mountains on all sides except the north. From the air, the vastness of the city sprawl is startling—a solid sea of buildings stretching across the valley floor to the distant horizon. The most conspicuous landmarks, however, are the snowcapped peaks of **Popocatépetl** and **Iztaccíhuatl** to the southeast. The looming mountains hemming Mexico City in are chiefly responsible for creating the smog problem that threatens the environment. And at elevations ranging from about 7,200 to 8,000 feet, this is one of the world's loftiest cities.

Much of the valley, including the area occupied by Mexico City, is an old lakebed with no underlying bedrock. The combination of unstable subsoil and the volcanic nature of the region makes sinking and earthquakes the two greatest threats to the city's buildings. The metropolis, in fact, is settling under its own weight even as it continues to rise story upon steel, glass and stone story—although it only yields about an inch each year. But despite the preponderance of stone and concrete, Mexico City is surprisingly green (when it rains). Tamarind, cypress and rubber trees lines the streets, date palms adorn parks, clipped shrubs border sidewalks.

Although located in a tropical latitude, the altitude usually makes it feel like spring. Days are pleasant, and nights, even in midsummer, are cool. Spring's actual arrival also signals a reduction of winter's severe pollution levels. There are distinct rainy (June through September or October) and dry (October or November through May) seasons.

Earthquakes—the result of unfortunate geography—are in the back of every resident's mind. Mexico City's greatest natural catastrophe in modern times was the massive earthquake and aftershocks on Sept. 19 and 20, 1985. Some 10,000 people died, and scores of buildings were destroyed or later razed. There are still abandoned, decrepit structures here and there that were ruined but never torn down. In October 1995 a powerful 7.6 magnitude quake centered near the Pacific Coast resort of Manzanillo, about 335 miles to the west, sent panicky office workers fleeing from high-rise buildings to the open spaces of the *Zócalo*, some no doubt reliving the terror of 10 years before.

Fast Facts

LOCATION: In south-central Mexico.

POPULATION: 10 million; metropolitan area 21 million (estimated).

ELEVATION: 2,240 meters (7,347 feet).

WHAT'S THERE: A treasure trove of museums, led by the National Museum of Anthropology's priceless collection of historical and cultural artifacts; magnificent colonial architecture, from ornate churches to stately mansions; the Polanco neighborhood's fashionable boutiques and fine dining; sidewalk vendors and markets galore; world-class performing arts, including music, theater, dance and folkloric productions; the massive pyramids at the nearby archeological ruins of Teotihuacán.

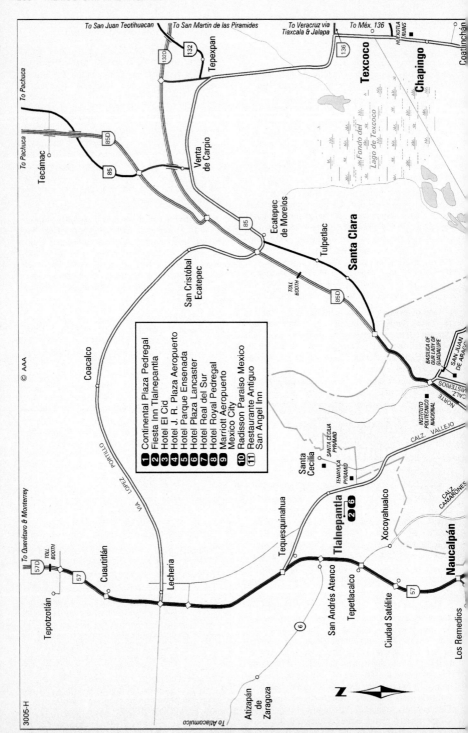

Legend:
1. Continental Plaza Pedregal
2. Fiesta Inn Tlalnepantla
3. Hotel El Cid
4. Hotel J. R. Plaza Aeropuerto
5. Hotel Parque Ensenada
6. Hotel Plaza Lancaster
7. Hotel Real del Sur
8. Hotel Royal Pedregal
9. Marriott Aeropuerto Mexico City
10. Radisson Paraiso Mexico
11. Restaurante Antiguo San Angel Inn

© AAA

3005-H

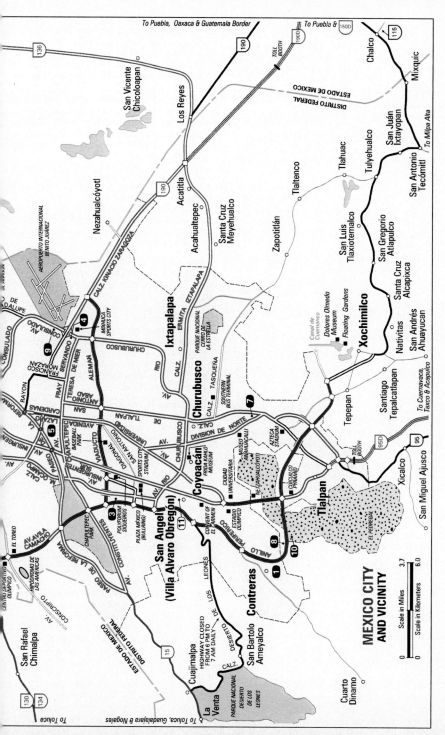

MEXICO CITY
AND VICINITY

Scale in Miles
0   3.7

Scale in Kilometers
0   6.0

Visitors will see sharp contrasts. Men and women conducting urgent business on cell phones and foreign diplomats dining in elegant restaurants give Mexico City a distinctly international air. In blatant contrast are ragged children and the destitute elderly begging for a few coins, sad reminders of the rampant poverty suffered by millions trying to eke out a life. The green expanses of **Chapultepec Park** and the charm of colonial plazas are counterbalanced by the ceaseless noise and congestion of the city's traffic, some of the worst anywhere.

And everywhere in Mexico City, people hustle. Captive audiences stopped at red lights are sure to be besieged by candy, flower and newspaper sellers, beggars, fire jugglers, kids playing trumpets, a man walking from car to car playing a violin.

Although it lacks a port, the capital is an industrial powerhouse where new factory construction pushes ever farther outward toward the surrounding mountains. Construction, textiles, chemicals, plastics, cement, iron and steel are among the major industries. Joining the city's own army of assembly plants are those established by large U.S. and other foreign companies. Tanneries prepare fine leather and workshops fashion it into beautifully crafted products. Silversmithing and glassmaking are other highly developed crafts.

The entire city is designated a national historic monument, and the enormous *Zócalo*, or main square, is its centerpiece. (Although most Mexican cities and towns have a central plaza that may be locally referred to as the *zócalo*, it is only Mexico City's that receives the official designation.) It is the world's second largest public gathering place after Moscow's Red Square. Once a verdant green common strolled by privileged aristocrats, the *Zócalo* is now a vast expanse of concrete (the plaza was paved over during the Revolution of 1910) that, appropriately, is best known as a very public stage for political rallies.

HISTORICAL OVERVIEW

Nomadic Indians from the north made their way to the Valley of Mexico in 1325 to fulfill a priestly prophecy: They were destined to settle where an eagle, carrying a serpent in its beak, was perched on a cactus (an image that appears on the Mexican flag). According to legend, that spot was an island in the middle of Lake Texcoco. Thus was the great capital of **Tenochtitlán** founded.

The Aztecs were named after their original homeland of Aztlán, thought by some archeologists to be the village of Mexcaltitán in the present-day state of Nayarit. Built on a manmade island in a swampy lagoon area near the Pacific Coast, Mexcaltitán's layout resembles that of ancient Tenochtitlán. Soon they controlled the riches of the Valley of Mexico, an important trade center. By the end of the 15th century Tenochtitlán was a beautiful and luxurious city of fountains, gardens and canals that encompassed the small islands dotting the lake. Eventual land reclamation resulted in the creation of one large island connected by causeways to the mainland and a political empire of Aztec nations. Tenochtitlán's population was about 300,000—possibly the world's largest city at its time. Then the Spanish arrived.

On Nov. 8, 1519, explorer Hernán Cortés became the first white man to enter Tenochtitlán's ceremonial center, today's *Zócalo*. One of world history's great mysteries is how an adventure seeker with a tiny band of followers could so successfully conquer the most aggressively warrior nation in the New World.

Although he led fewer than 400 men, Cortés was armed with formidable weapons; the sound of the Spanish cannons terrified the Aztecs. Furthermore, the Spaniards were aided by Indian allies only too eager to hasten the overthrow of their hated enemies. (The militant Aztecs exacted heavy payment from conquered tribes—gifts of tribute that in large measure subsidized the lavish lifestyle of Tenochtitlán's inhabitants.) The presence of 16 horses, which the Aztecs took to be some sort of god-monsters, further awed and frightened them as well.

Moctezuma II, the Aztec emperor, met Cortés with rich gifts and offered no resistance to his entry into the city. He believed the Spaniard to be a divine envoy of Quetzalcóatl, the fairskinned, golden-haired god of civilization who according to legend was to return in the year of One Reed (Ce Acatl). On the Aztec calendar, 1519 was that year. This case of mistaken identity brought about Moctezuma's downfall. Taking the ruler captive, Cortés and his troops remained in Tenochtitlán.

Sometime later, Moctezuma was wounded during a popular uprising by his people against the Spanish and died on June 30, 1520. On that evening, referred to as *La Noche Triste*, or "Night of Sadness," Cortés was driven from Tenochtitlán at the cost of about three-quarters of his force. The savagery of the hand-to-hand combat was horrific. It is said that Aztec warriors brandishing clubs embedded with shards of obsidian were able to decapitate the Spaniards' horses. The survivors, however, were allowed to escape, reaching Tlaxcala, an anti-Aztec stronghold. After refortifying, open warfare ensued, marked by naval attacks on Lake Texcoco that cut off Aztec supplies and fresh water. After a long siege, the vaunted empire of the Aztecs collapsed with the fall of Tenochtitlán on Aug. 13, 1521.

The Spaniards built their own city atop the ruins of the capital, leaving the outer periphery to the vanquished. Aztecs gradually intermingled with the Spanish, resulting in *mestizos*, persons of mixed Spanish and Indian blood who comprise the great majority of Mexico's present-day population.

Although Spanish colonial rule was harsh, Mexico City benefited from the crown, becoming the most important city in New Spain and the capital of Spain's far-flung empire in the Americas. Lake Texcoco was gradually filled. Working together, Spanish and Indian architects developed a wildly ornamental baroque style that frequently utilized a light, porous volcanic rock known as *tezontle*. The 18th century—the golden age of Mexican architecture—produced some of the city's most impressive buildings.

Mexico City remained in the iron grip of Spanish rule for exactly 3 centuries, culminating in the decade-long fight for independence that followed *Grito de Dolores*, Father Miguel Hidalgo's impassioned speech advocating Mexican freedom, in 1810. It was finally taken by an army of patriots under Gen. Agustín de Iturbide, who entered the city on Sept. 27, 1821. Iturbide, a man hungry for power, appointed himself emperor of the new nation in 1822 and was crowned in Mexico City as Agustín I. His empire was short lived; in December 1822 the republic was proclaimed and Iturbide was forced to abdicate.

The Federal District was created in 1824 to centralize Mexico's new government. Mexico City continued as capital of the republic until the French installed Archduke Maximilian as emperor in 1864. His unhappy reign lasted 3 years, when, deserted by his original backer, Napoleon III, Maximilian was captured and executed. During these years, Benito Juárez was the president

The Informed Traveler

Media

The News is the country's only English-language daily. It prints national and international news and has sections on sports, finance and the environment, as well as a calendar of community events, an entertainment guide, local TV listings and classified ads. The *Mexico City Times*, another English paper, is published every day but Sunday and contains excerpts from the *New York Times*. The *Daily Bulletin*, also in English, has a summary of world and local news and is distributed free daily except Monday. *Tiempo Libre*, published every Thursday, has information about restaurants, museums, galleries and cultural events. Major U.S. newspapers are available at many newsstands the day after they are printed.

The American Bookstore, Avenida Francisco Madero #25 near Bolívar (M: Allende, line 2), has U.S. newspapers and magazines, books and an extensive selection of travel guides. The Sanborn's chain of drugstores also carries newspapers, magazines and books. Mexico City has numerous branches; one is in the House of Tiles, Avenida Madero #4 (M: Bellas Artes, lines 2 and 8).

Weather

Being at a high altitude in a tropical latitude has a canceling effect, and Mexico City normally experiences no severe temperature extremes (although an El Niño-fueled heat wave in May 1998 sent the mercury soaring to 100 F, smashing the previous all-time high by 10 degrees). That anomaly aside, days are generally sunny and pleasant and nights comfortably cool throughout the year. The arrival of spring somewhat diminishes the severe smog problem, brought on by winter's thermal inversions and exacerbated by the city's tremendous amount of automobile traffic. Afternoon showers are likely from June through September.

Dress in the capital ranges from casual to elegantly formal, depending on your agenda. Expensive restaurants may require jackets and ties for men. A sweater, jacket or light topcoat is advisable for evenings or for trips to nearby mountain resorts, where temperatures may be cooler than in the city.

Staying Safe

Street crime—including armed robbery, pickpocketing and purse snatching—has risen dramatically. Two major factors contributing to this surge are low rates of apprehension and conviction, and the link between crime and police collaboration. No part of the city is immune, even the upscale Polanco neighborhood and other areas frequented by tourists. Do not wander around anywhere after dark, especially alone. If you're going out for the evening, arrange designated hotel taxi transportation to and from your destination, particularly if you're unfamiliar with your surroundings. If you start feeling uneasy on the street, go to the nearest hotel.

Taxi robberies are among the most frequently reported crimes; never hail a circulating cab on the street. The Zona Rosa and the area behind the U.S. Embassy are particularly vulnerable to street crime against foreigners. In addition, the capital's size and unfamiliarity can put you off your guard. Enjoy yourself, but stay alert at all times. Keep close watch over money, cameras or any other valuables in your possession, and avoid carrying large amounts of cash. *Also see "Taxis" under "Getting Around" and "Personal Safety," page 66.*

of Mexico's de facto liberal government, which instituted reform laws devoted to the separation of church and state. Besides raising living conditions in the country, he took major steps to improve the physical layout of the capital.

It was during the 1860s that the first *colonias*, or residential districts, began to appear. Modernization began on a large scale during the reign of dictator Porfirio Díaz from 1876 to 1910. Mexico City benefited from the establishment of such amenities as electric lighting, streetcars and a drainage system. The **Palacio de Bellas Artes** (Palace of Fine Arts) and other monumental public buildings were constructed, their design modeled after prevailing European neoclassical styles.

As the governmental seat, the capital's history has obviously paralleled the history of the entire nation. Consequently, the political unrest that culminated in the Mexican Revolution of 1910 centered in the city. The protracted conflict turned the capital into a battlefield. But with only anarchy as a cause, the rebels, under their leaders Pancho Villa and Emiliano Zapata, occupied Mexico City in December 1914 for only a month; President Venustiano Carranza and his army soon returned to power.

Modernization continued after adoption of the Constitution of 1917, bringing a steady stream of impoverished *mestizos* and Indians from the countryside into Mexico City. They crowded into working-class *colonias*, while the creation of such luxurious residential districts as Lomas de Chapultepec (Chapultepec Hills) housed the wealthy few. Skyscrapers began to define the city's skyline in the 1930s.

One early renewal project was the relief of the centuries-old water shortage in the capital. The springs of Laguna del Río Lerma, beyond the mountains west of the city in the Valley of Toluca, now bring water by aqueduct to reservoirs in Chapultepec Park. The first sections of a modern subway system were completed in 1971; today the Metro's nine lines provide efficient and inexpensive city transportation. Construction of the system also brought to light some ancient archeological treasures, notably the Templo Mayor, or Great Temple of the Aztecs.

Since German traveler Baron Alexander von Humboldt described 18th-century Mexico City as a city of palaces centered on the *Zócalo*, the capital has has expanded to become a metropolis. In addition to its business and commercial districts, Mexico City is honeycombed with hundreds of separate neighborhoods. In the last half of the 20th century the metropolitan area has exploded in all directions, incorporating such former close-in suburbs as **Churubusco, Coyoacán, Ixtapalapa, San Angel, Tlalpan, Villa de Guadalupe** and **Xochimilco**, each of which manages to maintain its own distinctive character.

APPROACHES

BY AIR

Benito Juárez International Airport is in the northeastern part of the city, about 6 kilometers (4 miles) east of the *Zócalo*. The five-floor International Terminal, opened in 1993, greatly increased the airport's available space. Some 35 airlines, both international and domestic, maintain regular flights to and from Benito Juárez.

The airport has numerous facilities catering to foreign travelers, such as lockers for storing baggage; Ladatel (long-distance) phones, including some that accept international credit cards; rental car agencies; ATMs and *casas de cambio* (currency exchange offices); branches of the Mexican banks Banamex, Bancomer and Banco Internacional; and a hotel reservations service, which can book a room according to location and price specifications. There is no charge for making a reservation, but advance payment for one night is required. Authorized baggage handlers are identified by the "Union" ID placard attached to their hand carts.

Contact the airline directly when making reservations for flights to other cities within Mexico, or if you need price or schedule information. This can be frustrating if you reach someone who doesn't speak good English; airline numbers also change frequently. If possible, make all flight arrangements prior to your departure; then the only reason you may need to call is to confirm times. When departing Mexico City, make sure to allow for sufficient travel time to the airport—a minimum of 45 minutes if you're based in the downtown area. Arrive at least an hour before departure for domestic flights, 90 minutes before departure for international flights. If you have an early morning flight, staying at the Marriott Aeropuerto is convenient; an elevated skywalk connects the hotel and Terminal B. For additional information about airlines *see "Arriving by Air," page 53.*

Authorized airport taxis are the safest way to reach the downtown area. The vehicles, sedans or minivans, have a black aircraft symbol on the door and are labeled *"Transportación Terrestre"* (Ground Transportation). Taxis require prepayment at the official airport taxi counter; look for the *"Transportación Terrestre"* sign inside or just outside the terminal. Prices are based on a zone system. Beware of overcharging; confirm the rate by consulting the posted map, or ask to see a map if one isn't posted. Yellow-outfitted escorts show you to an available taxi; tickets are given to the driver. Do not negotiate with anyone who approaches you with the offer of a ride into town.

If you're traveling light, you might consider using **Metro**, Mexico City's rapid transit system.

Large pieces of luggage aren't likely to be allowed on board, however, and riding a crowded subway car weighed down with anything more than an overnight bag is not only cumbersome but unsafe. The airport station is Terminal Aérea (Air Terminal Building, line 5) on Boulevard Puerto Aéreo, a few minutes' walk from the main terminal; follow the signs. To reach the downtown area, take the subway to the Pantitlán station and switch to line 1.

BY CAR

Mex. 15-D, 57-D and 85-D are the major highways approaching Mexico City from the west and north. From the south and east come Mex. 95-D and Mex. 150-D. Other routes are likely to be slow, winding or of substandard quality, and one—Mex. 134, which travels southwest from Mexico City to Mex. 200 along the Pacific Coast—should be avoided entirely.

Leaving the city, the main thoroughfares are Avenida Insurgentes Sur, which becomes Mex. 95-D as it heads south to Cuernavaca, Taxco and Acapulco; running north, Avenida Insurgentes Norte becomes Mex. 85-D/85 heading toward Pachuca. The Periférico, which loops around the city's western and southern sides, is called Avenida Avila Camacho within the city and becomes Mex. 57-D heading northwest toward Querétaro. Avenida Constituyentes runs west past Chapultepec Park and becomes Mex. 15 as it heads toward Toluca; Calzada Ignacio Zaragoza leads east out of the city, becoming Mex. 190-D as it heads toward Puebla.

Try to time both arrival and departure times into and out of Mexico City as early in the morning as possible to avoid the near-constant traffic.

Note: Seat belt use by the driver and all passengers is required within the Federal District.

BY TRAIN OR BUS

First-class train service (the only class recommended) is available to Mexico City only from Monterrey. Mexican rail lines connect with points at the U.S. border. Service is likely to be slow, and space should be reserved well in advance. The **Buenavista Railroad Station** is located on Avenida Insurgentes Norte at Mosqueta, directly north of the Monument to the Revolution and several long blocks from the nearest Metro station (M: Revolución, line 2). Passenger train travel in Mexico is problematic at present as the industry switches over from government ownership to privatization; travel by first-class bus is easier and more efficient.

With interconnections between Mexican and U.S. bus lines, it is possible to travel economically by bus from from several U.S. border cities to Mexico City. Transportes del Norte, Tres Estrellas de Oro, Transportes Chihuahuenses and Omnibus de México are linked with Greyhound

Vendor selling candles at the Guadalupe Basilica © Chris Sharp

Lines Inc. From Tijuana it takes about 40 hours to reach Mexico City; from Ciudad Juárez, across the border from El Paso, Tex., about 24 hours; from Matamoros, across the border from Brownsville, Tex., about 14 hours.

Bus travel is available from Mexico City to nearly every town in the republic, but reservations must be made. In the capital you can make them through Línea Gris, a travel agency at Calle Londres #166 in the Zona Rosa (see "Sightseeing," page 324). Most major Mexican lines offer "deluxe" (lujo) bus service; these companies include Autobuses Cristóbal Colón, Autobuses del Oriente (ADO), ETN, Omnibus de México, Primera Plus and Tres Estrellas de Oro. **Note:** Arrivals and departures at bus stations in Mexico are usually announced in Spanish only. For additional information about buses see "Bus Service," page 63.

Mexico City has four main bus terminals that correspond to the four compass points. By far the largest of the four is **Terminal Central de Autobuses del Norte**, Avenida Cien Metros #4907 (M: Autobuses del Norte, line 5). Most of the buses traveling from the northern border arrive at this terminal, also known as "Terminal Norte" or "Camiones Norte." From here, buses travel to almost every destination north of the capital, including the Pacific Coast resorts from Manzanillo northward; inland cities such as

"Don't Drive Today" Program

In a continuing effort to reduce air pollution, city government officials in 1989 established driving restrictions on all vehicular traffic, including vehicles carrying non-Mexican registration. The restriction is based on the last digit of a vehicle's license plate and pertains to the days of the week. It is in effect throughout the Mexico City metropolitan area, which includes the Distrito Federal (Federal District) and parts of the state of México.

Vehicles may not be driven on certain days according to the following schedule: MONDAY—license plates that end with 5 or 6; TUESDAY—license plates that end with 7 or 8; WEDNESDAY—license plates that end with 3 or 4; THURSDAY—license plates that end with 1 or 2; FRIDAY—license plates that end with 9 or 0. All vehicles may be driven SATURDAY and SUNDAY. The restrictions **do not** apply from 11 p.m. to 5 a.m. Failure to comply with "No Driving Today" regulations will result in vehicle impoundment and a hefty fine.

Personalized license plates containing only letters are assigned a number pertaining to the day on which the vehicle cannot be driven in the metropolitan area. To find out the designated day, contact the Secretaría de Turismo (the Ministry of Tourism, or SECTUR); phone 250-0123 (in Mexico City), 01 (800) 903-9200 (elsewhere within Mexico), or (800) 482-9832 (from the United States).

Signs explaining the "Don't Drive Today" program are posted along major highways entering the metropolitan area. Many of the signs, however, are in Spanish. Until further notice, the restrictions apply to all vehicles, regardless of license plate origin. Physically disabled drivers are not exempted from the regulation. If you are visiting Mexico City and plan to rent a car, contact the rental agency in advance and make certain the vehicle can be driven when you wish to use it.

Note: When pollution is extremely heavy (particularly during the winter months), emergency driving restrictions may be mandated. Before any such decision is made, announcements are broadcast on radio and TV specifying those digits and/or days that will be added to the normal restriction.

Aguascalientes, Guadalajara, Guanajuato, Monterrey, Morelia, Querétaro and San Miguel de Allende; and the nearby archeological sites of Teotihuacán and Tula.

The terminal offers currency exchange services (during normal banking hours) and has a hotel reservations booth. Taxis charge standard fares based on a zone system; tickets are purchased at booths inside the station. Count your change carefully, as overcharging is common.

Terminal de Autobuses de Pasajeros de Oriente (TAPO) is at Calzada Ignacio Zaragoza #200, near the airport (M: San Lázaro, line 1). The most modern of the four stations, it handles buses to and from such eastern destinations as Jalapa, Puebla, Veracruz, Villahermosa and cities on the Yucatán Peninsula, as well as Oaxaca, San Cristóbal de las Casas, Tuxtla Gutiérrez, Guatemala and other places to the south. Taxi ticket booths, a cafeteria, an ATM and currency exchange services are all available.

Terminal Central de Autobuses del Sur is at Avenida Taxqueña #1320 (M: Taxqueña, line 2). At the end of Metro's line 2, this also is a major terminus for local city buses from downtown and other points north. From here buses arrive and depart for Acapulco, Cuernavaca, Ixtapa/Zihuatanejo, Taxco and other points south of Mexico City. For day trips to Cuautla, Cuernavaca or

Tepoztlán, take one of the Pullman de Morelos buses, which leave frequently for each of these tourist destinations. Estrella de Oro has first-class service to Acapulco and Zihuatanejo. The terminal has long-distance (Ladatel) telephones, a post office and a travel agency.

The smallest of the four is the western station, **Terminal de Autobuses del Poniente**, Avenida Sur #122 at Tacubaya (M: Observatorio, line 1). This is the easiest way to take a day trip to Toluca by bus. Service also is available to Morelia and Guadalajara; the going is slow but the scenery is pleasant.

GETTING AROUND

CITY LAYOUT

Mexico City's *colonias*, or neighborhoods—more than 300 of them—are served by a maze of *calles*, *avenidas* and *calzadas*. Some narrow alleyways, or *callejones*, are cobblestoned relics from earlier days. Major thoroughfares, on the other hand, can have eight lanes. Most of the signs tend to be more confusing than enlightening. There is no real logic to the city's streets, which are named after rivers, mountains, foreign cities and countries, musicians, writers, doctors, composers, the states of Mexico and just about everything else. They also change names frequently.

A system of connected highways combine to form the **Circuito Interior**, which roughly encircles the central city. Beginning at the airport, on the east side of town, **Avenida Río Consulado** runs north and then west, becoming **Calzada Melchor Ocampo**. Ocampo swings south, passing east of Chapultepec Park and intersecting Paseo de la Reforma, at which point it continues as **Calzada Vasconcelos**. Angling off Vasconcelos is **Avenida de la Revolución**, which runs south to **Avenida Río Churubusco**. Churubusco then proceeds east before turning north to connect with Río Consulado, southwest of the airport, and completing the circuit. Theoretically, this loop provides a less congested alternative to the jam-packed streets within it. However, these roads themselves are usually crowded, particularly during the morning and evening rush hours.

Also within the Circuito Interior are axis roads *(ejes)*, a series of numbered boulevards running one way only, with special lanes reserved for trolleys and buses circulating in the opposite direction. East-west Eje 1 Norte and Eje 2 Norte are north of the *Zócalo*; Eje 2 Sur through Eje 8 Sur run progressively south of the *Zócalo*. North-south Eje 1 through 3 Oriente are east of **Eje Central Lázaro Cárdenas**, which divides the central city in half; Eje 1 through 3 Poniente are to the west.

The most magnificent of the broad principal arteries that intersect the central city is the **Paseo de la Reforma**. A legacy of French emperor Maximilian, it runs southwest to northeast for more than 7 miles. From the eastern end of Chapultepec Park to past Alameda Park, Reforma is exceptionally wide and beaded with monument-adorned *glorietas* (circles).

One good point of reference is the **Independence Monument** at the intersection of Reforma, Florencia and Tiber. The 150-foot-tall spire, topped by a gold angel, is easy to spot. Another is the major intersection at Paseo de la Reforma and **Avenida Insurgentes**, marked by the **Cuauhtémoc Monument**. Insurgentes, the capital's longest thoroughfare, runs north and south, bisecting western and eastern sections of the city. East-west **Viaducto Miguel Alemán** runs south of downtown, connecting Calzada Ignacio Zaragoza at the eastern end of the city with the Anillo Periférico at the western end.

Driving just about anywhere within Mexico City is a daunting prospect. The sheer number of vehicles makes for an extremely slow pace. Add to that aggressive tactics (the locals often disregard traffic signals), frequent construction, detours and a plethora of one-way streets, and visitors are far better off relying on taxi transportation provided by their hotel.

If circumstances dictate that you must drive, carry a good city map and always park the vehicle in a guarded lot. Street parking is not only rare but chancy, as vandalism often occurs. Any vehicle parked illegally is likely to have its license plate removed by police; expect to pay a fee to get it back. Never leave valuables in your car, particularly in plain view.

Note: Motorists in Mexico City who are stopped for a red light at many downtown intersections are besieged by everyone from beggars to performing children (whose parents are often sitting on a nearby corner) to vendors selling newspapers, flowers, candy and trinkets. The best defense if you're part of this captive audience is to keep your door locked, your window rolled up and look straight ahead, avoiding eye contact.

Speed limits are shown in kilometers. If a road, avenue or street is unmarked, follow these general guidelines: school zones, 20 km/h (10-12 mph); residential streets, 30 km/h (20 mph); main streets, 50 km/h (30 mph); avenues, bypasses, loop roads and overpasses within the city, 60 km/h (35 mph); main roads, 100 km/h (60 mph); selected main roads and toll roads, 110-120 km/h (65-75 mph).

TAXIS

Major hotels maintain fleets of *turismo* taxis associated specifically with the hotel. These can be used for short hops from your hotel to a nearby restaurant and back, or for longer excursions to shop or sightsee. For an hourly rate (and normally a 2-hour time minimum), you can arrange to have the driver wait at a specific location in addition to providing transportation. Rates for individual trips are negotiated with the driver; establish the fee for any excursion in advance. Although *turismo* taxis are expensive (a ride just a few blocks in length can cost several dollars), the peace of mind is well worth the cost.

If your hotel doesn't provide transportation or you otherwise need a cab, the U.S. Embassy strongly urges that you ride only in a taxi summoned by phone from a designated *sitio* (SEE-tee-oh) stand. They are considered safer than taxis that circulate because the driver can be easily traced back to the stand. Many of the stands list telephone numbers where the taxi can be called. Arrangements also can be made to have these cabs pick you up at a predetermined time and place.

Ask for the license plate number and the cab driver's name, and only use cabs with plates beginning with the letter "S," which are assigned to a particular site—such as a hotel—and registered. The number on the license plate should match the number painted on the side of the cab. Avoid the yellow and green Volkswagen Beetle taxis that constantly cruise the streets (often referred to as *ecologicos* or *magna sins*), or cabs with license plates containing the letter "L" (*libre* cabs).

Authorized taxis at the airport and at bus stations charge fees based on a zone system; tickets to pay the fee are purchased at booths inside the terminal. *Also see "Approaches—By Air," page 292.*

RENTAL CARS

There are many car rental agencies in Mexico City. The larger companies also have branches in major cities where you can leave your car at trip's end. Be sure you fully understand the terms of any rental contract, especially in regard to insurance coverage. It's much less expensive to reserve before you leave home; make reservations at least 1 week in advance. AAA/CAA members enjoy exceptional discounts through Hertz for vehicles booked in the United States. Consult your local AAA/CAA club or phone Hertz, (800) 654-3080.

Note: Although having a vehicle at your disposal can be convenient for sightseeing trips outside the metropolitan area, keep in mind that a rental car driven by a foreigner may unfortunately become a target for police who will try to extract a bribe.

Vehicles in the Mexico City metropolitan area, including the Distrito Federal (Federal District) and parts of the state of Mexico, may *not* be driven on certain days based on the last digit of the license plate. Make certain your rental car can be driven when you wish to use it. A rental agency may inadvertently provide a vehicle with a license plate with a last digit that corresponds to the day on which it cannot be driven. For additional information, *see the "Don't Drive Today Program" box on page 294.*

BUSES

City buses go just about everywhere and are inexpensive, but the system is not user-friendly for visitors. Routes and bus numbers change frequently, and route maps are practically nonexistent. Some signs at the downtown bus stops bear route descriptions. Buses run daily 5 a.m.-midnight, but show up much less frequently after 10 p.m.

Two major bus routes put visitors within walking distance of many of the city's attractions. The east-west route links the *Zócalo* with the National Auditorium in Chapultepec Park and continues to the Observatorio Metro station (line 1), traveling along avenidas Francisco Madero and Juárez and Paseo de la Reforma. These buses are usually marked "Zócalo." Buses running north-south along Avenida Insurgentes connect the huge Terminal Norte station with the southern suburbs of San Angel and University City via the Zona Rosa. These buses are usually marked "Indios Verdes-Tlalpan."

Never carry valuables onto a city bus, and know exactly where you're going before you board. But unless you simply want to have the experience, it's safer and much more convenient to use a taxi associated with your hotel for getting around.

PESEROS

These green-and-white vehicles resemble a minibus or van. *Peseros*, also called *colectivos*, travel along established routes and charged fixed rates (according to distance) that are a bit more than the bus but less than taxi fares. Route destinations (often a Metro station) are marked on the windshield or shown on a sign. Flag down a *pesero* as you would a bus, and tell the driver your destination when you board. Major routes include the principal east-west and north-south tourist corridors (the *Zócalo* to Chapultepec Park and Avenida Insurgentes Sur, respectively). This is an alternative to the crowded and often chaotic city buses, although using a designated taxi is still the safest way to travel.

METRO

Metro—one of the world's busiest subway systems—is faced with the formidable task of moving some 5 million riders daily over both surface and subterranean track. The nine lines cover most of the city. *Tren ligero* (light rail) lines connect with some of Metro's terminal stations, providing service to the popular tourist attraction of Xochimilco and other outlying areas.

Line 1 runs roughly west-east from the Observatory, near Chapultepec Park, to Pantitlán in the eastern suburbs, passing south of the Zona Rosa and the *Zócalo*. Subway riders bound for the airport switch to line 5 at the Pantitlán station. **Line 2** begins in the northwest part of the city at the Cuatro Caminos station, proceeds east, burrows under the *Zócalo* and then runs above ground due south to the Taxqueña station. **Line 3** runs from the Indios Verdes station, north of the Basilica of Guadalupe, south past Alameda Park to University City (National University of Mexico campus). **Line 4** runs north-south east of downtown, from the Martín Carrera to the Santa Anita stations. **Line 5** runs from the Politécnico station south to the La Raza station, then east and south to Pantitlán, with a stop (Terminal Aérea) at the airport. **Note:** To switch from line 3 to line 5—or vice versa—at the La Raza station requires a 10- to 15-minute walk through a long tunnel.

Line 6 runs north of downtown, proceeding east from the El Rosario station to the Martín Carrera station via the Instituto del Petróleo and Deportivo 18 de Marzo stations. **Line 7** runs north-south along the city's western edge from the El Rosario station to the Barranca del Muerto station. **Line 8** runs from the Garibaldi station (one stop north of the Bellas Artes station on line 2) south and east to the Constitución de 1917 station, in the southeast section of the city. **Line**

9 parallels line 1 and runs south of it, from the Tacubaya station in the west to the Pantitlán station in the east. In addition, **Line A** provides light rail service from the Pantitlán station (the eastern terminus of lines 1, 5 and 9) south to the La Paz station.

The fare, which includes transfers, is very inexpensive. Tickets are purchased at booths at the stations; the magnetically encoded stub allows passage through the turnstiles. Several tickets can be purchased at once to avoid spending time standing in lines. You also can purchase an *abono* ticket, which allows use of the entire system for a multiple-day period. (With this type of ticket, enter Metro stations only through the blue turnstiles; otherwise the ticket will be taken and not returned.)

At the stations, on signs and in guidebooks and brochures, Metro lines are designated by the following colors: line 1, bright pink; line 2, blue; line 3, olive green; line 4, light blue; line 5, yellow; line 6, red; line 7, orange; line 8, dark green; line 9, brown; and line A, purple. You can consult a color-coded subway guide at Metro information booths, or try obtaining a map of the system from the ticket booths at the larger stations.

Since Metro is used daily by millions for commuter travel, sardine-can conditions prevail. During weekday rush hours (both morning and evening) the trains are crammed and guards are

---

Visitor Services

Guides/Tours

The services of a good guide can be expensive but invaluable, particularly for the first few days in this huge city. If you go with this option, obtain the services of a bonded guide licensed by the Secretaría de Turismo (the Ministry of Tourism, or SECTUR). Ask to see his or her official guide card marked with "Departamento de Turismo" and take special note of the expiration date to the right of the photograph.

Additional fees are charged for guided trips outside Mexico City. SECTUR can provide assistance in obtaining a competent guide; phone (5) 250-0123 or 250-0151 (English spoken).

Taxi drivers also can function as a driver/bodyguard/guide, even if it means waiting by the car for an hour while you stroll one of the city's tourist-friendly neighborhoods. The average rate is about $10 an hour; it goes up if the trip ventures outside Federal District borders. The expense is well worth the peace of mind that comes from not having to negotiate city traffic or use public transportation. Never hail a cab on the street; instead, arrange an excursion with a driver affiliated with your hotel.

Information Sources

Contact SECTUR at (5) 250-0123 or 250-0151 (in Mexico City), 01 (800) 903-9200 (elsewhere within Mexico), or (800) 482-9832 (from the United States) for English answers to your questions about tourist protection laws and assistance. Phones are staffed 24 hours a day. SECTUR's offices are at Presidente Masaryk #172, near the northeastern edge of Chapultepec Park in the Polanco neighborhood (M: Polanco, line 7).

The Secretary of Tourism of the Federal District operates six tourist information modules staffed by English-speaking personnel. Two are conveniently located for visitors: Calle Amberes #54 (at Calle Londres) in the Zona Rosa (M: Insurgentes, line 1), and at the airport in the Domestic Arrivals Terminal. Phone (5) 525-9380 or (5) 762-6773, respectively.

The main post office (Correo Mayor) is at the corner of Tacuba and Avenida Lázaro Cárdenas in the first block north of the Palacio de Bellas Artes (M: Bellas Artes, lines 2 and 8). The U.S. Embassy is at Paseo de la Reforma #305, at the corner of Danubio. It is open for general business Mon.-Fri. 8:30-5:30; phone (5) 211-0042. The Canadian Embassy is at Schiller #529, just north of the National Museum of Anthropology (M: Auditorio, line 7). It is open Mon.-Fri. 8:30-2; phone (5) 254-3288. Both embassies are closed on U.S./Canadian and Mexican holidays.

The Asociación Mexicana Automovilística (Mexican Automobile Association, or AMA) may be able to assist visiting AAA/CAA members; for information phone (5) 588-7055 or 588-9355. AMA headquarters is located at Avenida Orizaba #7 near Avenida Chapultepec (M: Insurgentes, line 1).

Currency Exchange

While the rates charged by banks and *casas de cambio* (currency exchange offices) differ, they usually are better than the rates offered by hotels. Most banks exchange currency Mon.-Fri. 9-noon, but you may have to wait in line; exchange offices often are open weekdays until 5 and may be open Saturdays as well. Your hotel front desk is likely to be the most convenient option. Exchange offices are concentrated downtown near the major attractions, hotels and restaurants. There are ATMs on Paseo de la Reforma in the vicinity of the Zona Rosa and in the Historic Center; almost all take VISA and MasterCard. Only use ATMs inside commercial establishments and be alert for suspicious behavior around the machine—criminals may target tourists withdrawing cash. Above all, do not make street transactions at night.

METRO LINES

N

El Rosario
7 6
Tezozomoc
Aquiles Serdán
Azcapotzalco
Ferrería
Norte 45
Vallejo
Politécnico
5
Instituto del Petróleo
Lindavista
Indios Verdes
3
Basílica
La Villa
6
Martín Carrera
4
Talisman
Bondojito
Camarones
Autobuses del Norte
Potrero
Refinería
Cuatro Caminos
2
Tacuba
Panteones
Cuitlahuac
Popotla
Guerrero
Colegio Militar
La Raza
Misterios
Valle Gómez
Consulado
Eduardo Molina
Aragón
Oceanía
Tlatelolco
Garibaldi
8
Canal del Norte
San Joaquín
Normal
San Cosme
Revolución
Hidalgo
Bellas Artes
Allende
Morelos
Terminal Aérea
(Benito Juárez
International Airport)
Polanco
Juárez
San Juan de Letrán
Zócalo
Hangares
Auditorio
Salto del Agua
Pino Suárez
Merced
Candelaria
San Lázaro
Moctezuma
Balbuena
Aeropuerto
Balderas
Cuauhtémoc
Isabel la Católica
San Antonio Abad
Fray Servando
Pantitlán
1 5
Constituyentes
Insurgentes
Sevilla
Niños Héroes
Doctores
Gómez Farías
Zaragoza
9 A
Chapultepec
Obrera
Puebla
Tacubaya
Juanacatlán
Hospital General
Chabacano
Ciudad Deportiva
1
Observatorio
9
Patriotismo
Chilpancingo
Centro Médico
Lázaro Cárdenas
Jamaica
Mixihuca
Velódromo
San Pedro de los Piños
Etiopía
Viaducto
La Viga
Santa Anita
Coyuya
San Antonio
Eugenia
Xola
Tezontle
Apatlaco
Mixcoac
División del Norte
Villa de Cortés
Aculco
Nativitas
Escuadrón 201
7
Zapata
Portales
Atlalico
Barranca del Muerto
Coyoacán
Ermita
Iztapalapa
8
Viveros
General Anaya
Cerro de la Estrella
A
Miguel A. de Quevedo
La Purísima
Constitución de 1917
La Paz
Copilco
2
Taxqueña
Tren Ligero
Universidad
3

employed to control the crowds. Single women, unfortunately, may have to fend off unwelcome advances or inappropriate male conduct, and foreign visitors are prime targets for pickpockets.

Avoid using the subway for sightseeing (for safety's sake, hire a taxi affiliated with your hotel). If you do need to take Metro for any reason, make certain you know which direction the train is heading; check the signs on the loading platforms (andenes). They denote the last station on the line in each direction; for example, Dirección Pantitlán or Dirección Observatorio for line 1. Transfer gates, where more than one line shares a subway station, are marked correspondencia; exits, salida.

Metro is least crowded on weekends and holidays. In general trains begin running at 5 or 6 a.m. Mon.-Fri., 6 a.m. on Sat. and 7 a.m. on Sun. They run until at least 11:30 p.m. Sun.-Fri., later on Sat. **Note:** Luggage and backpacks are technically not permitted on any of the subway cars, nor is the taking of photographs allowed.

Points of interest and other locations described in the text include, where applicable, the name of the individual Metro station (M) and the subway line (1 through 9). Attraction listings without this designation are located away from Metro routes.

What To See

Note: To make it easier to plan a sightseeing itinerary in this sprawling city, the following attraction listings are grouped under nine separate, geographically based subheadings, and are spotted on three different maps. For a map of the greater Mexico City metropolitan area, see pages 288-289; for downtown Mexico City, see pages 304-305; for the Centro Histórico area, see page 313.

Around the Zocalo

CALLE MONEDA begins just east of the Zócalo at Avenida Seminario (M: Zócalo, line 2). It takes its name from the country's first mint, which now houses the **National Museum of the Cultures** (see attraction listing below). Many of the colonial-era buildings lining this thoroughfare, one of the city's oldest, are constructed of tezontle, the reddish volcanic rock used by the Maya to build their pyramids and temples. Near the Zócalo they are carefully refurbished but become more dilapidated as the street heads east. Vendors add to the bustle of this downtown corridor, which is closed to traffic and therefore pleasant to stroll.

At the corner of Moneda and Seminario is an outdoor model of Tenochtitlán as it might have appeared upon Hernán Cortés' arrival in 1519. The miniature temples and palaces are surrounded by a fountain's waters that simulate Lake Texcoco, in the middle of which the former Aztec capital resided; elevated causeways connected it to the mainland.

CATEDRAL METROPOLITANA (Metropolitan Cathedral), on the north side of the Zócalo (M: Zócalo, line 2), is one of the world's largest churches. A church built in 1525 was demolished in 1573 to make way for the present structure, which was not completed until 240 years later. The exterior presents a mingling of 16th-, 17th- and 18th-century architectural styles, from baroque ornamentation to a neoclassic clock tower.

The vast interior is shaped like a cross and has a central nave. Along the side aisles are 14 chapels variously adorned with statuary, ornate altars, paintings, gilded surfaces, priceless tapestries and various representations of Christ, including a black Christ figure. The **Chapel of the Kings**, at the end of the nave behind the main altar, is graced by gilded wood carvings and an extravagantly Churrigueresque altarpiece. Catacombs underneath the cathedral contain the tombs of many of Mexico's archbishops. Open daily.

The much smaller **El Sagrario** (Sacristy), adjoining the cathedral, was erected about 1750 and has an elaborate Churrigueresque facade. This parish church was originally built to house vestments and sacred relics.

Note: The interior of the cathedral is filled with enormous green scaffolds that provide support not only for restoration crews but also for the ceilings themselves. Both the cathedral and the Sacristy were damaged in the 1985 earthquake, and each has tilted noticeably as they ever so slowly sink into the underlying lakebed. The ongoing work doesn't deter worshippers, but the scaffolds obscure some of the interior architectural details.

CENTRO HISTORICO DE MEXICO (Historic Center of Mexico City) is the 668-block area radiating out from the Zócalo. This has been the city's hub since its founding by the Aztecs in 1325. Cortés and his followers decimated the Indian structures, building their own monuments atop the rubble. Today the district encompasses more than 1,500 historic structures, including the Templo Mayor, or Great Temple of the Aztecs (discovered during subway excavations), the National Palace and the Metropolitan Cathedral. Many of the private mansions and civic and religious buildings in the Historic Center date from the Spanish colonial period.

This area around the Zócalo is one of the city's liveliest. A multitude of businesses, including the National Pawn Shop, operate amid restaurants, museums, theaters, churches and the ubiquitous street vendors, who peddle everything from lottery tickets to holy water. Although the government maintains concerted effort to keep these roving entrepreneurs gathered in one place, they resist efforts at organization. Some of the streets around the Zócalo, where restoration efforts are ongoing, are closed to vehicular traffic.

Visitors, at any rate, will definitely want to explore on foot.

GRAN HOTEL, just west of the *Zócalo* at Avenida 16 de Septiembre #82 (M: Zócalo, line 2), is an example of turn-of-the-20th-century architecture. The grand lobby of this five-story marble structure is worth a peek; it features a spectacular Tiffany skylight and gilded, open-cage elevators.

MUSEO NACIONAL DE LAS CULTURAS (National Museum of the Cultures) is at Calle Moneda #13, near the cathedral and just east of the *Zócalo* (M: Zócalo, line 2). The Mexican archeological treasures once exhibited at this museum were moved to the National Museum of Anthropology in Chapultepec Park *(see attraction listing on page 311).* It now focuses on non-Mexican cultures, with exhibit halls grouped around a central patio. Especially notable are the African and South Seas groups. A striking Rufino Tamayo mural in the lobby depicts the 1910 Revolution. Open Tues.-Sat. 9:30-6, Sun. 9:30-4; several halls close for lunch between 2 and 3. Free. Phone (5) 512-7452.

NACIONAL MONTE DE PIEDAD (National Pawn Shop) is near the northwest corner of the *Zócalo* at Monte de Piedad and Avenida 5 de Mayo (M: Allende or Zócalo, line 2). The four-story, colonial-style structure stands on the site of Axayacatl, an Aztec palace occupied by the emperor Moctezuma and later entirely rebuilt by Hernán Cortés. The pawn shop was established in 1775 by the Count of Regla, who made his fortune from the Pachuca silver mines in the state of Hidalgo, to provide poor citizens with loans on personal property at low interest rates. Unredeemed articles can be bought cheaply at periodic auctions and at retail counters, and even those who don't intend to buy will enjoy browsing through the vast quantity of antiques and other merchandise. Open Mon.-Sat.

PALACIO DEL AYUNTAMIENTO (Municipal Palace), the City Hall, faces the *Zócalo's* south side (M: Zócalo, line 2). The original building at the square's southwest corner dates from 1724. On the front arcade are coat-of-arms mosaics depicting Mexican cities, states and regions, including Coyoacán, site of the first city hall in the Valley of Mexico; the 1325 founding of Aztec capital Tenochtitlán; and the Villa Rica de la Vera Cruz, said to be the first city hall in the continental Americas. Inside are archives and portraits of Mexican rulers. In front of the palace, bicycle-drawn carts can be hired to tour the Historic Center. The building east across Avenida 20 de Noviembre from the palace, also part of City Hall, is similar in appearance but was built in 1941 to provide more space for Federal District office workers.

PALACIO NACIONAL (National Palace), covering the east side of the *Zócalo* (M: Zócalo, line 2), occupies the site of Aztec emperor Moctezuma's palace. Built by slave labor under Hernán Cortés, the original structure was almost destroyed by anti-Spanish mobs in 1692 and had to be rebuilt. Portions of the original building still exist in the extreme rear.

This was the official residence of the viceroys from 1698 until the establishment of the republic in 1821; since then it has housed the offices of the president and other government officials. Changes to this immense complex of rooms, stairways and brass-adorned balconies have been made from time to time, the most recent being the addition of the top floor in the late 1920s.

The palace's chief attraction is the series of historical murals by Diego Rivera, which took some 25 years to execute. Those on the upper level of the central courtyard and decorating the walls of the main staircase provide a mesmerizing history lesson, depicting everything from the legend of Quetzalcóatl and romantically idealized views of Aztec life before the arrival of Cortés to the bloody 1910 Revolution. Major milestones in Mexican history are shown in imaginative detail, along with those individuals who helped shape the events—Spanish *conquistadores* (whom Rivera rendered in grotesque fashion) as well as such national heroes as Father Miguel Hidalgo, Benito Juárez and Emiliano Zapata. Karl Marx and surrealist Frida Kahlo, Rivera's wife, also appear.

Hanging over the central doorway is the Independence Bell. It was tolled by Father Miguel Hidalgo on the night of Sept. 15, 1810, in Dolores Hidalgo *(see separate listing under Central Mexico)* to call the Mexican people to arms. At 11 p.m. on Sept. 15 the president rings the bell in an annual re-enactment of the *Grito de Dolores*, Hidalgo's plea for freedom from Spanish rule. The former **Chamber of Deputies** on the second floor is preserved as it appeared when it was the location for the adoption of the liberal Constitution of 1857. Rooms around the chamber display historical items relating to the Mexican Congress. Guides are available for tours of the palace and the murals. Open daily. Free.

Museo Benito Juárez (Benito Juárez Museum) is on the palace's second floor. Juárez died in these living quarters, which display objects associated with his life and impact on Mexican history.

TEMPLO MAYOR (Great Temple of the Aztecs) encompasses several city blocks just north of the *Zócalo* and the National Palace; the site entrance is at calles Guatemala and Licenciado Verdad (M: Zócalo, line 2). The Great Temple, or Teocalli, was a monumental pyramid that served as the religious, political and sacrificial center of the Aztec empire. The ruins, located in the heart of today's metropolis, are striking evidence of a separate civilization that flourished hundreds of years earlier.

In Case of Emergency

Persons needing legal assistance should contact the Protección Legal al Turista (Tourist Protection) department at the Secretaría de Turismo (the Ministry of Tourism, or SECTUR). Headquarters is at Presidente Masaryk #172 (in the Polanco neighborhood); phone (5) 250-4434 or 250-6603 (English spoken). SECTUR'S 24-hour hotline can also help tourists in difficulty or coordinate aid in an emergency; phone (5) 250-0123 or 250-0151.

The U.S. Embassy, Paseo de la Reforma #305 (M: Sevilla or Insurgentes, line 1), phone (5) 209-9100, has a protection officer on 24-hour duty to advise you in case of such serious trouble as robbery, assault, major loss, accident, illness or death. In any event, Mexican law takes precedence and must be observed. The embassy also has lists of attorneys and translators on file.

In general, the police in Mexico City should be contacted only as a last resort. If your car is stolen, however, you must report it to the police, for you will be liable for any subsequent crimes committed in or with the vehicle. Phone (5) 588-5100 for police headquarters, or dial 06. An all-purpose emergency number (dial 08) can provide help to tourists who have been victims of a crime and need to file a police report; English is not likely to be spoken.

The city agency LOCATEL can help coordinate a search for missing persons and vehicles as well as provide assistance to those in need of public services; phone (5) 658-1111 (English may be spoken). For consumer protection issues, contact the Procuraduría del Consumidor (Consumer's Attorney); phone (5) 761-3811.

Medical assistance is available from the American British Cowdray (ABC) Hospital, in the southern part of the city at Calle Sur #136 and Avenida Observatorio (M: Observatorio, line 1, west bus terminal); phone (5) 230-8000. All major credit cards are accepted. The Mexican Red Cross (Cruz Roja), Ejército Nacional #1032 in the Polanco neighborhood, is open 24 hours; phone (5) 557-5757.

A list of English-speaking doctors, their locations and areas of expertise is normally available from the U.S. Embassy; the Canadian Embassy, phone (5) 254-3288; the British Embassy, Lerma #71 (2 blocks north of Paseo de la Reforma), phone (5) 596-6333; and your hotel desk.

The human sacrifices were performed as part of a ritual based on an Aztec legend involving Coyolxauhqui, goddess of the moon, and her brother Huitzilopochtli, a warrior and god of the sun. The daughter of Coatlicue, goddess of life and death, Coyolxauhqui was decapitated and dismembered by an avenging Huitzilopochtli for advocating to her 400 other brothers that their mother be murdered. Those brothers were wiped out as well and in the process became the planets and stars.

Steep steps led to twin shrines atop the Great Temple, one devoted to Huitzilopochtli and the other to Tlaloc, god of rain. Aztec citizens, as well as prisoners from other tribes captured during war, were killed and hurled down the temple's sides in a re-enactment of the battle between brother and sister; the blood of the sacrificial victims provided an offering for Huitzilopochtli and an assurance that the sun would again rise on a new day.

Demolished and buried by the conquering Spaniards, the structure—originally thought to be beneath the nearby Metropolitan Cathedral—was rediscovered in 1978 by a subway construction worker who stopped digging when his shovel struck a hard object—which turned out to be an 8-ton monolith of Coyolxauhqui, part of the pyramid's base. What at first glance appear to be simply demolished building foundations are actually the temple remains.

The excavated ruins reveal successive layers of older temples, each built atop the other as the Aztecs consolidated their empire. The site includes several other structures and sculptures scattered around the temple foundations as well as a *tzompantli*, or wall of skulls, an eerie reminder of the Aztecs' bloodthirsty nature. Signs in Spanish explain the origin of the different temples. English-speaking guides are available. Site open Tues.-Sun. 9-5. Admission is charged; free to all Sun. There is an additional charge to use a camera.

Museo Templo Mayor (Great Temple Museum), avenidas Guatemala and Seminario within the site, provides a valuable historical perspective, especially for those unfamiliar with Aztec lore. On display are more than 7,000 items recovered from the site and locations as far away as the present-day states of Veracruz and Guerrero. There are eight exhibit rooms (*salas*) on different levels, organized around a central open space dominated by the original discovery, the enormous stone depicting a beheaded and limbless Coyolxauhqui.

A scale reproduction of Tenochtitlán shows how the Aztec capital might have looked at its peak, and a cutaway model of the Great Temple illustrates its layers and methods of construction. A room devoted to war and human sacrifice helps convey the remarkable complexity of Aztec religious beliefs. The destruction of Tenochtitlán by Hernán Cortés and his followers is recounted, as are the commercial and governmental dealings of the Aztec empire. A motley group of stuffed animals represent those species known and utilized during Aztec times. Among the more impressive artifacts are life-size, terra-cotta eagle warrior statues and stone masks that were offered as tributes by subjugated tribes. Guided tours in English are available. Open same hours as the site.

ZOCALO (SOH-cah-loh), or Plaza de la Constitución, is at the east end of the main business district (M: Zócalo, line 2). Bounded by avenidas Corregidora, Seminario (Pino Suárez), Madero and Monte de Piedad, the *Zócalo* has been the center of national life and the scene of historical events since the Aztec era. This vast, bare, open expanse of concrete covers nearly 10 acres; only Moscow's Red Square is larger. Emperor Moctezuma's palace and the Templo Mayor stood on the site when the Spanish made their way into the city of Tenochtitlán and proceeded to tear it to the ground. *Zócalo*, which means "base of a pedestal," refers to a monument to independence commissioned by dictator Antonio López de Santa Anna in the mid-19th century; only its base was completed. The word was later used to denote the public square in the center of any Mexican village or town.

The *Zócalo* follows the Spanish blueprint for colonial settlements staked out in the Americas: a central plaza surrounded by a cathedral and government buildings. Some of the remains of pre-Conquest structures were used to build the Metropolitan Cathedral, the National Palace and the old mansions in the vicinity of the square. The renowned **Stone of the Sun** (Piedra del Sol), on display in the National Museum of Anthropology, was discovered in the churchyard of the cathedral in 1790.

A Mexican flag planted in the center of the plaza looks down on fluttering pigeons, scrambling children and embracing lovers, while traffic crawls unceasingly around its four corners. This is an uninhibitedly public meetingplace; Mexicans come here to protest and celebrate as well as to stroll. Destitute beggars outside the cathedral underscore life's harshness, and regular demonstrations are a reminder of the country's social inequities.

Even so, the *Zócalo* vibrates with everyday life. Vendors set up shop in front of the cathedral and along Avenida Seminario between the cathedral and the Templo Mayor site, selling everything from postcards to Mexican jumping beans. Frequently there are dancers and musicians performing for the crowds. Pungent aromas fill the block of Calzada Tacuba just north of the cathedral, which is dense with little shops and tiny takeout eateries. Old buildings hug this narrow thoroughfare, which is all clamor and hubbub. The commercial blocks around the *Zócalo*, long neglected, are slowly being restored to their colonial-era attractiveness.

Special events are held regularly. An elaborate flag-lowering ceremony performed daily at 6 p.m. is filled with the flourishes of formal pomp

A formal flag-lowering ceremony takes place daily at the Zócalo.   ©Chris Sharp

and circumstance. Hundreds of thousands of people flock to the square for the Sept. 15 and 16 Independence Day celebrations. (For a panoramic view of either proceeding, sit outside on the seventh-floor dining terrace at the **Majestic Hotel**, Avenida Madero on the west side of the Zócalo.) On other occasions protests and political rallies, accompanied by blaring megaphones and impassioned speechmaking, are an example of democracy at work in one of Latin America's most populous nations.

Note: This is a very crowded, congested part of the city. Do not even attempt to negotiate the traffic or find a place to park on your own. If you want to walk around and explore for an hour or so, hire a licensed guide, a private driver or a hotel taxi to drop you off, wait and then take you back to where you're staying. Avoid the Zócalo and surrounding streets after dark.

WITHIN THE HISTORIC CENTER

EX-COLEGIO DE SAN ILDEFONSO (Ex-College of San Ildefonso) is north of the Templo Mayor at Justo Sierra #16 (M: Zócalo, line 2). It occupies an outstanding colonial edifice built in 1749 as the Jesuit School of San Ildefonso. The building later housed the **Escuela Nacional Preparatoria** (National Preparatory School); after that college's educational programs were moved to other buildings it was converted to a museum. The renovated structure's three floors now contain colonial works of art; paintings by Fernando Leal and David Alfaro Siqueiros; and traveling exhibitions.

Especially worth seeing are the José Clemente Orozco murals depicting post-Revolutionary Mexico that surround the main patio. Some of his frescoes utilize the existing architecture as part of the overall design. Orozco's leftist politics are evident in such murals as "Return to the Battlefield," which strikingly conveys war's human tragedy. Open Tues.-Sun. 11-6 (also Wed. 6-9 p.m.). Admission is charged; over 59 and under 13 free. Free to all Sun.

EX-CONVENTO Y TEMPLO DE REGINA (Ex-Convent and Temple of Regina Coeli) is about 5 blocks southwest of the Zócalo at calles Regina and Bolívar (M: Isabel la Católica, line 1). It was founded by Conceptualist nuns in 1573 along the canals of Tenochtitlán. The sumptuous **Medina-Picasso Chapel**, built in 1733, capped 2 centuries of reconstructions and additions that left the convent encompassing an entire block. Marble altars, colonial-era paintings, and carved and gilded wooden statues of the saints grace its interior. On the left inside wall is a balcony once used by the nuns for Mass; an ancient organ is the centerpiece of the huge choir mezzanine.

IGLESIA DE SANTO DOMINGO (Church of Santo Domingo), on República de Venezuela (M: Allende, line 2), faces the north side of Santo Domingo Plaza. The original church, destroyed by a flood, was the first founded in Mexico by the Dominicans; it may have been the burial place of explorer Francisco Vásquez de Coronado. The present building, dating from 1736, has a beautiful baroque exterior highlighted by ornately carved Corinthian columns. Inside is a chapel containing milagros, offerings given by the devout in thanks for a miraculous cure from infirmity or disease.

IGLESIA Y HOSPITAL DE JESUS (Church and Hospital of Jesus) are 3 blocks south of the Zócalo on República del Salvador between 20 de Noviembre and Pino Suárez (M: Pino Suárez, lines 1 and 2). The first hospital in Mexico is said to stand on the site where Hernán Cortés and Aztec emperor Moctezuma first met in 1519; a stone monument on Pino Suárez next to the church commemorates the occasion. The chapel has an entrance on Salvador at Pino Suárez; inside are Cortés' remains. A plaque marking the tomb of the conquistador can be seen on the left wall of the main altar. The dramatic José Clemente Orozco mural "Apocalypse" covers the ceiling and upper walls of the church's choir mezzanine. Chapel open daily.

MUSEO DE LA CIUDAD DE MEXICO (Museum of Mexico City) is 3 blocks south of the Zócalo at Pino Suárez #30, near República del Salvador (M: Pino Suárez, line 2). Massive carved wooden doors open onto the central courtyard of this grand former mansion, built shortly after the Conquest as a private residence for the Count of Santiago de Calimaya. Constructed of reddish tezontle stone, it features timbered ceilings and friezes of cannons protruding from the outer walls. Supporting the building's northeastern corner, at Pino Suárez and Salvador, is a huge pre-Hispanic sculpture of a plumed serpent's head representing the god Quetzalcóatl.

In addition to some exhibits chronicling the city's history, the museum displays works by Mexican impressionist Joaquín Clausell. Tues.-Sun. 10-5:30. Admission is charged.

MUSEO JOSE LUIS CUEVAS (José Luis Cuevas Museum) is at Calle Academia #13, 2 blocks east of the Zócalo. This collection of modern art is housed in a restored ex-convent. One of the country's most highly regarded—and controversial—contemporary artists, the museum features his monumental sculpture "The Giantess." Temporary exhibitions feature emerging Latin American artists. Tues.-Sun. 10-6. Admission is charged.

PALACIO DE ITURBIDE (Iturbide Palace), west of the Zócalo at Avenida Madero #17 near Bolívar (M: Bellas Artes, lines 2 and 8), is a highly ornate neo-Renaissance mansion built in the late 18th century for a wealthy Spanish count. The palace, constructed of a combination of gray and volcanic tezontle stone, reflects the Italianate style and is highlighted by a huge archway over

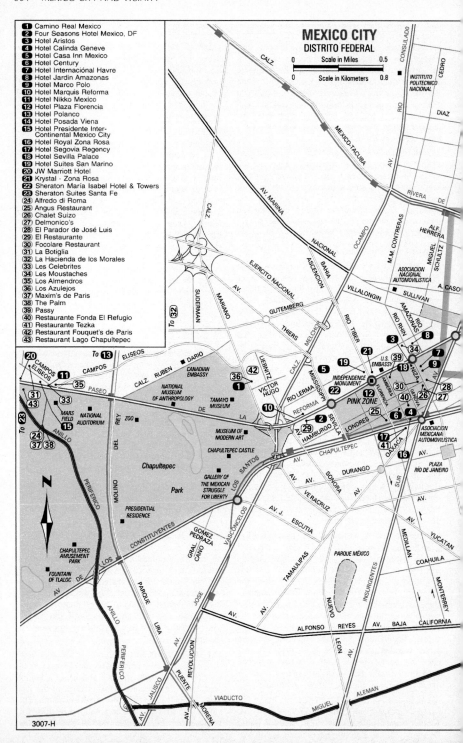

1 Camino Real Mexico
2 Four Seasons Hotel Mexico, DF
3 Hotel Aristos
4 Hotel Calinda Geneve
5 Hotel Casa Inn Mexico
6 Hotel Century
7 Hotel Internacional Havre
8 Hotel Jardin Amazonas
9 Hotel Marco Polo
10 Hotel Marquis Reforma
11 Hotel Nikko Mexico
12 Hotel Plaza Florencia
13 Hotel Polanco
14 Hotel Posada Viena
15 Hotel Presidente Inter-
   Continental Mexico City
16 Hotel Royal Zona Rosa
17 Hotel Segovia Regency
18 Hotel Sevilla Palace
19 Hotel Suites San Marino
20 JW Marriott Hotel
21 Krystal - Zona Rosa
22 Sheraton María Isabel Hotel & Towers
23 Sheraton Suites Santa Fe
24 Alfredo di Roma
25 Angus Restaurant
26 Chalet Suizo
27 Delmonico's
28 El Parador de José Luis
29 El Restaurante
30 Focolare Restaurant
31 La Botiglia
32 La Hacienda de los Morales
33 Les Celebrites
34 Les Moustaches
35 Los Almendros
36 Los Azulejos
37 Maxim's de Paris
38 The Palm
39 Passy
40 Restaurante Fonda El Refugio
41 Restaurante Tezka
42 Restaurant Fouquet's de Paris
43 Restaurant Lago Chapultepec

MEXICO CITY
DISTRITO FEDERAL

Scale in Miles
0   0.5

Scale in Kilometers
0   0.8

3007-H

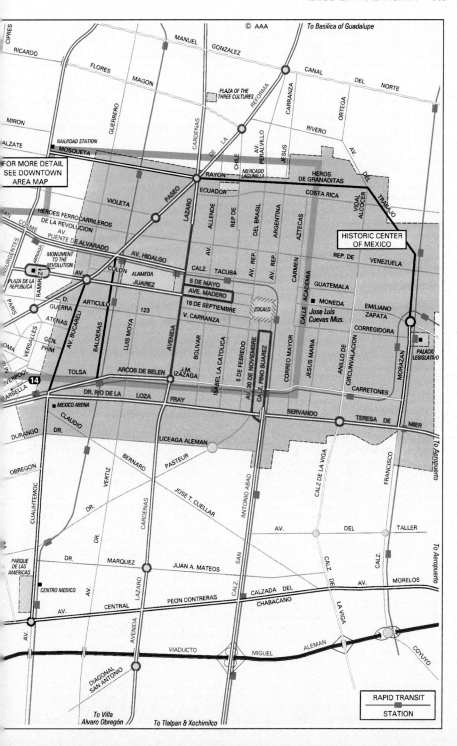

the front doors. It was occupied by self-proclaimed emperor Agustín de Iturbide 1821-23, and now houses a Banamex bank branch. Open to the public, the interior features a colonnaded courtyard with three tiers of balconies and is elegantly appointed with paintings and sculptures. A ground-floor gallery is the site of temporary art exhibitions. Open daily 10-6. Free.

PLAZA DE SANTO DOMINGO (Santo Domingo Plaza), 3 blocks northwest of the *Zócalo*, is bounded by República de Venezuela, República de Peru, República de Chile and República de Brasil (M: Zócalo, line 2). This is one of the best preserved colonial squares in the city. Dating from about 1550, the plaza is surrounded by charming old buildings. It is also the home of *los evangelistas*. These professional typists, writers and editors ply their trades from under arcades on the west side of the plaza, a service begun by public scribes in the 1850s for citizens unable to write. Typists produce everything from love letters to university term papers, and hand-operated presses churn out business cards, wedding invitations and other printed matter.

On the opposite end of the plaza at Brasil and Venezuela is the **Museo de Medicina Mexicana** (Museum of Mexican Medicine), in the former headquarters of the Palacio de la Inquisición (Inquisition Palace). For more than 2 centuries, Mexican heretics and those who opposed Spanish rule were punished in the palace's dungeons. Museum exhibits chart Mexico's medical advances from pre-Hispanic herbal cures to modern vaccines. Information is given in Spanish only. Open daily 10-6.

SECRETARIA DE EDUCACION PUBLICA (Ministry of Public Education) is north of the Templo Mayor at República de Argentina #28 (M: Zócalo, line 2). The walls of this building were perhaps Diego Rivera's greatest canvas; almost every space on the three floors is covered with murals symbolizing Mexican life, history and culture. While other artists contributed, it is Rivera's work that stands out. It was executed during the mid-1920s and commissioned by poet, philosopher and education minister José Vasconcelos as part of a program to promote the nation's heritage for a citizenry that was largely illiterate.

The first floor contains images of daily rural life, depictions of industry and the celebration of such truly Mexican festivities as the Day of the Dead. Notably missing from these scenes is Rivera's customary political satire; instead, he emphasized national pride. The muralist's habit of incorporating existing architectural details into his artworks also is evident. Panels on the second and third floors focus on Mexican workers, the nation's heroic leaders, the 1910 Revolution and such familiar Rivera targets as capitalist greed. Open Mon.-Fri. Free.

SUPREMA CORTE DE JUSTICIA (Supreme Court of Justice) is just south of the Palacio Nacional at Pino Suárez and Corregidora. Although built in the mid-1930s, it resembles the many colonial buildings found in this part of the city. The court's second-floor walls are covered with sardonic murals by José Clemente Orozco depicting workers' rights, nationalism and concepts of justice. Open Mon.-Fri.

Calle Corregidora runs between the court building and the Palacio Nacional. During pre-Conquest times a canal traversed this area, part of a system that connected Tenochtitlán to other Aztec centers around Lake Texcoco. Most of the canals disappeared as the lake diminished, although they are still in evidence around Xochimilco. Today evidence of the ancient waterway can still be seen, although Corregidora is now a pedestrian-only thoroughfare filled with vendor stalls.

ALAMEDA CENTRAL AND VICINITY

ALAMEDA CENTRAL (Alameda Park) is a green retreat in the middle of Mexico City's concrete jungle. This rectangular, centrally located park lies just west of the Palace of Fine Arts between avenidas Juárez and Hidalgo. Two Metro stations are close by: Hidalgo (lines 2 and 3) is at the intersection of Hidalgo and Paseo de la Reforma, a block off the park's northwest corner; Bellas Artes (lines 2 and 8) is at the park's northeast corner. The Alameda is surrounded by museums, theaters, cinemas, and first-class hotels and restaurants.

The Alameda is landscaped with poplars (*alamos,* from which the park received its name), as well as ash and willow trees, and contains fountains, 19th-century French sculptures and a Moorish kiosk. The land, originally the site of an Aztec market, was set aside in 1592 as a place for privileged Spanish aristocrats to stroll; more notoriously, it was the scene of burnings during the Inquisition. Today city dwellers of every description crowd this green space. Sundays typically bring out the crowds, with families, cotton candy and ice cream vendors, and lovers of all ages sharing the park. Organ grinders delight children, and there are free music concerts.

The **Juárez Hemiciclo** (Juárez Monument) faces Avenida Juárez along the park's southern boundary ("hemiciclo" refers to the monument's semicircular design). It honors the liberal president of Mexico (1858-72); his marble statue sits on a pedestal surrounded by columns. Juárez's March 21 birthday is celebrated at the park.

CASA DE LOS AZULEJOS (House of Tiles), Avenida Francisco Madero #4, about 2 blocks east of the Alameda (M: Bellas Artes, lines 2 and 8), is one of the city's finest colonial mansions. It was built in 1596 to be the residence of the Counts of Orizaba. A popular story relates that the son of one of the counts, considered a failure by his father, was told, "You will never build a house of tiles," meaning that he would never amount to anything. When success did come, the son had the entire exterior of the house covered with decorative blue and white tiles from Puebla. The bronze balustrade was brought from China. The flagship of the **Sanborn's** restaurant chain has occupied the building since 1919. Stop in for a look at the recently renovated main dining room and the Orozco mural that adorns the wall of the huge staircase. On the first floor is a drugstore selling everything from silver jewelry to personal toiletries. Open daily.

CORREO MAYOR (Main Post Office) is on the corner of avenidas Tacuba and Eje Central Lázaro Cárdenas across from the Palace of Fine Arts (M: Bellas Artes, lines 2 and 8). Built between 1902 and 1907, the handsome white stone building was designed by Italian architect Adamo Boari in the Renaissance style. The interior boasts richly carved woodwork. Within the building, a museum displays stamp collections and antique Mexican postal equipment, and a philatelic office sells selected Mexican stamps. Museum open Mon.-Fri. 9-6, Sat. 10-2.

IGLESIA DE SAN FERNANDO (Church of San Fernando), northwest of Alameda park at Guerrero #39 (M: Hidalgo, lines 2 and 3), is what remains of a former monastery built for Fernandino monks 1735-55. The Churrigueresque facade survived the monastery's dismantlement after the monks were expelled in 1860. The adjacent cemetery, the **Rotonda de los Hombres Ilustres** (Rotunda of Illustrious Men), holds the remains of several prominent figures in Mexican history, including former president Benito Juárez.

IGLESIA DE SAN FRANCISCO (Church of San Francisco) is on Avenida Madero, 2 blocks east of Alameda Park and almost directly across from Sanborn's (M: Bellas Artes, lines 2 and 8). Begun in 1524 with money granted by Hernán Cortés, it was long the center of Catholicism in America and headquarters of the Franciscan Order. The original complex, fragments of which are still visible, also comprised a monastery and training school for Franciscan missionaries. The present church dates from the 18th century and has an elaborately Churrigueresque facade.

MUSEO FRANZ MAYER (Franz Mayer Museum) is at Avenida Hidalgo #45 (Plaza de la Santa Veracruz), opposite the north side of Alameda Park (M: Bellas Artes, lines 2 and 8). This handsomely restored 16th-century building once served as a wheat-weighing station, hospital and convent. Today it houses one of the largest antiques collections in Mexico. The 10,000-odd pieces were amassed entirely by Mayer, a German immigrant who settled here in the early 20th century and donated the entire collection to his adopted country upon his death in 1975.

Because of Mayer's fondness for the applied arts, the items on view are all utilitarian in nature, though hardly ordinary. The treasures include ceramics, religious works in gold and silver, silver sculpture, wooden furniture, an impressive assortment of Talavera tiles, ceremonial crosses, textiles, rare timepieces, and a collection of more than 700 editions of "Don Quixote," many of them rare. Paintings by Mexican and European artists also are displayed. Guided tours are available. A pleasant café is located in the building's courtyard. Open Tues.-Sun. 10-5. Admission is charged; over 59 and under 13 free. Free to all Sun. Phone (5) 518-2265.

MUSEO MURAL DIEGO RIVERA (Diego Rivera Mural Museum) is at calles Balderas and Colón, just west of Alameda Park (M: Hidalgo, lines 2 and 3). It was built specifically to house Rivera's epic mural "Dream of a Sunday Afternoon in the Alameda Central," which had originally been painted on a wall of the Hotel del Prado across the street. Although the hotel was torn down following damage caused by the 1985 earthquake, the mural weathered the disaster and was carefully moved to this museum.

The central figures enjoying a Sunday promenade in the park are the artist (portrayed as a child); his wife, fellow painter Frida Kahlo; and a clothed skeleton representing satirist José Guadalupe Posada. They are surrounded by a gallery of Mexican historical characters—Hernán Cortés, Benito Juárez, Gen. António López de Santa Anna, Archduke Maximilian and Empress Carlota, Porfirio Díaz and others. Exhibits chronicle the mural's creation—Rivera provoked controversy by inscribing the words "God does not exist" on a placard held up by one figure—and the prodigious effort to transport it to its new home. Open Tues.-Sun. 10-2 and 3-6. Admission is charged; free to all Sun.

MUSEO NACIONAL DE ARTE (National Museum of Art) is at Calzada Tacuba #8, directly east of the Palace of Fine Arts (M: Bellas Artes, lines 2 and 8). Collections of sculpture, graphics and paintings trace the history and development of Mexican art from pre-Hispanic times up to 1950. The lobby features three late 19th-century sculptures created by Mexican artists, but with a decided French influence: "Aprés L'Orgie" (After the Orgy), "Desespoir" (Despair) and "Malgré Tout" (In Spite of It All).

The palatial building was designed by Italian architect Silvio Contri in 1904 to be the Palace of Communications; it was taken over by the museum in the early 1980s. Paintings by celebrated 19th-century landscape artist José María Velasco fill the third floor of this museum, including sweeping landscapes of Oaxaca and the Valley of Mexico. There also is a comprehensive overview of 20th-century painters. Open Tues.-Sun. 10-5. Admission is charged; over 59, students and under 13 free. Free to all Sun. Phone (5) 512-3224.

El Caballito (The Little Horse), in front of the museum, is the work of Manuel Tolsá. The 30-ton sculpture, showing King Charles IV of Spain astride his horse, is considered one of the world's finest equestrian statues. It was cast in 1803 from a single piece of bronze; the heat generated from the casting process was said to be so intense that the sculptor lost all his teeth.

Across Tacuba from the museum is the **Palacio de Minería**, another architecturally impressive building that dates from the early 19th century; it contains the offices of mining authorities and an engineering school.

MUSEO NACIONAL DE ARTES Y INDUSTRIAS POPULARES (National Museum of Popular Arts and Industries) is at Avenida Juárez #44, opposite the south side of Alameda Park (M: Bellas Artes, lines 2 and 8). The museum is in the old Church of Corpus Christi, part of a convent established in 1724 for Indian noblewomen. Almost everything is for sale as well as on display, and the exhibits encompass arts and crafts from throughout Mexico. Open daily. Phone (5) 521-6679.

MUSEO NACIONAL DE LA ESTAMPA (National Museum of Engraving), at Hidalgo #39 next to the Franz Mayer Museum (M: Bellas Artes, lines 2 and 8), focuses on the graphic arts. The second floor has permanent exhibits, notably the pointed political cartoons and cavorting skeleton figures of 19th-century Mexican artist José Guadalupe Posada. Temporary exhibits featuring the work of contemporary artists are mounted on the first floor. Open Tues.-Sun. 10-6. Admission is charged.

PALACIO DE BELLAS ARTES (Palace of Fine Arts) faces Avenida Juárez at the east end of Alameda Park (M: Bellas Artes, lines 2 and 8). A legacy of Porfirio Díaz's economically progressive but politically oppressive regime, the palace was begun in 1904, interrupted by the Revolution of 1910 and finally dedicated in 1934. This ornate, white marble structure was designed and executed mainly by Italian architects and sculptors; its exterior epitomizes the adoption of grand European styles characteristic of turn-of-the-20th-century public buildings in Mexico. Because of its enormous weight and the softness of the underlying soil, the building—like many others in the city—has settled considerably since its construction, and thousands of tons of concrete have been pumped underneath it to prevent further sinking.

Inside an art deco look prevails. This is the city's cultural center; it houses the national opera, national theater and the National Symphony Orchestra. The walls of the second and third floors are covered with outstanding murals by

Palacio de Bellas Artes　　　　　　　©John Neubauer

José Clemente Orozco, Diego Rivera, David Alfaro Siqueiros and Rufino Tamayo. Especially noteworthy is Rivera's work "Man in Control of His Universe," originally commissioned for New York City's Rockefeller Center in 1933 to illustrate the theme "Man at the Crossroads." His caustic rendering of capitalism and depiction of workers rallying behind socialist Vladimir Lenin angered the Rockefeller family, who had the mural destroyed; Rivera re-created it for the palace the following year.

In addition to the murals, there is a permanent collection of paintings, mostly by 19th-century Mexican artists. Major traveling art exhibitions also are mounted. Open Tues.-Sun. 10-6. Admission is charged to see the murals. Phone (5) 510-1388.

Ballet Folklórico is a theatrically colorful spectacle showcasing the legacy of Mexican folk music and dance. Two companies, one touring and the other resident, alternate performances in the palace theater, and their choreographed skills are indeed something to see. Shows take place Wed. and Sun. at 9 p.m.; also Sun. mornings at 9:30. Admission is charged. For ticket information phone (5) 510-1388 or 709-3111 *(also see "Concerts," page 326).*

The theater itself is famed for its 22-ton Tiffany glass curtain, designed by Mexican painter Gerardo Murillo (Dr. Atl) and executed by Louis

Comfort Tiffany in 1910. This art nouveau masterpiece is made of nearly 1 million pieces of colored glass and forms the backdrop for a spectacular illumination display. As lights play upon the multitude of glass pieces, the Valley of Mexico and twin volcanoes Popocatépetl and Iztaccíhuatl take shape. The half-hour show is given only on Sunday mornings before the matinee performance of the Ballet Folklórico.

PINACOTECA VIRREINAL DE SAN DIEGO (Museum of Colonial Painting) is on Dr. Mora #7, facing the west side of Alameda Park (M: Hidalgo, lines 2 and 3). It contains a display of primarily religious paintings by such 16th-, 17th- and 18th-century artists as Cristóbal de Villalpando, Miguel Cabrera, Simón Pereyns and José Juárez. A highlight is the Federico Cantú mural "Musician Angels and Indigenous Friars." The beautiful Franciscan church in which the artworks are displayed was once a monastery and dates from 1591. Open Tues.-Sun. 9-5. Admission is charged; teachers and students with ID, over 59 and under 13 free. Free to all Sun. Phone (5) 510-2793.

TORRE LATINOAMERICANA (Latin-American Tower), avenidas Madero and Lázaro Cárdenas (M: Bellas Artes, lines 2 and 8), is a 44-story glass skyscraper, at one time the city's tallest. Since Mexico City has no bedrock on which to build foundations, the tower rests on floating piers sunk deep into the underlying clay; it has survived every earth tremor occurring since its 1956 construction. Admission is charged to the observation area at the top of the structure, where rare smog-free days offer magnificent views of the city and its surrounding mountains; a better bet might be to take in the view at night, when a multitude of lights illuminate the metropolis. Open daily.

CHAPULTEPEC PARK AND THE ZONA ROSA

BOSQUE DE CHAPULTEPEC (Chapultepec Park) sprawls on either side of Paseo de la Reforma beginning about 4 blocks west of the Zona Rosa (M: Chapultepec, line 1; Auditorio and Constituyentes, line 7). It is the oldest natural park in North America and one of the largest and most varied in the world. The Aztecs, upon reaching the Valley of Mexico, first settled in this area. After the establishment of Tenochtitlán, Aztec emperors used Chapultepec Hill (within today's park) for summer relaxation, a practice continued after the Conquest by Spanish viceroys.

The *ahuehuetes* (cypresses) growing throughout the park were once used as a hunting preserve; many are centuries old, and some stand nearly 200 feet tall. One of the oldest, the **Tree of Moctezuma**, is 43 feet in circumference and stands near the main entrance.

Chapultepec Park is sometimes referred to as the lungs of the city, and indeed it takes a pounding. Grassy areas must endure the trampling of millions of feet, and the odd pile of litter can make it look somewhat run-down. But despite the wear and tear it's fascinating to stroll along the cobbled walkways, as much for the people-watching as anything else. You won't see many foreign tourists here; the park is very much a gathering place for city residents.

Sunday is the best day to visit. Almost everything is free, and families converge to enjoy their day off at this enormous green space and its zoo, lakes, botanic garden, museums and playgrounds—picnicking, listening to free concerts, or attending soccer games and other sporting events. Food cart vendors do a brisk business in sodas, ice cream, hamburgers, hot dogs, *churros* (a doughnut-like snack), homemade potato chips, pork rinds, cut-up fruit and candy. Other carts sell balloons, toys and stuffed animals.

Chapultepec is more or less divided into three sections. Near the main entrance of the eastern section (the oldest) is the **Monumento de los Niños Héroes** (Monument to the Child Heroes). The group of columns memorializes six cadets who were among those defending Chapultepec Castle, then a military college, against American troops at the height of the Mexican-American War in 1847. They reputedly leaped to their deaths wrapped in the Mexican flag rather than be captured. Some of the city's most notable cultural institutions are grouped here, including the **National Museum of Anthropology**, the **Museum of Modern Art**, the **Rufino Tamayo Museum** and the **National Museum of History** in Chapultepec Castle.

Rowboats can be rented at **Lago de Chapultepec** (Chapultepec Lake), in the heart of the old section. The **Casa del Lago** (Lake House), on the lake's western shore, functions as a cultural center and as a setting for public events. West of the lake is the **Jardín Botánico** (Botanical Garden). Just off Gran Avenida is the **Don Quixote Fountain**, which memorializes Cervantes' hero; his story is pictured in the tiles of the seats. A mural by Diego Rivera covering the bottom of the fountain depicts the evolution of life by water. The tanks in the vicinity receive water from the Río Lerma, west of Mexico City.

The section of the park west of Molino del Rey is newer. **Los Pinos** (The Pines), the president's residence, is just east of Molino del Rey; it is heavily guarded and cannot be visited. The **Chapultepec Amusement Park**, on the western side of the Anillo Periférico, is dominated by a giant roller coaster called "montaña rusa" (Russian mountain). The general admission charge includes a number of free rides.

South of the amusement park is the **Museo Tecnológico Moderno** (Museum of Modern Technology), a pyramidal structure with a planetarium and exhibits on aviation, energy, science and industry. Kids will enjoy the **Papalote Museo del Niño** (Children's Museum), at Avenida de los Constituyentes and the Anillo Periférico. Themed sections explore the human body, science, computers and artistic expression, among other subjects. In addition to numerous hands-on activities, it features an IMAX[theater. It is open daily 9-1 and 2-6 (also Thurs. 7-11 p.m.).

The park's newest section, which contains two man-made lakes, is less congested. The **Museo de Historia Natural** (Museum of Natural History) consists of 10 interconnecting domes that house nature dioramas and biological, geological and astronomical exhibits. A highlight is the museum's insect collection. Along the northern edge of the park, Paseo de la Reforma passes the 18,500-seat **National Auditorium**, high-rise hotels and office buildings before circling around **Plaza Petróleos**, where a monument pays tribute to the nationalization of the oil industry in the 1930s by President Lázaro Cárdenas. Farther west lies **Lomas de Chapultepec** (Chapultepec Hills), an exclusive residential area of walled estates.

Beyond the museums and amusements but still within the park is the national cemetery, where many of Mexico's noted artists, military leaders, political figures and important citizens have been laid to rest. A map is available at the entrance building. The cemetery is open daily.

If you plan to spend most of the day and would rather not sample the offerings of food vendors, bring a lunch. The park is open daily; most of its attractions are closed on Monday. Admission is free; separate admissions are charged for attractions. Most are free on Sunday.

Zoológico de Chapultepec (Chapultepec Park Zoo) is south of Paseo de la Reforma at Calzada Chivatito, near the National Museum of Anthropology. It was recently renovated and now displays giant pandas (this is one of the few zoos to have successfully bred them in captivity), a white tiger and other animals in natural habitats that have replaced the former steel cages. Children can ride ponies, a goat cart and a miniature train; train fare is charged. Open Tues.-Sun.

CASTILLO DE CHAPULTEPEC (Chapultepec Castle), in Chapultepec Park (M: Chapultepec, line 1), stands atop a 200-foot-high hill overlooking the central part of the city. This stony outcrop was once used by Aztec emperors as a summer retreat, and their likenesses were carved into it. Almost all traces of these carvings have vanished in the centuries since the conquering Spaniards tried to obliterate them.

Construction of the castle began in 1783. Completed in 1840, it was fortified and became a military college. When it was attacked and taken in 1847 by U.S. forces during the Mexican-American War, the castle was defended solely by its young cadets. The next occupants were Archduke Maximilian and his wife, Carlota, who remodeled it into a royal residence in 1866. After passing through a succession of leaders, the castle was finally bequeathed to the nation in 1939 by President Lázaro Cárdenas.

The climb to the castle along a paved walkway winding up Chapultepec Hill is fairly steep and takes about 20 minutes. En route there are frequent views of the downtown skyline. The rather dilapidated-looking castle houses the National Museum of History *(see listing below).*

Galería de la Lucha del Pueblo Mexicano por su Libertad (Gallery of the Mexican Struggle for Liberty), halfway up the hill, is popularly known as the Museo del Caracol for its architecture, which resembles the spiral shape of a snail's shell. The hallway leads past dioramas of decisive events in Mexican history, from the Spanish arrival to the creation of the Constitution of 1917. As the full name implies, the emphasis is on the numerous conflicts the country has endured. This walk through the past ends in a chamber of red *tezontle* (volcanic) stone dominated by three objects: the national flag, a carved-stone eagle and a facsimile of the 1917 Constitution. Explanations are in Spanish. Open Tues.-Sun. Admission is charged; free to all Sun.

Museo Nacional de Historia (National Museum of History) has 11 *salas* (halls) tracing Mexican history from the Conquest to the Revolution of 1910 and the adoption of the 1917 constitution. Weapons, paintings, clothing, furniture and maps are displayed, along with portraits of leading historical figures from Hernán Cortés to 20th-century presidents. Two striking Juan O'Gorman murals depict important events in the nation's history. Exhibit information is in Spanish. Open Tues.-Sun. Admission is charged; free to all Sun. Flash photography is not permitted.

LA ZONA ROSA (Pink Zone) is about halfway between Alameda Central and Chapultepec Park (M: Insurgentes or Sevilla, line 1). Roughly bordered by Paseo de la Reforma on the north, Avenida Chapultepec on the south, Insurgentes on the east and Sevilla on the west, this was long Mexico City's trendsetting neighborhood and favored tourist hotspot. In recent years, however, the Zona Rosa's popularity has been eclipsed by the Polanco area, which now has many of the city's best hotels, restaurants and retailers. Although still filled with shops, eateries and flashy nightspots, the Zona Rosa has become worn around the edges and also attracts groups of youth gangs who prey on anyone perceived to have money. Be careful if coming here for a night out, and arrange designated hotel taxi transportation both to and from your destination.

Zona Rosa streets are named after prominent world cities, and several are reserved for pedestrians. The principal thoroughfares—**Hamburgo, Londres, Liverpool, Amberes** and **Genova**—are lined with a mix of boutiques, outdoor cafés, fast-food franchises and T-shirt emporiums. You can still find high-quality clothing, jewelry, art, antiques, leather goods and silver here. When darkness falls, the Zona Rosa is crowded with visitors and locals seeking out tables at intimate restaurants; block-long **Calle Copenhague** consists entirely of eateries. Bars, discos and rock clubs draw weekend revelers.

MONUMENTO A LA INDEPENDENCIA (Independence Monument) is in the circle at Paseo de la Reforma and Tiber (M: Insurgentes, line 1). The 150-foot-high column, dating between 1901 and 1910, is topped by a winged statue of Victory. The central figure at the base is Father Miguel Hidalgo; he is flanked by other leaders in the war for independence, including José María Morelos Nicolás Bravo. The female statues represent Law, Justice, War and Peace. This is one of several commanding landmarks that stand in the middle of *glorietas* (traffic circles) at principal intersections along Reforma; locals and visitors alike use them as geographical reference points.

MUSEO DE ARTE MODERNO (Museum of Modern Art) occupies two circular buildings on the south side of Paseo de la Reforma, near the entrance to Chapultepec Park (M: Chapultepec, line 1). The works of Diego Rivera, David Alfaro Siqueiros, Rufino Tamayo and José Clemente Orozco—Mexico's "big four" of 20th-century painting—and other contemporary Mexican and international artists are represented. This museum contains Frida Kahlo's "The Two Fridas," one of the surrealist's best-known works. Temporary exhibitions also are presented. Open Tues.-Sun. 10-5. Admission is charged; free to all Sun.

MUSEO NACIONAL DE ANTROPOLOGIA (National Museum of Anthropology) faces the north side of Paseo de la Reforma at Calzada M. Gandhi, in Chapultepec Park (M: Chapultepec, line 1). A must-see stop for any Mexico City visitor, it is one of the world's finest museums. Construction was supervised by architect Pedro Ramírez Vazquez; the museum opened to the public in 1964. At the entrance looms a 217-ton, 25-foot-tall monolith of Tláloc, the Aztec god of rain; according to local legend, the stone sculpture's move to its new home was accompanied by a violent thunderstorm in the midst of the dry season.

The museum's design incorporates great open spaces, with a central patio of basalt rock onto which all of the *salas* (exhibit halls) open. This allows visitors the option of wandering at leisure among displays that document all of Mexico's important cultures, or exploring them chronologically, room by room. One end of the central courtyard is shaded by a huge square ceiling supported by a single column; when in use, a fountain sends water cascading over the four outer edges.

Radiating from this main-floor patio are 12 exhibition halls devoted to Mexico's early civilizations. Each room focuses on a separate period or culture. The exhibits encompass every conceivable type of artifact and include temple reconstructions, stone carvings, sculptures, ceramics, antique furniture, jewelry, pottery, masks, urns, decorative objects, and arts and crafts. Glass doors open onto verandas, where you can stand and contemplate replicas of significant archeological finds displayed in a parklike setting.

The first three rooms offer a general introduction to anthropology and the rise of Mesoamerican civilization. The next rooms survey the Pre-Classic and Classic periods. One room is devoted to Teotihuacán, the first of Mexico's great pre-Hispanic cities, and another focuses on Toltec culture. Objects on view include an acrobatic figurine from Tlatilco, a reproduction of Teotihuacán's Temple of Quetzalcóatl, a huge statue of Chalchiuhtlicue, the Teotihuacán goddess of the "running waters," and displays from Cholula *(see separate listing under Central Mexico)*. An Atlantean column (a warrior representation) and a reclining Chac Mool figure are among objects taken from the Tula ruins *(see separate listing under Central Mexico)*.

Perhaps the most spectacular is the **Mexica (Aztec) Hall**. It contains a number of treasures, occasionally reorganized to make room for new discoveries from the Templo Mayor. The room's focal point is the 24-ton Aztec calendar stone, the Piedra del Sol, or Stone of the Sun, with the face of the sun god carved in its center. Scholars consider it to be more accurate than European calendars of the same period.

Recurring motifs—eagles, serpents, skulls and human hearts—are symbols of the Aztec belief that human sacrifice was necessary to appease the gods. Also on view are a replica of Moctezuma's quetzal-feathered headdress (the original is in Vienna, Austria); a vivid statue of the goddess Coatlicue, rendered beheaded and wearing a skirt of snakes; and a scale model of the center of pre-Hispanic Tenochtitlán complete with hundreds of detailed miniatures and an accompanying mural depicting the lake that once covered the area. Here and in the other halls, dramatic lighting accentuates the remarkable artistry of the larger sculptures.

The exhibits devoted to Oaxaca move the focus away from the Valley of Mexico and the surrounding highland region. There are objects taken from the archeological zones of Monte Albán (Zaptoec) and Mitla (Mixtec). Vases and urns take the form of various gods, and one jade mask is shaped like a bat. Among the pottery pieces is a bowl with a hummingbird delicately perched on the rim. The **Gulf of Mexico Hall** is dominated by Olmec art, including a massive carved stone head with a typical combination of jaguar and human features. There also are some exquisite jade figurines. Particularly notable is the sculpted piece known as "The Wrestler" for its figure's stance.

Another highlight is the **Maya Hall**, which spotlights a culture that was arguably the most advanced in all Mesoamerica. While the artifacts displayed here may not equal the grandeur of their lavishly decorated temples—the singular Maya architectural achievement—they affirm the beauty of Maya art. Many of the ceramic figurines, pieces of jewelry and death masks were retrieved from burial sites. An outdoor garden features excellent reproductions of the famous murals found at Bonampak, in the state of Chiapas. The room devoted to northern and western Mexico contains figurines from the state of Colima, Tarascan objects, and examples of jewelry and pottery similar to those fashioned by Native American tribes in the southwestern United States.

The second floor has a series of rooms with ethnographic exhibits relating to Mexico's present-day Indian groups. Maps, photographs, regional costumes, re-creations of dwellings, dioramas showing day-to-day activities, and examples of arts and crafts all serve to remind visitors of the fact that despite tremendous modernization, many Mexicans still live in ways similar to those of their ancestors.

Dancers at the Guadalupe Basilica   ©Chris Sharp

Because the museum is so big, the main entrance hall is a good place to begin. Here, against the backdrop of a Rufino Tamayo mural depicting the battle between a snake and a jaguar, is the desk where guided tour tickets can be purchased, a library, a room featuring special temporary exhibits, a bookstore that has English-language guides to the museum, and an orientation theater showing a 20-minute audiovisual presentation that describes the principal Mesoamerican cultures. Most exhibit labeling is in Spanish; newer exhibits also include an English translation. Guided tours in Spanish, English and French are given Tues.-Sat. 9:30-5:30; a fee is charged.

To avoid museum overload, concentrate on the highlight rooms (Teotihuacán, Aztec and Maya), or arrange several shorter visits in order to see everything. The central courtyard is a pleasant place to relax if fatigue sets in, as is the restaurant on the lower level. Permission must be obtained to use a camera (without flash only); phone (5) 533-4976. Wheelchairs are available. Restrooms are provided. Open Tues.-Sun. 9-7, Mon. 9-7 on official festival days. Admission 20 pesos (about $2); free to all Sun. and on official festival days. Phone (5) 553-6381 or 553-6386.

MUSEO RUFINO TAMAYO (Rufino Tamayo Museum) is in Chapultepec Park, on the north side of Paseo de la Reforma and west of Calzada Gandhi (M: Chapultepec, line 1). It displays the personal modern art collection of the Oaxacan painter and muralist, who died in 1991. Although Tamayo's work was initially criticized for its lack of political content, his reputation as a key figure of 20th-century Mexican art has grown over the years. In addition to Tamayo's own paintings, there are works by Pablo Picasso, Francis Bacon, Salvador Dali and Joan Miró. The museum also mounts changing international exhibitions. Open Tues.-Sun. 10-6. Admission is charged; free to all Sun. Phone (5) 286-6519 or 286-6599.

UNITED STATES EMBASSY is at Paseo de la Reforma and Río Danubio, just north of the Zona Rosa (M: Insurgentes, line 1). Like many of the city's structures, it was built to withstand the impact of a powerful earthquake. Phone (5) 209-9100.

NORTH OF DOWNTOWN

BASILICA DE NUESTRA SEÑORA DE GUADALUPE (Basilica of Our Lady of Guadalupe) is about 10 kilometers (6 miles) north of downtown's historic center (M: Basílica or La Villa, line 3). The site is located off the northern extension of the Paseo de la Reforma, on a rocky hill in the suburb of Villa de Guadalupe (officially Villa Gustavo A. Madero). It honors the nation's patron saint and foremost iconic religious figure, the Guadalupe Virgin. One of Roman Catholicism's holiest shrines, it was visited by Pope

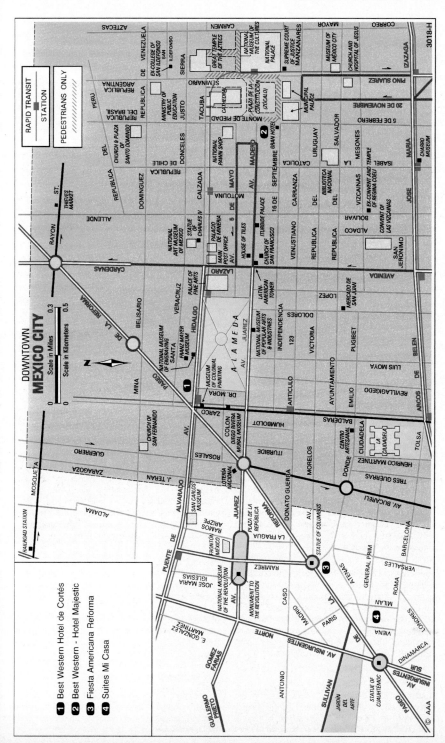

DOWNTOWN MEXICO CITY

Scale in Miles
0   0.3   0.5

Scale in Kilometers

RAPID TRANSIT
■ STATION
PEDESTRIANS ONLY

1 Best Western Hotel de Cortés
2 Best Western - Hotel Majestic
3 Fiesta Americana Reforma
4 Suites Mi Casa

© AAA

3018-H

John Paul II, revered in Mexico, in January 1999.

Mexican Catholics believe that at this site in December 1531 the Virgin appeared to Juan Diego, a peasant Indian, and asked him that a church be built. After hearing this story, the local bishop requested proof. Diego returned on Dec. 12, his cape filled with roses that the Virgin had directed him to pick (a rather miraculous occurrence itself, considering the time of year). When the cape was opened, the roses had disappeared and a vivid image of the dark-skinned Virgin appeared on the folds of cloth.

A basilica with an ornate colonial facade was built about 1709 to house the sacred image. So many devout believers made the pilgrimage, however, that a new structure was needed to replace the old church, which had been slowly sinking into the soft soil of the Texcoco lakebed. The original basilica houses a museum; it displays religious artworks, colonial-era paintings of the Virgin and a collection of *retablos*—small devotional paintings—along with choir seats and an impressive baroque altarpiece.

The new basilica opened in 1976 next to the older one. Daringly modern in design, it was completed under the direction of Pedro Ramírez Vásquez, architect of the National Museum of Anthropology, and can accommodate more than 10,000 people. The cloth hangs above the main altar in a gold frame; visitors can pass beneath it via a moving walkway.

Other shrines and chapels honor the Virgin's appearance. Up the hill is the **Capilla del Pocito** (Chapel of the Little Well) where, according to legend, a spring burst forth from the rock where the Virgin stood. The chapel has a Moorish-style tiled dome and a beautifully decorative interior. At the top of the hill is the **Capilla de las Rosas** (Chapel of the Roses), marking the spot where Juan Diego gathered his armload of flowers. An Aztec shrine dedicated to Tonantzin, the mother of Aztec gods, once stood on the hill as well; it was destroyed after the Conquest. Basilica open daily; museum open Tues.-Sun. Admission is charged to the museum.

The *Feast Day of the Virgin of Guadalupe*, held on Dec. 12, brings hundreds of thousands of pilgrims from all over the world to the huge square in front of the basilica. Here fervent prayer mixes with a carnival atmosphere. Many show their devotion by making the final approach to the basilica crawling on their knees. For others, the day is more of a party, with plenty of dancing, eating and merriment.

MONASTERY OF SAN AGUSTIN ACOLMAN— *see Acolman listing.*

PLAZA DE LAS TRES CULTURAS (Plaza of the Three Cultures) is north of the Historic Center and west of Paseo de la Reforma Norte, at Avenida Lázaro Cárdenas and Ricardo Flores Magón (M: Tlatelolco, line 3). The name comes from three vastly different influences—pre-Hispanic Aztec, colonial Spanish and contemporary Mexican—that have left their individual imprints on this plaza.

The ceremonial and trading center of Tlatelolco (tlah-tay-LOHL-koh) considerably predated the Aztec capital of Tenochtitlán. Even after it was absorbed by the Aztec empire in 1473, Tlatelolco continued to function as an important market; Hernán Cortés marveled at its size and organization, and historian Bernal Díaz described the vast array of goods and the hordes of buyers and sellers. It was from Tlatelolco that the Aztecs made their final stand against Spanish forces on Aug. 13, 1521. The bloody battle brought about the downfall of Tenochtitlán and the Aztec empire and signaled the end of the Conquest. A plaque in front of the plaza church commemorates the event.

Nearly 450 years later, the plaza was the scene of another massacre. On the eve of the 1968 Summer Olympic Games—with Mexico City in the world spotlight—a massive student protest over prevailing economic and social policies turned deadly when government troops were ordered to open fire. A simple monument, dedicated in 1993, recognizes the 25th anniversary of the tragedy.

The site ruins can be seen from raised walkways and give an indication of its former scale, for the main pyramid at Tlatelolco almost certainly rivaled the temples of Tenochtitlán in size. The **Church of Santiago Tlatelolco** dates from 1609. Constructed from *tezontle* rock, it has a restored interior that contains several frescoes and a strikingly simple stone altar. Next to the church are the remains of a monastery and former college where Franciscan friars taught the sons of Aztec nobility. Surrounding the plaza are a 1960s-era housing project and high-rise office buildings, such as the one housing the Ministry of Foreign Affairs. Several of the apartment buildings were demolished by the 1985 earthquake.

SANTA CECILIA PYRAMID is about 3 kilometers (2 miles) north of the Tenayuca Pyramid *(see next attraction listing)* via the road to Santa Cecelia Acatitlán. Both pyramids are located east of Tlalnepantla (tlahl-neh-PAHN-tlah), an industrial city just north of the Federal District in the state of México. Buses to the pyramids depart from Mexico City's Terminal Central de Autobuses del Norte. There is a Metro station at the terminal (Autobuses del Norte, line 5). Another way to reach them is by taxi.

The small Santa Cecelia pyramid, of Aztec origin, is remarkably well reconstructed and has a shrine dedicated to Huitzilopochtli, the war god and a dominant deity of the Aztecs. Beside this temple is the ruin of a shrine to the rain god Tláloc. Landscaped grounds surround the structures.

Also at the site is the **Dávalos Hurtado Museum**, named for Dr. Eusebio Dávalos Hurtado, an important Mexican anthropologist and former director of the Instituto Nacional de Antropología e Historia (National Institute of History and Anthropology). The museum contains several representations of Aztec gods; original sculptures, engravings and paintings; and a reproduction of a Mexica (Mexican-Aztec) temple. Site and museum open Tues.-Sun.

TENAYUCA PYRAMID is about 12 kilometers (7.5 miles) north of downtown Mexico City via Avenida Lázaro Cárdenas or Calzada Vallejo. This pre-Aztec site was once part of the 12th-century Chichimec empire. Passageways reveal the series of superimposed structures that excavations have uncovered within this pyramid, which is one of the most impressively reconstructed in the country. Its most striking features are the 52 plumed serpents that adorn three sides of the base, corresponding to the Aztec cycle of 52 years. At the foot of the stairway on the west side is a carved frieze of skulls; similar carvings are inside. Some archeologists believe that the pyramid was used as an astronomical observatory. Guide service is available. Site open Tues.-Sun. Admission is charged.

TEOTIHUACAN—*see Teotihuacán listing.*

West of Downtown

MONUMENTO A LA REVOLUCION (Monument to the Revolution) stands in the Plaza de la República, north of Paseo de la Reforma and west of the Alameda (M: Revolución, line 2). The massive building is topped by an imposing copper dome that surmounts four arches; the entire structure rises 250 feet. Under the four columns are the remains of four former presidents—Venustiano Carranza, Plutarco Calles, Lázaro Cárdenas and Francisco Madero—as well as revolutionary Pancho Villa. Porfirio Díaz, the dictator deposed by the Revolution of 1910, intended the building to house the government's legislative offices, but the uprising halted construction; the building was dedicated as a monument in the 1930s.

Inside the lower part of the monument is the **Museo Nacional de la Revolución** (National Museum of the Revolution). It houses a collection of weapons, along with paintings and sculptures depicting the revolution's leading figures. Open Tues.-Sat. 9-5, Sun. 9-3. Free. Phone (5) 546-2115.

MUSEO DE SAN CARLOS (San Carlos Museum) is about 3 blocks north of Plaza de la República at Puente de Alvarado #5 (M: Revolución, line 2). The impressive collection of paintings by European artists spans the 15th through the 19th centuries and includes works by Francisco José

Polyforum Siqueiros   ©John Neubauer

de Goya, Tintoretto, Titian, Anthony Van Dyck, Rembrandt, Pieter Breughel, Peter Paul Rubens, Joshua Reynolds and Camille Pissarro. The permanent collection occupies the top floor; temporary expositions are displayed on the ground floor.

The lovely neoclassic building, designed by the Spanish architect-sculptor Manuel Tolsá, was commissioned by the Count of Buenavista. It served as a private home for such notable military figures as Gen. Agustín de Iturbide and Gen. Antonio López de Santa Anna, and was offered to French forces by Archduke Maximilian during Mexico's occupation by France. Another resident was Countess Calderón de la Barca, author of "Life in Mexico," which described her experiences traveling through the country in the mid-19th century. A small public park off Puente de Alvarado faces the rear facade. Open Tues.-Sun. 10-6. Admission is charged; free to all Sun.

STATUE OF COLUMBUS stands within the *glorieta* (traffic circle) on Paseo de la Reforma at Avenida Morelos (M: Revolución, line 2). The work of Charles Cordier, it depicts the explorer (Cristóbal Colón in Spanish) and is one of several statues commissioned by Porfirio Díaz to grace major intersections along this stretch of the city's widest boulevard.

STATUE OF CUAUHTEMOC (or Cuauhtemotzín) is on Paseo de la Reforma at Avenida Insurgentes

(M: Insurgentes, line 1). Cuauhtémoc, the last Aztec emperor, was tortured by Hernán Cortés in an unsuccessful attempt to force him to reveal the hiding place of the vast treasure of Moctezuma. The statue, created by Miguel Moreña, shows the proud ruler garbed in a plumed robe and standing imperiously with his spear, surrounded by warriors. Pedestal engravings depict Cuauhtémoc's torture and the burning of his feet. The circle at Insurgentes and Reforma is a major crossroads for city traffic.

SOUTH OF DOWNTOWN

EL PEDREGAL is a great basaltic lava bed that covers 15 square miles at the southern end of Mexico City (M: Universidad, line 3, south terminal). It is crossed by the Anillo Periférico, the loop highway encircling the city, and surrounded by such suburban communities as Coyoacán, San Angel and Tlalpan. The lava flow is at its craggiest south of San Angel. West of the National University of Mexico campus is **Jardines del Pedregal** (Gardens of the Pedregal), an exclusive residential development. Beginning in the 1950s, ultramodern homes began cropping up in the middle of this barren rock landscape, incorporating the hardened lava formations to dramatic effect. Public transportation is scarce, although a taxi can be hired for a drive through the area.

El Pedregal is the result of the eruption of the volcano Xitle around A.D. 400. Excavations at the quarry of Copilco, just east of San Angel, have uncovered human remains and examples of primitive craftsmanship from a civilization that likely existed sometime during the Middle Preclassic period (1200-400 B.C.). Although Copilco had already been abandoned at the time of Xitle's eruption, the nearby religious, astronomical and commercial center of Cuicuilco was still active.

POLYFORUM SIQUEIROS, at Avenida Insurgentes Sur and Filadelfia, is on the grounds of the Hotel de México. An eight-sided, four-story exposition hall for the arts, it is the work of and a monument to muralist David Alfaro Siqueiros (1896-1974). Garish Siqueiros murals cover the building's exterior walls, and inside on the upper level a revolving floor permits an unimpeded view of his 26,150-square-foot ceiling mural "March of Humanity." Temporary exhibitions also are presented. In the basement a craft shop exhibits and sells high-priced handicrafts. Open daily. Admission is charged.

THE SOUTHERN SUBURBS

Churubusco, Coyoacán, Ixtapalapa, San Angel and **Tlalpan,** all within the Mexico City limits, were once individual *pueblos* (towns) that for the most part have maintained their distinct identities despite being swallowed up by the capital's rampant 20th-century growth. The Federal District, the 571-square-mile seat of national government, encompasses Mexico City and several separate municipalities, including **Xochimilco,** site of the popular floating gardens.

North-south Avenida Insurgentes Sur—a major thoroughfare lined with office buildings and commercial sprawl—is the easiest way to reach the southern suburbs, especially the tourist hotspots of San Angel and Coyoacán, both quietly well-to-do enclaves somehow removed from the rest of the city's clamor. Colonial charm, good restaurants, several museums, weekend arts and crafts shopping, and the cultural offerings of the **National University of Mexico** make this area a popular destination for visitors. City buses constantly run between downtown and the southern suburbs, and taxis come in handy for making short trips from one point of interest to another.

CHURUBUSCO, DISTRITO FEDERAL (C-10)

After having fought valiantly on the side of Gen. Antonio López de Santa Anna in several battles of the U.S.-Mexican War, members of St. Patrick's Battalion—a group of Mexican sympathizers—met disaster in Churubusco (choo-roo-BOOS-coh) in 1847. American forces captured and hanged most of the battalion of 260 Irish immigrants who had deserted the U.S. Army to fight for Mexico. Churubusco, thankfully, is much more tranquil today. The **Club Campestre** (Churubusco Country Club) is said to be the oldest golfing club in country. Mexico's major film studios also are concentrated in this suburb just east of Coyoacán.

EX-CONVENTO DE CHURUBUSCO (Ex-Convent of Churubusco) is at 20 de Agosto and General Anaya (M: General Anaya, line 2). It was built in 1678 over the ruins of an ancient Aztec temple. This former Franciscan convent, which includes the **Church of St. Matthew,** served as a fortress against invading U.S. forces in August 1847. There are lovely gardens on the grounds of the restored structure.

Museo Nacional de las Intervenciones (National Museum of Interventions) is within the convent complex. It chronicles the exploits of those adventurers, pirates and foreign armies—the United States and France chief among them—who have invaded Mexico over the past 4 centuries. Weapons, flags, medals and other war memorabilia make up the displays. Exhibit information is presented in Spanish. Guide service in English is available. Open Tues.-Sun. 9-6. Admission is charged; free to all Sun. Phone (5) 604-0699.

COYOACAN, DISTRITO FEDERAL (C-9)

West of Avenida Insurgentes Sur and about 10 kilometers (6 miles) south of downtown Mexico City, Coyoacán (coh-yoh-ah-KAHN) lies on the northern edge of the Pedregal. Established in 1521 by Hernán Cortés, Coyoacán was the third seat of Spanish government in New Spain. The name is loosely derived from the Náhuatl Indian term *coyohuacan,* or "place of the coyotes." **Francisco Sosa**, the main thoroughfare, connects the neighborhood with San Angel.

Coyoacán exudes upscale (by Mexico City standards) funkiness. Stucco buildings are painted bright purple, blue and yellow. Tall trees line the narrow streets. Bookstores, sweet shops, restaurants and sidewalk cafés all compete for the stroller's attention. The area is very congested; the easiest way to explore it is to hire a taxi driver who will drive you there, wait while you have a look around and then take you back to your hotel.

On Plaza Hidalgo stands the **Palace of Cortés**, now the Delegación de Coyoacán (Town Hall). The Spaniards allegedly tortured Aztec emperor Cuauhtémoc at the palace in an effort to obtain treasure.

Also of interest are the 1583 **Church of San Juan Bautista**, the 1530 **Dominican Monastery** and the **Alvarado House**, now a private home. The Alvarado House belonged to Pedro de Alvarado, Cortés' right-hand man in his conquest of Mexico and later governor of Guatemala. Two blocks east of Plaza Hidalgo on Calle Higuera is **Casa de la Malinche** (House of Malinche), the former home of Cortés' Indian mistress, interpreter and chief aide on his march through Mexico. Malinche, a major and much-maligned figure in Mexican legend, was supposedly condemned to 300 years of martyrdom for her act of betrayal. The solemn-looking dwelling sits across from **Plaza de la Conchita**, a peaceful little park.

Sunday is the best time to visit Coyoacán, when the plaza is the site of a lively street bazaar. City residents converge here against a heady backdrop of sights, colors and aromas. Vendors display their wares—clothing, jewelry, balloons, trinkets, plants, paintings, puppies, paper flowers, incense, carved figurines, housewares and myriad other items—in stalls or spread on the ground on blankets. Food carts are stacked with bags of homemade potato chips; *churro,* a doughnut-like pastry, in long strands coiled like snakes; *chincorros* (pork rinds) doused with hot sauce; fresh slices of watermelon and papaya standing upright in plastic cups; roasted corn on the cob flecked with butter; and cloudlike wads of cotton candy. Little kids hawk gum; sketch artists hunch over their work; traditionally dressed *señoras* with braided hair appraise the merchandise.

Street musicians, costumed dancers and performing animals provide entertainment, and the vendors' melodic cries punctuate the air. Underscoring this festival-like atmosphere, however, is the intense level of commerce and human enterprise that characterizes so much of Mexican life, as people ceaselessly endeavor to sell whatever others will buy.

MUSEO ANAHUACALLI (Diego Rivera Museum) is on the south side of the city, off Avenida División del Norte at Calle del Museo #150 (M: Coyoacán, line 3). The stark, pyramidal building, which incorporates Aztec and Maya influences, was designed by Rivera and constructed from black volcanic stone. It contains the muralist's vast personal collection of pre-Hispanic art. Dark, somber exhibit rooms are enlivened by many of the more than 60,000 items Rivera amassed. The Aztec and Toltec civilizations and the ancient city of Teotihuacán are well represented, and there is an outstanding collection of objects from the western states of Colima, Jalisco and Nayarit.

Rivera also set up a studio on the upper floor of the building, although he was barely able to use it before his death; mementos and works in progress now occupy the restored space. As spectacular as the building are the views from its hilltop location, particularly of the twin volcanoes Popocatépetl and Iztaccíhuatl. Open Tues.-Sun. 10-6 (closed 2-3 p.m.). Free. Phone (5) 617-4310.

MUSEO FRIDA KAHLO (Frida Kahlo Museum) is in a well-to-do residential area at Calle Londres #247, 5 blocks north of Plaza Hidalgo (M: Coyoacán, line 3). It is the birthplace and home

Day of the Dead exhibit, Frida Kahlo Museum ©John Neubauer

of Frida Kahlo, one of Latin America's most celebrated painters. The adobe house was Kahlo's lifelong residence; from 1929 until her death in 1954 she shared it with her husband Diego Rivera, Mexico's brilliant muralist. Through their tempestuous relationship Rivera and Kahlo forged the nucleus of contemporary Mexican art.

The renovated museum is an explosion of color, not the least of which is the cobalt-blue, red-trimmed exterior. The interior is preserved much as it appeared when Kahlo lived there. Personal possessions include the four-poster bed in which she was born and died. *Calaveras* (papier-mâché skeletons) and carved death masks are other reminders of the suffering that was part of Kahlo's everyday life and that provided the fuel for her creativity. About 50 of the self-taught artist's works are on display, including some surrealistic self-portraits reflecting an obsession with the health problems that plagued most of her life. A large Mayan urn behind glass contains Kahlo's ashes.

A spacious studio remains essentially as Kahlo left it and contains her wheelchair, paintbrushes and an easel on which rests an unfinished portrait of Joseph Stalin. The tiled kitchen features wooden spoons and Mexican ceramic jugs and bowls. Also displayed are an arrangement of miniature *retablos*, small devotional paintings executed on tin; a sampling of Rivera's drawings and murals; photographs, love letters, an address book and other personal effects; and a collection of pre-Hispanic pottery and ceramic figurines. There is a coffee shop on the basement level off the museum's interior patio. Open Tues.-Sun. 10-6. Admission is charged. Phone (5) 554-5999.

MUSEO LEON TROTSKY (Leon Trotsky Museum), north of Plaza Hidalgo at Río Churubusco #410 (M: Coyoacán, line 3), is the former residence of Russian revolutionary Leon Trotsky. Exiled from the Soviet Union in 1929 after losing leadership of the Communist Party to Joseph Stalin, he was murdered in his Coyoacán home on Aug. 20, 1940. An axe-wielding assassin (allegedly a Stalin ally) accomplished the deed, which had been attempted months earlier when a heavily armed group (thought to have included Mexican muralist David Alfaro Siqueiros) showered the residence with a hail of bullets. The high-walled, fortresslike dwelling is capped with turrets once occupied by armed guards. Inside are Trotsky's modest belongings, preserved largely as he left them, and newspaper clippings recounting the event. Open Tues.-Sun. 10-5. Admission is charged.

IXTAPALAPA, DISTRITO FEDERAL (C-10)

Long before it became a southeastern division of Mexico City, Ixtapalapa (ees-tah-pah-LAH-pah) was a flourishing Aztec town. Atop nearby **Cerro de la Estrella** (Star Hill), the Aztecs lighted fires to mark the beginning of their 52-year cycle. During the New Fire Ceremony, priests would ignite kindling on the chest of the unfortunate sacrificial victim. If the flame continued to burn, the continued existence of the world was assured. Flames would then be carried by runners to temples throughout the empire. Instead of human sacrifices, the hill today is the scene of a Passion Play performed on Good Friday.

The views of volcanoes Popocatépetl and Iztaccíhuatl are exceptional from the hilltop; a road leads to the summit. Many visitors ascend the hill by foot, as there are caves and small ruins that can be explored along the way.

SAN ANGEL, DISTRITO FEDERAL (C-9)

San Angel (sahn AHN-hehl) was once a small town far removed from colonial Mexico City. Like other southern suburbs, however, it has been overtaken by the capital's inexorable growth. Even so, a leisurely stroll past San Angel's elegant colonial mansions and bougainvillea-draped walls is a trip back through history and a welcome respite from downtown Mexico City's noise and congestion. The entire town is designated a national historic monument.

In the beautifully leafy **Parque de la Bombilla** (Bombilla Park), at the junction of avenidas La Paz and Insurgentes Sur, stands a granite monument honoring Gen. Alvaro Obregón. Obregón helped draft the Constitution of 1917 and was the first president of post-revolutionary Mexico. He was assassinated in San Angel by a religious fanatic in 1928. At one time the monument also featured his preserved arm, lost in battle during the Mexican Revolution; a wooden facsimile is now displayed on the monument's lower level.

A few blocks southwest of the park off Avenida La Paz is **Plaza San Jacinto**, a pleasant square bordered by cobblestone streets, tucked-away restaurants and outdoor cafés. A plaque in the square honors members of St. Patrick's Battalion, a group of Irish immigrants who deserted the U.S. Army and sided with Mexico during the Mexican-American War. The plaque lists the names of soldiers who were branded and hung by the Americans, and expresses gratitude for their loyalty to Mexico. Today the plaza is known for its **Bazar del Sábado** (Saturday Bazaar). All manner of artists, merchants and craftspeople set up shop in and around one of the elegant colonial-era mansions facing the plaza. Although prices tend to be high, so does quality *(see description under "Shopping," page 324).*

One of the capital's best-known restaurants, the **San Angel Inn**, occupies an opulent old hacienda at Calle Diego Rivera #50 (at Altavista). Lovely gardens and grounds please the eye as much as do the expertly prepared Mexican and international dishes. Lunch or dinner at the inn is a nice way to end a tour of San Angel, but keep in mind that reservations are advised (especially on weekends), prices reflect the restaurant's reputation, and the dress code is strictly enforced.

West of San Angel on the Mexico-Toluca Highway (Mex. 15) is **Parque Nacional Miguel Hidalgo** (Miguel Hidalgo National Park), known locally as La Marquesa for the name of the small town nearby. The battle of Monte de las Cruces, one of the many conflicts waged during the struggle for Mexican independence, took place here in the early 19th century. Surrounded by mountains, the park contains picnic sites, a government trout hatchery and a man-made lake stocked with trout. Horseback rides can be arranged at several park locations.

CASA DEL RISCO, Plaza San Jacinto #15 (Metro: Miguel A. de Quevedo, line 3), contains an extensive library and one of Mexico City's finest collections of European paintings from the 14th through the 17th centuries. Also of interest are the building's antique furnishings and a colorful, wildly abstract fountain in the patio that appears to be made primarily of broken crockery. The building is also referred to as the Centro Cultural Isidro Fabela. Open Tues.-Sun. Free.

DESIERTO DE LOS LEONES (Desert of the Lions) is about 24 kilometers (15 miles) west of San Angel on Mex. 15, just e. of the town of La Venta. This national park lies in a heavily wooded mountain area, and several walking trails wind through the pines. Within the park is a restored Carmelite monastery that was established in 1606. It is now the site of occasional concerts and exhibitions. This is a pretty spot for a picnic or a stop on the way to Toluca.

MUSEO DEL CARMEN (El Carmen Museum) is just south of Avenida La Paz at Avenida Revolución #4 and Monasterio (Metro: Miguel A. de Quevedo, line 3). The former Carmelite convent dates from 1615. Now a museum, the building is distinguished by carved doors, baroque altarpieces, a fine collection of religious paintings and three domes, each tiled in a different color. The cloister's garden has a tropical look, unusual for Mexico City. Open Tues.-Sun. 10-5. Admission is charged; free to all Sun.

MUSEO DE ARTE CARRILLO GIL (Carrillo Art Museum) is about 3 blocks north of Plaza San Jacinto at Avenida Revolución #1608 (Metro: Miguel A. de Quevedo, line 3). Carrillo Gil, a doctor, amassed the collection displayed in this museum, which focuses on paintings and graphics by noted 20th-century Mexican artists but includes European works as well. José Clemente Orozco, Diego Rivera, David Alfaro Siqueiros and Pablo Picasso are among those represented. Open Tues.-Sun. 10-6. Admission is charged; free to all Sun.

MUSEO ESTUDIO DIEGO RIVERA (Diego Rivera Studio Museum) is on Calle Diego Rivera, across the street from the San Angel Inn (Metro: Miguel A. de Quevedo, line 3). This studio, designed by Juan O'Gorman, is where the artist once lived and produced preliminary sketches for much of his work. On view are everyday objects, photographs and some unusual artworks. Open Tues.-Sun. 10-6. Admission is charged; free to all Sun.

UNIVERSIDAD NACIONAL AUTONOMA DE MEXICO (National University of Mexico, or UNAM) covers some 800 acres south of San Angel (M: Copilco or Universidad, line 3), roughly between avenidas Insurgentes Sur and Universidad. Its mosaic-covered modern buildings and academic reputation have made Ciudad Universitaria (University City), as the complex is commonly referred to, world famous. Originally known as the Royal and Pontifical University of Mexico, it was founded in 1553 by special charter from Philip II of Spain and is one of the oldest institutions of higher learning in the Americas.

The university's original site is marked by a plaque on the south side of the building at calles Moneda and Seminario, in the heart of Mexico City's historic center. The first school occupied several locations and closed down several times in the mid-19th century before finally reopening in the 1920s as today's university. With continued growth, its branches became scattered throughout the city.

The lack of a central campus was alleviated in 1950, when construction on University City began under the presidency of Miguel Alemán. Artists and architects alike worked on the design, attempting to integrate buildings and facilities into the volcanic landscape of the Pedregal. The result was a diverse group of modern architectural statements that remain striking (although no longer groundbreaking), despite more than 40 years of use by a student population that now numbers more than 300,000.

The best reason to visit the university is to see the murals that decorate the exterior of the main campus buildings, most of them concentrated just east of Insurgentes Sur. One of the most visually arresting is the **Biblioteca** (Main Library). This rectangular tower is covered with stone mosaic work, augmented in places by colored tiles. The frescoes, by Juan O'Gorman, vividly present stages of Mexican history, from the pre-Hispanic and colonial eras to the artist's vision of the future, depicted around a whirling atom.

Near the library is the **Rectoría** (Administration Building), dominated by a huge David Alfaro Siqueiros mural that incorporates pieces of colored glass to form a design stressing the importance of education. The mural has a three-dimensional effect that gives the impression of movement when viewed passing by on foot or in a vehicle. A mosaic that includes a three-headed mask symbolizing Indian, Spanish and *mestizo—*

the three peoples of Mexico—also adorns one wall of the **School of Medicine**.

Grassy, tree-lined quadrangles intersperse with the academic buildings. There are few dormitories; UNAM is primarily a commuter school. The **Museo de Mineralogía** (Museum of Mineralogy) and **Museo del Instituto de Geología** (Geology Institute Museum) contain geologic exhibits. The **Centro Cultural Universitario** (University Cultural Center), east off Insurgentes Sur in the southeast section of the campus, offers a full slate of performing arts programs within its several theaters and concert halls. The largest hall, Sala Nezahualcóyotl, is lauded as being acoustically perfect. The weekly publication *Tiempo Libre*, published on Thursdays, provides listings of scheduled events.

Some of the sports facilities and handball courts dotting the campus take their inspiration from the ancient pyramids. In stark contrast is **Estadio Olímpico** (Olympic Stadium), on the west side of Insurgentes Sur. It was reconstructed and enlarged for the 1968 Summer Olympics and can accommodate more than 100,000 people. The oval design somewhat resembles the crater of a volcano. A Diego Rivera mosaic of colored rocks, illustrating human endeavor in sports, covers the stadium's sloping walls.

The easiest way to get to the university is to take line 3 of the Metro and get off at one of the last two stops (traffic congestion along Insurgentes Sur can be daunting). City buses marked "Ciudad Universitaria" travel regularly down Insurgentes Sur and stop in front of the main complex of buildings. *Peseros* (minibuses) also cruise north-south along Insurgentes Sur; the fare is inexpensive. Buses operated by the university traverse the main sections of the campus and are free. If you only wish to view the major buildings, consider visiting on the weekend, when the student hordes are noticeably absent.

Tlalpan, Distrito Federal (C-9)

Tlalpan (TLAHL-pan), south of University City, can be reached by bus from the Taxqueña Metro station (line 2). This is another well-to-do suburb with many lovely homes scattered among the black volcanic rock of the Pedregal. The **Villa Olímpica** (Olympic Village), built to house athletes during the 1968 summer games, is now a residential area. Near **Plaza de la Constitución**, Tlalpan's main square, is the 1532 church of San Agustín de las Cuevas, which contains paintings by Miguel Cabrera. To the southwest is the extinct 13,097-foot Volcán Ajusco. Buses that leave from Azteca Stadium on Calzada de Tlalpan travel to the volcano, which offers excellent views of the surrounding area if the weather is clear.

CUICUILCO PYRAMID is near the intersection of Avenida Insurgentes Sur (Mex. 95) and the Anillo Periférico, close to Olympic Village. Be-

lieved to date back as far as 600 B.C., it is one of the oldest man-made structures in North America. The city of Cuicuilco, a religious and commercial center for the surrounding farm communities in the Valley of Mexico, predated Teotihuacán and was destroyed about A.D. 400 by the eruption of the volcano Xitle.

Today the site consists of a round platform, discovered in the early 1920s, and a ramp that once led to an altar at the temple's summit. The original structure was some 370 feet in diameter and 59 feet high; it was enlarged several times over the centuries. Much of the lava rock that once engulfed the pyramid has been removed, affording visitors a better view of the ruins. A small museum at the site has geologic exhibits and displays objects found during the excavations. Open Tues.-Sun. Admission is charged to the museum.

Xochimilco, Distrito Federal (C-10)

Xochimilco (soh-chee-MEEL-coh) is about 24 kilometers (15 miles) southeast of downtown Mexico City, within the Federal District but outside the city limits. The "place where the flowers grow" was once a Chichimec Indian stronghold. The city was captured by the Xochimilcas in the 13th century, and also was a popular residence for Aztec nobles. Flowers and vegetables grown here made their way to the Aztec capital Tenochtitlán via an intricate system of waterways. The Aztec tongue, Náhuatl, can still be heard today among the Indians who ply their canoes through the remaining canals.

The best way to reach Xochimilco is to take Mexico City's Metro (line 2) to the Taxqueña station, then board a light rail train *(tren ligero)* and get off at the Xochimilco stop. *Peseros* (minibuses) also make the trip from the Taxqueña Metro station to Xochimilco, as do buses that travel down Avenida Insurgentes Sur and Calzada de Tlalpan to the Anillo Periférico. By car, Xochimilco can be reached via the Periférico, exiting at Jardines del Sur. The tourist-oriented "floating gardens" area is busiest on Sunday, when Mexican families come on their traditional day off. It's much less crowded in the middle of the week.

Xochimilco is threaded by numerous waterways, the last remains of a once-extensive lake. Today's floating gardens were originally *chinampas*, or rafts woven of twigs, covered with earth and planted with flowers or vegetables. The rafts often carried a small hut and were propelled about the lake with oars. Gradually the roots of vegetation on the rafts attached to the lake bottom, and the gardens became islands threaded by canals. Other *chinampas* were anchored by planting willows or *ahuehuetes* (cypresses) around their perimeters.

Over the years the government has waged battle against tenacious water hyacinths, stagnation, pollution and falling water levels. Ongoing canal cleanup efforts seem to be proving successful, and Xochimilco continues to be a prime tourist attraction as well as a local weekend outing of choice. It also offers an approximation of what water commerce might have been like during Tenochtitlán's heyday.

For a real taste of Mexican merrymaking visit on Sunday, when Xochimilco is thronged by families and a freewheeling carnival atmosphere prevails. Signs marked "Embarcadero" point the way to the boat launches. The names of these hand-poled, bloom-bedecked, flat-bottomed barges are frequently spelled out with flowers. Boats come in varying sizes; most hold at least 10 people. The rental rate is per boat rather than per person, so it's cheaper—and more fun—to join a group.

Restaurants and souvenir stands line the canals. Everywhere there are hawkers, ashore and afloat in canoes, peddling tacos, beer, drinks, trinkets, balloons, flowers and fruit. Music is an integral part of the fun, and some boats are occupied by mariachi bands or guitar trios, in full costume and of varying degrees of polish, who paddle up to prospective customers and serenade them for a fee.

The government sets authorized rates for the different sizes of boats. If an operator tries to charge more, complain to the police, who usually patrol the principal pier. If a police officer is not available, you must resort to bargaining, at which the boat operators are uncannily skillful; many have learned some English for just this purpose. Be sure to agree on the price and the length of your ride before embarking. Bargaining is easier during the week when there are fewer visitors.

North of the town center is a more recently developed area of canals and *chinampas* where produce is raised, most of it bound for Mexico City markets. Boats can be hired to cruise these canals as well, although the area is kept separate from the tourist-targeted floating gardens. Picnicking is permitted along the banks of a manmade lake, where there also is a visitor center.

Although the floating gardens are the reason most people come here, Xochimilco has other attractions. Facing the main square is the early 16th-century **Franciscan Convent and Church of San Bernardino**, one of the first in New Spain. Stone carvings of angels and flowers adorn the church's exterior. Inside are several chapels and a main altar resplendent with gold gilt, sculptures and paintings. Also in the central part of town are garden centers and the market, liveliest on Saturdays when Indians come from miles around to sell their wares.

MUSEO DELORES OLMEDO (Delores Olmedo Museum) is at Avenida México #5843. Delores Olmedo Patino, a philanthropist, art collector and benefactor of Diego Rivera, bequeathed her hacienda, La Noria, as a museum. Rivera paintings on display include a portrait of Olmedo, portraits of Frida Kahlo, and drawings and engravings of Angelina Beloff, the artist's first wife. The collection also includes Mexican folk and religious art. Colonial furnishings and pre-Hispanic artifacts decorate the restored hacienda. The lovely grounds alone are worth a visit. Because the complex is spread out, it's easier to hire a taxi for the trip to Xochimilco. Tues.-Sun. 10-6. Admission is charged. Phone (5) 555-1016.

WHAT TO DO

DINING

Probably nothing emphasizes the cosmopolitan nature of Mexico City so clearly as do its innumerable restaurants and their international range of cuisines. For years, most of the best known and most elegant establishments specialized in French and Continental, those two benchmarks of fine dining. More recently, however, traditional Mexican cooking has taken center stage. Many of the newest and trendiest restaurants are serving time-honored dishes that originated during pre-Hispanic days, but with a contemporary twist.

This is not the cheese-slathered, spicy-hot food that many people still think of as generically "Mexican," nor is it necessarily reminiscent of regional specialties that have ended up on menus across the country. Ingredients are frequently exotic—*nopales*, fleshy pads of cactus; *huitlacoche*, the earthy black fungus that is Mexico's version of the truffle; or *cajeta*, a sweet caramel flavoring made from goat's milk. Preparation tends to be lighter and seasonings assertive, with liberal use of chilies and such Mexican herbs as epazote. Two popular spots featuring innovative Mexican cuisine are **Isadora**, in an art deco-style townhouse at Molière #50 in the Polanco neighborhood, and **Los Girasoles** (Sunflowers), which faces Plaza Manuel Tolsá on Calle Tacuba a few blocks east of Alameda Park (M: Bellas Artes, lines 2 and 8). The latter restaurant has a shaded terrace for outdoor dining.

Robustly traditional fare, of course, still has its aficionados, and numerous establishments that keep them happy. Here is where diners will find such reliable Mexican specialties as *sopa de tortilla* (tortilla soup); *chiles rellenos* (stuffed chilies); *huachinango a la Veracruzana* (a whole fish, usually sea bass or red snapper, awash in a sauce of tomatoes, onions, olives and capers); and *cochinita pibil* (pork wrapped in banana leaves and baked Yucatecan style). Restaurants serving authentic Mexican dishes include **Focolare**, Hamburgo #87, and **Fonda El Refugio**, Liverpool #166, both in the Zona Rosa.

In a class of their own are **La Hacienda de los Morales**, in the Polanco neighborhood, and the **San Angel Inn**, in the southern suburb of San Angel. La Hacienda de los Morales, in a beautifully restored former hacienda dating from the 16th century, features an "upscale colonial" decor, gardens and a lovely interior courtyard. The central dining room, noisy but convivial, has an exposed brick ceiling and a fireplace and is accented with art. A well-dressed, well-heeled professional crowd comes for good Mexican and international dishes, solicitous service and a notable tray of breads and rolls carted around by a waiter who serves them with tongs.

The San Angel Inn, also a former hacienda, is set in the midst of landscaped grounds. Long a favorite of well-to-do city residents for weekend lunches and elegant dinners, it also draws those who stop for an early-evening margarita sipped in serenity on the colonial patio. To dine here, you'll need to make reservations, dress up and be prepared to spend money, but the food and atmosphere are worth it.

For those who demand world-class haute cuisine (with prices to match), Mexico City has some dependable choices. Such restaurants are usually located in the big, expensive hotels. **Fouquet's de Paris**, in the Camino Real Hotel at Mariano Escobedo #700—a branch of the Parisian outpost—offers as refined and elegant a setting as you'll find in the capital for food that is a combination of international and Mexican flavors. Splurge at **Maxim's de Paris**, in the Hotel Intercontinental Presidente Mexico City at Campos Elíseos #218, which has a stylish art deco interior, an outstanding wine cellar and wonderfully attentive service. At these and other top-quality restaurants, reservations are required or advised, and a jacket and tie are *de rigueur* for men.

Other cuisines contribute to the city's reputation as a gastronome's delight. Spanish food, often more highly seasoned than Mexican, is particularly popular. At South American steak houses, beef dishes are grilled right at the table. Chinese, Japanese, German and Italian restaurants are readily available. For the homesick and/or unadventurous, there are plenty of American fast-food joints, including Burger King, McDonald's, Pizza Hut and Subway.

If you're in a hurry or just want a casual meal, eat at **Vips** or **Sanborn's**, both Mexican chains with numerous Mexico City locations. The food is dependably prepared and reasonably priced; they're good choices for breakfast. Another casual alternative is one of the sandwich stands that occupy almost every street corner. Try *tacos al pastor*—shreds of roast pork with grilled onions and cilantro heaped on a small tortilla, the whole thing rolled up burrito-style and popped in the mouth. At 5 pesos (about 50 cents) apiece, they're a popular late-night snack. The **El Globo**

bakery chain, with locations throughout the Federal District, offers good-quality breads and pastries at low prices.

Many of Mexico City's better restaurants are concentrated in the Polanco and Zona Rosa areas. Another cluster of good restaurants and cozy sidewalk cafés are in the suburbs of San Angel and Coyoacán. Casual neighborhood eateries and family-style places are the rule up and down Avenida Insurgentes Sur, in the downtown area and around the *Zócalo*. Keep in mind that many restaurants close on Sunday. Pay with a major credit card if possible, as the rate of exchange is better than that offered by banks or currency exchange offices.

Approach cocktails and liquors with caution if you are unaccustomed to the altitude. Also be aware that imported wines and spirits are heavily taxed; Mexican beers and wines are much less expensive. Although the better restaurants customarily use purified water, avoid green salads, unpeeled raw vegetables and unpeeled fruit if you have a sensitive stomach. To be completely safe, order drinks without ice cubes, or drink bottled water.

In general, restaurants cater to the local custom of eating the main meal of the day in the early afternoon, then a lighter supper around 9 p.m. or later. Most begin to serve breakfast around 7:30 a.m., *comida* (lunch) about 1 p.m. and dinner after 7:30 p.m. From 2 to 4, restaurants can be crowded with lingering diners; if you eat dinner before 9, on the other hand, you might have the place to yourself. Even in the finer establishments, don't expect every server to have a fluent command of English. A knowledge of basic Spanish or a handy phrase book not only helps in communication but also in deciphering menus. For a list of AAA-RATED establishments in Mexico City, *see the Lodgings & Restaurants section*.

SHOPPING

Malls, shops and markets not only line the streets but pop up in parks, subway stops and practically every neighborhood in the metropolis. The array of items for sale at these *mercados* is truly mind-boggling, and the bounty offered up by city merchants is matched only by their persuasive zeal for bargaining.

Whether it's a cheap souvenir or an expensive, finely crafted work of art, chances are you'll find it here. In particular, look for intricate silverwork, hand-carved masks, jewelry, tinted onyx and obsidian, carved wooden chests, boxes of inlaid wood, furniture, paintings, picture frames, fine glassware and pottery, lacquerware, handtooled leather and textiles—especially *sarapes*, *rebozos* (shawl-like garments), embroidery and fine table linens.

Merchandise is sold either in fixed-price shops where you pay the posted sale price or in markets where bargaining determines the cost. One of Mexico City's major shopping areas is the **Zona Rosa** (Pink Zone), off Paseo de la Reforma and encompassing calles Amberes, Génova, Hamburgo, Niza and Londres (M: Sevilla or Insurgentes, line 1). Galleries and boutiques abound, and outdoor cafés provide a relaxing break.

Another pricey shopping area is the **Polanco** neighborhood (M: Polanco, line 7). Armani, Cartier, Perry Ellis, Hermes and other chic fashion boutiques line a section of Avenida Presidente Masaryk that is Mexico City's version of L.A.'s Rodeo Drive. One of the city's biggest and most elegant malls is **Perisur**, located on the southern outskirts close to where the Periférico connects with Avenida Insurgentes Sur.

More modest shopping—and lower prices— prevail at hundreds of shops and vendor stalls along avenidas Juárez and Francisco Madero in the vicinity of the *Zócalo*. This old downtown section of Mexico City is packed with stores and shops. From the *Zócalo* west to Avenida Lázaro Cárdenas, every other side street is closed to traffic and paved with brick tiles. A government-run series of **FONART** shops offer a variety of arts and crafts—rugs, glassware, folk art, pottery— from all parts of the country at reasonable prices. Two centrally located outlets are at Londres #136A in the Zona Rosa (an upstairs space crammed with items) and at Avenida Juárez #89, just west of Alameda Park (also known as Exposición Nacional de Arte Popular).

Mexico City's *mercados* were once areas of stalls open to the weather, roving dogs, and plagues of insects and bacteria. Long on merchandise, they were short on sanitation. City officials stepped in, and the markets are now housed in clean, properly ventilated buildings. Here you can haggle to your heart's content—and should, for a vendor normally asks at least 25 percent more than he or she expects to receive.

A suitable arena in which to practice the art of bargaining is the **Mercado de Curiosidades** (San Juan Market). The principal section is in a modern three-story building at Ayuntamiento, Aranda and Buen Tono, 4 blocks south of Alameda Park (M: Salto del Agua, line 1). It offers an assortment of such wares as baskets, leather goods, jewelry, linens and shawls. The huge **Centro Artesenal Buenavista** (Buenavista Artisan Center), Aldama #187 near the Buenavista rail depot at the north end of the city, markets handicrafts from throughout Mexico. Specialties include leather goods, pottery, stained-glass lamps and clothing.

The city's biggest food market is **La Merced**, several blocks east of the *Zócalo* along Circunvalación (M: Merced, line 1). The huge buildings are crammed with a multitude of vendors selling

Dancers in Aztec regalia ©Chris Sharp

produce, housewares and other everyday items. The selection of fruits and vegetables in particular is staggering. While you're not likely to find many souvenirs, the sheer scope of the commerce that takes place here makes it a fascinating place to wander through.

The **Thieves' Market** is a popular flea market open only on Sundays. It adjoins the **Lagunilla Market**, on Rayón between Allende and Comonfort, east of the intersection of Lázaro Cárdenas and Paseo de la Reforma (M: Allende, line 2). A modern triple-roofed building of enormous proportions, Lagunilla is especially busy on Sunday, when vendors from all over the city set up tables or booths to sell used clothing, silver of varying quality and other goods. Antiques, coins, blankets and rare books are good buys here. Silver fanciers should head for **Tane**, Amberes #70 in the Zona Rosa and several other city locations, where the jewelry, candelabra and museum-quality reproductions are expensive but exquisitely crafted.

Handcrafted items from all over Mexico are sold at the **Mercado de la Ciudadela**, on Plaza de la Ciudadela at Avenida Balderas (M: Balderas, line 1). Dedicated shoppers will thrill to more than 300 booths where everything from leather moccasins to custom guitars is enticingly displayed. Glassblowers, weavers, saddlers, silversmiths and other artisans demonstrate their skills. Some of the most interesting items at La Ciudadela are the handcarved wooden masks, whose colorful and creatively rendered visages range from whimsical to demonic.

Scores of Mexican artists exhibit and sell paintings and sculpture in the city's many art galleries. Of special interest is the **Bazar del Sábado** (Saturday Bazaar) at Plaza San Jacinto #11 (M: Miguel A. de Quevedo, line 3) in the southern suburb of San Angel. Set up in a beautifully renovated 18th-century mansion—but usually spilling out of it as well—the bazaar is held only on Saturdays from 10-8. It specializes in art and features works by a tightly knit group of contemporary artisans, some of them U.S. expatriates. Paintings, sculpture, ceramics, textiles and garments, rugs and high-quality jewelry are sold. Among the fascinating handicrafts on display are the bizarrely carved and painted wooden creatures (animalitos) for which Oaxaca is famous, and "Tree of Life" candelabras exploding with flowers, animals and other figures.

Gilded statues of the Virgin Mary, Our Lady of Guadalupe and other Mexican patron saints are exquisite examples of handiwork and command high prices. More affordable merchandise—and a greater chance to bargain—can be found outside the bazaar, where merchants offer wooden toys, decorative gourds and beaded bracelets. Local artists exhibit their work, and the lively scene frequently includes dancers and other entertainment.

Sightseeing

Mexico City's enormous size makes it difficult to plan a sightseeing itinerary. Although many museums and other points of interest are concentrated in certain areas—the Historic Center, Chapultepec Park, the southern suburbs of San Angel and Coyoacán—getting to them can take effort, given the formidable traffic congestion. If the prospect of hitting the streets on your own seems too stressful, consider taking a guided tour.

Package tours accommodating various interests—architecture, the National University of Mexico, nightclubs, bullfights, archeological zones—are available from travel agencies throughout Mexico City. The larger hotels also can arrange sightseeing excursions.

Línea Gris, Londres #166 in the Zona Rosa (M: Sevilla, line 1), is the Mexican agency for Gray Line Tours and also serves as a clearinghouse for sightseeing information. Their city excursions take in all the major points of interest downtown and also travel to nearby destinations outside the city, including the ruins at Teotihuacán. Phone (5) 208-1163 (switchboard), 208-1415, 208-1505 or 208-1888.

As a service of the city government, free guided walking tours of the Historic Center are given Sundays at 10 a.m. The individual tours

vary from week to week but usually last 2 hours and focus on different parts of the area around the Zócalo and the Great Temple of the Aztecs (M: Zócalo, line 2). English-speaking guides are provided upon request. Phone (5) 510-2541 for details. For additional information about guided tours see the "Visitor Services" box.

Hands down, the best day to sightsee in Mexico City is Sunday: Most of the smoke-belching factories are closed, traffic eases somewhat as local residents escape for the weekend, and many attractions are free.

Sports and Recreation

For the spectator, opportunities in Mexico City are legion. Besides the major sports mentioned below, there are basketball games, boxing and wrestling matches and a growing collegiate schedule of American-style football. Refer to the sports pages of the newspapers for current activities and schedules. Your hotel can help you get tickets.

The best **bullfighting** in the republic can be found at the **Plaza México**, also known as the Plaza Monumental (M: San Antonio, line 7). Accommodating more than 50,000 spectators—the world's largest bullring—it is located off Avenida Insurgentes Sur, about 6 kilometers (4 miles) south of the circle at Paseo de la Reforma (the Cuauhtémoc Monument). Another ring is **El Toreo**, a short distance northeast of the Hippodrome of the Americas (M: Cuatro Caminos, line 2, west depot), although these days it is used primarily for wrestling and boxing tournaments.

The season for top matadors runs from December through March or April. During other months novice bullfighters (novilleros) take the ring. Bullfights start promptly at 4 p.m. on Sunday; buses marked "Plaza México" travel along Insurgentes Sur throughout the afternoon. Plan on arriving early to get a good seat, and hang on to your ticket stub so you can reclaim your seat if you need to leave it. The scene at these corridas is as rollicking as that at any American football or baseball game. Vendors hawk programs, gum and peanuts; hundreds of stalls outside the ring sell cold beer and snacks.

To avoid long lines at the bullring's ticket counter, buy tickets in advance or book a tour that includes a bullfight through your hotel or a travel agency. Ticket prices range from around $5 to $25; they vary according to proximity to the ring and the side on which you sit. Sun (sol) is cheap, shade (sombra) is expensive. Seats in the sun tend to attract the more unruly fans. For more information phone (5) 563-3959.

Jai alai, a fast-paced game that originated centuries ago in the Basque countries of Europe, is another popular spectator sport. The players compete by catching a small, hard ball in cestas (wicker baskets) worn on their arms, then slamming it back and forth on a 200-foot court. As much fun as watching the games is betting on them. With ever-changing odds, betting is intense and quite complex; bookies walk through the crowd carrying pads of betting slips.

Professional jai alai is played at the **Frontón México**, which faces the north side of Plaza de la República (M: Revolución, line 2). Several games are played evenings, Tues.-Sun.; box office opens at 6:30 p.m. Admission is charged. **Note:** Jackets and ties are normally required for men, dresses for women. **Frontenis** replaces *cestas* with rackets and employs a smaller court. It is played by women at **Frontón Metropolitano**, off Melchor Ocampo at Bahía Todos Santos #190. Admission is charged.

The country's most popular game is **soccer** *(fútbol)*. It is played almost every weekend by the big leagues at **Azteca Stadium**, in the southern part of the city on Calzada de Tlalpan, north of the Periférico Sur. Shuttles are available from the Taxqueña Metro station (line 2). Nearly 8,000 seats in this enormous facility are ensconced in plush boxes; many are air-conditioned and leased for 99-year terms. In August 1994, more than 112,000 fans crammed the stadium to watch the Houston Oilers defeat the Dallas Cowboys in an exhibition game. Professional soccer games also are played at the **Ciudad de los Deportes** (Sports City Stadium), near the Plaza México bullring (M: San Antonio, line 7), and at **Olympic Stadium** on the National University of Mexico campus. Minor leagues and amateur teams play at hundreds of fields throughout the city.

Professional **baseball** is popular in Mexico City, where there is league play during the summer months. Most games are played at the **Social Security Stadium**, Avenida Cuauhtémoc at Obrero Mundial (M: Centro Médico, lines 3 and 9). For a small admission fee you can enjoy the sweep and dash of **polo**. During the season matches are held on Sundays at **Mars Field** (Campo Marte) in Chapultepec Park (M: Auditorio, line 7).

Horse racing takes place at the lovely **Hipódromo de las Américas** (Hippodrome of the Americas). The track is in the northwestern part of the city on Avenida Conscripto, west of the Avenida Avila Camacho (the Periférico). Buses and *peseros* (minivans) marked "Hipódromo" travel west along Paseo de la Reforma to the track. Races are held throughout the year on Tuesday, Thursday, Friday and Saturday afternoons; races are not held Easter or Christmas weeks. Admission to the general admission section is free with the purchase of a program. There are several restaurants on the premises, including the fashionable Jockey Club. For further information phone (5) 557-4100.

Auto racing takes place at the **Autódromo Hermanos Rodríguez**, an exacting 3-mile course just off Viaducto Miguel Alemán in the Magdalena-Mixhuca Sports City complex, southwest of the airport (M: Ciudad Deportiva, line 9). Admission is charged. Also here is the **Palacio de los Desportes** (Sports Palace), Avenida Río Churubusco and the Viaducto (M: Velódromo, line 9). Designed by Félix Candela for the 1968 Olympic Games, it seats 25,000.

Wrestling matches of the fixed variety *(lucha libre)* attract hordes of fanatically loyal fans. The combatants take on the personas of heroes and villains, often wearing masks that conceal their identities as regular human beings. A massive suspension of disbelief helps in enjoying these flamboyant free-for-alls. Many matches take place at the **Arena Coliseo**, downtown at República del Peru #77 (M: Garibaldi, line 8). A visit is not for the faint of heart; the crowds are definitely on the rough side.

If you have more than a few days to spend in Mexico City, sightseeing can be alternated with your favorite activity. **Golf** and **tennis** can be arranged at private clubs except on weekends; hotels can assist in making arrangements. Several stables within Chapultepec Park rent horse for rides along the park's bridle paths. On weekends, many city residents venture to Cuernavaca, Cuautla *(see separate listings)*, Tequisquiapan and other nearby **swimming** resorts.

NIGHTLIFE

More often than not, nightlife in Mexico City means nightclubs—both independent establishments and the lobby bars in the big hotels. Nightclub tours are an easy way to visit some of the city's hot spots, since transportation and reservations are arranged for you. These tours usually last several hours and include dinner and a nice restaurant and perhaps a floor show or a stop at Plaza Garibaldi *(see below)*. For more information check with your hotel desk or contact Gray Line Tours; phone (5) 208-1163. The weekly publication *Tiempo Libre*, available at newsstands, provides entertainment listings.

Just as they do in Acapulco and Cancún, people in Mexico City tend to keep the evening going practically all night. Dinner might begin at 9 or 10 p.m., and most of the discos don't kick into high gear until midnight. Nearly every hotel has a bar where you can enjoy a quiet libation or nightcap. **Note:** Regardless of where you go after dark, use caution, and arrange for designated taxi transportation both to your destination and back to your hotel.

Hotel lobby bars offer an elegant atmosphere, a sophisticated clientele and music for dancing. Good bets include the bars in the **Intercontinental Presidente Mexico City**, Campos Elíseos #218, Colonia Polanco; the **Camino Real Mexico**, Mariano Escobedo #700 (near the main entrance to Chapultepec Park); the **Sheraton María Isabel Hotel and Towers**, Paseo de la Reforma #325 (opposite the Independence

Monument); and the **Westin Galería Plaza**, Hamburgo #195 in the Zona Rosa.

Avoid *cantinas*, small, dimly lit places that tend to attract hard-drinking patrons. An exception is the **La Opera Bar**, Avenida 5 de Mayo #10 at Filomeno Mata, 3 blocks east of Alameda Park (M: Bellas Artes, lines 2 and 8). By day this is a crowded lunch spot, with jacketed waiters and formal service. In the evening dinner is served, but the gilded ceiling, mirrored walls, dark paneled booths and clubby feel also make La Opera an intimate place for an early evening cocktail.

Elaborate floor shows are another option. International headliners appear at **El Patio**, an old-fashioned nightclub at Atenas #9 (east of the Zona Rosa and a block south of Paseo de la Reforma). **La Veranda**, in the Sheraton María Isabel, presents a Fiesta Mexicana show that includes dinner and dancing; phone (5) 207-3933. The rooftop bar at the **Hotel Majestic**, Avenida Francisco Madero #73 (M: Zócalo, line 2), often has live entertainment in a setting overlooking the *Zócalo*.

For those seeking an indubitably Mexican nightlife experience, **Plaza Garibaldi** offers it. Bounded by avenidas Lázaro Cárdenas and República de Honduras, about 5 blocks north of the Palace of Fine Arts (M: Garibaldi, line 8), this square is ruled by the city's mariachi bands, who serenade paying customers every night of the week. The typical outfit includes violin, trumpet, guitar and a heart-tugging vocalist, and the songs almost always address the travails of love (usually at the hands of an unfaithful woman—a nod to Mexican *machismo*). The name supposedly comes from the French word for marriage and the mid-19th-century custom of hiring a group of musicians to play at weddings. These days mariachis also appear at birthday celebrations and are hired out for parties.

Decked out in tight, silver-spangled costumes and wide-brimmed sombreros, the musicians unabashedly solicit business from the throngs of people crowding the plaza. Sunday night is the best time to hear music in the square itself. Mariachis also perform in the surrounding *cantinas* and clubs, which stay open into the wee hours. **Plaza Santa Cecelia** nightclub, across Calle Amargura from the plaza, puts on first-rate mariachi shows. At **El Tenampa** and **Tlaquepaque**, you can sit and listen to the mariachis while nibbling *botanas* (snacks). A less-raucous alternative is the **Jorongo Bar** in the Sheraton María Isabel, where mariachi trios play in luxurious surroundings.

Although Garibaldi is at its most exuberant late at night and is a traditional last stop for an evening on the town, the surrounding neighborhood is unsavory, filled with cheap hotels and gaudy burlesque theaters. Guard against pickpockets if the atmosphere is particularly rowdy,

and make sure you've arranged for safe transportation back to your destination.

Note: Always be careful when venturing out after dark anywhere in Mexico City, even in tourist-frequented areas like the Zona Rosa and Polanco. Metro is not recommended as a way of getting around, and never hail a taxi on the street. The safest way to travel is to make pickup and drop-off arrangements with your hotel taxi service.

CONCERTS

Music, being such an integral part of Mexican life, is celebrated in Mexico City throughout the year. The Sunday edition of *The News*, the city's English-language daily, includes a page listing current cultural offerings. Your hotel or a travel agency may be able to obtain tickets for major performances, which should be obtained in advance. Reservations also can be made through Ticketmaster; phone (5) 325-9000.

The **Palacio de Bellas Artes** (M: Bellas Artes, lines 2 and 8) is the home of the **National Symphony Orchestra**. The **National Opera** also stages productions here, usually January through March and August through October. The **Mexico City Philharmonic** gives concerts at **Ollin-Yolistli Hall**. It is located on the Anillo Periférico Sur just east of Avenida Insurgentes, at the city's southern end. International symphony, ballet and opera companies also perform at the **National Auditorium** in Chapultepec Park (M: Auditorio, line 7).

The acclaimed **National University Symphony** mounts its concert program at **Justo Sierra Auditorium** (M: Universidad, line 3, south terminal), on the National University of Mexico campus. The hall is famed for its acoustics. **Nezahualcoyotl Hall** regularly presents performing artists and groups, including the **State of Mexico Symphony**. It is located within the University Cultural Center, which is off Avenida Insurgentes south of the main campus buildings.

Music al fresco is particularly popular and can be heard on the street or at parks throughout the capital. Better yet, many of these performances are free. Styles range from Plaza Garibaldi's mariachi bands *(see "Nightlife")* to Mexican-style hard rock and heavy metal. Sunday concerts often take place in Alameda Park, usually around noon, and near the **Casa del Lago** (Lake House) in Chapultepec Park. The central plazas in the southern suburbs of Coyoacán and San Angel often are the scene of weekend musical offerings. Popular international artists appear at the National Auditorium, the **Palacio de los Desportes** (Sports Palace) and other large venues.

Some performances are to be seen as well as heard, especially the **Ballet Folklórico de México**. The ingredients for this elaborate 2-hour spectacle come from Mexico's rich heritage of traditional music and dance. The costumes in particular are flamboyantly colorful. Performances normally take place at the Palace of Fine Arts Wednesday at 9 p.m. and Sunday at 9:30 a.m. and 9 p.m. The famed Tiffany glass curtain at the **Palace of Fine Arts Theater** is lowered before the ballet's Sunday morning performances only. Although tickets are sold in advance at the box office, they may be difficult to obtain unless you purchase them at least a day ahead or book a tour that includes the ballet.

Note: The troupe is occasionally moved to another venue, usually the National Auditorium, to accommodate visiting performing arts groups. Check with the box office regarding specific schedule information; phone (5) 709-3111.

THEATER AND CINEMA

Stage productions of every imaginable genre can be found in Mexico City. Theaters are not centralized in an entertainment district but are located throughout the city. The **Teatro de los Insurgentes** (Theater of the Insurgents), Avenida Insurgentes Sur #1587, presents plays and musicals in a building that boasts a striking Diego Rivera mosaic on its facade. The **Teatro Blanquita** (Blanquita Theater), 4 blocks north of the Latin-American Tower on Avenida Lázaro Cárdenas (M: Bellas Artes, lines 2 and 8), offers variety shows performed by Mexico's top singers, dancers, comedians and magicians. Other theaters include the **Teatro de la Ciudad**, a block northeast of the Palace of Fine Arts at Calle Donceles #36 (due to reopen sometime in 2000 following a period of renovation); the **Hidalgo**, Avenida Hidalgo #23 (M: Hidalgo, line 2); and the **Virginia Fábregas Theater**, Calle Donceles #24-A (M: Allende, line 2). For listings, check *The News* or *Tiempo Libre*.

A complex of theaters cluster around the National Auditorium in Chapultepec Park. They include the **Teatro Granero** (Granary Theater), which is a theater-in-the-round, and the **Teatro del Bosque** (Theater of the Woods). Theatre Workshop, a local amateur group, stages productions in English at the **University of the Americas Theater**, Puebla #223, Colonia Roma, within walking distance of the Zona Rosa (M: Sevilla or Insurgentes, line 1).

Those with an understanding of the official language will have a much wider range of options, including works by American playwrights. Theaters presenting plays in Spanish include the **Teatro Casa de la Paz** (House of Peace), Cozumel #33, Colonia Roma (M: Sevilla, line 1); the **Foro la Gruta**, Avenida Revolución #1500 in San Angel; and the **Foro Shakespeare**, Zamora #7, Colonia Condesa, a few blocks southeast of Chapultepec Park's eastern end.

Most American and foreign films of any recognition are screened in Mexico City, with Spanish subtitles. Admission is inexpensive compared with that for theaters showing first-run films in the United States. Among the movie houses showing both arthouse and commercial fare are **Cineteca Nacional**, Calzada México-Coyoacán #389, the southern extension of Avenida Cuauhtémoc (M: Coyoacán, line 3), phone (5) 688-3272; **Cine Latino**, on Paseo de la Reforma between the Statue of Cuauhtémoc and the Independence Monument; **Cinematógrafo del Chopo**, Dr. Atl #37, Colonia Santa María de la Ribera; and **Sala José Revueltas** and **Sala Julio Bracho** in the Centro Cultural Universitario (University Cultural Center), Avenida Insurgentes Sur #3000 (south of the UNAM campus), phone (5) 685-2580.

SPECIAL EVENTS

Mexico City residents observe many of the celebrations listed in the "Fiestas and Holidays" section on pages 446-448. The capital also gives an extra flourish to historical commemorations that helped secure independence and pave the way for modern Mexico. Several religious holidays are of special importance as well.

Flower-garlanded cows, beribboned dogs and cats and irreverent roosters are paraded on Jan. 17 for the *Feast of San Antonio Abad*, or the "blessing of the animals." This whimsical ceremony takes place at the Metropolitan Cathedral on the *Zócalo*. On May 1, *Labor Day*, the president reviews a huge parade of workers from the central balcony of the National Palace. For the *Feast of Corpus Christi*, families dress children in native costumes or their Sunday best and gather at the Metropolitan Cathedral for a priest's blessing. The date is variable, occurring between late May and mid-June.

The fall of Tenochtitlán to Hernán Cortés and his followers is commemorated on *Cuauhtémoc Day*, Aug. 21, with wreath-laying ceremonies at the Plaza of the Three Cultures and the Cuauhtémoc Statue at the intersection of Paseo de la Reforma and Avenida Insurgentes. Father Miguel Hidalgo's "El Grito de Dolores," the rallying cry of Mexican independence, is repeated by the president of Mexico and echoed by hundreds of thousands on the evening of Sept. 15 in Plaza Constitución (the *Zócalo*). One of the year's biggest events, it is nationally televised. A morning military parade on *Independence Day*, Sept. 16, proceeds from the *Zócalo* to the Independence Monument, past buildings draped with streamers in the national colors of red, green and white.

Revolution Day, Nov. 20, features a spirited parade down avenidas Madero, Juárez and Reforma in commemoration of the start of the Revolution of 1910. The venerated Virgin of Guadalupe, patron saint of the country, is the focal point of a nationwide celebration of dancing, fireworks and religious processions on Dec. 12, the *Feast Day of the Virgin of Guadalupe*. Devout believers from throughout the country and abroad make the journey to the Basilica of Guadalupe, in the northern suburb of Villa de Guadalupe. Mexico City is decorated in high style for Christmas and the 9 days leading up to it, during which there are traditional re-enactments of the Holy Family's search for an inn *(posada)*.

WHERE TO STAY

BEST WESTERN HOTEL DE CORTES

▼▼ ▼▼   *Historic Hotel*   ((5)518-2182

All Year $95-$150   XP $20
Location: Across from Alameda Park. (Ave Hidalgo 85/ Paseo de La Reforma, 06300). Fax: 5/512-1863. **Facility:** Authentic 18th-century guest house with beautiful patio featuring rooms with fans, windows that open and disposable slippers. 29 units. 4 two-bedroom units. Some suites ($150). *Bath:* combo or shower only. 2 stories, exterior corridors. **Terms:** F12; cancellation fee imposed. **Amenities:** safes, honor bars, hair dryers. **Guest Services:** valet laundry. **Business Services:** meeting rooms. *Fee:* fax. **Cards:** AE, DI, MC, VI.

⬛ 🍴 🏋 🖨

BEST WESTERN-HOTEL MAJESTIC

▼▼ ▼▼   *Historic Hotel*   ((5)521-8600

All Year $88-$93   XP $10
Location: Facing Zocalo; in the heart of old Mexico City, adjacent to the Great Main Plaza. Madero 73 06000. Fax: 5/512-6262. **Facility:** Colonial-style hotel. Old World atmosphere. Public areas decorated with hand painted ceramic tiles from the 1700s. Teeming with Mexican diversity. Meets AAA guest room security requirements. 85 units. 5 two-bedroom units. 7 stories, interior corridors. **Parking:** extra charge or valet. **Terms:** cancellation fee imposed. **Amenities:** honor bars. *Some:* safes. **Guest Services:** valet laundry. **Business Services:** meeting rooms. **Cards:** AE, DI, MC, VI. *(See color ad below)*

⬛ 🍴 🏋 🎥

CAMINO REAL MEXICO

▼▼▼ ▼▼▼ *Hotel* ((5)263-8888

All Year $251 XP $35
Location: Between Victor Hugo and Kent, just n of Diana Cir; from Periferico, exit Masarik, then w. Mariano Escobedo 700 11590. Fax: 5/263-8889. **Facility:** Distinguished atmosphere. Expansive public areas. Very large rooms and bathrooms. Multi-lingual staff. 709 units. 9 two-bedroom units and 9 units with kitchen. Some suites ($399-$1109). 5 stories, interior corridors. **Parking:** extra charge or valet. **Terms:** F12; 7 day cancellation notice, package plans. **Amenities:** voice mail, safes, honor bars, hair dryers. *Some:* CD players. **Dining:** Los Azulejos, Restaurant Fouquet's de Paris, see separate listing. **Leisure Activities:** heated pool. *Fee:* 4 lighted tennis courts. **Guest Services:** gift shop, valet laundry. *Fee:* massage. **Business Services:** conference facilities, administrative services. *Fee:* PC, fax. **Cards:** AE, CB, DI, MC, VI. *(See color ad p 328 & opposite title page)*

🔣 🍴 24🕐 ⓨ 🏋 D 🏊 📺 📼 🖨
       FEE   FEE
📠 / ✖ 💻 🖵 🚹 /

CONTINENTAL PLAZA PEDREGAL

▼▼▼ *Hotel* (5/681-6855

All Year $150-$200 XP $12
Location: Just off Periferico Sur, exit Luis Cabrera. 3487 Periferico Sur 10400. Fax: 5/595-4394. **Facility:** European boutique-style hotel. Richly appointed rooms. Meets AAA guest room security requirements. 63 units. Some whirlpool units. *Bath:* shower only. 7 stories, interior corridors. **Parking:** extra charge. **Terms:** F12. **Amenities:** safes, honor bars. **Leisure Activities:** whirlpool, steamroom, rooftop sun deck, exercise room. **Guest Services:** valet laundry. **Business Services:** meeting rooms, fax. **Cards:** AE, DI, MC, VI.

                SOME UNITS
🍴 24🕐 D 📠 / ✖ /

FIESTA AMERICANA REFORMA

▼▼▼ *Hotel* ((5)140-4100

All Year $110-$125 XP $11
Location: Sw quarter of Glorieta Cristobal Colon. Paseo de la Reforma 80 06600. Fax: 5/140-4150. **Facility:** Fine public facilities. Some executive floor rooms with added amenities. 610 units. Some suites. 25 stories, interior corridors. **Parking:** valet. **Terms:** F12. **Amenities:** voice mail, honor bars, hair dryers. *Some:* safes. **Leisure Activities:** sauna, steamroom, exercise room. **Guest Services:** gift shop, valet laundry. *Fee:* massage. **Business Services:** conference facilities, administrative services, PC. *Fee:* fax. **Cards:** AE, DI, DS, MC, VI.

                  SOME UNITS
🔣 🍴 24🕐 D 📺 💻 📠 / ✖ /
                FEE

FOUR SEASONS HOTEL MEXICO D.F.

▼▼▼ ▼▼▼ *Hotel* ((5)230-1818

All Year $250-$360 XP $30
Location: On Paseo de la Reforma, adjacent to Chapultepec Park. Paseo de la Reforma 500 06600. Fax: 5/230-1817. **Facility:** Elegant and refined public areas. Spacious, tastefully appointed units. Most units overlook beautifully landscaped courtyard. 240 units. 2 two-bedroom units and 1 three-bedroom unit. 8 stories, interior corridors. **Parking:** extra charge or valet. **Terms:** F18; monthly rates available. **Amenities:** voice mail, safes, honor bars, hair dryers. **Dining & Entertainment:** dining room, coffee shop, 6:30 am-11:30 pm, $30-$70, cocktails, also, El Restaurante, see separate listing, entertainment. **Leisure Activities:** saunas, whirlpool, small heated rooftop pool. **Guest Services:** gift shop, afternoon tea, valet laundry. *Fee:* area transportation, massage. **Business Services:** conference facilities, administrative services. *Fee:* PC, fax. **Cards:** AE, DI, MC, VI.

➕ 🍴 24🕐 ⓨ 🏋 Ⓢ D 🏊 📺 📼
FEE   FEE   FEE
          SOME UNITS
🖨 📠 / ✖ 📼 /
            FEE

HOTEL ARISTOS

▼▼▼ *Hotel* (5/211-0112

All Year $80-$100
Location: In the Pink Zone. Paseo de la Reforma 276 06600. Fax: 5/514-4473. **Facility:** All rooms with king beds with separate sitting area with sleeper sofa. Complimentary bottled water in guest rooms. Junior, senior and residential suites available. 326 units. 1 two-bedroom unit. Some whirlpool units. 13 stories, interior corridors. **Parking:** extra charge. **Terms:** package plans. **Amenities:** honor bars, hair dryers. **Leisure Activities:** small pool, sauna, exercise room. **Guest Services:** gift shop, valet laundry. *Fee:* massage. **Business Services:** meeting rooms. *Fee:* fax. **Cards:** AE, DI, MC, VI.

                SOME UNITS
🍴 ⓨ 🏊 📺 / 📼 /

HOTEL CALINDA GENEVE

▼▼ *Hotel* ((5)211-0071

All Year $166 XP $12
Location: 0.5 km s of Paseo de la Reforma; in the Pink Zone. Londres 130 06600. Fax: 5/208-7422. **Facility:** Refined, Old World atmosphere. Some rooms, such as corner units, are larger than other rooms. Meets AAA guest room security requirements. 320 units. 10 two-bedroom units. 5 stories, interior corridors. **Terms:** F12. **Amenities:** honor bars. **Leisure Activities:** saunas, steamrooms. **Guest Services:** valet laundry. *Fee:* massage. **Business Services:** meeting rooms, administrative services, PC, fax. **Cards:** AE, DI, MC, VI. *(See color ad p 4 and p 329)*

SOME UNITS

HOTEL CASA INN MEXICO

▼▼ *Hotel* (5/211-0109

All Year $70-$80 XP $12
Location: Just n of Paseo de la Reforma, corner of Rio Lerma and Rio Mississippi. Rio Lerma 237 06500. Fax: 5/208-2014. **Facility:** Public areas with air conditioning. Meets AAA guest room security requirements. 165 units. Some suites. *Bath:* shower only. 13 stories, interior corridors. **Terms:** F12. **Amenities:** safes. **Guest Services:** gift shop, valet laundry. **Business Services:** meeting rooms. *Fee:* fax. **Cards:** AE, DI, MC, VI.

🅰🅰🅰 HOTEL CENTURY

▼▼▼ *Hotel* (5/726-9911

All Year $110-$130 XP $20
Location: In the Pink Zone. Liverpool 152 06600. Fax: 5/525-7475. **Facility:** Unique high-rise with oval shaped rooms, some older furnishings. 142 units. *Bath:* combo or shower only. 21 stories, interior corridors. **Parking:** extra charge or valet. **Terms:** F12; 3 day cancellation notice, package plans. **Amenities:** honor bars. **Dining & Entertainment:** coffee shop, 7 am-11 pm, $12-$15, cocktails, entertainment. **Guest Services:** valet laundry. **Business Services:** meeting rooms. **Cards:** AE, DI, MC, VI. *(See color ad below)*

SOME UNITS

🅰🅰🅰 HOTEL EL CID

▼▼ *Hotel* (5/277-6411

All Year $82-$90 XP $10
Location: Colonia San Pedro de Los Pinos; Ave Revolucion S and Periferico. Revolucion 583 03800. Fax: 5/272-2183. **Facility:** Attractive guest rooms. 184 units. Some whirlpool units. *Bath:* shower or tub only. 7 stories, interior corridors. **Parking:** valet. **Terms:** F12; 7 day cancellation notice. **Dining & Entertainment:** restaurant, 7 am-midnight, $10-$18, cocktails, entertainment. **Guest Services:** valet laundry. **Business Services:** conference facilities. *Fee:* fax. **Cards:** AE, MC, VI.

SOME UNITS

HOTEL INTERNACIONAL HAVRE

▼▼ *Hotel* (5/211-0082

All Year $50-$60 XP $15
Location: Just s of Paseo de la Reforma. Havre 21 06600. Fax: 5/533-1284. **Facility:** European atmosphere. Spacious rooms. 48 units. 14 stories, interior corridors. **Parking:** not available. **Terms:** F12 **Guest Services:** valet laundry. **Business Services:** fax. **Cards:** AE, CB, DI, MC, VI.

HOTEL JARDIN AMAZONAS

▼▼ *Motor Inn* (5/533-5950

All Year $50 XP $10
Location: Just n of Paseo de la Reforma. Rio Amazonas 73 06500. Fax: 5/514-2440. **Facility:** Some small rooms. 50 units, 3 with efficiency. *Bath:* shower only. 4 stories (no elevator), interior corridors. **Terms:** F12; 3 day cancellation notice. **Amenities:** honor bars. **Leisure Activities:** heated pool. **Guest Services:** valet laundry. **Cards:** AE, DI, MC, VI.

SOME UNITS

HOTEL J R PLAZA AEROPUERTO

▼▼▼ *Hotel* (5/785-5200

All Year $80-$110 XP $10
Location: Opposite international airport. Puerto Aereo Blvd 390 15500. Fax: 5/784-3221. **Facility:** Attractive guest rooms. Old World charm hotel with stained glass ceilings, rich wood accents, large junior suites. Older furnishing of excellent quality. Some three bedroom units. Complimentary bottled water. Some junior suites with separate sitting area and extra TV. 125 units. 4 stories, interior corridors. **Parking:** extra charge or valet. **Terms:** F12. **Amenities:** hair dryers. **Guest Services:** [CP] meal plan available, valet laundry. **Business Services:** meeting rooms. *Fee:* fax. **Cards:** AE, MC, VI.

SOME UNITS
[✈] [†↑] [✦] / [X̶] /

ⓐⓐ HOTEL MARCO POLO

▼▼▼ *Hotel* ((5)207-1893

All Year $145 XP $24
Location: In the Pink Zone. Amberes 27 06600. Fax: 5/533-3727. **Facility:** Boutique hotel with well-appointed rooms. Loaded with amenities like bath scale, clothes pressing machine, cosmetic mirror, robes and slippers. All double bedded units with sleeper sofa. All guests are greeted with a plate of fresh fruit and small chocolates. Meets AAA guest room security requirements. 64 efficiencies. Some whirlpool units. 6 stories, interior corridors. **Parking:** valet only. **Terms:** F12; 5 day cancellation notice-fee imposed. **Amenities:** safes, honor bars, hair dryers. **Dining:** restaurant, 7 am-midnight, $6-$14. **Leisure Activities:** *Fee:* in-room exercise machine. **Guest Services:** valet laundry. **Business Services:** meeting rooms, administrative services. *Fee:* PC, fax. **Cards:** AE, DI, MC, VI.

[†↑] [D] [✦] [▤] [▣] [▯] [DATA PORT]

HOTEL MARQUIS REFORMA

▼▼▼ ▼▼ *Hotel* (5/211-3600

All Year $265 XP $30
Location: 0.8 km sw of jct Insurgentes; opposite Chapultepec Park. Paseo de la Reforma 465 06500. Fax: 5/211-5561. **Facility:** Dramatic exterior of pink granite and blue glass. Expensive furnishings in public areas. Well-appointed rooms. Extensive business services available. Meets AAA guest room security requirements. 208 units. Some suites and whirlpool units. 11 stories, interior corridors. **Parking:** valet. **Terms:** F12; package plans - weekends. **Amenities:** voice mail, fax, safes, honor bars, hair dryers. *Some:* video games. **Leisure Activities:** saunas, whirlpools, outdoor terrace with whirlpool. **Guest Services:** gift shop, afternoon tea, valet laundry. *Fee:* massage. **Business Services:** conference facilities, administrative services, PC. *Fee:* fax. **Cards:** AE, DI, MC, VI.

[†↑] [24↑] [Y] [♠] [S] [D] [♦] [✦] [▤] [DATA PORT]
SOME UNITS FEE FEE
/ [X̶] [VCR] /

ⓐⓐ HOTEL NIKKO MEXICO

▼▼▼ ▼▼▼ *Hotel* ((5)280-1111

All Year $280 XP $15
Location: Polanco Zone; jct Campos Eliseos and Andres Bello sts; 1 blk from National Museum of Anthropology. Campos Eliseos 204 Col Polanco 11560. Fax: 5/280-9191. **Facility:** Elegance with modern architecture. 744 units, 10 with efficiency (no utensils). Some suites ($550-$2400) and whirlpool units. 38 stories, interior corridors. **Parking:** extra charge or valet. **Terms:** F12. **Amenities:** voice mail, safes, honor bars, irons, hair dryers. *Some:* CD players, fax. **Dining & Entertainment:** dining room, 3 restaurants, 6:30 am-1 am, $15-$30, cocktails, also, Les Celebrites, see separate listing, nightclub, entertainment. **Leisure Activities:** heated pool, saunas, steamrooms, putting green. *Fee:* golf practice range, 3 lighted tennis courts. **Guest Services:** gift shop, valet laundry. *Fee:* airport transportation-limousine, area transportation-limousine, massage. **Business Services:** conference facilities, administrative services, PC. *Fee:* fax. **Cards:** AE, DI, JC, MC, VI. *(See color ad p 332)*

[✈] [†↑] [24↑] [♠] [D] [🏊] [♦] [✦] [▤] [▣]
FEE FEE
SOME UNITS
[DATA PORT] / [X̶] [VCR] /

HOTEL PARQUE ENSENADA

▼▼ ▼▼ *Hotel* ((5)208-0052

6/1-11/30 $56-$69 XP $5
12/1-5/31 $53-$67 XP $5
Location: Colonia Roma; jct Cuauhtemoc y Alvaro Obregon aves; downtown area. Ave Alvaro Obregon 13 06700. Fax: 5/208-0052. **Facility:** Family ambience. Ask about their business section rooms. You'll find them a bit larger, with newer furnishings and better lighting. An excellent value. 132 units. *Bath:* shower only. 7 stories, interior corridors. **Terms:** F12. **Amenities:** safes. *Some:* honor bars. **Guest Services:** valet laundry. **Business Services:** administrative services, fax. **Cards:** AE, MC, VI.

SOME UNITS
[†↑] [✦] / [X̶] /

HOTEL PLAZA FLORENCIA

▼▼▼ ▼▼ *Hotel* (5/242-4700

All Year $130 XP $25
Location: In Pink Zone. Florencia 61 St 60006. Fax: 5/242-4785. **Facility:** Cozy ambience. Fifth floor rooms are for non-smoking guests. These rooms also have unique decorative wood accents. Hair dryers available at front desk. Meets AAA guest room security requirements. 142 units. 12 stories, interior corridors. **Parking:** extra charge or valet. **Terms:** F12; 7 day cancellation notice. **Amenities:** honor bars. **Leisure Activities:** *Fee:* exercise room. **Guest Services:** valet laundry. **Business Services:** meeting rooms, administrative services. *Fee:* PC, fax. **Cards:** AE, MC, VI.

[†↑] [✦] [▣] [DATA PORT]

HOTEL POLANCO

▼▼▼ ▼▼ *Hotel* (5/280-8082

All Year $73-$80
Location: Col Polanco opposite Chapultepec Park. (Edgar A Poe 8, at Campos Eliseos, 11560). Fax: 5/280-8082. **Facility:** Suburban quiet atmosphere, well appointed rooms. Meets AAA guest room security requirements. 77 units. *Bath:* shower only. 3 stories, interior corridors. **Amenities:** safes. **Dining:** La Botiglia, see separate listing. **Guest Services:** valet laundry. *Fee:* fax. **Cards:** AE, DS, MC, VI.

[†↑] [X̶] [✦] [DATA PORT]

HOTEL POSADA VIENA

◆◆ ◆◆ *Hotel*   ✆ (5)566-0700

All Year $65   XP $35
Location: Just off Dinamarca. Marsella 28 06600.
Fax: 5/592-7302. **Facility:** Modest to nicely furnished guest
rooms, featuring ceiling fans, bottled water and cosmetic
mirror. 88 units. 6 two-bedroom units. *Bath:* combo or
shower only. 4-5 stories, interior corridors. **Terms:** D10; 3
day cancellation notice. **Amenities:** irons, hair dryers. **Guest
Services:** valet laundry. **Business Services:** meeting rooms.
Cards: MC, VI.

SOME UNITS

⬛ 🍴 🍸 🎬 / 🐾 /

HOTEL PRESIDENTE INTER-CONTINENTAL MEXICO CITY

◆◆ ◆◆ ◆ *Hotel*   ✆ (5)327-7700

All Year $185-$205   XP $45
Location: On Paseo de la Reforma, 1.3 km w Periferico; in
Polanco, opposite Chapultepec Park and the National Audi-
torium. Campo Eliseos 218 Col Pol 11560. Fax: 5/327-7783.
Facility: Very modern hotel across from Chapultepec Park.
Impressive view from most rooms. Complimentary passes to
local museums and attractions. Some connecting rooms.
Outstanding business center services. Home to visiting
heads-of-state and rock stars, such as President Clinton,
Janet Reno, the King of Spain, Michael Jackson, Don King
and Gloria Estefan. Meets AAA guest room security requirements. 657 units. 2 two-bedroom units and 2 units with
kitchen. Some suites ($550-$1855) and whirlpool units. 42
stories, interior corridors. **Parking:** extra charge or valet.
Terms: F18; cancellation fee imposed. **Amenities:** voice
mail, honor bars, hair dryers. *Some:* fax, irons. **Dining:** Maxim's de Paris, Alfredo di Roma, The Palm, see separate listing. **Leisure Activities:** exercise room. **Guest Services:**
[BP] meal plan available, gift shop, valet laundry. *Fee:* area
transportation. **Business Services:** conference facilities, administrative services, PC. *Fee:* fax. **Cards:** AE, DI, MC, VI.

✈ 🍴 24🍴 🍸 🥂 Ⓢ Ⓓ 🐾 DATA PORT
FEE   FEE
SOME UNITS
/ ⊠ VCR 💻 /

HOTEL REAL DEL SUR

▼▼▼ *Hotel*   (5/610-4256

All Year $80-$90   XP $12
Location: Colonia El Reloj; 20 km s, jct Ave Division del Norte and Calzada de Tlalpan; Coyoacan. Ave Division del Norte 3640 04620. Fax: 5/617-1035. **Facility:** Comfortable guest rooms. Meets AAA guest room security requirements. 115 units. Some whirlpool units. *Bath:* some combo or shower only. 5 stories, interior corridors. **Parking:** valet. **Terms:** F12; 7 day cancellation notice. **Guest Services:** gift shop, valet laundry. **Business Services:** meeting rooms. **Cards:** AE, DI, MC, VI.

[⊤] [24↑] [⊤] [D] [♥]

▲▲▲ HOTEL ROYAL PEDREGAL

▼▼▼ *Hotel*   ((5)726-9036

All Year $220   XP $20
Location: Adjacent to main Periferico, in southern part of city, 0.5 km s from Peri Sur mall. Periferico Sur 4363 14210. Fax: 5/645-7964. **Facility:** Modern hotel with large rooms and elegant public areas. All rooms with bottled water and extra phone in all bathrooms. 326 units. Some whirlpool units ($220). *Bath:* combo or shower only. 5 stories, interior corridors. **Parking:** valet. **Terms:** F14; cancellation fee imposed. **Amenities:** safes, honor bars, hair dryers. **Dining & Entertainment:** dining room, coffee shop, 24 hours, $15-$25, cocktails, nightclub, entertainment. **Leisure Activities:** 2 heated pools, sauna. **Guest Services:** gift shop, afternoon tea, valet laundry. *Fee:* massage. **Business Services:** conference facilities, administrative services, PC. *Fee:* fax. **Cards:** AE, DI, MC, VI.

[S⊅] [⊤] [24↑] [⊤] [&] [D] [≥] [≋] [♦] [♥]
                                    FEE
        SOME UNITS
[DATA PORT] / [✕] /

▲▲▲ HOTEL ROYAL ZONA ROSA

▼▼▼ *Hotel*   ((5)228-9918

All Year $110-$130   XP $20
Location: In the Pink Zone, jct Chapultepec and Liverpool sts. Amberes 78 St 06600. Fax: 5/514-3330. **Facility:** Cheerful comfortable rooms. Attractive rooftop area. Most rooms with sleeper sofa. Some rooms with garden view. 162 units. Some whirlpool units. *Bath:* combo or shower only. 20 stories, interior corridors. **Parking:** valet. **Terms:** F14. **Amenities:** extended cable TV, safes, honor bars, hair dryers. **Dining:** dining room, restaurant, 7 am-1 am, $15-$25, cocktails. **Leisure Activities:** small heated pool, steamroom, exercise room. **Guest Services:** gift shop, valet laundry. *Fee:* massage. **Business Services:** meeting rooms, administrative services. *Fee:* PC, fax. **Cards:** AE, DI, MC, VI.

[S⊅] [⊤] [⊤] [D] [≥] [♥] [DATA PORT]
                        FEE

HOTEL SEGOVIA REGENCY

▼▼ *Hotel*   (5/208-8454

All Year $63-$66   XP $5
Location: Jct Monterrey and Oaxaca aves; adjacent to the Pink Zone. Ave Chapultepec 328 06700. Fax: 5/525-0391. **Facility:** Rooms with windows that open for fresh air. All bathrooms with bidet. 120 units. *Bath:* shower only. 7 stories, interior corridors. **Parking:** valet. **Terms:** F10. **Amenities:** safes. **Guest Services:** valet laundry. **Business Services:** meeting rooms. *Fee:* fax. **Cards:** AE, DI, MC, VI.

              SOME UNITS
[S⊅] [⊤] [⊤] [♥] / [Ⓜ] /

▲▲▲ HOTEL SEVILLA PALACE

▼▼▼ *Hotel*   ((5)566-8877

All Year $100-$260   XP $10
Location: Center; sw quarter of Glorieta Cristobal Colon Monumento. Ave Paseo de Reforma 105 06030. Fax: 5/703-1521. **Facility:** Panoramic rooftop pool and lounge. Comfortable guest rooms. Ample public areas. 414 units. Some suites and whirlpool units. *Bath:* combo or shower only. 23 stories, interior corridors. **Parking:** valet. **Terms:** F12; cancellation fee imposed. **Amenities:** voice mail, safes, honor bars. **Dining & Entertainment:** restaurant, 7 am-midnight, $10-$25, cocktails, entertainment. **Leisure Activities:** heated pool, whirlpool, exercise room. *Fee:* sauna. **Guest Services:** gift shop, valet laundry. *Fee:* massage. **Business Services:** conference facilities, administrative services. *Fee:* PC, fax. **Cards:** AE, MC, VI.

[S⊅] [⊤] [⊤] [D] [≥] [♥] [🖨]
                        FEE

HOTEL SUITES SAN MARINO

▼▼▼ *Extended Stay Motor Inn*   (5/525-4886

All Year $105   XP $20
Location: Just n of Paseo de la Reforma. Tiber 107 06500. Fax: 5/511-7800. **Facility:** Complimentary bottled water. Corner units larger than other rooms. Toasters available for a fee. 74 efficiencies. 1 two-bedroom unit. Some whirlpool units. *Bath:* combo or shower only. 12 stories, interior corridors. **Parking:** extra charge or valet. **Terms:** F12. **Leisure Activities:** exercise room. **Guest Services:** [CP] meal plan available, valet laundry. **Business Services:** meeting rooms, administrative services, PC. *Fee:* fax. **Cards:** AE, DI, MC, VI.

                          SOME UNITS
[⊤] [⊤] [♥] [DATA PORT] / [✕] [VCR] [▣] [🖨] /
                              FEE   FEE

▲▲▲ J. W. MARRIOTT HOTEL MEXICO CITY

▼▼▼ *Hotel*   (5/282-8899

8/1-11/30 $265
1/1-7/31 $260
12/1-12/31 $255
Location: On Reforma; opposite Chapultepec Park and the National Auditorium. Andres Bello No 29 11560. Fax: 5/282-8804. **Facility:** Cavernous entrance. Well appointed public areas. Very large rooms with oversize antique furnishings. Extensive state-of-the-art facilities. 312 units. 4 two-bedroom units. Some whirlpool units. 26 stories, interior corridors. **Parking:** extra charge or valet. **Terms:** check-in 4 pm. **Amenities:** safes, honor bars. **Dining & Entertainment:** dining room, restaurant, 24 hours, $18-$30, entertainment. **Leisure Activities:** heated pool, wading pool, sauna, whirlpool, steamroom. **Guest Services:** gift shop, afternoon tea, valet laundry. *Fee:* area transportation, massage. **Business Services:** conference facilities, administrative services, PC. *Fee:* fax. **Cards:** AE, DI, MC, VI. *(See color ad 2p 198)*

[✈] [⊤] [24↑] [⊤] [↑] [🎧] [S] [D] [≥] [♦]
FEE   FEE
                SOME UNITS
[♥] [DATA PORT] / [✕] [▣] [📞] /
FEE

▲▲▲ KRYSTAL-ZONA ROSA

▼▼▼ *Hotel*   (5/228-9928

All Year $130-$165   XP $20
Location: In the Pink Zone. Liverpool 155 06600. Fax: 5/511-3490. **Facility:** Modern high-rise. Many rooms with balcony. 302 units. Some whirlpool units. 18 stories, interior corridors. **Parking:** valet. **Terms:** F18; 3 day cancellation notice. **Amenities:** safes, honor bars. **Dining & Entertainment:** dining room, coffee shop, 7 am-1 am, $15-$30, cocktails, entertainment. **Leisure Activities:** heated pool, wading pool. **Guest Services:** gift shop, valet laundry. **Business Services:** conference facilities, administrative services. *Fee:* fax. **Cards:** AE, DS, MC, VI.

                          SOME UNITS
[✈] [⊤] [D] [≥] [♥] [▣] / [✕] /
FEE   FEE

MARRIOTT AEROPUERTO MEXICO CITY

Hotel (5/133-0033

All Year $205
Location: Adjacent to airport. Connected via skywalk in front of Terminal B. Fundidora Monterrey 89 15520. Fax: 5/133-0030. **Facility:** Rooms in series 51 or 57 are larger than other rooms. Rooms in series 56 or 06 with tight floor space. Boarding pass service for guests with carry-on luggage provided with specific airlines. Meets AAA guest room security requirements. 600 units. Some suites and whirlpool units. 8 stories, interior corridors. **Parking:** extra charge or valet. **Amenities:** voice mail, safes, honor bars, irons, hair dryers. **Dining & Entertainment:** dining room, coffee shop, 5 am-1 am, $5-$15, cocktails, entertainment. **Leisure Activities:** heated pool, steamroom. **Guest Services:** gift shop, valet laundry. *Fee:* massage. **Business Services:** conference facilities, administrative services. *Fee:* PC, fax. **Cards:** AE, DI, MC, VI. *(See color ad 2p 198)*

RADISSON PARAISO MEXICO

Hotel (5/606-4211

All Year $170-$190   XP $15
Location: Adjacent to main Periferico in southern part of city, immediately in front of Peri Sur shopping mall. Cuspide 53 14020 (Col Parques del Pedregal). Fax: 5/606-4006. **Facility:** Modern atrium lobby. Hotel offers beauty shop facilities, airline ticket office and car rentals. Some connecting rooms available. 236 units. *Bath:* combo or shower only. 14 stories, interior corridors. **Parking:** extra charge or valet. **Terms:** F12; small pets only. **Amenities:** voice mail, safes, honor bars, hair dryers. **Dining & Entertainment:** dining room, coffee shop, 7 am-11 pm, $8-$25, cocktails, entertainment. **Leisure Activities:** sauna, exercise room. **Guest Services:** gift shop, area transportation-local malls, valet laundry. *Fee:* massage. **Business Services:** conference facilities, administrative services. *Fee:* PC, fax. **Cards:** AE, DI, MC, VI.

SHERATON MARIA ISABEL HOTEL & TOWERS

▼▼▼▼▼ *Hotel* ((5)242-5555

All Year $250-$300 XP $40
Location: Next to US Embassy, opposite Angel de la Independencia Monument. Paseo de la Reforma 325 06500. Fax: 5/207-0684. **Facility:** Distinguished high-rise. Meets AAA guest room security requirements. 752 units. 28 two-bedroom units and 5 three-bedroom units. Some suites ($300-$1800) and whirlpool units. 19-22 stories, interior corridors. **Parking:** valet. **Terms:** F12. **Amenities:** safes (fee), honor bars. **Dining & Entertainment:** 2 dining rooms, coffee shop, 6:30 am-1 am, $10-$20, cocktails, entertainment. **Leisure Activities:** saunas, steamrooms, heated rooftop pool, 2 lighted tennis courts, exercise room. **Guest Services:** gift shop, valet laundry. *Fee:* massage. **Business Services:** meeting rooms, administrative services, PC, fax. **Cards:** AE, CB, DI, MC, VI. *(See color ad p 334)*

FEE
SOME UNITS

SHERATON SUITES SANTA FE

▼▼▼ *Hotel* ((5)258-8500

All Year $300 XP $40
Location: 12 km w of Paseo de la Reforma. 200 Guillermo Gonzalez Camar 01210. Fax: 5/258-8501. **Facility:** Dramatic steel glass high-rise. All units with separate sitting area. 194 units. 10 stories, interior corridors. **Parking:** valet. **Terms:** F12; 3 day cancellation notice-fee imposed. **Amenities:** voice mail, safes, honor bars, irons, hair dryers. **Leisure Activities:** whirlpools, steamroom, exercise room. **Guest Services:** gift shop, area transportation, valet laundry. **Business Services:** conference facilities, administrative services, PC. *Fee:* fax. **Cards:** AE, DI, MC, VI.

FEE
SOME UNITS

SUITES MI CASA

▼▼ *Apartment* (5/566-6711

3/1-11/30 $55 XP $11
12/1-2/1 $50 XP $9
Location: Just s of Paseo de la Reforma, at General Prim and Milan St. General Prim 106 06600. Fax: 5/566-6010. **Facility:** All rooms with fan. Ask for rooms facing the interior, much quieter than rooms facing the street. 27 units with kitchen. 1 two-bedroom unit. *Bath:* shower only. 7 stories, interior corridors. **Terms:** F7; open 12/1-2/1 & 3/1-11/30, 4 day cancellation notice-fee imposed. **Amenities:** safes. **Guest Services:** valet laundry. **Cards:** AE, MC, VI.

WHERE TO DINE

ALFREDO DI ROMA

▼▼ ▼▼ *Italian* (5/327-7700

L $12-$18 D $22-$38
Location: On Paseo de la Reforma, 1.3 km w Periferico; in Polanco, opposite Chapultepec Park and the National Auditorium; in Hotel Presidente Inter-Continental Mexico City. Campos Eliseos 218 11560. **Hours:** 1 pm-midnight. **Reservations:** required. **Features:** casual dress; cocktails; fee for parking; valet parking; a la carte. Elegant dining room and excellent service are combined with authentic Italian dishes. House specialties include imported prosciutto and fettucinni Alfredo prepared tableside. Extensive wine list. Hedonistic desserts. **Cards:** AE, CB, DI, MC, VI.

ANGUS RESTAURANT

▼▼ ▼▼ *Spanish* (5/520-2917

L $6-$12 D $6-$12
Location: Mex 57 and Paseo de la Reforma. Avila Camacho 1 11000. **Hours:** 7 am-midnight, Sun-6 pm. **Features:** casual dress; children's menu; cocktails; a la carte. Casual atmosphere. **Cards:** AE, MC, VI.

CHALET SUIZO

▼▼ ▼▼ *Ethnic* (5/511-7529

L $10-$16 D $16-$28
Location: Just s of Paseo de la Reforma; in the Pink Zone. Niza 37 06600. **Hours:** 12:30 pm-midnight, Fri & Sat-12:30 am. **Features:** semi-formal attire; cocktails; a la carte. Authentic Swiss decor. Variety of well-prepared German and Swiss food offered. This is a quaint Swiss restaurant with typical low ceilings, tudor style wood accents and the owners usually visiting each table, seeing after your needs. **Cards:** AE, CB, DI, MC, VI.

DELMONICO'S

▼▼▼ *Traditional Steak House* (5/207-4949

L $10-$15 D $15-$28
Location: Just off Niza. Londres 91 06600. **Hours:** 8 am-midnight, Sun-6 pm. Closed: 1/1, 12/25. **Features:** casual dress; cocktails & lounge; entertainment; fee for valet parking; a la carte. Saturday and Sunday brunch buffet, 9 am-2 pm. Similar to famous steak, this is a classic dining room with low lights, soft music, white linens and a formal staff. Some table side preparations. **Cards:** AE, DI, MC, VI.

EL PARADOR DE JOSE LUIS

▼▼▼▼ *Traditional Ethnic* (5/533-1840

L $15-$18 D $20-$30
Location: Just s of Paseo de la Reforma. Niza 15 06600. **Hours:** 1 pm-11 pm, Sun-6 pm. Closed major holidays; also Sun. **Reservations:** suggested; for dinner. **Features:** semi-formal attire; cocktails & lounge; fee for valet parking; a la carte. Long time popular restaurant with Old Spain atmosphere. Rich wood decor, white linen covered tables. Wide selection of classics from Spain is their focus, clearly. **Cards:** AE, DI, MC, VI.

EL RESTAURANTE

▼▼▼▼ *Nouvelle Specialty* (5/230-1818

L $10-$18 D $30-$60
Location: On Paseo de la Reforma, adjacent to Chapultepec Park; in Four Seasons Hotel Mexico D.F. 500 Paseo de la Reforma 06600. **Hours:** 1 pm-11 pm. **Reservations:** suggested. **Features:** dressy casual; cocktails; entertainment; fee for parking & valet parking; a la carte, also prix fixe. Culinary fantasy. Mediterranean concepts using premium local ingredients in complex and dazzling presentations. Refined courtyard dining. Impeccable service. A trio softly seranades from a terrace overlooking the courtyard. Some courtyard tables available. **Cards:** AE, CB, DI, MC, VI.

FOCOLARE RESTAURANT

▼▼▼ *Regional Mexican* (5/207-8055

L $8-$12 D $8-$12
Location: In the Pink Zone (Zona Rosa). Hamburgo 87, just off Niz 06600. **Hours:** 7:30 am-2 am, Sat & Sun from 9 am. **Reservations:** suggested; dinner. **Features:** casual dress; cocktails & lounge; entertainment; fee for valet parking; a la carte. Large, festive dining room. Hear the cocks crow as you select regional specialties from Puebla, Yucatan and Veracruz. Nightly folkloric show begins at 9 pm. Expect a night of fun and excellent Mexican food. **Cards:** AE, DI, MC, VI.

LA BOTIGLIA

 Italian (5/280-8082

L $10-$18 **D** $15-$24

Location: Col Polanco opposite Chapultepec Park; in Hotel Polanco. Edgar Allen Poe 8 11560. **Hours:** 8 am-11 pm. **Reservations:** suggested. **Features:** No A/C; semi-formal attire; cocktails & lounge; a la carte. Cozy European chalet ambience. Intriguing selection of anti-pastas, fine cheeses, regional specialties and a well rounded wine list. **Cards:** AE, CB, DI, DS, MC, VI.

LA HACIENDA DE LOS MORALES

 Regional Mexican (5/281-4554

L $7-$18 **D** $7-$18

Location: Just s of Ejercito Nacional. Vazquez de Mella 525 06300. **Hours:** 1 pm-1 am. Closed: 1/1, 12/25. **Reservations:** suggested. **Features:** semi-formal attire; cocktails & lounge; entertainment; valet parking; a la carte. Restored hacienda surrounded by beautiful gardens with fountains. Large courtyards and dining rooms for a relaxing, refined dinner. Excellent quality ingredients, large portions, formal staff. **Cards:** AE, CB, DI, MC, VI.

LES CELEBRITES

 Basque (5/280-1111

L $20-$40 **D** $30-$50

Location: Polanco Zone; jct Campos Eliseos and Andres Bello sts; 1 blk from National Museum of Anthropology; in Hotel Nikko Mexico. 204 Campos Eliseos 11560. **Hours:** 7-11 am, 1:30-4:30 & 7:30-11:30 pm. Closed: Sat. **Reservations:** suggested. **Features:** semi-formal attire; cocktails & lounge; fee for parking; valet parking; a la carte. Sophisticated dining comprises artistic presentation, highest quality ingredients and white gloved staff featuring Basque/French specialties. No charge for parking if within four hours. **Cards:** AE, CB, DI, MC, VI.

LES MOUSTACHES

 Nouvelle Continental (5/533-3390

L $15-$25 **D** $20-$40

Location: In the Pink Zone. 88 Rio Sena 06600. **Hours:** 1 pm-10 pm. Closed: Sun. **Features:** semi-formal attire; cocktails & lounge; fee for valet parking. Elegant surroundings. Refined atmosphere. Unique presentations. Various areas for dining: main dining room, garden courtyard or upstairs private dining. Coat and tie required Mon-Fri; casual attire on Sat. **Cards:** AE, DI, MC, VI.

LOS ALMENDROS

 Regional Mexican (5/531-7307

L $15-$25 **D** $20-$30

Location: Just e, corner of Campos Eliseos and Arquimedes; in Polanco district, within walking distance of Intercontinental, Nikko; Marriott Hotel. No. 164 Campos Eliseos 11560. **Hours:** 8 am-11 pm, Sun-9 pm. **Reservations:** suggested. **Features:** semi-formal attire; cocktails; entertainment; valet parking. Visit the Yucatan while in Mexico City and discover authentic, Mayan influenced cuisine. Dressy casual, yet not formal, this is a "must get to". Begin with panachos de cochinita pibil. Savory but not spicy. Move on to arroz con pollo con platanos fritos. Finish with a cerveza Leon. Unforgettable. **Cards:** AE, DI, MC, VI.

LOS AZULEJOS

 Continental (5/203-2121

L $10-$15 **D** $10-$15

Location: Between Victor Hugo and Kent, just n of Diana Cir, from Periferico, exit Masarik, then w; in Camino Real Mexico. 700 Mariano Escobedo 11590. **Hours:** 7-11:30 am, 1:30-5:30 & 7:30-11 pm. **Reservations:** suggested. **Features:** semi-formal attire; Sunday brunch; cocktails; fee for valet parking; buffet. Located on the 2nd floor, the garden level of a world famous hotel. Indoor or terrace seating. Wide selection of dishes with highest quality ingredients served in an upscale yet informal dining room. **Cards:** AE, DI, MC, VI.

MAXIM'S DE PARIS

 Traditional French (5/327-7700

L $25-$45 **D** $40-$85

Location: On Paseo de la Reforma, 1.3 km w Periferico; in Polanco, opposite Chapultepec Park and the National Auditorium; in Hotel Presidente Inter-Continental Mexico City. Campo Eliseos 218 Col Pol 11560. **Hours:** 1 pm-midnight. Closed: Sun. **Reservations:** suggested; weekends. **Features:** dressy casual; cocktails & lounge; fee for parking & valet parking; a la carte. Visit Paris while travelling in Mexico. The chef, the maitre d, the menu, the crystal, all French. Shimmering soups are ladled tableside from silver turines. Artistic and creative presentations. All items prepared "a la minute." Explore truffles, safron and caviar. Extensive wine list. **Cards:** AE, CB, DI, MC, VI.

THE PALM

 Steak House (5/327-7700

L $20-$40 **D** $20-$40

Location: On Paseo de la Reforma, 1.3 km w Periferico; in Polanco, opposite Chapultepec Park and the National Auditorium; in Hotel Presidente Inter-Continental Mexico City. Campo Eliseos 218 11560. **Hours:** 1 pm-midnight. Closed: Sun. **Features:** semi-formal attire; cocktails; fee for parking; valet parking; a la carte. House specialties include large steaks and huge live lobsters. Dining Room in rich woods, two tier seating, starched white table linens. Guests are girded for battle with huge bibs tied around their necks. **Cards:** AE, CB, DI, DS, MC, VI.

PASSY

 Traditional Continental (5/208-2087

L $10-$15 **D** $15-$35

Location: Just s of Paseo de la Reforma. Amberes 10 06600. **Hours:** 1 pm-11 pm. Closed major holidays; also Sun. **Reservations:** suggested. **Features:** semi-formal attire; cocktails & lounge; fee for valet parking; a la carte. Classic Continental selections. **Cards:** AE, CB, DI, MC, VI.

RESTAURANTE ANTIGUO SAN ANGEL INN *Historical*

 Provincial Mexican (5/616-2222

L $19-$40 **D** $25-$45

Location: 7 blks w of Insurgentes Sur; 5 blks e of Anillo Perferico; in Col San Angel Inn. Palmas & Altavista 01060. **Hours:** 1 pm-midnight, Sun-10 pm. Closed major holidays. **Reservations:** required. **Features:** No A/C; semi-formal attire; cocktails & lounge; entertainment; valet parking; a la carte. Renown dining room in renovated 18th-century hacienda, surrounded by gardens and patios. Relax first in any of the courtyard gardens or elegant rooms with a beverage. Then enjoy the large ornate main dining room and its excellent service. Haute Mexican cuisine. **Cards:** AE, CB, DI, MC, VI.

RESTAURANTE FONDA EL REFUGIO

 Regional Mexican   (5/525-8128

L $15-$39   **D** $20-$40

Location: In Pink Zone. Liverpool 166 06600. **Hours:** 1 pm-midnight, Sun-10 pm. Closed: 1/1, 12/25. **Features:** casual dress; cocktails; a la carte. Informal atmosphere. Quaint countryside decor. Excellent preparation of regional dishes. This long time local favorite offers a fun journey through the culinary regions of Mexico. **Cards:** AE, DI, MC, VI.

RESTAURANTE TEZKA

Continental   (5/228-9918

L $8-$15   **D** $10-$18

Location: In the Pink Zone. Jct Chapultepec and Liverpool sts; in Hotel Royal Zona Rosa. St 06600. **Hours:** 1 pm-5 pm, Thurs & Fri also 8 pm-11 pm. Closed: Sun & 12/25-1/1. **Reservations:** suggested. **Features:** dressy casual; cocktails; valet parking; a la carte. Continental cuisine infused with fresh regional ingredients. Elegant and refined dining room. Attentive, knowledgable and well trained staff. A well known local favorite. **Cards:** AE, DI, MC, VI.

RESTAURANT FOUQUET'S DE PARIS

French   (5/203-2121

L $30-$45   **D** $35-$50

Location: Between Victor Hugo and Kent, just n of Diana Cir; in Camino Real Hotel. Mariano Escobedo 700 11590. **Hours:** 7-11 am, 2-5 & 8-midnight, Sat from 8 pm. Closed major holidays; also Sun. **Reservations:** suggested. **Features:** dressy casual; cocktails & lounge; entertainment; fee for valet parking; a la carte. Large French dining room with matching lounge anteroom for relaxing with a drink. Classic French cuisine as creme potage and foie gras are dramatically presented. Refined atmosphere, formal staff. **Cards:** AE, CB, DI, JC, MC, VI.

RESTAURANT LAGO CHAPULTEPEC

Continental   (5/515-9586

L $20-$30   **D** $40-$65

Location: In new section of Chapultepec Park, near National Museum of Natural History. Chapultepec Park 11-870. **Hours:** 1:30 pm-9:30 pm. Closed major holidays. **Reservations:** suggested. **Features:** semi-formal attire; Sunday brunch; cocktails & lounge; entertainment; minimum charge-in evening; fee for valet parking; a la carte. Elegant dining spot overlooking lake. Sun buffet. **Cards:** AE, DI, MC, VI.

TENANCINGO, MEXICO (C-9) elev. 6,632'

Tenancingo (teh-nahn-SEEN-goh)—its name an Indian term meaning "place of little walls"—was founded in 1425. Overlooking the town from atop a hill is a large Christ statue; this vantage point provides a sweeping view. Tenancingo produces wood and palm furniture, *rebozos* (shawl-like woven garments) and fruit liqueurs, all of which are for sale at the huge open-air market held on Sundays.

MALINALCO is about 11 kilometers (7 miles) southeast of Tenancingo via a graded road to the village of Malinalco, then approximately 2 kilometers (1.2 miles) west on a good dirt road. Partially restored, the site is hewn into a cliffside. It was originally settled by the Matlazincas, who

were conquered by the Aztecs around 1476, and was still under construction when Hernán Cortés seized it.

The **Temple of the Eagles and Jaguars**, one of the world's few archeological remains carved from solid stone, has a reconstructed thatch and wood roof entrance, in front of which sits a headless stone figure. The doorway resembles an open-mouthed serpent. Beyond it is a circular chamber of solid rock decorated with sculptures of eagles and jaguars. A beautifully carved wooden drum retrieved from the **Temple of the Sun** (Building IV) resides in the Museum of Anthropology at the Mexiquense Cultural Center in Toluca.

The remains of frescoes also can be seen. The staircase that leads to the site is carved into the mountainside. It's an arduous climb of more than 400 steps that takes 30 minutes, but the view of the surrounding valley is magnificent. Buses from Toluca travel to Malinalco. Open Tues.-Sun. 10-4:30. Admission is charged.

SANTO DESIERTO DEL CARMEN MONASTERY NATIONAL PARK is about 10 kilometers (6 miles) southeast of Tenancingo on a graded road, a short distance from Malinalco. The park's main feature is a late 18th-century Carmelite monastery that sits in a lovely wooded setting.

TEOTENANGO ARCHEOLOGICAL ZONE, 25 kilometers (16 miles) north on Mex. 55, is one of the largest and most thoroughly reconstructed pre-Hispanic Indian cities in Mexico. It is attributed to the Matlazinca people and was probably a ceremonial center for nearby Malinalco. This walled site covers more than 2 square miles, spread across a flat bluff. The structures bear a direct influence to those at Teotihuacán—a good-sized ball court, large pyramids and squat temples faced with broad staircases. An uphill walk to the ruins passes a small museum displaying artifacts recovered during restoration efforts. Bus transportation to Teotenango is available from Toluca. Open Tues.-Sun. 9-5. Admission is charged.

TEOTIHUACAN, MEXICO (C-10) elev. 7,482'

The ruins of San Juan Teotihuacán (teh-oh-tee-wah-KAHN) are the most widely known and easily accessible of Mexico's major archeological zones. They also are among the most mysterious; very little is known about this religious center, the people who built it, or even what the city was originally called.

HISTORICAL BACKGROUND

Teotihuacán is thought to have been founded as early as 700 B.C., although it was not until around 100 B.C. that construction of its two great pyramids began. Archeologists estimate that at its height around A.D. 500, up to 200,000 people lived there, making it bigger than Rome at the time and one of the largest cities in the world. The city was burned and abandoned for unknown reasons around A.D. 750; it is believed the decline was gradual and perhaps facilitated by overpopulation and a resulting depletion of natural resources.

The area was later inhabited by the Toltecs; by the time the Aztecs discovered the site, it was in such an advanced state of ruin that they named it Teotihuacán, which means "place of the gods," or more broadly, "where men become gods." The gray stone structures seen today are to a large degree reconstructed, and the barren landscape barely hints at what the city must have looked like during its heyday some 1,500 years ago.

EXPLORING THE SITE

While Teotihuacán lacks the lush jungle backdrop of Palenque, it is the most monumentally scaled of all Mexico's ruins. The temple remains and two majestic pyramids rise from a flat, open plain, with little surrounding vegetation to obscure the view. The site was once paved with volcanic stone and mica slabs, and buildings were plastered with lime and mortar and then decorated with bas-relief sculptures and murals, often painted red; traces of the color are still discernible. The typical structural arrangement was

often a courtyard surrounded by several levels of temples and rooms.

The ruins are aligned along a north-south axis traversed by the **Avenida de los Muertos** (Avenue of the Dead). The name was given by the Aztecs, who believed that the low structures lining both sides of the avenue were burial sites. Some 80 of them, all similar in size and style, accentuate the grandness of the pyramids. Touches of paint can still be detected on some of the building fragments. This wide thoroughfare (paved for today's visitors) is more than a mile long; it seems even longer when you're trekking from one building to another.

The magnificent **Pyramid of the Sun**, on the east side of the Avenue of the Dead, dominates the ruins and is the oldest of Teotihuacán's structures. It is the world's third-largest pyramid; only those at Cholula and Cheops, Egypt, are bigger. The structure rises in five sloping levels to a height of more than 250 feet; each side of its base measures about 735 feet. Built of adobe brick faced with volcanic stone, it is visible for some distance from the highway approaching the site. When first discovered the pyramid was a gigantic mound covered with vegetation, but even the subsequent reconstruction fails to detract from the achievement of those who originally

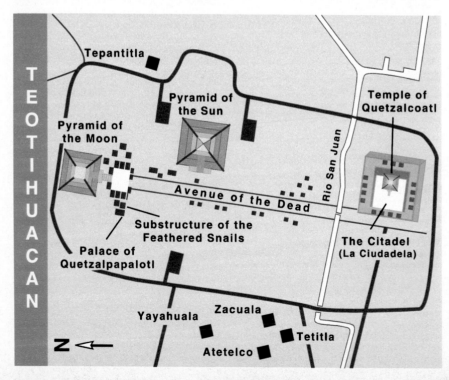

The Pyramid of the Moon, although huge, is the smaller of Teotihuacán's two pyramids. © Chris Sharp

built this enormous monument without benefit of the wheel or metal tools.

A stairway on the west flank begins at the pyramid's base and leads to the summit, where a temple probably once stood. The 248 steps make for an arduous climb, but the five levels each provide a chance to stop, take a breather and take in the view. In clear weather, the panorama from the top is simply breathtaking. Because of the gentle slope, descending is significantly easier than clambering down the steep sides of some of Mexico's other pyramids, such as El Castillo at Chichén Itzá. If you still feel vulnerable, hold onto the link chain that runs the length of the stairway.

The **Plaza of the Moon** constitutes a remarkable cluster of buildings. The plaza is surrounded by staired platforms and has a square altar in the middle. The **Pyramid of the Moon**, at the north end of the Avenue of the Dead, is 140 feet high; stairs scale its south face. It appears as tall as the Pyramid of the Sun because it was built on higher ground. The pyramid is connected to a temple with sloping walls. The climb to the summit of this pyramid is shorter (although no less taxing). It's worth the effort, though, for the panoramic vista of the Avenue of the Dead. **Note:** The apex is rocky and uneven; watch your footing.

At the southwest corner of the Plaza of the Moon is the restored **Palace of Quetzalpapalotl**, Teotihuacán's most elaborate building. Presumed to have been the home of a prominent citizen or supreme priest, it has some well-preserved murals. In the inner courtyard are pillars decorated with bas-reliefs depicting the *quetzal-papalotl*, a feathered butterfly, and various symbols related to water. Beneath this palace is the **Palace of the Jaguars**, so called because of the jaguar images in the rooms ringing the courtyard, and the **Substructure of the Feathered Snails**, part of a beautifully decorated temple beneath the Quetzalpapalotl Palace that features carvings of large snails garlanded with feathers.

In 1998 excavations uncovered a tomb and offerings inside the Pyramid of the Moon that archeologists hope will provide additional clues to help solve the riddle of the site's origination. Objects at what has initially been described as a burial site—most likely someone of high social standing—include obsidian and jade sculptures and skeleton fragments. In the last few years new stone remains also have been unearthed on the west side of the Avenue of the Dead; excavations are ongoing.

At the southern end of the zone is **La Ciudadela** (The Citadel). Teotihuacán was ruled from this vast sunken square, which encompassed nearly 17 acres and was surrounded by a low wall. The inner esplanade once held thousands of standing people. Within the courtyard are several temples; the most elaborate is the restored **Temple of Quetzalcóatl** (the Feathered Serpent). The god Quetzalcóatl was worshipped by the Maya, Toltec and Aztec civilizations, although it is unknown whether the inhabitants of

Teotihuacán paid tribute to the same being. Carved stone slabs face part of the structure; writhing serpents, their heads sticking out from ruffles of feathers, adorn some of the walls.

Other structures are located off the Avenue of the Dead. **Tepantitla**, east of the Pyramid of the Moon, may have been the residence of a high priest. Several walls have traces of paintings showing Tláloc, the rain god, amid swimming male figures and water imagery. **Tetitla**, west of the loop road that surrounds the archeological zone, has a labyrinthine maze of rooms with patchy murals depicting jaguars, snakes, quetzals and aquatic life. Also west of the loop road is **Atetelco**, another large-sized group of structures with murals that portray priests. Nearby are **Zacuala** and **Yayahuala**, fortresslike one-story structures with many rooms, halls and passageways.

The museum near the Pyramid of the Sun has archeological, historical and diagrammatic exhibits pertain to the peoples that once inhabited the area. Although the finest objects excavated at the site are displayed at the National Museum of Anthropology in Mexico City, the exhibits here offer a good introduction to Teotihuacán. Scale models of the zone can help orient the first-time visitor.

PRACTICALITIES

The ruins are about 49 kilometers (30 miles) northeast of downtown Mexico City. Buses for Teotihuacán depart regularly from the Terminal Central de Autobuses del Norte in Mexico City, on Avenida de los 100 Metros; Metro has a subway station at the terminal (Autobuses del Norte, line 5). The trip takes about an hour. Ascertain from the bus driver when the last bus returns to the city and where it picks up passengers. Numerous Mexico City travel agencies offer Teotihuacán sightseeing tours.

If driving, take Avenida Insurgentes Norte out of the city, which becomes Mex. 85-D. The four-lane, divided highway is in good condition, passing innumerable houses—cubes of gray concrete—perched in ascending rows on the hillsides. Take the exit for Mex. 132-D. From the toll plaza, the site entrance is about 22 kilometers (14 miles) east (about a 30-minute drive); signs along the way are marked "Piramides."

Wear sturdy, nonslip walking shoes if you plan to climb the pyramids, because the rocks can be slippery. On warm, sunny days wear lightweight clothing, sunscreen and a hat. During the summer months (June through September) afternoon showers are frequent. Fall and winter days can be cloudy, chilly and breezy. The altitude is more than 7,000 feet, so walk and climb at a relaxed pace.

Note: Numerous souvenir vendors roam the site, and you will be approached on many occasions to purchase items ranging from jewelry to carved figurines to lace shawls. The vendors are persistent but usually not aggressive. If you have no intention of buying anything, keep walking; a negative shake of the head and a polite "gracias" will convey a "thanks, but no thanks" response. If you stop, chances are you'll never get away. But if you want to buy something, by all means bargain; a vendor will initially offer three to four times what he or she is willing to settle for. Avoid weekends, which can be very crowded. Try to visit during the week and early in the day before the tour buses begin arriving.

Although snacks are available at the entrance and there are a few restaurants just outside the site, most hotels will pack a box lunch to take along on a bus tour. Bring bottled water, particularly if it's a hot day. There are very basic restrooms at the entrance. The archeological zone is open daily 8-5; the museum is open Tues.-Sun. Admission 20 pesos (about $2); free to all Sun. There is an additional fee for the use of a video camera.

TEPOTZOTLAN, MEXICO (C-10) elev. 7,577'

Tepotzotlán (teh-poht-soh-TLAHN), about 35 kilometers (22 miles) north of Mexico City, is an easy day trip destination from the capital. From the downtown area, take Avenida Avila Camacho (Mex. 57) northwest out of the city and watch for the Tepotzotlán turnoff; the town lies about a mile west. Buses also depart regularly for Tepotzotlán from the Tacuba Metro station (lines 2 and 7) and from the Terminal Central de Autobuses del Norte. The town is a good antidote for visitors tired of Mexico City's grinding congestion and noise: It has clear air, wonderful mountain views, colonial charm and a commercial yet laid-back atmosphere. After visiting the Church of San Francisco Xavier, Tepotzotlán's main attraction, have a relaxed lunch at one of the eateries surrounding the central plaza.

IGLESIA DE SAN FRANCISCO XAVIER (Church of San Francisco Xavier) faces the plaza. It was founded by the Jesuits in the late 16th century, serving as a seminary for the religious training of the children of Otomí Indians. Construction of the church began around 1670; it was subsequently expanded and embellished until just prior to the 1767 expulsion of the Jesuits from Mexico. The richly detailed stone carvings of angels and saints on the building's facade—a masterful example of Mexican baroque architecture—reflect the Jesuit order's wealth and influence.

A tree-lined atrium leads to the **Claustro de los Aljibes** (Aljibes Cloister), which contains paintings by Miguel Cabrera depicting the life of St. Ignatius of Loyola; Cabrera also painted portraits of many of the era's prominent Mexican citizens. The church's interior is even more elaborate than its exterior, a dizzying agglomeration of gold gilt, profuse carvings of cherubs and the saints, and five extravagantly appointed altarpieces. Sunlight coming through the windows bathes everything in golden light.

A highlight is the **Camarín de la Virgen**, or altar room, behind the **Capilla de la Virgen de Loreto** (Chapel of the Virgin of Loreto). This small, octagonal-shaped chamber is a jewel box of intricate interior design, with supporting columns taking the form of Indian-featured female figures and practically every inch of the walls adorned with fanciful carvings. Strategically placed mirrors make it easier to appreciate the painstaking work of native craftsmen.

Outside the **Claustro de los Naranjos** (Orange Cloister), which is planted with orange trees, are carefully tended gardens. Occasional concerts are given in the church. Church and National Viceregal Museum open Tues.-Sun. Admission is charged.

MUSEO NACIONAL DEL VIRREINATO (National Viceregal Museum), within the church's restored monastery, houses 3 centuries of colonial and religious art. Rare 16th-century vestments and altar hangings, gold and repoussé silver monstrances from the 17th century and a painting of the Virgin attributed to Bartolomé Esteban Murillo are among its many treasures. *Pastorelas*, passion plays incorporating local talent, and *posadas*, traditional re-enactments of Christ's birth, are performed during the Christmas season. Travel agencies in Mexico City can arrange for reservations, which should be booked well in advance. Admission is charged for the performances.

TEPOZTLAN, MORELOS (C-9) elev. 5,579′

Tepoztlán (teh-pohs-TLAHN), a name that means "place of copper," is secluded on the lush green slopes of the Sierra del Ajusco and protected by the Sierra de Tepoztlán. The latter's scarred cliffs constitute **Tepozteco National Park**, which surrounds the village of Tlalnepantla, northeast of Tepoztlán. Tepoztlán's sequestered location was perfect for Emiliano Zapata, regarded locally as a folk hero, who used the village as his revolutionary stronghold in 1910.

Despite proximity to modern Cuernavaca and Mexico City, traditional customs of the town's Aztec predecessors remain. Residents still speak Náhuatl, the ancient Aztec tongue, and mingle Christian and pre-Christian religious practices. A celebration held in early September honors both the Nativity of the Virgin and their patron god Tepoztécatl, the Mexican Bacchus credited with the perfection of pulque, the fermented drink extracted from the maguey plant. Tepoztlán's some-

what mystical environment also attracts those interested in new-age philosophies.

Other celebrations include *Mardi Gras*, held on the 3 days preceding Ash Wednesday, in which villagers perform Aztec dances and dress as Spanish *conquistadores*, and the town's weeklong fair, held annually during early May in the Ixcatepec *barrio*. Tepoztlán also has a colorful Sunday market overflowing with fruits, vegetables and regionally produced handicrafts.

CONVENT OF TEPOZTLAN, on the main plaza, is a national historic monument. Built by Dominicans in the 16th century, the massive structure has some walls that are more than 6 feet thick. The upper floor affords a fine view of the surrounding mountains.

TEPOZTECO PYRAMID, reached by a difficult climb, stands high on a hill overlooking the town. Now a ruin, this pre-Conquest monument, built by the Tlahuica Indians, honored the god Tepoztécatl. The vista from the hillside and the top of the pyramid is superb but the ascent is steep; make sure you wear comfortable hiking shoes. A play dramatizing Tepoztécatl's conversion to Christianity is presented in early September.

TEQUESQUITENGO, MORELOS (D-10) elev. 3,083′

South of Cuernavaca lies the resort area of Tequesquitengo (teh-kehs-kee-TEHN-goh), on **Lake Tequesquitengo**. The village was moved to its present location in 1820 when rising lake waters forced the abandonment of an earlier site. Between 1957 and 1958 the lake rose nearly 13 feet, inundating lakeside homes and the first floor of a hotel. To restore the water level, a 1.7-mile tunnel was bored through a nearby mountain rim.

The lake, about 3,000 feet above sea level, has calm, spring-fed waters ideal for water skiing; it is the site of championship exhibitions. Swimming, boating and fishing also are possible.

WHERE TO STAY

HOTEL HACIENDA VISTA HERMOSA

♦♦♦ *Classic Hotel*   ☎ 734/5-5361

All Year $130

Location: 8.5 km se of Alpuyeca interchange off Mex 95 and 95D; 1.5 km n of Lake Tequesquitengo. (Km 7, Carretera Alpuyeca, 62680). Fax: 734/5-5360. **Facility:** Historic. Magnificent 16th-century colonial sugar mill built by Hernan Cortes. Large and rustic rooms with period furnishings. Some rooms with private or semi-private pool and solariums. Many rooms with ceiling fans. Complimentary bottled water. Variety of suites available. 105 units. 19 two-bedroom units. *Bath:* combo or shower only. 2 stories, exterior corridors. **Terms:** 20 day cancellation notice-fee imposed. **Amenities:** no TVs. **Leisure Activities:** 2 pools, tennis court, playground, basketball. *Fee:* horseback riding. **Guest Services:** [AP] meal plan available, gift shop, valet laundry. **Business Services:** conference facilities. **Cards:** AE, DI, MC, VI.

SOME UNITS

TLALNEPANTLA, MEXICO

WHERE TO STAY

FIESTA INN TLALNEPANTLA
▼▼▼▼   *Motor Inn*   ((5)729-4100
All Year $90-$100   XP $10
Location: Downtown, 1.8 km e of jct Mex 57 and Tlalnepantla Baz; n of Mexico City limits. Ave Sor Juana Ines
de la Cruz #22 54000. Fax: 5/729-4121. **Facility:** Caters to
northern Mexico City. Compact business hotel with a decent
little restaurant and lounge. 131 units. 4 stories, interior corridors. **Parking:** valet. **Terms:** F12. **Leisure Activities:** exercise room. **Guest Services:** valet laundry. **Business
Services:** meeting rooms, administrative services. *Fee:* fax.
Cards: AE, CB, DI, MC, VI.

🍴 🍽 Ⓢ Ⓓ 🎦 [DATA PORT] / 🗙 💻 /   SOME UNITS

⨀ HOTEL PLAZA LANCASTER
▼▼▼▼   *Hotel*   (5/228-9500
All Year $160-$180   XP $20
Location: 0.5 mi e of jct Mex 57 at Tlalnepantla Baz, n of
Mexico city limits. Roberto Fulton No. 2-A 54000.
Fax: 5/228-9528. **Facility:** Large atrium lobby. All rooms
with sleeper sofa. Concierge level rooms with added amenities and services. Meets AAA guest room security requirements. 117 units. 6 two-bedroom units. Some whirlpool
units. *Bath:* combo or shower only. 7 stories, interior corridors. **Parking:** valet. **Terms:** F12. **Amenities:** voice mail,
safes, honor bars, hair dryers. **Dining & Entertainment:** dining room, restaurant, 6:30 am-midnight, $8-$23, nightclub,
entertainment. **Leisure Activities:** sauna, steamroom,
lighted tennis court, jogging, exercise room. **Guest Services:**
gift shop, valet laundry. **Business Services:** conference facilities, administrative services. *Fee:* fax. **Cards:** AE, MC, VI.

🍴 24🍴 🍽 Ⓓ 🗙 🎦 📠 💻 / 🗙 /   SOME UNITS

TOLUCA, MEXICO (C-9) elev. 8,790'

Capital of the state of México, Toluca (toh-
LOO-cah)—about 70 kilometers (43 miles) west
of Mexico City—is a commercial center in the
middle of the flat Toluca Valley. One of the highest Mexican cities in elevation, it thus enjoys
cool weather despite the tropical latitude. Although it is heavily industrial, low buildings
characterize Toluca's skyline, and there are many
little plazas and manicured parks.

Toluca was an Indian settlement as early as
1200; the name is derived from the Náhuatl Indian expression *tollocan*, or "those who bow
their heads." Spaniards under Hernán Cortés began settling the region in the early 16th century
after the conqueror was granted 22 towns in central and southern Mexico by King Carlos V.

Plaza de los Mártires (Plaza of the Martyrs),
the main plaza, is named for a group of revolutionaries who were executed in 1811 for their
part in Mexico's struggle to win freedom from
Spain, an uprising started by Father Miguel
Hidalgo. On the plaza's south side is the cathedral, where traditional dances are presented on
various Mexican holidays. Check with the State

Tourism Office for more information about these
colorful spectacles. Many of the facades of the
public buildings around the plaza were constructed from volcanic *tezontle* stone. Among
several downtown museums is the **Museo de
Bellas Artes** (Museum of Fine Arts), on Avenida
Santos Degollado a block north of the plaza. The
collection of paintings and sculptures spans the
16th through the 19th centuries.

A block or so south of the plaza along Avenida
Miguel Hidalgo is **Los Portales**, a pedestrian-
only walkway fronting an arcade of shops and
restaurants protected by arches and buzzing with
sidewalk vendors. It's an interesting place to
stroll. Here rows of candy stands offer Toluca's
local fruit confections, and liquor stores sell an
orange-flavored liqueur called *moscos*.

The Friday market (actually open every day of
the week), has long been considered one of
Mexico's largest and most colorful, although it is
now less a showcase for regional goods than a
conglomeration of flea market items such as
jeans, radios and used CDs. Indian villagers from
throughout the region gather at the market
(which is conveniently located near the main bus
station on **Paseo Tollocan**, the loop road that encircles Toluca) in a noisy cavalcade of buying
and selling. Sharp-eyed bargain hunters may un-
earth good buys on baskets, needlecraft, blankets
and pottery. For a better selection of native
handicrafts, try Casart *(see attraction listing)*.

Several towns and villages to the east and
south of Toluca offer a first-hand look at the way
Mexico's rural population has engaged in manufacturing and marketing since pre-Hispanic days.
Visiting these places during the morning is a
good way to acquire locally made items at the
various *tianguis* (open-air markets), even without
benefit of bargaining expertise.

East of Toluca on Mex. 15 to the paved turnoff for the village of San Pedro Cholula, then
south, is appropriately named **Tianguistenco**.
The Wednesday *tianguis* (open-air market) fills
roughly half of the village's streets with baskets,
sarapes and other crafts from throughout the
Toluca Valley. From Tianguistenco, follow the
signs to Mex. 55, which heads northwest toward
Mexicalcingo and Metepec. In **Metepec** *(see description below)*, renowned for its "Trees of
Life" and other colorful clay objects, Monday is
market day.

Inexpensive plastic shoes flow from countless
home workshops in nearby **San Mateo Atenco**,
to be sold at sidewalk stands and in the ubiquitous *zapaterías* (shoe stores). Sunday is market
day in San Mateo Atenco. The **San Mateo
Atenco Hacienda**, just south of Metepec off
Mex. 55, is where Mexico's first fighting bulls
were bred. Atenco bulls are still lauded for their
bravery, nearly 5 centuries after Mexico's first
bullfight took place in Mexico City in 1526.

From Mexico City, the easiest way to reach Toluca by car is to take toll highway Mex. 15-D. This direct route is expensive but fast. Buses to Toluca depart regularly from Mexico City's Terminal de Autobuses del Poniente, the western bus terminal; to get there, take Metro to the Observatorio station (at the western end of Line 1). Buses marked "Toluca—Directo" make the trip in the least amount of time. The State Tourism Office is in the Edificio Plaza Toluca building, downtown at Avenida Lerdo de Tejada (next to the Botanic Garden); phone (72) 14-1099.

WHAT TO SEE

CASART (Casa de Artesanías) is at Paseo Tollocan Oriente #700. The two-story building is a government-run outlet offering contemporary crafts produced in the state of México, including textiles, carved wood figures, ceramics and blown glass. It is also possible to watch the artisans as they work. The store is staffed with multilingual personnel. Daily 10-8.

CENTRO CULTURAL MEXIQUENSE (Mexican Cultural Center) is off the Paseo Tollocan loop road; from its southwest section (between the monument to Christopher Columbus, at the junction with Mex. 134, and the University of the State of México), follow the signs about 1.6 kilometers (1 mile) southwest to the cultural center. This large, spread-out complex is a mixture of architectural styles, from colonial to contemporary. The several museums here are dedicated to the conservation and exhibition of Mexican cultural traditions. The center can be reached from downtown Toluca via bus or taxi. Open Tues.-Sun. 9-5. Free. Guide service in English is available. Phone (72) 12-4074.

Museo de Antropología (Museum of Anthropology) exhibits artifacts from the state's archeological zones, including Malinalco and Calixtlahuaca. It was designed by Pedro Ramírez Vasquez, the architect who supervised construction of Mexico City's National Museum of Anthropology.

Museo de Arte Moderno (Museum of Modern Art) has works by Mexican muralists José Clemente Orozco, Diego Rivera and David Alfaro Siqueiros, among others.

Museo de Artes Popular (Museum of Popular Arts) is housed in a hacienda dating from the 17th century. Colorful murals decorate its walls, and a variety of regional handicrafts are on display. A huge "tree of life" that sits in the front hall. The museum's exhibits of saddles, clothing and other items used by *charros* (cowboys) are considered among the best of their type in the country.

COSMOVITRAL JARDIN BOTANICO (Botanic Garden), just east of the main plaza at calles Lerdo de Tejada, Degollado and Ignacio Rayón, was the site of the well-known Toluca market until 1975. Hundreds of plant species native to Mexico are exhibited within the walls of the Art Nouveau-style building. Most impressive, however, are the magnificent stained-glass panels, which replaced the original windows. Depicting the evolution of man and the universe, they were designed and built in 1980 by local artist Leopoldo Flores, who utilized some 45 tons of glass, 65 tons of metal and 25 tons of lead in their creation. Tues.-Sun. 9-5. Admission is charged.

MUSEO DE LA ACUARELA (Museum of Watercolor) is downtown at Calle Pedro Ascencio Norte #13, at the corner of Calle Nigromante. The museum occupies one of Toluca's oldest buildings, a two-story house with a central courtyard surrounded by exterior walkways and capped by a large skylight. It is known as "El Gallito," a reference to the brand of thread that was once distributed from the building. The permanent collection of 176 paintings is displayed in six halls, each named after a popular artist from the state of México. A documentation center chronicles the lives of the exhibiting artists. Guided tours are available. Tues.-Sun. 10-6. Free. Phone (72) 14-7304.

MUSEO FELIPE S. GUTIERREZ (Felipe S. Gutiérrez Museum) is downtown at Calle Nicolas Bravo #300, at the corner of Avenida Lerdo de Tejada. Gutiérrez, a 19th-century portrait painter, taught figure drawing to José María Velasco. He was one of the first Mexican artists who rendered his subjects' Indian lineage, making no attempt to give them European features. Such notable works as "La Cazadora de los Andes" show the influence of Gutiérrez's travels to South America and Europe. Guided tours are available. Open Tues.-Sun. 10-6. Free. Phone (72) 13-2814.

MUSEO JOSE MARIA VELASCO (José María Velasco Museum) is at Avenida Lerdo de Tejada #400, adjoining the Museum of Felipe S. Gutiérrez. It presents an overview of one of Mexico's most influential 19th-century painters, with both paintings and sculptures on display. One of Velasco's more notable works, "Vista desde Molino del Rey," was donated to the museum by President Ernesto Zedillo. One room contains a recreation of the artist's workshop. Guided tours are available. Open Tues.-Sun. 10-6. Free. Phone (72) 13-2814.

NEARBY DESTINATIONS

CALIXTLAHUACA ARCHEOLOGICAL ZONE is 8 kilometers (5 miles) north on Mex. 55 to the site turnoff, then about 3 kilometers (2 miles) west. The site is located on a hilltop above the village of the same name. Not much is known about its origins, although it was taken over by the Aztecs around 1476. Several buildings have been uncovered: the conical **Temple of Quetzalcóatl-Ehecatl;** the **Pyramid of Tláloc;**

and the **Tzompantli** (Altar of Skulls), which was probably used for human sacrifice. Buses make frequent trips from Toluca to Calixtlahuaca; there is a short uphill walk to get to the site entrance. Open daily 9-5. Admission is charged.

PARQUE NACIONAL NEVADO DE TOLUCA (Nevado de Toluca National Park) is south of Toluca; take Mex. 15 west about 13 kilometers (8 miles) to the village of Mextepec, then south on a paved road to another turnoff that leads east to Nevado de Toluca. This inactive volcano, also called Xinantécatl (which means "naked man" in the Náhuatl language), is the park's centerpiece and Mexico's fourth highest summit. At 15,032 feet, it towers above the city. The mountain's peak, snowcapped most of the year, is frequently obscured by clouds.

Within Nevado de Toluca's crater are two deep-blue lakes, the **Lake of the Moon** and the **Lake of the Sun**. On a clear day, the view from the crater is splendid. With care and a good guide, you can drive to the top of the mountain and then down into the crater. This is a popular weekend trip; check with the State Tourism Office in Toluca for information about guided excursions.

ZACANGO ZOO is about 7 kilometers (4 miles) southeast of the city via Mex. 55 to the Metepec exit, then approximately 6 kilometers (3.5 miles) west following signs. The zoo displays a number of species on the grounds of the former **Hacienda de Zacango**, home of the Order of Franciscan Priests in the 16th century. Features include an African compound with free-roaming animals, a walk-through aviary and a petting zoo. Food is available. Daily 9-5. Admission is charged.

METEPEC, MEXICO

About 8 kilometers (5 miles) southeast of Toluca and an hour west of Mexico City is the craft village of Metepec, best known for the *árboles de la vida* (trees of life) meticulously created by local artisans. Against a backdrop of clay trunks and branches, these delightful trees depict stories populated by a diverse cast of religious and secular characters.

Some 40 families in town are engaged in the craft, collectively turning out the majority of trees sold here and at shops in other parts of the country. Local pottery makers say the trees originated in the 1940s and that Mexican muralist Diego Rivera was an early aficionado. The basic design has remained the same: Clay is rolled into tubular shapes to form the trunk and branches, embellishments are added, and the trees are then fired in large kilns. Many include candlestick holders, reflecting their original function as candelabra.

The trees of life often feature Adam, Eve and a serpent as the central figures in an intricate tableaux that also may include animals, angels, birds, ears of corn, leaves and berries. Another popular depiction is Noah's ark and its resident menagerie. Some illustrate contemporary themes. Finished trees range in size from a few inches to as large as 5 feet. In Metepec's central plaza stands an 8-foot-tall tree with a cornucopia of branches decorated with flowers, cactuses, donkeys, angels, a replica of a local church and townspeople going about their daily business.

Buses depart frequently for Metepec from Toluca's central bus station. The town is an easy day trip from Mexico City as well. By car, leave the capital via Paseo de la Reforma or Avenida Constituyentes, picking up either toll Mex. 15-D or free Mex. 15 west toward Toluca. Take the Mex. 15-D exit for Taxco/Ixtapan de la Sal and follow signs for Metepec. Pottery shops line the main street; ask for directions to the artisans' workshops, where bargaining for purchases is expected. (**Note:** Many are closed from 2-4 for afternoon *siesta*.) The compact central section of town is easily strolled on foot.

WHERE TO STAY

DEL REY INN HOTEL

▼▼▼ *Motor Inn* ((721)2-2122

All Year	$100	XP $10

Location: 4 km e on Mex 15. Carretera Mex Toluca KM 63.5 50160 (PO Box 325, 50000). Fax: 721/2-2567. **Facility:** Large, modern facility; well appointed rooms; secure parking. 258 units. Some whirlpool units. 2-4 stories, interior corridors. **Terms:** F12. **Amenities:** extended cable TV, safes, irons, hair dryers. *Some:* honor bars. **Dining & Entertainment:** coffee shop, 7 am-midnight, $10-$20, cocktails, entertainment. **Leisure Activities:** 2 heated pools, wading pools, sauna, whirlpools. **Guest Services:** gift shop, valet laundry. **Business Services:** meeting rooms, administrative services. **Cards:** AE, DI, MC, VI.

SOME UNITS

QUINTA DEL REY

▼▼▼ *Hotel* (721/1-8777

All Year	$125-$130	XP $25

Location: 9.5 km e on Mex 15. Paseo Tollacan OTE km 5 52140. Fax: 721/6-7233. **Facility:** Charming colonial style rooms. Attractive courtyard with a small chapel. 66 units. 3 stories (no elevator), interior corridors. **Parking:** valet. **Terms:** F10. **Amenities:** extended cable TV, safes, irons, hair dryers. **Dining:** dining room, coffee shop, $10-$20, cocktails. **Leisure Activities:** heated pool, whirlpool, recreation program, playground, exercise room. **Guest Services:** gift shop, valet laundry. *Fee:* massage. **Business Services:** meeting rooms. **Cards:** AE, DI, MC, VI.

SOME UNITS

VALLE DE BRAVO, MEXICO (C-8) elev. 5,937'

Situated on a forested mountain slope about 140 kilometers (87 miles) west of Mexico City, Valle de Bravo (VAH-yeh deh BRAH-voh) overlooks large, man-made **Lake Avándaro**, part of a vast hydroelectric project serving the Valley of Mexico. The town is a popular weekend resort for well-to-do residents of Mexico City and Toluca. Boating, fishing, hiking, horseback riding, water skiing and windsurfing are among the recreational activities available. Nearby Avándaro Reort and Spa has an 18-hole golf course and extensive spa facilities. Valle de Bravo also hosts an international hang-gliding competition. Due to the elevation, the region is blessed with some of Mexico's nicest weather— mild, dry and sunny.

Buildings with whitewashed stucco walls and red-tiled roofs give the town an attractive colonial look. Further color is supplied by masses of bougainvillea cascading over walls and terraces, and—from November through May—fluttering clouds of monarch butterflies en route to their nearby wintering grounds *(see Angangueo listing under Central Mexico)*. In the vicinity of **Plaza Independencia**, the main square, are boutiques, restaurants, a two-story artisans' market and a bookstore.

CENTRAL MEXICO

The "heartland of Mexico" evokes more reminders of Spain's legacy than any other part of the country. It is in this region that Spanish explorers capitalized upon abundant mineral resources, particularly silver, and built Mexico's first colonial cities. History figures strongly here. It was in the town of Dolores Hidalgo that Father Miguel Hidalgo first declared Mexico's freedom from Spain in his 1810 proclamation *Grito de Dolores*—although independence would not be achieved until 11 long years later. The Treaty of Guadalupe Hidalgo, which ended the Mexican War and forced Mexico to give up its territory north of the Rio Grande to the United States, was signed in the city of Querétaro in 1848.

The colonial cities—including Guanajuato, Morelia, Puebla, Querétaro and Zacatecas—are noted for their carefully preserved centers, where venerable buildings, winding streets and shady plazas invite exploring. There are beautiful cathedrals and churches in Guanajuato, Morelia, Puebla, San Miguel de Allende and Zacatecas. Puebla also is known for buildings covered with geometrically patterned Talavera tiles—a Spanish import.

Guadalajara is Mexico's second city, a metropolis that preserves the past through lovely downtown plazas, imposing colonial architecture and such characteristically Mexican pleasures as the *jarabe*, or Mexican hat dance, the heartfelt strains of mariachi music and the flashy horsemanship on display at a *charreada*, or Mexican rodeo. Pleasant year-round weather plus cultural and recreational opportunities have helped make the resort towns along the shore of nearby Lake Chapala a major destination for U.S. and Canadian retirees.

ABASOLO, GUANAJUATO

WHERE TO STAY

HOTEL BALNEARIO SPA LA CALDERA

▼▼▼ *Resort* ((469)3-0020

| All Year | $71 | XP $15 |

Location: On Mex 110. (PO Box 16, 36970). Fax: 469/3-0020. **Facility:** Spacious, attractive grounds. 117 units. 4 two-bedroom units. *Bath:* combo or shower only. 2-3 stories, exterior corridors. **Terms:** 8 day cancellation notice. **Leisure Activities:** 9 pools, wading pools, whirlpool, 8 heated non-filtered mineral water pools; 1 large filtered pool, 2 tennis courts, playground. **Guest Services:** gift shop. **Business Services:** meeting rooms. **Cards:** MC, VI.

SOME UNITS

❙❙ 🍴 🎣 📷 / 🔀 🏷 /

AGUASCALIENTES, AGUASCALIENTES (G-6) elev. 6,193'

The name Aguascalientes (ah-guahs-ka-lee-EHN-tehs) its derived from nearby thermal springs, which were already known at the time of the city's founding. An extensive system of underground tunnels has earned Aguascalientes the nickname "La Ciudad Perforada" (the perforated city). This maze of catacombs, presumably excavated by an ancient people, has never been completely explored. Visitors, however, are not allowed in them.

Area records date from 1522, when Hernán Cortés sent Pedro de Alvarado to conquer Mexico's western territories. However, at the site where Aguascalientes now stands, attacks by native tribes forced Alvarado to turn back. The city was officially founded in 1575. It initially served as a rest stop along the silver route between Guanajuato and Mexico City to the south and Zacatecas to the north, and also functioned as an agricultural supply center for the mining region.

Modern Aguascalientes is a manufacturing center, and companies from Japan and the United States have set up operations here. Impressive reminders of a colonial past, however, can still be seen in the area around **Plaza de la Patria**, the main plaza. The city's warm, dry climate also makes it pleasant to explore on foot.

Aguascalientes' annual *Feria de San Marcos* (San Marcos Fair), honoring the city's patron saint, has been held since 1604. Mexico's oldest state fair, it takes place from late April to early May at the **Jardín de San Marcos**, a tree-shaded park west of the main plaza. The celebrations include fireworks, amusement rides, craft exhibits, agricultural and industrial expositions, parades, cultural events and the crowning of a festival queen. Bullfights and cockfights generate a great deal of wagering. Those planning a visit during this time should make reservations for accommodations well in advance. Also impressive are the city's Christmas celebrations.

THE INFORMED TRAVELER

The airport is about 34 kilometers (21 miles) south of the city. There is air service to Aguascalientes via Aero California *(see "Arriving by Air," page 53)*. Taxi service is available between the airport and downtown. The state tourist information office is located inside the Government Palace building on the main plaza and provides visitor information as well as maps.

Highway signs in and around Aguascalientes can be outdated, and it is easy to get lost; visitors should plan their itinerary and obtain specific directions before negotiating the city on their own. Roadways within the state are narrow, with little or no shoulders and much truck traffic, but are well maintained. Toll highway Mex. 45-D proceeds southeast, linking Aguascalientes with Lagos de Moreno.

WHAT TO SEE IN TOWN

The cathedral and various government buildings flank Plaza de la Patria. The **Palacio de Gobierno** (Government Palace), built of red sandstone, boasts hand-carved pillars and a fine interior patio. A highlight is the mural by Chilean painter Oswaldo Barra, which depicts all manner of mercantile scenes as well as miners grimly ascending from underground. Next door, the **Palacio Municipal** (City Hall), another imposing building, has an attractive fountain inside the entrance.

The baroque **Cathedral**, the oldest church in Aguascalientes, contains valuable religious paintings. The **Casa de la Cultura** (House of Culture), housed in an old colonial convent on Calle V. Carranza, is worth a stop for the beauty of the building, which has courtyards festooned with vividly colored bougainvillea. Other sights are within walking distance of the main plaza. The **Iglesia de San Antonio** (Church of San Antonio) has a cupola adorned with stained-glass windows.

MUSEO DE JOSE GUADALUPE POSADA (José Guadalupe Posada Museum) is about 6 blocks south of Plaza de la Patria on Plaza Encino, next to the **Templo del Encino** (Encino Church). The museum houses a collection of works by 19th-century Mexican engraver and cartoonist José Guadalupe Posada, who was born in the city. Posada was best known for his *calaveras*, skeletal-like figures that satirized events leading up to the Mexican Revolution of 1910. These humorous political scenarios influenced public opinion in their day.

MUSEO DE LA CIUDAD (City Museum), Calle Zaragoza #505, is opposite the Church of San Antonio. It exhibits 20th-century art, including a collection of paintings by Saturnino Herrán, whose work extolled the common people and fostered a sense of nationalist pride. Open Tues.-Sun.

DAY TRIPS

Although Aguascalientes is a fairly large city, the attractions of interest to tourists are concentrated around or near the main plaza. It should take no more than a day or two to see the sights. Another option is to stroll the plaza area in the morning and then arrange an afternoon excursion to a nearby winery or spa. **Peñuelas Hacienda** is a breeding ranch said to produce some of Mexico's most spirited bulls; make arrangements to visit beforehand, either through your hotel or the state tourism office.

Centro Deportivo Ojocaliente (Ojocaliente Sports Center) is about a kilometer east of downtown on Mex. 70. This spa has thermal pools, steam baths, saunas and tennis courts. **Plaza Vestir**, about 10 kilometers (6 miles) south on Mex. 45, is a collection of shops selling locally made clothing, embroidered items and shoes. A city bus or taxi will take you to the center.

In the nearby town of Pabellón de Hidalgo, 33 kilometers (20 miles) north of Aguascalientes on Mex. 45, then 5 kilometers (3 miles) west, is the Hacienda San Blas de Pabellón, which houses the **Museum of the Insurgency**. Here, after losing two important battles against the Spanish in 1811, insurgent leader Father Miguel Hidalgo y Costilla was relieved of his command and replaced by Ignacio Allende. The hacienda produces woolen goods on hand-powered looms.

The mining town of **Asientos**, easily reached by bus, is about 45 kilometers (28 miles) northeast. Many 16th- and 17th-century paintings are on display in the local churches, and a colonial atmosphere prevails. **Encarnación de Díaz**, about 42 kilometers (26 miles) south on Mex. 45, has old baroque churches and a central plaza with living trees sculpted into various shapes, including Christopher Columbus' ships the *Niña*, the *Pinta* and the *Santa María*.

WHERE TO STAY

HOTEL DE ANDREA ALAMEDA

◆◆◆◆ *Suite Hotel* ☎ (49)70-3800

All Year	$85	XP $15

Location: On east side, 3 blks e of Ave de la Convencion. Alameda Esq Tecnologico 20170. Fax: 49/70-3757. **Facility:** Elegant. Sumptuous Louis XVI style suites in miniature chateau. Courtyard. Quiet residential area surrounded by parks and tree-lined avenues. 48 units. *Bath:* combo or shower only. 2 stories, interior corridors. **Parking:** street only. **Terms:** F12. **Amenities:** honor bars, hair dryers. **Leisure Activities:** heated pool, wading pool, exercise room. **Guest Services:** gift shop. **Business Services:** meeting rooms. **Cards:** AE, MC, VI.

SOME UNITS

〔▮〕〔⛖〕〔📷〕 / 〔VCR〕 /

HOTEL FIESTA INN

◆◆◆◆ *Motor Inn* ☎ (49)78-0808

7/1-11/30	$106-$120	XP $12
1/1-6/30	$100-$114	XP $12
12/1-12/31	$90-$106	XP $12

Location: 1 km s on Leon Hwy (Mex 45). Mahatma Gandhi 302 S 20280. Fax: 49/78-0100. **Facility:** Adjacent to large shopping center. 125 units. 3 stories (no elevator). **Terms:** F12; cancellation fee imposed. **Leisure Activities:** heated pool, wading pool, exercise room. **Guest Services:** valet laundry. **Business Services:** meeting rooms, administrative services. **Cards:** AE, DI, MC, VI.

SOME UNITS

〔S▮〕〔▮〕〔Y〕〔⛖〕〔📷〕〔DATA PORT〕 / 〔✕〕〔VCR〕〔▭〕 /

QUINTA REAL AGUASCALIENTES

◆◆◆◆◆ *Hotel* ☎ (49)78-5818

5/16-11/30	$160-$190	XP $20
12/1-5/15	$152-$180	XP $20

Location: On south side, just e of jct Blvd Jos Chavez and Ave Aguascalientes, on highway to Leon. Ave Aguascalientes Sur 601 20270. Fax: 49/78-5616. **Facility:** Mexican colonial architecture. Luxurious units overlooking courtyard. Elegant atmosphere. 85 units. 1 two-bedroom unit and 1 three-bedroom unit. Some whirlpool units. 3 stories, interior/exterior corridors. **Parking:** valet. **Terms:** F12; 3 day cancellation notice. **Amenities:** honor bars, hair dryers. **Leisure Activities:** heated pool. **Guest Services:** gift shop, valet laundry. **Business Services:** meeting rooms, administrative services. **Cards:** AE, MC, VI.

〔S▮〕〔▮〕〔24▮〕〔Y〕〔▮〕〔D〕〔⛖〕〔📷〕〔DATA PORT〕
FEE
SOME UNITS
/ 〔✕〕 /

ANGANGUEO, MICHOACAN (C-8) elev. 7,997'

Angangueo (ahn-gahn-GEH-oh), which sits in a canyon carved by the Río Puerco, was a Tarasco pueblo long before the arrival of the Spanish. The name means "mouth of the cave." Towering above are the 10,000-foot peaks of Cerro de Guadalupe, El Campanario and Cerro de la Gotera. Angangueo has long been a mining town, although the silver mine in the vicinity—which began operations back in 1792—closed in 1990. At an altitude of nearly 8,000 feet and with abundant springs in the vicinity, the weather is always cool, the greenery lush. A love of bright colors also is apparent in Angangueo's homes, which are painted in every color of the rainbow.

SANTUARIO DE LAS MARIPOSAS MONARCA, EL ROSARIO (El Rosario Monarch Butterfly Sanctuary) is about 6 kilometers (4 miles) northeast of Angangueo, near the small village of El Rosario. The steep and rough dirt road to the sanctuary should be negotiated only in a truck or four-wheel-drive vehicle. An alternate entry can be made via a dirt road from the village of Ocampo, a few miles southwest of Angangueo; this route is longer but can be made adequately in a small car.

This is one of perhaps a dozen butterfly refuges in the highlands of Michoacán and México, some 100 miles west of Mexico City. Every winter an estimated 100 million monarchs—the last generation of butterflies that have spent the spring and summer in Canada and the United States—arrive as part of their remarkable migratory cycle. Scientists do not know for sure what inner navigational system guides the insects into making this 2,500-mile journey, although one possible explanation is that more than half of North America's species of milkweed—the caterpillars' food source—are native to Mexico, indicating that the urge to migrate is passed along genetically.

After reaching their wintering grounds the monarchs hibernate, forming enormous colonies in the sanctuary's tall pines and firs. In a semi-dormant state they burn almost no energy, which prepares them for the northward migration in the spring. Several generations hatch along the way, thus continuing the monarch's life cycle for another year.

Scientists did not discover the El Rosario refuge until 1974; it is now a designated nature preserve. Mexican government officials also impress upon residents and visitors the importance of maintaining the natural setting that the insects require for their annual stay. Those willing to make the effort will be rewarded by the spectacular sight of millions of monarchs at rest in the trees, some of which literally bend under their weight. Binoculars make it easier to observe them hanging from the tree branches.

Organized bus or van tours to the sanctuary can be arranged through travel agencies in Morelia, and while a tour saves time and effort, it also necessitates getting up before dawn. If you're spending the night in the nearby town of Zitácuaro, on Mex. 15 south of Angangueo, it is possible to catch a local bus from there to Angangueo. If you're driving, leave your car in Angangueo and ride in an open-air truck to the sanctuary. This is easier than it sounds; numerous trucks are available, and tourists are approached the moment they set foot in town. Truck rides also can be arranged from Ocampo. Guest rooms at local homes are another possibility; inquire at the Hotel Don Bruno in town.

For the truly fit and adventurous, the sanctuary can be reached on foot via an arduous hike along a rocky road with two river fordings and then up a steep 1-mile trail, all at an elevation of more than 8,500 feet. Villagers in the hamlet of El Rosario have cut steps into the steep slopes to help facilitate the climb. For directions and trip arrangements, check at the Hotel Don Bruno in Angangueo.

A nominal admission is charged. A vehicle access fee also is charged to help in maintaining the accessibility of the site. A guide leads groups of visitors along a loop trail; guide service is included in the admission, although a tip is appreciated. Wear sturdy, comfortable walking shoes and bring a jacket or sweater in case the weather is chilly. Weekends are crowded with Mexico City residents; go during the week if possible. The sanctuary is open daily Nov.-Mar.

CELAYA, GUANAJUATO

WHERE TO STAY

HOTEL CELAYA PLAZA

▼▼▼ *Motor Inn* ((461)4-6677
All Year $68-$75 XP $7
Location: Mex 45, west side of town; across from Pepsi Cola plant. Blvd A Lopez Mateos PTE S/N 38060. Fax: 461/4-6889. **Facility:** 130 units. Some whirlpool units. 3 stories (no elevator), interior/exterior corridors. **Terms:** F12. **Amenities:** *Some:* safes. **Leisure Activities:** heated pool, sauna, whirlpool, lighted tennis court, children's program, exercise room. **Guest Services:** gift shop, valet laundry. **Business Services:** meeting rooms. **Cards:** AE, MC, VI.

SOME UNITS

CHOLULA,
PUEBLA (C-10) elev. 7,039'

At the time of its destruction in 1519 by Hernán Cortés, Cholula (choh-LOO-lah) was an Aztec city built on the foundations of a great ceremonial center. At its peak 100,000 Cholultecs—a mixture of Olmec, Toltec, Aztec, Mixtec and Mazatec Indians—inhabited this city of shrines and temples. Archeological investigations indicate Cholula was first occupied about 400 B.C. and flowered about the second century A.D.—the same time Teotihuacán reached its peak. The Toltecs arrived about 1000 but were supplanted by the Aztecs about 1400.

When Hernán Cortés appeared in Cholula en route to Tenochtitlán, the Aztecs mistook the conqueror for the god Quetzalcóatl, which their mythology described as being fair skinned and with light hair. Consequently, the 100,000 inhabitants showed deference to Cortés and his band of 500 men. The conqueror promptly shattered this illusion by having his second in command,

Pedro de Alvarado, carry out the slaughter of 6,000 Indians and the destruction of their temples and shrines.

Following custom, the Spanish conquerors erected a church atop the rubble of each temple they razed. An example sits atop **Tepanapa Pyramid**, one of the New World's largest structures. Burrowing into the earth near the base of this brush-covered hill, archeologists have discovered that Cholula was a peer of Teotihuacán not only in time but also in size and grandeur. The Cholultecs, in fact, appeared to be better builders than the Aztecs who last occupied the city.

The vast complex of temples, altars and plazas has yielded significant finds. Among them are ceramics that pinpoint Cholula as contemporary with Teotihuacán. Although the buildings differ in style, the pottery found in the two centers is identical. A panel of polychromed symbols thought to pertain to Quetzalcóatl adorns the architrave of a temple platform. That human sacrifice was practiced, albeit on a more modest scale than that required by the Aztecs, has been revealed by the more than 300 burials found under the altars. Most were dedicated to the rain god Tláloc; others to Quetzalcóatl.

Cholula is said to have a church for each day of the year. There are actually 39 churches, and townspeople admit they include the churches of 18 nearby villages in their count. The city also is the site of the **University of the Americas**, a highly respected school founded in Mexico City in 1940 and originally called Mexico City College. The university moved to Cholula in 1968, offers courses in Spanish and English and is noted for its archeology program.

CAPILLA REAL (Royal Chapel), facing the main square, is within the walls of the Church of San Gabriel. Originally built for defensive purposes, the chapel has seven naves and 49 domes. It was damaged in the 1999 earthquake.

PIRAMIDE TEPANAPA (Tepanapa Pyramid), the focal point of the Cholula archeological site, rises near the main square. Its base length is about 1,315 feet—each side some 500 feet longer than the Pyramid of the Sun at Teotihuacán. An arduous stone trail leads to the **Santuario los Remedios**, which crowns the hill 230 feet above ground level. Climbers reaching the top are rewarded with excellent views. Some of the nearly 5 miles of tunnels are lighted; guides identify structures and decorative highlights. **Note:** The church was badly damaged by the 1999 earthquake and was closed at press time.

A museum near the entrance exhibits pottery and artifacts dating from pre-Hispanic times, Indian knives and arrowheads used in sacrifices, and a scale model of the pyramid as it is believed to have appeared prior to Hernán Cortés' arrival. Admission is charged.

ACATEPEC, PUEBLA (D-11)

The small villages of Acatepec (ah-kah-teh-PEHK) and Tonantzintla (toh-nahn-TSEEN-tlah) are just off Mex. 190 a few miles south of Cholula. Both are distinguished by baroque churches that are magnificent examples of Indian craftsmanship—local artisans employing pre-Hispanic imagery to depict Christian beliefs—and are well worth seeing for their visual splendor. The two towns are within walking distance of each other, and both churches can be visited by taking a local bus designated "Chipilo." Buses make the trip to Tonantzintla and Acatepec from either Cholula or Puebla.

The beautifully preserved and refurbished **Iglesia de San Francisco Acatepec** (Church of San Francisco Acatepec), in the center of town, is considered one of the most ornate in the Americas. The facade of this 18th-century church is an extravagantly colorful feast of blue, yellow and orange tiles fastidiously arranged in dazzling geometric patterns. The interior is somewhat more restrained but still lovely, with paneled doors, wall paintings and folk art decoration. The church's overall magnificence strongly reflects the culture of the Indians who labored to build it.

TONANTZINTLA, PUEBLA (D-11)

In nearby Tonantzintla is the **Iglesia de Santa María Tonantzintla** (Church of Santa María Tonantzintla), which dominates this tiny village. It exhibits visual splendor in reverse: while the church's yellowish exterior looks fairly disciplined, its interior is a definitive example of the riotously ornate Churrigueresque style. The walls and ceiling are completely covered with gilded decorations, painted cherubs and saints garlanded in plumed headdresses. The amazingly colorful motifs include fruits, flowers, birds and Christmas themes, and the faces and dress of the human figures are strongly Indian in character. Although it was under construction for nearly 300 years—from 1607 to 1897—the church exhibits such harmonious ornamental continuity that it all appears to date from the early 17th century.

DOLORES HIDALGO, GUANAJUATO (A-8) elev. 6,517'

Known in Mexico as "Cuna de la Independencia Nacional" (The Cradle of National Independence) and designated a national historic monument, Dolores Hidalgo (doh-LOH-rehs ee-DAHL-goh) lies in the valley of the Río Laja. Just before midnight on Sept. 15, 1810, Father Miguel Hidalgo y Costilla called together his parishioners by ringing the village church bell. He then gave the venerated *Grito de Dolores*, a speech announcing Mexican independence that ignited the 11-year war to achieve it. A statue of Hidalgo stands in the town's main plaza, where various vendors ply their wares among comfortable old benches and square-trimmed trees.

Dolores Hidalgo contains the former homes of other Mexican heroes; guides are available for tours of the town. The annual *Independence Day* celebrations held Sept. 15-16 re-create this historic event.

CASA DE DON MIGUEL HIDALGO (Home of Don Miguel Hidalgo), Morelos #1 at Hidalgo, contains many items relating to the life of the patriot priest, including paintings, portraits, books and period furniture. Admission is charged.

GUADALAJARA, JALISCO

To many people, Guadalajara (gwah-dah-lah-HAH-rah) embodies the essence of Mexico. Staunchly traditional and politically conservative while at the same time modern and progressive, the city is known for its flowers, gracious old buildings and the hospitality of its residents.

The capital of Jalisco, Guadalajara is a tourist and retirement center, as well as a commercial powerhouse. It also is a magnet for the Mexican poor, who pour into Guadalajara hoping for a better life and straining already overburdened public services. While visitors are likely to be enchanted by the city's colonial plazas and stately architecture, they must also contend with traffic jams, air pollution and other big-city ills.

Guadalajara's history dates to 1530, just 38 years after Christopher Columbus first reached North America and 9 years after the conquest of Mexico by Hernán Cortés. Another Spanish explorer, Nuño de Guzmán, founded the settlement. Guzmán was a cruel conqueror; he and his soldiers slaughtered entire Indian communities in

---

Fast Facts

LOCATION: In west-central Mexico, due east of Puerto Vallarta.

POPULATION: 1,628,600; metropolitan area 3,456,100 (1990 Census).

ELEVATION: 1,552 meters (5,091 feet).

WHAT'S THERE: A pedestrian-friendly historic center, sprinkled with colonial plazas, museums and architectural landmarks; Mercado Libertad, an enormous covered city market selling everything from pottery to dried iguanas; Plaza Tapatía, a seven-block-long promenade that is Guadalajara's best place for people watching; the suburbs of Tlaquepaque and Tonalá, where high-quality pottery and other handicrafts are produced and sold.

the course of exploring the lands west and north of Mexico City. He established Guadalajara—named for his hometown in Spain—at the site of present-day Nochistlán in the state of Zacatecas, about 60 miles to the northeast. Early settlers moved several times after Indian attacks before finally settling in the **Valley of Atemajac** in 1542. It was a wise choice, for the mile-high plateau ensured unimpeded expansion.

After the Spanish Crown learned of Guzmán's atrocities, he was deported back to Spain and the name of his self-appointed "country" was changed from La Gran España to Nuevo Galicia. Early on Guadalajara figured prominently in the history of this area. The town grew rapidly and by 1769 had become a provincial capital. Spanish expeditions left from Guadalajara to gain control of such far-flung lands as the Philippine and Molucca Islands and the island of Guam, and to establish missions in northern Mexico and present-day California. Wealth from the surrounding farms and silver mines was channeled into the construction of lavish churches, mansions and monuments.

After abolishing slavery and launching the War of Independence in September 1810, Father Miguel Hidalgo briefly occupied the city. In the late 1850s and early 1860s Guadalajara withstood army attacks led alternately by Archduke Maximilian and Benito Juárez, who made the city the capital of his reform government for a few months during his forced exile from Mexico City.

Guadalajara today is a sprawling metropolis, Mexico's second largest. It is estimated that more than 5 million residents jam the city and its suburbs. The surrounding high plains of the Valley of Atemajac, part of Mexico's great central plateau, are noted for fine horse, cattle and grain ranches. The city's factories convert metals, hides and foodstuffs into many different products. Guadalajara also has become an electronics center. Plants operated by Hewlett-Packard, IBM and Motorola produce cellular phones and desktop and laptop computers, leading some local business boosters to refer to the city as "Silicon Valley South."

A pleasant year-round climate no doubt has something to do with the fact that Guadalajarans are among the most active outdoor enthusiasts in the country. Good weather plus cultural and leisure opportunities has helped make the towns of **Ajijic, Chapala** and **Jocotepec**—all along the shore of nearby **Lake Chapala**—a major retirement destination for English-speaking residents from the United States and Canada.

Guadalajara even has its own word—*tapatío*. Reputedly derived from *tlapatiotl*, a term used to denote cacao or other small units of exchange frequently used in the Indian marketplace, it now refers to any person, thing or quality that is indisputably Guadalajaran. *Tapatío* indeed are such characteristically Mexican pleasures as the *jarabe*, or Mexican hat dance, and the music of the mariachis.

APPROACHES

BY AIR

Miguel Hidalgo International Airport is about 17 kilometers (11 miles) southeast of the city on Mex. 23. Aeroméxico, American, Continental, Delta and Mexicana airlines offer direct flights from U.S. cities. International connections are usually via Mexico City. Numerous half-hour flights connect Guadalajara with Puerto Vallarta *(see separate listing)*. Always check with a travel agency or the airline prior to booking a flight, as routes and direct-flight availability differs depending on the time of year. For additional information about airlines *see "Arriving by Air," page 53*.

Autotransportaciónes Aeropuerto (Airport Transportation) offers shared-ride shuttle van service to and from any place in the metropolitan area. Tickets are sold at a booth outside the terminal exit; fares are based on a zone system and can cost anywhere from $10-$15 per person. For details phone (3) 612-4278 or 612-4308. Taxis also take passengers to and from the airport.

BY CAR

Guadalajara's location between the Pacific coast and central Mexico makes it an ideal base from which to explore Jalisco and the surrounding states of Nayarit, Zacatecas, Aguascalientes, Guanajuato, Michoacán and Colima. Mex. 15/15-D is the major highway from the northwest; Mex. 54 from the north and northeast. Mex. 80 proceeds southwest to coastal Mex. 200, which heads south to Manzanillo or north to Puerto Vallarta. With the exception of Mex. 15-D, all of the above routes are old (free) highways.

The Guadalajara-Manzanillo toll highway, Mex. 54-D, begins at El Cuarenta, on Mex. 15 south of the city. Although the distance to Colima is not much shorter than that traveled on free Mex. 54, the toll road avoids the latter's narrow, winding stretches.

The Mex. 15-D toll highway is a multilane route linking Guadalajara with Mexico City. It takes between 5 and 6 hours to drive the 506-kilometer (316-mile) route, which runs south of Mex. 90, Mex. 45-D and Mex. 57-D via Irapuato and Querétaro—previously the most direct route between the two cities.

South of and roughly parallel to Mex. 15-D is old Mex. 15, a winding road that hugs the southern shore of Lake Chapala and passes through the cities of Morelia, Zitácuaro and Toluca on its way to Mexico City—a scenic but much more

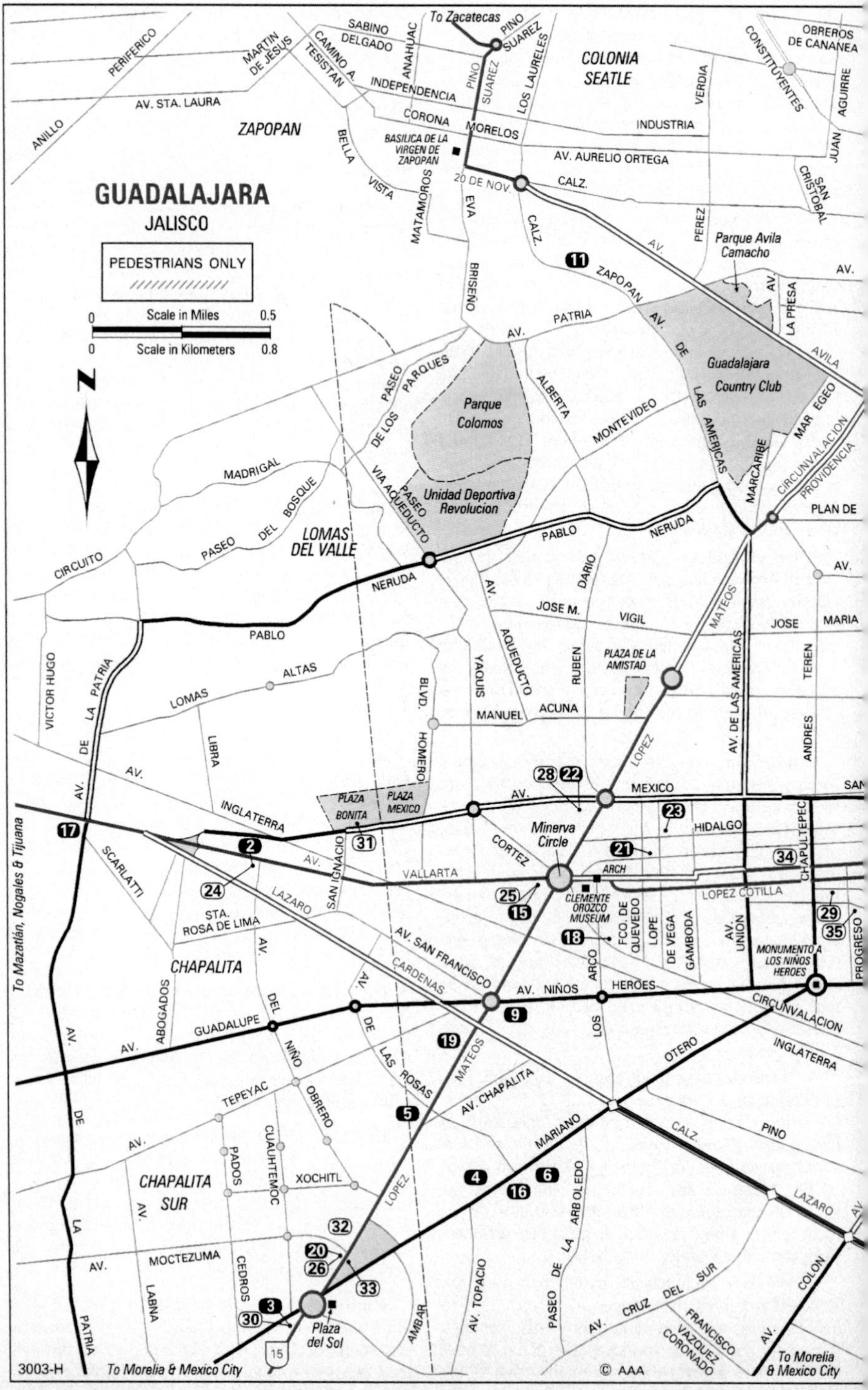

GUADALAJARA
JALISCO

PEDESTRIANS ONLY

Scale in Miles	
0	0.5

Scale in Kilometers	
0	0.8

N

To Zacatecas

COLONIA SEATLE

ZAPOPAN

OBREROS DE CANANEA

BASILICA DE LA VIRGEN DE ZAPOPAN

Parque Avila Camacho

Guadalajara Country Club

Parque Colomos

Unidad Deportiva Revolucion

LOMAS DEL VALLE

PLAZA DE LA AMISTAD

PLAZA BONITA

PLAZA MEXICO

Minerva Circle

CHAPALITA

CLEMENTE OROZCO MUSEUM

MONUMENTO A LOS NIÑOS HEROES

STA. ROSA DE LIMA

CHAPALITA SUR

Plaza del Sol

To Mazatlán, Nogales & Tijuana

To Morelia & Mexico City

To Morelia & Mexico City

3003-H

© AAA

Street labels: PERIFERICO, MARTIN DE JESUS, AV. STA. LAURA, ANILLO, BELLA VISTA, SABINO DELGADO, ANAHUAC, CAMINO A. TESISTAN, INDEPENDENCIA, CORONA, MORELOS, PINO SUAREZ, LOS LAURELES, VERDIA, INDUSTRIA, AV. AURELIO ORTEGA, CONSTITUYENTES, JUAN, SAN CRISTOBAL, JUAN AGUIRRE, MATAMOROS, EVA, BRISEÑO, 20 DE NOV., CALZ., AV. PATRIA, PEREZ, AV. ZAPOPAN, AV. DE LAS AMERICAS, LA PRESA, AV. AVILA, MAR EGEO, MAR CARIBE, CIRCUNVALACION PROVIDENCIA, PLAN DE, ALBERTA, MONTEVIDEO, PASEO DE LOS PARQUES, PASEO VIA AQUEDUCTO, PABLO, NERUDA, DARIO, JOSE M., VIGIL, JOSE MARIA, MADRIGAL, PASEO DEL BOSQUE, CIRCUITO, VICTOR HUGO, AV. DE LA PATRIA, LOMAS, ALTAS, LIBRA, BLVD. HOMERO, YAQUIS, AQUEDUCTO, MANUEL ACUÑA, RUBEN, LOPEZ, MEXICO, HIDALGO, JOSE, TEREN, ANDRES, CHAPULTEPEC, INGLATERRA, SCARLATTI, LAZARO, SAN IGNACIO, VALLARTA, CORTEZ, ARCH, LOPEZ COTILLA, FCO. DE QUEVEDO, DE VEGA, GAMBOA, AV. UNION, PROGRESO, ABOGADOS, GUADALUPE, DEL, NIÑO, OBRERO, AV. SAN FRANCISCO, CARDENAS, DE LAS ROSAS, AV. NIÑOS HEROES, LOS, ARCO, OTERO, CIRCUNVALACION, INGLATERRA, TEPEYAC, PADOS, CUAUHTEMOC, XOCHITL, LOPEZ, MATEOS, AV. CHAPALITA, MARIANO, CALZ., PINO, MOCTEZUMA, LABNA, CEDROS, AMBAR, AV. TOPACIO, PASEO DE LA ARBOLEDO, AV. CRUZ DEL SUR, FRANCISCO VAZQUEZ CORONADO, COLON, LAZARO, LA PATRIA

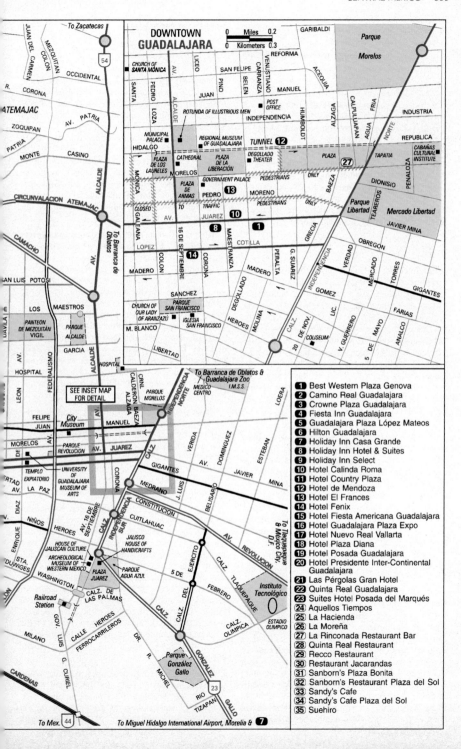

DOWNTOWN GUADALAJARA

0 Miles 0.2
0 Kilometers 0.3

1 Best Western Plaza Genova
2 Camino Real Guadalajara
3 Crowne Plaza Guadalajara
4 Fiesta Inn Guadalajara
5 Guadalajara Plaza López Mateos
6 Hilton Guadalajara
7 Holiday Inn Casa Grande
8 Holiday Inn Hotel & Suites
9 Holiday Inn Select
10 Hotel Calinda Roma
11 Hotel Country Plaza
12 Hotel de Mendoza
13 Hotel El Frances
14 Hotel Fenix
15 Hotel Fiesta Americana Guadalajara
16 Hotel Guadalajara Plaza Expo
17 Hotel Nuevo Real Vallarta
18 Hotel Plaza Diana
19 Hotel Posada Guadalajara
20 Hotel Presidente Inter-Continental Guadalajara
21 Las Pérgolas Gran Hotel
22 Quinta Real Guadalajara
23 Suites Hotel Posada del Marqués
24 Aquellos Tiempos
25 La Hacienda
26 La Moreña
27 La Rinconada Restaurant Bar
28 Quinta Real Restaurant
29 Recco Restaurant
30 Restaurant Jacarandas
31 Sanborn's Plaza Bonita
32 Sanborn's Restaurant Plaza del Sol
33 Sandy's Cafe
34 Sandy's Cafe Plaza del Sol
35 Suehiro

time-consuming alternative. The road is in poor condition in places, and driving the stretch from Morelia to Mexico City is not recommended because of the possibility of encounters with *banditos*.

Mex. 15-D begins east of Guadalajara near the suburb of Tonalá, bypassing cities and towns for the most part as it traverses rolling farmland and upland valleys and skirts the southern shore of Lake Cuitzeo. The route reaches its highest elevation near Atlacomulco, after which it descends into the Valley of Mexico and junctions with Boulevard Manuel A. Camacho (Mex. 57-D) on the northwestern edge of the capital. Toll charges are typically expensive, but toll highways in general are in much better condition than free roads throughout Mexico.

By Bus

Bus lines out of Guadalajara's **Nueva Central Camionera** (New Bus Station), about 10 kilometers (6 miles) east of downtown outside the suburb of Tlaquepaque (on the way to Tonalá), service all cities and most towns in the country. Several of the biggest lines are connected with Greyhound Lines Inc. Cross-country buses make frequent trips between Guadalajara and border points. "Deluxe" first-class travel compares favorably with major U.S. lines; these buses are the standard size but carry half as many passengers. "Deluxe" service is offered by Omnibus de México, ETN and Primera Plus.

The station is large and modern, with seven terminal buildings accommodating different lines. Amenities include shuttle bus service, luggage storage (referred to as *guarda equipaje*), restaurants, shops, Ladatel long-distance telephones and hotel information. City buses and *colectivos* designated "Centro" or "Central" travel between the bus station and downtown. You can also take a taxi from the station to the downtown area. Taxi tickets are sold inside each terminal building; fares are based on a zone system.

For shorter bus trips to Tequila, the Lake Chapala suburban communities or other towns within a 60-mile radius of the city, use the old **Central Camionera** (Central Bus Station), located off Avenida Dr. R. Michel at calles Los Angeles and 28 de Enero (just northeast of Parque Agua Azul). A convenient way to obtain route, schedule and fare information for the main Mexican lines is to stop at the **Servicios Coordinados** office, Calzada Independencia #254 in Plaza Tapatía. Reservations can also be made here. For additional information about buses *see* "*Bus Service*," page 63.

Getting Around

City Layout

For visitors, Guadalajara's chief attraction is the careful preservation of its **Centro Histórico**, the downtown historic district. Forming a shape somewhat like a giant cross are four different plazas, each offering a distinct personality: Plaza Tapatía, Plaza de la Liberación, Plaza de Armas and Plaza de los Laureles. They all surround the cathedral *(see attraction listing)*, which is the heart of the old city. Centuries of history unfold along the narrow cobblestone lanes and in the weathered two- and three-story buildings that constitute the center of old Guadalajara, where street vendors and shoeshine boys seem an immutable part of the landscape.

The plazas are perfect for strolling and observing the locals. **Plaza Tapatía** *(see attraction listing)* is Guadalajara's gathering place, conveniently located close to museums, monuments and grand examples of colonial architecture. Here are tree-lined parks, stone walkways, burbling fountains and a vast array of restaurants. On Sundays, throngs of dressed-up families parade up and down **Plaza de la Liberación**, just east of the cathedral and at the western end of Plaza Tapatía. A narrow waterway runs along this plaza, bordered on both sides by shops and more restaurants. A statue of Father Miguel Hidalgo shows the priest holding a broken chain, a symbol of his call to end slavery in Mexico.

Plaza de Armas, south of the cathedral, is the city's traditional main square, bordered on the east side by the Palacio de Gobierno *(see attraction listing)*. **Plaza de los Laureles** (west of the cathedral) is, as the name suggests, planted with Indian laurel trees. The church on the plaza's north side, built in the mid-20th century, is one of the newer buildings in the historic center.

West and south of the historic center the boulevards are wider, the buildings newer and taller. Around the intersection of avenidas Vallarta and Chapultepec and farther southwest—in the commercial development known as **Plaza del Sol**, along Avenida López Mateos—large malls and upscale shops cater to the city's wealthy business class. Here are expensive homes and many of Guadalajara's major hotels. Although Western culture is firmly entrenched throughout Mexico, it is particularly evident in these sections of the city, where such familiar stateside franchises as McDonald's and Radio Shack pop up on many corners.

Lending a unifying appearance to all the structural and human diversity are the vibrant purple of blooming jacaranda trees and cascading bougainvillea, which seems to grow just about everywhere. Fountains, most of them delightfully ornate, also are scattered throughout the city.

Sprawling Guadalajara is divided into four sectors; street names change when a new sector is entered. The major north-south routes are **Calzada Independencia/Gobernador Curiel** (which divides Guadalajara into east and west sectors), **Avenida Alcalde, Avenida Federalismo-Colón** and **Avenida López Mateos**. The major east-west routes are **Avenida Circunvalación, Avenida Avila Camacho, Avenida México/Juan Manuel-Federación, Avenida Vallarta/Juárez/Javier Mina** (which divides the city into north and south sectors) and **Avenida Guadalupe/Niños Héroes/Calzada González Gallo**.

Two thoroughfares loop around Guadalajara. The inner **Avenida Patria** travels around the western half of the city. The outer **Periférico** encircles the entire metropolitan area; navigating this two-lane route can be slow going, however, due to potholes and heavy truck traffic. **Note:** During and after the summer rainy season, roads both within the city and the state of Jalisco may develop dangerous breaks in the pavement and potholes that can cause accidents.

RENTAL CARS

It is said that Guadalajara has the highest car-per-capita ratio in Mexico: one car for every four citizens, about twice that of the rest of the country. Traffic is heavy and moves slowly, and many streets are equipped with *topes* (speed bumps). Significant truck traffic adds to the overall congestion. *Glorietas* (traffic circles) are common at busy intersections. **Note:** Air pollution levels have risen to the point where state officials have instituted a tune-up test that all vehicles with Jalisco license plates must pass. Vehicles with out-of-state plates, however, are exempted.

Hertz is one of many rental car agencies with offices at the airport and downtown. Be sure you fully understand the terms of any rental contract, especially with regard to insurance coverage. It's significantly less expensive to reserve before you leave home; make reservations at least 1 week in advance.

Note: AAA/CAA members enjoy exceptional discounts through Hertz for vehicles booked in the United States. Consult your local AAA/CAA club or phone Hertz, (800) 654-3080.

The Informed Traveler

Media

English-language newspapers, including the weekly *Guadalajara Colony Reporter*, are available at the Best Western Hotel Fenix, downtown at avenidas Corona and López Cotilla. *Let's Enjoy* and *Guest Huésped* are free magazines with information about Guadalajara and the Lake Chapala area.

Sandi Bookstore, Avenida Tepeyac #718 in the Chapalita neighborhood west of downtown, has English-language newspapers and books. The Sanborn's chain has several area locations and also offers books, newspapers and magazines in English; the downtown branch is at avenidas Juárez and 16 de Septiembre, a block south of Plaza de Armas.

Weather

Although Guadalajara is in the same latitude as tropical Honolulu, its altitude is comparable to Denver's. The result is springlike temperatures much of the year, along with abundant sunshine. Unlike the coastal and lowland areas, uncomfortably humid days are rare. High temperatures are normally in the 70s and 80s. In May, the warmest month, they can creep into the low 90s, but it always cools off in the evening. The rainy season is June through September. Air pollution in the city is a problem, although not as severe as in Mexico City.

Bring appropriate attire for an evening at the theater or dinner in a good restaurant. Otherwise, casual clothing is fine for sightseeing. A sweater or light jacket will come in handy on cool nights.

Staying Safe

The rules in Guadalajara are the same as those in any big city. At night, avoid urban neighborhoods that are away from the downtown core or other tourist areas; dark side streets in particular can be dangerous. If going out for the evening or taking a side trip during the day, it's a good idea to hire a taxi driver affiliated with your hotel. Keep an eye on personal items at all times, especially in the crowded shopping districts. Women are not welcome in *cantina* bars and other bastions of heavy drinking and *machismo* attitudes.

In Case of Emergency

To contact the city police department, phone (3) 617-6060 (no English spoken). Dial 06 to summon a police car (no English spoken). Better yet, try to avoid trouble.

Hospital México-Americano, Colomos #2110, provides full medical services and 24-hour emergency service; phone (3) 641-0089. The Cruz Roja (Red Cross) is also open 24 hours; phone (3) 613-1550 (English spoken). Major hotels and the U.S. Consulate can provide lists of doctors who are on 24-hour call.

BUSES

Buses are the preferred—and most economical—means of local transportation, for they cover every part of town. City buses run daily every few minutes from 6 a.m.-10 p.m. School bus-style vehicles are the cheapest (around 25c), but conditions tend to be substandard to what visitors are used to. They also are quite likely to be very crowded.

Tur buses (operated by Linea Turquesa), turquoise in color and with the letters "TUR" designated on the side, cost more but are air-conditioned, do not carry standing passengers and travel to such outlying tourist destinations as Tlaquepaque, Tonalá and Zapopan. *Par Vial* buses travel a central east-west route along avenidas Independencia/Hidalgo as far west as Minerva Circle (at Avenida López Mateos); from there, they double back along Avenida Vallarta/Juárez, a few blocks south. Privately operated *colectivos* (minivans) cost about the same as city buses; some have their destination marked on the windshield, although routes and pick-up points change frequently.

TAXIS

Compared to the bus, a taxi ride in Guadalajara is expensive. Even short 10-minute rides are likely to cost at least $5. Rates go up at night. Although all cabs must be equipped with a meter to determine the charge, make certain you agree on a destination and a fare with the driver before entering the cab. Check at your hotel's front desk for current fares; bellboys can often assist those who don't speak Spanish. Most cabs are found at or called from a cab stand *(sitio)*. *Sitios* are located near all the major hotels and attractions. The safest option is to stick with cab drivers who are affiliated with your hotel.

PARKING

On-street parking in the city center is scarce. Public parking garages generally charge a fixed rate per hour; few are insured for customers. Parking lots charge less than garages. An underground lot is below Plaza de la Liberación, just east of the cathedral. Always avoid areas marked *"No E," "Estacionamiento Prohibido"* (No parking) or *"Exclusivo"* (Reserved). License plates are removed from illegally parked vehicles, and a fine must be paid to retrieve them.

PUBLIC TRANSPORTATION

Guadalajara's *tren ligero* (light rail) rapid-transit system has two lines. Line 1 runs north-south along Avenida Federalismo-Colón for a distance of about 10 miles, between the northern and southern stretches of the Periférico. More helpful to visitors is Line 2, which runs east-west along avenidas Vallarta/Juárez and Javier Mina (the street name changes at Calzada Independencia). Trains run about every 15 minutes daily 6 a.m.-11 p.m.; the fare is inexpensive.

Cathedral   ©Chris Sharp

WHAT TO SEE

BARRANCA DE OBLATOS is 10 kilometers (6 miles) northeast of downtown Guadalajara via Calzada Independencia Norte. This 2,000-foot-deep gorge was cut by the Santiago and Verde rivers. Thermal rivulets plunge down the red walls (except during the dry season). The greater the depth, the more tropical the climate: Papayas, oranges, guavas, bananas, mangoes and other fruits grown at the canyon bottom are marketed in Guadalajara. A cable car leaves the rim daily at 8 a.m. to take workers to the power plant on the canyon floor. The best views are from the **Parque Huentitán el Alto Mirador** lookout area at the top of the gorge.

CASA DE LA CULTURA JALISCIENSE (House of Jaliscan Culture) is at avenidas 16 de Septiembre and Constituyentes, near Agua Azul Park. The building contains a movie theater, two art exhibition halls, artists' studios and the offices of various culture-oriented organizations. The 300,000-volume **Guadalajara Public Library** also is in this building.

CATEDRAL, facing Avenida Alcalde, is an intriguing mixture of Byzantine, Greek, Gothic, Churrigueresque and neoclassic architectural styles. Begun in 1561, it was consecrated in 1618. Its twin 200-foot towers were erected in

1848 after an earthquake destroyed the original, much shorter structures. Emblazoned with yellow and blue tiles, they are a Guadalajara landmark. Inside are three cavernous naves and 11 elegantly appointed altars, a gift from King Ferdinand VII of Spain. A lovely sculpture, "Our Lady of the Roses," was given to the city by the 16th-century Spanish king Carlos V. The priceless painting "The Assumption of the Virgin" in the sacristy is presumably by Bartolomé Murillo. Open daily.

IGLESIA DE NUESTRA SEÑORA DE ARANZAZU (Church of Our Lady of Aránzazu), avenidas 16 de Septiembre and Prisciliano Sánchez, borders the south side of **Parque San Francisco** (San Francisco Park). Although the exterior is plain, inside is an extravagantly ornate *retablo* (altarpiece) that is a dazzling example of Spanish baroque design; its niches contain life-size statues of the saints. Also impressive are the colorful walls and ceilings. Next to this church is **Iglesia San Francisco** (Church of San Francisco), which dates from the 16th century and has a tripletiered altar. The park is a shady green space frequented by food vendors and is a starting point for horse-drawn carriage rides.

IGLESIA DE SANTA MONICA (Church of Santa Monica) is at calles Santa Mónica and Reforma, about 4 blocks northwest of the cathedral. It dates from around 1720. The baroque facade features exquisite stone carvings in 18th-century Spanish style. The interior is elaborate as well.

INSTITUTO CULTURAL CABAÑAS (Cabañas Cultural Institute) is at the eastern end of Plaza Tapatía. Built in the early 19th century and financed by Bishop Juan Cruz Ruíz de Cabañas, it originally offered shelter for crippled, destitute or orphaned men, women and children. Later an orphanage, the building provided education and medical care for children up until the early 1970s before being renovated for use as a cultural center. The sprawling complex encompasses 23 patios linked by pink-tiled corridors. Known locally as El Hospicio Cabañas, it is the showplace for some of José Clemente Orozco's most powerful frescoes, notably *"El Hombre de Fuego"* ("Man of Fire"), which graces the lofty ceiling. His other projects, sketches and drawings are part of the institute's permanent collection.

Changing art exhibitions are mounted, and there is a movie theater, a performing arts theater and an outdoor patio where ballet, music and dance performances take place. Particularly interesting are the bronze sculptures by Alejandro Colungas that depict human figures transforming themselves into furniture. English-speaking guides are available. Tues.-Sat. 10:15-6, Sun. 10:15-3. Admission is charged; free to all Sun. Phone (3) 617-4440.

MUSEO CLEMENTE OROZCO is at Avenida Aurelio Aceves #27, just east of Minerva Circle off Avenida Vallarta. This is the former workshop and residence of Jalisco's leading muralist (1883-1949), who lived in the house for many years. Distinguished by a three-story window, it now displays photographs, tools, clothing and his personal easel. The wall facing the great window is covered by a huge mural entitled *"Alegoría del Vino"* ("Wine Allegory"). The museum also has a collection of documents, handwritten letters, posters, diplomas and other tributes to Orozco. Tues.-Sun. 10-2. Phone (3) 616-8329.

MUSEO DE ARQUEOLOGIA DEL OCCIDENTE DE MEXICO (Archeological Museum of Western Mexico) is on Plaza Juárez (at calzadas Independencia Sur and del Campesino), across from the entrance to Agua Azul Park. It exhibits a small but select group of figurines, pottery and other artifacts from sites in Colima, Jalisco and Nayarit. The museum is part of the University of Guadalajara. Tues.-Sat. 10-2 and 4-7, Sun. 11-4. Admission is charged.

MUSEO DE LA CIUDAD (City Museum) is west of the historic center at Avenida Independencia #684 (at Avenida Mariano Bárcenas). It opened in 1992 to commemorate Guadalajara's 450th anniversary. The old stone convent housing the museum is a fine example of late 17th-century colonial architecture. Eight *salas* (halls) present a chronological timeline of the city's history and development, from its founding by a handful of Spanish families to the dynamic present. Among the more interesting displays are equestrian trappings, reminders of Guadalajara's *charreada* tradition. Information is presented in Spanish. Tues.-Sat. 10-5, Sun. 10-3. Admission is charged; free to all Sun. Phone (3) 658-2531.

MUSEO REGIONAL DE GUADALAJARA (Regional Museum of Guadalajara), on Avenida Liceo 1 block north of the Government Palace, is housed in a former theological seminary dating from around 1700. It has been a museum since 1918. Exhibits focus on the history of Jalisco and western Mexico, and include pre-Hispanic artifacts, ethnological displays and a 1,715-pound meteorite discovered in the state of Zacatecas in 1792. A collection of Spanish and Mexican art on the second floor features paintings from the school of Bartolomé Murillo. Tues.-Sun. 9-3. Admission is charged; free to all Sun. Phone (3) 614-9957.

PALACIO DE GOBIERNO (Government Palace) faces the east side of Plaza de Armas. This Spanish baroque building dates from 1643. Note the stone gargoyles, used to divert water from the roof, and the pillared front entrance. Enormous murals by José Clemente Orozco depict Mexico's history using the themes of war, freedom and oppression. This building was the site of Father Miguel Hidalgo's decree abolishing slavery in 1810; a huge Orozco mural (in the stairwell to the right after entering) depicts the event. Another mural shows Benito Juárez and other political figures of his era; Guillermo Prieto's plea saving the people's president from assassination in 1858 was delivered here. The cannon and armor carved on the building's facade are a symbol of colonial authority. Daily 9-9.

PARQUE AGUA AZUL (Agua Azul Park), at the intersection of calzadas Independencia Sur and González Gallo, is the oldest of the city's parks. Trees, flowers, fountains and an artificial lake make this a popular spot for city residents and a pleasant place to while away an afternoon. On the grounds are an orchid house, an aviary and an outdoor theater. On the other side of Calzada González Gallo is **Plaza Juárez**, which has a monument encircled by the flags of other Latin American countries. Park open daily 8-6. Admission is charged.

Casa de las Artesanías de Jalisco (Jalisco House of Handicrafts) is just past the park entrance. This state-run store sells fixed-price regional handicrafts, including leather saddles, furniture, blown glass, ceramics, pottery, textiles, tinwork and woodcarvings. There also are museum displays of regional costumes and crafts from around the state. Mon.-Fri. 10-6, Sat. 11-5, Sun. 11-3.

PLAZA TAPATIA, along Avenida Hidalgo, is a seven-block-long pedestrian pathway connecting the Degollado Theater at the west end to the Cabañas Cultural Institute at the east end. The walkway enables visitors to see several of Guadalajara's downtown attractions without having to cross major streets. Underground parking lots also are along the route.

Plaza Tapatía is a prime spot for strolling and people watching. On weekend evenings it is filled with music and sights—old men tapping their walking sticks, grandmothers shepherding boisterous children, young women parading to the appreciative stares of young men. Vendors sell everything from candy to canaries. The festive atmosphere unfolds against a backdrop of flower beds, statues, fountains and reflecting pools, and there are myriad storefronts in which to browse or window shop.

An unusual but practical service is offered by the *escritorios* who set up shop in the arcade close to the State Tourism Office. For centuries these typists, writers and editors have helped illiterate people fill out documents or write messages and correspondence, particularly love letters. The *escritorios* have become experts in filling out official forms, and some have also learned English to help foreigners with Spanish translations.

ROTONDA DE LOS HOMBRES ILUSTRES (Rotunda of Illustrious Men) is north of the cathedral in a park bounded by Calle Hidalgo and avenidas Alcalde, Independencia/Industria and

Liceo. This mausoleum is where some of Jalisco's foremost native sons are buried. Most of those interred are intellectuals, artists, philanthropists and musicians; only two are military officials. Sculptures of the men are surrounded by a circular grouping of columns.

TEATRO DEGOLLADO (Degollado Theater) is on Calle Belén between Calle Morelos and Avenida Hidalgo. Completed in 1866, this impressive neoclassic building has been compared to Milan's La Scala Opera House. The relief above the columned entrance depicts Apollo and the Nine Muses. The bronze frieze on the theater's outside back wall illustrates Guadalajara's 1542 founding ceremony, which is believed to have taken place a short distance away.

Inside are opulent red and gold balconies and a dome with murals painted by Gerardo Suárez that depict Dante's "Divine Comedy." The remodeled theater is the home of the Jalisco Philharmonic Orchestra and presents operas, plays and concerts year-round. The best-known performances are given by the **University of Guadalajara Folkloric Ballet** every Sunday at 10 a.m.; tickets for each week's performance go on sale Thursday afternoon. If you can't attend an event, the theater is open Mon.-Sat. 10-1 for tours. Phone (3) 614-4773 for ticket information.

TEMPLO EXPIATORIO (Expiatory Temple) is a massive structure west of the historic center that covers a city block, bounded by avenidas López Cotilla, Juárez and Enrique Díaz de León. One balcony of this Gothic-style church, built at the turn of the 20th century, features mechanical representations of the 12 Apostles who make an appearance, accompanied by a carillon playing classical music, three times daily (9 a.m., noon and 6 p.m.). The clockwork figures can be viewed from the square in front of the church.

UNIVERSITY OF GUADALAJARA is on Avenida Juárez at Avenida Enrique Díaz de León, behind the Templo Expiatorio and 4 blocks west of Parque Revolución. The main building, French Renaissance in style, contains an Orozco mural. On the north side of Avenida Vallarta is the university tower, where cultural events are held regularly.

Museo de las Artes de la Universidad de Guadalajara (University of Guadalajara Museum of Arts), opposite the main building, is housed in a beautiful early 20th-century building that was once a primary school. The permanent collection consists primarily of contemporary Jaliscan and Mexican artists; traveling exhibitions are mounted regularly. Also here are early Orozco murals. Tues.-Sat. 10-8, Sun. noon-8.

ZOOLOGICO DE GUADALAJARA (Guadalajara Zoo) is about 6 kilometers (4 miles) north of Plaza Tapatía at the junction of Calzada Independencia Norte and Paseo del Zoológico. Covering 100 acres overlooking the Río Santiago Canyon, the zoo contains a variety of large mammals, birds, reptiles and monkeys. A train and well-marked footpaths allow access to the major viewing areas. Other facilities include a children's zoo, an auditorium for special presentations and snack stands. Next to the zoo is a planetarium and the **Selva Mágica** amusement park, which has a pool with performing dolphins. Parking is provided; guided tours are available. Tues.-Sun. 11-6. Admission is charged.

WHAT TO DO

DINING

Guadalajaran restaurants offer diners a number of meaty options. Typically *tapatío* fare includes grilled steaks; *carne asada a la tampiqueña*, spicy broiled or roasted meat served with bacon and beans; *pozole*, a thick, satisfying hominy-based soup with hunks of *carnitas* (pork), tomatoes, cilantro and frequently chickpeas; and *birria* (stewed goat or pork in a thick, spicy tomato broth). But the city also has elegant Conti-

nental dining rooms, vegetarian eateries, Italian-style trattorias and *loncherías*, stand-up lunch counters offering sandwich fixings piled on a fresh *bolillo* roll. Such options should satisfy anyone's taste and pocket.

Perhaps the most authentic of the city's eateries are the *restaurantes campestres*, country-style establishments serving big steaks with such hearty Mexican side dishes as beans, quesadillas and tortillas. The food is accompanied by mariachi music and entertainment. Some establishments also present a modified form of *charreada*, or rodeo, which gives willing customers the opportunity to fight a young bull; cheers or laughs ensue depending on the outcome. *Restaurantes campestres* are located within the city and also along main highways outside the urban area.

Gastronomic adventurers will be sorely tempted by the astounding variety of street food. Numerous inexpensive *taquerías* (taco stands) operate up and down the length of Plaza Tapatía; the freshly made corn tortillas are wrapped

Visitor Services

Guides/Tours

Tour guides with name tags who congregate at the bus terminal are likely to be agents on commission with hotels. The major hotels usually have a list of licensed bilingual guides. Bus tours of the downtown area and nearby points of interest are offered by Panoramex, Guadalajara's largest tour company; phone (3) 810-5005 or 810-5109 Mon.-Fri. 9-7, Sat. 9-2 (English spoken). For visitors without a car, this is the easiest way to explore the city and outlying suburbs.

Rides in horse-drawn *calandrias* (carriages) can be taken throughout the central downtown area and are a relaxing way to see the sights. Excursions depart from the Regional Museum of Guadalajara, Liberty Market and San Francisco Park. Few drivers speak English, so you may want to familiarize yourself with the layout of the city before embarking.

Information Sources

The Jalisco State Tourism Office, Calle Morelos #102 at Plaza Tapatía (behind the Degollado Theater), has lots of information about Guadalajara and other destinations within the state. It also provides listings for hotels, restaurants and cultural events, as well as walking tour maps of the historic center. Office hours are Mon.-Fri. 9-8, Sat.-Sun. and holidays 9-1; phone (3) 658-2222 (English spoken). A tourist information booth is inside the southern doorway of the Palacio de Gobierno (facing Plaza de Armas); it is open Mon.-Fri. 9-3 and 6-8, Sat. 9-1.

An information office maintained by the city's Convention and Visitors Bureau is at Avenida Vallarta #4095, across from the Camino Real Hotel; phone (3) 647-9281 (English spoken). Another office on Avenida Vallarta, on the ground level of the Los Arcos Monument Arch (just east of Minerva circle), provides guidebooks and maps and also handles service complaints; phone (3) 616-3332.

Mexico Retirement and Travel Assistance (MRTA) publishes the quarterly *Mexico Living and Travel Update*, which provides real estate, lifestyle, health, travel, cultural and entertainment information, much of it about the Guadalajara/Chapala area. For additional information contact MRTA, 6301 S. Squaw Valley Rd., Suite 23, Pahrump, NV 89048-7949.

The Citizens Consular Services office of the U.S. Consulate, Progreso #175 at Avenida López Cotilla, provides a reference list of English-speaking lawyers, doctors and translators for those in difficulty; a duty officer is available for after-hours emergencies. Phone (3) 825-2998 or 825-2700.

Currency Exchange

Casas de cambio (currency exchange offices) are located downtown along Avenida López Cotilla and in the vicinity of the Plaza del Sol mall. Cash and traveler's checks can be changed at branches of Banamex banks Mon.-Fri. 9-noon. A Banamex branch is at Calle Corona and Avenida Juárez.

around a wide variety of meat or vegetable fillings. The **Mercado Libertad** *(see "Shopping" below)* has hundreds of tiny stands offering full-course *comida corrida* meals, tamales, enchiladas, quesadillas and other treats. You can also find cheese, fruit and pastries. Cleanliness levels vary, however, and anyone planning to nibble their way from stall to stall should keep in mind the possibility of bacterial contamination, especially if the food has been sitting for a long time.

A less risky option is to try a place that specializes in regional fare. **La Chata**, on Calle Corona about 2 blocks south of Plaza de Armas, is an unassuming café specializing in roasted meats, *pozole* and other regional specialties. Breakfast is served as well. **Los Itacates**, Avenida Chapultepec Norte #110, serves similar traditional dishes in fancier surroundings. Many of the items can be ordered as taco fillings. The restaurant also offers a breakfast buffet. To get there, take a *Par Vial* route bus west on Avenida Independencia and get off at the Chapultepec stop.

If you prefer a more elegant night out, try **Maximino's**, at Avenida Lerdo de Tejada #2043 near the U.S. Consulate. Well-to-do Guadalajarans come to this restored two-story mansion for the French-influenced international cuisine and excellent service. This is one of the city's few restaurants where a jacket is recommended for men.

Travelers longing for a taste of home need not despair. Whether it's due to the many U.S. and Canadian expatriates residing in Guadalajara or the changing tastes of local residents, U.S. fast-food franchises have popped up everywhere. **Sandy's Café**, in the Plaza del Sol mall, features soups, sandwiches and pasta dishes in addition to more traditional Mexican dishes. The Mexican chain **Sanborn's** serves everything from pancakes to tacos; it also has a gift shop/bookstore with English-language newspapers and magazines. There are branches at Plaza Bonita on Avenida México and across from Plaza del Sol. And for a meal on the run, Guadalajara has a number of pizza carryouts.

Except at first-class hotels and restaurants where purified water is customarily used, be careful of drinking water; this includes the ice cubes in drinks. Avoid unpeeled raw vegetables and fruit as well as untreated milk and dairy products. For a list of AAA-RATED dining establishments in Guadalajara, *see the Lodgings & Restaurants section.*

Shopping

Guadalajara has a reputation as perhaps the country's best shopping city. Fashionable shops and boutiques line Avenida Chapultepec between avenidas México and Niños Héroes, west of the historic center. This is Guadalajara's **Zona Rosa** (Pink Zone), an upper-class area frequented by tourists. Malls dot the metropolitan landscape as well. The newest is **La Gran Plaza**, a sleek three-story collection of stores and a movie theater multiplex on Avenida Vallarta near the Camino Real Hotel. The largest is **Plaza del Sol**, at avenidas López Mateos Sur and Mariano Otero southwest of downtown. Restaurants and outdoor garden areas offer a break from shopping. City buses designated "Plaza del Sol" travel to the mall from Calzada Independencia in the vicinity of the Liberty Market.

Guadalajara also has an amazing number of shoe stores. **Calle Esteban Alatorre**, northeast of the historic center, is known locally as "shoe street." **Galería del Calzado**, at the corner of avenidas México and Yaquis (on the west side of town near Plaza México), is a shoe shopping center covering a square block. Shoe and boot prices at its stores are reputed to be among the best in Mexico.

Huge amounts of handicrafts are produced in the Guadalajara area; few other places in the world exhibit such a variety of styles and materials in such a large concentration of shops. Locally produced and nationally prized items include Guadalajaran glassware, home-spun textiles, and pottery from the craft villages of **Tlaquepaque** and **Tonalá** *(see "Sightseeing" below).* **Casa de las Artesanías de Jalisco** (Jalisco House of Handicrafts), on Calzada González Gallo in Agua Azul Park, is a state-operated craft shop with a fine selection of wares from throughout Jalisco, as well as other parts of the country. A second location is at avenidas Alcalde and Avila Camacho, north of the historic center.

Just off Calzada Independencia at Avenida Javier Mina is the **Mercado Libertad** (Liberty Market), a huge, timeless Mexican market under a 20th-century roof. Shoppers bargain for an encyclopedic array of tropical fruits and vegetables, like chewy *zapotes* (fruit from the sapodilla tree). Also available for haggling over are such handicrafts as baskets, woodcarvings and pottery; watches; chess sets; jewelry; leather goods; electronic gadgets; computer software programs; and such time-tested exotica as speckled quail eggs and herbal potions to cure impotence. The market also sells a tremendous variety of food, from tacos to the delicately carved mango slices sold by fruit vendors. Squeamish stomachs will want to avoid some of the more unappetizing stalls, which offer the likes of *menudo* (tripe stew) and calves' heads.

El Baratillo, Guadalajara's Sunday morning flea market, offers shopping that is more for fun than for serious purchasing, unless you're an expert haggler. It stretches for blocks along Avenida Javier Mina in an area east of the Liberty Market; take a local bus along Avenida Gigantes, 2 blocks south of the market, to get there. El Baratillo is an enormous melange of just about everything, most of it used.

A weekend art exposition sets up in the vicinity of the **Glorieta Chapalita** traffic circle, west of downtown at avenidas Guadalupe and de las Rosas. Scores of paintings and sculptures are sold by their creators in a festive atmosphere.

SIGHTSEEING

Guadalajara serves as a convenient base for day excursions to the Lake Chapala communities of **Ajijic, Jocotepec** and **Chapala;** to the pottery-making centers of **Tlaquepaque** and **Tonalá;** to the town of **Tequila,** known for the production of one of Mexico's more potent brews; and to the suburb of **Zapopan,** home of the revered Virgin of Zapopan. Casual attire is suitable for almost any sightseeing excursion in the Guadalajara area; shorts are frowned upon in churches, however.

AJIJIC, JALISCO (H-3)

Ajijic (ah-hee-HEEK) is about 8 kilometers (5 miles) west of Chapala on the northern shore of Lake Chapala. This artists' and writers' colony is populated by many former U.S. residents. Along **Calle Morelos** between the main square and the waterfront are shops and boutiques selling everything from local handicrafts to designer fashions. The picturesque waterfront area and the town's cobblestone streets make it a pleasant destination for shopping, strolling and perhaps lunch. Ajijic's *Fiesta of St. Andrew*, held in late November, is celebrated with parades, dancing and fireworks.

WHERE TO STAY

AJIJIC B&B
Bed & Breakfast   ((376)6-2377
All Year $45-$55
Location: Center. Calle Hidalgo 22 45920. Fax: 376/6-2331. **Facility:** Attractive Mexican decor throughout the property. Well appointed garden rooms. 6 units. *Bath:* shower only. 1 story. **Terms:** 3 day cancellation notice. **Guest Services:** [BP] meal plan available, valet laundry. **Cards:** MC, VI.

AJIJIC PLAZA SUITES
Motel   ((376)6-0383
All Year $34-$37   XP $6
Location: Center. Calle Colon 33 45920. Fax: 376/6-2331. **Facility:** Across the street from main plaza. 10 units. *Bath:* shower only. 1 story. **Terms:** F5; 3 day cancellation notice. **Amenities:** no TVs. **Guest Services:** [BP] meal plan available. **Cards:** AE, MC, VI.

INN AT SAN ANDRES
Bed & Breakfast   (376/6-1250
All Year $45-$55
Location: Center. 22A Galeana 45920. **Facility:** Attractive garden area. 5 units. Some whirlpool units. *Bath:* shower only. 2 stories, interior/exterior corridors. **Amenities:** no TVs. **Guest Services:** [CP] meal plan available.

LA NUEVA POSADA
Country Inn   ((376)6-1344
12/1-4/15 & 7/2-8/30 $65-$75   XP $8
4/16-7/1 & 8/31-11/30 $57-$68   XP $8
Location: 0.4 km se of main plaza. Donato Guerra 9 45920 (PO Box 30). Fax: 376/6-1444. **Facility:** Overlooking Lake Chapala. Some rooms with balcony. Mexican-Colonial decor. 23 units. 2 two-bedroom units and 4 units with kitchen. *Bath:* some shower or tub only. 3 stories (no elevator), interior corridors. **Terms:** F12; 15 day cancellation notice. **Amenities:** *Some:* irons. **Dining:** restaurant, see separate listing. **Guest Services:** [BP] meal plan available, gift shop. **Business Services:** meeting rooms. **Cards:** AE, MC, VI.

SOME UNITS
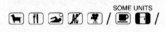

LOS ARTISTAS BED & BREAKFAST
Bed & Breakfast   (376/6-1027
All Year $45-$55
Location: Center. No. 105 Constitucion 45920 (Los Artistas B & B, PMB 71-387, LAREDO, TX, 78041-6010). Fax: 376/6-1762. **Facility:** Attractive gardens. Ample fenced parking area. Smoke free premises. 6 units. *Bath:* combo or shower only. 1 story, interior/exterior corridors. **Amenities:** no TVs. **Leisure Activities:** small pool. **Guest Services:** [CP] meal plan available.

POSADA LAS CALANDRIAS
Apartment   (376/6-1052
All Year $30
Location: 3 blks nw of Plaza Principal, Chapala Hwy, Jal 94. Carretera Poniente #8 (Apdo Postal 76, 45920). **Facility:** 30 units. 14 two-bedroom units, 14 efficiencies and 15 units with kitchen. *Bath:* combo or shower only. 2 stories, exterior corridors. **Terms:** 15 day cancellation notice, 30 day 12/1-4/1. **Amenities:** no TVs. **Leisure Activities:** heated pool. **Cards:** MC, VI.

WHERE TO DINE

RESTAURANTE LA NUEVA POSADA
Continental   (376/6-1344
L $10-$14   D $10-$14
Location: 0.4 km se of main plaza; in La Nueva Posada. Donato Guerra No. 9 45920. **Hours:** 8 am-10 pm, Fri & Sat-11 pm, Sun-9 pm. **Features:** cocktails; entertainment. Casual. **Cards:** AE, MC, VI.

CHAPALA, JALISCO (H-4)

Along with Ajijic and Jocotepec, Chapala (chah-PAH-lah) is the largest of several resort communities lining the northern shore of **Lake Chapala**. During the early 20th century it was the summer residence of dictator Porfirio Díaz. At that time the town attracted a rich international clientele who spent weekends at lavish estates, enjoying the area's tranquil beauty; D.H. Lawrence wrote "The Plumed Serpent" here in the mid-1920s. Today it caters to Mexican families and a resident population of American and Canadian retirees.

Commercial activity is centered along **Avenida Madero**, which leads to the lake and town pier. The street is lined with shops and small cafés. Near the pier is the main square, a pleasant spot to relax; band serenades are held here on Sunday evenings. Along the lakeshore is **Parque la Cristianíais**, where vendors gather on the weekend.

The lake itself, some 53 miles long and 18 miles wide, is the largest natural lake in Mexico, surrounded by lushly forested mountains. The weather is delightfully springlike all year, a bit cooler in summer and warmer in winter than Guadalajara. The lake, however, is the chief source of water for the city, and because of tremendous population growth in the surrounding area, the water level has dropped by half since the turn of the 20th century. Cutting down trees has caused millions of cubic feet of mud to seep into the lake over the years, and the stench of pollution is strongly evident in some areas. Engineers and Mexican environmental groups have worked to promote reforestation programs to reverse this trend.

Isla Mezcala (Mezcala Island) can be reached by boat from the Chapala pier. The ruins of a fort and bastion here date from the Mexican War of Independence, when rebels successfully defended the island against the Spanish army and navy from 1812-16. Hunger and sickness finally forced these 1,500 courageous souls to surrender, but their valor prompted the Spaniards to present them with an honor guard and a military pardon.

JOCOTEPEC, JALISCO (H-3)

Founded in 1528, Jocotepec (hoh-koh-teh-PEHK) sits at the western end of Lake Chapala. This popular retreat still manages to exude a relatively unspoiled Mexican atmosphere. It is known for handwoven items, which are still produced on old-fashioned looms. Local artisans turn out bedspreads, table coverings, wall hangings and *sarapes*. Several small shops line **Calle Hidalgo**, and it's possible to watch the weavers at work.

TEQUILA, JALISCO (F-3)

This typical Mexican town is located about 56 kilometers (35 miles) northwest of Guadalajara, just off Mex. 15. It sits amid extensive plantations devoted to the cultivation of the agave plant, from which the same-named beverage is extracted. Local distilleries (the major one is Sauza) have obtained a patent that prohibits other producers, even those within Mexico, from calling their drink tequila. A guided tour can be arranged; inquire at the main plaza. Tour buses to Tequila, a major highway bus stop, depart from Guadalajara's Central Camionera (bus station) on Calle Los Angeles, near Agua Azul Park. For additional information, contact a local travel agency.

Cultivated agave plants resemble a field of spiny blue bayonets. Although the region's indigenous peoples had long drunk the fermented sap, the Spaniards introduced the distilling process. The tough, swordlike fronds are stripped from the plant, exposing its "heart," which can weigh more than 100 pounds. The hearts are "cooked" in large copper kettles, and the resulting liquid is transferred to huge tanks. Clear tequila is bottled at once; the golden variety ages in oak casks for up to 7 years. From the Sauza Distillery it is possible to explore an abandoned old hacienda that was once occupied by the Sauza family.

Tequila lies at the northern base of extinct, 9,797-foot **Volcán de Tequila**, which has a stopper of hardened lava in its crater. Shards of obsidian, a volcanic glass, are visible in cuts flanking the highway near town. **La Toma**, a picnic spot with a waterfall and swimming pool, is about 4 kilometers (2.5 miles) northwest of Tequila off Mex. 15; the Santiago River Canyon, through which the river winds, is particularly scenic.

TLAQUEPAQUE, JALISCO (H-4)

This southeastern suburb is an important crafts center. Distinctive, hand-painted Tlaquepaque (tla-keh-PAH-keh) pottery is prized throughout Mexico. The fragile earthenware is decorated by hand. Many artisans still use the potter's wheel, and visitors can view the work in progress at some pottery shops. Tlaquepaque also is known for blown glass, textiles, jewelry, furniture, copperware and carved wood. The town is a tourist magnet and can get very crowded, but dedicated shoppers won't want to miss out on the huge selection of high-quality handicrafts.

Browsing is easiest along **Calle Independencia**, the pedestrian mall created in the early 1970s. Many of the shops and galleries are housed in refurbished old mansions with thick stone walls and iron gates. Dating from the late 17th to the early 20th centuries, most of these structures were built as weekend retreats for wealthy Guadalajaran merchants. Most of the larger shops accept U.S. dollars or payment by credit card, and will arrange to have purchases packed and shipped as well. Many are closed or open limited hours on Sunday.

The word "mariachi" seems to have originated in Tlaquepaque. French soldiers garrisoned in the city in the mid-19th century noted that the strolling troubadours performed primarily at weddings, or *mariages*, hence the possible derivation of the term. Mariachi bands are still very much a part of Tlaquepaque's social scene. They perform in the gazebo within **El Parián**, the main plaza (bounded by the streets Independencia, Guillermo Prieto, Morelos and Francisco Madero).

Under El Parián's circular roof are many sidewalk cafés, pleasant spots to relax over a leisurely lunch while the shops close for afternoon *siesta* (usually between 2 and 4). Other restaurants are scattered throughout town; one of the most popular is **Restaurante Sin Nombre** ("Restaurant With No Name"), at Calle Francisco Madero #80 less than 2 blocks north of the main plaza. The high walls of this restored mansion enclose a tropical garden complete with wandering peacocks. Bilingual waiters recite the menu of Mexican specialties, so ask about prices when ordering.

To learn more about the traditions associated with Jaliscan pottery, visit the **Museo Regional de la Ceramica** (Regional Museum of Ceramics), Calle Independencia #237 at Calle Alfareros. Housed in an 18th-century building that was formerly a private home, it contains several rooms displaying top-notch regional pottery pieces. Open Tues.-Sat. 10-4, Sun. 10-1. Free. Phone (3) 635-5404.

Across the street from the museum is **La Rosa de Cristal**, a glass factory where pole-wielding craftsmen and their young apprentices can be observed in the rear patio shaping molten glass into beautiful figurines, pitchers and other objects. Arrive in the morning; because of the heat generated by this process the blowers often quit early, particularly during the summer. The workshop is open Mon.-Fri. 9:30-2:30.

Sergio Bustamente's fanciful sculptures, known around the world, are featured at the **Galería Sergio Bustamente**, Calle Independencia #236. At Independencia #258 is **La Casa Canela**, with showrooms arranged around a lush garden patio. This tasteful shop offers Mexican furniture, papier-mâché artworks and antiques.

Bus #275 departs regularly for Tlaquepaque and Tonalá from the corner of avenidas Alcalde and Independencia in Guadalajara's historic center (near the cathedral); the trip takes about half an hour. Linea Turquesa buses carry only seated passengers; cheaper city buses carry both standing and seated passengers and are likely to be crowded. Tell the driver you want to get off at the stop nearest the main plaza (El Parián).

If driving, take Avenida Revolución off Calzada Independencia Sur, heading southeast away from downtown Guadalajara. This road becomes Boulevard Tlaquepaque as it heads into town. At the traffic circle, bear right onto Avenida Niños Héroes, which runs into Calle Independencia after a block. The tourist office is at Calle Guillermo Prieto #80, across from the main plaza. It is open Mon.-Fri. 9-3, Sat. 9-1; phone (3) 635-1503.

WHERE TO STAY

CASA DE LAS FLORES

▼▼▼▼   Bed & Breakfast   ((3)659-3186
All Year $60   XP $15
Location: Center; 4 blks s of Plaza Hidalgo. Santos Degollado #175 45500. Fax: 3/659-3186. **Facility:** Located near center of town. Restored historical home, colorful local decor and artwork. Relaxing, well cared for garden. Secure parking. Convenient to restaurants and craft stores. 7 units. *Bath:* shower only. 2 stories, exterior corridors. **Terms:** 7 day cancellation notice-fee imposed. **Amenities:** no TVs. **Guest Services:** [CP] meal plan available, valet laundry.

Ⓧ Ⓚ Ⓩ

LA VILLA DEL ENSUENO

▼▼   Bed & Breakfast   ((3)635-8792
All Year $75-$120   XP $15
Location: 1 km w of El Parian. Florida 305 45500. Fax: 3/659-6152. **Facility:** High wall surrounds property. Attractive grounds. 10 units. 2 two-bedroom units. *Bath:* combo or shower only. 2 stories, interior corridors. **Terms:** F15; 14 day cancellation notice-fee imposed, small pets only. **Amenities:** no TVs. **Leisure Activities:** heated pool, lighted tennis court. **Guest Services:** [CP] meal plan available, gift shop, valet laundry. **Cards:** AE, DS, MC, VI.

Ⓢ Ⓗ Ⓨ Ⓩ Ⓧ Ⓚ Ⓑ

MESON DON JOSE

▼▼▼   Bed & Breakfast   (3/635-7522
All Year $90   XP $15
Location: Center. Reforma #139 45500. Fax: 3/659-9315. **Facility:** Charming inn and gardens behind high nondescript wall. 9 units, 1 with kitchen. *Bath:* shower only. 2 stories (no elevator), interior/exterior corridors. **Terms:** F12. **Amenities:** safes. **Guest Services:** [BP] meal plan available, valet laundry. **Cards:** MC, VI.

Ⓚ Ⓗ Ⓓ Ⓩ Ⓚ Ⓨ Ⓑ

TONALA, JALISCO (G-4)

Tonalá (toh-nah-LAH), about 7 kilometers (4 miles east of Tlaquepaque, was the original site of Guadalajara until 1531, when the Spaniards, repeatedly harassed by hostile Indians, abandoned the area. This dusty village is another noted pottery-producing center, although it lacks Tlaquepaque's commercial flair. Some of the artisans who display their wares in Tlaquepaque live in Tonalá, where many of the homes double as family-run pottery workshops, or *talleres*.

The best days to visit are Thursdays and Sundays, when there is a large open-air *tianguis* (market). Savvy shoppers can obtain excellent buys on glassware, ceramics and papier-mâché crafts. Items are spread out on the sidewalks in a colorful hodgepodge, and street entertainers delight the crowds. Otherwise, most shops are open Mon.-Sat. 10-2 and 4-7; some close on Sunday.

Many of Tonalá's shops and restaurants are along north-south **Avenida de los Tonaltecas**; others are in the vicinity of the main plaza, at calles Juárez and Hidalgo. An excellent selection of ceramics can be found at **Casa de Artesanos**,

Avenida de los Tonaltecas #140 Sur. The workshop of Jorge Wilmot, who combined modern technology with traditional methods to produce distinctive ceramic designs, is at Calle Morelos #88. The shop/studio of Ken Edwards, Calle Morelos #184, features lovely stoneware items.

The **Museo Nacional de la Cerámica** (National Ceramics Museum) is at Avenida Constitución #104, 2 blocks north of the city hall. It displays pieces from pre-Columbian to modern times. It also contains a workshop where ceramics can be purchased. Tues.-Sat. 10-5, Sun. 10-2. Free.

The public buses that travel to Tlaquepaque go to Tonalá. You can also get there by taxi; one-way fare should average about $4 from Tlaquepaque, $7 from Guadalajara. If driving, take the Carretera Zapotlanejo (Zapotlanejo Highway) east out of Tlaquepaque. The tourist office is next to Casa de Artesanos on Avenida de los Tonaltecas Sur. It is open Mon.-Fri. 9-3, Sat. 9-1; phone (3) 683-1740. Inquire about the free walking tours on non-market days (Mon.-Wed. and Fri.-Sat.) that include visits to local workshops.

ZAPOPAN, JALISCO (G-3)

About 7 kilometers (4 miles) northwest of downtown Guadalajara via Avenida Avila Camacho, the suburb of Zapopan (sah-POH-pahn) is the home of the Virgin of Zapopan—often referred to as **La Zapopanita** ("Little Zapopaner") since her image, made of corn paste, stands a mere 10 inches tall. Legend alleges that Chimalhuacano Indians, awed by a Franciscan friar's display of La Zapopanita during the heat of battle against the Spanish, surrendered and were converted to Christianity. In 1734, at the height of an epidemic, she was taken to the towns and villages around Guadalajara. Wherever the virgin appeared, sickness reputedly ceased, and many miracles were subsequently attributed to her.

Each summer the statue of the virgin is encased in a protective glass shell and and embarks on a 4-month pilgrimage to the more than 100 parish churches throughout the state. Transported by special car, the virgin begins a final journey at dawn on Oct. 12 from Guadalajara's cathedral back to her home church, the massive 17th-century **Basilica de la Virgen de Zapopan** (Basilica of the Virgin of Zapopan), on the west side of Zapopan's central plaza.

Piety and merrymaking are both in evidence on this occasion. In addition to solemn marchers holding banners, there are marching bands, cowboys on horseback, police cars with screaming sirens, dancers in native costume and assorted revelers dressed up as if for a giant Halloween party. Many pilgrims show their devotion by crawling the last kilometer or two on their knees, underscoring the importance of this annual event for the nation's devout Catholics. The homecoming procession from the cathedral to the basilica—a 5-mile route—often involves more than 1 million participants and spectators and is a highlight of Guadalajara's *Fiestas de Octubre* (see "Special Events" below).

The basilica features an ornate Plateresque exterior and a tiled *mudéjar* dome. In the church courtyard a statue commemorates Pope John Paul II, who gave a mass at the plaza during his 1979 visit. Within the Franciscan monastery next door is the small **Museo Huichol**, which has displays of beadwork and other handicrafts (all for sale) made by the Huichol Indians of northern Jalisco, Nayarit and Zacatecas. City buses traveling northbound on Avenida 16 de Septiembre/Alcalde go to the basilica; the trip takes about half an hour.

SPORTS AND RECREATION

Bullfighting fans head for the 25,000-seat **Plaza Nuevo Progreso**, northeast of downtown on Calzada Independencia Norte (across from Jalisco Stadium). Bullfights *(corridas)* take place on Sunday afternoons starting at 4:30. Tickets are sold at the bullring and at the Plaza del Sol shopping mall. Spectators can opt for seats in the sun *(sol)* or shade *(sombra);* those in the shade are more expensive. For further information phone (3) 651-8506 or 637-9982, or ask at your hotel about dates and ticket prices.

Although they resemble the Western rodeos of the United States, **charreadas** are unmistakably Mexican. When Spanish explorers and conquerors reintroduced the horse (which had roamed the North American plains some 45,000,000 years earlier), only noblemen were permitted to ride. But the Indians soon acquired their own horseback skills, with the *charro* (male rider) evolving from the requirements of livestock raising in open country. *Charros* were resourceful, self-reliant men, familiar with the land and able to live off it. *Charro* contingents fought in the war to achieve Mexican independence, and *charreadas*, where native horseback riders gathered to show off their skills, became part of Mexican folklore. The National Association of Charros was founded in 1921, and in Guadalajara these events have remained particularly popular.

Both *charros* and *charras* (female riders) are expert at fancy horsemanship and roping. The focus is on style and finesse rather than competition, although some of the feats performed are of the daredevil variety. One of the chief pleasures of a *charreada* is viewing the elegantly ceremonial costumes on display. Men are decked out in white pleated shirts, black pants encrusted with silver buttons and a sombrero embroidered with gold or silver thread. *Charras*, female riders—often the daughters or wives of *charros*—wear lacy petticoats, brightly colored skirts decorated with lace and ribbons, and braided, beribboned hair.

Charreadas take place throughout the year. One easily accessible *charro* ring is located not far from downtown on Avenida Dr. R. Michel, on the east side of Agua Azul Park. These events are normally held Sundays beginning at noon. Admission is charged.

Soccer *(fútbol)* is the city's most popular spectator sport. Professional teams play at **Estadio Jalisco** (Jalisco Stadium), on Calzada Independencia Norte across from the bullring. Schedules vary; for ticket and other information, check with your hotel or the Jalisco State Tourism Office.

Guadalajara's year-round mild, sunny weather is ideal for **golf**, and several area courses accommodate both local duffers and the large contingent of American retirees. Some private courses allow visitors to play for a greens fee and proof of membership in a U.S. club; others are closed to nonmembers on weekends and holidays. Admittance to the immaculately maintained, 18-hole course at the **Guadalajara Country Club** is through a member, although the better hotels may be able to get their guests in. The country club is off Avenida Avila Camacho, about 8 kilometers (5 miles) northwest of the downtown historic center.

The **Atlas Golf Club** (18 holes) is southeast of the city, on Mex. 23 just south of Tlaquepaque (on the way to Lake Chapala); phone (3) 689-2620. The **San Isidro Golf Club** (27 holes) is about 15 kilometers (9 miles) north of the city on Mex. 54. The course is in the midst of an upscale residential development that includes tennis courts, horseback riding trails and a swimming pool; phone (3) 685-0512. The **Santa Anita Golf Club** is on Mex. 15, about 7 kilometers (4 miles) south of the Periférico loop road; phone (3) 686-1931.

Some of the larger hotels, such as the Crowne Plaza Guadalajara and the Camino Real Guadalajara, permit nonguests to use their **tennis** courts for a fee. There are public courts at **Parque Avila Camacho** (Avila Camacho Park), across Avenida Avila Camacho from the Guadalajara Country Club. **Parque Colomos** (Colomos Park), south of Avenida Patria and west of the country club in the city's western sector, has a track and tree-lined paths for **jogging**.

NIGHTLIFE

Unlike Mexico City or the big beach resorts, Guadalajara's nightlife is not particularly frenetic. Nightclubs, bars and discos tend to be concentrated in two places: downtown and in the Plaza del Sol area. Inquire at the front desk of your hotel or ask a bellboy what is happening in town during your stay. The lobby bar in the Fiesta Americana Hotel, Avenida Aurelio Aceves #225 on Minerva Circle, is a classy club/lounge with live music. **La Diligencia** in the Camino Real Hotel, Avenida Vallarta #5005, has a romantic atmosphere and music for dancing. **Maxim's Disco** in the Hotel Frances, Calle Maestranza #35 near downtown's historic center,

has live music and a dance floor. The Frances also has an intimate lobby bar with piano music.

Several theaters show U.S. and other foreign movies; check the newspapers for listings. Theaters showing foreign films include the **Cine Cinematógrafo**, a repertory house at Avenida Vallarta #1102 (2 blocks west of the University of Guadalajara Museum of Arts); **Cine Clemente Orozco**, in the Ex-Convento del Carmen at Avenida Juárez #638; and **Sala de Cine**, in the Cabañas Cultural Institute at the eastern end of Plaza Tapatía.

Soak up the local ambience at **Plaza de los Mariachis**, on Calzada Independencia Sur between avenidas Javier Mina and Alvaro Obregón (on the south side of the Mercado Libertad). This pretty plaza is staked out by the roving bands of musicians. For a fee (usually around $5) they will perform with guitar, violin, trumpet and an enthusiasm second to none. It costs nothing to listen to these serenades from another table, but if you're the one requesting a song, negotiate the price first. The music is at its best in the evening, but numerous sidewalk cafés clustered around the plaza also are pleasant places to relax during the day. Use the pedestrian overpass from the market to avoid the heavy traffic congestion. **Note:** Pickpockets frequent the plaza; keep an eye on your valuables.

On Thursday and Sunday evenings the **Jalisco State Band** gives free performances at Plaza de Armas, across from the Palacio de Gobierno. The music starts at 7 p.m., but if you want a seat at one of the benches arrive at least half an hour early. The **Municipal Band** performs Tuesdays beginning at 6:30 p.m.

THEATER AND CONCERTS

Probably the most cherished spectacle in town is the presentation of the **Ballet Folklórico de la Universidad de Guadalajara** in the Degollado Theater. Regional dances are complemented by *estudiantinas* or *rondallas* string ensembles, the Mexican counterpart of American high school marching bands or drum-and-bugle corps. Costumes, dance steps, musical instruments and melodies vary greatly from one Mexican state to the next. These lively, colorful affairs take place on Sunday mornings at 10 a.m. Tickets for each performance go on sale Thursday afternoon; phone (3) 614-4773. The **Jalisco Folkloric Ballet** performs at the Cabañas Cultural Institute Wednesdays at 8:30 p.m.

The **Orquesta Filarmónica de Jalisco** (Jalisco Philharmonic Orchestra) performs following the Ballet Folklórico on Sundays and seasonally at other times at the Degollado Theater. National and international artists appear at the theater as well. The **Cabañas Cultural Institute** presents various theater, dance and musical performances throughout the year. Chamber music recitals take place in the institute's **Tolsá Chapel**. The

English-language *Guadalajara Colony Reporter* publishes schedules of current events.

For something a little out of the ordinary, take in a performance at the **Teatro Experimental**, next to the entrance to Agua Azul Park. The season runs from February to November; performances are in Spanish.

SPECIAL EVENTS

Guadalajara's chief annual event is the *Fiestas de Octubre*, or October Fair. This monthlong artistic and cultural festival offers concerts, ballet, opera, theater, movies, *charreadas*, bullfights, folk art expositions and live music. Events take place at various locations, many in the vicinity of Plaza Tapatía, the city's pedestrian promenade, where outdoor stages and pavilions sprout. Hotel and ticket reservations are highly advised for the entire month of October and should be made in advance.

Guadalajarans celebrate many of the occasions listed in the "Fiestas and Holidays" section on pages 446-448. Some are of particular interest, such as *Independence Day* celebrations in mid-September, or the return of the Virgin of Zapopan to the Basilica of Zapopan on Oct. 12 *(see Zapopan listing under "Sightseeing" above)*. The city also sponsors a series of cultural events that take place the last 2 weeks of February before the beginning of Lent.

Other festivities with a special *tapatío* flavor are the *Day of the Three Wise Men* on Jan. 6; the *Tlaquepaque Ceramics Fair*, beginning June 15; the *Day of St. James the Apostle* in Tonalá on July 25, which features a mock battle between Indians and Spaniards; and *Day of the Dead* celebrations Nov. 1-2. Most of these are characterized by *tianguis* (open-air markets), *charreadas* (rodeos), fireworks, dancing, mariachi bands and tempting spreads of regional food.

The Christmas holidays in Guadalajara are celebrated with *pastorelas*, folk representations of the birth of Christ, and *posadas*, re-enactments of Mary and Joseph's search for an inn. The city's museums often participate, offering traditional dance programs and providing special refreshments. Families also get together to take part in candlelight processions to each other's homes, and nativity scenes are set up in churches and plazas. If you'll be visiting during December, check with your hotel, the Jalisco State Tourism Office or the bulletin boards at museums for further information.

WHERE TO STAY

BEST WESTERN PLAZA GENOVA
▼▼▼   *Hotel*   ((3)613-7500
All Year $65-$98   XP $8
Location: Center. Ave Juarez 123 44100. Fax: 3/614-8253. **Facility:** Near the historic district and the market. 197 units. 1 two-bedroom unit. *Bath:* shower only. 7 stories, interior corridors. **Parking:** extra charge. **Terms:** F12; 5 day cancellation notice. **Amenities:** honor bars. **Leisure Activities:** sauna, exercise room. *Fee:* steam rooms. **Guest Services:** gift shop. **Business Services:** meeting rooms, administrative services. **Cards:** AE, DI, MC, VI.

CAMINO REAL GUADALAJARA
▼▼▼ ▼▼▼   *Motor Inn*   ((3)134-2400
All Year $115   XP $15
Location: 6 km nw on Mex 15. Ave Vallarta 5005 45040. Fax: 3/134-2404. **Facility:** 205 units. 2 stories, interior/exterior corridors. **Parking:** valet. **Terms:** F12. **Amenities:** honor bars. *Some:* safes. **Dining:** Aquellos Tiempos, see separate listing. **Leisure Activities:** 4 pools (3 heated), wading pool, putting green, lighted tennis court, playground, exercise room. **Guest Services:** gift shop. **Business Services:** meeting rooms, administrative services. **Cards:** AE, DI, MC, VI.
(See color ad opposite inside front cover)

SOME UNITS

⚠ CROWNE PLAZA GUADALAJARA
▼▼▼ ▼▼▼   *Motor Inn*   ((3)634-1034
7/1-11/30 $190   XP $30
1/1-6/30 $180   XP $30
12/1-12/31 $160   XP $25
Location: 7.2 km s on Mex 15 and 80; off Glorieta Mariana Otero. Lopez Mateos Sur #2500 45050. Fax: 3/631-9393. **Facility:** Balconies or terraces. Very attractively landscaped grounds. 293 units. 5 two-bedroom units. 2-9 stories, interior/exterior corridors. **Parking:** valet. **Terms:** F12; 7 day cancellation notice. **Amenities:** safes, honor bars, irons, hair dryers. **Dining & Entertainment:** dining room, coffee shop, cocktails, also, Restaurant Jacarandas, see separate listing, entertainment. **Leisure Activities:** heated pool, wading pool, sauna, whirlpool, putting green, 2 lighted tennis courts, playground, exercise room. **Guest Services:** gift shop, valet laundry. **Business Services:** meeting rooms, administrative services. **Cards:** AE, DI, MC, VI.

SOME UNITS

FIESTA INN GUADALAJARA
▼▼▼   *Motor Inn*   (3/669-3200
7/1-11/30 $115-$140
12/1-6/30 $105-$128   XP $10
Location: 3.5 km w; near Expo Center. Mariano Otero 1550 45055. Fax: 3/669-3247. **Facility:** 158 units. 9 stories, interior corridors. **Parking:** valet. **Terms:** F12; cancellation fee imposed. **Leisure Activities:** heated pool, exercise room. **Guest Services:** valet laundry. **Business Services:** meeting rooms, administrative services. **Cards:** AE, DI, MC, VI.

SOME UNITS

GUADALAJARA PLAZA LOPEZ MATEOS

▼▼▼ *Hotel* ((3)647-5300

All Year $64-$88 XP $9
Location: 7 km s on Mex 15 and 80. Ave Lopez Mateos Sur 2128 45050. Fax: 3/122-1703. **Facility:** 142 units. *Bath:* shower only. 2-7 stories, interior/exterior corridors. **Terms:** F12. **Amenities:** *Some:* honor bars. **Leisure Activities:** heated pool. **Business Services:** meeting rooms. **Cards:** DI, MC, VI.

HILTON GUADALAJARA

▼▼▼ ▼▼ *Hotel* ((3)678-0505

All Year $135-$150 XP $20
Location: At Expo and World Trade Center. Ave de Las Rosas 2933 44540. Fax: 3/678-0521. **Facility:** Attractive public areas. Well appointed guest units. Guided tours of city with English speaking guides via hotel vehicles. 422 units. 20 stories, interior corridors. **Parking:** valet. **Terms:** F18; cancellation fee imposed. **Amenities:** voice mail, safes, honor bars, hair dryers. **Leisure Activities:** heated pool, steamroom, exercise room. **Guest Services:** gift shop, valet laundry. *Fee:* massage. **Business Services:** meeting rooms, administrative services, fax. **Cards:** AE, DI, MC, VI.

HOLIDAY INN CASA GRANDE

▼▼▼ *Motor Inn* ((3)678-9000

All Year $70-$90 XP $7
Location: At Guadalajara International Airport. Calle Interior Aeropuerto 45640. Fax: 3/678-9001. **Facility:** Connected to main terminal via a covered skywalk. 171 units. Some whirlpool units. *Bath:* shower only. 4 stories, interior corridors. **Terms:** F12. **Amenities:** irons. **Leisure Activities:** heated pool, exercise room. **Guest Services:** area transportation, valet laundry. **Business Services:** meeting rooms, administrative services. **Cards:** AE, DI, MC, VI.

HOLIDAY INN HOTEL & SUITES

▼▼▼ *Hotel* (3/613-1763

All Year $120-$150 XP $14
Location: Center. Ave Juarez 211-103 44100. Fax: 3/613-1763. **Facility:** In historic area of the city. 89 units, 20 with efficiency. Some whirlpool units. *Bath:* shower only. 5 stories, interior corridors. **Parking:** valet. **Terms:** F12; cancellation fee imposed. **Amenities:** honor bars. **Leisure Activities:** exercise room. **Guest Services:** gift shop, valet laundry. **Business Services:** meeting rooms. **Cards:** AE, MC, VI.

HOLIDAY INN SELECT

▼▼▼ *Hotel* ((3)122-2020

All Year $83-$90 XP $12
Location: 0.5 km s of Minerva Fountain. Ave Ninos Heroes 3089 44500. Fax: 3/647-7778. **Facility:** Well appointed units and public areas. Designed around the business traveler. 220 units. Some whirlpool units. 14 stories, interior corridors. **Parking:** extra charge or valet. **Terms:** F15. **Amenities:** honor bars, irons, hair dryers. **Leisure Activities:** heated pool, steamroom, exercise room. **Guest Services:** gift shop, valet laundry. **Business Services:** meeting rooms, administrative services, fax. **Cards:** AE, DI, MC, VI.

HOTEL CALINDA ROMA

▼▼▼ *Hotel* ((3)614-8650

All Year $45-$68 XP $10
Location: Downtown. Ave Juarez 170 44100. Fax: 3/614-2629. **Facility:** 127 units. *Bath:* combo or shower only. 5 stories, interior corridors. **Terms:** F16; 3 day cancellation notice. **Amenities:** honor bars. **Leisure Activities:** small heated pool. **Guest Services:** gift shop, valet laundry. **Business Services:** meeting rooms. **Cards:** AE, DI, MC, VI. *(See color ad p 4 and below)*

HOTEL COUNTRY PLAZA
Motor Inn   ((3)633-4633

All Year $148-$164   XP $13
Location: 8 km w. Prol Ave Americas 1170 45160. Fax: 3/656-2522. **Facility:** Parking with security. 115 units. Some whirlpool units. *Bath:* combo or shower only. 4 stories, interior corridors. **Terms:** D12. **Amenities:** safes, hair dryers. *Some:* honor bars. **Dining & Entertainment:** restaurant, 7 am-midnight, $6-$10, cocktails, entertainment. **Leisure Activities:** heated pool, wading pool, whirlpool, exercise room. **Guest Services:** gift shop, valet laundry. **Business Services:** meeting rooms. **Cards:** AE, MC, VI.

HOTEL DE MENDOZA
Hotel   ((3)613-4646

All Year $75-$97   XP $10
Location: Opposite Degollado Theatre. Venustiano Carranza 16 44100 (PO Box 1-2453). Fax: 3/613-7310. **Facility:** Some rooms with balcony. In the historic district. 104 units. *Bath:* combo or shower only. 5 stories, interior corridors. **Parking:** extra charge. **Terms:** F12; 15 day cancellation notice-fee imposed. **Leisure Activities:** small pool. **Guest Services:** gift shop, valet laundry. **Business Services:** meeting rooms. **Cards:** AE, DI, MC, VI.

HOTEL EL FRANCES
Historic Hotel   (3/613-1190

All Year $35   XP $4
Location: Center. Maestranza 35 44100. Fax: 3/658-2831. **Facility:** Located in historic district. Constructed in 1610. Old World charm. All rooms with ceiling fan. Some rooms can be noisy. 60 units. 10 two-bedroom units and 10 three-bedroom units. *Bath:* combo or shower only. 4 stories (no elevator), interior corridors. **Parking:** valet. **Terms:** F12; 3 day cancellation notice. **Business Services:** meeting rooms. **Cards:** AE, DI, MC, VI.

HOTEL FENIX
Hotel   ((3)614-5714

All Year $70   XP $6
Location: Just s of Plaza de Armas. Corona 160 44100. Fax: 3/613-4005. **Facility:** Some units with balcony. 257 units. *Bath:* combo or shower only. 12 stories, interior corridors. **Parking:** extra charge. **Terms:** F12. **Amenities:** *Some:* safes. **Guest Services:** gift shop. **Business Services:** meeting rooms. **Cards:** AE, CB, DI, MC, VI.

HOTEL FIESTA AMERICANA GUADALAJARA
Hotel   ((3)825-3434

All Year $134   XP $11
Location: On Minerva Cir, at jct aves Vallarta and Lopez Mateos. Aurelio Aceves 225 44110. Fax: 3/630-3725. **Facility:** 391 units. 18 stories, interior corridors. **Parking:** valet. **Terms:** F12. **Amenities:** honor bars. **Dining:** La Hacienda, see separate listing. **Leisure Activities:** heated pool, exercise room. **Fee:** 2 lighted tennis courts. **Guest Services:** gift shop, valet laundry. **Business Services:** meeting rooms, administrative services. **Cards:** AE, DI, MC, VI.

HOTEL GUADALAJARA PLAZA EXPO
Hotel   ((3)669-0215

All Year $76   XP $10
Location: At the Expo Center. Ave Mariano Otero 3261 44550. Fax: 3/122-2850. **Facility:** Walking distance to Expo Center. Attractive public areas, well appointed units. 204 units. 5 stories, interior corridors. **Parking:** valet. **Terms:** F12. **Leisure Activities:** heated pool, jogging, exercise room. **Guest Services:** gift shop. **Business Services:** meeting rooms, administrative services. **Cards:** AE, DI, MC, VI.

HOTEL NUEVO REAL VALLARTA
Motor Inn   (3/629-8610

All Year $52   XP $5
Location: 8 km w on Mex 15. Ave Vallarta 5549 45020. Fax: 3/629-0974. **Facility:** 62 units. *Bath:* shower only. 3 stories, exterior corridors. **Terms:** 7 day cancellation notice. **Leisure Activities:** whirlpool. **Business Services:** meeting rooms. **Cards:** AE, MC, VI.

HOTEL PLAZA DIANA
Hotel   ((3)615-5510

All Year $45-$70   XP $10
Location: 5 km n. Agustin Yanez 2760 44100. Fax: 3/630-3685. **Facility:** 158 units. Some whirlpool units. *Bath:* some combo or shower only. 6 stories, interior corridors. **Terms:** F12. **Leisure Activities:** heated pool, exercise room. **Guest Services:** gift shop. **Business Services:** meeting rooms, administrative services. **Cards:** AE, DI, MC, VI.

HOTEL POSADA GUADALAJARA
Hotel   ((3)121-2022

All Year $47   XP $7
Location: 5.2 km s on Mex 15 and 80. Ave Lopez Mateos 1280 Sur 45040 (Apartado Postal 1-1472). Fax: 3/122-1834. **Facility:** Some units with balcony. 170 units. 2 two-bedroom units and 18 units with kitchen. *Bath:* combo or shower only. 8 stories, interior corridors. **Terms:** F12. **Leisure Activities:** heated pool. **Guest Services:** gift shop. **Business Services:** meeting rooms. **Cards:** AE, DI, MC, VI.

HOTEL PRESIDENTE INTER-CONTINENTAL GUADALAJARA
Hotel   ((3)678-1234

All Year $235-$270   XP $45
Location: 7 km s on Mex 15 and 80; across from Plaza del Sol. (Ave Lopez Mateos Sur Y Moctezuma, 45050). Fax: 3/678-1222. **Facility:** Spectacular public areas, impressive facility, secured parking. Convenient to large shopping mall. 411 units, 1 with kitchen. Some whirlpool units. 13 stories, interior corridors. **Parking:** valet. **Terms:** F18. **Amenities:** extended cable TV, voice mail, safes, honor bars. *Some:* fax. **Dining:** La Morena, see separate listing. **Leisure Activities:** heated pool, whirlpools, exercise room. **Fee:** saunas. **Guest Services:** gift shop, valet laundry. **Fee:** massage. **Business Services:** meeting rooms, administrative services. **Cards:** AE, DI, MC, VI.

LAS PERGOLAS GRAN HOTEL
WWWW *Hotel*   📞 3/615-0088

All Year $60   XP $10
Location: 3 blks e of Minerva Cir, just n of Ave Vallarta. Ave Morelos 2244 44290. Fax: 3/630-0576. **Facility:** 158 units. *Bath:* shower only. 4 stories, interior corridors. **Terms:** F12; 30 day cancellation notice. **Amenities:** *Some:* safes, honor bars. **Leisure Activities:** heated pool. *Fee:* sauna. **Guest Services:** gift shop. **Business Services:** meeting rooms. **Cards:** AE, CB, DI, MC, VI.

SOME UNITS

QUINTA REAL GUADALAJARA
WWWW WWWW *Hotel*   📞 (3)615-0000

All Year $225   XP $30
Location: 2 blks n of Minerva Fountain near Lopez Mateos Ave. Ave Mexico 2727 44680. Fax: 3/630-1797. **Facility:** Elegant atmosphere, luxurious units. Manicured inner gardens. 76 units. Some whirlpool units. 3-5 stories, interior corridors. **Terms:** F12; cancellation fee imposed. **Amenities:** extended cable TV, voice mail, honor bars, irons, hair dryers. *Some:* CD players, safes. **Dining:** restaurant, see separate listing. **Leisure Activities:** small pool, whirlpool. **Guest Services:** valet laundry. **Business Services:** meeting rooms, administrative services, PC, fax. **Cards:** AE, DI, MC, VI.

SOME UNITS

SUITES HOTEL POSADA DEL MARQUES
WW WW *Apartment*   📞 3/630-3048

All Year $25   XP $5
Location: 0.5 km e of Minerva Cir, 0.3 km n. V Salado Alvarez 72 44290. **Facility:** In residential area. 23 units with kitchen. 2 two-bedroom units. 3 stories (no elevator), interior corridors. **Amenities:** no TVs. **Leisure Activities:** small heated pool.

WHERE TO DINE

AQUELLOS TIEMPOS
WWWW WWWW *Continental*   📞 3/134-2400
L $20-$40   D $20-$40
Location: 6 km nw on Mex 15; in Camino Real Guadalajara. Ave Vallarta 5005 45040. **Hours:** 7 am-1 am. Closed major holidays; also Sun. **Reservations:** suggested. **Features:** casual dress; cocktails & lounge; entertainment; fee for parking; valet parking; a la carte. An elegant fine dining restaurant, whose name means "The Golden Age," lives up to its title. Imaginative international and local cuisine. You'll find the food, service, and setting to be superlative. Exceptional salad and dessert offerings. **Cards:** AE, DI, MC, VI.

LA HACIENDA
WWW *Continental*   📞 3/825-3434
L $12-$24   D $12-$24
Location: On Minerva Cir, at jct aves Vallarta and Lopez Mateos; in Hotel Fiesta Americana Guadalajara. Aurelio Aceves 225-Glorie 44000. **Hours:** 1 pm-1 am. **Features:** cocktails; fee for parking; valet parking; a la carte. Fine dining service with both local and international fare. Enjoy their selection of appetizers, salads and imaginative entrees. Tempting desserts are also featured. **Cards:** AE, DI, MC, VI.

LA MORENA
WWW *Mexican*   📞 3/678-1234
L $12-$35   D $12-$35
Location: 7 km s on Mex 15 and 80; across from Plaza del Sol; in Hotel Presidente Inter-Continental Guadalajara. Lopez Mateos Sur Moctezuma 45050. **Hours:** 7 am-midnight, Sun-noon. **Features:** casual dress; cocktails; entertainment; valet parking. Enjoy Continental and local specialties in a modern, very well decorated atmosphere. Uniformed staff give professional service, talented food preparation. **Cards:** AE, DI, MC, VI.

LA RINCONADA RESTAURANT BAR   *Historical*
WW WW *Continental*   📞 3/613-9914
L $22-$38   D $22-$38
Location: Downtown in historical area. Morelos 86 44100. **Hours:** 8 am-9:30 pm. Closed major holidays. **Features:** No A/C; cocktails; fee for parking. Located in the historic center of the city, La Rinconada embodies its ambience. Enjoy Mexican and international cuisines in a splendid Spanish colonial setting. Enticing appetizers and salads, tender, flavorful steaks, artfully decorated desserts. **Cards:** AE, DI, MC, VI.

QUINTA REAL RESTAURANT
WWWW *Continental*   📞 3/615-0000
L $22-$40   D $22-$40
Location: 2 blks n of Minerva Fountain on Lopez Mateos Ave at Ave Mexico; in Quinta Real Guadalajara. Ave Mexico 2727 44680. **Hours:** 7 am-midnight. **Reservations:** suggested. **Features:** cocktails; entertainment; valet parking. Casual, elegant. Well-prepared meat, poultry and seafood selections. The most select and original Mexican recipes. **Cards:** AE, DI, MC, VI.

RECCO RESTAURANT
WW WW *Italian*   📞 3/825-0724
L $8-$15   D $8-$15
Location: Just e of Ave Chapultepec. Libertad 1981 44100. **Hours:** 1:30 pm-midnight, Sun-10 pm. Closed major holidays. **Reservations:** suggested. **Features:** No A/C; cocktails & lounge; a la carte. An Italian restaurant that is a good change of pace in Guadalajara. Enjoy a hearty portion of lasagna. The Caesar salad is magnifico! And so are their desserts. Moderate prices and pleasant service. **Cards:** AE, MC, VI.

RESTAURANT JACARANDAS
WWWW *Continental*   📞 3/634-1034
L $10-$22   D $10-$24
Location: 7.2 km s on Mex 15 and 80; off Glorieta Mariana Otero; in Crowne Plaza Guadalajara. Ave Lopez Mateos Sur 2500 45050. **Hours:** 8 am-noon & 1-1 am. Closed major holidays; also Sun. **Reservations:** suggested. **Features:** casual dress; cocktails; entertainment; valet parking. Enjoy the panoramic view of the city at Jacarandas, located atop the Crowne Plaza Guadalajara. This elegant restaurant serves imaginative salads, appetizers, high quality beef entrees and desserts prepared in both local and international cuisines. **Cards:** AE, DI, MC, VI.

SANBORNS PLAZA BONITA
WW *Mexican*   📞 3/813-2023
L $8-$18   D $8-$18
Location: 2 km w of Minerva Fountain. Ave Mexico 3370 34000. **Hours:** 7 am-1 am, Sun-midnight. **Features:** cocktails & lounge; entertainment. Sanborns has over 100 locations throughout Mexico and offers a good selection of US style sandwiches. Salad, soup and both Mexican and US entrees. Very good dessert selection, casual atmosphere. **Cards:** AE, MC, VI.

SANBORNS RESTAURANT PLAZA DEL SOL

 Mexican (3/121-3675

L $12-$22 **D** $12-$22

Location: 7 km s on Mex 15 and 80; across from Plaza del Sol Mall. Ave Lopez Mateos 2718 45050. **Hours:** 7 am-1 am. **Features:** cocktails & lounge; entertainment. Sanborns has over 100 locations throughout Mexico, and offers a good selection of US style sandwiches, salads, soups and both Mexican and US entrees. Very good dessert selection casual atmosphere. **Cards:** AE, MC, VI.

SANDY'S CAFE

 American (3/616-1841

L $5-$12 **D** $5-$12

Location: Ave Chapultepec and Pedro Moreno; just n of Ave Vallarta. Lopez Cotilla/Chapultepec. **Hours:** 8 am-10 pm. Closed major holidays. **Features:** cocktails; fee for parking; a la carte. Good selection of American style sandwiches, burgers and other entrees. Also has good local cuisine selections at attractive prices. Sandy's is a local chain with eight locations in the Guadalajara area. **Cards:** AE, MC, VI.

SANDY'S CAFE PLAZA DEL SOL

 American (3/121-9714

L $5-$12 **D** $5-$12

Location: Plaza del Sol Shopping Mall, west entrance. 13 Zone D. **Hours:** 8 am-10:30 pm. **Features:** casual dress; cocktails; a la carte. Good selection of American style sandwiches, burgers and other entrees. Also has good local cuisine selections at attractive prices. Sandy's is a local chain, with eight locations in the Guadalajara area. **Cards:** AE, MC, VI.

SUEHIRO

Ethnic (3/826-0094

L $15-$24 **D** $15-$24

Location: 4 blks e of Ave Chapultepec. Ave La Paz 1701 44100. **Hours:** 1:30 pm-5:30 & 7:30-11:30 pm. Closed: 1/1, 5/1, 12/25. **Reservations:** suggested. **Features:** cocktails & lounge; valet parking; a la carte. Features tableside food preparation of Japanese specialties. **Cards:** AE, MC, VI.

GUANAJUATO, GUANAJUATO (A-7) elev. 6,649'

Guanajuato (gwah-nah-HWAH-toh) is one of Mexico's most beautifully preserved colonial cities. Steeped in history, rich with culture and perched at the bottom of a delightfully scenic canyon, it offers numerous pleasures for the traveler. Leafy plazas, ornate mansions and flowerpot-bedecked alleyways add to Guanajuato's charm. So much of the city's colonial aspect endures, in fact, that it has been declared a national historic monument. Guanajuato also—in an age of global information sharing and pop culture predominance—remains thoroughly Mexican in character.

Capital of the state of the same name, Guanajuato (the name means "place of frogs") was founded in 1548. Silver is its reason for being. For a while the fabulous strike at La Valenciana Mine alone supplied more than half of all the silver received by the Spanish monarchs, yet it was claimed that the mother lode was never found. Several nearby silver mines as well as some gold and lead deposits are still producing.

This mineral wealth made Guanajuato the commercial and financial center of a region known as the **Bajío**, or heartland, for its green, rolling hills and fertile farmland. Along with Querétaro, San Luis Potosí, San Miguel de Allende and Zacatecas, it was one of Mexico's richest and most important colonial cities. The establishment of a university by the Jesuits in 1732 began Guanajuato's reputation as an intellectual center and seat of learning.

Ironically, the city which had become wealthy under Spanish rule took an integral role in the struggle for Mexican independence. In 1810, Guanajuato was invaded by a motley army of peasant farmers, miners and other disenfranchised citizens under the leadership of Father Miguel Hidalgo de Costilla, venerated as the "Father of Mexican Independence." Spanish Royalists—mining barons and the landowning elite—holed up in the massive town granary, **Alhóndiga de Granaditas**, which is now a museum *(see attraction listing below)*. Under orders from Hidalgo, a young miner nicknamed El Pípila heroically made his way to the wooden door of the fortresslike structure, setting it on fire and allowing the insurgents to storm the interior, giving them the first major military victory of the War of Independence.

Although Guanajuato was sacked and many of the town's Spanish aristocracy massacred, the revolutionaries did not remain in control for long. In 1811, Hidalgo and three of his leaders were executed near Chihuahua and their heads sent to Guanajuato to be hung on hooks protruding from the four outside corners of the granary, grisly reminders that this particular conflict was far from over. The heads remained impaled until 1821, when Mexico finally won its independence.

Happily, those Spanish legacies that remain add immeasurably to the city's picturesque air. It crowds the slopes of a dry, narrow, rugged canyon. Houses hug the canyon's different levels, with the foundation of one house sitting at the rooftop level of the one below. The Spanish architectural influence is unmistakably evident, but because Andalusians were among the early arrivals, there is a Moorish touch to some early buildings, which are painted in soft pastel colors and brightened with flower-filled window boxes.

Guanajuato's downtown core, like the centers of Oaxaca, Morelia, Querétaro and other Mexican colonial cities, maintains architectural integrity by restricting gas stations and other concessions to contemporary living to the suburbs and outlying areas. The city's twisting streets are interspersed with little plazas, perfect for relaxing on a shaded bench or perhaps chatting over coffee with one of the students who attend the prestigious **University of Guanajuato**. Narrow *callejónes* (lanes) shadowed by overhanging balconies follow the contours of the hills; some are so steep in places that stairways are built into the sidewalks.

PLANNING YOUR STAY

If you're basing a vacation in Guanajuato, plan on at least 2 days to fully appreciate the city's fine museums, colonial churches and outstanding university. A third day could be spent simply enjoying the compact city center—wandering from plaza to plaza, browsing through the **Hidalgo Market** and having a leisurely dinner at one of the outdoor cafés near the centrally located **Jardín de la Unión**, a park with an old-fashioned, romantic atmosphere.

Add another day for exploring attractions in the environs, such as the **Church of La Valenciana**, the **La Valenciana Mine**, **Cubilete Mountain** or the **Mummy Museum** *(see attraction listings below)*. Drive the **Carretera Panoramica** (Panoramic Highway), the loop road that roughly encircles the city and offers several memorably scenic vantage points, or have a picnic at **Presa de la Olla** (Olla Dam), site of a man-made lake and the pretty gardens at Acacia Park. Allow even more time to attend performances if your visit coincides with the **International Cervantes Festival** *(see "Special Events" below)*, held from mid- to late October; hotel reservations, however, should be booked up to 6 months in advance.

It's an easy trip from Guanajuato to several nearby colonial cities. **San Miguel de Allende** *(see separate listing)*, to the east, has a large community of American expatriates, a full slate of cultural events and a reputation as one of the best cities in Mexico to shop. **Querétaro** *(see separate listing)*, a bit farther southeast, is the capital of the same-named state. Another city filled with history, its colonial center has an elegant European look. **Dolores Hidalgo** *(see separate listing)* is where Father Miguel Hidalgo issued his impassioned cry for Mexican independence, the *Grito de Dolores*.

Northwest of Guanajuato is **León**, the state's largest city. It's a sprawling industrial center, but diehard shoppers should note that it is also the country's leading producer of shoes. Spend an afternoon bargaining for footwear and leather goods at several of the many downtown shops.

For those who cannot or would rather not negotiate Guanajuato's hilly streets, **Transportes Turísticos de Guanajuato** offers guided tours of such attractions as the Church of Valenciana, the Statue of El Pípila and the Mummy Museum. The office is underneath the Basilica Nuestra Señora de Guanajuato (Basilica of Our Lady of Guanajuato) on Plaza de la Paz; phone (473) 2-2838 or 2-2134.

THE INFORMED TRAVELER

The nearest airport is in León, about 56 kilometers (35 miles) northwest. Aeroméxico offers flights from Mexico City; the taxi ride to Guanajuato takes about an hour. For additional information about airlines *see "Arriving by Air," page 53*.

Central Camionera, the main bus station, is about 6 kilometers (3.5 miles) southwest of downtown. "Deluxe" bus service is offered by ETN and Omnibus de México. There is frequent service between Mexico City's Terminal del Norte (North Bus Terminal) and Guanajuato. The Flecha Amarilla line has service from Guanajuato to San Miguel de Allende several times daily. For additional information about buses *see "Bus Service," page 63*.

Local buses navigate several routes. One runs from downtown east along Mex. 110, passing several hotels along the way, and heads toward the La Valenciana Church and Mine and the town of Dolores Hidalgo. Buses designated "Presa-Estación" basically travel from one end of town to the other; they use the subterranean avenue if going toward the La Olla Reservoir and above-ground streets if going toward the train station. Another line takes tourists to the popular Mummy Museum. All schedules are subject to frequent change; double-check the itinerary at the main bus station.

The city's high altitude guarantees mild weather year-round. Daytime highs are usually in the low or mid 70s except in April and May, when they climb into the low 80s. Nighttime lows are usually in the 40s and 50s, although winter nights can be chillier. Showers or thunderstorms occur from June through September, but the weather is usually dry and sunny. Bring a couple of sweaters and a jacket or light coat if you're visiting in the fall or winter. Comfortable walking shoes are a must, not only for the cobblestoned street surfaces but for climbing the numerous hills.

Guanajuato has a large student population and an active social and cultural life. The city is small, and most establishments are casual and friendly. Tourist crime occurs infrequently, and personal safety is essentially a matter of taking the usual common sense precautions.

The tourism office is across from the Basilica of Our Lady of Guanajuato on Plaza de la Paz. It is open Mon.-Fri. 8:30-7:30, Sat.-Sun. 10-2; phone (473) 2-0086 or 2-1574. Another visitor information office is at Avenida Juárez and Calle 5 de Mayo near the old bus terminal.

CITY LAYOUT

Attempting to negotiate Guanajuato's narrow, congested and utterly illogical streets by car is a

To The Mummy Museum

© AAA

Avenida Subterránea Miguel Hidalgo is for inbound traffic only with street level exits just beyond the Hidalgo Market, at Plazuela de los Angeles, at Garden of the Union and terminus at Plaza de Allende. It is 3 km. long.

Hospital

Cantador Park

110

C. PARDO

To Mexico City, D.F. or León, Pípila Statue & Accommodation Number 3

ESCALERA SALGADO

5 DE MAYO

AV. SUBTERRANEA MIGUEL HIDALGO

JUAREZ

MENDIZABAL

Hidalgo Market

VALLE

Plazuela de los Angeles

JUAN

ALONZO

POCITOS

Plaza de la Paz

PARISH CHURCH (LA PARROQUIA)

Regional Museum (Alhóndiga de Granaditas)

Diego Rivera Museum

State Museum of Guanajuato

University of Guanajuato

Church of La Compañía

House of Crafts San Diego Church

Garden of the Union

TENAZA

EL SOL

Post Office

Juárez Theater Iconographic Museum of Don Quixote

MANUEL DOBLADO

HIDALGO

Plaza de Allende

CALLE BELAUNZARAN

CALLE SANGRE DE CRISTO

Las Embajadoras Park

GUANAJUATO

GUANAJUATO

C. SEBASTIAN

CALLE

San Jerónimo Park

PASTITA

0   Scale in Miles   0.2

0   Scale in Kilometers   0.3

PASEO DE LA PRESA

Government Palace

Antillón Park

Presa de la Olla

Acacia Park

3017-H

To Valenciana Church & Mine, Dolores Hidalgo, Cubilete Mountain & Accommodation Number 6

110

10

1 Hostería del Frayle
2 Hotel Hostel Cantarranas
3 Hotel Mision Guanajuato
4 Hotel Posada Santa Fe
5 Hotel San Diego
6 Parador San Javier Hotel
7 Quinta Las Acacias
8 Suites Casa de las Manrique
9 Restaurante Hotel Posada Santa Fe
10 Restaurante Real de la Esperanza

classic exercise in frustration. Furthermore, there are practically no local car rentals available. Most maps, including those available from the tourist information office, fail to show the winding, often unmarked streets in perspective. If you're staying at a hotel outside of the city, use local transportation for forays into and around downtown. Taxi stands *(sitios)* are located around Plaza de la Paz and the Jardín de la Unión, and taxis also can be hailed on the street. Always establish the fare before setting out.

Unlike many Mexican cities, where the streets are laid out in an orderly grid pattern radiating from a central plaza, downtown Guanajuato's twisting thoroughfares simply follow the dictates of the terrain. The two main streets, Avenida Juárez and Calle Pocitos, run roughly east-west; once past Plaza de la Paz, Avenida Juárez's name changes to Avenida Sopeña.

The **Jardín de la Unión** (Union Garden) is a delightful meeting place for locals, students and tourists. This elegant park has old-fashioned lampposts, tiled, tree-shaded walkways, outdoor cafés and a band shell that is the scene of frequent musical performances. Most of Guanajuato's downtown attractions are within easy walking distance. It's just off Avenida Juárez/Sopeña, which can be used as a point of orientation when exploring the downtown area.

Avenida Subterránea Miguel Hidalgo, an antiquated tunnel which in the mid-1960s was transformed into a vehicular subway for inbound traffic, follows the original course of the Río Guanajuato under the city—roughly parallel with Avenida Juárez/Sopeña—for about 1.5 miles. Mexican engineers rerouted the river into its own tunnel following a flood in 1905. The tunnel passes by the foundations of old buildings; street-level exits are just beyond the Hidalgo Market, at Plazuela de los Angeles, at Jardín de la Unión and at the subway terminus at Plaza Allende. Little more than illumination and paving stones were required to turn the tunnel into a traffic artery.

A confusing network of subsidiary tunnels have since been added in a not-too-successful effort to alleviate the heavy traffic; the city's layout was never intended to accommodate automobiles. Even horse-drawn carriages cannot fully negotiate the steep streets. It's best to travel on foot whenever possible, unless you want to experience an appropriately eerie night drive through the tunnel.

The best starting point for the **Carretera Panoramica** (Panoramic Highway), the scenic loop road that travels around Guanajuato's periphery, is from Mex. 110 just south of the Real de Minas Hotel (north of downtown). This route offers easy access to such attractions as the El Pípila Statue, Acacia Park, La Olla Dam, the Mummy Museum at the city cemetery (El Panteón) and the Church of La Valenciana.

EVENTS

Guanajuato's biggest cultural event is the annual *Festival Cervantino* (International Cervantes Festival). University of Guanajuato students first began presenting *entremeses*—skits—of Spanish author Miguel de Cervantes' work in the early 1950s at the Plaza de San Roque. The festival has grown ever since, and for 2 to 3 weeks in October, Mexican as well as international actors, dance companies and symphony orchestras perform at plazas and in theaters across the city. Theater performances are reserved, paying events, while the open-air performances in the plazas are sometimes free. The farcical *entremeses*, presented mostly in pantomime, are easily grasped even if you don't understand Spanish.

Ballet, films, and classical, jazz and rock concerts round out the festival offerings. Reservations need to be made months in advance for the top events; if Guanajuato hotels are full, an alternative is to stay in San Miguel de Allende. For information about the festival, contact the International Cervantes Festival, Alvaro Obregón #273, Colonia Roma, 06140 Mexico City, D.F.; phone 5514-7365.

The Juárez Theater *(see attraction listing below)* presents dramatic, dance, musical and operatic productions at various times throughout the year and also is the site for some events during the International Cervantes Festival.

Guanajuato residents observe several of the religious festivals celebrated in other Mexican cities, such as *Día de los Muertos*, or Day of the Dead (Nov. 1 and 2), and *posadas*, re-enactments of Mary and Joseph's search for an inn, during the Christmas season. The arrival of the Virgin of Guanajuato is commemorated in late May and again on Aug. 9. These festivals usually include fireworks, regional dance groups and sometimes a parade.

SHOPPING

Although shopping opportunities in Guanajuato are not as legion as in some Mexican cities, there are several options for browsers. The **Mercado Hidalgo** (Hidalgo Market) on Avenida Juárez occupies a hangarlike 1910 building that resembles, with its glass windows and elaborate iron grillwork, a Victorian train station.

The market has two levels. A peripheral walkway above is roamed by souvenir vendors and contains shops selling crafts, clothing and sombreros. Below are the produce, meat and sweet stands, where local families do their marketing, and little eateries offering quick bites of typical Mexican fare. Everything from fruit to honey-laced candy is offered along row after row of these tidy stalls. In contrast to the market's timeless look are the miniature-screen TVs hidden beneath some of the counters. Flower vendors congregate on the sidewalks outside. The market is open daily.

Bargainers may want to focus their skills on pottery purchases. Numerous types are sold, including the highly glazed, pale green and blue ceramic designs known as majolica or Talavera, a style introduced by the Spaniards. Ceramic mugs and other items fashioned by Gorky González, a local artisan renowned for his Talavera-influenced work, are available at lower prices here than at his studio, which is located on Calle Pastita near Parque de las Embajadoras (Embajadoras Park).

The government-run handicrafts shop, **Casa de Artesanías**, is behind the Juárez Theater, near the Jardín de la Unión; it offers a representative selection of pottery and other handicrafts. Committed shoppers based in Guanajuato may want to consider a jaunt to nearby San Miguel de Allende, where local artisans offer metalwork, jewelry, clothing and furniture. León, an easy excursion northwest of Guanajuato, specializes in shoes and leather goods.

WHAT TO SEE

DOWNTOWN

ALHONDIGA DE GRANADITAS (State Historical Museum), at Mendizábal and 28 de Septiembre (Calle Pocitos) near the center of the city, is one of Mexico's better museums. This massive 1809 structure was originally a seed and grain warehouse. During the War of Independence the Spanish Royalists of Guanajuato holed up in the building until its door was set afire by a patriotic mine worker nicknamed El Pípila (the young turkey). This victory was later avenged when the heads of the four insurgents—Hidalgo, Jiménez, Aldama and Allende—were gruesomely displayed on the corners of the building; the hooks from which they hung are still there. From the mid-19th to mid-20th centuries the building functioned as a prison.

The museum contains varied exhibits, including pre-Columbian stone artifacts, regional crafts and costumes, and items from the extensive art collection of muralist José Chávez Morado, most of which are displayed at the Museo del Pueblo de Guanajuato *(see attraction listing below)*. Morado murals depicting revolutionary themes embellish the Alhóndiga's stairwells. Bronze busts of the four revolutionary heroes preside in a hall illuminated by an eternal flame.

Permanent and temporary exhibitions feature the work of Mexican as well as international artists, and there is a fine exhibit that depicts Guanajuato's historical, social and mining importance through photographs and various artifacts. Tues.-Sat. 10-2 and 4-6, Sun. 10-4. Admission is charged; free to all Sun. There is an additional charge for using a camera. Phone (473) 2-1112.

HOTEL POSADA SANTA FE, Plaza Principal #12 at the Jardín de la Unión, houses a collection of paintings by Don Manuel Leal, a Guanajuatan who dramatically documented his perceptions of the city's history. The paintings hang in the hotel's lavishly appointed, colonial-style public areas. Phone (473) 2-0084.

IGLESIA DE LA COMPAÑIA (Church of La Compañía), at Calle Pocitos and Navarro near the University of Guanajuato, was built by the Jesuits 1747-65 and then abandoned when the order was expelled from New Spain. Restored in the 19th century, the church has a a lovely, typically ornate Churrigueresque exterior of rose-colored stone, intricately carved wooden doors and a large dome. The interior contains paintings by 18th-century artist Miguel Cabrera.

LA PARROQUIA (Parish Church), on Plaza de la Paz, is also known as the Basilica of Our Lady of Guanajuato. The church, which has a baroque facade that is an interesting yellow-orange in color, dates from 1671. The celebrated image of the Virgin of Guanajuato, brought from Granada, Spain, in 1557, was a gift from King Philip II. Mounted on a pedestal of solid silver, the jewel-bedecked wooden statue is said to date from the seventh century and is considered to be the oldest piece of Christian art in Mexico. The church also contains ornamental frescoes and Miguel Cabrera paintings.

MUSEO DEL PUEBLO DE GUANAJUATO (State Museum of Guanajuato), Calle Pocitos #7 near the University of Guanajuato, is an art museum housed in a 17th-century mansion. It has an extensive collection of religious paintings dating from the colonial era, amassed by muralist José Chávez Morado, as well as Morado murals. Also displayed are works by contemporary Mexican artists. Tues.-Sat. 10-2 and 4-7, Sun. 10-2. Admission is charged. Phone (473) 2-2990.

MUSEO DIEGO RIVERA (Diego Rivera Museum), at Calle Pocitos #47 just up the street from the Museo del Pueblo de Guanajuato, was the birthplace of the city's most celebrated native son. The first floor of the muralist's home has been restored and furnished with turn-of-the-20th-century antiques. The second and third floors contain more than 90 Rivera paintings, sketches and watercolors that trace the development of his style, influenced by both 20th-century Cubism and ancient Maya techniques. Included is a sketch for a 1933 mural commissioned by Rockefeller Center in New York City that was destroyed because it contained a portrait of Vladimir Lenin. Temporary exhibits by regional artists are presented on the top floor. Tues.-Sat. 10-1:30 and 4-6:30, Sun. 10-2:30. Admission is charged. Phone (473) 2-1197.

MUSEO ICONOGRAFICO DEL QUIJOTE (Iconographic Museum of Don Quixote), Manuel Doblado #1, is about 2 blocks southeast of the Jardín de la Unión. Some 600 pieces of art provide an immersion into the life of the enduring literary character created by Spanish author Miguel de Cervantes. Works by Pedro Coronel, Salvador Dalí, Pablo Picasso and others are executed in a variety of media, including paintings, sculpture, stained-glass windows and even clocks. Tues.-Sat. 10-6:30, Sun. 10-2:30. Free. Phone (473) 2-6721.

PALACIO DE GOBIERNO (Government Palace), Paseo de la Presa near the La Olla Dam, stands on the site of the old house of the Marqués de San Clemente. The original building was destroyed by a flood; the present structure was completed in 1903. It evokes a European elegance, enhanced by the use of Guanajuato green sandstone.

TEATRO JUAREZ (Juárez Theater), facing the Jardín de la Unión, is a deliciously opulent reminder of Guanajuato's late 19th-century prosperity; it was dedicated by dictator Porfirio Díaz in 1903 with a performance of the Guiseppe Verdi opera *Aida*. The theater's exterior is impressive, with tall columns, ascending steps, branching lampposts, bronze lions and statues of the Greek muses at the roof line.

Inside there are four levels of seating, private boxes, smoking rooms and dazzlingly intricate red-and-gold patterns on the walls and ceiling. The brocade and velvet as well as the Moorish-style ornamentation exemplify 19th-century romanticism. Staged productions—ranging from opera to the city's prestigious *Festival Internacional Cervantino*—are as colorful a spectacle as the theater itself. A nominal fee is charged for tours of the interior. Tues.-Sun. 9:15-1:45 and 5-7:45. Phone (473) 2-0183.

UNIVERSITY OF GUANAJUATO, Calle Pocitos and Lascurain de Retana, is one of Mexico's foremost universities. Since it was opened by Jesuits in 1732 at the request of Spain's King Philip V, it has been in almost continuous operation. In 1945 the school became a state university. Ten years later a modern new addition with interconnecting patios and open-air hallways was built, complete with Moorish-style facade. The city's cultural arts showcase, it offers theater, symphonies and student performances of Cervantes' "Entremeses," short comic presentations originally intended as intermission entertainment between plays.

TOURING GUANAJUATO'S PARKS AND PLAZAS

Guanajuato's meandering, often steep streets and tiny alleyways were made to be explored on foot. Several streets are closed to traffic, and those that aren't frequently are congested and filled with the fumes of idling vehicles. Strolling, therefore, is not only a more practical but a more pleasurable alternative. All you really need for a jaunt through the city's plazas is a good pair of shoes.

Although Guanajuato does not have a designated main square, the **Jardín de la Union** (Union Garden), in the center of town, is the city's lively focal point. This shady park draws residents and visitors alike. Band concerts are given Tuesday, Thursday and Sunday evenings, and there is always the chance that spontaneous musical performances will start up under the trees or at one of the outdoor cafés.

Facing one side of the triangle-shaped plaza are the opulent Teatro Juárez and the **Church of San Diego**, another of Guanajuato's picturesque colonial churches. Commissioned by Franciscan missionaries, it was almost destroyed by floodwaters and rebuilt in the late 18th century. The doorway in particular is representative of the flamboyant Churrigueresque architectural style.

Just off Jardín de la Unión is **Plazuela del Baratillo**, a peaceful spot for relaxing in the *sol* (sun) or *sombra* (shade) to the sounds of a gurgling fountain, a gift to the city from Emperor Maximilian.

Down Avenida Juárez from the Jardín de la Unión is **Plaza de la Paz**, anchored by the Basilica of Our Lady of Guanajuato, or La Parroquia (Parish Church). Behind the plaza is the University of Guanajuato. Palatial private residences dating from the 18th and 19th centuries surround the plaza, recalling the days when silver poured out of the region's mines. Continue down Avenida Juárez to **Plazuela de Los Angeles**, where the walls of the shops and houses are painted in bright colors. Close by is **Callejón del Beso** (Alley of the Kiss), an intimate passageway narrow enough to permit a smooch from balconies on either side of the street; according to local legend, two lovers who were kept apart did just that.

Near **Jardín de la Reforma**, a shady park along Avenida Juárez a block or so from the Hidalgo Market, is **Plaza de San Roque**, a small square that is the site of many of the *entremeses* presented by university students as part of the Cervantes festival in October. These rollicking skits, enhanced by the courtyard-like setting of the plaza, should not be missed if you're in town for the festival. At other times when classes are in session, student theatrical productions are often held in the plaza on Sunday evenings.

Equally engaging are the *callejoneadas* (kah-yeh-hoh-neh-AH-dahs) or serenades that take place at Guanajuato's plazas or in the city streets on various weekend evenings. During these frolics, strolling student ensembles called *estudiantinas* dress in medieval costumes and sing songs with guitar and mandolin accompaniment. The public is welcome to join in the merriment.

The reservoir impounded by **Presa de la Olla** (La Olla Dam), built in the mid-18th century, provides Guanajuato's supply of drinking water as well as a recreational setting favored by local weekenders. This residential area can be reached via Paseo de la Presa or by taking a city bus designated "Presa." **Antillón Park** is just below the dam. Flower gardens and a large statue of Father Miguel Hidalgo distinguish **Acacia Park**; picnicking is permitted, and rowboats can be rented for paddling around on the man-made lake.

NEARBY ATTRACTIONS

CERRO DEL CUBILETE (Cubilete Mountain) is about 16 kilometers (10 miles) west of Guanajuato off Mex. 110, on the way to Silao. It is said to be the geographical center of Mexico and draws many pilgrims. A gravel road climbs to the 9,440-foot summit, which is surmounted by an 80-foot-tall bronze statue of Cristo Rey (Christ the King). From here are superb views of the Bajío region, a fertile green plain dotted with lakes and isolated mountain peaks. An annual *Passion Play* takes place on Good Friday on the heights of Cubilete. City buses travel to the summit; the trip takes about 90 minutes.

ESTATUA DE EL PIPILA (Statue of El Pípila) overlooks Guanajuato from a hill to the east of the Jardín de la Unión. It immortalizes Juan José Martínez, a miner who set fire to the front door of the Alhóndiga de Granaditas, the massive granary where Spanish Royalists took refuge in 1810 during an attack on the city by Mexican revolutionaries. Although Martínez—nicknamed El Pípila—died during the daring raid, his courage helped lead the insurgents to victory. The dramatic, 30-foot-high figure, bearing a torch, keeps watch over the city below. This vantage point affords an outstanding view of Guanajuato's architectural landmarks and colorful pastel buildings, and is a nice spot for a picnic.

Buses designated "Pípila" take visitors to the monument; parking for other vehicles is free. El Pípila also is accessible by a steep climb on foot (wear sturdy walking shoes). To get there, take Calle Sopeña east to Callejón del Calvario and watch for the sign that says "Al Pípila."

IGLESIA DE LA VALENCIANA (Church of La Valenciana) is about 5 kilometers (3 miles) northeast of downtown on Mex. 110, toward Dolores Hidalgo. Actually the Iglesia de San Cayetano (Church of San Cayetano), it is commonly referred to as La Valenciana and is one of Mexico's finest colonial churches. Dating from 1788, it was constructed by the wealthy owner of the La Valenciana Mine, who later became the first Count of Valenciana.

The pink-stone facade, adorned with a profusion of delicate carvings, is a fine example of the grandly florid Churrigueresque style. The interior is a visual feast of floor-to-ceiling wood carvings overlaid with gold leaf and contains beautiful religious paintings. The three hand-carved wooden altars are encrusted with gilt decorations, and the inlaid pulpit was brought from China. On Dec. 8 a fiesta honors La Purísima (The Immaculate

Conception). Designated "Valenciana" buses take visitors to the church, which has been in continuous use since its inception.

LA VALENCIANA MINE is across the highway from the Church of La Valenciana. Discovered in 1760, it ranks as one of the greatest silver mines in history, at one point said to produce more than a fifth of the world's silver. The outer walls of the mine area are peaked to symbolize the crown of Spain. The shaft is exceptionally wide and and more than 1,500 feet deep; visitors can look down it but are not permitted to descend. The mine was reactivated in the late 1960s after decades of lying in ruin, and still brings up silver, lead and nickel.

MARFIL is a former mining town about 3 kilometers (2 miles) southwest of Guanajuato off Mex. 110; the old road to Marfil winds into a valley. At the height of this area's prosperity in the late 19th century, numerous silver mines operated and luxurious mansions lined the streets. Marfil was devastated in 1905 when La Olla Dam burst, killing many of the residents. The survivors moved uphill, many of the mines closed, and Marfil lapsed into obscurity. Abandoned buildings were later torn apart to retrieve the silver embedded in the structures' adobe and brick walls.

At Marfil is the restored **Ex-Hacienda de San Gabriel de Barrera**, now a museum. The former residence contains paintings and elegant period furniture as well as a lavishly decorated chapel. The beautiful grounds consist of manicured formal gardens in English, Italian and other styles, connected by walkways and accented with fountains and statuary. Admission is charged to the hacienda.

MUSEO DE LAS MOMIAS (Mummy Museum), the city's ghastliest attraction, is west of downtown on Calzada del Panteón, next to the city cemetery (El Panteón). Dryness, minerals and natural salts in the soil all helped preserve some 100 corpses, which escaped decomposition to a remarkable degree. The first exhumations were carried out in the 1860s when local citizens were unable to pay for a gravesite.

The mummies—men, women and children, some still with shoes and hair—are displayed behind glass with various frozen expressions, giving visitors the morbid thrill of viewing them face to face. This museum is not recommended for the squeamish or the claustrophobic (it's small and often crowded). True to Mexicans' fascination with death, outdoor vendors sell candy replicas of the mummies and young boys shout "Las momias!" in an attempt to be hired as tour guides. City buses and taxis that can be boarded or hailed along Avenida Juárez will stop within walking distance of the museum. Admission is charged; there is an extra charge for use of a camera. Phone (473) 2-0639.

WHERE TO STAY

HOSTERIA DEL FRAYLE
Historic Motel (473/2-1179

All Year $66 XP $10
Location: Center. Sopena 3 36000. Fax: 473/2-1179. **Facility:** Hotel converted from 17th-century gold and silver coin mint; some very steep steps. 37 units. 1 two-bedroom unit. *Bath:* shower only. 4 stories (no elevator), interior corridors. **Terms:**15 day cancellation notice. **Cards:** MC, VI.

HOTEL HOSTEL CANTARRANAS
Apartment ((473)2-5241

All Year $50 XP $10
Location: Center. Calle Cantarranas 50 36000. Fax: 473/2-1708. **Facility:** 200 year old building. Access to some units require walking up steep stairs. 10 units. 2 two-bedroom units and 8 efficiencies. *Bath:* shower only. 3 stories (no elevator), exterior corridors. **Parking:** extra charge. **Terms:** F12; 15 day cancellation notice, weekly & monthly rates available.

SOME UNITS

HOTEL MISION GUANAJUATO
Motor Inn ((473)2-3980

All Year $95 XP $10
Location: 2.5 km w; at the entrance to Guanajuato on Mex 110. Camino Antiguo A Marfil Km 2.5 36050. Fax: 473/2-3980. **Facility:** Part of the building dates to the 17th-century. Features immaculate grounds and several very attractive gardens. Pool area has murals by a local artist. Located on north end of town. 160 units. 1 two-bedroom unit. Some whirlpool units. *Bath:* combo or shower only. 2-3 stories (no elevator), interior corridors. **Parking:** valet. **Terms:** F12; 3 day cancellation notice. **Amenities:** *Some:* safes, honor bars. **Leisure Activities:** heated pool, lighted tennis court. **Guest Services:** gift shop, valet laundry. **Business Services:** meeting rooms. **Cards:** AE, MC, VI.

SOME UNITS

HOTEL POSADA SANTA FE
Historic Motor Inn ((473)2-0084

All Year $60-$100 XP $15
Location: Take vehicular subway to Jardin de la Union exit, left on Juarez 1 short blk, then right on Calle del Turco to hotel parking. Plaza Principal 12 36000. Fax: 473/2-4653. **Facility:** Restored 1862 building. 47 units. *Bath:* combo or shower only. 3 stories (no elevator), interior corridors. **Terms:** F12; 5 day cancellation notice. **Amenities:** *Some:* safes. **Dining:** restaurant, see separate listing. **Leisure Activities:** whirlpools. **Guest Services:** valet laundry. **Business Services:** meeting rooms. **Cards:** AE, MC, VI.

SOME UNITS

⟁ HOTEL SAN DIEGO

▼▼▼ *Hotel* ☏ (473)2-1300

1/1-6/30	$940-$1130	XP $100
12/1-12/31	$710-$860	XP $90
7/1-11/30	$130-$350	XP $120

Location: Center. Jardin de La Union 1 36000. Fax: 473/2-5626. **Facility:** Modernized 17th-century convent. Many units with semi-private balcony. Located in a historic commercial district that exudes local charm. Across from park and near cathedral and market, literally in the heart of Guanajuato. 43 units. 2 two-bedroom units. *Bath:* shower only. 4 stories, interior corridors. **Parking:** off-site. **Terms:** 3 day cancellation notice. **Dining & Entertainment:** dining room, 7 am-11 pm, $10-$25, entertainment. **Guest Services:** valet laundry. **Business Services:** meeting rooms. **Cards:** MC, VI.

PARADOR SAN JAVIER HOTEL

▼▼▼ *Hotel* ☏ (473)2-0650

All Year	$105	XP $10

Location: 2 km ne on Mex 110, Dolores Hidalgo Hwy. Plaza Aldama #92 36020. Fax: 473/2-3114. **Facility:** Old hacienda. Modern colonial style units, a few older ones with fireplace. Very attractive grounds and pool area. Colorful building with antique carriages in garden and public areas. 113 units. 2 two-bedroom units. *Bath:* combo or shower only. 6 stories, interior/exterior corridors. **Parking:** valet. **Terms:** F12; 8 day cancellation notice-fee imposed. **Amenities:** voice mail, safes. **Leisure Activities:** heated pool. **Guest Services:** valet laundry. **Business Services:** meeting rooms. **Cards:** AE, MC, VI.

SOME UNITS

QUINTA LAS ACACIAS

▼▼▼▼ *Bed & Breakfast* ☏ (473)1-1517

10/5-10/20	$220	XP $35
12/1-12/31	$160-$200	XP $30
1/1-10/4 & 10/21-11/30	$175	XP $30

Location: Center; across from Acacia Park. Paseo de la Fresa #168 36000. Fax: 473/1-1517. **Facility:** Restored 1890 mansion. Elegant, many antiques. Located near government palace, manicured garden, immaculate rooms and baths, Victorian woodwork, hardwood floors. 10 units. Some whirlpool units ($200-$250). 5 stories (no elevator), interior/exterior corridors. **Terms:** age restrictions may apply, 7 day cancellation notice. **Amenities:** voice mail, safes, hair dryers. **Leisure Activities:** whirlpool. **Guest Services:** [BP] meal plan available, valet laundry. **Cards:** AE, MC, VI.

SOME UNITS

SUITES CASA DE LAS MANRIQUE

▼▼▼ *Historic Hotel* ☏ 473/2-7678

All Year	$36-$50	XP $8

Location: Center; near Mercado Hidalgo. Ave Juarez 116 36000. Fax: 473/2-8306. **Facility:** Converted 1882 home. 8 units. 1 two-bedroom unit. Some whirlpool units. *Bath:* shower only. 3 stories (no elevator), interior corridors. **Terms:** F12; 15 day cancellation notice. **Amenities:** safes. **Leisure Activities:** rooftop sun deck. **Guest Services:** valet laundry. **Business Services:** meeting rooms. **Cards:** AE, MC, VI.

WHERE TO DINE

RESTAURANTE HOTEL POSADA SANTA FE

▼▼▼ *Mexican* ☏ 473/2-0084

L $10-$20   D $10-$20

Location: Take vehicular subway to Jardin de la Union exit, left on Juarez 1 short blk, then right on Calle del Turco; in Hotel Posada Santa Fe. Plaza Principal 12 36000. **Hours:** 7 am-11 pm. **Features:** No A/C; casual dress; cocktails. Indoor and sidewalk dining areas. **Cards:** AE, MC, VI.

RESTAURANT REAL DE LA ESPERANZA

▼▼▼ *Continental* ☏ 473/2-1041

L $10-$18   D $10-$18

Location: 5.5 km on the Dolores Hidalgo Hwy. 36000. **Hours:** 1 pm-9 pm. **Features:** No A/C; casual dress; cocktails. Replica of an old mission, located on a hill overlooking the city. **Cards:** AE, MC, VI.

IRAPUATO, GUANAJUATO

WHERE TO STAY

HOTEL REAL DE MINAS

▼▼▼ *Hotel* ☏ 462/6-2380

All Year	$65-$85	XP $15

Location: Center, just n of Zocalo; in Portal Carrillo Puerto. (PO Box 8, 36500). Fax: 462/6-7255. **Facility:** 75 units. *Bath:* combo or shower only. 9 stories, interior corridors. **Terms:** F12; 15 day cancellation notice. **Guest Services:** valet laundry. **Business Services:** meeting rooms. **Cards:** AE, DI, MC, VI.

SOME UNITS

MOTEL FLAMINGO

▼▼▼ *Motor Inn* ☏ (462)5-3646

All Year	$25	XP $5

Location: 2 blks from Flag Monument; 3 km se from Mex 45 W bypass jct. (Blvd Gustavo Diaz Ordaz 3472, 36660). Fax: 462/5-4517. **Facility:** Very well maintained units. 65 units. *Bath:* shower only. 2-3 stories, exterior corridors. **Terms:** F12 **Guest Services:** gift shop, valet laundry. **Cards:** AE, MC, VI.

LAGOS DE MORENO, JALISCO (G-4) elev. 5,917'

Lagos de Moreno (LAH-gos deh moh-REH-noh) is an attractive town in the Jaliscan highlands, strategically situated at the intersection of two major highways, Mex. 45 and Mex. 80. Though it is an important commercial hub, Lagos de Moreno retains a sense of timelessness. Designated a national historic monument, it has a downtown riverside park, colonial mansions with central patios, streets brightened by flowers and tiny plazas in unexpected places. Worth visiting are the **Montecristo House of Antiques**, downtown, and its remodeled Hacienda de Montecristo, just southwest of town on Mex. 80. Although the monastery that overlooks Lagos de

Moreno from a hillside perch is not open to visitors, those who make the climb will be rewarded with beautiful views, especially around sunset.

Leon, Guanajuato

Where To Stay

FIESTA INN LEON

▼▼▼ *Motor Inn*   ((47)10-0500

2/1-11/30	$119-$143	XP $12
12/1-1/31	$95-$131	XP $12

Location: 8 km se on Mex 45. Blvd Adolfo Lopez Mateos 2702 ote 37530. Fax: 47/10-0506. **Facility:** Attractive lobby and public areas, modern rooms on road to airport. 160 units. 3 stories, interior corridors. **Terms:** F12; cancellation fee imposed. **Leisure Activities:** heated pool, exercise room. **Guest Services:** valet laundry. **Business Services:** meeting rooms, administrative services. **Cards:** AE, DI, MC, VI.

SOME UNITS

HOLIDAY INN LEON

▼▼▼ *Motor Inn*   ((47)10-0003

All Year $80-$85   XP $10

Location: 3.5 km se on Mex 45. Blvd Lopez Mateos 1308 37270. Fax: 47/10-0003. **Facility:** Well-appointed rooms and public areas, modern facility is well-maintained, American style operation. 170 units. 5 stories, interior corridors. **Parking:** valet. **Terms:** F12; 3 day cancellation notice. **Amenities:** extended cable TV, irons, hair dryers. **Leisure Activities:** heated pool, exercise room. **Guest Services:** valet laundry. **Business Services:** meeting rooms, administrative services, PC. **Cards:** AE, DI, MC, VI.

SOME UNITS

⍟ HOTEL FIESTA AMERICANA-LEON

▼▼▼ ▼▼▼ *Hotel*   ((47)13-6040

All Year $209   XP $21

Location: Downtown on Mex 45; across from Centro Estrella. Blvd Adolfo Lopez Mateos 1102 37270. Fax: 47/13-5380. **Facility:** Very attractive, modern. Excellent and well-appointed rooms. Cordial, well trained staff. 211 units. Some whirlpool units. 6 stories, interior corridors. **Parking:** valet. **Terms:** F12; cancellation fee imposed. **Amenities:** voice mail, honor bars, hair dryers. **Dining & Entertainment:** 2 restaurants, 7 am-midnight, $8-$25, cocktails, entertainment. **Leisure Activities:** heated pool, saunas. *Fee:* 2 lighted tennis courts, tennis instruction. **Guest Services:** gift shop, valet laundry. *Fee:* massage. **Business Services:** meeting rooms, administrative services. **Cards:** AE, DI, MC, VI.

SOME UNITS
FEE

HOTEL LA ESTANCIA

▼▼▼▼ *Motor Inn*   ((47)16-3939

All Year $80   XP $12

Location: East entrance via Blvd Lopez Mateos, Mex 45; adjacent to Centro Estrella. Blvd Lopez Mateos 1311 Ote 37000 (PO Box 1-759). Fax: 47/16-3940. **Facility:** Ample parking with security. Rooms vary in size and decor; some excellent appointments. 76 units. 2 stories, interior corridors. **Parking:** valet. **Terms:** F12. **Amenities:** safes, hair dryers. **Leisure Activities:** heated pool, wading pool. **Guest Services:** gift shop, valet laundry. **Business Services:** meeting rooms. **Cards:** AE, DI, MC, VI.

SOME UNITS

Where To Dine

ARGENTILIA RESTAURANT

▼▼▼ *Argentine*   (47/18-3394

L $10-$20   D $10-$20

Location: 2 km n on Ave Lopez Mateos to Ave Campestre, then 0.5 km w. Blvd Campestre 901 37160. **Hours:** 2 pm-11 pm, Fri & Sat-midnight. **Reservations:** suggested. **Features:** casual dress; carryout; cocktails; entertainment; valet parking. Cuts of beef prepared Argentine style grilled over mesquite wood. Very good variety at pasta bar. **Cards:** AE, MC, VI.

FRASCATI RISTORANTE-PIZZERIA

▼▼▼ *Italian*   (47/73-7154

L $8-$18   D $8-$18

Location: 2 km on Ave Lopez Mateos to Ave Campestre, then 1 km w. Blvd Campestre 1403 37160. **Hours:** 2 pm-11:30 pm, Sun-6 pm. **Reservations:** suggested. **Features:** casual dress; cocktails; valet parking. Casual atmosphere. Wood burning pizza oven. **Cards:** AE, MC, VI.

LALO'S N CHARLIES

▼▼▼ *Continental*   (47/16-6668

L $6-$14   D $6-$14

Location: 3 km se. Blvd Lopez Mateos 4607 37000. **Hours:** 1:30 pm-midnight, Fri & Sat-1 am. **Features:** cocktails. Casual, good selection of meat, poultry and seafood. **Cards:** AE, MC, VI.

Matehuala, San Luis Potosi

Where To Stay

LAS PALMAS MIDWAY INN

▼▼▼ *Motor Inn*   (488/2-0002

All Year $58-$67

Location: On Mex 57, by north jct entrance road to Matehuala. 78700 (PO Box 73). Fax: 488/236-20. **Facility:** Great highway rest stop. Quiet garden courtyard. Good sized, well maintained units. 91 units. *Bath:* shower only. 1 story, exterior corridors. **Dining:** restaurant, see separate listing. **Leisure Activities:** wading pool, playground. *Fee:* miniature golf, bicycles. **Cards:** AE, DI, MC, VI.

SOME UNITS

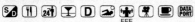

MOTEL EL DORADO

 Motel   (488/2-0174

All Year $35-$45
Location: On Mex 57; at Dr Arroyo Hwy jct. (PO Box 73,
78700). **Facility:** Older property with large units. Ask for
rooms in newer section that have ceramic tile flooring. 30
units. *Bath:* shower only. 1 story, exterior corridors.
Terms:pets (with prior notice). **Amenities:** no TVs. **Leisure
Activities:** playground. **Guest Services:** *Fee:* area transportation. **Cards:** AE, CB, DI, MC, VI.

WHERE TO DINE

LAS PALMAS RESTAURANT

 Continental   (488/2-0001

                              L $3-$8   D $3-$8
Location: On Mex 57, by north jct entrance road to Matehuala; in Las Palmas Midway Inn. **Hours:** 7 am-10:30 pm.
Features: casual dress; children's menu; cocktails &
lounge; a la carte. The place to stop and replenish. Continental menu, well-trained attentive staff, relaxing atmosphere. **Cards:** AE, CB, DI, MC, VI.

MORELIA,
MICHOACAN (B-7) elev. 6,399'

Capital of the state of Michoacán, Morelia
(Moh-REH-lee-ah) was founded in 1541. It was
first known as Valladolid, after the Spanish birthplace of New Spain's first viceroy, Antonio de
Mendoza. In 1828, the name was changed to
honor native son José María Morelos, who became a general for and hero of the Mexican War
of Independence.

An earlier priest, Bishop Vasco de Quiroga,
helped set in motion the region's development
soon after Mexico came under Spanish rule. As
the first bishop of Michoacán, Don Vasco introduced Christianity and various craft industries to
the Tarasco Indians, who revered him for his
kindness. "Tata Vasco," as the Indians called
him, also built hospitals and established Morelia's College of St. Nicholas *(see attraction listing),* one of the oldest state universities in the
Americas.

Today Morelia's city center retains a strong
Spanish flavor that has earned it the title "Aristocrat of Colonial Cities." In an effort to retain
this atmosphere of Old World charm, building
ordinances require that all new construction con-
form to the early colonial style. Many of the
city's richly decorated civil and religious buildings, however, were erected in the 17th and 18th
centuries. And Morelia's early planners had the
foresight to lay out wide, straight boulevards,
which for the most part accommodate today's
ever-present vehicle traffic.

Large, tree-lined **Plaza de Armas**, the main
square, is bounded on the north by Avenida Madero and on the south by Calle Allende. It also is
known as Plaza de los Mártires (Plaza of the

Martyrs) in honor of the rebel priests who were
executed during Mexico's War of Independence.
The square is surrounded by colonial-era buildings, and this part of the city is pedestrian-
friendly (although congested with vehicles and
vendors). Band concerts take place on Sundays.
(**Note:** Street names change frequently above and
below Avenida Madero, the principal east-west
artery.)

The architecturally striking **Casa de Cultura**
(House of Culture), 4 blocks north of the plaza
on Avenida Morelos Norte, was salvaged from
the ruins of a 350-year-old Carmelite monastery.
The peach-colored building serves as an open-air
theater for drama, dance and music groups, and
also provides studio space for artists. Within the
complex is a museum displaying a collection of
ceremonial masks from around the country.

The immense **Palacio Clavijero** (Clavijero
Palace), Calle Nigromante #79, is a former Jesuit
college that now functions as the state library.
Cultural events take place in the building's large
open-air gallery. At the southern end of the complex is the **Mercado de Dulces** (Candy Market).
Candy-making traditions begun by European
nuns are still carried out at this shrine to Mexican confections. Worth trying are the many flavors of *ate,* a pastelike concoction made with
fresh fruit to which sugar and water are added.
Perhaps the biggest holiday for sweets shops is
the *Day of the Dead* Nov. 1-2, when they turn
out an array of sugar skulls, skeletons and other
ghostly creations.

The city's famed Boy's Choir, which has sung
in Rome and Carnegie Hall, has its base in the
Templo y Colegio de las Rosas (Church and
College of las Rosas), established in the late 16th
century as a Dominican convent and the home of
the oldest school for liturgical music in the Western Hemisphere. Visitors are welcome to attend
the rehearsals at Las Rosas, which occupies a
magnificent colonial building on Avenida Santiago Tapia, 2 blocks north of the northwest corner
of Plaza de Armas. A statue of Vasco de Quiroga
stands opposite the statue of Cervantes in the
nearby **Jardín de las Rosas** (Garden of the
Roses).

Close by at Avenida Guillermo Prieto #176 is
the **Museo del Estado** (State Museum), which
offers an overview of Michoacáno history, from
pre-Columbian figurines to a collection of 18th-
century apothecary jars. The mansion in which
the museum is housed was once the residence of
self-designated Mexican emperor Agustín Iturbide. Open Mon.-Fri. 9-2, Sat. 9-7. Free.

Morelia's largest park, **Bosque Cuauhtémoc**
(Cuauhtémoc Woods Park), is east of downtown
off Avenida Acueducto (Mex. 15). This is a
popular Sunday picnic spot. On the park's northeast side, in the small **Plaza Morelos**, is a statue
of the patriot on horseback. At Avenida Acueducto #18, on the park's northern border, is the

Museo de Arte Contemporaneo (Museum of Contemporary Art). Works by both local and international artists are displayed in an early 19th-century mansion. Open Tues.-Sun. 10-1 and 4-7. Free.

The **Aqueduct**, dating from 1789, was once the primary means of bringing water to the city. It extends for more than a mile and is made up of 253 arches, the tallest 25 feet in height. They're impressively lit at night. Concealing small shops and private homes, some of the arches line two sides of **Parque Villalongín**. Extending east from this small park is **Fray Antonio de San Miguel**, a tree-shaded, two-block-long pedestrian street lined on both sides with stone benches. It runs to the **Iglesia Nuestra Señora de Guadalupe** (Church of Our Lady of Guadalupe), which has a highly ornate interior.

There is a modern side to Morelia as well. The **Centro de Convenciones** (Convention Center) is southeast of downtown, at the corner of Calzada Ventura Puente and the Periférico (loop road) that encircles the city. It houses a theater, planetarium and orchidarium. Planetarium programs are presented Sunday evenings; admission is charged. The orchid greenhouse contains more than 3,000 varieties that bloom at various times.

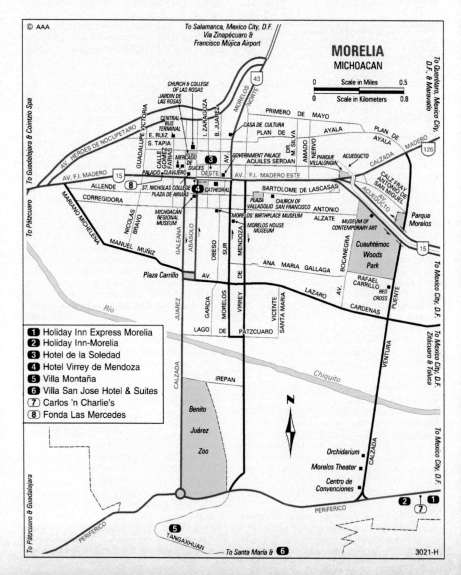

© AAA

To Salamanca, Mexico City, D.F.
Via Zinapécuaro &
Francisco Mújica Airport

MORELIA
MICHOACAN

Scale in Miles 0   0.5
Scale in Kilometers 0   0.8

❶ Holiday Inn Express Morelia
❷ Holiday Inn-Morelia
❸ Hotel de la Soledad
❹ Hotel Virrey de Mendoza
❺ Villa Montaña
❻ Villa San Jose Hotel & Suites
❼ Carlos 'n Charlie's
❽ Fonda Las Mercedes

3021-H

It is open daily; donations are accepted. Convention meetings and cultural events take place at the center's **Teatro Morelos** (Morelos Theater).

Thanks to the ministrations of Vasco de Quiroga, the state of Michoacán is a bountiful producer of crafts, and Morelia serves as its best showcase. Lacquerware, pottery, *sarapes*, woodcarvings and jewelry are typical items. Embroidered peasant blouses, for which this region is particularly noted, also can be purchased. The government-run museum and store in the Ex-Convent of San Francisco *(see attraction listing)* displays and sells handicrafts from all over the state.

Cultural events assume special importance in this university city. Folkloric dance performances and music recitals take place regularly at several locations around town. For schedule information, check with the State Tourism Office *(see "The Informed Traveler" below)* or at the Casa de Cultura. The *Feria de Morelia*, held in May, is an old-fashioned state fair showcasing livestock and produce displays. Musicians perform at various locations during the *International Music Festival*, which occurs in July and August. Michoacános also celebrate *Independence Day* Sept. 15-16, the *Birthday of José María Morelos* on Sept. 30, *Día de los Muertos* (Day of the Dead) Nov. 1-2 and the *Feast of the Virgin of Guadalupe*, honoring Mexico's patron saint, on Dec. 12.

THE INFORMED TRAVELER

Aeroméxico offers daily flights between Mexico City and Morelia's **Francisco Mújica Airport**, about 30 kilometers (19 miles) north of the city. Schedules change frequently, and flight times should be confirmed in advance. "Deluxe" bus service is offered by ETN between Morelia and Mexico City's Terminal de Autobuses del Poniente (Western Terminal), as well as to Guadalajara and Guanajuato. The central bus station is near the intersection of avenidas Eduardo Ruíz and Gomez Farias, a couple of blocks northwest of the main plaza.

Buses, taxicabs and *combis* all provide public transportation. Buses can be helpful for getting to and from Cuauhtémoc Woods Park and the Aqueduct via Avenida Madero, but they move slowly along the crowded streets during rush hours. *Combi* vehicles are different colors according to their destination. Taxis are not metered; agree on a fare before getting in the cab.

The State Tourism Office is in the Clavijero Palace, downtown at Calle Nigromante #79. In addition to maps and visitor information, the office can provide details about free guided walking tours of the city center. It is open Mon.-Fri. 9-8, Sat.-Sun. 9-4; phone (43) 13-2654.

WHAT TO SEE

CATHEDRAL is on the east side of Plaza de Armas and faces Avenida Madero. Considered by many to be among Mexico's most beautiful churches, it took more than a century (1640-1744) to build. Exterior highlights are the rose-colored stone facade, two elaborately decorated towers, and a colonial fence and gates. Inside are religious relics and paintings as well as a magnificent three-story organ with 4,600 pipes, reputed to be one of the world's largest. The cathedral is the site of the the *International Organ Festival*, held annually in early May.

COLEGIO DE SAN NICOLAS (College of St. Nicholas) is on Avenida Madero Poniente near the Mercado de Dulces. It is the oldest Mexican university still in operation and was the second educational institution to be established in the Americas. The first was founded by the Augustinian priest Alonso de la Veracruz in the town of Tiripetío, about 25 kilometers (16 miles) southwest of Morelia on Mex. 120. The convent of the former "University of Tiripetío" can still be seen.

Inaugurated in 1540 by Bishop Vasco de Quiroga, the Colegio de San Nicolás was transferred to Valladolid, later Morelia, in 1580. The school is now a division of Michoacán State University. Among its distinguished alumni were War of Independence leaders José María Morelos and Father Miguel Hidalgo. Interesting frescoes decorate the inner walls of the building's colonial patio. Open Mon.-Fri. Free.

EX-CONVENTO DE SAN FRANCISCO (Ex-Convent of San Francisco) is on Calle Bartolomé de las Casas at Plaza Valladolid, 2 blocks east of the cathedral. It dates from in 1531. The founding of Morelia took place in the square in front of it.

Casa de las Artesanías is in the church cloister. This combination museum and workshop displays lacquerware, woodcarvings, pottery, copper items, ceramics and other crafts from throughout the state. Artisans also can be observed at work. The quality of the handicrafts is excellent, and prices are accordingly high. Open daily 9-8.

MUSEO CASA DE MORELOS (Morelos House Museum) is on Avenida Morelos Sur at Calle Aldama. A typical example of domestic colonial architecture, it was José María Morelos' residence beginning in 1801. His descendants lived in the house until 1910, when it was converted into a museum. Inside are personal belongings, manuscripts and exhibits about the War of Independence. Open daily 9-7. Admission is charged.

MUSEO CASA NATAL DE MORELOS (Morelos' Birthplace Museum), Corregidora #113 at García Obeso, is where the Mexican revolutionary was born in 1765. The house, erected more than a century earlier, is a national monument and contains a public library. An eternal flame burns in a courtyard garden behind the building. Eight rooms are devoted to Morelos memorabilia, portraits and documents. Open Mon.-Sat. 9-2 and 4-8, Sat. 9-2. Free.

MUSEO REGIONAL MICHOACANO (Michoacán Regional Museum) is at Calle Allende #305 near the main plaza. This former 18th-century palace contains an art gallery, archeological exhibits, displays of colonial-era furniture and weaponry, and other historical items. Note the Alfredo Zalce mural depicting figures who have contributed to Mexico's national identity, as well as those who have not. Open Tues.-Sat. 9-7, Sun. 9-2. Admission is charged.

PALACIO DE GOBIERNO (Government Palace), the state capitol, faces the cathedral across Calle Allende. This baroque building, a former granary, is the colonial prototype for all new city edifices. Murals painted by Alfredo Zalce, Morelia's famed artist, depict scenes from Mexico's often violent history. Open daily.

PARQUE ZOOLOGICO BENITO JUAREZ (Benito Juárez Zoo) is about 3 kilometers (1.9 miles) south of the city center via Avenida Juárez. It houses an extensive collection of animals and birds amid landscaped grounds. The zoo also contains a small lake (rowboats are available for rent) and a children's playground. Open daily 10-6. Admission is charged.

NEARBY DESTINATIONS

The well-to-do hillside suburb of **Santa María**, just south of the Periférico (loop road) on the south side of Morelia, offers excellent views of the city and the valley beyond; several small resort hotels are in this area. About 32 kilometers (20 miles) north of Morelia on Mex. 43 is an unusual 19th-century causeway across Lake Cuitzeo. The town of **Cuitzeo**, on the lake's north shore, contains one of the region's two fortresslike 17th-century Augustinian monasteries; the other is in the city of **Yuríria**, north of Cuitzeo and a short distance east off Mex. 43.

Two national parks with scenic views are east of Morelia on Mex. 15. **Parque Nacional Insurgente José María Morelos** is about 26 kilometers (16 miles) east of the city. **Parque Nacional Cerro de Garnica**, which has two *miradores* (observation points) overlooking the rugged Mil Cumbres (Thousand Peaks) landscape, is another 24 kilometers (15 miles) further east. From here, Mex. 15 continues winding through steep mountains and dense forests to the town of Ciudad Hidalgo.

BALNEARIO COINTZIO (Cointzio Spa) is 9 kilometers (6 miles) west on Mex. 15, then about 6 kilometers (4 miles) south. At the base of a cliff where mineral waters of 100 F (37 C) emerge are two swimming pools, a wading pool, bathhouse, refreshment facilities and bungalows. Open Wed.-Mon. Admission is charged; there are additional fees for parking, pool and bungalows.

WHERE TO STAY

HOLIDAY INN EXPRESS MORELIA

▼▼▼ *Motel* ((43)15-7100

| 7/1-11/30 | $92 | XP $15 |
| 12/1-6/30 | $87 | XP $15 |

Location: 6.7 km se on Periferico. Ave Camelinas 5000 58270. Fax: 43/15-7257. **Facility:** Modern American style motel. Meets AAA guest room security requirements. 80 units. 2 stories, exterior corridors. **Terms:** F. **Amenities:** extended cable TV, voice mail, honor bars, irons, hair dryers. **Leisure Activities:** heated pool, wading pool. **Guest Services:** [CP] meal plan available, valet laundry. **Cards:** AE, DI, MC, VI.

SOME UNITS

HOLIDAY INN-MORELIA

▼▼▼ *Motor Inn* (43/14-3111

| 7/1-11/30 | $102-$120 | XP $12 |
| 12/1-6/30 | $95-$112 | XP $12 |

Location: 6.3 km se on the Periferico; opposite Plaza Las Americas. 3466 Camelinas Ave 58270. Fax: 43/14-3643. **Facility:** Near convention center. Ample fenced parking area and security. Meets AAA guest room security requirements. 123 units. 3 stories, interior corridors. **Parking:** valet. **Terms:** F19; 15 day cancellation notice. **Amenities:** voice mail, honor bars, irons, hair dryers. **Leisure Activities:** heated pool, wading pool, whirlpool, tennis court, jogging, exercise room. **Guest Services:** gift shop, valet laundry. **Business Services:** meeting rooms. **Cards:** AE, JC, MC, VI.

SOME UNITS

HOTEL DE LA SOLEDAD

▼▼ *Hotel* ((43)12-1888

All Year $50-$64 XP $6

Location: Just n of cathedral. Zaragoza 90 & Melchor Oca 58000. Fax: 43/12-2111. **Facility:** Converted monastery with landscaped patio. 58 units. *Bath:* combo or shower only. 2 stories, exterior corridors. **Parking:** extra charge. **Terms:** F12 **Guest Services:** [CP] & [MAP] meal plans available, gift shop, valet laundry. **Business Services:** meeting rooms. **Cards:** AE, CB, DI, MC, VI.

SOME UNITS
⏹ / ⏹ /

HOTEL VIRREY DE MENDOZA

▼▼▼ *Historic Hotel* ((43)12-0633

All Year $96-$217 XP $15

Location: Center; just w of cathedral. Ave Madero Poniente 310 58000 (Portal Matamdros 16). Fax: 43/12-6719. **Facility:** Old World elegance. Some units furnished in superb antiques. Few interior rooms. Original artwork, stained glass ceiling in central area. 55 units. Some whirlpool units ($96-$100). 3 stories, interior corridors. **Parking:** valet. **Terms:** F12; 7 day cancellation notice. **Guest Services:** valet laundry. **Business Services:** meeting rooms. **Cards:** AE, MC, VI.

⟨AAA⟩ VILLA MONTANA

▼▼▼ ▼▼▼   *Suite Motor Inn*   ((43)14-0231

All Year $130-$330   XP $30
Location: 3.3 km s off Mex 15, via Periferico and s on Tangaxhuan. Patzimba 201 58090 (PO Box 233). Fax: 43/15-1423. **Facility:** Cottages in landscaped garden, terraced on mountain slope above city. Refined atmosphere with fireplaces. Breathtaking views from garden and lounge. Spacious, very comfortable rooms and baths. 37 units. 4 two-bedroom units. 2 stories, exterior corridors. **Terms:** F8; age restrictions may apply, 15 day cancellation notice, $10 service charge. **Amenities:** safes, hair dryers. *Some:* honor bars. **Dining:** dining room, 7:30 am-11:30 pm, $10-$20, cocktails. **Leisure Activities:** heated pool, tennis court. **Guest Services:** gift shop, valet laundry. *Fee:* massage. **Business Services:** meeting rooms, PC. **Cards:** AE, MC, VI.

SOME UNITS
⟨🍴⟩ ⟨🏊⟩ ⟨AC⟩ ⟨📷⟩ ⟨🖨⟩ ⟨DATA PORT⟩ / ⟨VCR⟩ ⟨🔌⟩ /

⟨AAA⟩ VILLA SAN JOSE HOTEL & SUITES

▼▼▼ ▼▼▼   *Motor Inn*   ((43)24-4545

All Year $100-$120   XP $13
Location: 3.3 km s off Mex 15, via Periferico and s on Tangaxhuan. 77 Patzimba Col Vista Bella 58090. Fax: 43/24-4545. **Facility:** On a hillside, overlooking the city. 45 units. 4 two-bedroom units. Some whirlpool units ($250). **Bath:** combo or shower only. 2 stories, exterior corridors. **Parking:** valet. **Terms:** F12; 3 day cancellation notice. **Dining & Entertainment:** restaurant, 7 am-midnight, $10-$20, cocktails, entertainment. **Leisure Activities:** heated pool, whirlpool, tennis court. **Guest Services:** gift shop, valet laundry. **Business Services:** meeting rooms, administrative services. **Cards:** AE, MC, VI.

SOME UNITS
⟨S/D⟩ ⟨🍴⟩ ⟨🏊⟩ ⟨AC⟩ ⟨📷⟩ / ⟨✕⟩ ⟨🔌⟩ /

WHERE TO DINE

CARLOS 'N CHARLIE'S

▼▼ ▼▼▼   *American*   (43/24-3741

L $6-$14   D $6-$14
Location: Ave Camelinas 3340 58270. **Hours:** 1 pm-midnight. Closed: 1/1, 12/25. **Features:** No A/C; casual dress; children's menu; carryout; cocktails & lounge; valet parking; a la carte. Specializing in barbecue chicken, steak and ribs. Fun-type atmosphere. **Cards:** AE, DI, MC, VI.

FONDA LAS MERCEDES   *Historical*

▼▼▼ ▼▼▼   *Continental*   (43/12-6113

L $7-$15   D $7-$15
Location: In historic district, just w of the cathedral, corner of Ave Madero Pte. Leon Guzman #47 58000. **Hours:** 1:30 pm-midnight. Closed: 1/1, 12/25. **Reservations:** suggested. **Features:** No A/C; cocktails & lounge; street parking; a la carte. Contemporary colonial ambience. Extensive selection of intriguing international dishes. **Cards:** AE, MC, VI.

PACHUCA,
HIDALGO (B-10) elev. 7,957'

Capital of the state of Hidalgo, Pachuca (pah-CHOO-kah) is the center of a rich mining district that produces much of the world's silver. It is believed that silver was mined before the arrival of the Spanish, who founded the city in 1534. The surrounding hills are honeycombed with tunnels and heaped with slag piles, although industrialization has increased to counteract declining

mineral production. The Pachuca area also is known for the production of pulque, a mildly alcoholic drink made from the fermented juice of the maguey (mah-GAY) cactus.

Government offices are in the **Casas Coloradas** (Red Houses), a complex built as a school toward the end of the 18th century by the Count of Regla, who made his fortune from Pachuca's silver mines. Also of interest is the 1596 **Convent of San Francisco.** Housed within the convent is the **Archivo Casasola** (Casasola Archives), which contains an extensive collection of photographs chronicling Mexican history from the late 19th to early 20th centuries. The Mexican Revolution of 1910-20 is particularly well documented.

NEARBY DESTINATIONS

Northwest of Pachuca along Mex. 85 is the town of **Actópan** (ahk-TOH-pahn). The name, meaning "in thick and fertile soil," is appropriate, as the town lies in a rich agricultural region. It was founded July 8, 1546, 10 years after Augustinian friars had first journeyed to the area to Christianize the indigenous people. The Toltecs, meanwhile, had arrived even earlier—perhaps as far back as the seventh century.

In the nearby mountains are rock formations known locally as **Los Frailes**, or "The Friars." According to legend, these rocks were formed when God, angry with two friars who fell in love with a beautiful woman, turned all three people into stone.

Actópan's **Templo y Convento de San Nicolas** (St. Nicholas Church and Monastery), built in 1546, is distinguished by its massive and harmonious proportions. Among the building's impressive features are its patio, Renaissance-style doorway, frescoes and Gothic cloisters. The 125-foot-tall bell tower, between the church entrance and the door to the monastery, resembles a giant vertical prism and suggests a Moorish influence. In the chapel ruins outside the church, parts of a mural fresco painted on the walls and ceiling can still be seen. Painted to impress newly converted Indians, it depicts the various punishments their souls would receive in hell if they were not good Christians.

Further west along Mex. 85, between Actópan and Ixmiquilpan, is **El Mezquital,** an Otomí Indian region known for its embroidered clothing. **Ixmiquilpan** (ees-mee-KEEL-pahn) was once the Otomí capital. The town's **Church and Monastery of St. Michael the Archangel** is a huge, medieval-style fortress/complex and former monastery dating from 1550 and founded by the Order of St. Augustine. Inside the main church are Indian frescoes depicting imaginary beasts and warriors engaged in classic combat. The **Church of El Carmen,** graced by gilded altars, also is noteworthy.

Local handiwork on display in Pátzcuaro

©Chris Sharp

Monday is market day in Ixmiquilpan; beautifully worked bags, mother-of-pearl-encrusted miniatures, guitars, wine bottle racks and Otomí belts are all for sale. Maguey is an important local crop. From this versatile plant paper, vinegar, molasses, medicines, rope and thread all are made. More potent derivatives include such alcoholic drinks as aguamiel, pulque and mezcal.

About 11 kilometers (7 miles) northeast of Pachuca via Mex. 105 is **Mineral Real del Monte**, an old mining town that overlooks Pachuca. Its narrow, extremely steep cobblestone streets and old buildings are reminiscent of a Cornish village. Most of the houses were built more than 200 years ago, after the Count of Regla abandoned area mining operations and an English firm took over. Mex. 105 continues on to the picturesque town of **Omitlán**. About 3 kilometers (1.9 miles) past Omitlán a road branches eastward off Mex. 105 to **Huasca**, another village, and the nearby 18th-century smelting haciendas of **Santa María Regla** and **San Miguel Regla**. The two complexes have been converted into historical lodgings, with rooms, restaurants and other facilities occupying many of the original buildings.

From Mineral Real del Monte a paved road travels northwest to another old mining town, **Mineral El Chico**. En route is **El Chico National Park**, characterized by enormous rock formations and cool pine woods.

PÁTZCUARO, MICHOACAN (C-7)
elev. 7,131'

Pátzcuaro (PAHTZ-kwah-roh), built on the hills sloping back from Lake Pátzcuaro, has a 16th-century atmosphere. Along with its red and cream-colored churches, mansions and other buildings erected during 3 centuries of Spanish rule, the city boasts one of Mexico's loveliest colonial plazas.

Tarasco Indians from villages surrounding Lake Pátzcuaro bring handicrafts into town each Friday on market day. Available craftwork includes copper items from the nearby village of Santa Clara del Cobre (also known as Villa Escalante), as well as lacquerware, sisal mats and rugs, silver jewelry, pottery, fabrics and woodenware. The market is especially colorful during the fiesta celebrating the Virgin of Health that begins on Dec. 8. The city's commercial center, a block north of the main plaza, is filled with vendors and crowded with handicraft shops.

Many of the colorful native dances performed throughout Mexico originated in this area. One of the most widely known is "Los Viejitos" (the little old men), a witty commentary on the manners and foibles of age.

"Deluxe" bus service is provided by Herradura de Plata between Mexico City's Terminal de Autobuses del Poniente (Western Terminal) and Pátzcuaro's Central Camionera (Central Bus Station), south of town. The local tourism office is in a building diagonally across from the northwest corner of Plaza Vasco de Quiroga, at Calle Ibarra #2. The office is the third door on the right within the courtyard. It is open Mon.-Sat. 9-2 and 4-7, Sun. 9-2; phone (434) 2-1214 (English not likely to be spoken).

The village of **Tiripetío**, about 40 kilometers (25 miles) northeast of Pátzcuaro on Mex. 120, features an Augustinian church and monastery that once housed a school of higher studies for the Tarascos. Opened in 1540, the school offered courses in philosophy, arts, law and languages. The church, claimed to have been the first university in the New World by the village's proud residents, is open as a museum.

BASILICA, on a hill 2 blocks east of the plaza, dates from 1554. The venerated Virgin of Health, on the main altar, is made from a paste of crushed cornstalks mixed with a substance extracted from orchids. Created to attract the Indians of the region to Catholicism, the image is credited with miraculous healing powers. On Dec. 8 a fiesta honors the Virgin.

Every morning women set up shop in the church's park to serve a breakfast of *corundas*, triangular tamales wrapped in corn husks, and *atole*, a warm drink made of ground cornmeal or rice that has a thick consistency and often is flavored with vanilla.

CREFAL (Centro Regional de Educación Fundamental para América Latina), on Calzada de las Américas, is a training center for Latin American schoolteachers. It offers courses in hygiene, animal husbandry, horticulture, housing and crafts. Students from CREFAL have implemented community development projects in such countries as Guatemala and Uruguay.

EL ESTRIBO (Stirrup Peak), 3.5 kilometers (2.2 miles) west of the main plaza, overlooks the lake and surrounding villages. It is reached by a steep cobblestone road. Picnicking is permitted.

ISLA JANITZIO is in the middle of Lake Pátzcuaro. The town of the same name is built in terraced fashion. *Day of the Dead* ceremonies held Nov. 1-2 include an all-night candlelight vigil in the village cemetery. The island is accessible by launch.

Statue of Morelos dominates the town and has been called "quite an accomplishment in ugliness." José María Morelos' raised arm tops the 130-foot figure, which stands nearly as tall as the Statue of Liberty. A balcony offering a magnificent view of the lake is in the cuff of his sleeve. A spiral staircase leads to the top. The climb is arduous, but the stairway walls are adorned with more than 50 somewhat deteriorated murals depicting Morelos' life. In the head of the statue is a death mask of the priest turned freedom fighter. Admission is charged.

LA CASA DE LOS ONCE PATIOS (House of the Eleven Patios), half a block south of Plaza Vasco de Quiroga, was once a convent. It now houses the studios and galleries of painters and artisans, whom visitors can watch at work. The building also contains boutiques selling handicrafts. Phone (434) 2-1214.

LAKE PATZCUARO, its placid waters dotted with islands, is one of the highest lakes in the country. Around the lakeshore are a score or more of tiny Tarasco villages, many accessible only by boat. Fishing is the chief occupation. The distinctive "butterfly" nets that once were the main tool of local fishermen now appear mostly for photographers; the fishing fleet has adopted more modern means, although traditional canoes carved from a single tree trunk are still used. the lake still yields the *pescado blanco*, a small, almost transparent whitefish that has long been a local delicacy.

MUSEO DE ARTE POPULAR Y ARQUEOLOGIA (Museum of Popular Art and Archeology) is in the former Colegio de San Nicolás. English-speaking guides are available. On the museum grounds are remains of a pre-Columbian town and pyramid. Admission is charged.

WHERE TO STAY

POSADA DE DON VASCO-BEST WESTERN
◈◈◈ *Motor Inn* (434/2-2490
All Year $67-$85 XP $20
Location: 2.5 km n on Calz de las Americas. (PO Box 15, 61600). Fax: 434/2-0262. **Facility:** Colonial style. 103 units. 4 two-bedroom units. *Bath:* combo or shower only. 2 stories, exterior corridors. **Terms:** 3 day cancellation notice. **Leisure Activities:** heated pool, tennis court, playground. **Guest Services:** [CP] & [MAP] meal plans available, valet laundry. **Business Services:** meeting rooms. **Cards:** AE, MC, VI.

PUEBLA, PUEBLA (C-11) elev. 7,091'

Puebla (PWEH-blah), capital and commercial center of the state of Puebla, lies in a large valley that is flanked by four volcanoes: Popocatépetl, Iztaccíhuatl, Malinche and Citlaltépetl (Pico de Orizaba). A product of the Spanish Conquest, Puebla was established in 1531 by colonists to whom Spain had granted lands and Indian slaves. Strategically located between the Gulf of Mexico coast and Mexico City, the city protected the capital from military attack, became a stopover for the rich and famous, and developed into a major religious center.

History was made at forts Loreto and Guadalupe on May 5, 1862, when about 4,500 poorly armed Mexicans defeated some 6,500 French troops who were attempting to establish the reign of Archduke Maximilian. Maximilian, an Austrian related to then-emperor Napoleon III of France, was crowned the "ruler" of Mexico by

France, a nation eager to add to its own empire. The victory was a glorious one for the Mexican patriots and is still celebrated nationally.

Today, Puebla is a teeming city of more than 1 million, and cars and buses clog its streets. The city that was long second in importance in New Spain is bypassed by many travelers today. There is much to see here, however, and most of the major attractions are within a short walk of the main plaza. Architecturally, Puebla is a city of contrasts. Imposing glass towers stand side by side with churches and buildings featuring ornamental wrought-iron balconies and window gratings and walls adorned with Talavera tiles. Spanish and native artisans left behind a magnificent architectural legacy, and not surprisingly, Puebla is designated a national historic monument.

The main plaza is flanked with beautiful old colonial buildings and graced by iron benches and a large fountain. The surrounding streets, narrow and cobblestoned, form a grid pattern that adheres to the classic blueprint for cities built by the Spanish in Mexico. Noted for its French Renaissance design is the **Municipal Palace**, on the plaza at Avenida de la Reforma and Calle 2 Norte.

Vivid Talavera tile, used in combination with a dark red tile, is evident throughout Puebla. Tilemakers who settled from Talavera de la Reina, near Toledo, Spain, introduced this colorful form of decorative art. Puebla was the first city in Mexico to produce these handmade Spanish wares, and they are still made today.

Talavera tileworks include **Rugerio**, Avenida 18 Poniente #111, between Avenida 5 de Mayo and Calle 3 Norte; and **Cerámica Uriarte**, Avenida 4 Poniente #911. Visitors may observe at these workshops, where the ceramics are molded, painted by hand, fired and cooled. A particularly colorful example of the use of Talavera tile can be seen at the 17th-century **Casa de los Muñecos** (House of Dolls), just off the main plaza at Calle 2 Norte. Here the tiles are in combinations of blue and yellow and yellow and green. This house is known for its whimsical mosaic caricatures of the builder's supposed enemies.

Other products include carved onyx ornaments, pottery and cotton textiles. **El Parián Market**, Calle 6 Norte #200, has existed since 1796 and offers typical crafts from different towns in the state of Puebla. **Plazuela de los Sapos**, bounded by avenidas 3 and 5 Oriente and calles 4 and 8 Sur, is lined with shops offering antique furniture as well as new furniture made to look old.

The city's *moles* (mo-LEH), the Náhuatl word for sauces, are known throughout the republic. Many of these complex concoctions were painstakingly developed by convent nuns. Popular versions are poblano, a blend of chilies and bitter chocolate; pipian, which mixes chilies and pumpkin seeds; and adobo, an unlikely pairing of cumin and oranges. A signature dish created in the city is *chile en nogada*, a spicy mix of green chilies stuffed with ground beef and topped with walnut sauce and pomegranate seeds. Locally produced fruit and liqueur desserts called *nevados* are enjoyed at the end of a meal.

The *International Music Festival* in June and July draws artists from throughout the world. The antique **Teatro Principal**, at Avenida 8 Oriente and Calle de los Artistas, dates from 1760 and is among the oldest in the Americas. It can be toured by contacting the concierge; phone (22) 32-6085.

Water recreation is enjoyed at **Valsequillo Lake**, off the road to the Africam safari park *(see attraction listing)*. Formed by the Valsequillo Dam, the lake is lined with summer homes; boat rentals and restaurants are available. **Metepec** is a resort and convention complex with sports facilities, swimming pools and restaurants. To reach it, take Mex. 190 or Mex. 190-D about 32 kilometers (20 miles) south to Atlixco, cross the main square through town and then go north about 7 kilometers (4 miles) on a paved road.

In the town of **Atlixco** a huge Indian market sets up on Saturdays. Local celebrations include *Holy Week*, Palm Sunday to Easter Sunday, and the *Huey Atlixcóyotl Fiesta* during the entire month of September. The latter is a reunion of Indian towns and features music, dance and expressions of ancestral pride. On Sept. 30, on the *Day of St. Michael the Archangel*, there is a festival on top of a nearby hill.

The tourist information office is open daily 10-8; phone (22) 46-1285. There also is a visitor information office at Boulevard Hermanos Serdán and Avenida 6 Poniente, and another at Calle 24 Sur and Avenida 11 Oriente (third floor); the latter office is open Mon.-Fri. 8-3.

Note: An earthquake in June 1999 damaged a number of Puebla's churches and other historic structures. Several attractions were closed months after the earthquake, including the Palafox Library, the Bello González Museum, the Government Palace and the Church of La Compañia. Some places of interest to visitors may still be closed due to ongoing, extensive repair work.

WHAT TO SEE IN TOWN

CASA DE LA CULTURA (House of Culture), 1 block south of the main square at Avenida 5 Oriente #5, is in the former **Palacio del Obispado** (Archbishop's Palace). The building is in the classic poblano style—patterned red brick interspersed with glazed blue-and-white tiles, windows framed in white stucco, and a flat roof

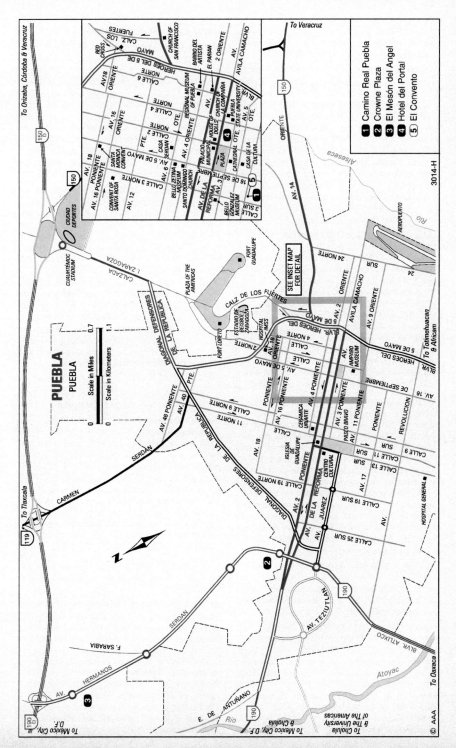

PUEBLA

Scale in Miles

Scale in Kilometers

1 Camino Real Puebla
2 Crowne Plaza
3 El Mesón del Angel
4 Hotel del Portal
5 El Convento

3014-H

© AAA

embellished with a row of white spikes. It contains a concert and lecture hall as well as the Palafox Library. Free maps of the city can be obtained here. Phone (22) 42-7692 or 46-5344.

Biblioteca Palafoxiana (Palafox Library), on the second floor, was founded in 1646 by Bishop Juan de Palafox y Mendoza. The immense room, just 20 feet wide but more than 200 feet long, contains thousands of volumes, mostly priceless bound manuscripts in Latin. Other valuable books include a 1584 atlas printed in Antwerp, Belgium, and a 16th-century Bible in four languages. Exquisitely carved cedar bookshelves protected by wire stand in three tiers above the worn red-tile floors. The reading tables are onyx with inlaid wood. Marble busts of Aristotle, Plato and other philosophers line one wall. Open Tues.-Sun. Admission is charged.

CASA DE LOS HERMANOS SERDAN (House of the Serdan Brothers), Avenida 6 Oriente between calles 2 and 4 Norte, houses the **Museum of the Revolution**. In their poblano-style home, which they had turned into an arsenal, the Serdán family played an important role in launching the revolution against dictator Porfirio Díaz. On Nov. 18, 1910, the house was surrounded by 500 federal army soldiers and policemen, who were alerted to the family's plot. During a 14-hour gunfight, several members of the family were killed; the rest were imprisoned. Bullet holes still scar the walls, floor and ceiling of the living room. Open Tues.-Sun. Admission is charged.

CATHEDRAL OF THE IMMACULATE CONCEPTION, one of the largest cathedrals in Mexico, stands on the main square. The plans were approved in 1562 by Philip II of Spain, but construction of the cathedral was not completed until 1641. The immense building is noted for its elaborately carved facade, great doors, 14 chapels and two bell towers that were erected in 1678. The interior features a gray onyx altar designed in 1799 by Manuel Tolsá, onyx sculptures carved by Tolsá, wood inlay in the choir, lovely tapestries and a collection of rare paintings. **Note:** The cathedral suffered earthquake damage, and extensive repair work is ongoing.

CENTRO CULTURAL POBLANO (Poblano Cultural Center), Reforma and Calle 13 Sur, is in the former Puebla penitentiary. It contains exposition and conference halls, a library and *hemeroteca* (newspaper collection).

CONVENTO DE SANTA ROSA, Calle 3 Norte near Avenida 12 Poniente, has a ceramics museum and a splendid 18th-century tiled kitchen. The convent has been mostly restored. According to legend, the traditional chocolate and chile sauce called *mole* was invented here by nuns who wanted to prepare a special dish for the saint's day of their bishop. The **Casa de las Artesanías** (House of Arts and Crafts), a government-sponsored craft shop, sells embroidery, onyx, lace, ceramics and other items representative of Puebla's rich cultural heritage.

FUERTES DE LORETO Y GUADALUPE (Forts Loreto and Guadalupe) commemorate the defeat of 6,500 French troops by a force of 4,500 Mexicans led by General Ignacio Zaragoza on May 5, 1862. Fort Loreto, which lies on a hill about 2.75 kilometers (1.5 miles) northeast of the main square, contains original cannons, a chapel that dates from 1780, and a museum dedicated to the battle as well as other aspects of Mexican history. Fort Guadalupe, also a site of the May 5 battle, stands just 1,500 feet away across the Plaza of the Americas. Admission is charged.

IGLESIA DE LA COMPAÑIA (Church of La Compañia), Avenida Avila Camacho, is done in the Churrigueresque style. The sacristy of the blue and white tiled church is the final resting place of a local legend, La China Poblana. Said to have been of Chinese descent, the girl was sold by pirates in Acapulco to a Puebla merchant, who adopted her and raised her as a daughter. In gratitude, La China Poblana devoted her life to helping the sick and the poor. Her standard dress, a white embroidered peasant blouse and a green and white skirt, is known as a *china poblana* dress and is the national costume for women. The skirt now includes a colorful, sequin-studded design of the Mexican eagle and is worn by young women dancing the *jarabe tapatío* (Mexican hat dance).

The church was heavily damaged by the 1999 earthquake and was closed at press time.

IGLESIA DE SAN FRANCISCO (Church of San Francisco), just off Avenida 10 Oriente at the south end of Paseo de San Francisco, is the oldest church in Puebla. It was founded in 1535; the present edifice was completed in 1667. Noted for its facade of colorful rectangular tiles, the church has a small chapel off the main altar that contains the remains of Franciscan friar Sebastián de Aparicio. Before taking his vows, Fray Sebastián was famed as the first roadbuilder in the Americas. He was beatified for his good deeds and purported miracles.

The church suffered major damage from the 1999 earthquake; only a small chapel was open at press time.

IGLESIA DE SANTO DOMINGO (Church of Santo Domingo), on 5 de Mayo between avenidas 4 Poniente and 6 Poniente, was completed in the early 17th century and features colorful tile decoration. Particularly noteworthy is the spectacularly ornate **Capilla del Rosario** (Chapel of the Rosary), which has walls and a ceiling completely covered with gold leaf and gilded stucco figures of angels, saints, children and animals. The extravagant altar features a statue of the Virgen del Rosario, crowned and adorned with jewels.

MUSEO AMPARO (Amparo Museum), Calle 2 Sur #708 at Calle 9 Oriente, contains one of the finest collections of pre-Hispanic art in Mexico, as well as colonial, modern and contemporary works. The exhibits are housed in a yellow stucco mansion—a hospital and college in former incarnations—that has a tranquil central courtyard. Near the museum entrance a 20-foot-tall stone sculpture pays tribute to corn's pre-eminent role in Mexico's early cultures.

Two floors of *salas* (halls) are filled with Olmec art, Nayarit clay figurines and other objects. In one hall a timeline charts the progression of Mesoamerican art over a 4,000-year period, comparing it to cultural developments in other parts of the world. One of the museum's most delightful works is a mural, completed in 1990 by Pedro Diego de Alvarado, that depicts four angels creating the colonial town of Puebla. Exhibit information is presented in both Spanish and English.

Large-screen televisions in the exhibit rooms broadcast explanations in English and several other languages. The musuem library contains 8,000 volumes specializing in Mexican art, archeology and history. Museum open Wed.-Mon. 10-6; library open Mon. and Wed.-Fri. 10-6, Sat. 10-4. Admission is charged; free to all Mon. Headphones that plug into the TV monitors can be rented for the pre-Hispanic exhibit areas. Phone (22) 46-4210.

MUSEO BELLO GONZALEZ (Bello González Museum), Avenida 3 Poniente #302, contains a collection of art and artifacts donated to the city by the son of José Luis Bello, a textile magnate and collector. Beautifully handcarved furniture, glassware, porcelain, gold and silver articles, paintings and ironwork from the 17th to 19th centuries are all on display. The museum's collection of Talavera pottery is among the largest in the country. Guided tours are available. Open Tues.-Sun. Admission is charged. Phone (22) 32-9475.

MUSEO BELLO ZETINA (Bello Zetina Museum), at 5 de Mayo #409 next to the Church of Santo Domingo, displays turn-of-the-20th-century antiques and religious art. Phone (22) 32-4720.

MUSEO REGIONAL DEL PUEBLA (Puebla Regional Museum), Avenida 4 Oriente and Calle 6 Norte, is in the **Casa de Alfeñique** (Sugarcake House), so called because of its ornate exterior. The 17th-century colonial mansion was a residence for visiting dignitaries. The first floor has an archeological and historical collection; the second floor is furnished in period. Admission is charged.

PLAZA OF THE AMERICAS is the exposition park complex that commemorates the centennial of the Battle of Puebla. The **Museo de Historia Natural** (Museum of Natural History), phone (22) 35-3419; **Museo de Antropología** (Anthro-

pology Museum), phone (22) 35-1478; **Planetarium**, phone (22) 35-2099; and **Escuela de Bella Artes** (School of Popular Arts) all are in the complex. A bubble-domed auditorium seats 2,000.

PUEBLA STATE UNIVERSITY, 1 block east of the cathedral, was founded in 1578 by the Jesuits. Its library contains priceless documents. The adjoining **Church of La Compañia** is one of the university buildings.

SANTUARIO DE GUADALUPE (Sanctuary of Guadalupe), on Reforma across from the Poblano Cultural Center, is one of the finest examples of the region's traditional architecture.

SECRET CONVENT OF SANTA MONICA is at Avenida 18 Poniente #103, just off 5 de Mayo. It was ordered closed when the 1857 Reform Laws abolished monasteries and convents in Mexico; the convent's nuns continued their work in semisecrecy until 1935. The museum preserves the dark corridors and austere rooms and includes a collection of religious art; the paintings on velvet by Rafael Morante have retained their brilliant colors after centuries. Guides are available. Entry to the museum is through a house and passageway. Open Tues.-Sun. Admission is charged.

NEARBY DESTINATIONS

AFRICAM, about 16 kilometers (10 miles) south and then east following the signs to Valsequillo, is a bit of Africa on the Mexican high plains. In this ecological park, such animals as lions, tigers, giraffes, buffaloes, deer and peacocks roam freely. Visitors can get out of their cars at certain locations for picture-taking opportunities. Guided tours are available. Buses to Africam depart frequently from Calle 4 Norte #1004 in Puebla. Admission is charged. Phone (22) 35-8700.

WHERE TO STAY

CAMINO REAL PUEBLA

▼▼▼ ▼▼▼   *Classic Hotel*   ((22)29-0910

7/16-11/30	$160	XP $70
12/1-7/15	$140	XP $60

Location: Just sw of the plaza. (7 Poniente 105 Centro Historico, 72000). Fax: 22/32-9251. **Facility:** Historic. Beautifully restored 16th-century convent with fountain courtyards. Individually appointed guest rooms include original colonial art, frescoes and high ceilings. 83 units. Some whirlpool units. *Bath:* combo or shower only. 4 stories, interior/exterior corridors. **Parking:** extra charge or valet. **Terms:** F. **Amenities:** honor bars. **Dining:** El Convento, see separate listing. **Guest Services:** gift shop, valet laundry. **Business Services:** conference facilities, administrative services, PC, fax. **Cards:** AE, DI, MC, VI.
(See color ad opposite inside front cover)

SOME UNITS

🆂🅳 🍽️ 🍸 ♿ 💥 📠 / ✕ 🅺 /

CROWNE PLAZA

 Hotel (22/13-7070

| All Year | $160-$180 | XP $15 |

Location: S of Mex 190D; Hermanos Serdan interchange. Ave Hermanos Serdan 141 72140. Fax: 22/13-7022. **Facility:** Attractive central pool courtyard. Contemporary-looking and well-equipped guest rooms. Meets AAA guest room security requirements. 214 units. Some whirlpool units. *Bath:* combo or shower only. 6 stories, exterior corridors. **Terms:** F12. **Amenities:** voice mail, honor bars, irons, hair dryers. *Some:* fax. **Leisure Activities:** heated pool, wading pool, playground, exercise room. **Guest Services:** gift shop, valet laundry. **Business Services:** conference facilities, administrative services. *Fee:* PC, fax. **Cards:** AE, DI, MC, VI.

EL MESON DEL ANGEL

Motor Inn (22/24-3000

| All Year | $130 | XP $8 |

Location: S of Mex 190D; Hermanos Serdan interchange. Hermanos Serdan 807 72100. Fax: 22/24-2227. **Facility:** Balcony or terrace, some with volcano view. Quiet garden areas. Meets AAA guest room security requirements. 192 units. Some whirlpool units. *Bath:* combo or shower only. 2-3 stories (no elevator), interior/exterior corridors. **Terms:** F12. **Amenities:** safes, honor bars, hair dryers. *Some:* irons. **Leisure Activities:** 2 heated pools, playground, exercise room. **Guest Services:** gift shop, valet laundry. **Business Services:** conference facilities, administrative services, PC, fax. **Cards:** AE, DI, MC, VI.

SOME UNITS

HOTEL DEL PORTAL

Hotel (22/46-0211

| All Year | $60 | XP $5 |

Location: Opposite Zocalo. (Juan De Palafox Y Mendoza 105, 72000). Fax: 22/32-3194. **Facility:** Rustic colonial decor. Some rooms with view of main city plaza. Older furnishings. Some small rooms. 98 units. *Bath:* shower only. 5 stories, interior corridors. **Terms:** 3 day cancellation notice. **Guest Services:** gift shop, valet laundry. **Business Services:** meeting rooms. **Cards:** AE, MC, VI.

WHERE TO DINE

EL CONVENTO

Continental (22/29-0909

| | L $10-$20 | D $10-$20 |

Location: Just sw of the plaza; in Camino Real Puebla. **Hours:** 1 pm-11:30 pm. Closed: Mon. **Reservations:** required. **Features:** No A/C; cocktails & lounge; valet parking; a la carte. This 16th-century ex-convent is an elegant specialty restaurant serving international fare. Surrounding walls and arches are adorned with beautiful hand painted frescoes. Some seating available facing the courtyard. **Cards:** AE, DI, MC, VI.

QUERETARO, QUERETARO (A-9) elev. 6,078'

Querétaro (keh-REH-tah-roh) lies in a valley at the base of a hill called the Sangremal. The city, founded by the Otomí Indians long before Europeans discovered the New World, became part of the Aztec Empire in the 15th century. It was captured by the Spanish in 1531 and developed as the headquarters for the Franciscan monks who established missions throughout Central America, Mexico and California.

Querétaro has played a pivotal role in Mexican history. The early 19th century saw the city as the center of rebellion against Spain. Doña Josefa (La Corregidora) and her husband, the local magistrate, formed the Society for the Study of Fine Arts to discuss poetry and politics; two of Mexico's greatest revolutionary heroes, Father Miguel Hidalgo and Capt. Ignacio Allende, often attended. In 1810, when budding plots for national independence were uncovered, Doña Josefa alerted the principal insurgents of their impending arrest.

Querétaro was the country's capital 37 years later when U.S. troops took over Mexico City; the Treaty of Guadalupe-Hidalgo, which ceded California, Arizona and New Mexico to the United States, was formulated in 1848 at the city's Academy of Fine Arts. During the War of Reform (1857-59), President Benito Juárez made Querétaro his headquarters.

Emperor Maximilian's headquarters was in the city as well; he ended his 3-year reign before a firing squad on nearby **Cerro de las Campañas** (Hill of the Bells), thus ending Europe's dream of controlling Mexico. The present Mexican constitution was drafted in Querétaro in 1917, and Mexico's dominant political party, the Partido Revolucionario Institucional (PRI), was organized in 1929.

Querétaro, a city of roughly half a million, is a manufacturing center with many industries on its outskirts. One of Mexico's largest exporters is a local company that makes transmission gearboxes for major U.S. automobile companies. Tractors, sewing machines, lift trucks, oil drilling rigs and food products also are produced. Visitors will also see pollution, congestion and poverty in this industrial city.

Most of the city's elegant colonial architecture can be found in the downtown area, where there are some shady parks and flower-filled gardens. The cobblestoned streets are narrow but well maintained. Among Querétaro's distinguished dwellings is the **Casa de la Marquesa**, at Madero #41. In the 18th century, this elegant mansion was the residence of a wealthy family of royal blood; it now houses the ISSSTE Cultural Center. Another noteworthy building is the **Convento de San Agustín**, now the Federal Palace, at Calle Allende Sur #14. This fine example of Mexican baroque architecture was built in 1731 by Ignacio Mariano de las Casas, one of Mexico's best known architects.

The city's 6-mile-long, 50-foot-high aqueduct, constructed by the Spanish more than 200 years ago, is still in use. Its 74 arches end at the **Fuente de Neptuno** (Neptune Fountain), at calles Madero and Allende.

Querétaro also is known for its gemstones, especially amethysts, opals and topaz. These should be purchased only at reputable shops; avoid sidewalk vendors. Other items associated with the area include colorful woolen articles woven in the towns of **Bernal** and **Colón**, reached by an 11-kilometer (7-mile) road leading north from an exit off Mex. 57 about 21 kilometers (13 miles) east of the city. The approach to Bernal is heralded by a 500-foot-high monolith weighing nearly 4 million tons, next to which the town lies.

The city's **Plaza de Toros Santa María** is one of the republic's best bullrings, drawing top matadors from Mexico and Spain. The main season runs from November through January.

The Secretaría de Turismo del Estado, Constituyentes Oriente #102, provides tourist information; phone (42) 13-8443, 13-8512, 13-9802, 13-9803 or 13-1311. The Casa Municipal de la Cultura, Avenida 5 de Mayo #4, can provide information on cultural events.

WHAT TO SEE

CERRO DE LAS CAMPANAS (Hill of the Bells) is on the western outskirts of the city. The hill seems to echo the pivotal role that Querétaro has played in Mexican history as witness to the ebb and flow of dictatorship and democracy. It was the site of Archduke Maximilian's last battle, and it was at this location that he was executed by a firing squad on June 19, 1867.

A monument erected by the government in honor of Benito Juárez, who defeated the ill-fated "Emperor of Mexico," is at the top of a hill behind the **Capilla de la Piedad**. This neoclassic chapel, erected by the Austrian government in 1901, is dedicated to Maximilian. Stelae mark the spots where Maximilian and his two Mexican generals, Miramón and Mejía, fell. In the **Museo del Sitio de Querétaro en 1867**, a small museum near the chapel, are several photographs taken in that year.

The Austrian nobleman once said that the letter "M" was his condemnation, and history seems to bear him out: His name, the name of the country he wanted to govern and the names of the three most important generals in his Mexican army all began with "M."

IGLESIA DE SAN FRANCISCO (Church of San Francisco), opposite the main square on Calle 5 de Mayo, dates from 1545 and dominates Plaza Obregón. The colored tiles of its dome were brought from Spain in 1540. It houses a collection of 17th-, 18th- and 19th-century religious paintings. A figure of Santiago adorns the doorway of the church.

IGLESIA DE SANTA CLARA (Church of Santa Clara) is on the Plaza de Santa Clara. Founded in 1633 and reconstructed during the 18th century by the architect Tresguerras, the church had one

of Mexico's richest nunneries. It is noted for its ornately carved interior and delicate exterior ironwork. The Fountain of Neptune in front of the building was also designed by Tresguerras.

IGLESIA DE SANTA ROSA DE VITERBO (Church of Santa Rosa de Viterbo), General Arteaga and Calle Ezequiel Montes, is an early reconstruction work by Tresguerras. Oriental influences are visible in the 1752 church's bell tower, fashioned after a pagoda, and in its flying buttresses, flanked by dragon faces. The interior is a mass of gilt, carved wood with inlaid marble and filigree work. The adjoining monastery is a hospital.

IGLESIA Y CONVENTO DE LA CRUZ (Church and Convent of the Cross), Avenida Venustiano Carranza and Calle Acuña, was one of the largest monasteries in the country. It played a prominent role in 17th- and 18th-century missionary activity in northern Mexico, the southwestern United States and Central America. As many as 200 monks lived in the mission compound, which consists of well-preserved cloisters, cells, an orchard, a kitchen with a cold storage chamber, several schools and an enclosed reservoir.

Standing watch over the church plaza are statues of Querétaro's founders and other figures important to the city's early history, including Fray Junípero Serra, the Jesuit who established nine of California's 22 missions. The monastery also served as Maximilian's army barracks and later, after his defeat in 1867, as his prison. The ashes of the heroine La Corregidora are encased in a monument behind the church.

MUSEO PIO MARIANO (Regional Museum) is in the former monastery next to the Church of San Francisco. It houses colonial relics; uniforms and weaponry; the desk at which sat the war council that sentenced Archduke Maximilian to death; the press that printed the first copies of the 1917 Political Constitution; 17th-, 18th- and 19th-century paintings by Juan Correa, Villalpando, Cabrera and Luis Rodríguez; and a library of more than 8,000 books, mostly parchment tomes from the 17th and 18th centuries.

The museum's huge, hand-lettered choir books were intended to be legible to singers in a gallery above the choirmaster. Adjoining the museum on the south is an artisans' cooperative where regional handicrafts are sold. Admission is charged.

PALACIO MUNICIPAL (Old City Hall), at the north end of Plaza de la Independencia, was the original Casas Reales of the Spanish governors and the former home of La Corregidora, the heroine of the 1810 War of Independence. Under house arrest, she whispered instructions through a keyhole to a messenger to warn insurgents Father Miguel Hidalgo and Capt. Ignacio Allende in the nearby town of Dolores. As a result, Hidalgo immediately issued his famous cry (*grito*) for independence. More than 50 years later,

Archduke Maximilian presided over many meetings in the building. Visitors are shown the keyhole. The building now serves as the governor's office.

PLAZA DE LA INDEPENDENCIA (Independence Plaza) is a little park surrounded by arcaded colonial buildings. Prominent among these is the **Casa Municipal de la Cultura** (Municipal House of Culture), a sumptuous 18th-century mansion. A monument commemorating the Marqués de la Villa del Villar del Aguila, who was instrumental in building the city aqueduct, is in the middle of the plaza.

PLAZA OBREGON (Obregón Plaza), in the center of the city, is the scene of band concerts and folk music on Thursday and Sunday evenings. A classical fountain is dedicated to Hebe, the Greek goddess of youth.

WHERE TO STAY

AZTECA PARADOR HOTEL
▼▼▼ *Motor Inn* (42/34-0592
All Year $25-$40 XP $5
Location: On Mex 57, 14.5 km n of Mex 45 interchange. (AP 98-C, 76000). Fax: 42/34-0592. **Facility:** In northern outskirts of city. Adjacent to Pemex station. 44 units. 4 two-bedroom units and 4 efficiencies. *Bath:* shower only. 2 stories, interior/exterior corridors. **Terms:** F12; utensil deposit required. **Leisure Activities:** heated pool. **Guest Services:** valet laundry. **Cards:** AE, MC, VI.

HOLIDAY INN - QUERETARO
▼▼▼▼ *Motor Inn* ((42)16-0202
All Year $135 XP $15
Location: On Mex 57, 1 km n of 45 and 45D interchange, exit Cinco de Febrero. Av 5 de Febrero 110 Col Ninos Heroes 76010 (Apartado Postal 95). Fax: 42/16-8902. **Facility:** Spanish colonial atmosphere with colorful gardens. Meets AAA guest room security requirements. 171 units. 3 stories, interior corridors. **Parking:** valet. **Terms:** F18; cancellation fee imposed. **Amenities:** voice mail, irons, hair dryers. *Some:* honor bars. **Leisure Activities:** heated pool, wading pool, whirlpool, 2 lighted tennis courts, playground, exercise room, sports court. **Guest Services:** gift shop, valet laundry. **Business Services:** conference facilities, administrative services, fax. **Cards:** AE, DI, MC, VI.

SOME UNITS

HOTEL HACIENDA JURICA QUERETARO
▼▼▼▼ *Historic Motor Inn* ((42)18-0022
9/1-11/30	$132-$150
5/1-8/31	$128-$145
1/1-4/30	$124-$140
12/1-12/31	$120-$135
Location: N Jurica exit Mex 57, then 4 km w. (PO Box 338, 76100). Fax: 42/18-0136. **Facility:** Converted 17th-century hacienda. Attractive landscaping. Artistic cobblestone walkways. 182 units. Some suites and whirlpool units. *Bath:* some shower or tub only. 2 stories, interior corridors. **Parking:** valet. **Terms:** 5 day cancellation notice. **Amenities:** honor bars, hair dryers. **Leisure Activities:** heated pool, wading pool, 2 lighted tennis courts, playground. *Fee:* golf-18 holes, horseback riding. **Guest Services:** gift shop, valet laundry. *Fee:* area transportation. **Business Services:** conference facilities. **Cards:** AE, DI, MC, VI.

FEE
SOME UNITS

HOTEL MESON DE SANTA ROSA
▼▼▼ *Classic Motel* (42/24-2623
All Year $90-$160 XP $15
Location: In center on Plaza de Independencia. (Pasteur Sur 17 Plaza de Independencia, 76000). Fax: 42/12-5522. **Facility:** Historic. Restored 18th-century guest house. Spacious rooms, a few with private balcony overlooking attractive inner courtyard. Meets AAA guest room security requirements. 21 units. 2 stories, interior corridors. **Parking:** extra charge or valet. **Terms:** F12. **Amenities:** safes, honor bars. **Leisure Activities:** heated pool. **Guest Services:** valet laundry. **Business Services:** meeting rooms. **Cards:** AE, MC, VI.

HOTEL MISION LA MANSION PARK PLAZA
▼▼▼▼ *Historic Motor Inn* (42/71-0030
All Year $98 XP $10
Location: On Mex 45 and 57, 37 km e at Km 172. 76800 (PO Box 128, SAN JUAN DEL RIO, QU). Fax: 42/31-0096. **Facility:** Sprawling 16th-century hacienda with extensive landscaped gardens. 134 units. Some whirlpool units. *Bath:* combo or shower only. 2 stories, interior corridors. **Terms:** 3 day cancellation notice. **Amenities:** *Some:* safes, honor bars, hair dryers. **Leisure Activities:** heated pool, 2 tennis courts, playground. *Fee:* golf-18 holes, bicycles. **Guest Services:** gift shop, valet laundry. **Business Services:** conference facilities, fax. **Cards:** AE, DI, DS, MC, VI.

HOTEL REAL DE MINAS
▼▼▼ *Motor Inn* (42/16-0444
All Year $75-$87 XP S7
Location: Off Mex 57; next to the Bull Ring. Libre Celaya Hwy 76140. Fax: 42/16-0662. **Facility:** Colonial atmosphere. Large pool and lawn area. 200 units. Some suites ($150-$190) and whirlpool units. *Bath:* combo or shower only. 2 stories, interior corridors. **Parking:** extra charge. **Leisure Activities:** heated pool, wading pool, 7 lighted tennis courts, playground. **Guest Services:** gift shop, valet laundry. **Business Services:** conference facilities. **Cards:** AE, DI, MC, VI.

LA CASA DE LA MARQUESA

▼▼▼ ▼▼▼   *Classic Country Inn*   (42/12-0092

12/1-1/4 & 3/16-11/30	$190	XP $35
1/5-3/15	$170	XP $30

Location: In downtown historic district. Madero 41 Esquina Allende 76000. **Fax:** 42/12-0098. **Facility:** Historic. Spectacular 1700s country inn, splendidly restored with beautiful courtyard, handpainted murals, elegant public areas and luxurious guest rooms. Formerly home to emperors and presidents. 25 units. Some whirlpool units. *Bath:* combo or shower only. 2 stories, exterior corridors. **Parking:** extra charge or valet. **Terms:** D6; age restrictions may apply, 3 day cancellation notice-fee imposed. **Guest Services:** [CP] meal plan available, complimentary evening beverages, valet laundry. **Cards:** AE, MC, VI.

WHERE TO DINE

EL COMEDOR DE LA MARQUESA   *Historical*

▼▼▼   *Continental*   (42/12-0092
                     L $10-$15   D $15-$20

Location: In downtown historic district; in La Casa de la Marquesa. Madero 41, Esq Allende 76000. **Hours:** 7 am-11 pm. **Reservations:** suggested. **Features:** No A/C; semiformal attire; cocktails & lounge; entertainment; valet parking; a la carte. Fine International cuisine including a few exotic game entrees. **Cards:** AE, MC, VI.

RESTAURANTE BAR 1810

▼▼ ▼▼▼   *Continental*   (42/14-3324
                      L $6-$8   D $6-$8

Location: Plaza Independencia; in historic district. Andador La Libertad 60 76000. **Hours:** 8 am-11 pm. Closed: 1/1, 12/24. **Reservations:** suggested. **Features:** No A/C; children's menu; cocktails & lounge; street parking; a la carte. International and Mexican specialties. Lively atmosphere that includes an outdoor patio in the main city plaza. Attentive, well-trained staff in white shirt and black vest round out your meal in the heart of this colonial city. **Cards:** AE, MC, VI.

SAN JUAN DEL RIO,
QUERETARO (B-9)   elev. 6,498'

San Juan del Río (sahn hwan dehl REE-oh), noted for semiprecious stones, woodcarvings, baskets and palm furniture, is located in a prosperous agricultural region that yields corn, dairy products and wine. This picturesque community was once an important stop on the stagecoach route to Mexico City. San Juan del Río features many buildings painted white and enhanced by decorative elements of dark brown carved stone.

Also near San Juan del Río are the Trinidad opal mines. Opals and amethysts are polished in town; gems should be purchased only at established shops. The town of Cadereyta, 50 kilometers (31 miles) north of Mex. 57-D on Mex. 120, has an extensive cactus nursery, one of Mexico's largest.

Nearby is **Hacienda Galindo**; to reach it, take the San Juan del Río exit off Mex. 57-D (at Km marker 172), then go about 6 kilometers (4 miles) south on two-lane Mex. 120 (follow the signs for Galindo/Amealco). Built in the mid-16th century, legend says the hacienda was a romantic gift from Hernán Cortés to his Indian

interpreter and mistress, La Malinche. During the 19th century it was the headquarters of a regional livestock breeding operation, and some of Mexico's best fighting bulls continue to be raised in this area. The building was converted to a colonial-style resort property in the 1970s and is popular as a weekend retreat for well-to-do Mexico City families. Breakfast on the veranda of the hacienda's sun-dappled courtyard is a delightful experience; follow it up with a stroll around the attractively landscaped grounds.

WHERE TO STAY

FIESTA AMERICANA HACIENDA GALINDO

▼▼▼ ▼▼▼   *Historic Motor Inn*   (42/75-0250

All Year	$111-$140	XP $10

Location: On Mex 45 and 57, exit km 172, 6 km s on Mex 120 toward Morelia. (PO Box 16, 76800). Fax: 42/75-0300. **Facility:** Large converted 16th-century hacienda, extensively decorated with period art. Beautiful grounds. 166 units, 1 with kitchen. Some suites ($120-$140) and whirlpool units. 3 stories, interior corridors. **Parking:** valet. **Terms:** F12. **Amenities:** honor bars. **Leisure Activities:** heated pool, wading pool, miniature golf, 6 tennis courts (Fee: 3 lighted), racquetball court, hiking trails, jogging, playground. *Fee:* horseback riding. **Guest Services:** gift shop, valet laundry. **Business Services:** conference facilities, administrative services. **Cards:** AE, DI, MC, VI.

SAN LUIS POTOSI,
SAN LUIS POTOSI (F-7)   elev. 6,157'

San Luis Potosí (sahn loo-EES poh-toh-SEE), capital of the state of the same name, dates from the late 1500s when it was established as a mining settlement. Today it is sprawling city with more than half a million residents, and the local economy is no longer based on gold, silver, lead and copper production.

The city was seat of the national government under President Benito Juárez in 1863 and again in 1867. While here in 1854, González Bocanegra wrote the Mexican national anthem, first sung in Mexico City's Santa Ana Theater on Sept. 15 of that year. The San Luis Plan, drafted by Francisco Madero while he was imprisoned in the city by dictator Porfirio Díaz, set the stage for the Revolution of 1910.

A distribution point for foreign and domestic merchandise, San Luis Potosí's atmosphere is largely industrial. Tanneries, flour mills, smelters, textile mills, breweries and furniture factories are among the manufacturing concerns, and highways around the city and within the state are busy with truck traffic.

San Luis Potosí is not all soot and smoke. It has a well-preserved colonial center, anchored by **Plaza de Armas**, the main square. The plaza is flanked by the city's 18th-century cathedral and the Government Palace. Among the wares on display at the **Mercado Hidalgo** (Hidalgo Market) are prized Santa María *rebozos* (shawl-like garments), which are so fine they can be pulled through a woman's wedding ring; pottery; and a candy called *queso de tuna* made from the fruit of the prickly pear cactus. Calle Hidalgo is a pedestrian mall flanked by some of San Luis Potosí's finest shops and stores.

The **Plaza España** bullring is on Avenida Universidad, near the southeastern corner of Alameda Park. Across from the north side of Alameda Park is the city's modern railway station, where a series of Fernando Leal frescoes depict the history of transportation in Mexico.

About 56 kilometers (35 miles) south of the city via Mex. 57 are two spas known for their medicinal waters. **Lourdes Spa**, just outside Santa María del Río, has strongly alkaline, radioactive waters that purportedly benefit intestinal ailments. **El Gogorrón National Park** is accessible from a paved road that branches southwest off Mex. 57 to the village of Villa de Reyes; its thermal pools and many springs are reputed to alleviate circulatory problems and rheumatism.

Since it can be difficult to drive on the potholed and cobblestoned streets in the older section of the city, one sightseeing alternative is a guided tour. City tours depart from Plaza Fundadores, behind the Government Palace, at 9 a.m.; to request one phone (48) 12-2178. For local tourist information contact SECTUR Mon.-Fri. 9-3 and 5-7; phone (48) 14-3692 or 12-0906 (English spoken). To contact the Green Angels phone (48) 12-6063.

WHAT TO SEE

CASA DE LA CULTURA (House of Culture), Carranza #1815, is an art museum that exhibits the work of both national and regional artists. Admission is charged. Phone (48) 13-2247.

CERRO DE SAN PEDRO, 8 kilometers (5 miles) east on Mex. 70 to signs, then 13 kilometers (8 miles) north, is a ghost town containing the ruins of shops, churches, estates and a hospital. It was founded in 1583 after several mines in the vicinity began operations. By the late 1940s, the gold, lead, iron, manganese and mercury deposits finally began to give out. The section of town known as "La Colonia de los Gringos" contains what once were company offices and living quarters of the American Smelting and Refining Co.

Local firms continue to extract limited quantities of minerals from the mines. Visitors can enter **La Descubridora**, the town's first mine. Guide service is available.

IGLESIA DE NUESTRA SEÑORA DEL CARMEN (Church of Our Lady of El Carmen), on Plaza del Carmen, is an ornate baroque structure with domes of blue, green, yellow and white tiles. The interior contains a carved pulpit, a reredos by Tresguerras, paintings by Vallejo and a baroque altar considered one of the most impressive in Mexico.

MUSEO DEL CENTRO TAURINO POTOSINO (Bullfighting Center Museum of San Luis Potosí), calles Universidad and López Hermosa, contains an extensive collection of such bullfighting memorabilia as photographs, posters, clothing and equipment of famous matadors. The museum also features a bullfighting archives. Spanish-speaking guides are available. Free.

MUSEO NACIONAL DE LA MASCARA (National Museum of Regional Masks) is at Villerías #2, between Calle Guerrero and Plaza del Carmen. Housed in an architecturally interesting pink mansion that dates from the 18th century, the museum displays an assortment of masks from throughout Mexico. Many of the masks, some of which date from pre-Hispanic times, are still used during fiestas and other celebrations. Open Tues.-Sun. Phone (48) 12-3025.

MUSEO REGIONAL (Regional Museum), Calle Galeana #450, is housed in the former Convent of San Francisco. It contains artifacts, historical documents and other items dating from the 16th century. The impressive 17th-century **Aranzazú Chapel** is in the rear of the museum. The adjacent church, which faces the plaza, is part of the building as well. Open Tues.-Sun. Admission is charged. Phone (48) 12-5185.

MUSEO REGIONAL DE ARTE POPULAR (Regional Museum of Popular Art), Parque Tangamanga #1, displays crafts from throughout the state, with emphasis on the Huastec region of northeastern Mexico. Displays include chairs, baskets, wooden items, pottery and a wax altar. There also is an exhibit pertaining to the creation of the area's celebrated Santa María shawls. Open Tues.-Sun. Phone (48) 12-7521.

PALACIO DE GOBIERNO (Government Palace), a neoclassic structure across the Plaza de Armas from the cathedral, dates from 1770. Here Benito Juárez, despite petitions for mercy from all over the world, denied clemency to Archduke Maximilian; the deposed emperor was subsequently executed at Querétaro. A wax tableau and a portrait gallery in the **Juárez Room** recall the event.

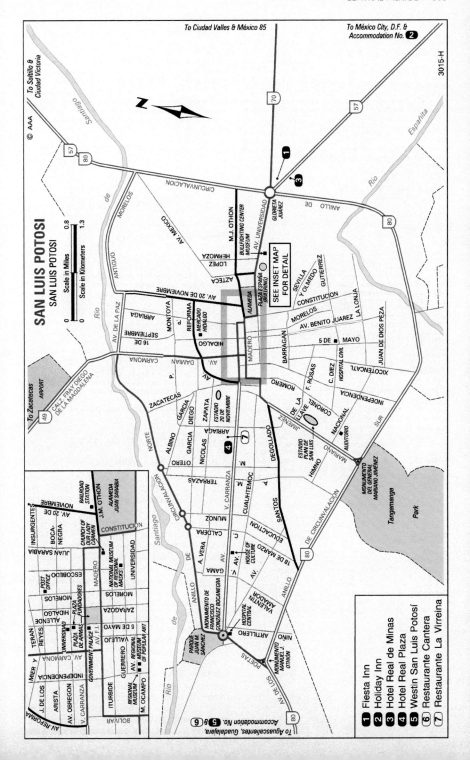

SAN LUIS POTOSI
SAN LUIS POTOSI

To Ciudad Valles & México 85

To México City, D.F. &
Accommodation No. 2

© AAA

To Saltillo &
Ciudad Victoria

3015-H

Scale in Miles
0   0.8
Scale in Kilometers
0   1.3

To Zacatecas

AIRPORT

CALZ. FRAY DIEGO
DE LA MAGDALENA

SEE INSET MAP
FOR DETAIL

Tangamanga
Park

To Aguascalientes, Guadalajara,
Accommodation No. 5 & 6

1 Fiesta Inn
2 Holiday Inn
3 Hotel Real de Minas
4 Hotel Real Plaza
5 Westin San Luis Potosí
6 Restaurante Cantera
7 Restaurante La Virreina

WHERE TO STAY

FIESTA INN

 *Motor Inn* ((48)22-1995

1/1-11/30	$120-$137	XP $14
12/1-12/31	$112-$127	XP $10

Location: On Mex 57; 1 km se of Glorieta Juarez. Carr 57 Lado Sur Dist Juarez 78390 (PO Box 393). Fax: 48/22-0550. **Facility:** Attractive rooms. Extremely well maintained. Meets AAA guest room security requirements. 105 units. 2 two-bedroom units. *Bath:* combo or shower only. 2 stories, exterior corridors. **Terms:** F12; cancellation fee imposed. **Amenities:** voice mail. **Leisure Activities:** heated pool, playground, exercise room. **Guest Services:** area transportation, valet laundry. **Business Services:** conference facilities, administrative services, fax. **Cards:** AE, DI, MC, VI.

SOME UNITS

HOLIDAY INN

 *Motor Inn* (48/34-4100

All Year	$96	XP $12

Location: 5 km se on Mex 57. (PO Box F-1893, 78090). Fax: 48/18-6105. **Facility:** Large pool and lawn areas. Walled-in parking. 210 units. Some suites ($150-$295) and whirlpool units. 2-3 stories, interior/exterior corridors. **Terms:** F15. **Amenities:** voice mail, honor bars. *Some:* irons, hair dryers. **Leisure Activities:** heated pool, wading pool, lighted tennis court, playground, exercise room. **Guest Services:** gift shop, valet laundry. **Business Services:** conference facilities, administrative services, PC, fax. **Cards:** AE, DI, MC, VI.

SOME UNITS

HOTEL REAL DE MINAS

 *Motor Inn* (48/18-2616

All Year	$89	XP $5

Location: On Mex 57; 1 km se of Glorieta Juarez. 78090 (PO Box F-1371). Fax: 48/18-6915. **Facility:** Quiet atmosphere, attractive landscaping. 178 units. *Bath:* combo or shower only. 2 stories, interior/exterior corridors. **Terms:** F11; 3 day cancellation notice. **Leisure Activities:** children's program. **Guest Services:** valet laundry. **Business Services:** conference facilities, administrative services. **Cards:** AE, MC, VI.

FEE

HOTEL REAL PLAZA

 *Hotel* (48/14-6055

All Year	$42	XP $6

Location: In heart of downtown. Ave Carranza 890 78250. Fax: 48/14-6639. **Facility:** Somewhat dated guest room furnishings and decor, yet comfortable and well-maintained. 270 units. *Bath:* shower only. 9 stories, interior corridors. **Terms:** F12; 3 day cancellation notice. **Guest Services:** gift shop, valet laundry. *Fee:* area transportation. **Business Services:** meeting rooms. **Cards:** AE, MC, VI.

FEE

WESTIN SAN LUIS POTOSI

 *Hotel* ((48)25-0125

7/1-11/30	$200	XP $25
2/1-6/30	$175	XP $25
12/1-1/31	$155	XP $20

Location: 3.5 km sw on Carretera SLP-Guadalajara. Real de Lomas 1000 78210. Fax: 48/25-0200. **Facility:** Upscale colonial themes. Quiet courtyard areas. 123 units. 1 two-bedroom unit. Some whirlpool units. 3 stories, exterior corridors. **Parking:** valet. **Terms:** F12; cancellation fee imposed, package plans. **Amenities:** honor bars. *Some:* safes. **Leisure Activities:** heated pool. **Guest Services:** gift shop, area transportation, valet laundry. **Business Services:** conference facilities, fax. **Cards:** AE, CB, DI, MC, VI.

FEE
SOME UNITS

WHERE TO DINE

RESTAURANTE CANTERA

 *Continental* (48/25-0125

L $6-$12　D $10-$30

Location: 3.5 km sw on Carretera SLP-Guadalajara; in the Westin San Luis Potosi. Real Lomas 1000 78210. **Reservations:** suggested. **Features:** dressy casual; cocktails & lounge; valet parking; a la carte, buffet. **Cards:** AE, CB, DI, MC, VI.

RESTAURANTE LA VIRREINA　*Historical*

 *Continental* (48/12-3750

L $8-$14　D $12-$22

Location: 1 km w on Mex 80; in center of downtown. Ave V Carranza 830 78230. **Hours:** 1:30 pm-11 pm. Closed: 1/1, 12/25. **Reservations:** suggested; for dinner. **Features:** semi-formal attire; children's menu; cocktails; entertainment; fee for area transportation. Elegantly styled in remodeled Maximilian-period mansion. **Cards:** AE, DI, MC, VI.

SAN MIGUEL DE ALLENDE, GUANAJUATO (A-8) elev. 6,134'

You sense that San Miguel de Allende (pronounced a-YEHN-deh) is special before you even get there. The feeling is reinforced in subtle ways: a family selling snacks along the roadside, a horse and rider clip-clopping contentedly in the distance, brown hills brightened by wildflowers. At this altitude the air has a refreshing coolness, even though the sun is bright. Small clusters of dwellings—tiny cement cubes with tin roofs—and dirt yards exhibit obvious poverty, but somehow seem less grim than the vast shantytowns ringing Mexico City.

Mex. 111, a local two-lane road that branches west off highway Mex. 57-D, is an unlikely gateway to the charm that defines San Miguel. Its outskirts have that everyday scruffiness common to most Mexican towns—dilapidated gas stations mix with newer commercial development in a small-scale version of "suburban sprawl." But as Mex. 111 twists and turns toward the center of town, things start to change. The street narrows and becomes cobbled. Aged buildings rub shoulders along a sidewalk barely wide enough for one pedestrian, let alone two. Open shop doorways offer quick glimpses of clothing and crafts.

Suddenly you're at a scenic overlook, a pulloff with a small parking area. A few vendors sit beside their wares—piles of woven baskets, perhaps, or neatly arranged rows of painted ceramic figurines. Below a protective wrought-iron fence the town spreads out, filling a bowl-shaped valley. Squat, flat-roofed, earth-toned buildings line the steep hillsides, interspersed with green clumps of trees. One structure towers above the others: multispired **La Parroquia**, the parish church *(see attraction listing)*, which functions as both visual landmark and spiritual focus for a venerable settlement founded in 1542 by the Franciscan monk Juan de San Miguel.

San Miguel began as a mission where Indians were evangelized and also taught European weaving and agricultural techniques. As it prospered, the settlement became a local market center for the surrounding haciendas trading in cattle and textiles. Historical significance made its mark as well: Here native son Ignacio Allende, along with Father Miguel Hidalgo y Costilla, a priest from the neighboring town of Dolores Hidalgo, planned the original uprising that led to Mexico's bitter and protracted War of Independence. When San Miguel officially became a city in 1826, "Allende" was added to its name to honor the freedom fighter.

This new status didn't stem the period of decline San Miguel endured for the remainder of the 19th century, a slow slide from prosperity related directly to the subsiding of mining operations. But exactly a century later, in 1926, the Mexican government designated it a national historic monument, and preservation measures began in earnest. Modern construction was prohibited in the city center; crumbling old buildings were carefully restored. Foreigners began moving in during the 1930s, and today there is an established North American expatriate community of artisans, teachers, writers and part-time residents.

THE INFORMED TRAVELER

The **Guanajuato/León Airport** is in León, about 2 hours away. Aeroméxico, American, Continental and Mexicana airlines offer flights from selected U.S. cities. Buses operated by AeroPlus meet all flights and shuttle passengers between the airport and San Miguel. More expensive taxi service also is available. For additional information about airlines *see "Arriving by Air," page 53*.

"Deluxe" bus service from Mexico City's Terminal Central de Autobuses del Norte is provided daily by ETN, Flecha Amarilla and Primera Plus. The trip takes about 4 hours, including a stop in Querétaro. Local buses covering the same route make numerous stops. Flecha Amarilla buses also provide frequent service between San Miguel and Guanajuato. The central bus station is on the westward extension of Calle Canal, about 3 kilometers (2 miles) west of the center of town. For additional information about buses *see "Bus Service," page 63*. Taxis provide flat-rate service between the bus station and downtown, as well as to other locations around the city. There is a *sitio* (cab stand) at the main plaza.

By car, the 180-mile journey from Mexico City takes 3 to 4 hours via Mex. 57-D to the Querétaro toll bypass (watch for the San Miguel exit). The bypass highway crosses Mex. 57-D north of Querétaro and connects with Mex. 111, which proceeds northwest to San Miguel. From Guanajuato, take Mex. 110 northeast to Dolores Hidalgo, then Mex. 51 south. As is the case with Mex. 111, the trip along these two-lane routes is slow but scenic, offering views of typical Mexican rural life.

Note: Street parking is scarce in the congested historic center, and local police do not hesitate to issue violators a ticket. If driving from Mexico City or elsewhere, you may have to park several blocks from the center. If you're staying in town and have a car, leave it at your hotel and use public transportation. The altitude may initially tire visitors not used to walking at higher elevations.

La Parroquia, San Miguel's parish church   ©John Neubauer

The tourist office is on the southeastern corner of the main plaza, next to La Parroquia. It is open Mon.-Fri. 10-2:45 and 5-7, Sat.-Sun. 10-noon; phone (415) 2-1747 (English spoken).

Banks along Calle San Francisco exchange currency Mon.-Fri. 9-1:30, but the *casas de cambio* (currency exchange offices) located in the center of town are a quicker alternative.

San Miguel's weather is similar to Guanajuato's: warm and dry most of the year. April and May are the warmest months, but the city rarely experiences the extremes of heat common to much of Mexico. Winter nights can be chilly, and many hotels aren't heated (although some have fireplaces). The rainy season is June through September.

EXPLORING AROUND TOWN

Some travelers complain that San Miguel's "gentrification," so to speak, has replaced authentic Mexican atmosphere with a touristy vibe—trendy restaurants, pricey boutiques and a lack of local grit. But a stroll through the historic center proves that these complaints are primarily quibbles. Here there is atmosphere to spare, whether it's intricate stone carvings adorning the doors and windows of handsome old buildings or the extravagant beauty of their sheltered inner patios, cool retreats filled with trees, burbling fountains, clipped hedges and flowerpot urns.

There's a sense of discovery along the narrow streets that sparks curiosity as to what's around the next corner. You'll see other tourists but also have plenty of opportunities to mingle with locals—perhaps children who shyly ask if you want to buy some gum (*"Chicle"?*), or an elderly gentleman whiling away the afternoon at **El Jardín**, the main plaza.

Make the plaza, located between calles San Francisco and Correo, your first stop. Shaded by Indian laurel trees, it's a great place to relax on a wrought-iron bench, listen to the tolling bells of La Parroquia and observe the local scene. Buy a cold drink from a vendor and plan the day's itinerary. Most of the city's attractions are within walking distance of the plaza, and the historic center is compact. **Note:** Wear comfortable shoes; the streets tend to be steep and cobblestoned.

San Miguel's reputation as an arts center was established by the opening of the **Allende Institute**, southwest of downtown at Calle Ancha de San Antonio #20. One of its American founders, Stirling Dickinson, came to Mexico as a tourist in the 1930s and fell in love with the city. A painter and engraver, he helped inaugurate the institute in 1950 and was its director until 1987.

The lovely old building housing the school was once owned by the wealthy Canal family. Fountains, arcades and courtyard gardens grace the grounds of the campus, which has extensive classroom space, two art galleries, a theater and a library. Students from throughout the Americas take advantage of the art and language classes offered, and the institute also functions as a campus abroad for several American and Canadian art schools.

The **Centro Cultural Bellas Artes** (Bellas Artes Cultural Center), about 2 blocks west of the main plaza at Calle Hernández Macías #75, also is called the Centro Cultural el Nigromante (its official name) and the Centro Cultural Ignacio Ramírez. It is a branch of the well-known Instituto Nacional de Bellas Artes (National Institute of Fine Arts) in Mexico City. The impressive building, which dates from the mid-18th century, was once the Convento de la Concepción (Convent of the Conception) and has an immense, tree-shaded courtyard. It offers music, dance and visual arts classes; a bulletin board lists lectures and concerts given both here and elsewhere in the city. Several murals also are exhibited, including one by David Alfaro Siqueiros.

Saturday morning "adventure" tours to local handicraft workshops and out-of-town points of interest such as haciendas, ranches, vineyards or a monastery benefit the **Centro de Crecimiento**, a school for handicapped children that is supported through donations. The 3-hour tour departs from the main square at 10:30 a.m.; tickets are sold beginning at 9:30. The cost is 150 pesos (around $15).

The **Travel Institute of San Miguel**, Calle Cuna de Allende #11, sponsors city walking tours and excursions to various local sites; phone (4) 152-1630. For information about local happenings, consult the weekly English-language newspaper *Atención San Miguel*, which is available at the El Colibri bookstore, about 2 blocks east of the main plaza at Calle Sollano #30.

Siesta Tours South, Inc. specializes in tours of San Miguel as well as nearby Guanajuato, Pátzcuaro and Morelia (*see separate listings*). For information phone (352) 371-4406 or (800) 679-2746.

Travelers who want to hook up to the Internet or send email while in San Miguel can do so at Unisono, in the heart of town at Hernández Macías #72B. It offers a local dial-up connection and full cyber cafe services, and the staff speaks English.

SHOPPING

San Miguel is known for the variety and quality of its regionally produced handicrafts. Metalwork—masks, trays, lanterns, picture frames and decorative objects made of tin, copper, brass, bronze and wrought iron—and the designs of local silversmiths are particularly worth seeking out. Also available are pottery, weavings, sculpture, straw items, hand-loomed *cambaya* cloth (a material frequently used to make skirts), and folk and traditional art. The colonial furniture is some of the finest produced in Mexico. Most craft and gift shops are open Mon.-Sat. 9-7 and close from 2-4 for the traditional *siesta;* a few may open briefly on Sunday. Many accept U.S. dollars and/or MasterCard and VISA, and some will pack and ship purchases.

Open-air **Mercado Ignacio Ramírez**, the city market, fills the plaza in front of the Oratorio de San Felipe Neri (Church of San Felipe Neri), northeast of the main plaza, and usually spreads onto the surrounding streets. Livestock and fresh produce share space with inexpensive everyday items and souvenirs at the cheaper end of the price scale. The **Mercado de Artesanías** (Crafts Market) consists of vendor stalls in an alley off Calle Loreto, near the Quinta Loreto Hotel (several blocks north of the main plaza).

Pricier boutiques are scattered throughout the downtown area. **Casa Cohen,** just north of the main plaza at Calle Reloj #12, carries furniture, brass and bronze bowls and plates, and objects made of carved stone. **Casa Maxwell**, Calle Canal #14, has an array of Mexican and Latin American folk art, plus ceramics, jewelry, glassware and furniture. **Veryka**, Calle Zacateros #6A, also sells Latin American folk art. **Casa Anguiano**, at the corner of calles Canal and Hernández Macías, features embroidered fabrics and copperware. If you're looking for silver jewelry, browse through **Joyería David**, Calle Zacateros #53.

Art galleries are concentrated around the main plaza, and exhibit openings are big social events. Two that showcase both regional and national talent are **Galería San Miguel**, Plaza Principal #14, and **Galería Atenea**, Calle Cuna de Allende #15.

Dining, Nightlife and Events

Despite its small size, San Miguel has a number of restaurants offering a wide range of cuisines—from reliable French and Italian to regional Mexican to such unexpected choices as Tex-Mex and vegetarian. Much of this variety has to do with the American expatriate community. Restaurants also open and close with regularity. The most expensive establishments are in upscale hotels like the Villa Jacaranda and the Casa de Sierra Nevada, where a jacket and tie for men may be advised.

If you want a change of pace from these restaurants' standard Continental offerings, there are plenty of options. **Fonda Mesón de San José**, Calle Mesones #38, offers al fresco dining in a shady courtyard; the menu includes both Mexican and German specialties. **Mama Mía**, 2 blocks southwest of the main plaza at Calle Umarán #8, is a casual place serving pasta and pizzas. Live flamenco and folkloric music is presented nightly on the outdoor patio.

After-dark entertainment usually revolves around restaurants that also feature live music,

such as Mama Mía. Jazz and blues can be heard at **Tío Lucas**, a restaurant at Calle Mesones #103 (at Hernández Macías). **La Fragua**, Calle Cuna de Allende #3, is a popular San Miguel gathering place housed in an old colonial building. Traditional Mexican music is performed evenings in the courtyard. Rock, country and blues bands play at **Pancho and Lefty's**, Calle Mesones #99 near the main plaza.

San Miguel's biggest event is the honoring of the town's patron saint on Sept. 29. The festivities, which extend from late September into early October, take place around the main plaza and along the adjoining streets and include parades, fireworks and regional dance performances.

Holy Week celebrations, which begin about 2 weeks before Easter Sunday, give visitors the opportunity to view elaborately decorated family altars in private homes. *Independence Day*, Sept. 15 and 16, is celebrated here with particular enthusiasm. The city's Christmas *posadas* also are well known. For information about event happenings and schedules, stop by the tourist office.

What To See

BIBLIOTECA PUBLICA (Public Library) is 2 blocks north of the main plaza at Calle Insurgentes #25. As a repository for some 22,000 English volumes and an equal number of books in Spanish, it is the second largest bilingual library in Latin America. The reading room has back issues of popular magazines. Also here are the offices of the weekly English-language newspaper *Atención*. Scanning the variety of notices posted at the entrance (many in English) is a good way to find out what's going on around town.

A 2-hour house and garden tour of selected homes departs from the library on Sundays at noon (doors open at 11), except three specified Sundays celebrating Mexican and religious holidays; phone (415) 2-0293. A fixed donation of about $15 ($20 for the annual Christmas tour) is charged, which benefits a scholarship fund for the education of San Miguel youth. Library open Mon.-Sat.

IGLESIA DE LA CONCEPCION (Church of the Conception) is a few blocks west of the main plaza at calles Canal and Hernández Macías. It was begun in the mid-17th century and financed partially through the support of the Canal family, who figured prominently in the town's early history. The domed roof, one of the largest in Mexico, was not completed until 1891. Supported by elegant Corinthian columns, it is believed to be the work of La Parroquia architect Zeferino Gutiérrez. Open daily.

IGLESIA DE SAN FRANCISCO (Church of San Francisco) is on Calle Juárez between calles San Francisco and Mesones. Built in the late 18th century, it is thought to be the work of Eduardo

Tresguerras, who contributed to the design of many churches in central Mexico. Construction was financed through donations from wealthy families and the proceeds from bullfights. The intricate stone carvings gracing the exterior are a fine example of the ornate Churrigueresque style. The high-ceilinged interior contains statues, paintings and more carved stone.

LA PARROQUIA (Parish Church) is on Calle Correo, facing the south side of the main plaza. It soars over the plaza and dominates the city. Originally built in the late 17th century in a plain Franciscan style, the church was given an imposing facelift 2 centuries later by an Indian artisan, Zeferino Gutiérrez. With no formal training, he added the present facade of pink-hued sandstone, allegedly using postcard pictures of French Gothic cathedrals as his inspiration.

Inside, neoclassic stone altars have replaced earlier gilded wood ones. A statue of St. Michael the Archangel, namesake of both town and church (its official name is Parroquia de San Miguel Arcángel), adorns the main altar. Chapels are located to the side and behind the main altar. The original bell, also referred to as St. Michael and cast in 1732, begins ringing early in the morning to summon parishioners; La Parroquia remains an active house of worship. Open daily.

MUSEO CASA DE ALLENDE (House of Allende Museum) is on Calle Cuna de Allende, a block west of La Parroquia. The birthplace of Ignacio Allende now houses a historical museum. A plaque hanging over the front door reads, "Here was born the one who was famous." Allende was one of the few early leaders of the War of Independence with actual military training. Together, he and Father Miguel Hidalgo organized a ragtag army and plotted strategies for overthrowing Spanish rule. Museum exhibits chronicle the region's history and Allende's role in the struggle for freedom. Tues.-Sun. 10-4. Free.

ORATORIO DE SAN FELIPE NERI (Church of San Felipe Neri) is at calles Insurgentes and Loreto, 2 blocks northeast of the main plaza. It was built by San Miguel's Indian population in the early 18th century. The original structure's facade of pink stone is still visible at the church's eastern end, along with a figure of Nuestra Señora de Soledad (Our Lady of Solitude). The southern exterior is newer and incorporates a baroque style. The church is notable for its differently shaped domes. The adjoining chapel, **Santa Casa de Loreto**, is behind the church. A grating blocks the chapel entrance, although its gilded altars can still be seen.

NEARBY DESTINATIONS

The springs of **Taboada**, about 8 kilometers (5 miles) north of San Miguel on Mex. 51, feed both temperate and hot-water pools. Bus service to the spa departs from Calle San Francisco near the city market, but a more reliable means of transportation is to hire a taxi.

The village of Atotonilco, known for its **Sanctuario de Jesús Nazareno**, is 15 kilometers (9 miles) north on Mex. 51, then about 3 kilometers (1.9 miles) southwest off the highway. The insurgent army under Father Miguel Hidalgo and Ignacio Allende stopped here to seize the banner of the Virgin of Guadalupe, which the two leaders appropriated as their emblem. The choice of such a revered religious figure was calculated, for it compelled the Indians to join the insurrection on the side of the rebels. The village itself is uninteresting, but the church contains lively frescoes depicting biblical scenes that were used to teach concepts of Christianity. Local buses also make this trip, leaving from the vicinity of the market.

WHERE TO STAY

ANTIGUA VILLA SANTA MONICA

▼▼▼▼▼   *Country Inn*   (415/2-0427

All Year $123-$163   XP $25
Location: Facing Benito Juarez Park. Baeza #22 37700 (APDO Postal 686). Fax: 415/2-0518. **Facility:** Very attractive intimate inn. All rooms unique; all facing interior courtyard. Well-landscaped. Building is over 200 years old. 13 units. Some whirlpool units. 1 story, exterior corridors. **Terms:** D12; 20 day cancellation notice-fee imposed. **Amenities:** *Some:* honor bars. **Leisure Activities:** small heated pool. **Guest Services:** [CP] meal plan available, valet laundry. **Cards:** AE, MC, VI.

SOME UNITS

CASA DE SIERRA NEVADA

▼▼▼ ▼▼▼   *Historic Cottage*   ((415)2-7040

All Year $170-$280   XP $30
Location: Just e of central plaza. Hospicio 35 37700 (Apartado Postal 226). Fax: 415/2-2337. **Facility:** Five 16th-century converted haciendas with a feeling of privacy but close to downtown. Elegant furnishings. Some private patios or terraces. 37 units. 1 two-bedroom unit. *Bath:* combo or shower only. 2 stories, exterior corridors. **Parking:** valet. **Terms:** 30 day cancellation notice. **Amenities:** safes, honor bars, hair dryers. **Dining:** restaurant, see separate listing. **Leisure Activities:** heated pool. **Guest Services:** valet laundry. *Fee:* massage. **Business Services:** meeting rooms. **Cards:** AE, MC, VI.

SOME UNITS

CASA MURPHY BED & BREAKFAST

▼▼▼▼▼   *Bed & Breakfast*   ((415)2-3776

All Year $70-$80   XP $20
Location: 3 blks w of main plaza. San Antonio Abad 22 37700. Fax: 415/2-3776. **Facility:** Attractive gardens, entire property surrounded by high wall. Well-appointed rooms and common areas. Smoking allowed in garden area only. Smoke free premises. 6 units, 2 with kitchen. *Bath:* combo or shower only. 1-2 stories, interior/exterior corridors. **Parking:** valet. **Terms:** 15 day cancellation notice-fee imposed. **Guest Services:** [BP] meal plan available, valet laundry. **Cards:** AE, DS, MC, VI.

SOME UNITS

CASA SCHUCK

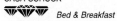 *Bed & Breakfast* ((415)2-0657

All Year $98-$150
Location: 4 blks e of main plaza. Bajada de la Garita #3 37700 (P APBO 180). Fax: 415/2-0657. **Facility:** Classic hacienda style home, beautiful garden, very well appointed rooms with high ceilings. Comfortable public areas. 6 units. *Bath:* combo or shower only. 2 stories, exterior corridors. **Parking:** street only. **Terms:** 30 day cancellation notice-fee imposed. **Amenities:** no TVs. **Leisure Activities:** heated pool. **Guest Services:** valet laundry. **Business Services:** meeting rooms.

GUADIANA BED AND BREAKFAST

 Bed & Breakfast ((415)2-4948

All Year $65 XP $10
Location: 0.5 mi s of main plaza. Mesquite #11 37700. Fax: 415/2-5171. **Facility:** In a quiet residential area. Modern, yet has local charm at a reasonable price. 8 units. *Bath:* shower only. 3 stories (no elevator). **Terms:** D12; 14 day cancellation notice. **Amenities:** no TVs. **Guest Services:** [BP] meal plan available, valet laundry. **Cards:** MC, VI.

◆◆◆ HACIENDA DE LAS FLORES

 *Bed & Breakfast* (415/2-1808

12/1-4/15 & 7/1-8/31 $75-$117 XP $25
4/16-6/30 & 9/1-11/30 $61-$102 XP $25
Location: 2.5 blks s from central plaza. Hospicio 16 37700. Fax: 415/2-1859. **Facility:** Colonial-style converted hacienda. Very pretty setting. Attractive, well maintained guest rooms. Overlooks bull ring. 18 units. *Bath:* combo or shower only. 2 stories, exterior corridors. **Parking:** extra charge. **Terms:** F12; 10 day cancellation notice-fee imposed. **Leisure Activities:** small heated pool. **Guest Services:** [BP] meal plan available, valet laundry. **Business Services:** meeting rooms. **Cards:** MC, VI.

SOME UNITS

HOTEL ARISTOS SAN MIGUEL

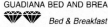 *Hotel* ((415)2-0149

All Year $50 XP $10
Location: 1.3 km s on Mex 49, Celaya Hwy. (PO Box 588, 37700). Fax: 415/2-1631. **Facility:** Lovely landscaped grounds. Quiet surroundings. Pleasant rooms with attractive Mexican decor. 60 units. *Bath:* combo or shower only. 2 stories, interior corridors. **Terms:** 5 day cancellation notice. **Leisure Activities:** heated pool. **Fee:** 2 tennis courts. **Guest Services:** valet laundry. **Business Services:** meeting rooms. **Cards:** AE, MC, VI.

◆◆◆ HOTEL HACIENDA TABOADA, GTO.

Motor Inn ((415)2-0850

All Year $140-$200 XP $56
Location: Km 8 on San Miguel de Allende Dolores Hidalgo Hwy Mex 51, 3 km w via signs. (APDO Postal 100, 37700). Fax: 415/2-1798. **Facility:** Peaceful setting, natural hot spring pools. Located north of town, nicely landscaped, modern facility away from traffic and noise. 70 units. 3 stories, exterior corridors. **Terms:** F3; cancellation fee imposed, package plans. **Dining:** restaurant, 8 am-10:30 pm, $7-$18, cocktails. **Leisure Activities:** 2 heated pools, wading pools, 2 tennis courts, horseback riding, playground, exercise room. **Guest Services:** [BP] meal plan available, gift shop, valet laundry. **Business Services:** meeting rooms. **Cards:** AE, DI, MC, VI.

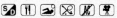

HOTEL LA SIESTA

 Motel (415/2-0207

All Year $59-$68 XP $10
Location: 2 km s on Mex 49, Celaya Hwy. (PO Box 72, 37700). Fax: 415/2-3722. **Facility:** Modest, rustic motel rooms with fireplace. 29 units. 2 two-bedroom units. *Bath:* shower only. 1 story, exterior corridors. **Terms:** F10; 7 day cancellation notice. **Guest Services:** [BP] meal plan available, valet laundry. **Cards:** AE, MC, VI.

HOTEL POSADA DE LA ALDEA

Motor Inn (415/2-1022

All Year $76 XP $20
Location: 1 km s on Mex 49, Celaya Hwy. Calle Ancha de San Antonio #15 37700 (APDO Postal 410). Fax: 415/2-1296. **Facility:** Walking distance to plaza, large parking lot and grounds on the east end of town. 66 units. *Bath:* combo or shower only. 3 stories, interior corridors. **Terms:** F10; 5 day cancellation notice. **Leisure Activities:** wading pool, 2 tennis courts. **Guest Services:** valet laundry. **Business Services:** meeting rooms. **Cards:** MC, VI.

SOME UNITS

HOTEL VERANDA SAN MIGUEL

 Motel ((415)2-1765

All Year $60 XP $10
Location: 2 km s on Mex 57. Camino Real a Queretaro 1 37700 (APDO Postal 301). Fax: 415/2-1765. **Facility:** Very attractive grounds, located on east end of town; outskirts. 50 units, 8 with kitchen. *Bath:* shower only. 2 stories, exterior corridors. **Terms:** F12; 3 day cancellation notice. **Leisure Activities:** Fee: miniature golf. **Business Services:** meeting rooms. **Cards:** AE, MC, VI.

◆◆◆ HOTEL VILLA JACARANDA

Motor Inn ((415)2-1015

Location: 3 blks s of main plaza. Aldama 53 37700. Fax: 415/2-0883. **Facility:** Attractive grounds, very nice landscaping. Very pleasant, well-furnished guest rooms with fireplace and patio. Movie theatre shows films most nights. 16 units. 2 stories, interior/exterior corridors. **Terms:** 30 day cancellation notice. **Amenities:** hair dryers. **Dining:** restaurant, see separate listing. **Leisure Activities:** whirlpool. **Guest Services:** valet laundry. **Business Services:** meeting rooms. **Cards:** AE, MC, VI.

SOME UNITS

◆◆◆ LA PUERTECITA BOUTIQUE HOTEL

Country Inn ((415)2-5011

All Year $165 XP $25
Location: From intersection w/Pedro Vargas (Queretero Hwy), 0.6 km e. Santo Domingo 75 37740. Fax: 415/2-5505. **Facility:** Beautiful secluded setting overlooking town. Handsome guest rooms and facilities. Language courses available on site. 34 units. Some whirlpool units. 3 stories, interior/exterior corridors. **Parking:** valet. **Terms:** F10; 15 day cancellation notice-fee imposed. **Dining:** dining room, 8 am-9:30 pm, $15-$20, cocktails. **Leisure Activities:** 2 heated pools, whirlpool, exercise room, billiard room, library, mountain bike tours, country club privileges offering golf, tennis, gym. **Guest Services:** valet laundry. **Business Services:** meeting rooms. **Cards:** AE, MC, VI.

SOME UNITS

FEE

MI CASA B & B

▼▼ *Historic Bed & Breakfast* ((415)2-2492

All Year $85-$100 XP $10
Location: 2.5 blks w of main plaza. Canal 58 APDO 496
37700. Fax: 415/2-0121. **Facility:** Located in the center of
town, close to main plaza in a 200 year old home. Pleasant
rooftop garden/lounging area. Unique decor and ambience.
4 units. *Bath:* combo or shower only. 2 stories, exterior corridors. **Parking:** street only. **Terms:** 14 day cancellation
notice-fee imposed. **Amenities:** no TVs. **Guest Services:**
[BP] meal plan available.

RANCHO HOTEL SAKKARAH

▼▼▼▼ *Country Inn* ((418)5-2061

All Year $53-$58 XP $11
Location: 13 km n on San Miguel de Allende Dolores
Hidalgo Hwy on Mex 51, 2 km e via signs. (APDO Postal
729, 37700). Fax: 418/5-2062. **Facility:** Fine, peaceful location. Handsome rooms and few distractions. 8 units. *Bath:*
shower only. 1 story, exterior corridors. **Terms:** F12; 15 day
cancellation notice. **Leisure Activities:** heated pool, whirlpool. **Guest Services:** valet laundry. **Business Services:**
conference facilities. **Cards:** AE, MC, VI.

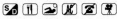

VILLA MIRASOL HOTEL

▼▼▼ *Bed & Breakfast* (415/2-6685

All Year $75-$95 XP $12
Location: Just w of main plaza. Pila Seca #35 37700.
Fax: 415/2-1564. **Facility:** Variety of rooms, private and
semi-private patios, newly tiled bathrooms, attractive decor,
hospitable local ambience. 10 units. *Bath:* combo or shower
only. 2 stories. **Parking:** street only. **Terms:** D12; 3 day cancellation notice-fee imposed. **Guest Services:** [CP] meal
plan available, valet laundry. **Cards:** AE, MC, VI.

*The following lodging was either not evaluated
or did not meet AAA rating requirements and
is listed for your information only.*

CASA DE LIZA VILLAS EN EL PARQUE

[fyi] *Bed & Breakfast* (415/2-0352

All Year $144-$288 XP $30
Too new to rate. **Location:** Bajada del Chorro #7 37700
(705 Martens Ct PMB 84-203, LAREDO, TX, 78041-6010).
Fax: 415/2-6144. **Amenities:** 6 units, pets, microwaves, re-
frigerators. **Terms:** F12; 7 day cancellation notice-fee imposed. **Cards:** MC, VI.

SOME UNITS

WHERE TO DINE

ANTIGUA TRATTORIA ITALIAN

▼▼ *Italian* (415/2-3790

L $7-$15 D $7-$15
Location: 3 blks s of main plaza. CODO #9 37700.
Hours: 1 pm-11 pm. Closed: Mon & 5/15-5/31.
Reservations: suggested. **Features:** No A/C; casual dress;
cocktails. Friendly atmosphere, very popular with the locals.
Nice selection of entrees from both the north and south of
Italy. **Cards:** AE, MC, VI.

SAN MIGUELITO

▼▼ *Mexican* (415/2-5393

D $8-$14
Location: Center. San Francisco #1 37700. **Hours:** 6 pm-
midnight, Sat & Sun from 1 pm. Closed: Mon. **Features:** casual dress; cocktails & lounge; entertainment. Festive
atmosphere. Average food. Favorite of locals. **Cards:** AE,
MC, VI.

SIERRA NEVADA RESTAURANT *Historical*

▼▼▼▼ *Continental* (415/2-0415

L $12-$20 D $12-$20
Location: Just e of central plaza; in Casa de Sierra Nevada. Hospicio 35 37700. **Hours:** 8-11 am, 1-4 & 7-10 pm,
Fri & Sat-10:30 pm. **Reservations:** required. **Features:** No
A/C; casual dress; cocktails & lounge; a la carte. Elegant
dining in converted historic hacienda. International specialties. Jacket is required in the dining room, casual in patio
area. **Cards:** AE, MC, VI.

VILLA JACARANDA RESTAURANT

▼▼▼ *Continental* (415/2-1015

L $8-$20 D $8-$20
Location: 3 blks s of main plaza; in Hotel Villa Jacaranda.
Aldama 53 37700. **Hours:** 7:30 am-10 pm.
Reservations: suggested. **Features:** No A/C; casual dress;
cocktails. Well-prepared international specialties.
Cards: AE, MC, VI.

Tlaxcala,
Tlaxcala (C-11) elev. 7,387'

A highland city in the middle of a wooded region, Tlaxcala (tlas-KAH-lah), the state capital,
is about 75 miles east of Mexico City. The Tlaxcala Indians, a Chichimec group, settled in this
region after defeating the Aztecs at Lake Texcoco. Alliance with the Otomí Indians provided
the military protection that gave the Tlaxcaltecs
the freedom to advance their civilization. Leaders
of this small, powerful nation were the second,
after the Totonacs, to align their forces with
Hernán Cortés.

Apparently, joining the wrong side has been
forgiven. This amiable colonial town, off the
usual tourist track, is one of Mexico's most picturesque and makes for a pleasant side trip from
Mexico City or Puebla. The downtown area is a
delightful assemblage of structures in shades of
sepia, deep red and orange. **Plaza de la Constitución,** the main square, is distinguished by
neatly trimmed trees, a bandstand and a burbling
fountain presented to the city by King Philip III.
Hundreds of cheering spectators stood on roof-
tops and lined the streets around the plaza in
May 1997, when U.S. President Bill Clinton included a stop at Tlaxcala on his first state visit to
Mexico.

Most points of interest in town surround the
plaza. On its north side is the **Palacio de Gobierno** (Government Palace), with a brick exterior
punctuated by ornately decorated windows and
doorways. Inside are extravagantly colorful murals depicting agricultural life and the history of

the Tlaxcaltec people, painted in the early 1960s by local artist Desiderio Hernández Xochitiotzin. Also on the plaza is the baroque **Palacio de Justicia** (Palace of Justice), with neoclassic touches added in the 18th century. Inside the **Parroquia de San José** (Parish Church of St. Joseph), a peach-colored building, is the **Capilla de San José** (Chapel of St. Joseph), which has an arched ceiling with plaster ornamentation and impressive altarpieces.

Near the plaza is the **Museo de Artes Populares** (Museum of Popular Arts), where a variety of artisans ply their trades. Visitors can observe such demonstrations as weaving and the preparation of pulque (a drink made from the fermented sap of the maguey plant). Many of the items are for sale. The museum is open Tues.-Sun.

The Secretaría de Turismo del Estado (State Tourism Secretariat) is located at Avenida Benito Juárez #18 (behind the Government Palace) and can provide visitor information; phone (246) 2-0027. The staff speaks English.

Near Tlaxcala are two vacation resorts. Both offer lodgings, sports facilities and medical services. **La Trinidad** is north of the city and east off Mex. 119, before the junction with Mex. 136. **Malintzin** lies at a 9,840-foot elevation on the northern slopes of La Malinche, an extinct volcano 14,632 feet high. From a marked exit on Mex. 136 between the towns of Apizaco and Huamantla, a road ascends 14 kilometers (9 miles) to this mountain retreat, which is at the entrance to La Malinche National Park.

EX-CONVENTO FRANCISCO DE LA ASUNCION (Ex-Convent of the Assumption) is southeast of the main plaza and off a smaller plaza, Plaza Xicoténcatl; a cobblestone path leads up a hill to the cathedral. Before leaving to conquer what is now Mexico City, Hernán Cortés ordered several Catholic rites held for his Tlaxcaltec allies, including the baptism of the king Xicoténcatl. The original chapel with its stone baptismal font can be seen. In the Franciscan church, which dates from the early 16th century, are gilded altars, 17th-century religious paintings and an intricately carved and decorated wooden ceiling in *mudéjar* (Moorish) fashion. A lovely open-air chapel displays Moorish-style pointed arches.

Occupying the church's cloister is the **Museo Regional de Tlaxcala** (Tlaxcala Regional Museum). Exhibits in the whitewashed rooms depict the state's history from prehistoric times to the present. Tues.-Sun. 10-5. Admission is charged.

SANTA ANA CHIAUTEMPAN is a weaving center less than 3 kilometers (2 miles) from Tlaxcala; it can be reached via the paved road that branches east from town. Artisans here and in Tlaxcala fashion hand-loomed *sarapes* and beautiful bolts of cloth. The village's main street is lined with shops selling rugs and *sarapes*. Native craftwork is supplemented by the tweeds and woolen bedspreads produced in the region's modern textile plants.

SANTUARIO DE LA VIRGEN DE OCOTLAN (Sanctuary of the Virgin of Ocotlán) sits atop a hill about a mile east of town. The shrine commemorates the supposed appearance of the Virgin of Guadalupe to the Indian Juan Diego Bernardino at this site in 1541. A masterpiece of baroque architecture in the indigenous Puebla-Tlaxcalan style, it has a dazzlingly white, elaborately carved stucco facade and towers supported by twin tiled bases of red clay. Conch shells and images of the Virgin and the archangels adorn the portal. The interior is a riot of gilded wood ornamentation on which Indian artist Francisco Miguel Tlayotehuanitzin labored 20 years. The octagonal **Camarín** (Dressing Room), a chamber where the Virgin's robes were said to be changed, explodes with carvings of angels and saints intertwined with garlands and other decorative accents.

Visitors can hike to the shrine from the center of town, or take an inexpensive *colectivo* (minivan) designated "Ocotlán"; the driver stops at the front steps and will wait while you tour the sanctuary.

TIZATLAN RUINS are north of Tlaxcala via Mex. 117 to Mex. 136, then east to the Tizatlán turnoff. A wool-weaving settlement established by the Tlaxcaltecs in the mid-14th century, Tizatlán developed into a major trade center. The ruins include a palace built on a small platform and small sanctuaries with colorful murals painted on the altars. These paintings depict wars with the Aztecs, who failed in their attempt to incorporate the Tlaxcaltec nation into their empire.

THE MURALS OF CACAXTLA

Perhaps the finest examples of pre-Columbian artwork in all of Mexico are on view at the **Cacaxtla Ruins**. The mural paintings decorating several of the buildings at this archeological site remain vividly colorful more than a thousand years after their execution. Archeological evidence suggests that the city that once stood here reached a peak of development between A.D. 650 and 900, and was abandoned by the beginning of the 11th century.

The rise of Cacaxtla corresponded to the fall of Teotihuacán *(see separate listing under Mexico City and Vicinity)* and the subsequent social upheaval and political instability. Cacaxtla is thought to have been the capital of the Olmecan-Xicalancas, one of several groups who moved into this region of Mexico during a period of widespread unrest. Their domain encompassed the Valley of Puebla and the southwestern corner of present-day Tlaxcala state. The city was built atop a rise that facilitated contact with other Mesoamerican tribes but was also vulnerable to raids. As a result, the perimeter was walled and moated to ward off attack.

The Cacaxtla murals were discovered only in 1975. Many are exceptionally well preserved and comparable to those at Bonampak, in the jungles of Chiapas near the Guatemalan border, although this site is considerably easier to reach. The mix of Maya, Aztec and Olmec characteristics confirms the existence of a pre-Hispanic commercial and cultural exchange between central Mexico and the Yucatán. Excavations at the site are ongoing.

Cacaxtla's earliest structures were a group of adobe edifices that over time were demolished and filled in to form a large platform. This process was repeated several times until the foundation reached its present height. Most of the structures that visitors see today are vestiges dating from the latest period of construction. Archeologists made a ghoulish discovery during the initial excavations: the remains of more than 200 children apparently sacrificed at the beginning of a new construction phase. **Note:** A crude wooden staircase ascends the platform to the murals; exercise care when climbing the steps.

The complex of ceremonial courtyards, tombs and enclosures known as the **Palace** were repeatedly reconfigured during the site's centuries of occupation, most likely as living quarters for the ruling class. Scattered throughout this area are the murals. The largest and most dramatic is the mythological **Mural of the Battle**, painted between A.D. 650 and 700. It depicts two groups of warriors—one outfitted in birdlike plumage, feather headdresses and jade jewelry, the other fiercely attacking with knives and spears, cloaked in the skins of jaguars. The colors—rich blues, reds, yellows and browns—and the depth of detail are startling.

Another concentration of murals can be seen in **Building A**. Here there are five murals, all characterized by themes of fertility and the continuation of life. The figure depicted on the

North Jamb is particularly striking—cloaked in jaguar skin and wearing a blue nose pendant, with a plant sprouting out of his stomach. The clawed hands grasp a snake and a receptacle with the face of Tlaloc, the rain god. The **South Jamb** figure, holding a seashell from which a human figure emerges, has hair pulled into a topknot and garlanded with beads and flowers.

In addition to the murals, there is at Cacaxtla a latticework construction, the only one of its kind at any archeological zone in Mexico. It was constructed with a core of mud-packed twigs, then coated with mortar made of lime and sand.

The Cacaxtla ruins are about 17 kilometers (12 miles) southwest of Tlaxcala. To reach them by car from town, take the road toward Nativitas (follow signs) to the village of San Miguel del Milagro. The hillside entrance to the site is about a 1-mile walk from the parking lot. From Mexico City, take Mex. 150-D east to the San Martín Texmelucan exit and head in the direction of Tlaxcala. Watch for the side road to Nativitas and follow the signs for Cacaxtla. City buses and *colectivos* also travel from Tlaxcala to San Miguel del Milagro and Nativitas.

Site open Tues.-Sun. 9-5. Admission is charged; free to all Sun. There is an additional charge for the use of a video camera. Flash photography is not permitted.

TULA, HIDALGO (B-10) elev. 6,776'

Tula (TOO-lah) was founded by Franciscans in the early 16th century; their fortresslike church, which also dates from that time, still stands. Tula, typical of smaller Mexican towns, has a busy market and a quiet central plaza bordered with taco stands. Evening band concerts occasionally take place in the square.

Archeologists long believed that the remains of the Toltec capital of Tollan, which means

The Legend of Quetzalcoatl

One of Mexican history's most intriguing mysteries surrounds Quetzalcóatl, a man known for his advocacy of peace and who was believed to have opposed the practice of human sacrifice. Over time, fact and myth have become almost impenetrably tangled, although certain events are reasonably established. The son of Toltec chieftain Mixcóatl, Quetzalcóatl took the full name Ce Acatl Quetzalcóatl (literally, "One Reed Feathered Serpent"). It is believed that he founded the Toltec city of Tollan (Tula); the plumed serpent motif is noticeably evident at this archeological site. A power struggle ensued, and according to legend Quetzalcóatl's rivals conspired to get him drunk and thereby shame him into exile. (A more likely scenario is that the continued invasion of warlike tribes caused a decline in Toltec power.) The king led his followers, it is said, out of Tula and east toward the Gulf coast, where he either sailed off, promising to return in a future era, or burned himself alive and was reincarnated as the morning star. Meanwhile, Quetzalcóatl the myth continued to be invoked, a personage described as light-skinned, blue-eyed and bearded—features different from those of any person the Indians had ever before seen. When Hernán Cortés arrived in the Aztec capital of Tenochtitlán, the emperor Moctezuma believed him to be the returning god—a case of mistaken identity the *conquistador* craftily used to his advantage.

"metropolis" or "large city," were somewhere in this region; however, the exact whereabouts remained a mystery until Tula was determined to be the site in 1938. More recent finds have enlarged the originally discovered area of 2.3 square miles almost threefold.

TULA RUINS, on a hill just north of the Río Tula, are about a mile from town. They constitute what is left of the capital and chief ceremonial center of the Toltecs. Tula is generally acknowledged to have been the next major city to emerge in pre-Hispanic Mexico after the fall of Teotihuacán. Its period of dominance was relatively brief—from about A.D. 950 to 1174, when the Chichimecs, forerunners of the Aztecs, attacked, sacked and burned it. Toltec stylistic and governmental influence spread as far as the great Maya center of Chichén Itzá, nearly 750 miles due east of Tula on the Yucatán Peninsula. However, it is thought unlikely that Tula ever achieved the prominence of either Teotihuacán or Chichén Itzá.

In contrast to the wealth discovered at such ruins as Monte Albán, in the state of Oaxaca, or Palenque, in the state of Chiapas, few precious objects have been retrieved from this site. It could well be that the invading Chichimecs plundered Tula in the process of destroying it. What building fragments remain seem to reinforce the Toltecs' militarism; stone carvings frequently display images of warriors outfitted for battle.

The sculptural figure known as Chac Mool, first found at this site, has since become an international artistic symbol of Mesoamerican culture. But the reclining figure—holding a vessel that presumably received still-beating hearts torn from victims' chests during Toltec sacrificial ceremonies—again points to the violent nature of their culture. On the other hand, the Toltecs were so highly developed in the areas of painting, sculpture, architecture and speech that in their time, the name was said to be synonymous with "artist."

The partially reconstructed ceremonial center is the most interesting section of this archeological zone; Tula's more outlying areas have yet to be excavated to any great degree. The focal point of the ruins is the five-tiered pyramid with a tongue-twisting name, the **Temple of Tlahuizcalpantecuitli** (Lord of the House of the Morning Star Venus). It dominates the north side of a plaza flanked by colonnaded buildings. On the east side once stood a smaller pyramid, now in ruins; on the west side is a ball court remarkably similar to the one at Chichén Itzá.

On top of the pyramid stand Tula's most intriguing creations, four colossal figures more than 15 feet tall. One is a replica; the original is displayed at the National Museum of Anthropology in Mexico City. Known as the Atlantes, they once supported the roof of a temple that stood atop the pyramid. They may be representations of the Toltec ruler Ce Acatl Quetzalcóatl, who

was named for the fair-skinned god of Mexican folklore. Each Atlantean is swaddled in a loincloth resembling a diaper. Their chests are protected by stylized butterfly breastplates, their backs by shields in the shape of the sun; headdresses are decorated with feathers. Each figure carries a spear-thrower in its right hand, a supply of spears in its left.

Some of the pyramid's stone slabs show relief carvings of jaguars, coyotes and eagles clutching hearts in their beaks. In front of it sits an L-shaped colonnade that once supported a great roof, perhaps to shade Tula's priests and nobility during ceremonial functions. Part of a long bench also remains, complete with carvings of warriors. The **Burnt Palace**, west of the pyramid, has three chambers, all with a central patio and more benches; paint still colors some of the bench carvings in the middle room, which is the best preserved.

North of the pyramid is the **Coatepantli** (Serpent Wall), a fragment decorated with elaborate carvings of rattlesnakes devouring skeletal human heads—yet another symbolic reference to Toltec fearsomeness—as well as another, smaller, ball court. A modern museum building near the entrance exhibits artifacts found at the site and has displays relating to the Toltecs.

Tula is about 80 kilometers (50 miles) north of Mexico City. To reach the ruins by car, take the Periférico Norte out of the city, which becomes Mex. 57-D (the toll highway) to Querétaro). Take the second Tula exit (Mex. 126) about 20 kilometers (12 miles) north to the town and the ruins. Buses depart for the town of Tula from Mexico City's Terminal Central de Autobuses del Norte, Avenida de los 100 Metros; Metro has a subway station at the terminal (Autobuses del Norte, line 5). Taxis departing from the main plaza drop visitors off at the ruins. Site open daily 10-5; museum open Tues.-Sun. 10-5. Admission is charged.

WHERE TO STAY

MOTEL QUINTA MITZI
◆◆◆ *Motel*   ☎ 715/5-0112
All Year $25   XP $5
Location: 1.5 km se. Mex 15 61420. **Facility:** Unit with fireplace. Unusual archeological exhibit. 9 units. *Bath:* shower only. 1 story, exterior corridors. **Terms:** F10; 8 day cancellation notice. **Amenities:** no TVs. **Cards:** MC, VI.

🅰️ 🆎

TZINTZUNTZAN,
MICHOACAN (C-8) elev. 6,724'

Once the capital of a powerful Tarascan kingdom, Tzintzuntzan (tseen-TSOON-tsahn) is now a small village on the shores of Lake Pátzcuaro.

The curious name means "the place of the hummingbirds" in the Tarasco Indian language. This area is one of the largest sources of inexpensive hand-painted pottery in Mexico. Local artisans decorate their pottery with simple, childlike drawings of swans, fish and native net fishermen. The Tarascan also weave figurines and table and floor mats out of reeds. Another cottage industry is woodcarving; items range from small wall decorations, dishes and flowerpots to doors, windows and columns.

The restored 16th-century Franciscan **Convent of Santa Ana** can be visited. The church courtyard is noted for its olive trees, which were planted by Don Vasco de Quiroga despite a Spanish injunction against planting the trees in the New World. Restored *yácatas*, ruins of Tarasco pyramids, are visible from Mex. 120; a paved side road leads to the edge of the site.

Holy Week ceremonies culminate with a series of concerts and performances of classical Spanish plays, staged by residents in the atrium of the Santa Ana Convent. The village's *pastorelas*, medieval dramas based on the Nativity, begin Dec. 16.

Tzintzuntzan also participates in *Day of the Dead* ceremonies Nov. 1-2. During this all-night vigil, families visit the local cemetery to bring food, drink and other *ofrendas* (offerings) to their deceased relatives. This ritual, as well as those observed during *Holy Week*, attract many visitors to towns on the islands of and around Lake Pátzcuaro. If you'll be visiting during either of these times, book hotel reservations in Pátzcuaro or nearby Quiroga well in advance.

URUAPAN,
MICHOACAN (I-4) elev. 5,491′

Uruapan (oo-roo-AH-pahn) means "place where the flowers bloom," and the lush vegetation seen throughout the city is a testament to the warm climate (it is nearly 2,000 feet lower in elevation than nearby Pátzcuaro). Orange groves and plantations growing coffee, avocados and bananas flourish in the fertile farmland that surrounds the city. Uruapan also is known for hand-painted lacquerware carved from cedar and other native woods.

Parque Eduardo Ruiz has lush vegetation along streamside paths and fountains with dancing waters propelled by gravity alone; no pumps are used. The park is better known as the National Park, as it and nearby Tzaráracua Falls are the most attractive portions of **Barranca del Río Cupatitzio National Park**; the river rises at **Rodilla del Diablo** (Devil's Knee) spring, also within the park. It is located off Calzada La Quinta on the northern edge of the city. The **Mu-**

nicipal Museum at the park entrance displays and sells lacquerware and other native crafts.

MUSEO DE LA HUATAPERA (La Huatapera Museum), facing Plaza Principal, is a fine example of 16th-century architecture. Originally a chapel and hospital, it now houses some of the region's most skillful examples of Tarasco Indian workmanship, including primitive dolls, statues, lacquerware and copper handicrafts.

PARICUTIN (pah-ree-koo-TEEN), a blunt-topped cone rising some 1,700 feet above the surrounding valley, is a now-dormant volcano that sprang from a cornfield in 1943. During its brief period of activity, Paricutín destroyed two villages and forced more than 4,000 people to abandon their homes.

The weirdly blackened landscape is accessible by going north on Mex. 37 for about 16 kilometers (10 miles) and then taking a paved road west 21 kilometers (13 miles) to the town of Angahuan. The volcanic cone and the lava fields around it can be reached on horseback; guided trips can be arranged in Angahuan.

TZARARACUA FALLS (tsah-RAH-rah-kwah) is about 10 kilometers (6 miles) south of town. Here the Río Cupatitzio rushes through a natural stone amphitheater, then drops about 90 feet into a pool. There is about a half-mile walk from the parking area down to the falls; horses also can be rented for a ride to the falls.

WHERE TO STAY

⟨AAA⟩ **HOTEL MANSION DEL CUPATITZIO**
▼▼▼▼ *Motor Inn* ((452)3-2100
All Year $710-$880   XP $110
Location: 0.5 km se of Mex 37 on Calz Fray Juan de San Miguel. Parque Nacional S/N 60000 (Apartado Postal 63). Fax: 452/4-6772. **Facility:** Old hacienda atmosphere. View of courtyard or adjacent park. 57 units. Some whirlpool units ($910-$1200). *Bath:* combo or shower only. 2 stories, exterior corridors. **Terms:** F12. **Amenities:** hair dryers. *Some:* safes, irons. *Dining:* restaurant, 7 am-10:30 pm, $5-$12, cocktails. **Leisure Activities:** heated pool, exercise room. **Guest Services:** gift shop, valet laundry. **Business Services:** meeting rooms. **Cards:** AE, MC, VI.

SOME UNITS
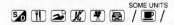

ZACATECAS,
ZACATECAS (F-6) elev. 8,115′

Zacatecas (sah-kah-TEH-kahs), capital of the state of the same name, is built in a ravine on the slopes of **Cerro de la Bufa**, a rock-crowned hill 8,748 feet high. Long a mining center, the settlement was taken by the Spaniards in 1548. In 1588, it was named "The Very Noble and Loyal City of Our Lady of the Zacatecas" because of the vast quantities of silver shipped from the region to Spain. Although now surrounded by agricultural and cattle-raising lands, Zacatecas continues to be a center for silver mining. The largest mine in the region is 200-year-old El Bote, which is still in operation.

Elaborate old mansions, an aqueduct and stone steps connecting steeply inclined flagstone streets lend the city a medieval atmosphere, and also attest to the ostentatious wealth generated by the mines. In contrast to this air of antiquity are the modern buildings of the University of Zacatecas; a mining museum on Avenida López Mateos lies at the foot of the hillside campus.

Within a 12-block area best explored on foot are several colonial buildings, including the baroque **Cathedral, Government Palace, Calderón Theater, Church of San Agustín** and **Church of Santo Domingo**. A tourism office is next to the Government Palace. The nearby public marketplace resembles a turn-of-the-20th-century shopping area.

The **Patrocinio Chapel**, erected in 1728 on the Cerro de la Bufa, offers an exceptional view of the town and its mountain setting. The crest of Cerro de la Bufa can be reached by a paved road. Several shops sell state-made crafts. The **Battle of Zacatecas Museum** at the summit chronicles Pancho Villa's capture of the city in 1914.

A wide, divided avenue 5 kilometers (3 miles) long leads east from downtown Zacatecas to the suburb of **Guadalupe**, the site of an early 18th-century convent. It once served as a base for Franciscan missions established to the north of Mexico in what is now the southwestern United States. The town is noted for colonial architecture as well as for marquetry and wool *sarapes* with portraits woven into their designs. Likenesses may include clients or such famous personages as John F. Kennedy.

Trancoso, 22 kilometers (14 miles) east off Mex. 45/49, has one of the most elegant and best preserved old haciendas in Mexico. In Bracho, on the north side of the loop road encircling the city, *La Morisma* is celebrated the last week in August. During this fiesta, hundreds of local boys and men dressed in Moorish-style costumes act out a battle against a European army for several consecutive days. Farther north, off the loop, are the ghost towns of Veta Grande and Pánuco; the former is the site of the main silver lode that began Zacatecas' mining operations.

For tourist information contact the Dirección de Turismo del Estado (State Tourism Bureau) in front of the railroad station; phone (492) 4-0393 or 4-0552. There also is a tourism information office across the street from the cathedral.

A toll highway links Zacatecas and Fresnillo. Mexicana Airlines offers direct flights from several U.S. cities. "Deluxe" bus service from Mexico City is provided by Omnibus de México, (492) 2-5495, Futura and Turistar.

WHAT TO SEE IN TOWN

CATHEDRAL, on the south side of the plaza, was begun in 1612 and completed in 1752. It is one of the ultimate expressions of the Mexican Churrigueresque style. Notable indeed is the exterior explosion of extravagant ornamentation, carved out of pink sandstone. The elaborate carvings, gold and silver ornaments and valuable artwork recall the city's days as a wealthy Spanish mining center.

MINA EL EDEN (Edén Mine) can be reached by car from Mex. 54; when entering the city, turn northeast at the Hotel Aristos Zacatecas and then proceed down the hill about half a kilometer, following signs. From downtown, go past Alameda Park and the Social Security building. First operated in the 16th century, the mine produced great quantities of silver, copper and zinc during its most active period.

A small powered train takes visitors through the mine's 1,950-foot-long tunnel entrance; a guided tour then travels through several other tunnels. Talks in Spanish tell of the gruesome living conditions of the original Indian miners. Admission is charged.

MUSEO FRANCISCO GOITIA (Francisco Goitia Museum), across from Sierra de Alica Park, is in the former Governor's Mansion. Works by Francisco Goitia (1882-1960) as well as sculpture and paintings by other contemporary Zacatecano artists are displayed.

MUSEO PEDRO CORONEL (Pedro Coronel Museum), on Plaza Santo Domingo near the main square, was originally a Jesuit monastery and later a jail. The museum now houses the outstanding private collection of noted Zacatecan artist and sculptor Pedro Coronel. On display are works by Pablo Picasso, Salvador Dalí, Joan Miró and Marc Chagall; Coronel's tomb and an exhibit of his own sculpture and paintings; pre-Columbian pieces and colonial-era works by Zacatecan artists; Chinese, Indian, Greek and Egyptian art; and a fine collection of Mesoamerican and African masks. Fri.-Wed. 10-2 and 4-7. Admission is charged. Phone (492) 2-8021.

MUSEO RAFAEL CORONEL (Rafael Coronel Museum) is north of the cathedral; take Hidalgo 2 blocks to Calle Abasolo, go left, then go right at the next fork. The museum is housed in the Convento de San Francisco, a gracious 18th-century edifice with an exterior colored in tones of mellowed pink. Lush flowering plants fill the gardens in the interior courtyard.

Inside is an amazing collection of several thousand masks, all donated by Rafael Coronel, younger brother of Pedro. They depict saints as well as grotesque-looking, devilish figures, *conquistadores* and bizarrely imaginative animals. Entirely handmade and decorated with everything from human hair to glitter, the masks are a remarkable testament to Mexican artistic ingenuity. There also are impressive dioramas of puppets engaged in such activities as warfare, a bullfight and a wedding. Tues.-Sun. 10-5. Admission is charged.

TELEFERICO ZACATECAS (Zacatecas Tramway), next to the Del Bosque Motel, can be reached from Mex. 54, following signs. Built by Swiss engineers, the tramway connects the hills Cerro de la Bufa and Cerro Grillo, spanning the northern section of Zacatecas. It overlooks the city from varying heights and covers a distance of 2,100 feet. The two enclosed cars are capable of holding six passengers at a time. Parking is available on either end of the run. Admission is charged.

NEARBY DESTINATIONS

CHICOMOSTOC RUINS, also known as La Quemada Ruins, lie on the hillside of a valley, about 56 kilometers (35 miles) southwest of Zacatecas off Mex. 54. Only partially restored, this archeological site bears traces of narrow streets and the foundations of homes and temples of the Náhuatlac Indians, who settled the valley around 1170. Thought to be destroyed by fire, the city was already a ruin when the Spaniards discovered it in 1535.

Among the remaining structures are a restored pyramid, a palace with 11 standing columns, and the substantial surrounding walls that have led some archeologists to believe that Chicomostoc was built as a fortress. Since local transportation is unreliable, the ruins are much easier to reach if you have your own vehicle. From the highway it's an uphill, 30-minute walk to the site entrance, past desert scenery characterized by stands of nopal cactus; visitors should wear comfortable hiking shoes and bring water. Open Tues.-Sun. 10-5. Admission is charged; free to all Sun.

CONVENTO DE GUADALUPE (Convent of Guadalupe) is about 7 kilometers (4 miles) southeast of the city via Mex. 45/49, in the village of Guadalupe. Local buses (*Ruta* 13) depart regularly for Guadalupe from the corner of Calle Salazar and Boulevard López Mateos, near the old bus terminal in downtown Zacatecas.

Dating from 1707, this enormous baroque church and former monastery once housed Franciscan monks who spread Christianity throughout the vast reaches of northern Mexico. Seemingly endless corridors, all lined with paintings and portraits, pass rows of cells where the monks spent their time when not ministering to the Indians.

The convent now houses the **Museo de Arte Virreinal** (Museum of Viceregal Art), which contains 18th-century Miguel Cabrera paintings of the Virgin of Guadalupe and other colonial religious art, as well as a library with a collection of hand-printed books. Especially noteworthy is the **Capilla de Napoles** (Chapel of Napoles), which has a domed roof covered with beautifully ornate gold-leaf decoration. The chapel is not always open, so a tip for the guide who grants entrance is appreciated. Guided tours of the museum also are available. Open Tues.-Sun. 10-4:30. Admission is charged; free to all Sun.

WHERE TO STAY

CONTINENTAL PLAZA ZACATECAS
▼▼▼▼   *Historic Hotel*   (492/2-6183
All Year $60   XP $10
Location: Center, on Plaza de Armas. Ave Hidalgo 703 98000. Fax: 492/2-6245. **Facility:** In historic district, opposite Cathedral and Governor's Palace. Many rooms overlooking fountain courtyard. Some with patio. 113 units. *Bath:* combo or shower only. 6 stories, interior corridors. **Terms:** F12. **Amenities:** extended cable TV. **Guest Services:** gift shop, valet laundry. **Business Services:** meeting rooms. **Cards:** AE, MC, VI.

SOME UNITS
🍴 🍸 🛗 D 🐾 🏃 / ✕ /

AAA HOTEL HACIENDA DEL BOSQUE
▼▼▼▼   *Motor Inn*   ((492)4-6666
All Year $126   XP $11
Location: 4 km ne of center on Gauadalajura Rd; at the crossroads on Hwy 54. Heroes de Chapultepec 801 98054. Fax: 492/4-6565. **Facility:** Located on north end of town; modern, well-appointed rooms, some with balcony. Very attractive grounds, secure parking. 80 units, 2 with efficiency. 2 stories, interior corridors. **Terms:** F12; 10 day cancellation notice. **Amenities:** *Some:* honor bars. **Dining:** restaurant, 7 am-11 pm, $5-$12, cocktails. **Leisure Activities:** playground. **Guest Services:** gift shop, area transportation, valet laundry. **Business Services:** meeting rooms. **Cards:** AE, MC, VI.

SOME UNITS
🆂 🚷 🛏 🍴 D 🏃 / ✕ /

HOWARD JOHNSON PLAZA HOTEL
▼▼▼▼   *Hotel*   (492/2-3415
All Year $100-$120
Location: Center, 3 blks s of cathedral, on Mex 45. (Blvd Lopez Mateos & Callejon del Barro, 98000). Fax: 492/2-3311. **Facility:** Well-appointed guest rooms and public areas. Meets AAA guest room security requirements. 126 units. Some whirlpool units. 5 stories, interior corridors. **Terms:** 21 day cancellation notice-fee imposed. **Amenities:** extended cable TV, hair dryers. **Leisure Activities:** heated pool, sauna, exercise room. **Guest Services:** gift shop, valet laundry. **Business Services:** meeting rooms, administrative services. **Cards:** AE, MC, VI.

SOME UNITS
🍴 24 🍸 🆂 D 🏊 🏃 DATA PORT / VCR /

QUINTA REAL ZACATECAS
▼▼▼▼   *Historic Hotel*   ((492)2-9104
All Year $110   XP $15
Location: 5 blks w of cathedral beside Elcubo Aqueduct on Ave Gonzalez Ortega. Ave Rayon 434 98000. Fax: 492/2-8440. **Facility:** Imposing and picturesque architecture, constructed around ruins of a 19th-century bull ring. Large, comfortable rooms and refined service. 49 units. Some whirlpool units. 5 stories, interior corridors. **Parking:** valet. **Terms:** F12. **Amenities:** voice mail, honor bars, irons, hair dryers. **Dining:** dining room, see separate listing. **Guest Services:** gift shop, valet laundry. **Business Services:** meeting rooms. **Cards:** AE, MC, VI.

SOME UNITS
🍴 🏃 DATA PORT / ✕ /

Where To Dine

QUINTA REAL DINING ROOM

 *Continental*   (492/2-9104

L $10-$15   **D** $10-$20

Location: 5 blks w of cathedral beside Elcubo Aqueduct on Ave Gonzalez Ortega; in Quinta Real Zacatecas. Ave Rayon 434 98000. **Hours:** 7 am-11 pm. **Reservations:** suggested. **Features:** casual dress; cocktails & lounge; valet parking; a la carte. Elegant, formal dining room overlooking picturesque bull ring ruins. Some seafood and Mexican menu items. Gastronomic events. **Cards:** AE, MC, VI.

Zamora, Michoacan

Where To Stay

HOTEL JERICO

 *Motor Inn*   (351/7-1212

All Year $50   XP $10

Location: On Mex 15. 2.5 km e on Carr Zamora-La Barca 59600. Fax: 351/7-0142. **Facility:** 172 units. *Bath:* combo or shower only. 2 stories, exterior corridors. **Terms:** F12; 3 day cancellation notice. **Leisure Activities:** wading pool, sauna, whirlpool, lighted tennis court, jogging, playground. *Fee:* exercise room. **Guest Services:** gift shop, valet laundry. *Fee:* massage. **Business Services:** meeting rooms. **Cards:** AE, DI, MC, VI.

SOME UNITS

SOUTHERN MEXICO

This is Mexico's most impoverished region economically but among its richest in cultural traditions. The states of Oaxaca and Chiapas are home to the country's largest concentration of Indian communities. Most of the people are descended from the Zapotec and Mixtec civilizations that flourished hundreds of years before the Spanish conquest of Mexico. Maya legacy is indelibly evident at the ruins of Palenque, in Chiapas. Mexico's southernmost state also made international headlines with the 1994 emergence of the Zapatista National Liberation Army, a guerrilla movement that has demanded greater opportunities for the region's Indians, or *indígenas*.

Oaxaca just might be the quintessential Mexican destination. It offers excellent museums; the Church of Santo Domingo, which has one of the most breathtakingly beautiful interiors of any religious building in Mexico; Plaza Prinicpal, the vibrant main square; the impressive archeological ruins of Monte Alban; a profusion of Indian markets overflowing with native handicrafts; and a distinctive regional cuisine incorporating everything from subtly spiced mole sauces to fried grasshoppers doused with a splash of lime.

For a different experience, head to Veracruz. It has the languorous ambience of a tropical port (Mexico's oldest and largest) as well as the energy provided by lively music, folk dances and a jolt of *café con leche*—strong black coffee laced with hot milk—that can be enjoyed at one of the city's sidewalk cafes. Taxco, a delightfully picturesque old silver-mining town in the state of Guerrero, is a designated national historic monument and a popular tourist stop between Mexico City and Acapulco.

CHILPANCINGO, GUERRERO (I-7) elev. 4,460'

Capital of the state of Guerrero and home to the University of Guerrero, Chilpancingo (cheel-pahn-SEEN-goh) is a bustling college town. It also has historical credentials—the first Congress of Mexico met here in 1813.

Points of interest include the **Casa del Primer Congreso Revolucionario** (House of the First Revolutionary Congress), **La Asunción Church**, the city's ancient cemetery and the **Palacio de Gobierno** (State Capitol), which has some fine murals. The Indian village of **Acatlán**, 55 kilometers (34 miles) northeast of Chilpancingo via a partially paved road, is noted for hand-loomed and embroidered shawls.

Travel Advisory

It is recommended that visitors check on current conditions before traveling to the states of Chiapas, Guerrero (outside the established tourist destinations of Acapulco, Ixtapa/Zihuatanejo and Taxco) and Tabasco. Civil unrest continues in the isthmus area of southern Mexico (Chiapas and Tabasco), and there is the possibility of sporadic violence in the more remote parts of these states. The most potentially dangerous areas in Guerrero are the mountainous, remote interior and undeveloped sections of the Pacific coast. For additional information, consult a Mexico Tourism Board Office *(see p. 39)*, a Mexican consulate *(see p. 40)* or the U.S. State Department's Bureau of Consular Affairs website *(see p. 33)*.

In Chilapa, 54 kilometers (33 miles) east of Chilpancingo, the *Day of St. Gertrude* on Nov. 16 features whimsically named native dances, including The Seven Vices, The Eight Lunatics, The Old Woman and The Mule. In Chichihualco, 33 kilometers (20 miles) northwest of Chilpancingo, the *Fiesta of St. James* Sept. 28-29 includes a parade, regional foods and such native dances as Fishermen and Devils.

JUXTLAHUACA CAVES are reached via a paved road that leaves Mex. 95 at Petaquillas, about 11 kilometers (7 miles) south of Chilpancingo. Rivaling the caves in Cacahuamilpa Caves National Park *(see Taxco listing)* in size and beauty, these caves are little known outside the region. They contain walls decorated with 3,000-year-old Olmec paintings and unusual geological formations, including translucent salt "veils" and flowerlike crystal formations.

Subterranean ponds and streams support a variety of sightless creatures. A lantern-lit guided tour takes about 5 hours. Explorers should wear comfortable, sturdy walking shoes and bring a light snack; rainwear is advised against spray from subterranean waterfalls. Admission is charged.

JALAPA,
VERACRUZ (C-12)   elev. 4,681′

Capital of the state of Veracruz, Jalapa (hah-LAH-pah) isn't on most Mexican tourist itineraries. But although little visited, it is an altogether charming blend of old and new. Built on the slopes of Macuiltépetl, a large, tiered hill, the city was a Spanish stronghold and an important stagecoach stop between Veracruz and Mexico City. The colonists who followed in the wake of Hernán Cortés found the higher altitude and cooler climate a welcome respite from steamy Veracruz. Jalapa is the capital of the state, a governmental center and a commercial hub for regional coffee and fruit growers.

Although it is home to nearly 300,000 people, Jalapa (spelled Xalapa in Mexico) doesn't seem like a big city. The natural setting is breathtaking—the black volcanic peaks of the Sierra Madre Oriental rise in the distance, towered over by Pico de Orizaba, Mexico's tallest mountain. Practically every corner offers a vista of the mountainous terrain that surrounds the city.

Jalapa's colonial legacy is evident in the structures flanking its older, cobblestone avenues; their red-tiled roofs, wrought-iron balconies, carved wooden doors and window grilles are unmistakably Spanish. Shops and homes are painted in vibrant shades of white, green and deep red. The streets are steep and curving, and also change names and directions frequently; a good city map is an effective navigational aid. Taxis and local buses provide inexpensive transportation to points within the city center.

Begin a morning stroll of downtown Jalapa at the **Café la Parroquia**, on Calle Zaragoza near the south side of the Palacio de Gobierno (Government Palace). A local meetingplace, it has an old-fashioned '50s look and attracts everyone from university professors to families. As in Veracruz, a favorite morning beverage is a *lechero*, a tall glass of strong espresso to which hot milk is added. Tapping your glass with a spoon signals the waiter, who pours the milk from a steaming kettle. In fact, this is a city made for drinking coffee, reading the newspaper and perhaps striking up a conversation with a new acquaintance.

At the corner of calles Enríquez and Revolución, just north of the Government Palace, stands the city's 18th-century **Cathedral**. Its plain white facade is accented by Moorish-style arches and a bell tower clock transported from London. The religious paintings inside are worth a look, as is the sloping floor.

The *chipichipi*, a light but persistent winter rain, and evening mists in summer contribute to Jalapa's reputation as the "flower garden of Mexico." The warmth and moisture create a natural greenhouse effect, and the city is filled with roses, bougainvillea and pine trees. Tree-shaded **Parque Juárez** (Juárez Park), across Calle Enríquez from the Palacio Municipal (City Hall), is representative of the prevailing lushness. White wrought-iron benches are scattered among pruned hedges and well-tended flower beds at this park, which also is the city's central plaza. It provides a restful spot to observe the comings and goings of Jalapeños.

Mexico's equivalent of Cambridge is a hip cultural center as well, being home to the University of Veracruz. The **Agora Arts Center**, just off Juárez Park, is a hangout for students and artists and has extensive events listings, including university lectures, performances by the Ballet Folklórico Veracruzana and the Jalapa Symphony Orchestra, and theater and film schedules, as well as books and recordings for sale. The **Teatro del Estado** (State Theater) on Ignacio de la Llave hosts performances by the ballet and the symphony. All Jalapa celebrates on Sept. 30, the *Day of St. Jerome*, when streets are bedecked with flowers and candlelight processions are held.

A few blocks south of Juárez Park on the grounds of an attractively landscaped lakeside park is the state-run **Casa de Artesanías**, where there are handicrafts for sale by Veracruzan artists, as well as packaged coffee beans. The indoor market on Calle Altamirano, about 2 blocks north of Juárez Park, is a typically colorful hodgepodge displaying assorted trinkets, heaps of dried chilies and beans, and containers of bubbling mole sauces. Street vendors frequent **Callejón Diamante**, a steep little alley off Calle Enríquez (a block or so east of Juárez Park), along which are several casual restaurants specializing in regional fare. Locals and visitors alike head to **La Sopa**, which serves a filling *comida corrida* (fixed-price lunch).

Parque Macuiltépetl (Macuiltépetl Park), north of downtown, is an ecological preserve that showcases indigenous flora and fauna. The winding paths are a bracing climb up one of Jalapa's hillsides, but the views are outstanding.

THE INFORMED TRAVELER

The nearest international airport is in Veracruz. From Veracruz, Jalapa is about a 2-hour drive north on Mex. 180 to the town of Cardel, then east on Mex. 140 past numerous coffee plantations.

The central bus station (CAXA) is on Avenida 20 de Noviembre, about a mile east of the downtown area. From this clean, modern building you can make first-class bus connections and long-distance phone calls, arrange for a taxi into town (an otherwise hilly walk) and even grab a bite to eat. It also has a tourist information booth that is open daily. "Deluxe" bus service is offered by Autobuses del Oriente (ADO).

WHAT TO SEE IN TOWN

MUSEO DE ANTROPOLOGIA (Anthropological Museum) is northwest of downtown at avenidas Jalapa and Aqueducto. Run by the University of Veracruz, it houses a superb collection of exhibits and artifacts encompassing most of Mexico's gulf coast Indian groups, with an emphasis on the Olmec, Totonac and Huastec cultures. Contrasting vividly with the antiquity of the objects on display is the ultramodern museum building, designed by Edward Durrell Stone, architect of the John F. Kennedy Center for the Performing Arts in Washington, D.C. A series of outdoor patios overlook the parklike grounds, which are landscaped with tropical vegetation.

A massive Olmec head is stationed at the museum entrance; several other heads, the largest almost 9 feet tall, are on display in outdoor gardens and indoor galleries. Additional highlights include dramatically lifelike ceramic statues of women wearing belts in the form of writhing serpents; a carved figure in green stone holding an infant with jaguar-like facial features that are characteristically Olmec; and beautifully crafted jade and bone jewelry. The carefully organized displays are augmented by maps that note excavation sites and show where the civilizations flourished.

Information about the exhibits is presented in Spanish only. Tues.-Sun. 9:30-5. Admission is charged; there is an extra fee for the use of a video camera. Phone (28) 15-4952.

PALACIO DE GOBIERNO (Government Palace), the State Capitol, is on the east side of Plaza Juárez. Ornate fountains face the long, pink, colonial-style building. Inside are murals by José Chávez Morado, including "Liberation," which depicts humanity's struggle for freedom.

NEARBY DESTINATIONS

Formal plantings, an arboretum and a palm collection make up **Clavijero Botanical Gardens**, about 3 kilometers (1.5 miles) south of downtown via the road to Coatepec. En route are views of coffee and banana plantations. **Coatepec**, a colonial town about 8 kilometers (5 miles) south of Jalapa, is known for the raising of ornamental plants, chiefly orchids. The main plaza is surrounded by small shops selling coffee beans and *heladerías* (ice cream parlors) dishing up exotic flavors.

About 11 kilometers (7 miles) past Coatepec is **Xico** (HEE-coh), a village where sacks of coffee beans are one of the most common sights. Nearby **Cascada de Texolo** (Texolo Waterfall) has been put to good scenic use in such films as "Romancing the Stone" and parts of the Harrison Ford espionage adventure "A Clear and Present Danger." The falls cascade into a gorge surrounded by lush greenery. A restaurant is at the site, and pathways allow visitors to observe the falls from different vantage points. Local buses to Coatepec and Xico depart from Jalapa's central bus station (*see "The Informed Traveler"*).

About 10 kilometers (6 miles) east of Jalapa on Mex. 140 (toward Veracruz) is **Hacienda Lencero**, a former inn for stagecoaches traveling between Veracruz and Mexico City. The estate was additionally a sugar plantation, a cattle ranch and for a time the home of Antonio López de Santa Anna, a little-loved politician who was president of Mexico on 11 different, short-lived occasions. A tour of the well-preserved buildings offers insight into 19th-century hacienda life, a relatively luxurious existence reserved for wealthy plantation owners. Particularly impressive are the finely crafted Mexican rugs and expensive imported furniture that fill the house, and the carefully tended gardens that surround it. Open Tues.-Sun. Admission is charged.

OAXACA, OAXACA (I-8)   elev. 5,084'

Oaxaca (wa-HAH-ka), the state capital, is situated in a high valley surrounded by the towering summits of the Sierra Madre del Sur. Many of the city's buildings are constructed of an unusual greenish volcanic stone that takes on a golden tone when the sun is low on the horizon. Others are painted bright turquoise or pink. Bougainvillea and roses tumble over walls, geraniums spill out of huge clay pots, and the blooms of jacaranda trees form masses of purple. Completing this colorful palette is the sky over the valley, which is usually an azure blue. Climb to the top of **Cerro del Fortín**, a hill north of the downtown area, for fine views of the city and its lush valley setting.

Oaxaca lies in the shadow of the Mixtec and Zapotec civilizations. Highly religious, these tribes erected elaborate ceremonial centers, were knowledgeable in astronomy and developed systems of writing that are reputed to be the oldest on the North American continent. Today's city is a mixture of pre-Conquest, colonial and modern periods, with a prominent Indian influence. Automobile traffic and industrial activity are reminders of contemporary Mexico, but the resplendently colonial central core exudes an atmosphere remarkably reminiscent of the 18th and 19th centuries. As a result, Oaxaca has been designated a national historic monument.

While the coastal areas of Oaxaca state are steamy and the low-lying Isthmus of Tehuantepec region hot and dry, the capital is protected by the encircling mountains. With an average

elevation of 5,000 feet, the climate of the plateau is mild and healthful. This fertile valley is one of Mexico's oldest continuously inhabited regions; evidence of human settlement dates back to 8,000 B.C. The first great civilization to flourish was that of the Zapotecs; their achievements are preserved at the ruins of **Monte Albán**.

Zapotec culture attained its zenith from about the third through the seventh centuries; it was challenged by the Mixtecs, who built their own center at **Mitla**. The two tribes fought for control of the valley until the Aztecs came and conquered in the late 15th century. The Spanish followed, and the city of Oaxaca was founded by Hernán Cortés in 1529.

Oaxaca has produced two of Mexico's best known presidents. Benito Juárez was born in the nearby village of Guelatao. A Zapotec with no

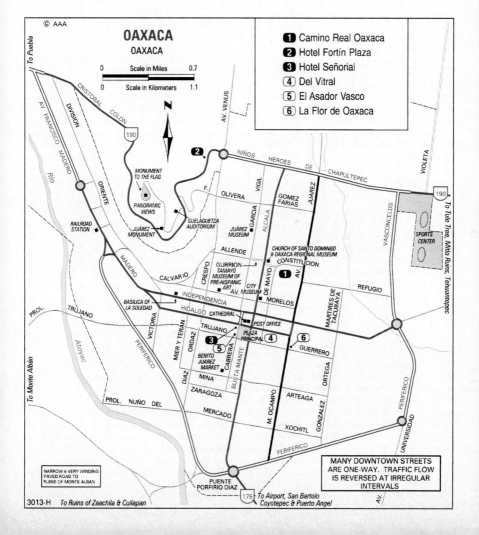

formal childhood education, he nevertheless entered politics, serving as governor of the state, chief justice of the Mexican Supreme Court and later as president of Mexico (1858-72). It was Juárez who led the drive against the French army and Archduke Maximilian's efforts to remain emperor of Mexico and create a Mexican monarchy; the empire was defeated in 1867. Juárez's humble background and subsequent accomplishments have invited comparisons with Abraham Lincoln. Regarded as a national hero, streets, statues and a university bear his name.

Porfirio Díaz, on the other hand, is not nearly so highly regarded. Of Mixtec rather than Zapotec heritage, Díaz embarked on a military career and assumed the presidency in 1876. The Díaz government soon took on the trappings of a dictatorship, however. Important Mexican advances in railroads, manufacturing, oil production and investment abroad were made during his regime, but at the expense of the country's poor and indigenous citizens. Opposition to his policies presaged the Revolution of 1910.

Indian traditions and heritage have remained largely intact in both Oaxaca and neighboring Chiapas, encouraging richness and diversity in handicrafts, ethnic celebrations and regional cookery. Descendants of the Zapotec and Mixtec peoples live in small villages throughout the valley and in the mountains. Regional dialects abound, and for many residents—known as Oaxaqueños—Spanish is a second language.

This strong cultural identity has made Oaxaca one of Mexico's leading art centers. In the last decade a group of artists, all native to the state, have converged here to produce artwork that is stylistically diverse but rooted in themes relating to the lives of the Indians who populate the many rural villages surrounding the city. Some of them first ventured to the city from local villages in the 1970s to study at a training studio sponsored by Oaxacan painter Rufino Tamayo. After dispersing to far-flung locales in Europe and the United States, many have returned to their homeland to create art that is being snapped up by serious Mexican collectors.

The city and the surrounding villages are filled with churches—colonial-era structures as well as cathedral-like edifices that manage to be simultaneously garish, ornate, shabby and splendid. There are more than two dozen in the city alone, including the **Church of Santo Domingo** *(see attraction listing under "What To See")*, which merits a special visit for its dazzling interior decoration. Oaxaca's cathedral, on one end of the main plaza, has a lovely baroque exterior and a wooden clock that still keeps accurate time.

Be sure to sample the local cuisine. The state is known in particular for *mole* sauces, which incorporate a number of spices. There are seven distinct varieties, only one employing the chocolate that also turns up in the *mole poblano* sauce of Puebla. Other specialties are meat-stuffed *tamales* steamed in banana leaves; *tlayudas*, king-size tortillas that should satiate the heartiest appetite; and assorted cheeses. The *comida corrida*, a fixed-item midday meal, is one way to enjoy Oaxacan cooking at reasonable prices. *Comida corridas* are offered at the outdoor cafés located around the main square.

PLANNING YOUR STAY

The peak tourist seasons in Oaxaca are Semana Santa, the week before Easter, and the Christmas season. But there are so many things to see and do that visitors could easily spend 4 or 5 days at any time of year. Allow at least a day to visit the principal downtown attractions; if you have a particular interest in colonial architecture, spend a day touring the cathedral and churches and another visiting the museums. The bustling city markets are certainly worth a visit, especially on Saturdays; spend the morning shopping and take in a few downtown attractions in the afternoon. For nighttime entertainment—music, atmosphere, people watching—there's no better place than the main plaza.

Bus tours to nearby craft villages or town markets will fill up a full day. Of the nearby archeological sites, Monte Albán and Mitla are the most significant; plan on a full day at Monte Albán and half a day at Mitla. Day trips to these two sites could also be combined with a visit to a nearby town. Tour Monte Albán, and then explore the craft village of **Arrazola** or the ruins of a Dominican monastery at **Cuilapan**. On the way to Mitla, stop at the village of **Santa María del Tule** for a look at the Tule Tree, a huge Mexican cypress. For those who want a more in-depth immersion in the region's culture, the **Instituto Cultural Oaxaca** (Oaxaca Cultural Institute), Avenida Juárez #909, offers workshops, cultural programs, Spanish language classes and the opportunity to live with a local family.

Many potholed detours lead in and out of Oaxaca; if you'd rather not drive, take a guided tour. Hotels and travel agencies offer various sightseeing packages. Itineraries include nearby market villages, craft centers and archeological sites, a general tour of the city or tours of churches and museums. A more expensive option is to hire a licensed guide, available through the state tourism office.

THE INFORMED TRAVELER

There are no direct U.S. flights to Oaxaca, but both Aeroméxico and Mexicana offer nonstop connecting flights from Mexico City. The domestic airlines Aero Caribe and Aviacsa have flights from nearby cities, including Cancún, Mérida, Tuxtla Gutiérrez and Villahermosa. Oaxaca's **Benito Juárez Airport** is about 8 kilometers (5 miles) south of the city. Taxi and minibus service between the airport and downtown hotels is easily arranged. For additional information about airlines *see "Arriving by Air," page 53.*

A recently opened toll road running north to the city of Tehuacán reduces the amount of time it takes to travel by car between Oaxaca and Mexico City. The two-lane roadway features wider lanes, fewer curves and better-engineered grades than most other routes that travel through the mountains. It parallels Mex. 190 from Oaxaca northwest to the town of Nochixtlán, then travels north-northwest to Tehuacán, paralleling Mex. 131 for part of the way. Northwest of Tehuacán the road ties into Mex. 150-D, which proceeds west to Mexico City.

First-class bus service is available to and from Mexico City, but there are many stops along the 565-kilometer (350-mile) route. "Deluxe" bus service is provided by ADO. The first-class bus station is north of downtown on Calzada Niños Héroes de Chapultepec. While in Oaxaca, local buses are an economical way to travel to the archeological ruins and Indian villages, although trips can be excruciatingly slow along the narrow, winding mountain roads. For additional information about buses *see "Bus Service," page 63.*

Taxis are another way to get around town, and the fare to nearby destinations can be shared among several riders; negotiate the rate before you set out. Taxis line up around the main plaza.

Personal safety while staying in Oaxaca means such common-sense precautions as keeping your car in a lot overnight rather than parking it on the street, storing all valuables out of sight, and staying alert in such public places as markets and bus stations—professional pickpockets can be very smooth. From a visitor's standpoint, the police usually aren't very helpful, and they tend to use strong-arm tactics to quell localized protests that erupt over such issues as land disputes. The often-violent business of producing illegal drugs also is conducted in remote mountain regions of the state. While foreign travelers are highly unlikely to experience any problems, it's best to stick to established tourist areas, and avoid driving late at night.

Because of the relatively high altitude, temperatures are mild to warm throughout the year, averaging in the 70s or 80s during the day and the 50s or 60s at night. May is the hottest month and the height of the dry season; the rainy season is from June through September. While precipitation is usually limited to afternoon showers, there may be heavy rains in July and August. At this tropical latitude the sun can be quite strong; take the necessary precautions if you'll be outside all day. Sturdy, comfortable walking shoes also come in handy for exploring the ruins and trekking around the village markets. Casual dress is appropriate just about everywhere in Oaxaca

©Chris Sharp

(but do not wear skimpy or revealing clothing inside churches).

The state tourism office is at Calle 5 de Mayo #200 at the corner of Morelos; phone (951) 6-4828. It is open daily 9-8. There also is a tourist information booth in the municipal palace at Avenida Independencia and García Vigil.

SPECIAL EVENTS

Oaxaca's festivals, like the city itself, are colorful and expansive. They draw big crowds, so hotel space should be booked well in advance for the Easter holiday and in July, November and December. Holy Week, beginning the Friday before Easter Sunday, brings parades and communion services, and local churches sponsor fairs, concerts and other activities.

The *Guelaguetza*, meaning "offering," is a centuries-old festival celebrated throughout the state of Oaxaca. Community troupes present their regional costumes, dances, songs and music in a specially designed, open-air theater built into the side of Cerro del Fortín, the hill north of the city. To reach the site, take Avenida Madero north to the Mex. 190 junction, then go east on Mex. 190 about 1.6 kilometers (1 mile). Performances are given on two successive Mondays, normally beginning in the latter half of July; check in advance with a travel agency or your hotel for the exact dates. Tickets are necessary for the main performances and should be reserved no later than May, preferably through a travel agent; confirm the exact festival dates when you make your reservations.

In addition to song and dance, the *Guelaguetza* includes staged re-enactments of battles between Zapotec and Mixtec warriors and presentations of the Aztec and Spanish conquests. Participating singers, dancers and musicians throw *guelaguetzas* (gifts) to spectators. This spectacle of color and sound should not be missed. **Note:** Wear a hat or appropriate headgear for protection from the strong Oaxacan sun.

Oaxaca celebrates the *Día de los Muertos* (Day of the Dead) Nov. 1 and 2 along with the rest of Mexico. The markets are ablaze with marigolds and sell all manner of offerings with which to decorate altars built to honor the deceased. The *Fiesta of the Virgen de la Soledad* in mid-December is a Christmas season highlight and honors the city's patron saint with processions, fireworks, floats and dances. Dec. 23 brings the *Night of the Radishes*. For this competition the main plaza is filled with booths displaying local radishes carved into every conceivable shape. Sweets are served in clay dishes; after finishing the treat, fling your dish to the ground so it smashes.

SHOPPING

Oaxaca is truly paradise for the dedicated shopper. Its markets are among Mexico's most exciting, with head-turning displays of crafts, foodstuffs, household products and curios. If you don't mind the crowds and noise, Saturdays provide the biggest spectacle, drawing Indians who come for miles around to buy and sell. Arrive unburdened so you can maintain your bearings amid the jostling, and prepare to be tempted by the sheer variety of goods on display. The more you bargain, the more you can purchase—begin by offering to pay half the selling price for any item.

The area is known for the production of leather goods, hand-loomed cottons, tempered machetes and daggers, jewelry, carved idols and black pottery from the village of **San Bartolo Coyotepec**. **Teotitlán** and **Ocotlán** are weaving and pottery centers, respectively. The handcarved handles of Oaxacan knives have an eagle surmounting the horn grip; the skillfully etched blades usually carry the maker's name on one side and a Spanish proverb on the other. Local artisans also create carved, brightly painted wooden animals that have whimsical or surreal expressions. Gold, silver and jade jewelry is often a reproduction of actual pieces found at Monte Albán or designed in a similar style.

CITY MARKETS

The **Mercado de Abastos** (Abastos Market), southwest of downtown, is one of Oaxaca's busiest. It is open daily but is most active on Saturday, when scores of Indian villagers dressed in native garb convene to display their merchandise in a huge warehouse and across blocks of open-air lots and canopied stalls. This market is crammed with such items as shawls, embroidered blouses, Oaxacan pottery, woven baskets, rugs, toys, religious ornaments, woodcarvings and jewelry. The air is filled with the smells of incense, chocolate and tortillas. Abastos is also a produce and livestock center, and there are piles of dried chilies in a rainbow of colors, mounds of garlic bulbs, herbs, unfamiliar vegetables and tropical fruits. Adding to the exotic atmosphere are the lilting sounds of Zapotec and Mixtec dialects.

One block south of Plaza Principal along Calle 20 de Noviembre is the **Mercado Benito Juárez**, which also is busiest on Saturday. A covered area is surrounded by open-air stands and street vendors selling everything from spices to *huaraches* (leather sandals) to live birds. The market has a notable crafts section which includes such clothing items as coarse-weave woolen sweaters, shawls and capes. There are numerous food stalls as well. Use appropriate caution when deciding whether or not to sample snacks; if you can see something being cooked it's usually safe to eat. **Mercado 20 de Noviembre**, just south of the Benito Juárez market, offers mole sauces, Oaxacan chocolate an dother foodstuffs.

The **Mercado de Artesanías**, about 2 blocks south of the Benito Juárez Market at the corner of calles José García and Zaragoza, specializes in textiles. The artisans can be observed as they weave rugs, wall hangings and *sarapes* on simple looms. Expect to bargain for any purchase.

SHOPS AND GALLERIES

If you don't relish the give-and-take of haggling, try one of Oaxaca's many stores. The government-run **FONART** store at García Vigil and Manuel Bravo #116 sells a variety of representative crafts from all over the country at fixed prices. The state-run **Artesanías y Industrias Populares del Estado de Oaxaca (ARIPO)**, Calle García Vigil #809, has rooms filled with Oaxacan black pottery, rugs and clothing. There are views of craftspeople at work on their looms.

The **Galería de Arte de Oaxaca**, Calle Trujano #102, is a gallery featuring the work of noted Oaxacan painters and sculptors. **Víctor Artes Regionales**, Porfirio Díaz #111, is housed in a 17th-century monastery and specializes in locally handcrafted dresses, masks and woven tablecloths.

Calle M. Alcalá between the main square and the Church of Santo Domingo is a pedestrian boulevard lined with high-quality shops. **La Mano Mágica**, Calle M. Alcalá #203, is a combination art gallery and crafts shop. Paintings by

Oaxacan artists are exhibited, and regional pottery, textiles and woodcarvings are available from artisans who usually work out of their homes. **Corazón del Pueblo**, Calle M. Alcalá #307-309, stocks a collection of ceramic figurines, decorative boxes and colorfully painted picture frames from all over Mexico, along with English- and Spanish-language art books.

Note: While it's easy to accumulate a trove of treasures, they may need to be shipped home. The better shops and stores can usually arrange for shipping, but this is not the case with items purchased at the markets or from craftspeople in the villages. The most important thing to remember in such cases is to procure a written receipt.

WHAT TO SEE

DOWNTOWN

BASILICA DE LA SOLEDAD (Basílica of Our Lady of Solitude) is a massive 17th-century building at Avenida Independencia #107 (at Avenida Galeana), about 5 blocks west of Plaza Principal. The basilica, actually a complex of several buildings and a garden, is dedicated to the Virgen de la Soledad (Virgin of Solitude). A statue of the Virgin, Oaxaca's patron saint, is displayed above the altar, draped in jewel-encrusted black velvet. According to legend, the stone effigy was found inside the pack of a dead mule; the church was built to commemorate the miracle. Devout believers claim the statue has supernatural healing powers.

The basilica's interior is an extravagant showcase of baroque ornamentation—chandeliers, paintings, statuary and a gilt ceiling. A museum to the rear of the church displays a replica of the Virgin statue. It also contains glass panels depicting the legend of her arrival in the city and an enormous assemblage of gifts (primarily miniature glass figurines) sent in tribute. Basílica and museum open daily. Admission is charged to the museum. Phone (951) 6-7566.

CATEDRAL, facing the north side of Plaza Principal, was begun in 1563 and completed about 2 centuries later. Although severely damaged by earthquakes, the rebuilt cathedral, which is constructed of the native greenish stone, still reflects much of its original grandeur. The clock, its works made of wood, was presented by a Spanish king. The facade bas-relief is a fine example of baroque craftsmanship.

CENTRO CULTURAL SANTO DOMINGO (Santo Domingo Cultural Center) is in the former monastery next to the Church of Santo Domingo. The principal exhibit showcases the beautiful pieces of jewelry and other priceless objects found in Tomb 7 of the Monte Albán ruins. The cultural center also contains fascinating, carefully organized collections of regional handicrafts, costumes worn by the different Indian groups within the state, and archeological artifacts. Information is presented in Spanish. Open Tues.-Sun. Admission is charged; free to all Sun. Phone (951) 6-2991.

IGLESIA DE SAN FELIPE NERI (Church of San Felipe Neri) is on Avenida Independencia at Avenida J.P. García, about 3 blocks northwest of Plaza Principal. The interior of this 17th-century baroque church features a lavish altar of carved, gilded wood and impressive wall frescoes. Open daily. Free.

IGLESIA DE SANTO DOMINGO (Church of Santo Domingo), at Gurrión, M. Alcalá, Berriozábal and Reforma, about 4 blocks from Plaza Principal, was founded by the Dominicans in the 16th century and has a well-deserved reputation as one of the most breathtaking churches in Mexico. Every square inch of the interior walls and ceilings is covered with magnificent gold leaf and polychrome reliefs. One particularly noteworthy decoration under the raised choir depicts crowned heads appearing on the branches of the genealogical tree of the family of Félix de Guzmán. It is dramatically floodlit at night. The adjoining monastery now houses the **Santo Domingo Cultural Center**.

INSTITUTO DE ARTES GRAFICAS DE OAXACA (Graphic Arts Institute of Oaxaca) is at M. Alcalá #507, across from the Church of Santo Domingo. Created primarily through the efforts of celebrated Oaxacan artist Francisco Toledo, the institute has a collection of more than 5,000 engravings that includes his work, that of fellow Mexicans Rufino Tamayo and José Guadalupe Posada, and international artists. There also is an extensive library of art-related volumes. Open Wed.-Mon. 10:30-8. Donations requested. Phone (951) 6-6980.

MUSEO CASA DE JUAREZ (Juárez House Museum) is at García Vigil #609. The museum is in a 19th-century colonial home once owned by Padre Antonio Sala Nueva, benefactor and teacher to one of Mexico's most popular presidents, Benito Juárez. The Sala Nuevas brought the young Oaxaqueño from the village of Guelatao to live with them; Juárez's resulting education was the springboard for his careers in law and politics. The house, representative of a 19th-century upper class lifestyle, contains period furniture, books and memorabilia associated with both men. Open Tues.-Sun. Admission is charged; free to all Sun. Phone (951) 6-1860.

MUSEO DE ARTE CONTEMPORANEO DE OAXACA (Museum of Contemporary Art of Oaxaca) is at Calle M. Alcalá #202, a couple of blocks north of Plaza Principal. It occupies a restored, 16th-century building also known as **Casa de Cortés** (House of Cortés), so named for supposedly being a former residence of the conqueror (historians insist otherwise). Changing exhibits in the beautifully restored colonial building feature the work of contemporary artists, both regional and international. Open Wed.-Mon. 10:30-8. Donations requested. Phone (951) 6-8499.

MUSEO RUFINO TAMAYO DE ARTE PREHISPANICO (Rufino Tamayo Museum of Pre-Hispanic Art), Avenida Morelos #503, is 4 blocks northwest of Plaza Principal. The private collection of artist Rufino Tamayo, which he donated to his native city, traces the development of art in Mexico from about 1250 B.C. to 1500. Housed in a restored, 16th-century colonial mansion, the collection is arranged chronologically and includes artifacts from Teotihuacán, Nayarit state, and the Olmec, Maya, Totonac and Aztec civilizations. Figurines, sculpture and other works are exhibited in a series of brightly colored rooms. Exhibit information is presented in Spanish. Open Wed.-Sat. and Mon. 10-2 and 4-7, Sun. 10-3. Admission is charged. Phone (951) 6-4750.

PLAZA PRINCIPAL, Oaxaca's main square, has an Old World charm and a reputation as one of Mexico's most enjoyable plazas. At its center is a wrought-iron gazebo; fountains decorate some of the walkways. Most of the city's attractions are within walking distance. Many of the museums and the better hotels and restaurants are north of the plaza; also to the north, a 3-block stretch of Calle Alcalá between Morelos and Allende is reserved for pedestrians only. The city's markets are to the south.

The square, shaded by Indian laurel trees, is a place of constant human activity. Traditionally garbed Indian families mix with sharply dressed businessmen and funky young backpackers. Sidewalk vendors peddle their wares and shoeshiners ply their trade. Café tables fill with customers. Protest groups congregate; in this city of students and *indígenas* (natives), much of the political gathering takes place in front of the **Palacio de Gobierno** (Government Palace), opposite the cathedral.

Busy as it it during the day, the plaza really comes alive after dark, when there are more foreigners out and about. Street musicians materialize and offer impromptu performances. Vendors hawk ice cream, roast corn, pineapple chunks, *chorizo* (sausage), blankets, baskets, masks, musical instruments, balloons, children's toys and tin skeletons dancing on the end of sticks. Band concerts, which always draw an appreciative crowd, are held at the bandstand almost daily during the summer, and on Tuesday, Thursday and Sunday evenings the rest of the year. The music varies from brass bands to marimba to Oaxacan rock.

TEATRO MACEDONIO DE ALCALA (Alcalá Theater) is on Avenida Independencia at Avenida 5 de Mayo, 2 blocks east of Plaza Principal. Built around the turn of the 20th century, it reflects the grandiose style public buildings took

under the rule of native son and dictator Porfirio Díaz. The interior in particular is plushly opulent. Occasional shows and concerts are given in the theater; check with the state tourism office for schedule information.

VILLAGE DAY TRIPS

Excursions to area villages can be as rewarding as shopping in the city. The second-class bus station has bus service to most of the villages; another option is to take an inexpensive taxi from a lot near the Abastos Market. Taxis serve the local population as well and fill up quickly in the morning; a per-person rate is charged. *Tianguis* (open-air markets) take place on the following days: Tuesday at **Atzompa**, about 3 kilometers (1.5 miles) southeast on Mex. 190; Wednesday at **San Pablo Etla**, 14 kilometers (9 miles) northwest on Mex. 190; Thursday at **Ejutla**, 61 kilometers (38 miles) south on Mex. 175, and at **Zaachila**, about 18 kilometers (11 miles) southwest; Friday at **Ocotlán**, about 40 kilometers (25 miles) south on Mex. 175; and Sunday at **Tlacolula**, about 32 kilometers (20 miles) southeast on Mex. 190.

Green-glazed pottery is the specialty at Atzompa, including bowls from which breasts or lilies whimsically sprout. Also look for clay dolls. A variety of cheeses and mole sauces can be purchased at San Pablo Etla's market; Ejutla's market is agriculturally oriented as well. Zaachila has a produce and livestock market that does not target tourists but is interesting for its slice of Mexican village life. Ocotlán's raucous Friday market is probably the busiest outside of Oaxaca. *Rebozos* (scarves or shawl-like garments), produce, leather goods, cutlery and ceramic figurines are among the many items for sale.

Other towns are known for a particular craft in which the entire populace seems to be involved. **Arrazola**, a tiny village southwest of Oaxaca near the ruins of Monte Albán, is noted for carvers who fashion fanciful wooden creatures painted in vivid colors. Second-class buses travel to Arrazola, and local youngsters will take you to the artisans' homes for a small tip. **San Bartolo Coyotepec** is the source of the distinctive black pottery sold in many Oaxaca shops. Buses and tours travel frequently to this village, about 37 kilometers (23 miles) south on Mex. 175. Items can be purchased at the local factory, in shops around the plaza or from the potters' homes.

Depending on how long you linger, a trip from Oaxaca to one of the villages and back could take the better part of a day. To maximize your time, combine two destinations; for instance, sample Ocotlán's market in the morning, then stop by San Bartolo Coyotepec on your way back to town.

MONTE ALBAN

The **Monte Albán Ruins**, one of Mexico's greatest pre-Columbian sites, preside over the valley of Oaxaca from a mountaintop location about 9 kilometers (6 miles) southwest of Oaxaca via a narrow, winding road. This major religious center was built by the Zapotecs around 600 B.C. on the deliberately flattened summit of a mountain. At its height around A.D. 300, Monte Albán supported 40,000 inhabitants. By the 10th century the city had been taken over by the Mixtecs, who essentially used it as a lavish burial ground. The Mixtecs were in turn conquered by the Aztecs, and Monte Albán fell into ruin around the time of the Conquest.

The site's focal point is the **Great Plaza**, a grassy area about 970 feet long and 650 feet wide, bounded by four large ceremonial platforms. It was leveled by hewing away rock outcroppings. All of the buildings are aligned on a precise north-south axis except for one, an observatory believed to be placed in relation to the stars rather than to compass directions.

An I-shaped ball court dominates one corner of the plaza. The game played on the court, somewhat similar to soccer and part of ancient religious ceremonies, involved two teams attempting to maneuver a rubber ball through rings placed at either end. Unlike ball courts at Maya and Toltec archeological sites, however, the one at Monte Albán does not have rings.

One of the most fascinating buildings is the **Temple of the Dancers**, on the west side of the plaza. The oldest building at the site, it is named for the elaborate figures carved into its stone slabs. Some of the writhing, nude bodies have twisted facial expressions. They were first thought to be dancers but may be representations of the diseased or cadavers used for study in a school of medicine. Other structures include pyramids and the remains of temples.

Some 170 subterranean tombs are scattered throughout the ruins. These contain numerous slab paintings, glyphs, frescoes and stone carvings. **Tombs 104** and **105** are guarded but can be entered by climbing down a ladder. In 1932, **Tomb 7** yielded a priceless collection of items, which are on display at the **Regional Museum of Oaxaca** (see attraction listing above). The riches include urns, goblets, masks, gold breastplates and jewelry made of jade, pearl and ivory.

Note: The ruins sustained some damage from an earthquake in September 1999. Approximately 30 percent of Monte Alban's restored structures were damaged to some extent. At press time the site was open and repair work was ongoing, although some pyramids may still be cordoned off.

Tour buses depart for Monte Albán from the Mesón del Angel Hotel at Calle Mina #518. The journey to the site is very slow but very scenic. If driving, take Calle M. Cabrera to the Periférico (loop) road at the southern edge of town; cross the Río Atoyac, then take the right fork to the ruins. Guide service is available. Open daily 8-5. Admission is charged; free to all Sun. and holidays.

MITLA, OAXACA (l-9)

The town of **Mitla** (MEE-tlah) is about 42 kilometers (26 miles) southeast of Oaxaca and about 1.9 kilometers (3 miles) off Mex. 190. It was inhabited by the Zapotecs as early as 800 B.C., abandoned more than 1,000 years later, and subsequently resettled by the Mixtecs. The original city, a religious and ceremonial center, prospered up until the time of the Conquest. The name means "place of rest" and refers to the catacombs beneath the Mitla ruins.

Weaving is the principal commercial activity today; woven goods can be purchased almost everywhere. Around Mitla and south along Mex. 190 are outlet stores selling mezcal, a locally produced liquor that packs a wallop. Derived from a variety of the maguey plant, mezcal is a specialty of the state of Oaxaca. The bottle often includes a pickled *gusano* (worm). If imbibed at all, mezcal is best diluted with fruit juice.

The **Museo Frissell de Arte Zapoteca** (Frissell Museum of Zapotec Art), just off the central plaza, is housed in a restored hacienda. It contains Zapotec and Mixtec relics. The museum is maintained by the University of the Americas. Exhibits are labeled in English.

The **Mitla Ruins**, about 1 kilometer (.6 mile) north of the central plaza following the main street, are elaborate cut-stonework ruins, considered to be one of Mexico's most important archeological sites. The mud and stone buildings are inlaid with small cut stones arranged in geometric patterns. The site was begun by the Zapotecs but taken over by the Mixtecs, and the architectural style reflects the latter group. Some buildings remained in use after the Spanish conquest. Unlike many Maya ruins, Mitla was never overtaken by devouring jungle, and the structures are well preserved.

The ruins are divided into five groups. In each group, rectangular patios are surrounded by various buildings or long, narrow rooms. Underground chambers and cruciform tombs honeycomb the soil beneath the structures. The **Hall of Columns**, the most important group, is supported by six enormous pillars, each a single stone, and more than 100,000 pieces of cut stones form the intricate mosaic decorating its walls. The most frequently seen design is a zigzag pattern that also appears on locally woven blankets. Incongruously, a Spanish colonial church occupies one of the site courtyards.

What sets Mitla apart from other North American archeological sites is the lack of human, animal or mythological figures—abstract representations predominate. Open Tues.-Sun.

Admission is charged; free to all Sun. and holidays.

Note: Vendors congregate outside the ruins, hawking fake archeological pieces and a variety of crafts. There also are open-air craft markets next to the ruins. Keep in mind that many of the same items can be purchased in town as well, sometimes at lower prices.

OTHER ARCHEOLOGICAL SITES

The ruins of **Dainzú** are about 24 kilometers (15 miles) southeast on a dirt road off Mex. 190, between Oaxaca and Mitla. They date from 600 to 200 B.C. and are believed to be one of the final evidences of Olmec civilization in the Oaxaca region. Excavations have unearthed an attractive pyramid structure, a ball court and artwork portraying ball players, although little restoration has been accomplished. A caretaker is available to guide visitors around the site. Admission is charged.

The **Zaachila Ruins** are in Zaachila, about 18 kilometers (11 miles) southwest of Oaxaca and past the village of Cuilapan. Archeologists exploring this final stronghold of the Zapotec empire uncovered a tomb built between 700 A.D. and 1050. It contained 11 burial mounds, original wall decorations, pottery and sculpture of major importance. The tomb's contents were transferred to the National Museum of Anthropology in Mexico City. While there are a few pyramids and tombs near the village plaza, they are not open to visitors.

TLACOLULA, OAXACA (I-8)

Tlacolula (tlah-coh-LOO-lah), dating from around 1250, is an important market center for the surrounding Indian communities and the area's mezcal and castor oil producers. Its *mudéjar* (Moorish-style), 16th-century chapel is one of the most ornate in the state of Oaxaca. Known as the **Chapel of Silver**, it is built of cut stone and decorated with intricate carvings. Tlacolula's Sunday market is notable for its size and selection, and all kinds of intriguing items turn up among the mundane housewares and utilitarian clothing. In mid-October a regional festival is held, highlighted by the celebrants' dancing from Tlacolula to nearby villages.

The **Yagul Ruins** are 2.75 kilometers (1.7 miles) east of town, then 2 kilometers (1.2 miles) north of Mex. 190 by paved road. This Zapotec-Mixtec city, with well-preserved tombs, mosaics and buildings, flourished about 500 B.C. Resembling a huge palace with six patios, the site may have served a civic rather than a religious function. The site's ball court is in excellent condition.

CUILAPAN, GUELATAO AND SANTA MARIA DEL TULE

Cuilapan, about 16 kilometers (10 miles) southwest of Oaxaca via a paved road, contains the ruins of a never-completed Dominican monastery that dates from 1555. In the cemetery is the tomb of Donaji, the Zapotec princess whose Christian name was Doña Juana de Cortés. A church has been restored and is in use; it has a Renaissance facade and a number of frescoes. Vicente Guerrero, one of Mexico's first presidents, was executed at this site on Feb. 14, 1831. His remains are interred in the base of the Independence Monument in Mexico City.

The village of **Guelatao,** 63 kilometers (39 miles) north on Mex. 175, is the birthplace of Mexican president Benito Juárez. Guelatao's monument-studded plaza honors this native son, and lively celebrations are held on his birthday, March 21. Although the journey to Guelatao offers impressive views at around 7,000 feet, motorists should exercise caution when negotiating the roadway's serpentine bends and potholes. Frequent drizzle also can make the road surface slippery. To fully enjoy the scenery, take a bus.

About 10 kilometers (6 miles) southeast on Mex. 190 in the village of **Santa María del Tule** is the imposing **Arbol del Tule** (Tule Tree), a giant *ahuehuete,* or Mexican cypress. Believed to be more than 2,000 years old, this colossal specimen stands in the local churchyard and measures some 150 feet both in height and around its base. Local youngsters act as guides, and for a few pesos will point out the tree's more interestingly shaped knots and branches.

WHERE TO STAY

CAMINO REAL OAXACA

▽▽▽▽ ▽▽▽▽   *Classic Country Inn*   (951/6-0611
All Year $155-$270   XP $25
Location: Center; 4 blks n of Zocalo; between Murguia and Abasolo sts. 5 De Mayo 300 68000. Fax: 951/6-0732. **Facility:** Historic. Picturesque 16th-century convent with colonnaded cloisters and fountain courtyard. High-ceiling, austere rooms. 91 units. 2 stories, interior/exterior corridors. **Parking:** valet. **Terms:** F18; 3 day cancellation notice. **Amenities:** honor bars. **Leisure Activities:** heated pool. **Guest Services:** gift shop, valet laundry. **Business Services:** conference facilities. **Cards:** AE, DI, MC, VI.
(See color ad opposite title page)

FEE

HOTEL FORTIN PLAZA

▽▽ ▽▽   *Hotel*   ((951)5-7777
12/1-12/31 & 7/16-8/20 $100   XP $10
1/1-7/15 & 8/21-11/30 $80   XP $10
Location: On north side; in Colonia Estrella on Mex 190. Av Venus 118 68040. Fax: 951/5-1328. **Facility:** Overlooking city. 93 units. *Bath:* shower only. 2 stories, interior/exterior corridors. **Terms:** F8; 7 day cancellation notice-fee imposed. **Amenities:** hair dryers. **Guest Services:** valet laundry. **Business Services:** meeting rooms. *Fee:* fax. **Cards:** AE, DI, MC, VI.

HOTEL SENORIAL

 Hotel (951/6-3933

All Year $48-$55 XP $4
Location: Facing Zocalo. Portal de Flores 6 68000.
Fax: 951/6-3668. **Facility:** Some very good rooms. 127
units. *Bath:* shower only. 3 stories, interior/exterior corridors.
Terms: F12; 15 day cancellation notice. **Guest Services:**
valet laundry. **Cards:** MC, VI.

WHERE TO DINE

DEL VITRAL

 Regional Mexican (951/6-3124

L $5-$13   **D** $5-$13
Location: Just e of Zocalo. Guerrero 201 68000. **Hours:** 1
pm-11 pm. **Features:** No A/C; casual dress; cocktails; street
parking; a la carte. On 2nd floor, older, formal looking decor.
Good selection of international dishes also offered. Great
view of the main plaza, teeming with reflections of Oaxaca.
Attentive, well-trained staff. **Cards:** AE, DI, DS, MC, VI.

EL ASADOR VASCO

Regional Mexican (951/4-4755

L $5-$15   **D** $10-$20
Location: On west side of Zocalo. Portal de Flores 11
68000. **Hours:** 1 pm-11:30 pm. **Features:** No A/C; casual
dress; cocktails; a la carte. On 2nd floor overlooking Zocalo.
Colonial restaurant offering a very good selection of regional
and international dishes. **Cards:** AE, DI, MC, VI.

LA FLOR DE OAXACA

 Regional Mexican (951/6-5522

L $4-$6   **D** $4-$6
Location: Just e of Zocalo, adjacent chapel. Armenta y Lopez 311 68000. **Hours:** 8 am-10:30 pm. **Features:** No A/C;
cocktails; a la carte. Predominantly beef and chicken Oaxacan specialties. **Cards:** DI, DS, MC, VI.

PALENQUE, CHIAPAS (H-10)

The Maya ruins of Palenque (pah-LEHN-keh)
are thought by many to be the most impressive
in Mexico. What they lack in sheer scope is
more than made up for by the site's haunting
presence. Swaddled in dense jungle, the crumbling but intricately decorated structures seem to
be inhabited by the ghosts of their distant past.
The primeval feeling is heightened by the occasional chattering of monkeys or the shriek of an
exotic bird. Similarities between the architecture
at Palenque and that of palaces in southeast Asia
hint at a possible link between Mexico and the
Orient, although the mysteries of Maya civilization related to this particular puzzle will probably
lay forever buried under the rubble of this former
ceremonial center.

The site, part of a national park, occupies the
lower foothills of the Sierra Madre in one of
Mexico's wettest, most lushly forested regions.
Palenque most likely began as a farming settlement around 100 B.C. and flourished between
A.D. 600 and 700, when the city ruled an area
covering much of the present-day states of Chiapas and Tabasco. It was abandoned around A.D.

800 for reasons unknown but still debated by
historians. The interpretation of inscriptions
carved into Palenque's structures have enabled
archeologists to discover the names of its rulers
and date the occurrence of birthdays, marriages
and even the start and finish of armed military
campaigns.

The ruins, named for the nearby town of
Palenque (also known as Santo Domingo de
Palenque), are some 145 kilometers (90 miles)
southeast of Villahermosa. As early as the end of
the 17th century, the vegetation-covered mounds
in the vicinity had been identified as vestiges of
a once-great city. It was not until the 1920s,
however, that large-scale excavations under the
supervision of Danish explorer Frans Blom *(see
San Cristóbal de las Casas listing)* began clear-
ing away centuries of earth and encroaching
jungle. Much of this archeological zone still remains unexplored, although extensive research
has brought to light significant knowledge about
Palenque, its inhabitants, its culture and its central role within the Maya empire.

The excavated section—small in relation to
the city's size during its heyday more than 1,000
years ago—spreads a mile or so from east to
west. The structures here are among the best preserved in Mesoamerica. Stone plaques at the individual temples offer descriptions in English,
Spanish and Maya. One of the most impressive
is the 90-foot-tall **Templo de las Inscripciones**
(Temple of the Inscriptions), to the right as you
enter the site. The name comes from three large
limestone tablets inscribed with hieroglyphics.
The climb to the top of this stairstepped, pyramidal structure is slow going but manageable, and
well worth the effort for the panoramic view of
the surrounding buildings, particularly the conglomeration known as the Palace.

This temple was the final resting place of
Pacal, the king who ruled Palenque for almost 70
years beginning at the ripe old age of 12. It is
believed to be one of the only temples in Mexico
constructed expressly to be a tomb. Discovered
in 1952 by Mexican archeologist Alberto Ruz,
the royal crypt is reached by descending a steep
flight of stone block stairs; its entrance was
blocked by tons of rubble that took several years
to clear. **Note:** The steps can be slippery, and
those subject to claustrophobia will want to
avoid the dank, stuffy atmosphere and stay above
ground.

The crypt's walls and the sarcophagus itself
are decorated with relief carvings. Most of the
crypt's contents—offerings for the king's journey
through the underworld that included a priceless
jade-encrusted mask—were transferred to the
National Museum of Anthropology in Mexico
City; the massive sarcophagus lid remains. A hollow stone duct running from the crypt to the
temple above, visible from the staircase, was

built to allow Pacal's soul to make its way to the underworld.

Next to the Temple of the Inscriptions is **Temple XIII**, where another tomb was discovered in 1995. Preliminary research indicates that the individual buried here also was important within Palenque's ruling hierarchy. Just east is the **Palace**, a complex of stepped buildings and four courtyards connected by corridors and an extensive system of underground passageways. The exterior walls are adorned with the beautifully carved, unusually well-preserved panels and stucco reliefs for which Palenque is famous. Most depict members of the Pacal dynasty. This cluster is capped by a watchtower of unknown function, although it may have been used for observing the heavens.

Other groups of structures are in various stages of restoration. Cross the Río Otolum (little more than a stream) to reach the **Temple of the Cross**, at the southeastern edge of the ruins. It is one of several structures ringing a spacious plaza. Projecting upward from the temple are vertical roof combs, a decorative architectural feature favored by Maya builders. Inside the building is a small shrine. Nearby are **Temple 14**, which contains more stone tablets with carved inscriptions; the **Building of the Foliated Cross**, with a largely obliterated facade; and the **Temple of the Sun**, which archeologists believe may contain the tomb of Pacal's son, Chan-Bahlum, his successor to the throne. Inscriptions here depict the passing of rule from father to son.

At the site's northern end is the **Northern Group** of buildings, including a ball court and the **Temple of the Count**, named for Frederick Waldeck, an early explorer. This structure, the best preserved of the group, is made up of five stepped tiers; its main facade faces east.

Near the Northern Group is a former museum that is now used to store artifacts unearthed during the ongoing excavations. Behind this building a pathway winds downhill toward the paved road to the ruins, passing cool pools of water and even a waterfall. While swimming is not permitted, the pools are ideal for refreshing tired feet. **Note:** Because of the dense vegetation, it is advisable not to wander off of the path alone, even if other people are nearby.

Several bus lines offer "deluxe" service to the town of Palenque. From Villahermosa, service is provided by ADO; the trip takes 2 to 3 hours. From Tuxtla Gutiérrez, service is provided by Autotransportes Cristóbal Colón; the trip takes about 6 hours. Travel agencies in Villahermosa, Tuxtla Gutiérrez and San Cristóbal de las Casas can provide information on reaching Palenque by bus. Although the ruins can be adequately toured in half a day, and some tourists treat Palenque as a day trip from Villahermosa, staying overnight makes for a less hurried agenda.

From Villahermosa, motorists should take Mex. 186 to Catazajá, then Mex. 199 south to the ruins. Passing through lush countryside, the roadway is generally straight, although slick during the June-through-October rainy season and potholed at any time of year. Mex. 199 forks just west of the town of Palenque; the fork is designated by a large statue. Palenque itself has little to offer tourists, although there are hotels and restaurants around the main plaza and more accommodations and campgrounds in the La Cañada area west of the main plaza and along the paved road to the ruins, which are about 8 kilometers (5 miles) to the southwest. For those arriving by first-class bus, *colectivo* shuttle buses and taxis run between the center of town and the ruins.

Summer is not a particularly good time to visit, as the heat and humidity are oppressive. The winter months—approximately November through February—are also humid, although somewhat cooler. Arrive early to avoid both the heat and the crowds, and wear a hat and sunblock for protection from the sun. An all-weather jacket or other rain gear will come in handy at any time. Insect repellent is necessary if you plan on doing any exploring or clambering around the ruins, particularly in the late afternoon.

A combined museum and visitor center, located on the highway about a mile before the main entrance, contains a refreshment stand and shops selling Chiapan handicrafts. The museum displays reproductions of hieroglyphic panels and other artifacts uncovered at the ruins, with explanations in both Spanish and English. Local vendors peddle souvenirs in the large parking lot at the site entrance, where the ticket booth is located. Site open daily 8-5; Temple of the Inscriptions crypt open daily 10-4; museum open Tues.-Sun. 10-5. The crypt may be closed in rainy weather. Admission to the ruins is charged; free to all Sun. There is a separate museum admission, and an additional charge for the use of a video camera.

AGUA AZUL WATERFALLS NATIONAL PARK

About 62 kilometers (39 miles) south of Palenque off Mex. 199 (toward the town of Ocosingo) is **Parque Nacional Cascadas de Agua Azul** (Agua Azul Waterfalls National Park). The park is about 4 kilometers (2.5 miles) off the highway via a turnoff. A landing strip for small planes is in the vicinity, and some garbage is visible in what has become a very touristy and crowded area. Highlighted by rapids, pools and cascades of various heights, the parkland extends some 5 kilometers (3 miles) through jungles of palm trees and exotic flowers. Swimming is permitted in Agua Azul's clean, blue waters (be careful of strong currents); outdoor restaurants serving fish dishes line the walking path (an up-hill trek) along the falls. Rustic cabins and a campsite are nearby.

The park is most pleasant during the drier months (November through May). However, intentional burning in April and May to clear the jungle can result in a thick haze of smoke. Admission to the park is charged (per person or per vehicle). Travel agencies in the town of Palenque offer day trip packages to Agua Azul and a closer waterfall, **Misol-Ha**; inquire along Avenida Juárez near the main plaza.

For adventurers, a dirt road runs east from Ocosingo to the ruins of **Toniná**, deep in the Chiapan jungle. Several pyramids and ball courts been uncovered here, along with numerous broken statues. Evidence links this former religious and administrative center to Palenque and Yaxchilán, all three cities part of the far-flung Maya empire. Taxi drivers charge an exorbitant fare to get to the ruins from Ocosingo, so you'll save this expense if you have a car. There are no explanatory plaques at the site; those interested in Toniná's history should inquire about the services of a guide in Ocosingo. The ruins are open daily; admission is charged.

BONAMPAK AND YAXCHILAN

From Palenque, Tenosique or San Cristóbal de las Casas it is possible to charter a plane or jeep to travel the some 120 kilometers (75 miles) southeast to **Bonampak**, site of some of the most sophisticated Maya murals yet found (A.D. 600). Unfortunately, many of them are notably deteriorated because of the constant humidity, and most visitors will gain just as much appreciation from the reproductions on view at the National Museum of Anthropology in Mexico City and the Museum of Anthropology in Villahermosa.

Not far from Bonampak is another Maya site, **Yaxchilán**, cradled in a horseshoe bend of the Río Usumacinta near the Guatemalan border. It was built at about the same time as Bonampak and contains temples, a palace and notable staircases. By chartered plane, Yaxchilán is about an hour distant from Palenque. Needless to say, the trip is only for true devotees of archeological ruins; make travel arrangements well in advance.

WHERE TO STAY

CHAN-KAH RESORT VILLAGE
▼▼ *Cottage*   ((934)5-1100
All Year $82   XP $15
Location: 3.5 km on hwy to archaeological ruins. Km 3 Carretera A Las Ruinas 29960. Fax: 934/5-0820. **Facility:** Individual cottages in tropical jungle setting at entrance to National Archaeological Zone. 72 units. 4 two-bedroom units. *Bath:* shower only. **Parking:** valet. **Terms:** F12; cancellation fee imposed. **Amenities:** no TVs. **Leisure Activities:** spring fed filtered pool, game room. **Business Services:** meeting rooms. **Cards:** MC, VI.

SOME UNITS

HOTEL CALINDA NUTUTUN PALENQUE
▼▼ ▼▼ *Motor Inn*   (934/5-0100
All Year $70-$80   XP $8
Location: 5 km s on Mex 199 to Agua Azul. Km 3.5 Carr Palenque-Oco 29960. Fax: 934/5-0626. **Facility:** Large rooms on spacious tropical grounds adjacent to mountain fed river. Meets AAA guest room security requirements. 57 units. *Bath:* combo or shower only. 2 stories, exterior corridors. **Terms:** F12. **Leisure Activities:** wading pool, river swimming, playground. **Guest Services:** gift shop, valet laundry. **Cards:** AE, MC, VI.

HOTEL MISION PALENQUE PARK PLAZA
▼▼ ▼▼ *Motor Inn*   (934/5-0241
All Year $120   XP $8
Location: 4 blks e of center, following signs. Rancho San Martin de Porr 29960. Fax: 934/5-0300. **Facility:** Quietly located on extensive grounds. Hacienda style with rooms furnished in simple modern style. 210 units. *Bath:* combo or shower only. 2 stories, exterior corridors. **Terms:** F12. **Leisure Activities:** 2 tennis courts, bicycles. **Guest Services:** valet laundry. **Cards:** AE, DI, MC, VI.

SOME UNITS

HOTEL PLAZA PALENQUE
▼▼ ▼▼ *Motor Inn*   (934/5-0555
All Year $70   XP $5
Location: 1 km n on Mex 199. 29960 (PO Box 58). Fax: 934/5-0395. **Facility:** 100 units. *Bath:* shower only. **Terms:** F12; 14 day cancellation notice. **Amenities:** Some: safes. **Guest Services:** gift shop, valet laundry. **Business Services:** meeting rooms. **Cards:** AE, MC, VI.

PAPANTLA, VERACRUZ (B-11)

Papantla (pah-PAHN-tlah) spreads out over the green foothills of the Sierra Madre Oriental, about 243 kilometers (150 miles) northwest of Veracruz. This was the capital of the Totonac kingdom in the mid-15th century, before it fell to the conquering Aztecs. The vanquished Totonacs extracted a revenge of sorts by aiding Hernán Cortés in defeating the Aztec empire. The city remains a center of Totonac culture today, and visitors are likely to see locals wearing native garb: billowing white pants and sailor shirts for men, lacy skirts and embroidered white blouses for women.

White-tiled, palm-shaded **Plaza Téllez**, the main plaza, is located in the center of town, which is at the top of a hill. Benches in the plaza are inlaid with tile mosaics. The **Catedral Señora de la Asunción** is on the plaza's south side. Carved into the church's north wall is a stone mural some 165 feet long. Called *Homenaje a la Cultura Totonaca*, the mural depicts Totonac folkloric figures and is dominated by a rendering of the plumed serpent Quetzalcóatl that runs its entire length. There is a tourist office in the **Palacio Municipal** (City Hall) building on the west side of the plaza, which is usually open only in the morning.

Downhill and north of the plaza is the first-class Autobuses del Oriente (ADO) bus station, at the intersection of avenidas Venustiano Carranza and Benito Juárez. From the station there is "deluxe" service to Poza Rica, Jalapa and Veracruz.

Papantla is Mexico's vanilla-producing center, and concrete memorials to the vanilla bean stand at opposite ends of the city. The distinctively sweet scent frequently hovers in the air. Vanilla bean pods are fashioned into small figures that are sold around town, along with textiles, embroidered clothing and baskets. In the morning, vendors sell tamales and *atole*, a thick, warm, vanilla-flavored drink, from stands at the **Mercado Juárez** (Juárez Market), opposite the cathedral. Produce and live poultry predominate. Souvenir hunters will have more luck at **Mercado Hidalgo** (Hidalgo Market), on Avenida 20 de Noviembre just off the northwest corner of the main plaza, where handmade men's and women's clothing can be found.

Papantla is celebrated for its **Voladores de Papantla** (Papantla Flyers)—Totonac Indians who give an exciting rendition of the "Flying Pole" dance. Ropes that have been wound around a 70-foot-tall pole are tied around their waists. Four dancers jump backward off a tiny revolving platform atop the pole, whirling downwards as the ropes unwind. A fifth man, who dances while playing a flute and beating a drum, remains on top of the platform. Each performer revolves around the pole 13 times; the total number of revolutions, 52, equals the number of years in the Aztec religious life cycle.

Before it evolved into a crowd-pleasing spectacle of its own, the dance was part of a pre-Hispanic agricultural ceremony designed to secure the favor of the rain gods and to celebrate the vanilla harvest. The *voladores* (flying pole dancers) perform in the courtyard of the cathedral, known as the Plaza de los Voladores, on Sundays, and up to three times a day during the *Festival of Corpus Christi* in late May or early June. Papantla's signature annual event, the festival is celebrated with art exhibitions, traditional dances, cockfights and fireworks displays. Overlooking the city from a hilltop is a giant likeness of a flute-playing *volador*, a monument erected in 1988. There are good views of the surrounding countryside from the base of the statue, which can be reached by walking up Avenida Reforma from the cathedral.

EL TAJÍN

The main reason to come to Papantla is to visit the ruins of **El Tajín** (tah-HEEN), about 13 kilometers (8 miles) west of town via a paved road. Generally ascribed to the Totonacs—although no one knows for sure who created it—

this ceremonial center (the name means "city of thunder") probably reached its peak about A.D. 800. Unidentified invaders from the north had destroyed it by 1200. Some of the site has been restored, although archeologists estimate that hundreds of ruined buildings remain hidden beneath the jungle growth that characterizes this coastal region of Mexico. For those interested in ruins, El Tajín's size and architectural legacy make it well worth exploring.

The El Tajín ruins were not discovered until the late 18th century. A major restoration project began in 1992 as part of the 500th anniversary of Christopher Columbus' discovery of the New World. More than 30 buildings have subsequently been restored, although many more hidden under grassy mounds await excavation. The entire archeological zone is thought to cover some 4 square miles. **Note:** Visitors should stay on the cleared pathways between the buildings; the thick underbrush in this part of Mexico is likely to be inhabited by poisonous snakes.

The excavated structures are divided into two main groups. In the main group is the most impressive structure, the **Pyramid of the Niches**. Its seven terraces are punctuated with a total of 365 corniced, deeply recessed square niches that were once painted bright red and blue. The overall appearance of this 60-foot-tall pyramid is somewhat similar to that of a colossal beehive. A steep staircase with bordering ramps ascends the east side. A smaller pyramid, **Building 5**, is located just to the south.

Several I-shaped ball courts of various sizes underscore the ceremonial significance of the ancient game that was played throughout Mesoamerica. Little is known about how it was played; participants probably maneuvered a rubber ball across the playing field by kicking it, along the lines of modern-day soccer. Death by sacrifice may have been the brutal outcome, although it is unknown whether the winners or the losers lost their lives. Carved panels depicting scenes relating to this ritual decorate the **South Ball Court** south of the Pyramid of the Niches, El Tajín's largest and best-preserved example.

North of the Pyramid of the Niches, an uphill pathway leads to a newer group of buildings called **El Tajín Chico** (Little Tajín). Separate from the ceremonial structures, this section is thought to be where the city's ruling elite once lived. Overlooking the complex is the **Building of the Columns**; the six richly carved column shafts—three on each side—once supported a ceiling. A Maya arch forms the entrance to **Building A. Building C**, a pyramid, features stone fretwork similar to that adorning the Pyramid of the Niches.

A museum at the entrance to the site displays pottery and other artifacts retrieved from the excavations. Also at the entrance area are a restaurant, souvenir stands and an informational plaque in English, among other languages, that tells what is known about El Tajín. The flying pole dance performed in town also takes place here (the pole is near the museum) whenever there are enough tourists—usually touring groups—to form an appreciative crowd. A fee is charged to watch the spectacle, which is not without risk to its daredevil performers.

Local buses depart for El Tajín from the Mercado Juárez (Juárez Market) on the main plaza. The Papantla tourist office can provide information about bus or minibus service to the ruins, although English is not likely to be spoken; it's easier to reach the site in your own vehicle or visit it as part of an organized bus tour. Ruins open daily 9-5. Admission is charged; free to all Sun. There is an extra charge for the use of a video camera.

In early 1994, archeologists discovered the ruins of a major city, **El Pital**, about 10 miles up the Nautla River from the Gulf of Mexico. The site, about 40 miles southeast of El Tajín, consists of dozens of mounds covered with orange and banana groves—local residents assumed they were natural hills—that hide the remains of large earthen pyramids and other structures. Researchers believe that the city flourished concurrently with Teotihuacán *(see separate listing under Mexico City and Vicinity)* and may have been part of a cultural link connecting the central gulf coast region with the ancient cities of central Mexico. Excavations have begun at this site, which is the most important archeological find in

Mexico since the late 1970s discovery during subway construction of the Templo Mayor (Great Temple of the Aztecs) in Mexico City.

SAN CRISTOBAL DE LAS CASAS, CHIAPAS (I-10) elev. 6,888'

San Cristóbal (sahn krees-TOH-bahl) de las Casas was settled in 1528 by troops of Hernán Cortés under the command of Diego de Mazariegos, who later became the governor of Cuba. In a fertile basin ringed by the Chiapas Mountains, it was once capital of the state. San Cristóbal, a beautiful colonial city that has been designated a national historic monument, is located in an especially scenic, though remote, part of Mexico where rain-laden clouds brush the tops of forested ridges.

San Cristóbal and Chiapas made headlines in 1994 when peasant rebels calling themselves the Zapatista National Liberation Army seized territory in this poverty-ridden state. The insurgents called for more democratic dealings on the part of the Mexican government, economic aid and health care for poor Chiapan farmers and greater rights for the country's indigenous peoples. While the conflict did not directly affect tourists, it has stirred debate regarding political reform measures and underscored the deep class divisions present in contemporary Mexican society.

Although well into the tropics, San Cristóbal's altitude and frequent heavy cloud cover lend it a decidedly nontropical feeling. The air is redolent

Brightly colored buildings enliven a San Cristóbal street. ©John Neubauer

with the smoky fragrance of burning *ocote* (a Náhuatl Indian word meaning "kindlewood"), a pitch-pine kindling sold in the markets. This also is the area where Central America begins, culturally if not politically; the border with Guatemala lies little more than 160 kilometers (100 miles) southeast.

Writers, artists and researchers have long made the pilgrimage here; more recently, European travelers have "discovered" it. **Centro Bilingue**, 2 blocks from the main plaza, is a school offering Spanish-language classes. It is housed in a colonial building that also includes the **Centro Cultural El Puente**, which has a café, information center, media room and bookstore; phone (967) 8-3723.

San Cristóbal's outskirts—like those of many Mexican cities—sprawl drearily along the highway, with billboards advertising Coke and Pepsi as a reminder of modern encroachment. Colonial charm is preserved, however, in the city center. The narrow streets were designed for carriages rather than cars. Old houses with grilled windows give it a look that is stylistically Spanish, although the atmosphere is definitely Indian. The local population supplies the markets with handwoven fabrics, handcrafted leather articles, ornamental candles, wooden toys, and earthenware jugs and vases. While most men in San Cristóbal wear contemporary-style clothing, older women still dress in traditional Maya garb.

The **Central Market**, on Avenida General M. Utrilla about 6 blocks north of the main plaza, stands out due to the many colorful costumes worn by merchants and customers. It's open every morning but Sunday, when the local village markets take over. Produce and household items dominate the open-air portion; if you're searching for handicrafts, try the shops east of the main plaza along Calle Real de Guadalupe. All of the market is fascinating, although the squeamish will want to avoid the gory butcher stalls within the covered section. **Note:** Avoid taking pictures of vendors or shoppers at the market.

Venerable churches contribute to the local character as well; many of these ornate structures were built by missionaries. Some of the carvings adorning San Cristóbal's 16th-century **Cathedral**, which flanks the main plaza, are missing their heads. The bright yellow exterior is particularly lovely in the late afternoon sun. Three blocks south of the plaza, just off Avenida Miguel Hidalgo, is the 1587 **Templo del Carmen** (Church of El Carmen), which has a street passing through the middle of its four-story arch. The **Templo de San Cristóbal** (Church of San Cristóbal) perches atop a hill at the end of Calle Hermanos Domínguez; walk 3 blocks south of the main plaza along Avenida Miguel Hidalgo, then turn right. Although you'll have to climb what seems like an endless series of steps up the hill to reach the church, the view of the city

from the top is worth it. In the hills east of the town center is the **Church of the Virgin of Guadalupe**.

The ancient ruins at **Moxquivil** are northeast of San Cristóbal; information about the site can be obtained at the Na-Bolom Museum *(see attraction listing below)*. The **Grutas de Rancho Grande** (San Cristóbal Caves) are 11 kilometers (7 miles) southeast of town just off Mex. 190; look for the sign that says "Rancho Nuevo" on the right-hand side of the road. The large cavern, which extends deep into the side of a mountain, is a short hike from the roadway. Another nearby destination is **El Arcotete**, a natural limestone arch that forms a bridge over a river. To get there, follow Calle Real de Guadalupe east out of town, which becomes the road to the village of Tenejapa; the arch is about 3.5 kilometers (2 miles) past the Guadalupe Church, following signs.

Excursions to these and other points of interest in and around San Cristóbal can be arranged through the tourist office, located in the City Hall building on the main plaza, opposite the cathedral. The office is open Mon.-Sat. 9-8 (may be closed 2-4), Sun. 9-2; phone (967) 9-1967 or 8-6570. Check the bulletin board there for notices pertaining to cultural events and guided tours. "Deluxe" bus service to and from Mérida, Oaxaca, Tuxtla Gutiérrez and Villahermosa is offered by Autotransportes Cristóbal Colón. The first-class bus station is at the intersection of Mex. 190 and Avenida Insurgentes, about 9 blocks south of the main plaza.

Although some of San Cristóbal's most intriguing events take place in the surrounding villages, several are celebrated in town. The *Feria de Primavera* (Spring Fair) takes place the week after Easter. The merriment includes parades, band concerts, handicraft exhibits, amusement rides and stalls serving an array of regional foods. The *Fiesta of San Cristóbal*, held July 22-25, honors the town's patron saint. Pilgrims carrying torches climb the steep hill to the Church of San Cristóbal to attend special services.

Mex. 190 from San Cristóbal west to Tuxtla Gutiérrez winds for some 81 kilometers (50 miles) in a series of S-curves around high mountain peaks, frequently above cloud level. The altitude drops some 5,000 feet between the two cities. A drive through this region passes beautiful, unspoiled scenery, but slippery pavement can make the roadway dangerous. Motorists should maintain a speed appropriate to conditions and exercise caution, particularly around curves.

WHAT TO SEE IN TOWN

MUSEO DEL AMBAR (Amber Museum) is 3 blocks north of the main plaza at Avenida General M. Utrilla #10 (Plaza Sivan). Pass through the clothing shop to reach the museum, which is perhaps the only one in Mexico devoted to amber, a brownish-yellow, translucent fossil resin that is mined in the nearby Simojovel Valley. On view are sculpted amber pieces carved by local artisans, as well as ancient chunks with fossilized insects inside. Amber jewelry is offered for sale. Open daily 10-6. Free.

MUSEO NA-BOLOM (Na-Bolom Museum) is northeast of the main plaza at Avenida Vicente Guerrero #33. It celebrates the work of Danish explorer and ethnologist Frans Blom, who first came to Chiapas in 1919 to study the region's people, archeological zones, history, flora and fauna. The colonial-style building, dating from 1891 and now a museum, was purchased by Blom in 1950. It became the headquarters from which his expeditions departed and a gathering place for archeologists, researchers and others interested in this remote region of Mexico.

Blom went on to conduct extensive research at the Maya ruins around Palenque, and oversaw some of the first excavations at Uxmal *(see separate listing under Yucatán Peninsula)*. His wife Gertrude, a journalist and photographer, devoted herself to preserving the rain forest homeland of the reclusive Lacandón Indians. After Blom died in 1963, Gertrude Blom continued her husband's support of the region's ecology and ethnic peoples until her own death in 1993. Na-Bolom continues to operate as a private, nonprofit institute dedicated to the preservation of the environment and native cultures.

Guided group tours of the home take in a collection of pre-Hispanic artifacts put together by Blom; the library, with thousands of volumes about the Maya and Chiapas; a walk through the extensive gardens; and a showing of the film "La Reina de la Selva," about the Lacandón forest and its inhabitants. Group tours are offered Tues.-Sun. beginning at 4:30. Admission is charged. Na-Bolom also functions as a guest house, with about a dozen rustic rooms; guests receive a free tour of the house and have access to the library. Make reservations well in advance. Dinner can be arranged at Na-Bolom as well, and dining companions are likely to include visiting anthropologists or researchers. Phone (967) 8-1418.

TEMPLE AND EX-CONVENT OF SANTO DOMINGO, about 5 blocks north of the main plaza, is entered from Avenida 20 de Noviembre. Construction of the church was begun in 1547; the extravagantly detailed carvings on its baroque exterior have weathered to a dusty pink. Inside are numerous representations of saints. People from the surrounding villages spread their wares—embroidered clothing, pottery, dolls outfitted like Zapatista guerrilla fighters—in the plaza in front of the church. An adjacent convent houses a handicraft museum selling such exquisite Indian-made items as wool capes adorned with down and feathers.

Santo Domingo market   © John Neubauer

SAN JUAN CHAMULA AND ZINACANTAN

The ethnic peoples populating the nearby communities north of San Cristóbal are among the most interesting in the country. They have managed—over hundreds of years and despite the drastic modernization much of Mexico has undergone—to maintain their cultural identity. Although almost all are members of the Tzeltal and Tzotzil tribes, the inhabitants of these mountain villages maintain a striking variety of differences in manner of dress, dialect, and religious customs and ceremonies.

At an altitude of some 7,000 feet above sea level, the area has a temperate climate and a local economy based on agriculture. Corn, beans and squash are grown, and chickens, turkeys, pigs, rabbits, sheep and some cattle are raised. Among the handicrafts produced by village artisans are wooden musical instruments, leather goods, ceramics, furniture and woven baskets. The best time to visit is during a fiesta or on Sunday, when most of the villages have their own market and tourists are most welcomed.

San Juan Chamula, about 12 kilometers (8 miles) north of San Cristóbal via a paved road, is the best known town. The municipality of Chamula is divided into three areas—San Juan, Sebastian and San Pedro—that are home to some

70,000 people. Spanish is not spoken, and English is rarely heard. Visitors must obtain permission to explore the town and pay a fee at the tourist office on the main plaza.

Perhaps the highest honor that a local citizen can obtain here is to assume "the change of authority," which occurs annually at the beginning of the year. Municipal leaders select a man to be the guardian of the town church and the events that occur within it for a full year; his family is cared for by the townspeople for the duration of his responsibility.

Shamans, or spiritual healers, come to San Juan Chamula's church to administer to families experiencing physical or mental problems. They may place a hand on the pulse of the sufferer and chant prayers, or break eggs over the heads of the troubled and wash their bodies with the raw contents, which act as a spiritual cleanser. "Posh," a decidedly alcoholic concoction extracted from fermented sugar cane, may be either consumed or sprayed over ailing body parts in the belief that it acts as a connection to the gods. Shamans also have extensive knowledge of the region's medicinal plants and herbs, and use them as healing agents.

The church itself has a beautifully carved wooden door. Inside the floor is strewn with pine needles, and the smell of incense wafts throughout. Kneeling in front of burning candles are men and women who chant, pray or simply sit and reflect while sipping a soft drink or the potent posh. Statues of saints line the walls, although they play a part in these rituals in name only; Catholicism is not observed by the Chamulas. Visitors may stand and observe quietly in the background.

The town is noted for its religious observances, particularly those celebrated during *Holy Week* (between Palm Sunday and Easter Sunday). A blend of Christian and pagan rites, the ceremonies take place both inside the church and in the plaza in front of it. On June 24, a Catholic priest visits the village to baptize newborn children.

Other events take place throughout the year. The *Feast of San Sebastian and Saint Paul* takes place Jan. 18-20. *Carnaval* celebrations, featuring a parade of vivid costumes, are held in February or March. March 17-19 marks the *Feast of St. Joseph*. The *Feast of the Holy Cross* occurs May 1-3, while the *Feast of the Angel St. Michael* takes place May 6-9. The *Feast of St. John the Baptist* (the patron saint of San Juan Chamula) is observed June 22-24. Additional events include the *Feast of St. Rose and St. Augustine* Aug. 28-30, the *Feast of St. Matthew and St. Nicholas* Sept. 19-21, and the *Feast of the Virgin of the Rosary of St. Francis* Oct. 5-7. San Juan Chamula also celebrates—along with the rest of Mexico—the *Day of the Dead* Nov. 2, the *Feast Day of the Virgin of Guadalupe* Dec. 12,

and celebrations of Jesus' birth during the Christmas season.

Note: A visit to any local village involves sensitivity, as you are an outsider and may well be made to feel like one. Picture taking is forbidden at most events, and particularly so inside churches; in fact, a special police force arrests violators. In any areas inhabited by *indígena* villagers, residents may not take kindly to being stared at, and photography of any sort will be objected to. Children may pose for pictures in exchange for a few pesos, but on the whole, keep cameras packed. Buying a trinket or souvenir provides a memory of the trip and also aids—however marginally—the local economy. Youthful vendors, many of whom live in desperate poverty, will hawk tourists aggressively.

Daily dress varies according to the village. In San Juan Chamula, men wear short or long white trousers secured by a leather belt and a black, grey or white wool *jorongo* (a sort of sleeveless jacket). Standard garb for women, regardless of the village, is the *huipil* (a white blouse with colorful embroidery), a black wool skirt and a blue or red shawl. Many women run colorful ribbons through their hair, which is traditionally worn in long braids. In **Zinacantán**, a nearby town that is wealthier than San Juan Chamula, villagers often sport red ponchos adorned with tassels. Zinacantán's church also has a floor covered in pine needles, but the rituals here incorporate Catholicism to a greater degree. Photography, both inside and out, is strictly prohibited.

WHERE TO STAY

HOSTAL FLAMBOYANT ESPANAL

♦♦ ♦♦   *Country Inn*   ((967)8-0045

All Year $50
Location: In town; just n of Parque Espinosa. Ave 16 de Septiembre & Primero 29200 (PO Box 12). Fax: 967/8-0514. **Facility:** Rustic colonial decor. Large rooms. 84 units. *Bath:* combo or shower only. 2 stories, exterior corridors. **Terms:** 30 day cancellation notice, 7 day in summer. **Leisure Activities:** exercise room. **Guest Services:** gift shop, valet laundry. **Cards:** AE, MC, VI.

[¶] [Ⓚ] [✦]

HOTEL BONAMPAK

♦♦   *Motor Inn*   (967/8-1621

All Year $29   XP $3
Location: On Mex 190, north entrance to town at statue. Calzada Mexico 5 29310 (Apartado Postal 75). Fax: 967/8-1622. **Facility:** 50 units, 1 with efficiency. *Bath:* shower only. 2 stories, interior/exterior corridors. **Terms:** F12; 15 day cancellation notice. **Leisure Activities:** miniature golf, tennis court, playground. **Guest Services:** gift shop, valet laundry. **Cards:** AE, DI, MC, VI.

SOME UNITS
[¶] [≋] [✕] [Ⓚ] / [🛏] /

POSADA DIEGO DE MAZARIEGOS

▼▼▼   *Country Inn*   ((967)8-0833

All Year $47   XP $20
Location: Just n of Parque Espinosa. Ma Adelina Flores 2
29240. Fax: 967/8-0827. **Facility:** Mexican colonial style architecture and decor. Many rooms with fireplace. 77 units.
Some whirlpool units. *Bath:* shower only. 2 stories, interior/
exterior corridors. **Terms:** F6; 30 day cancellation notice-fee
imposed. **Guest Services:** [MAP] meal plan available, gift
shop, valet laundry. **Business Services:** meeting rooms.
Cards: AE, CB, DI, MC, VI.

                        SOME UNITS
[$D] [🍽] [🍸] [AC] / [🅗] /

TAXCO, GUERRERO (D-9) elev. 5,897'

Probably the oldest mining town in North
America, Taxco (TAHS-coh) originated as the Indian village of Tlachco (place of ball game)
when Hernán Cortés' captains discovered rich
gold deposits. The restored **Hacienda del Chor-
rillo**, where they handled smelted silver ship-
ments, is now the governor's guest house and
can be visited. **Bermeja Hill** still bears the scar
of a cavernous mining shaft called the King's
Shaft, reputed to be the oldest on the continent.
The town's real development dates from the time

of José de la Borda, a French miner who arrived
in 1716 and amassed an immense fortune. Silver
mines that Borda opened still produce.

Borda's initial impact on the mining industry
was carried on by a young American named William Spratling, who came to Taxco in 1929 to
write a book. Stranded in Mexico after his pub-
lisher went broke, Spratling turned to the silver
business. He opened a retail outlet and found apprentices among the local youth, many of whom
are now proprietors of Taxco's silver shops.

Sprawled over a rugged hillside in the heart of
the Sierra Madre, Taxco has changed little in appearance since Borda's time. The Mexican government prohibits the building of modern
structures; older ones proliferate, in various
stages of preservation. Whitewashed houses, red-
tiled roofs and cobblestoned streets give Taxco
its colonial charm.

Only the facade remains of the **Figueroa
House**, completed in 1767 by the Count Cadena,
a friend of José de la Borda. It is said that the
count, a magistrate, required Indians to pay their
fines by working on the house. It was perhaps
for this reason it was called La Casa de las Lá-
grimas, "The House of Tears."

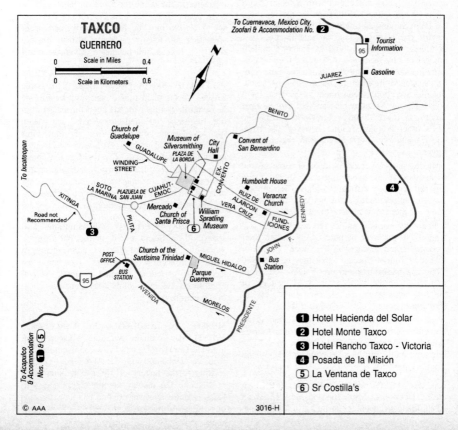

TAXCO
GUERRERO

Scale in Miles   0 — 0.4
Scale in Kilometers   0 — 0.6

1 Hotel Hacienda del Solar
2 Hotel Monte Taxco
3 Hotel Rancho Taxco - Victoria
4 Posada de la Misión
5 La Ventana de Taxco
6 Sr Costilla's

© AAA   3016-H

Taxco's main square is typical of those in other old Mexican towns, shaded by trees, offering benches for relaxation and providing a bandstand for musical performances. Sunday is market day; such wares as old-style *sarapes*, tin candlesticks, decorative mirrors and hand-carved furniture are displayed. Handcrafted silver items, jewelry, colonial-style furniture and wrought-iron articles are available at the market and in many shops.

The *Feria Nacional de la Plata* (National Silver Fair), held the first week in December and Mexico's most important silversmithing contest, is symbolic of the town's craft. Each year judges confer international recognition to artisans whose designs and workmanship are deemed superior.

Another annual event of interest to visitors is the *Jornadas Alarconianas* (Alarcón Days). This cultural and artistic festival offers painting expositions, band serenades in Borda Square and musical performances during the last three weekends in May. Presentations of plays by Juan Ruiz de Alarcón, a Taxco native born of noble Spanish parentage who wrote his works during the same period as Miguel de Cervantes, are given in plazas and city streets.

The pageantry associated with *Semana Santa* (Holy Week) is known throughout the republic. On Palm Sunday an image of Christ on a donkey departs the nearby village of Tehuilotepec, east of town, for a processional to Taxco. Candlelit processions by *penitentes* take place nightly, culminating on Holy Thursday, when the Last Supper is staged in front of Santa Prisca Church. The Resurrection re-enactment takes place at 9 or 10 p.m. on Saturday, and another processional occurs on Easter Sunday. Fireworks during the city's other holidays feature *castillos*, tall bamboo frameworks covered with firework-animated figures.

Steep, narrow roads, infrequent street name designations and many one-way streets make driving in Taxco difficult. Walking is the best way to explore it; taxis are available for visiting points of interest outside of town.

Federally licensed guides are usually available around the plaza or at hotels. Ask to see their credentials and beware of "freelance" guides or "Official Tourist Bureaus" that may be scattered along the major inbound city routes—these are seldom government sponsored. Walking tours of the city begin at the Hotel Loma Linda; for information phone (762) 2-0206 or 2-0753.

Taxco's state tourist office (Subsecretaría de Fomento Turístico) is located at Avenida John F. Kennedy Norte; phone (762) 2-2274 or 2-2279. For tour guide information phone (762) 2-0648 (English spoken).

CACAHUAMILPA CAVES NATIONAL PARK is at the intersection of Mex. 166 and Mex. 55, about 32 kilometers (20 miles) northeast of Taxco. Spe-

lunkers have burrowed more than 8 miles through the passageways of Grutas de Cacahuamilpa (kah-kah-wah-MEEL-pah) and still haven't reached the end. About half a mile of the vast labyrinth can be viewed from wide, paved pathways. Huge chambers—100 feet high, 200 feet long and nearly as wide—hold an array of fantastic formations, some of which are enhanced by lighting. Spanish-speaking guides lead regularly scheduled, 90-minute tours of the caverns. Comfortable walking shoes are recommended. Admission is charged.

CASA HUMBOLDT (Humboldt House), on Juan Ruíz de Alarcón, dates from the 16th century. German naturalist Baron von Humboldt spent the night in April 1803 while on a scientific journey that included South America and Cuba. The restored house, which boasts a rich Moorish facade, has also served as a convent, hospital and Taxco's first movie theater; it now houses the Museo de Arte Virreinal.

CONVENT OF SAN BERNARDINO, off the Plaza del Convento, is where the Plan of Iguala was drafted in 1821 by Agustín de Iturbide, a pivotal character in the battle for Mexican independence from Spain. The plan drew the various Mexican social classes into the freedom movement, consolidating previously ineffective efforts. Mexico finally achieved independence several months later.

IGLESIA DE SANTA PRISCA (Church of Santa Prisca), on the main square, was built by José de la Borda in gratitude for his good fortune in mining. Begun in 1751 and completed 7 years later, the carved stone edifice has twin 130-foot spires flanking a tiled dome. Profusely ornamented walls and confessionals, lovely Miguel Cabrera paintings and 12 altars affirm that Borda spared no expense in making this a beautifully appointed church. It is one of Mexico's finest examples of baroque architecture.

MUSEO DE PLATERIA (Silversmithing Museum), Plaza Borda #1, is in the Patio de las Artesanías in front of Taxco's main square. It houses a collection of exquisite silver items that have won prizes in national contests. Several craft shops are in a colonial-style mansion next to the exhibit hall.

MUSEO DE ARQUEOLOGIA GUILLERMO SPRATLING (William Spratling Museum), behind the Church of Santa Prisca on avenidas Porfirio A. Delgado and El Arco, has exhibits relating to the history of Taxco and other areas of Mexico. On display are pre-Columbian artifacts, samples of silver ore and paintings by various artists. Admission is charged.

WHERE TO STAY

HOTEL HACIENDA DEL SOLAR

▼▼ ▼▼ *Cottage*   (762/2-0323

All Year $76   XP $5
Location: 3.5 km s off Mex 95, opposite tourist office, just
e. (PO Box 96, 40200). Fax: 762/2-0323. **Facility:** On
mountaintop with panoramic view of city. Most rooms with
fireplace and balcony. 22 units. *Bath:* combo or shower only.
2 stories, exterior corridors. **Terms:** 10 day cancellation notice. **Amenities:** no TVs. **Dining:** La Ventana de Taxco, see
separate listing. **Leisure Activities:** tennis court. **Cards:** AE,
MC, VI.

⏐⊣ ⌻ ⟨⟨ ⦾

HOTEL MONTE TAXCO

▼▼ ▼▼ *Motor Inn*   (762/2-1300

All Year $110   XP $10
Location: On steep mountain overlooking city, just n of Mex
95 at entrance of city. Fracionamiento Lomas de T 40210
(PO Box 84). Fax: 762/2-1428. **Facility:** Panoramic view of
city. 156 units. 2 stories, interior corridors. **Terms:** F12; 3
day cancellation notice. **Amenities:** honor bars. **Leisure Activities:** 2 heated pools, wading pool, exercise room. *Fee:*
golf-9 holes, 3 tennis courts, horseback riding. **Guest
Services:** [AP] meal plan available, gift shop, valet laundry.
Fee: area transportation, massage. **Business Services:** conference facilities. **Cards:** AE, DI, MC, VI.

⏐⊣ ⟨⟨ ⌻ ⦾ ⊠

HOTEL RANCHO TAXCO-VICTORIA

▼▼ *Hotel*   (762/2-0004

All Year $42-S58   XP $5
Location: 2 1/2 blks s of Santa Prisca Church; on hill overlooking town. Carlos J Nibbi 5 & 7 (PO Box 83, 40200).
Fax: 762/2-0010. **Facility:** Some with balcony. Most rooms
with good view of Taxco and surrounding mountains. 64
units. *Bath:* combo or shower only. 2 stories, exterior corridors. **Amenities:** no TVs. **Cards:** AE, MC, VI.

⏐⊣ ⌻ ⟨⟨ ⦾

POSADA DE LA MISION

▼▼ ▼▼ *Hotel*   (762/2-0063

All Year $138   XP $20
Location: On Mex 95. Cerro de La Mision 32 40230 (PO
Box 88). Fax: 762/2-2198. **Facility:** Colonial-style. Tranquil
atmosphere. 150 units. 4 two-bedroom units and 1 unit with
kitchen (no utensils). *Bath:* combo or shower only. 1-3 stories (no elevator), exterior corridors. **Terms:** F12; 3 day cancellation notice. **Leisure Activities:** heated pool, whirlpool.
Guest Services: [MAP] meal plan available, gift shop.
Business Services: meeting rooms. **Cards:** AE, DI, MC, VI.

⏐⊣ ⌻ ⦾ ⟨⟨

WHERE TO DINE

LA VENTANA DE TAXCO

▼▼▼▼▼ *Continental*   (762/2-0587

                        L $12-$18   D $12-$18
Location: 3.5 km s off Mex 95, opposite tourist office, just
e; in Hotel Hacienda Del Solar. 40200. **Hours:** 8:30-11 am,
1-5 & 7:30-10:30 pm. **Reservations:** suggested.
Features: No A/C; casual dress; cocktail lounge; a la carte.
Panoramic view of city. International cuisine featuring Italian
specialties. Upscale Western decor reminiscent of Taxco's
rich silvermining days. An attentive staff ensures a memorable dinner. **Cards:** AE, MC, VI.

SR COSTILLA'S

▼▼ *Traditional American*   (762/2-3215

                        L $5-$10   D $5-S10
Location: In downtown; overlooking main plaza. **Hours:** 1
pm-midnight. **Features:** No A/C; casual dress; cocktails &
lounge; a la carte. Rustic decor. Informal atmosphere. Many
tables on balcony overlooking town square. Specializing in
barbeque chicken, steak and ribs. High energy, young staff,
fun place from which to see Taxco. **Cards:** MC, VI.

TUXTLA GUTIERREZ, CHIAPAS (H-9)

Tuxtla Gutiérrez (TOOX-tlah goo-TYEH-rehs)
replaced San Cristóbal de las Casas as the capital
of the state of Chiapas in 1892. The discovery of
vast oil reserves brought an influx of people and
wealth to this prosperous commercial hub, which
is lower in elevation and therefore steamier than
many of the surrounding mountain communities.
Tuxtla Gutiérrez also is a distribution point for
the region's coffee and tobacco plantations.

Mex. 190 passes through the city; its approach
from the west is cluttered with hotels. The hectic
downtown area is divided by Avenida Central,
the principal thoroughfare, which runs east-west.
The main square constitutes two plazas separated
by Avenida Central. It is fronted by imposing
government buildings, shaded by manicured trees
and filled with benches. In the marketplace and
in shops near the plaza, such articles as appli-
qued scarves, gold filigree jewelry, boxes of inlaid wood and brightly painted gourds are sold.

The local tourist information office is at the
western end of town on Boulevard Dr. Belisario
Domínguez #950; phone (961) 3-9396, 3-9397,
3-9398 or 3-9399, or 01 (800) 280-3500 (toll-
free long distance within Mexico). At Boulevard
Dr. Belisario Domínguez #2035 is the
government-run **Casa de las Artesanías**, which
has Chiapan handicrafts on display and for sale.
"Deluxe" bus service is provided by Autotransportes Cristóbal Colón. The first-class bus station
is 2 blocks west of the main plaza at Avenida 2
Norte and 2 Poniente; phone (961) 2-7777.

This is Chiapas' economic and transportation
center, and there is little for tourists to see. If
you're touring this part of Mexico, however, you
may need to spend the night here. The surrounding countryside is noted for lush scenery, including mountains, canyons, forests and such
waterfalls as El Chorreadero. Air tours to
Palenque, Bonampak, Yaxchilán, Lagunas de
Montebello National Park, and Presa de la Angostura and Netzahualcóyotl dams can all be arranged in Tuxtla Gutiérrez.

CAÑON DEL SUMIDERO (El Sumidero Canyon),
about 15 kilometers (9 miles) north, is reached
by a paved mountain road. Five different lookout
points provide spectacular views of the canyon's
sheer walls as they plunge to the Río Grijalva

below. During the Conquest, Indian warriors threw themselves into the canyon rather than surrender and become slaves of the Spanish. The once-churning rapids have been pacified by the construction of the Chicoasén Dam, down the river from the canyon. Boat tours can be arranged in the town of Chiapa de Corzo, east of Tuxtla Gutiérrez, to observe not only the canyon's gaping cliffs but the river's murky green waters and the surrounding forest's alligators, exotic birds and colorful butterflies.

ZOOLOGICO MIGUEL ALVAREZ DEL TORO (Zoomat), about 8 kilometers (5 miles) southeast of downtown, is one of Mexico's most noteworthy zoos. On exhibit is an impressive collection of more than 100 animal species native to Chiapas, including monkeys, tapirs, anteaters, eagles, boa constrictors, iguanas, scorpions and jaguars. The animals are housed in simulated habitats so roomy they appear to roam free through the lush vegetation. Open Tues.-Sun.

WHERE TO STAY

CAMINO REAL TUXTLA GUITIERREZ
▼▼▼ ▼▼▼   *Hotel*   ((961)7-7777
All Year $114-$134   XP $17
Location: 1.5 mi e. No 1195 Blvd Belisario Dominguez 29060. Fax: 961/7-7799. **Facility:** Striking architecture. 210 units. Some whirlpool units. 6 stories, interior corridors. **Parking:** valet. **Terms:** F12; 15 day cancellation notice-fee imposed. **Amenities:** safes, honor bars. **Dining:** Montebello, see separate listing. **Leisure Activities:** wading pool, sauna, whirlpool, steamroom, playground. *Fee:* 2 lighted tennis courts. **Guest Services:** gift shop, valet laundry. *Fee:* massage. **Business Services:** conference facilities, fax. **Cards:** AE, DI, MC, VI. *(See color ad opposite title page)*

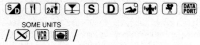

SOME UNITS
/ ⊠ VCR 🖥 /

HOTEL FLAMBOYANT
▼▼▼ ▼▼▼   *Hotel*   (961/5-0888
All Year $70   XP $7
Location: 4.5 km w on Mex 190. Blvd Belisario Dominguez 29000. Fax: 961/5-0087. **Facility:** Circular shaped property with lawn area in the center. 118 units. Some whirlpool units. **Bath:** shower only. 5 stories, interior corridors. **Terms:** F12. **Leisure Activities:** wading pool, tennis court, playground. **Guest Services:** gift shop, valet laundry. **Business Services:** meeting rooms, administrative services. **Cards:** AE, MC, VI.

SOME UNITS
 / 🛢 /
FEE

WHERE TO DINE

MONTEBELLO
▼▼▼ ▼▼▼   *Nouvelle Continental*   (961/7-7777
   D $12-$30
Location: 1.5 mi e; in Camino Real Tuxtla Guitierrez. No 1195 Blvd Belisario Dominguez 29060. **Hours:** 2 pm-11 pm. **Features:** semi-formal attire; cocktails & lounge; valet parking; a la carte. Comfortable dining with contemporary decor, high degree of table-side service. Artistic presentation of complex regional dishes. Sample regional Yucatecan or Chapeneco dishes as well as more Continental selections. **Cards:** AE, CB, DI, MC, VI.

⊠

VERACRUZ, VERACRUZ (H-9)

Mexico's oldest and largest port, Veracruz (veh-rah-CROOS) has played an important role in the country's history, from the arrival of Hernán Cortés through the Mexican Revolution of 1910. It is the principal port of entry along Mexico's Gulf of Mexico coast. Veracruz is noted for cigars, distinctive cuisine, coffee and the *quexquémetl*, a capelike garment decorated with multicolored embroidery. Totonac Indians produce some of the finest traditional designs.

Veracruz has long served as a doorway leading into the heart of Mexico. Spanish rule began in Veracruz in 1519 with the arrival of Cortés, who named his new settlement La Villa Rica de la Vera Cruz (Rich Town of the True Cross). Cortés then went inland to discover the Aztec capital and to launch the campaign that resulted in the colonization of the continental Americas.

Veracruz was the point of arrival for African slaves and served as a support base for Spanish colonial activities in Florida. Ironically, Spanish rule ended in the city as well. Three centuries after Cortés' landfall, the Spanish flag was lowered at the Fortress of San Juan de Ulúa across the bay.

Veracruz is the only place where the celebrated privateer John Hawkins, accompanied by his nephew Francis Drake, met defeat. His powerful fleet was thwarted at the hands of Spanish and Mexican men in 1568, many years before the construction of San Juan de Ulúa and other forts. Both pirates returned to England with a few survivors in their ship, the *Judith*, and were received as heroes.

U.S. forces also landed in Veracruz on their way to Mexico City during the Mexican-American War of 1846-48. In 1862, French troops marched inland from Veracruz to subdue the country for Archduke Maximilian's arrival. U.S. forces again landed in 1914 to protest the actions of the Mexican military under Victoriano Huerta, who had seized the presidency after assassinating President Francisco I. Madero. These three invasions, along with the city's role in the struggle for Mexican independence, earned it the title "Cuatro veces heroica Veracruz" (four times heroic).

The **Plaza de Armas**, the city's main square and one of the oldest Spanish plazas in North America, serves as a focal point for today's decidedly more peaceful activity. The sidewalk tables of the **Gran Café de la Parroquia**, on the plaza, are ideal for lounging and enjoying an order of *cafe con leche*, concentrated coffee mixed with boiled milk served in tall glasses, or perhaps a thick ice cream soda in a glass with inky black coffee at the bottom. For coffee refills, bang your knife against your glass.

The plaza is the site of strolling mariachi players, string trios—jarana, guitar and harp—and frequent band concerts. Music is a major contributor to the city scene; the popular song "La Bamba" originated in Veracruz. Crowds also gather to watch *jarocho* folk dances, part of a rich cultural tradition.

Buses depart a block south of the plaza on Avenida 5 de Mayo for points within the city and its outlying beaches; a block north a crafts market sells jewelry. West of the plaza, old buildings contrast with modern structures. On weekends downtown cafés and arcades are filled with white-uniformed cadets from the Mexican Naval Academy at nearby Antón Lizardo.

Extending a couple of miles from downtown along the Gulf of Mexico, the *malecón* seawall is a popular walkway from which to view such colonial buildings as the **Aduana Marítima** (customs house) and **La Parroquia Cathedral**, specialty shops and the bustling harbor. A few blocks from the Aduana Marítima are remnants of a protective wall that surrounded Veracruz in the 18th century.

A drive southward along the shore via Boulevard M. Avila Camacho leads to **Playa Villa del Mar**, about 3.5 kilometers (2.2 miles) from the Plaza de Armas, and **Playa Mocambo**, 10 kilometers (6 miles) south. Both beaches are somewhat muddy, and sharks sometimes lurk offshore. The beaches are, however, a pleasant place to stroll and watch fishermen mending their nets or making repairs on their boats. On weekends they are filled with bathers, dancers and vendors proffering beer and seafood, all against a backdrop of nonstop band music.

Beyond Playa Mocambo, at the mouth of the Río Jamapa, is **Boca del Río**, noted for its fine open-air seafood restaurants. Diners are frequently treated to performances of the *son jarocho* dance by local children, accompanied by harp players.

Interesting side trips include **La Antigua**, the original site of Veracruz, 32 kilometers (20 miles) north on Mex. 180. A small village shaded by big trees, it contains the headquarters of Cortés as well as **La Ermita** (Hermitage), reputed to be the oldest church on the American mainland. A black cannon guarding one corner of the ruin is a reminder of the fear Europeans brought to Mexican shores. The barracks that housed the army of Gen. Antonio López de Santa Anna, formed in 1835 to fight in Texas, is also at the site.

On **Isla de los Sacrificios**, one of three small offshore islands, is a 115-foot-tall lighthouse with a range of 50 nautical miles. The island was named for the human sacrifices that Cortés witnessed as he approached the shore. Today the annual rituals of Veracruz are a little less hazardous; the city's pre-Lenten *Carnaval* rivals

New Orleans' in spectacle and enthusiasm, if not in size. Boat trips to the island depart from the *malecón*.

Veracruz serves as the destination point of an annual ocean yacht regatta in early June. This 4-day event begins in Galveston, Tex., and features some 70 yachts traveling a distance of 620 miles. For local tourist information, phone (29) 32-1613 or 31-7026.

The toll highway between Veracruz and Córdoba completes Mex. 150-D, an expressway that links Mexico City with the country's most important port. Many potholes can mar Mex. 180, the coastal highway, after heavy rains.

CASTILLO DE SAN JUAN DE ULUA (Castle of San Juan de Ulúa), in the harbor on Gallega Island, is reached by car or foot over a free causeway from extensions of avenidas Morelos and República. The Spanish began the massive fort to protect their New World interests; construction took place 1582-1707. The dungeons and walks are open. The site holds a modern arsenal, drydock, shipyard and the Veracruz marine signal station. The fortress offers fine views of the port and also serves as the city's convention center.

HEROICA ESCUELA NAVAL (Mexican Naval Academy) is 34 kilometers (21 miles) south in the coastal village of Antón Lizardo. It is reached by paved Mex. 48, which branches off Mex. 150 at Boca del Río. The academy, surrounded by Australian pines, is about a third of a mile from the gulf. A statue commemorates Cadet Virgilio Uribe, who died during the April 21, 1914, bombardment by U.S. warships. Guided tours are available.

MANDINGA LAGOON, a brackish, mangrove-hidden lake, is reached by a 3-kilometer (2-mile) paved spur branching south from the Antón Lizardo route. Boats and motors can be rented. Rustic restaurants specialize in fresh catches from the sea and lagoon.

MUSEO DE ARTE E HISTORIA VERACRUZANA (Museum of the City of Veracruz), Calle Zaragoza #397, emphasizes the history and art of the Veracruz area. The ground floor concentrates on pre-Hispanic history with displays of clay figurines, Olmec and Huastec objects and Totonac *yugos,* the large horseshoe-shaped stones that were used in Indian ball games. The second floor contains artifacts from the Mexican Revolution and the American occupation of Veracruz in 1914. Open Tues.-Sun.

ZEMPOALA, VERACRUZ (H-8)

About 40 kilometers (25 miles) north of Veracruz off Mex. 180 lie the **Zempoala Ruins**, the remains of the ceremonial center and fortress of the Totonac Indians. The ruins are located on the northern edge of the town of Zempoala (sehm-poh-AH-lah), also known as Cempoala.

Zempoala was a Classic Period contemporary of El Tajín *(see Papantla listing)*, although it continued to thrive after the latter's abandonment sometime during the 13th century. It was here that Hernán Cortés gained the first Indian allies in his 1519 campaign to conquer the Aztecs. The *conquistadores* took note of the city because the white stucco buildings, gleaming in the tropical sun, most likely reminded them of silver. He gained the trust of the Totonac chief (reputedly celebrated for his enormous girth) and his followers, who had been under Aztec rule for the previous 50 years.

Six major structures remain, standing amid lush tropical vegetation. **La Gran Pirámide** (The Great Pyramid), constructed of riverbed stones, rises on 13 platforms to about 35 feet and probably resembled similar temples in the Aztec capital of Tenochtitlán. The **Templo de las Chimeneas** (Temple of the Chimneys) derives its name from a series of semicircular pillars. **Las Caritas** (The Little Faces), a three-story edifice of boulders and cement, is adorned with niches containing small carved faces. The site is open daily. Admission is charged; free to all Sun. There is an additional charge for the use of a video camera. First-class buses travel regularly from Veracruz north to the town of Cardel; from Cardel, *colectivos* (minivans) transport visitors to the ruins. The site is about a 45-minute drive from Veracruz; watch for the sign indicating the Zempoala turnoff.

WHERE TO STAY

 FIESTA AMERICANA VERACRUZ

Motel   (29/89-8989

All Year   S173   XP $17
Location: 6 mi sw on Ave Avila Camacho. Prol Blvd Avila Camacho 94299. Fax: 29/22-4343. **Facility:** 233 units. 7 stories, interior corridors. **Terms:** F12. **Amenities:** voice mail, safes, honor bars, irons, hair dryers. **Dining & Entertainment:** 2 restaurants, 2 coffee shops, deli, 7 am-midnight, $10-$20, entertainment. **Leisure Activities:** heated pool, wading pool, sauna, bicycles, exercise room. **Guest Services:** gift shop, valet laundry. *Fee:* massage. **Business Services:** meeting rooms, administrative services. *Fee:* PC, fax. **Cards:** AE, DI, MC, VI.
(See color ad below)

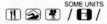
FEE

HOTEL COLONIAL

Hotel   (29/32-0193

All Year   S51-S65
Location: Opposite Plaza de Armas. Miguel Lerdo 117 Zona Centro 91700. Fax: 29/32-2465. **Facility:** Rooms in the remodeled section are a bit larger, have deadbolt locks and 24 hour air conditioning. Rooms in the older commercial section have air conditioning from 8-10 am and 1-5 pm. All rooms with ceiling fan. 174 units. *Bath:* shower only. 7 stories, interior corridors. **Parking:** extra charge. **Terms:** 15 day cancellation notice. **Leisure Activities:** heated pool, wading pool. **Guest Services:** complimentary laundry. **Business Services:** conference facilities. *Fee:* fax. **Cards:** AE, MC, VI.

SOME UNITS

HOTEL PLAYA PARAISO

Hotel   ((29)21-8600

3/1-5/31   S70   XP $6
12/1-2/28   S65   XP $6
6/1-11/30   S55-S60   XP $9
Location: 8 km sw on Blvd Veracruz Mocambo. Blvd Adolfo Ruiz Cortines 3500. Fax: 29/21-8699. **Facility:** One- and two-bedroom bungalows on the beach, with a view of the gulf. 108 units. 1 two-bedroom unit and 5 units with kitchen. *Bath:* shower only. 3 stories, exterior corridors. **Terms:** F12; 8 day cancellation notice-fee imposed. **Amenities:** voice mail, safes, honor bars. **Leisure Activities:** 2 pools, wading pools, beach, swimming. **Guest Services:** gift shop, valet laundry. **Cards:** AE, MC, VI.

SOME UNITS

TORREMAR RESORT

▼▼▼▼ *Hotel*   ((29)89-2100

All Year $130-$145   XP $11
Location: 8 km sw on Blvd Veracruz Mocambo. Blvd Al-
dolfo Ruiz Cortines 4300 94260. Fax: 29/89-2121.
Facility: Modern and spacious lobby and public areas.
Meets AAA guest room security requirements. 230 units. 3
two-bedroom units. Some suites ($170-$250) and whirlpool
units ($160-$175). 9 stories, interior/exterior corridors.
Terms: F12; cancellation fee imposed. **Amenities:** honor
bars. *Some:* safes. **Dining & Entertainment:** dining room,
coffee shop, 7 am-midnight, $8-$14, nightclub, entertainment. **Leisure Activities:** 2 pools, wading pool, beach,
swimming, playground. *Fee:* sailboating, windsurfing. **Guest
Services:** gift shop, valet laundry. **Business Services:** conference facilities, administrative services, PC, fax.
Cards: AE, DI, MC, VI.

SOME UNITS

[icons]

VILLAHERMOSA, TABASCO (H-10)

Villahermosa (vee-yah-ehr-MOH-sah) was
founded in 1519 under the name Santa María de
la Victoria. Hernán Cortés established the settlement to commemorate his defeat of an army of
Indian warriors who had attacked him during his
march toward the Aztec capital of Tenochtitlán.
In tribute to their conquerer, the Indians gave
Cortés an Indian princess. Baptized Doña Marina, she became Cortés' mistress and trusted
translator, an invaluable asset in his conquest of
Mexico.

Villahermosa's strategic location on the banks
of the navigable Río Grijalva, which flows northward out of rubber, cacao and coffee country,
makes it an important distribution center. This
river and the Río Usumacinta carry the largest
volumes of water in a country not known for extensive river systems.

For years the area suffered from a stagnant
economy. However, the 1970s discovery of some
of the world's richest oil fields, as well as the
development of extensive hydroelectric projects
and successful agricultural programs, energized
this hot, humid port. Villahermosa is sometimes
referred to as *"La Ciudad de dos Mentiras,"* or
"The City of Two Lies": It is neither a small
town, nor is it necessarily beautiful. Rather, it is
a hectic, congested business center and one of
Mexico's more prosperous cities. Oil drilling has
created blight as well as wealth, however, and
the quest for timber and rangeland has depleted
Tabasco's natural forests.

Flower-lined Paseo Malecón separates the
banks of the Río Grijalva from the shops, hotels
and restaurants of the downtown area. **Zona Re-
modelada**, abutting the business sector, has a
tropical look. Downtown seafood restaurants and
many seafood cocktail stands offer fresh catches
from the nearby gulf. Sightseeing boats depart
regularly from the *malecón* (waterfront promenade) for river excursions.

The tourism office is located in the modern
complex of buildings known as **Tabasco 2000**,
past the La Venta Museum and heading west out
of downtown. The office, at Paseo Tabasco
#1504 (opposite the Palacio Municipal), is open
Mon.-Fri. 9-3 and 6-8 p.m.; phone (93) 16-3633.
"Deluxe" bus service to Campeche, Mérida,
Mexico City, Palenque, San Cristóbal de las Casas, Veracruz and other cities is offered by ADO.
The ADO bus terminal is at Calle Javier Mina
#297.

NEARBY DESTINATIONS

From this transportation hub travelers can fly,
drive or, from Teapa (south of Villahermosa),
take a train to the Yucatán Peninsula. For motorists taking Mex. 180 northeastward along the
Gulf of Mexico coast, a toll bridge has replaced
the flat-bottom boats that used to ferry travelers
between the towns of Zacatal and Ciudad del
Carmen. The Villahermosa-Escárcega route—east
on Mex. 186 to the village of Francisco Escárcega, then north to Champotón via Mex.
261—is an inland alternative. Mex. 186 also offers direct access to the Palenque ruins *(see
Palenque listing)*, southeast of Villahermosa.

West of the city are prosperous cacao plantations and the important archeological site of **Comalcalco**. A driving tour of this region reveals a
lush Mexico that contrasts sharply with the country's arid expanses. Along Mex. 180 west toward
Cárdenas are masses of bright green banana
plants sporting clusters of the yellow fruit, which
is sold at roadside stands. Cárdenas itself is a cacao processing center, and some chocolate plantations and factories offer guided tours (check
with travel agencies in Villahermosa). Throughout the countryside grows the cacao tree; its
large, elliptical pods bear the seeds from which
cocoa and chocolate are made.

From Cárdenas, the ruins of Comalcalco can
be reached by taking Mex. 187 north about 35
kilometers (22 miles) to the town of Comalcalco;
the ruins are about 3 kilometers (2 miles) farther
on the right (watch for signs). Another way to
reach the ruins is to take Avenida Universidad
(the coastal route to Campeche) north out of Villahermosa and follow the signs for Comalcalco via
the town of Nacajuca, a distance of about 51
kilometers (32 miles). Although narrow and studded with *topes* (speed bumps), the road offers
pretty views of tropical vegetation. Descendants
of the Chontal Maya, who originally inhabited
Comalcalco around A.D. 600-900, still live in the
area and earn a livelihood as their ancestors did
by processing cacao and raising bananas and
other fruits.

This is the westernmost Maya archeological
zone and bears similarities to the architectural
style found at Palenque. The structures at Comalcalco, however, were constructed of kilned brick

rather than the stone used elsewhere in pre-Hispanic Mexico. The bricks, visible on a large pyramidal structure, were made of crushed oyster shells mixed with clay and sand. Also at the site are the ruins of several temples and tombs protected by thatched shelters; some are decorated with fragments of stucco masks. Around some of the ruins are signs warning *No Subir* (Do Not Climb). A small museum near the entrance exhibits site artifacts, including bricks that the Maya inscribed with painted messages and drawings before covering them with stucco. The site is open daily. Admission is charged.

About 25 kilometers (15 miles) farther north on Mex. 187 is the gulfside fishing village of **Paraíso**. The beaches here are not nearly as nice as those along the Yucatán Peninsula, and tourist amenities are few and far between. The town does have a scattering of restaurants if you're in the mood for a seafood lunch. Farther west on Mex. 180 and then north on a paved road is the scenic getaway of **Sánchez Magallanes**. About 118 kilometers (73 miles) south of Cárdenas via Mex. 187 is **Presa Netzahualcóyotl**, one of Mexico's notable engineering feats. The dam controls the flow of the Río Grijalva.

WHAT TO SEE IN TOWN

MUSEO DE ANTROPOLOGIA (Museum of Anthropology) is in the **Investigaciones de Culturas Olmeca y Maya** (Investigation Center for the Olmec and Maya Cultures, or CICOM); the cultural complex is south of downtown at Periférico Carlos Pellicer #511, along the left bank of the Río Grijalva. It is dedicated to Tabascan poet and historian Carlos Pellicer Cámara, who was largely responsible for amassing the outstanding collection of objects on display at the La Venta Museum *(see attraction listing below)*.

Exhibit halls in the spacious, modern building contain representative pieces from Teotihuacán and the Aztec, Totonac, Mixtec and Zapotec cultures, as well as artifacts from the states of Nayarit and Colima. Featured are jade, ceramic and clay figurines; stelae; burial urns; and gold objects. Special attention has been given to the Olmec and Maya civilizations, and many of the sculptures on view bear the jaguarlike facial features common to Olmec art. The museum also has reproductions of the Maya murals at Bonampak *(see Palenque listing)*.

The displays are complemented by photographs and maps of the archeological sites from which they were taken; descriptions are mostly in Spanish. The ground floor contains administrative offices, an auditorium and a restaurant; most of the exhibits are on the second and third floors. Daily 9-8. Admission is charged.

MUSEO LA VENTA (La Venta Museum) is west of downtown on Boulevard Ruiz Cortines/Grijalva (Mex. 180 bypass), just north of Paseo Tabasco. This open-air park-museum spreads along the shores of man-made **Laguna de las Ilusiones** (Lake of the Illusions). Its 30 monuments, some weighing as much as 30 tons, were discovered in the late 1930s at the ruins of **La Venta**, a principal Olmec ceremonial center in the river country near the Veracruz state line about 129 kilometers (80 miles) west of Villahermosa. When oil exploration threatened to destroy the archeological zone, most of the artifacts were transported to this site on the city's outskirts.

The park showcases some of the more monumental works produced by Mexico's first advanced civilization. Three colossal stone heads wear war helmets and display the characteristic facial features of Olmec art: wide noses, infantile expressions and full, downward-turning lips resembling the mouth of a jaguar. Other objects include sculptures, stone altars, stelae (stone tablets) and a tomb. All are scattered throughout junglelike grounds inhabited by free-roaming monkeys and deer, twittering birds, crocodiles (confined to a moat) and some caged animals. This lush sanctuary should be toured in the morning before it gets too hot. Insect repellent is strongly advised. A sound-and-light show is presented each evening (except Wed.). Open Tues.-Sun. Admission is charged. Phone (93) 15-2228.

WHERE TO STAY

CALINDA VIVA SPA VILLAHERMOSA

▼▼ 💎   *Motor Inn*   ((93)15-0000

All Year $62
Location: 1.5 km n on Mex 180; near Tabasco 2000 Commercial Complex. Adolfo Ruiz Cortinez con 86050. Fax: 93/15-3073. **Facility:** Balconies or patios. 240 units. *Bath:* shower only. 3 stories (no elevator). **Amenities:** safes. *Some:* honor bars. **Leisure Activities:** wading pool. **Guest Services:** gift shop, valet laundry. **Business Services:** conference facilities. **Cards:** AE, DI, MC, VI.
(See color ad p 4 and p 437)

[⊩] [⟟] [🏊] [🎥] [DATA PORT]

🔺 **CAMINO REAL VILLAHERMOSA**

▼▼▼   *Hotel*   (93/16-4400

All Year $135   XP $20
Location: 1.5 km n on Mex 180; in the Tabasco 2000 Commercial Complex. Ave Paseo Tabasco 1407 86030. Fax: 93/16-4540. **Facility:** Modern high-rise with direct access to mall. Meets AAA guest room security requirements. 190 units. 11 stories, interior corridors. **Parking:** valet. **Terms:** F12. **Amenities:** safes. **Dining & Entertainment:** restaurant, 6 am-midnight, $5-$12, cocktails, entertainment. **Leisure Activities:** wading pool. **Guest Services:** gift shop, valet laundry. **Business Services:** conference facilities. **Cards:** AE, DI, MC, VI. *(See color ad opposite title page)*

SOME UNITS
[⊩] [D] [🏊] [📶] [🎥] / [✕] /

HOTEL CENCALI

 Motor Inn   (93/15-1999

All Year $70
Location: 1.5 km n on Mex 180; near Tabasco 2000 Commercial Complex. Calle Juarez & Paseo Taba 86040. Fax: 93/15-6600. **Facility:** Overlooks Lake of the Illusions in a parklike setting. Meets AAA guest room security requirements. 113 units, 1 with kitchen. 3 stories (no elevator), interior/exterior corridors. **Terms:** check-in 6 pm. **Amenities:** *Some:* honor bars. **Leisure Activities:** wading pool. **Guest Services:** [CP] meal plan available, gift shop, valet laundry. **Business Services:** conference facilities, administrative services. **Cards:** AE, CB, DI, MC, VI.

HOTEL HYATT REGENCY VILLAHERMOSA

 *Hotel*   ((93)15-1234

All Year $95-$130   XP $15
Location: 1.5 km n on Mex 180, near Tabasco 2000 Commercial Complex. (Ave Juarez 106, LINDAVISTA, CL, 86050). Fax: 93/15-1235. **Facility:** 207 units. 9 stories, interior corridors. **Terms:** F12. **Amenities:** safes, honor bars. **Dining:** Bouganvillas Restaurant, see separate listing. **Leisure Activities:** wading pool, 2 lighted tennis courts, playground. **Guest Services:** gift shop, valet laundry. **Business Services:** conference facilities, administrative services. **Cards:** AE, CB, DI, MC, VI.

SOME UNITS

WHERE TO DINE

The following restaurant has not been evaluated by AAA and is listed for your information only.

BOUGANVILLAS RESTAURANT

[fyi]   (93/13-4444

Not evaluated. **Location:** 1.5 km n on Mex 180, near Tabasco 2000 Commercial Complex; in Hotel Hyatt Regency Villahermosa. Ave Juarez 106 86050. Elegant continental dining.

Speaking of Spanish

ON THE FOLLOWING PAGES are listed some of the Spanish phrases and sentences that are most useful to an English-speaking visitor in Mexico. Although not essential, a basic knowledge of the language will be helpful. Most Mexicans who deal with tourists speak at least some English, and those who don't will be only too glad to help you along with your attempts at Spanish. Fortunately, the language is not that difficult to speak. A little study of the following rules of pronunciation will be sufficient to make yourself understood.

Even if your knowledge of Spanish is rudimentary, using such everyday expressions as por favor (please), gracias (thank you), buenos dias (good morning), buenas tardes (good afternoon) and buenas noches (good evening) shows respect. Mexicans are very polite and use these terms all the time; you should also. Good manners mean more than being able to speak the language fluently.

Pronunciation

The pronunciation of the Spanish language presents very few difficulties. The spelling is almost phonetic; nearly every letter has one sound that it retains at all times.

Vowels
A—pronounced as "a" in father.
E—pronounced as "e" in them.
I—pronounced as "e" in me.
O—pronounced as "o" in hold.
U—pronounced as "oo" in food.

Consonants
The consonants do not differ materially from those in English. The few differences can be summarized as follows:

b and v—in Mexico are pronounced as in "boy."

c—is pronounced with an "s" sound before e and i. Otherwise it has a "k" sound. Ex. cinco—seen-koh.

g—is soft, like a strong English "h," when it precedes e and i. Ex. gente—hente. In all other cases, it is a hard "g" as in go. Ex. gato—gahtoh. If gu precedes an e or i, the "g" has a hard sound and the "u" is not pronounced. Ex. guerra—geh-rah, guiso—geeh-so. If the "u" has an umlaut it is pronounced güera—gweh-rah, güiro—gwee-roh.

h—always silent, except after c, which makes a "ch" sound as in English.

j—pronounced like the English "h."

ll—pronounced like the English "y." Ex. caballo—kah-BAH-yo.

ñ—combination of "n" and "y," like cognac. Ex. niño—neenyoh.

qu—pronounced like "k." Ex. que—keh.

r—in Mexico the "r" is trilled; the "r" at the beginning of a word and the double "rr" are trilled quite strongly.

x—pronounced as in English, and also pronounced like the English "s," as in Xochimilco (soh-chih-MEEL-coh), and the English "h," as in México (ME-hee-coh). In Mexico "x" also is used to represent the "sh" sound in native languages, as in Xel-Há (Shehl-AH).

z—in Mexico is always pronounced like the English "s."

ch, ll, ñ—these are all letters in the Spanish alphabet and are found after the single letter: "ch" after "c," "ll" after "l," "ñ" after "n."

Diphthongs
Spanish diphthongs are pronounced as very swift omissions of the component vowels.
Ex. "ue" as in weh—fuente.
Ex. "au" as in English ouch—gaucho.

Accent or Stress
1. The stress falls on the next to the last syllable when a word ends in a vowel, "n" or "s."
Ex. hombre—OHM-breh.
Ex. hablan—AH-blahn.
Ex. estos—EHS-tos.
2. The stress falls on the last syllable when the word ends in a consonant other than "n" or "s."
Ex. hablar—ah-BLAR.
3. In some cases an accent mark will be found over a vowel. This does not change the pronunciation of that vowel but indicates that the stress falls on that syllable.
Ex. gramática—grah-MAH-teeh-cah.

Words and Phrases

Note: All nouns in Spanish are either masculine or feminine, and there are two words meaning "the": el is used before masculine nouns, la before feminine nouns. Masculine words end with an o, feminine words end with an a (although there are a few exceptions). An adjective agrees in gender with the noun it modifies. The plural of el is los, of la is las. After words given on these pages the gender is indicated by (m.) for masculine, (f.) for feminine. For instance, say el hotel and los hoteles; la posada and las posadas. The word "usted," meaning "you," is always abbreviated Ud. (Vd. in old writings).

Language

Do you understand English?	¿Entiende Ud. el inglés?
I do not speak Spanish	No hablo español.
Yes, sir; no, madam	Si, señor; no, señora.
Very little	Muy poco.
I do not understand	No entiendo.
Do you understand me?	¿Me entiende Ud.?
Please speak slowly	Por favor hable despacio.
I wish to speak with an interpreter	Quisiera hablar con un intérprete.
What did you say?	¿Cómo dice?

Polite Phrases

Good morning	Buenos días.
Good afternoon	Buenas tardes.
Good night	Buenas noches.
Goodbye; see you later	Adios; hasta la vista.
Thank you	Gracias.
Yes; very good	Sí; muy bien.
Please	Por favor.
Excuse me	Perdóneme.
I am very sorry	Lo siento mucho.

To Explain Your Needs

I need; we need	Necesito; necesitamos.
I would like to telephone	Quisiera telefonear.
I am hungry; we are hungry	Tengo hambre; tenemos hambre.
I am thirsty; we are thirsty	Tengo sed; tenemos sed.
I am cold; we are cold	Tengo frío; tenemos frío.
I am warm; we are warm	Tengo calor; tenemos calor.
I am tired; we are tired	Estoy cansado; estamos cansados.
I am sick; we are sick	Estoy enfermo; estamos enfermos.
The child is sick; tired	El niño (la niña) está enfermo (a); cansado (a).
Men's room, ladies' room	El baño de hombres, de damas.
Fire	Fuego (m.).
Help	Auxilio; socorro (m.).

Time

today	hoy	the afternoon	la tarde
the morning	la mañana	tonight	esta noche
tomorrow	mañana	night	la noche
noon	el mediodía	last night	anoche
yesterday	ayer	midnight	la media noche

What time is it?	¿Qué hora es?
It is one o'clock	Es la una.
It is ten minutes past two	Son las dos y diez.
It is quarter past three	Son las tres y cuarto.
It is a quarter of five	Es un cuarto para las cinco.
It is 25 minutes of six	Son veinticinco para las seis.
It is half past four	Son las cuatro y media.

Days of the Week

Sunday	domingo (m.)	Thursday	jueves (m.)
Monday	lunes (m.)	Friday	viernes (m.)
Tuesday	martes (m.)	Saturday	sábado (m.)
Wednesday	miércoles (m.)		

Months of the Year

January	enero (m.)	August	agosto (m.)
February	febrero (m.)	September	septiembre (m.)
March	marzo (m.)	October	octubre (m.)
April	abril (m.)	November	noviembre (m.)
May	mayo (m.)	December	diciembre (m.)
June	junio (m.)		
July	julio (m.)		

Colors

white	blanco	blue; dark blue	azul; azul oscuro
black	negro		
gray	gris	green; light green	verde; verde claro
brown	café		
red	rojo	purple	morado
pink	rosa	yellow	amarillo

Useful Adjectives

Note: These adjectives are in their masculine forms. End them with an "a" if you want the feminine form (except for grande, tarde and fácil, which are used for both genders).

bad	malo	sharp	agudo
high	alto	easy	fácil
beautiful	bello	slow	lento
kind	bondadoso	expensive	caro
cheap	barato	small	pequeño
large	grande	fast	rápido
clean	limpio	ugly	feo
late	tarde	good	bueno
difficult	difícil	unkind	despiadado, duro
low	bajo	long	largo
dirty	sucio	short	corto
polite	cortés	narrow	angosto
early	temprano	dangerous	peligroso

Numerals

1. uno	8. ocho	15. quince	30. treinta	90. noventa
2. dos	9. nueve	16. diez y seis	31. treinta y uno	100. cien
3. tres	10. diez	17. diez y siete	40. cuarenta	200. doscientos
4. cuatro	11. once	18. diez y ocho	50. cincuenta	500. quinientos
5. cinco	12. doce	19. diez y nueve	60. sesenta	1,000. mil
6. seis	13. trece	20. veinte	70. setenta	1,000,000. un millón
7. siete	14. catorce	21. veintiuno	80. ochenta	

Points of the Compass

north.....norte (m.)   south.........sur.(m.)   east........este (m.)   west..................oeste (m.)

Note: In addresses, east is oriente, abbreviated Ote.; west is poniente, abbreviated Pte.

At the Border

passport	pasaporte
tourist card	tarjeta de turista
age	edad
marital status	estado civil
single	soltero
married	casado
widowed	viudo
divorced	divorciado
profession or occupation	profesión; ocupación
vaccination card	certificado de vacuna
car owner's title (registration)	título de propiedad (registro)
driver's license	licencia de manejar
year of car	modelo (o año)
make (Ford, Plymouth, etc.)	marca
license plate number and state	número y estado de placa
chassis and motor number	número de chasis y motor
number of doors	número de puertas
number of cylinders	número de cilindros
number of passengers	número de pasajeros

On the Road

highway	carretera (f.)	street	calle (f.)
road	camino (m.)	avenue	avenida (f.)

boulevard	bulevar (m.)	left side	lado izquierdo (m.)
corner	esquina (f.)	right side	lado derecho (m.)
kilometer	kilómetro (m.)		
block	cuadra (f.)		

Please show me the road to	Enséñeme el camino a. . . .
How far is?	¿Qué tan lejos está. . . .
Can we get to. . .before dark?	¿Podemos llegar a. . . .antes del anochecer?
Is this road dangerous?	¿Es peligroso este camino?
Is that road in good condition?	¿Está en buen estado ese camino?
Is it paved or is it a dirt road?	¿Está pavimentado o es de tierra?
Go straight ahead.	Siga adelante.
Turn to the right; left.	Vuelta a la derecha; izquierda.
What city, town, is this?	¿Qué ciudad, pueblo, es éste?
Where does this road lead?	¿A dónde va este camino?

In Case of Car Trouble

I want to ask you a favor.	Quiero pedirle un favor.
My car broke down.	Se me descompuso el carro.
I need a tow truck.	Necesito una grúa.
My lights don't work.	Mis faros no funcionan.
My engine's overheating.	Mi motor se está sobrecalentando.
I have run out of gasoline.	Se me acabó la gasolina.
Is there a gasoline station near here?	¿Hay alguna gasolinería cerca de aquí?
Is there a garage near here?	¿Hay algún taller cerca?
Please send a mechanic.	Por favor mándeme un mecánico.
May I go with you to get a mechanic?	¿Puedo ir con usted a conseguir un mecánico?
Do you have a rope to tow my car?	¿Tiene un cable para remolcar mi carro?
The starter does not work.	El arranque no funciona.
Can you help me push the car to one side of the road?	¿Puede ayudarme a empujar el coche a un lado del camino?
Do you want to be my witness?	¿Quiere ser mi testigo?
Do you want to help me change a tire?	¿Quiere ayudarme a cambiar una llanta?

Arriving in Town

Is English spoken here?	¿Se habla inglés aquí?
Where is the center of town?	¿Dónde está el centro de la ciudad?
May I park here?	¿Puedo estacionarme aquí?
Could you recommend a good restaurant; a good small hotel; a first class hotel?	¿Puede Ud. recomendar un buen restaurante; un buen hotel pequeño; un hotel de primera clase?
Please direct me to the nearest post office	Por favor diríjame a la oficina de correos mas cercana.
I wish to telephone, to telegraph, to cable	Quiero telefonear, telegrafiar, cablegrafiar.
Please direct me to the railroad station, the bus station	Por favor diríjame a la estación del ferrocarril, a la estación del autobús.
Where is X Street, X Square, the X Hotel?	¿Dónde está la Calle X, la Plaza X, el Hotel X?
How often does the bus go by?	¿Que tan seguido pasa el autobús?
Does the streetcar stop here?	¿Para aquí el tranvía?
I wish to change some money.	Quiero cambiar dinero.
What is the rate of exchange?	¿Cuál es el tipo de cambio?
I want to cash a check.	Quiero cambiar un cheque.
I have lost my traveler's checks.	He perdido mis cheques de viajero.
Where can I find a policeman, a hairdresser, a doctor, a drug store?	¿Dónde puedo hallar un policía, un peinador, un médico, una farmacia?
Where is the police station; the chamber of commerce; the automobile club?	¿Dónde está la comisaría, la cámara de comercio, la asociación automovilística?
Where can I find guidebooks, road maps, postcards, American newspapers?	¿Dónde se pueden hallar guías turísticas, mapas de carreteras, tarjetas postales, periódicos norteamericanos? icanos?

At the Hotel

hotel	hotel (m.)	air conditioning	aire acondicionado
inn	posada (f.)	room	cuarto (m.)
guesthouse	casa de huéspedes (f.)	hot water	agua caliente
apartment house	apartamentos (m.)	office	oficina (f.)
		elevator	elevador (m.)
furnished room	cuarto amueblado (m.)	dining room	comedor (m.)
		guest	huésped (m.)
stairway	escalera (f.)	manager	gerente
bedroom	recámara (f.)	office employee	empleado de oficina
bathroom	cuarto de baño (m.)	maid	camarera (f.)
kitchen	cocina (f.)	key	llave (f.)
towel	toalla (f.)	porter	mozo (m.) de servicios
washcloth	toallita facial (f.)	bellboy	botones (m.)
soap	jabón (m.)	ice water	agua con hielo

I want a single room, with bath .....Deseo un cuarto para una persona, con baño.
I want a room for two, with twin beds .....Deseo un cuarto para dos, con camas gemelas.
I want two connecting rooms .....Deseo dos cuartos comunicados.
On the lower floor; upper floor .....En el piso bajo; piso alto.
A front room; a back room .....Un cuarto al frente; al fondo.
Do you have hot running water? .....¿Hay agua corriente y caliente?
What is the price? .....¿Cuál es el precio?
What is the minimum rate? .....¿Cuál es el precio mínimo?
Do you accept checks in payment? .....¿Acepta Ud. cheques en pago?
Is there a garage? .....¿Hay garage?
Please call me at six o'clock .....Hágame el favor de llamarme a las seis.
Where is the ladies' room, men's room? .....¿Dónde está el lavabo de señoras, de señores?
Will you have the baggage brought up? down? .....¿Quiere Ud. hacer subir. . . .bajar el equipaje?
We are leaving tomorrow .....Partimos mañana.
We are staying several days. . . .Just tonight. .....Nos quedaremos aquí unos pocos días. . . .solamente esta noche.
Please send these clothes to the laundry .....Hágame el favor de mandar esta ropa a la lavandería.
Please clean and press this suit .....Hágame el favor de limpiar y planchar este traje.
I want it today; tomorrow. .....Lo quiero hoy; mañana.
Where is a barber shop? .....¿Dónde hay una peluquería?
I wish my bill, please. .....Quiero mi cuenta, por favor.
Please forward my correspondence to this address. .....Por favor reexpida mi correspondencia a esta dirección.
Do you want to prepare a lunch for us to carry with us? .....¿Quiere Ud. prepararnos un almuerzo para llevárnoslo?

At the Garage

Fill up the gasoline tank; the radiator .....Llene el tanque de gasolina; el radiador.
Give me five, ten, fifteen, twenty liters .....Deme cinco, diez, quince, veinte litros.
Do you have unleaded gasoline? .....¿Tiene gasolina sin plomo?
How much is gasoline per liter? .....¿Cuánto vale el litro de gasolina?
Check the oil; change the oil, antifreeze .....Vea el aceite; cambie el aceite, anticongelante.
Please lubricate the car; wash the car .....Favor de lubricar el automóvil; lavar el automóvil.
Please tighten the brakes; adjust the brakes .....Favor de apretar los frenos; ajustar los frenos.
Please tune the engine; change the spark plugs .....Favor de afinarme el motor; cambiar las bujías.
My tire has a puncture. Can you repair it? .....Mi llanta está picada. ¿Puede repararla?
The tire is flat. .....La llanta está desinflada.
Put water in the battery. .....Por favor, póngale agua en la batería.
The horn is not working. .....La bocina no funciona.
The battery needs charging .....La batería necesita carga.
Please replace this headlamp .....Por favor, cámbieme este farol.
  the fan belt .....la banda del ventilador.
  the radiator hose .....la manguera del radiador.
The gas line is clogged .....La tubería de gasolina está tapada.
My engine's overheating .....Mi motor se está sobrecalentando.

The exhaust is choked ....Está obstruido el tubo de escape.
The steering gear is out of order.................................La dirección está descompuesta.
The radiator leaks ....El radiador gotea.
The clutch slips ....El clutch se derrapa.
The gasoline tank is leaking..El tanque de gasolina está goteando.
There is a short circuit ....Hay un cortocircuito.
The windshield wiper does not work ....El limpiavidrios del parabrisa no funciona.
The taillight does not work ....La calavera no funciona.
The water pump does not work....................................La bomba de agua no funciona.
Please clean the windshield..Favor de limpiar el parabrisa.
When will the repairs be finished? ....¿Cuándo terminará la reparación?
How much do I owe you? ....¿Cuánto le debo?

In Restaurants

breakfast ....desayuno (m).
lunch ....almuerzo (m.)
midday meal ....comida (f.)
dinner; supper..cena (f.); merienda (f.)
spoon ....cuchara (f.)
cup...taza (f.)
glass ....vaso (m.)
napkin ....servilleta (f.)
bill ....cuenta (f.)
tip...propina (f.)
knife ....cuchillo (m.)
fork...tenedor (m.)

Meat, Eggs, Fish

bacon ....tocino (m.)
beef..carne (f.) de res (m.)
beefsteak ....bistec (m.)
chicken ....pollo (m.)
duck ....pato (m.)
egg..huevo (m.)
   fried ....frito
    soft-boiled...tibio
    hard-boiled..duro
fish ....pescado (m.)
ham...jamón (m.)
lamb ....carne (f.) de carnero (m.)
lamb chops ....chuletas (f.) de carnero (m.)
meat..carne (f.)
omelette ....omelete de huevo (m.)
pork...carne (f.) de puerco (m.)
roast..asado (m.)
sausage ....salchicha (f.)
turkey..guajolote (m.); pavo (m.)
veal...ternera (f.)

Vegetables

salad ....ensalada (f.)
beans..frijoles (m.)
beets...betabeles (f.)
cabbage ....repollo (m.); col (f.)
corn; young corn ....maíz (m.); elote (m.)
lettuce ....lechuga (f.)
onion ....cebolla (f.)
peas..chícharos (m.)
potatoes ....papas (f.)
rice..arroz (m.)
string beans ....ejotes (m.)
sweet potatoes..camotes (m.)
tomatoes ....jitomates (m.)
vegetables..legumbres (f.); verduras (f.)

Bread

bread	pan (m.)
crackers	galletas (f.)
toast	pan tostado (m.)

Beverages, Liquors

beer	cerveza (f.)
brandy	brandy (m.)
coffee	café (m.)
with cream	con crema (f.)
without cream	sin crema
gin	ginebra (f.)
juice	jugo (m.)
milk	leche (f.)
rum	ron (m.)
tea	té (m.)
whiskey	whisky (m.)
table wine	vino de mesa (m.)

Sweets

dessert	postre (m.)
sweet rolls	pan dulce (m.)
cake	pastel (m.)
candies	dulces (m.)
cookies	galletas (f.)
custard	flan (m.)
ice cream	helado (m.)
sherbets	nieves (f.)
pastries	pasteles (m.)
pie	pastel (m.)

Fruits, Nuts

apple	manzana (f.)
avocado	aguacate (m.)
banana	plátano (m.)
cantaloupe	melón (m.)
figs	higos (m.)
fruit	fruta (f.)
grapes	uvas (f.)
guava	guayaba (f.)
grapefruit	toronja (f.)
lemon	limón amarillo (m.)
lime (sweet)	limón (m.)
nuts	nueces (f.)
olives	aceitunas (f.)
orange	naranja (f.)
peach	durazno (m.)
peanuts	cacahuates (m.)
pecans	nueces (f.)
pineapple	piña (f.)
strawberries	fresas (f.)
walnut	nuez (f.) de castilla
watermelon	sandía (f.)

Miscellaneous

sugar	azúcar (m.)
salt	sal (f.)
pepper	pimienta (f.)
butter	mantequilla (f.)
soup; broth	sopa (f.); caldo (m.)
cheese	queso (m.)
honey	miel de abejas (f.)
cigarette; cigar	cigarrillo (m.); puro (m.)
Please bring me the menu	Por favor tráigame el menú.
I like my meat rare, medium, well done	Quiero la carne roja, término medio, bien cocida

FIESTAS AND HOLIDAYS

NOTE: The dates listed here for local celebrations are often variable and may be moved forward or back when the fiesta must be celebrated on a specific day of the week or time of the month or year. Confirm dates in advance with your hotel, at a local tourist information office or at city hall. For background information about widely observed events see "Celebrations," page 28.

NATIONAL FIESTAS AND HOLIDAYS

All banks and most businesses close on these days.

Jan. 1	New Year's Day (Año Nuevo)
Feb. 5	Constitution Day (Día de la Constitución) commemorates the Constitutions of 1857 and 1917, by which Mexico is now governed.
Mar. 21	Birthday of Benito Juárez, Mexican president and national hero.
May 1	Labor Day (Día del Trabajo), with workers' parades throughout the country.
May 5	Battle of Puebla (Batalla de Puebla) commemorates the Mexican victory over the French at Puebla in 1862.
Sept. 1	The president of Mexico delivers the annual State of the Nation Address (Informe Presidencial).
Sept. 16	Independence Day (Día de la Independencia). The president presides at the ceremony of the *Grito de Dolores* in Mexico City's Constitution Square (*Zócalo*); or sometimes at the parish church in Dolores Hidalgo, Gto., where Father Miguel Hidalgo y Costilla issued the *Grito* in 1810. Special celebrations take place in each state capital and start the night of Sept. 15.
Oct. 12	Discovery of America by Columbus, known as Día de la Raza (Day of the Race).
Nov. 20	Revolution Day (Día de la Revolución). Anniversary of the Mexican Revolution of 1910.
Dec. 25	Christmas Day (Navidad). Plays, religious ceremonies.

FIESTAS AND FAIRS IN MEXICO

The following fiestas and holiday periods are celebrated almost everywhere in the country.

Feb. 2	Candlemas (Día de la Candelaria) is celebrated with processions, bullfights, dancing and the blessing of the seeds and candles. The festivities are especially colorful in San Juan de los Lagos, Jal., Talpa de Allende, Jal., and Santa María del Tule, Oax.
Mar. 19	St. Joseph's Day (Día de San José). Especially colorful in Tamuín, S.L.P.
3 days preceding Ash Wednesday	Carnaval. Especially colorful in Acapulco, Gro.; Angahuan, Mich.; Cozumel, Q.R.; Ensenada, B.C.; Huejotzingo, Pue.; Ixtapalapa, D.F.; Jalapa, Ver.; Jarácuaro, Mich.; Larraínzar (San Andrés Chamula), Chis.; Mazatlán, Sin.; San Cristóbal de las Casas, Chis.; San Juan Chamula, Chis.; Tepoztlán, Mor.; and Veracruz, Ver.
Holy Week (Semana Santa)	Holy Week runs from Palm Sunday to Easter Sunday. Particularly impressive are the candlelight processions in Taxco, the Passion Play in Ixtapalapa (Mexico City), and the Processions of Silence in San Luis Potosí and San Miguel de Allende. Other notable observances occur in Atlixco, Pue.; Catemaco, Ver.; Cusárare and San Ignacio Arareco, Chih. (Tarahumara rituals and races); Jérez, Zac.; Huajicori and Mesa del Nayar, Nay.; Ocoyoacac, Mex.; Pátzcuaro, Mich.; Purísima de Bustos, Gto.; Querétaro, Qro.; San Pedrito, Jal.; Santa Teresa, Nay.; Temascalcingo, Mex.; Tzintzuntzan, Mich.; and Zinacantán, Chis.
Holy Saturday	Judas Day. Grotesque papier-mâché figures representing Judas are burned. Especially colorful in Mexico City and vicinity.
May 3	Holy Cross Day (Día de la Santa Cruz). Construction workers mount decorated crosses atop unfinished buildings. Fireworks, picnics at building site. Especially colorful in El Ocotito, Gro.
June 24	Saint John the Baptist Day (Día de San Juan Bautista) is celebrated with popular fairs, religious festivities and practical jokes associated with dunking.
June 29	Fiesta of St. Peter and St. Paul. Especially colorful in Mexcaltitán, Nay., and Zaachila, Oax.
Oct. 4	St. Francis' Day. Especially interesting in Real de Catorce, S.L.P., and San Francisquito, Son.
Nov. 1-2	Day of the Dead (Día de Muertos). A 2-day religious festival marked by visits to cemeteries, flower and culinary offerings, candlelight vigils, elaborately decorated home altars and general merrymaking. It is especially impressive in Janitzio, Mich. Other noteworthy observances take place in Huáncito, Ihuatzio and Tzintzuntzan, Mich.; Jesús María, Nay.; Oaxaca, Oax.; Chiapa de Corzo, Chis.; Huejutla, Hgo.; Míxquic, D.F.; and Centro Ceremonial Mazahua, Mex.

Dec. 8	Immaculate Conception. Almoloya, Hgo.; San Juan de los Lagos, Jal.; Pátzcuaro, Mich.; and Zacatlán, Pue. are among the many towns with noteworthy celebrations.
Dec. 12	Feast Day of the Virgin of Guadalupe. Religious festival that pays tribute to the Guadalupe Virgin. This is Mexico's largest religious pilgrimage. Especially dramatic in Mexico City, but celebrations take place throughout the country.
Dec. 24-25	Christmas. Celebrations usually begin on Dec. 16 with the *posadas*. At Salamanca, Gto., the fiesta lasts until Feb. 2 and includes numerous Nativity scenes enhanced by moving parts and sound-and-light effects. Other well-known celebrations take place in Aguascalientes, Ags.; Chínipas, Chih.; Escuinapa, Sin.; Oaxaca, Oax.; San Juan del Río, Qro.; San Luis Potosí, S.L.P.; San Miguel de Allende, Gto.; Santiago Tuxtla, Ver.; Tepotzotlán, Mex.; Tuxpan, Jal.; Villa Coronado, Chih.; Villa de Reyes, S.L.P.; and Uruáchic, Chih.
Dec. 31	New Year's Eve and Thanksgiving (Fin de Año y Día de Gracias).

OTHER SELECTED LOCAL FESTIVALS

Dec. 30-Jan. 6	Tlaxcala, Tlax.	Walking Cane Fair (Feria del Bastón) includes a *tianguis* (market) that displays and sells the colorful canes made in nearby Tizatlán.
Jan. 1	San Juan Chamula, Chis.	New Year's celebration includes change of tribal governors and Chamula Indian traditional ceremonies.
Jan. 2-6	Tizimín, Yuc.	Fair of the Three Kings features *pastorelas*, a cattle fair and *jaranas*, the uniquely Yucatecan dances. On Three Kings Day (Día de Reyes), Jan. 6, gifts are exchanged as on Christmas in other parts of the world.
Jan. 15-23	Chiapa de Corzo, Chis.	Fiesta of St. Sebastian the Martyr includes a naval battle on the river; lavish costumes.
Jan. 17	Taxco, Gro.	St. Anthony's Day. Blessing of pets and other animals in the parish church.
Jan. 18	Taxco, Gro.	Day of Santa Prisca, town patroness, begins with parishioners singing early morning wake-up songs *(mañanitas)* to the Virgin. Celebration and dancing last all day.
Jan. (second Monday)	Lo de Villa, Col.	A festival in this village near the city of Colima includes a *Toro de Once*, a bullfight open to any and all who want to try their hand at the sport. Another festival with dancing, fireworks and the coronation of a festival queen begins the week before the second Tuesday in January and continues until the following Sunday.
Feb. 1-3	San Blas, Nay.	Blessing of the Sea. Dancing and horse races.
Mar. 6	Taxco, Gro.	Day of Our Lord of Xalpa. Indian dances include Los Tlacololeros, Santiagos, Diablos and Pescadores.
Mar. 18-Apr. 4	Tonalá, Jal.	Ceramics Fair. Handicrafts.
Mar. 21	Guelatao, Oax.	Birthday of Benito Juárez.
Mar. or Apr.	Uruapan, Mich.	Palm Sunday celebration with a huge crafts display and *tianguis*.
Apr. 1-7	Cuernavaca, Mor.	Flower Fair. Exhibits and competitions in floriculture and gardening. Sound-and-light show; popular entertainers.
Apr. 16-May 6	Aguascalientes, Ags.	San Marcos National Fair. A major commercial, industrial and agricultural exposition. Handicrafts.
Apr. 20-26	Tuxtla Gutiérrez, Chis.	Fiesta of St. Mark the Evangelist. A regional commercial and crafts fair, with *charreadas*, theatrical presentations, marimba contests and sports events.
Apr. (last week)	Villahermosa, Tab.	Tabasco State Fair. People from throughout the state present their music, dances and traditions. Folkloric ballet.
Apr. (late)	Ensenada, B.C.	Newport Beach, Calif., to Ensenada Hobie Cat Regatta.
May (last three weekends)	Taxco, Gro.	Alarcón Days. Cultural and artistic festival with band serenades, musical performances and presentations of plays by Taxco-born playwright Juan Ruiz de Alarcón.
May 1-19	Morelia, Mich.	Michoacán State Fair.
May 3-15	Tepic, Nay.	Fiesta of St. Isador the Farmer. A commercial and cultural fair that includes the blessing of seeds, animals and water.
May 19-22	Chihuahua, Chih.	Fiesta of Santa Rita. A major fair with commercial exhibits, cultural events, food and Indian dances.
May 20-June 10	Monterrey, N.L.	Commercial and agricultural fair.
May 20-28	Magdalena, Son.	Father Kino Day and Fair.
May 20-30	Tequisquiapan, Qro.	Grand National Cheese and Wine Fair. Tastings and sales, *tianguis*, cultural events.
June (movable)	Ciudad Juárez, Chih.	Expo-Juárez, a fair with commercial, industrial, agricultural, livestock and craft exhibits.
June 1	Guaymas, Son.	Mexican Navy Day features a naval battle with fireworks.

June (1st Thurs.)	Temascalcingo, Mex.	Corpus Christi Thursday. Blessing of farm animals and equipment; children in Indian costumes.
June 15-July 2	Tlaquepaque, Jal.	National Ceramics Fair and June Fiestas. Craft competitions, exhibits and demonstrations; cultural events.
June 15-July 15	Santa Ana Chiautempan, Tlax.	National Sarape Fair.
June 18	Papantla, Ver.	Corpus Christi Day and Vanilla Festival. The famous Flying Pole dancers perform in their place of origin.
June 29	Zaachila, Oax.	Festival of Saint Peter and Saint Paul. Includes stilt dance and other Indian dances.
July 15	Catemaco, Ver.	Day of Our Lady of Mount Carmel. Native costumes.
July 25	Santiago Tuxtla, Ver.	Day of St. James the Apostle. Líseres, Negritos and other local Indian dances.
Mid- to late July (two successive Mondays)	Oaxaca, Oax.	Guelaguetza (Festival of Cooperation). Elaborate, colorful folkloric festival with dances, regional costumes and music.
Aug. (movable, first half)	Oxkutzcab, Yuc.	Popular fair; Maya traditions.
Aug. 2	Mexico City, D.F.	Cuauhtémoc Day. Dances and ceremonies at Cuauhtémoc Circle honor the last Aztec emperor.
Aug. 5-20	Huamantla, Tlax.	Celebration for the Day of the Virgin of Charity and Assumption Day. Flowers and sawdust adorn the streets for processions and for the running of the bulls, also held in Pamplona, Spain. Fair, Indian dances, *tianguis*.
Aug. 11-22	Santa Clara del Cobre, Mich.	Copper Fair. Copper handicrafts. Indian dancers, floats.
Aug. 18-31	San Luis Potosí, S.L.P.	National Fair of Potosí (Feria Nacional Potosina) on the Day of St. Louis the King.
Aug. 27- Sept. 1	Zacatecas, Zac.	Festival of La Morisma. Re-enactment of a 3-day battle between Moors and Spaniards. *Pastorelas;* Indian dances.
Sept. 1-16	Zacatecas, Zac.	National Fair. Agriculture and livestock, handicrafts, bullfights, art exhibitions and sports.
Sept. 10-17	Dolores Hidalgo, Gto.	Independence Fair and Regional Exposition. *El Grito de Dolores* is reissued by the president on Sept. 15 of most years; there is television coverage of the Mexico City ceremony.
Sept. 15-Nov.	Puebla, Pue.	International Fair, a major cultural event focusing on music. The Regional Fair of Hard Cider is an industrial, agricultural and handicrafts exposition.
Sept. 22-Oct. 4	Magdalena, Son.	Fiestas of St. Francis Xavier. Attended by Seri, Yaqui, Pápago, Pima and Sioux Indians.
Sept. 25- Oct. 10	Real de Catorce, S.L.P.	Fiesta of St. Francis and Regional Fair. Among the many pilgrims are the Huichol, who cross the Zacatecas Desert on foot from their Jalisco homeland. Religious and traditional ceremonies.
Oct. (all)	Guadalajara, Jal.	October Festivals (Fiestas de Octubre). Major fair with many shows, races and other events in the arts and sports.
Oct. (most)	Guanajuato, Gto.	Cervantes International Festival. One of Mexico's leading cultural events, it draws participants from many countries. *Entremeses*, skits based on the author's work, are featured.
Oct. 1-19	Pachuca, Hgo.	Hidalgo State Fair.
Dec. (1st week)	Taxco, Gro.	National Silver Fair. Show and sale of silver items by craftsmen from throughout the world.
Dec. 10-12	San Cristóbal de las Casas, Chis.	Fiesta of the Virgin of Guadalupe. Tzotzil and Tzeltal Indians in procession; marimba music, equestrian parades.
Dec. 23	Oaxaca, Oax.	Night of the Radishes features radish figurines and thin, fried radish cakes covered with molasses. The cakes are served in a clay dish that must be broken after the cakes are finished.

The World at Your Fingertips

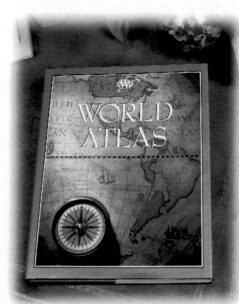

O pen up a world of knowledge with the AAA World Atlas. This comprehensive atlas is completely revised, reflecting the most up-to-date boundaries and political designations possible. Each section of the atlas provides extensive information regarding each country or U.S. state featured, with detailed maps, demographic figures, geographical facts, economic data, and much more.

Take a peek at what the world has to offer. Purchase a copy of the **AAA World Atlas** at your local AAA office today.

450

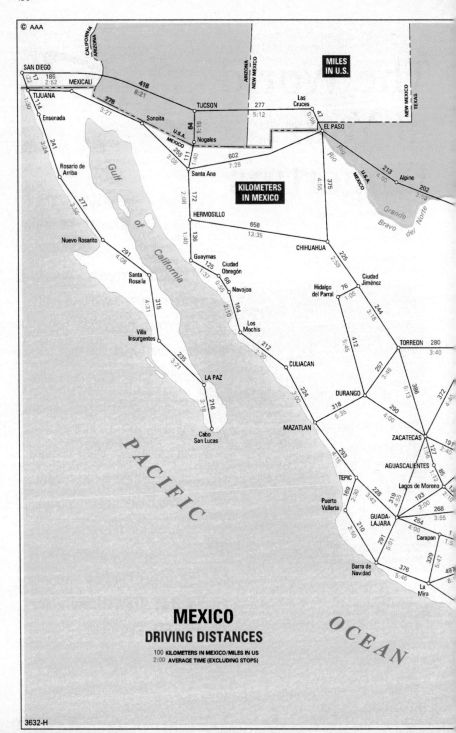

© AAA

CALIFORNIA / ARIZONA

ARIZONA / NEW MEXICO

NEW MEXICO / TEXAS

MILES IN U.S.

SAN DIEGO
17 / :22
185 / 2:52
MEXICALI
418 / 8:21

TUCSON
277 / 5:12
Las Cruces
47 / 0:58
EL PASO

TIJUANA
114
1:30
278 / 3:27
Sonoita
64 / 1:16
U.S.A. / MEXICO

Ensenada
241 / 3:24
Nogales
255 / 3:08
111 / 1:40
602 / 7:28
213 / 4:00
Alpine
202 / 3:50

Rosario de Arriba

Santa Ana
375 / 4:55

Rio

Grande / Bravo / del Norte

Gulf

277 / 3:46
172 / 2:08
KILOMETERS IN MEXICO

Nuevo Rosarito
291 / 4:08
HERMOSILLO
136 / 1:40
658 / 13:35

of

CHIHUAHUA
225 / 2:59

Santa Rosalia
315 / 4:31
Guaymas
125 / 1:37
Ciudad Obregón
68 / 0:55
Navojoa

Ciudad Jiménez
Hidalgo del Parral
76 / 1:05
244 / 3:18

California

164 / 2:10

412 / 5:45

Villa Insurgentes
235 / 3:21
Los Mochis
212 / 2:30

TORREON
280 / 3:40

LA PAZ
216 / 3:18
CULIACAN
224 / 3:00
DURANGO
257 / 3:46
386 / 5:13
372 / 4:40

318 / 5:35
290 / 4:00

Cabo San Lucas
MAZATLAN
ZACATECAS
191 / 2:40
127 / 1:56

AGUASCALIENTES
85 / 1:12

293 / 4:15
Lagos de Moreno
193 / 3:00
268 / 3:55

TEPIC
169 / 2:30
228 / 3:42
319 / 4:55
254 / 4:00
Carapan

Puerto Vallarta
GUADA-LAJARA
210 / 2:50
291 / 5:01

Barra de Navidad
376 / 5:46
329 / 5:47
497 / 8:

La Mira

PACIFIC

OCEAN

MEXICO
DRIVING DISTANCES

100 KILOMETERS IN MEXICO/MILES IN US
2:00 AVERAGE TIME (EXCLUDING STOPS)

3632-H

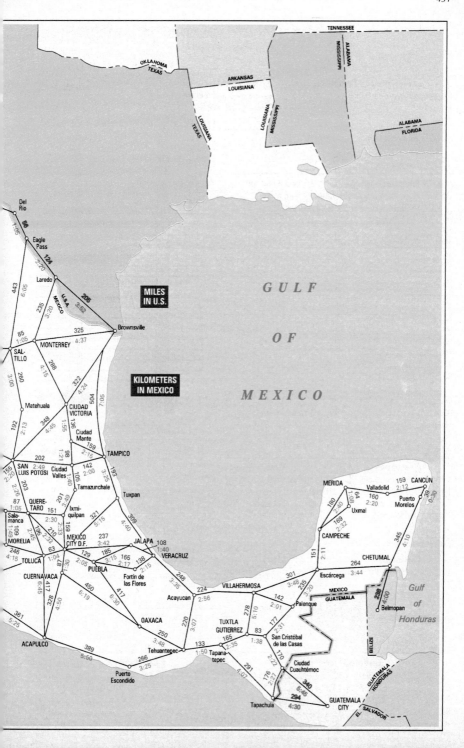

Metric Equivalents

TEMPERATURE

To convert Fahrenheit to Celsius, subtract 32 from the Fahrenheit temperature, multiply by 5 and divide by 9.
To convert Celsius to Fahrenheit, multipy by 9, divide by 5 and add 32.

ACRES

1 acre = 0.4 hectare (ha)	1 hectare = 2.47 acres

MILES AND KILOMETERS

Note: A kilometer is approximately 5/8 or 0.6 of a mile.
To convert kilometers to miles multiply by 0.6.

Miles/Kilometers		Kilometers/Miles	
15	24.1	30	18.6
20	32.2	35	21.7
25	40.2	40	24.8
30	48.3	45	27.9
35	56.3	50	31.0
40	64.4	55	34.1
45	72.4	60	37.2
50	80.5	65	40.3
55	88.5	70	43.4
60	96.6	75	46.6
65	104.6	80	49.7
70	112.7	85	52.8
75	120.7	90	55.9
80	128.7	95	59.0
85	136.8	100	62.1
90	144.8	105	65.2
95	152.9	110	68.3
100	160.9	115	71.4

Celsius° / Fahrenheit°

Celsius °		Fahrenheit °
100	BOILING	212
37		100
35		95
32		90
29		85
27		80
24		75
21		70
18		65
16		60
13		55
10		50
7		45
4		40
2		35
0	FREEZING	32
-4		25
-7		20
-9		15
-12		10
-15		5
-18		0
-21		-5
-24		-10
-27		-15

LINEAR MEASURE

Customary	Metric
1 inch = 2.54 centimeters	1 centimeter = 0.4 inches
1 foot = 30 centimeters	1 meter = 3.3 feet
1 yard = 0.91 meters	1 meter = 1.09 yards
1 mile = 1.6 kilometers	1 kilometer = .62 miles

WEIGHT

If You Know:	Multiply By:	To Find:
Ounces	28	Grams
Pounds	0.45	Kilograms
Grams	0.035	Ounces
Kilograms	2.2	Pounds

LIQUID MEASURE

Customary	Metric
1 fluid ounce = 30 milliliters	1 milliliter = .03 fluid ounces
1 cup = .24 liters	1 liter = 2.1 pints
1 pint = .47 liters	1 liter = 1.06 quarts
1 quart = .95 liters	1 liter = .26 gallons
1 gallon = 3.8 liters	

PRESSURE

Air pressure in automobile tires is expressed in kilopascals. Multiply pound-force per square inch (psi) by 6.89 to find kilopascals (kPa).

24 psi = 165 kPa	28 psi = 193 kPa
26 psi = 179 kPa	30 psi = 207 kPa

GALLONS AND LITERS

Gallons/Liters				Liters/Gallons			
5	19.0	12	45.6	10	2.6	40	10.4
6	22.8	14	53.2	15	3.9	50	13.0
7	26.6	16	60.8	20	5.2	60	15.6
8	30.4	18	68.4	25	6.5	70	18.2
9	34.2	20	76.0	30	7.8	80	20.8
10	38.0	25	95.0	35	9.1	90	23.4

Highway Signs

Stop

No Passing

Horizontal Clearance

Maximum Weight (Metric Tons)

No Pedestrians

Parking Limit

One-Hour Parking

No Left Turn

No U Turn

No Parking

Keep to the Right

Inspection

No Trucks

Pedestrians Keep Left

Speed Limit (In K.P.H.)

Right Turn on Red Permitted

No Bicycles

Keep Right

Do Not Enter

Road Signs In Spanish	_Descriptions In English_
Topes, Vibradores	Speed Bumps
Un Solo Carril	One Lane
Pavimento Derrapante	Pavement Slippery
Prohibido Seguir de Frente	Do Not Enter
Vado	Dip

For Hassle-Free International Travel...

Put AAA First on Your Itinerary

When traveling south of the border, carry an **Inter-American Driving Permit...** even if you're not planning to drive. Should you need to communicate with foreign authorities, this recognizable form of identification can help you get on your way more quickly. Valid in more than 15 countries, the permit contains your name, photo, and driver information translated into three foreign languages.

Before you travel south, travel to any AAA office for your Inter-American Driving Permit. Bring your valid U.S. driver's license, $10, and two passport-size photos (also available at AAA offices).

Travel With Someone You Trust®

ALPHABETICAL LISTING OF CITIES, TOWNS AND PLACES

POINTS OF INTEREST INDEX

ART GALLERIES

ARTS & CRAFTS

AUDITORIUMS

BATTLEFIELDS

BEACHES

Bridges

Buildings, Office

Buildings, Public; Capitol; City Hall

BULL RINGS

CANYONS

CARILLONS

CAVES

CEMETERIES

Children's Attractions

Churches, Cathedrals & Basilicas

Churches-Chapels

Churches-Missions

Events-Sports

Exhibits & Collections-General

Exhibits & Collections-Historical

EXHIBITS & COLLECTIONS-INDIAN

EXHIBITS & COLLECTIONS-SCIENCE

EXHIBITS & COLLECTIONS-WARS

EXHIBITS & COLLECTIONS-WEAPONS

EXPERIMENTAL FARMS & STATIONS

FORTS & MILITARY INSTALLATIONS

FOUNTAINS

GARDENS

Museums & Public Buildings

Music Events

Music Halls & Opera Houses

Paintings

Parks, City

Parks, National

PENINSULAS

PLAZAS

RACETRACKS-AUTO

RACETRACKS-AUTO

RACETRACKS-HORSE

RESORT, RECREATION & SIGHTSEEING AREAS

RUINS

SCENIC DRIVES

SCHOOLS

SCHOOLS-ACADEMIES

SCHOOLS-COLLEGES & UNIVERSITIES

SCHOOLS-INSTITUTES

SHOPS, FIRMS & STORES

Sightseeing Tours

Towers

Trees

Views

Visitor Centers

Bed & Breakfast Lodgings Index

Some bed and breakfasts listed below might have historical significance. Those properties are also referenced in the Historical index. The indication that continental [CP] or full breakfast [BP] is included in the room rate reflects whether a property is a bed-and-breakfast facility.

Country Inns Index

Some of the following country inns can also be considered as bed-and-breakfast operations. The indication that continental [CP] or full breakfast [BP] is included in the room rate reflects whether a property is a bed-and-breakfast facility.

HISTORICAL LODGINGS & RESTAURANTS INDEX

Some of the following historical lodgings can also be considered as bed-and-breakfast operations. The indication that continental [CP] or full breakfast [BP] is included in the room rate reflects whether a property is a bed-and-breakfast facility.

RESORTS INDEX

Many establishments are located in resort areas; however, the following places have extensive on-premises recreational facilities.

Resorts (cont'd)

Baja California

Accommodations

Casa Del Mar Golf Resort
& Spa .... San José del Cabo, **Baja California Sur** 158

Estero Beach Resort
Hotel .... Ensenada, **Baja California** 167

Fiesta Americana Grand Los
Cabos .... Cabo San Lucas, **Baja California Sur** 155

Hotel Presidente Inter-Continental Los Cabos All
Inclusive Exclusive
Resort .... San José del Cabo, **Baja California Sur** 158

Hotel Buena Vista Beach
Resort .... Buenavista, **Baja California Sur** 151

Hotel
Finisterra ... Cabo San Lucas, **Baja California Sur** 156

Hacienda Bajamar .... Ensenada, **Baja California** 167

La Concha Beach
Resort .... La Paz, **Baja California Sur** 175

Melia Cabo Real Beach & Golf
Resort .... San José del Cabo, **Baja California Sur** 159

Melia Los
Cabos .... San José del Cabo, **Baja California Sur** 159

Melia San
Lucas .... Cabo San Lucas, **Baja California Sur** 156

Pueblo Bonito
Resort .... Cabo San Lucas, **Baja California Sur** 156

Pueblo Bonito Rose
Resort .... Cabo San Lucas, **Baja California Sur** 156

Rosarito Beach Hotel
& Spa .... Rosarito, **Baja California** 180

Sheraton Hacienda Del Mar Resort &
Spa .... Cabo San Lucas, **Baja California Sur** 156

Solmar Suites
Resort .... Cabo San Lucas, **Baja California Sur** 156

Westin Regina Golf & Beach Resort, Los
Cabos .... San José del Cabo, **Baja California Sur** 159

The Pacific Coast

Accommodations

Allegro Resort Nuevo Vallarta
All Inclusive .... Nuevo Vallarta, **Nayarit** 267

Barcelo Huatulco Beach
Resort .... Bahías de Huatulco, **Oaxaca** 240

Camino Real Mazatlan .... Mazatlán, **Sinaloa** 264

Camino Real Puerto Vallarta ...... Puerto Vallarta, **Jalisco** 276

Hotel Pierre Marques .... Acapulco, **Guerrero** 235

Hotel Playa Mazatlán .... Mazatlán, **Sinaloa** 265

Las Brisas .... Acapulco, **Guerrero** 235

Magnihotel Huatulco Suites
Resort .... Bahías de Huatulco, **Oaxaca** 240

Qualton Club & Spa An All Inclusive
Resort .... Puerto Vallarta, **Jalisco** 278

Sierra Hotel Manzanillo .... Manzanillo, **Colima** 255

The Fairmont Acapulco
Princess .... Acapulco, **Guerrero** 234

Vista Club Hotel Playa de Oro-All
Inclusive .... Puerto Vallarta, **Jalisco** 278

Westin Regina Resort Puerto
Vallarta .... Puerto Vallarta, **Jalisco** 279

Central Mexico

Accommodations

Antigua Villa Santa
Monica .... San Miguel de Allende, **Guanajuato** 400

Fiesta Americana Hacienda
Galindo .... San Juan del Río, **Querétaro** 393

Hotel Balneario Spa La
Caldera .... Abasolo, **Guanajuato** 346

Hotel Hacienda Vista
Hermosa .... Tequesquitengo, **Morelos** 341

Hotel Meson de Santa Rosa .. Querétaro, **Querétaro** 392

La Casa de la Marquesa .... Querétaro, **Querétaro** 393

ABOUT CAMPGROUNDS

For regulations on entering Mexico, see "Arriving in Mexico," page 52.

The camping and recreational vehicle areas listed in this section must meet high standards of cleanliness, maintenance and facility development. Privately owned campgrounds are labeled "Private." Any campgrounds run by national parks or local governments are labeled "Public." Areas are listed alphabetically under the nearest city. Unless a mailing address is given in parentheses following the location, mail is sent to the town under which the campground is listed.

In individual listings, the total site count, seasonal and transient, is shown to the left of the rate lines. The number of transient sites by category is shown in the body of the listing. The figure following "T" indicates the number of transient sites exclusively for TENT campers; the figure following "T/RV," the number of interchangeable TENT or RV sites; and the figure following "RV," the number of sites exclusively for recreational vehicles.

ACAPULCO, GUERRERO

ACAPULCO TRAILER PARK NO. 1
Private   60 Sites
All Year $10.00 for 2   60EWS   XP S2
Location: 14.5 km nw off Mex 200 on Pie de la Cuesta Beach Dr. 39300 (PO Box 1). Fax: 74/60-2457. **Terms:** Res dep req, 14 day refund notice; A/C $1.50, 30 amps; pets. **Facility:** 2 acres; T/RV-60. On strong surf beach. Palm tree shade. Most sites face ocean. Brick or gravel patios. Flush toilets; wading pool, small pool; boat ramp. **Services:** groceries. **Leisure Activities:** *Fee:* water skiing. *Rental:* boats.
☏ 74/60-0010

HOW THE RATES ARE QUOTED

All rates are quoted in approximate U.S. dollars. Much of the information in this book is necessarily compiled some time in advance of publication. Rates are subject to change and are for information only.

Current rates (in pesos) may or may not be posted at the campground's front office. Any violations of posted rates should be reported along with documentation—either the bill itself or a photocopy—to AAA/CAA and to PROFECO (Procuraduría Federal del Consumidor). This en-

ables both agencies to make a full investigation on your behalf. Rate complaints should be directed to the attention of the PROFECO representative at the Mexico Tourism Board office nearest your place of residence. For addresses of Mexico Tourism Board offices in the United States and Canada, *see page 39.*

DAILY camping fees quoted reflect the base rate for the number of persons specified. Where the term "Fam" is used, it generally refers to parents and unmarried children under a certain age, usually 18. If off-season fees are significantly lower during specified periods, the lower fees and their effective dates are shown.

Fees for extra persons ("XP") also are listed; an **F** means that under the campground's family plan, the extra person charge is reduced for children.

HOOKUPS: Electric, water and sewer hookups are indicated by the letters E, W and S preceded by the number of each available for transient campers. If there is a charge for their use in addition to the basic site fee, it is shown immediately following the appropriate letter. In the example:

25 E $1.00   W 20 incl   10 S $.75

there are 25 electric hookups with an additional charge of $1, 20 water with the charge included in the electric hookup fee, and 10 sewer with an additional charge of 75c.

Air conditioning (A/C) and/or heaters are listed only when a fee is charged for the use of the camper's own equipment in addition to the basic electric hookup fee. There may or may not be a fee charged for cable TV and phone hookups.

MAJOR CREDIT CARDS honored by campgrounds are indicated in individual listings by the following symbols: AE (American Express), CB (Carte Blanche), DI (Diners Club), DS (Discover), MC (MasterCard) and VI (VISA).

Each listing also includes campground location, telephone number (if applicable) and a description of its facilities, services and recreational offerings.

Terms Used in Listings

CHECKOUT TIME: Given in listing only if campers must check out before noon.

DISPOSAL FACILITIES: If applicable, the type of disposal service available to registered campers is indicated as follows: dump station—a fixed facility; portable disposal service—on-site holding tank service provided by the campground; complete disposal facilities—both types are available. There may or may not be a fee.

LOCATION: Distances are given in kilometers from the center of town, unless otherwise indicated.

PETS: Most campgrounds permit pets on a leash; pets are not mentioned unless other restrictions apply. Proof of current rabies vaccination shots may be required.

RV LIMITATION: Restrictions on the type or length of recreational vehicles accepted at individual areas.

SHOWERS: Not mentioned if hot showers are available; hot showers are required at privately owned campgrounds. There may or may not be a fee.

TOILETS: Noted in listing if all are flush toilets.

Campgrounds

Acapulco, Guerrero

KOA ACAPULCO WEST
Private   110 Sites   (74/44-4062
All Year $11.50-17.25 for 2 110EWS   XP $3
Location: 15 km nw off Mex 200 via Pie de la Cuesta Beach Dr, 4 km ne on Barra de Coyuca. Carr Pie de la Cuesta 39580. Fax: 74/83-2281. **Terms:** 50 amps, wkly/mthly/seasonal rates; pets. **Facility:** 4 acres; T/RV-110. Partially shaded sites, some pull-thru. A few with ocean view. Strong surf beach. Tent sites, $8. Lounge; snack bar; flush toilets; pool, wading pool; basketball, soccer, volleyball, view dolphins daily, whale (May & June), beautiful sunsets. **Services:** groceries. *Fee:* coin laundry. **Recreation:** fishing.

PLAYA SUAVE TRAILER PARK
Private   38 Sites   (74/85-1885
All Year $11.50 for 2   38EWS
Location: 0.5 km e; corner Diego H de Mendoza; entrance on Calz Vasco Nunez de Balboa. Ave Miguel Aleman No 276 39300 (A P 165). **Terms:** Reserv deposit; no pets. **Facility:** 3 acres; T/RV-38. In shaded coconut grove in western bayfront hotel zone. Dump station; cold showers; flush toilets.

Bahia Kino, Sonora

KINO BAY TRAILER PARK
Private   200 Sites   (624/2-0216
All Year $18.00 for 2   200EWS   XP $3
Location: 8 km nw on Beach Hwy. Mar de Cortez S/N 83340 (PO Box 57). Fax: 624/2-0083. **Terms:** Reserv deposit, 14 day refund notice, 10/1-4/11; 30 amps, mthly rates; pets. **Facility:** 4 acres; T/RV-200. Across from beach. Covered patios. Inviting common room with patio overlooking the beach. Dump station; flush toilets. **Services:** propane. *Fee:* coin laundry. **Recreation:** boat storage facilities. **Cards:** MC, VI.

Bucerias, Nayarit

BUCERIAS TRAILER COURT
Private   47 Sites   (329/8-0265
12/1-6/1 & 11/1-11/30 $20.00 for 2   47EWS   XP $4
Location: 11 km n of Puerto Vallarta on Mex 200 at Km 143, follow signs. Lazaro Cardenas y Javier SN Mina 63732 (PO Box 148). Fax: 329/8-0300. **Terms:** Open 12/1-6/1 & 11/1-11/30; mthly rates; pets. **Facility:** 2 acres; RV-47. On beach. Dump station; flush toilets; pool, wading pool.

Cabo San Lucas, Baja California Sur

VAGABUNDOS DEL MAR RV PARK
Private   65 Sites   (114/3-0290
All Year $14.50-16.00 for 2 65EWS   XP $3
Location: 3 km e on Mex 1. (APDO Postal 197). Fax: 114/3-0511. **Terms:** Reserv deposit, 30 day refund notice, handling fee; wkly/mthly rates; pets. **Facility:** 3 acres; RV-65. Reservations (707) 374-5511; Fax (707)374-6843. Flush toilets; cable TV hookups; pool; restaurant 1 pm-10 pm. **Services:** *Fee:* coin laundry.

Cancun, Quintana Roo

CANCUN MECOLOCO TRAILER PARK
Private   100 Sites   (98/50-3200
All Year $13.00 for 4   70EWS
Location: On beach road between Puerto Juarez and Punta Sam. Km 3 carr Puerto Juarez-Punta Sam 77500. Fax: 98/80-2376. **Terms:** Pets. **Facility:** 5 acres; T/RV-100. Rural location across road from Caribbean sandy beaches. Adjacent to Mayan ruin excavation. Verify rate information when making reservation. Dump station; flush toilets. **Services:** groceries; laundry. **Recreation:** fishing, scuba diving, snorkeling.

CHAPALA, JALISCO

PAL TRAILER PARK
Private   105 Sites   (37/66-0040
All Year $14.00 for 2   105EWS   XP $3
Location: On Chapala-Ajijic Hwy Jal 94. Allen W Lloyd
#149 45915 (PO Box 84, 45900). Fax: 37/66-0040.
Terms: Reserv deposit, 7 day refund notice; 30 amps, mthly
rates. **Facility:** T-3, RV-105. Flush toilets; cable TV hook-
ups; heated pool, wading pool; rec room. **Services:** Fee:
coin laundry.

CIUDAD CONSTITUCION, BAJA CALIFORNIA SUR

MANFRED'S RV PARK
Private   80 Sites   (113/2-1103
All Year $12.00-15.00 for 2 80EW   50S   XP $3
Location: On Mex 1, 1 km n of town. Hwy 1 (Apartado
Postal 120, 23600). Fax: 113/2-1103. **Terms:** Pets.
Facility: 5 acres; RV-80, T/RV-80. Nicely landscaped with
flowering plants and trees. 2 motel rooms $35 for up to 2
persons, extra person $5. Flush toilets; pool; restaurant
open for dinner serving authentic Austrian dishes.

CREEL, CHIHUAHUA

KOA
Private   104 Sites   (145/6-0665
All Year $22.00 for 2   74E   25S
Location: Center. Adolfo Lopez Mateos S/N 33200.
Terms: 50 amps; no pets. **Facility:** T-30, RV-74. Restaurant
8 am-10 pm. Very nicely done campground. Also, has 20
Kabins with baths and heaters, some have efficiency kitch-
ens and will sleep 4-6 persons. All sites have picnic table
and charcoal grill. Tent sites, $10 US dollars/day; cabanas
$710 pesos/day. Dump station; lounge; flush toilets; play-
ground, rec room. **Services:** groceries. Fee: coin laundry.
Recreation: hiking trails. **Cards:** AE, MC, VI.

CUERNAVACA, MORELOS

CUERNAVACA TRAILER PARK DIAMANTE
Private   153 Sites   (73/16-0761
All Year $10.00-15.00 for 2 153EWS   XP $3
Location: On Hwy 95D, exit Calle Diana, 0.4 km w, s on
Mesalina. (Mesalina 3, Colonia Delicias, 62250).
Fax: 73/16-0761. **Terms:** 30 amps; pets. **Facility:** 2 acres;
RV-153. Country setting. Flush toilets; heated pool; 1 tennis
court; playground, fronton court, pool table. **Services:**
groceries.

ENSENADA, BAJA CALIFORNIA

BAJA SEASONS RV BEACH RESORT
Private   133 Sites   (615/5-4015
3/16-11/30 $50.00-67.00 for 2 133EWS   XP $10
12/1-3/15 $40.00-50.00 for 2   XP $10
Location: On Hwy 1D; northbound exit Alisitos, make
U-turn, then 10 km s; 42 km n of town. Carretera Escencia
Tijuana Ensenada 72.5 (Aportado Postal 1492, LA SALINA).
Fax: 615/5-4019. **Terms:** Reserv deposit, 14 day refund no-
tice; 30 amps, wkly/mthly rates; pets $1 extra charge.
Facility: 50 acres; RV-133. Beachfront RV park between
Rosarito and Ensenada. Restaurant 7:30 am-10 pm. Open,
dry tent sites, $10 per person; motel rooms, $56-$76; Villas,
$151-$224. Lounge; flush toilets; cable TV hookups; pool,
saunas, whirlpool; 2 lighted tennis courts; rec room, restaurant & bar, steam room. miniature golf. **Services:** groceries.
Fee: coin laundry. Fee: horseback riding. **Cards:** MC, VI.

ESTERO BEACH RV PARK
Private   100 Sites   (617/6-6225
12/1-9/30 $16.00-30.00 for 2 50EWS   XP $5
10/1-11/30 $16.00-25.00 for 2   XP $5
Location: 10.5 km s of town on Hwy 1, then 1.5 km w on
Ave Jose Ma Moreles and Ave Lupita Novelo O; at Estero
Beach Resort Hotel. (PMB 1186, 482 W San Ysidro Bl, SAN
YSIDRO, 92173). **Terms:** Reserv deposit, 3 day refund notice, handling fee; mthly rates; pets. **Facility:** 4 acres; 35m
limit, T-50, RV-50. Open sites. Restaurant & lounge at resort, 7:30 am-10 pm. Extra vehicle, $5 extra charge. Dump
station; lounge; flush toilets; beach, swimming; boat ramp;
playground. 3 lighted tennis courts. **Services:** Fee: coin
laundry. **Recreation:** fishing, water skiing. Fee: boating,
jetskis & waverunners, 4/1-10/1; horseback riding. Rental:
paddleboats; bicycles. **Cards:** MC, VI.

GUADALAJARA, JALISCO

HACIENDA TRAILER PARK
Private   98 Sites   (3/627-1724
All Year $14.00 for 2   98EWS   XP $3
Location: 9.5 km nw; 0.5 km sw of Mex 15. (PO Box 45,
45000). Fax: 3/627-2832. **Terms:** Reserv deposit, 15 day
refund notice; pets. **Facility:** Alt 1568m; 4 acres; RV-98.
Nicely designed sites in quiet location; patios. Some shaded
sites. Flush toilets; cable TV hookups; heated pool; rec
room. **Services:** Fee: coin laundry.

SAN JOSE DEL TAJO
Private   150 Sites   (3/686-1738
All Year $16.00 for 2   150EWS   XP $2
Location: 15.5 km s on Mex 15 and 80. Ave Presidente Lo-
pez Mateos 45560 (PO Box 31-242, 45051).
Fax: 3/686-1738. **Terms:** Reserv deposit, 30 day refund no-
tice, handling fee; 50 amps, mthly rates; pets. **Facility:** 16
acres; RV-150. Secluded. Some shaded sites. Flush toilets;
cable TV hookups; pool; 1 tennis court; rec room. **Services:**
Fee: coin laundry. **Recreation:** rec program.

LA PAZ, BAJA CALIFORNIA SUR

AQUAMARINA RV PARK
Private   19 Sites   (112/2-3761
All Year $16.50 for 2   19EWS   XP $2
Location: 3 km w on Hwy 1, then 1 km n on Calle Navarit.
(APDO Postal 133, 23094). Fax: 112/5-6228. **Terms:** A/C
$1.20, elec heaters $1.20, wkly/mthly rates; pets. **Facility:** 5
acres; RV-19. On La Paz Bay, enclosed park with many
trees. 2 apartments & mobile home, $34-$50. Flush toilets;
pool; boat ramp, marina. **Services:** Fee: coin laundry. **Recreation:** fishing, charter trips. Fee: mooring, storage.

CASA BLANCA RV PARK

Private   47 Sites   (112/4-0009

All Year $15.00 for 2   47EWS   XP $3
Location: On Hwy 1, at km 4.5, west entrance to town. Ave Delfines (Apdo Postal 681, 23094). Fax: 112/4-0009. **Terms:** Mthly rates; pets. **Facility:** T/RV-47. Enclosed park with modest restrooms. Tents $10. Flush toilets; pool; 1 tennis court. **Services:** Fee: coin laundry.

LA PAZ TRAILER PARK

Private   35 Sites   (112/2-8787

All Year $15.00 for 2   35EWS   XP $5
Location: 4 km w on Hwy 1, turn n, just w of Volkswagen Agency, 1.2 km n, then 0.4 km e. Brecha California #1010 23094 (Apdo Postal 482). Fax: 112/2-9938. **Terms:** Reserv deposit, 3 day refund notice; wkly/mthly rates; pets. **Facility:** 6 acres; RV-35. 9 pull-thru sites, walled park. Tent sites, $11 for 2 persons. Flush toilets; cable TV hookups; pool, wading pool. **Services:** Fee: coin laundry. **Recreation:** 0.5 km from beach & boat ramp, fishing trips. **Cards:** AE, MC, VI.

LORETO, BAJA CALIFORNIA SUR

LORETO SHORES VILLAS & RV PARK

Private   37 Sites   (113/5-0629

All Year $14.00 for 2   37EWS   XP $4
Location: 1 km s of town center via Francisco Madero. Colonia Zaragoza 23880 (Apdo Postal 219). Fax: 113/5-0711. **Terms:** Reserv deposit; wkly rates. **Facility:** 5 acres; RV-37. At the beach; open, mostly pull-thru sites, modest restrooms. Tent sites, $5 per person; RV site without hook up, $11; villas $65-$120. Dump station; flush toilets; beach. **Services:** Fee: coin laundry. **Recreation:** fishing.

TRIPUI RESORT RV PARK

Private   31 Sites   (113/3-0818

All Year $14.00 for 2   31EWS   XP $5
Location: 20 km s via Hwy 1 and 1 km e, 0.8 km from Puerto Escondids. (Apdo Postal 100, 23880). Fax: 113/3-0828. **Terms:** Reserv deposit, 3 day refund notice; wkly/mthly rates; pets. **Facility:** 5 acres; RV-31. Open sites at the edge of a mobile home park. Campsite, $5 per person; 1 pallapa shaded RV site, $20; motel rooms $50 for up to 2 persons, extra person $5. Lounge; flush toilets; cable TV hookups; pool, wading pool; boat ramp; playground, restaurant 8 am-9 pm. marina. **Services:** groceries. Fee: coin laundry.

VILLAS DE LORETO

Private   9 Sites   (113/50-586

All Year $15.00 for 2   9EWS   XP $5
Location: 1 km s of town center via Franciso Madero. Colonia Zaragoza 23880 (Box 132). **Terms:** Reserv deposit, 30 day refund notice, handling fee; wkly rates. **Facility:** 4 acres; RV-9. At the beach in walled park. Smoke free premises. Motel rooms $70 for 2 persons, $15 extra person. Flush toilets; beach, pool, swimming; mountain bike & local tours. **Services:** Fee: coin laundry. **Recreation:** kayak rentals. **Cards:** MC, VI.

LOS BARRILES, BAJA CALIFORNIA SUR

MARTIN VERDUGO'S BEACH RESORT

Private   94 Sites   (114/1-0054

All Year $11.00-13.00 for 2 69EWS   XP $4
Location: 1 km e of Hwy 1. Bahia de Palmas 23501 (Apdo Postal 17). Fax: 114/1-0054. **Terms:** Mthly rates. **Facility:** 5 acres; T-25, RV-69. Partially shaded sites. Restaurant (6:30-11 am) and palapa bar. Motel rooms, $44-$46, with kitchens, $51. Lounge; flush toilets; beach, pool; boat ramp. **Services:** Fee: coin laundry. **Recreation:** boating. Fee: charter fishing.

LOS MOCHIS, SINALOA

HOTELES COLINAS DEL VALLE RV TRAILER PARK S.A. DE CV

Private   56 Sites   (681/1-8111

All Year $14.00 for 4   56EWS
Location: On Mex 15, 2 km s of Los Mochis exit. Blvd Macario Gaxiola y Carrete 81200 (A P 600). Fax: 681/1-8181. **Terms:** 30 amps; pets. **Facility:** 3 acres; RV-56. Small amusement park with ferris wheel, kid's train and merry-go-round. Some pull-thru sites. Closed Mon. Flush toilets; pool, 2 wading pools, large water & metal slides; 4 lighted tennis courts; volleyball & basketball courts. **Cards:** AE, MC, VI.

MATEHUALA, SAN LUIS POTOSI

LAS PALMAS TRAILER PARK

Private   35 Sites   (488/2-0001

All Year $20.00-25.00   35EWS
Location: On Mex 57, by north jct entrance road to Matehuala; on grounds of Las Palmas Hotel and Restaurant. (PO Box 73, 78700). **Terms:** Wkly/mthly rates; pets. **Facility:** Alt 1524m; 4 acres; RV-35. Quiet well-maintained grounds. Valet laundry service. Dump station; lounge; flush toilets; pool, wading pool. miniature golf; bowling. **Cards:** AE, MC, VI.

MONTERREY, NUEVO LEON

MOTEL NUEVA CASTILLA TRAILER PARK

Private   6 Sites   (8/385-0258

All Year $7.00-11.00 for 2   6EWS   XP $3
Location: 15.5 km n on Mex 85; on north/south hwy leading to toll road to Nuevo Laredo. Fax: 8/385-0265. **Facility:** 10 acres; RV-6. Fenced lot, open sites. Lounge; flush toilets; pool. **Cards:** AE, MC, VI.

MULEGE, BAJA CALIFORNIA SUR

THE ORCHARD (HUERTA SAUCEDO) RV PARK

Private   76 Sites   (115/3-0300

All Year $17.55 for 2   46EWS   XP $2
Location: 2 km s on Hwy 1. (Apdo Postal 24, 23900). **Terms:** Sr disc; **Terms:**wkly rates. **Facility:** 15 acres; T-30, RV-46. At the river; many shade trees. Tents & dry camping available at extra charge, for up to 2 persons; cabanas, $65 small; $110 large for up to 4 persons. Dump station; flush toilets; boat ramp; barbecue area, horseshoes, local tour arrangements, pig roast fiestas in season. **Recreation:** fishing. Rental: canoes, paddleboats; bicycles.

VILLA MARIA ISABEL RECREATIONAL PARK

Private   58 Sites   (115/3-0246

All Year $14.00 for 2   33EW   25S   XP $2
Location: 3 km s on Hwy 1. (Apdo Postal 5, 23900). Fax: 115/3-0246. **Terms:** Wkly rates. **Facility:** 5 acres; T-25, T/RV-33. At the river. Pull-thru sites. Tent sites with palapa, $4.50 per person. Dump station; flush toilets; pool; boat ramp; bakery 11/1-5/31, local tour arrangements. **Services:** Fee: coin laundry.

PATZCUARO, MICHOACAN

EL POZO TRAILER PARK
Private   20 Sites   ☎ 434/2-0937
All Year $12.00 for 2   20EWS   XP $2
Location: 1.5 km ne on Mex 120, Morelia Hwy. (PO Box 142, 61600). Fax: 434/2-0937. **Terms:** Reserv deposit; 15 amps; pets. **Facility:** Alt 2154m; 3 acres; RV-20. Large open spaces. Flush toilets; playground.

PUEBLA, PUEBLA

TRAILER PARK LAS AMERICAS
Private   60 Sites   ☎ 22/47-0134
All Year $8.00-10.00 for 2   60EWS   XP $2
Location: 10 km sw on Mex 190, Cholula-Puebla Hwy, opposite the Glaxo Factory. (PO Box 49, CHOLULA). **Terms:** Pets, dog kennel avail. **Facility:** Alt 7200m; 3 acres; T/RV-60. Quiet location with open sites. Large lawn areas and walled perimeter. Rate spread according to length of trailer. Flush toilets; pool, wading pool; rec room, party room with barbecue pit. **Services:** *Fee:* coin laundry.

PUERTO VALLARTA, JALISCO

LAURIES "TACHOS" TRAILER PARK
Private   125 Sites   ☎ 322/4-2163
All Year $16.00 for 2   125EWS   XP $5
Location: 6.3 km n on Airport Rd (Mex 200), 1 km e on paved road. Camino Nuevo al Pitillal S/N 48300 (Apartado Postal 315, PUERTA VALLARTA). **Terms:** Reserv deposit; wkly rates; pets. **Facility:** 10 acres; RV-125, T/RV-100. Good selection of sites, some pull-thru sites, some with shade trees. Flush toilets; pool.

QUERETARO, QUERETARO

AZTECA TRAILER PARK
Private   30 Sites   ☎ 42/34-0592
All Year $6.00-8.00 for 2   30EWS   XP $3
Location: On Mex 57; 14.5 km n of Mex 45 and 45D interchange; on grounds of Azteca Parador Motor Inn. (PO Box 4, Juriquilla, 76230). **Terms:** Reserv deposit; 20 amps; no pets. **Facility:** Alt 6160m; 15 acres; RV-30. Open sites on grounds of motel. Flush toilets; heated pool. **Cards:** AE, MC, VI.

ROSARITO, BAJA CALIFORNIA

OASIS RESORT
Private   53 Sites   ☎ 663/1-3250
Fri & Sat $59.00 for 4   53EWS   XP $10
Sun-Thurs $49.00 for 4   XP $10
Location: On Hwy 1D (toll road), southbound exit El Oasis; northbound exit Rancho Delmar, just s, 8 km n of town. Km 25 Carr Escenica Tijuana-Ensenada (PO Box 158, IMPERIAL BEACH, 91933). Fax: 663/3-3252. **Terms:** Check-in 3 pm; reserv deposit, 3 day refund notice; 50 amps; no pets. **Facility:** 10 acres; RV-53. Beachfront RV park. Concrete and grass sites with built-in barbecue. Rental RV's, $99-$142. Lounge; flush toilets; putting green; beach, pool, wading pool, sauna, whirlpools; 1 tennis court; playground, rec room, exercise room, 2 restaurants. **Services:** groceries. *Fee:* coin laundry. **Cards:** AE, MC, VI.

SAN CARLOS, SONORA

TETA KAWI TRAILER PARK
Private   45 Sites   ☎ 622/6-0220
All Year $9.00-20.00 for 2   45EWS   XP $3
Location: 10.7 km nw on Mex 15, 9.3 km w on San Carlos turn-off. Across from Bahia de San Carlos (PO Box 71, GUAYMAS, 85506). Fax: 622/6-0248. **Terms:** Reserv deposit, 14 day refund notice; 30 amps, mthly rates; pets. **Facility:** 3 acres; T/RV-45. Open sites across from beach, behind motel. Concrete patios. Lounge; flush toilets; pool. **Cards:** AE, MC, VI.

SAN CRISTOBAL DE LAS CASAS, CHIAPAS

BONAMPAK TRAILER PARK
Private   30 Sites   ☎ 967/8-1621
All Year $5.00-10.00 for 2   20EWS   XP $5
Location: On Mex 190, north entrance to town, at statue; on grounds of Hotel Bonampak. Calzado Mexico 5 29310 (PO Box 75). **Terms:** Reserv deposit, 15 day refund notice; pets. **Facility:** Alt 2113m; T-10, T/RV-20. At entrance to ruins. Lounge; flush toilets; playground. **Cards:** AE, CB, DI, MC, VI.

SAN FELIPE, BAJA CALIFORNIA

SAN FELIPE MARINA RESORT RV PARK
Private   136 Sites   ☎ 657/7-1435
All Year $22.00 for 4   136EWS   XP $5
Location: 4.5 km s on road to airport. Km 4.5 Carr San Felipe AeroPuerto 21850 (233 Pauline Ave, PMB 8518, CALEXICO, 92231). Fax: 657/7-1566. **Terms:** Reserv deposit, 3 day refund notice; 50 amps; pets. **Facility:** 4 acres; RV-136. Unshaded sites overlooking the marina. For US reservations: (800) 291-5397. Dump station; flush toilets; pool; hotel facilities available to guests. **Services:** groceries; laundry. **Cards:** AE, MC, VI.

SAN MIGUEL DE ALLENDE, GUANAJUATO

LAGO DORADO
Private   35 Sites   ☎ 415/2-2301
All Year $10.00-12.00   35EW   8S   XP $3-3
Location: 3.8 km s on Mex 49 to Villa De Los Frailes, 2 km w following signs. (PO Box 523, 37700). **Terms:** Pets. **Facility:** Alt 1800m; 10 acres; RV-35. Some shaded sites. Dump station; flush toilets; pool.

TRAILER PARK LA SIESTA
Private   70 Sites   ☎ 415/2-0207
All Year $11.00 for 2   70EWS   XP $2
Location: 2 km s on Mex 49, Celaya Hwy. (PO Box 72, 37700). **Terms:** Reserv deposit, 7 day refund notice; A/C $2.50, elec heaters $2.50; pets. **Facility:** Alt 1800m; 3 acres; RV-70. Open sites on grounds of motel. Flush toilets; playground, facilities of motel available to guests.

TECATE, BAJA CALIFORNIA

TECATE KOA ON RANCHO OJAI

Private   41 Sites   ☎ 66/53-3014
All Year $25.00-35.00 for 2 41EWS   XP $6
Location: On Hwy 2, 20 km e of town near Km 112. Carr Mexicali-Tijuana Km 112 (PO Box 280, TECATE, 91980). Fax: 66/55-3015. **Terms:** Reserv deposit, 4 day refund notice; 50 amps, wkly/mthly rates; pets. **Facility:** 40 acres; T/RV-41. At a ranch in the mountains. Log cabins, $40-$50; Tent sites, $28 for 4 persons, $6 extra person. Dump station; flush toilets; heated pool; playground, barbecues, clubhouse, horseshoes, picnic tables, volleyball. **Services:** groceries. *Fee:* coin laundry. **Recreation:** hiking trails. *Fee:* horseback riding. *Rental:* bicycles.

ZACATECAS, ZACATECAS

HOTEL HACIENDA DEL BOSQUE RV PARK

Private   34 Sites   ☎ 492/4-6666
All Year $18.00 for 2   34EWS
Location: 4 km ne of center on Guadalajara Rd; at the crossroads on Hwy 54. Heroes de Chapultepec 801 98054. Fax: 492/4-6565. **Terms:** Sr disc; reserv deposit, 15 day refund notice; 50 amps; pets. **Facility:** Alt 5000m; 2 acres; RV-34. Adjacent Hotel Hacienda del Bosque. Flagstone paved sites; back in. Lounge; flush toilets; playground. **Cards:** AE, MC, VI.

The Symbols of Quality

*D*iamond ratings provide you an easy way to elect quality lodgings and restaurants with the amenities and degree of sophistication you desire. Each property receiving a Diamond rating is thoroughly inspected and rated using consistent, objective criteria.

One Diamond–This means an establishment meets our members' basic requirements. Lodgings are good but modest and designed for the budget-minded. Restaurants are clean, casual, and family-oriented.

Two Diamond–These establishments meet all of the One-Diamond requirements with enhanced furnishings for lodgings and broader menu selections for restaurants.

Three Diamond–They offer guests a degree of sophistication. Lodgings feature more luxury and amenities, while restaurants provide extensive menus and a skilled service staff.

Four Diamond–This rating is given to those establishments that create a truly memorable experience for guests. Lodgings feature a high level of service amid luxurious surroundings. Restaurants are geared toward an adult dining experience with a highly skilled staff and elegant atmosphere.

Five Diamond–AAA's highest award is given to those rare luxury establishments that are world-renowned. The service, quality, and sophistication are exceptional, creating an unforgettable experience.

Trust AAA to provide you objective and accurate ratings of thousands of lodgings and restaurants throughout North America. Know before you go what to expect when you get there.

Travel With Someone You Trust

491

Every ten minutes someone traveling in America loses their cash.* If American Express® Travelers Cheques are lost or stolen, they can be replaced, usually within 24 hours. Cash can't. And they're available at no fee for AAA members at AAA offices.

  Travelers Cheques

*1998 US Statistical Abstract
© 2000 American Express. Payment methods vary from club to club.

NOTES

NOTES

NOTES